Actors &
Performers'
YEARBOOK
2020

Actors' & Performers'

YEARBOOK

2020

Edited by Lloyd Trott

methuen | drama

LONDON · NEW YORK · OXFORD · NEW DELHI · SYDNEY

METHUEN DRAMA
Bloomsbury Publishing Plc
50 Bedford Square, London, WC1B 3DP, UK
1385 Broadway, New York, NY 10018, USA

BLOOMSBURY, METHUEN DRAMA and the Methuen Drama logo are
trademarks of Bloomsbury Publishing Plc

Sixteenth edition published in Great Britain 2020

Project editor: Judy Tither

A catalogue record for this book is available from the British Library.

A catalog record for this book is available from the Library of Congress.

ISBN: PB: 978-1-350-10757-1
ePDF: 978-1-350-10759-5
eBook: 978-1-350-10758-8

Printed and bound in Great Britain

To find out more about our authors and books visit www.bloomsbury.com
and sign up for our newsletters.

About the Editor

Lloyd Trott is the Academy Dramaturg of the Royal Academy of Dramatic Art, London. He has taught actors at RADA for 43 years. He helps to plan and cast the Academy's public repertoire with the Academy's Director. He has two main teaching strands, Dramaturgy and Professional Development. Lloyd is the Academy's primary liaison with actors' agents and casting directors in the UK and shepherds the acting students through their third year and into the profession. Alongside his RADA commitments Lloyd has worked as an Arts researcher and lobbyist and been an elected politician. He represented Dulwich in the last years of the Inner London Education Authority (1986–90) where he set up and chaired a Cultural Review of Inner London, as well as chairing the Arts and Libraries Committee of the Association of Metropolitan Authorities. In the mid-nineties he was Dramaturg at Theatr Clwyd. He taught dramaturgy on the MA Writing for Performance at Goldsmiths College 1998–2005, since when he has worked full-time at RADA. Lloyd was the 2011 Winner of the Kenneth Tynan Award for services to dramaturgy in the UK.

Contents

Foreword ix
Introduction xi

Training
Introduction 1
Training for the under-18s 2
Arts Emergency – Julie Hesmondhalgh 5
Pop-up youth theatre in Yorkshire
  – Nick Evans 8
Drama schools 13
Checklist of drama school deadlines,
  audition requirements, audition fees
  and funding systems – Lloyd Trott 25
What are drama schools looking for?
  – Geoffrey Colman 28
Short-term and part-time courses 32
Private tutors and coaches 43
An actor's toolkit – Simon Dunmore 51

Agents and casting directors
Introduction 53
Agents 54
Being an agent – Howard Roberts 96
CPMA: the Co-operative Personal
  Management Association 99
Voice-over agents 101
Presenters' agents 105
Casting directors 106
Casting for the stage – Anne McNulty 126
Casting for musical theatre
  – David Grindrod 128
Woman in a brown skirt
  – Sophie Stanton 130

Theatre
Introduction 133
Dramaturg at HOME
  – Petra Jane Tauscher 134

Producing theatres 138
Effective audition speeches
  – Simon Dunmore 157
Understudying – Andrew Piper 166
Independent managements/theatre
  producers 170
Ignition, inspiration and the imposter
  – Scott Graham 179
Middle and smaller-scale companies 183
Starting your own theatre company
  – Pilar Ortí 224
Finding funding for projects
  – Sinead Mac Manus 228
The multi-hyphenate comedy actor-
  performer-writer – Chris Head 232
Pantomime 235
The art and craft of pantomime
  – Iain Lauchlan 243
English-language European theatre
  companies 246
A touring actor's survival guide
  – Maev Alexander 249
Fringe theatres 254
To fringe, or not to fringe
  – Simon Dunmore 265
Edinburgh or bust: is it worth it?
  – Shane Dempsey 267
Open Book: fairer finances for fringe
  theatre – Piers Beckley 270
Children's, young people's and theatre
  in education – Paul Harman 273
Shakespeare changes prisoners' lives
  – Bruce Wall 295
Festivals 298
Role-play companies 303
Professional role-playing
  – Robbie Swales 309

Media
Introduction 312
Television companies 313

Casting for television – Janie Frazer 316
Auditioning for camera
  – Nancy Bishop 320
Self-taping auditions – Ros Hubbard 323
Are you ready for Pilot Season?
  – Brendan Thomas 326
Independent film, video and TV
  production companies 330
Film schools 342
Actors and video games –Mark Estdale 344
Radio and audio book companies 347
Acting for radio – Gordon House 353
Media festivals 356

Disabled actors

Introduction 359
Training 359
Sources of work 359
Arts organisations 364
Rights, advice and support 366
Opportunities for disabled actors
  – Jamie Beddard 368

Resources

Introduction 371
Equity 372
Act For Change
  – Kobna Holdbrook-Smith 373
Beyond #metoo – Kelly Burke 376
Spotlight, casting directories and
  information services 380

'Point me in the right direction':
  navigating the casting services
  – Isabelle Farah 384
Be prepared for publicity
  – Jayne Trotman 388
Photographers and repro companies 391
Getting the most from your
  photographs – Angus Deuchar 409
Making money from your voice
  – Marina Caldarone 412
Showreel, voicereel and website
  services 415
Showreels: creation and maintenance
  – Anthony Holmes 422
Digital wellbeing for actors
  – Sinead Mac Manus 426
Accountants 430
Tax and National Insurance for actors
  – Philippe Carden 436
Equity Pension Scheme
  – Andrew Barker @ First Act 440
Physical and mental fitness for actors
  – Alex Caan 443
Funding bodies 447
Publications, libraries, references and
  booksellers 452
Organisations, associations and
  societies 457
Bibliography 466
Webography 473

Foreword

Equity (see page 372) is a relatively small union covering a wide variety of issues – not just contracts – of importance to those working in the performing arts. Despite our size we are expert in all the issues we cover, thanks to a dedicated staff with a wide variety of specialist knowledge to support our members.

However, you, as lone actor, also have a range of other concerns that are outside Equity's remit. For instance, how do you go about finding a specialist photographer capable of capturing the essential 'you'? What unforeseen pitfalls can you expect to encounter on a small-scale tour? Which agents and casting directors are happy to receive unsolicited showreels?

The joy of this wonderfully comprehensive book is that it gives you not only detailed listings for every aspect of work-related issues, but also great insights into the experiences of seasoned practitioners. The really helpful introductions and articles are written with warmth and humour. It is a valuable companion and an essential tool for all actors at whatever stage in their careers.

Christine Payne
General Secretary of Equity

Introduction

Being all too aware that the majority of the Yearbook's contents remains firmly focussed on actors, I am pleased that we have two new articles for 2020 from Scott Graham and Chris Head, which have relevance for a wider group of performers, as well as actors wanting to enhance their performance abilities.

On the 25th anniversary of his co-founding Frantic Assembly with Steven Hoggett, I invited Scott Graham to reflect on his achievements and continuing practice, especially that he is now sole Artistic Director of the company. It was rather a surprise on first reading his article, 'Ignition, inspiration and the imposter' to find that Scott is still haunted by the knowledge he did not undergo a formal training, even though he has made such a lasting impact on both audiences and performers. It seemed a strange contradiction given sharing skills and ideas, is a first principle of Frantic Assembly's practice, whether this is in the very act of discovering them in research and development, in the rehearsal room with collaborators, or in the wider world of Frantic Assembly's outreach work, particularly its programme Ignition aimed directly at young men, who otherwise would never have thought of themselves as actors or dancers. This sharing goes hand in hand with a desire 'to puncture the mystique around theatre and dance'. Scott's elegant articulation of tackling self-doubt should be inspiring for any performer to read.

It was my intention in writing the article 'Routes into comedy' for the 2017 Yearbook that it should be the first in a series of cabaret/comedy articles to mark the importance of this field. The publication of Chris Head's book *A Director's Guide to the Art of Stand-up*, by Methuen Drama in this month of writing, seemed too good an opportunity to miss for the first handover. 'Routes to comedy' concentrated on just two comedians and, a producer, whereas Chris's 'The multi-hyphenate comedy actor-performer-writer' is bursting with comedians just as he reports comedy festivals are swarming with producers. I have observed over the last 15 years or so, one, two, sometimes three, extremely funny women in my RADA classes and yet, apart from one five-week Restoration Comedy project, there is no component of the BA Acting course that directly cultivates this gift, as Daisy May Cooper reprimanded us in a newspaper interview, earlier this year. Daisy, and Phoebe Waller-Bridge are just the most prominent of a host of RADA graduates, who have ventured into comedy and as Chris notes found a quick path from writing for themselves in live performance to television and other media, as well as fuelling an uplift in their casting in dramatic roles: Yasmin Akram, Lily Bevan, Karen Cogan, Lu Corfield and Louise Ford, to mention but a few. This much I knew, but it has taken Chris to enlighten me to the fact that our universities now award degrees in comedy.

The key linking factor between comedy, particularly stand-up, and enhanced performances in dramatic roles, is confidence. As Chris notes, often stand-up involves a heightened presentation of the self, but what happens when at a meeting about acting work, it is the true self that the director/casting director wants to see? This question also applies to actors' publicising a new film, TV series or play which features them, which is why I asked Jayne Trotman to contribute her article 'Be prepared for publicity' to the Yearbook. During my early years at RADA in the later 1970s, early '80s I was staggered to find that so many fine acting students were poor public speakers. This became very evident when for a while I co-ordinated touring productions to London schools, which involved the students giving Q&A sessions after performances. In subsequent years, as my own experience and understanding of actors grew, increasing numbers of directors, some of them very senior, began asking me to give second opinions, when they couldn't make their mind up about a particular casting. Rarely was I asked to comment on an actor's talent, the phone calls wouldn't have been made had that been in question. The two most frequently asked questions are: 'Brilliant audition, but am I going to be able to direct them? They don't seem to be able to string two words of conversation together' and 'But will they be good company members?' While most of Jayne's publicity experience comes from working at the high end of feature films, her advice to actors can apply just as well to a local newspaper interview or local radio broadcast in the town, where for the duration of the run you can easily become temporary celebrities. Breaking Jayne's recommendations down further you can see how they apply equally well to the presentation of self at 'meetings'.

Since the government introduction of Auto-Enrolment requiring all UK employers to establish a pension scheme for their workers, we have been wanting the Yearbook to return to publishing a detailed explanation of pensions for actors and in particular, the Equity Pension Scheme. On the whole, Auto-Enrolment is a good thing for most employees, but can become problematic for actors given the peripatetic nature of their work. As an interim measure Philippe Carden has provided a little note at the end of his 'Tax and Insurance' article for the last few years. Now we have the benefit of the advice of a leading expert in the field: Andrew Barker, who has provided a free-standing article on the Equity Pension Scheme, of which he is very much custodian.

Our team continues with Anna Brewer, as Senior Commissioning Editor, Judy Tither as Managing Editor, and myself, while Meredith Benson has joined us, as Assistant Editor during the last year.

Lloyd Trott
Consultant Editor
July 2019

Training
Introduction

This section is largely devoted to those who are 18 and older. This is not to dismiss the fact that there is training (of varying kinds) for those under that age. However, the field is so wide that the confines of this book limit listings only to the major organisations.

In spite of the fact that a minority of well-known actors did not formally train, it is very important for today's aspirant to do so. An ever-increasing number of people want to become actors, so those with 'casting clout' (agents, casting directors and directors) have more and more people to choose from. Doesn't it make sense to select from those who've undergone the rigours of a respected training process? It is an essential fact that the acting industry works on very tight time-scales and budgets – trained actors should be quicker, more reliable and, usually, more inventive than their untrained counterparts. For instance, an untrained voice that cracks up after a few days of live performance is time-consuming and costly for a management – only the larger productions can afford understudies. An untrained actor, who may look good on camera, will take time to learn how to work on a television set, where time spent keeping technicians waiting is very, very expensive. A fight (in a theatre or on camera) has to be staged so that it (a) looks real, (b) is safe for the participants and (c) can be seen properly by camera and/or audience – actors who've been trained in the essentials of combat will make this staging process much quicker. Moving correctly in period costumes, performing all kinds of formal dance and using microphones properly are just a few of the other time-saving skills that the trained actor can bring to a production. It is only an exceptional few who, nowadays, have the opportunity to 'learn on the job'.

For today's aspiring actor, it is important to train on a professionally recognised course. The established drama schools are the focus of such training. There are acting-related university degree courses which have a reasonable proportion of vocational training (as well as academic work) and there are numerous part-time, short-term and 'foundation' courses which will give you basic insights into the many crafts involved in acting. However, because of the intense competition, a full-time drama school course of at least a year is essential for most people.

For those who have already trained, there are opportunities to learn new skills and refine those already acquired, or simply to keep them in trim when the acting work is not coming in. The latter is very important, as you can be asked to demonstrate your skills at very short notice. Being an actor is a bit like being a fireman – without the regular salary. Also, the more you can legitimately add to the 'Skills' section of your CV, the more you can enhance your chances of finding work.

Editor's Note: It is especially important to **check for the latest information on all fees listed** under all headings in this section. *Actors and Performers Yearbook* makes every effort to ensure that such information is correct and up-to-date, but prices are especially liable to ongoing amendment.

Training for the under-18s

It is a fact that many child stars do not succeed as adult actors. There are notable exceptions – Emma Watson and Leonardo di Caprio, for instance – but they are the exceptions that prove the rule. I also wonder whether a childhood largely devoted to performing is entirely healthy: what about learning about life? And what about learning other essential skills in order to earn one's living when the acting work is not coming in?

Generally speaking, the best thing for the stage-struck child is to send him or her to one of the numerous youth theatre groups and drama workshops that exist in almost every town and city. These are often listed in *Yellow Pages*, and many are members of the National Association of Youth Theatres – see below. Public productions are often the last priority of such groups – especially for the younger ages – but a terrific amount can be learnt by the young from what seem like simple, make-believe games. Children in such groups won't learn many of the technical skills necessary to acting, but they will learn a lot of important social skills and the fundamental business of 'interacting' that is so important to an acting ensemble – that it's not just what you can create that matters, but what you can create with other people. Some youth theatres are allied to agencies who will promote their members for professional work, but it is important to note that employment of the under-16s is very strictly regulated.

National Association of Youth Theatres (NAYT)

c/o Friargate Theatre, Lower Friargate, York YO1 9SL
tel 03302 290820
email info@nayt.org.uk
website www.nayt.org.uk

Founded in 1982, the National Association of Youth Theatres (NAYT) is the development agency for youth theatre practice in England. The organisation supports the development of youth theatre activity through training, advocacy, participation programmes, and information services. Registration is open to any group or individual using theatre techniques in their work with young people, outside formal education. NAYT is an educational charity (No. 1046042) and a company limited by guarantee (No. 2989999).

NAYT responds to enquiries from young people, teachers, parents, carers, youth workers and social services looking for information and advice about youth theatre provision or career or educational opportunities. This free service puts young people in direct contact with youth theatres.

National Youth Arts Wales (NYAW)

245 Western Avenue, Cardiff CF5 2YX
tel 029 2026 5060 *fax* 029 2026 5014
email nyaw@nyaw.co.uk
website www.nyaw.co.uk/e_nytw.html

NYAW represents the National Youth Brass Band of Wales, National Youth Wind Orchestra of Wales, National Youth Jazz Wales, National Youth Choir of Wales, National Youth Chamber Ensemble of Wales, National Youth Dance Wales, National Youth Orchestra of Wales, and National Youth Theatre of Wales (NYTW).

The National Youth Theatre of Wales was founded in 1976 and has since provided opportunities for hundreds of young people, many of whom are now actively involved with the theatre as professional actors, directors, writers, designers and stage managers. The NYTW is aimed at young people aged 16-21 who are drawn from all over Wales. With guidance from its Creative Activist, the youth theatre prepares and rehearses during the summer of each year for a series of high-profile public performances.

In addition, the NYTW spearheads a development programme of workshops and education activities, designed to increase interest and participation in youth theatre.

National Youth Music Theatre (NYMT)

Adrian House, 27 Vincent Square, London SW1P 2NN
email enquiries@nymt.org.uk
website www.nymt.org.uk

The National Youth Music Theatre offers exceptional opportunities in pre-professional, musical theatre training for talented young people of all backgrounds aged 10 to 23 years through skill workshops, master classes and residential courses led by industry professsionals, through commissioning and presentation of exciting new work and — in collaboration with some of the UK's leading creative minds — producing bold, new realisations of major works of the core repertoire.

These opportunities exist for stage performers, musicians, technicians, musical directors, choreographers and designers.

The National Youth Music Theatre represents the very best in work with young people through musical theatre, enabling thousands of youngsters across the UK to develop both their creative and personal potential, leading Andrew Lloyd-Webber to dub it 'the best youth music theatre in the world'.

National Youth Theatre of Great Britain (NYT)

443-45 Holloway Road, London N7 6LW
tel 020 3696 7066
website www.nyt.org.uk
Artistic Director Paul Roseby *Executive Director* Karen Turner

Founded in 1956 as the world's first youth theatre, the National Youth Theatre of Great Britain is a world-leading youth arts organisation. Delivering free performance opportunities, courses and masterclasses, it nurtures and showcases exceptional performers and theatre technicians from Great Britain and Northern Ireland.

Every year the National Youth Theatre visits over 70 arts venues and schools across the UK in the search for young people aged between 14-25 to join their company. Once successfully auditioned, members can be involved with ambitious productions both on stage and backstage, as well as developing skills in facilitation and creative leadership. The National Youth Theatre also runs a social inclusion programme featuring long-term engagement with SEN schools, and accredited courses for those not in education or training, as well as many open access projects and community productions.

The National Youth Theatre's world renowned alumni include: Helen Mirren, Daniel Craig, Colin Firth, Rosamund Pike, Daniel Day Lewis, Zawe Ashton, Chiwetel Ejiofor, Orlando Bloom, Catherine Tait, Ben Kingsley, Ashley Jensen, Derek Jacobi, Timothy Dalton, David Walliams, Matt Lucas, Hugh Boneville, Matt Smith, Adeel Aktar and David Harewood.

Scottish Youth Theatre

The Old Sheriff Court, 105 Brunswick Street, Glasgow G1 1TF
tel 0141 552 3988 *fax* 0141 552 7615
email info@scottishyouththeatre.org
website www.scottishyouththeatre.org
Artistic Director Mary McCluskey

Founded in 1977, Scottish Youth Theatre is Scotland's national theatre for and by young people.

Using the youth theatre/drama process to develop not only creativity and performance skills but also transferable skills in participants, Scottish Youth Theatre puts particular emphasis on each individual's personal and social development. It offers weekly drama and dance classes for young people aged $2\frac{1}{2}$ to 25, performances for all the family and the flagship Summer Festival, which includes performance and technical theatre courses, open to young people across Scotland aged 8 to 25.

For participants who have shown promise and are interested in a career in any aspect of theatre, film and television, there is Scottish Youth Theatre's high-quality, high-profile project and performance group, SYT Productions.

Scottish Youth Theatre also works in partnership with schools, youth theatres, youth groups and national agencies to deliver tailor-made Special Projects.

Youth Music Theatre UK

The Hub, St Alban's Fulham, 2 Margravine Road, London W6 8HJ
tel 020 8563 7725
email mail@ymtuk.org
website www.youthmusictheatreuk.org

Youth Music Theatre UK (also known as YMT) is the UK's national company providing musical theatre activities for young people across the UK. It is one of the nine National Youth Music Organisations (NYMOs) supported by Arts Council England and the DfE (Music and Dance Scheme); its core programme links young people from local/regional productions into formal training at drama school – so successful auditionees will be talented, with many going on into the creative industries. YMT has a strong relationship with the UK's largest teaching union, the NASUWT, who are its principal sponsors, and with Trinity College London, who formally assess the activities.

Auditions for young performers take place around the UK in January and February, and successful applicants join the companies of 8 fully staged productions at venues and festivals around the country in the summer holidays.

YMT The Explore Programme is a series of workshops, courses and projects that help young people develop their skills and abilities in the performing arts. This includes the opportunity to work with artistic teams to create new music theatre. YMT also creates similar pathways for young writers, composers and musicians as well as those interested in technical theatre. YMT offer a wide range of outreach opportunities with schools, youth services and cross-cultural groups.

Training opportunities for graduate directors, assistant directors, assistant MDs, designers and choreographers working alongside its professional staff are also available.

Youth Theatre Ireland

7 North Great George's Street, Dublin 1
tel +353 (0) 1 878 1301
email info@youththeatre.ie
website www.youththeatre.ie
Facebook @YouthTheatreIreland
Twitter @YouthTheatreIrl
Instagram @youththeatreireland

Youth Theatre Ireland is the national development organisation for youth theatre. It supports a network of youth theatres which deliver year-round programmes of drama workshops and performance opportunities to young people aged 12–21 from cities, towns and villages across Ireland.

Youth Theatre Ireland advocates the inherent value and the unique relationship between young people and theatre as an artform, and is committed to extending and enhancing young people's understanding of theatre and to raising the artistic standards of youth theatre across the country. The organisation supports youth drama in practice through an annual programme that includes the National Youth Theatre, National festivals of youth theatres, commissioning new writing, publications, resources, training and other services, as well as research and policy development.

With a membership of 55 youth theatres throughout the country, Youth Theatre Ireland supports the sustained development of youth theatres in partnership with local authorities, youth services, theatres and arts centres. Its productions are of a professional standard and are cast from youth theatres around Ireland. Previous productions include: the world premiere of Carmel Winters' *Salt Mountain* (2015), directed by Jo Mangan; *R.U.R. – Rossum's Universal Robots* by Karel Čapek, directed by Cáitriona McLaughlin (2017); and the world premiere of Dylan Coburn Gray's *Ask Too Much of Me*, directed by Veronica Coburn (2019). For further details about Youth Theatre Ireland's work, please refer to the website.

Arts Emergency

Julie Hesmondhalgh

The crisis in arts education: how working-class artists are being squeezed out of the industry

I had an unexpectedly lovely train journey recently. Lucky enough to have managed to reserve a seat at a table in a typically over-crowded carriage, I was planning to shove my earphones in, bury my head in a book and disengage from my fellow passengers. So, when the strangers at my table started to chat to one another – and to me – my heart sank a bit. But it ended up being one of the most interesting and engaging journeys I've ever had.

My cross-country companions were Alan, a middle-aged gay actor; Kate, a young maths teacher at a struggling comprehensive school in West London; and Henry, a Ghanaian-born scientist working in Washington DC. We covered so much in that two hours between London and Manchester: childhood, sexuality, racism, Trump and perhaps inevitably – there being a teacher amongst us – education. Kate talked with sadness about how the new GCSEs were taking their toll on teachers and pupils alike at her school and how she'd been working every evening and weekend to try to get her Year 11s through them. She said that the school was already feeling the effects of the cuts in arts subjects; that although she was a maths teacher, the erosion of subjects that had enhanced her students' creativity and awakened their minds to the wider world was already taking its toll on the mental health of the young people. Henry talked passionately about how, although he was a scientist by trade, it was the arts that gave him joy, that refreshed him and rebooted him after long days at the lab. Music venues, theatres, cinemas: these were his hang-outs of choice. Alan and I both talked about the opportunities that we had taken for granted as we started out in the performing arts – opportunities that no longer exist for young people growing up in towns like ours; from families like ours.

I, along with a dozen of my mates, left my hometown of Accrington at the age of 18 to go to drama school in London, after a brilliant theatre studies teacher at our local Further Education college inspired us all to make a go of it and audition. There were five of us from that course at LAMDA at the same time at the end of the 1980s, all on *full grants* from our Local Education Authority. That FE performing arts course, I found out this week, no longer exists. Neither does the full local authority grant, of course. And nor, I'd venture, does the philosophy that an education in the arts, or a desire to have a career in the arts, is a worthwhile pursuit for people from backgrounds like mine.

There has been an insidious mindset creeping into our national psyche, no doubt massively exacerbated by the prohibitive costs of higher education tuition fees, that some-how a career in the arts is pie-in-the-sky and unrealistic, and that an arts or humanities degree or drama/art school training is not worth the investment. God forbid that anyone should be enthusiastic about learning for learning's sake and want to study philosophy or classics, never mind acting or dance because of a personal passion for the subject, without wondering and worrying about how to make that choice economically viable in the long term. As Nicky Morgan, the then Conservative Education Minister famously said in 2014, 'Arts subjects limit career choices', warning young people that studying arts at higher education could 'hold them back for the rest of their lives'.

The majority of educationalists, of course – even those working in Science and Maths subjects like my travelling companion Kate – would disagree. The study of the arts, and in particular the performing arts, are partly encouraged in top public schools, I'm sure, because of the confidence, social skills and interpretative thinking that develop as a result. The wealthy have never been discouraged from indulging their passion for music, film, painting, theatre and dance. A government report in November 2017 recorded that the creative industries were indeed thriving with the '£92bn sector growing at twice the rate of the economy' (**www.gov.uk** *Creative industries' record contribution to UK economy*, 29 November 2017).

But it appears that a huge swathe of the population, namely the state educated, the less well-off, the working class, for whom the decision to saddle oneself with over £27,000 debt at the start of their adult life is a major consideration, are being massively disincentivized to engage with the arts and humanities, from school onwards. It starts with funding cuts and continues as arts subjects are moved into a more theoretical and less practical curriculum framework at GCSE level. The controversial English Baccalaureate and its exclusion of arts is seen by many as the nail in the coffin of any meaningful creative education. Drama, art, dance and music at school have often been the only access young people have had to learning those skills.

There are, luckily, amazing organisations picking up the pieces and attempting to fill the gaps that current government policy is leaving. There is hope. Groups of people are crowdfunding to create bursaries to allow students from less privileged backgrounds to access arts and performance degrees. Theatres and art spaces are investing in outreach work to pull hard-to-reach communities into their buildings through youth theatre and specialised groups. Teachers and directors are setting up free training programmes, and watching their talented students overcome sometimes unbelievably challenging personal circumstances to thrive and succeed in an arts industry that they have been told is not for them: organisations like Alt, Nottingham-based Talent First and the mighty Arts Emergency.

Set up in 2011 by comedian Josie Long and campaigner Neil Griffiths, the Arts Emergency philosophy and aim are simple and effective: to create an 'Alternative Old Boys' Network'; to open up the same opportunities naturally afforded to those privileged few, who grow up with those school and family connections firmly in place, to everyone. They have pulled together an enormous number of experts and practitioners from a vast array of specialised areas and connected them with young people from backgrounds that have meant they have little access to the arts. Free talks and events are regularly made available, and when the scheme spread to the North a couple of years ago I became involved as a supporter and speaker in schools and colleges.

There is an incredibly successful mentoring scheme that I have witnessed first-hand as my husband, the writer Ian Kershaw, has been a mentor for over a year now. His first mentee, a sparky seventeen-year-old aspiring writer and the first in her family to access higher education, won't mind me saying that she thrived under the programme. Together, they saw theatre, attended talks by leading writers, met people in the industry and visited studios and rehearsal rooms. She grabbed the opportunity she was offered to write for a local theatre-in-education tour and did work experience at CBBC. She is now at university studying English with a creative writing pathway as part of her BA.

Maisie (not her real name) was clear about what she wanted to do from the off and Arts Emergency enabled her, creating networks that simply don't ordinarily exist for people like her. But sometimes the work they do is about opening up unknown worlds to their participants. Another young person might, for example, be passionate about, and fascinated by, films and filmmaking, but have no access to the world of the studio floor or editing suite or post-production house. He or she might be a fantastic and naturally gifted vision mixer or a sound recordist, but unless they're given the opportunity to experiment in these roles, they'll never know. As Arts Emergency say: 'You can't be what you can't see.'

The working-class artists who were encouraged and supported by the state from the 1950s through to my generation growing up in the 1980s and early 1990s, who are now part of the cultural landscape of the UK as writers, actors, directors, dancers, visual artists, musicians, directors, etc. are the last of their kind. Or could be, if we don't act to change the current climate of exclusion. A culture without diversity is a sick one. If our future artists only come from a narrow stratum of society (the most well-off and privately educated) then who will be left to tell the stories of the rest of us? Who will hold a mirror to our world and ask the important questions about how we live now? Because art exists not only to entertain, but to reflect and inform and inspire. At its best, it can be transcendent and transformative and completely democratic; in that it is, or should be, available to us all, regardless of where we're from and who we are. The more diverse our culture, the wider the world of the stories we experience, the richer we all are for it. Perhaps most importantly, it creates, as I experienced on that Pendolino train a few weeks back, a point of connection in an increasingly isolating and fractured world.

Arts Emergency, Unit C8, 3 Bradbury Street, London N16 8JN, info@arts-emergency.org

Julie Hesmondhalgh is a television and theatre actress and co-creator of the theatre company Arts Threshold. Her TV roles have included appearances in *The Bill*, *The Dwelling Place*, *Pat and Margaret*, *Dalziel & Pascoe*, *Cucumber*, *Happy Valley* and *Broadchurch*. Her most famous role to date has been as Hayley Cropper in the soap *Coronation Street*. Her theatre work includes: *Black Roses: The Killing of Sophie Lancaster* (Royal Exchange, 2012); *Blindsided* (Royal Exchange, 2014); *God Bless the Child* (Royal Court, 2014); Margaret Edson's *Wit* (Royal Exchange, 2016). She is a founder member of Manchester-based grassroots theatre company Take Back and a member of The Gap collective in Manchester. Her *Working Diary* will be published with Methuen Drama in 2019, royalties of which will go to Arts Emergency.

Training

Pop-up youth theatre in Yorkshire

Nick Evans

If a key purpose of the arts is to provide an escape and alternative to the difficult and sometimes disappointing world that we live in, then it is also true that sometimes the stark reality of that world can seem so overpowering that nothing else really matters. So, it was in the early summer of 2016, when I found myself in Southampton as part of the creative team for Cameron Mackintosh's colourful production of *Mary Poppins*, which acted as a sublime hymn to playfulness and possibility. It was tempting, in a world of umbrellas, sweet shops and dancing chimney-sweeps to soak in a childlike innocence and escapism that felt a million miles from everyday life.

That all changed on 16 June 2016.

MP attacked on street in Yorkshire constituency dies

Over the hours and days that followed, we came to hear the details of the dreadful murder of Jo Cox, the forty-one-year-old MP, mother, wife, sister and campaigner. The nation seemed stopped momentarily by the awfulness of the event. The sudden attack by one of her constituents, a far-right terrorist, was horrific in its nature. How could this happen, on British streets, in broad daylight, to a person so obviously trying to do good? It felt like something had changed in who we were. A question I found myself thinking was: is there anything that those of us working in theatre could do to arrest the horrible feeling that things were breaking apart in our country?

A few weeks later, my friend Carolyn Harris, the Labour MP for my hometown, Swansea, explained to me that she had often sat with her friend Jo Cox as Jo talked of her love of theatre, in particular *Les Misérables*. Carolyn wondered whether we could perhaps conjure a night at a London theatre that would pay tribute to Jo and celebrate her life. My response was almost immediate. It was clear Jo had had a passion for politics, an ability to connect with young people and a fierce pride – not only in her home constituency – but also for Yorkshire in general. I knew that I had to find a response that brought all these things together. I therefore proposed that we should stage *Les Misérables* in a disused mill in Jo Cox's constituency, Batley and Spen, and cast it with 120 teenagers from Yorkshire.

How might we make something of such a significant scale happen? My aims for the project were, firstly, to provide an opportunity for young people in Jo's constituency and the neighbouring areas to experience professional-level theatre. Secondly, to encourage participants and audiences across the diverse communities of Batley and Spen; and, thirdly, to celebrate the impact of the arts and its capacity to bring joy after so much darkness and loss had been felt on the streets of Batley and Spen.

I would need a fair amount of good fortune to pull off such a huge undertaking in a part of the country I knew little about. The first and one of the most significant moments of that good luck came with the election of the brilliant Tracy Brabin as successor to Jo Cox as MP for Batley and Spen. Tracy had grown up in the area and had been a professional actor. She made it clear not only how daunting it was to follow in the footsteps of someone as unique as Jo, but also how utterly she believed in the arts as a vehicle to change communities and empower young people.

Soon after, the other key player fell into place. Tracy Brabin hosted a meeting in Parliament with community activists and educators from Yorkshire to discuss the arts, at which I pitched the idea for *Les Mis Batley and Spen* or, as it was now becoming known, the *Hear the People Sing* project. I invited Donna Munday, who had been a general manager on Billy Elliot in London. Donna's experience, huge energies, determination, fight and passion as a producer had been proved time and again, but she also offered something far more important: a conviction that the arts should be for everyone and that our industry succeeds when it finds roots in communities – especially working-class communities – across the whole nation. She was a perfect ally.

Much of the model for the project came from my own upbringing in South Wales. As a teenager in the late 1980s, from a relatively poor background, I found huge opportunities at my comprehensive school. At thirteen, I stumbled upon the council-run, free-at-the-point-of-access West Glamorgan Youth Theatre Company. This wonderful organisation has trained hundreds of young people who have gone on to work in the industry (most famously Russell T. Davies and Michael Sheen), and an equal number of brilliant young people who have gone on to be business leaders, police officers, teachers, carers and self-employed business people, who would all point to the impact of the company and its values on their lives and development. WGYTC had produced professional-standard productions of works as diverse as *Hamlet* and *Into the Woods* for over four decades. I knew that its basic practices and the principles of its founder, Godfrey Evans, were the foundations on which I should build. The company had been a key education for me twice over: as a student, it had taught me the foundations of working in theatre and fostered a passion for theatre that exists to this day. In 2000, I was lucky to be invited to become Artistic Director of the company and benefitted hugely as a teacher and a director from an eight-year period honing directing skills, forging my own leadership style and, most importantly, sharing practice with other creatives in what can sometimes be an isolating industry.

Godfrey's foundations were: to believe that young people, from whatever background, can achieve anything if challenged to excellence. To place an equal emphasis on young people interested in performance as those interested in technical stagecraft. To encourage a respectful working environment in which the opinions and ideas of young people can flourish. To do so in a residential education environment where people of the widest range of social and economic background could live and learn together.

Over an intense five months in 2017, Donna Munday and I, with the support and advice of Tracy Brabin, undertook to raise a significant sum of money to not only build a traverse theatre in an empty industrial space, but to secure a residential setting for rehearsal, kindly organised by the University of Leeds, and to build a team to deliver the project. We focussed constantly on ensuring that all the young people involved could access the four weeks of rehearsal and performance without paying a fee.

Having gone into local schools, distributed leaflets and held three separate open auditions in Batley and Spen, the company of over 100 young people started to emerge. They were proving to represent the richness and diversity of that area in all its glory. Ranging in age from thirteen to nineteen, we had some young people who had proven talent and needed to be shown a route to take it further, sharing corridors with young people who had never stepped on a stage before. We had participants from all the different faith communities of the area and some who had no faith at all. Many were accessing the project for very personal reasons – for example, a young person who had faced the onset of significant illness that year and a young woman who had faced the trauma of being in the

Manchester Arena when a bomb exploded that same summer. Many had known Jo Cox personally and saw the project as a way of dealing with a personal grief connected to her death. What was humbling was their common purpose. All talked about wanting to do the project to prove something, not just to themselves but to the wider world about what their generation could achieve. There was a palpable sense of this young company of actors, designers, stage managers and musicians burning to provide a sense of purpose and hope when so many media commentators said there was none.

The theatrical community stepped up to send a message to Batley and Spen that their community, Jo and the efforts of these young people mattered. Major suppliers of lighting, sound and costume all provided equipment and expertise that allowed us to build the pop-up Jo Cox Theatre in an empty Oxfam warehouse in the heart of Batley. As the producer of the show, Sir Cameron Mackintosh was a source of real encouragement, even allowing us to borrow West End costumes and props for use in our alternative version (a generosity matched by that other great producer Lord Andrew Lloyd Webber who supported it financially). Performers in the West End shook buckets to raise funds, and singers and actors gave up a valuable day to stage a fundraiser cabaret. The on-the-ground staffing of the project was made up of theatre educators and professionals drawn from a range of West End shows. Perhaps most humbling was the number of times I checked into our Just Giving page to find donations from friends in the theatre industry, many of whom I knew to be struggling or out of work, but who still found a not-insignificant amount of money to help the project happen. Many did so because they were moved by what happened to Jo. Many more left comments suggesting they valued the opportunity to give these young people from an economically challenged area the same experience, and opportunity, to fall in love with theatre that they had once had.

In the first days of rehearsal I found myself with just a nagging feeling that the pace of work lacked a little urgency. The focus of our brilliant young participants was impressive but not quite yet of professional standard. Then one week in, that all changed when we were joined in rehearsals by Gordon and Jean Leadbeater, the parents of Jo Cox, and her sister Kim. They sat and watched as we staged and ran several numbers. They revelled in a sharing of our second workshop piece, 'More in Common', a piece devised and written by our young people when they were not called to rehearsals. Created around the themes of political voice, equality and citizenship, and how that what we have in common is far more important than what divides us, this was as vital as any work undertaken in the main rehearsals. Something changed in that morning. Gordon, Jean and Kim chatted with our young company openly about their wonderful daughter. Rehearsals after that morning took on a new purpose.

There were five performances of the Batley and Spen *Les Misérables*. When the fifteen-piece orchestra, all of whom had played in the show in London, struck up the overture in this warehouse in Batley, an audible gasp went around the space. A nightly ovation was given when the kabuki cloth dropped away in Act 2 and a thirty-foot barricade, built and painted by our young production team, rolled into the space. I cannot give enough credit to the professional approach of the 100 or so young people, all of whom took notes after every show and got better and better with every performance.

Something special happened on that barricade in Batley and I can't quite explain rationally just how wonderful, moving and engaging the production was. I know that it's what that community needed and deserved. I know that it's what happens when you expose hungry, driven young people who have not had fair opportunities to brilliant educators and professionals. I also know the special nature of the show owed something to Jo, to what happened to her and to how that made us even more determined to pursue a narrative of togetherness, reject a narrative of hate and replace it with a sense of hope and optimism. Theatre made that happen.

There is a moment late in *Les Misérables* where the one student to have survived the battle, Marius, sings 'Empty Chairs at Empty Tables'. It is a song about grief and about the guilt of grief and about confronting grief. Sung beautifully by sixteen-year-old Ewan Jones, I knew I had to think carefully about how this song worked, in this community, on this very poignant occasion. I decided to direct a moment that spoke more widely than just the story. As the 'ghosts' of the students left the space littered with empty chairs and as Ewan sang the poignant final lyrics, I brought onstage the youngest company member, Bilal Khan. From Batley's strong and vibrant Muslim community, and a pupil at the Batley Boy's School where Jo Cox was a regular visitor, Bilal had never acted before, but in our production played the cheeky-chappie Gavroche. Now, as the ghost of the character he had played, Bilal walked with control, detail and dignity into the space and, with perfect actor's timing, laid the white rose of Yorkshire (Jo's favourite flower) onto Marius's lap as the final notes of the song died away.

I imagine that some of the young participants will become actors, some will work in the production departments of our major theatres, some will become politicians or writers or campaigners. I suspect many will become more engaged citizens, more present parents, more thoughtful neighbours because they have had this experience. What I am sure of, right now, is this. As I stood atop that barricade on the final morning, just before it was dismantled, I was reminded of a very real fight worth having. All of us in this industry should be climbing onto a different kind of barricade to ensure the fight for access to the arts remains a right for all young people, regardless of their economic background. That fight will produce a more robust industry. But, more importantly, it will produce a more reflective, emotionally intelligent and engaged society.

The truth is that there is significant arts provision run by excellent people all around the country, but with a year-on-year attack on local government funding having taken place for the best part of a decade, it's becoming harder and harder for young people from economically challenged households to get anywhere near it. As schools find themselves in an increasingly competitive environment, where the league-table is king, it is unsurprising to find hard-pressed head teachers searching for money to support academic subjects that are double-weighted for league-table points whilst allowing drama, music, dance and art to slip from the curriculum. Even the West Glamorgan Youth Theatre Company has been under threat in recent years. Finally, this year Swansea Council cut their annual grant entirely with its partner local authority, Neath Port Talbot, having done the same three years earlier.

We urgently need a national convention to put the issue on the table and come up with concrete plans to move forward. Our arts councils, national theatre companies, head teachers, education unions and leading drama schools need to sit in a room for seventy-two hours and thrash out solutions to the vacuum left by our short-sighted government. What should be on the table? Obviously, the creation of a vocal and angry campaign to put arts back into core education policies and to embarrass any government that fails to do so is very necessary. The campaign should promote the creation of a national feeder system of regional youth theatres under the auspices of the national theatre specialists to work as peripatetic staff within individual schools across the nation to inject drama skills into after-school optional classes as core preparation for performing in local youth theatre company productions (part-funded by tax breaks to actors; match-funded by government). All of which would be a drop in the ocean – but, as a formulated, joined-up approach to practical theatre education for those who need it most, it would at the very least ensure an emergency Elastoplast to a very immediate injury.

Nick Evans is a director, who has worked extensively as a creative and, associate, on a range of major productions nationally and internationally. His higher education took place at the University of Warwick and the Royal Central School of Speech and Drama. He continues to direct the West Glamorgan Youth Theatre, when he can. He is the founder and Artistic Director of the Batley and Spen Youth Theatre.

Drama schools

Currently there is a core of established drama schools which belong to an organisation called the Federation of Drama Schools (**www.federationofdramaschools.co.uk**) which was formed after the closure of Drama UK in 2016. The twenty drama schools which are members of the Federation all run courses that were formerly accredited by Drama UK, offering practice-based, vocational training courses, quality assured by experienced professionals. Upon graduating from any of these schools you will be eligible for Spotlight and Equity membership. There are also a few well-respected courses that are not part of the Federation of Drama Schools.

It is important to check the current funding arrangements for each course you intend applying for. Don't simply rely on what arrangements were in place last year, as things have a habit of changing. Almost all of the drama schools offer a three-year BA degree in acting – in spite of the fact that there is little or no written component to the courses, let alone formal, written exams. Historically, the schools took the 'degree' route to help students get funding on the same basis as those following conventional academic courses. Degree status actually means very little in the acting profession, and courses with degree status are not necessarily better than those without it. Funding for some accredited one- and two-year courses is available, but not with the same frequency as for three-year courses.

It is worth spending time checking through all the courses listed below – also, read through the *Guide to Professional Training in Drama and Technical Theatre,* which although slightly out of date is very helpful. You can still access if from Drama UK's website: **www.dramauk.co.uk/writeable/custom_uploads/cf2d39883ed11eabda225ee8dfe99a7f.pdf**. Look, too, at **www.theessentialsguide.co.uk** for a very thought-through list of what to look for in a course. Look at the online prospectuses for any school that you feel could be viable for you – and read each one thoroughly. Important considerations include whether you could be eligible for funding whether student loan, scholarship or DaDA award for your fees and maintenance. Central London is significantly more expensive to live in than out of London schools.

Above all, it's important to try to assess which schools and courses you feel would suit you best and to apply, via UCAS **www.ucas.ac.uk** or **www.cukas.ac.uk**, to as many as you can afford the audition fees and travel costs for. Some schools offer means-tested audition fee waivers. Don't forget to factor in the cost of overnight accommodation, if necessary. The plain truth is that competition for places is so intense, especially for women, that you need to audition for as many places as possible. Every time you do another audition you will learn more about the techniques of auditioning than any book or class can teach you. It is important to appreciate that many people take two or three years of auditioning, and sometimes more, before they get places. If you are determined to become a professional actor, you have to take rejection in your stride – learn from it, and keep on trying until you succeed.

Finally, carefully check the application deadlines, funding details and audition specifications of each school to which you intend to apply – there are some considerable variations. See the Checklist following the listings given below. Many schools will have audition guidelines and advice for applicants on their website.

Notes:
• For general information on funding for fees and maintenance loans, see **www.gov.uk/browse/education/funding-and-finance-for-students**.
• Places on some courses are currently funded through Dance and Drama Awards (DaDAs). These were introduced in the late 1990s, and provide funding for about two-thirds of successful applicants. For more details, check each relevant school's prospectus and website – also look at **www.gov.uk/dance-drama-awards**.
• For the latest details on member of the Federation of Drama Schools please see FDS website **www.federationofdramaschools.co.uk**.
* denotes membership of the Federation of Drama Schools

The Academy of Live and Recorded Arts (ALRA)*

alra Academy of Live & Recorded Arts

ALRA South campus, Main Reception,
The Royal Victoria Patriotic Building,
John Archer Way, London SW18 3SX
tel 020 8870 6475
email info@alra.co.uk
ALRA North campus, Mill at the Pier, Trenchfield
Mill, Heritage Way, Wigan WN3 4BL
website www.alra.co.uk
Principal Adrian Hall

Acting courses

• BA (Hons) Acting. A full-time, 3-year course to prepare students for a varied career as a professional actor.
• MA Acting. A full-time, intensive, 15-month course to prepare students for a career in acting. This course is also available at both ALRA North and South.
• Foundation Courses in Acting. Available part-time and full-time, aimed at those considering full-time actor training and those considering a career change.

Directing courses
• MA Directing. A 2-year course with international placement. Only available at ALRA North.

Other short courses and workshops available periodically.

See **www.alra.co.uk** for more details.

American Musical Theatre Academy London (AMTA)

68 Wallis Road, Hackney Wick, London E9 5LH
tel 020 7253 3118
email info@theamta.com
website www.theamta.com
Principals/Directors Kenneth Avery-Clark, Christie Miller

Courses offered:
• One Year Full-Time Musical Theatre Programme.
• Two Year Full-Time Musical Theatre Programme.
• One Year Part-Time Musical Theatre Foundation Course.

No specific academic requirements, entry is by audition only. Applicants must be skilled in at least 2 of the 3 disciplines: acting, singing, dance. Train for a week in New York (one year course).

Welcomes candidates with disabilities and will consider each on a case-by-case basis, according to the strength of their audition. Please note that current premises are not wheelchair accessible.

ArtsEd*

14 Bath Road, London W4 1LY
tel 020 8987 6666
email info@artsed.co.uk
website www.artsed.co.uk
Principal and Director of the School of Musical Theatre Chris Hocking *Director of the School of Acting* Julie Spencer

ArtsEd is one of the UK's leading drama schools, offering outstanding conservatoire training on the BA (Hons) courses in Acting and Musical Theatre. Winner of TEF Gold for delivering outstanding teaching, learning and student outcomes 2018 and 2019. ArtsEd was ranked as the top school for overall student satisfaction in the 2018 and 2019 National Student Survey.

Degree courses are validated by City, University of London. Dance and Drama Awards are available, linked to the Level 6 approved Trinity College London diplomas and ArtsEd also awards bursaries from its own funds. Applications for courses and awards should be made direct to the school.

Acting courses:

• BA (Hons) Acting/Level 6 Diploma in Professional Acting (3 years). Applicants must be aged 18 or over.
• BA (Hons) Musical Theatre/Level 6 Diploma in Musical Theatre (3 years). Applicants must be aged 18 or over.
• MA Acting (1 year postgraduate). Applicants must be aged 21 or over.

• Foundation Musical Theatre (1 year). Applicants must be aged 18 or over.
• Foundation Acting (1 year). Applicants must aged 18 or over.
• Part-time Foundation Musical Theatre (2 terms). Applicants must be aged 18 or over.
• Part-time Foundation Acting (2 terms). Applicants must be over 18 or over.

The Birmingham Theatre School
The Old Fire Station, 285-287 Moseley Road, Highgate, Birmingham B12 0DX
tel 0121 440 1665
email info@birminghamtheatreschool.co.uk
website www.birminghamtheatreschool.co.uk
Principal Chris Rozanski

Full-time acting courses:

• HND Performing Arts/Theatre Acting (2 years). Applicants must be aged 18 or over with BTEC level 3 or A level qualifications.
• BTEC Extended National Diploma in Performing Arts (Acting) (2 years). Applicants must be aged 16 or over.
• Professional Acting Diploma (1 year). Applicants must be aged 18 or over.
• Part-Time Evening Acting Diploma. Termly.
• Acting for Beginners. Autumn, spring and summer terms, 11 weeks per term.

The Bridge Theatre Training Company
Admin: Harrow Business Centre, 429-433 Pinner Road, Harrow, Middlesex HA1 4HN, Courses: The Academy Mews, 15 Pratt Mews, Camden, London NW1 0AD
tel 020 7424 0860
email admin@thebridge-ttc.org
website www.thebridge-ttc.org
Joint Artistic Directors Mark Akrill and Judith Pollard

The Bridge is a non-profit organisation which provides intensive training for a professional acting career. Courses include comprehensive career guidance, and a graduating season of public productions in London theatres, with a West End showcase in front of agents, directors and casting directors.

Full-time acting courses:

• Professional Acting Course (2 years). Applicants must be aged 18 or over.
• Professional Acting Course (1 year postgraduate/post-experience). Applicants must be aged 21 or over, with a university degree or significant relevant experience.

Bristol Old Vic Theatre School*
2 Downside Road, Clifton, Bristol BS8 2XF
tel 0117 973 3535
email enquiries@oldvic.ac.uk
website www.oldvic.ac.uk
Facebook BOVTS

Twitter @BOVTS
Instagram @bovtsbristol
Principal Paul Rummer *Artistic Director* Jenny Stephens

Member of the Conservatoire for Dance and Drama. All courses are entirely vocational and are validated by the University of the West of England.

Full-time acting courses: Applications for BA Hons and MFA through UCAS. All applicants are auditioned - please see our sebsite for details of regional audition locations.

• BA Hons Professional Acting (3 years).
• MFA in Professional Acting (1 year, 40 weeks, for international students).
• Summer Foundation Course in Acting (10 weeks) - apply directly to the School.

City Lit
Keeley Street, Covent Garden, London WC2B 4BA
tel 020 7492 2542
email drama@citylit.ac.uk
website www.citylit.ac.uk/courses/acting-diploma-level-3
Patron Jonathan Miller

An intensive year-long course will provide students with a thorough foundation in actor training. Course starts mid-Spetember and runs Thursday evenings and all day Saturdays. Please contact the department for details.

Working with industry professionals and experienced teachers, candidates will develop skills in actor's voice, movement, physicality and singing. Students will hone their craft across a range of specialisms, from classical training through to screen performance. Students will perform in a full-scale theatre production at the end of the course. Graduates from this course gain the Diploma in Performing Arts (level 3), accredited by Open College Network London, with UCAS points for college of university entry.

The course timetable is designed to fit around part-time employment.

Applicants for the course will ideally have completed a full level 2 Foundation course or equivalent (at least one years' actor training).

Entry is by audition. Please prepare two two-minute monologues (one classical, one contemporary) and be prepared to attend a day-long workshop.No audition fee. Auditions in July, August and early September.

Students can apply for ann Advanced Learner Loan from Student Finance England for all or part of the fees for this course. For more information contacct the Drama department Monday-Friday 10:00-16:00 on 020-7492 2582 or email drama@citylit.ac.uk.

Court Theatre Training Company
The Courtyard Theatre, Bowling Green Walk, 40 Pitfield Street, London N1 6EU

tel 020 7739 6868
email info@courttheatretraining.org.uk
website www.courttheatretraining.org.uk
Principal/Director June Abbott *Key contact* Sarah Meadows

As well as the BA (Hons) Acting 2 Years (see below), offers a postgraduate acting course and training for directors and stage managers – please consult the website for further details. The site has wheelchair access and there is a support system for students who are dyslexic.

Full-time acting courses:

• BA (Hons) Acting (2 years) – a distinctive course specially designed for the practical training of the actor; work can take place within the professional environment of an acclaimed working theatre. Applicants must be aged 19+ with 120 UCAS points. Some public funding is available. Applications should be made directly or via UCAS/CUKAS by the end of July.

Cygnet Training Theatre*

Cygnet Theatre, Friars Gate, Exeter EX2 4AZ
tel 01392 277189
email info@cygnettheatre.co.uk
website www.cygnettheatre.co.uk
Principal Rosalind Williams *Artistic Director* Alistair Ganley

Cygnet offers 3-year full-time training based in its own studio theatre alongside a 1-year foundation course and post-graduate options. Ensemble training: delivering technical skills in acting, voice, movement and singing through dedicated workshops, one-to-one tutorials, and an ongoing commitment to public performance and touring.

Functions as a small touring company, drawing its members from all over the UK and abroad. Successful applicants demonstrate talent, flexibility, maturity, awareness and self-discipline. Applicants must be aged 18 or over. Professional Acting Certificate; ATCL & LTCL as appropriate. Stage Combat (BADC) exams.

The Dorset School of Acting

Lighthouse, 21 Kingland Road, Poole, Dorset BH15 1UG
tel 01202 922675
email admin@dorsetschoolofacting.co.uk
website www.dorsetschoolofacting.co.uk
Co-founders/Principals James Bowden & Laura Roxburgh

The 1 year diploma course in Acting & Musical Theatre has a 100% success rate in placing students at reputable drama schools for further training or into professional work. It is designed to provide a real insight into the rigours of drama school training, giving classes in acting, dance, voice and singing, tutorial sessions, theatre visits and business advice. Holds at least 3 masterclasses a year, taught by major,

current industry professionals who are leaders in their field. The school welcomes applications from students with disabilities, and is happy to make adjustments to ensure that its courses are inclusive. It does not expect applicants to be strong in all disciplines when they audition.

Acting courses offered:

• 1 Year Diploma in Acting & Musical Theatre (30 weeks) – the qualification gained is Trinity ATCL Level 4 in Drama & Speech. Applicants should be aged 16+. Applications should be made directly to the school by the end of July.
• 2 Year Diploma in Acting & Musical Thatre (78 weeks) – the qualification gained is Trinity LTCL Level 6 in Drama & Speech. Applicants should be aged 18+. Applications should be made directly to the school by the end of July.
• Fully funded 2-year vocational sixth form (level 3) in Acting (72 weeks) – the qualification is an extended diploma equivalent to 3 A levels. Funding is only available for students 16–19 years. Applications should be made directly to the school by the end of July.

Drama Centre London*

Granary Building, 1 Granary Square, London N1C 4AA
tel 020 7514 7023
email drama.centre.admissions@csm.arts.ac.uk
website www.arts.ac.uk/csm/drama-centre-london
Programme Director, Drama and Performance Fred Meller *BA Acting Course Director* David Jackson

Trains students to become professional actors, directors and writers. Established in 1963, it is now part of the University of the Arts London, and is a member of Drama UK. The school awards 3 Foundation Scholarships; 1 Reeves Scholarship; 5 UK/EU Leverhulme Scholarships; and 2 International Leverhulme Scholarships. For detailed information on Scholarships and Bursaries, see the website under 'Apply and Funding'.

Full-time acting course:

• BA (Hons) Acting (3 years). Applicants must have 2 A levels or equivalent. 16 places are available. Public funding/student loans available for all UK/EU students doing their first degree. Applications should be made through UCAS.
• MA Acting (45 weeks). 20 places are available.
• MA Screen: Acting (60 weeks over 16 months). 18 places are available.

Note that applicants for both MA courses must have a related degree, a diploma in dance or drama, an honours degree in another discipline supported by performance-related experience (professional, amateur or student), or significant professional experience. Applications are made direct to the school.
• Diploma in Foundation Studies (Performance) (30 weeks). Applicants must have 1 A level or a BTEC

National Diploma in Performing Arts or equivalent. 20 places are available. Applications are made direct to the school.

Drama Studio London (DSL)*

1 Grange Road, London W5 5QN
tel 020 8579 3897
email admin@dramastudiolondon.co.uk
website www.dramastudiolondon.co.uk
Managing Director Kit Thacker *Head of Degree Acting* Aileen Gonsalves

Drama Studio London (DSL) provides full time, professional acting training for the profession by the profession, for anyone over 18 with passion, talent and an open-minded approach. Auditions and open days are held from September onwards. For a prospectus or more information and to apply, visit the website or contact **admissions@dramastudiolondon.co.uk**. Diploma students have the option of taking the Trinity College London National Certificate in Professional Acting,along with their DSL Diploma.

• 1 Year Diploma in Professional Acting
• 2 Year Diploma in Professional Acting
• 3 Year BA (Hons) in Professional Acting validated by De Montfort University
• Short Evening Courses and summer schools

E15 Acting School*

Hatfields, Rectory Lane, Loughton IG10 3RY
tel 020 8508 5983 *fax* 020 8508 7521
email east15@essex.ac.uk
website www.east15.ac.uk
Director Chris Main *Key contact* Lindsay Rule (Executive Assistant)

Full-time acting courses: All BA courses are 3 years. Deadline for applications in June.

• BA Acting, BA Acting (International), BA Acting and Community Theatre, BA Acting and Contemporary Theatre, BA Acting and Stage Combat, BA Physical Theatre
• BA World Performance

All acting courses require a successful audition. For additional academic requirements see course setails on the website.

Other full time undergraduate courses:
• Certificate of Higher Education in Theatre Arts (1 year)
• BA Stage and Production Management (3 years)
• BA Theatre Making and Producing
• MA Acting (1 year). Selection for this course is based upon experience and potential. All applicants must be over the age of 21; there is no upper age limit. Applicants must hold a BA degree (normally at least a 2:1) or have suitable previous life professional or academic experience
• MA/MFA in Acting (International)

Please see the website for details of the above courses.

École Internationale de Théâtre Jacques Lecoq

57 Rue du Faubourg Saint-Denis, 75010 Paris
tel +33 (0) 1 4770 4478 *fax* +33 (0) 1 4523 4014
email contact@ecole-jacqueslecoq.com
website www.ecole-jacqueslecoq.com
Principal Mrs Pascale Lecoq

Founded in Paris in 1956, with the aim of producing a young theatre of new work, generating performance languages which emphasise the physical playing of the actor. Focuses on art theatre, but with the view that theatre education is broader than the theatre itself: "It is a matter not only of training actors, but of educating theatre artists of all kinds." Provides as broad and durable a foundation as possible for every student. Also offers part-time courses. See also the company's entry under *Short-term and part-time courses* on page 36.

Full-time acting courses:
• Professional Course (Certificate – Master Level; 2 years). No public funding available. Applications should be made direct to the school from November to June (generally after June there is a waiting list). Applicants must be aged 21+ with initial theatre training and stage experience.

Fourth Monkey

The Monkey House, 97-101 Seven Sisters Road, London N7 7QP
tel 020 7281 0360
email office@fourthmonkey.co.uk
website www.fourthmonkey.co.uk
Artistic Director Mr Steven Green

A training provider with a difference, offering full- or part-time ensemble-based contemporary Rep training and professional performance opportunities. Shortlisted for *The Stage*'s School of the Year award.

Full-time acting courses:
• Two Year Rep (2 year full-time actor training programme, 40 hours per week. Based in London and includes a month-long residential programme in Italy). Applicants must be aged 18 and over. Performance experience and A-Level qualifications or similar desirable, but not compulsory.
• Year of the Monkey (1 year full-time actor training programme, 20-35 hours per week variable, concluding at the Edinburgh Fringe Festival). Applicants must be aged 18 and over. Performance experience and A-Level qualifications or similar are desirable, but not compulsory.

Fourth Monkey accepts applications from all areas of society; the only factor impacting suitability on any training programme is the presence of talent, a desire to learn and develop and an equal desire to work as an ensemble company member.

The Giles Foreman Centre for Acting

Studio Soho,
entrance in Royalty Mews (next to Quo Vadis),
22-25 Dean Street, London W1D 3AR

tel 020 7437 3175
email info@gilesforeman.com
website www.gilesforeman.com
Director Giles Foreman *Key contact* Lindsay Richardson

An exciting professional acting studio housing some of the country's top coaches in the disciplines of screen- and theatre-acting, movement, voice, improvisation, on-camera, Meisner technique, movement psychology and character analysis – directing and text analysis.

Comprises 2 easy-access large bright air-conditioned studios plus changing room, chillout area and kitchen, props store. (Wheelchair-accessible, entrance lift and step-free studio facilities.) Plus separate airy daylight-studio and meeting-rooms. Wi-Fi throughout. Offers the opportunity for professional actors to develop their skills through regular acting classes and workshops, and to create projects in both film and theatre. Specialised intensive masterclass short courses offered by internationally renowned practitioners from all over the world. Due to its location at the heart of the the UK film, TV and theatre industry, also offers many opportunities to meet casting directors, directors and producers through industry showcases, casting-network and Q&A evenings.

Professional coaches available to prepare actors for auditions and self-tapes, and develop characters for projects they have secured.

Full-time courses:

• Post-Graduate-Equivalent Intensive Diplomas in Acting and Directing (15 months). One half-scholarship available. Applicants should be aged 20 or over. PCDL registered.
• Foundation ATCL Diploma (11 months, evening and weekend-mode). Validated by Trinity College London. Applicants should be aged 17 or over.

GSA, Guildford School of Acting*

University of Surrey, Stag Hill Campus, Guildford GU2 7XH
tel 01483 560701 *fax* 01483 535431
email gsaenquiries@gsa.surrey.ac.uk
website www.gsauk.org
Facebook @theGSA
Head of GSA Sean McNamara

Guildford School of Acting was founded in 1935 and is part of the University of Surrey. GSA is a vibrant community of performers, performance makers, creative practitioners and technicians graduating from a wide variety of programmes each year. from 1964 onwards has concentrated on the vocational training of actors and stage managers.

Full-time acting courses: Applications for undergraduate courses should be made via UCAS. Applications for the BA (Hons) Theatre (conversion by distance learning) and for Foundation and Postgraduate courses should be made direct to the University of Surrey.

• Foundation Acting (1 year).
• Foundation Musical Theatre (1 year).
• BA (Hons) Acting (3 years). Applicants must be aged 18 or over, with 3 A levels.
• BA (Hons) Musical Theatre (3 years). Applicants must be aged 18 or over, with 3 A levels.
• BA (Hons) Actor Musician (3 years). Applicants must be aged 18 or over, with 3 A levels.
• BA (Hons) Theatre Production. Applications must be aged 18 or over, with 3 A levels.
• BA (Hons) Actor Musician (3 years) Applicants must be 18 or over, with 3 A levels.
• BA (Hons) Theatre and Production (3 years). Applicants must be 18 or over, with 3 A levels.
• BA (Hons) Dance. Applicants must be aged 18 or over, with 3 A levels.
• BA (Hons) Theatre (1 year on-line learning conversion programme).
• MA in Acting (1 year) Applicants must be aged 21 or over.
• MA in Musical Theatre (1 year). Applicants must be aged 21 or over.
• MA Stage Management and Production (1 year). Applicants must be aged 21 or over.

Guildhall School of Music & Drama*

Silk Street, Barbican, London EC2Y 8DT
tel 020 7628 2571 *fax* 020 7256 9438
email registry@gsmd.ac.uk
website www.gsmd.ac.uk
Vice Princiapl and Director of Drama Orla O'Loughlin
Head of Acting Brodie Ross

Full-time acting courses:

• BA (Hons) Acting (3 years). Applicants must normally be at least 18 years old at the start of the course with a minimum of 2 A-level passes or equivalent. Students on the course undertake classes in voice, movement and acting technique, and work on a variety of extended rehearsal projects which include modern plays, Restoration, musical theatre, Russian naturalism and Shakespeare.
• MA in Acting (3 years). Designed for students who have a university honours degree and wish to have a full professional training in acting. The MA students work in the same classes, rehearsals and performances as the students on the 3-year BA in Acting course. They take additional modules developing their critical and reflective skills and are required to achieve more demanding learning outcomes and a higher standard overall. Throughout the 3 years clear guidance is given on starting in the acting profession. There are regular talks from alumni of the School, and visits by regional theatre directors, agents, casting directors, tax advisers and representatives from Equity. In the third year all students take part in a showcase performance in the West End which is open to agents, casting directors and industry professionals.

Entrance for both the BA and MA course is by audition. Applications should be made direct to the School as early as possible and by mid-January at the latest. At the point of audition, no distinction is made between applicants to the BA and the MA. Student Support from the UK Government is available for most EU students.

We consider diversity to be an enriching and vital part of theatre-making. We welcome applications from individuals with disabilities and encourage them to disclose relevant information regarding any disability when completing their application form, to enable us to provide support during the audition process.

International School of Screen Acting
The Old Lab, 3 Mills Studios, Three Mills Lane, London E3 3DU
tel 020 8709 8719
email enquiries@screenacting.co.uk
website www.screenacting.co.uk
Facebook www.facebook.com/screenactingUK/
Twitter @ScreenActingUK
Instagram @ScreenActingUK
*Key contact*James Berkery

Founded in 2001, ISSA is the leading specialist screen acting school in the UK. It runs as a full time drama school dedicated to preparing actors for today's TV and filmindustry.Based within 3 Mills Studios, the school is at the heart of a creative and successful media village.

Full-time acting courses:
• One Year Full Time Advanced Screen Acting.
• Two Year Screen Acting.

Italia Conti Academy of Theatre Arts*
'Avondale', 72 Landor Road, London SW9 9PH
tel 020 7733 3210
email acting@italiaconti.co.uk
website www.italiaconti-acting.com
Director of Acting Programmes Chris White

A member of FDS, the Academy offers a 3-year BA (Hons) Acting Degree, validated by the University of East London, as well as a 1-year CertHE Introduction to Acting course which is in preparation for full-time actor's training. Italia Conti Academy of Theatre Arts is a world-renowned centre for actor training. Its graduates populate the performance industries and it is this commercial edge that makes the BA (Hons) Acting course unique. It is one of the country's leading vocational acting courses with an emphasis on professional development and employability.

Full-time acting courses:
• BA (Hons) Acting (3 years). Applicants must be aged 18 or over with 5 GCSEs (grade C or above), including English and maths, and 2 A levels (grade E or above) or equivalent.
• CertHE Introduction to Acting (1 year). Applicants must be aged 18 or over with 5 GCSEs (grade C or above), including English and maths.

Kogan Academy of Dramatic Art
9-15 Elthorne Road, Archway, London N19 4AJ
tel 020 7272 0027 *fax* 020 7272 0026
email info@scienceofacting.com
website www.scienceofacting.com
Principal Neil Sheffield *Office Manager* Dennis McGeown

Formerly known as The Academy of the Science of Acting and Directing.

Full-time acting courses: No public funding is available for the courses listed below, but students may apply for a limited number of scholarships. There are daytime and evening courses.

• Three Year Acting Course. offering a BA (Hons) in Acting accredited by Kingston University. Applicants must be aged 18 or over. Offers 30 places each year.
• Two Year Acting Course. Applicants must be aged 18 or over. Offers 30 places each year.
• One Year Acting Course. Applicants must be aged 18 or over. Offers 30 places each year.
• Evening Courses. "One to One" sessions, workshops and other training also available.

LAMDA (London Academy of Music & Dramatic Art)*
155 Talgarth Road, London W14 9DA
tel 020 8834 0500 *fax* 020 8834 0501
email admissions@lamda.ac.uk
website www.lamda.ac.uk
Principal Sarah Frankcom

LAMDA (London Academy of Music & Dramatic Art) is a world-leading conservatoire, providing exceptional vocational training in the dramatic arts. We prepare actors for sustainable careers in the industry. You can see our alumni at the National Theatre, the RSC, Shakespeare's Globe, on London's West End, on Broadway and on big and small screen worldwide.

As part of the Conservatoire for Dance and Drama, LAMDA receives funding from the Higher Education Funding Council for England (HEFCE). This means that eligible UK/EU students are able to access loans to assist with their tuition fees. LAMDA and the Conservatoire also have a range of scholarships and bursaries available to ensure that the most talented students can access training, regardless of their financial circumstances.

Committed to recruiting on talent alone, LAMDA auditions and/or interviews everyone who submits an application by the advertised deadline, providing they meet the age requirements for the training. We do not ask applicants for specific academic qualifications; we ask only for talent, passion and a commitment to learn.

Full-time acting courses:
• BA (Hons) Professional Acting (3 years). Minimum entry age is 18. Admission is by audition and interview.

• MFA Professional Acting (2 years). Minimum entry age is 18, but due to the experience necessary for this course, most students will be 21 and over and hold a first degree in a relevant subject.
• MA Classical Acting for the Professional Theatre (1 year). This course is for international students with a BA or BFA degree or equivalent. Students without this qualification must demonstrate a comparable level of knowledge and experience gained in a professional company or vocational drama school. Admission is by audition and interview.
• Foundation Diploma (1year). Minimum entry age is 18. Admission is by audition and/or interview dependent on experience and career intent. This course is not validated by a higher educstion institution; it is part of LAMDA's own range of non-accredited diplomas.
• LAMDA Semester Diploma in Classical Acting (14 weeks). Minimum entry age is 18 and admission is by application only. International applicants may apply to LAMDA directly or through their home university or college.

Please visit **www.lamda.ac.uk** for further details, application deadlines and fees, as well as information on all other LAMDA courses.

The Liverpool Institute for Performing Arts (LIPA)*

Mount Street, Liverpool L1 9HF
tel 0151 330 3000
email admissions@lipa.ac.uk
website www.lipa.ac.uk
Facebook @LIPALiverpool
Twitter @LIPALiverpool
Instagram @lipaliverpool
Principal Mark Featherstone-Witty

LIPA offers a Foundation Certificate in Acting, BA (Hons) Acting, BA (Hons) Acting (Screen & Digital Media) and MA in Acting (Company.

Full-time acting courses:

• Foundation Certificate in Acting (1 year). This highly practical course aims to provide you with the skills, tools and knowledge to stand out from the crowd and improve your chances of securing a place at one of the top drama schools. Apply direct to LIPA.
• BA (Hons) Acting (3 years). Offers training that prepares actors for rehearsal, performance, production, interdisciplinary creation and industry engagement. Working with traditional and innovative approaches, you expand your phychological and physical processes to hone your acting methodology. Apply to LIPA via UCAS and a LIPA application form.
• BA (Honss) Acting (Screen & Digital Media) (3 years). LIPA's intensive and practical training prepares actors to work across established mediums and emerging digital story-telling platforms. Also learning off-camera skills (including scriptwriting and

filmmaking techniques) enables the student to create a digital portfolio. Apply to LIPA via UCAS, followed by an online LIPA form.
• MA Acting (1 year). On this course you will create original ensemble work to perform and tour as a professional company, supported by funding from us. You will also receive advanced training to further your technical skills and approach. Apply direct to LIPA.

London Academy of Radio, Film & TV

1 Lancing Street, London NW1 1NA
tel 0870 626 5100
website www.media-courses.com
Director of Courses Andy Parkin *Key contact* Estelle Burton

The school has more than 30 teaching staff; around 1,200 students take one or more of its 100+ courses. It is situated opposite Euston Station.

Full-time acting courses:

• Diploma in Screen Acting. Application deadline is June. Age range: 16+. Entry is by audition: 1 modern and 1 classical speech.

London School of Dramatic Art

4 Bute Street, London SW7 3EX
tel 020 7581 6100
email enquiries@lsda-acting.com
website www.lsda-acting.com
Principal Jake Taylor *Administrator* Misha Arntsen

Offers a range of comprehensive courses designed to develop individual creative talents, and to provide a thorough grounding in all aspects of performance as part of a student's preparation for a working life as an actor. There is currently no wheelchair access to the main building or training rooms: if this affects applicants who would like to know when these spaces become accessible, please let the school know. All auditions are free and no international student fees are charged. No formal qualifications are required as the training is vocational: "We look more at potential and at levels of creativity."

Full-time courses:

• Advanced Diploma in Acting (1 year). No public funding available. Applications should be made to the school by the end of September. Applicants must be aged 18 or over.
• Foundation Diploma in Acting (1 year). No public funding available. Applications should be made direct to the school by the end of September. Applicants must be aged 18 or over.

London School of Musical Theatre

83 Borough Road, London SE1 1DN
tel 020 7407 4455
email info@lsmt.co.uk
website www.lsmt.co.uk
Twitter @TheLSMT

Training

Principal/Course Producer Adrian Jeckells

Full-time courses:

• Musical Theatre Diploma Course (1 year). Age range for entry is 18-35.

London Studio Centre (LSC)
Artsdepot, 5 Nether Street, Tally Ho Corner, North Finchley, London, N12 0GA
tel 020 7837 7741
email info@londonstudiocentre.ac.uk
website www.londonstudiocentre.org
Facebook www.facebook.com/LdnStudioCentre
Twitter @LdnStudioCentre
Director Nic Espinosa *Admissions Manager* Sarah Tudor *Dean of Studies & Programme Leader* Robert Penman

London Studio Centre is a professional dance college accredited by the Council for Dance Education and Training. Courses include: BA (Hons) Theatre Dance (validated by Middlesex University), a Foundation Course, LSC Diploma and Saturday Associate Programmes.

LSC's facilities include state-of-the-art dance and drama studios and access to fully equipped theatres. LSC graduates are regularly seen performing on stage in London's West End and in international dance companies.

Manchester School of Theatre at MMU*
School of Theatre, 70 Oxford Street, Manchester M1 5NH
tel 0161 247 1933 *fax* 0161 247 6875
email msaprogteam1@mmu.ac.uk
website www.theatre.mmu.ac.uk
Programme Leader BA (Hons) Acting David Salter

Full-time acting courses:

• BA (Hons) Acting (3 years). Applicants must be aged 18 or over with 2 A levels or equivalent. Applications should be made through UCAS by January.

Mountview*
Peckham Hill Street, London SE15 5JT
tel 020 8881 2201 *fax* 020 8829 0034
email enquiries@mountview.org.uk
website www.mountview.org.uk
Facebook /mountviewLDN
Twitter @mountviewLDN
Instagram @mountviewldn
Principal Stephen Jameson

Full-time acting courses: Applications for the courses listed below should be made direct to the school.

• BA (Hons) Acting (3 years). Applicants must be aged 18 or over, usually with A levels but these are not essential. Dance and Drama Awards are available for a significant number of students.

• BA (Hons) Actor Musician (3 years). Applicants must be aged 18 or over, usually with A levels but these are not essential. Dance and Drama Awards are available for a significant number of students.
• BA (Hons) Musical Theatre (3 years). Applicants must be aged 18 or over, usually with A levels but these are not essential. Dance and Drama Awards are available for a significant number of students.
• PG Dip in Acting/MA in Performance (1 year). Applicants must be aged 21 or over, usually with a university degree.
• PG Dip in Musical Theatre/MA in Performance (1 year). Applicants must be aged 21 or over, usually with a university degree.

The MTA (The Musical Theatre Academy)
Bernie Grant Arts Centre, Town Hall Approach Road, Tottenham Green, London N15 4RX
tel 020 8885 6543
email info@theMTA.co.uk
website www.theMTA.co.uk
Principal Annemarie Lewis Thomas

The MTA run the UK's first accelerated learning programme for multi-disciplinary performers, meaning that their students are industry-ready in 2 years as opposed to the more traditional 3. The acting component of the musical theatre course is split 50/50 between stage and screen acting. The college only employs working professionals ensuring that students are taught current and relevant industry thinking. The college has received industry plaudits for its work and is extremely successful at gaining students agent representation on completion of the course, with nearly three-quarters of graduates still in the industry carving out careers.

Oxford School of Drama*
Sansomes Farm Studios, Woodstock, Oxford OX20 1ER
tel 01993 812883 *fax* 01993 811220
email info@oxforddrama.ac.uk
website www.oxforddrama.ac.uk
Principal Edward Hicks

The smallest of the drama schools, it has a 94% employment rate and an 'Outstanding' Ofsted rating. Provides a significant number of Dance and Drama Awards and Advanced Learning Loans for its 1- and 3-year courses. Also offers its own Hardship fund which is distributed each year to students on full-time courses at the school. Students not in receipt of a DaDA are prioritised for funding. The Sir John Gielgud Charitable Trust currently supports the school and, in addition, students have also won the Laurence Olivier Bursary, the Spotlight Prize, the Alan Bates Award, and the BBC Carleton Hobbs bursary award.

Full-time acting courses: Applications for the courses listed below should be made direct to the school by 31 May.

• Three Year Acting Course. Applicants must be aged 18 or over.
• One Year Acting Course. Applicants must be aged 21 or over.

Poor School

242 Pentonville Road, London N1 9JY
tel 020 7837 6030 *fax* 020 7837 5330
email acting@thepoorschool.com
website www.thepoorschool.com
Principal Paul Caister

The school was created in 1986 with the aim of providing high-quality acting training that is financially within the reach of all, or almost all. Training lasts 2 years and operates in the evenings and at weekends until the final 2 terms, when daytime work is involved. Since March 1993 the Poor School has owned its own theatre, the Workhouse; this is a flexible studio theatre seating 50-80.

Full-time acting courses:

• Two Year Acting Course (6 terms). Most students are in their early 20s but the school offers many places to older and younger people. Auditions are held throughout the year. In their graduating year, students present 2 showcases for the profession only as well as a season of plays for the public.

RADA (Royal Academy of Dramatic Art)*

62-64 Gower Street, London WC1E 6ED
tel 020 7636 7076
email enquiries@rada.ac.uk
website www.rada.ac.uk
Facebook /Royal Academy of Dramatic Art
Twitter @RADA_London
Instagram @royalacademyofdramaticart
Director Edward Kemp

RADA offers vocational training for actors, stage managers, designers and technical stage craft specialists.

Train in acting full-time
• BA (Hons) in Acting
• MA Theatre Lab
• Foundation Course in Acting (non-HE)

Train in theatre production full-time
• Foundation Degree (FdA) in Technical Theatre and Stage Management
• BA (Hons) in Technical Theatre and Stage Management (progression year)
• Post-graduate Diploma (PgDip) in Theatre Costume

RADA also offers an MA in Text and Performance in partnership with Birkbeck, University of London as well as short courses throughout the year in acting and theatre production. RADA training is practical, intensive and rigorous, and offers the highest level of teaching with unparalleled links to the industry, and

an impressive track record of graduate employment as award-winners and leaders in their field.

More details on all the courses are available on the RADA website **www.rada.ac.uk**.

The REP College

17 St Mary's Avenue, Purley on Thames, Berks RG8 8BJ
email tudor@repcollege.co.uk
website www.repcollege.co.uk
Key contact David Tudor

Provides acting students with 1 year of practical education, including 14 public performances.

Full-time acting courses:

• Acting Course (1 year plus shorter courses). Applicants must be aged 18 or over.

Rose Bruford College*

Lamorbey Park, Burnt Oak Lane, Sidcup DA15 9DF
tel 020 8308 2600 *fax* 020 8308 0542
email enquiries@bruford.ac.uk
website www.bruford.ac.uk
Principal and CEO Clarie Middleton

Full-time acting courses: Applicants for the BA degree courses listed below must be over the age of 18 with the equivalent of a minimum of 2 A levels at grade C or above. BA Applications should be made through UCAS and MAs through the college website.

• BA (Hons) Acting (3 years)
• BA (Hons) Actor Musicianship (3 years)
• BA (Hons) American Theatre Arts (3 years)
• BA (Hons) European Theatre Arts (3 years)
• MA Ensemble Theatre (1 year)
• MA Theatre for Young Audiences (1 year)

Royal Academy of Music

Musical Theatre Department, Marylebone Road, London NW1 5HT
tel 020 7873 7483 *fax* 020 7873 7484
email d.bowling@ram.ac.uk
website www.ram.ac.uk/mth
Head of Musical Theatre Daniel Bowling MMus
Programme Leader Louise Shephard *Musical Theatre Company Coordinator* Stephen Minay

Students are enrolled at the Royal Academy of Music, an institution of world renown, training students for more than 190 years. Students study for University of London degrees. Fellow students include instrumentalists, composers, jazz and commercial musicians, pianists and opera singers.

Full-time acting courses:

• One Year Musical Theatre Programme. Aimed at graduates, mature students and experienced performers wishing to undertake a career in musical theatre. The course provides an intensive training in singing, acting, movement and voice to students of postgraduate (or equivalent) level. Includes extensive one-to-one tuition with expert tutors and industry showcase, projects for invited industry guests and public performances.

Royal Birmingham Conservatoire*

Jennens Road, Birmingham B4 7XG
tel 0121 331 5901
email info@bsa.bcu.ac.uk
website www.bsa.bcu.ac.uk
Principal Julian Lloyd Webber *Vice Principal – Acting, Professor of Acting Training* Stephen Simms

Full-time acting courses:

• BA (Hons) Acting (3 years). Applicants must be aged 18 or over by the time the course commences with 2 A levels (grade E or above) or equivalent. Admission is by two-stage audition.
• MA/PgDip Acting (1 year). Applicants must have a first degree and some relevant experience. Admission is by audition.
• BA (Hons) Applied Performance (Community and Education) (3 years). Applicants must be aged 18 by the time the course commences with a minimum of 2 A levels or equivalent (240 points). Candidates will be invited to an interview and workshop assessment.
• BA (Hons) Stage Management (3 years). Applicants must be aged 18 by the time the course commences, with a minimum of 2 A Levels or equivalent (240 points). Candidates will be invited to interview.
• MFA Acting (The British Tradition) (2 years). Applicants must have a first degree and some relevant experience. Admission is by audition in the USA, Birmingham or by DVD.
• MA/PgDip Professional Voice Practice (1 year). Applicants must have a first degree and some relevant experience. Admission is by audition.

The Royal Central School of Speech and Drama*

64 Eton Avenue, London NW3 3HY
tel 020 7722 8183 *fax* 020 7722 4132
email enquiries@cssd.ac.uk
website www.cssd.ac.uk
Principal Gavin Henderson *Head of Acting* Geoffrey Colman

Scholarships/Bursaries Central has a range of scholarships, bursaries and awards available for students on its undergraduate and postgraduate programmes. Visit the website for further details.

Undergraduate courses:

BA (Hons) Acting – Offers three specialist courses Acting, Acting Collaborative and Devised Theatre and Acting Musical Theatre. Entry requirements are 2 A levels at grade C, 3 GCSEs at grade C and selection by audition. Normal offers may be higher and depend upon expected grades and audition performance. Exceptionally, applicants who do not meet this requirement, but demonstrate appropriate potential, may be accepted. Applications should be made through UCAS by January.

BA (Hons) Theatre Practice (Performance Arts) – 3 A Levels at BBC and subject to an interview and participation in a selection day. Normal offers may be higher and depend upon expected grades, their portfolio and performance at interview. Exceptionally, applicants who do not meet this requirement, but demonstrate appropriate potential, may be accepted. Applications should be made through UCAS by January.

Postgraduate courses:

All MA courses listed below are for postgraduates or actors (aged 21 or over) with significant professional experience. Applications for all postgraduate courses should be made direct to the school:

• Acting
• Acting for Screen
• Actor Training and Coaching
• Movement Studies
• Musical Theatre
• Performance Practices and Research

Royal Conservatoire of Scotland*

100 Renfrew Street, Glasgow G2 3DB
tel 0141 332 4101 *fax* 0141 332 8901
email admissions@rcs.ac.uk
website www.rcs.ac.uk
Principal Jeffrey Sharkey

Full-time acting courses: Applications for the undergraduate courses listed below should be made via **www.ucas.com/ucas/conservatoires** by 15 January 2020 (UK/EU) or International (non-EU) by 31 March 2020. Applications for postgraduate courses listed below should be made via **www.ucas.com/ucas/conservatoires** by 31 March 2020. Please email admissions@rcs.ac.uk for more information.

Courses available:

• BA Acting (full-time, 3 years)
• BA Musical Theatre (full-time, 3 years)
• BA (Hons) Contemporary Performance Practice (full-time, 4 years)
• MA Musical Theatre - Performance/Musical Directing (full-time, 1 year)
• MA Classical and Contemporary Text - Acting/Directing (full-time, 1 year)

Royal Welsh College of Music and Drama*

Castle Grounds, Cathays Park, Cardiff CF10 3ER
tel 029 2039 1361
website www.rwcmd.ac.uk
Principal Helena Gaunt *Head of Actor Training* David Bond *Drama Admissions Officer* Luise Moggridge

Full-time acting courses:

• BA (Hons) Acting (3 years). Applicants should normally be at least 18 years old by the time of enrolment. There is a range of support in place to help cover the cost of tuition, the details of which will

depend on where the student normally lives. Applications should be made through CUKAS.
• Postgraduate Diploma in Acting for Stage, Screen and Radio (1 year). Applicants should normally be at least 21 years old by the time of enrolment. Applications should be made directly to the college.
• MA in Acting for Stage, Screen and Radio (4 terms – September until January). Applicants should

normally be at least 21 years old by the time of enrolment. Applications should be made directly to the college.
• MA in Musical Theatre (3 terms – January until December). Applicants should normally be at least 21 years old by the time of enrolment. Applications should be made directly to the college.

Checklist of drama school deadlines, audition requirements, audition fees and funding systems

Postgraduate courses often have different application deadlines and funding systems. Compiled by Lloyd Trott.

School	Definition of 'Classical'	Definition of 'Modern/ Contemporary'	Other Parameters	Audition Fee	Funding System	Application Deadline
ALRA	Shakespeare/Jacobean	After 1980	No longer than 2mins each	£45	DaDA/ student loans	End of March
1ArtsEd	Classical (preferably Shakespeare) "8-10 lines of heightened text"	Written after 1980 – no more than 2mins	Short dialogue at recall stage – provided by school – to camera	£45	DaDA or student loans	Late February
Birmingham School of Acting	Elizabethan/Jacobean (they provide you with a list that you MAY choose from)	"Last 20 years"	No longer than 2mins each; a song for the recall, with sheet music – no more than 3mins	£46	Maintained	Mid-May
Bristol Old Vic Theatre School	Pre-1800	Post-1956	Speeches should not exceed 2mins. You also need an unaccompanied song. A piece of sight reading will be given to you with a few minutes to prepare	£50	UCAS Conserva- toires	Last working day in February
Royal Central School of Speech and Drama	Two from supplied list	After 1960	None	£55	Maintained	Mid-January – via UCAS
Drama Centre	Shakespeare/His Contemporaries	After 1830	Speeches should not exceed 3mins	£50	Maintained	Mid-January – via UCAS

School	Definition of 'Classical'	Definition of 'Modern/ Contemporary'	Other Parameters	Audition Fee	Funding System	Application Deadline
Drama Studio	Classical	After 1955		£45	DaDA	No set deadline
East 15	Shakespearean/Jacobean – "no more than 1.5mins&rdquo	After 1950 – "no more than 2mins"	A 3rd speech that contrasts well with the modern speech – no longer than 2mins	£55	Maintained	Mid-April – via UCAS
Guildford (GSA)	Written before 1800	Written after 1950	A Shakespeare sonnet	£45	DaDA/ Maintained	Mid-January – via UCAS
Guildford School	Shakespeare/Jacobean – verse (blank or rhymed)	Written after 1956	And a contrasting speech from a 20th or 21st century play; speeches no longer than 2mins each; a short unaccompanied song sung in English	£64	HEFCE	24th January
Italia Conti	One from supplied list	Post-1950	No more than 1.5mins each	£45	Maintained	Late March – via UCAS
LAMDA	Elizabethan/Jacobean	Modern	No longer than 3mins each and clearly contrasting; asked to sing at recall	UK/EU £54; non-EU £85	Maintained	Early March
LIPA	One from supplied list	After 1960	2min devised piece	£40	Maintained	Mid-January – via UCAS
Manchester School of Theatre	Shakespeare – blank verse	After 1970	And a contrasting speech from any published play; no more than 2mins each	£45	Maintained	15th March
Mountview	Blank verse prior to 1800. Translations permitted	After 1997	No longer than 2mins each	£45	DaDA	Mid-February
Oxford	Elizabethan/Jacobean	After 1950	No more than 2mins each	£45 (EU) £55 (non-EU)	DaDA and Advanced Learner Loans	31st May

School	Definition of 'Classical'	Definition of 'Modern/ Contemporary'	Other Parameters	Audition Fee	Funding System	Application Deadline
RADA	Elizabethan/Jacobean	After 1960	Second Classical speech may be required; a song in recall	£45 until 10th December, £86 after that	Maintained	End February
Rose Bruford	16th/17th/18th century or Ancient Greek	After 1960 – "not verse"	No more than 1.5mins each	£45	Maintained	Mid-January – via UCAS
Royal Conservatoire of Scotland	Shakespeare – "preferably in verse"	A contrasting contemporary speech from a play published in the last 30 years	No less than 1min and no more than 3mins each; song	£55 + admin £2	Maintained	UK/EU 15th January. International 31st March both via UCAS conservatoires
Royal Welsh	(Recall only) Elizabethan/ Jacobean	From 1956	No longer than 2mins each	£47 (may be waived where there is proof of exceptional hadrship)	Maintained	15th January – via CUKAS

Notes:
• When only 'Classical' is specified, this can mean anything written before about 1800.
• When only 'Modern' or 'Contemporary' is specified, you should be fine with anything written after 1945 – and speeches written between 1900 and 1945 have often proved acceptable in this category.
• 'Verse' is sometimes specified – this doesn't mean that it necessarily needs to rhyme. In fact, some schools specify 'blank' (i.e. non-rhyming) verse.
• You'll find various definitions in the 'Classical' column – "Shakespearean/ Jacobean", "Elizabethan/Jacobean", "Shakespeare/Contemporaries". Strictly, these all imply slightly different (but overlapping) periods in history. In practice, anything written between about 1560 and 1640 should be fine.
• All schools ask that there is sufficient contrast between 'Classical' and 'Modern/ Contemporary' speeches.

• See individual schools' websites for more detailed audition requirements and advice.
• UCAS & CUKAS (www.cukas.ac.uk) fee (where appropriate) is in addition to each school's audition fee.
• Musical Theatre & other specialist courses usually have additional audition requirements.
• Some schools will allow late applications, but they can't guarantee you an audition and may charge a higher audition fee.
• Some schools offer free auditions to those from low-income households.
• Also see *Effective audition speeches* on page 157.

Warning:
Some of these details may change for entry in future years. Please inform the Editor of any such changes at **lloydtrott@rada.ac.uk**.

What are drama schools looking for?

Geoffrey Colman

A lifelong contract

Many drama school applicants underestimate the fact that becoming an actor is about signing a sort of lifelong and extraordinary contract that contains the most incredible clause – one that requires the artist to metaphorically go to places both dark and light, to represent, live and die for us. Seven times a week or in fourteen takes. To successfully navigate such challenges one must possess a licence, for to 'go there' is not something that everybody can or wants to do. Not everybody has the talent. Not everybody is prepared to dedicate the years of preparation required to become an actor. Alas, many also underestimate the phenomenal personal responsibility of such an undertaking and delude themselves that it can be achieved by just wanting it very much – like a child wants ice-cream. I have not found this to be the case.

In the last ten years there has been significant expansion in the field of actor-training. The professional or conservatoire sector comprises schools that subscribe to, and are measured by, a set of overarching industry-approved principles held by the Federation of Drama Schools (FDS) **www.federationofdramaschools.co.uk** (the individual FDS schools are listed on the checklist preceding this article). The core principles state that the selection process is by audition, and that training will be professionally aligned, intensive, and delivering at least 900 hours of practical contact teaching a year. Many thousands apply to the FDS schools each year, for a precious few places. Of course, conservatoire training is not for everyone. There are many university drama departments where the courses, whilst not offering 30+ professional contact hours per week, do offer a vast range of performance-related academic disciplines that can be studied both theoretically and practically. Such programmes, though perhaps less specialist, do offer the student excellent opportunities to act, write, and direct whilst developing their own individual performance interests and skills.

Recent years have seen emerge a vast catalogue of non-professional diploma and degree-awarding courses offering performance-related study and preparation. Often curated by established conservatoires, such courses give the less experienced performer invaluable insight into the ways of the conservatoire system, and are particularly useful when considering whether professional actor training is a viable option.

What are you looking for? Do your research

Despite the existence of excellent regulating bodies such as the Quality Assurance Agency – which sets important benchmarks for the delivery of training, published student surveys and the names of famous alumni – across the conservatoire drama schools there is significant variation in terms of funding (including tuition top-up fees), quality of training, award outcomes (certificate, diploma, degree), and most certainly graduate employment prospects, which differ from school to school. So never mind the question about what are drama schools looking for – what are *you* looking for? Most candidates have such a limited, almost passive, expectation about what drama schools want at audition, and of the actual training itself. The first task is, therefore, not to perfect some extraordinarily well-honed accent or radical audition monologue interpretation, but rather, many months prior to this process, to undertake a sleeves-rolled-up systematic approach to a lot of very necessary research into the sector itself. If you are going to commit three years of your life to something, you really should find out what that something is!

All drama schools and university drama departments publish their entry requirements in either a glossy prospectus or more typically on a website, but, as such, these only really describe required entry criteria, a brief course outline and, in the case of some drama schools, a list of suggested classical audition speeches. Drama schools require potential students to audition, whilst it is not unusual for the university sector to offer some, but not all, candidates an interview and workshop. Entry requirements and selection criteria vary from institution to institution, but in general terms, the university sector is looking for well-qualified students with excellent A-level or equivalent qualifications. The conservatoire sector, on the other hand, bases its selection much more on audition success than exam grades, and is looking for 'evidence of ongoing commitment to acting' (such as having played featured roles in youth theatre production companies), 'evidence of a trainable voice and body', 'evidence of intellectual, emotional and physical skills', and so on. These competencies are all there waiting on the audition panellist's check list. There is not a section that refers to 'tingle factor' or 'star quality' because this is only found on the fame TV panellist's laminated sheet. Equally, there isn't an additional sub-criteria requirement listing particular body types to balance future casting designs not yet discussed.

The choice of audition speech preoccupies many candidates who unearth an astounding range of two-minute extracts – often inappropriately sourced from internet material that disallows any creative placement of their own heart and mind. Don't obsess about contrasting this or the other. Just select an extract from a play that is simple, clear, unfussy and – most important of all – one that allows for you to enter its world without a fight (and most certainly without the need to show that you are entering it). People do bring much worked-upon accents, props, shouts, peculiar moves, glances and screams, as though volume alone will do the trick. This should be avoided. Remember, too, that audition panellists experience the gamut of human suffering in two-minute chunks. But emotion in itself is not the gold medal if it is false, inappropriate or showy (especially without real context). The audition day is not merely there to equip the candidate with a jolly site tour or a space within which to recite a contrasting classical and contemporary speech. It might even, just possibly, offer some sort of snatched insight into how the course might be taught. To enter the world of drama school depends upon something far more fundamental than a set of well-worn, clichéd, seen-it-in-the-movies assumptions.

Both the conservatoire and university sector see the value of Open Day events – and so should you. The real answers required are sometimes just a little bit more abstract. Open Days afford a terrific and all-important onsite 'experience' of the building, its community of staff and students, and general but –nevertheless important – 'feel' of the place. Training institutions have rightly been questioned about how they construct their communities and, in particular, what they are doing to increase diversity. A recent parliamentary enquiry into access and diversity in the performing arts concluded that, despite many positive initiatives, drama schools needed to reform. One long-held perception that is difficult to dispel is that the whole audition process is very expensive. Whereas university drama departments accept applications via a centralised UCAS system, drama schools also ask for an additional fee. Many of the conservatoires within the Federation of Drama Schools now offer audition-fee waivers – offering free or heavily subsidized auditions to those facing the greatest barriers to attending.

If possible, attend a few plays or musicals performed by final-year students from different schools or departments as this can be extremely useful in that it demonstrates a very public slice of the quality of teaching and professional guidance offered. Once started, this level of cultural forensic work will certainly enable you to identify at least where you would like to study. But why do you want to become an actor? This is the real question that you must ask. Not so that you can decorate your application form or personal statement with incredible, but quite useless, prose (as often audition candidates do), but rather, align all future coordinates to it. You will need to refer to this answer for the rest of your life.

Audition actively, with clarity and commitment

It was the jaded theatre producer Emmanuel Azenberg who pessimistically described how successful entry into the ranks of the professional Broadway musical chorus required an alarming, but necessary, process of becoming a kind of *fabulous invalid* – a gradual giving up of self and becoming unable to do or cope with anything other than being in the chorus itself – never really knowing who deals the cards – and, in fact, never really knowing what the game is in the first place! Having been involved with drama school auditions for many years, I would suggest that his observation might just as well apply as a cautionary tale to those many thousands of audition candidates that approach the day with all-too-little consideration for the task and commitment ahead.

The craft of acting is not limited to a single method or approach; it is joyfully promiscuous. But for every actor we witness on our screens or in the theatre itself we also encounter a different sort of promiscuity. Some actors are famously trained and some are just famous, possessing a peculiar, but much desired, cultural tag. The 'celebrity' is often 'untrained', but connected to the performance industry by events that afford measurable charisma, enigma or sensation. As such celebrities may not in the short term need a drama school training, but rather, a constant stream of tabloid stories showing hasty late-night retreats from exclusive bars and restaurants. Such activities can (and occasionally do) open doors and give entry into the industry – but the hinges that hold them are tissue-thin – and the doors will not always remain permanently open!

Look diligently before you leap

Training is not casual, but quite conservative and very ordered indeed. One class follows another and then another. How do you fit into this delightful regime? It can be repetitive and exhausting. The panel will look for signs of someone who can cope with this or not. A professional training is a physical, emotional, muscular assimilation of many processes. Learning lines is not the issue – but learning the difficult routine and discipline of acting can be. The audition is as much about assessing this point as to whether a given Juliet or Hamlet is believable.

Like many momentous occasions in life the drama school audition can be so very memorable. Like the first day of the school summer holidays or the first page of a new novel or even your first kiss. For there to be a first day at drama school is an achievement in itself. And yet to audition is to be part of an occasion mixed with both excitement and fear. Excitement in that all the waiting and preparation is over – but also fear regarding what happens if a place is not offered. To be an acting student at a conservatoire drama school is not to be part of something that is either casual or meaningless. But success in the current climate is now also measured by other indictors. Most students juggle outside work commitments with a very heavy workload of study and somehow exist on far less money than is possible. Drama school training is impacting – it marks all those who experience it. Yes every move, every gesture and vocal shift is catalogued for later dissection. But this is why to be trained is not to take an unfathomable leap in the dark. Sacrifices will have to be made and we must ensure that in the new funding climate becoming an artist will not render a fearful voiceless future to all but a privileged few.

What drama schools want is to restore the helplessness of our own lives through the long productive and meaningful careers of future artists like you. Don't take an unfathomable leap. Only if you're utterly convinced should you sign the training contract – but prepare for this moment with diligence, care and humility. Good luck!

Geoffrey Colman is Head of Acting at The Royal Central School of Speech and Drama.

Short-term and part-time courses

This section lists both 'taster' opportunities for drama school aspirants, and further training for professional actors.

Pre-drama-school courses

Competition for drama school places seems to be growing even more ferocious, and many applicants will enhance their chances if they go on a pre-drama-school course. You may, for example, have done A level Drama, but the actual acting training on such courses is often limited – generally geared more towards the exam-passing university entrant than auditioning for drama school. Whatever your acting background, a 'taster' course (for just a week, for instance) can give you a good idea of what further help/training you need in order to prepare you properly for drama school auditions.

Additional skills

As well as the organisations listed below, there are periodic 'one-off' workshops around the country. These are usually 'trailed', and sometimes advertised, in *The Stage*. Equity occasionally subsidises such enterprises (some, away from the major cities), so it is worth checking with your local Branch/Organiser. Actors Centres are not just places to sharpen up your existing skills and develop new ones, but also great meeting places for actors to exchange ideas and information.

Academy of Creative Training

8/10 Rock Place, Brighton, East Sussex BN2 1PF
tel 01273 818266
email info@actbrighton.org
website www.actbrighton.org
Principal/Director Janette Edisford

All classes are in the evenings and at weekends to allow students to undertake actor training whilst maintaining their domestic and financial commitments. Monthly payment options are available by arrangement. Entry onto long courses is via audition (*Fee*: £30) or attendance on a 2-week intensive workshop (*Fee*: £100) held monthly throughout the year and designed as an introduction to actor training. Students embarking on the Diploma in Acting are eligible to audition for a bursary. Range of short courses and Summer Schools. The school operates an equal opportunities policy that includes disabled students, but there is limited access to the dance studio and washroom facilities.

Courses offered:

• ATCL Diploma in Acting (2 years). For students aged 18+. *Audition requirements*: as above
• Intensive Foundation Course (1 year, 10 hours per week). For students aged 16+. *Audition requirements*: as above
• Creative Playground (12 weeks of 3 hour Masterclasses, runs each term)
• Introduction to Playwriting (2 terms)
• Musical Theatre (12 weeks of 3 hour classes, runs each term).

Academy of Performance Combat (APC)

mobile 07963 206803
email info@theapc.org.uk
website www.theapc.org.uk

APC is dedicated to bringing combat in any form in any media into the 21st century. "We are absolutely committed to safer, more exacting techniques than any other organisation." Please see the website for more details of courses and qualifications offered.

Actor Works

First Floor, Raine House, Raine Street, Wapping, London E1W 3RJ
tel 020 7702 0909
email ask@actorworks.org
website www.actorworks.org
Director Daniel Brennan

Full-time evening and weekend course: This course is designed for those who may:

• need to work during the day to pay for their training;
• have family commitments that prevent them from studying in the day;
• be considering changing their career and need to keep 'the day job' until the acting bug finally bites for good.

It is an intensive, 2-year vocational training, which covers all aspects of an actor's work. Subjects covered include: acting for stage, screen acting, actors' movement, speech, voice, reading, audition technique, stage combat, dance, singing and theatre history. During the course students will take part in up to 5 different productions, normally at the end of every term.

The course culminates in an agents' showcase at a major theatre and a season of graduation plays on the London fringe.

Students on this course must be aged 20+. There is no upper age limit.

There are 6 terms in all.

Postgraduate course: This course is designed for those who:
• studied drama at university and would like some more 'hands on' experience;
• have had actor training and would like to hone their skills.

This is a 1-year daytime course, which offers full actor training. Subjects covered include: acting for stage, screen acting, actors' movement, speech, voice, reading, audition technique, stage combat, dance, singing and theatre history. During the course students will take part in up to 4 different productions, normally at the end of every term.

The course culminates in an agents showcase at a major theatre and a season of graduation plays on the London fringe.

Students on this course must be aged 21+. There is no upper age limit.

There are 3 terms in all.

Foundation course: This course is designed for younger students who:
• need guidance and support through the gruelling process of auditioning for major drama schools;
• have not yet decided whether acting is for them;
• want to do something productive with their gap year.

This 1-year daytime course is not full actor training as such, but it prepares students for what they will experience should they choose to take up acting as a career. Emphasis is placed on preparation, application and discipline. We encourage confidence and a feeling of self-worth which helps students through the audition process. Subjects covered include: voice, speech, actors' movement, audition preparation, stage combat, theatre history and reading. Students can expect to take roles in 3 different productions over the year.

Students on this course must be between the ages of 17 and 20.

There are 3 terms in all.

Other courses offered: Also now runs a part-time course designed for those who wish to pursue acting as a leisure interest. "You may wish to 'test the water' before considering full-time training; to improve your self-confidence in group situations; to improve your public-speaking skills; or perhaps simply enjoy a new activity one night a week." These qualifications are currently NVQ Level 3 equivalent and from 2008 count for between 20 and 65 points towards UCAS tariffs. The cost for 10 Tuesday evenings is £350. For LAMDA tuition on Thursdays, an extra £100 (plus the cost of exam – £40-£50).There is no need to audition, though "please phone us in the first instance to reserve a place, before sending payment".

Actors Centre
1A Tower Street, Covent Garden,
London WC2H 9NP
tel 020 3841 6600
email reception@actorscentre.co.uk
website www.actorscentre.co.uk
Facebook www.facebook.com/The ActorsCentrel
Chief Executive Louise Coles

Founded in 1978. The Actors Centre runs workshops and courses from its venue in the heart of the West End. The Centre boasts five studios, a Green Room Cafe and Bar, and incorporates the Tristan Bates Theatre. Their members-only professional workshop programme is unrivalled and covers all aspects of performance and business skills development for the working actor. Membership is assessed and approved against a professional criteria that demands a level of training, experience and/or affiliation with recognised industry bodies. Membership comes with a host of of benefits including access to the building, studio/ theatre hire discounts, perks, free opportunities and access to workshops and courses in the quarterly programme. The Actors Centre also runs workshops and courses for non-members, programmed throughout the year and on a bespoke basis.

Regular workshops include Acting, Screen Acting, Shakespeare, Auditioning, Improvistion, Voice, Dialect, Voiceovers, Stage Combat, Physical Theatre, Musical Theatre, Writing and Career Advice. In addition, members can book individual sessions to work on Audition Technique, Accents, Marketing/ Branding, Voice and Singing.singing, acting,

Please see the website for more information.

Actors Temple
13-14 Warren Street, London W1T 5LG
tel 020 3004 4537
email bookiings@actorstemple.com
website www.actorstemple.com
Co-founders Mark Wakeling and Ellie Zeegen
Managing Director Ashlie Walker

Actor training studio, offering part-time, ongoing and flexible courses, classes and workshops for actors of all levels and experiences. Influenced by Sanford Meisner, the training has been extensively developed over the past 15 years. An inclusive and supportive community of creatives, their ethos is to create an atmosphere which inspires confidence and to equip

Training

actors to build a career in the world of acting. Weekly taster sessions are open to all. Contact to book a place and for more information.

ArtsEd*

Cone Ripman House, 14 Bath Road, Chiswick, London W4 1LY
tel 020 8987 6666
website www.artsed.co.uk

Courses offered:

• Post-Diploma BA (Hons) in Musical Theatre or Acting. Validated by City University. A three-year course.
• Foundation in Musical Theatre or Acting (1-year full-time).

EXCELerate Part-Time Courses in Acting or Musical Theatre. 3 evenings per week running over 3 terms, starting in Spetember.

Part-time evening and holiday courses for 17+ years:
• Various courses in acting and musical theatre disciplines, including stage, screen, voice, dance and audition technique, are offered for varying skill levels throughout the year.

For full details on all courses offered at ArtsEd, please visit **www.artsed.co.uk**.

Associated Studios Performing Arts Academy

The Hub, St Alban's Fulham,
2 Margravine Road London W6 8HJ
tel 020 7385 2038
email info@associatedstudios.co.uk
website www.associatedstudios.co.uk
CEO/Founding Principal Leontine Hass

Founded in 2007, Associated Studios offers professional development and training for musical theatre performers. For those interested in training, there is a two-year felxible and one-year full-time Musical Theatre course (4 days per week). There are also several professional development programmes, masterclasses and short courses throughout the year, giving professional and/or experienced performers the opportunity to work on their skills. Applicants for all courses must be 18+ and all applicants must audition for a place on the course. Visit the website for regular updates.

Full-time courses:
• 1 Year Musical Theatre Diploma (full-time, 4 days per week)
• 2 Year Musical Theatre programme (Flexible: Year 1: 4 days per week, Year 2: 2 days per week)
• 1 Year Musical Theatre Foundation course (part-time, 1 day per week)
• 7 Month Musical Theatre Course (part-time — 2 days per week)
• 4 Month Musical Theatre Course (part-time — 2 days per week)

• 1 Year Opera (part-time, 2 days per week)
• 4 Month Opera (part-time, 2 days per week, September and February intake)
• Open masterclasses also offered

The Birmingham Theatre School

The Old Fire Station, 285-287 Moseley Road, Highgate, Birmingham B12 0DX
tel 0121 440 1665
email info@birminghamtheatreschool.co.uk
website www.birminghamtheatreschool.com
Principal Chris Rozanski *Key contact* Fiona Allison (Arts Admin Manager)

Courses offered:

• Part-time Professional Diploma (Evenings & Weekends). Applicants must be aged 18 years or over.
• Acting for Beginners (11 weeks). Covers the basics of character creation, voice, improvisation and performance discipline for acting beginners. Students participate in all aspects of the creative process, from basic exercises to final presentations. Classes take place in the evening.
• Creating Performance (11 weeks). Each term, students will create and perform using a variety of techniques and using both texts and devised work. All aspects of character creation and working with an audience will be explored. Suitable for people with previous experience in acting. Classes take place in the evening.

The Bloomsbury Alexander Centre

Bristol House, 80A Southampton Row, London WC1B 4BB
tel 020 7404 5348 020 8374 3184
email info@alexcentre.com
website www.alexcentre.com
Directors Stephen Cooper, Natacha Osorio

The centre specialises in teaching the Alexander Technique. Teachers are available for private lessons, with discounts available for students and actors. There are ongoing introductory workshops and courses, as well as drop-in vocal work for actors with experience of the AT. The introductory course runs for 4 weeks (1.5 hours a week) and costs £80. The drop-in AT vocal work classes are £15 per session. *Note for disabled actors:* "Our premises are on the ground floor with one step up onto the main entrance and one other just inside."

Boden Studios

99 East Barnet Road, New Barnet, Herts EN4 8RF
tel 020 8447 0909 *fax* 020 8449 5212
email info@bodenstudios.com
website www.bodenstudios.com
Director Adam Boden

Established in 1973. A part-time performing arts school offering 1 full scholarship each year.

Courses offered:

• Acting Performance – 12 weeks, 1.5 hours per week

• Guildhall Drama Exams – 12 weeks, 1 hour per week

British Academy of Dramatic Combat

website www.badc.co.uk

Offers a Performance Certificate in Stage Combat at Foundation, Basic, Basic Level 2, Recommended and Advanced levels. Training is available in the following methods: Broadsword & Shield, Double Handed Broadsword, Quarterstaff, Rapier & Dagger, Rapier & Cloak, Rapier & Buckler, Smallsword, Unarmed Combat. Programmes of workshops are arranged throughout the country, and anyone with suitable venue spaces or wanting to be added to the workshop mailing list should email **workshops@badc.co.uk.**

The British Academy of Stage & Screen Combat

Kemp House, 152 City Road, London EC1V 2NX
email info@bassc.org
website www.bassc.org
Facebook www.facebook.com/TheBASSC
Twitter @TheBASSC
Instagram @the_BASSC

The British Academy of Stage & Screen Combat was founded in 1993 with the aim of improving the standards of safety, quality and training of stage combat, and promoting a unified code of practice for the training, teaching and assessing of stage combat within the United Kingdom.

All BASSC teachers have undergone a rigorous training programme and the examining members of the BASSC are highly qualified, experienced professionals with a tradition of working in theatre throughout the UK, including the National Theatre, RSC, Royal Opera House, Donmar Warehouse, Liverpool Everyman, Theatre Royal York and Newcastle and Shakespeare's Globe, and television and film productions such as: *Vikings* (Seasons 1-5), *Dawn, Fallen, Berserk, American Patriot, Anna Karenina, Ironclad, The Eagle, Hammer of the Gods, Alexander, Troy, Stardust, The Last Legion* and *Sherlock Holmes* 1 & 2.

BASSC teachers train students in stage combat at numerous drama schools, universities and colleges including: RADA, the Royal Central School of Speech and Drama, the Royal Birmingham Conservatoire, Drama Studio London and Bath Spa University. They also teach students outside of drama courses at independently run classes and workshops including the annual British National Stage Combat Workshop. Teachers run classes and workshops in the USA, Germany, Spain and the Ukraine.

Since its formation the BASSC has established a reputation as the invigorating driving force behind stage combat in the United Kingdom, and is respected, both nationally and internationally, as the leading provider of professional-level stage combat training.

As a result of this, British Equity, in 1997, recognised the BASSC's Advanced Certificate as a valid qualification for entry onto the Equity Fight Directors' Training Scheme, and in 2001 the BASSC was appointed by the Equity Council for the training and assessment of Fight Director candidates applying to join the Equity Fight Directors' Register.

The BASSC now has training schemes in place which allow for development from actor/combatant to Certified Teacher, as well as assessment and training of Fight Directors for the Equity register.

The City Lit

Keeley Street, Covent Garden, London WC2B 4BA
tel 020 7492 2542
email drama@citylit.ac.uk
website www.citylit.ac.uk
website www.cltheatre.co.uk
Head of Drama, Dance & Speech Vivienne Rochester

The college offers an eclectic mix of disciplines such as acting, movement, voice, musical theatre, teaching, media, mime, circus, stage fighting, magic, comedy, dance, self-presentation, debating, accents, sight-reading and pronunciation for speakers of other languages, etc., which develop vocational, social and personal skills.

There are various small grants that might cover travel, books or child-care. Students may ring or come into the office for an interview between 12.30pm and 1.30pm (Monday and Wednesday), or 5.30pm and 6.30pm (Monday, Tuesday and Thursday).

The City Lit Theatre Company was set up to train a company of actors to produce work of the highest professional standard, providing a platform for its members to hone their skills and display their talents. Directors, teachers and practitioners are invited and engaged to facilitate. Its members are made up of a combination of graduates from the accredited courses, or from the advanced/professional provision in the Drama, Dance & Speech department's programme, and experienced practitioners who wish to further their experience with the college. Auditions are held annually. The college has awarded associate status to a number of actors who have produced an excellent body of work with the company. All company members are eligible for the 3 productions staged each year, and some productions transfer on to other venues. Also, artists are invited, if appropriate, to professional castings that are occasionally held at The City Lit. Professional Masterclasses are held throughout the year.

The accredited courses are as follows (Drama UK recognised):

• Professional Acting Diploma (2 year full-time). Entry is by audition
• Drama Foundation course (1 year part-time). Entry is by audition

• Access to HE Diploma (drama) (1 year part-time). Entry is by audition
• Stage Fighting (1 year part-time, plus a number of shorter courses). Applicants must be aged 19 or over. Entry is by interview

A range of acting, voice, movement, TV and film, radio presenting classes and other related disciplines are also available. Courses run for 10-12 weeks or shorter with entry at various points throughout the year as well as a summer school throughout the months of July and August. Contact The City Lit for a prospectus and visit **www.citylit.ac.uk/ dramaschool.**

Drama Studio London (DSL)*
1 Grange Road, London W5 5QN
tel 020 8579 3897 *fax* 020 8566 2035
email admin@dramastudiolondon.co.uk
website www.dramastudiolondon.co.uk
Managing Director Kit Thacker

Courses offered:

• Acting Summer School
• Adult Evening Acting Beginners Course (10 weeks)
• Adult Evening Acting Intermediate Course (10 weeks)

E15 Acting School*
Loughton Campus: Hatfields, Rectory Lane, Loughton IG10 3RY; Southend Campus: Elmer Approach, Southend-on-Sea, SS1 1LW
tel 020 8508 5983 *fax* 020 8508 7521
email east15@essex.ac.uk
website www.east15.ac.uk
Facebook @east15actingschool
Twitter @E15actingschool
Instagram @east15actingschool
Director Chris Main *Key contact* Beth Mathieson (Executive Assistant)

Courses offered:

For details of all summer programmes please visit the website **www.east15.ac.uk**

Applicants must be aged 17 years or over.

École Internationale de Théâtre Jacques Lecoq
57 Rue du Faubourg Saint-Denis, 75010 Paris
tel +33 (0) 1 4770 4478 *fax* +33 (0) 1 4523 4014
email contact@ecole-jacqueslecoq.com
website www.ecole-jacqueslecoq.com
Principal Mrs Pascale Lecoq

Founded in Paris in 1956, with the aim of producing a young theatre of new work, generating performance languages which emphasise the physical playing of the actor. Focuses on art theatre, but with the view that theatre education is broader than the theatre itself: "It is a matter not only of training actors, but of educating theatre artists of all kinds." Provides as broad and durable a foundation as possible for every

student. As well as the part-time courses listed below, offers a 2-year full-time Professional Course resulting in a Master Level Certificate. See also the company's entry under *Drama schools* on page 17. As a movement school, all classes require a great degree of physical movement, so applicants must be physically fit.

Courses offered:

• LEM (1 season October-June). 7 hours per week. Entry by file
• Introductory Course (1 season October-June). 5 hours per week. Entry by file
• Workshops online on the website

Fourth Monkey Actor Training Company
The Monkey House, 97-101 Seven Sisters Road, London N7 7QP
tel 020 7281 0360
email office@fourthmonkey.co.uk
website www.fourthmonkey.co.uk
Artistic Director Mr Steven Green

A training provider with a difference, offering full- or part-time ensemble-based contemporary rep training and professional performance opportunities.

Courses offered:

• Two Year Rep. Two year, full-time actor training programme, 40 hours a week. Based in London and includes a second year spent predominantly working as a professional rep company, concluding at the Camden Fringe. Applicants must be aged 18 and over. Performance experience and A-level qualifications or similar desirable but not compulsory.
• Year of the Monkey. One year course, full-time actor training programme, 22-40 hours a week variable, concluding at the Camden Fringe Festival. Applicants must be aged 18 and over. Performance experience and A-level qualifications or similar desirable but not compulsory.
  Accepts applications from all areas of society; the only factor impacting suitability on any training programme is the presence of talent, a desire to learn, enthusiasm to develop and a willingness to work as an ensemble company member.

The Giles Foreman Centre for Acting
Studio Soho,
entrance in Royalty Mews (next to Quo Vadis), 22-25 Dean Street, London W1D 3AR
tel 020 7437 3175
email info@gilesforeman.com
website www.gilesforeman.com
Director Giles Foreman *Key contact* Lindsay Richardson

An exciting professional acting studio housing some of the country's top coaches in the disciplines of screen- and theatre-acting, movement, voice, improvisation on-camera, Meisner technique movement psychology and character analysis, directing and text analysis.

Comprises 2 easy-access large bright air-conditioned studios plus changing room, chillout area and kitchen, props store. (Wheelchair-accessible, entrance lift and step-free studio facilities.) Plus separate airy daylight-studio and meeting-rooms. Wi-Fi throughout.

Courses offered (many run throughout the year):

All ages from 17+.

• Complete Beginners/Introduction to Acting (10 weeks – 3 hours per week). Open entry.
• Intermediate Acting (12 weeks – 4 hours per week). Entry by application.
• Advanced Acting (12 weeks – 4 hours per week). Entry by application.
• Professional Acting (12 weeks – 4 hours per week). Entry by interview/audition.
• Movement (10 weeks – 2 hours per week). Entry by application.
• Voice (10 weeks – 2 hours per week). Entry by application.
• On-Camera (10 weeks – 3 hours per week). Entry by application.
• Meisner Technique (10 weeks – 3 hours per week). Entry by application.

Other courses offered:

• Meet the Industry Evenings (2 hours), September-July. Application via Spotlight or relevant CV.
• Workshops – specialised subjects (12 hours over 2 days). Application by appropriate previous study and/or performing experience.

GSA, Guildford School of Acting*

Stag Hill Campus, Guildford GU2 7XH
tel 01483 560701
email info@gsauk.org
website www.gsauk.org
Head of GSA Terrie Fender

Courses offered:

• Singing in the Theatre (1 week). A summer course designed for students over the age of 17 who wish to improve their singing. Other disciplines relating to the voice will also be explored. Entry is in July.
• Musical Theatre (2 weeks). Culminating in a performance in the Bellairs Playhouse, this course is open to students aged 17 or over and takes place in July/August.
• Audition Techniques (1 week). Course takes place in August and is geared towards students aged 17 or over.
• Intensive Musical Theatre Dance for Beginners (1 week). An intensive course to discover what your body is capable of doing. Explore the foundations of tap, jazz and ballet and get guidance and expert advice on what you need to work on and hopefully gain the confidence to compete in a dance class

situation. The course takes place in August and is open to students 17 years and over.
• Acting for Camera (1 week). The course takes place in August and is open to students 17 years and over.

Other summer schools: Courses are offered at a reasonable cost and provide either a stimulating refresher course or an introduction to basic theatre training. There is no audition procedure, and everyone is welcome. All courses are staffed by members of the GSA faculty.

July/August:
• Youth Theatre (9 days).
• Musical Theatre (2 weeks).
• Intensive Musical Theatre Dance (5 days).
• Intensive Musical Theatre Acting (5 days).
• Intensive Musical Theatre Singing (5 days).
• Audition Technique (2 x 5-day sessions).
• Directing a Musical (5 days).
• Acting for Camera (5 days).

For further information or to download an application form, please refer to the website, or telephone or email (**summerschool@gsauk.org**) for a brochure.

Guildhall School of Music & Drama*

Silk Street, Barbican, London EC2Y 8DT
tel 020 7628 2571 *fax* 020 7256 9438
email dramasummerschool@gsmd.ac.uk
website www.gsmd.ac.uk
Vice-Principal and Director of Drama Orla O'Loughlin
Head of Acting Brodie Ross

Founded in 1880, the Guildhall School is acknowledged internationally as a leading conservatoire for both music and drama.

Courses offered: The 2 adult summer school courses (Acting in Shakespeare & Contemporary Theatre; and Acting in Musical Theatre) each offer 3 weeks of stimulating and inspiring training in acting. Both will include class work or workshops with many of the school's core staff.

• Acting in Shakespeare & Contemporary Theatre. 3 weeks of intensive tuition, workshops and rehearsals. Students have craft-based classes for half of the day; for the other half they work with a director and explore short scenes from Shakespeare and contemporary plays, investigating the texts through group exercises and improvisation. The aim is to demystify Shakespeare and provide a challenging insight into modern drama. The course concludes with a presentation of work-in-progress to students and staff (not open to the public) which may take the form of a workshop or open class.
• Acting in Musical Theatre. 3 weeks of intensive tuition, workshops and rehearsals. Students have craft-based classes for half the day; for the other half they work as an ensemble with a director on a musical project, exploring a selection of scenes, songs and dances based around a theme. The focus of the

course will be upon the craft of acting within the context of musical theatre. It will conclude with a presentation of work-in-progress to students and staff (not open to the public) which may take the form of a workshop or open class. The course is led by Guildhall School tutor Martin Connor, who directs the School's annual musical.

Craft-based classes for both courses include: Acting, Voice, Movement, Improvisation, Mask, Combat, Historical, Dance and Audition Technique. At least 2 visits to attend performances in London theatres are included in the fees of both courses. Applicants must be at least 18 years old by the start of the course; there is no upper age limit. A good standard of English is essential. Accommodation is available. Please consult the website (**www.gsmd.ac.uk/ dramasummerschool**) for up-to-date information on fees, curriculum and application procedure, or telephone 020-7382 7183 for details of the application procedure. Email enquiries to **dramasummerschool@gsmd.ac.uk**
• Drama Summer School (16-17 years). This 2-week course mirrors the approach of our adult summer school and is designed to appeal to various levels of experience, including beginners and those who wish to pursue full-time drama training.

"There is no application deadline but, in view of the limited number of places, applicants are strongly advised to book early. If the summer school is full, you will be placed on a waiting list."

The Impulse Company
Classes in central London
mobile 07525 264173
email info@impulsecompany.co.uk
website www.impulsecompany.co.uk
Principal/Director Scott Williams *Key contact* Lindsay Mohun

Established for over 20 years in the UK, Scott Williams' Impulse Company provides Meisner-rooted core training for the adult actor within a supportive and positive atmosphere. It is currently focusing on its Modular part-time Year course. It also offers short courses, a summer rehearsal and performance programme, and workshops in New York.

Principal course offered:
• Modular Year course. 3 self-contained 8-week terms. Entry is by interview, in October and January each year. 8+ hours per week.
• Second Year Rehearsal & Performance course. 3 self-contained 11-week rehearsal and performance periods per year. Entry is by completion of the Year course, or by invitation. 7+ hours per week.

International School of Screen Acting
3 Mills Studios, Three Mill Lane, London E3 3DU
tel 020 8709 8719
email enquiries@screenacting.co.uk
website www.screenacting.co.uk
Facebook screenactingUK/

Twitter @ScreenActingUK
Key contact Mark Normandy

Founded in 2001 to specialise in offering full-time training specifically in television and film acting, taking a holistic approach to creativity in relation to students' personal development.

Courses offered:
• 'Crash Course' – week-long course offered at various times throughout the year. No audition required.
• Summer Course – week-long course offered in Aug/ Sept. No audition required.
• Weekend Course – ISSA's weekend Screen Acting & Self Taping Course is a two-day intensive to enhance improve and develop performance on screen.

Kogan Academy of Dramatic Art
First Floor, Dwell House, 637 Holloway Road, London N19 5SS
tel 020 7272 0027 *fax* 020 7272 0026
email info@scienceofacting.com
website www.scienceofacting.com
Facebook @koganacademy
Twitter @koganacademy
Head of School Nick Cawdron

Courses offered:
• Three Year Full Time Acting Course. Applicants must be aged 18 or over. This is a BA (Hons) accredited by Kingston University. *Audition requirements/fee*: see entry on
• Three Year Evening Acting Course. Applicants must be aged 16 or over. Offers 14 places each year. *Audition requirements/fee*: see entry on page 19 for details.
• Two Year Evening Acting Course. Applicants must be aged 16 or over. Offers 14 places each year. *Audition requirements/fee*: see entry on page 19 for details.
• One Year Evening Acting Course. Applicants must be aged 16 or over. Offers 14 places each year. *Audition requirements/fee*: see entry on page 19 for details.
• 6 Month Intensive Acting Course for International Students.
• Spring Workshop (2 weeks). Course takes place in March. No audition required.
• Summer Workshop (2 weeks). Course takes place in July. No audition required.

LAMDA (London Academy of Music & Dramatic Art)*
155 Talgarth Road, London W14 9DA
tel 020 8834 0500 *fax* 020 8834 0501
email enquiries@lamda.ac.uk
website www.lamda.ac.uk
Principal Sarah Frankcom *Admissions Assistants* Amy Richardson, Hannah Hurt

Courses offered: Short-term courses are offered in the following areas:

- ShakespeareSummer School (8 weeks)
- Shakespeare (4 weeks)
- English Communication Skills Through Drama (EFL – 3 weeks)
- Audition Technique (2 weeks)
- Introduction to Drama School (2 weeks)
- Introduction to Screen Acting (2 weeks)

The Introduction to Drama School, Introduction to Screen Acting and Audition Technique courses are open to students aged 16 and over; the Shakespeare Short Course is for those aged 17 and over; and the Shakespeare Summer School and EFL courses are both for students 18 years and over. For more information on all LAMDA's courses, including fees and deadlines, please visit the website.

London Academy of Radio, Film & TV

1 Lancing Street, London NW1 1NA
tel 0870-626 5100
website www.media-courses.com
Director of Courses Andy Parkin *Key contact* Estelle Burton

The academy has more than 30 teaching staff; around 1,200 students take one or more of its 100+ courses. It is situated opposite Euston Station.

Courses offered:

- Acting Masterclass (1 week – 30 hours). No audition required
- Acting for Film & TV (9-week course – 9 x 3 hours). No audition required (*Note*: 2 versions of this course exist – 1 on a weekday evening; 1 on a Saturday)

London School of Dramatic Art

4 Bute Street, London SW7 3EX
tel 020 7581 6100
email enquiries@lsda-acting.com
website www.lsda-acting.com
Principal Jake Taylor *Administrator* Misha Arntsen

Offers a range of comprehensive courses designed to develop individual creative talents, and to provide a thorough grounding in all aspects of performance as part of a student's preparation for a working life as an actor. There is currently no wheelchair access to the main building or training rooms: if this affects applicants who would like to know when these spaces become accessible, please let the school know. All auditions are free and no international student fees are charged. No formal qualifications are required, as the training is vocational: "We look more at potential and at levels of creativity."

Part-time 18+ acting courses:

- Diploma in Acting (2 years, 7.5 hours per week). Entry is by audition
- Access to Acting (8 weeks, 2.5 hours per week)

Short-term 18+ acting courses:

- Introduction to Drama School (2 weeks in July)
- Introduction to Drama School (2 weeks in August)

- Screen Acting (1 week in September)
- Audition Techniques (1 week in September)

Manchester School of Acting

14-32 Hewitt Street, Manchester M15 4GB
tel 0161 238 8900
email info@manchesterschoolofacting.co.uk
website www.manchesterschoolofacting.co.uk
Key contact Mark Hudson

High-profile acting school offering part-time training for actors.

Method Acting London

16-18 Heneage Street, London E1 5LJ
tel 020 7622 9742
email main@methodacting.co.uk
website www.methodacting.co.uk
Principal/Director Sam Rumbelow

Within the specifically defined and well-established structure of the classes, provides a grounded, conscious understanding of the craft of acting is facilitated, while unlocking powerful creativity of your thoughts, impulses and emotions. Entry is after a detailed talk and discussion of class and the applicant, conducted by phone.

Part-time/short-term 16+ acting courses:

- Main Class (4 weeks, 16 hours per week)
- Mid Class (4 weeks, 3 hours per week)

Michael Chekhov Studio London

48 Vectis Road,
London SW17 9RG (Administration Office)
tel 020 8696 7372
email info@michaelchekhovstudio.org.uk
website www.michaelchekhovstudio.org.uk
Director Graham Dixon *Key Contact* Ian Bevins

Founded in 2003, the MCSL provides actors (and directors) an opportunity to explore Michael Chekhov's unique approach to the art of acting. Many drama trainings are based upon 'closed systems' that look inside one's own psychology to create a character but Chekhov created an 'open system' that permits actors to enter immediately an objective creative world immediately using an increased ability to imagine and sense. Yearly programs of workshops, intensives on the basic techniques of Chekhov leading to more advanced work including ensemble initiatives and private coaching on the Chekhov approach to the art of acting and directing.

Morley College

61 Westminster Bridge Road, London SE1 7HT
tel 020 7450 1832
email drama@morleycollege.ac.uk
website www.morleycollege.ac.uk
Key contact Dominic Grant

Offers part-time acting classes from entry-level to advanced. Classes are led by specialist acting tutors

Training

with extensive professional experience. An Access Hardship Fund and concessionary fees are available to some students.

Courses offered:

• A range of evening and part-time acting skills courses are available, including: Acting level 1, 2 and 3; Acting: The Company; courses in Physical Theatre, Directing, Playwrighting, Voice, Devising, Mask, Mime, and Clowning. Drama skills including courses for actors with moderate learning disabilities, Confidence through Acting Courses, Public Speaking courses and many others. Morley College also now offers an HND in Performing Arts. Some courses require tutor approval.

Mountview*

120 Peckham Hill Street, London SE15 5JT
tel 020 8881 2201
email enquiries@mountview.org.uk
website www.mountview.org.uk
Facebook /mountviewldn
Twitter @mountviewLDN
Instagram @mountviewldn
Principal Stephen Jameson

Courses offered:

• Foundation Acting (1 year). 9 hours of classes per week. Entry is by audition.
• Foundation Musical Theatre (1 year). 9 hours of classes per week. Entry is by audition.
• Foundation Acting (30 weeks). Full-time. 30 hours of classes per week. Entry is by audition.
• Foundation Musical Theatre (30 weeks). Full-time. 30 hours of classes per week. Entry is by audition.
• Actors' Masterclass (3 weeks), Course takes place in July/August. No audition required.
• Musical Theatre Bootcamp (3 weeks). Course takes place in JulyAugust. No audition required.
• Amateur Directors' Weekend (2 days). Course takes place in July. No audition required.

Oxford School of Drama*

Sansomes Farm Studios, Woodstock,
Oxford OX20 1ER
tel 01993 812883
email info@oxforddrama.ac.uk
website www.oxforddrama.ac.uk
Principal Edward Hicks

Course offered:

• Six Month Foundation Course in Acting, runs from September to March. Aimed at students aged 18 and over. The course covers acting methods and technique, movement, voice, singing, film and television and stage fighting. 32 hours of classes per week for 22 weeks. Graduates include Philip McGinley (regular in *Game of Thrones*) and Lydia Rose Bewley (regular in *The Royals* and *Drifters*). Entry is by audition.

Pineapple Dance Studios

7 Langley Street, London WC2H 9JA
tel 020 7836 4004 *fax* 020 7836 0803

email studios@pineapple.uk.com
website www.pineapple.uk.com

Pineapple offers more classes than any other studio throughout Europe, and the widest variety of dance styles. The philosophy behind the creation of the Pineapple Dance Studios was to break down the elitist barriers surrounding dance, making it available to everyone – from the absolute beginner to the advanced and the professional dancer. All classes are open, so you do not need to book; you can just come along at any time and join a class. Everybody is welcome: Pineapple offers classes for all levels and all ages. Approx. 200 classes per week, ranging from classical ballet to street jazz, hip hop to Salsa, Egyptian dance to Bollywood grooves plus many more. Opening hours: Mon to Fri: 9am–9pm; Sat: 9am–6pm.

Poor School

242 Pentonville Road, London N1 9JY
tel 020 7837 6030 *fax* 020 7837 5330
email acting@thepoorschool.com
website www.thepoorschool.com
Principal Paul Caister

The school was created in 1986 with the aim of providing high-quality acting training that is financially within the reach of all, or almost all. Training lasts 2 years and operates in the evenings and at weekends until the final 2 terms, when daytime work is involved. Since March 1993 the Poor School has owned its own theatre, the Workhouse; this is a flexible studio theatre seating 50-80.

Short courses:

The Poor School runs 4-day courses through the year, and many take these as an alternative to audition. There is also a summer programme of short acting courses from June to September, incorporating 3-week, 4-day and shorter courses. Accommodation in London may be booked through the school.

The Questors Theatre Ealing

12 Mattock Lane, London W5 5BQ
tel 020 8567 0011 *fax* 020 8567 2275
email enquiries@questors.org.uk
website http://www.questors.org.uk/
Principal David Emmet *Key contact* Andrea Bath (Executive Director)

Provides part-time training for actors in the context of a working theatre. Financial support is available from a private trust fund for a limited number of students.

Courses offered:

• Acting: Foundation and Performance (2 years). 6 hours of classes per week. Entry is by audition.
• Introduction to Acting (1 year). Age range for entry is 17-20. 3 hours of classes per week. Entry is by audition.

Royal Academy of Dramatic Art (RADA)*

62-64 Gower Street, London WC1E 6ED
tel 020 7636 7076 *fax* 020 7323 3865

email sallypower@rada.ac.uk
website www.rada.ac.uk
Instagram @royalacademyofdramaticart
Director Edward Kemp

Courses offered:

• Acting Shakespeare (8 weeks). Designed for experienced actors, this course offers an opportunity to expand, explore and deepen awareness of Shakespeare's texts. During the first 6 weeks, you will have classes in physical performance, Alexander Technique, stage fighting, period dance, choral singing of the period, voice, voice and text, character in text, sonnets, monologues and scenes, as well as weekly workshop sessions.The last 2 weeks of the course are spent in full-time rehearsal for a workshop production culminating in 3 performances in a RADA theatre. Entry is by audition. This course takes place in June and July. *Audition requirements*: 1 speech from Shakespeare and 1 from a modern play, each lasting no longer than 3 minutes.
• The RADA Shakespeare Summer School (4 weeks). Based on exploring Shakespeare from an actor's point of view, this course mixes rehearsing scenes and speeches with intensive classes in essential acting skills. Students below the age of 18 are not normally accepted; most students are in their 20s. Course takes place in July and August. No audition required.
• Musical Theatre Intensive (5 weeks). This innovative course is for experienced performers who are intending to pursue a career in musical theatre. You will work with the Academy's staff on singing, voice, movement, acting, combat, clown, dance and much more. The first 3 weeks of the course will focus on skill development, culminating in informal presentations. In the final 2 weeks, you will work with a director and musical director on an abridged musical which you will perform for an invited audience. This performance, though deliberately minimal, and witha concentration on the work of the participants, may serve as a useful showcase for your further professional work. Throughout the course you will be given guidance from our highly experienced teaching team on technique, casting and on developing your personal audition repertoire.
• The RADA Contemporary Drama Summer School (10 days). This course provides the opportunity to work on modern or contemporary texts. Students work in groups led by a director, with support from a voice and a movement instructor. Other playwrights talk about their work during special evening sessions, describing their experience of working with actors and what they expect from them, following presentations of excerpts from their plays by RADA graduates. Students present rehearsed material and receive feedback from the director and the voice and movement teachers on the last day of the course. Students below the age of 18 are not normally accepted; there is no upper age limit.
• European Greats. This 5-day course examines scenes from Chekhov and Ibsen. Fresh approaches to the work of these authors is encouraged, along with looking at how the themes of these plays are still urgent and relevant to us today. Scenes are explored with a director, and participants are asked to thoroughly review their process of rehearsal in accordance with the material. The course is aimed at those with some experience of acting who want the opportunity to explore these writers from the point of view of the performer.
• We run numerous other courses throughout the year. Please check the website.

Richmond Drama School

RACC, Parkshot, Richmond TW9 2RE
tel 020 8891 5907
email art@racc.ac.uk
website www.RACC.ac.uk

Courses offered:

Richmond Drama School offers established courses; including Access to Drama (HE), Foundation Year in Acting, Audition Techniques, Stage Combat, Improvisation, and many others. With an exceptional reputation for outstanding teaching and a strong history of placing students in the country's top CDT drama schools; these include RADA, Central, Guildhall, LIPA and ALRA amongst others. Many previous students, who have not desired an academic pathway, have been able to step straight into the professional industry. Up-to-date details are available from the website.

Rose Bruford College*

Lamorbey Park, Burnt Oak Lane, Sidcup DA15 9DF
tel 020 8308 2600 *fax* 020 8308 0542
email enquiries@bruford.ac.uk
website www.bruford.ac.uk
Principal and CEO Clarie Middleton

Courses offered:

• Acting Summer School (2 weeks). Designed for participants over the age of 18 (16+ for non-residential students), this programme includes classes, rehearsals and workshops on voice, movement, acting and improvisation.
• Acting Advanced Intensive (12 weeks). Designed for professionals wanting additional training.
• MA Ensemble Theatre (full time, 13 months). Designed for professional practitioners to develop their practice as a researcher through experiential learning.
• MA Theatre for Young Audiences (part or full time). Designed to work and study with leading TYA figures.

Royal Birmingham Conservatoire*

200 Jennens Road, Birmingham B4 7XG
tel 0121 331 7200
email info@bsa.bcu.ac.uk
website www.bsa.bcu.ac.uk
Principal Stephen Simms *Admissions Manager* Roger Franke

Courses offered:

• Creative Drama (30 weeks part-time). 3 hours of classes per week
• Acting Summer School. 2 weeks in August
• Shakespeare Summer School. 4 days in August
• Musical Theatre Week. 6 days in August
• Musical Theatre Weekend. 2 days in August

The Royal Central School of Speech and Drama*

64 Eton Avenue, London NW3 3HY
tel 020 7722 8183 *fax* 020 7722 4132
email short.courses@cssd.ac.uk
website www.cssd.ac.uk
Principal Gavin Henderson,

A selection of courses offered:

Evening Courses (3 terms a year)

(18+ years)

• Acting – An Introduction
• Acting – Working with Text
• Acting – The Play
• Acting for Camera
• Acting – Shakespeare
• Audition Technique
• Directing – An Introduction
• Voice for Performance – An Introduction
• Playwriting – An Introduction
• Saturday Youth Theatre for 6-17 year olds

Diplomas

(18+ years)

• Gap Year Diploma (September start)
• Acting Diploma (January start)
• Musical Theatre Diploma (January start)

Summer School (from July to August)

Acting

(17+ Years)

• StageCombat
• Musical Theatre
• Acting for Beginners
• Acting with Text
• Actors' Audition Pieces
• Directed Scenes
• Summer Shakespeare
• Summer Theatre Company
• Acting for Camera for Beginners

Voice

(18+ Years)

• Voice Fundamentals 1: Good Voice Use
• Voice Fundamentals 2: Voice in Performance

Youth Theatre

(Ages 6-17 years)

• Youth theatre for Actors (Age 6-17) (1 week)
• Preparing for Higher Education: Studying Drama (Age 15-17)

Theatre Royal Haymarket Masterclass Trust

Theatre Royal Haymarket, London SW1Y 4HT
tel 020 7389 9660
email info@masterclass.org.uk
website www.masterclass.org.uk
Twitter @Masterclasstrh
Patrons Dame Judi Dench, Sir Peter Hall, Sir David Hare, Maureen Lipman CBE, Elaine Page OBE

Masterclass is a theatre charity based at the Theatre Royal Haymarket that opens doors to young people from all backgrounds, aged 16-30, who are interested in the performance industry. The programme provides workshops and talks with leading actors, directors, designers and writers working in theatre today, alongside unique performance experiences, apprenticeship opportunities and community projects.

Previous Masters have included Danny DeVito, Simon Callow, Mike Leigh, Alan Rickman, Joanna Lumley, Idris Elba, Bradley Cooper and Damian Lewis. For details of forthcoming events, consult the website.

Theatre Workout Ltd

41A Granville Park, Blackheath, London SE13 7DY
tel 020 8144 2290
email enquiries@theatreworkout.com
website www.theatreworkout.com
Facebook TheatreWorkoutAcademy.com
Twitter @theatreworkout
Director Adam Milford

Theatre Workout is the centre for education in London's West End offering official West End workshops, summer schools, short courses and other bespoke workshops.

Youngblood

Top Floor, 57 Paddington Street, Marylebone, London W1U 4HZ
tel 020 7193 3207
email info@youngblood.co.uk
website www.youngblood.co.uk

A company of fight directors and stage-combat teachers. Runs ongoing classes for professional actors in various locations around London. Also provides fight directors and trainers for film, television and theatre projects, including low-budget productions.

Private tutors and coaches

ABI Acting

email abiacting@gmail.com

Specialises in audition technique, relaxation, unlocking and analysing Shakespeare, text preparation and voice training for professional actors and drama school candidates. Also presentation and public speaking skills. Charges a basic rate of £35 per hour, but is happy to discuss with each individual client how a session can be made to meet their specific needs. Is happy to provide material for private students to use, and to answer minor follow-up queries after a lesson.

Teaches at home but is happy to travel to a client's home for a small extra cost. The nearest station is Kensal Green tube or Kensal Rise overground station. – a 7-minute walk. Bus routes are 452, 187, 52 and 6. Is a visiting lecturer and audition panelist at several top London drama schools, tutor and private coach. Is also an actress in TV, film and theatre for over 20 years. "My extensive experience means I understand, and can effectively address, both the actor's needs and the industry's demands."

Acting Audition Success (Philip Rosch)

53 West Heath Court, North End Road, Golders Green, London NW11 7RG
tel 020 8731 6686 *mobile* 07429 255829
email philiproschactor@gmail.com
website actingauditionsuccess.co.uk
Facebook philip.rosch
Twitter @philiprosch
Instagram Philip RoschExceptional numbers of students gain drama school entry having been given great audition speeches; teaches effective sight-reading, powerful improvisation and makes Shakespeare easy. Gives expert career advice to get a superb agent. Also teaches brilliant technique for camera auditions and how to make a spell-binding self-tape. Philip is happy to answer minor follow-up queries at no extra charge.

Charges £70 per hour (with generous extra time for free at the end of almost every lesson). First lesson includes a free extra half hour. All payment methods accepted.

Teaches from home, not wheelchair accessible. Nearest station is Golders Green, then 3-minute walk. Main buses: 13, 82, 83, 102, 183, 210, 226, 240, 245, 260, 268, 328 and 460. Happy to take phone calls to discuss details of his services. Has taught approx. 1,300 actors since 1985.

Philip Rosch is a highly experienced British-American actor and acting tutor with 34 years' experience. He has worked with Timothee Chalamet, Joaquin Phoenix, John C. reilly, Antonio Banderas, Meryl Streep, Idris Elba, John Simm, Luke Evans and Stephen Frears, having numerous high-profile roles in TV, film, theatre, voice-overs, radio, commercials and video-games including: *The King*; *Misfits*; *Mr Selfridge*; *Law & Order: UK*; *The Secret Agent*; *Florence Foster Jenkins*; *Human Traffic*; Shakespeare's Globe Theatre, Old Vic Theatre; Radio 4; Hitman and Hitman 2 (video games).

"Truthful acting is simple and involves just two things: how your character feels and what your character wants. My teaching methods are highly effective in helping any actor give captivating, truthful performances."

Acting Coach Scotland

Unit 21, 6 Harmony Row, Govan Workspace, Glasgow G51 3BA
tel 0141 440 1272
email hello@actingcoachscotland.co.uk
website www.actingcoachscotland.co.uk
Facebook www.facebook.com/ActingCoachScotland
Twitter @hello_acs
Instagram Weareactingcoachscotland
Principals Mark Westbrook and Nick J. Field

Established in 2008, with the aim of making high quality professional training available to all. Acting Coach Scotland offers a bespoke 1-year full time diploma in Stage and Screen Performance and a 3-year part-time option. Staff are working actors, producers, writers, directors and other specialists. No scholarships are currently available.

There are no specific academic requirements for entrance, acceptance is by audition and interview. Applicants should be 17 years or older. The average age of the students is 27. Application should be made directly to the school.

Intensive training in Acting, Improvisation, Acting for Camera, Voice, Accents and Performance Psychology. Students experience 25 public performances, including a 3-week run at the Edinburgh Fringe, and 3 professionally produced short films. Training for the BASSC Actor Combatant (Unarmed and Rapier & Dagger) exam is part of the course.

Students who complete the course are entitled to Graduate Membership of Spotlight.

Applications from applicants with disabilities are welcome. Successful candidates with disabilities will have a full needs assessment before the course begins.

Audition Doctor

South East London
mobile 07764 193806
email tilly.blackwood@gmail.com
website www.auditiondoctor.co.uk

A bespoke service that provides invaluable help for auditions, whether you are a professional actor dealing with confidence issues or a Drama School applicant. Charges £80 per hour. Students bring their own material to work from. Answers minor follow-up queries at no extra charge. Teaches from a home location with weekly surgeries conducted at The Actors Centre (both are wheelchair accessible). The nearest station is Borough on the Northern Line, around a 4-minute walk away. "I have been, and continue to be, a professional working actor for the last 20 years, and have been teaching for the last 3. With my sanity intact and an undwindled passion for the business, I am perfectly placed to give up-to-date assistance, direction and information in an ever-changing profession." Audition Doctor has been listed in the top 10 Acting Coaches on the Acting in London website

Barbara Berkery

London N19
tel 020 7281 3139
email barbaraberkery@hotmail.com

Specialises in accents, voice and text. Details of fees and discounts are available upon enquiry. Happy to provide material for private students to use, and to answer minor follow-up queries at no extra charge. Teaches from home and/or studio, both of which are wheelchair accessible. Main teaching location is 10 minutes' walk from Holloway Road tube (bus routes 17, 43, 271 and 263). Further details are available from IMDb. Has taught hundreds of actors/aspiring actors over a period of 30 years, and possesses extensive experience both as an actress and as a director. Works with her Associates at Vox Barbarae, Elspeth Brodie and Eleanor Boyce, which is often more convenient both financially and logistically.

Nancy Bishop Casting

18 Hanover Street, 4th Floor, London W1S 1YN
email workshops@nancybishopcasting.com
website www.nancybishopcasting.com

Specialises in on-camera audition coaching. Nancy Bishop is primarily a casting director, but sometimes also works as a coach for on-camera auditioning. She is the founder of the Acting for Film department at the Prague Film School, and teaches her technique in masterclasses throughout Europe, as well as in New York, Los Angeles and internationally. She has lectured at the Actors Centre in London, the National Theater Institute in the US, and the Royal Scottish Academy of Music and Drama. Subject to availability, she can coach in London or via Skype, provided it is not for a film she is casting. For more information, see her book, *Auditioning for Film and TV* (Bloomsbury Methuen Drama). Check her website for an audition masterclass schedule.

Main areas of work are film, TV and commercials. Prefers to meet actors during the production process. Welcomes invitations to theatre or screening in London by email.

Irene Bradshaw

Flat F, Welbeck Mansions, Inglewood Road, West Hampstead, London NW6 1QX
mobile 07949 552915
email eyebraddas@gmail.com
website www.voice-power-works.co.uk
Facebook www.facebook.com/VoicePowerWorksIreneBradshaw

Specialises in audition technique, voice/production, RP and accents. Charges £50 per hour, which is a special rate for actors. Provides material for students to use, and all lessons can be recorded on your iPhone or smart phone. She is happy to answer minor follow-up queries. Teaches from home (unless a client is disabled, in which case will travel to theirs); the nearest tube is West Hampstead, a 5-minute walk. Bus routes are C11, 139 and 328.

Has taught "countless" actors and aspiring actors over 43 years. An actress for more than 20 years in film, television and theatre, she trained in the Linklater method of voice production at LAMDA with Kristin Linklater, sponsored by the Arts Council of Great Britain. Has taught at the City Lit, the Actors Centre and most of the leading stage and drama schools, as well as running her own theatre company, where she directed several plays in new writing as well as classics. Has trained numerous students for entry into drama school with considerable success, and has helped many actors find their voice.

Ross Campbell

Private Fulham/West Kensington Studio, London SW6 and Farnborough, GU14
mobile 07956 465165
email rosscampbell@ntlworld.com
website wwwrosscampbelle.biz
website www.dailysingingtips.com, www.thesingersportal.com
Facebook www.facebook.com/rosscampbelluk, www.facebook.com/SingingAnExtensiveHandbook
Twitter @rosscampbelluk

Specialises in singing and acting techniques, audition preparation, college entrance and related examinations and diplomas. Charges £80 per hour. Is happy to provide material for private students to use, and to answer minor follow-up queries after a lesson.

Teaches in a private studio at home in Surrey and a private London studio. The nearest stations are West Brompton and Barons Court – a 7-minute walk. Has taught many actors, singers, triple threat performers for 30 years, and has professionals in every West End show on a continuous basis. Ross is a professor at the Royal Academy of Music London, Director and Head of Singing and Musical Theatre at Musical Theatre UK (MTUK), a former head of music and singing at Guildford School of Acting (GSA) and a consultant to Musical Theatre Poland (MTP). He is also an award-winning author for the ABRSM.

Mel Churcher

mobile 07778 773019
email melchurcher@gmail.com
website www.melchurcher.com

website www.actinganddrama.com

Teaches in Central London and by Skype. More details are available from www.imdb.com and from own websites.

Has taught thousands of actors and aspiring actors over 30 years. Has worked as an actor and theatre director; taught at most major UK drama schools and at the Actors Centre; coached on more than 50 films; run national and international workshops; and authored 2 books: *A Screen Acting Workshop plus DVD* (Nick Hern Books, 2011), and *Acting for Film: Truth 24 Times a Second* (Virgin Books, 2003). Holds an MA in Performing Arts (Middlesex) and in Voice Research (CSSD). "I am happy to help with most aspects of auditioning and working in theatre and film. I can can advise on understanding the differences between film and theatre, film technique, and building confidence and overcoming nerves."

MJ Coldiron

54 Millfields Road, London E5 0SB
mobile 07941 920498
fax 020 8533 1506
email mcoldiron@mac.com

Offers audition coaching for professional and aspiring actors; advice about theatre and performance training in the US and the UK; and coaching in acting technique, public speaking and presentation skills. Charges £45 per hour (3 sessions for £120). Occasional group workshops. Can provide material for clients and is happy to receive minor follow-up queries. Teaches from home studio, with the nearest rail station being Hackney Central Overground. Has taught hundreds of aspiring actors over 25 years: please make contact for more details. Advises clients: "The theatrical profession is very demanding and is not to be sought for fame or fortune. It is also very competitive and you must work hard, but if you have talent, desire and discipline I can help you to improve your technique and gain in confidence."

The Confident Voice

School of Economic Science Building,
11-13 Mandeville Place, London W1V 3AJ
mobile 07976 805976
email neville@speakwell.co.uk
website www.speakwell.co.uk

Specialises in audition technique and voice. Dialogue coach, Shakespeare, musical comedy and lyrical interpretation. Services include coaching in elocution, communication techniques and self-awareness; also the establishment of confidence and natural performance. Fee details are available on application. Offers special packages and coaching in stage, TV and radio techniques. Teaches from the Mandeville Place address, which is wheelchair-accessible. The nearest station is Bond Street underground, around 3 minutes' walk away (bus route 10). Has taught hundreds of actors and directors over 20 years.

Advises clients: "Have complete faith and confidence in *yourself*. Continual work on voice and movement and penetration of Shakespeare – the greatest master Teacher."

Jerry Cox, MA BA PGCE

4 Stevenson Close, Barnet, Herts EN5 1DR
mobile 07957 654027
email jerrymarwood@hotmail.com

Specialises in audition technique and voice. Charges £25 per hour or £40 for 2 hours. Is happy to provide material for private students to use, and to answer minor follow-up queries. Teaches from home or from the client's home. The nearest railway is Oakleigh Park/Totteridge & Whetstone – a 10-15 minute walk from the main teaching location. Bus route 383. Has taught 300-500 actors and aspiring actors over 8 years, and worked as an actor, deviser and director; lots of film, theatre, TIE and touring experience. Advises clients: "To paraphrase Bella Merlin, get the process right, and the results look after themselves."

Bridget de Courcy

19 Muswell Road, London N10

Taught singing at the Actors Centre, Covent Garden for 19 years.

Jane de Florez, LGSM PGDip

West Kensington/Barons Court, London W14
tel 020 7602 0741
email janedeflorez@gmail.com
website www.thetutorpages.com/tutor/jane-de-florez-singing-teacher-earls-court

Specialises in singing technique, repertoire, performance, auditions. Charges £35 per hour. Is happy to provide material for private students to use, and to answer minor follow-up queries at no extra charge. Teaches from home studio, which is 5 minutes' walk from West Kensington and Barons Court tube stations. Has taught hundreds of actors and aspiring actors for the past 20 years, and now sees at least 10 pupils each week who are performers or aspiring performers. Teaches a strong, versatile technique that is suitable for all types of music. Most students go into classical, musical theatre and cabaret.

Antonia Doggett

1 Brading Crescent, Wanstead, E11 3RT
tel 07814 155090
email antoniadoggettcontact@gmail.com
website www.antoniadoggett.co.uk

Specialises in audition preparation, cold reading, text, Shakespeare, voice, LAMDA/Trinity examinations, one to one, courses and workshops. Charges £30 per hour and prefers payment by PayPal or electronic transfer. Is happy to provide material for private students to use, and to answer minor follow-up queries after a lesson.

Teaches at home, or happy to travel to central, south or south east London or client's home. The location is wheelchair accessible and the nearest station is Holborn – a 3-minute walk away. Has taught around actors and aspiring actors for 7 years and previously trained with Teatr Piesn Kozla, Poland, assistant director for Stathis Livathinos, National Theatre of Greece. Also an examinar for London College of Music and New Era examinations. Currently a voice coach for *Waterloo Road*.

Drama School Auditions

mobile 07862 255402
email matt@dramaschoolauditions.co.uk
website www.dramaschoolauditions.co.uk

Specialises in audition technique (particularly for drama schools), casting, performance confidence and personal management. Offers a range of course options with different pricings; please consult the website for details. Bursaries may be considered in extreme circumstances. Preferred payment methods are cheque or BACS transfer. Has an extensive database of both classical and modern speeches, which are used in conjunction with the courses. Minor follow-up queries are addressed at no extra charge. Courses take place at various studios, and wheelchair-accessible locations can be organised with advance notice. The company has been running for more than 3 years and has taught many actors and aspiring actors. Details about the tutors are available from the website.

Ben Eedle

273 Camberwell New Road,
London SE5 0TF or Flat 12, Dorryn Court,
Trewbury Road, London SE26 5DR
mobile 07587 526286
email ben@theenglishbears.com
website www.theenglishbears.com

Specialises in voice into acting. Charges £40 per session (min 1.5hr), and offers a free 30-minute consultation. Happy to provide material for private students to use and will answer minor follow-up queries at no extra cost. Teaches at home (not wheelchair accessible) or at the client's home. The nearest tube is Oval on the Northern line, about a 15-minute walk away. Buses are 436, 185, 36 (all direct from Oval tube). Has taught more than 100 actors or aspiring actors. Trained at Webber Douglas and CSSD. Still works as an actor. Has also directed theatre productions. Advises actors: "Your authentic voice is central to the successful playing of any character."

Prue Gillett Actor Training

Staffordshire
email prue@pruegillett.com
website www.pruegillett.com

Specialises in the Meisner Technique, Received Pronunciation and Accent Reduction. Charges from £25 per 3-hour session for group classes, and £35 per hour for private sessions. When possible will provide material for students' use, and will answer minor follow-up queries at no extra cost. Teaches from home in Leek, North Staffordshire. Workshops at drama schools and other locations are arranged on request. Please see website for further details.

John Grayson

2 Jubilee Road, St Johns, Worcester WR2 4LY
mobile 07702 188031
email jgbizzybee@outlook.com
website www.JohnLGrayson.com

Specialises in audition technique, voice, accents, singing, public speaking and coaching. Charges £25 per hour. Can provide material for students and is happy to receive minor follow-up queries. Can teach from home or from a client's house. The nearest station is Worcester Foregate Street (there is a good service from Birmingham), from which the house is 10-15 minutes' walk away. Has taught around 20 aspiring actors in about 6 years. Please see website for more details. Is happy to advise students on how to survive when not working.

Martin Harris

17 Groveland Road, Wallasey, Merseyside CH45 8JX
tel 0151 637 1481 *mobile* 07788 723570
email martin@auditioncoach.co.uk
website www.auditioncoach.co.uk

Specialises in audition technique and selection and direction of audition pieces. Offers group acting classes as well as one-to-one tuition for aspiring and professional actors. Also teaches sight reading and gives advice about CVs, agents and jobs. Charges £30 per hour, with a discount of 20% if the client pays for 10 sessions in advance. Accepts payment with cash or cheque, or via Internet banking.

Is happy to provide material for private students to use, and will answer minor follow-up queries at no extra charge. Teaches at home, or at the client's home (with a small extra charge).Wallasey Grove Road is the nearest train station. The home/office is literally next to the station. Has taught more than 200 actor clients over 10 years. Trained as an actor at Birmingham School of Acting, and has worked as an actor and director since 1995. Currently also Artistic Director of Rocket Theatre.

Daniel Hoffmann-Gill

London
mobile 07946 433903
email danielhg@gmail.com

Specialises in actor confidence-building, improvisation technique, removing actors' blocks, audition technique, casting technique and various practitioner-centred methods such as Guskin, Meisner, Lecoq and Donnellan. Has been a professional actor for more than 19 years, working in film, TV and theatre, and has taught actors for over 16 years. Focuses on one-to-one work, aimed at enabling the actor to do themselves and their imagination justice – also, on practical assistance in audition technique and how to do the very best you can in any casting situation, "no matter how bizarre". Uses real casting briefs and exercises, for students to try out their ideas.

Has previously taught at the Royal Central School of Speech and Drama, East 15, the Actors Centre, the National Theatre, as well as for numerous London agents. References from previous students are available on request. Charges £50 per hour, with special packages available for long-term work or working towards drama school entry: these are tailored on an individual basis, so please email for details. Works from home or from the client's home, and occasionally uses performance spaces, depending on the project. All locations used are wheelchair-accessible. Has taught around 300 actors. Advises clients that "hard graft and positive attitude go a long way in a tough, tough industry".

Jennifer Jane Hooker

Based in Central London
mobile 07725 977146
email jj@jjhooker.com
website www.jjhooker.com

Specialises in character work, scene breakdown, emotional and sensory work, and audition technique. Charges £50 per hour with a free introductory meeting. Teaches both known actors and new students with emphasis on practical work – proven results in both drama school entry and auditions. Trained with Susan Batson of Susan Batson Studios, NYC, who sends her actors to JJ when they are in Europe. Certified practitioner of Core Competency Coaching, an effective technique to get rid of fears and judgements that stop us from reaching our true potential. Can provide material for use by private students. Closest tubes: Baker Street, Bond Street.

Mark Hudson

MSA, 14-32 Hewitt Street, Manchester M15 4GB
tel 0161 238 8900
email mark@manchesterschoolofacting.co.uk
website www.manchesterschoolofacting.co.uk

Film, television and theatre - acting, dialogue and dialect coach.

Charlie Hughes-D'Aeth

Based in Brighton and London
mobile 07811 010963
email chdaeth@aol.com

Text and Voice Coach. Currently consultant text and voice coach on RSC's *Matilda the Musical* and resident voice coach on Warner Bros' *Charlie and the Chocolate Factory*.

   Offers coaching on practical voice technique for text and singing.

Desmond Jones

20 Thornton Avenue, London W4 1QG
tel/fax 020 8747 3537
email enquiries@desmondjones.com
website www.desmondjones.com

Specialises in physical audition techniques and mime and physical theatre. One of the founders of physical theatre; has run his own School of Mime and Physical Theatre for 25 years, with expertise in all aspects of movement. Charges are negotiable, with various packages and discounts available; please make contact for more information. Will provide clients with occasional worknotes and is happy to answer minor follow-up queries. Teaches out of home (a 3-minute walk from Turnham Green station, bus routes 94, 27, H91, 191, 267), or the home of the client – whichever is more suitable. Has taught more than 2,500 aspiring actors over 40 years. Advises clients: "Do it now!"

Lawrence Lambert

c/o The Actors Centre, 1A Tower Street, London WC2H 9NP
email lawrielambo@yahoo.co.uk

Audition, creating character, improvisation, text and voice. Specialist in Method Acting. Work detail can be for beginners, professionals or individuals returning to the profession. Charges £30 per hour, with a discount for block bookings. Happy to provide material for private students to use, and to answer follow-up queries after a lesson.

Will teach at home, or at the client's home, or at the Actors Centre; all are wheelchair-accessible. Nearest tube/railway station is Arsenal (home) or Leicester Square (Actors Centre). Bus route is 19.
   Is currently teaching ACting for Film at the Met Film School, Ealing, and Introduction to Acting at the City Lit, Holborn. Has taught professional actors and aspiring actors for over 25 years. Experienced in stage, television and feature film, and is an East 15 acting school graduate. "I cater for all types of experience – from novice to seasoned professional."

Marj McDaid

Stoke Newington, London N16
tel 020 7923 4929 *mobile* 07815 993203
email marjmcdaid@hotmail.com
website www.voicings.co.uk

Specialises in voice for speech and singing (Estill method – safe techniques for shouting, screaming, etc.), character work, and accents (especially Irish and American). Charges £40 per hour; discounts can be arranged when a number of sessions paid for in advance. Prefers cash or interbank transfer. Is happy to provide audition speeches (not songs) for private students to use, and will answer minor follow-up queries at no extra charge. Teaches from home, which is 10 mins from Dalston or Stoke Newington (overground) and not far from Highbury & Islington tube. Bus routes include 67, 73, 76, 149, 243, 393 and 476. Has taught hundreds of actors and aspiring actors over 20 years.

Martin McKellan
Covent Garden, London WC2
mobile 07425 204070
email dialectandvoice@yahoo.co.uk
website www.martinmckellan.com

Specialises in auditions, acting classes and all aspects of voice work (accent and dialogue a particular area of expertise). Rates are negotiable and offers are available; please make contact for full details. Is happy to provide material for private students to use, and to answer minor follow-up queries at no extra charge. Will teach from home, from a client's home or at another location. Covent Garden is the nearest tube station, 3 minutes' walk away. Has taught thousands of actors and aspiring actors over the past 15 years, and has extensive experience as a freelance acting/voice coach working in the West End and in Regional Theatre and for both film and television.

Alison Mead
9 Victorian Road, Chislehurst BR7 6DE
020 3601 7022 *mobile* 07770 672589
email alison.mead49@gmail.com
website www.alisonmead.com

Specialises in audition technique, accent work, sight reading, acting through song, Shakespeare, character building, Stanislavski, Meisner and Laban techniques. Also happy to teach all areas of acting and text work, specifically designed for schools, colleges and theatre groups. Charges are negotiable, but there is a basic rate of £40 per hour for private tuition (£60 for 2 hours). Sessions can be also be shared by two people for £60 per hour. Alison is happy to provide material for private students to use, and to answer minor follow-up queries after a lesson.

Teaches at home, which is wheelchair-accessible or is happy to travel to student's home for a small extra charge. The nearest station is Elmstead Woods, 20 minutes from London Bridge. Trains to Bickley from Victoria run twice per hour and take 25 minutes. Alison is happy to collect her student from either station for each lesson. Bus routes are 314 and 161 from Elmstead to Chislehurst (Canterbury towards Whistable) or 162 from Bickley towards Chislehurst. She has taught many actors and aspiring actors for over 25 years. Alison has taught Drama and Theatre Arts at degree level, A-Level and GCSE. She has adjudicated at 6 drama festivals for both adults and young people. "Make sure this is the career for you and that it is what you want above all else."

Robin Miller
London
mobile 07957 627677
email robinjenni@hotmail.com
website www.mandy.com/uk/robin.miller and www.spotlight.com/0632-4531-6660

Specialises in audition speeches, accents and dialects. Charges £20 per hour (special packages negotiable; preferred payment methods are cash or cheque), and is happy to answer minor follow-up queries at no extra charge. Teaches at home – no steps up to the house – or at the client's home. Nearest station is St Margaret's, 12 minutes away, or Twickenham, 10 minutes away. Bus routes are H37, 110 or 267. Has 30 years' experience in the acting profession as an actress, writer, workshop leader, teacher and director; please see Spotlight and Mandy for further details. Advises actors that "choosing the right speech is incredibly important".

Sally Mortemore
7 Groton Road, Earlsfield, London SW18 4ER
tel 020 8576 2192 *mobile* 07973 835292
email mortemores@aol.com
website www.sallymortemore.com

Fully qualified voice coach and professional actress; specialises in Shakespeare and is very experienced in voice, audition coaching, text and accent softening. Charges £30 per hour or £40 for 1.5 hours. Offers a free half-hour consultation for new students, and a discounted rate of £20 per hour for drama school leavers in their first year as a professional. Is happy to provide material for students to use, and to answer minor follow-up queries. Teaches from home, which is wheelchair-accessible; the nearest station is Earlsfield, only 2 minutes away. Has taught 200+ actors and aspiring actors over 6 years.

Frances Parkes
Suite 5, 3rd Floor, 1 Harley Street,
London W1G 9QD
tel 020 8542 2777
email frances@maxyourvoice.com
website www.maxyourvoice.com

Specialises in vocal technique, including accents, dialects and dialogue. Also coaches acting on film and preparing for TV/film roles. Charges £95 per hour and may offer reductions for students and Actors Centre members, rates are negotiated for each production. Is happy to provide material for private students to use, and to answer follow-up queries after a lesson.

Teaches at The Actors' Centre, Diorama and Harley Street studios, though is happy to travel to the client if this is more suitable, dependent on the situation. Diorama studios and Harley Street rooms are wheelchair-accessible at all times. The nearest stations are Oxford Street and Warren Street – both a 5-minute walk from each location. The studios are also served by multiple bus routes. Has taught for over 10 years and has dealt with many actors and aspiring actors during this time. Trained at the Guildhall and worked in the acting profession for 7 years at the same time as coaching for film, TV and theatre work and audios/voice overs. "Use your inspiration to fuel your work and your commitment to learn your craft."

Richard Ryder

9 Kamen House, 17-21 Magdalen Street, London SE1 2RH
mobile 07967 352551
email richard@therichervoice.com
website www.therichervoice.com
website www.theaccentkit.com

Specialises in accents, voice and text coaching. Charges £90 per hour with a discount for 6 or more sessions booked in advance. Cash or direct payment to bank. Happy to provide material for private students to use, and to answer minor follow-up queries at no extra cost. Teaches at home (wheelchair accessible) or at the client's home (time charged for travel). The nearest station is London Bridge, 6 minutes' walk from the main teaching location (buses 47, RV1 and many others pass through this area). Has more than 14 years' teaching and coaching experience, at the RSC, National Theatre, West End theatre, TV and film.

You can also download The Accent Kit app for iPhone and Android

Rebecca Semark

Epping, Essex
mobile 07956 850330
email rebecca@semark.biz
website www.semark.biz

Specialises in audition technique, monologues and voice technique. Stage and drama school entrants includes singing. Offers discounts to sibling groups and students. Fortnightly teaching is preferred, as this gives more time to practise work and allows for other commitments. Is happy to provide material for students to use, and to answer minor follow-up queries. Teaches from home; the closest station is Epping on the Central Line, which is a 5-10 minute walk. Has taught many performers, actors and aspiring actors over a 20-year period. Since 1973 has worked extensively in theatre and television as a dancer, actress and singer in many genres, including Musical Theatre.

Ros Simmons

120 Hillfield Avenue, Crouch End, London N8 7DN
tel 020 8347 8089
email ros@rossimmons.co.uk
website www.rossimmons.co.uk

Coaching Rates:

• 1 hour £65.00
• 1.5 hours: £90.00
• 2 hours: £120.00

Specialises in accents and dialects, voice and auditions, as well as Spoken English skills for those with English as a second language. Provides full accent breakdowns and is happy to answer minor follow-up queries. Teaches mainly from home base, with Finsbury Park the nearest tube (overground, Hornsey Station on Tottenham Lane, just around the corner from the premises). Buses from Finsbury Park tube are W3 to Tottenham Lane or W7 to Crouch End Broadway. Has taught around 1,000 actors and aspiring actors, in drama schools and privately, over a period of 15 years. Trained as an actor at the Polytechnic School of Theatre in Manchester, and has worked extensively in theatre, film, TV and radio.

Giles Taylor

mobile 07973 960681
email gilestaylor@ukgateway.net

Specialises in Shakespeare and audition speeches. Is a verse specialist, but works too on prose texts – classical and modern. Charges £40 per hour. Discounts are available: 3 sessions for £100, and students £30 per hour. Is happy to provide material for private students to use, and to answer minor follow-up queries after a lesson.

Teaches from home, but other locations can be arranged (please note that these may incur travel costs). The nearest tube station is Highgate and bus routes are 43 and 134. Has taught more than 100 actors and aspiring actors over 6 years. "I have been in the business for nearly 20 years, working in theatre, music theatre, television, film and radio. I am a regular teacher at the Actors Centre."

Paul Todd

3 Rosehart Mews, London W11 3JN
tel 020 7229 9776 *mobile* 07813 985092
email paultodd@talk21.com

Specialises in singing, acting, piano, music theory and voice. Charges £30 per hour; discounts are available on application. Happy to provide material for students to use, and to answer minor follow-up queries at no extra charge. Teaches from home, the nearest tube stations are Notting Hill/Bayswater/Queensway around 8-9 minutes away. Bus routes are 7, 23, 27, 28, 31 and 328. More details about services offered are available from Forward Talent/Yellow Pages. Has taught very many actor/singers and aspiring actor/singers over 40 years. Has extensive experience as Musical Director at numerous theatres around the UK, including Theatre In The Round, Scarborough and The Royal National Theatre. Advises: "Get on with it. Get the right teacher. Do it."

Vocal Confidence with Alix Longman

Melbourne, Australia
mobile +61 (0) 401 798 258
email alix@vocalconfidence.com
website www.vocalconfidence.com

Skype: Sessions available worldwide.

Alix Longman's "Vocal Confidence technique is a

unique, fast and effective method that fixes all vocal problems with speech, presentation and singing." Audition technique and dialect work also offered. Charges £50 (AU$100) per hour. 10% discount for students and members of Equity/Spotlight. Initial and follow-up queries provided for no extra fee. Has successfully reconnected thousands of actors and singers to their Vocal Confidence over 25 years. "Vocal Confidence reconnects the voice to the tone of emotional integrity which instantly connects and pulls every person in the audience, both personally and professionally." Further details and testimonials available on website.

Genevieve Walsh

37 Kelvedon House, Guildford Road, Stockwell, London SW8 2DN
mobile 07801 948864

Specialises in coaching for auditions and public speaking (presentation technique). Charges £30 per hour (£20 for students). Happy to help in the selection of material for students' use, and to answer minor follow-up queries, time permitting. Teaches from home (nearest station is Stockwell, a 5-minute walk away; bus routes 2 or 88). Has taught dozens of actors and aspiring actors over a 35-year period, and has extensive experience as an actor, teacher and director. "Know your material inside out and all the background to the speech. It is very basic advice, but it is essential."

Mark Westbrook – Acting Coach Scotland

ACS Studio, 2nd Floor, 19 Queen Street, Glasgow G1 3ED
tel 0800 756 9535
email mark@actingcoachscotland.co.uk
website www.actingcoachscotland.co.uk

Areas of specialism are practical aesthetics, audition technique and group acting classes. Charges £30 per hour for private tuition, and £125 for a 10-week evening class. Packages are available (£75 for 3 hours, £130 for 6 hours). Preferred payment methods are PayPal or cash. Provides audition material for students to use, and is happy to give feedback after lessons at no extra charge. Teaches at a city-centre studio, but would travel to the home of wheelchair users. The closest station is St Enochs tube or Queen Street station (5 and 10 minutes away respectively). Has taught hundreds of actors over a period of 10 years. Wide experience as a professional theatre director, former lecturer in acting and head of acting at a conservatory for musical theatre. Advises actors: "You can unlock any scene if you know the right questions to ask."

Anne Wittman

North London
mobile 07956 602508

email info@spokenstates.com
website www.spokenstates.com

Specialises in coaching British and other non-US actors in a range of American dialects for audition and performance. Also works with accent correction for foreign speakers who would like to attain greater clarity of speech and to correct or soften their existing accent towards General American. Coaches RP for both native and foreign speakers; also coaches acting for audition and performance. Enjoys working with poets and other writers on presentation of their own material at readings.

Charges £75 per hour and a half session, £100 for two hours. Happy to provide material for private students to use, and to answer minor follow-up queries at no extra cost. Teaches from home (wheelchair accessible), but is also connected with various institutions. Nearest tube stations are Finsbury Park or Highgate: the most direct route to the main teaching location is the W3 or W7 bus from Finsbury Park. Has taught at least 500 actors since 1994. Further details are available from the website – also see Anne's article on dialect published in the 2013 edition of *Contacts*, under Drama Training.

Tessa Wood

43 Woodhurst Road, London W3 6SS
tel 020 8896 2659 *mobile* 07957 207808
email TessaRosWood@aol.com

Specialises in physical voice including centring, alignment, tension release, breath, articulation, range, projection, tone. Also Standard English, RP and period RP, and audition technique. Fee is negotiable and there is a 20% discount for students and sometimes for actors who aren't working. Can provide copies of audition material, but generally does not lend books as they never seem to be returned. Will give minor follow-up advice for no extra charge. Teaches from home or the client's home (for an additional charge). Nearest train link is the Silverlink (North London Line) and the station, Acton Central, is 5 minutes away. Acton Town (Piccadilly/District Lines) is about 15-minutes' walk, and Acton Mainline (1 stop from Paddington) is about 10 minutes away. Many of the buses from Shepherd's Bush going in the direction of Ealing pass within 5-6 minutes of the house (route 207 plus others).

Has taught well over 3,000 actors and aspiring actors over a 20-year period. Pursued a full-time acting career for 15 years, and still does some acting every year. Has coached well-known TV presenters and actors on a one-to-one basis. "Whether or not an actor has full-time training (which I would highly recommend), they should keep up their process with classes, both one-to-one and in the form of group workshops."

An actor's toolkit

Compiled by Simon Dunmore

You need to organise the following essential items before you even get your first interview, let alone an agent and/or your first job. You should start planning for all these in good time, before the end of your training – ready for your first public production.

1 Join Equity! You can join (very cheaply) as a student member (see **www.equity.org.uk/ about-us/join-us**) and, for a small extra fee, reserve your professional name: details of how to go about this are on the website.

2 A good, strong professional name. If you can't (or don't want to) use your real name, it's important to select an alternative that you're completely comfortable with.

3 Well-designed headed paper. Beatrice Warde, the passionate typography expert, said, "Typefaces are the clothes words wear." Find a typeface that 'dresses' your professional name well.

4 Secure and reliable telephone and Internet connections for professional use. *Note*: It is very important that your outgoing message and email address sound professional and not like hangovers from your adolescence.

5 A reliable computer with printer. *Tip*: Laser printers provide a much crisper quality when printing text – and laser toner is much cheaper, per page, than ink.

6 An up-to-date copy of *Actors and Performers Yearbook*. *Tip*: It is worthwhile not only reading the rest of this book to get a feel for how different parts of the profession function, but also reading through websites.

7 A good set of photographs and sufficient copies. See Angus Deuchar's article and the introduction to Photographers and Repro Companies starting on page 391.

8 A well-laid-out and up-to-date CV. *Notes*: It's important to ensure that all spellings of proper names (directors, play titles, etc.) are correct. Also, to understand how to convert your CV into Portable Document Format (PDF) for email transmission.

9 A good standard letter that you can adapt for individual circumstances, and use in emails, etc.

10 Half-a-dozen (or more) varied audition speeches. See my *Effective Audition Speeches* article on page 157.

11 Half-a-dozen (or more) varied audition songs.

12 A mental list of things (not just acting ones) you could talk about in order to respond to the almost inevitable question(s), "What have you been doing recently?" and/or "Tell me a bit about yourself."

13 An entry in *Spotlight* – details at **www.spotlight.com/join**. *Note*: Entry into *Spotlight* is strictly limited to professionally trained and/or professionally experienced performers, and applications are always vetted.

14 A reasonable selection of clothes for interviews and auditions. Essentially, you need to feel comfortable and appropriately dressed for each individual circumstance … and you will face a wide variety of such circumstances.

15 An up-to-date passport – jobs which require travelling abroad at short notice are becoming more frequent.

16 A budget. The costs of the above can accumulate quite quickly – before you've earned a penny. And there are many other minor things not listed: postage; Equity entry fee and annual subscription; subscriptions to *The Stage* and other professional publications; travel costs to interviews, and so on. All the above items can easily add up to much more money than you might think: you need to calculate your potential professional expenses and budget for them. *Notes*: Although many of the above are allowable against tax (see Philippe Carden's article *Tax & National Insurance for Actors* on page 436), don't forget to include your potential tax bill! Also, at the outset of your career, consider carefully the cost-effectiveness of items like personal websites, show-reels, etc. These are only worthwhile if you have sufficient high-quality material that makes you look 'professional'.

17 Sources of non-acting income that are flexible enough for you to drop at 24 hours' notice. At an educated guess, only about 10 per cent of the profession earn a living *solely* from acting. And, even for those, incomes can be incredibly variable – £200 one year to over £20,000 the next.

18 A working knowledge of the nation's transport systems (especially London's): you will often not know where you might be required for audition/interview (even work) until very late in the day. *Tip*: As a general rule it is wise to double your estimated travelling time to allow for the almost inevitable foul-ups.

19 A great deal of patience, persistence, determination, cunning and resourcefulness.

20 A stoical source of solace for the bad times. *Tip*: Find another activity that absorbs you as much as acting does.

21 A copy of my *An Actor's Guide To Getting Work* for reading on the loo (published by Methuen).

General points:

(a) Can you organise yourself? Acting can be an instant business. For days/weeks/months/years nothing happens, and then a few minutes/hours/days/weeks/months/years later it can *all* be happening. You must always be ready, but not constantly on tenterhooks. In spite of the popular image of the chaotic, dizzy actor, you have to be personally organised or you could significantly harm your employment prospects.

(b) As an actor you are your own business. You are not only your own work-force, but also your publicity and public relations office, accountancy division, transport manager, and – above all – your managing director. Of course, you may well have an agent, an accountant, etc., but none of these people can do anything unless you give them clear direction. You are finally responsible for your success or failure in the business.

Simon Dunmore has been directing productions for over 30 years – nearly 20 years as a resident director in regional theatres and, more recently, working freelance. In that time there have been more than 200 productions (of all styles, colours, shapes and sizes), most recently several Drama School Showcases, Maugham's *Home and Beauty* and new plays about sex, WB Yeats' up-and-down relationship with Maud Gonne, one set inside a pyramid, and another about Bismarck. Past favourites include: *The Promise* (Alexei Arbuzov), *Antigone* (Jean Anouilh), a seven-handed version of *Antony & Cleopatra* and too many others to mention. He also teaches acting, and has worked in many drama schools and other training establishments around the country. He has written several books: *An Actor's Guide to Getting Work* (fifth edition, 2012), the *Alternative Shakespeare Auditions* series, and was formerly the Consultant Editor for *Actors' Yearbook*.

Agents and casting directors
Introduction

Actors have probably existed since before the invention of writing; actors' agents have only been around since the invention of the telephone, just over a century ago. Prior to this, work-seeking actors had to make themselves known in person to potential employers – for instance, certain hostelries in the Covent Garden area of central London were well-known 'talent-spotting' haunts. Actors would also 'catch a ride' with one of the touring companies in the hope of proving themselves to the manager – and then being put on the payroll. Others would pay managers to let them play small parts, in the hope of being noticed. All this meant a lot of hard work and/or expense (let alone the time needed to earn their living by other means) for the pre-electronic-age actor. The invention of actors' agents seemed to fill a vital gap.

In the 1970s, a number of actors, dissatisfied with the (by then) traditional agent system, formed the first co-operative agencies (see page 89). This apparently simple idea – with all members taking turns to 'man' the office – took a while to become established. Like many 'simple ideas', the pioneers found that there were more complications involved than they'd initially envisaged, and employers were slow to accept the idea. Nearly forty years later, the best 'co-ops' have as much professional credibility as their conventional counterparts.

It used to be the case that only the biggest companies used casting directors. The administrative burden inherent in running such a company (let alone directing productions) meant that assistance in the casting process became essential. The 1990s saw a rise in the use of casting directors and in the number of freelancers working on short-term contracts: most of the latter work in a wide variety of fields.

The simple fact is that a significant proportion of properly paid acting work is 'brokered' by casting directors and agents.

Agents and casting directors have very distinct functions – see the articles. The term 'casting agents' is used to describe walk-on agents who take the responsibility for casting walk-ons/extras in television and film. They have client bases comprising lots of different types, and on request can supply a suitable crowd for any occasion. Thus they fulfil the roles of both agent and casting director for non-speaking parts that don't need to be auditioned.

Agents

A good agent understands contracts, knows the current rates in every field of work and – most importantly – has plenty of professional contacts and access to far more casting information than most individuals can ever possess. Directors and casting directors rely on the agents they know and trust to help with the filtering process of whom to interview. A good agent will work hard at promoting each of his/her clients; in return, it is not unreasonable that they charge commission on every contract they negotiate for you – generally, 10-20 per cent (plus VAT, if appropriate). A good agent will also (a) have only as many clients as they can reasonably handle, and (b) ensure that they have a good range of ages and types of actors in order to cover as many casting opportunities as possible.

When you are seeking representation, it is advisable to contact agents by post in the first instance – unless specifically informed otherwise. It is a good idea to include a separate 10x8in (25x20cm) photograph, and it is important that all your enclosures give your name and the best way to contact you (not a long list of confusing alternatives). Agents receive many requests for representation, and photographs can become separated from their accompanying letters and CVs, so proper labelling is essential.

Use the listings that follow to (a) target your submission as accurately as possible (for example, by writing to a specific, named person – unless advised otherwise), (b) check for any details that could inform the content of your letter, and (c) find out whether each would be interested in any extras, like a showreel. Time spent checking such details can save money and enhance your chances of being noticed more than the next person. Unless you have a good collection of professional credits, it is generally best to write to agents when there's an opportunity for them to see you performing in something.

If you are invited to meet an agent, that is often a good sign. You should approach the occasion in much the same way as you would an interview for a production. The major difference is that you should be prepared to ask (reasonable) questions – rates of commission, for instance.

When seeking representation, it can be a good idea to target only those agencies that you think might suit you. For instance, might you feel lost in a large agency, but feel more comfortable with a smaller one? On the other hand, some larger agencies have huge 'clout' and can be the first 'port of call' for the casting of prestigious productions.

When you've been taken on by an agent, it is important to establish how your working relationship will function. Be clear about any areas of work that you don't want to be suggested for, discuss your availability for auditions and interviews, agree how much promotion you should do for yourself, and so on.

These listings only contain agents who represent adult actors – there are many others who represent children, models, extras and so on.

PMA following an agency's name denotes membership of the Personal Managers' Association, the leading professional body of talent agencies in the UK. It was set up more than 60 years ago with the intention of encouraging good practice among agents through better communication between agents and from agents to the industry.

42 PMA

Palladium House, 1-4 Argyll Street,
London W1F 7TA
tel 020 7292 0554
email info@42mp.com
website www.42mp.com
Partner Kate Buckley, assisted by Kelly Byrne and
Hannah Roeg; *Managers* Ness Evans, Molly Cowan,
Molly Wansell and Harrison Davies

Established 2013. Main areas of work are theatre, TV
and film. Represents actors, directors, casting
directors, writers and producers. Welcomes
performance notices nationwide given a week's
notice. Welcomes letters (with CVs and
photographs), CVs and photographs sent by email
and show reels. Represents actors with disabilities.

A&J Management

56 Park Avenue, Enfield EN1 2HW
tel 020 8004 3367
email info@ajmanagement.co.uk
website www.ajmanagement.co.uk
Managing Director Jo McLintock *Key contact* Jo
McLintock

Established in 1984. 2 agents represent actors. Areas
of work include theatre, musicals, television, film and
commercials.

Will consider attending performances with a
minimum of 2 weeks' notice. Accepts submissions
(with CVs and photographs) from actors previously
unknown to the company if sent by email. Invitations
to view individual actors' websites are also accepted.

Chris Abakporo

47 Chatsworth Road, Stratford, London E15 1RB
mobile 07903 192413
email chrisabak@hotmail.co.uk
Agent Chris Abakporo

Established in 2010. Areas of work include TV, film
and commercials. Welcomes CVs and photographs
sent by email. Also accepts showreels and invitations
to view actors' websites.

Access Artiste Management Ltd

The Bloomsbury Building, 10 Bloomsbury Way,
London WC1A 2SL
tel 020 3916 0270
email mail@access-uk.com
website www.access-uk.com
Manager Sarah Bryan

Established in 1999. Areas of work include theatre,
musicals, television, film, commercials, corporate.
Also represents directors, musical directors,
choreographers, composers, playwrights and musical
works.

Will consider attending performances in Greater
London and elsewhere with 1 month's notice.
Accepts submissions (with CVs and photographs)
from professional actors previously unknown to the
company. Showreels, voicereels and details of
individual actors' websites should only be sent upon
request. Welcomes enquiries from disabled actors.

Actors International Ltd

Soho, London
tel 020 7118 2278
email mail@actorsinternational.co.uk
website www.actorsinternational.co.uk
Facebook www.facebook.com/actorsintl
Twitter @ACTORSINTL
Agents Caroline Taylor, Lee Thomas

Established in 2000. 2 agents represent around 70
actors. Areas of work include theatre, musicals,
television, film, commercials and corporate.

Will attend showcases/performances within Central
London given as much notice as possible. Accepts
email submissions ONLY; no postal submissions will
be considered.

Actors World Casting

13 Briarbank Road, London W13 0HH
mobile 07960 332846
email katherine@actors-world-production.com
Agent Katherine Pageon

Established in 2005. 1 agent represents 40 actors.
Areas of work include theatre, musicals, television,
film, commercials, corporate, voice-overs.

Will consider attending performances in Greater
London with at least 2 weeks' notice. Notices of
performances should be sent via email only. Accepts
submissions sent via email (with CVs and 1
photograph only) from actors previously unknown to
the company. Invitations to view individual actors'
websites also accepted, as are enquiries from disabled
actors. *Commission*: Theatre 15%; Other 20%.

AFA Associates

Unit 101A, Business Design Centre, 52 Upper Street,
London N1 0QH
tel 020 7682 3677 *mobile* 07904 962779
email afa-associates@hotmail.com
Agent Rhiannon Mosson

Established in 2009. Works in theatre, film, TV,
commercials, corporate, musicals and promos.

Welcomes performance notices within the Greater
London area if given at least 7 days' notice. Accepts
approaches from actors by post and email, and
welcomes showreels and invitations to view
individual actors' websites. Represents actors with
disabilities.

The Agency PMA

25 Leeson Street Lower, Dublin D02 XD77, Ireland
tel +353 1 661 8535
email office@theagency.ie
website www.theagency.ie
Directors Karl Hayden

The Agency has been representing Ireland's foremost acting talent for stage and screen since its establishment 30 years ago. In that time its multi-award-winning clients have appeared in numerous productions worldwide, and the company continues to set the standard for excellence in acting.

AHA Talent Ltd PMA

2 Percy Street, London W1T 1DD
tel 020 7250 1760 *mobile* 0788 540159
email mail@ahatalent.co.uk
website www.ahatalent.co.uk
Twitter @AHActors
Agents Amanda Fitzalan Howard, Mark Price, Darren Rugg, Kirsten Wright, Kevin Brady, Chloe Brayfield
Assistant Amy Clarke

8 agents represent around 200 actors and creatives working in theatre, musicals, television, radio, film, commercials, corporate role-play and voice-overs. Other clients include writers, broadcasters, designers, directors and composers.

Will consider attending performances within Greater London given 2-3 weeks' notice. Welcomes submissions (with CVs, photographs, showreels, voicereels and sae) from actors previously unknown to the agency if sent by post. Does not accept email applications or invitations to view an actor's website. *Commission*: 10-15% depending on the medium.

All Talent Agency Ltd

Unit 2.7 The Hub, 70 Pacific Drive,
Glasgow G51 1EA
tel 0141 418 1074 *mobile* 07971 337074
email info@alltalentagency.co.uk
website www.alltalentagency.co.uk

Established in 2005. 2 agents represent 50-60 actors. Also represents other skills within the profession.

Will consider attending performances in Central London and Glasgow with at least 2-3 weeks' notice. Accepts submissions (with CVs and photographs) from actors previously unknown to the company; postal submissions preferred. Invitations to view showreels or voicereels and individual actors' websites also accepted, and follow-up calls welcomed. Welcomes enquiries from disabled actors. *Commission*: 15%

Anita Alraun Representation

1A Queensway, Blackpool,
Lancashire FY4 2DG (correspondence address)
tel 01253 343784
Sole Proprietor/Agent Anita Alraun

1 agent represents 30 actors. Areas of work include theatre, musicals, film, television, commercials, radio drama, corporate and some voice-overs.

Accepts submissions (with CV, photograph and SAE – essential for reply) by post only from trained/experienced actors previously unknown to the company. Emailed submissions will not be considered. Please do not send showreels or voicereels unless requested. *Commission*: Radio 10%; Theatre 12.5%; Film and TV 12.5%; Commercials 15%

Jonathan Altaras Associates Ltd PMA

53 Chandos Place, London WC2N 4HS
tel 020 7812 6461/2/3
email info@jaalondon.com
Agents: Wim Hance, Helen Filmer

Established in 1991. Areas of work are theatre, musicals, TV, film, commercials, corporate and voice-over.

Welcomes performance notices in the Greater London area, given as much notice as possible. Welcomes letters with CVs, photographs, showreels, voice tapes with sae. Invitations, CVs, photographs, showreel link by email. No follow-up phone calls please. Does not currently represent actors with disabilities but is open to the idea of representing disabled actors.

ALW Associates

1 Grafton Chambers, Grafton Place,
London NW1 1LN
tel 020 7388 7018 *fax* 020 7813 1398
email alw_carolpaul@talktalk.net

Established in 1977 as Vernon Conway Ltd. Sole representation of 50 actors. Areas of work include theatre, television, film and commercials.

Will consider attending performances at venues within Greater London and occasionally elsewhere with 1 week's notice. Accepts submissions (with CVs and photographs) from actors previously unknown to the company, sent by post or email. Also accepts invitations to view individual actors' websites. Showreels and voicereels should only be sent on request. *Commission*: Theatre and Radio 10-12.5%; Film and TV 12.5%; Commercials 15%

Amber Personal Management Ltd PMA

2nd Floor, 52 Port Street, Manchester M1 2EQ
tel 0161 228 0236 *fax* 0161 228 0235
email info@amberltd.co.uk
website www.amberltd.co.uk
Twitter @ambermgmt
Agents Sally Sheridan, Jasmine Parri, Estelle Jenkins

Works in theatre, musicals, television, film, commercials, corporate and voice-over. 3 agents represent 90-100 actors. Will consider attending performances in Manchester, Leeds and Liverpool if given a minimum of 2 weeks' notice.

Welcomes applications via email at apply@amberltd.co.uk. Encourages enquiries from actors with disabilities. Will accept showreels, voicereels and invitations to view individual actors' websites. *Commission*: Recorded Media (TV/Film/Commercial) 15%; Theatre, Musicals, Corporate 10%

The American Agency

14 Bonny Street, London NW1 9PG
tel 020 7485 8883

email americanagency@btconnect.com
Agent Ed Cobb

Areas of work include theatre, musicals, television, film, commercials, corporate and voice-overs. 2 agents represent 80 actors.

Will consider attending performances within the Greater London area. Accepts submissions (with CVs and photographs) from actors previously unknown to the agency if sent by post or email. Invitations to view individual actors' websites, showreels and voicereels are also accepted. Welcomes enquiries from disabled actors. *Commission*: Theatre 10%; Other 15%

Angel & Francis Ltd PMA

1st Floor, 12 D'Arblay Street, London W1F 8DU
tel 020 7439 3086 *fax* 020 7437 1712
email submissions@angelandfrancis.co.uk
Director Kevin Francis

Established in 1976. 2 agents represent about 80 actors andleading TV/film casting directors and creatives. Areas of work include theatre, television, film and commercials. *Commission*: 10-12.5%

Christopher Antony Associates

Building 3, 566 Chiswick High Road,
London W4 5YA
tel 020 8994 9952
email info@christopherantony.co.uk
website www.christopherantony.co.uk
Agents Chris Sheils, Kerry Walker

Christopher Antony Associates has been operational since 2006. Offers a personal management service specialising in Musical Theatre. As theatre agents, represents a small and diverse list of artistes in the West End, UK Tours and Overseas.

APM Associates

Elstree Film Studios, Shenley Road,
Borehamwood WD6 1JG
tel 020 8953 7377
mobile 07918 166706 or 07760 625551
email apm@apmassociates.net
website www.apmassociates.net
Twitter @apmassociates
Managing Director Linda French

APM Associates represent clients in all fields of the entertainment industry, including television, film, theatre, musical theatre, commercials and dance.

Welcomes applications from both experienced performers and graduates of accredited drama schools via post or email. *Commission*: Brochure and specimen contract available upon offer of interview.

ARG (Artists Rights Group Ltd) PMA

4A Exmoor Street, London W10 6BD
tel 020 7436 6400
email comiskey@argtalent.com
website www.argtalent.com

Agents Sue Latimer (assisted by Sarah Spahovic), Claire Cominsky (assisted by Katherine Darke), Tiffany Grayson

Established on 2001, main area of work are theatre, musicals, film, TV and corporate. Represent approximately 60 actors, as well as presenters amd production.

Welcome performance notices UK wide, ideallly with a week or more notice. Welcomes letters (with CV and photographers), CVs, showreels and photographs by email.

Argyle Associates

43 Clappers Lane, Fulking, West Sussex BN5 9ND
mobile 07905 293319
email argyle.associates@me.com
Director Richard Linford *Key personnel* Geraldine Pryor

Established in 1995. 2 agents represent 30 actors. Areas of work include theatre, musicals, television, film, commercials and corporate.

Will consider attending performances at venues in Sussex and Surrey (e.g. Eastbourne, Brighton, Guildford, Dorking, Windsor) with 2 weeks' notice. Accepts submissions (with CVs and photographs) from actors previously unknown to the company if sent by post. Invitations to view individual actors' websites are also accepted. "Be clear about what you think you have to offer the agency – your type and roles. Your photograph should look like you and be a high-grade holiday snap." *Commission*: Theatre and Radio 10%; TV 12.5%; Commercials, Film, Corporate and CD Rom 15%

The Artists Partnership PMA

21-22 Warwick Street, London W1B 5NE
tel 020 7439 1456 *fax* 020 7734 6530
email email@theartistspartnership.co.uk
website www.theartistspartnership.co.uk
Managing Director Roger Charteris; *Agents* Alice Coles, Kimberley Donovan, Annalisa Gordon, Emily Hayward-Whitlock, Miranda Hefferman, Saskia Mulder, Leigh Rodda, Zoe Stoker, Robert Taylor, Lottie Champness, Harry Wilson, Sarah Vignoles

Represents actors, directors, writers, experts and speakers for theatre, television, film, commercials, voice-overs, speaking and literary opportunities.

Jonathan Arun Group (JAG) PMA

37 Pearman Street, London SE1 7RB
tel 020 7840 0123
email info@jag-london.com
website www.jag-london.com
Agents Jonathan Arun, Amy O'Neill, Max Latimer, Rachel Chambers, Maria Girod-Roux (Commercials)

Established in 2007. Main areas of work are theatre, film, television, musical theatre, commercials, and American TV/film. 2 agents represent 80 actors plus a commercials list of 35. Will consider attending performances if given at least 3 weeks' notice.

Please approach the agency by email only, with Spotlight link and showreel. Tries to respond to all, but if interested in taking further will always respond within 2 weeks. Will consider representing actors with disabilities.

Asquith & Horner

The Studio, 14 College Road, Bromley BR1 3NS
tel 020 8466 5580 *fax* 020 8313 0443
website www.spotlightagent.info (view PIN 9858-0919-0728)
Senior Partner Anthony Vander Elst *Partner* Helen Melville

Established 1989. 2 agents represent 70 actors. Also represented are directors, choreographers, presenters, singers, dancers and commercial models. Areas of work include theatre, musicals, television, film, commercials, corporate and voice-overs.

Will consider attending performances at venues within Greater London and elsewhere, but requests as much notice as possible. Accepts submissions (CVs and photographs) from actors previously unknown to the company; also accepts showreels and voicereels, and invitations to view actors' websites. "Unsolicited enquiries should always be accompanied by an appropriately stamped and addressed envelope for return of answer, photo, voicereel, etc." Email applications are discouraged.

Associated International Management (AIM) PMA

Studio 405, The Print Rooms, 164-180 Union Street, London SE1 0LH
tel 020 7831 9709
email info@aimagents.com
website www.aimagents.com
Key contacts Stephen Gittins, Susan Galimberti

An international management established in 1984. Agents represent around 60 actors. Areas of work include theatre, television, film and commercials.
Will consider attending performances within the Greater London area with at least 3 weeks' notice. Accepts submissions (with CVs and photographs) from actors previously unknown to the agency if sent by post, but not by email. *Commission*: 12.5%

BAM Associates (UK) Ltd

Benets, Dolberrow, Churchill, Bristol BS25 5NT
tel 01934 852942
email casting@ebam.tv
website www.ebam.tv

2 agents represent 80 actors. Areas of work includetelevision, film, commercials, theatre, musicals, corporate, radio and voice-overs.

Welcomes hardcopy or emailed submissions from actors seeking representation. *Commission*: Theatre 10%; Mechanical Media 15%

Gavin Barker Associates Ltd PMA

2D Wimpole Street, London W1G 0EB
tel 020 7499 4777 *fax* 020 7499 3777

email assistant@gavinbarkerassociates.co.uk
website www.gavinbarkerassociates.co.uk
Managing Director Gavin Barker *Associate Director* Michelle Burke *Senior Assistant* James Evans *Junior Assistant* Frazier Wearne

Established in 1998. 3 agents represent 60 actors and a handful of creatives. Areas of work include theatre, musicals, television, film, commercials, corporate and voice-overs. Also represents directors and choreographers.

Will consider attending performances at venues in Greater London given at least 3 weeks' notice. Accepts submissions (with CVs and photographs) from actors previously unknown to the company if sent by email. Follow-up calls are not welcome. Happy to receive showreels and voicereels. "We do not currently represent any disabled actors, but would consider each applicant on a case by case basis." *Commission*: 10-12.5%

Becca Barr Management

Lower Ground Floor, 73 Wells Street, London W1T 3QG
tel 020 3137 2980
email info@beccabarrmanagement.co.uk
website www.beccabarrmanagement.co.uk
Facebook /Beccabarrmanagement
Twitter @BeccaBarrmgmt
Instagram beccabarrrmanagement

BBM represents an eclectic mix of talent ranging from presenters to experts, actors and social influencers.
Accepts submissions by email (with CVs and photographs). Showreels and voicereels are also welcome.

Becky Barrett Management PMA

Southern branch: Windsor
tel 020 3773 9590
email info@bbm.agency
website www.beckybarrettmanagement.co.uk
Facebook /BBMAgents
Twitter @BBMAgents
Managing Director/Agent Becky Barrett, *Junior Agent* Danielle Crockford

Established in 2014. Main areas of work are theatre, film, TV and commercials. BBM offers a personal management service with a strong focus on triple thrreat performers. The company represents 120 actors.
Performance notices are accepted and will consider attending perfomances UK-wide, given as much notice as posible. Welcomes applications from both experienced performers and new graduates from accredited schools. Please send submissions to representation@bbm.agency including your CV Spotlight link and showreel links.
Commission: Theatre 12.5%; television commercials 20%; all other entertainment activites 15%.

EBA (Eamonn Bedford Agency)
2nd Floor, 10 Warwick Street, London W1B 5LZ
tel 020 7734 9632
email info@eamonnbedford.com
(enquiries@eamonnbedford.com for Submissions)
website www.eamonnbedford.com

Agents Eamonn Bedford, Charlie Cox, Katie McCord

Established in 2012. 3 agents represents 100 clients. Areas of work include theatre, film and TV.

Accepts CVs with photographs from those seeking representation, via email. *Commission*: TV and Film 12.5%, Theatre 10%

Olivia Bell Management PMA
193 Wardour Street, London W1F 8ZF
tel 020 7439 3270 *fax* 020 7439 3485
email xania@olivia-bell.co.uk
Managing Director Xania Segal; *Agents* Robin Hudson, Gavin Mills, Antony Read, Harriet Kingdon, Julie Gordon, Ellie Nelson

Established in 2001. 7 agents represent 130 actors. Areas of work include theatre, musicals, television, film and commercials.

Will consider attending performances at venues within Greater London with a minimum of 1 week's notice. Accepts submissions (with CVs and photographs) from actors previously unknown to the company if sent by post. Invitations to view individual actors' websites and showreels or voicereels are also accepted. *Commission*: 12.5-20%

Jorg Betts Associates PMA
2 John Street, London WC1N 2ES
tel 020 3405 4546
email agents@jorgbetts.com

Established in 2001. Areas of work include theatre, musicals, television, film, commercials and corporates. Also represents directors, casting director, choreographers and presenters.

Accepts submissions (with CVs and photographs) from actors previously unknown to the company if sent by post.

Billboard PM Ltd
45 Lothrop Street, London W10 4JB
tel 020 8960 9393 *mobile* 07791 970773
email daniel@billboardpm.com
website www.billboardpm.com
Twitter @billboardpm
Agent Daniel Tasker

Established in 1985. 1 agent represents 50 actors. Areas of work include theatre, musicals, television, film, commercials, corporate and voice-overs.

Will consider attending performances at venues in Greater London given a minimum of 4 weeks' notice. Accepts submissions by email only, no bigger than 1MB, from actors if they are currently performing.

Commission: Commercials 16%; Film and TV 13.5%; Other 11%

Rebecca Blond Associates PMA
69A Kings Road, London SW3 4NX
tel 020 7351 4100 *fax* 020 7351 4600
email info@rebeccablond.com
Agent Rebecca Blond

Established in 1991. 2 agents represent around 60 actors in all areas of acting work; also represents directors.

Welcomes performance notices for shows within Greater London with 2 weeks' notice. Welcomes representation enquiries (with CV and photographs) by post or email, as well as showreels and invitations to view individual actors' websites. Does not welcome follow-up calls. *Commission*: Varies

Bloomfields Welch Management PMA
2.5 Lafone House, The Leathermarket, Weston Street, London SE1 3ER
tel 020 7659 2001
email submissions@bloomfieldswelch.com
website www.bloomfieldswelch.com
Twitter @bwmgt
Director Emma Bloomfield *Agent* Barnaby Welch
Assistant Oliver Sands

Established in 2004. Areas of work include theatre, musicals, television, film, commercials and corporate. 3 agents represent 40 actors.

Will consider attending performances anywhere, given at least 2 weeks' notice. Accepts submissions (with CVs and photographs) from actors previously unknown to the company if sent by email, but not by post. Invitations to view individual actors' websites, showreels and voicereels are also accepted. Welcomes enquiries from disabled actors.

Blue Star Associates
7-8 Shaldon Mansions, 132 Charing Cross Road, London WC2H 0LA
tel 020 7836 6220
email bluestar.london.2000@gmail.com
Directors Barrie Stacey, Keith Hopkins

Established in 2007 (formerly Barrie Stacey Promotions, established 1960). Works in theatre, musicals, pantomime, television, film and commercials. Around 70 actors represented. Will consider attending performances in the Greater London area.

Welcomes letters (with CVs and photographs) sent by post or email. Does not represent actors with disabilities. *Commission*: Theatre 10%; TV/Film 15%

Sandra Boyce Management PMA
125 Dynevor Road, London N16 0DA
tel 020 7923 0606 *fax* 020 7241 2313
email info@sandraboyce.com
Agent Sandra Boyce (MD)

2 agents represent 50 actors in all areas of acting work; directors also represented.

Welcomes performance notices if given at least 2 weeks' notice, and is prepared to travel within the Greater London area. Happy to accept letters (by post, enclose SAE) with CVs and photographs from individuals previously unknown to the company, but does not welcome follow-up calls. Encourages approaches from disabled actors. Also welcomes showreels and voicereels.

Michelle Braidman Associates Ltd PMA

2 Futura House, 169 Grange Road, London SE1 3BN
tel 020 7237 3523
email info@braidman.com
website www.braidman.com
Twitter @TeamBraidman
Agents Michelle Braidman, Nicola Whitworth, Rebecca Kirby

Established in 1983. A leading international theatrical agency representing actors, directors adn creative talent.
     Submissions should be sent electronically to representation@braidman.com

Eva Bridge Management

Ryden Grange, Bisley, Surrey GU21 2TH
tel 01635 799454 *mobile* 07788 725164
email info@evabridge.com
website www.evabridge.com
Agent Eva Bridge *Assistants* Jessica Galt, Leanora Adds

Established in 2012. Main areas of work are theatre, musicals, film, television, commercials and voice-over.

Will consider attending performances in London and in the Surrey/Berkshire areas, given 2 weeks' notice. Is happy to receive approaches by actors previously unknown to the agency. Does not currently represent actors with disabilities, but would certainly consider it. *Commission*: Commercials 15%; Film, TV, Voice-overs, Corporate 12%; Theatre 10%

BROOD PMA

49 Greek Street, London W1D 4EG
tel 020 7998 7861
website www.broodmanagement.com
Twitter @broodlondon
Main Agent Brian Parsonage-Kelly

Represents 60 actors and personalities. Clients work throughout the industry from Hollywood to Fringe, corporates to cruises and soaps to commercials. Prospective clients please visit the website, apply by email only **broodapplication@aol.com**.

Valerie Brook Agency

10 Sandringham Road, Cheadle Hulme, Cheshire SK8 5NH
tel 0161 486 1631
email colinbrook@freenetname.co.uk

2 agents represent 25 actors. Areas of work include theatre, musicals, television, film, commercials and corporate role-play.

Will consider attending performances at venues outside Greater London with 2 weeks' notice. Accepts postal submissions (with CVs and photographs) from actors previously unknown to the company. Invitations to view individual actors' websites are also accepted. *Commission*: Negotiated with clients individually

Brown, Simcocks & Andrews LLP PMA

504 The Chandlery, 50 Westminster Bridge Road, London SE1 7QY
tel 020 7953 7484 020 7953 7494
email info@bsaagency.co.uk
website www.brownsimcocksandandrews.co.uk
Partners Carrie Simcocks (retired), Kelly Andrews

Established in the 1970s. Areas of work include theatre, musicals, television, film, commercials and corporate.

Please visit our website to see more information about us and how best to approach us for representation. *Commission*: 10-15%

Brunskill Management Ltd

Suite 8A, 169 Queen's Gate, London SW7 5HE
tel 020 7589 8668 *mobile* 07788 101881
email mark@brunskill.com
Director Mark Holden-Hindley

For artist representation see Stranton Davidson Associates.

BBA Management Ltd

4th Floor, Joel House, 19 Garrick Street, London WC2E 9AX
tel 020 3077 1400
email office@bba.management
website www.bba.management
Director Bronia Buchanan *Agents* Jess Reid, Gails Smith, Sarah Sparrow, Carley Tauchert, Olivia Gould Hutchins

Sole representation of approximately 40 creatives and 224 actors. Areas of work include theatre, musicals, television, film and commercials.

Will consider attending performances at venues within Greater London and elsewhere, but requests as much notice as possible. Accepts submissions by email (with CVs and photographs) from actors previously unknown to the company. Showreels and voicereels are also encouraged. *Commission*: 12.5% +VAT for stage and 15% +VAT for TV and film.

Burnett Crowther Ltd PMA

10 Golden Square, London W1F 9JA
tel 020 7437 8008 *fax* 020 7287 3239
email associates@bcltd.org
website www.bcltd.org
Agents Barry Burnett, Lizanne Crowther

Established in 1965. 2 agents represent 125 actors.

Will consider attending performances at venues within Greater London, with 3 weeks' notice. Accepts submissions by email (with CVs and photographs) from actors previously unknown to the company. See website for further details on how to apply. *Commission*: 10-12%

Burningham Associates
4 Victoria Road, Twickenham TW1 3HW
mobile 07807 176287
email info@burnassoc.org
website www.burnassoc.org
Director Susan Burningham *Associate (Germany)* Margaret Nieman

Established in 2012. Main areas of work are theatre, film, television, radio, commercials, voice-over and corporate (films and training). Also represents playrights.

Accepts letters (with CV and photographs and sae) only. Actors with disabilities are welcome to apply. The agency will only consider actors who have attended a full-time accredited drama school, who are members of Spotlight and intend to become full members of Equity. All actors are expected to have a showreel and voicereel. *Commission*: Theatre, 10%, Film, Television, Radio, Voice Overs Commercials, Corporate 15%

The BWH Agency Ltd PMA
5th Floor, 35 Soho Square, London W1D 3QX
tel 020 7734 0657 *fax* 020 7734 1278
email info@thebwhagency.co.uk
website www.thebwhagency.co.uk
Agents and Company Directors Joe Hutton, Bill Petrie, Lisa Willoughby and Andrew Braidford *Agent* Holly Davidson, all assisted by Nicole Robinson, Oliver Campbell and Maddie Burdett-Couts (accountant)

Established in 2004, main areas of work are theatre, musicals, TV, film, commercials and radio. Welcomes submissions by email onyl, CVs, photographs and showreels.

Paul Byram Associates (THE AGENCY) PMA
Suite B0079, The Long Lodge,
265-269 Kingston Road, Wimbledon, SW19 3FW
tel 020 3137 3385
email contact@paulbyram.com
website www.paulbyram.com
Senior Agent Paul Byram *Agent* Jason Jenkins

Established in 2010 main areas of work are TV, theatre, film, commercials, corporate and musicals. Represents 50 actors, as well as casting directors and directors. Charges commission on a sliding scale.

Welcomes perfomance notices within central London and Fringe venues with 2 weeks' notice; will occasionally go further afield with greater notice.All

contact via the company website contact page or, worst case, vai email only. No post please. Represents actor with disabilities.

CAM (Creative Artists Management) PMA
55-59 Shaftesbury Avenue, London W1D 6LD
tel 020 7292 0600
email reception@cam.co.uk
website www.cam.co.uk
Twitter @CAM_London
Agents Michael Wiggs, Dawn Green, Peter Brooks, Samantha Boyd, Bex Elliff, Lucy Doyle; *Assistants* Alex Scanlan, Lucinda Francis, Caitlin O'Farrell, Kev Reddington, Laura Fowler-Watt

Founded in 1988. Main areas of work include film, television, theatre, musical theatre, commercials, corporate and voice over. Represents about 280 actors; also represents directors. Welcomes performance notices if given about a week's notice, mainly in London, but will consider travelling further afield depending on show/venue/agent availability. Welcomes CVs and photos, and showreels sent by email. Follow-up phone calls not necessary.
Commission varies depending on contract.

Carey Dodd Associates PMA
78 York Street, London W1H 1DP
tel 020 7993 4992
email agents@careydoddassociates.com
email applications@careydoddassociates.com
Agents Christopher Carey, Samantha Dodd

Jessica Carney Associates PMA
4th Floor, 23 Golden Square, London W1F 9JP
tel 020 7434 4143
email assistant@jcarneyassociates.co.uk
website www.jessicacarneyassociates.co.uk

Established in 1950. Areas of work include: theatre, television, films, commercials and musicals. Also represents technicians and craftspeople.

Cannot consider actors for representation unless they can be seen in performance (not showcase) within Greater London (requires 2-3 weeks' notice), or possess good mainstream TV credits. Only accepts submissions if sent by email to **representation@jcarneyassociates.co.uk**. Emails should contain a link to their Spotlight CV and showreel. *Commission*: TV/Film 12.5%; Theatre 10%; Commercials 15%

CBL Management PMA
20 Hollingbury Rise, Brighton BN1 7HJ
mobile 07956 890307
email enquiries@cblmanagement.co.uk
website www.cblmanagement.co.uk
Facebook www.facebook.com/cblmanagement
Twitter @cblmanagement
Agents Claire Carpenter, Beth Eden, Linda Edwards

Established in 2007. 3 agents represent 90 artistes. Works in theatre, musicals, television, film, commercials, corporate and voice-over. Directors, choreographers and musical director also represented.

Welcomes CVs and photographs by email only.

CDA PMA
167-169 Kensington High Street, London W8 6SH
tel 020 7937 2749 *fax* 020 7373 1110
email cda@cdalondon.com
Agents Belina Wright, Theresa Hickey

3 agents represent 60 actors.

Will consider attending performances at venues within Greater London with 3 weeks' notice. Accepts submissions (with CVs and photographs) from actors previously unknown to the company if sent by post. Showreels, voicereels and invitations to view individual actors' websites are also accepted. *Commission*: Variable

Center Stage Agency
7 Rutledge Terrace, South Circular Road, Dublin 8
tel +353 1 453 3599
email geraldinecenterstage@eircom.net
website www.centerstageagency.com

Founded 1994, areas of work include theatre, television, film, musicals, voice-over, commercial and web-based work.

Will consider attending performances at venues in Dublin with 1 weeks' notice. Accepts submissions by email (with CVs and photographs). Showreels are also welcome. *Commission*: 10-15%.

Esta Charkham Associates
16 British Grove, Chiswick, London W4 2NL
tel 020 8741 2843
email office@charkham.net
website www.charkham.net

Boutique talent agency established in 2010. Areas of work include theatre, film, TV, radio, voice-over and comedy.

Will consider attending performances at venues in Greater London area with at least 2 weeks' notice. Accepts submissions of CV and photograph along with a covering letter by way of a request for representation. Does not welcome email enquiries.

Sharry Clark Artists
tel 020 8349 9824; Welsh office 01792 401112
email info@petercharlesworth.co.uk
email sharryclarkeartists@gmail.com
Facebook Sharry Clark Artists
Twitter @SharryCArtists
Director Sharry Clark

Does not welcome unsolicited contact – including performance notices – from actors previously unknown to the company.

Cinetea
9 rue des Trois Bornes, 75011 Paris
tel +33 (0) 1 4278 1717
email cinetea@orange.fr
website www.cinetea.fr
Agent Marie Claude Schwartz

Will accept European actors speaking French; CVs and photographs should be sent by email. Showreels and voicereels also accepted.

Claypole Management
Kemp House, 152-160 City Road,
London EC1V 2NX
tel 0845 650 1777
email info@claypolemanagement.co.uk
website www.claypolemanagement.co.uk

Established in 2000. Areas of work include: theatre, musicals, television, film, commercials and corporate.

Will consider attending performances. Welcomes Spotlight, Catsing Network and Casting Call Pro links to showreels via email. Also welcomes invitations to view individual actors' websites, showreels or Spotlight links. Happy to receive applications for representation from disabled actors.

Clic Agency
7 Ffordd Seion, Bangor, Gwynedd LL57 1BS
tel 01248 354420
email clic@btinternet.com
website www.clicagency.co.uk
Facebook https://facebook.com/groups/
168535334204/
Twitter @clicagency
Proprietor Helen Pritchard

Established in 2008. Represents around 50 actorsfrom all over the UK. Also carries out casting for productions being filmed in North Wales.

Accepts submissions (with CVs and photographs) from actors previously unknown to the company, sent by email. Encourages enquiries from disabled actors and welcomes showreels, voicereels, follow-up calls and invitations to view individual actors' websites. *Commission*: Varies, but not more than 15%

Elspeth Cochrane Personal Management
Now amalgamated with Asquith & Horner. See the company's entry under *Agents* on page 58.

Cole Kitchenn Personal Management Ltd PMA
See the entry for InterTalent Rights Group on page 72 .

Shane Collins Associates PMA
Suite 112, Davina House, 137-149 Goswell Road, London EC1V 7ET

tel 020 7253 1010
email info@shanecollins.co.uk
website www.shanecollins.co.uk
Agent Shane Collins

Established in 1986, the agency represents around 85 actors working in all areas of the industry.

Will consider attending performances within Greater London given as much notice as possible. Accepts submissions from actors previously unknown to the company sent to submissions@shanecollins.co.uk.

Conway Van Gelder Grant PMA

3rd Floor, 8-12 Broadwick Street, London W1F 8HN
tel 020 7287 0077 *fax* 020 7287 1940
Agents Nicholas Gall; Nicola van Gelder and Kat Oliver, assisted by George Davies and Rachael Swanson; John Grant, assisted by Deborah Charlton and Alice Smith and Liz Nelson, assisted by Vena Dacent.

5 agents represent actors working in all areas of the industry.

Will consider attending performances within Greater London and occasionally elsewhere, given 3-4 weeks' notice. Accepts postal submissions (with CVs, photographs and sae to ensure reply) from actors previously unknown to the agency, along with invitations to view an actor's website. Showreels and voicereels should only be sent if requested after initial contact has been made. Follow-up telephone calls and emails are not welcomed. *Commission*: Varies according to contract

Howard Cooke Associates (HCA) PMA

19 Coulson Street, London SW3 3NA
tel 020 7591 0144
Managing Director/Senior Agent Howard Cooke
Associate Agent Bronwyn Sanders

2 agents represent 40 actors. Areas of work include theatre, musicals, television, film, commercials and corporate.

Will consider attending performances at venues within Greater London and elsewhere (if within easy travelling distance) with 3 weeks' notice. Hard-copy applications (with CVs, photographs and sae) from actors previously unknown to the company are welcome, but email submissions are not accepted. *Commission*: 10-20%

Cooper Searle Personal Management Ltd

3rd Floor, 207 Regent Street, London W1B 3HH
tel 020 7183 4851
email admin@coopersearle.com
website www.coopersearle.com
Twitter @CooperSearle
Director/Agent Emily Rose, *Agent* Paul Rose

Established in 2010. Represents around 75 clients. Main areas of work are theatre, musicals, television, film, commercials, corporate, and stills.

Emily and Paul will try to attend performances if it is possible, but welcomes approaches from actors. Emily and Paul will always see clients perform. Applications should be via email containing actor's CV, headshots, and any material or links that can help the agency see their work. The agency considers every application based on performance ability and marketability. *Commission*: 12.5-15%

Clive Corner Associates

'The Belenes', 60 Wakeham, Portland DT5 1HN
tel 01305 860267
email cornerassociates@aol.com
Key personnel Clive Corner, Duncan Stratton

Established in 1988. 2 agents represent 40 actors. Areas of work include theatre, musicals, television, film, commercials and corporate.

Will consider attending performances at venues within Greater London if given 3 weeks' notice. Rarely prepared to travel elsewhere. Accepts submissions by email. *Commission*: 20%

Lou Coulson Associates Ltd PMA

37 Berwick Street, London W1F 8RS
tel 020 7734 9633
email lou@loucoulson.co.uk
Agents: Lou Coulson, Tom Reed, Megan Wheldon, Hattie Windsor, Anne-Rose Yuill, Naomi Downham, Amy Higgins *Assistant*: Kim Wiles

Represents actors working in all areas of the industry and has strong relationships with US agencies and managers.

Will consider attending performances within Greater London and occasionally elsewhere, given notice. Accepts postal submissions (with CVs, photographs and SAE to ensure reply) from actors previously unknown to the agency, along with invitations to view an actor's website. Showreels should only be sent if requested after initial contact has been made. Follow-up telephone calls and emails not welcome.

Commission varies according to contracts.

Coulter Management Agency PMA

Suite 418, The Pentagon Centre, Washington Street, Glasgow G3 8AZ
tel 0141 204 4058
email info@coultermanagement.com
website www.coultermanagement.com
Agent Julie Hamilton *Young Performers Agent* Gary Hamilton *Assistants* Angela Cummiskey, Fran Bloomer

Areas of work include theatre, television, film, commercials, corporate and voice-overs.

Will consider attending performances at venues in Scotland with 3 weeks' notice. Accepts submissions (with CVs and photographs) from actors previously unknown to the company if sent by email. Showreels and voicereels are also accepted. *Commission*: 7.5-15% (sliding scale)

Covent Garden Management

Cida, 7-15 Greatorex Street, London E1 5NF
tel 020 7392 7324 *fax* 020 7240 8409
email info@coventgardenmanagement.com

Established in 2002. The agency represents around 30 actors. Areas of work include theatre, musicals, television, film, commercials, corporate and voice-overs. Also represents directors.

Will consider attending performances at venues within Greater London with 2 weeks' notice. Accepts submissions (with CVs and photographs) from actors previously unknown to the company if sent by post. *Commission:* 10-15%

Cowley, Knox & Guy

3rd Floor, 207 Regents Street, London W1B 3HH
tel 020 3507 1897
email office@ckg.management
website www.ktalent.co.uk
Agents Mel Wildey, Stephanie Fisher, David Stoller

Areas of work include theatre, musicals, television, film, commercials, corporate and voice-overs.

WelcomesCVs and letters from established performers. These should be sent via email. Also welcomes showreels and voice tapes.

Curtis Brown Ltd PMA

Haymarket House, 28-29 Haymarket,
London SW1Y 4SP
tel 020 7393 4400 *fax* 020 7393 4401
email info@curtisbrown.co.uk
website www.curtisbrown.co.uk
Agents Tiffany Agbeko, Debi Allen, Lara Beach (*Assistant* Ashleigh Hall); Kate Buckle, Jacquie Drew (*Assistants* Emma Power and Madeleine Newman-Suttle); Oriana Elia (*Assistants* Jack Collins and Isabelle Whitaker); Mary Fitzgerald and Lucy Johnson (*Assistant* Inez Baxter); Sophie Holden, Cordelia Keaney, Alistair Lindsey-Renton and Helen Clarkson (*Assistants* Emma Bennett and Ronan McCabe); Sarah MacCormack and Emma Higginbottom (*Assistant* Josh Byrne); Charlene McManus (*Assistant* Jessica Lax); Adam Maskwell, Grant Parsons, Joe Powell, Kate Staddon (*Assistants* Abigail Millar and Isabelle Sweetland); Frances Stevenson and Jessica Jackson (*Assistant* Emily Hughes); Sam Turnbull, Olivia Woodward (*Assistant* Alex Sedgley).

One of Europe's oldest and largest independent literary and media agencies. Established over 100 years ago, there are now more than 20 agents within the Book, Media, Actors and Presenters Divisions, 5 of whom represent actors. Also represents writers, directors, playwrights and celebrities.

Submissions should be sent by post and addressed to 'Actors Agents'. They should include a covering letter with email address, CV, photograph, showreel (if actor has one) and sae for the return of the showreel.

Tries to respond within 4-6 weeks. Does not meet potential clients before viewing their work. Does not accept email or faxed submissions. *Commission:* 12.5-15%

David Daly Associates

586 King's Road, London SW6 2DX
tel 020-7384 1036 *fax* 020-7610 9512
email agent@daviddaly.co.uk
Manchester office: 16 King Street, Knutsford WA16 6DL
tel tel 01565 631999 *fax* 01565 755334
email north@daviddaly.co.uk
website www.daviddaly.co.uk
Twitter @DavidDalyAssoc
Agents David Daly, Rosalind Bach (London); David Daly, Mary Ramsay (Manchester)

An established actors' agency bring 30 years of experience to the entertainment industry.

Elizabeth Davies Associates

Suite 279, 116 Ballards Lane, Finchley,
London N3 2DN
tel 020 3138 0950 *mobile* 07534 196166
email edaviesassociates@yahoo.com
Agents Elizabeth Davies, Omar Hunte

Established in 2007. Areas of work include theatre, musicals, TV, film, commercials, corporate, voice-over, touring, booker, PR and marketing. Books are currently closed.

Will consider attending performances at venues within Greater London. Accepts submissions (with CVs and photographs), showreels, voice tapes and invitations to view individual actors' websites. *Commission:* 20-25%

Chris Davis Management PMA

Tenbury House, 36 Teme Street, Tenbury Wells,
Worcestershire WR15 8AA
tel 01584 819005 *fax* 01584 819076
email cdavis@cdm-ltd.com
website www.cdm-ltd.com
Managing Director Chris Davis

Areas of work are theatre, musicals, television, film, commercials and corporate. 2 agents represent 80 actors; directors, choreographers, designers and musical directors are also represented.

Will consider attending performances within Greater London and elsewhere, given as much notice as possible. Welcomes letters (with CVs and photographs) from actors previously unknown to the agency, sent by post or email. Does not welcome follow-up calls. Accepts showreels, voicereels and invitations to view individual actors' websites. Encourages applications from actors with disabilities.

Davis Bishop Associates

Cotton's Farmhouse, 28 Whiston Road, Cogenhoe,
Northamptonshire NN7 1NL

tel 01604 891487
email admin@cottonsfarmhouse.org
Agents Lena Davis, John Bishop

Established in 1986. Areas of work include theatre, musicals, television, film, commercials, corporate, voice-overs. Also represent other skills within the profession.

Will consider attending performances in Greater London with plenty of notice. Accepts submissions (with CVs and photographs) from actors unknown to the company. Follow-up calls and email submissions are not welcomed. *Commission:* 10-20%

Denton Brierley PMA

82 Rivington Place, London EC2A 3AZ
tel 020 3866 5747
email info@dentonbrierley.com
Agents Gavin Denton-Jones, Suzy Brierley and Sofe Goodwin

Three agents represent actors working in all areas of the industry. Will consider attending performances within Greater London, given 2 weeks' notice. Accepts email submissions (with CVs, photographs and showreels) from actors previously unknown to the agency. Commission: varies according to contract.

Devine Artist Management

115 Tempus Building, 9 Mirabel Street, Manchester M3 1NP
tel 0161 726 5726
email manchester@devinemanagement.co.uk
website www.devinemanagement.co.uk

Works in all areas. A paperless office which only accepts applications by email. Prefers to view showreels via a link. Does not welcome follow-up calls. Welcomes applications from young performers. Currently represents several disabled actors and presenters, and encourages applications from such individuals.

Diamond Management PMA

31 Percy Street, London W1T 2DD
tel 020 7631 0400
email agents@diman.co.uk
website www.diamondmanagement.co.uk
*Agents:*Lesley Duff, Jean Diamond, Clare Partridge

Established in 2003. Main areas of work are TV, theatre, commercials and film; also represents directors, MDs, writers and costume designers.

Welcomes letters (with CVs and photographs), follow-up phone calls, CVs and photographs sent by email, showreels, voice tapes and invitations to view actors' websites. Represents actors with disabilities. *Commission* 12.5%

DQ Management

27 Ravenswood Park, Northwood, Middlesex HA6 3PR

tel 01273 721221 *mobile* 07713 984633
email dq.management1@gmail.com
website www.dqmanagement.com
Senior Partners Peter Davis, Kate Davis

Established in 2003. Areas of work include theatre, musicals, television, film, commercials and corporate. 2 agents represent 80 actors.

Will consider attending performances within the Greater London area and elsewhere with at least 2 weeks' notice. Accepts submissions (with CVs and photographs) from actors previously unknown to the company if sent by post. Invitations to view individuals' websites, showreels or voicereels are also accepted. Welcomes enquiries from disabled actors. *Commission:* Theatre 10%; West End 12.5%; TV/Film/Commercials 15%

Kenneth Earle Personal Management

214 Brixton Road, London SW9 6AP
tel 020 7274 1219 *fax* 020 7274 9529
email kennethearle@agents-uk.com
website www.kennethearlepersonalmanagement.com

Established in 2000. 3 agents represent around 40 actors. Areas of work include theatre, musicals, television, film, commercials, corporate and voice-over.

Accepts submissions (with CVs and photographs) from actors previously unknown to the company if sent by post or email. No telephone calls. Please include any showreels, voicereels, demos, links, websites and invitations. *Commission:* 15%

Susi Earnshaw Management

The Bull Theatre, 68 High Street, Barnet, Herts. EN5 5SJ
tel 020 8441 5010 *fax* 020 8364 9618
email casting@susiearnshaw.co.uk
website www.susiearnshawmanagement.com
Agents Susi Earnshaw, Melissa Gillespie, Jessie Tsang, Robin Parsons

Established in 1989. 4 agents and bookers represent 30 adult actors, 60 child performers, and various tribute bands. Areas of work include theatre, musicals, television, film, corporate, live entertainment, dance videos, radio and commercials.

Prefers submissions via email (with CVs and photos). *Commission:* Theatre 10%; TV, Film and Commercials 15%

Elite Talent

54 Crosslee Road, Blackley, Manchester M9 6TA
mobile 07787 342221
email paul@elitetalent.co.uk
website www.elitetalent.co.uk
Twitter @eliteactorsuk
Senior Agent Paul Newbery

Established in 2007. London and Manchester representation. Main areas of work are theatre, musicals, television, film, commercials and corporate.

Will consider attending performances in Manchester/ Northern areas, given 14 days' notice. Welcomes letters (with CVs and photographs) sent by post or email, but prefers email submissions. Also accepts showreels, voicereels (online only), and invitations to view actors' websites. Encourages submissions from actors with disabilities. *Commission*: Theatre 10%, TV, Film, Corporate 15%, Commercials 20%

Emptage Hallett PMA

2nd Floor, 3-5 The Balcony, Castle Arcade, Cardiff, CF10 1BU
tel 02920 344205
email cardiff@emptagehallett.co.uk
website www.emptagehallett.co.uk
Agents Claire Symons, Gemma McAvoy

Founded in 1999, main area of work is theatre, musicals, TV, film, commercials, voice-over and corporate. Represents around 90 actors, and also directors, presenters, writers, fight directors and casting directors. Charges standard PMA rates. They will make every effort to attend performances in Cardiff and surrounding areas. Happy to receive emails with links to view showreels, voicereels and Spotlight CV link. Also welcome applications from actors with disabilities who have a link to their showreel and Spotlight CV.

June Epstein Associates

62 Compayne Gardens, London NW6 3RY
tel 020-7328 0864 or 020-7372 1928
fax 020-7328 0684
email june@june-epstein-associates.co.uk

Established in 1973; represents approximately 40 actors working in theatre, musicals, television, film commercials and corporate role-play. Recommends the photographers Jonathan Dockar-Drysdale (**fact-d@lineone.net**) and Peter Simpkin (**petersimpkin@aol.com**).

Will consider attending performances within Greater London given 2-3 weeks' notice. Accepts postal submissions (with CVs and photographs) from actors previously unknown to the agency. Welcomes voicereels from singers, follow-up telephone calls and showreels, but prefers not to receive emails. *Commission*: 10%; Commercials 15%

The Jane Estall Agency

37 Madeira Drive, Hastings TN34 2NH
mobile 07703 550006
email thejaneestallagency@gmail.com
website www.thejaneestallagency.webeden.com
Owner/Director Jane Estall

Established in 2010. Represents around 25 actors. Areas of work include theatre, musicals, TV, film, commercials, corporate and voice-over. Also represents stand-up comedians and chaperones.

Will consider attending performances, given 1 week's notice. Welcomes submissions (with CVs and

photographs) from actors previously unknown to the agency, sent by post and email; also accepts showreels, voice tapes and invitations to view individual actors' websites. Represents actors with disabilities.

Stephanie Evans Associates

Rivington House, 82 Great Eastern Street, London EC2A 3JF
tel/fax 0870 609 2629
email steph@stephanie-evans.com
website www.stephanie-evans.com
Director Stephanie Evans

Established in 2003. 1 agent represents 60 actors. Areas of work include theatre, musicals, television, film, commercials and corporate.

Will consider attending performances in England and Wales with at least 1 month's notice. Accepts submissions (with CVs, photographs and showreels) from actors previously unknown to the company if sent by post. Invitations to view individual actors' websites are also accepted. Welcomes enquiries from disabled actors. *Commission*: 12%

Paola Farino

109 St George's Road, London SE1 6HY
tel 020 7207 0858
email info@paolafarino.co.uk
website www.paolafarino.co.uk

Established in 2007. Sole agent, works in theatre, TV, film, commercials, corporate and photography. Will consider attending performances within Greater London. Prefers to receive performance notices and all other approaches by email – include Spotlight PIN. "Check website first to see if there is anybody else represented with a similar MO."

Feast Management PMA

1st Floor, 34 Upper Street, London N1 0PN
tel 020 7354 5216
email office@feastmanagement.co.uk
Agents Sadie Feast, Helen Seagriff, Lisa Stark

Three agents represent actors. Areas of work include theatre, musicals, television, film, commercials, corporate and voice-overs.

Will consider attending performances in the London area if plenty of notice is given. Accepts submissions (with CVs and photographs) from actors previously unknown to the company.

First Act Personal Management

2 St Michaels, New Arley, Coventry CV7 8PY
tel 01676 540285 *fax* 01676 542777
email firstactpm@aol.com
website www.spotlightagent.info/firstact
Agent John Burton

Established in 2003. 1 agent represents 25 actors. Areas of work include theatre, musicals, television, film, commercials, corporate and voice-overs.

Will consider attending performances in England and Wales with at least 2 weeks' notice. Accepts submissions (with CVs and photographs) from actors previously unknown to the company if sent by post. Invitations to view individual actors' websites, showreels or voicereels are also accepted. Welcomes enquiries from disabled actors. *Commission*: 10-15%

Flatlined Talent

Unit 2, Campbell Street, Preston PR1 5LX
tel 07557 434680
email office@flatlinedtalent.co.uk
website wwwflatlinedtalent.co.uk
Agents Jacklyn Cooksley-Pekepo, Kay Purcell

Established in 2011. Main areas of work are theatre, musicals, television, film, commercials and corporate. 2 agents represent 20 actors.

Will consider attending performances anywhere in Great Britain, and preferably in the North West, given at least 2 weeks' notice. Accepts letters and emails from individuals previously unknown to the agency, if accompanied by CVs and photographs. Currently represents no disabled actors, but offers positive discrimination to all. *Commission*: Rep Theatre/Corporate/low-paid work 5-10%; TV/Film 15%

Kerry Foley Management Ltd

Holly Bush House, 3 Rennison Drive, Wombourne, South Staffordshire WV5 9HW
mobile 07747 864001
email kerry@kfmltd.com
website www.kfmltd.com
Twitter @KFM_Agency
Director Kerry Foley

Established in 2011. Main areas of work are theatre, musicals, television, film, commercials and corporate. Also represents creatives, including directors, musical directors and choreographers. Will consider CVs and photographs sent by email. Agency is open to all actors on their merits.

James Foster Ltd

G33, Waterfront Studios, 1 Dock Road, London E16 1AG
tel 020 7434 0398
email info@jamesfosterltd.co.uk
website www.jamesfosterltd.co.uk
Twitter @JamesFosterLTD
Managing Director/Senior Agent James Foster

Originally Jeremy Brook Limited and Jean Clarke Management (established in 1995). Areas of work include theatre, musicals, television, film, commercials, corporate and radio.

Will consider attending performances in Greater London with at least 3-4 weeks' notice. Accepts submissions from actors previously unknown to the agency by email (see website for further details). Showreels, voicereels and invitations to views an

actor's website are also accepted, but follow-up calls and emails are not welcome.

Julie Fox Associates

tel London 020 3092 1512 North 01270 780880
email agent@juliefoxassociates.co.uk
website www.juliefoxassociates.co.uk
Agents Julie Fox, Corrine Murray

Agency works in all areas of live and recorded media. 2 agents represent 50 actors; directors and casting directors also represented. Accepts email approaches only (letters, CVs, showreels or links to Spotlight).

Hilary Gagan Associates PMA

187 Drury Lane, London WC2B 5QD
tel 020 7404 8794 *fax* 020 7430 1869
email hilary@hgassoc.co.uk
Assistant Shiv Coard

3 agents represent approximately 100 actors. Areas of work include theatre, musicals, television, film, commercials, corporate, voice-overs. Also represents directors and choreographers.

Will consider attending performances in Greater London with at least 2 weeks' notice. Accepts submissions (with CVs and photographs with name on back of photograph) from actors previously unknown to the agency (include sae). Invitations to view individual actors' websites, showreels and voicereels are also accepted. Follow-up calls are welcomed, as are enquiries from disabled actors. *Commission*: 7.5-15%

Galloways PMA

Suite 410, Henry Wood House, 2 Riding House Street, London W1W 7FA
email info@gallowaysagency.com
website www.gallowaysagency.com
Head Agent Jilly Moore; *Agent* Romany Hoyland; *Commercials Agent* Miranda Heffernan

Established in 1985, and represents actors for stage, screen, radio and commercials.

Galloways is a small, close-knit team who focus on the individual needs of our actors. Many of our clients have been with us since the inception of the company but we are also constantly looking for fresh talent to add to our list. We also work with agents in New York and Los Angeles.

Submissions for representation can be made either by post or email. No phone calls please. We will respond to all postal applications which include a self-addressed envelope.

Gardner Herrity PMA

24 Conway Street, London W1T 6BG
tel 020 7388 0088 *fax* 020 7388 0688
email info@gardnerherrity.co.uk
Key contact Andy Herrity

Areas of work include feature films, television, theatre and radio drama.

Will consider attending performances within the Greater London area with at least 3 weeks' notice. Accepts submissions if sent by email representation@gardnerherrity.co.uk. Welcomes enquiries from disabled actors. *Commission*: 10%

Garricks PMA

Angel House, 76 Mallinson Road,
London SW11 1BN
tel 020-7738 1600
email info@garricks.net
Key contact Megan Willis

Established in 1981. Areas of work include theatre, television, film, commercials and corporate.

Will consider attending performances at venues within Greater London and elsewhere. Accepts submissions (with CVs and photographs) from actors previously unknown to the company, sent by post or (preferably) email. Invitations to view individual actors' websites are also accepted. *Commission*: TV, Film and Theatre 10%; Commercials 15%

Gilbert & Payne Personal Management

Room 404, 4th Floor, Linen Hall,
162-168 Regent Street, London W1B 5TB
tel 020 7734 7505 *fax* 020 7494 3787
email ee@gilbertandpayne.com
Director Elena Gilbert *Key personnel* Elaine Payne

Established in 1996. 2 agents represent 50 actors. Areas of work include theatre, musicals, television, film, commercials and corporate, with a particular emphasis on musical theatre. Also represents choreographers.

Will consider attending performances at venues in Greater London with a minimum of 1 week's notice. Accepts submissions (with CVs and photographs) from actors previously unknown to the company if sent by post. Follow-up telephone calls are also accepted. *Commission*: Theatre 10%

Global Artists PMA

6th Floor, 41-44 Great Queen Street, Covent Garden,
London WC2B 5AD
tel 020 7839 4888 *fax* 020 7839 4555
email info@globalartists.co.uk
website www.globalartists.co.uk

A personal management company representing professional actors and actresses. Areas of work include theatre, musical theatre, television, film, commercials and corporate. Also represents a limited number of theatre designers, choreographers, directors and musical directors.

Accepts submissions from actors previously unknown to the company, sent by post or email. Does not welcome telephone enquiries.

Gordon & French PMA

12-13 Poland Street, London W1F 8QB
tel 020 7734 4818 *fax* 020 7734 4832

website www.gordonandfrench.co.uk
Agents Kate Bryden, Christina Cooke, Donna French

Established in 1972. Main areas of work are theatre, TV, film commercials and voice-over. Represents 70 performers.

Accepts requests for respresentation by post or email; the email address for submissions is representation@gordonandfrench.co.uk. If applying by post and would like material returned please enclose an sae. Every representation reuest is read but owing to the volume of material received the company is only able to respond to those submissions it would like to pursue. The company only caters for voice work for thier existing clients and therefore are unable to accept these representation requests.

Grantham-Hazeldine Ltd PMA

Suite 427, The Linen Hall, 162-168 Regent St,
London W1B 5TE
tel 020 7038 3737
email agents@granthamhazeldine.com
website www.granthamhazeldine.com
Agents Gina Rowland and Nicholas Errington

Established in 1984. The agents represent actors and creatives. Areas of work include theatre, musicals, television, film, commercials, corporate and voice-overs. Also represents writers and stunt co-ordinators.

Accepts submissions (with CVs, photos and showreel) from actors previously unknown to the company if sent by email. *Commission*: Radio 10% plus VAT; Theatre 12.5% plus VAT; TV and Film 15% plus VAT

Darren Gray (Management)

2 Marston Lane, Portsmouth, Hampshire PO3 5TW
tel 023 9269 9973 *fax* 023 9267 7227
email darren.gray1@virgin.net
website www.darrengraymanagement.com
Managing Director Darren Gray

Established in 1994. 2 agents represent 60 actors in both England and Australia. Agency mainly represents Australian actors, the majority of whom come from Australian soap operas. Areas of work include theatre, musicals, television, film, commercials, corporate and voice-overs. Also represents directors, producers, writers and presenters.

Will consider attending performances at venues within Greater London and elsewhere at whatever notice possible. Accepts submissions (with CVs and photographs) from actors previously unknown to the company, sent by post or email. Showreels, voicereels and invitations to view individual actors' websites are also accepted. Welcomes enquiries from disabled actors. *Commission*: 10%

Louise Gubbay Associates

69 Paynesfield Road, Tatsfield, Kent TN16 2BG
tel 01959 573080

email alex@louisegubbay.com
website www.louisegubbay.com
Managing Director Louise Gubbay

Founded in 2006. Works in theatre, musicals, television, film, commercials and corporate. LGA represents 40 actors.

Welcomes CVs from professionally trained actors only, by post or email. LGA is a full member of the Agents Association (London region) and now has an LA division. *Commission:* Varies

Hall James Personal Management
12 Melcombe Place, London NW1 6JJ
tel 020 3036 0558
email info@halljames.co.uk
website www.halljames.co.uk
Directors Sam Hall, Stori James

Established in 2006. Areas of work include musicals, television, film, commercials and corporate. 2 agents represent around 50 actors; also represents theatre directors and choreographers.

Welcomes performance notices and letters (with CVs) from individual actors previously unknown to the agency, as well as showreels. *Commission:* 10%

Hamilton Hodell Ltd PMA
20 Golden Square, London W1F 9JL
tel 020 7636 1221 *fax* 020 7636 1226
email info@hamiltonhodell.co.uk
website www.hamiltonhodell.co.uk
Agents Alexander Cooke, Madeleine Dewhirst, Christopher Farrar, Elizabeth Fergusson, Christian Hodell, Hannah O'Sullivan, Sian Smyth, Joshua Woodford

The agency represents 150 actors, working in leading roles in film, television, theatre and radio productions.

The Harris Agency Ltd
71 The Avenue, Watford, Herts WD17 4NU
tel 01923 211644
email theharrisagency@btconnect.com
Agent Sharon Harris

In association with The Harris Drama School. Evening acting workshops for all clients and actors seeking representation. Established in 1977. 2 agents represent 40 clients.

Accepts invitations for productions at any time of year. Welcomes letters (with CVs and photographs) from actors previously unknown to the agency, sent by post or email. Also accepts follow-up calls, showreels, voicereels, and invitations to view individual actors' websites. Encourages enquiries from actors with disabilities. *Commission:* Theatre 10%; TV, Film, Commercials 15%

Harvey Stein Associates Ltd
tel 020 7175 7937
email info@harveystein.co.uk
website www.harveystein.co.uk
Managing Director Lois Harvey

Established in 2015, with 1 agent and 1 assistant, managing a small client list working throughout the industry. Happy to receive respresentation requests by email, but no large files, just links.

HATCH Talent Ltd PMA
113 Shoreditch High Street, London EC1 6JN
tel 020 3950 6333
email info@hatchtalent.co.uk
website www.hatchtalent.co.uk
Agents Vic Murray, Michael Ford, Becky Williams, Lucy Nooshin; *Agent's Assistants:* Clarissa Efthymaides, Buffy Watling

Established in 2017, and currently representing over 150 clients. Areas of work include theatre, TV, film and radio; also represents presenters, comedians and writers. Welcomes CVs, photographs and showreels sent by email. Committed to a policy of equal opportunity.

Hatton McEwan Penford PMA
Studio 11.B.1 The Leather Market, Weston Street, London SE1 3ER
tel 020 3735 8278
email mail@hattonmcewanpenford.com
website www.hattonmcewanpenford.com
Agents Aileen McEwan, James Penford, Jess Francis

Established in 1988, the agency represents actors working in theatre, musicals, television, film and commercials.Actors will consider short film work if paid; submit a CV and script with enquiries.

Representation Cannot accept postal submissions. Only attach one small image to emails. Please don't send show-reels as files, links to Spotlight, Vimeo etc are the best way. Due to a high number of submissions the company will only respond it wishes to take things further. Please give as much notice as possible for invitations to performances; unlikely to be able to travel outside of London.

Cheryl Hayes Management
85 Rothschild Road, London W4 5NT
tel 020 8994 4447 *mobile* 07767 685560
email cheryl@cherylhayes.co.uk
website www.cherylhayes.co.uk

Established in 2008. Primarily represents comedy writer/performers.

Will consider attending performances if given 2-3 weeks' notice. Welcomes approaches from actors, comedy writers and performers with CVs and photographs by post or email, and will accept showreels, voicereels and invitations to view individual actors' websites. *Commission:* 15%

Henry's Agency
53 Westbury, Rochford, Essex SS4 1UL
tel 01702 541413 *fax* 01702 541413
email info@henrysagency.co.uk
website www.henrysagency.co.uk

Established in 1995; 1 agent represents 35 actors. Areas of work include theatre, musicals, television, film, commercials and corporate.

Will consider attending performances at venues within Greater London with 2 weeks' notice. Accepts submissions (with CVs and photographs) from actors previously unknown to the company if sent by post. Emails are accepted if attachments consist of Word documents or small jpeg files. Follow-up telephone calls, showreels and voicereels are also accepted. Recommends the photographer Ash (**ash@ashphotomedia.com**). *Commission*: Varies

Hobson's Actors

62 Chiswick High Road, Chiswick, London W4 1SY
tel 020 8995 3628 *fax* 020 8996 5350
website www.hobsons-international.com
Drama Agent Christina Beyer *Commercial Agent* Linda Sacks

Areas of work include theatre, musicals, television, film, commercials and corporate.

Will consider attending performances at venues within Greater London given 2 weeks' notice. Accepts submissions (with CVs and photographs) from actors previously unknown to the company if sent by post. Showreels are also accepted.

Jane Hollowood Associates Ltd

10 Bradley Street, Mancheser M1 1EH
tel 0161 237 9141 *tel* 020 8291 5545
mobile 07712 436566
email info@janehollowood.co.uk
website www.janehollowood.co.uk
Agents Jane Hollowood, Frankie Stoner

Established in 1998; 2 agents represent approx. 85 actors working in many areas of the industry.

Will consider attending performances within Greater London and potentially elsewhere, depending on diary commitments and provided that 2-3 weeks' notice is given. Accepts postal and email submissions (with CVs and photographs) from actors previously unknown to the agency. Showreels and voicereels should only be sent on request, and follow-up telephone calls are unwelcome. *Commission*: Theatre 10%; Radio, Role-play and Voice-overs 12%; Television, Film and Commercials 15%

HR Creative Artists (HRCA)

tel 020 3286 8830
email contact@hrca.eu
website www.hrca.eu

Representing a culturally rich mix of artists from across Europe and worldwide. Applications must be made electronically via email, following the submissions guidelines on the website.

Nancy Hudson Associates PMA

50 South Molton Street, London W1K 5SB
tel 020 7499 5548

email agents@nancyhudsonassociates.com
website www.nancyhudsonassociates.com
Twitter @NHALtd
Director/Agent Nancy Hudson; *Agent* Hana Voyce

Established in 1999. 2 agents representing 80 actors. Areas of work include theatre, television, film, commercials, radio, corporate and voice-overs.

Welcomes submissions by email with Spotlight link.

Steve Hughes Management Ltd

tel 0844 5564670
email management@stevehughesuk.com
website www.stevehughesuk.com
Artist Manager Steve Hughes

Founded in 2012. Management company and theatre producer based in London, with an extensive network of contacts in all areas of the entertainment and music business. Client portfolio includes a range of high-profile celebrities. A strong emphasis on developing new and exciting talent.

Welcomes letters (with CVs and photographs) from individual actors previously unknown to the agency, sent by post but not email. Will consider invitations to view actors' websites and to visit productions.

Hunwick Associates PMA

3F1, 44 Howe Street, Edinburgh EH3 6TH
tel 0131 667 0530
email maryam@hunwickassociates.com
website www.hunwickassociates.com
Actors Agent Maryam Hunwick *Writers/Directors Agent* Lisa Nicoll

Personal management agency established in 1999. 1 agent represents actors in all media including several BAFTA and BIFA award-winning stage, screen and television artists.

Will consider attending performances at venues within Greater London and in Scotland given 4 weeks' notice. Accepts submissions (with CVs and photographs) from actors previously unknown to the company if sent by post. Will also accept showreels. *Commission*: Theatre 10%; TV and Broadcast Media 12.5%; Commercials 15%

IAMBE Productions Ltd

376 London Road, Hadleigh, Essex SS7 2DA
mobile 07834 584977
email admin@iambeproductions.com
website www.iambeproductions.com
Twitter @Acts4events
Agent IAMBE Productions

Established in 2015. Areas of work include theatre, film, corporate and festivals.

Will consider attending performances, though this is dependent on client. Accepts submissions by email (with CVs and photographs) and links to showreels. Happy to consider applications for representation from disabled actors. *Commission:* Varies

Icon Actors Management
Tanzaro House, Ardwick Green North,
Manchester M12 6FZ
tel 0161 273 3344
email info@iconactors.net
website www.iconactors.net
Agent Kirstie Jones

Established in 2000. Areas of work include theatre,
musicals, television, film, commercials, corporate and
voice-overs.

iD Agency Limited
6 Paramount Court, 41 University Street,
London WC1E 6JP
mobile 07528 381833
email info@theidagency.co.uk
website www.theidagency.co.uk
Company Directors Hannah Burt, Barbara Adie

Established in 2011. Works in theatre, musicals, TV,
film, commercials, corporate and presenting. 2 agents
represent 30 clients (actors and presenters).

Will consider attending performances in London.
Actors should send CVs and photographs by email to
info@theidagency.co.uk. *Commission*: 12.5%, 20%
for commercial

IDAMOS Agency
1 Frederick Court, London E18 1LE
tel 020 3318 0244
email idamosagency@gmail.com
website www.idamos.com
Director Liz Isaac *Head Agent* Phillip Barnes

Established in 2012, IDAMOS represents actors with
unique skills in a variety of performance fields,
including theatre, musicals, film, TV, commercials,
corporate and voice-over. 2 agents represent 55
actors.

Will consider attending performances at venues
within Greater London with 2 weeks' notice. Accepts
submissions (with CVs and photographs), and also
happy to receive showreels, voicereels and invitations
to view individual actors' websites, all via email. Does
not currently represent disabled actors.

Identity Agency Group (IAG) PMA
95 Gray's Inn Road, London WC1X 8TX
tel 020 7504 2510
email casting@identityagencygroup.com
website www.identityagencygroup.com
Agents in theatre, film and TV: Femi Oguns (CEO),
Jonathan Hall and Ikki El-Amriti *Agent for
Commercial Division* Eleanor Kirby

Established in 2006, offers personal management in
London, Los Angeles and Toronto.
    Full respresentation with IAG is by invitation only.
Does not accept submissions via email or post.

Imperial Personal Management Ltd
102 Kirkstall Road, Leeds LS3 1JA
tel 0113 244 3222

email katie@ipmcasting.com
website www.ipmcasting.com
Managing Director Katie Ross

Established in 2007. 4 agents represent 30-50 actors
working in television and film; also has a subsidiary
company, IPM Crew. Recommends Imperial
Photography (**info@ipmcasting.com**).

Welcomes performance notices within the Greater
London and Northern areas (within 50 miles of the
company's postcode), and prefers 1 month's notice if
possible. Welcomes letters (with CVs and
photographs) from individual actors previously
unknown to the agency, sent by post or email.
Accepts follow-up telephone calls, showreels and
voicereels, and welcomes invitations to view
individual actors' websites. Encourages enquiries
from actors with disabilities. *Commission*: 10-15%

Independent Talent Group Ltd PMA
40 Whitfield Street, London W1T 2RH
tel 020 7636 6565

Areas of work include theatre, musicals, television,
film, commercials, corporate and voice-overs. Also
represents directors, writers, technicians and
presenters.

Will consider attending performances at venues
within Greater London. Accepts submissions (with
CVs and photographs) from actors previously
unknown to the company if sent by post. SAE must
be included. We do not accept email submissions.
Commission: 12.5%

Inter-City Casting
27 Wigan Lane, Wigan,
Greater Manchester WN1 1XR
tel 01942 321969
email intercitycasting@btconnect.com
Agent Caroline Joynt

Established in 1983. 2 agents represent approximately
60 actors. Areas of work include theatre, musicals,
television, film, commercials and corporate.

Will consider attending performances at venues in
Manchester and Liverpool. Accepts submissions (with
CVs and photographs) from actors previously
unknown to the company if sent by post. Showreels,
voicereels and invitations to view individual actors'
websites also accepted. Recommends the
photographer Michael Pollard (see entry under
Photographers and repro companies on page 391).
Commission: 10-12.5% plus VAT

International Actors London (IAL)
Penthouse 11, Bickenhall Mansions,
London W1U 6BR
tel 020 7125 0539
email ialagents@gmail.com
website www.ialagency.com
Key contact John Riordan

Established in 2011. Works in theatre, TV, film and commercials. 2 agents represent ethnically diverse and international actors based in the UK.

Will consider attending performances within the Greater London area, given 2-4 weeks' notice. Actors should apply by emailing their Spotlight link, which should have their showreel attached. Does not currently represent actors with disabilities, but applications are welcome. *Commission*: Theatre 10%; Voice-over, Commercial Theatre 12.5%; TV, Film, Commercials 15%

InterTalent Rights Group PMA (incorporating Cole Kitchenn Management Ltd)

InterTalent House, 46 Charlotte Street, London W1T 2GS
020 7427 5681
email actors@intertalentgroup.com

Managing Directors/Agents Oliver Thomson (*Associate* Marcus Ellard), Alex Segal (*Associate* Martha Atack), Ashley Valence (*Assistant* Bex Severn) *Agent* Brooke Kinsella (*Associate* Alexandra MacMillan), *Assistant* Zach Brown

Welcomes performance notices within Greater London given 2–3 weeks' notice.

For prospective clients who would like to submit their CVs for representation, please enclose an SAE if you would like your photo/CV returned. Prefers email submissions. Please include any links and show-reels. Unfortunately, cannot guarantee a reply.

Irish Actors London Ltd

Penthouse 11, Bickenhall Mansions, London W1U 6BR
tel 020 7125 0539
email irishactorslondon@gmail.com
website www.irishactorslondon.co.uk
Key contact John Riordan

Established in 2010. 2 agents represent Irish actors working in theatre, TV, film and commercials.

Will consider attending performances within the Greater London area, given 2-4 weeks' notice. Actors should apply by emailing their Spotlight link, which should have their showreel attached. Does not currently represent actors with disabilities, but applications are welcome. *Commission*: Theatre 10%; Voice-over/Commercial Theatre 12.5%; TV, Film, Commercials 15%

JB Associates

PO Box 173, Manchester M19 0AR
tel 0161 249 3666
email info@j-b-a.net
website www.j-b-a.net
Proprietor John Basham

Established in 1996. 2 agents represent 65 actors. Areas of work include theatre, musicals, television, film, commercials, corporate and voice-overs.

Will consider attending performances at venues in the North and occasionally elsewhere, given 3-4 weeks' notice. Accepts submissions (with CVs and photographs) from actors previously unknown to the company preferably by email. Will also accept showreels, voicereels, and invitations to view individual actors' websites. *Commission*: Theatre 10%; TV 15%

Jeffrey & White Management Ltd PMA

7 Paynes Park, Hitchen, Hertfordshire SG5 1EH
tel 01462 429769
email info@jeffreyandwhite.co.uk
Partners Gemma Towersey and Ellie Goodhew

Established in 1986. 2 agents represent 70 actors. Areas of work include theatre, musicals, television, film, commercials and corporate.

Will consider attending performances given as much notice as possible. Accepts submissions (with CVs and photographs) from actors previously unknown to the company if sent by post or email. *Commission*: Theatre, Film and TV 12.5%; Commercials 15%

Mark Jermin Management

University of Wales, Trinity Saint David, Mount Pleasant Campus, Swansea SA1 6ED
tel 01792 458855
email info@markjermin.co.uk
website www.markjermin.co.uk
Agents Mark Jermin, Charlotte Robb, Kelly Smith

Established in 2007. Areas of work include theatre, musicals, television, film, commercials, corporate and voice-overs.

Will consider attending performances at venues within London, Manchester and south and west Wales, given 2 weeks' notice. Accepts submissions by email (with CVs and photographs) for actors unknown to the agents. Also accepts unsolicited CVs (with photgraphs), via email. Happy to receive invitations to view actors' websites and to consider applications for representation from disabled actors. *Commission*: Negotiable

Jewell, Wright Ltd

22 Upper Ground, London SE1 9PD
tel 020 3865 0932
email agents@jwl-london.com
website www.jwl-london.com
Twitter @JewellWrightLtd
Director/Agent Jimmy Jewell *Agent* Neal Wright
Junior Agent Connie Woodall

Established in 2005. Main areas of work are theatre, musicals, television, film, commercials and radio. 3 agents represent 100 actors.

Will attend performances in Greater London only, if given at least 2 weeks' notice. Welcomes letters (with CVs and photographs, plus showreel) from individual actors previously unknown to the company if sent by email. Actively encourages enquiries from actors with disabilities. *Commission*: Theatre 12.5%; Television/Film 15%; Commercials 17.5%

Johnston & Mathers Associates Ltd

PO Box 3167, Barnet, London EN5 2WA
tel 020 8449 4968 *fax* 020 8449 4968
email Johnstonmathers@aol.com
website www.johnstonandmathers.com
Key personnel Dawn Mathers, Suzanne Johnston

Established in 2001. Areas of work include theatre, musicals, television, film, commercials and corporate. A small agency of around 40 actors.

Will consider attending performances within the Greater London area with at least 1 month's notice. Accepts submissions (with CVs and photographs) from actors previously unknown to the company if sent by email. Invitations to view individual actors' websites are accepted, as are showreels and voicereels. Welcomes enquiries from disabled actors.

JPA Management PMA

30 Daws Hill Lane, High Wycombe,
Buckinghamshire HP11 1PW
tel 01494 520978
email agent@jpaassociates.co.uk
website www.jpaassociates.co.uk
Agent Marylyn Phillips

Established in 1995, main areas of work are theatre, musicals, TV, film, commercials, corporate, voice overs and radio. Represents over 40 actors. *Commission*: 10%-15%. Does not welcome performance notices. Welcomes CVs and photographs sent by email. Represents actors with disabilities.

KAL Management

95 Gloucester Road, Hampton,
Middlesex TW12 2UW
tel 020 8783 0039 *fax* 020 8979 6487
email kaplan222@aol.com
website www.kaplan-kaye.co.uk
Key personnel Kaplan Kaye

Established in 1982. Sole representation of approximately 25 actors. Areas of work include theatre, musicals, television, film, commercials, corporate and voice-overs.

Will consider attending performances at venues within Greater London given as much notice as possible. Accepts submissions (with CVs and photographs) from actors previously unknown to the company if sent by post. Showreels and voicereels should only be sent on request. *Commission*: Theatre 10%; TV 15%

Roberta Kanal Agency

82 Constance Road, Twickenham,
Middlesex TW2 7JA
tel 020 8894 2277 *fax* 020 8894 7952
email roberta.kanal82@gmail.com
Director Roberta Kanal

Established in 1972; 1 agent represents approximately 30 actors working in all areas of the industry.

"Take a simple approach: phone first; send a CV if requested, with a clear letter and one photograph, along with an sae for their return. As with casting directors, only use email if requested. Unsolicited items will be ignored due to the growing number of applications becoming impossible to handle."

Keddie Scott Associates PMA

31 Hatton Garden, London EC1N 8DH
tel 020 3490 1050 *fax* 020 7147 1326
mobile 07786 070543
email info@keddiescott.com
website www.keddiescott.com
Managing Director Fiona Keddie-Ord assisted by Jonathan McHardy and Richard Vincent. *Scottish Book* Paul Harper assisted by Tamsin Pollock (email scotland@keddiescott.com. *Northern Book* Anthony Williams assisted by Sue Avanson (*email* north@keddiescott.com)

Keddie Scott Associates Ltd has been established since 2003. Works in all areas of the performing arts industry, including TV, film, commercials, theatre, musical theatre (small- mid- large-scale) and corporate assignments of every nature. Please note that KSA operates on a Personal Exclusive Management basis.

Robert Kelly Associates PMA

10 Greek Street, London, W1D 4DH
email rep@robertkellyassociates.com
website www.robertkellyassociates.com

Established in 2006. Robert Kelly represent clients in television, film, theatre, musical theatre, radio and commercials. Recommends the photographer Brandon Bishop (**www.brandonbishopphotography.com**). Will consider attending performances within Greater London, at repertory theatres nationally and at Number 1 touring venues in the South East if given 4-6 weeks' notice.

Welcomes letters (with CVs) from individual actors previously unknown to the agency. Submissions should be sent by post or email. Showreels, voicereels and invitations to view individual actors' websites are also accepted. *Commission*: Theatre 10%; Corporate & Radio 12.5%; TV & Film 15%

Steve Kenis & Co PMA

95 Barkston Gardens, London SW5 0EU
tel 020 7434 9055 *fax* 020 7373 9404
email sk@sknco.com
Agents Steve Kenis, Karen Holmes

Founded in 2000. 2 agents represent 14 actors, as well as writers, directors and technicians. *Commission*: 10%

Kew Personal Management

PO Box 765, Redhill, Surrey RH1 9HB
mobile 07876 457402
email info@kewpersonalmanagement.com
website www.kewpersonalmanagement.com
Company Manager Kate Winn

Works in theatre, musicals, TV, film, commercials, corporate, voice-over and presenting.

Will consider attending performances in the Greater London area. Accepts letters (with CVs and photographs) from actors previously unknown to the company, but email is preferred. Accepts showreels, voicereels and links to Spotlight pages. Also represents children. Happy to accept submissions from disabled actors.

LA Management

10 Fair Oak Close, Kenley, Surrey CR8 5LJ
tel 020 7183 6211
email lee-ann@lamanagement.biz
website www.lamanagement.biz
Actors' Agent/Talent Director Lee-Ann Robathan

Established in 2006. Main areas of work are television, film, commercials, corporate, theatre and radio. Also represents presenters, singers and voice-over artists. Will see actors perform, but requires 1 week's notice.

Welcomes letters with follow-up calls, emails, showreels and voicereels. LA Management is open to representing all actors, with or without disabilities.

Laine Management

131 Victoria Road, Salford M6 8LF
tel 0161 789 7775 *fax* 0161 787 7572
email info@lainemanagement.co.uk
website www.lainemanagement.co.uk
Company Director Samantha Greeley

Areas of work include theatre, television, film, commercials and corporate.

Will consider attending performances at venues in Manchester and the surrounding area with 2-4 weeks' notice. Accepts CVs and photographs from individuals previously unknown to the agency, but emails, showreels and invitations to view individual actors' websites are not welcomed. *Commission*: 15%

Langford Associates Ltd

17 Westfields Avenue, Barnes, London SW13 0AT
tel 020 8878 7148
website www.langfordassociates.com
Key personnel Barry Langford, Simon Hayes

Established in 1987. 1 agent represents 40-45 actors. Areas of work include theatre, television, film, commercials, corporate and voice-overs.

Will consider attending performances at mainstream venues within Greater London, given 2 weeks' notice. Accepts submissions (with CVs and photographs) by

post or email. Email submissions should include no more than 1 small image (emails with multiple attachments will be deleted unread). 'Name' actors seeking representation may ring and speak to Barry Langford in complete confidence.

"I am always happy to receive details by post and I regularly meet with new actors. When writing, please include an sae if you would like your details to be returned. Please do not send unsolicited showreels. I prefer to receive 10x8in photographs, and would suggest that you use a good photographer and update your photo at least every 18 months. Make sure you are listed in Spotlight, as this is a prerequisite for all professional actors."

Nina Lee Management PMA

Suite 36, 88-90 Hatton Garden, London EC1N 8PN
tel 020 3375 6269
email nina@ninaleemanagement.com
website www.ninaleemanagement.com
Agent Nina Lee

Areas of work include theatre, TV, film, commercials, corporate and radio.

Welcomes performance notices, each one will be considered on its individual merits. Accepts submissions by email (with CVs and photographs).

Mike Leigh Associates

11-12 Great Sutton Street, London EC1V 0BX
tel 020 7017 8757 *fax* 020 7486 5886
email mail@mikeleighassoc.com
website www.mikeleighassoc.com
Agents Mike Leigh, Janie Jenkins

Established in 2007. Works in all areas except voice-over. 2 agents represent 60 actors; also represented are presenters, comedians, DJs and writers. Recommends the photographer Steve Ullathorne (**steve@steveullathorne.com**).

Will consider attending performances within Greater London given 1 month's notice. Welcomes letters (with CVs and photographs) from actors previously unknown to the agency if sent by post, but not by email. Will accept showreels, voicereels, and invitations to view individual actors' websites.
Commission: 15%

Leno Martin Associates Ltd

Personal Management/Theatre Production/Casting,
3B Nettlefold Place, London SE27 0JW
tel 020 8655 7656
email info@lenomartinassociates.com
website www.lenomartinassociates.com
Twitter @LMAagents
Senior Agent Antony Stuart-Hicks (Theatre/Screen)
Senior Agent Paul Leno (MT/Commercials/International/Cruise)*Senior Agent* Leon Kay (Musical Theatre)

Established in 2014. Main areas of talent management are theatre, musical theatre, television, film, commercials, cruise ships, UK/International tours and pantomime. Will consider attending performances within the London/Greater London area, given 2-4 weeks' notice.

Welcomes letters and emails (with CVs and headshots); also accepts showreels and invitations to view individual actors' websites. Emails accepted. "We would prefer, where possible, to attend a performance." Currently looking to expand representation of versatile performers. An Equal Opportunities company. *Commission*: Stage 12.5%; Screen 15%; Self-sourced 10%. Contract: 12 month minimum term.

Lime Actors Agency & Management Ltd

Nemesis House, 1 Oxford Court, Bishopsgate, Manchester M2 3WQ
tel 0161 236 0827 *fax* 0161 228 6727
email georgina@limemanagement.co.uk
Director Georgina Andrew

Established in 1999. 1 agent represents 70 actors. Areas of work include theatre, musicals, television, film, commercials, corporate and voice-overs. Also represents musical directors.

Will consider attending performances at venues within Greater London and elsewhere given 4 weeks' notice. Accepts submissions (with CVs and photographs) from actors previously unknown to the company if sent by post. Follow-up telephone calls, showreels, voicereels and invitations to view individual actors' websites are also accepted.

Linkside Agency

57 High Street, Ashford, Kent TN24 8SG
tel 020 7384 1477 *fax* 01372 801972
email info@linksideagency.com

Established in 1986. 2 agents represent 40 actors. Areas of work include theatre, musicals, television, film, commercials, corporate and voice-overs.

Will consider attending performances at venues within Greater London given a minimum of 2 weeks' notice. Accepts submissions (with CVs and photographs) from actors previously unknown to the company if sent by email. Showreels and voicereels are also accepted.

Gina Long (Longrun Artistes)

71-75 Shelton Street, Covent Garden, London WC2H 9JQ
tel 01843 639747 *mobile* 07748 723228
email longrunartistes@icloud.com
website www.longrunartistes.com
Twitter @longrunartistes
Founder/Director Gina Long

Established in 2005. Works in theatre, musicals, TV, film, commercials, corporate, voice-over and dance. 2 agents represent 120 clients. Will accept unsolicited applications from actors previously unknown to the agency, as hard copy (with photographs).

Eva Long Agents

107 Station Road, Earls Barton, Northants NN6 0NX
mobile 07736 700849
fax 01604 811921
email EvaLongAgents@yahoo.co.uk
Key personnel Eva Long

Established in 2003. 1 agent represents 40 actors. Areas of work include theatre, musicals, television, film, commercials, corporate and voice-overs.

Will consider attending performances within the Greater London, Midlands and East Anglia areas, with at least 1 month's notice. Prefers to receive submissions (with CVs and headshots) by email, rather than by post. Showreels, voicereels and invitations to view individual actors' websites are also accepted. Welcomes enquiries from disabled actors. *Commission*: 15%

Lovett Logan Associates PMA

2 Riding House Street, London W1W 7FA
tel 020 7495 6400 *fax* 020 7495 6411
email london@lovettlogan.com (London)
email edinburgh@lovettlogan.com (Edinburgh)
Scottish office: Fourth Floor, 5 Rose Street, Edinburgh EH2 2PR
tel 0131 478 7878
website www.lovettlogan.com

Established in 1981. Areas of work include theatre, musicals, television, film, commercials, corporate and voice-overs.

Will consider attending performances at venues in Greater London and Scotland (handled by Scottish office) with 2-3 weeks' notice. Accepts submissions (with CVs and photographs) from actors previously unknown to the company if emailed to **representation@lovettlogan.com**. Invitations to view individual actors' websites are also accepted.

LSW Promotions

PO Box 31855, London SE17 3XP
tel 020 7793 9755 *fax* 020 7793 9755
email londonswo@hotmail.com
website www.londonshakespeare.org.uk
Executive Director Bruce Wall *Development Associate* James Croft

Established in 1998. 2 agents represent 20 actors. Areas of work include theatre, musicals, television and film.

Will consider attending performances at venues within Greater London and elsewhere, given 2 weeks' notice. Accepts submissions (with CVs and photographs) from actors previously unknown to the company, sent by post or email. Invitations to view individual actors' websites are also accepted. *Commission*: 10% donation to charity (LSW Prison Project)

MacFarlane Chard Associates PMA

113 Kingsway, London WC2B 6PP
tel 020 7636 7750 *fax* 020 7636 7751

email enquiries@macfarlane-chard.co.uk
website www.macfarlane-chard.co.uk
Twitter @MacFarlaneChard
Agents (actors) John Setrice, Charlie Metcalf, Gabriel Pac

Founded in 1994. Works in all areas. 3 agents represent 120 actors, as well as directors, writers, producers, technicians and authors.

Will consider attending performances in Greater London, given as much notice as possible. Welcomes letters or emails (with CVs and photographs) from actors previously unknown to the agency if sent by post, and encourages enquiries from actors with disabilities. Does not welcome follow-up calls, invitations to view individual actors' websites, or unsolicited approaches by email. Will accept showreels and voicereels. *Commission*: Varies

MacFarlane Doyle Associates

90 Long Acre, Covent Garden, London WC2E 9RZ
tel 020 3600 3470
email enquiries@macfarlanedoyle.com
website www.macfarlanedoyle.com
Agents Ross MacFarlane, Niei Morgan, Alys Drew

Established in 2009. Main areas of work are theatre, musicals, television, film, corporate, commercials and voice-overs. Each agent represents around 20 actors; directors and choreographers are also represented.

Welcomes performance notices and will travel to any area, given 3 weeks' notice. Prefers submissions by email. Represents actors with disabilities.
Commission: Theatre, TV & Film 15%; Commercials 20%

John Mahoney Management

Concorde House, 18 Margaret Street,
Brighton BN2 1TS
tel 01273 685970
email info@johnmahoney.management.co.uk
website www.johnmahoney.management.co.uk
Key personnel Stephen Holroyd, Alan Kite

Established in 1960. Represents 60-70 actors. Areas of work include theatre, musicals, television, film, commercials and corporate.

Please check submission details on website prior to seeking represention. Will consider attending performances at venues within Greater London and on the South Coast with 1 month's notice. Accepts submissions (with clearly written CVs and photographs) from actors previously unknown to the company if sent by post. Photographs should be of a good quality. Enclose an sae for return of personal details. Showreels, voicereels and invitations to view individual actors' websites are also accepted.
Commission: 10-17% depending on the type of work

Management 2000

11 Well Street, Treuddyn, Flintshire CH7 4NH
tel 01352 771231 *fax* 01352 771231

email jackey@management-2000.co.uk
website www.management-2000.co.uk

Established in 2000. 1 agent represents 30 actors. Areas of work include theatre, musicals, television, film, commercials, corporate and voice-overs.

Accepts submissions (with CVs and photographs) from actors previously unknown to the company if sent by post. Follow-up telephone calls, showreels and voicereels are also accepted. *Commission*: 10-15%

Marcus & McCrimmon Management

Winston House, 3 Bedford Square,
London WC1B 3RA
tel 020 7323 0546
email info@marcusandmccrimmon.com
website www.marcusandmccrimmon.com

Founded in 1999. Main areas of works are film, theatre, musicals, television and commercials. 2 agents represent around 100 actors.

Submissioms for representation should be made by email only, including headshot and link to Spotlight CV.

Markham, Froggatt & Irwin PMA

4 Windmill Street, London W1T 2HZ
tel 020 7636 4412 *fax* 020 7637 5233
email admin@markhamfroggattirwin.com
website www.markhamfroggattirwin.com
Twitter @MFandI_Talent
Agents: Film, TV and Theatre Alex Irwin, Jonty Brook, Anna Dudley, Richard Gibb, Emily MacDonald,Tom Christensen, Isabella Riggs
Commercials, Voice and Radio Ryan Wheeler

Works in theatre, musicals, television, film, commercials, corporate and voice-overs.

Ronnie Marshall Agency

66 Ollerton Road, London N11 2LA
tel 020 8368 4958

Established in 1970. 2 agents represent 20 actors in theatre, musicals, television, film, commercials, radio, corporate work and voice-overs.

Will consider attending performances at venues within the Greater London area subject to 2 weeks' prior notice. Accepts businesslike submissions (with CVs and photographs) from actors previously unknown to the agency if sent by post. Photographs should be a good likeness and accompanied by an sae for their return. Follow-up telephone calls and invitations to view individual actors' websites are also accepted. *Commission*: 5% if instigated by the client; 20% otherwise

Scott Marshall Partners PMA

Holborn Studios, 49/50 Eagle Wharf Road,
London N1 7ED
tel 020 7637 4623
email info@scottmarshall.co.uk
website www.scottmarshall.co.uk
Twitter @smpagency

Agents Amanda Evans, Manon Palmer, Craig Sills, Adrianna Tsigara

Areas of work include theatre, musicals, television, film, commercials, corporate and voice-overs. Also represents directors (theatre and TV) and creatives.

Accepts submissions (with CVs and photographs) from actors previously unknown to the company if sent by email only to **submissions@scottmarshall.co.uk**. No postal submissions accepted.

McLean-Williams Ltd PMA

Chester House Unit 2:15 Kennington Park, 1-3 Brixton Road, London SW9 6DE
tel 020 3567 1090 *fax* 020 7631 3739
email info@mclean-williams.com

Established in 2002; agency representing clients working in theatre, musicals, television, film, commercials and corporate role-play.

Will consider attending performances within Greater London given 2 weeks' notice. Welcomes submissions (with CVs, photographs, showreels and voicereels) from actors previously unknown to the agency. Will also accept follow-up telephone calls, emails and invitations to view an actor's website.

Bill McLean Personal Management

23B Deodar Road, London SW15 2NP
tel 020 8789 8191 *fax* 020 8789 8192

Established in 1972. Will consider attending performances in Greater London with sufficient notice. Accepts submissions (with CVs and photographs) from actors previously unknown to the company if sent by post. Follow-up telephone calls are also accepted. *Commission*: Theatre 10%; TV 12.5%; Commercials 15%

McMahon Management

28 Cecil Road, London W3 0DB
tel 020 8752 0172
email mcmahonmanagement@hotmail.co.uk
website www.mcmahonmanagement.co.uk
Twitter @McMahonMgmt
Agent Thomas McMahon *Assistant Agent* Brian Morse

Established in 2009. Works in theatre, TV, commercials, corporate and film. Will consider attending performances within London and Greater London given 2 weeks' notice. Welcomes letters (with CVs and headshots) from individuals previously unknown to the agency; these can only be returned with an appropriate sae. Happy to receive email requests with Spotlight link included. Does not welcome follow-up phone calls. *Commission*: Theatre 12.5%; TV, Film, Commercial and Corporate 15%

MCS Agency

47 Dean Street, London W1D 5BE
tel 020 7734 9995 *fax* 020-7734 9996

email info@mcsagency.co.uk
Key contact Fay Carnell

Established in 1994. 2 agents represent actors. Areas of work include theatre, musicals, television, film, commercials and voice-overs. Also represents presenters.

Will consider attending performances at venues within Greater London with 2 weeks' notice. Accepts submissions (with CVs and photographs) from actors previously unknown to the company if sent by post. Showreels, voicereels and invitations to view individual actors' websites are also accepted. *Commission*: 15-20%

Middleweek Newton Talent Management PMA

3rd Floor, 47 Bedford Street, London WC2A 9HA
tel 020 3394 0079 (Office)
email agents@mntalent.co.uk
website www.mntalent.co.uk
Agent Lucy Middleweek

Established in 2013. Areas of work include theatre, television, film and commercials.

Accepts submissions by email (with CVs and photographs). Also welcomes showreels and invitations to view individual actors' websites.

Milburn Browning Associates PMA (MMB Creative)

The Old Truman Brewery, 91 Brick Lane, London E1 6QL
tel 020 3582 9370
email michele@mmbcreative.com
Managing Director Michelle Milburn *Agents* Malcolm Browning, Tara Lynch, Nicola Bailey-James

Milburn Browning Associates became part of the umbrella group MMB Creative in 2016 at the same time a new voice-over agency, Fuller Voices with Becky Fuller as MD also joined MMB Creative. Manages a select client list providing a first-rate service and offers the clout and reputation that only comes with decades of experience and proven success.

Mitchell Maas McLennan Ltd

29 Thomas Street, Woolwich, London SE18 6HU
tel 020 8301 8745
email agency@mmm2000.co.uk
website www.mmm2000.co.uk

Established in 2005. 2 agents represent approximately 60 actors. Areas of work include theatre, musicals, television, film, commercials, corporate. Also represents choreographers. Recommends the photographer John Clark (see entry on page 397).

Will consider attending performances in Greater London and elsewhere with at least 2-4 weeks' notice. Accepts submissions (with CVs and photographs)

Agents and casting directors

from actors previously unknown to the agency. Showreels, voicereels and invitations to view individual actors' websites also accepted. Follow-up calls are welcomed. *Commission*: 10%

Morello Cherry Ltd

Morello Cherry Studios, 3rd Floor, Deansgate Mews, The Great Northern Warehouse, Manchester M3 4EN
tel 020 7993 5538 *mobile* 07886 846938
email applications@mcaa.co.uk
website www.mcaa.co.uk

Established in 2007. 2 agents represent 40 actors. Areas of work include film, television, SVOD, theatre, television, film, commercials, corporate and voice-overs.

Accepts submissions via email with links to online CV, footage and images. Does not welcome postal applications and requests no large file downloads. *Commission*: Standard Equity rates

Lee Morgan Management

The William IV Suite, 7-9 Henrietta Street, London WC2E 8PS
tel 020 7430 1006 *mobile* 07949 729639
email lee@leemorgan.biz
website www.leemorgan.biz

Established in 2005. Represents clients working in musicals, television, film and commercials.

Welcomes performance notices in the London areas, given 2 weeks' notice. Is happy to receive letters (with CVs and photographs) from individual actors previously unknown to the agency, sent by post or email. Accepts showreels and voicereels, and encourages enquiries from actors with disabilities.

MR Management PMA

67 Great Titchfield Street, London W1W 7PT
tel 020 7636 8737
email info@mrmanagement.net
website www.mrmanagement
Mark Pollard, Ross Dawes

Established in 2001. Main areas of work are theatre, musicals, TV, film and commercials. Also represents directors, presenters and writers. Welcomes CVs and photographs sent by email, showreels and voice tapes. Open to clients with disabilities but not currently representing any disabled actors. *Commission* 10-12.5% theatre, 15% film and TV

Mrs Jordan Associates PMA

4 Old Park Lane, London W1K 1QW
tel 020 3151 0710
email apps@mrsjordan.co.uk
website www.mrsjordan.co.uk
Associates Sean D. Lynch & Guy Kean

Established in 2008. Areas of work include stage, television, film, commercials, corporate and voice-

overs. Represents some regionally based actors. Does not represent walk-ons, extras, models or under-16s. 2 principal agents plus associates represent around 75 actors.

Will consider attending performances but would need to meet in advance. Unsolicited applications accepted by email only. Spotlight link imperative. Happy to consider applications from actors with disabilities. Advises actors: "We have a very small client list. Check our website's New Applicants page for advice before you email us. *Commission*: 10-15%

MSFT Management PMA

Tottenham Green Enterprise Centre, Town Hall Approach Road, London N15 4RX
tel 07917 157748
email msftmanagement@gmail.com
website www.msftandmanagement.com

MSFT Management (Management in Stage, Film & Television) is a fast-growing personal management agency representing multi-skilled artists, dedicated to the progression of their clients. MSFT Management seeks to work with 50 new clients by 2020 and is specifically looking for mid-career actors to join the London-based agency.

Requirements: actors must be registered with Spotlight, have a showreel and ideally be a member of Equity to apply for representation.

Elaine Murphy Associates

Suite 1, 50 High Street, London E11 2RJ
tel 020 8989 4122 *fax* 020 8989 1400
email elaine@elainemurphy.co.uk
Director Elaine Murphy

Established in 1990. 2 agents. Areas of work include film, TV, theatre, musicals, television, commercials, corporate and voice-overs.

Will consider attending performances within Greater London with plenty of notice. Accepts submissions (with Spotlight link) from actors previously unknown to the agency; showreels, voicereels and invitations to view individual actors' websites are also accepted.

Steve Nealon Associates PMA

3rd Floor, International House, 1-6 Yarmouth Place, London W1J 7BU
tel 020 7125 0468 *mobile* 07904 671877
fax 020 7629 1317
email admin@stevenealonassociates.co.uk
website www.stevenealonassociates.co.uk
Agents Steve Nealon and Alexis Conway Keane

Works in theatre, film, television, commercials, musicals and corporate.

Depending on the production and the actor, will attend performances anywhere in the UK, given a week's notice. Welcomes letters, with CVs and photographs, sent by post and email, and accepts showreels. Plans to represent actors with disabilities. *Commission*: 10-15%

Nelson Browne Management Ltd PMA
2nd Floor, 9 Savoy Street, London WC2E 7EG
mobile 07796 891388
email enquiries@nelsonbrowne.com
website www.nelsonbrowne.com
Company Director Mary Elliott Nelson

Established in 2007. 2 agents represent 80-90 actors working in musicals, television, film, commercials, corporate and voice-over; also represents directors and actor/musicians.

Welcomes performance notices within the Greater London area, given 2 weeks' notice. Welcomes letters (with CVs and photographs) from individual actors previously unknown to the agency, sent by post or email. Accepts follow-up telephone calls and invitations to view individual actors' websites. No showreels or voicereels. Encourages enquiries from actors with disabilities. *Commission*: Theatre 10%; TV and Film 15%

North West Actors – Nigel Adams
64 Nuttall Street, Bury, Manchester BL9 7EW
tel 0161 761 6437
email nigel.adams@northwestactors.co.uk
website www.northwestactors.co.uk
Proprietor Nigel Adams

Established in 2007. Main areas of work are theatre, television, film, commercials, corporate, radio and voice-overs. 1 agent represents 32 actors. Recommends the photographer Michael Pollard (**info@michaelpollard.co.uk**).

Will consider attending performances within the Greater Manchester area, given 2 weeks' notice, or London, given 4 weeks' notice. Welcomes letters (with CVs and photographs) from individual actors previously unknown to the agency, sent by post or email. Also accepts showreels, voicereels and invitations to view individual actors' websites.

Northern Lights Management
Dean Clough Mills, Halifax,
West Yorkshire HX3 5FD
tel 01422 382203
website www.northernlightsmanagement.co.uk
Twitter @NLightsActorsM
Agents Maureen Magee, Angie Cowton

Established in 1998. 2 agents represent Northern and Northern-based actors. Areas of work include theatre, musicals, television, film, commercials, corporate and voice-overs.

Accepts submissions (with CVs and photographs) from actors previously unknown to the company if sent by post. Showreels and voicereels are also accepted. Enclose an sae for reply and the return of items sent. Telephone calls and emails with attachments are not accepted.

NS Artistes' Management
10 Claverdon House, Hollybank Road, Billesley, Birmingham B13 0QY
tel 0121 684 5607 *mobile* 07870 969577
email administrator@nsartistes.co.uk
website www.nsartistes.co.uk
Managing Director Neale Stephen McGrath *Director* Arali Niamh McGrath

Founded in 2004, and representing 75 actors in all areas of acting work including role-play, presenting and training, the company also represents individuals for writing, consultancy, design, stage management, presenting, drama tutoring and fight arranging. "If you have a talent in the business, even if I have not mentioned it, then I am interested – no matter what age, creed or colour you are, or whether you are disabled or able-bodied."

Welcomes performance notices a fortnight in advance; will consider attending performances around the UK. Welcomes letters (with CVs and photographs) from actors previously unknown to the company if sent by post, but not by email. Does not welcome unsolicited showreels or invitations to view individual actors' websites. *Commission*: Theatre 12.5%; Stage Management 10%; Other 15%

Nyland Management
93 Kinder Road, Hayfield, High Peak SK22 2LE
tel 01633 745629 *mobile* 07902 246157
email casting@nylandmanagement.com
website www.nylandmanagement.com

2 agents represent 60 actors. Areas of work include theatre, musicals, TV, film, commercials, motion capture, corporate, role-play, promotions and voice-overs.

Accepts submissions from Spotlight members. Email only.

Otto Personal Management Ltd
Hagglers Corner, 586 Queen's Road,
Sheffield S2 4DU
tel 0114 372432 *mobile* 07587 133212
email admin@ottopm.co.uk
website www.ottopm.co.uk

Established in 1985. 41 actors. Areas of work include theatre, musicals, television, film, commercials, corporate and voice-overs.

Will consider attending performances at venues in the UK with approximately 1 month's notice. Accepts submissions (with CVs and photographs) from actors previously unknown to the company, sent by post or preferably by email. Will also accept showreels, voicereels and invitations to view individual actors' websites.*Commission*: 10-13%

Pan Artists Agency
Cornerways, 34 Woodhouse Lane, Sale M33 4JX
tel 0161 969 7419

email panartists@btconnect.com
website www.panartists.co.uk

Established in 1973. Accepts submissions (with CVs and photographs, "which must be up to date") from actors previously unknown to the company, sent by post or email. Postal submissions must be accompanied by an sae.

Paul Pearson – London Theatrical
18 Leamore Street, London W6 0JZ
tel 020 8748 1478
email agent@londontheatrical.com
website www.londontheatrical.com
CEO Paul Pearson *Head of Media* Chris Read

Established in 2009. 2 agents represent 35 clients. Main areas of work are film, television, theatre and commercials.

Only accepts CVs and photographs sent by email. Has an equal opportunities policy. *Commission:* 15%

Pelham Associates PMA
Citibase, Suite 25, 95 Ditchling Road,
Brighton BN1 4ST
email petercleall@pelhamassociates.co.uk
website www.pelhamassociates.co.uk
Agents Peter Cleall, Dione Inman

Established in 1993. Areas of work include theatre, musicals, television, film, commercials, corporate and voice-overs.

Will consider attending performances at venues within Greater London and elsewhere, given at least 2 weeks' notice. Accepts submissions (with CVs and photographs) from actors previously unknown to the company if sent by post. *Commission:* 8-12.5%

Pemberton Associates Ltd
50 Liverpool Street, London EC2M 7PY
tel 020 7224 9036 *fax* 0161 235 8442
www.pembertonassociates.com
Twitter @PembertonAssocs

Established in 1989. 3 agents represent 150 clients. Areas of work include theatre, musicals, television, film, commercials, corporate and voice-overs.

Will consider attending performances at venues in the North West, with 2-3 weeks' notice, if looking for new clients. Accepts submissions (with CVs and photographs) from actors previously unknown to the company if sent by post.

Frances Phillips PMA
89 Robeson Way, Borehamwood, Herts. WD6 5RY
tel 020 8953 0303 *mobile* 07957 334328
email frances@francesphillips.co.uk
website www.francesphillips.co.uk

Established in 1983 and representing 50 actors aged 16 upwards. Areas of work include theatre, musicals, television, film, commercials, corporate and voice-overs. Submissions by email only considered if

Spotlight View PIN number and date of birth details are included. CVs and photos will be requested at a later date if required.

Piccadilly Management
23 New Mount Street, Manchester M4 4DE
tel 0161 212 8522 *mobile* 07930 834891
tel 020 3322 7457 London office
email info@piccadillymanagement.com
website www.piccadillymanagement.com
Agent Peter Foster

Established in 1985. Main areas of work include television, theatre, stage, commercials, corporate and voice-overs. Represents around 50 actors.

Welcomes approaches from actors previously unknown to the company, sent by post or email. Accepts invitations to view individual actors' websites and welcomes enquiries from actors with disabilities.

Janet Plater Management Ltd
Floor D, Milburn House, Dean Street,
Newcastle upon Tyne NE1 1LF
tel 0191 221 2490
email info@jpmactors.com
website www.jpmactors.com

Established in 1997. 1 agent represents approximately 65 actors. Areas of work include theatre, musicals, television, film, commercials, corporate and voice-overs Extras department has over 800 extras in the North East region.

Will consider attending performances with a few weeks' notice. Accepts submissions (with CVs and or photographs or Spotlight link) from actors previously unknown to the company if sent via email. Links to showreels welcome; if applying by email no large attachments. *Commission:* Maximum of 15%

Premier Acting
tel 0141 255 0255
email info@premieracting.com
website www.premieracting.com
Agent Allan Jones

Established in 2013. Based in Glasgow, Premier Acting is an amalgamation of Glasgow Acting and the Cairns Agency.

Will consider attending performances at venues in Scotland with 3-4 weeks' notice. Accepts submissions (with CVs and photographs) from actors previously unknown to the agency. A Spotlight Link should be included if possible. Also welcomes showreels.

Morwenna Preston Management
tel 020 8835 8147
email info@morwennapreston.com
website www.morwennapreston.com
Facebook @MorwennaPreston

Three agents represent 100 actors for theatre, musicals, television, film and commercials.

Welcomes performance notices 4 weeks in advance, and is prepared to travel within the Greater London area. Welcomes letters (by email) from individuals previously unknown to the company. Does not welcome follow-up calls. Welcomes showreels and invitations to view individual actors' websites. *Commission*: 12.5%

Price Gardner Management PMA
BM 3162 London WC1N 3XX
tel 020 7610 2111
email info@pricegardner.co.uk
website www.pricegardner.co.uk
Contact Sarah Barnfield

Television, film, theatre, musical theatre, commercials, radio, voice-over and corporate. Submissions can be made via the website contact form or via email.

Principal Artistes
Suite 1, 57 Buckingham Gate, London SW1E 6AJ
tel 020 7637 2120 *mobile* 07881 623708
email info@principalartistes.co.uk

Established in 1993. 2 agents represent 60 actors. Areas of work include theatre, musicals, television, film, commercials and corporate.

Will consider attending performances at venues in Greater London with at least 1 week's notice. Accepts submissions (with CVs and photographs) from actors previously unknown to the company if emailed to enquiries@principalartistes.com or uploaded to the website www.principalartist.com. If sent by post please ensure it bears the correct posage. *Commission*: Theatre 10%; Other 15%

Pure Actors Agency & Management Ltd
4th Floor, 20-22 High Street, Manchester M4 1QB
tel 0161 832 5727
email enquiries@pure-management.co.uk
website www.pure-management.co.uk
Director Debbie Pine

Established in 2005. 1 agent represents 40 actors. Areas of work include television, film, theatre, commercials, radio and corporate.

Will consider attending performances within the Manchester area, given at least 6 weeks' notice. Recommends the photographer Michael Pollard (see entry on page 403). Accepts submissions (with CVs and photographs) from actors previously unknown to the agency – but be sure to include an sae. Showreels, voicereels and invitations to view individual actors' websites are also accepted. Welcomes enquiries from disabled actors. *Commission*: 15%

Qtalent PMA
2nd Floor, 161 Drury Lane, Covent Garden, London WC2B 5PN

Qtalent, which was incorporated with International Artistes, have over 50 years' experience and know-how in the British entertainment industry. This combined management resource now forms a unique and powerful force in the fields of film, television, and theatre in the UK and beyond. Qtalent are part of Qdos Entertainment, which is one of the largest entertainment groups in the UK. Together they represent a diverse client base, including numerous high-profile performers and actors.

Accepts submissions via email with CVs and headshots. For further information on how to apply, please visit: **www.qtalent.co.uk**.

RBM Actors
3rd Floor, 1 Lower Grosvenor Street, London SW1W OEJ
tel 020 7976 6021
email info@rbmactors.com
website www.rbmactors.com
Agent Sarah London

Works mainly in theatre, television, film and commercials. 2 agents represent around 30 actors, and comedians/writers.

Will consider attending performances within Greater London, given 2-3 weeks' notice. Welcomes letters (with CVs and photographs) from individual actors previously unknown to the company, sent by post only, but not follow-up calls. Accepts showreels and voicereels, as well as invitations to view individual actors' websites. Encourages enquiries from actors with disabilities. "We advise you to contact us when you are appearing in something. We don't represent actors we don't know or haven't seen."

Redeeming Features
i Primrose Street, London EC2 2EX
tel 020 3740 3338
email artists@redeemingfeatures.co.uk
website www.redeemingfeatures.co.uk
CEO and Founder Nathanael Wiseman *Head of Talent* Danielle Whiteman *Head of Development* Isabel Pastor *Casting Director* Andrew Fawn *Agent* Donovan Simmons and Zack Miller *Assistant Agent* Georgina Lest

Redeeming Features is an award-winning film and television production company with a boutique talent agency; an offshoot of a production company with an understanding of the realities of the industry from the point of view of scheduling, budgeting, casting and shooting.

Main areas of work are stage, film, TV, online, commercials, shorts, music videos emerging platforms.

Will consider attending performances within Greater London, given as much notice as possible. Can only represent actors who have a head shot and showreel, and are on Spotlight. *Commission*: around 20% across the board

Redroofs Associates
26 Bath Road, Maidenhead, Berkshire SL6 4JT
tel 01628 674092

email agency@redroofs.co.uk
website www.redroofs.co.uk

Established in 1947, the agency only represents Redroofs graduates and current students. It does not, therefore, welcome performance notices or representation enquiries from actors unknown to the school. Areas of work include theatre, musicals, television, film, commercials, corporate and voice-overs. *Commission*: 15%

Redrush Talent

37 Main Street, Killinchy, Co. Down BT23 6PN
tel 02891 878 146 *mobile* 07803 594961
email janice@redrushtalent.com
website www.redrushtalent.com
Founder and Agent Janice Rush *Assistant* Louise Statham

Founded in 2009, 1 agent represents 10 actors and also represents presenters and writers. Main areas of work include film, theatre, musicals, TV, commercials, corporate and voice-over.

Will consider attending performances at venues within Greater and Central London, given at least 1 weeks' notice. Accepts submissions (with CVs and photographs) from actors previously unknown to the company if sent by email. Showreels, voicereels and invitations to view individual actors' websites are also accepted. Redrush are happy to consider applications for representation from disabled actors. *Commission:* 15%

Lisa Richards Agency PMA

108 Upper Leeson Street, Dublin 4
tel +353 1 637 5000 *fax* +353 1 667 1256
email info@lisarichards.ie
website www.lisarichards.ie
Managing Director Lisa Cook *Agents (Actors)* Lisa Cook, Richard Cook, Jonathan Shankey, *(Voice-over)* Lorraine Cummins *(Literary)* Faith O'Grady *(Comedy)* Ami Burke, Christina Dwyer *(Corporate)* Eavan Kenny

The Lisa Richards Agency was founded in 1989 by Lisa and Richard Cook. Originally established as a theatrical agency, Lisa Richards now provides representation for actors, comedians, voice-over artists, authors, playwrights, directors and designers. The company employs a staff of 13 people across the different departments. 3 agents and 1 assistant represent 90-100 actors, and there is 1 voice-over agent, 2 comedy agents, and 1 literary agent as well as 1 receptionist.

Welcomes performance notices if sent 3 weeks in advance, and is prepared to travel around Ireland. Welcomes letters (with CVs and photographs) from actors previously unknown to the company if sent by post, but not by email; does not welcome follow-up calls. Happy to receive showreels and invitations to view individual actors' websites. Welcomes enquiries from disabled actors. Submission guidelines on site

for authors. Also operates a London office (details on website).

Room 3 Agency Ltd

Head Office: The Old Chapel, 14 Fairview Drive, Redland, Bristol BS6 6PH
tel 0845 5678 333 / 020 7183 1872 / 0117 944 1477
email kate@room3agency.com
website www.room3agency.com
Director Kate Marshall

Established in 2009. Main areas of work are television, film, commercials, corporate, voice-overs. 1 agent represents 20 actors; presenters also represented.

Will consider attending performances in London and the South West, with 1 month's notice. Accepts letters, CVs and photographs sent by post or email, showreels and invitations to view actors' websites. Does not represent actors with disabilities. *Commission*: 20%

Rossmore Management PMA

Broadley House,
48 Broadley Terrace. London NW1 6LG
tel 020 7258 1953
email agents@rossmoremanagement.com
website www.rossmoremanagement.com

Established in 1993. 2 agents and an assistant represent 70 actors. Areas of work include theatre, musicals, television, film, commercials, radio and voice-overs.

Will consider attending performances at venues within Greater London. Accepts submissions (with CVs and photographs) from actors previously unknown to the company by post or email, preferably submitted to online form at the company's website. Please include sae. *Commission*: Theatre and Radio 10%; Film, TV and Commercials 15% plus VAT

Royce Management

121 Merlin Grove, Beckenham BR3 3HS
tel 020 8650 1096
email office@roycemanagement.co.uk
website www.roycemanagement.co.uk

Established in 1980. 2 agents represent 50-60 actors. Areas of work include theatre, musicals, television, film, commercials, corporate and voice-overs.

Will consider attending performances at venues within Greater London with a minimum of 1 weeks' notice. Accepts submissions with a link to actors' Spotlight page by email. No attachments. *Commission*: Commercials 15%; All other work 10%

St James's Management

7 Smyatts Close, Southminster, Essex CM0 7JT
tel 01621 772183
Managing Director Jacqueline Leggo

Established in 1965. 1 agent represents approximately 40 actors. Areas of work include theatre, musicals, television, film, commercials, corporate and voice-overs. Actors should approach the company by letter and enclose an sae.

Saraband Associates
39-41 North Road, London N7 9DP

Areas of work include theatre, musicals, television, film and commercials.

Will occasionally consider attending performances at venues in Greater London, given 1 month's notice. Accepts submissions (with CVs and photographs) from actors previously unknown to the company if sent by post. An sae should be included with CVs and photographs. *Commission*: Varies

Savages Personal Management
67 Queens Wharf, Riverside Studios, 2 Crisp Road, London W6 9NE
tel 020 7348 7875
email info@savagespm.co.uk
website www.savagespm.co.uk
Facebook Savages Personal Management
Twitter @SAVAGESLondon
Agents: Justin Savage, Sarah Savage

Established in 2016. Areas of work are theatre, film, TV, musicals, commercials, corporate presenting and events. Represents more than 70 actors, presenters and directors. Will consider attending performances, given 3 weeks' notice. Welcomes enquiries from artists not previously known to the company by email with a link to a showreel and Spotlight page only. Cannot consider artists without a showreel. Will try to respond to all applications. Represents actors with disabilities and from every sphere of life. *Commission*: theatre 12.5%, plus VAT; everything else 15% plus VAT

Tim Scott
PO Box 63856, London N6 9BQ
tel 020 8347 8705
email timscott@btinternet.com

Established in 1988. Areas of work include theatre, television, film, and commercials.

Accepts postal submissions (with CVs and photographs) from actors previously unknown to the company.

SDM (formerly Simon Drake Management)
14 Ivor Court, Gloucester Place, London NW1 6BJ
tel 020 7183 8995 / 020 7183 9013
email admin@simondrakemanagement.co.uk
website www.simondrakemanagement.co.uk
Agent Simon Drake

Established in 2007. Works in theatre, musicals, TV and film. Unsolicited approaches should be made via email only, giving Spotlight PIN.

Dawn Sedgwick Management
3 Goodwins Court, London WC2N 4LL
tel 020 7240 0404 *fax* 020 7240 0415
email dawn@dawnsedgwickmanagement.com
website www.dawnsedgwickmanagement.com
Key contact Dawn Sedgwick

Established in 1992. 3 agents represent 15 actors. Areas of work include theatre, television, film, commercials, corporate and voice-overs. Also represents presenters, comedians and writers.

Accepts submissions (with CVs and photographs) from actors previously unknown to the agency if sent by post, but not by email. Showreels, voicereels and invitations to view individual actors' websites are also accepted. Welcomes enquiries from disabled actors. *Commission*: 15%

Select Management
PO BOX 748, London, NW4 1TT
mobile 07956 131494 and 07855794747
email mail@selectmanagement.info
website www.selectmanagement.info
Agent Venetia Suchdev

Established in 2008. Areas of work include theatre, TV, film, commercial, voice over, print, modeling, corporate, dance, presenting.

Will consider attending performances at venues within Greater London with at least 1 week's notice. Accepts CVs and photographs if sent by email. Also welcomes voice tapes and showreels or invitations to view individual actors' websites as well as applications for representation from disabled actors. *Commission*: 20%. No commission on any work obtained by actors themselves.

Sharkey & Co. Ltd PMA
44 Lexington Street, London W1F 0LW
tel 020 7287 1923
email info@sharkeyandco.com
website www.sharkeyandco.com
Agent Simon Sharkey

Established in 2012, main areas of work are theatre, TV, film, musicals, cabaret, radio, commercials, voice-over, talking books and corporates. Represents 85 actors. Does not represent children. *Commission* 12.5% for everything except feature films and commercials which are 15%.

Welcomes CVs and photographs sent by email with links to showreels and websites. Welcomes perfomance notices with a minimum of two weeks' notice, Greater London preferred.

Shepherd Management Ltd PMA
3rd Floor, Joel House, 17-21 Garrick Street, London WC2E 9BL
tel 020 7420 9350
email info@shepherdmanagement.co.uk
Agents: Drama Christina Shepherd, Sandra Chalmers,

Jeanette Hunter, James Beresford *Commercials* Karen Hough *Associate Agent* Clare Thomas

5 agents and 2 junior agents represent 120 actors, 1 director and 1 designer. Areas of work include theatre, musicals, television, film, corporate and voice-overs.

Will consider attending performances within Greater London given as much notice as possible. Showreels and voicereels will also be accepted. Emails and follow-up telephone calls are not welcomed.

Shepperd-Fox PMA
2nd Floor, 47 Bedford Street, London WC2E 9HA
tel 020 7240 2048
email info@shepperd-fox.co.uk
website www.shepperd-fox.co.uk
Twitter @shepperdfox
Agents Jane Shepperd, Jenny Rhodes, Gabriel Pac, Claire Cosgrove

A boutique theatrical agency based in Covent Garden, representing a select list of clients in theatre, TV, film, musical theatre, commercials and radio.

Rebecca Singer Management
79 Sutton Court Road, London W4 3EQ
tel 020 8742 7747 *mobile* 07801 259963
email office@rebeccasingermanagement.com
website www.rebeccasingermanagement.com
Twitter @rsm_office
Agent Rebecca Singer

Established in 2016, after 23 years with the Richard Stone Partnership. Main areas of work are theatre, musicals, TV, film, commercials, corporate work, radio and audio books. Does not do commercial voice-overs. Represents 42 actors and one fight director, and would be happy to represent actors if they move in to directing.

Welcomes performance notices, prefereably with a month's notice. Happy to travel within the London area if a theatre is accessible by public transport. Welcomes (with CVs and photographs), CVs and photographs sent by email, showreels and voice tapes. Would happily represent actors with disabilities. *Commission*: 12.5%

Sandra Singer Associates
21 Cotswold Road, Westcliff-on-Sea, Essex SS0 8AA
tel 01702 331616
email sandrasingeruk@aol.com
website www.sandrasinger.com
Key personnel Sandra Singer

Main areas of work are with leads and featured artists for feature films, film, television, commercials and musical theatre. Specialises in artistes under 25 years of age, but is also a boutique agency of established artistes.

Accepts applications by email. No zip files, jpgs, or emails with large files unless requested. Showreels should only be sent on request.

Camilla Storey Management
30 Percy Street, London W1T 2DB
tel 020 3051 8360 *mobile* 07870 281241
email darren@csmagt.com
Twitter @CamStoreyMagt
Agent Darren Chadwick-Hussein

Areas of work include TV, film, theatre, commercials, corporate, musicals and pantomimes.

Accepts submissions by email (with CVs and photographs), and also welcomes showreels.

Smart Management
PO Box 64377, London EC1V 1ND
tel 020 7837 8822
email smartmanagement@btconnect.com
Agent Mario Renzullo

Established in 2000. Areas of work include theatre, musicals, television, film, commercials, corporate and radio.ntact by post/email.

Will consider attending performances given 1 month's notice.

Paul Spyker Management
PO Box 48848, London WC1B 3WZ
tel 020 7462 0046
email belinda@psmlondon.com

Works in all areas of the entertainment industry; also represents directors and choreographers. Recommends the photographer Jorge de Reval.

Will consider seeing performances given a month's notice. Welcomes letters (with CVs) from individual actors previously unknown to the agency, if sent by post or email; also accepts invitations to view individual actors' websites. Encourages enquiries from actors with disabilities.

Stanton Davidson Associates PMA
St Martin's House, 59 St Martin's Lane, London WC2N 4JS
tel 020 7581 3388
email contact@stantondavidson.co.uk
website www.stantondavidson.co.uk
Twitter @SDALondon
Agents Geoff Stanton, Roger Davidson, Beth Gavin

Agency represents approximately 100 clients, actors, singers, producers, directors, designers, composers and musical directors. Areas of work include theatre, musical theatre, opera, film, television, radio, commercials, corporate and voice-overs.

Will consider attending performances both in and outside of Greater London, but request as much notice as possible. Accepts submissions from actors previously unknown to the company, preferably by email with a limited number of small attachments. If you can't resist the temptation to send a CV and photograph by post, please include an appropriately sized envelope for their return.

Stevenson Withers Associates PMA
Studio 7C, Clapham North Arts Centre,
Voltaire Road, London SW4 6DH
tel 020 7720 3355 *fax* 020 7720 5565
email talent@stevensonwithers.com
website www.stevensonwithers.com
Twitter @StevensonWither
Agents Natasha Stevenson, Jennifer Withers, Lindsay
Kutner, Tom Norcliffe *Assistants* Perry Antoniou,
Jamie Nash

3 agents represent over 100 actors. Areas of work
include theatre, musicals, television, film,
commercials, corporate and voice-overs. Actors
should approach the company by email.

Stirling Management Actors Agency
490 Halliwell Road, Bolton, Lancashire BL1 8AN
tel 01204 848333
email admin@stirlingmanagement.co.uk
website www.stirlingmanagement.co.uk
Agents Glen Mortimer, Karen Mortimer, Nathan
Wedge

Established in 2008. 3 agents represent 80-100 actors
and performers.Also agency for 40-60 children. Areas
of work include theatre, TV, film, commercials,
corporate, voice-overs and photo shoots. Also
represents cruise-ship singers and entertainers.

Will consider attending performances at venues in
the north west given at least 1 weeks' notice, though
preferably more. Accepts submissions by email (with
CVs and photographs). Asks that Spotlight links and
showreels be included if available. *Commission:*
Theatre 10%, TV, film and commercials 15%, Voice-
over and photoshoots 20%

Stiven Christie Management
1 Glen Street, Tollcross, Edinburgh EH3 9JD
tel 0131 228 4040
email info@stivenchristie.co.uk
website www.stivenchristie.co.uk
Proprietor Douglas Stiven

Founded in 1983 (and incorporating The Actors
Agency of Edinburgh). Agency represents actors for
theatre, musicals, television, film, commercials,
corporate and voice-overs.

Katherine Stonehouse Management
PO Box 64412, London W5 9GU
tel 020 8560 7709
email hello@katherinestonehouse.co.uk
website www.katherinestonehouse.co.uk
Senior Agent Katherine Stonehouse

Established in 2008. Works in theatre, musicals, TV,
film, commercials, corporate, voice-over, commercial
partnerships and TV presenting.

Will consider attending performances in Greater
London. Welcomes letters sent by post or email.

The Talent Agency Ltd
Freshwater House, Outdowns, Effingham KT24 5QR
tel 01483 281500 *fax* 01483 281501

email info@thetalentagencyltd.co.uk
Managing Director Mike Smith *Producer* Daryl Smith
Consultant Sally James

A management company established in 1974 and
covering all aspects of clients' career and long-term
development; represents around 10 actors. Areas of
work include television, film, commercials, corporate
and voice-overs. Also represents radio and TV
presenters and sports stars.

Will consider attending performances at venues in
Greater London and elsewhere, given 2-3 weeks'
notice. Accepts submissions (with CVs and
photographs) from actors previously unknown to the
company, sent by post or email. Also accepts
showreels and voicereels. Invitations to view
individual actors' websites are only accepted if sent
via email. Submitted CVs should be as complete as
possible, and separate clearly professional experience
from student productions. Applicants should always
state if they have yet to acquire a professional role.
Commission: 15-20% according to press,
accountancy, and PR agreements

Talent Artists Ltd
59 Sydner Road, London N16 7UF
tel 020 7923 1119 *fax* 020 7923 2009
Director Jane Wynn Owen

Talent Artists Ltd represents actors working in all
fields of the industry, with a particular emphasis on
musical theatre.

British Talent Agency
email agents@britishtalent.net
website www.britishtalent.net

Established in 2009. Main areas of work are film,
theatre and television – primarily in London, Los
Angeles and New York. Represents actors, writers,
models, recording artists and bands.

Welcomes contact by actors previously unknown to
the agency, if made by email with cover note, links to
online CVs, photos, websites and reels. No
attachments. Please visit our website and read our
contact policy before approaching. "Invitations to
shows are always welcome."

Tavistock Wood PMA
Tavistock Wood, 45 Conduit Street,
London W1S 2YN
tel 020 7494 4767 *fax* 020 7434 2017
email info@tavistockwood.com
website www.tavistockwood.com
Agents Angharad Wood, Charles Collier, Bella
Wingfield, Chloe Burrows, Grace Cavanagh-Butler,
Jethro Thompson

Specialist boutique agency and management
company representing around 100 clients across the
fields of acting, writing and direction. The agency is
now well known for an approach which places a

strong focus on pan-European talent. Accepts submissions, (with CVs and photographs), from actors previously unknown to the company by post only – these should be accompanied by a covering letter and a sae.

TCG Artist Management Ltd
14A Goodwin's Court, London WC2N 4LL
tel 020 7240 3600
email info@tcgam.co.uk
website www.tcgam.co.uk

Established in 1998. 1 agent represents 70 actors, with 2 assistants and an accounts manager. Areas of work include theatre, musicals, television, film and commercials. Accepts submissions via email with Spotlight link.

Lisa Thomas Management
Unit 10, 7 Wenlock Road, London N1 7SL
tel 020 7490 5546
email lisa@lisathomasmanagement.com
website www.lisathomasmanagement.com

Represents only comedians.

Katie Threlfall Associates PMA
13 Tolverne Road, London SW20 8RA
tel 020 8879 0493
email katie@ktthrelfall.co.uk
Twitter @KTThrelfall
Agent Katie Threlfall

Founded in 1996 as Hillman Threlfall; changed its name in 2006 to Katie Threlfall Associates. 1 agent represents 90 actors in theatre, musicals, television, film, commercials and corporate.

Will attend performances at venues within Greater London if given 1 month's notice. Accepts submissions (with CVs and photographs) from actors previously unknown to the company. Welcomes showreels and invitations to view individual actors' websites. "Address letters correctly to the agent. Only write in if you have a showreel, or with an invitation to a show: we do not take on or meet people whose work we do not know." *Commission*: Commercials 15%, Television 12.5%, Theatre 10%

Tildsley France Associates PMA
8 Northumberland Avenue, London WC2N 5BY
tel 020 8521 1888
email info@tildsleyfrance.co.uk
website www.tildsleyfrance.co.uk
Agent/Director Alex France *Director* Kathryn Kirton

Established in 2003 as Janice Tildsley Associates and relaunched as Tildsley France Associates in 2017. Areas of work include television, film, commercials and theatre.

Please check website for information before approaching for representation. *Commission*: 10-15%

TMG London
Adam House, 7-10 AdamStreet, The Strand, London WC2N 6AA

tel 020 7437 1383 *mobile* 07866 589905
email tanya.greep@googlemail.com
Proprietor Tanya Greep *Key personnel* Natalie Elliott

Established in 1981. 2 agents and 1 assistant represent 70-80 actors. Areas of work include theatre, musicals, television, film, commercials, corporate and voice-overs.

Will consider attending performances at venues within Greater London with 2 weeks' notice if an actor is playing a substantial role. Accepts submissions by email. Showreels and voicereels should only be sent on request. *Commission*: 12.5%

Total Vanity Ltd
15 Walton Way, Aylesbury, Bucks HP21 7JJ
mobile 07739 381788
email richardwilliams@totalvanity.com
website www.totalvanity.com
Agent Richard Williams

Established in 2000. 1 agent represents 50 actors. Areas of work include theatre, musicals, television, film, commercials, corporate and voice-overs. Also represents presenters.

Will consider attending performances within the Greater London area with at least 1 week's notice. Accepts submissions (with CVs and photographs) from actors previously unknown to the company if sent by post. Showreels, voicereels and invitations to view individual actors' websites are also accepted. Welcomes enquiries from disabled actors. *Commission*: 20%

Troika PMA
108 Great Portland Street, London W1W 5QZ
tel 020 7336 7868
email casting@troikatalent.com
website www.troikatalent.com
Agents Michael Duff and Sarah Stephenson *Associate* Heather Walsh assisted by Richard Johnston; Kat Gosling, *Associate* Tom Holcroft assisted by Alisha Bappoo; Gary O'Sullivan, assisted by Allie Sumners and Alexi Stylianou; Conor McCaughan and Sam Fox, Associate Leah Weerasinghe assisted by Elliot Keefe; Kate Morrison Associate Leah Weerasghe, assisted by Elliot Keefe; Melanie Rockcliffe assisted by Hannah Fletcher and Rebekka Taylor;Dylan Hearn assisted by Hannah Fletch adn Rebekka Tayor and Sophie Chapman, assistaed by Rhonda Lidgold

Established in 2005, main areas of work are film, theatre, TV and musicals. Represents approximately 250 clients, includng actors, directors, presenters, writers, comedians, casting directors and producers. Welcomes performance notices for productions in London. Accepts email submissions only with a showreel link if possible. Represents actors with disabilities. *Commission*: 12.5%

TTA (Top Talent Agency)
PO BOX 860, St Albans, Hertfordshire AL1 9BR
tel 01727 855903

email admin@toptalentagency.co.uk
website www.toptalentagency.co.uk
Director & Head Agent Warren Bacci *Child & Teen
Commercial Division* Toni Thorpe *TV, Film &
Theatre Adult Agent* Leoni Morris *MT Division* Mel
Cursons, Jo Bispham *Adult Commercial Division* Jakes
James *Junior Agent* Pauline Nakirya *Office Assistant*
Caarrie Bunyan *Head of HR & Director* Andy
Musgrove *Head of Finance* Nicola Tomlin

Established in 2008. 8 agents represent 300 actors
(children and adults). Areas of work include theatre,
musicals, television, film, commercials, corporate and
voice-overs.

Will consider attending performances with 1 week's
notice. To be considered for representation, please
apply through the Top Talent website,
www.toptalentagency.co.uk, and go to the 'join us'
page. *Commission*: 15% for adults and 23% for child
actors. Can represent disabled actors.

United Agents PMA
12-26 Lexington Street, London W1F 0LE
tel 020 3214 0800 *fax* 020 3214 0802
email info@unitedagents.co.uk
website www.unitedagents.co.uk
Agents Jess Alford, Sophie Austin, Julia Charteris,
Kate Davie, Charlotte Davies, Lorna Fallowfield, Sean
Gascoine, Olivia Homan, Lindy King, Kitty Laing,
Thea Martin, Stephanie Moore, Lucia Pallaris, Helen
Robinson, Dallas Smith, Lisa Toogood, Maureen
Vincent, Kirk Whelan-Foran, Ruth Young;
Commercials Sarah Armitage, Joanna Scaratt;
Television Writers/Performers and Presenters Duncan
Hayes; Voices Kate Davie, Rebecca Haigh.

Established in 2007. Represents about 500 actors. The
agency also represents writers, directors, producers,
designers and other creatives.

"We now only accept submissions by email. Please
email your CV and headshot to
submissions@unitedagents.co.uk and expect a reply
within 4-6 weeks. Any physical submissions will not
receive a response."

Universal Artists
Blick Studios, 46 Hill Street, Belfast BT1 2LB
mobile 07838 235792
email allie@universalartists.co.uk
website www.universalartists.co.uk
Agent Allie Ford

Established in 2005. Main areas of work are film, TV,
theatre, commercials, voice-over and radio. 1 agent
represents 65 artists.

Will consider attending performances within
Northern Ireland and Greater London. Welcomes
applications as emailed CVs, showreels and voice
tapes. Is open to representing actors with disabilities.
Commission: 12%

Urban Talent
Nemesis House, 1 Oxford Court, Bishopsgate,
Manchester M2 3WQ

tel 0161 228 6866 *fax* 0161 228 6727
email liz@nmsmanagement.co.uk
Key contact Liz Beeley

Urban Talent represents 30-50 actors. Areas of work
include theatre, television, film, commercials,
corporate and voice-overs. Also represents presenters.

Will consider attending performances at venues in
the North West with 2 weeks' notice. Accepts
submissions (with CVs and photographs) from actors
previously unknown to the company, sent by post or
email. Also accepts invitations to view individual
actors' websites. *Commission*: 15%

UVA Management
Pinewood Studios, Pinewood Road, Iver Heath,
Buckinghamshire SL0 0NHL
tel 0845 370 0883
email info@uvamanagement.com
website www.uvamanagement.com
Head agent Wayne Berko

Established in 2004. Main areas of work are theatre,
musicals, television, commercials and corporate. 2
agents represent around 8 actors; also represents
presenters.

Welcomes letters (with CVs and photographs) from
actors previously unknown to the company if sent by
post or email, but prefers not to receive invitations to
view individual actors' websites. Does not accept
showreels or voicereels. Welcomes enquiries from
actors with disabilities. *Commission*: Theatre 10%; TV
and Film 13%

VSA Ltd PMA
186 Shaftesbury Avenue, London WC2H 8JB
tel 020 7240 2927
email info@vsaltd.com
website www.vsaltd.com

VSA has a long and very fine heritage as an agency,
having been created by the theatrical agent and
impresario Vincent Shaw back in the 1950s. Since
then the agency has maintained its position as a top
theatrical management looking after many successful
artists, including the legendary Jessie Matthews, as
well as giving many industry leaders such as Bill
Kenwright an opportunity to get started in the
industry.

Andy Charles took over the agency in 2002, after
working alongside Vincent Shaw as his head agent,
and today runs VSA with fellow agent and business
partner Tod Weller. Their combined experience of
the industry from both sides of the fence (Andy's
from his career as an actor, and Tod's from his career
in TV, advertising and commercials production)
ensures an in-depth understanding of the demands of
an ever-changing business, as well as an empathy and
insight into the daily challenges of an artist's life.
"Our continued success depends on our relationships
with our clients and with casting professionals –

relationships we nurture and never take for granted; friendly, professional and very personal management is paramount to all that we do."

Roxane Vacca Management PMA

73 Beak Street, London W1F 9SR
Agents Dane Millard, Roxane Vacca

2 agents represent 45 actors. Does not welcome performance notices, but will accept letters (with CVs and photographs) from individual actors previously unknown to the agency if sent by post. Also accepts showreels, voicereels, and invitations to view individual actors' websites. *Commission*: Film & TV 12.5%; Theatre 10%; Commercials 15%

Louise Dyson at VisABLE People Ltd

31 Broad Street, WR10 1BB
tel 020 3488 1998 *mobile* 07729 738317
email office@visablepeople.com
website www.visablepeople.com
Agents Louise Dyson and Kate Ellison

Founded in 1994, VisABLE is the world's first agency representing only disabled people for professional engagements. It represents artistes with a wide range of impairments and in every age group, including children. 2 agents represent around 150 artistes in all areas of acting, including presenting.

Does not welcome performance notices: "Sorry, usually no time to get out and see them; unless existing clients." Happy to receive applications from disabled actors via VisABLE website only. Showreels should always be via a l ink sent by email. Also happy to receive invitations to view individual actors' websites. Recommends the photographer Richard Bailey. *Commission*: 10%-17.5% (commercials: 20%)

Suzann Wade PMA

9 Wimpole Mews, London W1G 8PB
tel 020 7486 0746 *fax* 020 7486 5664
email admin@suzannwade.com
website www.suzannwade.com
Director Suzann Wade & Assistants

Areas of work include theatre, musicals, film, TV, commercials, corporate, animation, computer games and voice-over. Talent agency also offering personal management.

Please, no direct emails or follow-up calls, representation interest via website contact form at www.suzannwade.com. Encourages enquiries from disabled actors, American and Oriental actors based in the UK, linguists and high-physicality actors via website only.

Waring & McKenna Ltd PMA

17 South Molton Street, London W1K 5QT
tel 020 7836 9222 *fax* 020 7836 9186
email dj@waringandmckenna.com
website www.waringandmckenna.com
Twitter @WaringMcKenna

Instagram @waringandmckenna
Agents Daphne Waring, John Summerfield, Matt Chopping, Charlie Wilson, Kelly Rowden and Liz Ekberg

Established in 1993. 6 agents represent approximately 80 actors. Areas of work include film, television, theatre, commercials, corporate and voice-overs both nationally and internationally.

Will consider attending performances at venues within Greater London and occasionally elsewhere, given at least 1 month's notice. Accepts postal submissions (with CVs and photographs) from actors previously unknown to the company. Follow-up telephone calls are also accepted. Showreels and voicereels should only be sent on request. *Commission*: Theatre and Radio 10%; TV and Low-Budget Films 12.5%; Commercials, Voice-overs and Feature Films over £4 million 15%

Janet Welch Personal Management

Old Orchard, The Street, Ubley, Bristol BS40 6PJ
tel 01761 463238
email info@janetwelchpm.co.uk

Established in 1990. Areas of work include theatre, musicals, television, film, commercials, corporate and voice-overs.

Will consider attending performances at venues within Greater London and sometimes elsewhere, given sufficient notice. Accepts submissions (with CVs and photographs) from actors previously unknown to the company if sent by post.

Meredith Westwood Management Ltd

Suite A, 236 Cambridge Heath Road, Bethnal Green, London E2 9DA
mobile 07411 503007
email meredithwestwoodmanagement@gmail.com
website www.meredithwestwoodmanagement.co.uk
Senior Casting Agent and Primary Enquiries Contact Tara.

Established in 2011. Works in film, TV, commercials, theatre, musicals, events, corporate, presenting and voice-over (does not represent sole voice-over or presenting clients). 2 agents represent 30 clients.

Will consider attending performances in London, for which short notice is encouraged. Welcomes emails from actors with links to showreels and websites or dates of performances. No follow-up phone calls, although follow-up emails are accepted. Happy to hear from actors with disabilities; all are judged equally regardless of disabilities or race. *Commission*: 20% across filmed and digital media, 15% across theatre and events.

Wilde Management

11 Wilton Road, Manchester M21 9GS
mobile 07759 567639
email info@wildemanagement.com
website www.wildemanagement.co.uk
Agent Rebecca Jenner *Assistant Agent* Phil Minns

Established in 2010. Main areas of work are theatre, TV and film. 1 agent represents approximately 10 actors. Welcomes CVs and photographs sent by email only. *Commission*: 10-15%

Williamson & Holmes

5th Floor, Sovereign House,
212-224 Shaftesbury Avenue, London WC2H 8PR
tel 020 7240 0407
email info@whlondon.co.uk
website www.whlondon.co.uk
Agents Jackie Williamson, Michelle Holmes, Danica Pickett, Hugo Harrison and Charlotte Watts

Established in 2005, the agency represents 80 actors. Areas of work include theatre, musicals, television, film, commercials and corporate.

Will consider attending performances at venues within Greater London with 2 weeks' notice. Accepts submissions (with CVs and photographs) from actors previously unknown to the company if a link to Spotlight page is emailed (no large attachments). *Commission*: Theatre 10%; TV/Film/Commercials/Radio 15%

Willow Personal Management

151 Main Street, Yaxley, Peterborough PE7 3LD
tel 01733 240392
email office@willowmanagement.co.uk
website www.willowmanagement.co.uk
Director Peter Burroughs

Established in 1995. 1 agent represents more than 150 actors. Specialises in the representation of short actors (under 5ft) and tall actors (over 7ft). Areas of work include theatre, musicals, television, film, commercials, corporate and voice-overs.

Accepts submissions (with CVs and colour photographs) from actors previously unknown to the company if sent by email. *Commission*: 15%

Wintersons PMA

59 St Martin's Lane, London WC2N 4JS
tel 020 7836 7849
email info@nikiwinterson.com
website www.nikiwinterson.com
Agents Niki Winterson, Lawrence James and David O'Hanlon *Chief Operations Officer* Alasdair Cameron *Financial Executive* Mithra Harding *Junior Agent* Faye Timby *Assistants* Shauna Kiernan, Dom Valentino, Aleks Rusic

Established in 2011. Main areas of work are theatre, TV, film, commercials and corporate. Represents 100 actors. Also represents directors, writers and casting directors. Welcomes performance notices and will attend whenever possible within London. Welcomes letters, CVs via email with Spotlight links only. Please do not attach images or large files to emails.

Felix de Wolfe PMA

20 Old Compton Street, London W1D 4TW
tel 020 7242 5066 *fax* 020 7242 8119
email info@felixdewolfe.com
Agents Caroline de Wolfe, Wendy Scozzaro

Areas of work include film, television, theatre, musicals, commercials, corporate and radio. Also represents directors, producers and writers.

Accepts submissions by email to **info@felixdewolfe.com** which must be marked Re: representation.*Commission*: Variable

Edward Wyman Agency

23 White Acre Close, Thornhill, Cardiff CF14 9DG
tel 029 2075 2351
email wymancasting@yahoo.co.uk
website www.wymancasting.co.uk
Managing Director Judith Gay

Areas of work include television, film, commercials, corporate, photo shoots and voice-overs.

Accepts submissions from actors previously unknown to the company. Application forms can be downloaded from the website. All submissions should include CVs and photographs and a valid DBS certificate. Welsh actors are particularly welcome. Most work South Wales-based. *Commission* 15%

CO-OPERATIVE AGENCIES

Before making an approach, it is important to understand what being a member of one of these entails, and to be clear about your reason(s) for wanting to join. Many Co-ops have clear details for applicants on their websites.

21st Century Actors Management

5 Crowndale Road, Camden Town,
London NW1 1TU
tel 020 3033 0062
email 21centuryactors@gmail.com
website www.21stcenturyactors.co.uk

Co-operative management established in 1992. Represents 21 actors. Areas of work include theatre, musicals, television, film, commercials and corporate. Members are expected to work 3 days in the office per month.

Will consider attending performances at venues in and around London. Accepts submissions (with CVs and photographs) from actors previously unknown to the company if sent by email. Actors requesting representation should write stating why they wish to join a co-operative, and outlining their casting type and skills. *Commission*: Theatre, TV, Commercials & Film 10%

1984 Personal Management Ltd

Suite 508, Davina House, 137 Goswell Road,
London EC1V 7ET

tel 020 7251 8046
email info@1984pm.com
website www.1984pm.com
Twitter @1984pm_actors

Co-operative management (CPMA member) representing 25 actors. Areas of work include theatre, musicals, television, film, commercials, and corporate. Members are expected to work 4 days in the office per month unless paying commission.

Will consider attending performances at venues in Greater London with 1 month's notice. Accepts letters and emails (with CVs, photographs or link to Spotlight CV). Please see website Apply section first. Will also accept showreels and follow-up telephone calls. *Commission*: 5%

Actors Alliance

KP CH3 28, Chester House, Kennington PArk, 1-3 Brixton Road, London SW9 6DE
tel 020 7407 6028
email actors@actorsalliance.co.uk
website www.actorsalliance.co.uk

A co-operative group of actors established in 1976 to advance one another's careers. Currently there are 19 members, who are all in Spotlight and belong to Equity. Areas of work include theatre, musicals, television, film, commercials, corporates and voice-overs. Members are expected to work in the office at least 1 day a week.

When interested, and given a minimum of 2 weeks' notice, will attend an applicant's performance in Greater London. Welcomes applications (with CV and photograph) by email or post (with a postal application it is useful to send an sae) Happy to accept links to showreels or voicereels. Actors Alliance is not funded from commission.

Actors' Creative Team

44-48 Bloomsbury Street, London WC1B 3QJ
tel 020 7462 4514
email office@actorscreativeteam.co.uk
website www.actorscreativeteam.co.uk
Twitter @ActorsCreativeT

Founded in 2001, this co-op agency has members working in theatre, musicals, television, film, commercials and corporate projects. Members are expected to work 3 days in the office each month and attend fortnightly meetings. Welcomes performance notices for events, given at least 2 weeks' notice. Will also accept emails (with links to Spotlight, cover letter and headshots), see website for more details. Prospective clients need to include their reasons for choosing a co-operative agency in a covering email. Commission: Theatre up to 10%; Recorded Media up to 12.5%

Actors Direct Ltd

Number 5, 651 Rochdale Road, Manchester M9 5SH
tel 0161 277 9360 *tel* 020 7206 2759

email info@actorsdirect.org.uk
website www.actorsdirect.org.uk
Administrators J. Langford

Established in 1994. Personal management. Sole representative of approximately 60 actors. Areas of work include theatre, musicals, television, film, commercials, corporate and voice-overs.

Will consider attending performances if given 2 weeks' notice. Accepts submissions (with CVs and photographs) from actors previously unknown to the company if sent by post or email. Also accepts showreels and voicereels.

Now has offices in Manchester and London.

The Actors File

The White House, Oval House, 52-54 Kennington Oval, London SE11 5SW
tel 020 7582 7923
email theactorsfile@btconnect.com
website www.theactorsfile.co.uk
Twitter @The_Actors_File

Established in 1983. Co-operative management representing 20-25 actors. Areas of work include theatre, musicals, television, film, commercials, corporate and voice-overs. Members are expected to work 4 days in the office per month and to attend business meetings.

Will attend performances at venues in Greater London and occasionally elsewhere. Accepts submissions by post or email which include CV, photograph and covering letter detailing interest iin a co-op. Will also accept showreels.

The Actors' Group

Swan Buildings, 20 Swan Street, Manchester M4 5JW
tel/fax 0161 834 4466
email enquiries@theactorsgroup.co.uk
website www.theactorsgroup.co.uk
Twitter @TheActorsGroup1

Established in 1980. Co-operative management representing actors. Member of CPMA and Co-operatives UK.

Areas of work include stage, television, film, commercials, radio, voice-overs, roleplay and corporate. Members are expected to carry out various office duties.

Will consider attending performances at venues in the North with 2-4 weeks' notice. Accepts submissions (by email) from actors previously unknown to the co-operative. Will also accept follow-up telephone calls, showreels, voicereels and invitations to view individual actors' websites.

Actors Network Agency

55 Lambeth Walk, London SE11 6DX
tel 020 7735 0999
email info@ana-actors.co.uk
website www.ana-actors.co.uk

Established in 1985. Co-operative personal management representing 35-40 actors. Areas of work include theatre, musicals, television, film, commercials, corporate and role-play. Members are expected to work up to 4 days in the office per month.

Will consider attending performances at venues in Greater London and occasionally elsewhere, given as much notice as possible. Accepts submissions (link to Spotlight entry or CV and photograph together with any showreels) via email. *Commission* 10%; Commercials 12.5%

Actorum Ltd

Unit 5, 11 Mowll Street, London SW9 6BG
tel 020 7636 6978
email info@actorum.com
website www.actorum.com

Co-operative management representing 35 actors. Operates on the principle of collective self-determination in the entertainment business with each actor working 4 days a month in the office when not working professionally.

Will consider attending performances at venues in Greater London and elsewhere, given 4 weeks' notice. All applications sent to **newaps@actorum.com**. Showreels, voicereels and invitations to view individual actors' websites accepted. *Commission*: Theatre 10%; TV, Commercials and Film 15%

Alpha Actors

8 Woodberry Down, London N4 2TG
tel 020 7241 0077 *fax* 020 7241 2410
email alpha@alphaactors.com
website www.alphaactors.com

A co-operative agency established in 1983, Alpha Actors currently represents 23 actors working in theatre, musicals, television, film, commercials and corporate work. Members are expected to work 4 days in the office each month.

Welcomes submissions by email or by post with letter, CV and photograph, and will consider attending performances within Greater London, given as much as notice as possible.

Arena Personal Management Ltd

139 Collingwood Road, Surrey SM1 2QW
tel 020 3741 8061
email info@arenapmltd.co.uk
website www.arenapmltd.co.uk

A hybrid co-operative of working and client members representing c. 20 London and south east actors. Areas of work include theatre, musicals, television, film, commercials, corporate and voice-overs. Working members are expected to work one day in their home office per week and benefit from some preferred consideration for doing so.

Will consider attending showcases at venues in Greater London given 3-4 weeks' notice and if invited

personally by an actor interested in a co-operative agency. Accepts submissions (with CVs and photographs) from actors previously unknown to the company by email only. Will also accept follow-up telephone calls, showreels, voicereels and invitations to view individual actors' websites. *Commission*: rates dependent on member status with both considered attractive

AXM (Actors Exchange Management Ltd)

Unit J302, J Block, Biscuit Factory,
100 Clement's Road, London SE16 4DG
tel 020 7837 3304
email info@axmgt.com
website www.axmgt.com
Twitter @AXMgt

Established in 1983. Co-operative management representing over 20 actors. Areas of work include theatre, musicals, television, film, commercials, corporate and voice-overs. Members are expected to work 3-4 days in the office per month.

Will consider attending performances at venues in Greater London, given sufficient notice. Accepts submissions (with CVs and photographs) from actors previously unknown to the company if sent by post or email. Showreels and voicereels should only be sent on request following an interview. *Commission*: Variable depending on work type

Bridges: The Actors' Agency Ltd

Studio S12, Out of the Blue Drill Hall,
36 Dalmeny Street, Edinburgh EH6 8RG
tel 0131 5543073
email admin@bridgesactorsagency.com
website www.bridgesactorsagency.com

Established in 2008. At present the only co-operative agency active in Scotland. Areas of work include theatre, television, film, commercials, radio and corporate. Members are expected to contribute to the running of the office, and to attend meetings; therefore all prospective members must be based a commutable distance from Edinburgh.

Accepts submissions via letters and emails: include a CV and headshot. Will also accept showreels, voicereels and invitations to view individual actors' websites. Welcomes invitations to attend performances and showcases.

Entry to the agency is via audition. If successful, a stakeholder donation of £100 is required to join the agency which is refundable when memership is terminated. Prospective members must also be registered with Spotlight. *Commission*: Non-Electronic 10%; Electronic 12%

Castaway Actors Agency

30-31 Wicklow Street, Dublin 2
tel +353 1 671 9264/9059

email office@castawayactors.com
website www.castawayactors.com

Established in 1989. A co-operative agency representing 29 actors. Members are expected to fulfil office duties throughout the year. Areas of work include theatre, musicals, television, film, commercials, corporate and voice-overs. Accepts submissions with CVs, photographs and a cover letter from Dublin-based actors.

CCM

Suite 22, Argyll House, All Saint's Passage, London SW18 1EP
tel 020 3697 1961
email casting@ccm.com
website www.ccmactors.com

Secretary Lucy Aley-Parker *Administrator* Roger Thomson

Established in 1993. Co-operative management representing up to 30 actors. Areas of work include theatre, film, television, musicals and commercials. Members are expected to work up to 3 days in the office per month, and need office skills.

Members will consider attending performances, with notice. The agency accepts letters and emails (with photographs and CVs – hard-copy submissions preferred) from actors previously unknown to the membership, and will also accept invitations to view actors' personal websites. Entry to the agency is via audition, which prospective members will be invited to attend. Actors must be aware of how co-operatives work, and their role within them. Please see our website for application procedure. Information is available from Equity and Spotlight. A Training Fee of £250 (in 2 instalments) is required to join the agency. Prospective clients must also be registered in *Spotlight*.

Central Line

129a Middleton Boulevard, Nottingham NG8 1FW
tel 0115 941 2937
email agents@thecentralline.co.uk
website http://thecentralline.co.uk
Facebook www.facebook.com/centralactors
Twitter @centralactors

Co-operative management agency established in 1984. Areas of work include theatre, musicals, television, film, commercials, corporate and voice-overs. Also represents directors. Members are expected to work in the office as and when appropriate.

Will consider attending performances at venues in Greater London and elsewhere. Accepts submissions (with links to Spotlight) from actors previously unknown to the company, sent by email only. Will also accept follow-up telephone calls, showreels, voicereels and invitations to view individual actors' websites. *Commission*: 8-15%

Circuit Personal Management Ltd

Suite 31 Progress Centre, Charlton Place, Ardwick Green, Manchester M12 6HS
tel 0161 425 0763
email mail@circuitpm.co.uk
email circuitpresentation@gmail.com
website www.circuitpm.co.uk
Twitter @CircuitPM
Editor Instagram: @Circuitinsta

Established in 1988. Co-operative management primarily representing actors in the North West area. Areas of work include theatre, musicals, television, film, commercials, corporate and voice-overs. Members are expected to work approximately 4-5 days quarterly in our Manchester office and to attend monthly meetings.

Will consider attending performances at venues within the operating area, preferably with 3-4 weeks' notice. Accepts submissions from actors (with CVs and photographs) sent by post or email. Will also accept follow-up telephone calls.

City Actors' Management

Oval House, 52-54 Kennington Oval, London SE11 5SW
tel 020 7793 9888
email info@cityactors.co.uk
website www.cityactors.co.uk

Co-operative management representing 38 actors with 1 full-time, office-based agent. Areas of work include theatre, musicals, television, film, commercials and corporate. Members are expected to work 3 days in the office per month.

Will consider attending performances at venues in Greater London with a minimum of 2 weeks' notice. Submissions (with CVs and photographs) should be sent by post or email. Advises actors to contact the agency when appearing in a show, or with a showreel, as new members will not be considered without their work being seen. Will also accept follow-up telephone calls. *Commission*: Theatre 12.5% depending on income; Media 15%

Crescent Management

China Works, Black Prince Road, London SE1 7SJ
tel 020 8987 0191
email mail@crescentmanagement.co.uk
website www.crescentmanagement.co.uk

Established in 1991, the agency has 20-25 members working in theatre, musicals, television, film, commercials and corporate drama. Members are expected to work 3 days in the office each month.

Will consider attending performances within Greater London given 2 weeks' notice. Accepts submissions (with CVs and photographs) from actors previously unknown to the agency: please read the advice on how to apply given on the website. Will also accept follow-up telephone calls, showreels, voicereels and invitations to view an actor's website. *Commission*: Theatre 10%; Television 12.5%; Film 15%

Denmark Street Management

Unit 77b, Eurolink Office Building, 49 Effra Road, Lambeth, London SW2 1BZ
tel 020 7700 5200 *fax* 020 7084 4053
email mail@denmarkstreet.net
website www.denmarkstreet.net

Established in 1985. Co-operative management representing up to 30 actors working in theatre, musicals, television, film, commercials, corporate and voice-overs. Members are expected to work 1 office day per week.

Will consider attending performances if given notice. Accepts submissions via the 'apply' link on the website only (applicants must be members of Spotlight) from actors previously unknown to the company. Showreels and voicereels should only be sent on request. Applicants should state why they would like to join a co-operative. Ethnic-minority and older actors are particularly welcome. *Commission*: 10% for all work.

Direct Personal Management

c/o Yorkshire Dance, 3 St Peter's Building, St Peter's Square, Leeds LS9 8AH
tel/fax 0113 266 4036
email office@directpm.co.uk
St John's House, 16 St John's Vale, London SE8 4EN
tel/fax 020-8694 1788
website www.directpm.co.uk
Twitter @DPMActors
Instagram @DPMActors

Established in 1984 (formerly Direct Line Personal Management). Co-operative management representing 25 actors. Areas of work include theatre, musicals, television, film, commercials, corporate, role-play and voice-overs. Members are expected to work 2 days in the office each month.

Will consider attending performances at venues within Greater London and elsewhere, with 1 month's notice. Accepts submissions (with CVs and photographs) from actors previously unknown to the company, sent by post or email. Follow-up telephone calls, showreels, voicereels and invitations to view individual actors' websites are also accepted. "Please consult our website before applying. Every applicant's enquiry is discussed at a monthly meeting. We do reply, but would appreciate it if actors enclosed an sae to help reduce our costs." *Commission*: 5-15%

Frontline Actors' Agency

30-31 Wicklow Street, Dublin 2
tel +353 1 635 9882
email contact@frontlineactors.com
website www.frontlineactors.com
Facebook @FrontlineActorsAgency
Twitter @FrontlineActors

Chair Shane Whisker

Established in 2000. Main areas of work are theatre, television, film, commercials, corporate and voice-overs. Co-operative agency with 24 actor members who are expected to work approximately 1 week per quarter in the office. Will attend performances in Ireland only, given 2 weeks' notice.

Welcomes letters (with CVs and photographs), showreels, and invitations to view actors' websites. Encourages submissions from actors with disabilities.

IML

The White House, 52-54 Kennington Oval, London SE11 5SW
tel 020 7587 1080 *fax* 020 7587 1080
email info@iml.org.uk
website www.iml.org.uk

Co-operative management established in 1980. Represents 22 actors. 2 members work in the office each day on a rotational basis. Areas of work include theatre, musicals, television, film and commercials. Members are expected to work 4 days in the office per month.

Will consider attending performances at venues in Greater London given 3 weeks' notice. Accepts submissions (with CVs and photographs) from actors previously unknown to the company if sent by post. Will also accept follow-up telephone calls. Showreels and voicereels should only be sent on request. *Commission*: 5-15% depending on the job

Inspiration Management

3.3 Hoxton Works, 128 Hoxton Street, London N1 6SH
tel 020 7012 1614
email mail@inspirationmanagement.org.uk
website www.inspirationmanagement.org.uk

Established in 1986, Inspiration is a co-operative actors' agency. Areas of work include theatre, television, film, commercials, corporate, audio and role-play. Members work 36 days in the office per year, when not engaged in professional acting work, and attend meetings once a month.

Actors can apply to join by email or post, with details of their shows where applicable, and are encouraged to consult the website prior to applying. Successful applicants will be invited to interview and audition. *Commission* 10% across the board

MV Management

Ralph Richardson Memorial Studios, Kingfisher Place, Clarendon Road, London N22 6XF
tel 020 8889 8231 *fax* 020 8829 1050
email theagency@mountview.org.uk
website www.mvmanagement.org.uk

Represents actors in all areas of the industry: television, film, theatre, musicals, commercials, radio and voiceover. "MV Management is a co-operative agency exclusively for actors who attended and have graduated from Mountview Academy of Theatre Arts. Please do not contact the agency regarding representation unless you are a Mountview graduate."

North of Watford Actors Agency

The Creative Quarter, The Town Hall,
St George's Street, Hebden Bridge,
West Yorks HX7 7BY
tel 01422 845361 or 020 3143 5648
email info@northofwatford.com
website www.northofwatford.com
Facebook North of Watford Actors Agency
Twitter @NorthofWatford
New Applications Coordinator James Colley

Established in 1984. North of Watford is a long-standing actor's agency with over 35 years' industry experience. Provides accurate recommendations to casting professionals. Represents fresh new talent and seasoned actors. Areas of work include film, television, theatre, radio, multimedia, commercials, voice-over, corporate, education/business training and role play. Clients work nationally and internationally.
    Please check website and social media for changes to their books.

NorthOne Management

53 Lambeth Walk, Lambeth, London SE11 6DX
tel 020 7735 5061
email actors@northone.co.uk
website www.northone.co.uk
Twitter @N1Management

Established in 1987. Co-operative management representing up to 30 actors. Areas of work include theatre, television, film, commercials and corporate. Members are expected to work 2-3 days in the office per month.

Will consider attending performances at venues within Greater London given at least 1 week's notice. Accepts submissions (with CVs and b&w 10x8in headshots, and Spotlight link) from actors previously unknown to the companyvia their website, with an explanation of why they wish to be representd by a co-operative agency. Will also accept follow-up telephone calls, showreels and voicereels. Prefers to hear from actors when currently performing. Administration and technical skills are advantageous. Applicants must be on Spotlight. *Commission*: 10%

Oren Actors Management

Chapter Arts Centre, Market Road, Cardiff CF5 1QE
tel 02920 233321
email info@orenactorsmanagement.co.uk
website www.orenactorsmanagement.co.uk
Facebook @OrenActors Management
Twitter @Oren_Actors
Instagram @oren_actors

Established in 1981. Co-operative management representing 20-25 actors. Areas of work include theatre, musicals, television, film, commercials, corporate and voice-overs. Members are expected to work 4 hours in the office per week when not in commissionable work.

Will consider attending performances at venues in Greater London, Cardiff, South West England and Wales given 2 weeks' notice. Accepts submissions (with CVs and photographs) from actors previously unknown to the company. Will also accept follow-up telephone calls, showreels, voicereels and invitations to view individual actors' websites. Applicants are asked to state clearly why they have approached a co-operative. *Commission*: Theatre 8%; Mechanical Media 10%

Performance Actors Agency

137 Goswell Road, London EC1V 7ET
tel 020 7251 5716
email info@performanceactors.co.uk
website www.performanceactors.co.uk
Key personnel Lionel Guyett

Established in 1984. Co-operative management representing 30+ actors. Areas of work include theatre, musicals, television, film, commercials, corporate and voice-overs. Members are expected to work 3-4 days a month in the office.

Will consider attending performances at venues within Greater London and occasionally elsewhere. Accepts submissions by email from actors previously unknown to the company. Will also accept showreels and voicereels. "We only recruit new members when specific categories are required. Call or email first." *Commission*: 10%

RbA Management Ltd

37-45 Windsor Street, Liverpool L8 1XE
tel 0151 708 7273
email info@rbamanagement.co.uk
website www.rbamanagement.co.uk

Established in 1995, RbA is a co-operative management representing up to 20 actors. Areas of work include theatre, musicals, television, film, radio, commercials, corporate and voice-overs. Many of the actors have other, additional skills. Members are expected to contribute 5 working days in the office every 2-3 months.

Will consider attending performances at venues in the North West (Manchester, Liverpool, North Wales) and nationally with 3-4 weeks' notice. Accepts brief, straightforward submissions (with CVs and photographs along with a covering letter) from actors previously unknown to the company if sent by post or email. Showreels, voicereels and invitations to view individual actors' websites are also accepted. *Commission*: 15%

Rogues & Vagabonds Management

Community Room 2, 2nd floor, Deptford Lounge,
Giffin Street, London SE8 4RJ

tel 020 7254 8130
email rogues@vagabondsmanagement.com
website www.vagabondsmanagement.com
Twitter @RandVManagement

Co-operative management representing 28-30 actors. Areas of work include theatre, television, film, commercials and corporate. Members are expected to work in the office 3 days per month.

Will consider attending performances anywhere, if given at least 3-4 weeks' notice. Accepts submissions (with CVs and photographs) from actors previously unknown to the company if sent by post or email to joinrogues@gmail.com. Showreels, voicereels and invitations to view individual actors' websites are also accepted. Welcomes enquiries from disabled actors. Commission: TV/Film 10% over £200, 15% over £300; Theatre 10% over £200.

Rosebery Management Ltd
87 Leonard St, London EC2A 4QS
tel 020 7684 0187
email admin@roseberymanagement.com

Established in 1984. Represents 45 actors in theatre, musicals, television, film, commercials, corporate work and voice-overs. Rosebery has a full-time Lead Agent.

Stage Centre Management Ltd
41 North Road, London N7 9DP
tel 020 7607 0872
email info@stagecentre.org.uk
website www.stagecentre.org.uk

Established in 1982. Co-operative management agency. Areas of work include theatre, musicals, television, film, commercials and corporate. Members are expected to work 1 day in the office per week when not acting.

Will consider attending performances at venues within Greater London and elsewhere, given at least 2 weeks' notice. Accepts submissions (with CVs and photographs) from actors previously unknown to the company, sent by post or email. Will also accept follow-up telephone calls, showreels, voicereels and invitations to view individual actors' websites. Applicants should not apply if they are unable to provide visible evidence of their work (e.g. performance notice, showcase or showreel). Commission: 10-15% depending on job

West Central Management
E4 Panther House, 38 Mount Pleasant, London WC1X 0AN
tel 020 7833 8134 fax 020 7833 8134
email mail@westcentralmanagement.co.uk
website www.westcentralmanagement.co.uk

Established in 1984. Co-operative management representing 15-20 actors. Areas of work include theatre, musicals, television, film, commercials and corporate. Members are expected to work 4 days in the office per month.

Will consider attending performances at venues within Greater London with 2 weeks' notice. Accepts submissions (with CVs and photographs) from actors previously unknown to the company, sent by post or email. Will also accept invitations to view individual actors' websites. "We would need to see an applicant's live performance or showreel, but only after an initial meeting/audition." Commission: 10%

Being an agent

Howard Roberts

There are a number of unfortunate stereotypes of agents, and – particularly among younger actors – misconceptions about an agent's role. Whilst popular belief would have us all enjoying long lunches between bouts of shark-like behaviour, the truth is somewhat more akin to that of any other hard-working facilitator.

What does an agent do?

There is no definitive job description for an agent; you will find that different agents have different styles, and work in different ways. Broadly speaking, however, we can divide the agent's role into four broad aims, as follows:
• to maintain contacts across the industry, in order to secure work for their clients – most commonly in terms of obtaining casting information;
• to negotiate fees on behalf of those clients, in order to maximise rewards for the artist, and to ensure that those fees are paid;
• to manage the artist's diary in order not to miss the next job opportunity; and
• to advise the artist on their career choices and options.

Bear in mind that your agent is working for you all the time, even when you might not be earning. It is for this reason that you pay them commission for all performing work in which you are engaged whilst they represent you.

When you see agents at showcases and first nights, or when you hear that an agent is coming to your production, remember that this is usually after they have already worked a full day in the office. Attending these events is a key part of their business: it is their opportunity to network, to keep abreast of new developments and new performers, and to maintain good relationships – for example, with a casting director. The job of an agent can be immensely rewarding, but those rewards come as a result of long hours and hard work.

How do I get an agent?

Sadly, anyone can call themselves an agent, because there are no entry restrictions to the profession. In this book, you will find more than 50 pages listing agents: some of them belong to the Personal Managers' Association (PMA), a body that requires members to have at least three years' trading in the industry prior to joining. However, many other established and reputable agents choose not to belong to the PMA. So take advice. Talk to other performers, to casting directors and to established industry advisers like John Colclough, and endeavour to establish a shortlist of suitable contacts.

A phone call or an email may establish whether an agency is currently considering new clients. Don't be too disheartened if they say that their list is full – persevere with other approaches. And do be careful with emailed requests: many agents now find themselves inundated with email traffic from actors seeking representation, and could choose not to respond.

If an agency asks you to send in your details, check what they require: this will usually be a current CV, a clear 10x8in head shot and a covering letter. See if they want a DVD showreel, or a CD voicereel, but be careful of sending these unsolicited. I would suggest that you always send a correctly stamped and addressed envelope with your submission, as this will make it easier for the agent to respond.

The CV should contain your relevant professional experience, details of where you trained, and any other marketable skill(s) you may possess (for example, a clean driving licence, sports at which you are proficient, languages you might speak, musical instruments you can play, whether you can safely ride a horse, and anything else that might add to your performance).

Photographs should be clear and as up to date as possible. Remember, on the Spotlight site your photo will appear slightly smaller than a passport photo, so you want the best possible definition, at the smallest size. You are in an image-led profession, and your picture is likely to be the first point of contact. Always go to a professional photographer, but be careful of spending too much money on photos until you have an agent; chances are, they might want something different. And always put your contact details on the back of your photo; in a busy office it can get separated from your letter and CV.

Keep your letter businesslike: check to whom you are writing, date the letter and spell their name correctly. Finally, ensure that you use the correct postage: it will not improve your chances if the agent has to pay a surcharge on your letter. Of course, the agent might be happy to receive an emailed submission, using your Spotlight PIN number to access your details. Always ensure that your Spotlight entry is up to date with your correct playing age, latest credits and full list of marketable skills.

Interviews

Turn up on time – never late, but not too early either. Check where you are going in advance so that you don't arrive flustered. You are going to see a busy person, who may be in a position to help your career, so treat the meeting seriously. If you fail to attend at the agreed time, they may think that you will treat castings in a similar manner.

Before 'the day', have your questions ready and prepared in your mind. How long have you been established? How many agents work here? How many clients do you represent? What are your commission rates? (It is unusual for these to be higher than 15% – and be very wary of any agency who would charge you for enrolment.) Are you VAT registered? (If so, remember that this means you will be paying VAT on top of your commission.) Where would you fit in with this agency, and would you clash with any of their existing clients?

This is all information that you need to glean – but at interview, do be careful *how* you ask your questions. Some agents might be more reticent than others; you will need to carefully judge the mood and tone of the meeting. The agent might want to make it clear that they are interviewing you, and not the other way round. Remember, agents will vary in their style and way of working: you must be sensitive and able to adapt.

Offers of representation

Agencies come in all shapes and sizes. Larger, well-established West End concerns certainly have the attraction of the star names they represent, and if they offer you a place it could work for you. They will have the first look at film scripts, and the international cachet. However, what are sometimes referred to as the 'boutique agencies' might also be advantageous: with them, you are likely to have direct access to the principal partners, and you are more likely to be important to them. Smaller agencies have the motivation to secure as much work as possible for their clients, for as much time as possible. They will not want 'passengers'.

If you do get an offer, or offers, of representation, take time to think about it, and *always* seek advice. This is an important decision. Remember that you are entering into a business relationship, not looking for a new best friend. Of course, the best sort of actor to be is a working actor, and so the agency that works best for you is the one that helps you to keep working, irrespective of its size and location or how long it has been established.

Contracts

A contract should place your business relationship on a professional basis, clearly stating not just commission rates, but also such important issues as the required notice period for terminating your agreement. Don't be afraid of being contractually committed, but neither should you ever sign a contract on the spot. Take it away and get a second opinion, be it from another performer, from Equity, or from someone with specialist knowledge.

Problems?

How often do agents hear actors complain that their agent never puts them up for anything – or that they are not seen, even though they are ideal for a part? The harsh reality is that it is a buyer's market. You face vast amounts of competition for every job, and despite your agent's best efforts, the casting director still might not want to see you.

If you really do feel that the actor-agent relationship is not working, the first person you should talk to is your agent! Try to work out if there has been any misunderstanding about your skills, or playing age, or photo; often such issues can easily be resolved by honest discussion.

If there are irreconcilable differences, then try hard to part amicably. It's a small profession, and agents do talk to one another. Attempt to secure new representation before you move, but first check any obligations you have to your existing agent in terms of period of notice, or ongoing work, or work for which you have been submitted.

And finally ...

Always try and work with your agent. Establish how proactive they want you to be. If there are areas of work you do not wish to pursue, make sure that you let your agent know. Always ensure that you keep your agent fully aware of your availability – weekends and holidays included.

Remember: actors face huge amounts of competition, and it is the agent's job to improve the odds in a client's favour. It is a very tough profession, and experience often indicates that you have to work very hard just to be lucky.

Howard Roberts MSc is a partner in Sandra Griffin Management Ltd. He has been an actors' agent for more than 20 years, initially as an assistant and then as a co-director. Prior to this he was a lecturer in Economics and Politics in Further Education. He lives in West London.

CPMA: the Co-operative Personal Management Association

Almost all actors' co-operative agencies belong to the Co-operative Personal Management Association (CPMA), which was created in 2002 to promote co-op agencies in the profession, encourage the highest professional standards, and represent the interests of co-op agencies to outside bodies, such as Equity and Government departments.

Actors represented by co-operative agencies run the agency themselves, through a democratic structure, and work as unpaid agents for each other. Some co-ops employ a co-ordinator or administrator (who is not an actor). Co-op agencies are non-profit-making, and any surplus funds are put back into the business. Co-op agencies began in the UK in 1970, since when many more have been established and thrive. Co-ops access the same casting information as conventional agents and suggest actors for jobs, negotiate contracts and fees, take commission on jobs, and recommend and promote their clients to casting directors (CDs) and others. There is often a fee to join a co-op, which is refunded when you leave. Other, non-refundable, fees may be charged, and there could also be a voluntary monthly levy to cover office costs, co-ordinator's fees, etc. Co-op members work in the office (typically two to four times a month), attend business meetings (usually monthly) to discuss aspects of running the agency, oversee the work of other co-op members (often with CDs), and consider the work of applicants.

Belonging to a co-op has many advantages: ·
• You quickly learn how the industry works, which can be very useful for newcomers and those returning to the profession.
• You are in contact with many industry professionals, which could help you get work.
• You are supported by other actors in the agency, some of who will have a lot of experience.
• You know which jobs you have been suggested for, and can monitor them.
• You have more influence over how you are represented, and can be more pro-active in your career.
• You can say which type of work you will or won't do, without fear of being asked to leave the agency.
• Usually, more than one person decides whom to suggest for a job. Many CDs acknowledge that co-ops often know their clients much better, and can sell them with honesty and confidence.
• Co-ops have smaller lists of clients, tend to avoid clashes, and commission rates are lower.

However, you should be aware that there can be drawbacks to being part of a co-op. As with conventional agents, standards vary; a co-op is only as good and professional as its members. Can you be sure that other members are working as hard for you, as you are for them? Continuity can also be a problem, with so many people involved. Although co-ops with a co-ordinator may have an advantage in this respect, measures such as detailed note-taking and not changing negotiators on a contract still need to be taken. And CDs tend to send breakdowns for major TV and film roles to the top agencies in the industry – although other parts will be sent to good co-ops.

To join a co-op you need to be a good agent (not just a good actor), committed, reliable and keen to support fellow actors. You must be able to use a computer and learn the software the agency uses. You must be prepared to get on the phone, talk to CDs, and sell your clients with knowledge and conviction, making intelligent and credible suggestions for roles. Consider, too, your personal commitments, such as doing non-acting jobs to earn money, and expenses, such as travel to and from the office, and joining/training fees.

If you are thinking of applying to a co-op, first ask if applications are being considered – and if so, how they should be submitted. Many co-ops, like conventional agents, do not accept email applications. Check CVs and photos on the agency's website to identify potential gaps. Send your photograph and CV, saying why a co-op agency interests you, and stressing skills and any contacts you have which could be useful. Co-ops usually want to see an applicant's work, so send a showreel or details of the show you're in (they tend not to go to drama school shows or showcases, unless someone has expressed interest).

To find out more about the agency, talk to current and former members. You might want to know when the agency was established; if any ex-members have returned; the extent of their contacts with CDs and with theatres; the range of casting information they receive; and whether they belong to the CPMA, which has a code of conduct (Equity particularly welcomed the creation of the CPMA for this reason). If the co-op is interested in your application, you will be interviewed by all available members. If offered a place, you will usually have a three- to six-month trial period. After discussion to see how both sides feel, you may then be offered full membership.

Please visit **www.cpma.coop** for further information.

Voice-over agents

This section lists agencies that specialise in voice-overs. Check the details of how each wishes to be approached, and refer to the 'Showreel, Voicereel and Website Services' section for more about getting a voicereel (or 'voice demo') made. Some of the larger conventional agencies have their own voice-over departments – generally for their existing clients only.

Accent Bank
420 Falcon Wharf, 34 Lombard Road, London SW11 3RF
tel 020 7223 5160
email enquiries@accentbank.co.uk
website www.accentbank.co.uk
Director Lisa Paterson

Areas of work include television, film, commercials, audio books, radio, corporate and training material. 3 agents represent more than 200 clients. Has in-house facilities to produce voicereels for clients and other actors. See the website for current rates.

Accepts submissions from actors previously unknown to the agency. Will also accept submissions sent via email. Voicereels and invitations to view individual actors' websites are also accepted. Follow-up calls are welcome. Will consider representing disabled actors. *Commission*: 15%

Ad Voice
40 Whitfield Street, London W1T 2RH
tel 020 7323 2345 *fax* 020 7323 0101
email info@advoice.co.uk
website www.advoice.co.uk
Key personnel Susan Barritt

Two agents represent clients working in television and radio commercials, documentaries, corporate, animations and audiobook recordings. Submission via **info@advoice.co.uk**

Calypso Voices
27 Poland Street, London W1F 8QW
tel 020 7734 6415 *fax* 020 7437 0410
email calypso@calypsovoices.com
website www.calypsovoices.com
Manager Jane Savage

2 agents represent 80 clients for voice-over work. Areas of work include television and radio commercials, documentaries, animation, corporate, audio books and on-air promotions.

Conway Van Gelder Grant
Third Floor, 8-12 Broadwick Street, London W1F 8HW
tel 020 7287 1070 *fax* 020 7287 1940
email voices@conwayvg.co.uk
website www.conwayvangeldergrant.com
Agents Kate Pulmpton, Hayley Ori, Neil McNulty

Areas of work include animated film, commercials, documentary, audio books, gaming and camapigns. *Commission*: 15%

Damn Good Voices
112 Chester House, 1-3 Brixton Road, London SW9 6DE
mobile 07702 228185 079809 549887
email damngoodvoices@me.com
website www.damngoodvoices.com
Facebook @damngoodvoices
Twitter @damngoodvoices
CEO Simon Cryer *Agent* Chris Davies *Agent's Assistant* Maddy Harland

Established in 2010, Damn Good Voices is a multi-award-winning voiceover agency, specialising in UK and US voice talent, working across all media including TV, film, radio, online, gaming and corporate.

Represents over 200 actors and singers. Welcomes performance notices with 7 days' notice where possible. Represenation requests should be made via the website only. Go to Representation in FAQs on the website. All submissions for representation are tracked and responded to personally. Submissions by email will not be accepted.

Commission: 15%

Earache Voices
177 Wardour Street, London W1F 8WX
tel 020 7287 2291 *fax* 020 7287 2288
email enquiries@earachevoices.com
website www.earachevoices.com
Agent Alex Lynch-White

Provides voice-overs for commercials, documentaries, audio books and animation.

Accepts voicereels via email only. *Commission*: 15%

Foreign Versions
tel 0333 123 2001
email info@foreignversions.co.uk
website www.foreignversions.com
Directors Margaret Davies, Anne Geary *Project Manager* Bérangère Capelle

Foreign Versions works with advertising agencies for foreign markets, corporate clients, companies producing audio guides, and film and television companies.

As the agency specialises in foreign languages, all voices must be mother-tongue speakers. Voice samples should be sent on MP3 (or similar) via email, together with a CV.

Hamilton Hodell Ltd

20 Golden Square, London W1F 9JL
tel 020 7636 1221 *fax* 020 7636 1226
email info@hamiltonhodell.co.uk
website www.hamiltonhodell.co.uk
Head of Voice and Commercials Louise Donald

Main areas of work are television, film, commercials and audio books. 1 agent in the Voice department and 4 in the Acting department represent around 124 clients in total.

Welcomes letters (with CVs) from individual actors previously unknown to the agency, sent by post only. Will accept follow-up telephone calls, unsolicited voicereels, and invitations to view individual actors' websites. Currently represents, or plans to represent, actors with disabilities. *Commission*: 15%

Hobson's Voices

2 Duke's Gate, Chiswick, London W4 5DX
tel 020 8995 3628 *fax* 020 8996 5350
email voices@hobsons-international.com
website www.hobsons-international.com
Managing Director Donna Lampton *Company Co-ordinator* Sue Horrix

6 agents represent 160 artists. Welcomes submissions for representation *by email only*. MP3 files to **submissions@hobsons-international.com**.

iCan Talk Ltd

tel 01858 466749
email hello@icantalk.co.uk
website www.icantalk.co.uk
Key contact Katie Matthews

Established in 2009. Voice-over agency.

Inter Voice Over

3rd Floor, 207 Regent Street, London W1B 3HH
tel 020 7262 6937
email info@intervoiceover.com
website www.intervoiceover.com
Casting Director Liliane Goudriaan

Established in 1998. Main areas of work are voice-over, voice acting, television, film, commercials and corporate videos. Welcomes voice demos by email to **casting@intervoiceover.com**. Does not currently represent actors with disabilities.

Lip Service

53A Brewer Street, London W1F 9UH
tel 020 7734 3393 *fax* 020 7734 3373
email bookings@lipservice.co.uk
Managing Director Alex Mactavish

4 agents solely represent over 100 clients and a number of foreign clients. Areas of work include television, film, commercials and audio books.

Accepts submissions (with CVs and voicereels) from individual actors previously unknown to the company, sent by email or post. Please enclose an sae for their return.

Kate Moon Management

PO Box 648, Harrington, Northampton NN6 9XT
Voice-Overs & Corporate Television Agent Kate Moon (*Director*)

Areas of work include television, commercials and audio books.

Accepts submissions (with CVs and voicereels) from individual actors (experienced only) previously unknown to the company, if sent by email.

Rabbit Vocal Management

180 Great Portland Street, London W1W 5QZ
tel 020 7287 6466 *fax* 020 7287 6566
email info@rabbitvocalmanagement.co.uk
website www.rabbitvocalmanagement.co.uk
Head of Rabbit Vocal Management Amy Howell

Representing 200 artists. Covers all areas of voice work including TV and radio, commercial, documentaries, audio books, promos and continuity, and animation.

Accepts submissions (with CVs) from actors previously unknown to the agency if sent by email but not by post. Invitations to view individual actors' websites are also accepted. Represents disabled actors.

Red 24 Voices

The Hospital Club, 3rd Floor, 24 Endell Street, London WC2H 9HQ
tel 020 7559 3611
email info@red24management.com
website www.red24management.com
Managing Director Paul Weedon

Main areas of work are television, commercials and radio. 2 agents represent around 50 clients. Recommends the company The Showreel for the production of voicereels.

Welcomes letters (with CVs) from individual actors previously unknown to the agency, sent by post or email. Will accept unsolicited voicereels and invitations to view individual actors' websites. Currently represents, or plans to represent, actors with disabilities. *Commission*: 20%

Rhubarb Voices

1st Floor, 1A Devonshire Road, Chiswick, London W4 2EU
tel 020 8742 8683 *fax* 020 8742 8693
email enquiries@rhubarbvoices.co.uk
website www.RhubarbVoices.co.uk
Key contact Johnny Garcia

Leading UK voice talent agency with experience casting voices into all platforms of the spoken word, including commercials, continuity & promos, corporate pieces, animation, games, ADR/lip-synch and more. Represents around 90 exclusive UK and North American artists, and more than 100 foreign-language artists.

Actors seeking representation should email their CV (including any voice-over work to date), a photo and an MP3 showreel. Please note that the agency prefers not to receive follow-up calls.

Shining Management Ltd
81 Oxford Street, London W1D 2EU
tel 020 7734 1981 *fax* 020 7734 2528
Director Clair Daintree *Key contact* Jennifer Taylor

2 agents represent 55 clients. Areas of work include voice-overs for television, film, commercials and audio books.

Accepts submissions (with CVs and voicereels) from individual actors previously unknown to the company if sent by post. Include an sae for the return of submissions. "Please do not ring with submission enquiries." *Commission*: 15%

Talking Heads
Argyll House, All Saints Passage, London SW18 1EP
tel 020 7292 7575
email voices@talkingheadsvoices.com
website www.talkingheadsvoices.com

Areas of work include commercials, television, film, animation, corporate videos, audio books and foreign voices.

Accepts submissions (with CVs and voicereels) by email or post. Invitations to view websites are also accepted. *Commission*: 15%

Sue Terry Voices Ltd
4th Floor, 35 Great Marlborough Street, London W1F 7JF
tel 020 7434 2040
email sue@sueterryvoices.com
website www.sueterryvoices.com
Managing Director Sue Terry

8 agents represent around 400 actors working in voice-overs only. Does not welcome unsolicited approaches by actors without performing agents. *Commission*: 15%

Tongue & Groove
PO Box 173, Manchester M19 0AR
tel 0161 249 3666
email info@tongueandgroove.co.uk
website www.tongueandgroove.co.uk
Producers Bev Ashworth, John Basham

2 agents represent 50 clients. Areas of work include voice-overs for television, commercials and audio books.

Accepts submissions (with CVs and voicereels) from individual actors previously unknown to the company if sent by post. Also accepts voicereels and invitations to view individual actors' websites.

Vocal Point
131 Great Titchfield Street, London W1W 5BB
tel 020 7419 0700 *fax* 020 7419 0699
email enquiries@vocalpoint.net
website www.vocalpoint.net
Agent Ben Romer Lee

Areas of work include television, commercials and audio books. 2 agents represent approximately 85 clients.

Accepts submissions from actors previously unknown to the company. Invitations to view individual actors' websites are also accepted. Follow-up calls are not welcomed. *Commission*: 15%

VoiceBank Ltd
PO Box 825, Altrincham, Cheshire WA15 5HH
tel 0161 973 8879
email elinors@voicebankltd.co.uk
website www.voicebankltd.co.uk
Director Elinor Stanton

Works in all areas: musicals, television, film, commercials, audio books and radio. Represents 42 clients.

Welcomes unsolicited voicereels and invitations to view individual actors' websites. Does not currently represent any actors with disabilities, but "this would not be a barrier to joining the company".

Voice Shop
First Floor, 1A Devonshire Road, London W4 2EU
tel 020 8742 7077 *fax* 020 8742 7011
email info@voice-shop.co.uk
website www.voice-shop.co.uk
Key contact Maxine Wiltshire

3 agents represent 42 clients working in television, film, commercials and audio-book recording.

Welcomes emails with MP3 audio samples from new actors, but prefers not to receive follow-up telephone calls or voicereels. All audio samples should contain appropriate material, and be professionally produced. *Commission*: 15%

Voice Squad
76 Park Avenue North, London NW10 1JY
tel 020 8450 4451
email voices@voicesquad.com
website www.voicesquad.com
Director Neil Conrich

4 agents represent more than 700 clients. Areas of work include television, film, commercials and audio books.

Accepts submissions (with CVs and voicereels) from individual actors previously unknown to the company if sent by email. *Commission*: 15%

Voicebank, The Irish Voice-Over Agency
35 Thomastown Rd, Dun Laoghaire, Co. Dublin
tel +353 1 235 0838

email info@voicebank.ie
website www.voicebank.ie
Company Manager/Owner Deborah Pearce

Voicebank are a voice-over agency only and represent actors, comedians and presenters for all aspects of voice work. Main areas of work include musicals, television, film, commercials, audio books and radio. 3 agents represent more than 120 clients.

Welcomes letters (with CVs and photographs) from individual actors previously unknown to the agency, sent by post only. Accepts unsolicited voicereels and invitations to view individual actors' websites. Voice-over demos of no longer than 2 minutes should be submitted on MP3 to info@voicebank.ie. Currently represents, or plans to represent, actors with disabilites. *Commission*: Varies

The Voiceover Gallery

110 Timberwharf, 32 Worsley Street,
Manchester M15 4NX
tel 0161 881 8844 *fax* 0161 881 8951
email info@thevoiceovergallery.co.uk
77 Blythe Road, London W14 0HP
tel 020 7987 0951
email info@thevoiceovergallery.co.uk
website www.thevoiceovergallery.co.uk
London: *Director* Marylou Thistleton-Smith *Voice Agent* Roddy Norris; Manchester: MD: Jason Thorpe *Vendor Manager* Hannah Ralph *Agency Manager* Judith Summerton *Voice Agent* Katie Berkes

Areas of work include corporate, documentary, new media, television and radio advertising. 3 agents represent 60 English voices and multiple foreign voices.

For all representation enquiries and instructions for submissions to the agency, visit the 'Our Services' section of the website, and click on 'Artist Services'. *Commission*: 15%

VSI (Voice & Script International)

Aradco House, 132 Cleveland Street,
London W1T 6AB
tel 020 7692 7700 *fax* 020 7692 7711
email info@vsi.tv
website www.vsi.tv
Head of Voice-Over Department Jose Alonso jose.alonso@vsi.tv/Isobel George isobel.george@vsi.tv
Voice-Over Project Managers Giovanna Molinelli giovanna.molinelli@vsi.tv, Giulia Parker giulia.parker@vsi.tv, Kirsty Walter kirsty.walter@vsi.tv, Marc van Moorsel marc.van-moorsel@vsi.tv, Matthew Howell matthew.howell@vsi.tv.*Key contact* Jose Alonso

7 voice-over agents represent approx. 1500 foreign-language voice-over clients. Areas of work include voice-overs for television, film, corporate and commercials.

Accepts submissions (with CVs) from individual actors and presenters previously unknown to the company, sent by post or email (**voices@vsi.tv**). Also accepts voicereels and invitations to view individual actors' websites. "We only use mother-tongue foreign-language speakers."

Yakety Yak All Mouth Ltd

56 Broadwick Street, London W1 7AJ
tel 020 7430 2600 *fax* 020 7404 6109
email info@yaketyyak.co.uk
website www.yaketyyak.co.uk
Proprietor Jolie Williams

3 agents represent 177 clients. Areas of work include voice-overs for television, film, commercials, animation and audio books.

Books are currently closed, but submissions can be sent to **submissions@yaketyyak.co.uk** in MP3 format. *Commission*: 15%

Presenters' agents

James Grant Media
94 Strand on the Green, London W4 3NN
tel 020 8742 4950 *fax* 020 8742 4951
website www.jamesgrant.co.uk

5 agents represent 21 presenter clients; also represents television presenters and stage actors.

Welcomes letters (with CVs and showreels) from individuals previously unknown to the agency, sent by post or email.

Jeremy Hicks Associates Ltd
15 Arlington Road, London NW1 7ER
email info@jeremyhicks.com
website www.jeremyhicks.com
Agents Jeremy Hicks, Sarah Dalkin and Charlotte Leaper*Agents' Assistant* Julie Dalkin

Represents presenters, writers and chefs.

Welcomes letters (with CVs and showreels) from individuals, and emails. *Commission*: 15% (10% for scriptwriters)

Red 24 Management
First Floor, Kingsway House, 103 Kingsway, London WC2B 6QX
tel 020 7559 3611
email info@red24management.com
website www.red24management.com
Managing Director Paul Weedon

Welcomes letters (with CVs and showreels) from individual presenters previously unknown to the company, sent by post or email, and accepts invitations to view individuals' websites.

Sandra Singer Associates
21 Cotswold Road, Westcliff on Sea, Essex SS0 8AA
tel 01702 331616
email sandrasingeruk@aol.com
website www.sandrasinger.com

2 agents represent approximately 40 main clients. "We are a specialist boutique agency representing some of the best talent in the UK for Acting and Musical Theatre." Also a leading Young Performers agency. Email requests in the first instance regarding representation. *Commission*: 10% Stage; 20% Screen

Triple A Media
Suite 23, 264 Lavender Hill, London SW11 1LJ
tel 020 7228 9007
email info@tripleamedia.com
website www.tripleamedia.com
Owner/Agent Andy Hipkiss

Established in 2007. Areas of work include television, radio and corporate. Also represents a number of other media professionals, including DJs, presenters and experts. Member of the Personal Managers Association (PMA).

Accepts submissions by email (with CVs and photographs), and welcomes showreels. Happy to represent actors with disabilities.

Jo Wander Management
110 Gloucester Avenue, London NW1 8HX
tel 020 7209 3777 *fax* 020 7209 3770
email jo@jowandermanagement.com
website www.jowandermanagement.com
Managing Director Jo Wander

1 agent represents 15-20 presenter clients.

Welcomes letters (with CVs and showreels) from individual presenters previously unknown to the agency, sent by post or email; will accept invitations to view individuals' websites.

Casting directors

Essentially, casting directors take on the 'nitty-gritty' work involved in the casting process – it is usually the director, and sometimes the producer, who actually 'directs' the casting decisions. The crucial thing to remember is that each one is employed – by someone else. Some casting directors are employed on a full-time basis; a significant number work freelance and can be as concerned about where their next job is coming from as you are. Therefore, if one gets you to meet their director-employer, it is important that you live up to that casting director's expectations: carefully absorb any brief that they give you. If you suddenly decide to take a radically different approach, they will be put into a difficult position with that director-employer.

Fundamental to the job of being a casting director is a wide knowledge of all kinds of actors. Therefore a good one will have seen as many productions as possible. Like squirrels storing nuts for the winter, they keep extensive notes and are continually adding to their collections of actor-profiles. An empathetic, intuitive and imaginative casting director has immeasurable value to both actors and director.

You should approach casting directors in much the same way as you would agents: however, it's even more important that there's something they can see you in. It's also important to remember that they are more project-oriented than talent-oriented. In other words, whilst an agent is looking for talent to add to their client list, a casting director is usually concentrating on specific talent for a specific project. Research what the casting director is currently casting, and target them accordingly. You can keep reasonably up to date with the activities of some casting directors by looking at the website of the Casting Directors Guild (CDG) – **www.thecdg.co.uk**.

Jo Adamson-Parker
mobile 07787 870211
email jo@northerndrama.co.uk

Main areas of work are theatre, television and film. Casting credits include: *The Bill, Chucklevision, Red Riding*, and theatre for Hull Truck, Pilot Theatre Company.

Will consider attending performances given 1-2 weeks' notice. Accepts submissions (with CVs and photographs) from actors previously unknown to the casting director sent by email. Will also accept showreels – preferably an emailable link. "I am eager to arrange general meetings with actors."

Pippa Ailion CDG
Unit 62A, Eurolink Business Centre, 49 Effra Road, London SW2 1BX
tel 020 7492 0709
email enquiries@pippaailioncasting.co.uk
Casting Directors Pippa Ailion CDG and Natalie Gallacher CDG *Assistant* Katherine Skene

Established in 1991, main areas of work are musical theatre and theatre. Casts on a case-by-case basis. Most recent productions: *Tina The Musical, Motown* (UK and Ireland tour) and *Dreamgirls*.

Welcomes perfrance notices within London given 4 weeks' notice. Welcomes CVs and pohotgraphs sent by email.

Dorothy Andrew Casting CDG
Kings Cottage, 409 Kings Road, Ashton-Under-Lyne, Lancashire OL6 9EX
tel 0161 344 2709
email dorothyandrewcasting@gmail.com

Casts mainly for television, film and commercials. Recent credits include: *Hollyoaks, Grange Hill* and *Court Room*.

Will accept postal submissions (with CVs and photographs) from actors previously unknown to the company, but unsolicited emails and showreels are not welcomed. "When writing, make your letter short and to the point. Always include a photograph (10x8in b&w) and a CV. Only send in a showreel if requested."

Ashton Hinkinson Casting
Unit 15, Panther House, 38 Mount Pleasant, London WC1X 0AN
tel 020 7580 6101

email casting@ahcasting.com
website www.ashtonhinkinson.com
Casting Directors Emma Ashton, Debs Hinkinson

Areas of work include television, film and commercials. Recent credits include: *Brother* (commercial for Bacon, Copenhagen); *Galaxy* (commercial for RSA, London); *Hostel 1 & 2* (for International Production Co.).

Will consider attending performances in Greater London with at least 1 week's notice. Invitations to showcases are also welcomed. Accepts submissions (with CVs and photographs) from actors previously unknown to the company; invitations to view individual actors' websites are also accepted.

Shaheen Baig Casting CDG

tel 020 7272 0522
email info@shaheenbaigcasting.com
website www.shaheenbaigcasting.com
Twitter @sbaigcasting

Recent film work includes *Lady Macbeth*, *God's Own Country*; Carol Morley's *The Falling*; Ben Wheatley's *Free Fire*; Paddy Considine's *Journeyman* and the debut features of Stephen Merchant *Fighting with My Family* and Idris Elba *Yardie*. Shaheen has also worked on several acclaimed television projects including *Marvellous*, *Peaky Blinders*, *Black Mirror* (for Channel 4); *Guerrilla*, *National Treasure*, *Damilola: Our Loved Boy*; Philip K. Dick's *Electric Dreams* for Channel 4/Sony & Amazon, and Shane Meadows' *The Virtues* for Channel 4.

Amy Ball CDG

See the entry for the Royal Court Theatre under *Producing theatres* on page 150.

Derek Barnes CDG

BBC Drama Series Casting, BBC Elstree, Room N221, Neptune House, Clarendon Road, Borehamwood WD6 1JF
tel 020 8228 7096 *fax* 020 8228 8311
email derek.barnes@bbc.co.uk

Main areas of work are film and television. Casting credits include: *Casualty*, *Holby City*, *Doctors* (BBC Drama Series) and *Down To Earth* (Series 5, BBC).

See also the entry for BBC (Drama Production) under *BBC network television* on page 313.

Briony Barnett Casting CDG

11 Goodwin's Court, London WC2N 4LL
tel 020 7836 3751
email briony@brionybarnettcasting.co.uk

Recent credits include, theatre: the Oliver award-winning *Handbagged*; the Olivier-nominated *The House That Will Not Stand* and *A Wolf in Snakeskin Shoes* starring Lucian Msamati (all for Tricycle Theatre). Film credits include *The Knot* and *Common People*. TV credits include the BBC Drama series *Dickensian*.

Lesley Beastall Casting

41E Elgin Crescent, London W11 2JD
tel 020 7727 6496
email lesley@lbcasting.co.uk
Casting Director Lesley Beastall

Works in commercials. Recent credits include: *Sunshine* (ITV1); *Built with You in Mind* (Thompson's Holidays); and voice-overs for The Natural Confectionary Company.

Does not welcome performance notices or unsolicited submissions by actors previously unknown to the company, but will accept invitations to view individual actors' websites. Any such approach should be made by email only.

Lauren Beauchamp Casting

34A Brightside, Billericay, Essex CM12 0LJ
mobile 07961 982198
email laurenbeauchamp@talktalk.net
Head Casting Director Lauren Beauchamp *Assistant Casting Director* Dee Atkins

Main areas of work are theatre, television, film and commercials. Recent casting credits include: *Itch* (short film; Director, Antony Gallagher for Itchka Productions); and *Bacon Sandwich* (theatre; Director, Emily North for Interact Productions).

Will consider attending performances within the Greater London and Essex areas, given at least 2 weeks' notice. Welcomes unsolicited CVs and photographs, sent by email only. Accepts showreels and invitations to view individual actors' websites.

Rowland Beckley

See the entry for BBC (Drama Production) under *BBC network television* on page 313.

Leila Bertrand Casting CDG

Jazz Productions Ltd, 53 Hormead Road, London W9 3NQ
tel 020 8964 0683 *mobile* 07976 187638
email leila@leilabcasting.com

Leila Bertrand has been a casting director for 15 years. Casts across theatre, film, TV and commercials. Credits include, theatre: *Macbeth* at Arcola Theatre, Wilton's Music Hall and international tour; film: *Sea Monster* (dir. Mark Walker) BAFTA nominee.

Actors should send headshots and CVs by post.

Lucy Bevan CDG

Ealing Studios, Ealing Green, London W5 5EP
tel 020 8567 6655
email lucy@lucybevan.com

Main areas of work are film and television. Credits include: *An Education* (BBC films), *Pirates of the Caribbean: On Stranger Tides* (Walt Disney Pictures), *300: Rise of an Empire* (Warner Bros.) and *Quartet* (Headline Pictures).

BBC Drama Series Casting

See the entry for BBC (Drama Production) under *BBC network television* on page 313.

Sarah Bird CDG

PO Box 32658, London W14 0XA
tel 020 7371 3248 *fax* 020 7602 8601
email sarah@sarahbird.com

Casts for film, television, theatre and commercials. Casting credits include: *You Don't Have To Say You Love Me*, directed by Simon Shore (Samuelson Productions); *Ladies in Lavender*, directed by Charles Dance (Scala Productions); *Fortysomething* (Carlton TV); and *Calico*, directed by Edward Hall (Sonia Friedman Productions).

Nicky Bligh CDG

mobile 07968 788561
email nicky@nickyblighcasting.com
Twitter @nickybligh

Covers TV and film, especially comedy. Has worked for numerous TV channels: BBC, SKY, Channel 4 and Comedy Central; and, production companies such as Tiger Aspect, Hat Trick and Universal Films. TV credits include *Bad Education*, *Psychobitches* and *Mrs Brown's Boys*.

Siobhan Bracke CDG

Basement Flat, 22A The Barons, St Margaret's, Middlesex TW1 2AP

Main area of work is theatre. Theatre credits include: Head of Casting for the RSC (1986-91); Shakespeare's Globe for Mark Rylance; Lyric Hammersmith for Neil Bartlett; Hampstead Theatre for Tony Clark/ Lucy Bailey; Cheek By Jowl for Declan Donnellan; Chichester – *Nicholas Nickelby* for Philip Franks; *I Am Shakespeare* for Mark Rylance; *When We Are Married* for Ian Brown, West Yorkshire Playhouse. Television credits include: *A Doll's House* and *Measure for Measure* for David Thacker; *Buddha of Suburbia* and *Persuasion* for Roger Michell.

Will consider attending performances at venues in Greater London and occasionally elsewhere, given as much notice as possible (preferably 4-5 weeks). Accepts submissions (with CVs and photographs) from actors previously unknown to the casting director if sent by post. Does not welcome email enquiries.

Andy Brierley CDG

email andy@andybrierley.com
Twitter @AndyBCasting

Andy has worked in casting for over a decade across a wide range of television, film and theatre projects such as *The Scandalous Lady W* and *Remember Me* (starring Michael Palin) for the BBC; *Top Boy* and *Run* (starring Olivia Colman) for Channel 4; and *Our Town* (Almeida Theatre). Recent credits include *Silent Witness* (2018) and *The Tunnel* (2017–18).

Jo Buckingham Casting CDG

tel 020 8568 5274 *mobile* 07753 605491
email jo@jobuckinghamcasting.co.uk

Jo has been a freelance casting director since 2011 having previously worked as an in-house casting director for BBC Comedy for nine years.

Credits include *Boy Meets Girl* (Tiger Aspect); *Way to Go* (BBC); *Miranda* (BBC); *Pulling* (Silver River); *Beautiful People* (BBC).

Aisha Bywaters Casting CDG

The Factory, 120 Lonodon Road, London SE1 6LF
mobile 07786 815109
email info@aishabywaters.com

Aisha has worked in casting since 2007 and worked for Shaheen Baig Casting for six years as an associate on numerous projects including *The Impossible* (starring Naomi Watts, Ewan McGregor); *Starred Up* (starring Jack O'Connell); *Locke* (starring Tom Hardy); *Black Mirror* (written by Charlie Brooker) and *Peaky Blinders* (starring Cillian Murphy). As a Casting Director she jointly cast many projects including *My Brother the Devil*. Since leaving, her credits as a Casting Director include the film *The Possibilities Are Endless* and TV projects *Youngers*, *Cyberbully* (starring Maisie Williams) and *The Watchmen* (starring Stephen Graham).

Happy to attend theatre in Greater London area with 4 weeks' notice. Accepts submissions from actors via email only.

Candid Casting

tel 020 7490 8882
email mail@candidcasting.co.uk
website www.candidcasting.co.uk
Facebook www.facebook.com/candidcasting
Twitter @candidcasting
Casting Director Amanda Tabak CDG CDA

Main areas of work are television, film and commercials. Casting credits include: *Kidulthood*, *Find Me in Paris* and *Honeytrap*, *Toni Erdmann*.

Will consider attending performances at venues in central London given at least 2 weeks' notice.

Cannon, Dudley & Associates

Dean Hill, Dean Street, East Farleigh ME15 0HT
tel 01622 720740
email cdacasting@blueyonder.co.uk
website www.facebook.com/cannon.dudley
Casting Director Carol Dudley CDG, CSA *Casting Associate* Helena Palmer

Main areas of work are film, theatre and television. Recent credits include: *The Third Mother – Mother of Tears* (Director: Dario Argento); *Master Harold and the Boys* (Director: Lonny Price); and theatre productions for Hampstead, Edinburgh and the West End.

Will consider attending performances at venues in Greater London given as much notice as possible.

Accepts submissions (with CVs and photographs) from actors previously unknown to the casting director if sent by post. Does not welcome email enquiries. CVs which are not submitted for specific projects or with reference to current shows or television performances cannot be kept for future reference. Telephone enquiries about current casting projects or progress of mailed submissions are not welcomed.

John Cannon CDG

BBC Elstree, (Rm N202) Neptune House, Eldon Avenue, Borehamwood WD6 1NL
tel 020 8228 7122
email john.cannon@bbc.co.uk

Currently Casting Director for *Holby City*.

Other recent television credits include: *Silent Witness*, *Mr Stink*, *Gangsta Granny*, *The Boy in the Dress*, *Grandpa's Great Escape*, *Big School*, *WPC 56*, *32 Brinkburn Street*, *The Coroner*, *Shakespeare and Hathaway* and *Father Brown* – all BBC. Was Resident Casting Director for the Royal Shakespeare Company. Recent theatre credits include: *See How They Run* (tour, W/E); *Hedda Gabler* (WYP/Liverpool Playhouse); and *Yellowman* (tour for Liverpool Everyman).

Welcomes performance notices with at least 2 weeks' notice. Also happy to receive emails (or letters with CVs and photographs) from actors, as well as invitations to view individual actors' websites or online showreels.

See also the entry for BBC (Drama Production) under *BBC network television* on page 313.

Anji Carroll CDG

email anji@anjicarroll.tv

Over 50 plays for the New Vic Theatre, including the award-winning *Snow Queen* and *Around the World in 80 Days*. The transfer of *Around the World ...* to the Royal Exchange and UK tour and in 2019 it's off to Broadway; *The Jungle Book* (Northampton and UK tour); *Before the Party*, *Echos End*, *Aladdin* (Salisbury Playhouse; *The Ladykillers* (New Wolsey Theatre); *The Lost Boy*, *Alice in Wonderland* (Theatre in the Quarter; *The Giant Jam Sandwich*, *Hood* (New Perspectives); *Judgement Day* (The Print Room); *Precious Little Talent* (Best Play at the London Theatre Festival Awards 2011, Trafalgar Studios).

Television credits include: BBC2's comedy drama series *The Cup*; *The Bill* (over 50 episodes); *The Sarah Jane Adventures: Invasion of the Bane*, 2 series of *London's Burning* (32 episodes), *The Knock* (4x90-minute episodes).

Other credits include: *Papadopoulos and Sons*; *West Is West*; *Mrs Ratcliffe's Revolution*; *Out of Depth* and *The Jolly Boys' Last Stand*; drama-documentary: *Curiosity — What Sank Titanic?' Mayday* and *Joan of Arc*.

Radio castings include: BBC 4's political drama series *Number Ten*.

The Casting Angels (London and Paris)

Suite 4, 14 College Road, Bromley BR1 3NS
fax 020 8313 0443
Director Michael Ange
Key personnel Michael *(Big Decisions)*, Gabriel *(Announcements)*, Raphael, Uriel *(The Daily Grind)*, Lucifer *(Special Consultant)*

Main areas of work are television, musicals, film and commercials with "casting across the board". Casts for the UK and other countries within Europe.

Will consider attending performances at venues in Greater London and elsewhere, given as much notice as possible. Accepts showreels.

Casting Couch Productions Ltd

213 Trowbridge Road, Bradford-on-Avon, Wiltshire BA15 1EU
mobile 07932 785807
email moira@everymansland.com
Casting Director/Producer Moira Townsend

Moira Townsend is currently producing children's shows but is still available for casting. Main areas of work are television, film and commercials. Casting credits include: *Who Killed Tutankhamen?* (documentary) and advertisements including British Airways, Curry's Electrical Stores, Heal's, Sugar Puffs, DVLA and Lunn Poly. Producers, please call for Bristol/Bath-based castings.

Will consider attending performances at venues in Greater London and elsewhere (especially Bath/Bristol area), given 2-3 weeks' notice. Accepts submissions from actors previously unknown to the casting director if sent by email. Actors will only receive a response if the casting director is able to attend a performance.

Suzy Catliff CDG

email soosecat@mac.com

Casting director and theatre director. Casts for television, film and theatre. Co-author of *The Casting Handbook* published by Routledge. Recent casting credits include: for theatre: Changeling Theatre: *The Winter's Tale*; *Nell Gwynne*; *Measure for Measure*; *Blithe Spirit*; *Hamlet*. Television: *Departure* - 6-part drama series; UK associate *The Murdoch Mysteries*; *Frankie Drake*. UK casting on *Primeval New World* and final two series of *Primeval UK* (ITV); *Silent Witness* (Series IX & X); *Blitz* (Channel 4); *D-Day* (BBC 1); *Sir Gadabout* (ITV); *Casualty* (3 series); *Ny-Lon* (associate). For film: *A Bunch of Amateurs*, *Stormbreaker*, *The Swimming Pool*, *Sense and Sensibility*, and *The English Patient* (associate).

Urvashi Chand CDG

Cinecraft, 69 Teignmouth Road, London NW2 4EA
tel 020 8208 3861
email urvashi@chandcasting.com
website www.chandcasting.com

Main area of work is film. Recent credits include: *Daylight Robbery* (directed by Barry Leonti), and *Red Mercury* (directed by Roy Battersby).

Will consider attending performances within the Greater London area and elsewhere with at least 2 weeks' notice. Accepts submissions (with CVs and photographs) from actors previously unknown to the agency, by email. Showreels, voicereels and invitations to view individual actors' websites are also accepted.

Charkham Casting

Suite 361, 14 Tottenham Court Road,
London W1T 1JY
tel 020 7927 8335 *fax* 020 7927 8336
email charkhamcasting@btconnect.com
Casting Directors Beth Charkham, Gary Ford

Areas of work include theatre, musicals, television, film and commercials. Recent credits include: *Charlie and the Chocolate Factory*, *Silent Witness* and *The Bill*.

Andrea Clark Casting

tel 020 7381 9933
email andrea@aclarkcasting.com
website www.aclarkcasting.com
Casting Director Andrea Clark

Works mainly in film, television and commercials.

Accepts showreels, links and invitations to view individual actors' websites or links to view Spotlight, Casting Call Pro or IMDb pages. Emails with multiple or very large attachments cannot be viewed. "When an actor has an agent, I prefer contact to be made via the agent."

Sam Claypole

email contact@samclaypolecasting.com
website www.samclaypolecasting.com
Casting Director Sam Claypole

Established in 2005. Works in film, TV, theatre, corporate and commercials. Recent credits include: *Giantland*, *Two Graves*, *Let's Be Evil*, *Almost Married* and *In Our Name* (all feature films).

Welcomes Spotlight, Casting Network, Casting Call Pro links to showreels, invitations to view actors' websites, and performance notices.

Ben Cogan

See the entry for BBC (Drama Production) under *BBC network television* on page 313.

Jayne Collins CDG

The Price Building, 110 York Road,
London SW11 3RD
tel 020 7223 0471 *fax* 020 7240 5323
email info@jaynecollinscasting.com
website www.jaynecollinscasting.com

Areas of work include theatre, musicals, television, film and commercials.

Will consider attending performances within the Greater London area and elsewhere, given at least 1 week's notice. Accepts submissions (with CVs and photographs) from actors previously unknown to the company if sent by post, but not by email. Welcomes showreels.

Alistair Coomer

See the entry for the National Theatre under *Producing theatres* on page 141.

Anna Cooper

Donmar Warehouse, 41 Earlham Street,
London WC2H 9LX
tel 020 7240 4882
email acooper@donmarwarehouse.com

Currently Casting Director at the Donmar Warehouse. Anna was previously a freelance casting director. She started work at the Almeida Theatre in 2003 and then worked independently – largely in theatre.

Recent theatre includes *A Number* (Nuffield, Southampton/Young Vic); *Tonight at 8.30*, *The Hudsucker Proxy* (Nuffield, Southampton) and *Multitudes* (Tricycle). As Associate to Toby Whale, TV includes *Capital*, *Doc Martin*, *Arthur and George*, *Atlantis*; film includes: *The Lady in the Van* and *Belle*.

Lin Cordoray

66 Cardross Street, London W6 0DR

Main areas of work are television and commercials.

Will consider attending performances at venues in Greater London. Accepts submissions (with CVs and photographs) from actors previously unknown to the casting director if sent by post. Does not welcome email enquiries.

Irene Cotton Casting

25 Druce Road, Dulwich Village, London SE21 7DW
tel 020 8299 1595 *fax* 020 8299 2787
email irenecotton@btinternet.com
Director Irene Cotton CDG

Recent credits include: *Jungle Tribes*; *Charlotte's Song*; Oscar-winning short 2016 *Stutterer*; *Above the Clouds*; *This is Axiom*; *A Thousand Leaves*;*Americus* (RAI Feature); *The Little Mermaid* (Feature); *Done 4* ,*Jobs Dinner* (Malcrazo Films); *The Little Black Book* (Park Theatre); Dirty Dancing (Aldwych Theatre and tour), *Long Lonely Walk* (film), *Why We Went To War* (Channel 4), *The Bill* (ITV); *The Countess* (Criterion Theatre, London); *Bang Bang* (dir. John Cleese and Nicky Henson); *Panorama* (BBC); and *Caffe Latte* commercial (Home Productions). Welcomes performance notices as far in advance as possible, and is prepared to travel to performances within Greater London. Does not welcome any other unsolicited form of approach, including CVs, photographs, showreels or invitations to view individual actors' websites. Advises actors to make contact only to inform the casting director "when their work can be seen – TV, film or stage".

Margaret Crawford

92 Castelnau, London SW13 9EU

Casts mainly for television. Casting credits include: *Bad Girls* (Series 2-8); *Footballers' Wives* (Series 1-5); *Footballers' Wives Extra Time* (Series 1 & 2); *Waterloo Road* (Series 1) and *Bombshell* (Series 1).

Will consider attending performances at venues in Greater London and occasionally elsewhere, given as much notice as possible. Accepts submissions (with CVs and photographs) from actors previously unknown to the casting director if sent by post. Does not welcome email enquiries. Also accepts showreels, voicereels and invitations to view individual actors' websites.

Kahleen Crawford Casting CDG

Film City Glasgow, Govan Town Hall, 401 Govan Road, Glasgow G51 2QJ
tel 0141 425 1725
email casting@kahleencrawford.com
website www.kahleencrawford.com
Casting Directors Kahleen Crawford, Danny Jackson and Caroline Stewart

Main areas of work include film, TV and commercials. Recent productions include: Outlaw King (dir. David Mackenzie); The Miniaturist (dir. Guillem Morales); I, Daniel Blake (dir. Ken Loach); *Under the Skin* (dir. Jonathan Glazer) and *45 Years* (dir. Andrew Haigh).

Welcomes CVs and photographs from actors previously unknown to the casting director (of a reasonable file size), if sent by email. Happy to receive invitations to view productions in London, Glasgow and the surrounding areas, provided 1 week's notice is given. Also accepts links to online showreels. Only grants a general interview in special circumstances.

Crocodile Casting

9 Ashley Close, Hendon, London NW4 1PH
tel 020 8203 7009 *fax* 020 8203 7711
email croccast@aol.com
website www.crocodilecasting.com
Casting Directors Tracie Saban, Claire Toeman

Established in 1996 with the aim of constantly accessing new faces and fresh talent. The company casts mainly for commercials, pop videos and corporate work; sometimes holds general auditions to meet new actors and models.

Sarah Crowe Casting CDG

92-96 De Beauvoir Road, London N1 4EN
tel 020 7286 5080
email info@sarahcrowecasting.co.uk
website www.sarahcrowecasting.co.uk
Twitter @scrowecasting

Sarah has worked extensively in both TV and film specialising in comedy. Her credits include *The Death of Stalin* and *The Thick of It*, both directed by Amando Iannucci; and *Rev* (dir. Peter Cattaneo).

Gary Davy CDG

17 Remington Street, London N1 8DH
tel 020 7253 3633
email casting@garydavy.com

Casts for film and television. Casting credits include: *Britannia* (SKY/Amazon); *Marcella* (ITV); *The Frankenstein Chronicles* (ITV); *The Woman in White* (BBC); *The Living and the Dead* (BBC); *The Enfield Haunting* (SKY); *Strike Back* (HBO/SKY); *Death Comes to Pemberly* (BBC); and UK casting on *Band of Brothers* (HBO/BBC).

Film casting credits include: *Woman in Gold*, Steve McQueen's *Hunger*, *The Sweeney*, *Revenger's Tragedy*, *The Proposition*, *44 Inch Chest* and *Streetdance 3D*.

Stephanie Dawes CDG

13 Nevern Square, London SW5 9NW
tel 07802 566642
email stephaniedawes5@gmail.com

Works in television and voice-over. Recent credits include: *Saved*, *Blue Murder*, *Stockwell*, and *Britannia High* (all ITV1).

Gabrielle Dawes CDG

PO Box 52493, London NW3 9DZ
tel 020 7435 3645
email gdawescasting@gmail.com

Gabrielle is a freelance Casting Director and Creative Associate for Jonathan Church Productions. As an Associate of Chichester Fesitval Theatre 2006–16 she cast over 45 prodictions.

Theatre includes: *The Norman Conquests*, *All About My Mother*, *New Voices 24-Hour Plays* (Old Vic); *Cat on a Hot Tin Roof*, *Three Days of Rain*, *Treasure Island* (West End); Rupert Goold's *Macbeth* (Chichester/West End/Broadway); *Wallenstein*, *The Grapes of Wrath*, *Separate Tables*, *Hay Fever*, *Aristo*, *Funny Girl*, *The Circle*, *Taking Sides/Collaboration* (and West End); *Hobson's Choice*, *The Waltz of the Toreadors*, *Twelfth Night* (all Chichester); *The English Game* (Headlong Theatre); *The Elephant Man* (Sheffield); *As You Like It* (Watford).

As Deputy Head of Casting at the National Theatre 2000–2006, award-winning productions included *Caroline, or Change*; *His Dark Materials*; *Elmina's Kitchen*; *The Pillowman* and *Coram Boy*.

Television credits include: Harold Pinter's *Celebration* and *Elmina's Kitchen* by Kwame Kwei-Armah. Films include *Perdie* (BAFTA award for Best Short Film) and *The Suicide Club*.

Recent casting includes TV development for Hat Trick Productions on *Whatever Happened to Zimraan* by Alistair Beaton; Season Casting Associate for the 2017 Theatre Royal Bath Summer Season.

Agents and casting directors

Kate Day CDG

Pound Cottage, 27 The Green South, Warborough, Oxfordshire OX10 7DR

Main areas of work are television, film and commercials.

Will consider attending performances at venues in Greater London and occasionally elsewhere, given as much notice as possible. Accepts submissions (with CVs and photographs) from actors previously unknown to the casting director if sent by post. Does not welcome email enquiries.

Paul De Freitas CDG

16 Wimpole Mews, London W1G 8PE
tel 020 7486 5407 *fax* 020 7486 1817
email info@pauldefreitas.com
website www.pauldefreitas.com

Main areas of work are film, television and commercials. Casting credits include: *Dog Boy* (BBC2); *Lazarus & Dingwall* (BBC2); *Bernard & The Genie* (Talkback/Attaboy); *The Princess Academy* (Weintraub Productions); and *What Larry Says* (Platypus Productions).

Kate Dowd Casting CDG

Lyric Hammersmith, Lyric Square, King Street, London W6 0QL
tel 020 7828 8071
email kate@katedowdcasting.com

Credits include: film *Mad Max, The Bourne Identity, Eye in the Sky* and *The Hurricane Heist*; TV series *The Assets, Galavant* and *Still Star-Crossed*.

Carol Dudley CDG, CSA

See entry for Cannon, Dudley & Associates.

Julia Duff CDG

First Floor, 11 Goodwins Court, London WC2N 4LL
tel 020 7863 5557
email julia@juliaduff.co.uk

Casts mainly for television. Casting credits include: *New Tricks, Hotel Babylon, Secret Diary of a Call Girl, Persuasion, Monarch of the Glen,* and *The Amazing Mrs Pritchard.*

Maureen Duff CDG

PO Box 47340, London NW3 4TY
tel 020-7586 0532 *fax* 020-7681 7172
email info@maureenduffcasting.com

Main areas of work are film, television and theatre. Credits include: *Closing The Ring* (Richard Attenborough); *The History of Mr Polly* (Granada Media); *Poirot* (several episodes for Granada Media); and *Dancing At Lughnasa* (and several other productions for the Northcott Theatre, Exeter).

Jennifer Duffy CDG

11 Portsea Mews, London W2 2BN
tel 020 7262 3326

email casting@jennyduffy.co.uk

Main areas of work are film and television. Credits include: *Life 'n' Lyrics* (Fiesta Productions, BBC Films, Universal); *Wallace & Gromit: The Curse of the Wererabbit* (Aardman/Dreamworks); *Macbeth* (BBC) and *Dunkirk* (BBC2, Huw Wheldon BAFTA Award 2005).

Irene East Casting CDG

40 Brookwood Avenue, Barnes, London SW13 0LR
tel 020 8876 5686 *fax* 020 8876 5686
email IrnEast@aol.com

Main areas of work are theatre and film. Casting Director for Love and Madness Productions. Theatre credits include: Rising Tides/High Tides Festival, *Bunny's Vendetta* (Derry); *Aristocrats* (Letterkenny); *Richard III* (Riverside and Tower of London); *Fool for Love, Macbeth, Ajax* (dir. Jack Shepherd); *A Skull in Connemara, The Tempest, The Playboy of the Western World*. Features include: *Begin* (Jack Shepherd); *A Distant Mirage* (Harbajan Verdi); *A Small Dot on the Landscape* (Alice D. Cooper), *If You Can Hear Me* (Jesse Lawrence).

Reader on panel for script-writing award.

Will attend performances at venues in Greater London and occasionally elsewhere, given a couple of days' notice. Please, no showreels unless requested.

Daniel Edwards CDG

tel 020 7078 7451/020 7096 8936
email daniel@danieledwardscasting.com
Twitter @dedwardscasting

Daniel worked as an actor for over 20 years in film, TV and theatre (under the name Danny Edwards) before moving into casting in 2005. Casts independently as well as being Casting Associate to Kate Rhodes James. Recent TV credits include: *Mr Selfridge* (2015–16), *Him* (2016), *Ripper Street* (2016), *Line of Duty* (2017), *Born to Kill* (2017).

EJ Casting

PO Box 63617, London W9 1AN
tel 020 7564 2688 *mobile* 07891 632946
email info@ejcasting.com
Director Edward James

Casts for theatre, musicals, film, commercials and corporate work. Casting credits include: *Into the Woods* and *Sweet Charity* (theatre); commercials for AOL, Lloyds Bank, Sony BMG, Universal Music, and Cadbury's Fingers; and *Air on a G String* (film).

Will consider attending performances at venues in Greater London and occasionally elsewhere. Accepts showreels containing work that has been broadcast. Due to the overwhelming number of CVs sent, is unable to accept general enquiries. "Please only send an application if it is a performance notice or in response to a specific breakdown."

ET Casting Ltd.

Unit 2G, Woodstock Studios, 36 Woodstock Grove, London W12 8LE

tel 020 3010 3030
email info@etcasting.com
website www.etcasting.com
Casting Director Emily Tilelli *Casting Associates* Zita Zutic-Konak

Established in 2011. Main areas of work are commercials, digital content, stills and feature films. Recent credits include: *Tucked* (feature film), *Nina Forever* (feature film) and *Social Suicide* (feature film). Will consider attending performances in the Greater London area, with a minimum of 3 weeks' notice.

Welcomes CVs and photographs sent by email, showreels and voice tapes, and invitations to view individual actors' websites.

Richard Evans CDG
10 Shirley Road, London W4 1DD
tel 020 8994 6304
email richard@evanscasting.co.uk
website www.evanscasting.co.uk and www.auditionsthecompleteguide.com

Main areas of work are theatre, musicals, television, film and commercials. Casting credits include: *The Rat Pack – Live From Las Vegas* (theatre).

Will consider attending performances at venues in Greater London and occasionally elsewhere, given sufficient notice. Requests 1-2 weeks before the opening night for theatre productions, and 2-3 days prior to transmission for television shows. Accepts follow-up telephone calls after a production has opened. Welcomes submissions (with CVs and photographs) from actors previously unknown to the casting director if sent by post, and email enquiries with links to Spotlight page, online showreel, etc. (but no large attachments).

Advises actors to: "Be specific, find out what people cast and their current projects, suggesting yourself for particular roles whenever possible. When inviting casting personnel to see your work, always ensure that the part you are playing is worth them coming to see, and offer complimentary tickets. Unless a part is very specific or hard to cast, we usually only invite artists in to audition whose work we have seen or have met, as this enables us to speak honestly and accurately about them to the creative teams with whom we are working. It is worth keeping in touch when you have something to say as your career progresses especially if you have met or know someone."

Fawn Casting Ltd
86-90 Paul Street, London EC2A 4NE
mobile 07766 501553
email andrew@fawncasting.com
website www.fawncasting.com
Owner/Casting Director Andrew Fawn

Established in 2012. Main areas of work are television, film, commercials, corporate, voice-over

and shorts. Recent credits include: *The Craftsman*, *The Watcher Self*, and *Drive-Thru*. Will consider attending performances in Greater London/Brighton given a minimum of 1-2 days' notice – 2 weeks preferred.

Susie Figgis
19 Spencer Rise, London NW5 1AR
tel 020 7482 2200

Known for *Ghandi* (1982), *Cry Freedom* (1987), *Interview with a Vampire* (1994), *The Full Monty* (1997), *Sleepy Hollow* (1999). Recent credits include: *The Pirates of the Caribbean: Dead Men Tell No Tales*, *Colette, Tom Raider, The Guernsey Literary and Potato Peel Pie Society*.

Bunny Fildes Casting CDG
56-60 Wigmore Street, London W1U 2RZ
tel 020 7935 1254 *fax* 020 7298 1871

Casts mainly for theatre, television, film and commercials.

Will consider attending performances within Greater London given 2 weeks' notice. Accepts postal submissions (with CVs and photographs) from actors previously unknown to the company. Unsolicited emails and showreels, however, are not welcomed.

Sally Fincher CDG
tel 020 8347 5945
email sallyfincher@btinternet.com

Main area of work is television. Credits include: *Murder In Suburbia, Sweet Medicine, Barbara, Kiss Me Kate, Outside Edge* and *The Upper Hand*.

Rachel Freck CDG
tel 020 8673 2455 *mobile* 07980 585607
email casting@rachelfreck.com

Credits include: film *Confetti, The Mask of Cain*, and *Housewife*; TV series *Little Dorrit, The Office, Toast, Mrs Wilson, W1A, Quacks* and *Howards End*.

Fruitcake London
Studio 125, 77 Beak Street, London W1F 9DB
tel 020 7993 5165
email casting@fruitcakelondon.com
Casting Directors Andrew Mann

Casts mainly for TV commercials and digital media. Casting credits in 2012 include: commercials for San Miguel, Vauxhall, Sky TV, M&S and Nike; and pop promos for Chase & Status, Paulina Rubio and Ayumi Hamasaki.

Will consider attending performances at venues in Greater London given 2 weeks' notice. Accepts submissions (with CVs and photographs) from actors previously unknown to the casting directors if sent by post. Does not welcome email enquiries.

Caroline Funnell
25 Rattray Road, London SW2 1AZ
tel 020 7326 4417

Areas of work include theatre and musicals. Will consider attending performances within the Greater London area with at least 2 weeks' notice.

Artistic Director of Sixteenfeet Productions (25 Rattray Road, London SW2 1AZ, info@sixteenfeet.co.uk).

Martin Gibbons Casting
Manchester & London
email info@martingibbons.com
website www.martingibbons.com
Casting Director Martin Gibbons CDG and Alex Wheeler

Established in 2011. Main areas of work are film, television, commercials, theatre, music videos, corporate and voice-over. Will consider attending performances in Manchester and London.

Welcomes CVs and photographs sent by email, as well as showreels and voice tapes.

Tracey Gillham CDG
tel 020 3778 0441
email tracey@traceygillhamcasting.co.uk
email michelle@traceygillhamcasting.co.uk
website www.traceygillhamcasting.co.uk
Associate Michelle Cavanagh

Main areas of work are film and television. For recent credits, please see Spotlight or the CDG website.

Nina Gold CDG
117 Chevening Road, London NW6 6DU
tel 020 8960 6099 *fax* 020 8968 6777
email info@ninagold.co.uk
Casting Directors Nina Gold, Robert Sterne

Main areas of work are film, television and commercials. Recent film credits: *The Man Who Would be King* (2018); *The Little Stranger* (2018); *Mama Mia! Here We Go Again* (2018); Recent TV credits: *Chernobyl* (2019); *Brexit* (2019); *King Lear* (2018); *Succession* (2018); *Patrick Melrose* (2018). Other casting credits include: *Vera Drake*, directed by Mike Leigh (Thin Man Films); *The Life and Death of Peter Sellers*, directed by Stephen Hopkins; *The Jacket*, directed by John Maybury (Warner Bros); *Daniel Deronda*, directed by Tom Hooper (BBC TV); *Amazing Grace* and *Rome* both directed by Michael Apted; *Starter for Ten* directed by Tom Vaughan; *The Illusionist* directed by Neil Burger; and *Brothers of the Head* directed by Keith Fulton and Louis Pepe.

Miranda Gooch
102 Leighton Gardens, London NW10 3RP

Casts mainly for feature films. Recent credits have included: *True Story* and *Tooth*.

Will consider attending performances within Greater London given as much notice as possible. Accepts submissions (with CVs and photographs) from actors previously unknown to the company, sent by post or email. Showreels are also accepted.

Jill Green CDG
Jill Green Casting, 37-41 Gower Street, London WC1E 6HH
tel 020 7299 7729

Casts for theatre and musicals. Casting credits include: *Jane Eyre* (UK tour); *Disney's Aladdin* (Prince Edward Theatre); *Kinky Boots* (Adelphi Theatre); *Beautiful - The Carole King Musical* (Aldwych Theatre); *The Curious Incident of the Dog in the Night-time* (Gielgud Theatre and UK tour); *Jersey Boys* (Piccadilly Theatre and UK tour); *La Strada* (The Other Place);*War Horse* (2015/16, New London Theatre and 2017/18 tour); *The Lion King* (international tour 2014-15); *The Scottsboro Boys* (Garrick and Young Vic Theatres); *I Can't Sing!* (London Palladium); *Rock of Ages* (Garrick and Shaftesbury Theatres and UK tour); *Finding Neverland* (Leicester Curve); *The Producers* (Drury Lane Theatre); and *Contact* (Queens Theatre.

Will consider attending performances within Greater London and occasionally elsewhere, given a minimum of 4 weeks' notice. Accepts email submissions (with Spotlight links, CVs and photographs attached) from actors who are currently appearing in a production, but does not welcome blanket mailings, unsolicited emails or showreels (unless an sae is enclosed for their return).

David Grindrod CDG
4th Floor, Palace Theatre, Shaftesbury Avenue, London W1D 5AY
tel 020 7437 2506 *fax* 020 7437 2507
email dga@grindrodcasting.co.uk

Casts for musicals and films. Film credits: Dance casting *Nine*, Ensemble casting *Mamma Mia!* and *The Phantom of the Opera*. West End casting: *Chicago*, *Mamma Mia!*, *Ghost*, *Hairspray*, *Love Never Dies*, *Sister Act*.

Will consider attending performances within Greater London and possibly elsewhere, given as much notice as possible. Does not welcome unsolicited submissions from actors. Casting breakdowns are released via Spotlight, therefore actors should only write in with reference to specific productions. See also David's article *Casting for musical theatre* on page 128.

Angela Grosvenor CDG
66 Woodland Road, London SE19 1PA
tel 020 8244 5665
email angela.grosvenor@virgin.net

Established in 1990. Main areas of work include TV and film. Recent credits include: The *Tractate Middoth*, *Topsy and Tim* and *The Cafe*.

Welcomes invitations to productions to view actors for consideration, and casting interviews can be arranged dependent on the situation.

Janet Hall
3 Shaw Road, Littleborough, Oldham OL15 9LG

Main areas of work include television, film and commercials. Casting credits include: AXA commercial, and *The Sound of Music* (theatre).

Will consider attending performances at venues in Greater London and in Manchester, Liverpool and Leeds, given 1 week's notice. Accepts submissions (with CVs and photographs) from actors previously unknown to the casting director, sent by post or email. Also accepts showreels, voicereels and invitations to view individual actors' websites.

Louis Hammond CDG

tel 020 7610 1579
email louis@louishammond.co.uk

Main areas of work are theatre, television and film. Casting credits include: *Barber Shop Chronicles* (Roundhouse/UK tour); *Beautiful Thing*, *Macbeth* (Bristol Tobacco Factory);*Kanye the First*, *Heroine* (High Tide); *The Sugar-Coated Bullets of the Bourgeoisie* (Arcola/High Tide); The 5 Plays Project (Young Vic); *Inkheart* (HOME Manchaester); *The Distance* (Sheffield Crucible/Orange Tree Richmond); *Romeo and Juliet* (Sheffield Crucible); *Creditors* (Young Vic); *Harrogate* (High Tide Festival); The Fun Fair (HOME Manchester); Primtime, *Creditors* (Young Vic); *Romeo and Juliet* (Sheffield Crucible); *The Funfair* (HOME Manchester); *Primtime*, *Violence and Son*, *Who Cares*, *Fireworks* (Casting Associate at the Royal Court); *Romeo and Juliet* (HOME, Manchester); *Amadeus* (Chichester Festival Theatre); *The History Boys* (Sheffield Crucible); *The Winter's Tale* (Open Air Theatre, Regents Park); *Driving Miss Daisy* (UK); *Rough Cuts/International Residencies* (Royal Court); *The Resistible Rise of Arturo Ui* (Liverpool/Nottingham); *Batman Live* (World Arena Tour). Film – *Mirrormask* and *Arsene Lupin*. TV – *The Bill* (Head of Casting).

Hammond Cox Casting

17a Clerenwell Green, London EC1R 0DP
tel 020 7734 3335
email office@hammondcoxcasting.com
website www.hammondcoxcasting.com
Casting Directors Michael Cox, Thom Hammond

Established in 2012. Works in film, commercials, music video and theatre. Recent credits include: Beady Eye (Music Video); Robinsons (Commercial) and *Flight of the Pompodour* (Short Film).

Gemma Hancock CDG

North Lodge, Weald Chase, Staplefield Road, Cuckfield, West Sussex RH17 5HY
email gemma@hancockstevenson.com
website www.hancockstevenson.com

Main areas of work are theatre, television and film.

Julie Harkin Casting CDG

17 Remington Street, London N1 8DH
tel 020 7336 0433
email info@julieharkincasting.com

Specialises in TV and film. Recent TV credits: *War and Peace*, *Cuffs*, *Fortitude*, *Utopia*, *Misfits*, *Kiri* and

Informer. Film credits: *War Book*; *Monsters*, *Dark Continent*, *The Woman in Black*, *Angel of Death*, *The Scouting Book for Boys*, *Eden Lake*, *Beast*, *The Titan*, and *The Ritual*.

Accepts links to view CVs, and on-line profiles or showreels via email. Welcomes performance notices via email, if given 2 weeks' notice.

Judi Hayfield CDG / Judi Hayfield Ltd

6 Richmond Hill Road, Gatley, Cheshire SK8 1QG
mobile 07919 221873
email judi.hayfield@hotmail.com

Former Head of Casting for Granada.

HB Casting

tel 020 7871 2969
email hannah@hbcasting.com
Casting Director Hannah Birkett

Previously awarded British Arrows, a CDA and a Film Craft Cristal for best casting. Areas of work include television, film, commercials. Recent credits include work for Snickers (Elton John), Playstation and Amazon Prime.

Will consider attending performances with one week's notice via email. Accepts CVs and photographs via email only.

Serena Hill

22a Whitehall Gardens, Acton, W3 9RD
mobile 07425 710707
email serenahillcasting@gmail.com

Serena Hill has returned from Australia and is currently working as a freelance Casting Director. She began her Casting Director career at the Royal Court Theatre from whence she moved to the National Theatre as Head of Casting under the successive artistic directorships of Richard Eyre, Trevor Nunn and Nicholas Hytner. She then took up the position of Casting Director at Sydney Theatre Company for artistic director Robyn Nevin, followed by co-artistic directors Cate Blanchett and Andrew Upton, and finally Kip Williams. As a freelance casting director in the UK, Serena worked on BBC Television Film's *Heading Home*, written and directed by David Hare; and, *Tumbledown* by Charles Wood, directed by Richard Eyre. As a freelance director in Australia Serena has worked on the Australian productions of *War Horse* for the National Theatre/ Global Creatures (2013), *Les Misérables* for Cameron Mackintosh/ Michael Cassel Group (2014) and the adult cast of *Matilda the Musical* for the Royal Shakespeare Company and Louise Withers Associates (2015). Recent credits include: *Dealing with Clair* by Martin Crimp (Orange Tree Theatre and English Touring Theatre).

Accepts links to view actors' CVs, on-line profiles, and showreels via e-mail.

Lotte Hines CDG

Horan & Hines, 26 Falkland Road,
London NW5 2PX

Agents and casting directors

tel 020 7267 5261 *mobile* 07793 966457
email lotte@lottehinescasting.com

Lotte was the Deputy Casting Director at the Royal Court between 2007 and 2014.

Subsequent credits include: *The Glass Menagerie* (Headlong), *Brenda* (Hightide Festival), *La Musica* (Young Vic), *The Weir* (The Lyceum, Edinburgh).

Polly Hootkins Casting CDG

tel 020 7692 1184 *mobile* 07545 784294
email phootkins@clara.net
website www.thecdg.co.uk
Key personnel Polly Hootkins

Prefers all submissions (CVs, photographs, showreels, etc.) via email.

Julia Horan CDG

Horan & Hines, 26 Falkland Road,
London NW5 2PX
tel 020 7267 5261 *mobile* 07967 356869
email julia@horanandhines.com

Julia has worked at the Young Vic, Royal Court, Almeida, Tricycle, extensively in the West End and beyond. She is an Associate Artist at the Young Vic. Recent theatre casting credits include: *Harry Potter and the Cursed Child* (Palace Theatre London, Lyric Theatre New York), *Fun Home*, *The Inheritance*, *The Jungle* (Young Vic), *Hamlet*, *Summer* and *Smoke* (Almeida). Film credits include *The Exceptions*.

Will consider attending performances within the Greater London area and elsewhere. Accepts submissions (with CVs and photographs) from actors previously unknown to the casting director, via email only.

Juliet Horsley

See the entry for the National Theatre under *Producing theatres* on page 146.

Amy Hubbard CDG

tel 020 3567 1210
email amy@amyhubbardcasting.com
Twitter @amyhubcast
Casting Director Amy Hubbard

Amy is an award-winning casting director with extensive experience on both blockbuster features (*Lord of the Rings*, *The Hobbit*) and TV series (*Homeland*). Recent credits include, film: *Dark River*, *Mary Shelley*, *The Man Who Invented Christmas*; TV: *Hatton Garden*.

Dan Hubbard CDG

The Chandlery, 50 Westminster Bridge Road,
London SE1 7QY
tel 020 3874 5270
email dan@danhubbardcasting.com
Casting Director Dan Hubbard *Casting Associate* Claire Robinson

Film credits include: *The Bourne Ultimatum*, *The Bourne Supremacy*, *Six Days*, *Captain Phillips*; TV credits include: *American Odyssey*, *Downtown Abbey*.

Accepts actor submissions by email only. Will accept invitations to performances in the London area, availability permitting.

Hubbard Casting

47 Bedford Street, London WC2E 9HA
tel 020 7631 4944 *fax* 020 7636 7117
email ros@hubbardcasting.com
email john@hubbardcasting.com
Casting Directors John Hubbard, Ros Hubbard

Known for films: *The Da Vinci Code* (2006), *Lara Croft: Tomb Raider* (2001), *The Mummy* (1999).

John Hubbard's recent credits include, film: *Hurricane*, 2018.

Ros Hubbard's recent credits include films: *The More You Ignore Me* (2018), *Journey's End* (2017), *Interlude in Prague* (2017), *The Time of Their Lives* (2017).

Sue Jackson

53 Moseley Wood Walk, Leeds LS16 7HQ

Freelance casting director.

Trevor Jackson CDG

1 Bedford Square, London WC1B 3RA
tel 020 7637 8866 *fax* 020 7436 2683

Casts mainly for musicals produced by Cameron Mackintosh Ltd. Casting credits include: *My Fair Lady*, *Les Miserables*, *Miss Saigon*, *Phantom of the Opera*, *Mary Poppins*, *Avenue Q* and *Oliver!*

Will consider attending performances at venues in Greater London given as much notice as possible. Accepts submissions (with CVs and photographs) from actors previously unknown to the casting director if sent by post, but does not welcome email enquiries. Showreels, voicereels and invitations to view individual actors' websites are also accepted.

Janis Jaffa Casting

London W12
email janis@janisjaffacasting.co.uk

Works mainly in television, film and commercials.

Will consider attending performances within Greater London. Welcomes emails (with CVs and photographs attached) from individual actors previously unknown to the agency. Will accept showreels and invitations to view individual actors' websites by email.

Jina Jay CDG

2 Sound Centre, Twickenham Film Studios,
The Barons, St Margaret's, Middlesex TW1 2AW
tel 020 8607 8888
email jinajay@gmail.com
Twitter @jinajaycasting

Known for films and TV: *Tinker, Tailor, Soldier, Spy* (2011), *The Grand Budapest Hotel* (2014), *Rogue One: A Star Wars Story* (2016), *Black Mirror* (2016–17), *Darkest Hour* (2017).

Lucy Jenkins (Jenkins McShane Casting)
74 High Street, Hampton Wick,
Kingston on Thames KT1 4DQ
tel 020 8943 5328 *fax* 020 8977 0466
email lucy@jenkinsmcshanecasting.com

Casts mainly for film, television, theatre and
commercials. Casting credits include: *Babyfather*
(BBC); *The Bill* (television); *Top Dog* (short film) and
Emma (theatre).

Victor Jenkins Casting CDG
Albert House, 256-260 Old Street,
London EC1V 9DD
tel 020 3457 0506 *mobile* 07919 207492
email victorjenkins@me.com
Twitter @verbalictor

Recent TV credits include: *Humans*, *The Last
Kingdom* and *Grantchester*.

Rebecca Jenner
All enquiries via email
email casting@rebeccajenner.com
website www.rebeccajenner.com
Casting Director Rebecca Jenner

Established in 2011. Main areas of work are theatre,
TV and film. Recent credits include: (as Casting
Director) *JB Shorts* (Manchester); *The Seagull*
(Library Theatre); *Wanted! Robin Hood* (Library
Theatre).

Will consider attending performances within Greater
London and in Manchester/the North West, given at
least 1 week's notice. Accepts CVs and photographs
sent by email only.

Priscilla John Casting CDG
tel 020 8741 4212
email priscilla@priscillajohn.com
Priscilla John, Orla Maxwell and Francesca Bradley
have worked together as a casting team since 2009 on
diverse and exciting film and international TV
projects. Priscilla leads the team with a wealth of
experience including the Royal Court Theatre in the
1970s, Granada TV, and an independent career
casting for David Lean, Steven Spielberg, Gore
Verbinski, Terence Davies and Andrei Tarkovsky.
Always on the hunt for new UK talent, the team are
passionate theatregoers attending West End and
graduate shows.

Sam Jones CDG
37 Pearman Street, London SE1 7RB
tel 020 7803 9523 *mobile* 07941 960998
email sam@samjonescasting.co.uk

Previously Head of Casting for the RSC, Sam cast the
first two award-winning years for the newly formed
National Theatre Wales. Her extensive theatre credits
include work for Peter Hall, Stephen Berkoff,
Kneehigh, Shared Experience, Told By An Idiot, The

Opera Group, Lyric Hammersmith, Hampstead
Theatre, the Almeida, The Royal Court, Young Vic,
Sheffield Crucible and the West Yorkshire Playhouse
among others. Her West End work includes: *Another
Country*, *Journey's End*, *Dinner*, *A Day in the Death of
Joe Egg*, *Up for Grabs!*, *After Mrs Rochester*, *The
Children's Hour*, *Betrayal* and *Old Times*. Her recent
television work includes: *Love and Marriage*, several
series of *Trial and Retribution*, *The Commander* and
Above Suspicion all for ITV, and the BAFTA award-
winning *Occupation*, *Lennon Naked* and *Prisoners'
Wives* for the BBC. Recent film work includes:
Resistance, *Jadoo*, *The Father* and *Panda Eyes*.

Sue Jones CDG
24 Nicoll Road, London NW10 9AB
tel 020 8838 5153 *fax* 020 8838 1130
email sue@suejones.net

Main areas of work are film, television, theatre and
commercials. Casting credits include: *The Virgin of
Liverpool*, starring Ricky Tomlinson and Imelda
Staunton (MOB Films); *The Sound of Thunder*, with
Ed Burns, Ben Kingsley and Catherine McCormack;
The Origins of Evil (CBS/Alliance Atlantis); *Messiah*
and *Coriolanus* (both plays directed by Stephen
Berkoff); *The Vicar* (BBC television); and *The
Politician's Wife* (Channel 4).

Kate and Lou Casting
1st Floor, 59 Charlotte Street, London W1T 4PE
tel 020 323 1952 *mobile* 07976 252531
website www.kateandloucasting.com
Facebook @kateandlou
Twitter @kateandloucast

Casts for commercials, still photography, online
content and short films. Recent credits include: AA,
Specsavers, McDonald's, Virgin Trains, Sky,
Cadbury's and Volvic.

Does welcome performance notices. Will accept
letters (with CVs and photographs) from individual
actors previously unknown to the company, and
unsolicited CVs and photographs, sent via email.
Does welcome showreels or invitations to view
individual actors' websites.

Anna Kennedy Casting
8 Rydal Road, London SW16 1QN
email anna@kennedycasting.com
website www.annakennedycasting.com

Welcomes performance notices, for productions
within the Greater London area, with 2 weeks' notice.
Will accept letters, but not emails, with CVs and
photographs from individuals previously unknown to
the casting director; also welcomes showreels and
invitations to view actors' websites.

Beverley Keogh CDG
29 Ardwick Green North, Ardwick,
Manchester M12 6DL

Agents and casting directors

tel 0161 273 4400 *fax* 0161 273 4401
email beverley@beverleykeogh.tv

Main areas of work are television, film and
commercials. Casting credits include: *The Village, In
The Flesh, Last Tango in Halifax, Scott & Bailey* and
The Mill.

Accepts submissions (with CVs and photographs)
from actors previously unknown to the casting
director, sent by post or email.

Belinda King Creative Productions
Casting Department, BK Studios,
157 Clarence Avenue, Northamptonshire NN2 6NY
tel 01604 720041
email casting@belindaking.com
website www.belindaking.com
*Casting Director*Joe Finn

Producers of shows at sea for luxury cruise brands
including Seabourn and Holland America Line.
International casting with auditions worldwide
including London, New York, Sydney, Moscow, Kiev.

Primary casting requirements: West-End and
Broadway calibre singers and classically-trained
dancers.

Jerry Knight-Smith CDG
tel 0161 615 6761
website www.royalexchangecasting.co.uk

Head of Casting at the Royal Exchange Theatre,
Manchester. See entry under *Producing theatres* on
page 150 for further details.

Suzy Korel CDG
mobile 07973 506793
email suzy@korel.org

Would consider attending performances at venues in
London given as much notice as possible. Accepts
submissions (with CVs and photographs) from actors
previously unknown to the casting director, and
receives pictures and CVs via email.

Karen Lindsay-Stewart CDG
PO Box 2301, London W1A 1PT
email asst@klscasting.co.uk

Known for *Harry Potter and the Sorcerer's Stone*
(2001); *Penny Dreadful* (2014–16). Main areas of
work are television and film. Recent films: Eternal
Beauty (2017); How to Talk to Girls at Parties (2017);
The Secret of Marrowbone (2017). Other casting
credits include: *Sylvia, Harry Potter and the Chamber
of Secrets,* and *Cambridge Spies.*

Will consider attending performances at venues in
Greater London with sufficient notice. Accepts
submissions (with CVs and photographs) from actors
previously unknown to the casting director if sent by
post, but does not welcome email enquiries. Do not
send sae(s) for replies.

Kay Magson Casting CDG
PO Box 175, Pudsey, Leeds LS28 7LN
tel 0113 236 0251

email kay.magson@btinternet.com
Casting Director Kay Magson

Recent credits include *Bollywood Jane, Twelfth Night,
Alice in Wonderland, Duchess of Malfi* (West
Yorkshire Playhouse); national tours of *Singin' In the
Rain, Aspects of Love, Round the Horne...Revisited* and
*Dracula, Noises Off, Billy Liar, The Flint Street
Nativity, The Electric Hills* (Liverpool); *A Model Girl*
(Greenwich); *One Last Card Trick, Aladdin*
(Watford); *Merrily We Roll Along, Importance of
Being Earnest, As You Like It* (Derby); *The Way of the
World, Follies* (Northampton); *East Is East* (York/
Bolton); *Rosencrantz & Guildenstern Are Dead, Much
Ado About Nothing* (Manchester Library).

Will consider attending performances within the
Greater London area and elsewhere, with at least 4
weeks' notice. Accepts submissions (with CVs and
photographs) from actors previously unknown to the
casting director, via email only.

John Manning
4 Holmbury Gardens, Hayes, Middlesex UB3 2LU
tel 020 8573 5463

Works in theatre and musicals. Recent credits
include: *The 39 Steps* (Criterion Theatre); *Turandot*
(Hampstead) and *An Inspector Calls* (national tour).

Will consider attending performances within the
Greater London area, and regularly attends regional
theatre – but does request 4 weeks' notice. Welcomes
letters (with CVs and photographs) from individual
actors previously unknown to the company, sent by
post only; will also accept invitations to view
individual actors' websites.

Carolyn McLeod
c/o 2nd Floor, 191 Wardour Street,
London W1F 8ZE
mobile 07946 476425
email info@cmcasting.co.uk
website www.cmcasting.co.uk
Facebook www.facebook.com/carolynmcleodcasting

Main areas of work are film and television. Recent
projects include: *A Christmas Prince: The Royal
Wedding* and *The Christmas Princess, Switch* for
Netflix, along with numerous projects for US TV
networks including Hallmark, Cinemax, SyFy
Channel and projects with the BBC. Independent
features include: *Bruno* and *Six From Eight* Films
currently in development include transgender road
movie *Violets are Blue* and *Blood and Stone.*

Given sufficient notice will consider attending
performances at venues in and around Greater
London. Will accept emailed broadcast or show
notifications, also emailed submissions from actors
previously unknown to the casting director.
Showreels, voicereels and invitations to view
individual actors' websites are also accepted, but
receipt may not be acknowledged.

Chrissie McMurrich

16 Spring Vale Avenue, Brentford, Middlesex TW8 9QH

Main areas of work are theatre and television. Recent casting includes: the tour of *Scooby Doo and the Pirate Ghost Live on Stage*; the Ludlow Festival/Exeter Northcott Theatre production of *Romeo and Juliet*; *Original Sin*, *The Blue Room*, *A Christmas Carol* and *Cyrano de Bergerac* for the Haymarket Basingstoke; and the tour of *Thomas the Tank Engine and Friends*.

Will consider attending performances at venues in Greater London given 2 weeks' notice. Accepts submissions with performance notices (containing photos and CVs) from actors previously unknown to the casting director if sent by post. No unsolicited emails are accepted. "Please be aware of the new postage rates for A4 envelopes. Not everyone will pay the Royal Mail handling charge to get unsolicited photos and CVs."

Anne McNulty CDG

email mcnulty19@gmail.com

Former Resident Casting Director for Donmar Warehouse. Now working as a freelance casting director, mainly in theatre. See Anne's article on page 126 for advice on casting for the stage.

Sooki McShane (Jenkins McShane Casting)

8A Piermont Road, East Dulwich, London SE22 0LN
tel 020 8693 7411 *fax* 020 8693 7411
email sooki@jenkinsmcshanecasting.com

Works mainly in theatre, film and television. Casting credits include: *Rainbow Room* (Granada television); *My Brother Rob* (feature film); and casting for the Warehouse Theatre Croydon.

Currently Resident Casting Director for the Nottingham Playhouse. See entry under *Producing theatres* on page 138 for further details.

Debbie McWilliams CDG

Lower Ground Flat, 69 Camberwell Grove, London SE5 8JE
tel 020 7207 7322
email debbie@castingconsultancy.com

Debbie McWilliams has cast the last 13 James Bond films. The diverse range of directors she has worked with include Derek Jarman, Roman Polanski, Stephen Frears, Anthony Minghella, Sam Mendes, Martin Campbell, Marc Foster and Ron Howard. Recent credits include: *Robin Hood* (2018), *Iron Sky: The Coming Race* (2018), *Stratton* (2017), *The Foreigner* (2018), *Film Stars Don't Die in Liverpool* (2017), *The Birth of Boxing* (2017).

Thea Meulenberg Casting

Keizersgracht 116 Amsterdam Postal address: Jacques Veltmanstraat 263, 1065DC Amsterdam
tel 0031 20626 5846 *mobile* 0031 654798109
email info@theameulenberg.com
website www.theameulenberg.com
website www.kftv.com/thea-meulenberg-casting
Facebook Thea Meulenberg Casting

Established in 1980 by Thea Meulenberg, the family company is now run by Laurens Meulenberg and Sevina Stapert-Meulenberg. Works in TV, film, commercials, corporate, print and photography. Provides casting solutions to the highest level of craftsmanship and creativity. Worldwide clients from teh USA, Dubai, India, the UK, Germany and the Netherlands.

Hannah Miller

See the entry for the Royal Shakespeare Company under *Producing theatres* on page 151.

Stephen Moore CDG

tel 020 8241 6713
email stephen@stephenmoorecasting.co.uk
website www.stephenmoorecasting.co.uk
Twitter @StephenRMoore

Main areas of work TV, film and theatre. Recent credits include, for TV: *Father Brown* (BBC1); *Casualty* (BBC1); *Doctors* (BBC1). For theatre: 49 Donkeys Hanged (dir. Simon Stokes); *Loot* (dir. Michael Fentiman); *The Boys in the Band* (dir. Adam Penford); *Monster Raving Loony* (dir.Simon Stokes; *The Exonerated* (dir. Bob Balaban).

Will consider attending performances in Greater London with a few weeks' notice. Welcomes CVs, photographs and links to showreels sent by email.

Benjamin Newsome Casting

15 Donne Court, Bollo Bridge Road, London W3 8YG
mobile 077480 20027
email ben.newsome@hotmail.co.uk
website www.newsomecasting.co.uk
Facebook /benjaminnewsomecasting
Twitter @newsomecasting
Instagram @newsomecasting
Casting Director Benjamin Newsome

Established in 2012. Main areas of work include theatre, musicals, film and corporate. Welcomes performance notices and will travel outside of London if travel costs are covered; 3-4 weeks' advance notice required.

Welcomes letters, emails and showreels from actors unknown to the company but preferably with a specific role in mind in a specific production. Does not hold general interviews.

Recent credits include *HAIR* (Hope Mill Theatre, Manchester), Bridlington Spa Repertory Season, *Rumpy Pumpy* (UK tour), *The Mystery of Edwin Drood* (Arts Theatre, London), *RAGS* (Lyric Thatre, London), *Dessa Rose* (Trafalgar Studios). Now also works with Theatrical Rights Worldwide representing musicals such as *Grease*, *We Will Rock You*, *Ghost*, *Saturday Night Fever*, *Flashdance* etc. Also joint owner of talent agency Alexander Baker Management.

James Orange Casting CDG

Linear House, Peyton Place, Greenwich,
London SE10 8RS
tel 020 3393 2612
email casting@jamesorange.com

James established James Orange Casting in 2007. He was Casting Director for Cameron Mackintosh Ltd 2010–14. Recent projects include: *An American in Paris* (West End), *On the Town* (Regents Park), *The Addams Family* (UK tour), *Strictly Ballroom the Musical* (West Yorkshire Playhouse and Toronto), *Shirley Valentine* (UK tour).

Accepts submissions (with CVs and photographs) from actors previously unknown to the casting director, via email only. Does not accept invitations to attend performances.

Helena Palmer

See the entry for the Royal Shakespeare Company under *Producing theatres* on page 151.

Theo Park Casting

465A Hornsey Road, London N19 4DR
tel 020 7419 1159
email theo@theoparkcasting.com

Recent films include: *The Current War* (2017); *Action Point* (2018); *Calibre* (2018); *The Spy Who Dumped Me* (2018); *Overlord* (2018) *Darkness Visible* (2019); *The Hustle* (2019); *Frankie* (2019). Recent TV includes *Vanity Fair* (mini-series 2018).

Susie Parriss Casting

1 Leamington Avenue, Morden SM4 4DQ
tel 020 8543 3326
email susieparrisscasting@gmail.com
website www.susieparrisscasting.com

Known for *Naked* (1993); *Secrets and Lies* (1996); *Hugo* (2011); and *Endeavour* (2012–19).

Recent TV includes: *Goodnight Sweetheart* (1993–2016); *Lewis* (2006–15); *Whitechapel* (2012); *Poldark* (2015–18); *Agatha Raisin* (2016–18) and *Victoria* (2016–19).

Simone Pereira Hind Casting CDG

Summerhall, Summerhall Place, Edinburgh EH9 1PL
tel 0131 290 2526
email anna@sphcasting.com
website www.simonepereirahind.com

Simone has been a casting director for 25 years, working mainly in film and television. Most recent credits include five series of *Outlander*, *Good Omens*, *Moondogs*, *The Replacement*, *I Love My Mum*, *Marionette* and *The Troll*.

Is able to attend performances in Edinburgh, Glasgow and sometimes London. Accepts CVs with photographs and showreels via email only. Happy to receive enquiries from actors previously unknown to her, particularly those based in Scotland. She is not always able to respond though may keep details on file for future reference.

Kate Plantin CDG

4 Riverside, Lower Hampton Road,
Sunbury on Thames TW16 5PW
tel 01932 782350
email kate@kateplantin.com
website www.kateplantin.com
Key Contact Kate Plantin

Established in 2000. Main areas of work include: theatre, film, television, corporate and commercials. Recent castings include: Theatre: *The Rise and Fall of Little Voice* (dir. Tom Latter); *The Unexpected Guest* (dir. Brian Blessed); *The Gulf* (dir. Matthew Gould); *Hammer House of Horror* (dir. Anna Soderblom); *The Trial of Jane Fonda* (dir. Joe Harmston); *All or Nothing* (dir. Tony McHale); *Dracula* (dir. Joe Harmston); *McQueen* (dir. John Caird); *Sweeney Todd* (dir. Bill Buckhurst). Film: *The Bromley Boys* (dir. Steve M. Kelly) and *Tango One* (dir. Sacha Bennett)).

Will consider attending performances at venues outside of London given 3 weeks' notice and 2 weeks' notice if within Greater London. Accepts submissions by email (with CVs and photographs). Also welcomes showreels and invitations to view actors' websites.

Gilly Poole CDG

11 Goodwins Court, London WC2N 4LL
tel 020 7379 5965
email gilly@crowleypoole.co.uk

Known for: *Titanic* (1997), *A Knight's Tale* (2001).

Recent credits include, TV: *Killing Eve* (2018), *The Durrells* (2016–2018); *Trollied* (2012–18), *The White Princess* (2017), *Indian Summers* (2015–16), *Outnumbered* (2007–16); theatre: *Sunny Afternoon* (Hampstead Theatre 2014, West End 2014–16).

Carl Proctor CDG

15B Bury Place, London WC1A 2JB
tel 020 7681 0034 *mobile* 07956 283340
email carlproctorcasting@gmail.com
website www.carlproctorcasting.com

Casts mainly for film and television. Casting credits include: *Son of God* (Christopher Spencer); *Blood Creek* (Joel Schumacher); *Shadow of the Vampire* (E. Elias Merhige); *The Wedding Date* (Clare Kilner); *Mrs Palfrey at the Claremount* (Dan Ireland) and *Twelfth Night* (Trevor Nunn).

Asks that actors only contact by email. CVs and photographs are no longer kept on file as these details are available on Spotlight Interactive.

Andy Pryor CDG

31-35 Kirby Street, London EC1N 8TE
tel 020 7851 8535 *fax* 020 7836 8299

Casts mainly for film and television. Casting credits include: *Glorious 39* (dir. Stephen Poliakoff); and *Doctor Who* and *Life on Mars* (for BBC Television*).*

Gennie Radcliffe CDG

Casting Department, ITV Coronation Street, Trafford Wharf Road, Trafford, Manchester M17 1FZ
tel 0161 952 0580
email gennie.radcliffe@itv.com

Casting Director for *Coronation Street* (since 2004), *Island at War, Blue Murder*. See entry for ITV Granada under *Independent television* on page 313 for further details.

Leigh-Ann Regan Casting (LARCA) Ltd

The Old Rectory Coach House, Leckwith Road, Llandough, Penarth, CF64 2LY
mobile 07779 321954
email leigh-annregan@btconnect.co.uk

Areas of work include television, film, commercials and theatre. Recent credits include: 21-part drama series for S4C/Fiction Factory (Ypris); 4 years casting *Caerdydd* for S4C/Fiction Factory.

Will consider attending performances in Greater London and elsewhere with at least 1 week's notice. Accepts submissions (with CVs and photographs) from actors previously unknown to the casting director.

Nadine Rennie

See the entry for the Soho Theatre under *Producing theatres* on page 152.

Simone Reynolds CDG

60 Hebdon Road, London SW17 7NN
email simonemreynolds@gmail.com

Main areas of work are film, television, theatre and commercials. Casting credits include: *The 39 Steps* (Olivier Award for Best Comedy); *The Vicar of Dibley* (TV); *The Politian's Wife*, BAFTA and Emmy Awards (TV); *Love of my Life* (film); *Happily Ever After* (film); *Jack and Sarah* (film); *Shining Through* (film).

Will consider attending performances at venues in Greater London and elsewhere, given as much notice as possible. Accepts postal submissions (with CVs and photographs) from actors previously unknown to the casting director, but does not welcome email enquiries. Advises actors to: "Keep CVs clear (separate out the part from the director and venue) and keep covering submissions brief."

Kate Rhodes-James CDG

78 Kingston Road, Teddington TW11 9HY
tel 020 8943 3265 *mobile* 07967 077256
email office@krjcasting.com

Kate trained as an actress. After three years she decided it wasn't for her. She assisted the casting on *The Young Indiana Chronicles* and then assisted Debbie McWilliams on three Bond films. Her first solo project was *Cold Feet* (ITV) and then *The Lakes* (BBC). Recent credits include, film: *Their Finest* (2016); TV: *Sherlock* (2010–17), *A Discovery of Witches* (2018), *Bodyguard* (2018).

Vicky Richardson CDG

email vrichardson.casting@gmail.com

Vicky Richardson was previously Casting Associate at the Donmar Warehouse. Since becoming a freelance casting director, she has worked with the National Theatre, Royal Exchange (Manchester), Nuffield Theatre (Southampton), The Orange Tree and Cleanbreak.

Danielle Roffe Casting

71 Mornington Street, London NW1 7QE
email danielle@danielleroffe.com
website www.danielleroffe.com

Works in film and television. Recent credits include: *The Upside of Anger, She's Gone,* and *Holy Cross.*

Welcomes performance notices and is prepared to travel within Greater London. Does not welcome unsolicited CVs, photographs or showreels, but is happy to receive invitations to view individual actors' websites.

Jessica Ronane CDG

See the entry for the Old Vic under *Producing theatres* on page 148.

Annie Rowe CDG

98 St Alban's Avenue, London W4 5JR
tel 020 8354 2699 *mobile* 07734 809597
email annie@annierowe-casting.com
website www.annierowecasting.com
Twitter @AnnieRoweCasts

Established in 2009. Main area of work: short and feature film, theatre, commercials, corporate film. Most recent work: *Late Company*, Trafalgar Studios, London.

Best known for casting: multi-award-winning short film *Waiting for Dawn, Yellow Face* at the NT Shed.

Happy to receive performance notices, given 2 weeks' notification. Showreels and invitations to view actors' websites welcome, preferably by email. Please submit via Spotlight link for a specific job, rather than unsolicited.

Neil Rutherford Casting

mobile 07960 891911
email neil@neilrutherford.com
website www.neilrutherford.com

A casting director since 2000, working mainly in theatre in the West End and internationally, having been Head of Casting at ATG until 2012 and now freelance.

Welcomes CVs and letters (with photographs), via email. Also happy to receive casting interview enquiries via the same method.

Jane Salberg

86 Stade Street, Hythe, Kent CT21 6DY
tel 01303 239277
email janesalberg@aol.com

Works in theatre and musicals. Recent credits include: UK Casting Director for Jean Ann Ryan (Cruise Musicals); *Horrid Henry Live and Horrid* (UK tour); and *The Wizard of Oz* (Royal Festival Hall).

Prefers not to receive performance notices or unsolicited submissions, but will consider invitations to view individual actors' websites.

Ginny Schiller CDG

9 Clapton Terrace, London E5 9BW
tel 020 8806 5383
email casting@ginnyschiller.co.uk
website www.ginnyschiller.co.uk

Main area of work is theatre, but has also cast for television, film, radio and commercials. Recent work includes: *The Starry Messenger* (Wyndhams); *Admissions* (Trafalgar); *The Cherry Orchard* (BOV and Royal Exchange); *Richard III* (Almeida); *The Father* and *Bad Jews* (Ustinov, West End and tours); multiple West End transfers or original productions, over 20 shows at the Rose Theatre Kingston, 30+ for Theatre Royal Bath, and the Ustinov Studio seasons 2011-2019.

Accepts links to view actors' CVs and online profile or showreel via email. Welcomes performance notices via email, if given 2 weeks' notice.

Laura Scott CDG

56 Rowena Crescent, London SW11 2PT
tel 020 7978 6336 *fax* 020 7924 1907
email laurascottcasting@mac.com

Main areas of work are film, television, theatre and commercials. Casting credits include: *Bonekickers* (BBC TV); *William and Mary* (Series 1-3, TV); *Trial and Retribution XIV* (TV) and *The Time of Your Life* (TV).

The Searchers

70 Sylvia Court, Cavendish Street, London N1 7PG
email casting@thesearchers.net
website www.thesearchers.net
Directors Wayne Waterson, Ian Sheppard

Casts mainly for television, film and commercials. Recent credits include: commercials for Pepsi, Nike, Kellogg's and Royal Mail. Has worked for directors including Terry Gillingham, Tarsem and Earl Morris.

Will consider attending performances within Greater London given 1 week's notice. Accepts submissions

(with CVs, showreels and photographs) from actors previously unknown to the company, but does not welcome unsolicited emails or invitations to view an actor's website.

Nadira Seecoomar CDG

tel 020 8892 8478
email nadira.seecoomar@gmail.com

Known for *The Inbetweeners 2* (2014), *The Inbetweeners Movie* (2011), *My Summer of Love* (2004), *Jump Tomorrow* (2001).

Recent credits include, film: *The Festival* (2018); TV: *The Windsors* (2016–18), *People Just Do Nothing* (2017), *Ill Behaviour* (2017), *White Gold* (2017), *Chewing Gum* (2017)

Select Casting Ltd

PO Box 748, London NW4 1TT
mobile 07956 131494
email info@selectcasting.co.uk
website www.selectcasting.co.uk
website http://pro.imdb.com/name/nm3052115/
Twitter @selectcasting
Casting Venetia Suchdev

In 2004 Select Casting Ltd started up as an in-house extras agency for an already established production house. It gained independent status as a casting agency as well as an extras agency for actors and background supporting artistes in 2007. Select Management was established in 2008 to look after a handful of professional actors, dancers, presenters and models who are registered on Spotlight.

Initially specialising in the Bollywood market it quickly progressed to more regional film productions by film-makers from other regions in the Indian subcontinent. Also offers services to film-makers from the Middle East and Russia and a wider global market, allowing production companies to make one call and fulfil all their requirements for an international cast and grew globally.

Provides line production services and full accounting packages (including tax credits and day-to-day cash flow services etc).

Recent filmography: Bollywood films include: *Bhagam Bhag, Namastey London, Salaam-E-Ishq* and *Patiala House*; Russian films include: *Platon*; Middle Eastern productions include: *El Malik Farourk (King Farouk)*; Hungarian-US productions include: *Magic Boys*; Chinese productions include: *Dual Crisis, Triumph in the Skies II, Passage of my Youth, Finding Mr Right 2, Flying Tiger 2, Impman 4, Vanguard* starring Jackie Chan; British feature films include: *Keith Lemon - The Film* and *Kick*; Canadian TV series *The Frankie Drake Mysteries*. Has also worked on several music videos, commercials, idents and promos etc. Works in all forms of media - film, TV, online, modelling in print or on stage.

Phil Shaw

Suite 476, 2 Old Brompton Road, South Kensington, London SW7 3DQ
tel 020 8715 8943
email philshawcasting@gmail.com

Main areas of work are theatre, television, film and commercials. Casting credits include: Originating Co-Exec Producer: *Wire in the Blood* (ITV pilot)*Deckies* (Channel 4 series pilot); *Days in the Trees* (BBC Radio); *The Bill* (Thames TV); *Body Story* (BBC TV doc/drama series); *Romans 12:20* (BAFTA nominated; Grand Jury Prize, ARPA, Los Angeles); *Winter Fiction* (NFTS); *The Killing of Sister George* (Oldham Coliseum); *The Turn of the Screw* (No. 1 tour); *Billy Liar; The Chalk Garden; People Are Living There* (King's Head Theatre); *Cock & Bull Story* (Old Red Lion); *Enjoy* (Watford Palace); *Angels in America* (Lyric, Hammersmith); *The Last Post* (BAFTA nominated; Grand Prize, Berlin Film Festival); *Italian Movies* (Indiana Productions, feature - UK casting); currently, *Albion* (US/UK TV mini-series); NY Times best-seller *Darkness Falls*, and *The Trip to Bountiful* (West End).

Will consider attending performances at Central London venues, and also West End No. 1 tour, NT and RSC understudy runs, given a minimum of 2 weeks' notice. Accepts postal submissions (with resume/photograph) from actors previously unknown to the casting director, but does not welcome unsolicited showreels or email enquiries (unless a performance notice).

Michelle Smith CDG

220 Church Lane, Woodford, Stockport SK7 1PQ
tel 0161 439 6825 *fax* 0161 439 0622
email michelle.smith18@btinternet.com

Specialising in film, television and commercials. Recent TV casting credits include: *Reg* (BBC1), *Common* (BBC1), *Moving On* (BBC). Recent film credits include: *The Messenger, Electricity, The Violators* and *Lies We Tell*.

Suzanne Smith CDG

3rd Floor, 15 Crinan Street, York Way, London N1 9SQ
tel 020 8993 8118 *fax* 020 7436 9690
email zan@dircon.co.uk

Main areas of work are film and television. Credits include: *Dracula* (NBC/Sky); *Black Sails* for Starz; *Band of Brothers* and *The Pacific*. Films include: *Three Musketeers* and *Mariah Mundi*.

Emma Stafford

FLIX Facilities, 112 Broadway, Media City M50 2UW
mobile 07841 03069
email assistant@emmastafford.tv
website www.emmastafford.tv

Areas of work include television, film and commercials. Recent credits include: *200 Magazine*, Co-op Bank, Robinsons, *If I Were a Butterfly*.

Will consider attending performances within the North West area with at least 2 weeks' notice. Accepts letters (with CVs and photographs) from actors previously unknown to the agency; will also accept CVs and photographs sent by email, and view showreels.

Helen Stafford

14 Park Avenue, Enfield, London EN1 2HP
tel 020 8360 6329
email helenstaffordcasting@gmail.com

Casts in film and theatre, in both the UK and the USA. Recent credits include: films: *Big City Dreams, Somking Guns aka A Punter's Prayer*, and *Red Devil* both produced by Sony Pictures USA; theatre: New York Broadway production transfers to London West End.

Will consider seeing actors perform in Central and Greater London, with 1 week's notice.

Robert Sterne

See the entry for Nina Gold CDG under *Casting directors* on page 114.

Gail Stevens & Rebecca Farhall Casting

84-85 London Lane, London EC1A 9ET
email office@gailstevenscasting.com

Main areas of work are television, film and commercials. Casting credits include: *Zero Dark Thirty, Slumdog Millionaire , Trainspotting* and *Babylon*.

Sam Stevenson CDG

email sam@hancockstevenson.com
website www.hancockstevenson.com

See entry for National Theatre in *Producing theatres* on page 146.

Liz Stoll CDG

email liz.stoll@lizstollcasting.co.uk

Has worked in all areas of actor casting and has recently left the BBC after casting BBC1 drama for the past 18 years. Work for the BBC includes the series *One Night*, the film *The Night Watch*, 5 series of *Judge John Deed*, 5 series of *Down To Earth*, various episodes of *Dalziel and Pasco, Waking The Dead*, over 300 episodes of *Holby City*, plus *Father Brown, The Coroner* and *Shakespeare and Hathaway*.

Happy to receive performance notices at least 2 weeks in advance, and is prepared to travel within Greater London (sometimes further, work permitting) to see shows. Welcomes emails with CVs and photographs from actors previously unknown to the casting director; prefers Spotlight showreels, and is happy to receive invitations to view individuals' websites.

Syson Grainger Casting

Rooms 7&8, 2nd Floor, 83-84 Berwick Street,
London W1F 8TS
tel 020 7287 5327 *fax* 020 7287 3629

Recent feature films include: *Children of Men*,
directed by Alfonso Cuaron; *Syriana*, directed by
Stephen Gagan; *Batman Begins*, directed by Chris
Nolan; *Troy*, directed by Wolfgang Petersen; *Snatch*,
directed by Guy Ritchie; *Spygame*, directed by Tony
Scott; and *Fifth Element*, directed by Luc Besson.

Amanda Tabak CDG

See the entry for Candid Casting under *Casting
directors* on page 108.

Topps Casting

The Media Centre, 7 Northumberland Street,
West Yorkshire HD1 1RL
tel 01484 511988 *fax* 01484 483100
email nicci@toppscasting.co.uk
website www.toppscasting.co.uk
Twitter @niccitopping
Casting Director Nicci Topping

Works in television, film and commercials. Recent
work includes: feature films *Speak No Evil* and *Tribe*;
feature trailer *Storage*.

Welcomes performance notices within Greater
London and elsewhere (Manchester, Leeds, Sheffield)
if given 2 weeks' notice. Accepts letters (with CVs &
photographs) from individual actors previously
unknown to the agency, sent by post or email.

Moira Townsend

See the entry for Casting Couch Productions Ltd
under *Casting directors* on page 109.

Jill Trevellick CDG

92 Priory Road, London N8 7EY
tel 020 8340 2734
email jill@jilltrevellick.com

Main areas of work are film and television. Casting
credits include: TV – *Dickensian*, *Downton Abbey*
(series 1-3, 5 & 6); *The Hour*, *White Heat*, *Merlin*,
Vanity Fair, *North and South*, *The Canterbury Tales*,
Merlin (series 1-5). Film – *What We Did On Our
Holiday* (Andy Hamilton & Guy Jenkin, 2013); *Fish
Tank* (Andrea Arnold, 2009); *I Know You Know*
(Justin Kerrigan, 2009).

Sally Vaughan CDG

2 Kennington Park Place, London SE11 4AS
tel 020 7735 6539

Main area of work is theatre. Credits include:
Porridge (No. 1 UK tour); *'Allo, 'Allo* (No. 1 UK
tour); *Dad's Army – The Lost Episodes* (No. 1 UK
tour); *Sweet Charity* (Victoria Palace Theatre), *Of
Thee I Sing* and *Sweeney Todd* (Bridewell Theatre);
and *Anna Weiss* (Whitehall Theatre).

Anne Vosser

156 Lower Farnham Road, Aldershot,
Hampshire GU12 4EL
tel 01252 404716 *mobile* 07968 868712
email anne@vosser-casting.co.uk
website www.vosser-casting.co.uk

Main areas of work are theatre and musicals. Casting
credits include: *What The Butler Saw*, *Zorro*, *Taboo*,
Fame, *Saturday Night Fever*, *Footloose*, *Never Forget*
(all in the West End).

Fiona Weir CDG

2nd Floor, 138 Portobello Road, London W11 2DZ
tel 020 7727 5600 *mobile* 07980 285607
email fweir@icloud.com

Known for *Brooklyn* (2015), *Fantastic Beasts and
Where to Find Them* (2016), *Harry Potter and the
Deathly Hallow Part I* (2010), *Harry Potter and the
Goblet of Fire* (2005).

Recent credits include, film, *Fantastic Beasts: The
Crimes of Grindelwald* (2018), *My Cousin Rachel*
(2017), *The Light Between the Oceans* (2016), *Room*
(2015), *Pride* (2014)

June West

email junewest@junewestcasting.com
website www.junewestcasting.com

Having enjoyed a career as Casting Director at ITV
Granada, June has worked on numerous award-
winning dramas, comedy series, drama-
documentaries and, of course, the longest-running
soap in history – *Coronation Street*.

June is now a freelance Casting Director, and with the
benefit of more than 30 years' experience working
with some of the most celebrated talent in our
industry.

Recent credits include: theatre, *The Family Way*
(Bolton Octagon 2016), *The Ancient Search of Youth
and the Five Tibetans* by Jim Cartwright (Bolton
Octagon 2015).

Only accepts contact by email. Send show-reels or
details of forthcoming TV or theatre appearances.
Tries to cover as many productions as possible
between projects and will be in touch if they are able
to cover your production. Cannot reply to every
email so do not get disheartened if they do not reply
to your email.

Matt Western

150 Blythe Road, London W14 0HD
tel 020 7602 6646 *mobile* 07740 70207
email matt@mattwestern.co.uk
website www.mattwestern.co.uk

Main areas of work are film, television and
commercials. Recent casting credits include, film:
Three Acts (2018), *The Holly Kane Experiment* (2017),
Susu (2017), *Golden Years* (2016), *Boys Will Be Boys*

(2016); TV: *Missing* (series 1, 2014 and series 2, 2016).

Tara Woodward

Top Flat, 93 Gloucester Avenue, Primrose Hill, London NW1 8LB
tel 020 7586 3487 *fax* 020 7681 8574

Main areas of work are film, television, theatre and commercials. Casting credits include: *The Early Days*, *Post* and *Hello Friend* (all for Shine/Film Four Lab); *Chasing Heaven* (for Venice Film Festival); *The Browning Version* and *Romeo and Juliet* (theatre); and commercials for Parmalat Aqua and Royal Danish Post. Has worked as Casting Assistant to Nina Gold on films including *All Or Nothing* (directed by Mike Leigh) and *Love's Labour's Lost* (directed by Kenneth Branagh).

Jeremy Zimmermann Casting

36 Marshall Street, London W1F 7EY
tel 020 7478 5161 *fax* 020 7437 4747
email jeremy@zimmermanncasting.com

Main areas of work are film and television. Recent casting work includes: *Keeping Mum*, *The Contract*, *Van Wilder 2*, *Dog Soldiers* and *Blood And Chocolate*.

Will consider attending performances at venues in Greater London and elsewhere. Accepts postal submissions (with CVs and photographs) from actors previously unknown to the casting director, but does not welcome email enquiries. Invitations to view individual actors' websites are also accepted.

Casting for the stage

Anne McNulty

If the essence of acting on stage is the gathering of a group of people to share a story, then the work of a casting director is to guide and support the director in meeting and choosing the actors to make up that group. The director will have ideas and expectations and it's my job to share the widest possible range of acting talent to achieve the cast. The choice is wide open until we have seen all our actors.

The play, the director, the venue, the timescale, the salary – these are the first things to take into consideration when I am approached to work with a director on a play. We will both read the script in depth. We produce a breakdown describing each of the roles and I may send this out to agents via a Spotlight link; it will depend on size of cast and if the director has strong initial ideas. I will check CVs and perhaps go straight to an offer for the key roles in a production.

I will also compile a list of actors for each of the roles based on my knowledge of their work, details from their agents and their CVs. We will also receive individual submissions and will read these too. The decisions about who and how many actors to meet will depend on the director's schedule and who we feel is suitable. We will also be speculative if there is a credit that interests us on an actor's CV, or if we have seen a review that describes a particular actor who we like the sound of. It is not necessary to have an agent to be considered for casting but sometimes if may be a stipulation that the actor has some professional experience. It all depends on the role and the director.

I may work with an assistant and between us we will book rooms, liaise with the director about the text you should prepare, fix the meetings and read in, if required.

You will be invited to audition because you have been singled out as a potential for the role and one of a small group being met. A fixed time has been allocated for your meeting and you need to use it to show your skills. Please don't make excuses. You should have been given enough time to prepare, but if you are called in at short notice then do all you can and share that in the meeting.

Know the story of the play. The internet can offer a precis for existing texts, and if it is a new play you may be sent the script – if not, interpret what you can from the sides you are sent. It is vital to prepare well and bring your sense of the character into the meeting. You are coming into the room to get the job, so a sense of who you are as a person and as a company member is important. Expect to be asked a question about any shows you have seen lately, or if you have a favourite writer or actor, who they are and why you chose them.

If the role requires an accent then prepare in that accent and also be ready to use your own accent. The director could ask you to give an extreme interpretation of the character to see how far you can stretch in trying something. Do think about how you dress, as being too relaxed and informal can suggest you're not taking the meeting seriously. Shorts and flip-flops simply do not work.

One other crucial piece of advice is to listen carefully and be succinct. The urgency and nerves of wanting to do a good audition can mean you don't hear properly or reply quickly, meaning you may not hear everything that the director has said. Often, this clarity is vital and you can always ask for them to say it again. If you are asked if you have any questions, it usually means 'do you understand?' and it is not an opportunity to stall or to ask the director how they see the part.

You may meet directors who are less forthcoming and simply want you to work on the text. They may give you a note but will not really engage in chat. Don't be alarmed, they will be considering your work just the same and that is their style.

If the meeting does not lead to you getting the role, your work and the inspiration you offered will be recorded by the team and hopefully they will think of you for future projects. You may feel you are totally right for a role but there are many considerations in balancing a company, casting a family, the siblings – even twins! Also, the relationship of the parents, best friend, rival or lover, will decide how the choice is made. I always feed back to agents and actors after their auditions. This can take time but gives you an indication of how it went so you can use that in the future.

When I am in the midst of a casting, the priority will always be the meetings. I will give you as much information as possible, to ensure that your meeting can be open, investigative and a time to really work the text. Make the most of it.

My other source of insight is to see as many shows as I can – every evening and sometimes on the weekend. I will go to regional productions and shows on tour, to watch as many actors, interpretations and styles of direction and production, as they give me lots of information. I cover many of the drama school shows and share the progress of new graduates as they find their first jobs in theatre. I will also see all the current television and films – so there's plenty of input going into each new casting.

I think William Shakespeare sums it up perfectly: 'the readiness is all'. Keep it simple, prepare well and good luck.

Anne McNulty, CDG, is originally from Manchester and moved to London in 1986 to work for a charity, then joined the Young Vic in 1990 as PA to the Artistic and Administrative Directors. This was where she met Sam Mendes and joined the Donmar Warehouse as Casting Director, plus administrative support, in May 1992. After working with both Michael Grandage and Josie Rourke, she left in 2012 to pursue a freelance career and to work in drama schools, with a particular interest in audition workshops.

Agents and casting directors

Casting for musical theatre

David Grindrod

The process of producing/casting a musical can be a very long and costly affair. Everyone is looking for the next *Phantom of the Opera* or *Mamma Mia!*; years of work can go into the production you see on stage today. Workshops have now become a necessity in order to see if a show 'has legs', without spending too much money. In consultation with the producer and creative team, I will assemble a group of actors who may not be totally right for the roles but who work well in a workshop situation. If the green light is given after the workshop presentation, the casting process – in conjunction with everything else – begins.

A casting breakdown is drawn up: this consists of all the details required by agents and artists about the characters, vocal ranges, etc. plus the proposed dates of the production. Open calls are sometimes organised for specific roles, but normally the breakdown gets sent to agents via the Spotlight link, which reaches 500 agents/representatives at the touch of a button.

There is always a 'wish list' of actors whom producers would like in their production, but the bulk of submissions will come through agents, in the form of photos and CVs. Unsolicited mail is also received; sometimes it is difficult to keep all this on file due to sheer number of submissions. Either I or my associates will also attend college shows and presentations to look for specific talent.

When preparing your photos and CVs, always remember that these are the calling cards with which you promote yourself! A good photograph is not 'artistic' (i.e. showing a face half in shadow); rather, it should always present a good full face that really does look like you. Your CV should ideally be just one page stapled to the back of your photograph. It should include all relevant details (*not* forgetting contact details) to show your skills. Make this information clear and precise. If you feel that you are suitable for musical casting, be very accurate and truthful about your vocal range: don't make it complicated – basically, tenor or soprano, with the top of your range noted. We can normally tell your style by the shows you have appeared in.

The audition process normally begins with artists performing two contrasting songs that show range and personality. Make an effort to pick a song that is suitable for the show – not pop, for example, when you are up for Rogers & Hammerstein. Nerves will take over; therefore, don't sing the song you learnt yesterday, but perform something tried and tested (something you would be happy singing naked in Trafalgar Square!). When we ask, "Have you got something else?" we don't want the answer, "My agent said you only wanted two songs,"; have your book of audition pieces with you and give us the chance to choose an alternative. Actors often ask whether I have favourite songs that I like to hear – or songs that I don't: I only really mind when they come in with completely the wrong song for the production.

If an actor is successful, they will receive a call-back for a dance/movement call. This normally causes concerns, but actually it is not usually that specific; we only want to see whether a person is happy with his/her body. If the audition is for a major dance show, hopefully you will know your limitations, and either not audition at all, or be ready to throw yourself into the routine. Again, be honest: then you won't upset the creative team.

Further recalls take place with music and script from the show: the musical supervisor or associate director normally takes these calls. If you come in for the musical supervisor, come back with music prepared and your own song. *Always* bring your own song – it's a good reminder for the team. In addition to any script you are asked to read, you may get asked for a speech: have a couple of acting pieces prepared, and again, nerves will take over, so make sure you know them properly. Remember that these speeches are also to allow the director to assess how well you can respond to direction, and how readily you can take a note.

The culmination of the casting process – 'the finals' – is the most nerve-wracking experience, even for a highly experienced artist. Bring everything with you that you have been given. You may not get *asked* for everything, but have it just in case. You may have been asked to dress in a certain way; always put some thought into that, as directors can be blinkered at times ... I have known artists to arrive with a couple of outfits and ask me to pick one! The panel will consist of the whole creative team and the producers. At this stage I can't do any more for you – though hopefully I can keep the atmosphere in the room happy and 'up'. Stay calm, don't change anything that you have been told, and audition to the best of your abilities.

Now the wait to see if you have the role. Always remember that you have got this far in the process because you can sing and act far better than anyone else. In the end, the decision could come down to height, look, hair colour; funnily enough it may not have anything to do with your singing/acting skills at this point. And you may not get an instant answer; you may have to wait until other meetings have taken place. You may get put on 'hold': normally that means you are not first on the list, but if somebody above you declines the offer you may move up. If you are lucky, the phone call will come with a straight offer. How exciting is that ... Contractual details are then advised and, if all that is agreed, your date for first rehearsal is given. Always remember that you are a small part of the bigger picture – a small part of the jigsaw puzzle that goes together to form: The Musical.

David Grindrod founded David Grindrod Associates (DGA) with Stephen Crockett in January 1998, after 20 years' experience in the theatre in various roles ranging from assistant stage manager to general manager. Current West End casting includes *Chicago*, *Evita*, *The Lord of the Rings*, *Mamma Mia!* (worldwide), *Spamalot*, *The Sound of Music*. Films include *The Phantom of The Opera*. DGA are also casting consultants for *On The Town* and *Kismet* at the English National Opera, and belong to the Casting Directors Guild of Great Britain.

Woman in a brown skirt

Sophie Stanton

Sophie Stanton reflects on the Donmar Warehouse's pioneering commitment to providing more opportunities for female actors in its all-women Shakespeare Trilogy, which helped her to land her most significant roles to date: Falstaff in the Donmar's *Henry IV* and Mrs Rich in the RSC'S revival of *The Fantastic Follies of Mrs Rich* by Mary Pix (1700).

I mourned my training when it ended. I consider myself fortunate that I did, but it was painful. Perhaps that's why for many years I compulsively enrolled on courses in whatever subject piqued my interest at the time.

On the cartoon course, perhaps a couple of years out of drama school, I titled one project, 'The Seven Stages of Wan'. It's a portrait of an actress as she journeys through her career from early childhood to old age, sans everything. I revisit it now with one question in mind – how prophetic was I in those early years?

The first three frames are self-explanatory: 'I wanna be Mary' depicts a child of nursery school age in the school nativity (I was always a shepherd in ours); 'I wanna be picked', aged fourteen she's auditioning for a production of Romeo and Juliet – we did *A Midsummer Night's Dream*. I was Puck. We also did The Mikado. I played Koko, the Lord High Executioner. A pattern was emerging. 'I wanna be unpicked' sees the young drama student suffering 'first-term fatigue syndrome' at the fictitious Deptford Academy of Dramatic Art, (DADA)… Whilst training, I played a wealth of older ladies – drunks, eccentrics, power-houses of motherhood – and was all the better for it as a young mind at the very start of a career. Of course, there was no way I was going to get an agent from it, but I was truly stretched in most disciplines and, therefore, ironically, in my creative prime upon graduation.

The first couple of years were paltry. I played a mouse, Pimple, someone who'd been abused on *The Bill*. The worst corpse of my entire life occurred in a 'reminiscence show' we inflicted on older members of the community round various care homes, when one woman screamed, 'Oh, shut up! You are getting on my nerves' in the middle of my solo. Which rather hit the nail on the head and drove it into my heart. But it got me my Equity card.

'I wanna work' was the frame I saw myself in at the time of drawing the cartoon. Our female protagonist sits in a coffee shop with a male actor friend sharing a conversation she has had with her agent, desperate to get a job *of any description*. Both are smoking (how times have changed). She asks how his career is going. 'Well, great. But then, I'm a boy' is the response. (Or have they?) We fast-forward to the middle-aged actress outside a Winnebago. 'Love, I'm a bloody joke,' she says on the phone, 'I've got two sodding lines and some business with a rhino! It would be *nice* to play Lady M before it's too late, frankly!' In a letter to my former self I might comment that this insight into life for an actress of a certain age is uncanny. To which, my former self would undoubtedly reply, 'That's not me being insightful, it's the truth.' Which of course it is, unless you are exceptionally lucky. Or unless you get cast as a man. I wonder what I would have felt had I known then that I'd wait twenty-odd years to play a major role and that that major role would be an old fat bloke. I'm sure the old fat bloke bit of the equation wouldn't have been an issue having cornered the market in shepherds, traditionally male fairies, executioners and old ladies. But the wait?

And so to Falstaff in the Donmar Warehouse's all-female Shakespeare Trilogy (St Ann's Warehouse, New York, 2015; Donmar King's Cross, 2016). In one, rare twenty-four-hour period, I landed two smashing theatre jobs and was on a 'pencil' (they do fall through, don't ever trust a pencil) for a TV series that has so far run to three seasons and would no doubt have made a healthy dent in my mortgage. But it had been too long since I'd played a part I'd really had to work at. There is a rose called Falstaff. It is unmissable in a border – bold, broad, robust, its petals seem infinitesimal and it's almost the colour of electricity, at once mesmerising and repellent. Its lust for the world strikes me as so enormous that all that energy simply cannot last. Which is probably all I need to say about the role. It undoubtedly changed the landscape for me as an artist. You cannot turn that down. It just doesn't come around very often if you're a bird.

Don't get me wrong: many of the roles I have played have been absolute gems – in *Mercury Fur, England People Very Nice, Dying for It, Beautiful Thing, Ding Dong the Wicked, Nut, Ink, Made in Dagenham: The Musical* – in bastions of new writing: the Almeida, the Royal Court, the National, the Bush. Just too, too many to mention, providing exceptional material with which to carve out a notably varied career. But, still, a lot of them amount to cameos as they're in relief of the male protagonist, which is often all we can expect as 'character actresses'.

Falstaff gave me no choice but to step up as an artist. To stride out, to claim space and make noise unapologetically in a manner which is simply foreign to us as both women and as female actors. It was a language that I had barely spoken since childhood, in fact, when I had been permitted to play the noisy parts in school plays. I took inspiration from John Travolta strutting through the streets of NYC to the sound track of 'Staying Alive' – just feeling great about himself. I studied men who walk only in straight lines, taking for granted that the rest of us will step aside. I dropped my voice an octave and hit maximum volume. And, of course, I embraced the male spread. Falstaff gives it large.

Women, to this day, tend to be written small. Even the female juvenile lead is often written with a bias towards making the bloke-part look tender when he falls in love with her (which isn't a terribly progressive representation of men either, might I add, we must fight for both genders). Obviously, I get cast as the juve lead's mum or just that woman who's complaining in a shop. I call them the 'brown skirt parts'.

God forbid they should dress you in anything interesting; you might upstage the lead. Yesterday's conversation with a costume designer – 'I'm going to make you downbeat, muted. In contrast to, you know, *the politicians.*' The film is about the politicians, need I say, all male.

Unsurprisingly, Falstaff was the best possible preparation for the biggest female role I have played to date – Mrs Rich in *The Fantastic Follies of Mrs Rich*, an adaptation of Mary Pix's lost play *The Beau Defeated* of 1700 (RSC, Stratford, 2018). Mrs Rich is writ large, oh, yes she is. The delicious absurdity of her social pretension, the enormity of her wit, her kitsch, her pain and her glory, the cabaret, the vaudeville demanded by the writing – none of it could I draw on from having played the brown-skirt parts. All of my references were male. I spent a lot of time researching the work of drag queens. We just don't have permission to display as women. At best, it is not female tradition. At worst it is unsavoury.

I had four soaring solos written by Grant Olding scored for four saxophones aspiring to be a string quartet (not since I was heckled by an old lady had I sung solo), I was gifted endless innuendos, ad libs, exquisite soliloquies and audience collusion. I learnt the harpsichord, how to vogue, wolf whistle, had costumes made which really should be behind glass at the Victoria and Albert museum and finally – finally — I got to perform my first professional sword fight. That part was Falstaffian.

God forbid this swathe of women in significant male roles should be relegated to a thing of the past because look at where it can lead. It would be nice not to have to play a man in order to fulfil an epic role of a lifetime, but those female roles are painfully rare. Women have to be represented bigger – not just more, but bigger. We cannot let this work fade. Do not go gentle into that good night. Thank you, Mr Dylan Thomas. I shall try very hard not to.

In the penultimate frame of my cartoon, our now older protagonist has indeed won the part of Lady M, but it's too late as her memory has gone and she suffers a mammoth dry in the 'dashed the brains out' speech. Two walk-on actors mutter bitchy comments behind her. It's bleak. And finally, we come to 'Dribble Hall; retirement home for dear old thesps'. We find the elderly woman at what is possibly her final Christmas, being entertained by Naff Theatre Company. Her face is full of loss, *wan*, but there's a soupçon of defiance left about the eyes. She says to herself, 'And so it came to pass'... This, the last frame, is again titled, 'I wanna be Mary'.

Perhaps this has answered my question. Perhaps I should've been delighted to know that I'd play an old bloke in twenty or so years because evidently in my mid-twenties I was already resigned to a life of artistic frustration simply because of my gender.

When the time comes, if I reach an age when I can expect to spend time somewhere like Dribble Hall, I do hope I have wits enough not to be saying, 'I wanna be Mary.' Mary's a dull part. Mary's basically there to give birth to one of the lead guys. Mary is Woman-in-a-Brown-Skirt. I hope, in my dotage, that I'm aiming higher than Mary. I wanna be saying, I dunno, 'I wanna be the Angel Gabriel.' Or I wanna be... !

God?

Now, God's a good part.

Sophie Stanton graduated from RADA in 1991 and has worked extensively in British theatre, television, film and radio ever since. She also sometimes writes and occasionally directs. Her first play *Cariad* was published in 2007. She is currently working on her second play with the generous support of the Arts Council England. Amongst other things.

Theatre
Introduction

Theatres and theatre companies/managements abound in all kinds of different forms, and paid opportunities for live performance are not restricted to putting on productions. The days of the permanent repertory company are almost gone, but there is a much wider diversity of work available. The larger companies/managements often use casting directors (see page 106), who should usually be your first port of call with your letter, CV and photograph. However, it can be worth exploiting any personal contacts that you may have.

For all approaches, it is important to send your submissions to the person named – unless you have a personal contact.

Dramaturg at HOME

Petra Jane Tauscher

The growth in the number of visible dramaturgs in British theatre in the last 25 years has been remarkable. Their emergence in this country has often been greeted with suspicion, particularly in and around the new theatre writing community, which is far larger here than in most other European countries. Some playwrights thought being assigned a dramaturg by a commissioning theatre was an unhelpful control mechanism, an infringement of their creativity. Some artistic directors associated dramaturgs with the American prevalence of work-shopping plays in development with actors (28 workshops in the case of Tony Kushner's *Angels in America*) as risible and other playwrights saw dramaturg-led workshops as excuses for theatres not committing to the production of more new plays. This was to dismiss out of hand the enhancement that positive support from an informed specialist, the dramaturg, and actors' creativity can bring to the writing process.

The British resistance to this principle is partly understandable given the traditional under resourcing of theatre here in comparison with many other European countries, and its success in new theatre writing drawn from a very rapid turnover in the initial presentation of new product with on average four-week runs, and the same amount of time, or less, for rehearsal. It is interesting to note the rise of work-shopping in the more commercially lucrative musical theatre sector. *Made in Dagenham* received four major workshops over a couple of years. On the continent new productions can rehearse for six months and stay in the repertoire for several years. The German premiere production of Mark Ravenhill's *Shopping and Fucking* began its life at the Baracke in January 1998, then transferred to the Schaubühne, where it remained in the repertoire for over a decade. Nevertheless the original resistance to dramaturgs in Britain demonstrated a lack of understanding of their wider responsibilities beyond support to new writing. In fact the breadth of the field of dramaturgy is such that any one dramaturg's relationship to it at any one time is akin to any one doctor's relationship to the whole of medicine. However, unlike doctors, dramaturgs can shift between different aspects of dramaturgy fairly readily, particularly if they are, like myself at HOME in Manchester, employed full time by one theatre company. To make the function of my role more clear my job title is Creative Producer and Dramaturg.

In my role as creative producer I am concerned with making things happen, such joint productions with other theatre companies; liaising with potential visiting companies; relating to other theatre-makers across Greater Manchester and helping to manage programmes within the building such as the assistant directors we nurture on lengthy placements from the two-year MA in Directing at Birkbeck College, University of London. As dramaturg, in addition to our own productions, there is only time for me to be deeply involved in one or two other productions at a time, though I can give notes to any production visiting HOME. For his first production in the new building Artistic Director Walter Meierjohann asked playwright Simon Stephens to adapt Odon von Horvath's *Kasimir and Karoline* into a local contemporary setting, *The Funfair*. The play, set in 1929 just after the worldwide financial crisis, had a strong resonance with current times. The three of us put a lot of work into ensuring the translation of every sentence was correct and relevant and Simon managed to stay faithful to the original at the same time as making the play very much his own. Next season, I am working with writers on two key projects: Ibsen's *Ghosts* in a new version by David Watson directed by Polly Findlay, and with 59 Productions on an adaptation of Paul Auster's novella, *City of Glass* by Duncan Macmillan which opens here and transfers to the Lyric, Hammersmith in London and then New York.

Much of my work with the director and writer is in the preparation of a piece, but the role of dramaturg during a production is often underestimated. The production dramaturg acts as a partner to the director throughout a process, which always throws up questions, surprises and change! My involvement is strongest at the start and at the end of the rehearsal process. In rehearsals actors are encouraged to approach me to seek support, particularly on creating back stories and other psychological aspects of their character. In 'tech' rehearsal – particularly with a show that has high visual ambition - a director's focus has to be on the technical team. Occasionally actors may feel they have 'lost' the director, and having bonded with the dramaturg over the early work, it is useful that I am present to address their concerns in those long tech days when nerves are bubbling before an opening. Likewise the preview period is key in the director/dramaturg relationship as this is the critical period where there is so much to digest. Directors' notes are technical and for the actors and contain much detailed observation. The dramaturg feeds their own notes to the director and always has the whole piece in mind. Is the rhythm of the play correct? Is the story clear? What are we saying with this play? Is the original conceptual ambition of the piece coming through? Where are the audience confused or bored? What can be changed?

It has helped my work as a dramaturg that I trained for three years at the prestigious Ernst Busch Theatre Academy in Berlin, extending my study abroad year from reading Modern Languages at Oxford. Not long after the fall of the Berlin Wall, I arrived from Oxford with a very academic approach to theatre making. When I was cast as Queen Elizabeth I in Schiller's *Mary Stuart* I spent a lot of my pre-rehearsal preparation time on the eighteenth-century German cultural and philosophical context in which Schiller was writing. I remember reading a great deal of Immanuel Kant. I had to learn how not to let all that interesting work block my own creativity. My fellow student, Nina Hoss (now one of Germany's most celebrated actors on stage and screen), cast opposite me as Mary, spent much of her preparation time contemplating and simulating the spatial dynamics of the rooms that the two queens would have occupied. I learnt fast the importance of a sensual, physical way into material alongside the more cerebral. It is from this training perhaps that I discovered a love of theatre that understands and utilizes space, and how the visual tension of the stage supports an actor and a story as well as adding layers of possibility. Interestingly the first three months of actor and director training at the Ernst Busch is improvisation without words. This was the foundation of theatre training for me, and an experience I cannot recommend enough to young actors and directors fresh from the verbal world of schools and universities. It was here I learnt to observe and articulate observation with precision, which is perhaps the most important skill of production dramaturgy.

It was at Ersnt Busch that I encountered my first dramaturg, as the Head of the school; Dr Klaus Voelker was an eminent dramaturg who had worked as the resident dramaturg in major producing houses in Germany and Switzerland and with Samuel Beckett in France. The role always intrigued me, and in my first professional years as a member of the Peter Stein Ensemble and then at the Berlin Ensemble, I began to understand the different functions and the variety of the role within an organization. In the UK the dramaturg is often seen as a new name for a literary manager. That is certainly one aspect of a dramaturg's responsibility, but on the continent a dramaturg is key in planning ahead, co-curating seasons, discovering directorial, design and acting talent, nurturing relationships and generally supporting the vision the artistic director has for a building.

HOME was formed in 2012 by merging two arts institutions, one which had already lost its original building, the Library Theatre, and one which was to lose its larger cinema, Cornerhouse (also an art gallery, bookshop and cafe). The wonderful award winning new building has two theatre spaces – a 450-seat theatre – and a fully flexible studio space for 150, five cinemas showing independent films and a large gallery. The central staircase of the whole building was designed deliberately to bring the audiences of the different art forms into direct contact, with the hope that it would help create in all of them an interest in what the other audiences were enjoying.

It is a thrilling place for a dramaturg, with exciting challenges. Over the last year the theatre team has worked successfully on establishing a new identity for the theatre work as well as developing a relationship with the other art forms and the different audiences. Traditionally in Britain there is an odd lack of overlap between audiences for film and theatre and this is something we are working on. Already in one year we see the cinema and visual arts audiences investing in our theatre work – perhaps attracted by the visual sophistication of much of the work in the programme, by companies such as 1927, Philippe Quesne, Peeping Tom, Hofesh Shechter. We are creating a new audience beyond traditional theatre-goers. This is key to the future and we look to ways to connect our audiences. Much of my programming time is in co-curating festivals which bring the art forms together. For example every April our Viva Festival celebrates Spanish and Latin American theatre, film and art. The theatre work in the festival is a mix of invited international companies and newly commissioned work. This year we were able to provide a residency for Cuban playwright, Abel Gonzalez Melo and we staged the UK premiere of his first, 2006, success *Chamaco* (*Kiddo*) alongside a newly commissioned work *Weathered* (both plays were cast with local actors). I am currently working with the other departments on a 2017 Russian season to coincide with the centenary year of the Russian Revolution.

An interest in international work connects all our art forms and is a key part of HOME's identity. In theatre we look to ways to connect the international and local. An example of this is our collaboration with the Irish theatre company ANU productions. The first project, *Angel Meadow*, was an immersive piece in an abandoned pub as part of our site-specific season in 2014, giving tiny fractions of audiences very close encounters and experiences with actors in confined spaces. Angel Meadow no longer exists. It was a part of the old Ancoats' district of inner Manchester. In the nineteenth century Angel Meadow was a steaming sordid hell on Earth at the centre of the industrial world. Small groups of audience were moved through the old Ancoats pub, layered with the various lives of people who had passed through the doors of Angel Meadow: lodgers in a night asylum, working men in a pub, dead bodies laid out for an inquest and scuttling gangs fighting for their territory. They not only saw the world of Irish immigrants, they heard it, touched it, and tasted it, encountering landlords, butchers, devils and angels along the way, moving in an instant from present-day Ancoats to its violent, sordid past, and back again, and even inhabiting both at once.

Angel Meadow became a sell-out success and the team decided to invite ANU back this year to mark the 20th anniversary of the bombing of Manchester by the Provisional IRA. The bomb, the largest detonated in mainland Britain since the Second World War, devastated the city centre and injured 212 people. We were not aiming to forefront the political historical analysis and context, but to capture the impact on Mancunians lives 1996, and their reflections two decades later. *On Corporation Street* was based on a hundred testimonies from those involved and collected by Manchester's Mighty Heart Theatre. The testimonies were performed by the cast, word for word, copy in hand, in Manchester Town Hall at the end of May in front of a small audience. It was a powerful collection of reminiscences given further status through public performance. ANU's production, cast with Irish and Manchester actors, distilled those stories and reactions to their essentials, preserving recognisable elements of the original wording and enhancing these through sensitive and imaginative performance to give a heightened sense of reality and considerable time for reflection. We housed the production inside HOME itself with an audience moving around the building and scenes taking place in back corridors, storage spaces and surreal small rooms built into our studio. The show's audience was a fascinating mix of theatre lovers who came for the immersive promenade experience and Mancunians drawn by the material who had never experienced theatre other than from a seat.

Funding has now materialized to fully equip the facilities within our smaller, second theatre space, and we are planning a more focused and responsive programming policy for it. We have already christened the space with a number of exciting pieces of theatre that have emerged on the scene (*The Beanfield, Beyond Caring*), but the new fully flexible seating creates great opportunities. This will include two festivals of new work: the two-week-long Orbit festival in October will bring together leading emerging UK theatre companies; and Push in January–February, which will be specifically for theatre-makers from Greater Manchester building on the success of the former Re:play festival of the Library Theatre. Nurturing emerging companies and artists is an essential part of what we do. We have a full development programme alongside our produced work and we use every opportunity to provide young theatre-makers with space and dramaturgical support. Now that our second space is fully operational, our collaborative programmes and projects with emerging local and national writers, directors and companies will increase. Our second year feels as challenging and exciting as our first!

After graduating from Oxford, **Petra Jane Tauscher** spent her first professional years in Europe: three years with Peter Stein, then at the Berlin Ensemble as an assistant director. Upon returning home to the UK, she had an opportunity to work in film and later became Head of Drama Development for Atlantic Productions, alongside her work as a freelance dramaturg for theatre. Petra joined HOME's theatre team in 2013 as creative producer and dramaturg. She co-curated the site-specific and opening season, and has been the resident production dramaturg for all HOME-produced shows until 2018. From late 2018, Petra has been Director of the International Youth Arts Festival, Kingston upon Thames.

Theatre

Producing theatres

Included in this section are the national and regional building-based companies that mount their own productions – sometimes in co-operation with others, and sometimes sending out tours. (Almost all also receive touring productions.) The majority are subsidised by the national and regional Arts Councils (and use Equity's regional theatre contract), but a few are not (and use Equity's commercial theatre contract), and a few have their own contractual arrangements. Almost all have websites which can be very useful for keeping track of their activities. A little extra insight into a theatre – beyond that listed on the following pages – might just tip the balance in your favour.

In real terms, rates of pay are better than they were a decade and more ago, but they are still only 'adequate' – especially if you are incurring the extra costs of living away from home. However, rehearsing and performing a production in such a theatre can be an exhilarating experience. A well-run theatre has a wonderful 'family' atmosphere, and in the close-knit working environment you can often make friendships which sustain for many years afterwards – as well as contacts who might be useful in years to come. It is well worth checking each theatre's 'casting procedures' very carefully as there are significant variations between them. It is also worth familiarising yourself with their programmes of productions via *The Stage* and/or their websites.

Abbey Theatre Amharclann na Mainistreach

26/27 Lower Abbey Street, Dublin 1, Ireland
tel +353 (0) 1 878 7222 *fax* +353 (0) 1 872 9177
email info@abbeytheatre.ie
Directors Graham McLaren Neil Murray *Associate Director* Caitriona McLaughlin *Casting Director* Sarah Jones

Production details: The Abbey Theatre produces an ambitious annual prgramme of Irish and international theatre across its two stages and on tour in Ireland and internationally. The Abbey Theatre is committed to building the Irish theatre repertoire, through commissioning and producing new Irish writing, and re-imagining national and international classics in collaboration with leading contemporary talent.

Casting procedures: The Abbey Theatre is the only theatre in Ireland with a full time in-house casting department dedicated to seeking out new and emerging talent, as well as keeping abreast of the continued work and development of previously established actors from all over the country and abroad. The Abbey Theatre holds general auditions bi-annually. The casting department attends performances throughout the year, nationally and internationally, as well as drama school showcases in Dublin and London.

Almeida Theatre

Almeida Street, London N1 1TA
tel 020 7359 4404

email info@almeida.co.uk
website www.almeida.co.uk
Artistic Director Rupert Goold

Production details: A small room with an international reputation. The Almeida makes brave new work that asks big questions of plays, of theatre and of the world around us. It brings together the most exciting artists to take risks; to provoke, inspire and surprise audiences; to interrogate the present, dig up the past and imagine the future. Stages approximately 6 productions each year. Recent West End transfers include *Ink*, *Hamlet*, *Mary Stuart* and *Summer and Smoke*.

Casting procedures: Productions are cast by external freelance casting directors on a project-by-project basis. Uses the TMA/Equity Subsidised Rep contract and subscribes to the Equity Pension Scheme. Actively promotes the use of inclusive casting.

Arcola Theatre

24 Ashwin Street, London E8 3DL
tel 020 7503 1645
email production@arcolatheatre.com
website www.arcolatheatre.com
Artistic Director Mehmet Ergen

Production details: Founded in 2000 by Artistic Director Mehmet Ergen and Executive Producer Leyla Nazli, Arcola Theatre is now one of the most respected arts venues in the UK, "blazing a trail in artistic excellence and innovative management from the outset". Housed in a converted factory in

Hackney, Arcola is a favourite of established theatre literati as well as young, upwardly mobile innovators. London's largest theatre studio, it has become well known for the variety of its programming, from new writing to classic drama, music and comedy.

Arcola has staged work by some of the best living actors, writers and directors, including productions by William Gaskill, Timberlake Wertenbaker, Ariel Dorfman, Sean Holmes, Dominic Domgoole, Max Stafford-Clark and Frank McGuinness, among others. 2 studio theatres and 4 other spaces suitable for rehearsals and other events.

Yvonne Arnaud Theatre

Millbrook, Guildford, Surrey GU1 3UX
tel 01483 440077
website www.yvonne-arnaud.co.uk
Facebook www.facebook.com/GuildfordYAT
Twitter @YvonneArnaud
Theatre Administrator and Associate Programmer Jamie Smith

Production details: The Yvonne Arnaud Theatre is a busy producing and presenting house, creating shows in Guildford and touring nationally, with many productions transferring to the West End. On both the main stage and in the Mill Studio an eclectic mix of classical and contemporary work by new, lesser-known and established writers is staged.

The Youth and Education facility offers an exciting mix of activities for young people and adults all year round. The Yvonne Arnaud opened the 80-seat Mill Studio in 1993, to provide a venue for work that would not otherwise be seen in Guildford. It also forms the base for the Youth Theatre's activities.

Belgrade Theatre

Belgrade Square, Coventry CV1 1GS
tel 024 7625 6431
email admin@belgrade.co.uk
website www.belgrade.co.uk
Theatre Director & Chief Executive Hamish Glen
Associate Director – Community & Education Justine Themen

Production details: Recent productions include: *One Night in November* (about the Coventry Blitz); *Scenes from a Marriage* (directed by Trevor Nunn); and 'legendary' annual pantomimes.

Birmingham Repertory Theatre

Centenary Square, Broad Street,
Birmingham B1 3AH
tel 0121 245 2000
email info@birmingham-rep.co.uk
website www.birmingham-rep.co.uk
Artistic Director Roxana Silbert *Associate Director Learning & Participation* Steve Ball *Casting Co-ordinator* Alison Solomon

Production details: Stages 15 productions in the main house each year, and 6 in the studio. Also runs Outreach, Community and Education programmes.

Casting procedures: "The play's director, a casting director and sometimes a producer handle casting for all Main House and Studio productions. We currently make use of freelance casting directors, specific to each production, administered by our in-house Casting Co-ordinator."

Birmingham Stage Company (BSC)

Suite 228, 162 Regent Street, London W1B 5TB
tel 020 7437 3391 *fax* 020 7437 3395
email info@birminghamstage.net
website www.birminghamstage.net
Actor/Manager Neal Foster

Production details: Founded in 1992, the BSC stages 5 shows each year, 4 of which tour nationally. Produces a range of plays with particular emphasis on new writing, and is recognised for its children's shows, which visit 60 venues around the UK. Recent productions include: *Proof* (West End); *Horrible Histories* (UK tour); *The Jungle Book* (UK tour); *Treasure Island* (UK tour); *Danny the Champion of the World*. Offers TMA/Equity approved contracts and subscribes to the Equity Pension Scheme.

Casting procedures: Uses freelance casting directors and sometimes holds general auditions. Casting breakdowns are published on the website, and in *Spotlight*. Submissions by hard copy only – no phone calls. "Do as much research as you can before submitting." Actively encourages applications from disabled actors.

The Bridge Theatre

3 Potters Field Park, London SE1 2SG
email info@bridgetheatre.co.uk
website www.bridgetheatre.co.uk
Artistic Director Nicholas Hytner

Production details: Founded by Nicholas Hytner and Nick Starr on leaving the National Theatre after 12 years, The Bridge focuses on the commissioning and production of new shows, as well as staging the occasional classic. The new 900-seat adaptable auditorium is designed to answer the needs of contemporary audiences and theatre-makers and respond to shows with different formats (end-stage, thrust stage and promenade). It is the first wholly new theatre of scale to be added to London's commercial sector in 80 years. Opening productions included *Young Marx, Julius Caesar, Nightfall, Allelujah!*

Bristol Old Vic

King Street, Bristol BS1 4ED
tel 0117 949 3993 *fax* 0117 949 3993
email admin@bristololdvic.org.uk
website www.bristololdvic.org.uk
Artistic Director Tom Morris

Production details: Bristol Old Vic is a theatre company founded in 1946 and based in a complex which includes the unique Theatre Royal, opened in

1766 – the oldest theatre auditorium in the UK, which many think the most beautiful. Bristol Old Vic is also unique in its close working relationship with the Bristol Old Vic Theatre School.

The Bush Theatre

7 Uxbridge Road, London W12 8LJ
tel 020 8743 3584
email info@bushtheatre.co.uk
website www.bushtheatre.co.uk
Facebook www.facebook.com/bushtheatre
Twitter @bushtheatre
Artistic Director Lynette Linton *Associate Director* Daniel Bailey *Producer* Jessica Campbell *Assistant Producer* Oscar Owen

Production details: Founded in 1972, the Bush specialises in developing and producing new writing from the widest range of perspectives. Stages 10 productions a year, totalling around 289 performances. Also tours productions, although the bulk of performances are at the Bush itself. Up to 8 actors are employed on each production, and the company offers TMA/Equity approved contracts. Recent productions include: *Guards at the Taj* and *HIR*.

Casting procedures: Employs freelance casting directors and does not hold general meetings or issue public casting breakdowns. Welcomes letters and emails from actors previously unknown to the company. Does not welcome showreels or invitations to view actors' websites. Actively encourages applications from disabled actors and promotes the use of inclusive casting.

Chichester Festival Theatre

Oaklands Park, Chichester PO19 6AP
website www.cft.org.uk
Artistic Director Daniel Evans *Executive Director* Kathy Bourne

Production details: Chichester Festival Theatre is one of the UK's flagship theatres, renowned for the exceptionally high standard of its productions as well as its work with the community and young people. The 1,300-seat Festival Theatre's bold thrust stage design makes it one of England's most striking playhouses; the 300-seat Minerva Theatre sits nearby. The annual Festival season runs from April to November, during which productions originated at Chichester reach an audience of over 230,000. Year-round programming continues through the winter with high-class touring productions. Recent West End transfers from Chichester (as originating producer) include the musical *Caroline, or Change*; Ian McKellen in *King Lear*; and James Graham's new play *Quiz*.

Casting procedures: Casting is done on a production-by-production basis.

Citizens Theatre

Gorbals, Glasgow G5 9DS
tel 0141 429 5561 *fax* 0141 429 7374
email info@citz.co.uk
website www.citz.co.uk
Artistic Director Dominic Hill *Production Administrator (Casting & Contracts)* Jacqueline Muir

Production details: Internationally renowned producing theatre, producing work in Glasgow and on tour as well as a pioneering year-round Citizens Learning and TAG programme for participants of all ages. Stages 7 productions a year, and undertakes 2 tours per annum. Offers TMA/Equity approved contracts.

Casting procedures: Does not use freelance casting directors. Holds limited general auditions once a year in June, and specific casting for individual shows as and when required. Welcomes emails from actors (with CVs and photographs), which should be submitted to **jackie@citz.co.uk**.

Coliseum Theatre

Fairbottom Street, Oldham OL1 3SW
tel 0161 624 1731
email mail@coliseum.org.uk
website www.coliseum.org.uk
Acting Associate Director Chris Lawson

Production details: A traditional repertory theatre producing 8 shows each year, with additional incoming tours and one-off special events. Also runs Outreach and Community programmes (contact Carly Henderson). Recent productions include: *Chicago, Boeing Boeing, Our Day Out* and *Hobson's Choice*.

Casting procedures: Does not use freelance casting directors. Casting breakdowns are available from the website. Welcomes letters and email submissions for specific roles (with CVs and photographs). Also accepts invitations to view individual actors' websites. Offers TMA/Equity approved contracts and subscribes to the Equity Pension Scheme. Will consider applications from disabled actors to play characters with disabilities.

Contact Theatre

Oxford Road, Manchester M15 6JA
tel 0161 274 3434 *fax* 0161 274 0640
website www.contactmcr.com
Artistic Director Matt Fenton

Production details: Since re-opening in 1999, Contact has emphasised its work with young adults (aged 13-30), putting participation at the heart of its ethos and activities. Contact is also one of the most culturally diverse theatres in the country; it was awarded the inaugural ECLIPSE award for cultural diversity, as well as the Arts Council's ART04 Award Northwest for 'outstanding achievement in the arts'.

Contact has striven to rewrite the rulebook on what 'theatre' can be. A wide range of touring theatre, music, dance and mixed-media work complements the theatre's in-house productions. The huge variety of participatory work with young people is integrated as closely as possible with the company's 'professional' programme. High quality and innovation are key to Contact's participatory work; leading companies working with young people at Contact have included: Frantic Assembly, RJC Dance, Quarantine, and Nitro – as well as a huge range of artists from hip hop to forum theatre and from verse drama to contemporary dance. Recent productions include: *Perfect* (Kaite O'Reilly and Paul Clay); *Slamdunk* (Felix Cross, Benji Reid with Nitro); *Dancing within Walls* (by Rani Moorthy with Rasa); *Dreaming of Bones* (with Red Ladder).

Casting procedures: Uses freelance casting directors and does not advertise casting breakdowns publicly. Welcomes letters (with CVs and photographs) from actors, but warns that it is unable to reply to unsolicited submissions. The theatre prefers not to receive showreels, emails and invitations to view actors' websites. Offers TMA/Equity approved contracts. Actively encourages applications from disabled actors and promotes the use of inclusive casting.

Curve

60 Rutland Street, Leicester LE1 1SB
tel 0116 2423560
email contactus@curvetheatre.co.uk
website www.curveonline.co.uk
Artistic Director Paul Kerryson *Associate Director (Community Engagement)* Suba Das *Associate Director (Participation & Learning)* Tim Ford

Production details: A new state-of-the-art theatre designed by world-renowned architect Rafael Vinoly. Has 2 auditoria, one with 750 seats and the other providing a 350-seat flexible smaller space. "A stunning glass façade encloses a magnificent foyer and mezzanine walkway, with views onto the café, bars, dressing rooms and workshop areas. The stage is placed at street level between the 2 auditoria."

Casting procedures: Uses both in-house and freelance casting directors. Holds general auditions; actors may write in for casting breakdowns as soon as productions are announced. Does not welcome unsolicited approaches by post or by email, showreels, or invitations to view individual actors' websites. Offers Equity-approved contracts as negotiated through TMA. Actively encourages applications from disabled actors and promotes the use of inclusive casting.

Derby Theatre

15 Theatre Walk, St Peter's Quarter, Derby DE1 2NF
tel 01332 593939
website www.derbytheatre.co.uk
Twitter @derbytheatre
Artistic Director Sarah Brigham

Production details: Derby Theatre has a long and rich history of delivering high-quality drama to audiences. Previously Derby Playhouse, Derby Theatre, which sits at the heart of the city, is now owned and run by the University of Derby. The theatre is rooted in the local community but international in its outlook, producing and presenting performances working with the best local, regional and national talent.

In 2012 Derby Theatre was awarded strategic funding by Arts Council England to develop a new model for regional theatre in the 21st century. From 2013, under the new artistic directorship of Sarah Brigham, who works alongside General Manager Gary Johnson, the theatre is transforming from a traditional producing house to an organisation of training, mentorship and artistic excellence. Its aim is to be an examplar – a new way of looking at the role and responsibility of theatre to its community. Derby's focus will ensure that each part of the theatre's process will be open to public learning opportunities, building the organisation's ability to take artistic risks by bringing creatives and audiences along on a creative path via the co-production of narratives.

Stages 6 productions annually in the Main House, and also works in youth theatre and TIE. Offers Equity-approved contracts as negotiated through UK Theatre, and subscribes to the Equity Pension Scheme. Recent productions include (from 2013): *Cooking with Elvis*, *The Seagull*, *Kes* and *The Odyssey*.

Casting procedures: Uses freelance casting directors. Actors are invited to email enquiries to **casting@derbytheatre.co.uk**. Welcomes letters (with CVs and photographs) from individual actors previously unknown to the company, sent by post or email, and accepts showreels as well as invitations to view actors' websites and visit productions. Applications from disabled actors are actively encouraged.

Donmar Warehouse

41 Earlham Street, London WC2H 9LX
tel 020 7240 4882
website www.donmarwarehouse.com
Artistic Director Michael Longhurst *Casting Director* Anna Cooper CDG

Production details: Independent producing house located in Covent Garden. The building originally served as a vat room and hop warehouse for the local brewery. In 1961 it was purchased by Donald Albery and converted into a rehearsal studio for the London Festival Ballet, which he formed with ballerina Margot Fonteyn. The theatre takes its name from them.

In the 1990s the Donmar was redesigned. The current theatre space retains the characteristics of the former warehouse while incorporating a new thrust stage. Recent productions include: *The Prime of Miss Jean Brodie*, *Aristocrats*, *Measure for Measure*, *Sweat*, *Sweet Charity* and *Appropriate*.

Casting procedures: Casting breakdowns are not publicly available. Offers TMA/SOLT/Equity

Theatre

approved contracts. Rarely has the opportunity to cast disabled actors.

The Dukes

Moor Lane, Lancaster LA1 1QE
tel 01524 598500
website www.dukes-lancaster.org
Director Joe Sumison *Theatre Secretary* Jacqui Wilson

Production details: A producing theatre with an independent cinema. Stages several home-produced shows each year in the main house (313 seats) and 1 in the studio (178 seats), with a focus on contemporary drama and outdoor, site-specific productions. Also runs a Youth Arts programme. Recent productions include: *The Life And Times Of Mitchell & Kenyon*, *No Fat Juliets*, *Sabbat* and *Robin Hood* (outdoor walkabout production).

Casting procedures: Does not use freelance casting directors. Casting breakdowns are obtainable through the website, postal application (with sae) and Spotlight. Welcomes letters (with CVs and photographs) but not email submissions. Showreels and invitations to view individual actors' websites are also accepted. Offers TMA/Equity approved contracts. Actively encourages applications from disabled actors and promotes the use of inclusive casting.

Dundee Rep and Scottish Dance Theatre Ltd

Tay Square, Dundee DD1 1PB
tel 01382 227684
website www.dundeerep.co.uk
Joint Chief Executive/Artistic Director (Dundee Rep) Andrew Panton *Executive Director/Joint Chief Executive* Liam Sinclair

Production details: Producing theatre housing Dundee Repertory Ensemble – Scotland's only permanent acting company. Stages 6 shows each year in the main house. Home also to Rep Engage, Scotland's largest permanent Creative Learning Department (contact Gemma Nicol). Recent productions include: *Much Ado ABout Nothing* and *Witness for the Prosecution*.

Casting procedures: Does not use freelance casting directors. Welcomes letters (with CVs and photographs) but not email submissions.

East Riding Theatre

10 Lord Roberts Road, Beverley,
East Yorkshire HU17 9BE
tel 01482 874050
email boxoffice@eastridingtheatre.co.uk
website www.eastridingtheatre.co.uk
Facebook www.facebook.com/ertheatre
Twitter @ertheatre
Artistic Director Adrian Rawlins

Founded in 2014, ERT is a professional producing and receiving house. It is managed by a voluntary board and run by community volunteers. ERT employs creative artists on a regular basis, building on its growing reputation as a high-quality performance venue. Minimum Equity rates apply. ERT also has a resident company: She Productions, an all female professional company who writes their own work and provides outreach work and in-house workshops. They are touring their original musical musical, *It's Different for Girls,* developed at ERT, to northern theatres in the autumn.

The main house, stages at least 4 productions a year and 5 or 6 small in-house events in the café bar (seats 50). Summer schools/community cast appear in some in-house productions. Recent productions include: *Goodnight Mister Tom* and *Beryl. Beryl* will be transferring to the Arcola Theatre in October and November 2019. ERT hosts the John Godber Company at least once a year.

Young People's Theatre and TIE: ERT performs 2 projects. Audience age range is 40-60. Additional skills required from actors include singing, the ability to play a musical instrument and to understake physical theatre. Actors are sometimes asked to lead workshops. Other Lives productions are an associated company bringing acccessible classics to ERT such as *Under Milkwood.*

Gate Theatre

Above Prince Albert Pub, 11 Pembridge Road, London W11 3HQ
tel 020 7229 5387 *fax* 020 7221 6055
email gate@gatetheatre.co.uk
website www.gatetheatre.co.uk
Artistic Director Ellen McDougall

Production details: Presents new writing and undiscovered classics from around the world in original and visually imaginative productions. Stages 5-6 shows each year. Also runs a Community/ Education programme. Ellen McDougall's inaugural season includes: The Unknown Island, Suzy Storck, Twilight, Trust, and a collaboration with ENO.

Casting procedures: Does not accept unsolicited CVs/submissions. "Individual directors tend to cast from their own lists – contact with the director is the best way to ensure that your application is considered. The Gate Theatre Company is committed to promoting theatre as an activity for all."

Greenwich Theatre

Crooms Hill, Greenwich, London SE10 8ES
tel 020 8858 4447 *fax* 020 8858 8042
email info@greenwichtheatre.org.uk
website www.greenwichtheatre.org.uk
Facebook www.facebook.com/ GreenwichTheatreLondon
Artistic & Executive Director James Haddrell

Production details: Currently mainly receiving touring productions, but occasionally produces shows in-house. Specialises in emerging companies, children's theatre and classic drama. Produces occasional showcases and semi-staged readings at different points of the year; these often involve professional performers. Recent productions include: Under My Thumb (London and Ed Fest Fringe); Grazing at a Distant Star (London and Ed Fest Fringe); Octopus (London and regional tour). Offers TMA/Equity approved contracts and subscribes to the Equity Pension Scheme.

Casting procedures: Generally uses freelance casting directors. "Please don't send unsolicited applications; do look at the casting section on the website, as we aim to provide advance information on our future productions, and answer standard questions. Most casting is concerned with the pantomime, so the best time to enquire is between May and July. We are keen to hear from locally based musical performers and especially anyone who has experience of working with young people." Does not have a specific policy on casting disabled actors, as the stage is not wheelchair accessible: "It depends on the actor's particular needs."

Hampstead Theatre
Eton Avenue, London NW3 3EU
tel 020 7722 9301
email info@hampsteadtheatre.com
website www.hampsteadtheatre.com
Artistic Director Roxana Silbert

Production details: Hampstead Theatre is a new-writing producing house, featuring new, mid-career and established writers. Plays are bold, original and entertaining. Presents at least 7 productions on the Main Stage each year, and 7 in the Downstairs studio. Recent productions include: The Olivier Award-nominated *The Phlebotomist* by Ella Road; the Pulitzer-winning *Cost of Living* by Martyna Majok; *I and You* by Lauren Gunderson (shown on Instagram for free in association with Instagram); the Olivier-winning *Caroline or Change* by Tony Kushner (transferred to the West End); Prism by Terry Johnson (UK no. 1 tour). Studio shows include *The Firm* by Ifeyinwa Frederick; *Every Day I Make Greatness Happen* by Richard Molloy and *The Strange Death of John Doe* by Fiona Doyle.

Casting procedures: Casting Director is Juliet Horsley with the use of other casting directors, depending on the play's director.

Harrogate Theatre
Oxford Street, Harrogate, North Yorks HG1 1QF
tel 01423 502710 *fax* 01423 563205
email info@harrogatetheatre.co.uk
website www.harrogatetheatre.co.uk
Chief Executive David Bown

Production details: Stages 3 productions annually in the main house; also works in Outreach and Community (key contact, Hannah Draper). Recent productions include: *Private Lives*, *The Emperor's New Clothes*, and *Dick Whittington*.

Casting procedures: Uses freelance casting directors and sometimes holds general auditions. Offers Equity approved contracts as negotiated through TMA, and participates in the Equity Pension Scheme. Will consider applications from disabled actors to play characters with disabilities. Harrogate Theatre has no resident Artistic Director, and so unsolicited approaches are not welcome. Please check the website for any casting opportunities.

HOME
2 Tony Wilson Place, Manchester M15 4FN
tel 0161 228 7621
email info@homemcr.org
website www.homemcr.org
Head of Programme Kevin Jamieson *Assistant Producer* Amanda Fawcett *Associate Companies* 1927, Quarantine

Production details: HOME was formed by the merger in 2012 of the Library Theatre Company and Cornerhouse, HOME produces the best in contemporary theatre, visual art and film, learning and participation, creative industries and digital innovation. The company's venue, opened in spring 2015, comprises a 500-seat theatre, a 150-seat flexible studio space, a 500m², four metre-high gallery space, five cinema screens, education spaces, digital production and broadcast facilities, a café bar, restaurant and offices. HOME provides new opportunities for artists and audiences to create work in different ways together and serves as a social and cultural hub – in one building visitors can see original new work across the visual arts, theatre and film.

Offers TMA/Equity-approved contracts.

Casting procedures: Uses freelance casting directors; casting breakdowns are available from the website and Spotlight. Also holds a limited number of general auditions/interviews in the summer. Actors requesting inclusion in these are advised to write in March or April. HOME encourages applications from actors with disability, and promotes inclusive casting.

Hull Truck Theatre
50 Ferensway, Hull HU2 8LB
tel 01482 224800
email admin@hulltruck.co.uk
website www.hulltruck.co.uk
Artistic Director Mark Babych *Casting* Enquiries to Administration Department

Hull Truck Theatre is a pioneering theatre with a unique Northern voice, locally rooted, global in outlook, inspiring artists, audiences and communities to reach their greatest potential.

It produces and presents inspiring theatre that relects the diversity of a modern Britain. It provides the resources, space and support to grow people and ideas, it is an ambassador for Hull, a flagship for the region and a welcoming home for local communities.

Through work with schools and local communities Hull Truck Theatre engages with thousands of young people, disabled groups and adults, offering opportunities to participate in the arts, whether as the first step into a career, a way to build confidence and meet new people, or as part of a rounded education.

"We tell inspiring stories dug from the heart of our city, alongside tales from the wider world, that reflect the diverse range of communities and creative voices that populate our nation. We produce exceptional drama made here in Hull, often showcasing new talent, and continuing the momentum of Hull UK City of Culture 2017.

We are ambitious and bold, committed to our core values of Inclusion, Innovation and Integrity." Mark Babych, Artistic Director

Key Theatre

Embankment Road, Peterborough, Cambridgeshire PE1 1EF
tel 01733 207237
website www.peterboroughkeytheatre.co.uk
Artistic Director Michael Cross *Youth Theatre/TIE Officer* Paul Collings

Production details: Mainly a receiving house with occasional in-house productions including an annual pantomime and TIE tours. Stages up to 4 shows each year with co-production opportunities.

Casting procedures: Does not use freelance casting directors. Occasional general auditions. Unsolicited communications are not advised. Casting requirements are sometimes available through the website, but usually through professional casting services, Spotlight link and *The Stage*. "Actors working in the area (and especially touring to the Key) are always encouraged to make contact with the Artistic Director and introduce themselves. Invitations to see artists working in productions are always welcome, and, wherever possible, accepted!" Offers TMA/Equity contracts and does not subscribe to the Equity Pension Scheme. Rarely (or never) has the opportunity to employ disabled actors.

The Kiln (formerly Tricycle Theatre)

269 Kilburn High Road, London NW6 7JR
tel 020 7372 6611
email info@kilntheatre.com
website www.kilntheatre.com
Artistic Director Indhu Rubasingham

Production details: Based in Kilburn, Kiln Theatre creates internationally renowned, high-quality, engaging and innovative work which presents the world through a variety of different lenses, amplifying unheard voices into the mainstream. Led by Artistic Director Indhu Rubasingham and Executive Director Daisy Heath, it makes theatre that crosses continents and tells big stories about human connections across cultures, race and languages.

Recent productions include *White Teeth* by Zadie Smith, adapted by Stephen Sharkey, *Holy Sh!t* by

Alexis Zegerman, *Approaching Empty* by Ishy Din, *The Son* by Florian Zeller and *The Half God of Rainfall* by Inua Ellams. Recent collaborations include the National Theatre, Tamasha and Sundance Theatre Lab (US).

Education details: The ambitious Creative Learning programme aims to champion the imagination, aspiration and potential of the Brent community young and old. Invests in creating meaningful relationships with young people to inspire and encourage their creativity, their confidence and self-esteem. Works with older people to create a thriving community around the theatre.

Casting details: Kiln Theatre encourages artists of all ages and backgrounds. Uses freelance casting directors for main house productions. For casting information contact the team at artistic@kilntheatre.com.

Leeds Playhouse (formerly West Yorkshire Playhouse)

Playhouse Square, Quarry Hill, Leeds LS2 7UP
tel 0113 213 7800 *fax* 0113 213 7250
website www.wyp.org.uk
Artistic Director James Brining

Production details: Leeds Playhouse opened nearly 50 years ago. It is a cultural hub, a place where people gather to tell and share stories and to engage in world class theatre. The Playhouse makes work which is pioneering and relevant, seeking out the best companies and artists to create inspirational theatre in the heart of Yorkshire. From large-scale spectacles to intimate performance, the Playhouse develops and makes work for the stage, found spaces, touring, schools and community venues. As dedicated collaborators, Leeds Playhouse works regularly with other organisations from across the UK, and some of the most distinctive and original voices in theatre today.

Through its Artistic Development programme Furnace, the Playhouse develops work with established practitioners and finds, nurtures and supports new voices, as well as cultivating artists by providing creative space for writers, directors, companies and individual theatre-makers to refine their practice at any stage of their career. The Playhouse's sector-leading Creative Engagement team works with over 10,000 people aged 0–95 every year through a range of weekly workshops and exciting creative projects using theatre to open up possibilities, reaching out to refugee communities, young people, students, older people and people with learning disabilities.

Leeds Playhouse's Autumn/Winter 2019 season will take place back in the redeveloped theatre following a £15.8 million transformation. The new building will have a new city-facing entrance improved access to and around the theatre in its brand-new foyer spaces, and a new studio theatre, the Bramall Rock Void.

Offers TMA/Equity contracts and does not subscribe to the Equity Pension Scheme. Casting procedures: Currently Leeds Playhouse casts through agents' submissions and works with casting directors on productions on a show-by-show basis. Casting information is available on the website. Leeds Playhouse is an equal opportunities employer in relation to casting.

Live Theatre
Broad Chare, Quayside,
Newcastle upon Tyne NE1 3DQ
tel 0191 261 2694 *fax* 0191 232 2224
email info@live.org.uk
website www.live.org.uk
Artistic Director Joe Douglas

Production details: New writing theatre established in 1973. Produces 8-10 shows each year in the main house. Also runs TIE, Outreach and Community programmes.

Casting procedures: Does not use freelance casting directors. Welcomes submissions (with CVs and photographs), sent by post or email. Actors may write at any time. Showreels and invitations to view individual actors' websites are also accepted. Offers ITC/Equity approved contracts. Actively encourages applications from disabled actors and promotes the use of inclusive casting.

Liverpool Everyman & Playhouse Theatres
5-11 Hope Street, Liverpool L1 9BH
tel 0151 708 3700 *fax* 0151 708 3701
email info@everymanplayhouse.com
website www.everymanplayhouse.com
Artistic Director Gemma Bodinetz

Production details: The Everyman's acting company runs from January until July each year. This is followed by an autumn season featuring co-productions with theatre companies which share a similar ethos. This approach aims to inspire and nurture local actors, writers, creatives and audiences, and to have an impact internationally.

'Residences' at the Playhouse allow the theatre to regularly host a selection of the finest national and international companies, to help form bonds with audiences, communities, young people and artists in Liverpool.

The theatres' award-winning Young Everyman Playhouse scheme provides young people with practical training across all aspects of theatre.

Lyric Hammersmith Theatre
Lyric Square, King Street, London W6 0QL
tel 020 8741 6850 *fax* 020 8741 5965
email enquiries@lyric.co.uk
website www.lyric.co.uk
Artistic Director Rachel O'Riordan *Executive Director* Sian Alexander

Production details: The Lyric Hammersmith Theatre is one of the UK's leading producing theatres, creating world class theatre from the heart of Hammersmith, the theatre's home for more than a 130 years.

The Lyric has two stages – a 130 seat contemporary Studio and 590 seat Frank Matcham-designed Main House. It makes work that rejoices in the unique relationship these theatres have with their audience – theatre that is bold, brave and humane.

Central to the Lyric's values and ethos is a commitment to providing opportunities for children and young people from disadvantaged and difficult circumstances. It has gained a national reputation for its ground breaking work that creates pathways into the arts for young talent from all backgrounds, helping to diversify our industry.

Casting procedures: Different directors cast their own productions, using freelance casting directors.

Lyric Theatre
55 Ridgeway Street, Belfast BT9 5FB
email info@lyrictheatre.co.uk
website www.lyrictheatre.co.uk
Executive Producer Jimmy Fay *Casting Director* Clare Gault *Producer* Bronagh McFeely

Production details: Northern Ireland's leading full-time producing house for professional theatre. Presents a distinctive, challenging and entertaining programme of new writing as well as contemporary and classic plays by Irish, European and American writers. Recent productions include: *Educating Rita*, *The 39 Steps*, *Here Comes the Night* and *Smiley*.

Casting procedures: *Casting Director* Clare Gault
Does not normally use freelance casting directors. Welcomes submissions (Spolight or online CVs preferred), sent by post or email. Actors may write in at any time. Advises actors to check the website for its future programme. Offers TMA/Equity approved contracts. Will consider applications from disabled actors to play characters with disabilities.

Manor Pavilion Theatre
Manor Road, Sidmouth, Devon EX10 8RP
tel 020 7636 4343 *fax* 020 7636 2323

Since the death of Charles Vance, the management of the summer season has been taken over by Paul Taylor Mills Ltd.

Menier Chocolate Factory
51/53 Southwark Street, London SE1 1RU
tel 020 7907 7060
email info@menierchocolatefactory.com
website www.menierchocolatefactory.com
Artistic Director David Babani

Production details: The Menier Chocolate Factory, which opened in 2004, is an award-winning 180-seat off-West End theatre which stages plays and musicals, live music and stand-up comedy. "There's nowhere

Theatre

quite like the Chocolate Factory anywhere … the bubbliest kid on the block and one of London's great theatre hopes." (*Daily Telegraph*)

Mercury Theatre

Balkerne Gate, Colchester, Essex CO1 1PT
tel 01206 577006 *fax* 01206 769607
email info@mercurytheatre.co.uk
website www.mercurytheatre.co.uk
Creative Director Ryan McBryde

Production details: The Mercury is a regional theatre based in Colchester which creates, hosts, and tours performances nationally. Staging classic and contemporary drama, musical theatre, new writing, panto, dance, and comedy, the Mercury also supports new talent and runs a Community programme (contact Thomas Freeth). Recent productions include: *The Butterfly Lion*, *Dial M For Murder* and *Betty Blue Eyes*.

Casting procedures: For all casting enquiries, email **casting@mercurytheatre.co.uk**

The Mill at Sonning Theatre

Sonning Eye, Reading RG4 6TY
tel 0118 969 6039
email admin@millatsonning.com
website www.millatsonning.com
Artistic Director Sally Hughes

Production details: Popular 'dinner theatre' venue, producing a range of plays for audiences to watch while eating a meal. Recent productions include: *French Without Tears*, *Time to Kill*, and *It Runs in the Family*.

Casting procedures: Forthcoming productions are listed on the website. Actors should send their details, along with specific casting suggestions, to the Artistic Director 2 months before each show.

National Theatre

South Bank, London SE1 9PX
tel 020 7452 3178
email casting@nationaltheatre.org.uk
website www.nationaltheatre.org.uk
Artistic Director Rufus Norris *Head of Casting* Alastair Coomer CDG *Senior Casting Associate* Isabella Odoffin CDG *Senior Casting Assistant* Bryony Jarvis-Taylor *Casting Assistant* Naomi Downham

Production details: The National Theatre's mission is to make world class theatre that's entertaining, challenging and inspiring – and to make it for everyone. It aims to reach the widest possible audience and to be as inclusive, diverse and national as possible with a broad range of productions that play in London, on tour around the UK, on Broadway and across the globe. The National Theatre's extensive UK-wide learning and participation programme supports young people's creative education through performance and writing programmes like Connections, New Views and Let's

Play. Its major new initiative Public Acts creates extraordinary acts of theatre and community; the first Public Acts production was 2018's *Pericles*. The National Theatre extends its reach through digital programmes including the free streaming service National Theatre Collection, and NT Live, which broadcasts some of the best of British theatre to over 2,500 venues in 65 countries. The National Theatre invests in the future of theatre by developing talent, creating bold new work and building audiences, partnering with a range of UK theatres and theatre companies.

Casting details: Actors known to the theatre may be approached directly, but casting is predominantly carried out through agents. The NT will first approach agents to check actors' availability, then audition a shortlist. New talent is actively sought out, and the casting team sees several performances a week within London and (less frequently) outside. The Casting Department champions diversity in all forms within casting decisions and is dedicated to creating a safe and supportive audition environment where actors are empowered to do their best work. It also attends drama schools' showcases and will sometimes approach other casting directors known to the NT.

National Theatre of Scotland (NTS)

Civic House, 26 Civic Street, Glasgow G4 9RH
tel 0141 221 0970 *fax* 0141 248 7241
email info@nationaltheatrescotland.com
website www.nationaltheatrescotland.com
Artistic Director Laurie Sansom *Associate Director* Graham McLaren *Artistic Development Producer* Caroline Newall

Production details: The National Theatre of Scotland launched to the public in February 2006. It has no building, and instead takes theatre all over Scotland and beyond, working with new and existing venues and companies to create and tour theatre of the highest quality. This theatre takes place in the great buildings of Scotland, but also in site-specific locations, community halls and drill halls, car parks and forests. To date, over 130,000 people have seen or participated in its work. NTS has produced 28 pieces of work in 62 locations, from the Shetlands to Dumfries, and from Belfast to London. In 2007/8 NTS toured to the USA and Australasia.

Scottish theatre has always been for the people, led by great performances, great stories and great playwrights. The National Theatre of Scotland exists to build a new generation of theatregoers, as well as reinvigorating the existing ones; to create theatre on a national and international scale that is contemporary, confident and forward-looking; to bring together brilliant artists, designers, composers, choreographers and playwrights; and to exceed expectations of what and where theatre can be.

Offers actors in-house ITC/Equity approved contracts and does not subscribe to the Equity Pension Scheme.

Casting procedures: Each casting process is led by the director of each production, with advisory support from the NTS Artistic Team and Casting Director. When casting for specific shows, the Casting Director puts out a call to agents through *Spotlight.*

The NTS Artistic team makes every effort to see every theatrical event produced in Scotland, maximising the number of actors that NTS sees. The team also responds to individual requests to see actors' work. All actors' CVs and headshots that NTS receives are acknowledged and kept on file in the NTS office. The NTS Casting Director reviews these files at regular intervals, and Directors are encouraged to go through these files before casting their productions. In addition, NTS holds an annual 2-day casting workshop to connect with actors who have sent in CVs but whose work it has been unable to see during the year. Actively encourages applications from disabled actors and promotes the use of inclusive casting.

National Theatre Wales
30 Castle Arcade, Cardiff CF10 1BW
tel 029 2035 3070
email admin@nationaltheatrewales.org
website www.nationaltheatrewales.org
Artistic Director Kully Thiarai

Production details: National Theatre Wales has been making English-language productions in locations all over Wales, the UK, internationally and online since 2010. It operates from a small base in Cardiff's city centre, but works all over the country and beyond, using Wales' rich and diverse landscape, it's towns, cities and villages, its incredible stories and rich talent as its inspiration.

Casting procedures: See **http:// community.nationaltheatrewales.org/group/actors**

The New Wolsey Theatre
Civic Drive, Ipswich IP1 2AS
tel 01473 295900
email info@wolseytheatre.co.uk
website www.wolseytheatre.co.uk
Artistic Director Peter Rowe *Associate Director* Rob Salmon *Chief Executive* Sarah Holmes

Production details: Mixed producing/receiving house, staging 3-4 productions a year in the main house and specialising in musical theatre using actor-musicians. Alongside these productions, the theatre also produces 4 plays per year in our studio space with its Young Company and Youth Theatres. It also works in creative learning and community outreach; the contact for this is Rob Salmon, Associate Director.

Casting procedures: Uses freelance casting directors and does not hold general auditions. Does not welcome unsolicited approaches from actors, unless in response to a casting breakdown. Offers TMA/ Equity-approved contracts. Actively encourages applications from disabled actors and promotes the use of inclusive casting.

New Vic Theatre
Etruria Road, Newcastle-under-Lyme ST5 0JG
tel 01782 717954 *fax* 01782 712885
email admin@newvictheatre.org.uk
website www.newvictheatre.org.uk
Facebook @NewVicTheatreStaffordshire
Twitter @NewVicTheatre
Instagram @New_Vic_Theatre
Artistic Director Theresa Heskins

Production details: Purpose-built theatre-in-the-round with a full programme of in-house drama, concerts and occasional touring productions. Stages 10 shows each year in the main house. Also very active with Outreach and Education programmes (contact Sue Moffat and Jill Rezzano respectively). Recent productions include: *The Wind in the Willows*, *Intemperance, The 39 Steps* and *Brassed Off.*

Casting procedures: Theatre uses an associate casting director through Spotlight link. Casting breakdowns are posted in the casting section of the website. Submissions should be specific and referenced to a particular role.

Northern Stage (formerly Newcastle Playhouse)
Barras Bridge, Newcastle NE1 7RH
tel 0191 242 7200 *fax* 0191 242 7257
email directors@northernstage.co.uk
website www.northernstage.co.uk
Artistic Director Lorne Campbell

Production details: Northern Stage is the largest producing theatre company in the North East of England. The building, formerly known as Newcastle Playhouse & Gulbenkian Studio, re-opened in summer 2006 as Northern Stage following a £9m redevelopment programme. The new building has 3 stages and presents and produces a wide repertoire of UK and international theatre. Staging 6 shows a year, the company also works on participatory projects, with Kylie Lloyd as the lead contact. Touring productions in 2009/2010 included: *Oh What A Lovely War* and *Apples*; 2012 touring *Close the Coalhouse Door*. Offers TMA/Equity-approved contracts and subscribes to the Equity Pension Scheme.

Casting procedures: Casting breakdowns, when available, are published on the website. Actively encourages applications from disabled actors and promotes the use of inclusive casting.

Nottingham Playhouse
Wellington Circus, Nottingham NG1 5AF
tel 0115 947 4361
email enquiry@nottinghamplayhouse.co.uk
website www.nottinghamplayhouse.co.uk

Theatre

Artistic Director Adam Penford *Associate Director* Fiona Buffini *Casting Director* Sooki McShane

Production details: Nottingham Theatre Trust was founded in 1948 and moved to its current location in 1963. Stages 10 shows each year in the main house, two own-produced shows in the studio. Also runs Participation programme. Recent productions include: *Touched, East is East, The Grapes of Wrath*, and *Sleuth.*

Casting procedures: Does not use freelance casting directors. Casting breakdowns are available from the casting director, Sooki McShane. Welcomes letters (with CVs and photographs) but not email submissions. Showreels and invitations to view individual actors' websites are also accepted.

Nuffield Southampton Theatres

142-144 Above Bar Street, Southampton SO14 7DU
tel 023 8031 5500 *fax* 023 8031 5511
email info@nstheatres.co.uk
website www.nstheatres.co.uk
Director and Chief Executive Sam Hodges

Production details: A regional theatre producing a range of modern classics, adaptations and new writing. Stages shows in the main house. Recent productions include: *The Shadow Factory, A Streetcar Named Desire* and *Fantastic Mr Fox.* Offers UK Theatre/Equity-approved contracts and subscribes to the Equity Pension Scheme.

Casting procedures: Uses freelance casting directors. Casting breakdowns are sometimes available through the Equity Job Information Service. "We consider applications from disabled actors in exactly the same way as applications from able-bodied actors."

Octagon Theatre

Howell Croft South, Bolton BL1 1SB
tel 01204 529407
email info@octagonbolton.co.uk
website www.octagonbolton.co.uk
Facebook /OctagonBolton
Twitter @octagontheatre
Instagram @octagontheatre
Artistic Director Lotte Wakeham

Production details: Stages 8-9 shows each year in the main auditorium, currently producing a season of off-site work while the theatre building is closed for redevelopment. Also runs Education, Outreach and Community programmes. Recent productions include: *And Did Those Feet, The Wonderful Wizard of Oz, The Rise and Fall of Little Voice* and *The Importance of Being Earnest.*

Casting procedures: Occasionally uses freelance casting directors. Actors should refer to the casting page of the company's website.

The Old Vic

The Cut, London SE1 8NB
tel 020 7928 2651 *fax* 020 7261 9161
email enquiries@oldvictheatre.com
website www.oldvictheatre.com
Artistic Director Matthew Warchus *Casting Director* Jessica Ronane (020 3362 0408)

Production details: The Old Vic is London's independent not-for-profit theatre, a world leader in creativity and entertainment. The Old Vic is mercurial: it can be transformed into a theatre in the round, a space for music and comedy, has played host to opera, dance, cinema, music hall, classical dramas, variety, clowns, big spectacles and novelty acts. It was the original home of the English National Opera, the Sadler's Wells dance company and the National Theatre. It's also been a tavern, a college, a coffee house, a lecture hall and a meeting place.

All of this is now in the bones of the building and is as important a part of its open-armed, inclusive, welcoming personality as its grand historic decor and the iconic performances and famous productions it has housed.

Today, Artistic Director Matthew Warchus is building on 200 years of creative adventure, with the Old Vic recently being hailed as London's most eclectic and frequently electrifying theatre. Under his leadership, we aim to be a surprising, unpredictable, ground-breaking, rule-breaking, independent beacon of accessible, uplifting and unintimidating art.

Recent productions include *Girl from the North Country, Woyzeck, King Lear* (Glenda Jackson), *Fanny and Alexander*, and *Wise Children.*

Open Air Theatre

Inner Circle, Regent's Park, London NW1 4NR
website www.openairtheatre.org
Artistic Director Timothy Shaeder

Production details: Stages 4 shows each year in the main house, including 1 family show. Recent productions include: *Much Ado About Nothing; The Tempest* re-imagined for everyone aged 6 or over; *The Importance of Being Earnest;* and *Hello, Dolly!*

Casting procedures: Uses freelance casting directors, who send full casting breakdowns to agents as required for each production. "Unfortunately we are unable to consider unsolicited CVs."

Orange Tree Theatre

1 Clarence Street, Richmond TW9 2SA
tel 020 8940 0141 *fax* 020 8332 0369
email admin@orangetreetheatre.co.uk
website www.orangetreetheatre.co.uk
Artistic Director Paul Miller

Production details: The Orange Tree produces and co-produces a mixture of new writing, re-discoveries, contemporary revivals in its uniquely intimate theatre in the round. Education and Participation work forms a major area of activity. Stages 8/9 shows each year.

Casting procedures: Please email **admin@orangetreetheatre.co.uk** for casting

Producing theatres 149

enquiries. Actively encourages applications from disabled actors and promotes the use of inclusive casting.

Park Theatre

Clifton Terrace, Finsbury Park, London N4 3JP
tel 020 7870 6876
email info@parktheatre.co.uk
email hire@parktheatre.co.uk
website www.parktheatre.co.uk
Artistic Director Jez Bond *Executive Director* Rachael Williams

Production details: Park Theatre programmes a balance of new writing and classics, plays and musicals across its two theatres - Park90 and Park200.

Looks for work that has a strong narrative and emotional drive and plays that can flourish within the intimacy of smaller theatres. Maintains a good gender balance of male and female roles on stage within a season as well as generally encouraging BAME stories and casting.Generally prefers productions with smaller casts and high production values. Recent productions include: *Boys in the Band* by Matt Crowley starring Mark Gatiss, *Madame Rubinstein* by John Misto starring Miriam Margolyes, and Ian McKellen in *Shakespeare, Tolkien, Others & You.* *Toast* by Richard Bean starring Matthew Kelly (UK tour and New York transfer), *An Audience with Jimmy Savile* by Jonathan Maitland starring Alistair McGowan (Edinburgh transfer) and *The Patriotic Traitor* by Jonathan Lynn starring Tom Conti and Laurence Fox.

Both produces and receives Equity-approved contracts and subscribes to Equity pension scheme, with UK Theatre agreement where applicable.

Casting procedures: Uses freelance casting directors, but does not hold general auditions. Casting breakdowns are periodically available via Spotlight. Due to small staff, unsolicited CVs cannot be responded to.

Perth Theatre, Horsecross Arts

Horsecross Arts Ltd, Perth Theatre & Concert Hall, Mill Street, Perth PH1 5HZ
tel 01738 472700
email info@horsecross.co.uk
website www.horsecross.co.uk
Artistic Director Lu Kemp

Production details: Perth Theatre, Horsecross Arts produces 4 shows a year and programmes work from independent touring companies and producing houses under the Artistic Directorship of Lu Kemp. Co-produces work with both Scottish and UK venues and produces a family pantomime. Runs Perth Youth Theatre, a vibrant Creative Learning programme, and is committed to providing innovative and relevant work for Scottish audiences.

The Casting process is under review, with a view to reflecting greater diversity and stronger representation of local artists (email: casting@horsecross.co.uk).

Pitlochry Festival Theatre

Port-Na-Craig, Pitlochry PH16 5DR
tel 01796 484600
email admin@pitlochryfestivaltheatre.com
website www.pitlochryfestivaltheatre.com
Artistic Director Elizabeth Newman

Production details: Founded in 1951, Pitlochry Festival Theatre is a producing and presenting theatre located in the Perthshire Highlands. Comprises the main house (capacity 538), an extensive production facility, and *Explorers*: The Scottish Plant Hunters Garden, containing open-air performance spaces. Between May and October each year a 14-18 strong acting ensemble presents a season of 6 major productions performed in day-change repertoire. An autumn production is presented in October/November and a winter, large-scale musical is presented in December. Visiting theatre, music, dance, opera and other activities are presented during the winter months. Also runs Creative Learning programmes. Recent productions include: *Chicago, Singin' in the Rain, The Rise and Fall of Little Voice, Quality Street, Travesties* and *Before the Party*. TMA/Equity contracts are offered.

Casting procedures: Sometimes uses freelance casting directors. Recruits new members of the acting ensemble each autumn and winter, with a detailed casting breakdown published each spring-summer and autumn direct to agents and via Spotlight. The closing date for applications is usually in mid-November; auditions are then held in London and Edinburgh in November, December and January. Submissions at any other time – or not in response to the casting breakdown – will not be considered. The theatre actively encourages applications from disabled actors and promotes the use of inclusive casting.

Queen's Theatre

Billet Lane, Hornchurch, Essex RM11 1QT
website www.queens-theatre.co.uk
Artistic Director Douglas Rintoul

Production details: Has been a producing theatre since it was first established in 1953. Currently works with actor-musicians in a permanent repertory company model. Stages 8 shows each year in the main house. Also runs TIE, Outreach and Community programmes. Recent productions include: *Return to the Forbidden Planet, The Great Gatsby* and *Godspell*.

Casting procedures: Does not use freelance casting directors. Holds general auditions; actors should write in April or May requesting inclusion. Welcomes letters (with CVs and photographs) from actor-musicians only.

Rose Theatre Kingston

24-26 High Street, Kingston-upon-Thames, Surrey KT1 1HL

Theatre

tel 020 8546 6983
email admin@rosetheatrekingston.org
website www.rosetheatrekingston.org
Chief Executive Robert O'Dowd *Executive Producer* Jerry Gunn

The Rose Theatre Kingston opened its doors to the public in January 2008 with English Touring Productions' production of *Uncle Vanya*, directed by Sir Peter Hall. The design of the theatre was inspired by the Elizabethan Rose on London's Bankside; Kingston's Rose has the same horse-shoe shaped auditorium and an open lozenge stage, creating a sense of intimacy between actors and audiences. The Rose auditorium has a capacity of more than 850 across 3 tiers of seating, including a pit area where audiences can sit on cushions for just £7. In addition to the main space there is a studio, capacity 120, and a gallery, capacity 60. These spaces host a variety of talks and workshops led by theatre writers and practitioners. The theatre also has a strong connection with Kingston University, where it facilitates the University's MA in Classical Drama.

The Rose presents a combination of home-produced drama and received work. Since opening, it has produced 16 home-grown productions, including *Love's Labour's Lost* and *A Midsummer Night's Dream*, directed by Sir Peter Hall; *The Winslow Boy* and *The Lady from the Sea*, directed by Stephen Unwin; and two rep seasons.

Royal & Derngate Theatres

Guildhall Road, Northampton NN1 1DP
tel 01604 626222 (Admin), 01604 627566 (TIE)
website www.royalandderngate.com
Artistic Director James Dacre *Associate Director* Dani Parr

Recently the subject of a £15 million redevelopment project, the theatre offers 2 auditoria and 'Underground', a creativity centre that is home to the Youth Theatre and a wide range of workshops and projects for the local community. The theatre's annual pantomime is produced by Qdos (see entry under *Pantomime producers* on page 237).

Royal Court Theatre

Sloane Square, London SW1W 8AS
tel 020 7565 5050 *fax* 020 7565 5001
email info@royalcourttheatre.com
website www.royalcourttheatre.com
Facebook www.facebook.com/facebook.com/royalcourttheatre
Twitter @royalcourt
Artistic Director Vicky Featherstone *Executive Director* Lucy Davies *Casting Director* Amy Ball *Associate Directors* Lucy Morrison, Hamish Pirie, John Tiffany, Graham Whybrow *Associate Playwright* Simon Stephens *Associate Artists* Carrie Cracknell, Simon Godwin, Katie Mitchell

Production details: Since 1956 the English Stage Company at the Royal Court has focused on developing, funding and producing new writing. Productions frequently transfer to the West End and Broadway. Stages about 14 productions a year. Also presents an extensive play development programme incorporating workshops and rehearsed readings. Recent productions include: *X* by Alistair McDowall, *Hangmen* by Martin McDonagh, *Escaped Alone* by Caryl Churchill, *Cyprus Avenue* by David Ireland, *I See You* by Mongiwekhaya, *YEN* by Anna Jordan, *Linda* by Penelope Skinner, *Plaques and Tangles* by Nicola Wilson, *Violence and Son* by Gary Owen. Offers SOLT/TMA/UK Theatre/Equity-approved contracts and does not subscribe to the Equity Pension Scheme.

Casting procedures: Welcomes submissions (with CVs and photographs) by post or email all year round.

Royal Exchange Theatre

St Ann's Square, Manchester M2 7DH
tel 0161 833 9833
website www.royalexchange.co.uk
Joint Artistic Directors Roy Alexander Weise, Bryony Shanahan *Head of Casting* Jerry Knight-Smith *Director of Creative Learning and Engagement* Inga Hirst

Production details: Manchester's leading producing theatre company, comprising a main theatre and studio space. Presents 8-9 productions, on average, in the main theatre and 3-4 in the studio each year. The programme is a mixture of reimagined classics from the repertoire, musicals and an ambitious programme of new plays and contemporary theatre. Also runs Creative Learning and Community Engagement programmes involving schools, young people, community groups and theatre enthusiasts of all ages. Work is based around the theatre's repertoire and its unique building. Where possible, the department leads sessions in the theatre, and frequently works with other departments around the building to give participants an insight into how theatre, and particularly the Royal Exchange, work. Recent productions include: *Our Town*, *Happy Days*, *Guys and Dolls* and *Jubilee*.

Casting procedures: Head of Casting works with a freelance associate who together coordinate casting for each show. Actors are contracted for individual plays rather than for a season of work. Releases advance production information to around 200 agents on the website. Detailed casting breakdowns are only available for some shows.

Will consider attending performances at venues in the North West and London with sufficient notice. Accepts submissions (with CVs and photographs), but actors should bear in mind that the department expects to receive more than 2000 CVs and photos each season – and more in the summer months following graduation at the drama schools. All submissions are considered but they are not kept on file indefinitely.

Royal Lyceum Edinburgh

Grindlay Street, Edinburgh EH3 9AX
tel 0131 248 4800 *fax* 0131 228 3955
email info@lyceum.org.uk
website www.lyceum.org.uk
Artistic Director David Greig

Production details: The Royal Lyceum is one of
Scotland's largest producing theatre companies with a
season of in-house drama productions and co-
productions running from September to June. In
addition, the theatre stages a Christmas show.
Occasionally tours in Scotland and abroad, limited
hosting of touring companies, and runs an ambitious
and acclaimed Creative Learning Department. Recent
productions include: *The Duchess of Malfi, Local
Hero, Touching the Void,* and *Wendy and Peter Pan.*

Casting procedures: Does not offer general
auditions. "Casting depends on individual directors'
choices."

Royal Shakespeare Company

Royal Shakespeare Theatre, Waterside,
Stratford-upon-Avon, Warwickshire, CV37 6BB
tel 020 7845 0500
London Office: 1 Earlham Street, London WC2H 9LL
website www.rsc.org.uk
Artistic Director Gregory Doran *Deputy Artistic
Director* Erica Whyman *Head of Casting* Hannah
Miller *Casting Director* Helena Palmer

Production details: The Royal Shakespeare Company
creates Shakespeare for everyone, made in Stratford-
upon-Avon and shared around the world. The
Company produces an inspirational artistic
programme each year, setting Shakespeare in context,
alongside the work of his contemporaries and today's
writers. Productions begin life at the RSC's Stratford
workshops and theatres, and are brought to the
widest possible audience through touring, residencies,
live broadcasts and online activity.
    The RSC is at heart an ensemble company, with
actors most often being contracted to perform in
several productions in a season of work.

Casting procedures: We welcome performance
notices sent 4-6 weeks in advance, and travel all over
the UK. Please send correspondence including
invitations and submissions for specific productions
to **suggestions@rsc.org.uk**, and preferably in relation
to specific productions.

Shakespeare's Globe

21 New Globe Walk, Bankside, London SE1 9DT
tel 020 7902 1400 *fax* 020 7902 1401
email info@shakespearesglobe.com
website www.shakespearesglobe.com
Artistic Director Michelle Terry *Head of Casting*
Karishma Balani *Casting Associate* Rebecca Murphy

Production details: A reconstruction of
Shakespeare's Globe, the theatre has a repertoire

which includes the work of Shakespeare, his
contemporaries and new writing. The season runs
from April to October with up to 10 productions
staged each year. Opened second theatre in 2014, The
Sam Wanamaker Playhouse, a reconstruction of an
indoor Jacobean theatre. Recent productions
include: *The Merchant of Venice, Nell Gwyn, The
Taming of the Shrew* and *Imogen.*

Casting procedures: Welcomes letters (with CVs and
photographs) but not email submissions: prefers
invitations to see actors in performance. Actors
should write to the Casting Department. Offers actors
Equity-approved contracts through an in-house
agreement. Actively encourages applications from
disabled actors and promotes the use of inclusive
casting. The website has more information about
casting procedures.

Sheffield Theatres

55 Norfolk Street, Sheffield S1 1DA
tel 0114 249 5999
email info@sheffieldtheatres.co.uk
website www.sheffieldtheatres.co.uk
Artistic Director Robert Hastie

Production details: Comprises 3 theatres: the
Crucible Theatre (thrust stage, 960 capacity), the
Studio Theatre (200-400 capacity) and the Lyceum
Theatre (pros. arch, 1,168 capacity). Stages 5-6 shows
each year in the Crucible, 3-4 in the Studio and 1-2 in
the Lyceum. Also runs learning programmes. Recent
productions include: *Standing at the Sky's Edge* and
Life of Pi.

Casting procedures: Uses freelance casting directors.
Welcomes letters (with CVs and photographs). Offers
TMA/Equity approved contracts.

Sheringham Little Theatre

2 Station Road, Sheringham, Norfolk NR26 8RE
tel 01263 822117
email enquiries@sheringhamlittletheatre.com
website www.sheringhamlittletheatre.com
Artistic Director Debbie Thompson

Production details: A professional seaside repertory
summer season which runs for 10 weeks from July to
September, comprising 5 plays which are traditional
comedies, farces, thrillers and classics.

Casting procedures: Holds general auditions. Actors
should write between January and March, sending a
CV and *recent* photograph. Email submissions not
welcome. "As a small venue we are non-Equity, but
we do work with Equity to pay a realistic wage; we
also pay for accommodation and towards travel
costs." Actively encourages applications from
disabled actors and promotes the use of inclusive
casting.

Sherman Theatre

Senghennydd Road, Cardiff CF24 4YE
tel 029 2064 6901 *fax* 029 2064 6902

website www.shermantheatre.co.uk
Artistic Director Joe Murphy

Production details: Stages 4 shows each year and specialises in work for young audiences. Often uses actor-musicians.

Casting procedures: Does not use freelance casting directors. Sometimes holds general auditions. Welcomes letters (with CVs and photographs) but not email submissions. Also accepts invitations to view individual actors' websites.

Soho Theatre

21 Dean Street, London W1D 3NE
tel 020 7287 5060 *fax* 020 7287 5961
email hires@sohotheatre.com (for hirings)
website www.sohotheatre.com
Executive Director Mark Godrey *Creative Director* David Luff *Head of Comedy* Steve Lock

Production details: Soho Theatre + Writers' Centre aims to discover and develop new playwrights, produce a year-round programme of new plays, and attract new audiences. Founded in 1972, the company premiered the early work of such playwrights as Caryl Churchill, David Edgar, Hanif Kureishi, Tanika Gupta, and Timberlake Wertenbaker; more recently it has presented new plays by Laura Wade, Will Eno, Adriano Shaplin, Debbie Tucker Green, Matt Charman, Rebecca Lenkiewicz and Toby Whithouse.

Soho Theatre + Writers' Centre includes a flexible 144-seat theatre, a large self-contained studio space with 85-seat capacity, theatre bar, restaurant, offices, rehearsal, writing and meeting rooms. All spaces are accessible and available for hire. For bookings and general information, please visit **www.sohotheatre.com**.

Casting procedures: Casting is carried out in-house by Nadine Rennie.

Southwark Playhouse

77-85 Newington Causeway, London SE1 6BD
tel 020 7407 0234 *fax* 020 7407 8350
email admin@southwarkplayhouse.co.uk
website www.southwarkplayhouse.co.uk

Production details: Southwark Playhouse's central vision is that of a vibrant theatre in the heart of the London Borough of Southwark, serving the widest possible constituency within the Borough and beyond, providing a platform for emerging theatre practitioners and a programme of performance, education work and community drama.

Southwark Playhouse will be moving to a location in the London Bridge Station development, which completes in 2018. Please see the website for the latest details.

Stephen Joseph Theatre

Westborough, Scarborough YO11 1JW
tel 01723 370540 *fax* 01723 360506

email enquiries@sjt.uk.com
website www.sjt.uk.com
Artistic Director Paul Robinson

Production details: Stages 6-7 productions each year with lunchtime shows, late nights, rural and national touring. Most work is new writing. Recent productions include: *Improbable Fiction*, *Playing God*, and *Villette*.

Casting procedures: Sometimes holds general auditions; actors may write at any time requesting inclusion. Welcomes submissions (with CVs and photographs) by post or email. Also accepts showreels and invitations to view individual actors' websites. Offers TMA/Equity approved contracts. Will consider applications from disabled actors to play characters with disabilities.

"Casting Director Sarah Hughes is not resident at the SJT. Casting normally only takes place 2-3 times a year. Please note that unsolicited CVs/photos/showreels will only be returned if with an sae to the same value as the original."

Storyhouse

Hunter Street, Chester CH1 2AR
tel 01244 409113
email info@storyhouse.com
website www.storyhouse.com
Artistic Director Alex Clifton

Founded in 2017, Storyhouse is Chester's award-winning theatre, library, cinema and arts centre. It presents a year-round programme of theatre, comedy, dance and music events alongside a raft of creative festivals.

Storyhouse also produces the much-loved Grosvenor Park Open Air Theatre, Moonlight Flicks outdoor cinema in Chester's Roman Gadrens, the Chester Music Festival and Literature Festival.

Produces 5 productions in the main house a year. Equity approved contracts.

Suffolk Summer Theatres (Southwold & Aldeburgh)

St Edmund's Hall, Cumberland Road, Southwold IP18 6JP
mobile 07930 530948
email peter@southwoldtheatre.org
website www.southwoldtheatre.org
Producers: Peter Adshead and Mark Sterling

Production details: Summer theatre with an extensive programme. Stages 5 productions each year playing in 2 venues and occasional tours. Recent productions include: *Arsenic and Old Lace*, *Dick Barton – Special Agent*, *Move Over Mrs Markham*, *Five Finger Exercise*, *Taking Steps*, *Sleuth* and *The Late Edwina Black*.

Casting procedures: Does not use freelance casting directors. Holds general auditions; actors should write in November requesting inclusion. Does not issue casting breakdowns. Welcomes letters (with CVs and photographs) or email submissions, and advises that it is not possible to see everyone who writes in. Offers non-Equity contracts. Rarely (or never) has the opportunity to cast disabled actors.

The Library Theatre

See the entry for HOME under *Producing theatres* on page 143.

Theatr Clwyd

Mold, Flintshire CH7 1YA
tel 01352 756331 *fax* 01352 701558
email mail@clwyd-theatr-cymru.co.uk
website www.clwyd-theatr-cymru.co.uk
Artistic Director Tamara Harvey *Producer* William James

Production details: The major drama-producing company in Wales. Although most work is presented in English, some pieces are performed in Welsh. Stages 5-6 shows in the main house, and 5-6 in the studio each year, with some mid- large-scale productions touring Wales and England. Also runs TIE programmes.

Recent productions include: *Aristocrats, Season's Greetings, Copenhagen, Under Milk Wood* and *Arms and the Man*. Offers TMA/Equity approved contracts and subscribes to the Equity Pension Scheme.

Casting procedures: Theatr Clwyd employs freelance casting directors. For further information contact William James at the address above.

Theatre By The Lake

Lakeside, Keswick, Cumbria CA12 5DJ
website www.theatrebythelake.com
Artistic Director Liz Stevenson *Associate Producer* Zoe Bailey

Production details: Each year, Theatre by the Lake produces a Summer Season of 6 plays in repertoire, an Easter production/Spring Season, and a Christmas production. Also promotes a touring programme of visiting professional work across all artforms, and runs Education and Outreach programmes. Recent productions include: *A Chorus of Disapproval, Blackbird, The Memory of Water*, and *A Midsummer Night's Dream*. Offers TMA/Equity-approved contracts and subscribes to the Equity Pension Scheme.

Casting procedures: Auditions are held 3 times a year. All casting is in-house; does not use freelance casting directors. Casting breakdowns can be obtained by postal application with sae. Does not accept general submissions from actors. Further information about the casting process can be found on the website.

Theatre Royal Bath

Sawclose, Bath BA1 1ET
tel 01225 448815

website www.theatreroyal.org.uk
Twitter @TheatreRBath
Director Danny Moar

One of the oldest theatres in Britain. Comprising three auditoria – the Main House, the Ustinov Studio Theatre and the Egg theatre for children and young people – the Theatre Royal offers a varied programme of entertainment all year round.

Theatre Royal, Bury St Edmunds

Westgate Street, Bury St Edmunds, Suffolk IP33 1QR
tel 01284 829945
email Sharron@theatreroyal.org
website www.theatreroyal.org
Artistic Director and CEO Karen Simpson

Production details: Seating capacity 358. Built in 1819, the theatre is the only surviving Regency theatre in the country. Produces an annual pantomime at Christmas and 2 other shows a year – a rural tour in the spring and an in-house production in the autumn, often from or about the Regency period. Offers non-Equity contracts.

Casting procedures: Casting breakdowns are published via Spotlight only. Actors wishing to be considered for the pantomime should write to the theatre in August. (The spring and autumn shows are cast in January/February and June/July respectively.) Only welcomes letters and emails (with CVs and photographs) from actors previously unknown to the company during these casting periods. Does not welcome showreels, but is happy to receive performance notices. Rarely or never has the opportunity to cast disabled actors.

Theatre Royal Plymouth

Royal Parade, Plymouth PL1 2TR
tel 01752 668282
website www.theatreroyal.com
Twitter @TRPlymouth
Producer Louise Schumann

Specialises in the production of new plays. Its engagement and learning work engages young people and communities in Plymouth and beyond. The award-winning waterfront production and learning centre, TR2, offers set, costume, prop-making and rehearsal facilities.

Theatre Royal Stratford East

Gerry Raffles Square, London E15 1BN
tel 020 8534 7374 *fax* 020 8534 8381
email theatreroyal@stratfordeast.com
website www.stratfordeast.com
Artistic Director Nadia Fall

Production details: Committed to new work which portrays the experiences of different social and ethnic communities, the theatre is constantly striving to present shows which resonate with its diverse local audiences. Stages 8 shows each year. Also runs Young

People's, Outreach and Community programmes. Recent productions include: *Janis Joplin Full Tilt, The House of Inbetween* and *Love N Stuff.*

Casting procedures: Casting opportunities are advertised on the website. Welcomes submissions (with CVs and photographs) sent by post. Advises actors to research the theatre's work before writing, and to think carefully about their own suitability. Invitations to view individual actors' websites also accepted. Actively encourages applications from disabled actors and promotes the use of inclusive casting.

Theatre Royal Windsor

Thames Street, Windsor SL4 1PS
tel 01753 863444 *fax* 01753 831673
email info@theatreroyalwindsor.co.uk
website www.theatreroyalwindsor.co.uk
Chief Executive Bill Kenwright *Executive Director* Robert Miles

Production details: A long-standing, non-subsidised producing theatre. Shows run for 1-2 weeks. Stages new productions each year with some going on to tour. Recent productions include: *The Best Man, How the Other Half Loves* and *This is Elvis.*

Casting procedures: Does not use freelance casting directors. Welcomes letters (with CVs and photographs) but not email submissions. Offers TMA/Equity-approved contracts. Will consider applications from disabled actors to play characters with disabilities.

Tobacco Factory Theatres

First Floor, Tobacco Factory, Raleigh Road, Southville, Bristol BS3 1TF
tel 0117 902 0345 *fax* 0117 902 0162
email theatre@tobaccofactorytheatres.com
website www.tobaccofactorytheatres.com
Artistic Director Mike Tweddle

Production details: Stages 6-8 productions a year in the theatre space and touring work, and also works with the local community. Does not always offer Equity-approved contracts. Offers contracts where possible.

Casting procedures: Casts in-house and does not hold general auditions. Casting breakdowns are available from the website, and via postal application (with sae). Welcomes emails from actors previously unknown to the company, but does not welcome showreels or invitations to view individual actors' websites. Actively encourages applications from disabled actors and promotes the use of inclusive casting.

Torch Theatre

St Peter's Road, Milford Haven SA73 2BU
tel 01646 694192 *fax* 01646 698919
email info@torchtheatre.co.uk
website www.torchtheatre.co.uk

Artistic Director Peter Doran *PA to Artistic Director* Janine Grayshon

Production details: Stages 4-5 productions each year. Recent productions include: *Brief Encounter, One Flew Over the Cuckoo's Nest* and *Woman in Black.*

Casting procedures: Sometimes holds general auditions; actors should write in June requesting inclusion. Casting breakdowns are available by postal application (with sae) and Equity Job Information Service. Welcomes submissions (with CVs and photographs), sent by email. Showreels and invitations to view individual actors' websites are also accepted. Advises actors to join the mailing list so they know what is being planned 6 months in advance. Offers TMA/Equity approved contracts. Actively encourages applications from disabled actors and promotes the use of inclusive casting.

Traverse Theatre

Cambridge Street, Edinburgh EH1 2ED
tel 0131 228 3223
email casting@traverse.co.uk
website www.traverse.co.uk
Interim Artistic Director Gareth Nicholls

Production details: Scotland's only theatre committed to new writing. Presents a mixed programme of in-house productions and visiting companies and festivals, across its two theatre spaces. Also runs Engagement Projects and Script Development programmes; see website for more details.

Casting procedures: Welcomesemail submissions. Particularly interested to hear from Scotland-based actors.

Tricycle Theatre

See the entry for Kiln Theatre under Producing theatres on page 144.

Tron Theatre

63 Trongate, Glasgow G1 5HB
tel 0141 552 3748 *fax* 0141 552 6657
email casting@tron.co.uk
website www.tron.co.uk
Artistic Director Andy Arnold *Outreach* Lisa Keenan

Production details: The Tron Theatre Company is currently under the leadership of Andy Arnold. The Tron presents the people of Glasgow and Scotland with outstanding professional productions of the finest new writing and contemporary adaptations of classic texts, with an emphasis on world, UK and Scottish premieres. The Tron also provides a supportive environment for emerging and established theatre talent, nurturing the future voices of Scottish Theatre. (Seating capacity: main house 230, studio 50.) 6 Tron productions are staged annually in the main house (including co-productions) and 1 production is staged annually in the studio. Other areas of work include our Education & Outreach programme. Recent productions include: World premiere stage adaptation of *Ulysses* by James Joyce; John Byrne's new adaptation of *Three Sisters; Dreams and Other Nightmares of Edwin Morgan* by Liz Lochhead; and in autumn 2015, contemporary adaptation of Ibsen's *Ghosts* by Megan Barker.

Casting procedures: Casting is done by liaising with show director and casting directors, and using details of actors on file. Actors can write at any time to request inclusion, as their submissions will be kept on file. Accepts submissions (with CVs and photographs) from actors unknown to the company. Actors are employed under Equity-approved contracts, and the theatre participates in the Equity Pension Scheme. Encourages applications from disabled actors and promotes the use of inclusive casting.

Watermill Theatre

Bagnor, Newbury RG20 8AE
tel 01635 45834 *fax* 01635 523726
website www.watermill.org.uk
Facebook The Watermill Theatre
Twitter @watermillTh
Artistic and Executive Director Paul Hart *Associate Director* (New Working and Touring) Abigail Pickhard Price *Casting and Producing Assistant* Kezia Buckland Matt Ray *Outreach Director* Heidi Bird

Production details: A producing theatre where actors live onsite. Stages 9 shows each year with runs of 6-8 weeks, 1 Outreach tour and 2 Youth Theatre shows. Recent productions have included: Shakespeare, Music Theatre, New Writing and Classics.

Casting procedures: Does not use freelance casting directors. Welcomes emails (with CVs and photographs) with reference to specific castings only. Offers TMA/Equity-approved contracts and subscribes to the Equity Pension Scheme. The Watermill Theatre is committed to equality of opportunity for all.

Watford Palace Theatre

20 Clarendon Road, Watford WD17 1JZ
tel 01923 235455 *fax* 01923 819664
email enquiries@watfordpalacetheatre.co.uk
website www.watfordpalacetheatre.co.uk
Artistic Director and Chief Executive Brigid Larmour

Production details: Producing theatre built in 1908 and refurbished in 2002-2004. The theatre presents a varied programme including inventive, ambitious and inclusive drama, new plays, musicals, dance and family shows. All programme enquiries should be send to **programming@watfordpalacetheatre.co.uk**.

Casting procedures: Casts in-house and uses freelance casting directors. Enquiries should be sent to **casting@watfordpalacetheatre.co.uk**. Unable to respond to individual CVs. Will consider applications from disabled actors to play disabled characters.

Offers UK heatre/Euity agreements. Also involved in Education and Community theatre, for which enquiries should be sent to **participation@watfordpalacetheatre.co.uk**.

Wiltshire Creative

Malthouse Lane, Salisbury SP2 7RA
tel 01722 320117
email info@salisburyplayhouse.com
website www.salisburyplayhouse.com
Artistic Director Gareth Machin

Production details: Pan-arts organisation incorporating Salisbury Playhouse, Salisbury Arts Centre and Salisbury International Arts Festival. Produces a winde range of theatre and cross art work throughout the year, alongside an extensive Take Part programme and Theatre For Young People.

Casting procedures: Offers TMA/Equity-approved contracts. Most productions are cast using freelance casting directors although occasionally in-house. Submissions for specific productions by email are welcome. Promotes inclusive casting, and actively encourages applications from disabled actors.

Worcester Repertory Company

The Swan Theatre, The Moors, Worcester WR1 3ED
tel 01905 726969
email info@worcester-rep.co.uk
website www.worcester-rep.co.uk
Artistic Director Ben Humphrey

Production details: Originally founded in 1968 and the breeding ground for directors such as David Wood OBE, John Doyle, Phyllida Lloyd CBE and Rufus Norris (Director of the National Theatre), the Worcester Rep. now produces between four and seven productions a year. Productions include small-scale touring shows, site-specific Shakespeare and classical work, new studio work and main house pantomine. As with most companies, contracts are offered on a show-by-show basis but most actors work on more than one production with the company. The company is based at the Swan Theatre, Worcester.

Casting procedures: Casting is handled in-house. The comapny is happy to receive submissions from actors previously unknown to the company either by post of email. Most casting occurs between January and April of each year. Please addess all casting submissions to Ben Humphrey (Artistic Director).

York Theatre Royal

St Leonard's Place, York YO1 7HD
tel 01904 623568 (Box Office)
website www.yorktheatreroyal.co.uk
Facebook @yorktheatreroyal
Twitter @YorkTheatre
Instagram @yorkthreaterroyal

Production details: One of the oldest theatres in the country; seats 760 in the Main House and 102 in the

Studio. Productions include classics, new writing and the famous York pantomime every Christmas. Also hosts touring companies, premières and has partnerships with tutti frutti, Wise Children, Shakespeare's Rose Theatre and Pilot Theatre Company, who are resident at the theatre. Runs Outreach, Community programmes and Youth Theatre. Recent productions include: *Swallows and Amazons*, *Driving Miss Daisy*, *A View from the Bridge*, Olivier-Award Winning *The Railway Children*, *The Grand Old Dame of York* and *Sleeping Beauty*.

Casting procedures: Occasionally uses freelance casting directors.

Young Vic

66 The Cut, London SE1 8LZ
email info@youngvic.org
website www.youngvic.org
Artistic Director Kwame Kwei-Armah

Production details: The Young Vic presents a wide variety of classics, new plays, forgotten works and music theatre. The theatre is especially concerned with the art of directing. The Directors Programme is the most comprehensive in the UK. This fusion makes the Young Vic one of the most exciting theatres in the world. "Our audience is famously the youngest and most diverse in London. We encourage those who don't think theatre is 'for them'". Recent productions include: *Yerma*, *Fun Home*, *The Convert*, *Death of a Salesman*, *Tree*, *Blood Wedding* and *Portia Coughlin*.

Casting procedures: Uses freelance casting directors. Does not welcome direct submissions from actors. Offers TMA/Equity approved contracts. Actively encourages applications from disabled actors and promotes the use of inclusive casting.

Theatre

Effective audition speeches

Simon Dunmore

Audition speeches may be a fundamental part of the actor's 'toolkit', but a surprising number of otherwise good actors are not very good at doing them – and many make poor choices of material to use. It's true that most castings involve a reading, but sometimes audition speeches are asked for in advance, and occasionally you'll get, 'We'd just like to see something else; what can you show us?' It would be very silly to be caught out because you haven't done an audition speech since drama school.

Essentially, audition speeches should be self-contained, well chosen, well researched, well staged and well gauged for the space you are in and for whoever is watching you – just like a good production of a play. In fact an audition speech should be a 'mini-production' (of a 'mini-play') in its own right.

Essential parameters

Length

An audition piece should be no more than two or two-and-a-half minutes long (that's roughly 300 words, depending on pace). Two minutes (or less) can be very effective provided that it contains all the parameters listed elsewhere in this article.

How many?

The important thing is to have a good range of audition material so that you've got a library to choose from to suit each given circumstance. I suggest at least half a dozen.

What types?

Your collection should consist of a good variety of characters you could credibly play. They should be within your 'playing range' and appropriate to your appearance: an audition speech is not an acting exercise; it's part of your marketing portfolio.

You should also aim to find material that rarely (if ever) appears elsewhere on the audition circuit. Judging acting is a highly subjective business, so it is generally better to find 'original' material to heighten your chances of not being compared to others. I suggest that you only use material that is popular if you feel sure you can perform it (them) extremely well – on a bad day ...

Accents

If you choose to do a speech written in a regional accent, make sure you can do that accent well enough to convince a native. (It is important to have at least one in your repertoire that features your own accent if it is a strong and 'characterful' one.) Some people choose to 'translate' a speech into an accent with which they are more comfortable, and this can work. However, watch that in doing this you are not sacrificing too much of the quality of the original language.

Sources of speeches

Don't just rely on plays that you know; you should be steadily expanding your knowledge of dramatic literature. Seeing, reading, sitting in libraries and bookshops (especially secondhand ones); even picking up an audition book to find inspiration for a playwright (previously unknown to you) whom you could explore further.

Theatre

Look in novels, less well-known films, and good journalism (for instance) for material that could be made into good 'drama'. For example, Shakespeare copied (almost word-for-word) Queen Katherine's wonderful speech beginning 'Sir, I desire you do me right and justice ...' (*Henry VIII,* Act II, Scene 4) from the court record.

It's generally inadvisable to write your own speech(es). This rarely works, because very few actors are good playwrights. If you do decide to use a self-written piece, it can be a good idea to use a *nom de plume;* you're selling yourself as an actor, not as a playwright. You should also be prepared to talk about the whole play, even if you haven't written it yet.

Content

Too many people fail because they choose to do an indifferent speech. Even if they do it well, it somehow doesn't have much impact because of indifferent writing, lack of depth, and so on. Essentially you should go for pieces that have good 'journeys' – just like a good play.

It can be useful to find speeches that enable you to show your special skills (singing or juggling, for instance), but don't try to cram so much in that the sense is lost in a firework display of technical virtuosity. At the other extreme, avoid something that requires performance at one pace or on one note.

And, never set out to shock deliberately through content and/or crude language. That is not to say don't do 'shockers'; rather, don't set out with the specific idea of shocking your interviewer(s) as many people seem to intend. We've heard most of it before. I cannot describe how mind-numbingly tedious audition-days can become when peppered with such speeches.

Warning: There is now a lot of free audition material available on the Internet. Much of it is indifferently written; however, I have come across the occasional 'gem'.

Shape

Make sure that each of your pieces has a decent shape. In a sense it should be like a good play, with a beginning, middle and ending. Even if the character ends up back where he/she started, so long as he/she has travelled a 'journey' then that's fine.

Shakespeare and the classics

Traditionally you need to have at least one of these in your armoury. The fact is that most people perform them indifferently. Too many renditions seem as dead as their writers. The problem is that they are remote – in language and in content – from our direct experience, and therefore usually require much more research, thought and preparation than a modern speech.

NB It's very tedious to see comedy Shakespeare speech done in a 'cod' West Country accent. If you can genuinely do one of the many variants of this accent, then that's fine, but his language works in every other regional accent in which I've heard it done.

'Trying on'

Try reading any speech that looks good to you (on the page) out loud, in front of someone else, before you start rehearsing it. If you do this, you'll get an even better idea of whether each speech really suits (and 'grabs') you. It's a bit like buying clothes: you see a pair of trousers (say) that look good on the hanger; sometimes you will feel completely different about them when you try them on. The opposite can also occur: you feel indifferent about a speech on the page; you read it out loud and it feels much, much better.

Rehearsing your speeches
'What are you bringing on stage?'
You must bring your character's life history (gleaned from the play and supplemented by your imagination) into your performance. [As the character (i.e. in the first person), write notes of all the bits of information (big and small) that you find, in order to build his/her life.] Most of what you 'bring' won't be obvious to your auditioner(s). However, it will be immediately obvious if that 'life history' is not present. Just as 90% of an iceberg is underwater, a similar proportion of a good performance is also hidden ... but must be there, underneath, to support that performance.

It is particularly important to be clear about what actually provokes the character to start speaking – the 'ignition' that kicks your 'engine' into life. Try running a brief 'film' in your imagination, culminating in the event (for instance, a statement or a gesture from someone else) that is your cue.

Your invisible partner(s)
If you choose a speech addressing another character, then it is vital that that other person (and how they are reacting through the speech) is clear to you. It is generally better to imagine an adaptation of someone you know rather than to 'borrow' someone you've only seen on a flat screen. There can be a huge difference in how we perceive others between two and three dimensions.

It's not just them (and how they are reacting); it's also important to be clear about your relationship. As well as imagining what your character's lover looks like (for instance), you must also know the feel of their touch, their smell, and so forth – and many more personal aspects.

It is also important that any other people, places and events mentioned in the speech are similarly 'clear' in your imagination.

Your invisible circumstances
You should also bring the setting, clothes and practical items with you – in your imagination. (NB I could have written 'set, costumes and props', but I believe that it's important to think of everything being 'real' and not items constructed for a production.) I believe that actors neglecting these is the cause of a high proportion of failed and indifferent speeches. It's not just the visual images, it is also what the other senses give you: the 'brush' of a summer breeze across your face, for instance. Plays are not performed in 'real' rooms (there will be at least one wall missing) and every play has at least one non-appearing character mentioned. These absences are filled by the actors' imaginations. Do the same with these 'absences' in the audition circumstances.

It isn't just the major features that you should think about, but also the apparently minor details – for instance, the mark on a wall that suddenly catches your character's eye. It can be a good idea to draw a map (or groundplan) so that the whole 'geography' of your 'circumstances' is clear for you. Then fill out your imaginary location with as much detail as possible.

Interpretation
As you are creating a 'mini-production' of a 'mini-play' (the 'child' of its 'parent-play'), I believe that it's legitimate to make changes to the given circumstances of the speech when

Theatre

it occurs in the play, especially if such changes enhance your audition performance. (After all, a 'child' can never lose the genetic code of its 'parents', but he/she will evolve their own personality, which will be different.) However, be prepared to justify it – and don't get defensive. There's usually no harm in honest disagreement.

That voyage of discovery

Be aware of the 'voyage of discovery' that shapes your speech. Don't anticipate the end at the beginning. This is a common fault in rehearsal, which is easily corrected – but a remarkable number of people fall into this trap when performing their audition speeches.

It can be very useful to write out a speech with each sentence (or even each phrase) on a separate line. It then appears less of a 'block' of words on the page and more a series of separate, but connected, thoughts and ideas. It is also a good idea to leave sufficient space between each line to write notes on what is the impulse to go on to say the next thing, and the next, and...

Beginnings

If you start your speech nebulously, your interviewer probably won't take in what you are doing for the first few seconds and may miss vital information that could make the rest of it a complete puzzle to them. You need to find a way of starting your speech that will grab their attention from the very beginning. This doesn't mean that the beginning has to be loud, simply that it should be positive and effective – almost as if the house lights were faded down and the curtain rising on... You!

NB It can also be very useful to incorporate a simple movement to start a speech; a turn of the head, for instance.

Endings

It's also important to be clear as to why a character stops speaking after talking for two minutes. You need to be clear what your character's final thought is – crucially stopping his/her flow.

Finally

Ask yourself: 'Are my speech and my presentation of it a good piece of "Theatre?"'

Some practical considerations

Staging

Once you've done all the work set out in the previous paragraphs, you need to think carefully about how you stage each piece. Too many people seem inclined to put in extraneous moves either to compensate for the lack of the other character(s), or because they think the speech is boring if it doesn't contain enough movement. If you are properly 'connecting' to character and 'circumstances', the moves will follow naturally from each 'impulse'. However, much of the effect of your performance will be dissipated if your auditioners don't see enough of your face, and especially your eyes. In general (unless it is an address to the audience), they should be able to see three-quarters of your face for at least half the duration of the speech. To achieve this, orientate the other character(s) and 'circumstances' to suit the audition situation. For instance, place the imaginary person to whom you're talking at around 45 degrees to left or right in front of you. If your map (or groundplan) is clear in your mind, then it should be simple to angle it appropriately.

There is no point in placing a chair specifically to mark another character – or even the hat-stand which I once saw used as the object of some singular passions. If you do use such objects you'll usually find yourself concentrating on that object rather than your 'partner(s)'. They should be clearly lodged in your imagination so that the interviewer can 'see' them through you. Also, don't think that you have to stare at one place continually just to make it clear that he or she is there.

Chairs

A warning about chairs. There is a common variety of chair, as familiar as the bollard is to the motorway, that inhabits many popular audition venues. It can serve all kinds of functions as well as the simple one of being sat upon. However, don't rely on the well-known weight and balance of these plastic and steel functionaries for crucial elements of your well-prepared speech. You may suddenly find only chairs with arms or a room filled with wobbly ones. Be prepared to adapt to whatever form of seating is available.

Tip 1 Do a brief check on the mechanics of your audition-chair before you start your speech. For instance, you don't want to be thrown by the fact that the back is lower than that of the chair you rehearsed with...

Tip 2 If your audition-chair represents a different type of seat (a low, backless bench, for instance), sit on the chair as though you're sitting on that 'bench'.

Props

Avoid using props. As you haven't got a proper set, costume or lighting, too much of the visual emphasis goes on to the prop and consequently away from you. It is amazing how riveting even a small piece of paper produced for one of the numerous 'letter' speeches can become.

Props can be mimed: that mime doesn't need to be brilliant. And think how much easier it is to put down an imaginary glass on an imaginary table, without making a sound at the wrong moment. In using any imaginary prop, remember not just the shape as you 'hold' it in your hand but also its weight and its impact on your sense of touch.

The only exception to this can be a prop introduced briefly and then quickly discarded. Even then, make sure its impact doesn't take the focus from the rest of the speech.

Performing your speeches

Each presentation of a speech has to have the raw energy of a first performance. Unlike a first night, where the only new factor (in theory, at least) is the audience, you have to face numerous new and possibly unexpected factors when doing your audition speech. You need to be not only well rehearsed but also well prepared for how to cope with all the peripherals that are other people's responsibilities when you are actually doing a production. You are your own stage-management, wardrobe department, front-of-house manager, and so forth.

'Act in here?'

I don't think any audition-room is entirely satisfactory. They can be dirty and unkempt, too hot or too cold, too big or too small, have inconvenient echoes, have barely adequate waiting facilities and/or be hard to find down a maze of corridors. You'll be very fortunate if the whole session has only road traffic as a background noise. You have to be prepared to adjust the presentation of your speech(es) to each context – by fractionally slowing down and enhancing your diction slightly if there's an unavoidable echo, or scaling down your movement in a small room, for instance.

Theatre

It's your space

You should regard the space in which you are doing your speech as your stage with which to do whatsoever you wish – as long as you have due reverence for the fabric of the building, for your interviewers and their goods and chattels. Move the chairs if you need to, take your shoes off if that's necessary, and so on ... but don't ask if it's 'all right' to do so. It can get very tedious for an interviewer if you keep on asking permission every time you want to change something. Providing it doesn't affect your audience directly, just get on with what is necessary for your performance.

Don't ask where to stand; your actor's instinct should tell you the optimum place for what you are about to do. Especially, don't ask permission to start, even if it's only with one of those pathetic little enquiring looks – another way of undermining yourself in your interviewer's eyes. Once you've been given your cue, it's all yours and in your own time.

Natural hazards

Be aware of natural hazards in the room: for example, a low afternoon sun pouring through the windows that blinds you as soon as you happen to turn into it. Don't, on the other hand, stand in the deepest shadow; nobody wants an actor who cannot find his or her light.

Your interviewer will probably be sympathetic if the unexpected suddenly interrupts you, but it really is your responsibility to spot this kind of thing beforehand and adjust accordingly. If it is something impossible to anticipate, then aim to recover as quickly as possible and get back into your speech. After all, if something goes wrong during a performance, you don't just stop until it's put right; you continue as best you can, and 99.9% of the time nobody in the audience will notice that anything went wrong.

Explanations

Minimise explanations about your speech. Ask yourself if you need them at all. In fact the best speeches are self-contained and don't need explanation beyond the character's name and possibly the title and the writer of the play. Whatever their individual faults, most directors do know a lot of plays, the characters within them and who wrote them. Be careful not to insult directors by telling them what they already probably know. (For example, 'Hamlet from *Hamlet* by William Shakespeare.') On the other hand, make sure you know the title and writer of more obscure plays and be prepared to discuss them.

Sometimes, in the process of getting inside the character, actors forget to give these basic details. I don't think this matters (I enjoy trying to work them out for myself), but some directors have a nasty habit of interrupting actors' preparations with demands like 'What are you doing, then?' If you do forget and are so interrupted, don't be so thrown that you rush into your speech.

Your interviewer as the other character

Some people try to use their interviewer as the other character for the purposes of their speech. This is not necessarily a good idea. It can work but is fraught with pitfalls.

First of all, do you need to ask permission beforehand? Politeness dictates that you should. After all, you are asking the auditioner to do the job of being in your play. He or she may say, 'Yes, of course', but has probably been asked the same question in every other session of the day; it can get very tedious. Even if it is all right, the auditioner is probably not an actor, will become self-conscious in the process, not react in the way you anticipated, may well want to drop out of character to write notes and consequently won't be a con-sistent partner.

Preparation
Do give yourself a moment to position and check your chair and to check the 'geography' of your performance in this particular space.

A pause for thought
Then, also do give yourself that moment of thought before starting a speech – a moment to immerse yourself within your character and circumstances. Almost everybody under-stands that it can be hard to change gear from chatting to acting. Don't think that you are wasting time; it'll only be a few seconds, and your interviewer will almost certainly have something else to write down before concentrating on you again. (For most actors a 'few seconds' feels much, much longer in these stressed circumstances.)

However, don't take too long to wind up into your speech with lots of heavy breathing or pacing about or even just standing quietly in a corner. That may be what you have to do before you go on stage, but most directors, however understanding, will begin to wonder what kind of lunatic you are and are you going to take up precious rehearsal-time with these warm-ups? Your 'pause for thought' should be as brief as you can make it without showing your inner turmoil. Properly done, this can be riveting to watch.

Starting
One of the hardest aspects of doing a speech is starting it from cold. If you are onstage at the beginning of a stage-production (especially on a first night), you'll experience an im-mense, and for some, terrifying, feeling of excitement and power as the audience goes quiet. You should aim to recreate this feeling just before you start your speech. It'll give you tingles up your spine and put a real 'kick' into your speech. This will 'communicate' to your auditioners and make them really look at you – even if they've had their heads down scribbling in the preceding seconds.
Tip To help stimulate this process, get the smell of dust into your imagination – it's the pervading smell of any theatre.

Communication
You may well 'feel' your speech, but are you communicating it? Just because you are in a small room with only one person watching, don't mutter your speech at below conver-sation-level. How do I know you can fill a stage, however small, if you are not filling the room we're in? You have to make that room your stage, the interviewer(s) your audience. Think of them as being in the best seats in the stalls (the ones reserved for the critics on a first night) and aim just beyond the limits of the space. Only a lazy actor will give a smaller performance on stage just because there is a small audience.

Don't blast your interviewer out of his seat, either. Measure the acoustics: a lot of audition-rooms are part of church-hall complexes and tend to have high ceilings with the inevitable echo.

The 'need'
There is a 'need' that drives any speech; two minutes is a long time for someone to keep on talking. A long speech is a series of connected thoughts and ideas; underneath there has to be the 'need' to talk at such length. We all know people who 'go on' too much in

Theatre

everyday life – the odd person is able to sustain attention because of the energy and 'need' to communicate. The same is true on stage and in the audition.

Also, remember that your character hasn't usually planned to say so much. Essentially, the circumstances provoke the 'need' for them to add more, and more, and ...

Stopping

If you do need to stop during a piece – you've dried or it's started badly – do it positively and calmly, and do it without a grovelling apology. You may feel terrible but you have to get yourself out of the mess without becoming embarrassing. You can even capitalise on having handled it well. A brief (and positive) 'I'll start again' or whatever won't be held against you. If you dry or make a mistake significantly into a speech, just pause briefly and find your way back, just as you would in a public performance.

Bear in mind that most interviewers do not know how acting works. So if, say, your breathing starts going haywire, that's not a reason to stop unless it really is affecting the speech badly. You have left your teachers behind at drama school.

Finishing

When you finish you should keep the final thought in your mind and gently freeze for a moment, just as you would if you're left onstage at the end of a scene in a play. Then fade the imaginary stage-lighting (and close the curtains) at a suitable rate. (That 'moment' should last about a second. If you're unsure, say a multi-syllable word like 'Mississippi' in your head.) Then – without looking your interviewer(s) in the eye – relax back to your normal self, ready to move on to whatever your interviewer wants to do next. Many find the not 'looking your interviewer(s) in the eye' difficult, and a few even think that it might seem rude. However, if you do make eye contact at that crucial moment, you'll probably start to feel very vulnerable – and give out the 'vibe' that you're unconfident about your performance. Whatever you may really feel about that performance, there's nothing else that you can now do, except wait.

There may be a silence; your interviewer(s) may well want to write notes on what you've done. Just settle down and let them get on with it. Don't be thrown by that aching pause; you should quietly wait. The 'ball' is now very definitely in the interviewer's 'court' to restart the conversation.

'Thank you' (a)

There may be a vague 'Thank you' or 'Right', even 'Mmmm' from the interviewer at the end of your speech. Don't read anything in to these vague expostulations. If you do you'll start to undermine yourself. We directors are usually thinking about what we're going to write down about your efforts. That thinking process is dominant and what comes out of our mouths is merely our acknowledgement that you've finished – an attempt at politeness that doesn't come out quite right. (I hear myself doing this constantly, but have never found a way round it.)

'Thank you' (b)

Some actors opt for a 'Thank you', or 'That's it', at the end. Sometimes this sounds pathetic; on others it comes across as sheer arrogance (watch the way some actors do curtain calls). If you've got a good enough 'ending', you've given the cue. The director may not respond to it immediately, but you should have clearly established that the 'ball' is now firmly in his or her 'court'. It's much better to say nothing.

Switching off

It is respected that it can take a few seconds to come back to reality, particularly if it's a very emotional speech. But it's fundamental to acting that just as you can 'switch on', you can 'switch off' with apparent ease. I will never forget a woman who did a wonderfully passionate speech from Arnold Wesker's *Four Seasons* and ended up in buckets of tears. She had done it extremely well but when it was over she simply could not stop crying and had to be taken from the room and given time to recover. What would have happened if she'd had to get similarly emotional on stage and then immediately go on to do a comic scene, as can occur? This is an extreme example which exemplifies the need to look very carefully at how you change back to reality.

'Why don't you try that again? This time standing on your head'

Don't get so stuck into a way of doing a speech that you cannot do it in any other way put to you. Some directors like to work on speeches. You should understand the insides of each speech so well that you could do it 'standing on your head'.

Advice

Some directors give constructive advice. In general, take that as a compliment, even if they are critical. Nobody will waste time and energy giving notes if they didn't at least like some aspect of you and your work. However, one director's constructive notes can become another's criticisms. In rehearsal an actor will take a note and try it out. Sometimes it doesn't work, and the moment has to be looked at again. Maybe it was only half-right. In an audition there is usually no time to rehearse that note to see if it works for you. So, when you do try it, and it perhaps doesn't quite work, you have no recourse to its originator for further amplification. Take such notes as suggestions to be utilised or discarded as suits you and your speech. That's how rehearsals should be anyway.

Final note

Working on audition speeches can be a wonderful way of keeping your 'acting juices' flowing through periods of unemployment.

Simon Dunmore has been directing productions for over 30 years – nearly 20 years as a resident director in regional theatres and, more recently, working freelance. In that time there have been over 200 productions (of all styles, colours, shapes and sizes) – recently: several Drama School Showcases, Maugham's *Home and Beauty* and new plays about sex, WB Yeats' up-and-down relationship with Maud Gonne, one set inside a pyramid and another about Bismarck. Past favourites include: *The Promise* (Alexei Arbuzov), *Antigone* (Jean Anouilh), a seven-handed version of *Antony & Cleopatra* and too many others to mention. He also teaches acting and has worked in many drama schools and other training establishments around the country. He has written several books: *An Actor's Guide to Getting Work* (fifth edition, 2012), the *Alternative Shakespeare Auditions* series, and was formerly the Consultant Editor for *Actors' Yearbook*.

Theatre

Understudying

Andrew Piper

Some Frequently Asked Questions

Why would I want to do it?

What's not to like? Reasonable money, loads of free time, very few responsibilities, and the possibility of playing a meaty role alongside some of your theatrical heroes or belting out the solo of a show-stopper in a West End or major provincial theatre.

What are the 'down sides'?

If you're looking for a fast-track to stardom or are in this job for the glamour and glory, then this is not the job for you. There is no getting away from the fact that the understudies are the B-team. Understudying can be a thankless task – no one pays you much attention unless the actor you're covering is off (which may be never), there's very little to do, and most of the time you're essentially getting paid *not* to act – rather like a tuneless busker being given a tenner to go and play *somewhere else*!

Perhaps more so than almost any other acting job, this is very much 'a job'. If you can squeeze some art or advancement out of it too then that's great (in some cases miraculous), but this is definitely not a contract to go into with starry-eyed optimism.

How should I prepare?

Learn the lines! The amount of actual rehearsal time (as opposed to just watching the principal cast) may be fairly minimal. When you do get to rehearse there will be a lot to learn in a very short space of time, so the more solid you are on lines the more productive your rehearsal time will be, and the sooner you'll feel confident about being ready to go on. Do as much of the usual homework – character, historical research, cultural background, etc. – that you would do for any other part. You'll get less opportunity to discuss this in rehearsal (more on that later), but again it means you'll enjoy yourself more in the rehearsal room.

How much rehearsal will I get?

In short, not a lot – certainly not as much as the principal actors will have – but (depending how soon you're called to go on) enough to get you through. You probably won't start rehearsals at all until the main cast have been rehearsing for a while – at the very least the blocking needs to have been decided before you arrive – so the chances are you'll just get a few days (at best) before production week.

During production week itself, expect to be pretty much ignored completely by everyone: their focus is now purely on the principal cast and the technical running of the show. The job of the understudy during this period is to make notes on changes to his or her blocking, become familiar with lighting, sound and other stage effects, keep working on lines, stay available … but generally just stay out of the way. Keep working on your part(s); you may only have had a few days' rehearsal by this point, but there have been enough instances of principal actors injuring themselves during a tech for you not to be complacent at this point!

Rehearsals are likely to be taken by the assistant director, or possibly even the company manager. If you're lucky, you'll have a little time for discussion about character and intentions (the more homework you've done before rehearsals, the more time you'll have), but an awful lot will be down to you to work out for yourself, simply by working on the script and watching the main cast at work.

Do I have to copy the principal actor's performance?

Understudy rehearsals differ from normal rehearsals in one important respect: all your moves (and many of your character choices) have already been decided and cannot be changed by you. In some ways this can be quite liberating – someone else has done all the hard work for you – but it can be challenging to take on these choices and make them your own. What you certainly don't want to do is produce a 'photocopy' of the principal actor's performance, which risks feeling like a hollow caricature; the challenge is to develop a performance which can slot in seamlessly to the main production, but which nevertheless feels like it's your creation. It can be disheartening to be so restricted in your choices, but trust that the principal actor's (and director's) instincts are good, and find a way to make it work for you.

Once the show is open, what are my responsibilities?

Most of your time will be spent either doing ensemble stuff on stage, or simply waiting in the dressing room. Apart from understudy rehearsals (one a week, perhaps, or possibly once a fortnight; if you're working for the RSC you may not have any understudy rehearsals at all once the show is up) your time is your own. If you're not needed for the curtain call, you may not be required to stay until the very end of the show. The rule of thumb is that you're free to go once the character you're covering has made his or her final entrance, but this can vary from production to production.

How often will I go on?

If you're working on a musical, the vocal demands of the piece will probably mean that principal performers will need to take occasional shows, or even just musical numbers, off to rest their voices, and so an understudy on a musical is pretty much guaranteed to be going on fairly frequently. In a straight play there is the distinct possibility that you will never go on at all, unless it's a long and demanding run. Even in the middle of a flu epidemic, the actor(s) you are covering may have a 'show must go on' mentality. They may be secretly hoping that the company manager will send them home, but will not voluntarily go off unless they are on the verge of being hospitalised.

It won't hurt to develop a good relationship with the actor you're covering, so that (a) they know that you actually want to go on (assuming you do; many understudies are quite happy not to) and (b) they may be more inclined to give you your moment in the sun when illness strikes and they're deciding whether or not they're fit enough to go on.

Incidentally, no company manager will allow a healthy principal to take a show off to give their understudy the chance to go on – that would be breach of contract – but I've heard stories of a few who may be wilfully credulous if the principal calls in sick for a matinee in the understudy's home town.

What's it like to go on?

When you get the call to go on, then just about everyone in the company – including the principal actors – will be focusing their energies on making sure that you have everything you need to give a good performance. Depending on how much notice you are given, you may have an opportunity to run through bits of business on stage with the principals, and they may well offer you notes on how to play it. Some of these notes may be helpful, others won't be; take what you need and discard the rest. For the next few hours you are 'one of them', playing for the A-team, and you have to trust that your skill as an actor and all the preparation you've done will get you through. This isn't the time to try anything new; just do what you've rehearsed and everything will be fine.

Don't get star-struck about the people you're on stage with. These are your colleagues, your fellow artists, and whatever your relationship off stage might be, right now they are your equals, so don't be afraid to give a full-blooded performance. Some nerves are completely understandable, so if you know you tend to rush or be a bit quiet, say, when you're nervous, be aware of this and make a conscious effort to slow down or speak up, as appropriate.

Once the nerves have started to subside, allow yourself to enjoy it. Stay focused and in the moment, remembering all the things you've rehearsed, but now that you're playing with the A-team, take on the energy of the other actors and allow it to lift your own performance. Producers are generally happy if you can just get the lines out in the right order and hit your mark – as far as they're concerned you're just there to stop too many people asking for their money back – and if you can do that, then you've done your job, but if you've done your homework, then there's no reason why you can't take it further than that and give a bloody good performance.

Will I get an understudy matinee?

Depending on the agreement you have with the producers, there may be an opportunity for an understudy performance, especially if not all the understudies have had the chance to go on during the run of the show. It's not guaranteed, but if it is going to happen, it will usually be one afternoon when there's no public performance in the theatre (or a theatre on the tour that's reasonably close to London).

All the understudies will play their covered role (or sometimes roles), and may ask supporting members of the principal cast to come in and play the others. They are not obliged to say yes, since it's not in their contract to give up their afternoon off, and they're not getting paid for it; but if asked nicely, most actors are generally happy to help out if they can. If one of them isn't available for some reason, there may need to be some nifty doubling, or the company manager may go on with a book.

Who should I invite to see me?

The understudy matinee is your chance to invite all your friends, family, former colleagues, potential employers, casts from nearby theatres – just about anyone! – to come and see your performance. Tickets will usually be free, but there may be a limit on the number of tickets available to keep front-of-house staff costs down.

I mention inviting potential employers: this can be tricky, even if the show is in the West End. Excuses for casting directors' non-attendance may be along the lines of "Oh, it's so hard to get away from the office [50 yards from the theatre!] during the day," but in reality, producers' frequent indifference to the actual acting talent of the understudy – or, for that matter, the malaise that can set in in the understudy after years sitting in a dressing room doing crosswords – can result in some really quite uninspiring performances during these matinees, and the casting directors know it. (I'm talking about straight plays here; it's a rather different story in musical theatre, where understudies are usually working members of the ensemble and more regularly pressed into service in principal roles.) It's worth asking, nevertheless, although only if you're confident in giving them a show they'll be impressed with. Don't however think that this is your moment to get seen by every casting director in town – it won't be.

Should I do it again?

A good, reliable understudy is highly prized by producers, and may even be offered work on a new production before the principal actors are cast. But once known as an understudy (with the exception, perhaps, of the RSC), it can be hard to get them to see you as someone they might want to cast in a principal role. That may not be a problem for you – in the West End, at least, it gives you terrific freedom to do other things, especially if you have family commitments or are developing another career as a writer or voice-over, say – but a life of waiting in the wings is not for everyone. If you're coming to the end of one understudy job, you must think carefully (and discuss with your agent) about how much and what kind of understudy work you'd like to be put up for in the future. Regular understudying is not the occupation of the ambitious actor, so think carefully about what the benefits and pitfalls of taking a particular understudy job might be.

Andrew Piper trained at Bristol Old Vic Theatre School and edited *Actors' Yearbook* for the 2007 and 2008 editions. He understudied the role of Bernard Woolley in the original West End transfer of Chichester Festival Theatre's production of *Yes, Prime Minister*. Thanks are due to the more experienced understudies who offered their comments on early drafts of this article. More information about Andrew can be found at **www.andrew-piper.com**.

Theatre

Independent managements/theatre producers

This section mostly lists commercial organisations that mount West End and touring productions to larger-scale venues – some of which originate in the subsidised sector. Most such productions will be led by well-known actors, but they will usually need supporting actors who can also understudy those leads. (In long-running West End productions, the understudies get a chance to do their own performance – a useful opportunity to 'showcase' for agents and casting directors.) Sometimes, such a production will tour in order to try it out before (hopefully) coming into the West End; at others, a management will tour to 'milk' further profits from a West End success.

On tour, apart from 'Acting ASMs' (assistant stage managers who also understudy), you shouldn't be asked to do any of the graft of get-ins and get-outs – unlike on smaller-scale touring. However, if you are also understudying, you will be expected to do an understudy rehearsal every week until the last stages of the tour. This rehearsal will probably be taken by the company manager (rarely, the director) and the whole ambience will feel very unsympathetic to good acting. Despite this, it is very important to be as fully prepared as possible for the chance that the 'name' you are understudying will be unavoidably delayed one night. Touring is fraught with potential delays, and a reputation for being able to 'deliver the goods' at very short notice will enhance future employment prospects. The downside of playing small parts and understudying is that you can become stuck doing this – a good agent will be able to advise in this area.

Touring is not for everyone: long periods away from home, wide variations in the quality of digs (often costing more in holiday resorts during the 'season'), and the fact that you could miss opportunities to be seen for other work are some of the potential disadvantages. On the plus side, contracts for large-scale tours are usually at least three months with a minimum of a week in each venue, and you should have time to see some of the most beautiful sights in the UK (if not Europe and further afield).

Although not as expensive as major films, such productions do cost a lot of money to mount, and productions have been known to collapse suddenly without any warning. When accepting work in this area it is important to have a proper Equity contract.

Ambassador Theatre Group (ATG)

39-41 Charing Cross Road, London WC2H 0AR
tel 0844 871 7627
CEO Mark Cornell Executive *Vice President* Adam Kenwright *Casting Associate* Ellie Collyer-Bristow

Production details: ATG is the largest owner and operator of theatres in the UK, with 40 venues, rising to 50 across the world. It produces across the UK, Japan, Europe and New York. Anywhere between 3 and 30 actors work on each production. Recent productions include: *Guys and Dolls*, *Sweeney Todd*, Matthew Bourne's *Nutcracker* and *Highland Fling*, *The New Statesman* and *The Rocky Horror Show*.

Offers Equity approved contracts and is "happy to make contributions [to the Equity Pension Scheme] on behalf of any members of the scheme that we employ".

Casting procedures: Uses freelance casting directors. Welcomes letters (with CVs and photographs), but not email submissions. Actors may write at any time, but prefers contact to be made via an agent and preferably during pre-production. Advises actors against sending expensive photos 'on spec', especially if unaccompanied by a letter. Actively encourages applications from disabled actors and promotes the use of inclusive casting.

Andy Barnes Productions

5A Irving Street, London WC2H 7AT
tel 020 7839 9003
email andy@andybarnesproductions.com
website www.andybarnesproductions.com
Director Andy Barnes *Associate Producer* Wendy Barnes

Production details: Founded in 2005. Primarily a producer of new musicals with Fringe and West End experience; also produces small plays. Founder and producer of Perfect Pitch Musicals Ltd – a development network for new musical theatre. Stages 2-3 productions each year at various venues, which include arts centres and theatres. Number of actors going on tour varies, and regions covered include London, the South East and New York. Recent productions include: *When Harry Met Sally* (UK Tour); *Days of Hope* (King's Head); *Departure Lounge* (Arts Theatre & Edinburgh Festival); and *Someone Who'll Watch Over Me* (Gene Frankel, NY).

Casting procedures: Uses freelance and in-house casting directors. Holds general auditions; actors should write in March and September to request inclusion. Casting breakdowns are available via Spotlight. Welcomes letters (with CVs and photographs) from individual actors previously unknown to the company. Also welcomes email submissions and showreels, but will not accept invitations to view individual actors' websites.

Blue Star Productions

7-8 Shaldon Mansions, 132 Charing Cross Road, London WC2H 0LA
tel 020 7386 6220/4128 *fax* 020 7836 2949
email hopkinstacey@aol.com
Directors Barrie Stacey, Keith Hopkins *Stage Director* Tony Joseph

Production details: Founded in 1966. Specialises in children's musicals and songbook concerts. Stages 24 productions annually with 100 performances during the course of the year. Tours to 8 different theatres in Southern England, including the London area. In general 8 actors are involved in each production. Recent productions include: *West End to Broadway* and *Movie Memories*. Offers non-Equity contracts and does not subscribe to the Equity Pension Scheme.

Casting procedures: All casting is done in-house. Holds general auditions. Casting breakdowns are available on request. Welcomes letters (with CVs and photographs) but not email submissions. Advises actors: "Don't be grand when just starting." Actively encourages applications from disabled actors and promotes the use of inclusive casting.

Jonathan Church Productions

Noel Coward Theatre, 85-88 St Martin's Lane, London WC2N 4AU
tel 020 7812 7474
email office@jonathanchurchproductions.com
website www.jonathanchurchproduction.com
Director Jonathan Church

Jonathan Church Productions was established in 2015 in association with Delfont Mackingtosh Theatres to produce and general manage high-quality plays and musicals on tour, internationally and in the West End. On average plays 12 venues per tour (1 week at each venue) in Scotland, the North-West, London, the Midlands, and the South-East in theatres and arts centres.

Letters, unsolicited CVs and showreels are not welcomed but invitations to view individual actors' websites and to visit productions are welcome. Also encourages applications from disabled actors and promotes the use of inclusive casting. Casting is at the discretion and choice of the individual cast director per project, usually on Spotlight.

Recent productions include the National Theatre/Headlong production of *This House* by James Graham (UK tour); Bath Thatre Royal/JCP procution of *The Price* by Arthur Miller (Bath Theatre Royal and Wyndham's) and West End transfer of Bush Theatre's *Misty* to Trafalgar Studios.

Offers Equity contracts and is a UK Theatre member and SOLT member.

Contemporary Stage Co

9 Finchley Way, London N3 1AG
email contemp.stage@hotmail.co.uk
Artistic Director David Graham-Young

Production details: Founded in 1993, The Contemporary Stage Company focus on presenting plays and adaptations of novels, with an emphasis on work from cultures outside the English-speaking world. Recent productions include: *The Master and Margarita* (Almeida Theatre), *Flight* (Lyric Theatre), *Potestad* (Gate, Glasgow Mayfest, BBC Radio 3), *Regressions* (Donmar Warehouse, RSC) and *The Tunnel* (Croydon Warehouse).

Casting procedures: Occasionally uses freelance casting directors and holds general auditions. Casting breakdowns are available via PCR. Welcomes CVs and letters from actors previously unknown to the company. Also welcomes invitations to view individual actors' websites and performance notices. Rarely has the opportunity to cast disabled actors.

Vanessa Ford Productions Ltd

Upper House Farm, Upper House Lane, Shamley Green GU5 0SX
tel 01483 278203 *fax* 01483 271509
email vanessa@vanessafordproductions.co.uk
Managing Director Vanessa Ford

Production details: Founded in 1979. Tours to approximately 30 theatres throughout the UK each year. On average, 14 actors work on each production. Recent productions include: *The Hobbit, A Christmas Carol* and *Shirley Valentine*. Offers ITC/Equity-

Theatre

approved contracts and does not subscribe to the Equity Pension Scheme.

Casting procedures: Occasionally uses freelance casting directors, and sometimes holds general auditions. Casting breakdowns are available on the website and through Spotlight. Welcomes submissions (with CVs and photographs) by post and email. Invitations to view individual actors' websites are also accepted. Will consider applications from disabled actors to play disabled characters.

Robert Fox Ltd

email info@robertfoxltd.com
website www.robertfoxltd.com
Director Robert Fox

Production details: Founded in 1980. Theatre and film production company specialising in large-scale theatre productions and musicals as well as feature films. Performances are staged in the West End and on Broadway. Recent theatre productions include: *South Downs* and *The Browning Version* (West End) and *Hugh Jackman Back On Broadway* (Broadway). Also co-produced the films *Atonement* and, more recently, *Wilde Salome*.

Casting procedures: Employs casting directors for specific projects and does not welcome unsolicited submissions from actors.

Sonia Friedman Productions

5th Floor, 65 Chandos Place, London WC2N 4HG
tel 020 7854 8750 *fax* 020 7854 7059
email queries@soniafriedman.com
website www.soniafriedman.com
Twitter @SFP_London
Producer Sonia Friedman *Executive Producer* Pam Skinner *Executive Director* Diane Benjamin *Associate Producers* Ross Brooke-Taylor, Lucie Lovatt, Ben Canning and David Nock

Production details: Sonia Friedman Productions is one of the West End's most prolific and significant theatre producers, responsible for some of the most successful theatre productions in London and on Broadway over the past few years. Since 1990 SFP has produced more than 170 new shows.

Current productions include: the UK premiere of *The Book of Mormon*, *Harry Potter and the Cursed Child* in London, New York and Melbourne, *Mean Girls* at the August Wilson Theatre, New York, *The Ferryman* at the Bernard B. Jacobs Theatre, New York, *Ink* at Samuel J. Friedman Theatre, New York, *Fiddler on the Roof* at the Playhouse Theatre, London, *Rosmersholm* at the Duke of York's Theatre, London.

Forthcoming productions include: *Harry Potter and the Cursed Child* at the Curran, San Francisco and Mehr! Theatre am Großmarkt, Hamburg, *The Book of Mormon* at Palace Theatre, Manchester, Sunderland Empire Theatre, Royal Theatre Carreé, Amsterdam, Musikhuset, Aarhus and Theater 11, Zurich, Musical Dome, Cologne

David Graham Entertainment Ltd

3rd Floor, 14 Hanover Street, London W1S 1YH
tel 020 7175 7170
email david@davidgraham.co.uk
website www.davidgrahamentertainment.com
Director David Graham

Production details: Theatre producer and concert promoter. Stages around 4 productions in 80 theatres and concert halls on an annual basis, with more than 300 performances per year. Countries covered include Britain, Holland, Germany, Canada, Spain, Norway and Ireland. In general, 12 performers work on each production. Recent productions include: *Rising Damp*, *Birds Of A Feather*, *The Wonderful West End* and *Hold Tight, It's 60s Night.*

Casting procedures: Does not use freelance casting directors or hold general auditions. Casting breakdowns available via Script Breakdown, CastCall and other casting publications.

Michael Grandage Productions

Fourth Floor, Wyndham's Theatre,
Charing Cross Road, London WC2H 0DA
tel 020 3582 7210
email mm@michaelgrandagecompany.com
Producer Nick Frankfort *Artistic Director* Michael Grandage *Executive Director* Stella McCabe *Assistant Producer* Molly McCarthy

Production details: Following his hugely successful, 10-year reign at the Donmar Warehouse, director Michael Grandage set up at the Noel Coward Theatre for a 15-month run of plays 2012–13. During 2018, the company revived *Red* by John Logan and a new production of *The Lieutenant on Inishmore* by Martin McDonagh. The company also produces films, has a general management service and looks after a select group of creative practitioners.

The Derek Grant Organisation

13 Beechwood Road, West Moors, Dorset BH22 0BN
tel 01202 855777
email admin@derekgrant.co.uk
website www.derekgrant.co.uk
Directors/Producers Derek Grant, Michael Jones

Production details: Producer of nationwide theatre tours, celebrity 'evening withs', children's shows, comedy, concerts and plays. On average stages 3-4 projects annually, with around 80 performances in arts centres, theatres and community venues across the UK. In general 6 actors are involved in each production. Recent productions include: Hans Andersen's *The Snow Queen* (13 performances at Lichfield Garrick Theatre); *Pinocchio* (at Bolton Albert Halls); Vince Hill in Concert (at North Pier Blackpool); and *Goldilocks and the Three Bears* (nationwide tour).

Casting procedures: Does not use freelance casting directors. Sometimes holds general auditions and actors are advised to write in September and January requesting inclusion. Welcomes letters (with CVs and photographs) from individual actors previously unknown to the company, sent by post or email. Accepts showreels and will consider invitations to view individual actors' websites. Considers applications from disabled characters to play characters with disabilities. "We treat all our artistes with respect and have a high reputation in the business."

Hartshorn Hook
Arts Theatre, 6-7 Great Newport Street, London WC2H 7JB
email louis@hartshornhook.com
website www.hartshornhook.com
Directors Louis Hartshorn, Brian Hook

Production details: Founded 2007, Hartshorn Hook Productions is a commercial theatre company based in the West End. It provides general management services to theatre companies across the UK, whether professional productions or community projects. Recent productions include: *American Idiots* (Arts); *Richard II* (House of Commons); *Murder Ballad* (Arts); *Away From Home* (UK tour), *The Blues Brothers – A Tribute* (Lowry Theatre, Manchester and West End) and *Beulah* (UK tour). Hartshorn Hook also leads workshops and contribute to events such as the 2014 UK Theatre Touring Symposium.

Casting procedures: Welcomes invitations to attend productions in Greater London.

Hiss & Boo Theatre Company Ltd
Nyes Hill, Wineham Lane, Bolney, West Sussex RH17 5SD
tel 01444 881707
email email@hissboo.co.uk
website www.hissboo.co.uk
Artistic Director Ian Liston

Production details: Established in 1977. Pantomime producers also specialising in touring plays and revues in the UK and overseas.

Casting procedures: Works with a known pool of performers. Casting and auditions are only available via Spotlight Interactive Casting. Does not welcome unsolicited CVs by post or email. Offers actors UK Theatre/Equity contracts.

Paul Holman Associates
Morritt House, 58 Station Approach, South Ruislip, Middlesex HA4 6SA
tel 020 8845 9408 *fax* 020 8582 2557
email enquiries@paulholmanassociates.co.uk
website www.paulholmanassociates.co.uk
Directors Paul Holman, John Ogle, Lee Waddingham

Production details: Established in 1990. Produces pantomimes, summer shows and one-night attractions. See entry under *Pantomime producers* on page 236 for more details.

Thelma Holt Ltd
Noel Coward Theatre, 85-88 St Martin's Lane, London WC2W 4AU
tel 020 7812 7455
email tholt@dircom.co.uk

Recent productions: *Macbeth* direction by Yukio Ninagawa, Barbican Theatre, 2017; *Imperium* by Robert Harris adapted by Mike Poulton, a RSC production, Gielgud Theatre, 2018; *Don Quixote* by Cervantes adapted by James Fenton, a RSC production, Garrick Theatre, 2018.

Image Musical Theatre
23 Sedgeford Road, Shepherd's Bush, London W12 0NA
tel 020 8743 9380 *fax* 020 8749 9294
email brian@imagemusicaltheatre.co.uk
website www.imagemusicaltheatre.co.uk
Producer/Director Brian Thresh *Composer/Lyricist* Robert Hyman

Production details: Founded in 1988. Stages 4 productions annually, with around 900 performances in 70 venues including arts centres, theatres, schools and other educational venues throughout the UK. In general 3-4 actors are involved in each production. *Recent productions* include: *The Jungle Book*, *The Secret Garden*, *Tom's Midnight Garden*, *The Snow Queen*, *The Wind in the Willows*, and *Alice in Wonderland*.

Casting procedures: Sometimes holds general auditions. Actors should write in June, October and late January to request inclusion. Casting breakdowns are publicly available via the website, from Equity Job Information Service, and from CastNet and Castweb. Welcomes letters (with CVs and photographs) from individual actors previously unknown to the company only if sent by post. No emails and no showreels, but will accept invitations to view individual actors' websites. Rarely (or never) has the opportunity to cast disabled actors.

Colin Ingram Ltd
Suite 526, Linen Hall, 162-168 Regent Street, London W1B 5TE
tel 020 7038 3905 *fax* 020 7038 3907
email info@coliningramltd.com
website www.coliningramltd.com
Director Colin Ingram *Production Associate* Simon Ash

Production details: Theatrical producers and general managers. The company offers Equity-approved contracts and participates in the Equity Pension Scheme. "Please see the website for details of recent productions and venues."

Casting procedures: Uses freelance casting directors. Does not welcome unsolicited approaches from individual actors previously unknown to the company.

Theatre

Jendagi Productions Ltd

PO Box 5597, Glasgow, G77 9DH
tel 0141 533 5856
email robert@robertckelly.co.uk
website www.robertckelly.co.uk
Managing Director Robert Kelly

Production details: The company has over thirty five years' experience hosting productions across the UK, Ireland, Australia and New Zealand, with over 200 performances each year. Recent productions include: *Menopause the Musical*, *Mum's the Word*, *51 Shades of Maggie* and *Fame the Musical*. Each year the company produces multiple pantomimes in the UK and Ireland. Offers Equity-approved contracts and subscribes to the Equity Pension Scheme.

Casting procedures: Uses freelance casting directors. Actively encourages applications from disabled actors and promotes the use of inclusive casting.

Gareth Johnson Ltd

Plas Hafren, Eglwyswrw, Crymych,
Pembrokeshire SA41 3UL
tel 07770 225227 and 01239 891368 *fax* 01239 800089
email gjltd@mac.com
website www.garethjohnsonltd.com

Production details: Founded in 2000, this general management company produces (for a client) up to 6 shows a year, West End, UK and overseas. Recent productions include *Chess* (Coliseum); *42nd Street* (Drury Lane); *Carousel* (Coliseum); *Eifman Ballet* (Coliseum); *Sunset Boulevard* (Coliseum); *Beyond Bollywood* (London Palladium); *The King's Speech* (tour); *Oh What a Lovely War* (tour); Mossovet State Theatre Chekhov Season (Wyndham's Theatre); *From Here To Eternity* (Shaftesbury Theatre); *Wonderful Town* (Royal Exchange, Hallé and Lowry – tour); *Journey's End* (tour and West End); *Cowardy Custard* (tour); *Touched* (Trafalgar). Offers Equity contracts.

Casting procedures: Uses freelance casting directors and does not welcome unsolicited contact of any kind from actors. Policy on disabled actors as instructed by client.

Andy Jordan Productions Ltd

16 Prior Street, Lincoln LN5 7SW
mobile 07775 615205
email andyjandyjordan@aol.com
Director Andy Jordan

Production details: Founded in 2000. Commercial production company, largely producing new plays of all genres. Stages 1-2 productions annually with 50-100 performances per year. Performs annually in 4-10 theatres across the UK. Also tours overseas. On average, 3-7 actors work on each production. Recent work includes: Strindberg's *Women* (Jermyn Street Theatre (2016), *Foreplay* (King's Head Theatre, 2014), *Lies Have Been Told: An Evening with Robert*

Maxwell (2 seasons in West End, 2006), *2Graves* (West End 2006), *Worlds End* (Edinburgh Festival). Usually offers Equity-approved contracts (either TMA or ITC).

Casting procedures: Uses freelance casting directors. Supports diversity in casting. Casting breakdowns are published on Spotlight Link. Welcomes submissions (with CVs and photographs) sent by post and email.

Richard Jordan Productions Ltd

Mews Studios, 16 Vernon Yard, London W11 2DX
tel 020 7243 9001 *fax* 020 7313 9667
email info@richardjordanproductions.com
Director Richard Jordan

Production details: Founded in 1998. Produces theatre in the West End, throughout the UK and internationally. Main area of work is new writing and revivals of plays; occasionally produces musicals. Company works as general managers and consultants for a wide range of producers and theatres in the UK and abroad. Stages around 10-20 productions annually with 300 performances during the course of the year. The company has produced and developed over 230 productions in 27 different countries including 83 world premieres and 92 US, UK and Australian premiers by both new and established writers. Richard has been at the forefront of developing and presenting works by a diverse range of established and emerging writers and artists from around the world. He is the recipient of numerous major awards including the TONY and Olivier.

Casting procedures: Welcomes letters (with CVs and photographs) but not email submissions. Applications are particularly welcome if actors are currently in a production that the company can go and see. Advises that applicants should have an awareness of the type of work produced by the company before sending CVs.

Bill Kenwright Ltd

BKL House, 1 Venice Walk, London W2 1RR
tel 020 7446 6200
email info@kenwright.com
website www.kenwright.com
Twitter @BKL_Productions

Award-winning prolific commercial theatre and film production company, presenting revivals and new works for the West End, international and regional theatres. Productions include: *Blood Brothers*, *Heathers*, *Joseph and the Amazing Technicolor Dreamcoat*, *Evita*, *Cabaret* and *The Sound of Music*. Films include: *My Pure Land*, *Another Mother's Son*, *Broken*, *Cheri* and *Don't Go Breaking My Heart*.

Casting procedures: In-house and freelance casting directors. Enquiries (with CVs and photographs) to **info@kenwright.com**.

Limelight Productions Ltd

Unit 13, The io Centre, The Royal Arsenal, Seymour Street, London SE18 6SX

tel 020 8853 9570 *fax* 020 8853 9579
email enquiries@thelg.co.uk
website www.thelimelightgroup.co.uk or
www.thlg.co.uk
Facebook @thelimelightgroup
Twitter @Limelight_Group
Artistic Director Richard Lewis *Executive Producer*
Martin Ronan

Production details: Established in 1996. Stages 2-3
productions annually, touring the UK and
internationally.

Recent productions include: *LazyTown Live,
Octonauts Live, Peppa Pig Live* and *Ben and Holly's
Little Kingdom Live* and *Some Mothers Do 'Ave 'Em.*
Offers Equity-approved contracts.

Cameron Mackintosh Ltd

1 Bedford Square, London WC1B 3RB
tel 020 7637 8866 *fax* 020 7436 2683
Chairman Cameron Mackintosh *Managing
Director* Nicholas Allott *Executive Producer and Head
of Casting* Trevor Jackson *Casting Director* James
Orange *Casting Assistant* Paul Wooller

Production details: Stages musical theatre
productions worldwide. Recent productions include:
*Les Miserables, Miss Saigon, The Phantom of the
Opera, Oliver!, Betty Blue Eyes, Avenue Q.*

Casting procedures: In-house casting. Does not hold
general auditions. Welcomes letters (with CVs and
photographs) but not email submissions. Also accepts
showreels and invitations to view individual actors'
websites.

Johnny Mans Productions Ltd

PO Box 196, Hoddesdon, Herts. EN10 7WG
tel 01992 470907 *mobile* 07974 755997
email johnnymansagent@aol.com
website www.johnnymansproductions.co.uk
Key contact Johnny Mans

Production details: Originally founded as a limited
company in 1989, activities include producing and
promoting one-night stands, celebrity concerts,
musicals and touring productions; casting for
television, pantomime and cruise ships; and artiste
and personal management for Sir Norman Wisdom's
estate, Max Bygraves' estate, Nicholas Parsons, Frank
Ifield, Nicki Gillis and the Rainmakers, Trace Dann,
Lezlie Anders, Dave Prowse, Issi Dye, Georgia
Tuohey, Jeremy Spake, Jess Conrad, Leah Bell,
Duncan Norvelle, Steve Barclay and many others.
Stages about 30 different productions annually,
totalling around 250 performances during the course
of the year. Tours concert productions to more than
300 different theatres and arts centres across the UK
and Ireland each year. Recent productions include:
*Just A Laugh A Minute, Frank Ifield Remembers,
Tapestry - The Carole King Story, Calamity Jane,
Beatlemania, The Spirit of Pavarotti, Rock'n'Roll
Paradise, A Slice of Nostalgia Pie, Jukebox & Bobbysox,*

*Be Bop A Lula, Silver Belles, Follow the Herd, Nights
on Broadway (The Bee Gees Story).* Johnny Mans
Productions also publish and edit *Encore Magazine,*
the popular light-entertainment magazine for the
showbusiness professional, which is a bi-monthly,
full-colour periodical. For details contact
encoremags@aol.com or telephone 0845-4670792.

Casting procedures: In the first instance, contact
johnnymansagent@aol.com by email, or write in
with photograph and CV/biography to the address
given above. Prospective future clients will then be
contacted accordingly. Johnny Mans Productions
offers Equity-approved contracts.

Meadow Rosenthal Limited

26 Goodge Street, London W1T 2QG
tel 020 7436 2244 *fax* 0870 762 7882
email info@meadowrosenthal.com
website www.meadowrosenthal.com
Producers Jeremy Meadow, Suzanna Rosenthal

Production details: The company produces West
End, Off-West End and touring theatre shows both
nationally and internationally. Also runs Something
for the Weekend which promotes, tours and manages
comedy and festival shows.

Casting procedures: Uses freelance casting directors
and Spotlight. Actors should only apply in response
to advertisements.

Middle Ground Theatre Co.

3 Gordon Terrace, Malvern Wells,
Malvern WR14 4ER
tel 01684 577231 *fax* 01684 574472
email middleground@middlegroundtheatre.co.uk
website www.middlegroundtheatre.co.uk
Artistic Director Michael Lunney

Production details: Theatre company producing
drama to tour No. 1 UK theatre venues and arts
centres. Stages 1 or 2 productions a year with 180
performances across around 25 venues. Covers the
whole of Britain and Northern Ireland. Size of cast
varies from show to show. Offers actors non-Equity
contracts and does not participate in the Equity
Pension Scheme. Recent productions include:
*Meeting Joe Strummer, The Importance of Being
Earnest, Billy Liar, Dial M for Murder,* and *Tunes of
Glory.*

Casting procedures: Casts in-house. Casting
breakdowns are not publicly available (Spotlight
only). Welcomes submissions from actors (with CV
and photograph) if sent by post or email. Also
welcomes showreels and invitations to view
individual actors' websites. Will consider applications
from disabled actors to play disabled characters.

Mischief Theatre

c/o Kenny Wax Ltd, 3rd Floor,
62 Shaftesbury Avenue, Londond W1D 6LT
tel 020 7437 1736

Theatre

Theatre

email sarah@mischieftheatre.co.uk
website www.mischieftheatre.co.uk
Artistic Director Henry Lewis *Company Director*
Jonathan Sayer *Administrator* Sarah Whiteside

Production details: Mischief Theatre is a comedy
theatre company based in London, first formed by a
group of LAMDA graduates. Mischief is dedicated to
creating engaging and exciting, improvised and
scripted comedy theatre of an excellent standard
through well-honed improvised and comedic
technique and strong theatrical ensemble work.

Current productions: *The Play that Goes Wrong*,
Duchess Theatre; *The Comedy About a Bank Robbery*,
Criterion Theatre; *Groan Ups*, Vaudeville Theatre,
2019; *Magic Goes Wrong*, Vaudeville Theatre, 2019.
Touring: *Peter Pan Goes Wrong*.

Norwell Lapley Productions Ltd
Tenbury House, 36 Teme Street, Tenbury Wells,
Worcestershire WR15 8AA
tel 01584 819005 *fax* 01584 819076
email info@cdm-ltd.com
website www.norwelllapley.com
Director Chris Davis *Artist Manager* Triona Adams

Production details: Produces theatre in the West
End and touring productions. Stages 4-5 productions
annually and gives 40-50 performances during the
course of the year at theatres nationwide. Recent
productions include *Zipp*. Offers TMA/SOLT/Equity-
approved contracts and subscribes to the Equity
Pension Scheme.

Casting procedures: Uses freelance casting directors
and does not deal directly with actors. Rarely has the
opportunity to cast disabled actors.

Playful Productions
41-44 Great Queen Street, London WC2B 5AD
tel 020 7811 4600
email aboutus@playful.com
website www.playfuluk.com

Production details: Directors Matthew Byam Shaw,
Nia Janis and Nick Salmon work within a team of 24.
Produces plays and musicals for the West End,
Broadway and on tour. Also provides general
management and production accountancy services to
other producers. 'The adventure of finding,
nurturing, and shaping an idea all the way through to
a production is incredibly rewarding. Ideas have
sprung from modern fiction, documentary television,
music we have listened to, conversations with our
peers, and overheard conversations on the tube. They
would remain ideas if we weren't fortunate enough to
collaborate with talented playwrights, composers,
designers, directors and actors at the top of their
game, who help us realise each project's ambition.'

Long-running productions: *Wicked*, Apollo Victoria.
Touring productions: *Kinky Boots*, *Dirty Dancing*,
Shrek the Musical. Recent productions: *Quiz*, Noel

Coward Theatre, 2018; *The Moderate Soprano*, Duke
of York's Theatre, 2018; *Imperium*, Gielgud Theatre,
2018; *Come from Away*, Phoenix Theatre, 2019.

Popular Productions Ltd
27 Old Gloucester Street, London WC1N 3AX
tel 01268 907458
email lm@popularproductions.com
website www.popularproductions.com
Producers John Payton, Lucy Magee

Production details: International theatre producer.
Stages 4-6 productions annually, with around 80
performances in 4 theatres in the UK and Dubai.
Anything from 2 to 100 actors may be involved in
each production. Recent productions include: *The
Sound of Music* (International; Middle East
Premiere); *When Harry Met Sally* (Dubai); *The
Woman in Black* (Dubai).

Casting procedures: Uses freelance casting directors.
Sometimes holds general auditions. Casting
breakdowns are available from Spotlight and Casting
Call Pro. Does not welcome unsolicited approaches
by actors unknown to the company, but will consider
invitations to view individual actors' websites. Rarely,
or never, has the opportunity to cast disabled actors.

David Pugh & Dafydd Rogers
Wyndham's Theatre, Charing Cross Road,
London WC2 0DA
tel 020 7292 0390 *fax* 020 7292 0399
Directors David Pugh, Dafydd Rogers

Production details: Theatre production company
staging 2-3 productions annually in the West End
and Broadway, and touring to theatres throughout
the UK. Recent productions include: *Art*, *The Play
What I Wrote* and *Blues Brothers*.

Casting procedures: Sometimes holds general
auditions. Actors should address requests for
inclusion to Sarah Bird CDG (see entry under *Casting
directors* on page 106), who is responsible for all
casting.

PW Productions Ltd
2nd Floor, 80-81 St Martin's Lane,
London WC2N 4AA
tel 020 7395 7580 *fax* 020 7240 2947
email info@pwprods.co.uk
website www.pwprods.co.uk
Facebook PW Productions Ltd
Twitter @PWProds
Chairman Peter Wilson *Managing Director* Iain Gillie

Production details: The company, which Peter
Wilson founded in 1983, specialises in the
production, general management and bookkeeping/
accountancy for theatre presentations. Recent
productions include: *The Woman in Black*, Stephen
Daldry's production of *An Inspector Calls*, Sting's
musical *The Last Ship*, Nigel Slater's *Toast* and James
Graham's *Sketching*.

James Quaife Productions

London
website www.jamesquaife.com
Producer James Quaife

Production details: Established in 2008, James Quaife is an independent theatre producer and general manager working in the West End. Works mainly in theatre with new writing, and employs actors in drama, comedy and musicals. Committed to producing high-quality theatre in the UK; dedicated to the production and staging of ambitious theatre and, by doing so, contributing to the vibrancy and development of the theatre industry. Recent productions include: *Good People* starring Imelda Staunton (Noël Coward Theatre); *Barking In Essex* starring Lee Evans, Sheila Hancock and Keeley Hawes (Wyndham's Theatre); *Happy Never After* (Edinburgh Fringe Festival 2013, Pleasance Courtyard); the world premiere of *People Like Us* and *Happy Never After* (Pleasance Theatre, London); *Step 9 (of 12)* starring Blake Harrison (Trafalgar Studios); the London premiere of *Precious Little Talent* by Ella Hickson (Trafalgar Studios, 2011 London Theatre Award for Best New Play); *Molière*, *Little Fish* and *Death Of Long Pig* (Finborough Theatre).

Casting procedures: Uses freelance casting directors. Casting breakdowns are sent to agents and available from Spotlight.

The Really Useful Group Ltd

17 Slingsby Place, London WC2E 9AB
tel 020 7240 0880 *fax* 020 7240 1204
website www.reallyuseful.com

Production details: The Really Useful Group (RUG) was founded in 1977 by Andrew Lloyd Webber. It is an international entertainment company actively involved in theatre ownership and management, theatrical production, film, television, video and concert productions, merchandising, records and music publishing.

Rho Delta Ltd

66 Constantine Road, London NW3 2NE
tel 020 7485 1356 *fax* 020 7436 1395
email info@ripleyduggan.com
Director Greg Ripley-Duggan

Production details: Founded in 1991. Produces West End and touring commercial theatre. Stages 1 production annually which tours to 6 theatres. Recent productions include: *The Old Masters*, *Life x 3* and *The Memory of Water*. Offers actors TMA/SOLT/Equity-approved contracts and subscribes to the Equity Pension Scheme.

Casting procedures: Uses freelance casting directors and does not deal directly with actors. Will consider applications from disabled actors.

Showcase Entertainments Productions Ltd

2 Lumley Close, Newton Aycliffe,
Co. Durham DL5 5PA

Managing Director/Executive Producer Geoffrey JL Hindmarch *Director/Choreographer* Paul W Morgan

Production details: A professional theatrical touring company. Stages 5 productions annually, with around 100 performances in 60 theatres across England, Scotland and Wales. In general 10 actors are involved in each production. Recent productions include: *Musical Magic* starring Paul Daniels and full showcase company (Harlow Playhouse, Litchfield Garrick, Palace Theatre Mansfield).

Casting procedures: Sometimes holds general auditions; actors may write at any time to request inclusion. Welcomes letters (with CVs and photographs) from individual actors previously unknown to the company, sent by post or email. Also welcomes showreels. Rarely, or never, has the opportunity to cast disabled actors.

Marc Sinden Productions Group of Companies

1 Hogarth Hill, London NW11 6AY
tel 020 8455 3278
website www.sindenproductions.com,
www.onenightbooking.com,
www.uktheatreavailability.co.uk,
www.montecarlotheatre.co.uk
Director Marc Sinden

Production details: A West End and touring theatre producer, reaching theatres and arts centres across the UK and Europe. For details of recent productions, please consult the website. Also runs the UK Theatre Availability System (**www.uktheatreavailability.co.uk**) which allows touring companies to check the availability and suitability of theatre spaces.

Casting procedures: Uses freelance casting directors and does not welcome casting enquiries and submissions from actors.

Squaredeal Productions Ltd

tel 020 2358 4496
email jenny@jennytopper.com
website www.jennytopper.com
Director Jenny Topper

Production details: Established in 2003. An independent theatre producer staging on average 2 productions annually and performing in the West End and 20 theatre venues across the UK. Also Consultant Producer to Theatre Royal, Plymouth. Recent productions include: *The Clean House* (10-week tour); *Martha, Josie and Chinese Elvis* (12-week tour); *Duet for One* (West End); *End of the Rainbow* (West End, tour and Broadway); *Daytona*; *The Three Lions* and *The Nightingales* (with Theatre Royal Bath). As Consultant Producer to Theatre Royal Plymouth, productions included: *Grand Guignol* by Carl Gross; *After Electra* by April de Angelis; *Monster, Raving, Loony* by James Graham.

Casting procedures: Does not hold general auditions. Will accept letters (with CVs and photographs) from actors previously unknown to the company, sent by post or by email. Offers Equity-approved contracts as negotiated through TMA. Rarely has the opportunity to cast disabled actors.

Stanhope Productions Ltd

4th Floor, 80/81 St Martins Lane,
London WC2N 4AA
tel 020 7240 3098 *fax* 020 7504 8656
email admin@stanhopeprod.com
Producer Kim Poster

Production details: Founded in 2001. Theatrical producing company. Stages 4-5 productions annually and gives 576 performances during the course of the year. Tours to 2-4 different theatres, primarily in the West End and London area. In general 18 actors are involved in each production. Recent productions include: *All My Sons, A View from the Bridge, Prick Up Your Ears, Carousel, Fiddler on the Roof, Summer and Smoke, Epitaph for George Dillon, A Woman of No Importance,* and *Brand.* Offers SOLT/Equity-approved contracts.

Casting procedures: Uses freelance casting directors. Holds general auditions. Casting breakdowns are available via Equity Job Information Service. Will consider applications from disabled actors to play disabled characters.

UK Productions

Brook House, Mint Street, Godalming,
Surrey GU7 1HE
tel 01483 423600 *fax* 01483 418486
email mail@ukproductions.co.uk
website www.ukproductions.co.uk
Managing Director Martin Dodd

Production details: Established 1995. Produces pantomime, musicals and drama for No. 1 touring, nationally and internationally. (See entry under *Pantomime producers* on page 238.) Offers non-Equity contracts ("roughly in line with Equity") and does not subscribe to the Equity Pension Scheme. Recent productions include: *The Kite Runner, Oklahoma!, Seven Brides for Seven Brothers, 42nd Street, Disney's Beauty & The Beast, South Pacific,* plus many pantomimes.

Casting procedures: Casting is done in-house. Does not hold general auditions. Casting breakdowns are distributed via Spotlight or direct to agents. Welcomes performance notices but not any other unsolicited form of correspondence. "Unsolicited CVs are generally a waste of time." Will consider applications from disabled actors to play characters with disabilities.

Ulster Theatre Company

17 Duncrun Road, Limavady,
Co. Londonderry BT49 0JD
tel 028 7775 0240
email michaelpoynor@hotmail.com
website www.ulstertheatrecompany.com
Artistic Director Michael Poynor

Production details: Originally set up as a training company touring mid-scale musical productions in the UK and Ireland. The Company also produces an annual original pantomime, and tours other productions from time to time. Recent productions include: *Comedy of Errors: The Musical, Jonathan Harker and DRACULA, Scrooge's Christmas* and *The Long Now.*

Each production consists of around 8 actors and, on average, the company present 2-3 productions per year. This equates to between 60 and 100 performances annually at venues across the UK and Ireland, mainly small theatres and arts centres. The Company offers Equity/ITC-approved contracts.

Casting procedures: Uses in-house casting directors and holds auditions as required. Casting breakdowns are available via email. Welcomes both CVs and letters from actors previously unknown to the Company, and unsolicited CVs and photographs. These should be sent via email. Also asks that applicants are aware that actors based locally are preferred due to inability to pay travel costs. Welcomes invitations to view individual actors' websites, but only attends invitations to productions within Ireland. Does not welcome showreels. Rarely has the opportunity to cast disabled actors due to the physical nature of most productions.

Anthony Vander Elst Productions

The Studio, 14 College Road, Bromley BR1 3NS
tel 020 8466 5580
Director Anthony Vander Elst

Productions details: Established in 1977. Produces 1-2 productions per year touring the UK.

Recent productions include: *Appearances* (Mayfair Theatre, London); *The Teddy Bears Picnic* (Chester Gateway Theatre); and *Last of the Red Hot Lovers* (London). Unsolicited approaches from actors are discouraged. Offers TMA/Equity-approved contracts.

West End International

The Old Brewhouse, Chesham Road, Wigginton,
Hertfordshire HP23 6EH
tel 01442 824557
email info@westendinternational.com
website www.westendinternational.com
Directors Martin Yates, Alison Price

Production details: Concert and theatre producers. Will accept casting enquiries and letters (with CVs and photographs) from actors previously unknown to the company, sent by post or email. Does not welcome unsolicited showreels.

Ignition, inspiration and the imposter

Scott Graham

I have been lucky enough to have been the artistic director of Frantic Assembly, the company I co-founded, for the past 25 years. It frustrates and savages me from time to time, but that is all part of the relationship with a job that also sustains, educates and consistently surprises me. To be in a rehearsal room with a playwright and other fascinating humans is to engage in literary and historical analysis, sociology, philosophy, poetry, anthropology, politics, psychology, etc. Admittedly, we might not be talking as experts, but the breadth of that conversation, in pursuit of a better understanding of a character's predicament or the experience of an audience, is an invigorating privilege and often inspirational.

Having said that, my relationship with this career is complex.

Serendipity saw me being put forward for a play by a schoolteacher against my will and yet enjoying it immensely. Then I discovered a fascination for movement when I stepped in to help choreograph a physical scene between an Oberon, who did not turn up, and Titania, who was my first proper girlfriend. (It was not all good luck as Titania actually left me for Oberon!). When I plucked up the courage to join a drama society at university I was fortunate enough to meet people who would become some of my closest friends and allies, with whom we would have the audacity to form a company based on very little experience, a hell of a lot of energy and a sense of, well, why not?

Even back then, as soon as we learned something, we would try to teach it, to pass it on. I think this meant that we were always breaking processes down into their component parts to see how they really worked (my dad was a motor mechanic and this metaphor is as close I have got to following in his footsteps). As we had zero training, we did not have a short hand or vast technique to fall back on. If I was falling back on anything it was my years of playing sport. I could see the similarities. Sport and martial art gave me a good sense of my own balance and physicality and that awareness really helped, not only in making it more likely that I could achieve the movement, but also in puncturing some of the mystique around theatre and dance.

Sport has had a profound effect on how the company operates. We would do hundreds of workshops in schools and I would always attempt to make the students feel like they could be part of a games lesson or the best part of the playground. We were aiming for that euphoria of scoring a goal or winning as a team. I think I was trying to keep the people who might think this drama lark was not for them in the room in the hope that they, like me, would experience that revelation, see the similarities and apply their skills within the theatre studio.

When we created our free training programme, Ignition, it was with the purpose of attracting young men into our type of theatre. It was not created simply by feeling their absence, but by the strong belief that they were out there with all of their crossover skills, applying them elsewhere. They were never going to come to us because we were terrifying them. We had to look at the language we used and how we presented ourselves if we were to be an attractive proposition to these young men.

We trawled the country trying to get a diverse mix of young men who had little or no engagement in the arts and put them through an intense training programme where, in four days, they met for the first time and by the end had made and performed a show for a public audience. They were nurtured and supported by professionals at every step, but it was their bravery, generosity and commitment that got them through what can be a transformative week in their lives. Many graduates have gone on to work in theatre. Paapa Essiedu played Hamlet at the RSC in 2016. There might not be a more high-profile symbol of the success of this programme than this. Across the country, young men returned to their towns invigorated and empowered and I am immensely proud of that.

The success of Ignition has been extraordinary and in 2019 we launched our female version with a similar drive to bring new voices and energy into our theatre. Again, the focus is on the energy and ethics I have found in sport.

One of my most illuminating rehearsal periods was the creation of Frantic's boxing show, *Beautiful Burnout*. We had already researched the boxing world extensively and found intense, sensitive relationships at the heart of what might appear to be the coldest, loneliest and most brutal of sports. There is so much respect and care to be found inside these gyms. So much to learn and so much to be taught. There is something really beautiful to see how that boxer between rounds, sweating, gloves on, cannot drink or even pick up their bottle of water without a friend unscrewing it and holding it to their mouth.

We wanted to take some of that encouraging culture back into the rehearsal room for this show. In fact, we turned the room into a gym with weights, skipping ropes and punch bags set up. The effect on the performing company was startling. The room became so positive and energised. People would choose to train during their breaks. No one collapsed onto a sofa and bitched about agents. The focus was absolute.

All of this was born out of the intense circuit training and boxing warm ups. It had built a team and vast amounts of mutual respect. It was so successful that versions of it have been employed on most subsequent Frantic shows to build a culture of support, application and community. It builds the ensemble.

All of this validated my instinct about what sport could bring to theatre and how crossover skills were valuable. This was me bringing a world I felt comfortable with into the theatre experience.

My lack of training or what I might have considered a proper theatre background has, at times, made me feel an imposter. I felt unsure, that I had no right to be right. I questioned my authority to write the *Frantic Assembly Book of Devising Theatre*[1] and needed some convincing. When I was invited to speak to academics as part of my role as Visiting Professor at Coventry University I initially felt a paralysing sense that I was a charlatan and had nothing to say.

But I have also found a lack of training has been liberating, allowing me to be inspired by a vast range of stimuli. I embraced my limitations and developed a way of working that suited me and those that might be like me. I have seen that method empower skilled actors and dancers too. I have seen how they break free from their training and technique and are refreshed.

Knowledge creeps up on you. It can take a long time to recognise that you have something to say and the authority to say it. I have seen plenty of people make all the right noises and present a veneer of authority. I have been intimidated by it but I have ultimately seen through it. It comes from the same place as my imposter syndrome. It comes from our fear of the world looking at us and seeing that we might not know the answers. In theatre, what is so wrong about that? Just like my initial inexperience and limitations I have learnt to use this to my advantage. It is an exciting place to be.

When I was part of the creative team making *The Curious Incident of the Dog in the Night-Time*[2] I went through that initial fear of being found out, of being out of my depth, but what was so illuminating and empowering was seeing that same look on other people's faces. They were not trying to hide the fear that is an essential part of the creative process. We were all taking ourselves to places we were not sure about. We were taking risks, trying something new and encouraging each other to be brave. Seeing these respected and award-winning artists work in such an honest and relentless fashion was a formative creative experience that helped me deal with (accept rather than crush) my imposter syndrome and redefined my relationship with the rehearsal room.

It is now so clear to me that we enter a rehearsal room to find out what we don't yet know rather than enter to tell the world what we do know. I tell my MA students when they are setting up devising tasks, be the bad scientist, not the good scientist. The bad scientist mixes ingredients and blows their eyebrows off. As long as they remember that that concoction can do that then they have learnt something. They can use that again when the time is right. Don't be the good scientist who merely acts to prove their theory. They have not moved forward through the task. They have not discovered something new.

Training opportunities are the same. As we walk in through the door we should be asking, what can we take with us as we leave? Too often we enter with a mask and just pray it does not slip. I know I have.

This is why I love working with actors. Initially many hide behind that mask, but when you can help them to get to that place of truth you see how empowering that can be. I have seen the tiniest moment of physicality become the breakthrough for an actor to base a whole character on. Not a tic or an affectation. I mean a moment that links to the tension held within and makes sense of their interaction with the world around them. It feels seismic. It also comes from an understanding of the text. There is often a perception that physical work is not cerebral. This is a damaging miscalculation. We live the majority of our lives reading the world physically, displaying and reading nuance. I consider my move-ment direction to be 'direction through movement' and its ambition is to open up the text. I think it is so important that performers are open to the potential the physical approach can bring. Try not to hide what you think are your deficiencies, don't think of movement as something that you can or cannot do, it is what we *all* do! We tell and read stories physically all through our waking hours. Exploring this and embracing this nuance can only empower the actor.

This is why I love my job. I learn something every day. I learn about you, I learn about characters and I learn about me. When I get asked a question at a post-show discussion, I often think that the student believes they are asking me what I know without realising that the act of asking is helping me form those thoughts. Those thoughts can surprise me. I would not know that I thought that if they had not asked me that question.

I think it is important to recognise that. We can crush ourselves under the expectation that we should know all the answers. This can close us off from meaningful collaboration and kill a rehearsal room or drama studio. Sometimes holding up your hands and saying, 'I don't know what to do here' is not an admission of defeat. It is the invitation to your collaborators to step up. It often takes that explicit moment of honesty.

[1]*Frantic Assembly Book of Devising Theatre* by Scott Graham and Steven Hoggett, 2nd edition, Routledge, 2014.

[2] The National Theatre's Olivier and Tony Award-winning production of *The Curious Incident of the Dog in the Night-Time* (2012) has been seen by over 3 million people in nine countries around the world, most recently completing a smash-hit UK and International Tour at the Piccadilly Theatre in London's West End in 2019. Directed by Marianne Elliott and adapted by playwright Simon Stephens.

Scott Graham is co-founder and artistic director of Frantic Assembly. Further information about Frantic Assembly and contact details can be found in their entry in our Middle and smaller scale theatre company listings on page 193 of this Yearbook. The extensive Frantic Assembly website (**www.franticassembly.co.uk**) gives details and illustrations of their previous productions, and how to apply to take part in Ignition.

Middle and smaller-scale companies

This section covers a huge range of companies, from the very prestigious, often subsidised (like Out of Joint), which usually only perform in theatres with around 500 seats (or more), to the very small, which frequently have little or no public subsidy and perform wherever they can find a paying audience. The bigger companies operate much like the commercial 'big boys' in the previous section – except they tend to have longer rehearsal periods. The smaller companies rarely use casting directors, tend to do only one or two performances in each venue, and often pay below Equity rates – and it's probable that you'll have to help with get-ins and get-outs. It's very hard work and you have to rise to the peak of performance every time, in spite of travelling in cramped vans, sharing unsatisfactory digs and rarely, if ever, being seen by anyone who could advance your career. However, some very prestigious companies have grown from such very small beginnings, and a number of now highly respected directors, playwrights and actors have started this way. It is important to assess the potential quality of the product (as well as the pay, and terms and conditions) before accepting such a job.

As such companies tend to come and go with great rapidity, the listings only contain companies that have been in existence for three years or more.
Note Some of the companies listed are members of the Independent Theatre Council (ITC) – **www.itc-arts.org**.

20 Stories High
Toxteth TV, 37-45 Windsor Street, Liverpool L8 1XE
tel 0151 708 9728
email info@20storieshigh.org.uk
website www.20storieshigh.org.uk
Co-Artistic Directors Julia Samuels, Keith Saha
Executive Director Leanne Jones

Production details: Established in 2006. Creates dynamic, challenging theatre which attracts new audiences, artists and participants. Arts Council NPO from April 2012. Generally stages 1 project annually, with around 40 performances in 20 theatres, schools and youth clubs in the North West and nationally. In general 2-5 actors are involved in each production. Offers Equity-approved contracts as negotiated through ITC. Recent productions include: *She's Leaving Home* by Keith Saha (directed by Julia Samuels – commissioned as part of Culture Liverpool's Sgt Pepper at 50 celebrations); *I Told My Mum I Was Going on an RE Trip...* (written and directed by Julia Samuels – co-production with Contact Theatre); *The Broke 'n' Beat Collective* by Keith Saha (directed by Julia Samuels – national tour co-production with Theatre Rites); *Tales from the MP3* verbatim production edited by Julia Samuels (directed by Julia Samuels – national tour); *Melody Loses Her Mojo* by Keith Saha (directed by Keith Saha – co-production with Liverpool Everyman Playhouse and Curve Theatre – national tour); *Whole* by Philip Osment (directed by Juia Samuels – national tour);

Blackberry Trout Face by Lawrence Wilson (directed by Julia Samuels – national tour); and *Ghost Boy* by Keith Saha (co-production with Contact Theatre and Birmingham Rep – national tour).

Casting procedures: Holds general auditions. Casting breakdowns are available from the website and Equity Job Information Service. Welcomes letters (with CVs and photographs) from individual actors previously unknown to the company, sent by post or email, and is happy to consider invitations to view individual actors' websites. Actively encourages applications from BME and disabled actors and promotes the use of integrated casting.

1623 Theatre Company
QUAD Market Place, Cathedral Quarter, Derby DE1 3AS
tel 01332 285434
email ben.spiller@1623theatre.co.uk
website www.1623theatre.co.uk
Artistic Director Ben Spiller

Production details: 1623 aspires to widen horizons and challenge preconceptions in response to Shakespeare and the world today. Its mission is to make great theatre, support artists, inspire learners and engage with communities and champion diversity. Recent productions include: *Lear/Cordelia* (Derby Theatre), *Queer Lady M* (Atteborough Arts Centre), *Hamlet Off The Wall* (Sheffield Museums), *unclepandarus.com* (World Shakespeare Festival) and

Emergency Shakespeare (*Watch This Space* at the National Theatre).

Casting procedures: Welcomes both CVs and letters from actors previously unknown to the Company and unsolicited CVs and photographs. These should be sent via email. Also welcomes invitations to view individual actors' websites or productions. Happy to accept showreels. Actively encourages applications from actors who self-define as D/deaf, disabled, emerging, female, LGBT++, people of colour and working class.

Accidental Theatre

4thFloor, Wellington Buildings,
2-4 Wellington Street, Belfast BT1 6HT
email info@accidentaltheatre.co.uk
website www.accidentaltheatre.co.uk
Artistic Director Richard Lavery

Production Details: Accidental's theatre is a collision of perspectives, art forms and unusual collaborations — curious stories told through vibrant, ambitious performances. Accidental works with playwrights, actors, filmmakers, DJs, choreographers, musicians, poets, painters, technicians and curators to craft plays for Ireland and the world stage. Every production is a fresh invention, each play's architecture defined by the artists with whom we build it. Collective risk-taking is the inspiration that jolts our work into new theatrical territories and opens it up to new audiences. Accidental walks the tightrope between the unexpected and the impossible, exploring the intersection between British narrative and European aesthetic styles of theatre.

Recent productions include: Gordon Osràm's *Funeral* (Dave Kingham), *The Lost Martini (devised)*, *The Kitchen, the Bedroom and the Grave* (by Donal O'Hagan), *DEATH (on a shoestring)* (by Dave Kinghan) and *The Writers' Room* (by Michael Shannon).

"Collective risk-taking is the inspiration that jolts our work into new theatrical territories and opens it up to new audiences. Accidental walks the tightrope between the unexpected and the impossible, exploring the intersection between British narrative and European aesthetic styles of theatre."

Casting Procedures: Uses in-house casting directors and hold general auditions. Welcomes enquiries, CVs and letters from actors previously unknown to the theatre. Also happy to receive unsolicited CVs, letters, showreels and invitations to view individual actors websites. Casting breakdowns are available from the theatre's website, Spotlight and *The Stage*. Promotes inclusive casting, actively encourages applications from actors with disabilities to play characters with disabilities.

Actors of Dionysus (AOD)

25 St Luke's Road, Brighton BN2 9ZD
tel 01273 673691

email info@actorsofdionysus.com
website www.actorsofdionysus.com
Facebook www.facebook.com/ActorsOfDionysus
Twitter @aodtheatre
Instagram @actorsofdionysus
Artistic Director Tamsin Shasha; *General Manager* Megan Rogers; *Education Officer* Mark Katz *Associate Director* Katherine Sturt-Scobie

Production details: National and international touring company founded in 1993. Not regularly funded. **aod** productions specialise in performing new adaptations of Ancient Greek drama and new writing inspired by myth (often with an aerial dimension), through a fusion of poetry, music and movement. "Our mission statement is to make magic from myth, creating beautiful work that transforms, resonates and inspires a wide range of audiences." Via its outreach arm, aodEducation, we offer an established educational programme of workshops, pre-show talks, publications, audio-CDs and DVDs. Can tour througout the year; venues include national and international touring venues. In general 1-5 actors work on each production. Recent productions include: *Lysistrata* (2018); *Savage Beauty* (2017); *Antigone* (2017); *Lysistrata* (2016), *Helen* (2016), *Bacchae* (2016), *Paris Alexandros* (2015); *Helen* (2014); *Medea* (2013); *Lysistrata* (2010-2011), *Bacchic* (2006-2008). Recent DVDs include: *Antigone* (2017), *Helen* (2014) and *Medea* (2013). Recent Audio CDs include *Sappho: The Sweetness of Honey* (2014). Also holds one-off high-profile events as part of **aod** events.

Casting procedures: Does not use freelance casting directors. Holds general workshop auditions; actors should write to request inclusion in early spring and summer. Casting breakdowns are available via the website and Spotlight. Does not welcome general submissions from actors but will accept invitations to view individual actors' Spotlight links and websites.

Actors Touring Company (ATC)

Institute of Contemporary Arts,
12 Carlton House Terrace, London SW1Y 5AH
tel 020 7930 6014
email atc@atctheatre.com
website www.atctheatre.com
Artistic Director Matthew Xia

Production details: Established in 1979. 2 productions are staged annually, touring to theatres in the UK and internationally, employing roughly 4-6 actors. Offers ITC/Equity-approved contracts. Recent productions include: *The Golden Dragon* (UK, India, Iraq, Ireland), *The Events* (UK/International), *The Suppliant Women* (UK/International), *Living with the Lights On* (UK, Spain, Finland), *Winter Solstice* (UK).

Casting procedures: Unsolicited approaches from actors are discouraged. Works with specified casting directors on casting productions.

APL Theatre Ltd

3rd Floor, 207 Regent Street, London W1B 3HH
tel 020 7692 8722

email info@apltheatre.com
website apltheatre.com
Facebook apltheatreproductions
Twitter @apltheatreltd
Instagram apltheatreltd

UK, nationwide and international productions. Casting services. Consultancy and general management, tour booking, costume/properety and scenery hire. UK Theatre and SOLT member. Mental health advocates.

ARC Theatre Ensemble

PO Box 1146, Barking, Essex IG11 9WB
tel 020 8594 1095
email carole@arctheatre.com
website www.arctheatre.com
Chief Executive Officer/Artistic Director Carole Pluckrose *Creative Director* Clifford Oliver (Olly)

Production details: Founded in 1984, Arc has built a strong core Management and Associate team bringing together an exceptional range of creative skills, educational experience and business and social expertise. The company is governed by an equally diverse and committed Board of Management. "We also benefit from a first-class pool of highly skilled, trained actors, storytellers, facilitators, workshop leaders, production managers and designers who are individually hand-picked to suit each programme or bespoke project." See the website for more details of its work.

Casting procedures: "To register your interest in working with Arc, please submit your details via the website. We will keep your details on record and contact you when a suitable opportunity arises. Alternatively you can email your details to our General Manager, Nita Bocking: **nita@arctheatre.com**."

Attic Theatre Company

Mitcham Library, 157 London Road, Mitcham CR24 2YR
tel/fax 020 8640 6800
email info@attictheatrecompany.com
website www.attictheatrecompany.com
Artistic Director Jonathan Humphreys

Production details: Attic was founded over 25 years ago when two actors and a musician created a theatre in the ballroom next door to Wimbledon Theatre. From its current base above Mitcham Library, Attic makes theatre for both traditional and non-traditional theatre spaces and ccommissions new work as well as classic adaptations. Many of Attic's productions are staged within Merton in theatres, parks and historic buildings. Attic also runs an extensive community programme. It has produced over 50 productions including world premieres, revivals and new work. For recent and forthcoming poductions see (**www.attictheatrecompany.com**).

Casting procedures: Uses freelance casting directors. Does not hold general auditions and does not accept casting enquiries or submissions from actors.

Badapple Theatre Company

PO Box 57, Green Hammerton, York YO26 8WQ
tel 01423 339168
email office@badappletheatre.com
website www.badappletheatre.com
Director Kate Bramley

Production details: Founded in 1998. Specialises in new comedy. Stages between 2 and 5 productions per year at a local rural touring level and/or national arts centre/small- to mid-scale theatre level. Uses 6-8 actors per year.

Casting procedures: Uses direct mail castings to agencies. Actors with an interest in the company are free to contact the office at any time. Directors prefer to see actors in performance prior to castings, so welcomes updates of performances in the Yorkshire region that company directors would be able to attend.

Big Telly Theatre Company

c/o Flowerfield Arts Centre, 185 Coleraine Road, Portstewart, Co. L'Derry BT55 7HU
tel 028 7083 2588 *fax* 028 7083 2588
email info@big-telly.com
website www.big-telly.com
Twitter @BigTellyNI
Director Zoë Seaton

Production details: Big Telly Theatre Company is Northern Ireland's longest established professional, not-for-profit theatre company, formed in 1987 and based in Portstewart on the North Coast. The company produces theatre, interactive workshop programmes and community creativity projects, which tour throughout Great Britain, Ireland and internationally. It concentrates on the visual potential of theatre through fusion with other art forms such as dance, music, circus, magic and film to create a unique sense of spectacle. "Big Telly's work is driven by a determination to offer audiences entertainment that surprises, stimulates and ignites the imagination."

Casting procedures: Does not use freelance casting directors. Casting breakdowns are available through Spotlight, Equity and other job-information services, and are also released to agents. Welcomes submissions (with CVs and photographs) from actors previously unknown to the company sent by post or email. Invitations to view individual actors' websites are also accepted. Offers ITC/Equity contracts, and endeavours to employ disabled actors when casting for disabled characters.

Border Crossings

13 Bankside, Enfield EN2 8BN
tel 020 3146 8788
email info@bordercrossings.org.uk
website www.bordercrossings.org.uk
Director Michael Walling

Production details: Established in 1995. International company, working in theatre and combined arts, that creates dynamic performances by fusing many forms of world theatre, dance and music. Stages 1 or 2 productions per year touring to up to 15 venues including arts centres and theatres. Roughly 3-9 actors are used in each production. Recent credits include: *The Flesh in Mine* (2014); *Consumed* (UK tour 2013); *Re-Orientations* (Soho Theatre 2010); *The Dilemma of a Ghost* (2007); *Bullie's House* (Riverside Studios); *Orientations* (Oval House); *Dis-Orientations* (Riverside Studios); and *Double Tongue* (UK tour). "We don't offer Equity contracts, although our own contracts are modelled on the ITC/Equity contract, and we usually pay above the minimum." Does not subscribe to the Equity Pension Scheme.

Casting procedures: Welcomes letters (with CVs and photographs) from actors previously unknown to the company if sent by post, but not by email. Invitations to view individual actors' websites and showreels are accepted. Actively encourages applications from disabled actors and promotes the use of inclusive casting.

Borderline Theatre Co.

Gaiety Theatre, Carrick Street, Ayr KA7 1NU
email enquiries@borderlinetheatre.co.uk
website www.borderlinetheatre.co.uk
Producer Dave Shea, Rishaad Moudden, Lauren McLay

Production details: Founded in 1974, the company is the longest running touring theatre in Scotland. It currently stages one touring production each year, with around 25 performances at 15-20 different venues. Venues include small to mid-scale arts centres, theatres and village halls across Scotland. In general 3-4 actors work on each production. Recent productions include: *Uncanny Valley*, *The Straw Chair* and *A Slow Air*.

Casting procedures: Does not use freelance casting directors. Currently releases casting breakdowns to agents, but may publish these on the website in future. Welcomes submissions (with CVs Spotlight links, showreels and photographs) from actors previously unknown to the company sent by post or email. Also accepts showreels.

Boundless Theatre

Unit J307, The Biscuit Factory, 100 Clement's Road, London SE16 4DG
tel 020 7928 2811
email admin@boundlesstheatre.org.uk
website www.boundlesstheatre.org.uk
Artistic Director Rob Drummer *Executive Producer* Zoe Lally

Production details: Established in 2001 (as Company of Angels). New and experimental work for young audiences. Offers Equity approved contracts as negotiated through ITC. Recent productions include: *Natives* (Southwark Playhouse); *World Factory*

(Young Vic and New Wolsey Theatre) and Theatre Cafe Festival (venues include The Tramshed and York Theatre Royal).

Casting procedures: Actors may write at any time to request inclusion on the database for future reference. Performers previously unknown to the company should contact Boundless Theatre with their CV by email only. Boundless Theatre is an equal opportunities employer and actively encourages applications from BME and disabled actors in line with their policy on inclusive casting.

Bruiser Theatre Company

BEAT Carnival Centre 11-47 Boyd Street, Belfast BT13 2GU
tel 028 9024 3731 *mobile* 07540 477055
email info@bruisertheatrecompany.com
website www.bruisertheatrecompany.com
Artistic Director Lisa May *Company Manager* Andrew Hume

Production details: Founded in 1997, Bruiser focus on producing exciting and innovative theatre, presenting existing texts using physical theatre techniques. Recent productions include: *The Importance of Being Earnest, Cabaret, Sweet Charity* and *The 25th Annual Putnam County Spelling Bee* (in association with The MAC, Belfast); *The Complete Works of William Shakespeare (Abridged)* and *Playhouse Creatures*. Each production consists of 2-14 actors and musicians and, on average, the company present 2 productions per year. This equates to a tour of around 45 performances at 16 venues across Ireland and Scotland.

Casting procedures: Uses in-house casting directors; casting breakdowns are available on the website. Welcomes both CVs and letters from actors previously unknown to the Company and unsolicited CVs and photographs throughout the year. These should be sent via email. Also welcomes performance notices, invitations to view individual actors' websites and showreels. Rarely has the opportunity to cast disabled actors.

Cahoots Theatre Company

St Martin's Theatre, West Street, London WC2H 9NZ
mobile 07711 245848
email ds@denisesilvey.com
website www.cahootstheatrecompany.com
Artistic Director Denise Silvey

Production details: Founded in 1999. Produces theatre, cabaret and CD recordings, as well as acting as a general management and press agent (see also !!Link!! entry under Agents). Stages 3-4 productions a year, with 100 performances over 15 venues (arts centres, theatres and cabaret venues) in London, Edinburgh and New York. Productions may involve from 1 to 17 performers. Offers Equity approved and non-Equity contracts. Recent credits include: *Dead*

Sheep and *An Audience with Jimmy Savile* at Park Theatre, and *The Man Called Monkhouse* on tour.

Casting procedures: Casting in in-house. Also publishes casting breakdowns on the Equity JIS. Welcomes emails (but not letters) with CVs and photographs from individuals previously unknown to the company. Does not welcome showreels, but is happy to receive invitations to view actors' websites. Will consider applications from disabled actors to play characters with disabilities.

Cambridge Shakespeare Festival
11 Crossways House, Anstey Way, Trumpington, Cambridge CB2 9JZ
mobile 07955 218824
email mail@cambridgeshakespeare.com
website www.cambridgeshakespeare.com
Artistic Director Dr David Crilly *Associate Directors* Simon Bell, David Rowan

Production details: The Festival Company was established in Oxford in 1988 by Artistic Director Dr David Crilly. The main focus for the Company is the annual Cambridge Shakespeare Festival, which runs throughout July and August. Situated in the gardens of the Colleges of Cambridge University, its pastoral setting is one of the loveliest in the world.

Cardboard Citizens
77a Greenfield Road, London E1 1EJ
tel 020 7377 8948
email mail@cardboardcitizens.org.uk
website www.cardboardcitizens.org.uk
Artistic Director Adrian Jackson

Production details: The UK's only homeless people's professional theatre company. Specialises in making forum theatre, but has broadened its scope to the provision of a range of performance-based cultural actions with, for and by homeless and previously homeless people. Productions include: *Cathy Come Home, Benefit Meta, Glasshouse, A Few Man Fridays, Mincemeat, Woyzeck* – national tour; *Timon of Athens* – national tour with RSC; *Visible* – national tour, 'down and out' community production.

Casting procedures: Uses in-house casting directors. Holds general auditions; actors may write at any time requesting inclusion. Welcomes letters, CVs and photographs from individual actors previously unknown to the company, sent via post or email. Also welcomes showreels and invitations to view individual actors' websites. Offers Equity-approved contracts. Actively encourages applications from actors with experience of homelessness, disabled people and promotes the use of inclusive casting.

The Castle Players
c/o Tilly Bailey & Irvine, 8 Newgate, Barnard Castle, County Durham, DL12 8NG
mobile 07748 708619
email info@castleplayers.co.uk
website www.castleplayers.co.uk
Chair Laurence Sach

Production details: An amateur community theatre company limited by guarantee. Established in 1987. Undertakes major open-air summer productions in specially constructed tiered-seat theatre. Also stages minimum of 1 touring production annually. Recent productions include: *Macbeth, Henry V, Twelfth Night, When We Are Married, Flarepath* and *The Adventures of Oliver Twist*. A participating company in the 2016 RSC *A Midsummer Night's Dream – A Play for the Nation*.

Casting procedures: Productions are cast from the local community at open auditions. Subscribe to the newsletter via the company website for regular updates. Uses in-house casting directors and holds general auditions; actors should write in January to request inclusion. Will accept unsolicited CVs and photographs sent by email only.

Chain Reaction Theatre Company
Millers House, Three Mill Lane, London E3 3DU
tel 020 8981 9527
email mail@chainreactiontheatre.co.uk
website www.chainreactiontheatre.co.uk
Artistic Director Sarah Smit

Production details: Established in 1994. An award-winning theatre company producing informative, entertaining and thought-provoking theatre, workshops and video productions for people of all ages. Aims to create quality accessible theatre experiences, and engage audiences with writing and performances that explore contemporary issues and perceptions of everyday life. Currently has 12 educational shows in its repertoire, each designed for a specific age range from 5 to 16 years. Performances tackle sensitive and controversial topics including drug-awareness, sexual health, bullying, healthy eating and exercise, and emotional wellbeing. Also designs bespoke pieces of theatre and video productions for a range of professionals, which may be used at corporate workshops, training events and conferences, and also works in TIE and Outreach.

Since 2003 has produced original musical theatre for adult audiences. Its first production, *Everyone Loves Me*, won an award for best musical, and its most recent production, *Pretty Please*, premiered in London in 2007.

Tours up to 4 shows each year. Recent productions include: *Food 4 Thought*; *It's Your Body*; *Movin' On Up*; and *Totally Together*. For more information, contact Sarah Smit.

Casting procedures: Uses freelance casting directors and sometimes holds general auditions. Check website for details of when applications will be accepted.

Cheek by Jowl
Stage Door, Barbican Theatre, Silk Street, London EC2Y 8DS
email info@cheekbyjowl.com
website www.cheekbyjowl.com
Facebook www.facebook.com/cheekbyjowl

Theatre

Twitter @CbyJ
Editor Instagram @wearecheekbyjowl
Artistic Directors Declan Donnellan, Nick Ormerod

Production details: The company was founded in 1981 by Declan Donnellan and Nick Ormerod. The name conveys an intimacy between the actors, the audience and the text; the phrase 'cheek by jowl' is quoted from *A Midsummer Night's Dream* ("Follow! Nay, I'll go with thee cheek by jowl" (Act III Sc II)) Recent productions include: *Pérèclès*, *Prince de Tyr* (in French), *The Winter's Tale* (in English), *Measure for Measure* (in Russian), *Ubu Roi* (in French) and *Tis Pity She's a Whore* (in English).

Casting procedures: "Like the vast majority of other British theatre companies, our actors are on fixed-term contracts. However, many actors come back regularly to work with us. For each new Cheek by Jowl production, a Casting Director is appointed. Please do not send unsolicited CVs as we are unable to accept them."

Chickenshed Theatre

290 Chase Side, Southgate, London N14 4PE
tel 020 8292 9222 *fax* 020 8292 0202
email susanj@chickenshed.org.uk
website www.chickenshed.org.uk
Artistic Director: Lou Stein; *Managing Director*: Louise Perry; *Creative Directors*: Dave Carey, Joseph Morton and Christine Niering; *Casting Director*: Fiona Carey

Founded in 1974, Chickenshed is a company that makes inspirational theatre, where imagination translates into empowerment. Bringing together people of all ages and from all backgrounds to produce outstanding theatre that entertains, inspires, challenges and educates both audiences and participants alike.

By using the power of performing arts, Chickenshed helps people reach their full potential and feel accepted. Creates a truly inclusive environment where people don't stigmatise, label or disregard, but accept and welcome difference.

Chickenshed encourages high profile and sustainable partnerships with the companies and professionals throughout the UK. Chickenshed runs children's and youth theatres for over 800 young people, operates three nationally accredited education courses, engages in community outreach projects and has established a growing network of 'sheds' both nationally and internationally.

The Rayne Theatre is an attractive and modern theatre space seating 300. The seating can be retracted to the rear wall creating a large, flat open space for performance or workshops. The Studio Theatre is 12m x 12m and is extremely versatile with seating for up to 140.

Most shows run from 3–6 weeks while the Christmas show runs for 7. Chickenshed has four performance spaces which are used during the Christmas show run but at other times performance spaces are available.

Hire rates: the Rayne: minimum £150/hr (depending upon requirements); Studio: minimum £100/hr (depending upon requirements).

Premises are accessible to disabled performers.

Recent productions include:*Rapunzel, One Flew Over the Cuckoo Nest, The Midnight Gang, Don't Stop Thinking About Tomorrow, Monolog.*

Casting procedures: Chickenshed generally produces in-house shows. Occasionally holds general auditions. Occasionally uses website breaksown services. please submit CVs throughout the year. Occasionally uses website breakdown services. Welcomes letters from individual actors previously unknown to the company and welcomes invitations to view individual actros' website and to visit other productions.

Actively promotes inclusive casting and believes that all of their actors should have access to all parts that are required. Usually casts from their own pool of actors but if there is a specific artistic casting requirement open calls may be considered.

Clean Break

2 Patshull Road, London NW5 2LB
tel 020 7482 8600 *fax* 020 7482 8611
email general@cleanbreak.org.uk
website www.cleanbreak.org.uk
Facebook www.facebook.com/cleanbreak
Twitter @CleanBrk
Executive Director Erin Gavaghan *Joint Artistic Directors* Anne Herrmann Roisin McBrinn *Producer* Mimi Fandlay

Production details: Clean Break was founded in 1979 by 2 women prisoners at HMP Askham Grange. The company's artistic mission is to create bold new plays by the best women playwrights, telling the stories about women and crime that are not being told elsewhere, and taking this work into prisons and onto stages across London, the UK and the world. The company generally stages 1 production, presenting 35 performances each year. Tours to around 5 theatres and prisons across England and Scotland annually. The average cast size is 3-4. Recent productions include: *House/Amongst the Reeds* (Edinburgh Festival Fringe), *Joanne* (RSC).*Dream Pill* (Edinburgh Festival Fringe), *Recharged* (Soho Theatre, Latitude festival), *Charged* (Soho Theatre), *it felt empty when the heart went at first but it is alright now* (Arcola Theatre), and *This Wide Night* (Soho Theatre). Offers ITC/Equity- approved contracts and does not subscribe to the Equity Pension Scheme.

Casting procedures: Uses freelance casting directors. Does not issue breakdowns. Auditions are organised via actors' agents and personal management. Unable to accept unsolicited CVs or showreels from actors. "Clean Break employ only women to deliver our services in accordance with our exemption under the Equality Act 2010, Part 1 Schedule 9. We also actively seek to work with artists who have lived experience of the criminal justice system." Actively encourages applications from disabled actors and promotes the use of inclusive casting.

Clod Ensemble

Unit 3, The Laundry, 2-18 Warburton Road, London E8 3FN
tel 020 7749 0555 *fax* 020 7749 0597
email admin@clodensemble.com
website www.clodensemble.com
Artistic Directors Suzy Willson, Paul Clark

Production details: A small- to mid-scale company established in 1996. Creates theatre, music and performance events, workshops and courses in London, the UK and internationally. Stages on average 1 production each year in the main house; also works in Outreach and Community. Recent productions include: *Under Glass* and *On the High Road*.

Casting procedures: Producer does the casting. Sometimes holds general auditions and actors should write to request inclusion. Welcomes unsolicited CVs and photographs if sent by email. Also accepts invitations to view individual actors' websites. Offers Equity-approved contracts as negotiated through ITC. Actively encourages applications from disabled actors and promotes the use of inclusive casting.

Close for Comfort Theatre Company

34 Boleyn Walk, Leatherhead, Surrey KT22 7HU
tel 01372 378613
email close4comf@aol.com
website www.closeforcomforttheatre.co.uk
Director Janet Gill *Co-director* Glenn Johnson

Production details: Founded in 2001. "Takes theatre to living rooms across the south of England."

Casting procedures: Does not use freelance casting directors or hold general auditions.

Cloud Nine Theatre Productions

5 Marden Terrace, Cullercoats, North Shields NE30 4PD
tel 0191 253 1901
email cloudninetheatre@blueyonder.co.uk
website www.cloudninetheatre.co.uk
Artistic Director Peter Mortimer *Associate Director* Colette Stroud

Production details: Established in 1997. Dedicated to commissioning and producing new work from Northern playwrights. Has produced plays by more than 24 Northern dramatists, in leading North-East venues. On average stages 2-3 productions each year. Recent productions include: *Death at Dawn - A Soldier's Tale from the Great War* (2014), *A Parcel for Mr Smith* (2015) and *The End of the Pier* (2016).

Casting procedures: Uses in-house casting directors. Depends on production; our small-scale productions tend to use members of our ensemble, but we audition for larger scale productions. Enquire first. As a North East-based company, we tend to cast with actors from this region, and generally would not encourage other actors to apply unless specifically requested.

The Common Players

72 West End Road, Exeter
email anthony@common-players.org.uk
website www.common-players.org.uk
Artistic Director Anthony Richards

Production details: Founded in 1989, The Common Players focus on presenting both original productions and the classic texts for, and in partnership with, the communities of the West Country. Recent productions include: *Jerusalem* (by Jez Butterworth), *Educating Rita* (Willy Russell) and *Smuggler's Gold* (an educational programme). Each production consists of 2-16 actors and, on average, the company present 2-3 productions per year. This equates to 30-40 performances at 30 venues across the south west, ranging from small theatres, to arts centres, community spaces, schools and outdoor venues.

Casting procedures: Uses in-house casting directors, but does not hold general auditions. A casting breakdown is available on the website. Rarely has the opportunity to cast disabled actors.

Communicado Productions

The Old Schoolhouse Newlandrig, Midlothian EH23 4NS
mobile 07525 181183
email gerrymulgrew@yahoo.co.uk
website www.communicadotheatre.co.uk
Artistic Director Gerry Mulgrew

Production details: Founded in 1983, Communicado is a theatre company that has presented the classics and new stories, live music and visual and physical theatre for over 20 years. It also holds teaching workshops and does exploratory theatre work. Its productions include: *Tam O Shanter* (with Assembly Productions), *The Government Inspector* (with Aberystwyth Arts Centre) and *Calum's Road* (with National Theatre of Scotland).

Each production consists of around 10 actors and, on average, the Company present 2 productions per year. This equates to around 60 performances across Scotland, mainly arts centres, theatres and community spaces. Communicado also take their work to the Edinburgh Fringe Festival. Offers Equity/ITC approved contracts.

Casting procedures: Welcomes invitations to view individual actors' websites and to attend performances. Actively encourages applications from disabled actors and promotes the use of inclusive casting.

Complicité

14 Anglers Lane, Kentish Town, London NW5 3DG
tel 020 7485 7700 *fax* 020 7485 7701

Theatre

email email@complicite.org
website www.complicite.org
Facebook @TheatredeComplicite
Twitter @complicite
Instagram @complicitetheatre
Artistic Director Simon McBurney

Production details: Award-winning theatre company founded in 1983. Constantly evolving its ensemble of performers and collaborators. Work ranges from entirely devised pieces to theatrical adaptations and revivals of classic texts. Recent productions include: *everything that rises must dance, A Pacifist's Guide to the War on Cancer The Encounter, Beware of Pity, The Master and Margarita, A Dog's Heart, Shun-kin, A Disappearing Number, Endgame, The Elephant Vanishes* and *Measure for Measure*. Contracts vary.

Casting procedures: Invites performers to casting auditions through agents or Spotlight. Welcomes invitations to see work (accompanied by a CV and photograph), but unable to respond to everyone. "We are always more inclined to meet actors previously unknown to us if they are familiar with our work (i.e. if they have seen a Complicité show or participated in an Open Workshop). Complicité's Creative Learning Department programmes up to 2 Open Workshop seasons for actors each year." Join the mailing list at **www.complicite.org**. Actively encourages applications from disabled actors and promotes the use of inclusive casting.

Concordance

Finborough Theatre, 118 Finborough Road, London SW10 9ED
tel 020 7244 7439
email admin@concordance.org.uk
website www.concordance.org.uk

Production details: Concordance is a theatrical production company, founded by Neil McPherson in 1981, and is resident at the Finborough Theatre, London – see entry under *Fringe theatres* on page 257. The company presents new writing, revivals of neglected work and music theatre.

CragRats Theatre

Suite 23, Finch's Yard, Eastwick Road, Bookham, Surrey KT23 4BA
tel 01372 457968 *fax* 01372 459808
email enquiries@cragrats.com
website www.cragrats.com

Company's work: A workshop delivery company founded in 1989, specialising in training in the education sector. Events draw on a unique mix of live theatre, dynamic workshops, e-learning, video and inspirational ambassadors with every element supported by in-depth research.

Employs 70 freelance actors a year. Project managers and facilitators are trained in-house. Clients include: schools across the UK, ASDA, NHS, British Airways, Learning & Skills Councils and the Royal Bank of Scotland.

Recruitment procedures: Extends its actor-base each month. Recruits actors through the website and through agents, Equity Job Information Service and advertisements in The Stage. Welcomes submissions (with CVs and photographs) by post or email from actors with at least 3 years of training at an approved drama school. Accepts invitations to view individual actors' websites and showreels. Actively encourages applications from disabled actors.

Creation Theatre Company

3rd Floor, Cherwell House, 1-5 London Place, Oxford OX4 1BD
tel 01865 761393 *fax* 01865 245745
email enquiry@creationtheatre.co.uk
website www.creationtheatre.co.uk
Director David Parrish *Associate Director* Charlotte Conquest

Production details: Produces site-specific Shakespeare. Stages 2-5 productions annually in unusual, non-traditional theatre venues (e.g. open air shows in parks, factory spaces, and a spiegeltent) with approximately 150 performances per year, mostly in Oxford. 8 actors work on each production. Recent productions include *The Snow Queen* and *King Lear*.

Casting procedures: Does not use freelance casting directors or hold general auditions. Casting breakdowns are available by postal application (with sae) and via Castcall. Welcomes letters and emails (with CVs and photographs) from actors previously unknown to the company at any time of year.

Dark Horse

Lawrence Batley Theatre, Queen's Street, Huddersfield HD1 2SP
tel 01484 484441 *fax* 01484 484443
email info@darkhorsetheatre.co.uk
website www.darkhorsetheatre.co.uk
Artistic Director Vanessa Brooks

Production details: Established in 2000. Production company exploring a range of projects that include actors with learning disabilities and promote inclusive working practices. Approximately 1 production per year touring to 10-15 venues, including arts centres and theatres in Yorkshire, the North West and internationally. Roughly 5-8 actors are used in each production.

Casting procedures: Occasionally uses freelance casting directors. Does not welcome unsolicited CVs. Actively encourages applications from disabled actors and promotes the use of inclusive casting. Offers Equity-approved contracts.

Dead Earnest Theatre

The Workstation, 15 Paternoster Row, Sheffield S1 2BX
tel 0114 221 0225 *mobile* 07855 866292
email info@deadearnest.co.uk
website www.deadearnest.co.uk
Facebook www.facebook.com/deadearnesttheatre

Twitter @deadearnest
Creative Director Charlie Barnes *Project Manager* Blue Merrick *Associate Team* Gareth Bennet-Ryan, Eleanor Curry, Penny Capper, Corinne Sue Mitchell, Rachel Newman, Nick Nuttgens, Fiona Paul, Victoria Roberts, Sarah Sayeed, Kitty Randle, Stacey Sampson

Production details: Dead Earnest is an Applied Theatre company based in Sheffield. Since forming in 1993, the company has delivered touring shows, commissioned performances and creative projects in South Yorkshire and across the UK. The company uses a variety of theatre techniques to explore social issues, with a particular focus on Forum Theatre.

Dead Earnest Theatre's work broadly fits into three categories: health and well-being (forum theatre for health professionals and service users); creative learning (working with universities, colleges and schools), and community theatre (working with community organisations and groups exploring issues around inequality and diversity). Has strong links with both Sheffield Hallam University, where the original Artistic Director, Ashley Barnes, is now Head of Stage and Screen, and the University of Sheffield, creating original plays based on academic research.

Stages around 20 productions each year (mainly forum theatre), which all rehearse in Sheffield but are shown throughout the country. Dead Earnest is a member of ITC and supplies Equity-approved contracts but does not subscribe to the Equity pension scheme.

Casting procedures: Uses pool of northern actors. Sometimes holds general auditions. Welcomes postal or email submissions (with CVs and photographs) from actors previously unknown to the company. Actively encourages applications from under-represented groups (including disabled and BAME performers).

Dirty Market Theatre Company
6 Grace's Mews, Camberwell, London SE5 8JF
tel 020 7701 8429
email info@dirtymarket.co.uk
website www.dirtymarket.co.uk
Co-directors Georgina Sowerby, Jon Lee

Production details: A collective of theatre makers with classical training; aims to integrate classical backgrounds with contemporary practice to create imaginative and exciting live performance. Applies for funding on a project-to-project basis, and is a member of ITC.

Casting procedures: Uses freelance casting directors. Casts from open workshops, and actors are advised to participate in these to get to know the company's work. Advertises via the website, Casting Call Pro, agents, SPF, etc. Welcomes approaches by actors by post and by email, but prefers to receive showreels by website link. Actively encourages applications from disabled actors.

DV8 Physical Theatre
Toynbee Studios, 28 Commercial Street, London E1 6AB

email dv8@artsadmin.co.uk
website www.dv8.co.uk
Twitter @DV8PhysTheatre
Artistic Director Lloyd Newson

Production details: Recent productions include: *JOHN* (2014, verbatim theatre production); *Can We Talk About This?* (2012, verbatim theatre production). Other productions include: *To Be Straight With You* (verbatim theatre production); *Just for Show* (stage production); *The Cost of Living* (film); *Living Costs* (stage production); *Enter Achilles* (film/stage); *Strange Fish* (film/stage).

Casting procedures: Uses in-house casting directors. Performers should write in and submit videos when auditions are advertised.

Eastern Angles Theatre Company
Sir John Mills Theatre, Gatacre Road, Ipswich IP1 2LQ
tel 01473 218202 *fax* 01473 384999
email info@easternangles.co.uk
website www.easternangles.co.uk
Director Ivan Cutting *Executive Director* Kate Sarley

Production details: Founded in 1982, the company tours theatre productions around East Anglia. New writing and a flavour of the region colour all of its original work. Stages 4-5 pieces each year, with an average annual total of 220 performances at 80 different venues. These include arts centres and theatres, educational and community venues, and site-specific locations. Tours mainly to East England but also nationally on occasion. In general, 6 actors work on each production. Offers ITC/Equity contracts; does not subscribe to the Equity Pension Scheme.

Casting procedures: Does not use freelance casting directors or hold general auditions. Casting breakdowns are not publicly available but may occasionally be posted on the website. Welcomes letters (with CVs and photographs, but not saes); email attachments will not be opened. Advises applicants to consult the website to get an idea of the sort of work the company produces. Applicants should only write once and should specify in their letter if they are local or native to the region. Will consider applications from disabled actors to play characters with disabilities.

The Edge Theatre
Manchester Road, Chorlton, Manchester M21 9JG
tel 0161 2829 776
email info@edgetheatre.co.uk
website www.edgetheatre.co.uk
Facebook /theedgetheatre
Twitter @theedgemcr
Editor Instagram edgemanchester
Artistic Director Janine Waters

Production details: The Edge is Manchester's award-winning theatre for participation and is a receiving

Theatre

and a producing house. They are members of Paines Plough Small Scale Touring Network and have a particular interest in participatory theatre, musical theatre, new writing and theatre for children. Recent productions include: *Love Shift* (Royal Exchange Theatre 2010), *Spinach* (Royal Exchange Theatre, 2011 and Kings Head, 2012) and *Dreaming Under a Different Moon* (Edge Theatre, 2012). Edge stage 1 in-house production every 2 years. Edge offer Equity/ITC-approved contracts.

Casting procedures: Uses in-house casting directors, but does not hold general auditions. Welcomes unsolicited CVs and photographs and showreels from actors who are strong singers only. Also happy to receive invitations to view productions in the north-west. Actively encourages applications from disabled actors and promotes the use of inclusive casting.

English Touring Theatre

25 Short Street, London SE1 8LJ
tel 020 7450 1990
email admin@ett.org.uk
website www.ett.org.uk
Artistic Director Richard Twyman

Production details: English Touring Theatre was founded in 1993 to create outstanding theatre and tour it to the widest possible audience. ETT is recognised as one of the UK's most successful and influential touring production companies. It tours to mid-large scale venues nationwide. It works with leading artists to stage an eclectic mix of new and classic work; theatre that is thrilling, ground-breaking and entertaining.
. Offers UK Theatre/Equity contracts and subscribes to the Equity Pension Scheme.

Casting procedures: Uses freelance casting directors and does not encourage unsolicited submissions from actors.

European Theatre Company

39 Oxford Avenue, London SW20 8LS
tel 020 8544 1994 *fax* 020 8544 1999
email admin@europeantheatre.co.uk
website www.europeantheatre.co.uk
Directors Adam Roberts, Jennie Graham

Production details: Founded in 1992, the company produces French-language theatre which tours the UK. Stages 3 or more productions a year, with around 250 performances in arts centres, theatres, schools and community venues. Normally employs 5 actors for each production.

Casting procedures: Casts in-house. Welcomes letters (not emails) with CVs and photographs from French-speaking actors previously unknown to the company.

The Faction

17 Vanbrugh Park, London SE3 7AF
email info@thefaction.org.uk
website www.thefaction.org.uk

Artistic Director Mark Leipacher *Co-Artistic Director* Rachel Valentine Smith

Production details: Founded in 2008, an independent theatre company dedicated to innovative revivals of classical texts. Aims to generate and sustain an ensemble of actors who share and develop skills, and who can explore a 21st-century solution to the extinct repertory system. "We question what constitutes a 'classical text', and work to determine which authors' works complement and enhance our understanding and enjoyment of Shakespeare and his contemporaries and thus should be a permanent part of the repertoire."

Stages 3+ productions annually, with around 120 performances at 4 venues (arts centres/theatres/outdoor/educational). In general 8-20 actors are involved in each production. Recent productions include: Highsmith's *The Talented Mr Ripley* (Greenwich Theatre); Shakespeare's *Romeo and Juliet* (Greenwich Theatre); Schiller's *Joan of Arc* (New Diorama Theatre); Lorca's *Blood Wedding* (New Diorama Theatre); Schiller's *Mary Stuart* (New Diorama Theatre/UK tour/Qatar).

Casting procedures: Casts in-house. Casting breakdowns are available from the website, mailing list, email and Casting Call Pro. Welcomes letters (with CVs and photographs) from individual actors previously unknown to the company, sent by email. Also accepts showreels and invitations to view actors' websites and visit other productions. Encourages applications from disabled actors and promotes the use of inclusive casting.

Fluellen Theatre Company

14 Devon Place, Swansea SA3 4DR
tel 01792 368269
email fluellentheatre@aol.com
website www.fluellentheatre.co.uk
Artistic Director Peter Richards *Associate Director* Claire Novelli

Production details: Fluellen is a small-scale classical theatre company producing work from Greek drama to Harold Pinter via Shakespeare. Recently included new drama into programming. All productions premiere at the Grand Theatre Swansea. Recent productions include: *The Merry Wives of Windsor* (Shakespeare), *Antigone* (Sophocles) and *The Late Marilyn Monroe* (a new play by Francis Hardy). Each production consists of a variable number of cast members and, on average, the company present 4 main productions per year, alongside 9 shorter 'Lunchtime Theatre' productions. This equates to around 60 performances at 10 venues in Wales, including arts centres, theatres and outdoor community spaces.

Casting procedures: Uses in-house casting director. General auditions are held several times throughout the year. Welcomes both CVs and letters from actors previously unknown to the Company and unsolicited

CVs and photographs. These should be sent via email. Also welcomes invitations to view individual actors' websites and showreels. Happy to consider applications from disabled actors and will consider inclusive casting.

Forbidden Theatre Company

56 Handsworth Road, London N17 6DE
email info@forbidden.org.uk
website www.forbidden.org.uk
Artistic Director Steve Brownlie

Production details: Physical and visual theatre company. Produces small-scale productions of adaptations of classics and devised work. Stages 1 production annually and gives approximately 40 performances per year. Tours 2 venues on average and performs in arts centres and theatre venues in London and Scotland. In general, 4-6 actors work on each production. Recent productions include: *Goddess, Stung,* and *Mrs Wobble the Waitress and Friends.*

Casting procedures: Does not use freelance casting directors. Sometimes holds general auditions. Actors can write at any time requesting inclusion. Welcomes letters (with CVs and photographs) but not email submissions. Advises that the company will only reply to actors if inviting them to audition. CVs are kept on file.

Forced Entertainment

The Workstation, 15 Paternoster Row, Sheffield S1 2BX
tel 0114 279 8977
website www.forcedentertainment.com
Key personnel Tim Etchells (*Artistic Director*), Robin Arthur, Richard Lowden, Claire Marshall, Cathy Naden, Terry O'Connor

Production details: Since forming the company in 1984, the 6 core members of the group have sustained a unique artistic partnership, confirming their position as "trailblazers in contemporary theatre". The company's substantial canon of work reflects an interest in the mechanics of performance, the role of the audience, and the machinations of contemporary urban life. Its work, framed and focused by Artistic Director Tim Etchells, is distinctive and provocative, delighting in disrupting the conventions of theatre and the expectations of audiences. Forced Entertainment's trademark collaborative process – devising work as a group through improvisation, experimentation and debate – has made them pioneers of British avant-garde theatre, and touring all over the world has earned them an unparalleled international reputation. Visit the website for a full archive of work.

Forest Forge Theatre Co.

The Theatre Centre, Endeavour Park, Crow Arch Lane, Ringwood, Hants BH24 1SF
tel 01425 470188 *fax* 01425 471158
email info@forestforge.co.uk
website www.forestforge.co.uk
CEO/Artistic Director Kirstie Davis *Associate Director* David Haworth

Production details: Tours 3 productions a year into studios, village halls and arts centres, and has a large Creative Learning programme. The company is particularly interested in commissioning new work with rural or regional themes, and second productions. Recent commissions include: *Free Folk* by Gary Owen, and *For the Record* by Joyce Branagh.

Found Theatre

The Byways, Church Street, Monyash, Derbyshire DE45 1JH
tel 01629 813083
email found_theatre@yahoo.co.uk
website www.foundtheatre.org.uk
Artistic and Casting Director Simon Corble

Production details: Small-scale touring and site-specific theatre.

Casting procedures: Does not hold general auditions; actors should write for specific projects only, when advertised. Welcomes unsolicited CVs and photographs sent via email and invitations to view individual actors' websites.

Frantic Assembly

31 Eyre Street Hill, London EC1R 5EW
tel 020 7841 3115
email admin@franticassembly.co.uk
website www.franticassembly.co.uk
Facebook www.facebook.com/franticassembly
Twitter @franticassembly
Artistic Director Scott Graham *Executive Director* Kerry Whelan

Production details: Award-winning theatre company Frantic Assembly's method of devising theatre has been impacting theatrical practice and unlocking the creative potential of future theatre-makers for 25 years. One of the most exiting theatre companies in the UK, Frantic Assembly has toured extensively across Great Britian, and has worked in 40 countries internationally collaborating with some of today's most inspiring artists. Frantic Assembly are currently studied as leading contemporary theatre practitioners on five British and international academic syllabuses, and in the last year introduced over 15,000 workshop participants to the company's process of creating theatre. With a history of commissioning writers such as Mark Ravenhill, Abi Morgan and Bryony Lavery, the company has been accclaimed for its collaborative approach. In 2016, the company started delivering practical modules on a new Collaborative Theatre-Making MA it has created with Coventry University.

In 2018 Frantic Assembly launched the Frantic Assembly Podcast which is hosted by Scott Graham and gives insight to the work and practices of Frantic

Assembly, it includes relevant guests and collaborators.

Casting procedures: Does not hold open auditions. Does not accept unsolicited CVs. External casting directors are used to cast for productions.

Frantic Theatre Company

32 Wood Lane, Falmouth TR11 4RF
tel 0870 165 7350
email bookings@frantictheatre.com
website www.frantictheatre.com

Production details: Founded in 1990. Stages 2 productions annually with around 900 performances in venues throughout the UK and Ireland every year. Venues include arts centres, village halls, theatres, outdoor venues, educational and community venues, private homes and hospitals. On average 2 actors work on each production. Recent productions include: *You Hum It, I'll Play It.*

Casting procedures: Holds general auditions. Actors should write in May and November to request inclusion. Casting breakdowns are available at Call Pro. Actors are advised not to telephone and to send their details only when they have researched the company's very specific work and explain their suitability

Freedom Studios

Bradford Design Exchange, 34 Peckover Street, Little Germany, Bradford BD1 5BD
tel 01274 730077
email hello@freedomstudios.co.uk
website www.freedomstudios.co.uk
Creative Producer Deborah Dickinson

Production details: Established in 2007. A national touring, devising theatre company. Stages theatrical events and experiences at arts centres, theatres and outdoor venues across the UK. In general 2-4 actors are involved in each production. Offers Equity-approved contracts as negotiated through ITC. Recent productions include *Street Voices 2*. Also holds the Asian Theatre School for a 15-week period each year, for aspiring Yorkshire British Asian, Black and ethnic minority artists; and Unit 4, "a twice-yearly platform event for some of the most exciting voices in the UK contemporary arts scene".

Casting procedures: Sometimes holds general auditions. Welcomes letters (with CVs and photographs) from individual actors previously unknown to the company, sent by post or email; also accepts showreels and invitations to view individual actors' websites. Will consider applications from disabled characters to play characters with disabilities.

Galleon Theatre Company Ltd

50 Openshaw Road, London SE2 0TE
tel 020 8310 7276
email boxoffice@galleontheatre.co.uk
website www.galleontheatre.co.uk

Artistic Director Alice de Sousa *Theatre Director* Bruce Jamieson

Production details: For recent productions, please see the website. Also has a film company, Galleon Films Ltd, which is developing a slate of 4 feature films.

Casting procedures: Uses an in-house casting director. Holds general auditions; actors should write to request inclusion when the company is casting for a specific project. Casting breakdowns are available through CastNet and advertisements in *The Stage*. Welcomes letters (with CVs and photographs) but not email submissions. Showreels and invitations to view individual actors' websites are also accepted.

Goat and Monkey

email info@goatandmonkey.co.uk
website www.goatandmonkey.co.uk
Director Joel Scott *Producer* Sally Scott

Production details: Founded in 2004, Goat and Monkey create immersive and site-specific theatre that is highly visual, detailed and ambitious. Their work pushes the boundaries of audience interaction and theatrical form and looks to provide a unique experience for audiences in a variety of different environments. Recent productions include: *The Devil Speaks True* (tour), *The Moonlight Club*, *The Perils of Poisonous Plants* (Kew Gardens) and *The Seed* (live performances, online story and real-world treasure hunt. Each production can include 1-45 actors and, on average, the company present 1 production and several smaller research-based projects per year. Performances take place in theatres, found sites and outdoor venues across London and the south-east. Offers ITC-based contracts.

Casting procedures: Uses freelance casting directors and only holds production specific auditions. Welcomes both CVs and letters from actors previously unknown to the company if sent by email. Also welcomes invitations to view individual actors' websites, but does not welcome showreels. Casting breakdowns are available through the website and Spotlight. Would welcome the chance to cast disabled actors.

Gomito Productions

email sam@gomito.co.uk
website wwww.gomito.co.uk
Producer Sam Worboys

Production details: Founded in 2001, Gomito is a collaboration of artists making new visual theatre. The company is an ever-changing family of performers, designers, directors, musicians and writers who want to share stories in a certain way; with creativity, entertainment, humour, emotion and homespun roughness; with theatricality at its simplest. Recent productions include: *The Achemystorium, Woodland* and *Chester Tuffnut*. Each production consists of 3-6 actors and, on average, the company present 1-3 productions per year. This equates to over 50 performances at over 25 venues, including art centres, theatres and educational establishments. Productions also tour nationally.

Casting procedures: Gomito primarily uses its open workshops for casting at various times throughout the year. Email or join the mailing list on the website for details. Welcomes both CVs and letters from actors previously unknown to the company and unsolicited CVs and photographs. Also welcomes invitations to view individual actors' websites and showreels.

Graeae Theatre Company

Bradbury Studios, 138 Kingsland Road,
London E2 8DY
tel 020 7613 6900
email info@graeae.org
website www.graeae.org
Artistic Director Jenny Sealey

Production details: Founded in 1980 and artistically led by Jenny Sealey, Graeae boldly places D/deaf and disabled actors centre stage.

Graeae's signature aesthetic is the compelling creative integration of sign language, captioning and audio description, which engages with both disabled and non-disabled audiences. Championing accessibility and providing a platform for new generations of artists, Graeae leads the way in pioneering, trail-blazing theatre. Graeae also run an extensive programme of creative learning opportunities throughout the year, training and developing the next generation of D/deaf and disabled artists. These programmes include Write to Play and Ensemble.

Recent productions and co-productions include: *Reasons to be Cheerful*, *Cosmic Scallies*, *The House of Bernarda Alba*, *The Solid Life of Sugar Water*, *Blood Wedding*, *The Threepenny Opera*, *Belonging*, *Blasted* and *Bent*. Spectacular outdoor productions include *This is Not for You*, *The Limbless Knight*, *Prometheus Awakes* and *The Iron Man*.

Graeae are strategic partners on the Ramps on the Moon consortium and are a National Portfolio Organisation (NPO) of Arts Council England.

Grassmarket Project

email info@grassmarketproject.org
website www.grassmarketproject.org
Director Jeremy Weller

Production details: Founded in 1989. Independent theatre company producing new work in theatres across Europe, USA and the UK. Stages 2 productions annually and gives 30-40 performances every year. On average, 5-6 actors work on each production. Recent productions include: *De Andre (The Others)*; *Fathers & Sons* (Betty Nansen Theatre, Copenhagen); *Bus Stops* (Glasgow); and *The Foolish Young Man* (Roundhouse Theatre, London). Has also

worked in film, notably on Lars von Trier's *Limboland*.

Casting procedures: Productions are cast by freelance casting directors or the company's artistic director. Sometimes holds general auditions. Employs a mixture of trained and untrained actors. Welcomes letters (with CVs and photographs) by post or email. Showreels and invitations to view individual actors' websites are also accepted. Offers non-Equity contracts. Will consider applications from disabled actors to play characters with disabilities.

Green Ginger

Unit 18, Albion Dockside Estate, Hanover Place,
Bristol BS1 6UT
mobile 07977 465850
email mail@greenginger.net
website www.greenginger.net
Facebook www.facebook.com/greengingertheatre
Twitter @greenginger
Artistic Director Chris Pirie *Patron* Terry Gilliam

Production details: Founded in 1978, Green Ginger is a theatre company based in Bristol, UK and Wiseppe, France that creates and tours original theatre with complementary educational activities for most ages and all abilities. Green Ginger collaborates with major arts organisations, including Welsh National Opera and Aardman Animations. Its members teach at University of Bristol, École Supérieure Nationale de la Marionette (France) and the Royal Welsh College of Music and Drama. Recent productions include: *Lionel the Vinyl* (2013), *Outpost* (2014) and *Intronauts* (2018).

Each production consists of 3-4 actors and, on average, the company presents 2 productions a year. The company tours extensively, having performed around the world for 40 years. Touring productions can be adapted to a variety of venues including schools, theatres, community spaces and outdoor and non-traditional theatre spaces. Offers Equity/ITC approved contracts at above minimum rates.

Casting procedures: Uses freelance casting directors and occasionally holds general auditions. Casting breakdowns are available online and on social media. Welcomes both CVs and letters from performers previously unknown to the company and unsolicited CVs and photographs. Also welcomes invitations to view individual actors' websites and showreels. The company welcomes the opportunity to cast disabled actors.

Grid Iron Theatre Company

Suite 4/1, 2 Commercial Street, Edinburgh EH6 6JA
tel 0131 555 5455
email admin@gridiron.org.uk
website www.gridiron.org.uk
Director Ben Harrison

Production details: Founded in 1995. Produces new writing and site-specific theatre. Stages 1-3 productions annually and gives 20-50 performances every year. Performs in theatres, outdoor and site-specific venues in Scotland, England and Northern and the Republic of Ireland. Recent productions include: *Huxley's Lab, Barflies, Once Upon a Dragon* and *Roam*.

Casting procedures: Sometimes holds general auditions. Actors may write requesting inclusion at any time throughout the year. Welcomes submissions (with CVs and photographs) sent by post and email. Showreels and invitations to view individual actors' websites are also accepted.

Happystorm Theatre
11 Old Mill Close, Pendlebury, Salford M27 4DW
mobile 07547 711839
email info@happystormtheatre.co.uk
website www.happystormtheatre.co.uk
Joint Artistic Directors Susi Wrenshaw, Matthew Ganley

Production details: Established in 2010. Award-winning production company specialising in immersive, site-specific theatre. 360-degree adventures that cut to the core of contemporary Salford. Recent productions include *Borderline Vultures* and *The Crypt Project*.

Casting procedures: Uses in-house casting directors and does not hold general auditions. Casting breakdowns are available as Spotlight submissions or by email and via the Equity Job Information Service. Actors should approach the company only for specific casting requirements. Will consider individual performance notices. Actively encourages applications from disabled actors and promotes the use of inclusive casting.

Headlong Theatre
3rd Floor, 34-35 Berwick Street, London W1F 8RP
tel 020 7478 0270 *fax* 020 7434 1749
email info@headlongtheatre.co.uk
website www.headlongtheatre.co.uk
Artistic Director Jeremy Herrin *Key contact* Henny Finch

Production details: National touring theatre company dedicated to new ways of making theatre by exploring revolutionary writers and practitioners of the past, present and future. Stages 4-6 projects annually, performing 24-32 weeks of the year. Tours nationally and internationally. Recent productions include: *Romeo and Juliet* (UK Tour); *Decade* (St Katharine Docks); *Earthquakes in London* (National Theatre/UK Tour); and *ENRON* (Chichester Minerva/Royal Court/West End/Broadway/UK Tour).

Casting procedures: Offers TMA/Equity approved contracts. Casting not dealt with in-house. Independent casting directors used on a show-by-show basis. Show invitations can be sent via email.

Hidden Talent Productions Ltd
50D Wickham Road, Brockley, London SE4 1NZ
mobile 07905 175934

email info@hiddentalent.org.uk
website www.hiddentalent.org.uk
Artistic Director Adam Linsson *Casting Director* Andrew Miller

Production details: Established in 2006 as a not-for-profit, small-scale theatre producing company. Stages primarily new musicals and cabarets. Aims to raise the profile of musical theatre in the community by producing new works. Tours to small venues across the UK. Offers closed workshop performances and readings through to fully staged musical productions in larger theatres. Stages on average 1 production in the main house and 2 in the studio each year. Recent productions include: *Heaven Sent, A New Musical Comedy* (World Premiere – New Wimbledon Studio); *Manhattan Melodies in the West End* (Dominion Theatre Studio) and numerous cabarets.

Casting procedures: Uses in-house casting directors. Sometimes holds general auditions; actors may write in at any time, but preferably when the company is casting specific projects. Casting breakdowns are available via the website or on postal application with an sae. Welcomes letters (with CVs and photographs) from individual actors previously unknown to the company sent by post or email. Accepts showreels and invitations to view individual actors' websites. Will consider applications from disabled actors to play characters with disabilities.

Highly Sprung Performance Company
Studio 3, 54 Grafton Street, Coventry CV1 2HW
tel 07810 267660
email mail@sprunghq.fsnet.co.uk
website www.highlysprungperformance.co.uk
Co-Artistic Directors Sarah Worth, Mark Worth

Production details: Founded in 1999. Aims to create original and innovative performances exploring the relationship between dance, text and physical theatre. Also runs community and educational activities alongside productions. Stages 1 production annually with 25 performances every year. Tours 10-15 venues annually: these include arts centres, theatres, outdoor and educational venues in the West Midlands, London, Manchester and Edinburgh. On average 2-8 actors work on each production. Recent productions include: *Pretend I'm Not Here* and *More Than Kisses*.

Casting procedures: Holds general auditions. Actors should send CVs and photographs by post or email. These will be kept on file for future auditions. Casting breakdowns are available on the website, by postal application and via Equity Job information Service and advertisements in *The Stage*. Showreels and invitations to view individual actors' websites are also accepted.

Hijinx Theatre
Wales Millennium Centre, Bute Place, Cardiff CF10 5AL
tel 029 2030 0331

email info@hijinx.org.uk
website www.hijinx.org.uk
Artistic Director Ben Pettitt-Wade

Production details: Founded in 1981, the company makes professional theatre performed by actors with and without learning disabilities which tours globally.

Offers ITC/Equity-approved contracts and does not subscribe to the Equity Pension Scheme.

Casting procedures: Shows are cast by the Artistic Director. Welcomes letters, CVs and photographs from actors previously unknown to the company. Welcomes applications from disabled and non-disabled actors.

Historia Theatre Co

8 Cloudesley Square, London N1 0HT
tel 020 7837 8008
email historiatheatre@yahoo.co.uk
website www.historiatheatre.com
Facebook @theatrecompanyhistoria
Artistic Director Catherine Price

Production details: Established in 1997. "Historia presents plays that have their source or inspiration in history." 1 production annually with 20-30 performances. Plays in small theatres in Londn mainly for short runs; touring productions visit theatres, arts venues, National Trust houses, museums, churches, schools and village halls both nationally and in London. Roughly 6-8 actors are used in each production. Recent productions include: *Dear Chocolate Soldier* (World War One play); *Fire and Phoenix* (about the Great Fire of London) 2016; *Magna Carta* (2015); 4-week run of *Queen Anne* (2014); schools tour of *The Sound of Breaking Glass* by Sally Sheringham (about the Suffragettes) 2012-2013; *Judenfrei: Love and Death in Hitler's Germany* (2011 – New End Theatre, Hampstead; 2010 – Henley Fringe Festival and tour); *An African's Blood* (2007, and a limited season in 2008; tour); *Five Eleven or the Powder Treason* (2005; tour), and *Evelina* (2004; Pentameters Theatre). Offers ITC/Equity rates where possible.

Casting procedures: Does not use freelance casting directors or hold general auditions. Breakdowns are published via Equity's Job Information Service and Spotlight link. Unsolicited approaches from actors are discouraged. Will consider applications from disabled actors when casting for characters with disabilities.

Hoipolloi Theatre

Office F, Dale's Brewery, Gwydir Street, Cambridge CB1 2LJ
tel/fax 01223 322748
email info@hoipolloi.org.uk
website www.hoipolloi.org.uk
Director Shôn Dale-Jones *Associate Director* Stephanie Müller

Production details: Founded in 1994, the company creates visually and physically dynamic, imaginative and comic work which tours to small-and middle-scale theatres and arts centres throughout the UK. It is also involved in educational work. Stages 1-2 productions annually, presenting 100 performances every year at 60-70 venues. On average 4-5 actors work on each production. Recent productions include *My Uncle Arly*.

Casting procedures: Sometimes holds general auditions. Actors may write at any time requesting inclusion. Welcomes letters (with CVs and photographs) but not email submissions. Invitations to view individual actors' websites are also accepted. Advises actors approaching the company to have some knowledge of its work.

Hollow Crown Productions

Rose Cottage, Stone Street, Spexhall, Halesworth, Suffolk IP19 0RN
mobile 07930 530948
email peter@hollowcrown.co.uk
website www.hollowcrown.co.uk
Artistic Director Peter Adshead

Production details: A theatrical production company with a difference. Provides an extension to the young graduate actor's training through the professional production experience. Offers ongoing vocational support to develop and enhance the foundation skills conferred through recognised drama school training, so that each company member may achieve their full potential.

Casting procedures: Uses in-house casting directors. Sometimes holds general auditions via workshops; actors may write in at any time. Casting breakdowns are available from CastNet. Welcomes letters (with CVs and photographs) from actors not previously known to the company if sent by post; no email submissions. Does not accept showreels. Offers own contract based on Equity Fringe/TMA. Will consider applications from disabled actors to play characters with disabilities. "The company is especially keen to hear from actors whose philosophy/approach to text resonates with its artistic policy, and who would be keen to explore often neglected classical texts – including Shakespearean texts in their quarto/folio forms."

Horse + Bamboo Theatre

The Boo, 679 Bacup Road, Waterfoot, Rossendale, Lancashire BB4 7HQ
tel 01706 220241
email info@horseandbamboo.org
website www.horseandbamboo.org
Facebook TheBooWaterfront
Twitter @horseandbamboo
Instagram @horseandbamboo
Key contacts Esther Ferry-Kennington, Phil Milston

Production details: Established in 1978. A visual touring theatre using masks, puppets and with a specialism in the folk arts. Tours to venues, including arts centres and outdoor venues in the UK. Performers must have mask/puppetry experience to a professional level. Offers Equity contract. Members of ITC.

Casting procedures: Welcomes letters from actors, makers and socially engaged artists.

Icarus Theatre Collective

5 Elephant Lane, London SE16 4JD
tel 020 7998 1562
website www.icarustheatre.co.uk
Facebook www.facebook.com/icarustheatre
Twitter @icarustheatre
Instagram @icarustheatre
Artistic Director Max Lewendel

Production details: Icarus creates theatre that is kinetic, intellectual, and visceral: theatre that moves. We choose to relish what others shy away from, destroy boundaries when others would create rules. We explore harsh, brutal themes with a modern exploration of Theatre of the Absurd in classic and contemporary storytelling. We are changing our focus this year to tackle the increasingly dangerous nativist, misogynist, and racist rhetoric. We will:
– Put female, EU, and BAME artists in staff positions and the central role of new productions
– Ensure disability and demographic are no barrier to making art
– Defy the stigmas surrounding mental health, proving it is a prevalent issue in our society and one that all our central characters live with.
Also work in Education, Outreach & Community, for which the key contact is edu@icarustheatre.co.uk. Recent productions include: *How to Be a Bad Girl* by Sabrina Chap, *Macbeth* and *Hamlet* by William Shakespeare; *The Trials of Galileo* by Nic Young; *H.P. Lovecraft's At the Mountains of Madness* adapted by Max Lewendel; *The Lesson* by Eugène Ionesco; *Journey's End* by R.C. Sherriff and *Vincent in Brixton* by Nicholas Wright.

Casting procedures: Uses in-house casting directors. Holds general auditions; actors should write in when advised to do so by the company's newsletter. Casting breakdowns are available from the website and are advertised in Spotlight. Welcomes letters (with CVs and photographs) sent by post or email but no attachments via email. Accepts showreels or invitations to view individual actors' websites or performances.

Ichiza Theatre Company

2 Bradford Court, Bloxham, Oxon OX15 4RA
tel 01295 720500 *fax* 01295 722118
email office@ichiza.co.uk
website www.ichiza.co.uk
Artistic Director Togo Igawa *Associate Director* Masumi Kako

Production details: Established in 2007. Produces Japanese plays, from traditional theatre to contemporary works, in collaboration with artists from different backgrounds. Recently completed its first production, *The Face of Jizo* by Hisashi Inoue, at Arcola Theatre, to acclaim from wide audiences. Plans to start work in TIE/Outreach in the near future.

Casting procedures: Uses in-house casting directors and holds general auditions; actors are advised to write in only when auditions are announced. Casting breakdowns are available from Equity Job Information Service and *The Stage*. Does not welcome unsolicited approaches by email, but will accept letters (with CVs and photographs) and showreels sent in response to specific, announced auditions. Actively encourages applications from disabled actors and promotes the use of inclusive casting.

Incisor

41 Edith Avenue, Peacehaven, East Sussex BN10 8JB
mobile 07979 498450
email sarahmann7@hotmail.co.uk
website www.theatre-company-incisor.com
Artistic/Casting Director Sarah Mann *Associate Director* James Madden

Production details: Recent productions include: *Pinter's People*, *The Odd Couple* and *Abigail's Party*.

Casting procedures: Uses in-house casting directors and does not hold general auditions. Casting breakdowns are available from Casting Call Pro/ Castweb/CastNet. Welcomes letters (with CVs and photographs) from actors previously unknown to the company, sent by post or by email. Does not accept showreels but will respond to invitations to view individual actors' websites. Actively encourages applications from disabled actors and promotes the use of inclusive casting. "Incisor's style is big and bold, especially as a lot of our work is outdoors. Large characters and voices needed."

Jam Theatre Company

45a West Street, Marlow, Buckinghamshire SL7 2LS
tel 01628 483808
email office@jamtheatre.co.uk
website www.jamtheatre.co.uk
Artistic Director Jo Noel-Hartley *Producer, Production Design and Management* Mark Hartley

Production details: Founded in 2006, Jam Theatre Company is a professional theatre company writing and producing original productions for their own studio theatre and for transfer to commercial theatres. Shows are available for co-productions and licensing in the UK and America with Samuel French, London or via the Jam Theatre website. Jam also offer full-time and e-learning programmes in theatre and performing arts. Jam pays above Equity minimums, but doesn't offer approved contracts. Recent productions include: *Cinderella and the 7 Dwarfs*, *Santa's Secret Escape* and *Spots and Stripes*.

Casting procedures: Casting breakdowns are available through the website, Spotlight and Castweb. Welcomes CVs and letters from actors previously unknown to the company via email and online links to showreels. Also happy to receive production notices and invitations to view individual actors' websites. Will consider applications from disabled actors to play characters with disabilities.

Jasperian Theatre Company

Milsrof, Eglos Road, Ludgvan Churchtown, Penzance TR208HG
tel 01736 740907 *mobile* 07941 616177
email jasperiantheatre@mac.com
website www.jasperian.org
Artistic Director Tony Jasper *Production Directors* Kenneth Pickering, Peter Moreton, Harry Gostelow, Clare Davidson

Production details: Founded in 1992, JTC specialises in plays and revues that have a religious underpinning and/or deal with the human condition. The company casts all shows on artistic ability – not on any religious affiliation. Normally stages 2-3 productions each year with possibly a total of around 100 performances. Tours to a variety of different venues including theatres, churches and private houses across the UK. In general 3-7 actors work on each production. Recent productions include: *Charles Wesley 1707* (100 venues), *Stories of Grace*, *It Happened One Friday* and *God's Trombones*.

Casting procedures: Uses freelance casting directors. Actors may write requesting inclusion in the next round of auditions at any time, but the beginning of February, June and September are normally good times. Casting breakdowns are available through casting agencies. Prefers actors to send in their details by post but will accept the occasional email. Showreels are also accepted. Advises actors to read audition notices carefully and only come if suitable and available over the time period specified. Offers non-Equity contracts; however, "Apart from usually £250-£350 I also offer all accommodation and meals paid, and in some instances this is better than a basic Equity contract. I attempt to cast only Equity members. In 18 years, no-one has been owed money [by me]." Encourages applications from disabled actors and promotes the use of inclusive casting.

Kabosh

The Old Museum Arts Centre,
7 College Square North, Belfast BT1 6AR
tel 028 9024 3343 *fax* 028 9023 1130
email artisticdirector@kabosh.net
website www.kabosh.net
Artistic Director Paula McFetridge

Production details: Founded in 1994. Produces innovative physical and visual theatre for local, national and international touring and site-specific work. Stages 2-4 productions annually with 56

performances during the course of the year. Tours to around 30 venues annually, including arts centres and theatres, and site-specific locations. In general 2-6 actors are involved in each production. Countries covered include Northern Ireland, Republic of Ireland, England (including London), Scotland, Wales, parts of Europe and North America. Recent productions include: *Rhinoceros* and *Todd*.

Casting procedures: Auditions are by invitation only. Actors should write requesting inclusion in July (for autumn productions) and November (for spring productions). Welcomes applications (with CVs and photographs) sent by post and email. Also accepts invitations to view individual actors' websites. Any actor known to the company is welcome to send a CV and headshot (which will be kept on file) and to notify the director of performances where their work may be seen. The director will endeavour to see new actors. Any unseen actor who has sent a CV will be notified of open auditions, should they arise.

Kali Theatre Company

The Albany, Douglas Way, Deptford,
London SE8 4AG
tel 020 8694 6033
email info@kalitheatre.co.uk
website www.kalitheatre.co.uk
Artistic Director Helen Bell

Production details: Founded in 1991 to encourage, support and promote new writing by Asian women. "We focus on content and ideas as much as style, aiming to present memorable theatre events based on challenging and innovative ideas." One touring production each year, playing to diverse audience. Nurtures novice playwrights through its two level Writer Development Programme, culminating in public readings of new plays. Has worked with writers such as Tanika Gupta, Rukhsana Ahmad, Gurpreet Bhatti and Shelley Silas among others. Recent productions include: *Mustafa*, *The Husbands*, *The Dishonoured*, *Ready Or Not*, *My Big Fat Cowpat Wedding* and *Bitched*. See website for further details.

Casting procedures: Welcomes letters (with CV and photograph) from South Asian actors previously unknown to the company by email. Does not accept showreels or invitations to view individual actors' websites. Rarely (or never) has the opportunity to cast disabled actors. "Phone to find out what we are casting before sending CVs and photos".

Kneehigh Theatre

14 Walsingham Place, Truro, Cornwall TR1 2RP
website www.kneehigh.co.uk
Artistic Director Mike Shepherd

Production details: Stages 3 productions annually with 130 performances during the course of the year. On average tours to 15 venues annually. Performs in arts centres, theatres, outdoor and "out of the ordinary" indoor venues across the UK and

Theatre

internationally. Recent productions include: *A Matter of Life and Death*, *Cymbeline*, *Rapunzel* and *Brief Encounter*. Offers ITC/Equity-approved contracts but does not subscribe to the Equity Pension Scheme.

Casting procedures: Does not hold general auditions. Advises that the company works with a pool of performers, but is interested in meeting new actors – either by personal recommendation or by seeing their work. Actively encourages applications from disabled actors and promotes the use of inclusive casting.

Language Laid Bare Productions
Top Floor, 298 Brockley Road, London SE4 2RA
mobile 07545 704016
email languagelaidbare@yahoo.co.uk
Producer Darren Batten

Production details: Aims to produce high-quality performances of new writing and rarely played drama from the UK and overseas. To discover and develop new work and playwrights, and to provide a platform for new and emerging actors and creatives. Stages around 2 productions each year, with 30 performances in 6 arts centres/theatres nationwide. In general 5 actors are involved in each production. Recent productions include: *Deirdre & Me*, *You Don't Kiss*, and *Nina and Shaz*.

Casting procedures: Uses in-house casting directors. Casting breakdowns are available from Castweb, Castnet and Casting Call Pro. Does not welcome unsolicited approaches by actors, but will accept invitations to view individual actors' websites. Actively encourages applications from disabled actors and promotes the use of inclusive casting.

LipService
Z-Arts, 335 Stretford Road, Manchester M15 5ZA
tel 0161 232 6093/4 *fax* 0161 881 0061
email info@lip-service.net
website www.lipservicetheatre.co.uk
Joint Artistic Directors Sue Ryding, Maggie Fox

Production details: Over the past 20 years, LipService has established itself as one of the leading comedy touring companies, producing shows for the theatre which have a strong base in popular culture. These include: *The Picture of Doreen Gray*; *Inspector Norse* (a self-assembly Swedish crime thriller); *Desperate to be Doris*; *Jane Bond* (blonde and dangerous; a spoof of all things Bond); *Very Little Women* (a comic version of Louisa May Alcott's *Little Women*); *Hector's House* (an epic tale of togas and taramasalata); *The Importance of Being Earnest* (a trivial comedy for serious people); *Women on the Verger* (a hilarious look at romantic women's fiction); *Move Over Moriarty* (an impenetrable case for Sherlock Holmes and Doctor Watson); and *Withering Looks* (a slice of life with the Brontë Sisters).

LipService attracts audiences from a wide social mix and age range. Based in Manchester, the company has built up a solid touring circuit in the North of England and throughout the rest of Britain. Challenges its audience by setting up a recognisable form and subverting it. This is partly achieved by two women playing all the characters, but also by ingenious theatrical surprises. "Along with the National Theatre of Brent, LipService is one of our great 2-person ensembles." (*Guardian*)

Casting procedures: Uses casting directors of co-producing venue. Does not hold general auditions. Actors should write requesting inclusion when extra performers are needed for a new production. Casting breakdowns are available direct from the co-producing theatre; details of co-producers are available via the website. Welcomes invitations from actors to view their work and from actors familiar with the company's work. Offers TMA/Equity-approved contracts.

London Actors Theatre Co.
Unit 5A, Spaces Business Centre, Ingate Place, London SW8 3NS
tel 020 7978 2620 *fax* 020 7978 2631
email latchmere@fishers.org.uk

Production details: Founded in 1987 and normally stages 1-2 productions annually, employing 6-8 actors on non-Equity contracts.

Casting procedures: Casting breakdowns are published in *The Stage*. Any approaches not relating to a specific breakdown are discouraged.

London Bubble Theatre Co.
5 Elephant Lane, London SE16 4JD
tel 020 7237 4434
email admin@londonbubble.org.uk
website www.londonbubble.org.uk
Creative Director Jonathan Petherbridge *Associate Director, Creative Learning* Adam Annand

Production details: The company's mission is "to attract and involve a wide range of audiences and participants, particularly those experiencing theatre for the first time, to inventive and unpredictable events that reflect the diversity of our city and its people".

To this end, the company has the following aims:

• To work particularly with and for people who do not normally have access to theatre for geographical, financial or cultural reasons
• To encourage and enable people to develop their own theatre and related skills
• To work to create a popular theatre form which is open, exciting and accessible
• To produce events which demonstrate and celebrate the creative abilities of all those taking part
• To examine issues of common concern to all those involved through the choice of material for workshops, projects and professional performances
• To challenge prejudice and bigotry through the company's organisation, working processes and final product

• To achieve a diversity of influence that is discernible throughout the company's work and consciousness

Recent productions include: *Primary, Tales from the Arabian Nights, After Hiroshima, Hopelessly De-Voted* and *From Docks to Desktops*.

Louche Theatre

Oakleigh, Waun Fawr, Aberystwyth SY23 3QD
tel 07949 667343 (Admin) and 01970 612617 (Box Office)
email louche.theatre@hotmail.co.uk
website www.louchetheatre.com
Artistic Director Harry Durnall *Production Manager* Anwen Howard

Production details: Founded in 1981, Louche Theatre presents 3-4 productions per year which are performed in Aberystwyth then tour Wales. Most years, one of theses are taken to the Edinburgh Festival Fringe. Recent productions include: *The Erpingham Camp, Peter Pan, The Merchant of Venice, A Christmas Carol* and *Kindertransport*. Each production consists of 10 actors and this equates to around 30 performances; including a tour of 5 venues, specifically small theatres and community centres.

Casting procedures: Uses in-house casting directors and holds general auditions in January. A casting breakdown can be requested by email. Welcomes both CVs and letters from actors previously unknown to the company and unsolicited CVs and photographs. These should be sent via email. Also welcomes invitations to view individual actors' websites and showreels. Encourages applications from disabled actors.

Lurking Truth

Gwynfryn, Newtown Road, Machynlleth, Powys SY20 8EY
tel 01654 702 200
email ddr@aber.ac.uk
website www.theatre-wales.co.uk/companies/company_details.asp?ID=21
Artistic Director and Secretary David Ian Rabey

Production details: Founded in 1986, Lurking Truth present contemporary work and premieres by dramatists such as Howard Barker, David Ian Rabey, David Rudkin and Arnold Wesker. This is sometimes done in association with Aberystwyth University Department of Theatre, Film and Television Studies, and several alumni of the department have gone on to work with the company.

Casting procedures: Uses in-house casting directors. Welcomes unsolicited CVs (with photographs) sent by email. Also welcomes invitations to view individual actors' websites, but does not welcome showreels.

Mad Dogs and Englishmen

The Old Post Office, Green Lane, Quidenham, Norfolk NR16 2AP
tel 01953 888499 *fax* 01953 888499
email info@mad-dogs.org.uk
website www.mad-dogs.org.uk
Director Ann Courtney

Production details: Founded in 1995. Theatre company based in Norfolk whose policy is to provide well-balanced, entertaining and educational drama. Main areas of work are new writing, adaptations and classical work. Stages 2 productions annually with 70 performances during the course of the year, plus 30 workshops for schools. Tours to rural venues (churches, public houses) as well as arts centres, theatres, outdoor venues, educational venues, and community venues. On average 4-9 actors are involved in each production. Recent productions include: *The Magician's Box*, commissioned by Wilkin and Sons of Tiptree and *David Copperfield*, celebrating the Charles Dickens bicentennial.

Casting procedures: Sometimes holds general auditions.

Magnetic North Theatre Productions

Summerhall, Summerhall Place, Ediburgh EH9 1PL
email mail@magneticnorth.org.uk
website www.magneticnorth.org.uk
Director Nicholas Bone; *Producer* Verity Leigh; *Marketing* James Coutts

Production details: Founded in 1999. Commissions and produces new plays: 12 full productions and 1 film have been produced. Also runs a cross art form Artist Development programme for early- and mid-career artists. Stages 1-2 productions annually and gives 20-40 performances during the course of a year. Tours on average to 12 venues annually. About 5 actors are involved in each production. Recent productions include: *Our Fathers, A Walk at the Edge of the World, Sex and God, Pass the Spoon* and *Walden*.

Casting procedures: Sometimes holds general auditions. Actors should write to request inclusion when productions are announced on the website. Casting breakdowns are publicly available through the website. Welcomes submissions (with CVs and photographs) sent by post or email. Also accepts invitations to view individual actors' websites. Advises that the company has a low turnover of productions and a small staff, and finds it difficult to respond to general enquiries about available work.

MANACTCO (formerly Manchester Actors Company)

31 Leslie Street, Manchester M14 7NE
tel 0161 445 8477 *fax* 0161 332 7867
email admin@manactco.org.uk
website www.manactco.org.uk
Artistic Director Stephen Boyes

Production details: Established in 1980 and now the North West's leading provider of theatre in schools.

Theatre

"We are emphatically *not* a TIE company." Reaches well over 80,000 young people each year with around 6 touring productions. Recent productions include: *The Tempest, Of Mice and Men, The Pirate Queen, Much Ado About Nothing,* and *Poetry in Motion.*

Casting procedures: Uses in-house casting directors and sometimes holds general auditions. Actors may write in June/July requesting inclusion. Casting breakdowns are available via Equity Job Information Service and specific casting websites, for example Casting Call Pro. Welcomes letters (with CVs and photographs) from individual actors previously unknown to the company, sent by post or email; also welcomes showreels and invitations to view individual actors' websites. Actively encourages applications from disabled actors and promotes the use of inclusive casting. "We give priority to formally trained actors who have completed recognised courses at drama school. We like actors who can face the rigours of touring with good humour!"

Guy Masterson Productions

email guy@guymasterson.com
Artistic Director Guy Masterson

Production details: Olivier Award-winning producer of small- to mid-scale touring theatre work. Stages 4-6 productions annually with up to 400 touring performances a year. Touring access to 500 different national and international venues, including arts centres, theatres, arts festivals and outdoor, educational and community venues. Recent productions include: *Morecambe* (Olivier Award for Best Entertainment), *Shylock, The Odd Couple, Twelve Angry Men, Animal Farm* and *Under Milk Wood.*

Casting procedures: Rarely holds auditions. Mainly works with actors seen previously or by invitation.

Meeting Ground Theatre Co.

4 Shirley Road, Nottingham NG3 5DA
tel 0115 962 3009
website www.meetinggroundtheatrecompany.co.uk
Artistic directors Tanya Myers and Stephen Lowe

Production details: Work is based on the belief that, by taking artistic work across barriers and frontiers – whether they be national, psychological, intellectual, cultural, spiritual or disciplinary – new sources of energy and creativity can be engendered.

Since 1985 Meeting Ground has been celebrating the meeting of artists from different disciplines and cultures. Administered from its Nottingham base, the company draws together writers, actors, musicians, directors, puppeteers, designers and digital artists, and encourgaes community participation. At the heart of the company's artistic policy and vision is the theatrical exploration of what we call the 'politics of the imagination; issues and questions that control the imagination and shape all our destinies. We actively seek to listen and give voice to the unheard.'

Casting procedures: Offers ITC/Equity contracts and does not subscribe to the Equity Pension Scheme. Actively encourages applications from disabled actors and promotes the use of inclusive casting.

Midland Actors Theatre (MAT)

25 Merrishaw Road, Northfield,
Birmingham B31 3SL
tel 0121 608 7144 *fax* 0121 608 7144
email news@midlandactorstheatre.co.uk
website www.midlandactorstheatre.com
Director David Allen *Associate Director* Gillian Adamson

Production details: Founded in 1999. Produces classics and new work. Specialises in theatre tours, community productions and schools-based projects. Stages 1-2 productions annually with 30-40 performances during the course of the year. Tours on average to 40 different theatres, schools, and other venues in the West Midlands, East Midlands, and nationally each year. Around 2-5 actors are involved in each production. Recent productions include: *Macbeth, Prospero's Island, The Children, The Mothers, The Good Person of Sezuan* and *The White Shining Land.* Offers ITC/Equity-approved contracts and does not subscribe to the Equity Pension Scheme.

Casting procedures: Sometimes holds general auditions. Actors should write requesting inclusion when auditions are advertised; general casting enquiries are most welcome in January and June. Casting breakdowns are publicly available via Equity Job Information Service. Advises that the company is primarily interested in actors who are Midlands based. Actively encourages applications from disabled actors and promotes the use of inclusive casting.

Mikron Theatre Company

Marsden Mechanics, Peel Street, Marsden,
Huddersfield HD7 6BW
tel 01484 843701
email admin@mikron.org.uk
website www.mikron.org.uk
Twitter @mikrontheatre
Artistic Director Marianne McNamara

Production details: Theatre anywhere for everyone, by canal, river and road. Has been touring for 46 years: "Mighty little Mikron" (*Guardian*). Tours on Tyseley, the company's historic narrowboat, on the inland waterways of Britain in the summer, and by road in the autumn months. Recent productions include:*Best Foot Forward* by Maeve Larkin and *In at the Deep End* by Laurence Peacock.

Casting procedures: Does not hold general auditions. Actors may write in Dec/Jan to request inclusion, and are strongly advised to keep an eye on the website. Casting breakdowns are publicly available from the website, via Spotlight. Welcomes letters and emails (with CVs and photographs) from actor musicians only. Does not accept showreels, but accepts invitations to view individual actors' websites. Asks actors to "please bear in mind that this is a hard tour: boating all day and shows and get-ins every night. Do consult the website before applying".

Mimbre

Unit 4, Energy Centre, Bowling Green Walk, London N1 6AQ
tel 020 7613 1068
email info@mimbre.co.uk
website www.mimbre.co.uk
Artistic Directors Lina Johnansson, Silvia Fratelli, *Associate Artistic Director* Emma Norin

Production details: A local and international circus and street theatre company, using circus skills and dance to produce innovative work and promote a strong, positive image of women. Works in unconventional settings, creating moments of the unexpected and reclaiming some beauty in the urban environment. Mimbre's performances and participation programme are designed to reach beyond social, financial and cultural boundaries and find fresh ways to engage, encourage and inspire audiences, both nationally and internationally. Stages 1-2 main shows and works in collaboration with 50-60 performances in 15-20 arts centres, outdoor and festival venues, and theatres across the UK and Europe. In general 3-6 performers are involved in each production. Latest productions: *Lifted* (premiered June 2019); *Fierce Sisters* (premiered 2018) and *The Exploded Circus* (premiered May 2018).

Casting procedures: Uses in-house casting directors; holds general auditions only when producing a new show. Welcomes letters (with CVs and photographs) from individual actors previously unknown to the company, sent by email. Accepts showreels, performance notices and invitations to view performers' websites. Actively encourages applications from disabled actors and promotes the use of inclusive casting.

New Perspectives Theatre Co.

8 Park Lane Business Centre, Park Lane, Nottingham NG6 0DW
tel 0115 927 2334 *fax* 0115 927 1612
email info@newperspectives.co.uk
website www.newperspectives.co.uk
Artistic Director Jack McNamara

Production details: Founded in 1973. A leading East Midlands touring theatre company; also tours nationally. On average stages 3-5 productions each year, touring all over the county including theatres, arts centres and rural venues. Equity-approved contracts as negotiated through ITC. Recent productions include: *The Lovesong of Alfred J Hitchcock* (Leicester Curve, regional tour); *The Boss Of It All* (Assembly, Edinburgh); *Farm Boy*

(Edinburgh Festival, national tour); *Dolly* (Curve, regional tour); *Those Magnificent Men* (regional tour) and *Lark Rise to Candleford* (national tour).

Casting procedures: Does not welcome unsolicited approaches. Promotes the use of inclusive casting. Casting breakdowns are available through Spotlight Link and from the website.

New Shoes Theatre

mobile 07972 395634
email admin@newshoestheatre.org.uk
website www.newshoestheatre.org.uk
Facebook NewShoesTheatre
Twitter @newshoestheatre
Artistic Director Nicolette Kay

Production details: The company stages 1 or 2 productions annually: *Hurried Steps* by award-winning writer Dacia Mariani, which is performed in arts centres, theatres, educational and community venues. The latest show is *Jeannie* by Aimée Stuart produced in association with Neil McPherson for the Finborough Theatre. Up to 8 actors can be involved in eahc production.

Casting procedures: Uses in-house casting directors. Casting breakdowns can be found on-line on sites such as the webpage, *The Stage*, Spotlight, Casting Call Pro and Arts Jobs and/or social media such as Twitter and Facebook.

NITRO

Unit 36, 88-90 Hatton Gardens, London EC1N 8PG
tel 020 7609 1331
email info@nitro.co.uk
Artistic Director Felix Cross

Production details: Founded in 1978; formerly known as Black Theatre Co-operative Ltd. National touring theatre company that generates and produces contemporary black musical theatre. First established to provide training for black writers, directors and artists. Aims to explore ways of using black music as a means of attracting new audiences to theatre. Stages 1-2 productions annually with 1-2 performances during the course of the year. Recent productions include: *Nitrobeat* and *A Nitro at the Opera*.

Casting procedures: Sometimes uses agents when casting. Also holds general auditions; actors should write at the start of the year to request inclusion. Welcomes submissions (with CVs and photographs) sent by post or email. Accepts invitations to view individual actors' websites. Advises that the company keeps an up-to-date catalogue of black actors and would particularly welcome CVs from actors of different ethnic backgrounds. Offers TMA/Equity-approved contracts and does not subscribe to the Equity Pension Scheme. Actively encourages applications from disabled actors and promotes the use of inclusive casting.

No Limits Theatre

Studio 2, Arts Centre Washington, Fatfield, Tyne & Wear NE38 8AB

Theatre

tel 0191 4154966 *fax*
email info@nolimitstheatre.org.uk
website www.nolimitstheatre.org.uk
Artistic Director/Chief Executive Janet Nettleton
Associate Director Alan Parker

Production details: Founded in 1995, No Limits is a touring theatre company that works with adults with and without learning disabilities. Aims to produce high-quality, devised work that challenges traditional perceptions of theatre and disability, staging 1 production in 20 different venues across the UK each year. It also has a strong commitment to outreach and development work. In general 5-8 actors work on each production. Recent productions include: *Attic*, *The Winged State* and *Cuckoo Jack*.

Casting procedures: Welcomes letters, CVs and photographs from actors previously unknown to the company, but does not accept emails or unsolicited showreels. Advises that the company already has a core acting team but often takes on new actors in workshop training sessions.

Northern Broadsides

139 E Mill, Dean Clough, Halifax HX3 5AX
tel 01422 369704
website www.northern-broadsides.co.uk
Founder Barrie Rutter *Artistic Director and Composer* Conrad Nelson *Executive Director* Kay Packwood

Production details: Formed in 1992 by Barrie Rutter, Northern Broadsides is a multi-award winning touring company based in the historic Dean Clough Mill in Halifax, West Yorkshire. The company has built up a formidable reputation performing Shakespeare and classical texts with an innovative, popular and regional style. The company tours extensively in the UK, and has delighted audiences across the world, touring to India, Brazil, the USA, Greece, Cyprus, the Czech Republic, Poland, Germany, Austria and Denmark.

The company repertoire consists mainly of Shakespeare and classical texts. These plays possess a timeless resonance and their universal exploration of the human condition has currency in any day and age, appealing directly to the soul, the emotions and the imagination. Northern Broadsides are dedicated to interpreting the classics in a manner which makes what is often regarded as 'difficult' work extremely accessible. Their lively 'no frills' approach, with simple storytelling and minimal sets, has not only won the company many plaudits and awards, but enabled both established and new audiences to enjoy Shakespeare regardless of language or theatrical convention.

Northern Broadsides' work is characterised by its vitality, humour and passion.

NTC Touring Theatre Company

The Dovecote Centre, Amble,
Northumberland NE65 0DX

tel 01665 713655
email admin@northumberlandtheatre.co.uk
website www.northumberlandtheatre.co.uk
Artistic Director Gillian Hambleton

Production details: Founded in 1978 as Northumberland Theatre Company. Small-scale touring theatre company performing at village halls, small theatres and community venues in predominantly rural areas. Main areas of work are new writing and physical theatre pieces. Stages 2+ productions annually with more than 90 performances during the course of the year. Up to 5 actors are involved in each production.

Casting procedures: Holds audition workshops for locally based actors, usually in the spring. Casting breakdowns are available on the website, Facebook via Equity and Arts Jobs. Welcomes submissions (with CVs and photographs) by email. Also accepts invitations to view individual actors' performances and will always reply to individual actors. Particularly interested in locally based actors or actors with local origins, and will keep details on file for future reference unless requested to do otherwise. Actively promotes the use of inclusive casting.

The Okai Collier Company Ltd

39 Morris House, Roman Road, Bethnal Green, London E2 0HP
tel 020 8980 5716
email info@okaicollier.com
website www.okaicollier.com
Artistic Directors Omar F. Okai, Simon James Collier

Production details: The Okai Collier Company was formed in 1994 by artistic directors Omar F. Okai and Simon James Collier to explore and push the boundaries of everyday ideas, opinions and opportunities in the creative arts: music, theatre, dance, painting and the written word. Using a variety of media including IT, the company aims to break down contemporary social barriers and encourage new talent by developing a range of projects in this field. These projects include award-winning theatrical productions, opera, creative writing with young people, exhibitions for new artists and community arts projects, as well as its innovative publishing division. Okai Collier is committed to maintaining a balanced portfolio of work, divided between the commercial and charitable spheres and drawing on a diverse range of people and disciplines.

Open Clasp Theatre Company

The Stephenson Building, 173 Elswick Road, Newcastle-upon-Tyne NE4 6SQ
tel 0191 272 4063 *fax* 0191 272 4137
email info@openclasp.org.com
website www.openclasp.org.uk
Facebook Open Clasp Theatre co
Twitter @OpenClasp
Artistic Director Catrina McHugh MBE

Production details: Open Clasp makes truthful, risk-taking and award-winning theatre informed by the lived experiences of working-class women, women disenfranchised in the theatre and society, those from minority communities and women affected by the criminal justice system. They take a special interest in women and young women from the North, shining a light on their experiences through our work. Open Clasp make space for debate, encouraging audiences to walk in the shoes of the most disempowered women in society. Their work is performed in theatres, prisons, village halls, schools, conferences and community centres and most recently, the Edinburgh Fringe and off-Broadway to national and international acclaim. It resonates deep into the communities where it is created and outside ensures the under-respresented are seen in a new light by women, men and those with the power to make a difference.

On average stages 1 touring production per year, usually in Oct-Nov, first stage developments in March and one-off project commissions. Tours/previews include approx. 30 performances in 20+ arts centres, theatres and educational and community venues in the North East, South East, Yorkshire and London. Recent productions include: *Rattle Snake*, *Key Change*, *Sugar* (preview tour), *The Space Between Us*, *Swags & Tails*, *BlueGiro*, and *Rattle & Roll*.

Casting procedures: Sometimes holds general auditions; actors requesting inclusion should write in January. Casting breakdowns are available from the website, by postal application with sae, and from online casting services. Welcomes letters (with CVs and photographs) from individual actors previously unknown to the company, sent by post or email, but does not accept showreels. Will consider invitations to view individual actors' websites if accompanied by a full CV. Encourages applications from disabled actors. "It is paramount that our actors share the ethos of the company. Open Clasp ensures that casting is representative of the diverse groups we work with, the issues explored, and the characters they have created."

The Original Theatre Company
Dovedon Hall Office, Chedburgh Road, Whepstead, Bury St Edmunds, Suffolk IP29 4UB
tel 0870 803 0158
email info@originaltheatre.com
website www.originaltheatre.com
Director Alastair Whatley

Production details: Established in 2004. Stages 3-4 productions annually, with 200 performances in 40-50 mid to large-scale theatres across the UK. In general 8-13 actors are involved in each production. Offers Equity-approved contracts. Recent productions include: Sebatian Faulk's *Birdsong* (2013 and 2014), *Private Ear & The Public Eye* (Yvonne Arnaud Theatre and tour), *Three Men in a Boat* (Yvonne Arnaud Theatre and tour), *Our Country's Good* (Kingston Rose, Theatre Clywd and tour); *Dancing at Lughnasa* (Glasgow Citizens and tour); *See How They Run* and *Twelfth Night* (produced in rep and touring); *Vincent in Brixton* (Yvonne Arnaud, Theatre Royal Windsor, Northcott Exeter); *Othello* (Harrogate Theatre, Buxton Opera House).

Casting procedures: Sometimes holds general auditions; actors may write in March and July to request inclusion. Casting breakdowns are available from the website, by postal application with sae, and from Spotlight. Welcomes letters (with CVs and photographs) from individual actors previously unknown to the company, sent by post only. Also welcomes showreels and invitations to view individual actors' websites. Actively encourages applications from disabled actors and promotes the use of inclusive casting.

Out of Joint
3 Thane Works, Thane Villas, London N7 7PH
tel 020 7609 0207 *fax* 020 7609 0203
email hello@outofjoint.co.uk
website www.outofjoint.co.uk
Operations Assistant Thomas Ryalls

Production details: Stages 2 productions annually with approximately 230 performances during the course of the year. Tours nationally playing to around 15 arts centres and theatres each year. Recent productions include: *The Remains of the Day*, *Close Quarters* and *Rita, Sue and Bob Too*.

Casting procedures: Welcomes email submissions from individual actors. Also accepts performance notices from individual actors. Offers Equity-approved contracts.

Ovation
Upstairs at the Gatehouse, Highgate, London N6 4BD
tel 020 8340 4256
email events@ovationproductions.com
website www.upstairsatthegatehouse.com
Artistic Directors John and Katie Plews

Established in 1997, Upstairs at the Gatehouse offers a varied programme of drama, musicals and fringe theatre productions.

The main theatre has flexible seating configurations: thrust has seating for 122, L-shaped has seating for 108, cabaret has seating for 140 and traverse (for in-house productions only) has seating for 116. The usual duration of a run for a show can be between one night and six weeks. Subsidised rates are not available. Hire rates are available on application.

Produces three in-house shows a year. Castings are announced on the website. General auditions are not held. Casting breakdowns are available on the website and Spotlight. Letters (with CVs and photographs) from invidivual actors not previously known to the company are only welcome when casting. Unsolicited CVs and photographs sent by email are only welcome when casting. Showreels are not welcome.

Ovation Productions

Upstairs at The Gatehouse, Highgate,
London N6 4BD
tel 020 8340 4256
website www.ovationtheatres.com
Directors John Plews, Katie Plews

Production details: Founded in 1985. Owns and
operates Upstairs at the Gatehouse, a fringe theatre in
North London (see entry under *Fringe theatres* on
page 255). Recent productions include: *Anything
Goes, Return to the Forbidden Planet, Top Hat, Flat
Out* and *Nice Work If You can Get It.*

Casting details: Casting breakdowns are always
posted on **www.upstairsatthegatehouse.com** and on
Spotlight. Welcomes email submissions. Offers non-
Equity contracts. Will consider applications from
disabled actors to play characters with disabilities.

The Oxford Shakespeare Company

98 Galloway Road, London W12 0PJ
tel 07581 751198
email info@osctheatre.org.uk
website www.oxfordshakespear.co
Directors Nicholas Green, Emma Randle, Charlotte
Windmill

Production details: Founded in 2001. Stage
Shakespeare and other classic plays. The OSC are
celebrated for their open air, site-specific
performances both at their summer residency at
Wadham College and across the Historic Royal Palaes
sites of Hampton Court, Kensington Palace, Tow of
London and the Banqueting House, Whitehall. Stages
3 productions with up to 100 performances during
the course of the year. Acting company of up to 12
including actor/musicians. Recent productions
include: *Much Ado About Nothing, Love's Labour Lost,*
and *Twelfth Night* (Nicholas Green and Nick Lloyd
Webber), *As You Like It* (Michael Oakley and Nick
Lloyd Webber); *A Midsummer Night's Dream*
(Gemma Fairlie and *The Tempest* (Mick Gordon and
Nick Lloyd Webber).

Casting procedures: Casting breakdowns are released
to agents and are available via Spotlight.

Oxfordshire Theatre Company

c/o Mercer Lewin, 41 Cornmarket Street,
Oxford OX1 3HA
mobile 07802 287703
email info@oxfordshiretheatrecompany.co.uk
website www.oxfordshiretheatrecompany.co.uk
Artistic Director Karen Simpson

Production details: Tours high-quality, challenging,
entertaining and accessible theatre to audiences in
Oxfordshire and beyond. The company has a unique
reputation for taking theatre to non-theatre venues,
especially in rural areas. Creates a minimum of 3
productions each year, each of which has a resonance
with both adults and younger audiences. The autumn
production appeals to families with young children;
the spring show embraces narratives that challenge,
engage and excite adult audiences. From 2009 the
company has produced a summer production that
actively encourages both young people and older
people to become a more prominent part of its
audience.

Casting procedures: The company casts by audition.
Breakdowns are published on the website as well as in
Castcall and Casting Call Pro, among others. Is
unable to consider unsolicited submssions at other
times. Actively encourages applications from disabled
actors and promotes the use of inclusive casting.

Paines Plough

4th Floor, 43 Aldwych, London WC2B 4DN
tel 020 7240 4533 *fax* 020 7240 4534
email office@painesplough.com
website www.painesplough.com
Artistic Directors James Grieve, George Perrin

Production details: Founded in 1974, the company is
dedicated to producing and touring new writing.
Recent work includes: Vinay Patel's *Stick and Stones;*
Simon Longman's *Island Town* and George
Christous' *How To Spot An Alien* (all part of the
Roundabout season); Anna Jordan's *Pop Music* and
Simon Stephens' *Sea Wall.*

Casting procedures: Casts all productions in-house.
Does not accept unsolicited CVs or photographs, but
holds open auditions throughout the year to meet
new actors.

Pendle Productions

Bridge Farm, 249 Hawes Side Lane, Blackpool,
Lancashire FY4 4AA
tel 01253 839375 *fax* 01253 792930
email admin@pendleproductions.co.uk
website www.pendleproductions.co.uk
Director TS Lince

Production details: Touring professional theatre
company. Stages between 10 and 15 productions each
year, with 600 performances nationally in 300 venues
of all types. Recent productions include: *Cinderella,
Sinbad* and *Treasure Island.*

Casting procedures: Sometimes holds general
auditions; actors should write in April-June
requesting inclusion. Casting breakdowns are publicly
available via the usual channels. Welcomes letters
(with CVs and photographs) from individual actors
previously unknown to the company sent by post or
email. Accepts showreels but prefers not to receive
invitations to view individual actors' websites.
Actively encourages applications from disabled
actors, and promotes the use of inclusive casting.

Pentabus Theatre Company

Bromfield, Ludlow, Shropshire SY8 2JU
tel 01584 856564
email info@pentabus.co.uk
website www.pentabus.co.uk
Artistic Director Sophie Motely

Production details: Pentabus is the nation's rural theatre company and the only professional theatre company in the UK whose vision is singularly rural. Tours new plays about the contemporary rural world to new audiences in village halls, fields, festivals and theatres, telling stories with local relevance, plus national and international impact. Believes that every person living in an isolated rural community has a right to exceptional theatre. Pentabus is based on a farm in Shropshire, and to date all of their work has been made there. It then tours village halls and theatres locally and nationally. Over four and a half decades they've produced 171 new plays, reached over 550,000 audience members, won a prestigious South Bank Show award for their show about racism, a Fringe First for their play about climate change and were the first to live stream from a village hall.

The Company produces 3 new shows a year and has previously commissioned Robert Alan Evans, Deirdre Kinahan, Matt Hartley, Sian Owen, Simon Longman, Rory Mullarkey, Duncan Macmillan & Jonny Donahoe, Alecky Blythe and Julian Gardner, amongst others.

Casting procedures: Occasionally uses freelance casting directors. Casting breakdowns are available via Spotlight. No CVs or email enquiries; instead invite to see in a show.

The People's Theatre Co
69 Manor Way, Guildford, Surrey GU2 7RR
email ptc@ptc.org.uk
website www.ptc.org.uk
Facebook /peoples.theatre.company
Twitter @the_ptc
Director Steven Lee

Production details: Established in 2003. The company has built an international reputation for its unique brand of sophisticated original pop musicals. Stages 120+ performances per year, touring across theUK and abroad to Receiving Houses and number 1/number 2 venues. 2-7 actors are generally involved in each production. Recent productions include: *How The Koala Learnt To Hug*, *There Was An Old Lady Who Swallowed A Fly*, *Don't Dribble on tghe Dragon* and the award-winning Bink trilogy of full-scale family musicals.

Casting procedures: Casting is done in-house. Holds general auditions. Actors should only write requesting inclusion in response to casting calls. Actors can also follow the company on social media for first alerts to castings. Casting breakdowns are obtainable via the usual array of sources including Spotlight and Mandy.com. Accepts submissions (with CVs and photographs) from individual actors previously unknown to the the company; submissions sent by email are also accepted. Applications from disabled actors are considered to play disabled characters. "We want a well-presented CV with personal information, training, experience

and detailed skills – particularly singing, as most of our work is musicals. New actors and recent graduates welcome."

People Show
Brady Arts Centre, 192-196 Hanbury Street, London E1 5HU
tel 020 7729 1841 *fax* 020 7739 0203
email people@peopleshow.co.uk
website www.peopleshow.co.uk
Company: Fiona Creese, Gareth Brierley, George Khan, Jessica Worrall, Mark Long, Sadie Cook

Production details: The longest-running experimental theatre company in the UK, touring nationally and internationally since 1966, creating devised work for arts centres, theatres, and outdoor and site-specific venues. Anything from 3 to 65 actors are involved in each production. Offers Equity-approved contracts as negotiated through ITC. Recent works includes: 50th Year – Anniversary Celebrations at Artsadmin and*People Show 127:The Last Straw at Ovalhouse*.

Casting procedures: People Show is an ensemble company with a core group of 7 artists, and an extended network of 45 plus associate artists. Does not use freelance casting directors or hold general auditions. Welcomes approaches from performers previously unknown to the company.

Pilot Theatre
York Theatre Royal, St Leonards Place, York YO1 7HD
tel 01904 635755
email info@pilot-theatre.com
website www.pilot-theatre.com
Artistic Director Marcus Romer

Production details: Pilot Theatre is an international touring theatre company based in York, UK. They devise and develop projects with particular focus on working for and with young audiences. They also work across platforms to produce and distribute work digitally, run training conferences, livestream events and performances, provide a wide range of online educational resources.

A wide range of work over the last few years includes the six-camera livestream of the York Myserty Plays for The Space and a range of specially commissioned plays including: *Loneliness of the Long Distance Runner*, *Running on the Cracks*, *Blood + Chocolate* and more recently the new adaptation of *Antigone* by Ry Williams.

"We work with established artists, leading practitioners and diverse teams alongside nurturing young and emergent talent to develop our practice across all platforms of delivery. The audiences and communities we aim to reach are reflected by the diverse teams who make and deliver our work."

Casting procedures: The company regularly posts casting information online. "Please try and avoid

Theatre

sending surface mail for casting, as we are trying to minimise wastage and energy usage." Please email your details to: **casting@pilot-theatre.com**.

Point Blank

The Riverside, 1 Mowbray Street, Sheffield S3 8EN
tel 0114 249 3650/51 *fax* 0114 249 3655
email info@pointblank.org.uk
website www.pointblank.org.uk
Creative Director Steve Jackson

Production details: Established in 1999. Small-scale national touring theatre producing new work, devised, physical theatre and new writing. Stages 1 production annually. 30-60 performances per year touring 18 venues which include art centres, theatres, outdoor venues, educational and community venues. Regions covered include North, North West, Yorkshire, West Midlands, South East, London, Scotland, Ireland and Wales. 2-4 actors are involved in each production. Actors are employed under Equity approved contracts negotiated through ITC. Recent productions include: *Operation Wonderland* (15 venues including The Crucible, Latchmere and The Traverse); *Roses and Morphine* (18 venues including The Crucible, Royal Exchange and Aberystwyth Arts Centre); and *Last Orders* (Sheffield, site-specific).

Casting procedures: Casting is carried out by in-house casting director. Hold general auditions. Actors can write at anytime to request inclusion; details will be kept on file. Casting breakdowns are obtainable via casting websites. Accepts submissions (with CVs and photographs) from individual actors previously unknown to the company. Applications from disabled actors are considered to play disabled characters wherever possible.

"Research the company first to check it's appropriate. We will get back with details of shows as appropriate. Yorkshire-based actors are particularly welcome to apply".

Powerhouse Theatre Company

58 Oak Hill, Wood Street Village,
Guildford GU3 3ER
mobile 01483 232690
email powerhousetheattre@hotmail.co.uk
website www.powerhousetheatre.co.uk
Artistic Director Geoff Lawson

Production details: Founded in 2007, Powerhouse focuses on presenting high quality, accessible and entertaining productions that deal with important social issues, as well as as well as educational history shows for young people and site-specific work. Recent productions include: *Our Tudors*, *Suffragette* and *Pretty Ugly*. Each production consists of 3-4 actors and, on average, the company tours 3-4 productions per year. This equates to around 50 performances at 4-5 venues, mainly theatres, arts centres, schools and community spaces.

Casting procedures: Uses in-house casting directors, but does not hold general auditions. Casting breakdowns through Casting Call Pro and individual agents. Welcomes both CVs and letters from actors previously unknown to the company and unsolicited CVs and photographs. Also welcomes invitations to view individual actors' websites and showreels. Happy to consider applications from disabled actors and promotes inclusive casting.

Primecut Productions

285A Ormerth Road, Belfast BT7 3GG
tel 028 906 45101 *fax* 028 906 45101
email info@primecutproductions.co.uk
website www.primecutproductions.co.uk

Production details: Established in 1992, Prime Cut Productions is an independent theatre producing organisation based in Belfast. We are committed to producing excellent contemporary theatre that is accessible and entertaining for as wide an audience as possible, forge artistic links locally and internationally, and continue to nurture the development of theatre practice and artists in Northern Ireland. We have produced 50+ highly acclaimed Irish premieres of the best of international theatre as well showcasing the work of Northern Irish theatre artists across the Island of Ireland and beyond.

Since 2014 Prime Cut have been the recipients of the BBC Performing Arts Fellowship, two Weston Jerwood Creative Bursaries, the Allianz Arts & Business Board Member of the Year Award (2015), Artistic Director Emma Jordan received the Paul Hamlyn Foundation Breakthrough Award and the 2015 Spirit of Festival Award at Belfast International Arts Festival. Our production of *Scorch* has played to overwhelming critical acclaim at the Adelaide Fringe, Edinburgh Fringe, across Ireland, UK, Sweden and Germany winning seven international awards including an Irish Times Theatre Award, an Irish Writers' Guild Award the Holden St Award, a Fringe First, an Adelaide Fringe Best Theatre Award and an Adelaide Critics' Choice Award. Our 2017 production of *Red* was the recipient of four awards at the recent Irish Times Irish Theatre Awards including Best Production, Best Director for Emma Jordan, Best Actor for Patrick O Kane and Best Set Design for Ciaran Bagnall.

Prime Cut delivers under three main strands: CREATE; INNOVATE and PARTICIPATE.
• CREATE: an artistic programme of two professional productions annually of the best of international drama featuring casts and creative teams of the highest quality.
• INNOVATE: our Annual Artistic Development Programme. It drives forward the development of Northern Irish professional theatre through the provision of the finest international training and professional development opportunities for Northern Irish artists.

• PARTICIPATE: our Community Engagement Programme providing year-round opportunities for arts access and participation for young people, older people, disadvantaged people and people from minority groupings, through a range of arts including theatre, dance, movement, film, music and visual art.

Proteus Theatre Company

Proteus Creation Space, Council Road, Basingstoke, Hants RG21 3DH
tel 01256 354541
email info@proteustheatre.com
website www.proteustheatre.com
Facebook www.facebook.com/proteustheatrecompany
Twitter @proteustheatre
Artistic Director Mary Swan

Production details: Established in 1981. Touring theatre company operating nationally. Stages 2-3 productions annually touring to 80 venues including arts centres, theatres, outdoor venues, educational and community venues. Recent credits include: *Becoming Hattie* and *Macbeth*.

Casting procedures: Casting breakdowns available via the website and Equity Job Information Service. Does not welcome unsolicited CVs. Actively encourages applications from disabled actors and promotes the use of inclusive casting. Offers ITC/Equity-approved contracts.

Punchdrunk

Canon Factory, Ashley Road, London N17 9LH
tel 020 7655 0940
email punchdrunk@punchdrunk.org.uk
website www.punchdrunk.org.uk
Facebook www.facebook.com/punchdrunkuk
Twitter @PunchdrunkUK
Artistic Director Felix Barratt *Director of Enrichment & Punchdrunk Village* Peter Higgin *Associte Director & Choreographer* Maxine Doyle *Associate Director* Hector Harkness *Associate Artist* Katy Balfour

Since 2000, Punchdrunk has pioneered a game-changing form of theatre in which roaming audiences experience epic story-telling inside sensory theatrical worlds. Blending classic texts, physical performance, award-winning design installation and unexpected sites, the company's format rejects the passive obedience ususally expected of audiences. Much of the work has a strong and choreographic focus.

Punchdrunk has developed a reputation for transformative productions that focus as much on the audience and the performance space as on the performers and narrative. Inspired designers occupy deserted buildings and apply a cinematic level of detail to immerse the audience in the world of the show.

This is a unique theatrical experience where the lines between space, performer and spectator are constantly shifting. Audiences are invited to rediscover the childllike excitement and anticipation of exploring the unknown and experience a real sense of adventure. Free to encounter the installed environment in an individual imaginative journey, the choice of what to watch and where to go is theirs alone.

Offers Equity-approved contracts through ITC; does not subscribe to the Equity Pension Scheme.

Punchdrunk Enrichment works with schools, colleges, community groups and partner organisations. Recent productions include: *Lost Lending Library* (2013—current); *Against Captain's Orders* (2015), *The Drowned Man* (2013—2014).

Casting procedures: Apply for auditions when advertised, following the instructions. Advertises on website, social media, arts job- and dance-specific websites. Unable to view productions for casting purposes but encourages aplpications from all.

Purple Fish Productions

22 Newton Avenue, London W3 8AL
mobile 07976 809693
email info@purplefishproductions.co.uk
website www.purplefishproductions.co.uk
Artistic Director Michelle Seton

Production details: Founded in 2001. Aims to produce both established work and exciting devised pieces for adults and children. Michelle Seton trained in London and at Le Coq in Paris. Stages 3 productions with 75 performances during the course of the year. Tours to 20 different arts centres, theatres, educational and community venues annually. Tours have covered Greater London, Ireland and Canada. In general 2 actors are involved in each production. Recent productions include: *Told by a Dodo* and *The Two of Us*.

Casting procedures: Casting breakdowns are available via the website. Welcomes letters (with CVs and photographs) but not email submissions. Actors should write only when the company advertises. Invitations to view individual actors' websites are also accepted.

Pursued by a Bear Productions

The Maltings, Bridge Square, Farnham, Surrey GU9 7QR
email pursuedbyabear@yahoo.co.uk
website www.pursuedbyabear.co.uk
Artistic Director Helena Bell

Production details: Theatre and digital film company specialising in new writing commissions. PBAB produces and tours 1 new (Arts Council funded) theatre production annually and creates large-scale community and educational film (most recently funded by Heritage Lottery). Recent theatre tours include: *Kalashnikov: In the Woods by the Lake* by Fraser Grace (Theatre 503 & South East Tour); *Footprints in the Sand* by Oladipo Agboluaje and Rukhsana Ahmad (Oval House & South East tour). Forthcoming theatre production: *Kabaddi-Kabaddi-*

Theatre

Kabaddi by Satinder Chohan (National UK Touring 2012/13). Forthcoming Film: *On Hungry Hill* (Screening November 2012).

Casting procedures: Welcomes submissions (with CVs and photographs) sent by post or email.

Raised Eyebrow Theatre Company

Low Hall Cottage, Carr Lane, Brompton, Scarborough YO13 9DH
tel/fax 01723 850538
email lizipatch@aol.com
website www.raisedeyebrow.co.uk
Artistic Director Lizi Patch *Associate Director* Jon Stokes

Production details: A community and TIE company staging 2-3 productions each year and presenting approximately 220 performances in schools and community venues across England. The company also runs youth theatres and workshops. In general 5 actors work on each production. Recent productions include: *Farmer Charles*, Raised Eyebrow Youth Theatre; *Destination 2014*, for Capacity Builders conference in Birmingham; *The Street Never Ends* and *The Wave*, Filey Festival; *The Past on Your Doorstep*, Chaddeston Park and Osmaston Park, Derby; *A Midsummer Murder*, The Old Mill, Langtoft Abbey House (in partnership with Derbyshire-based Orange Box Design); *Space Pirates – Adventures on Planet Maths*, tour; *Spike* (in partnership with Scarborough Safer Communities); and *A Midsummer Night's Dream* (Raised Eyebrow Youth Theatre).

Casting procedures: Casting is done in house and with the help of freelance casting directors. Casting breakdowns are available by postal application (with sae), and in *The Stage*. Welcomes letters and emails (with professional CVs and 10x8 photographs) from actors previously unknown to the company. Will also accept showreels and emails. Advises that professional applications will be given priority over photocopies, passport photos and holiday snaps.

Real Circumstance Theatre Company

22 Erle Havard Road, West Bergholt, Colchester CO6 3LH
email info@realcircumstance.com
website www.realcircumstance.com
Artistic Director Dan Sherer *Creative Producer* Anna Bewick

Production details: Real Circumstance is an East of England theatre company dedicated to exploring new ways of playmaking; to working with new writers and emergent artists; and to raising the profile of the East as a source of creative work. Tours 1 studio production each year, to the community. Recent productions include: *Our Share of Tomorrow* by Dan Sherer, *LOUGH/RAIN* by Declan Feenan and Clara Brennan, and *LIMBO* by Declan Feenan (all co-produced with York Theatre Royal and ran at the Edinburgh Fringe).

Casting procedures: Uses in-house casting directors. Sometimes holds general auditions; actors may write at any time to request inclusion. Welcomes letters (with CVs and photographs) from actors previously unknown to the company, and accepts submissions by email. Welcomes showreels and invitations to view individual actors' websites. Offers Equity-approved contracts negotiated through ITC.

Red Ladder Theatre Co.

3 St Peter's Buildings, York Street, Leeds LS9 8AJ
tel 0113 245 5311 *fax* 0113 245 5351
email rod@redladder.co.uk
website www.redladder.co.uk
Twitter @redladdertheatr
Artistic Director Rod Dixon

Production details: Red Ladder's mission is to create theatre based around, and influenced by, human struggle. They aim to create galvanising and life-affirming productions that redefine and reclaim notions of the popular, the political and the radical in a theatre context. The company, founded in 1968 in London, has a colourful history. It spans 50 years, from the radical socialist theatre movement in Britain known as agitprop, to its current position.

The company moved to Leeds in the 70s and is still based in the city. During the 80s it redefined itself, changing its cooperative structure to a hierarchy. Acknowledged today as one of Britain's leading national touring companies producing high-quality new plays.

Recent productions include:*The Damned United* (Anders Lustgarten from the David Peace novel, co-production with the Leeds Playhouse), *Glory* by Nick Ahad (co-produced with The Dukes Theatre, Lancaster).

The Red Room

Garden Studios, 71-75 Shelton Street, Covent Garden, London WC2H 9JQ
tel 020 7470 8790 *fax* 020 7379 0801
email info@theredroom.org.uk
website www.theredroom.org.uk
Artistic Director Topher Campbell

Production details: Founded in 1995. Produces new theatre and film work which frees the imagination to challenge the status quo. Creates groundbreaking collaborations between writers, artists and communities to provoke and influence wider social debate. Engages in cultural activism, including bi-monthly RRPlatform events. Stages 1-2 productions annually with 25-50 performances during the course of the year. Tours to international and national locations. In general, fewer than 5 actors (often with ability to work in a devised way) are involved in each production. Recent productions include: *Unstated*, *Journeys to Work, Hoxton Story, Animal, The Bogus Woman* and *Stitching*.

Casting procedures: Accepts emailed CVs and photographs – no letters or telephone enquiries, please. Offers ITC/Equity-approved contracts where possible. Does not subscribe to the Equity pension scheme. Actively encourages applications from disabled actors and promotes the use of inclusive casting.

Red Rose Chain

Gippeswyk Hall, Gippeswyk Avenue, Ipswich, Suffolk IP2 9AF
tel 01473 603388 *fax* 01473 601122
email info@redrosechain.com
website www.redrosechain.com
Directors Joanna Carrick, David Newborn, Jimmy Grimes

Production details: A film and theatre company which spends every summer outdoors with its theatre-in-the-forest event. Runs workshops and develops new writing. "Our diverse work all serves to underpin Red Rose Chain's aim: to use theatre and film to challenge thinking and make connections with those who are normally ignored or avoided by mainstream arts." Stages 4 productions annually, with 50 performances in 20 venues including arts centres, theatres, and outdoor, educational and community venues in East Anglia. In general 3-12 actors are involved in each production. Recent productions include: *A Winter's Tale* (Rendlesham Forest); *Slide Down the Rainbow* (Nowton Park); and *I love Kitkats* (Red Rose Chain).

Casting procedures: Sometimes holds general auditions; casting breakdowns are available via the website. Welcomes letters (with CVs and photographs) from individual actors previously unknown to the company, sent by post or email. Also welcomes showreels and invitations to view individual actors' websites. Actively encourages applications from disabled actors and promotes the use of inclusive casting.

Reveal Theatre Company

The Creative Village,
Staffordshire University Business Village,
72 Leek Road, Stoke on Trent ST4 2AR
tel 01782 294871
email enquiries@revealtheatre.co.uk
website www.revealtheatre.co.uk
Creative Director Robert Marsden *Director of Productions* Julia Barton

Production details: Established in 1999. A professional small- to middle-scale producing company for touring and residency. Also has a strong outreach department. Stages on average 3 productions each year. Recent productions include: *Beauty and the Beast* (directed by Alex Shepley) and Stephen Sondheim's *Into The Woods* (directed by Robert Marsden).

Casting procedures: Uses in-house casting directors; casting breakdowns are available via the website. Actors may write at any time requesting inclusion.

Welcomes submissions (with CVs and photographs) sent by post, but not by email. Also welcomes showreels, and invitations to view individual actors' websites. Offers Equity-approved contracts as negotiated through ITC. Will consider applications from disabled actors to play characters with disabilities.

Richmond Productions

47 Moor Mead Road, St Margaret's,
Twickenham TW1 1JS
website www.richmondproductions.co.uk
Director Alister Cameron

Production details: Founded in 1993. International touring company producing small-cast comedies. Stages 2 productions annually. Tours to hotels in the Middle East and Eastern Europe. Offers non-Equity contracts. Rarely (or never) has the opportunity to cast disabled actors.

Casting procedures: Advises that the company only uses actors already known to it.

Riding Lights Theatre Company

Friargate Theatre, Lower Friargate, York YO1 9SL
tel 01904 655317
website www.ridinglights.org
Artistic Director Paul Burbridge *Artistic Associates* Sean Cavanagh, Bridget Foreman

Production details: Initially a community theatre project founded in York in 1977, today Riding Lights is touring up to 3 diverse companies simultaneously throughout the UK and abroad. The company is recognised both as a pioneer in reinstating the value of theatre in Christian communication and for significant original and artistic achievement. Recent productions include: *Flight Cases* and *African Show* (co-production with York Theatre Royal).

Rifco Theatre Company

Watford Palace Theatre, 20 Clarendon Road,
Watford WD17 1JZ
tel 01923 810305
website www.rifcotheatre.com
Artistic Director Pravesh Kumar

Production details: Rifo Theatre Company develops, produces and tours vibrant, accessible and high-quality theatre locally from its base in Watford. The company develops both new plays and musicals of scale and spectacle, and works alongside a wide range of artistic collaborators. The work is developed to encourage and engage new and diverse audiences, reflecting and celebrating contemporary British Asian experiences, culture and society.

Offers UK Theatre/Equity-approved contracts. Recent productions include: *Laila The Musical*, *The Masala Queens* and *Dishoom*.

Casting procedures: via casting directors and professional agents. Welcomes letters (with relevant links) from individual actors previously unknown to the company, via email **casting@rifotheatre.com**.

Theatre

Rocket Theatre

17 Groveland Road, Wallasey, Merseyside CH45 8JX
tel 0151 637 1481 *mobile* 07788 723570
email martin@rockettheatre.co.uk
website www.rockettheatre.co.uk
Director Martin Harris

Production details: Rocket Theatre was set up in 1995. It has produced work and toured throughout the UK with completely new work and regional premieres of work originally staged by some of London's new-writing venues (particularly the Royal Court, the Bush and the National). The company has won several awards. Previous productions include: Oscar Wilde's *Lord Arthur Savile's Crime, I Licked a Slag's Deodorant* by Jim Cartwright; *Howie the Rookie* by Mark O'Rowe; *A Skull in Connemara* by Martin McDonagh and *Dealer's Choice* by Patrick Marber, as well as several new plays by Jim Burke. The company is currently working on a production of Spoonface Steinberg By Lee Halland a brand new musical based on the life of Fred Dibnah – see the website for details. Rocket Theatre is keen to hear about any interesting collaboration opportunities with other companies or individuals.

Casting procedures: Casting breakdowns are available on the Rocket website and through various industry casting resources. Does not welcome applications from actors unless casting is called for specific parts.

Scamp Theatre Ltd

42 Church Lane, Arlesey, Bedfordshire SG15 6UX
tel 01462 734843 *fax* 01462 730878
email admin@scamptheatre.com
website www.scamptheatre.com
Director Louise Callow

Production details: Established in 2003. An independent production company staging 3-4 shows annually, with more than 100 performances in the same number of theatres across the UK. In general 3 actors are involved in each production. Offers Equity-approved contracts as negotiated through ITC. Recent productions include: *The Scarecrows' Wedding* (West End, UK tour); *Private Peaceful* by Michael Morpurgo (West End, UK tour); *Pirate Gran* (UK tour); *Tiddler and Other Terrific Tales* (UK tour) and *Stick Man* (West End, UK tour).

Casting procedures: Uses freelance casting directors. Scamp do not accept unsolicited CVs. Scamp consider applications from disabled actors to play characters with disabilities.

Scarlet Theatre

Studio 4, The Bull, 68 High Street, Barnet EN5 5SJ
tel 020 8441 9779 *fax* 020 8447 0075
email admin@scarlettheatre.co.uk
website www.scarlettheatre.co.uk
Director Gráinne Byrne

Production details: A touring theatre company founded in 1982 which stages between 2 and 6 productions each year. On average the company tours annually to 10 venues across the UK, Ireland and the rest of Europe, with anywhere between 2-10 actors working on each production. Recent productions include: *The Chair Women* (Riverside Studios and Traverse Theatre) and *The Wedding* (Southwark Playhouse).

Casting procedures: Casting is done in house and actors are welcome to write or email with their CVs and photographs. The company prefers not to receive showreels unless it has requested them.

Scene Three Creative

5 Gold Street, Stalbridge, Dorset DT10 2LX
tel 07899 825152
email info@scenethreecreative.co.uk
website www.scenethreecreative.co.uk
Directors Philip Dart, Claudia Leaf

Production details: A creative production company making work for many different venues and communities.

Casting procedures: "We regret that we are unable to hold general auditions or see actors outside of designated casting periods. Agents' information services such as Spotlight are normally supplied with casting breakdowns."

Shakespeare at The Tobacco Factory

Raleigh Road, Southville, Bristol BS3 ITF
tel 0117 963 3054
email office@stf-theatre.org.uk
website www.stf-theatre.org.uk
Artistic Director Andrew Hilton

Production details: Established in 2000. 2 productions staged annually with 80 performances in Bristol. Up to 18 actors used in each production. Recent productions include: *Hamlet* and *All's Well That Ends Well*.

Casting procedures: Casting breakdowns available via the website. Accepts electronic submissions (with CVs and photographs) from actors previously unknown to the company. Invitations to view individual actors' websites are also accepted. Actors writing to request inclusion should make contact in August. Rarely has the opportunity to cast disabled actors.

Shared Experience

Oxford Playhouse, 11-12 Beaumont Street, Oxford OX1 2LW
tel 01865 305321
email admin@sharedexperience.org.uk
website www.sharedexperience.org.uk
Artistic Director Polly Teale

Production details: An award-winning theatre company founded during the 1970s, Shared Experience stages 2-3 productions annually and tours to different arts centres and theatres in the UK and abroad. In general 6-10 actors are involved in each production. Recent productions include: *Mermaid, Mary Shelley, The Caucasian Chalk Circle,, A Passage to India, Jane Eyre, Kindertransport* and *War and Peace.*

Casting procedures: Uses freelance casting directors. Advises that actors should contactthe office by phone to enquire about the current casting director. "Please do not send unsolicited mail." Offers TMA/Equity-approved contracts. Actively encourages applications from disabled actors and promotes the use of inclusive casting.

Simple8 Theatre Company

Heath House, Lyneham Road,
Milton-under-Wychwood, OX7 6LW
mobile 07710 174717
email chris@simple8.co.uk
website www.simple8.co.uk
Twitter @simple8theatre
Simple8 is a collective, run by Chris Doyle, Sebastian Armesto, Emily Pennant-Rea, Dudley Hinton, Hannah Emanuel & Mat Wandless

Production details: Simple8 is a critically-acclaimed and award-winning ensemble based theatre company who specialise in creating innovative, bold new plays using large casts – all performed on a shoestring. Their approach is rooted in 'poor theatre', which focuses on the story and revolves around the ensemble, who create the atmosphere and setting without relying on extravagant lighting, scenery, props or sound. Simple8 have produced 8 productions to date, at Arcola Theatre and Park Theatre. Simple8 is an associate company of Shoreditch Town Hall. Winners of the Peter Brook Award for Best Ensemble 2013 and 2015.

Casting procedures: Uses freelance casting directors, but does not hold general auditions. Instead Simple8 recommend actors submit their details for consideration once they have seen a Simple8 production, attended a workshop, or introduced themselves in person. Welcomes both CVs and letters from actors previously unknown to the company and unsolicited CVs and photographs. These should be sent via email. Also welcomes invitations to view individual actors' websites and attend productions, but does not welcome showreels. Happy to consider disabled actors, though this is dependent on each individual project.

Sky Blue Theatre Company

14 Hayfield Avenue, Sawston, Cambridge CB22 3JZ
tel 01223 529491 *mobile* 07941 012293
email admin@skybluetheatre.com
website www.skybluetheatre.com
Directors Anne Bartram, Frances Brownlie, John Mitton

Production details: Founded in 2007. A Cambridge-based company touring schools, theatres and community venues with new plays, Shakespeare productions and workshops. Founded the British Theatre Challenge, an international playwriting competition. Works with young people through its own theatre school and with colleges developing skills in performing arts. Stages 6 productions for young people's theatre and TIE annually, giving around 100 performances in 40 venues nationally. In general,4 actors ago on tour, playing to audiences aged 7 to 18. Actors are sometimes expected to lead workshops. Recent productions include: *That Catholic Thing*, ten new one act plays and Romeo and Juliet workshops.

Casting procedures: Holds general auditions, for which breakdowns are available via Casting Call Pro and the website. Welcomes letters (with CVs and photographs) from individual actors previously unknown to the company, sent by post or email. Does accept showreels and will consider invitations to view actors' websites and performances. Will consider applications from disabled actors for any role.

Small World Theatre

Theatr Byd Bychan, Bath House Road, Cardigan, Ceredigion SA43 1JY
tel 01239 615952
email info@smallworld.org.uk
website www.smallworld.org.uk
Facebook facebook.com/SmallWorldTheatre
Director Ann Shrosbree *Artistic Director* Bill Hamblett
Administrator Helen Groth

Production details: Small World Theatre is an arts sustainability organisation housed in a near zero carbon venue with 4 areas of work: production house (making original performances and touring theatre) presenting house; project work including theatre for development, theatre forum; education and training, outdoor street spectaculars and giany lantern parades.

Casting procedures: Uses in-house casting directors, issues rare casting calls. Will consider submissions (letters, CVs and photographs) from actors previously unknown to the company, sent by post or email. No unsolicited showreels. Casts actors with disabilities in inclusive roles, and to play differently able roles.

Sole Purpose Productions

The Playhouse, Artillery Street, Derry, Londonderry BT48 6RG
tel 028 7127 9918
email solepurpose@mac.com
website www.solepurpose.org
Facebook www.facebook.com/solepurposeproductions
Twitter @SolePurpose_
Artistic Director Patricia Byrne

Production details: Founded in 1997, Sole Purpose Productions creates new professional theatre on social and public issues. The company has toured extensively throughout Ireland and the UK, and has had work staged in New York, San Francisco and Seattle. Recent productions include: *Mothers Out Front* by Edie Shillue (a tragicomedy on climate change) and *Blinkered* by Patricia Byrne (a play on mental health and suicide) which won the Special Jury Prize at Origin Theatre's First Irish Festival in New York and had four nominations.

Each production consists of 3-5 actors and, on average, the company presents 1-2 productions per year, touring to theatres and community venues nationally and internationally.

Casting procedures: Holds general auditions at various times throughout the year and a casting breakdown is available via the Sole Purpose website when a production is coming up. Welcomes both CVs and letters from actors previously unknown to the Company and unsolicited CVs and photographs. Also welcomes invitations to view individual actor's websites and showreels. Promotes inclusive casting and welcomes applications from disabled actors to play characters with disabilities.

Spanner in the Works

95 Old Woolwich Road, London SE10 9PP
tel 020 7193 7995
email info@spannerintheworks.org.uk
website www.spannerintheworks.org.uk
Artistic Director Darren Rapier

Production details: Spanner in the Works produce plays and films, as well as running workshops in all media disciplines for a variety of clientele. The company produces films and books in partnership with Tualen Pictures and Tualen Press. Primarily, Spanner in the Works concentrate on stage productions and workshops. They have produced musicals, plays, short films and audio drama, as well as community theatre pieces. Recent productions include: *Riverscross* (online soap), *Blind Man's Bluff* (short film) and *Worlds Apart* (theatre).

Casting procedures: Uses in-house and freelance casting directors. Casting breakdowns are available, although this is dependent on the project. Will happily consider applications from disabled actors, but their inclusion is dependent on the nature of each individual project.

Sphinx Theatre Company

78 Lyford Road, London SW18 3JW
tel 020 3669 8210
email info@sphinxtheatre.co.uk
website www.sphinxtheatre.co.uk
Artistic Director Sue Parrish

Production details: Established 40 years ago, the company specialises in writing, directing and developing roles for women. Recent productions include: *Women Centre Stage, Heroines* and *Women Centre Stage: Power Play* festivals and *A Berlin Kabaret.*

Casting procedures: Casting breakdowns are available via email (with CVs and photographs). Offers Equity-approved contracts.

A Stage Kindly

7 Northiam, Cromer Street, London WC1H 8LB
mobile 07947 074887 07909 884386
email mail@astagekindly.com
website www.astagekindly.com
Co-founders and Artistic Directors Giles Howe, Katy Lipson

Production details: Founded in 2008. Aims to enthuse about, advocate and help develop new musical theatre. Stages new-writing revues, feature-length and showcase presentations of new works, and offers services specific to writers creating new MT such as translation, appraisal, demos, etc. Also holds workshops for performers with a focus on new musicals. Recent productions include: UK premiere of *Ballets Russes*; preview showcase of *Soviet Zion*; and tour of international new-writing revue *Bravo*. Stages around 5 productions annually, with 25 performances in venues including theatres, bars, clubs, halls and arts centres. In general 6 actors are involved in each production.

Casting procedures: Audition information is posted on the website, as are casting breakdowns (also available from Casting Call Pro, Arts Jobs, etc.). Welcomes letters (with CVs and photographs) from actors previously unknown to the company, sent by post or email. Also accepts showreels and invitations to view individual actors' websites.

Ed Stephenson Productions

7 Hawthorn Road, Little Sutton, Cheshire CH66 1PR
tel 0151 339 6145
email roger@edstephensonproductions.co.uk
website www.edstephensonproductions.co.uk
Company Administrator Diane Barker

Production details: Founded in 2004. Stages on average 1 production every 1-2 years; has evolved from stage to film production. Recent films include: *A Quiet Night In* (2009), *The Weekend Hostage* (2011), *A Matter of Principle* (2015) and *Burning Grief* (2017).

Casting procedures: Uses in-house casting directors. Sometimes holds auditions. Uses casting agencies for auditioning. Welcomes letters (with CVs and photographs) from individual actors previously unknown to the company, sent by post or email. Accepts showreels and invitations to view individual actors' websites. Will consider applications from disabled actors where appropriate for the role. "Our contracts are heavily based on ITC/Equity contracts."

Suspect Culture

Kinning Park Complex, 40 Cornwall Street, Glasgow G41 1AH
tel 0141 419 9666
email info@suspectculture.com
website www.suspectculture.com
Director Graham Eatough

Production details: Suspect Culture was formed in 1990 by Graham Eatough, David Greig and Nick

Powell. Early productions include: *One Way Street* (1995), *Airport* (1996), *Timeless* (1997) and *Mainstream* (1999). The company is based in Glasgow and tours 1-2 productions throughout Scotland and internationally each year. Generally uses 2-6 actors on each production. Recent productions include: *8000m* (Tramway, Glasgow) and *One-Two* (Traverse, Edinburgh; Contact Theatre, Manchester; MAC, Birmingham; Tron, Glasgow; Byre Theatre, St Andrews; Lemon Tree, Northampton; Tolbooth, Stirling and Paisley Arts Centres).

"To us, a collaborative approach means giving text, design, music and performance equal weight in all our work. The director, writer, designer and composer are involved from the very beginning of each new idea, which is then developed through a long process of workshops and rehearsal before being presented to an audience. This emphasis on collaboration is reflected in the way we credit artists and assign authorship, which is always shared among the artistic team."

Casting procedures: Suspect Culture does not hold formal auditions, but rather open workshops which are by invitation. This gives the company a chance to meet practitioners it hasn't worked with before (and vice versa). The company welcomes letters, emails, showreels, invitations to view actors' websites, CVs and photographs from actors – but asks all applicants to gain a full understanding of Suspect's particular working methods before writing. Only rarely employs actors who have not seen at least some of Suspect's work.

TABS Productions

57 Chamberlain Place, London E17 6AZ
tel 020 8527 9266
email adrianmljames@aol.com
website www.tabsproductions.co.uk
Directors Adrian Lloyd-James, Karen Henson

Production details: Founded 15 years ago, the company stages approximately 6 productions each year totalling around 300 performances. It has produced No. 1 and middle-scale tours and has co-produced with repertory theatre companies. Generally tours to about 45 different arts centres, theatres and outdoor venues across the UK annually. The average cast size is 4-8 actors.

Casting procedures: Welcomes letters, CVs and photographs from actors previously unknown to the company, but does not accept emails or showreels. Actors should only write when a job has been advertised to agents. Occasionally offers Equity-approved contracts. Rarely (or never) has the opportunity to cast disabled actors.

Taking Flight Theatre Company

Chapter Art Centre, Cardiff CF5 1QE
tel 029 202 30020
email beth@takingflighttheatre.co.uk
website www.takingflighttheatre.co.uk
Directors Beth House, Elise Davison

Production details: Established in 2007. Accessible, professional promenade productions with integrated casts/support teams. Stages 1-2 productions annually, with around 80 performances in 40 outdoor venues across Wales and England. In general 6-10 actors are involved in each production. Recent productions include: *The Tempest* and *You've Got Dragons*.

Casting procedures: Sometimes holds general auditions and actors may write at any time to request inclusion. Casting breakdowns are publicly available via the website, Equity Job Information Service and Casting Call Pro, as well as from the Disability Arts Cymru site. Welcomes letters (with CVs and photographs) from individual actors previously unknown to the company sent by post or email, as well as showreels and invitations to view individual actors' websites. Actively encourages applications from D/deaf and disabled actors. "We are very eager to hear from D/deaf, disabled and/or sensory impaired actors."

Talawa Theatre Company

35-47 Bethnal Green Road, London E1 6LA
tel 020 7251 6644
email hq@talawa.com
website www.talawa.com
Artistic Director Michael Buffong

Production details: Founded in 1986, Talawa is Britain's leading Black Theatre company. "We give voice to the Black British experience and nurture, develop and support talent. We cultivate Black audiences for Black work, and by doing so we enrich British theatre."
  Offers ITC/Equity contracts and does not subscribe to the Equity Pension Scheme.

Casting procedures: Welcomes submissions (with CVs and photographs) sent by email. Actively encourages applications from disabled actors and promotes the use of inclusive casting.

Tamasha Theatre Company

RichMix, 35-47 Bethnal Green Road, London E1 6LA
tel 020 7749 0090 *fax* 020 7729 8906
email admin@tamasha.org.uk
website www.tamasha.org.uk
Artistic Director Fin Kennedy

Production details: Founded in 1989. Produces 'untold stories' in mainstream theatre venues. Stages 1-3 productions annually and gives approximately 60 performances during the course of the year. Tours annually to small- and mid-scale theatre venues in London and regionally In general 2-15 actors are involved in each production. Recent productions include: *The Arrival, Snookered, Wuthering Heights, The Trouble with Asian Men* and *Strictly Dandia*.

Casting procedures: Only holds auditions when casting for a specific production. Uses Spotlight and own files when inviting people to audition plus casting director on specific projects. Welcomes CVs

Theatre

and headshots by post at any time; these will be kept on file and looked at afresh during each casting process. Also runs professional artist development scheme: Tamasha Developing Artists – see website for details. Offers ITC/Equity-approved contracts.

Tara Theatre

356 Garratt Lane, London SW18 4ES
tel 020 8333 4457 *fax* 020 8870 9540
email tara@tara-arts.com
website www.tara-arts.com
Artistic Director Jatinder Verma

Production details: Founded in 1977, the company's range of in-house and touring work spans European and Asian classics through to new plays. Recent productions include: *Macbeth, The Miser, Bollywood Jack, Paradise of the Assassins, Chigger Foot Boys* and *Combustion*. The new Tara Theatre, opened in September 2016 by the Mayor of London, Sadiq Khan, is Britain's first multi-cultural theatre. Its cross-culture architecture is echoed by a diverse programme of classic and new plays produced by Tara and visiting companies, connecting worlds of imagination.

Theatr Pena

19 Boverton Street, Cardiff CF23 5ES
mobile 07572 489455
email info@theatrpena.co.uk
website www.theatrpena.co.uk
Artistic Director Erica Eirian *Producer* Ceri James

Production details: Theatr Pena is a project-funded company established in 2008 out of a desire to celebrate text and to create opportunities for women in theatre. The Company's mission is to make literary theatre a vibrant part of 21st-century theatre in Wales.

Currently 1 production is staged per year. This consists of 3-6 actors and, on average, the company gives 18-25 performances annually. Nest production (spring 2018, national tour of Wales) Woman of Flowers by Siôn Eirian, after Saunders Lewis.

Casting procedures: In-house casting directors, but does not hold general auditions. Company members offered first refusal of appropropriate roles. Welcomes letters (accompanied by CVs and headshots). Actively encourages applications from disabled actors and promotes the use of inclusive casting.

Theatr Genedlaethol Cymru

Y Llwyfan, College Road, Carmarthen SA31 3EQ
tel 01267 233 882
email thgc@theatr.com
website www.theatr.com
Artistic Director Arwel Gruffydd *Associate Director* Sara Lloyd

Production details: Founded in 2003, Theatr Genedlaethol Cymru is the Welsh-language national theatre of Wales. Its work includes national tours, community projects and site-specific work. Recent productions include *Y Bont, Blodeuwedd, Y Negesydd* (*The Messenger*) and *Chwalfa*. Each production consists of 6 or more actors and, on average, the company present 5-7 productions per year. This equates to over 70 performances across the UK hosted at various venues, including arts centres, theatres and community spaces. Offers Equity-approved contracts negotiated through UK Theatre.

Casting procedures: Uses in-house casting directors, but does not hold general auditions. Welcomes both CVs and letters from actors previously unknown to the company and unsolicited CVs and photographs only when casting. These should be sent via email. Also welcomes invitations to view individual actors' websites, productions and showreels. Actively encourages applications from disabled actors.

Theatre-Rites

Unit 206, E1 Business Centre, 7 Whitechapel Road, London E1 1DU
tel 020 7164 6196
email info@theatre-rites.co.uk
website www.theatre-rites.co.uk
Facebook www.facebook.com/TheatreRites
Twitter @TheatreRites
Instagram @theatrerites
Artistic Director Sue Buckmaster

Production details: Committed to creating challenging productions which push the boundaries of theatrical form by experimenting to combine different artistic disciplines. Highly imaginative visual experiences for families to share together. Stages two productions annually, with around 45 performances in 12 arts centre and theatres across all English regions, in Scotland and internationally. In general 4-8 actors go on tour, playing to audiences of various ages, often 5+.Actors are sometimes expected to lead workshops; singing, musical instrument, dance physical theatre and puppetry skills, depending on the project. Recent productions include: Big Up!; Siyanda: *The Welcoming Party, Beasty Baby, The Broke 'n' Beat Collective* and *Rubbish*.

Casting procedures: Casting breadowns are available via the website and artsjobs. Welcomes letters (with CVs and photographs) from actors previously unknown to the company. Also welcomes showreels and invitations to view individual actors' websites. Offers Equity-approved contracts as negotiated through ITC. Promotes the use of inclusive casting. Multi-disciplined performers are always very welcome.

Theatre Absolute

Shop Front Theatre, 38 City Arcade, Coventry
email info@theatreabsolute.co.uk
website www.theatreabsolute.co.uk
Artistic Director/Writer Chris O'Connell
Producer Julia Negus

Production details: Founded in 1992, the company commissions, develops and produces new work for theatre. In 2009, Theatre Absolute founded the UK's first professional Shop Front Theatre in Coventry, West Midlands. Work includes performances, script readings, writing workshops, and mentor support for actors, writers, producers and emerging theatre makers.

Casting procedures: Actors should consult the website for details of the next project. 'If you are a local actor, do come to a show/event or drop in and introduce yourself in the first instance'.

Theatre Alibi

Emmanuel Hall, Emmanuel Road, Exeter EX4 1EJ
tel/fax 01392 217315
email info@theatrealibi.co.uk
website www.theatrealibi.co.uk
Facebook www.facebook.com/TheatreAlibiUK
Twitter @TheatreAlibi
Artistic Director Nikki Sved

Production details: Founded in 1982, the company creates new work for all ages that is physically and visually inventive and often enriched by other art forms including music, animation, film, puppetry, dance and photography. Stages 2 productions a year, with a total of around 130 performances. Tours theatres and arts centres as well as schools and community venues, the nature of the venue depending on the individual show. The company offers ITC/Equity-approved contracts and is an ITC Ethical Manager.

Recent productions include: *Falling* (small-scale national tour of theatres and arts centres for adult audiences) and *Table Mates* (tour of primary schools, community venues and theatres for 5-11-year-olds, mainly in the South West).

Casting procedures: Casts in house as well as welcoming new performers. Runs occasional general auditions and for some productions publishes casting breakdowns and is instigating open auditions. Welcomes letters and emails with CVs and photographs at any time of year. Also welcomes links to showreels and individual websites.

Theatre Broad

Easter Ballat, Balfron Station, Nr Glasgow G63 0SQ
tel 01360 440480
email info@theatrebroad.co.uk
email actors@theatrebroad.co.uk
website www.theatrebroad.co.uk
Artistic Director Carol Metcalf *Executive Director* David Reid-Kay

Production details: An innovative theatre company dedicated to providing regular, affordable, quality theatre to people in the Stirling area, then touring throughout the country. Aims to provide audiences with the opportunity to see the best available plays, from a broad range of styles, writers and cultures.

In addition to its mainstream productions, the company's award-winning Community Roots programme is in association with Forth Valley College, Stirling, Falkirk and Clackmannan. Disabled adult students appear in specially devised productions where they are supported in the rehearsal room and in performance by professional actors and practitioners.

Tours 2-4 projects annually, with around 20-40 performances at 6-12 venues in Stirling, Central Scotland, Dumfries and Aberdeenshire. Venues include mid-scale theatres, arts centres, village halls and art galleries. In general 2-15 actors go on tour, depending on the production. Recent productions include: *An Afternoon Delight* by Ross Mather and Gordon Reid (Stirling's Studio Theatre); *Ludus – PlayfulLlove*, devised and directed by Carol Metcalf (Scottish and Cumbria tour); *Bruce's Quest – The Musical* by Gareth Candy; *Our World* (a community productions on global warming) by Carol Metcalf; *Brush Up Your Shakespeare* (celebrating Shakespeare's 400th anniversary) devised by Carol Metcalf; *Prelude and Fugue* by Clifford Bax; *SuperNatural* by Gareth Candy. A Scottish and Cumbria tour of Ira Levin's *Deathtrap*; *3 Stars and a Quest: Tron Labyrinth* (by Gareth Candy and Carol Metcalf); a Scottish tour of *J. M. Barrie: Peter Pan Man* (by Anne Stenhouse and J.M. Barrie); *When Santa Got Lost In Space* (a pantomime by Carol Metcalf).

Casting procedures: Casting is done in-house by the Artistic and Executive Directors, and actors may write at any time to request inclusion. Casting breakdowns are available from the website, Equity Job Information Service and Casting Call Pro. No hard copy submissions, but will accept CVs and photographs sent by email, as well as showreels and invitations to view individual actors' websites/other productions. Encourages applications from disabled performers and promotes the use of inclusive casting. Theatre Broad is a member of The Federation of Scottish Theatre.

Theatre Is

The Hat Factory, 65-67 Bute Street, Luton, Bedfordshire LU1 2EY
tel 01582 481221 *fax* 01279 506694
email info@theatreis.org
website www.theatreis.org

Production details: Established in 2006. Challenging and creating new models of live performance by, with and for young audiences across the East of England and beyond. 3 productions are staged annually touring East of England, London, Midlands, North West and Wales. 50 performances per year at an average of 20 venues. Types of venue include: arts centres, theatres, outdoor venues, educational and community venues. 4 actors are generally involved in each production. Actors are employed under ITC/Equity-approved contracts. Recent productions include: *Master Juba* (Hackney Empire, Norwich Playhouse); *Claytime* (New Wolsey Theatre, Lyric Hammersmith, Unicorn Theatre).

Casting procedures: Casting is done by an in-house casting director. Casting breakdowns are only available to agents via the Spotlight link. Does not welcome individual submissions from actors. Actively encourages applications from disabled actors and promotes the use of inclusive casting in new writing productions.

Theatre Lab Company

76 St Dunstan's Avenue, London W3 6QJ
mobile 07958 4048806
email anastasia@theatrelab.co.uk
website www.theatrelab.co.uk
Director Anastasia Revi

Production details: Established in 1997. Stages 1 production annually, with around 20 performances in 3 theatres in the Midlands and South East, and abroad. In general 4-6 actors are involved in each production. Offers Equity-approved contracts as negotiated through ITC "when funded". Recent productions include *Velvet Scratch* (Prague Festival 2007; Edinburgh Festival 2007; Greek tour 2008; New York Fringe Festival 2008).

Casting procedures: Uses freelance casting directors. Holds general auditions and actors may write to request inclusion when advertised. Casting breakdowns are available from the website, by postal application (with sae) and in *The Stage*. Welcomes letters (with CVs and photographs) from individual actors previously unknown to the company, sent by post or email. Also welcomes showreels and invitations to view individual actors' websites. Will consider applications from disabled actors to play characters with disabilities.

Théâtre Sans Frontières

2a Tanner's Yard, Hexham,
Northumberland NE46 3NL
tel 01434 603114 *fax* 01434 607206
email info@tsf.org.uk
website www.tsf.org.uk
Facebook @theatresansf
Twitter @theatresansf
Instagram theatresansf*Artistic Directors* Sarah Kemp (CEO), John Cobb

Production details: Founded in 1991. Set up by former students of Philippe Gaulier and Monika Pagneux. Specialises in physical theatre and stages texts in different languages for adults and children using international performers. Stages 2-3 productions annually with 60-100 performances in venues including arts centres, schools and theatres. In general 3-6 actors are involved in each production. Recent productions include: *Lipsynch* (co-produced with Robert Lepage and Ex Machina, toured internationally); *La Chanson du Retour* (with Sage

Gateshead); *Canary Gold* (collaboration with Teatro Tamaska), Le Moulin Magique. *Heaven Eyes, Lorca: Amor en el Jardin, Chernobyl@30* (with Theatre Arabesky, Ukraine), *A Frog Called Woanda* (with Theatre À L'Envers, Quebec) and UK schools' tour Ti Jean et La Chèvre (for children aged 8 to 12 years).

Casting procedures: Sometimes holds general auditions. Actors may write at any time requesting inclusion. Casting breakdowns are available on request. Welcomes submissions (with CVs and photographs) sent by post or email. Invitations to view individual actors' websites are also accepted. "We are usually looking for actors who have languages other than English (especially French, Spanish or German), and who have a clear physical theatre training (i.e. Le Coq, Gaulier, Pagneux or Complicite)."

Theatre Set-up

12 Fairlawn Close, Southgate, London N14 4JX
website www.ts-u.co.uk
Charitable Director Wendy Macphee

This company has been taken over by the Festival Players **www.thefestivalplayers.org.uk**.

Theatre Without Walls

Forwood House, Forwood, Gloucestershire GL6 9AB
mobile 07962 040441
email hello@theatrewithoutwalls.org
website www.theatrewithoutwalls.org
Directors Jason Maher, Genevieve Swift

Production details: Established in 2002. Award-winning theatre company specialising in forum, education and new writing. Productions represent only one-fifth of its output; also produces television and corporate films. 2 productions are staged annually with 60 performances per year, touring to 20 venues including arts centres, theatres and outdoor venues. Tours cover the UK, Ireland and Europe. 3 actors are involved in each production. Actors are employed under ITC/Equity-approved contracts. Recent productions include: *Don Quixote* (Banbury Mill); *The Hold* (Cheltenham Everyman) and *The Plant Hunters* (National Trust).

Casting procedures: "We cast mostly through agents and our own knowledge/word of mouth/ recommendations. We sometimes post casting information via Equity JIS and other 'freely available resources'. We never use casting services which actors have to pay for, except for Spotlight. Any information obtained via paid-for services has simply been copied from another source. Please don't send us any information (such as photos, CVs, showreels, etc.) unless we have requested it. We regularly hold actors' labs and often cast from them." Theatre Without Walls is a member of ITC and most of its work is undertaken using Equity contracts. Those working with vulnerable adults or children must have a current enhanced Criminal Record Bureau/Police

Check and hold full insurance equal or greater than that provided by Equity for its members. Considers applications from disabled actors to play disabled characters.

See also the company's entry under *Role-play companies* on page 307.

Theatre Workshop

34 Hamilton Place, Edinburgh EH3 5AX
tel 0131 225 7942 *fax* 0131 220 0112
email afleming@twe.org.uk
website www.theatre-workshop.com
Artistic Director Robert Rae

Production details: Founded in 1965; stages 4 productions a year with around 60 performances across 2 theatre venues. Occasionally tours internationally. Employs an average of 5 actors on each production, using ITC/Equity-approved contracts. Recent productions include: *The Jasmine Road* (No Limits International Theatre Festival, Berlin) and *The Threepenny Opera* (Edinburgh Festival Theatre & Tramway, Glasgow).

Casting procedures: Casting breakdowns are available from the website and Equity Job Information Service. Welcomes letters and emails (with CVs and photographs) from individuals previously unknown to the company. Also happy to receive showreels and invitations to view individuals' websites. Encourages applications from disabled actors and promotes the use of inclusive casting. "Theatre Workshop casts both disabled and non-disabled actors in all our productions."

Third Party Productions Ltd

81 Braybrooke Road, Hastings, East Sussex TN34 1TF
tel 01424 436149 *mobile* 07768 694211/694212
email gleave@thirdparty.org.uk
website www.thirdparty.org.uk
Joint Artistic Directors Anthony Gleave, Nicholas Collett

Production details: Established in 1992. A UK and International touring theatre company. Work is usually based on classic plays which are deconstructed and re-imagined during the rehearsal process, and given a contemporary and experimental vitality. Currently working with John Wright – founder of Trestle Theatre and co-founder of Told By An Idiot – and co-producing work with French company BordCadre and Galician clown company Macquinaria Pesada. Stages 1-3 productions annually with around 40-120 performances at 30-90 venues of all types. In general 3-7 actors are involved in each production. Recent productions include: *Noggin the Nog* (based on the TV series created by Oliver Postgate and Peter Firmin), *The Tragicall History of Dr Faustus – A Damned Fine Play* (New Diorama, London), and *La Fausse Suivante/The False Servant* (Café de la Danse Paris and UK tour).

Casting procedures: Auditions by invitation only. May advertise for certain projects through various publications and websites. Welcomes unsolicited CVs and photographs, and invitations to view individual actors' websites, if sent by email only. Actively encourages applications from disabled actors when advertising for casting.

Tilted Wig Productions

tel 07837 912285/07843 092783
email katherine@tiltedwigproductions.com
Producers Matthew Parish, Katherine Senior

Production details: Tilted Wig Productions was formed in 2017. Has 12 years' experience producing and touring plays throughout the UK both as Tilted Wig and Creative Cow – a Devon-based theatre company we co-founded in 2007. An ensemble of actors, crew and creatives has taken over 20 productions on the road, touring in the depths of the British countryside, setting up shows in pubs and skittle alleys. Shows now tour to some of the biggest theatres in the UK yet that same ethos is still the driving force behind the company.

Recent productions: *Great Expectations*, 2018; *The Picture of Dorian Gray*, 2019.

Casting procedures: Does not hold general auditions; the company works with a pool of performers, but is always interested in meeting new actors – either by personal recommendation or by seeing their work. Casts for some roles via agents through Spotlight. Encourages applications from disabled actors and promotes the use of inclusive casting.

Tin Shed Theatre Company

46 Lennard Street, Newport, NP19 0EJ
mobile 07921 366038 or 07511 139773
email tinshedtheatre@gmx.com
website www.tinshedtheatrecompany.com
Company Directors Georgina Harris, Justin Cliffe, Antonio Rimola

Production details: Established in 2008. Specialises in devised theatre which lends itself to performance in unusual spaces. High-energy, high-impact work that focuses on many different genres. Also has an educational programme with an emphasis on the English curriculum.

Stages 1 production each year in the main house and 3 in the studio. Recent productions include: Brighton Fringe 2012, Edinburgh Fringe 2013 and national tour of *Dr Frankenstein's Travelling Freakshow*; *The Ritual*; *An Immersive* and Halloween Experience 2013.

Casting procedures: Uses freelance directors; actors may write at any time to request inclusion. Casting breakdowns are available from the website. Welcomes unsolicited approaches by post and email, and accepts showreels and invitations to view individual actors' websites/visit other productions. Encourages applications from disabled actors and promotes the use of inclusive casting.

Theatre

Tinderbox Theatre Company
Crescent Arts Centre, 2-4 University Road,
Belfast BT7 1NH
tel 028 9043 9313
email info@tinderbox.org.uk
website www.tinderbox.org.uk
Artistic Director Patrick J. O'Reilly *Producer* Jen
Shepherd

Production details: Founded in 1988. Produces,
develops and stages new work and provides
professional theatre training. Stages 2-3 productions
and tours annually, including arts centres, theatres
and site-specific locations in the UK and Ireland.
Recent productions include: *The Man Who Fell To
Pieces*, *Ubu the King* and *Hubert and the Yes Sock*.

Casting procedures: Holds open calls for auditions.
Welcomes letters (with CVs and photographs) and
email submissions. Invitations to view individual
actors' websites are also accepted. Offers Equity-
approved contracts. Encourages applications from
disabled actors and promotes the use of inclusive
casting.

Told by an Idiot
St Martin's House, 59 St Martin's Lane,
London WC2N 4JS
tel 020 7407 4123
email info@toldbyanidiot.org
website www.toldbyanidiot.org
Artistic Director Paul Hunter

Production details: Founded in 1993, the company
tours to theatres nationally and internationally.

Casting procedures: Casting is either in-house or
with a freelance casting director, depending on the
project. Offers ITC/Equity contracts.

TOSG Gaelic Theatre Company
Sabhal Mor Ostaig, Sleat, Isle of Skye IV44 8RQ
tel 01471 888542 *fax* 01471 888542
email tosg@tosg.org
website www.tosg.org.uk
Artistic Director Simon Mackenzie

Production details: Founded in 1996. Professional
Gaelic Theatre Company producing theatre for both
adults and children. Also runs a new writing scheme.
All productions are performed in Gaelic. Stages 2
productions annually and gives 50 performances per
year. Tours to 30 different venues annually, including
arts centres, theatres, educational and community
venues in Scotland. In general 5 actors are involved in
each production.

Casting procedures: Sometimes holds general
auditions. Gaelic-speaking actors can write in May
requesting inclusion. Welcomes letters (with CVs and
photographs) but not email submissions. Invitations
to view individual actors' websites are also accepted.

Trestle Theatre Company
Trestle Arts Base, Russet Drive, St Albans AL4 0JQ
tel 01727 850950

email admin@trestle.org.uk
website www.trestle.org.uk
Twitter @TrestleTheatre
Artistic Director Emily Gray

Production details: Founded in 1981 as a touring
theatre company, now also with a home venue
(Trestle Arts Base), national and international
workshop programme and a global business making
and selling handcrafted theatre masks. Performers/
facilitators used across all areas of the company. All
projects concentrate on new, devised or
commissioned work, incorporating mask, text,
physical theatre, dance and other movement forms,
storytelling, puppetry, music and song. Currently 2
shows touring schools with high quality
performances, workshops and resources – national
and international tours. In general 2-5 performers are
involved in each project. Offers ITC/Equity contracts.

Casting procedures: Rarely holds general auditions.
Does not welcome on-spec CVs. Will consider
invitations to see actors in shows if the performance
style is relevant to the way in which Trestle works. If
looking for suggestions, casting breakdowns will be
posted on the website. Usually casts actors with
strong physical/visual theatre acting training or
experience. Actively encourages applications from
disabled actors and promotes the use of inclusive
casting.

Triangle Theatre Company
email office@triangletheatre.co.uk
website www.triangletheatre.co.uk
Joint Artistic Directors Carran Waterfield, Richard
Talbot

Production details: Runs performances and talks for
conferences, schools and colleges, and heritage sites as
well as collaborations with academics and researchers
contributing to the ongoing dissemination of
Triangle's method of extended and immersive play
with character, personal biography and history. Stages
on average 1 major original production each year,
including studio and site-specific situations. Studio
work is actor-centred and scripted from lengthy,
devised rehearsals. Site-specific work is experimental
and participatory, and developed in partnership with
universities and local authorities. Recent productions
include: *The Last Women* (2009) and *Knickers and
Vests* (part of the Cultural Olympiad to London
2010).

Winner of the UK Museums & Heritage Award for
excellence, and the Roots & Wings Award for
performance and interactive projects in response to
museum collections. Also Fringe First and
Independent Theatre Award Short List, Best
Production/Actress, Festival of Experimental Theatre,
Volgograd, Russia.

Casting procedures: Casting and contracts agreed by
Artistic Directors. Triangle holds ensemble auditions
and training workshops to develop material, generate

ideas and employ associate artists. Actors are advised to consult the website for detailed information and to approach the company regarding specific, relevant projects. Does not welcome unsolicited submissions by post or by email, or showreels, but will accept invitations to view individual actors' websites. Offers independent contracts based on ITC. Actively encourages applications from disabled actors and promotes the use of inclusive casting.

Two's Company

244 Upland Road,London SE22 0DN
tel 020 8299 3714
email graham@2scompanytheatre.co.uk
website www.2scompanytheatre.co.uk
Facebook /2sComp
Twitter @2sComp
Artistic Director Tricia Thorns *Producer* Graham Cowley

Production details: Founded in 1999, Two's Company focus on presenting 'new plays of the past', forgotten plays from earlier times which depict events or people contemporary with them. For example, they produced a series of plays about the First World War, originally written at the time. Recent productions include: *A Day by the Sea* by N.C. Hunter, *The Fifth Column* by Ernest Hemingway, *The Cutting of the Cloth* by Michael Hastings, *What The Women Did* (Southwark Playhouse), and *London Wall*, by John van Druten (Finborough Theatre and St James Theatre). Each production consists of 8-10 actors and usually the company presents 1 production per year. This equates to around 26 performances at 1 London venue, mainly small London theatres. Occasionally, a tour will go out to small theatres and arts centres.

Casting procedures: Hardly ever uses freelance casting directors, and does not hold general auditions. Welcomes both CVs and letters from actors previously unknown to the company and unsolicited CVs and photographs but only when casting. These should be sent via email. Also welcomes invitations to view individual actors' websites, especially if they include showreels. Rarely has the opportunity to cast disabled actors.

TYPE (The Yellowchair Performance Experience)

89 Birchanger Lane, Birchanger, Bishop Stortford, Herts CM23 5QF
email contactTYPE@gmail.com
website www.wix.com/yellowchair/type
Key contact Hugh Allison

Production details: Aims to give new talent their first break on the UK Fringe (not limited to actors). Recent productions include: *A Midsummer Night's Dream, What Andrew Heard, The Bear*.

Casting procedures: Does not use freelance casting directors or hold general auditions. Actors may write

in at any time. Casting breakdowns are usually available on CCP and at **mandy.com**. Welcomes letters (with CVs and photographs) from individual actors previously unknown to the company, sent by post. May cast disabled actors, depending on the role.

UK Arts International

6 Fort Crescent, Margate CT9 1HN
website www.ukarts.com

Production details: Mainly presents productions from overseas and tours them throughout the UK.

Casting procedures: Does not hold general auditions and does not welcome submissions from actors previously unknown to the company.

Unlimited Theatre

Unit 21, Munro House, Duke Street, Leeds LS9 8AG
tel 01138 805682
email unlimited@unlimited.org.uk
website www.unlimited.org.uk
Creative Director Jon Spooner

Production details: Founded in 1997. Creates work intended to "explore how personal experience can illuminate political debate, and which puts marginalised voices centre-stage". Stages 1-2 productions annually with 50-100 performances. Tours to 10-20 different venues each year, including arts centres and theatres throughout the UK (including Glasgow, Edinburgh and Belfast) and overseas. In general 4-6 actors are involved in each production. Recent productions include: *Money the Gameshow, Play Dough, Am I Dead Yet?, The Astro Science Challenge* and *How I Hacked My Way Into Space.*

Casting procedures: Sometimes holds general auditions. Welcomes responses to casting calls but not email submissions. Follow **@untheatre** on Twitter or sign up to newsletter for info on casting calls. "We are a small- to middle-scale organisation and only occasionally employ freelance actors. We are always interested in hearing from potential new collaborators." Offers ITC/Equity-approved contracts. Actively encourages applications from disabled actors and promotes the use of inclusive casting.

Unrestricted View

109 St Paul's Road, Islington, London N1 2NA
tel 020 7704 2001
email felicity@henandchickens.com
website www.unrestrictedview.co.uk
Artistic Directors Felicity Wren, James Wren *Theatre Manager* Mark Johnson

Production details: Unrestricted View produce new writing and comedy. Run by actors for actors, the company offer a safe, supportive space for creative people to work in. The theatre is also a cinema space. The theatre hosted 3 productions in 2014 and offers financial and professional support to 3 resident acting companies. Theatre productions are hosted on 3-week runs and comedy shows are hosted on an individual basis, with the theatre in use as a performance space 355 days per year. Recent productions include: *Get It Seen* (a month of feature films and shorts from independent producers – affliated with the BFI) and *A May's Plays* (a 15-year celebration of the theatre with 10 new 15-minute plays supplied by the company's sister theatre in New York City – The WorkShop Theater).

The main theatre space has 54 seats, which can be arranged in a number of different configurations. Hire-rates are as follows: £1,200 per week, or on a day-by-day basis of £120 (until 7.30pm) or £150 (until 9.30pm).

Casting Procedures: Uses in-house casting directors. A casting breakdown is available on Casting Call Pro and the website, with details of upcoming productions on Twitter and Facebook. Happy to consider applications from disabled actors.

Vanguard Productions
30 Coombe Rise, Findon Valley, Worthing, West Sussex BN14 0ED
tel 01903 872982
email vanguard.productions@ntlworld.com
website www.vanguardproductions.co.uk
Artistic Directors Nelson. E.Ward, Amaryllis Crooke and Rachel Ward

Production details: Founded in 1996, Vanguard take theatre and entertainment to areas of the community that are socially excluded. These include residential/nursing homes, day centres, museums and village halls as well as smal-scale theatre venues. An outreach programme also exists for schools and colleges. Recent productions include: *Maxie: The Life of Max Miller*, *What A Swell Party* and *Magic Moments*. Each production contains 3-4 actors and Vanguard present 4 productions per year. This equates to 50-70 performances annually at venues across the south of England, including residential/nursing homes, day centres, museums, schools, colleges and art centres.

Casting procedures: Uses in-house casting directors and only holds general auditions periodically. The best time to contact regarding roles is during the summer for parts in the Christmas production. Casting breakdowns are put on Mandy.com and Equity job information service. Welcomes both CVs and letters from actors previously unknown to the Company and unsolicited CVs and photographs. These should be sent via email.

Volcano Theatre Company
229 High Street, Swansea SA1 1NY
tel 01792 464790
email paul@volcanotheatre.co.uk
website www.volcanotheatre.co.uk
Directors Paul Davies, Fern Smith

Production details: Original theatrical productions and site-specific events. Small-scale national and international touring company based in Wales. Devised and collaborative work, physical theatre, new writing, adaptations/deconstructions of classics. Stages 2-4 productions and gives 50-80 performances each year. Venues include arts centres and theatres in the UK, Europe and worldwide. Usually 2-8 performers per production. Recent productions include: *i-witness*, *Dead Cat Bounce* and *A Few Little Drops*.

Casting procedures: There are no casting breakdowns. Performers are selected through workshops and invited auditions. Unsolicited admissions are read but not held on record.

Waking Exploits
15 Windsor House, Westgate Street, Cardiff CF10 1DG
email info@wakingexploits.co.uk
website www.wakingexploits.co.uk
Producer Iain Goosey *Associate Producer* Michael Salmon

Production details: Established in 2010. Produces high-quality, innovative work by contemporary playwrights from across the UK, in theatres and site-specific locations. Stages 1-2 productions each year, with 20-40 performances in 10-20 venues (England and Wales) including mid-scale arts centres and theatres. In general 5-10 actors are involved in each show. Recent productions include: *Serious Money* by Caryl Churchill and *Pornography* by Simon Stephens.

Casting procedures: Uses freelance casting director. General submissions from actors are encouraged only during casting period (published on the website). Breakdowns are displayed on the site and via Spotlight, Equity Job Information Service and Ideas Tap. Offers Equity TMA contracts. Does not welcome unsolicited approaches by post, but actors may email CVs, photographs, showreels and invitations to view websites or visit productions. Actively encourages applications from disabled actors and promotes the use of inclusive casting.

Walk the Plank
72 Broad Street, Salford, M6 5BZ
tel 0161 736 8964
email info@walktheplank.co.uk
website www.walktheplank.co.uk

Production details: Founded 2001, Walk the Plank are outdoor arts experts, who create events with mass appeal. Walk the Plank present over 10 productions per year, hosting outdoor productions at various locations across England and internationally. Recent production locations include: UK City of Culture – Londonderry, Manchester Day Parade and Hull's Freedom Festival.

Casting procedures: Uses in-house casting directors. Welcomes both CVs and letters from actors previously unknown to the company, but will not accept unsolicited CVs and photographs. Also welcomes showreels and invitations to view individual actor's websites or invitations to view specific productions. Actively encourages applications from disabled actors and promotes the use of inclusive casting.

Keith Whitall

25 Solway, Hailsham BN27 3HB
tel 01323 844882
Director Keith Whitall

Production details: Founded in 2000. Produces revues, small-scale musicals and occasionally plays and one-person shows. Stages 2-3 productions annually with 20 or more performances in theatres in Brighton and the South East. So far has only toured to 1 arts centre. In general 9-10 actors are involved in each production. Recent productions include: *Broadway Calling, The Pleasure of Your Company* and *Noel Coward & Cole Porter Revisited.* Offers non-Equity contracts and does not subscribe to the Equity Pension Scheme.

Casting procedures: Sometimes holds general auditions. Actors may write at any time requesting inclusion. Casting breakdowns are usually made available to casting directors or actors seen in a production. Welcomes letters (with CVs and photographs) but not email submissions. "In my revues I usually use 3-4 experienced artistes plus new young artistes in whom I am especially interested." Musical theatre experience is preferable. Rarely has opportunity to cast disabled actors, but "possible in future depending on backstage access".

The Wrestling School

42 Durlston Road, London E5 8RR
tel 020 8442 4229
website www.thewrestlingschool.co.uk
Director Howard Barker

Production details: Founded in 1988. "Develops ways of presenting complex ideas in the theatre through the work of Howard Barker." Stages 1 production annually; in general 5-7 actors are involved in each production.

Casting procedures: Sometimes holds auditions. Welcomes letters when casting (with CVs and photographs) but not email submissions. Actors should telephone in late July, or consult the website, to find out if the company is casting.

Y Touring Theatre Company

One KX, 120 Cromer Street, London WC1B 8BS
tel 020 7520 3090

email d.jackson@ytouring.org.uk
website www.theatreofdebate.com
Artistic Director Nigel Townsend

Production details: Award-winning professional touring company for young people and adults. Produces 2 tours per year in the UK. Offers ITC/Equity-approved contracts and does not subscribe to the Equity Pension Scheme.

Casting procedures: Uses freelance casting directors and publishes casting breakdowns through Spotlight. Does not hold general auditions. Will accept CVs and photos at any time of year to be held on file for consideration. Please do not send showreels or unsolicited scripts. Will consider applications from disabled actors.

Yellow Earth Theatre

The Albany, Douglas Way, Deptford, London SE8 4AG
tel 020 8694 6631
email admin@yellowearth.org
website www.yellowearth.org
Artistic Director Kumiko Mendl

Production details: Yellow Earth Theatre was established by a group of British East Asian (BEA) performers in 1995. It develops and presents new theatre work by BEA artists. It engages new mainstream and BEA audiences in fresh, vibrant work that reflects the BEA experience and creates high profile opportunities for BEA actors, writers and directors. It has presented 22 high profile productions in London and on tour in the UK, including performances at the RSC, Barbican and Soho Theatres. It tours work nationally and shows are designed to tour easily. Detailed technical requiremetns are provided along with a touring stage manager. Yellow Earth is a member of ITC.

Casting procedures: Casts in-house. Sometimes holds general auditions. Welcomes emails with CVs and photographs from actors with East Asian heritage only. Accepts invitations to view individual actors' websites, but not showreels. Promotes the use of inclusive casting.

East Asian includes: Brunei, Burma, Cambodia, China, East Timor, Hong Kong, Indonesia, Japan, Laos, Malaysia, Mongolia, North Korea, Philippines, Singapore, South Korea, Taiwan, Thailand, Vietnam and their diasporas.

Theatre

Starting your own theatre company

Pilar Ortí

The first question you should ask yourself before starting a theatre company is – do you really need to set up a company, or do you just want to put on a show? In order to put on a show you don't need to go through all the hassle of setting up a company. If you *do* want to set up a company – why? In some cases this might be as difficult a question to answer as, "Why do you want to act?", but it's worth having an idea of why you want to invest so much time and energy in setting up and running an organisation rather than looking for acting work. Whatever your answer, be honest with yourself. And the clearer you can be, the better, as your answers will affect the kind of organisation you end up creating.

Of course, many companies emerge after a group of actors produce a show together: at some point, someone decides that, as a company of people, you are worth keeping together. If this is the case, then you are ready to run a company of your own. But there are many ways of making theatre, as you well know, and the range of theatre produced is also vast. What kind of work do you want to do? At this point it is worth bearing in mind your 'artistic policy', and coming up with a couple of sentences that describe the work you do. I know that 'policy' sounds dry, but if you end up constituting yourself as a non-commercial organisation and applying to public funds (or trusts and foundations), you will need to learn a whole new vocabulary which seems to have little to do with your art. You should never lose sight of your artistic dreams and ambitions – but you may need to talk about them in terms of policy, objectives, qualitative evaluation, benefits, management structure, cultural diversity, contingency ... the list goes on and on. This article is meant to inspire you, not send you off to sleep, so don't despair: learn the language and then use it in a creative way that makes sense to you.

Allow yourself to dream

Long-term plans are necessary – so learn to dream. (Okay, give it a try in the first instance by putting on a show. Then, if you enjoy it, carry on!) Plans, of course, can change along the way: I suggest that you have an absolutely ambitious dream plan and a let's-try-and-see-what's-possible-now plan. Opportunities arise when you least expect them, and if you know where you are heading, you can grab them without letting them throw you off-course.

I view running a theatre company rather like directing a show: the more theatre you watch, the stronger the idea you will have of what *you* want the show to be, what is unique about it, and what you can realistically achieve. So if you, like me, trained as an actor or actress and suddenly find yourself running a company, seek advice and look at how others operate. If you consider how other people do things, you will be able to adapt the bits you like and which make sense to you. In a sector such as ours, it is not difficult to find those who are pleased to help – and the freshness of people just starting out reminds us all of how much can be achieved when we don't know our limitations.

Seek help

There is an awful lot of free/cheap advice out there. During the year in which we focused on building the administrative foundations for our company, my colleague and I talked to as many consultants, local authority officers, venue managers, etc. as we could. Some of these conversations came about through informal meetings; others, by taking part in official programmes. We found out what funders were really looking for, and what other companies were doing in our area; we learnt to draw up business plans with budgets covering three and five years; and we discovered what our strengths and weaknesses were, and what threats and opportunities exist 'out there'.

A word of warning: take *all* advice (including that which I am giving you now) with a pinch of salt, especially from those who hardly know you and your work. Follow your gut instinct. When we were in pre-production for *Antigone*, a business consultant suggested that we invite Funeral Services to advertise in our programme, "seeing as how they all die in the end". Mmm.

The best consultancies are those which have been carefully structured so that the consultant spends time with you, getting to know you and your plans, and then helps you find your own answers by providing their expertise. Arts & Business's 'Business in the Arts' programme is worth checking out, although you need to have a very definite idea of what you need help with. (To see what else Arts & Business do, check out their website, **www.aandb.org.uk**.)

Making it 'proper'

Once you have decided on the work you want to do and how you want to go about producing it, you will need to find a legal structure for your company. This shows outsiders that you are serious, and it also makes monetary transactions easier.

Forbidden's first show was produced in Edinburgh: the only 'proper' thing the company had was a bank account (and a name!). We then registered the name and became a limited company, and after our first London show, became a registered charity. This was a good idea as our income mainly comes from trusts and foundations (most of which require you to be a charity in order to receive their grants, for tax purposes); it also allows us to claim Gift Aid when we receive donations from individuals. (Gift Aid is great: the donor claims their donation as tax-deductible, and you receive an extra 23 per cent from the Inland Revenue.)

Setting up a charity still allows you to pursue your own artistic programme: making theatre for the public is considered to 'advance education', which is a charitable objective. So you can still run your company as a business, drawing salaries, etc. and making sure that any annual profits stay within the company.

Just like a limited company, a registered charity is governed by a Board. The main difference between the two set-ups is that those who sit on a charity's Board (the Trustees) do so on a voluntary basis. It therefore would make no sense for *you* to be part of the Board (although there is talk of a possible change in the law to allow Trustees to be remunerated for their work). This means that, in theory at least, you are putting the fate of your company in the hands of other people. So choose your Trustees very carefully, and try to include people who have some knowledge of legal matters and accountancy.

This set-up has worked for Forbidden, as we have been extremely lucky: we have managed to find experienced individuals with integrity and a passion for what we do. You might prefer a different kind of set-up which gives you more legal control: banks and Business Links offer free advice on the different options. If you want some focused advice and have a bit of cash to spare, you might attend the Independent Theatre Council's (ITC)

Theatre

seminar on 'Starting a Theatre Company'. And when you have a bit more cash, you might want to join the ITC – membership is bound to come in handy when questions on legal matters arise. (Have a look at the website, **www.itc-arts.org.uk**.)

Learn as you go along

Know your strengths and weaknesses. Setting up a theatre company will involve doing ten thousand things you might never have done before; however, a lot of it can be learnt along the way, and much of it is common sense. It won't take you long to discover those things you are useless at, and those that you absolutely hate. You then have two choices: do them anyway, or find someone else to do them for you/with you.

If there are more than two of you running the company, decide who will be in charge of what. Certain things, like fundraising, might be too daunting for one person to do on their own, but you can break it down into more manageable pieces. Someone might have a clearer head for numbers and can prepare the budget, and someone else can write the description of the show and why it will make a huge contribution to theatre in this country.

Let's talk about money

And seeing that I've come to fundraising, I shall dwell on it. You can't escape it. No matter how much your company grows, no matter how successful you are, no matter how large your staff is – if you are in charge, you will worry about it, so learn to enjoy it. I know that this sounds perverse, but fundraising applications are your chance to enthuse someone else about what you do. To tell them about your plans – about what you want to do and why you want to do it. Tell them how you want to make a difference; about *why* you think it's different; about how it will help you, and others, grow. And yes, you will need to learn some new vocabulary, and be able to distinguish between qualitative and quantitative evaluation, but it helps if you see this as a game with which you have to keep up. (At the last ITC annual general meeting, I found out that 'well-being' is a new way of convincing funders that theatre is necessary to people's lives!) What's really important is to convince funders that you really want to do the work, and that you want to do it well. (When I talk about funders, I am referring to anyone who might want to donate to or invest in your company. I have no experience of commercial deals, but I imagine that these work in a similar way: you find out what it is that people want in return for their money, and then convince them that you can provide it – as well as putting on a really good show.)

This is also where having long-term plans comes in handy: funding applications usually take between six weeks and three months to be assessed. Sometimes, even more: our first successful application for an Education Officer took more than one year from the date on which I sent it to the day the letter of acceptance came through. While I'm on the subject of those who will give you money – *nurture your relationships with them*. We have found that those trusts, foundations and individuals who are willing to help us out once, are likely to do so again.

I have also discovered that funding applications help you plan in detail how you are going to realise a production or a project. Good funding applications might come in useful even if you don't get the money – they will probably provide a good description of your plans, which you can then show others interested in your work. (For books and directories on fundraising, check out the Directory of Social Change's website, **www.dsc.org.uk**. They also have a small bookshop in Stephenson Way, near Euston Square in London NW1.)

Final words

I have left the most important thing until last. *Treat those working with you well, especially your actors.* Make working with you an enjoyable experience. If you hold auditions, make them worthwhile for those attending. When you are able to pay your personnel, pay them on time. Treat them like the professionals that they are. And when things go wrong, as they inevitably will, take responsibility for your company and make up for the hassle with a gesture, however small – custard creams work for me!

When I first started running Forbidden, I kept hearing that I should treat it like running a business. What I have discovered is that it is an exercise in people management. Forbidden exists because people have believed in our work and are willing to invest their time and money in what we do. Different organisations work in different ways: I hope these words have helped you find one that will work for you.

After running Forbidden Theatre Company as Artistic Director for seven years, Pilar now uses her people management skills to facilitate learning in leaders and in teams. She is director of Unusual Connections, a company which uses theatre-based training to deliver Leadership Programmes and Strategic Team-Away days. She also freelances as workshop leader and voice-over artist, and can be contated via **info@unusualconnections.co.uk**

Finding funding for projects
Sinead Mac Manus

Finding funding for projects is an essential part of the subsidised theatre scene. Unless you are working in the commercial sector, most theatre productions do not generate enough income to cover their costs. Fundraising provides the shortfall. The funding landscape in the UK is wide and varied, and can seem to the beginner to be an impossible terrain to navigate. However, as with most things, there are tricks of the trade that you can learn, and the process *does* get easier with practice.

Starting points

There are two good starting publications that I would recommend for fledging arts fundraisers: the first entitled 'Guide to Arts Funding in England', is an excellent overview of arts funding available to download for free from the Department for Culture, Media and Sport (DCMS) website (**www.culture.gov.uk**). Also recommended is Susan Forrester's and David Lloyd's *The Arts Funding Guide* published by the Directory of Social Change in 2002 (**www.dsc.org.uk**), which may be available in your local library. These guides take the user through the areas where you can find funding for projects, such as Government grants including Arts Council funding, Lottery funding, funding from your Local Authority, grants from charitable trusts and foundations, and bursaries.

Research, research, research

Successful fundraising is all about research, and matching available funds to your projects. If you approach fundraising creatively you should be able to adapt projects to available funds while still retaining your artistic integrity. So how do you discover what is out there? Get on the arts mailing lists to find out about new rounds of funds. Research the funding bodies and their criteria. Talk to your local Council about what funds they can offer you and your project. Find out what venues support new work with bursaries, or support in kind such as free space. Find out what trusts and foundations there are and who they give money to. Look up fundraising directories in your local library or one of the resource centres at organisations such as CIDA in east London (**www.cida.co.uk**), the Directory of Social Change (**www.dsc.org.uk**) or Arts and Business (**http://aandb.org.uk**).

The Funder Finder website (**www.funderfinder.org.uk**) features downloadable resources including a handy budget tool and grant application tool. Their cd-rom with details of hundreds of grants can be found in some resource centres or libraries for free use. They also have a free comprehensive advice pack on their website which has downloadable leaflets on areas such as budgeting, planning a funding strategy and tips for successful applications. The website also has a comprehensive A–Z list of trusts and foundations that have available funds.

It is important to research the funder that you are applying to, in order to find the 'essence' of the funder. This is essential so that you can match your projects to the relevant funder. For example, a Lottery Funding scheme such as Awards for All (**www.awardsforall.org.uk**) distributes public money for the benefit of local communities. Therefore any application to them must be for a project that demonstrates clear benefit to an identified community or body of people.

Similarly, the Arts Councils of England, Wales, Scotland and Northern Ireland all distribute public funds and have to be very open and transparent about how their funds are distributed.

Arts Council England (ACE) is the development and funding agency for the arts in England. You can apply to ACE as an individual for funding between £200 to £30,000. Organisations can receive up to £100,000. You can apply any time and there are no deadlines. A decision will be forthcoming within six weeks for grants under £5,000 and twelve weeks for grants over £5,000. ACE set aims every three years which form the basis of their grant-making policy, so it is important for applicants to think about how their project will fit into these aims. As with any funding body, building a relationship is paramount. Even before you approach ACE for funding, you should be inviting them to your productions and telling them about your projects. Full details of how to apply, including guidance notes, are on the website (**www.artscouncil.org.uk**).

The Arts Council of Wales (**www.artswales.org.uk**) has a similar funding system and structure to England, but there are regular funding deadlines throughout the year. Creative Scotland (formerly The Scottish Arts Council; **www.creativescotland.com**) has a slightly more complicated funding system with deadlines for different funding streams. The Arts Council of Northern Ireland (**www.artscouncil-ni.org**) has different funding schemes for individuals and organisations, and different closing dates for individual schemes.

In contrast to the Arts Councils in the UK, many charitable trusts and foundations only distribute funds to limited companies, and, in some cases, registered charities. Some can fund individuals, but they are not many. When applying to trusts and foundations, it is important to remember they were usually set up to address an issue or problem. You will need to identify what this is and ensure that your project addresses this.

Find out what you can about the funding body that you are applying to and what their funding priorities are. Make sure you fit into their guidelines and that you are eligible to apply. Remember that all funders have agendas – they do not give money away for nothing. For example, many Local Authority arts funding schemes usually look for local projects that impact on the community and have public benefit. View researching and applying for funding as you would looking for a job. You would not apply to a company if you did not think you were qualified. Similarly, you are wasting your time and theirs if you apply for funding that you are not eligible to get, e.g. your theatre company is not a registered charity, or they only fund work with older people and you work with children.

The proposal

An easy to read guide on writing funding proposals is Tim Cook's *Avoiding the Wastepaper Basket – A practical guide to applying to Grant Making Trusts* (LVSC, 1998). The book is written from the perspective of the funding body, and looks at examples of good and bad funding proposals.

If there is no application form, write a clear and concise (2 x A4 page) proposal. Write in plain English and do not use jargon. Find what the 'grain' of the funding body is. Do their work for them. Show in your funding application exactly how you meet their criteria and fit into their funding policy. Again to use the analogy of applying for a job, use the exact wording of the guidelines in your application when you are talking about your project, much in the way you would use the wording in the Person Specification when you are applying for a job. You can even highlight their criteria in bold or italics to make it stand out.

Theatre

Follow the guidelines of the fund to the letter – supply all the information that they require but do not add in additional information if it is not requested. If you have something that you think may be of interest to them, mention in your application that this is available on request. Convey your enthusiasm and passion for your project and your belief in yourself and/or your company. Show how the project will be successful. Funders like to back winners.

When you are finished, show your finished application to a non-arts person and ask them to read it for clarity. If you do get a grant, remember to say thank you! Start to build a relationship with the funder and keep them updated on progress with the project. If you are not successful, ask for feedback from the funder on why.

Business sponsorship

Business sponsorship can be a useful way of raising funds for projects if you are not eligible to apply for grant project funding. Business sponsorship is where a company gives your organisation or project cash, or support in kind, in exchange for publicity for their product or service. It is important to remember that businesses will not give you money or support for nothing – they will require something in return. Sponsorship is essentially a commercial deal between yourself and the business, and therefore there should be a clear exchange of benefits, e.g. advertising benefit for the company and monetary benefit for the arts organisation, and there should be a value to the benefit given or received.

Arts & Business is the leading agency for bringing business and the arts together in the UK. Their website provides valuable information about building relationships between the arts and business, including details of investment schemes such as *Read* and *Invest*. They also publish an essential guide to business sponsorship entitled *Arts Business Sponsorship Manual,* which is included when you book on their Arts & Business Sponsorship Seminar – held regularly around the UK. The guide and other resources on sponsorship can also be read at their free resource centre in London (**http://aandb.org.uk**).

Income generation

An important part of finding funding for projects is generating your own income. Income can be earned or generated from a number of different sources: venues can pay you a fee or share the box office receipts of a production. They can also commission or co-produce a work. You can sell merchandise such as programmes, t-shirts or postcards at your events. You can generate income through education work including fees for workshops and residencies. Individuals can give you money for your projects (angels) or they can invest in your work and expect (or not!) a return. You can also raise funds through events ranging from theatre related events such as benefit performances and cabarets to 'fun' events such as sponsored walks to parachute jumps.

Creative thinking

When you are starting out, it can be difficult to see where you can obtain the money for projects. The Arts Council do prefer to fund artists or organisations with a track record, and therefore you may have to find alternative funding initially for your productions or projects. Trusts and foundations tend to only fund limited companies or registered charities, and so again this may not be an area of funding that you can tap into immediately.

Therefore it is important to think of ways of funding your work outside the traditional funding system. In many cases, this may mean that you have to fund your work yourself and hope that you can get a return on it, or at least break even. This is how the majority of companies fund their Edinburgh Festival Fringe run – by investing the money upfront in the hire of the venue, the accommodation and travel and the cost of the production and hoping that the take at the box office will cover these costs and give everyone involved in the production some wages. If you are using your own money to mount a production, you need to be able to assess what level of risk you are willing to accept and think of ways of lessening this risk. Examine your budget and see where you can reduce or cut costs. You could try to get free rehearsal space from a local school in exchange for workshops or use a local printer for your flyers in exchange for advertising in your programme. Consider sharing your venue with another company for a double bill (check that this is acceptable to the venue in advance) to halve the costs of the hire. Book a venue in your local area that you know so that you can at least invite friends and family to have a guaranteed audience. Ask friends and family to invest small amounts of money in your production. This can be done as a gift or on an investment and return basis e.g. an individual invests £100 and is guaranteed a return of £75 or an amount above £100, depending on how well the show does. Offer credits for purchase in the production as gifts – purchasers get credit in the publicity material, and an invitation to a performance.

There are many examples of artists and companies that have used creative ways to get their projects up and running. One company sold performances in the customer's sitting room on eBay for cash. Another company raised the money for a string of rural performances by doing a sponsored walk from venue to venue. Another company raised the money for a production by offering to do up a local community centre – they got free rehearsal space and a venue as part of the deal.

Remember that you are a creative individual! Use some of that creativity to think outside the box when it comes to finding money for projects.

Sinead Mac Manus has worked for a wide range of arts organisations, including Frantic Assembly, Tall Stories and Mimbre. She is currently a freelance creative business consultant and trainer, and has many years of experience working with and training creative entrepreneurs. She is the author of *eVolve Graduate Handbook: a practical guide to producing performance*, and founder of **StartaTheatreCompany.com** – an online guide to starting a performing arts company. Her activity in developing new business models around the idea of e-learning for creative entrepreneurs using web 2.0 tools and social media led her to be chosen this year as one of the Courvoisier: Future 500 to watch.

The multi-hyphenate comedy actor-performer-writer

Chris Head

In my view the best thing you can do to develop as a comedy actor-performer is to become a comedy actor-writer-performer. Writing for yourself makes you proactive, generating your own projects, and it gives you a way to showcase yourself which is not dependent on waiting for others. Then, when you do audition you will be a more attractive, match fit proposition. There are so many ways you can write and perform your own comedy. In this article I am going to draw on my own work as a director, coach and comedy consultant to hopefully inspire you with a range of real world examples.

If you haven't already started writing for yourself, an easy, but admittedly scary, start is to do five-minute stand-up open spots. You might shudder at the thought of stand-up, but it's the quickest and most direct way to get yourself in front of audiences and – with luck and persistence – there's a clear progression to paid gigs. Stand-up courses (ahem, like my own in London) can help ease you into it, and there are many supportive and friendly new act nights, especially in cities. Why as an actor might you do stand-up? It shows gumption and bravery, and it means you are getting regular stage time in front of audiences. All far more attractive than 'resting' between jobs. It also opens up other avenues such as presenting and compering.

The default in stand-up is to appear as a heightened version of yourself. In this case, you become a character; you're playing a version of yourself. As part of your act you can also deliver act-outs and dialogue as other characters thereby showcasing your acting and vocal talents. I coach an actor-stand-up, Ben Keenan, who makes a point of getting as many voices into his act as he can. This year he is also doing a group show at the Edinburgh Festival Fringe where he and two other comics share an hour-long slot. So alongside (or even instead of) club gigs you can develop a festival show. These are typically an hour and can take you to many agreeable places and the major festivals are swarming with producers.

At the time of writing I'm directing the Hollywood actor and producer Hopwood DePree in a festival show for Brighton, Manchester, Camden and Edinburgh Fringes. Researching his ancestry online he discovered that via the long-lost British branch of the family he is heir to a crumbling stately home outside Rochdale! Putting his acting on hold he relocated to the UK to pursue this passion project of restoring Hopwood Hall. ('Hopwood' being the original family name.) He didn't want to totally neglect his performing whilst in the UK, but at the same time had to juggle the restoration project. So the simple and direct form of stand-up was the perfect vehicle, and when he approached me for help it was a no-brainer to develop a festival show with him telling his amazing true story.

If you don't like the idea of being yourself on stage, however, you can also perform as a fictional character in stand-up contexts. I have worked for a number of years with character comic-actor-film maker Steve Whiteley. On the live stage he has found success performing in character as the spoken word artist Wisebowm. Initially performing short sets in comedy clubs in character, he progressed with me as director to doing full-length festival shows. To make the leap to this broader canvas, we fleshed out the wider world of characters around Wisebowm, treating the one-man show in effect like a sitcom. This then made the next step to a BBC Radio 4 sitcom pilot (that I script-edited) a natural one. It also showed the value of live performances as the producer sold the idea to the BBC using live footage.

Someone else I have worked with as director and coach over a number of years is Katia Kvinge. This Scottish-Norwegian comedian-writer-actor began doing stand-up as herself, but felt more at home performing characters. This eventually developed into full-length festival shows where she interacts with the audience as herself and showcases a range of character performances. For her this is the best of both worlds. The audience can meet her and hear her story and she gets to perform a range of character pieces too. This is true too of actor-writer Helen Wood who I direct in autobiographical one-woman shows on her idiosyncratic passions. Her most recent show on Ordnance Survey maps was seen at Edinburgh, on a national tour and at OS HQ! When she'd previously performed in acting roles she had to hide her glee at playing a role, but in these shows her joy at taking on a character is all part of the charm of the piece.

A perhaps more sociable way to showcase a range of characters of your own devising is in sketch comedy. Stand-up Janine Harouni writes and performs with the sketch group Muriel alongside Meg Salter and Sally O'Leary, all three of whom I have intensively coached in sitcom writing. The discipline of creating characters and sketches is a great grounding for the longer form of sitcom narrative and there are many examples of sitcoms that had their beginnings in sketch work. And what a great opportunity sketch shows present to you, the actor, to show your versatility and range and to try out characters and situations in short form.

Then there's long-form improv, which gives you a great chance to explore narrative on stage. All the writer-performers in this article have done improv. And, of course, there are comedy stage plays, which are a great format for showcasing your writing and performing in longer form narrative. One-hour plays have become very popular and in demand at arts festivals and can be a great springboard to broadcast media. For example, I have directed two such plays written and performed by Roxy Dunn and Alys Metcalf, *In Tents & Purposes* and *You Only Live Forever*, which have been seen at Assembly in Edinburgh and at the Soho Theatre.

Roxy and Alys have combined their comedy plays with developing work online, the combination of which has greatly increased their exposure as actors and writers. Muriel also make sketches for online consumption, racking up millions of views, and this I feel is the optimum approach giving you invaluable immediate feedback from live audiences alongside a potentially vast online audience. As well as producing your own work and having a YouTube channel you can also submit work to established channels that have a significant audience as Steve Whiteley did with his online comedy short that I script edited and helped develop, *Swiped* (2019). It quickly reached hundreds of thousands of views (which is very hard to do from a standing start) alongside millions of views for excerpts on social media.

Then there are the conventional broadcasters who are commissioning online material. The Muriel girls have produced sketches for BBC3 as has Katia, who has also made online shorts for Comedy Central. Another outlet for these kinds of filmed sketches and shorts is to submit them to film festivals. Steve has taken that route with *Swiped* and it is now an official selection at the Palm Springs International Shorts Festival. When we developed this 12-minute short we also had one eye on the potential of the characters and world to support a full-length narrative comedy series and the success of the short has led to considerable interest in the TV series idea. Fresh back from Palm Springs, Steve told me that in the States they are very engaged with the kind of 'multi-hyphenate' artists we have been discussing. Among UK artists Phoebe Waller-Bridge being someone they are very excited about (whose very name is a hyphen!).

I asked Steve if he had any thoughts for someone looking to branching out into the world of comedy writing and performing and I think his insights are the perfect way to end this piece: 'Be courageous. Don't be afraid to experiment and try new things. Dying on stage is a rite of passage and every time you die, you are reborn (deep) with a new-found knowledge on what you can do differently next time. Be persistent. It takes a long time to develop your act and material, the likelihood of overnight success is slim, but if you have a passion for it and you're half decent then stick with it and good things will eventually happen. Collaborate. The more you workshop your ideas with others the more likely it is that you'll develop your act-material-content quicker and have some thing more rounded. Don't be precious about getting feedback. Finally enjoy it! Otherwise what's the point? You may as well be handsomely paid (or not) and be miserable at a real job.'

Chris Head is a director, coach and comedy consultant. He teaches on the BA Comedy Degree at Bath Spa university, at Bristol Improv Theatre and independently in London. www.chrishead.com. He is the author of *A Director's Guide to the Art of Stand-up*, published by Methuen Drama (2018).

Pantomime

This section lists some of the major pantomime producers and some of the theatres and arts centres that produce their own pantomimes. These latter (often subsidised by a local authority) largely present touring and (sometimes) amateur productions. However, a number do mount their own professional pantomimes and it can be useful to look through the Theatres & Provincial/Touring section of *Contacts* to check which. Many have websites.

Another way of finding out is to check through the listings and reviews in *The Stage* every Christmas. (Also look at **www.its-behind-you.com** which lists forthcoming pantomimes.) Pantomimes in such theatres will often be directed by the resident director, and usually cannot afford the services of a casting director.

Some of these theatres occasionally produce their own shows throughout the year, especially as part of the work of their Education departments. Where possible we have included this information in each entry, but it is also worth visiting the theatre's website for further details.

PANTOMIME PRODUCERS

Chaplins Entertainment Ltd
Chaplins House, The Acorn Centre, Roebuck Road, Hainault, Essex IG6 3TU
tel 020 8501 2121
email fun@chaplinspantos.co.uk
website www.chaplinspantos.co.uk
Directors Mr J Holmes *Productions Manager* Jessica Djemil

Production details: A touring pantomime and theatre-in-education company which also works in film and television production. Stages 26 productions annually, performing in small theatres, schools, social clubs and community centres.

Casting procedures: Uses freelance casting directors and holds general auditions; actors requesting inclusion are asked to write from July until the end of October only. Casting breakdowns are publicly available from the website, by postal application (with sae), in *The Stage* and via Casting Call Pro. During the period specified, the company welcomes letters (with CVs and photographs) from individual actors previously unknown to them, sent by post or email, and will accept showreels and invitations to view individual actors' websites. Rarely or never has the opportunity to cast disabled actors.

Evolution Productions
Little Statenborough House, Sandwich Road, Eastry, Kent CT13 0DH
tel/fax 01304 615333
email emily@evolution-productions.co.uk
email paul@evolution-productions.co.uk
website www.evolution-productions.co.uk
Facebook /evolution.pantomimes
Twitter @pantomimes
Directors Emily Wood, Paul Hendy

Production details: Founded in 2004 and run by husband-and-wife team, Emily Wood and Paul Hendy. Produces pantomimes and Large-scale productions (recently produced *Mister Maker!* and *The Shapes Live!* (UK tour), *Morcambe* (UK tour), *Dear Santa* (UK and Singapore tour) and *Oliver!* at The Central Theatre, Chatham. Stages 8 pantomimes a year: The Marlowe Theatre, Canterbury; The Hawth Theatre, Crawley; The Grove Theatre, Dunstable; Lichfield Garrick, Lichfield; Lyceum Theatre, Sheffield; Theatre Severn Shrewsbury; Alban Areana, St Albans and the Octogan Theatre, Yeovil. Offers non-Equity, in-house contracts ("Equity equivalent") and does not subscribe to the Equity Pension Scheme.

Casting procedures: Casts in-house – all casting enquiries should be addressed toKate Roddy (**casting@evolution-productions.co.uk**). Holds general auditions; the best time to write to request inclusion is March/May. Casting breakdowns are published via Spotlight and through agents. Welcomes letters (with CVs and photographs) and performance notices from actors previously unknown to the company, sent by post or email. Happy to receive appropriate showreels and invitations to view individual actors' websites. Will consider applications from disabled actors to play disabled characters.

Extravaganza Productions
Old Ferry House, 4 London Road, Boston, Lincs PE21 8AA
tel 01205 355978
email extravaganza@panto-mime.co.uk
website www.panto-mime.co.uk
Directors David Vickers, Richard Chandler

Production details: Established in 1995. Presenting Pantomimes for The Plaza, Stockport and Middlesborough Theatre. Number of productions staged annually varies.

Casting procedures: Casting is carried out in house; actors can write at any time to request inclusion. Submissions (with CVs and photographs) should be addressed to Richard Chandler, Casting Director. Also accepts invitations to view individual actors' websites, and showreels. Applications from disabled actors are considered to play disabled characters.

First Family Entertainment

Fortune Theatre, Russell Street, London WC2B 5HH
tel 020 7010 7890 *fax* 020 7010 7899
email casting@ffe-uk.com
website www.ffe-uk.com
Chief Executive Kevin Wood *Production Co-ordinator* Jamie Taylor

Production details: Produces large-scale pantomimes. Venues include: Theatre Royal, Brighton; Churchill Theatre, Bromley; The King's Theatre, Glasgow; Milton Keynes Theatre, Richmond Theatre, Regent Theatre, Stoke on Trent; New Wimbledon Theatre; New Victoria Theatre, Woking; Opera House, Manchester; Sunderland Empire. Offers Equity-approved contracts and subscribes to the Equity Pension Scheme.

Casting procedures: In-house casting director is Scott Mitchell. Does not hold general auditions: only write in response to a specific breakdown. Breakdowns are published in February on Castweb, CastNet and direct to agents. Welcomes letters (with CVs and photographs) from actors previously unknown to the company if sent by post, but not by email. ("Please do not phone!") Happy to receive appropriate showreels, invitations to view individual actors' websites and performance notices. Actively encourages applications from disabled actors and promotes the use of inclusive casting.

Paul Hammond Productions

271 Regent Street, London W1B 2ES
tel 020 7084 6378
email production@hftm.co.uk
website www.paulhammondproductions.com
Director Paul Hammond *Casting* Ruth Langridge

Production details: Produces 4 pantomimes annually: Victoria Theatre, Halifax; Hazlitt Theatre, Maidstone; Pavilion Theatre, Worthing; and Drayton Manor Big Top. Offers actors non-Equity contracts and does not subscribe to the Equity Pension Scheme.

Casting Procedures: Casts in house. Actors should write to or email Ruth Langridge (with CVs and photographs) between February and July. Casting breakdowns are published in *The Stage*, Castweb and Entsweb. Welcomes CVs and photographs from actors previously unknown to the company. Happy

to receive appropriate showreels, invitations to view individual actors' websites and performance notices. Will consider applications from disabled actors to play disabled characters.

Hiss & Boo Theatre Company Ltd

1 Nyes Hill, Wineham Lane, Bolney,
West Sussex RH17 5SD
tel 01444 881707
email email@hissboo.co.uk
website www.hissboo.co.uk
Artistic Director Ian Liston

Production details: Established in 1977. Pantomime producers also specialising in touring plays and revues in the UK and overseas. Actors are employed under UK Theatre Ltd/Equity-approved contracts. The company subscribes to the Equity Pension Scheme. See also entry under *Independent managements/theatre producers* on page 173.

Casting procedures: Casting is done in house. Casting breakdowns are only available to agents via Spotlight Interactive. Does not welcome unsolicited CVs and photographs by post or email. Rarely has the opportunity to cast disabled actors.

Paul Holman Associates

Morritt House, 58 Station Approach, South Ruislip, Middlesex HA4 6SA
tel 020 8845 9408 *fax* 020 8839 3124
email enquiries@paulholmanassociates.co.uk
website www.paulholmanassociates.co.uk
Directors Paul Holman, Adrian Jeckells, John Ogle
Artistic Director/Associate Producer Lee Waddingham

Production details: Produces Pantomimes, Summer Seasons, Tours and other commercial projects. Stages between 10-15 productions annually. Venues where productions are staged include: Bridlington, Aylesbury (Civic), Catford (Broadway), Derby (Assembly Rooms), Leeds (Carriageworks), Newark (Palace), Redditch (Palace), Weston-super-mare (Playhouse). Summer Seasons: The Pier Theatre (Bournemouth), Princess Theatre (Hunstanton). Offers non-Equity (Variety) contracts and does not subscribe to the Equity Pension Scheme.

Casting procedures: Casting is done by in-house casting director. Occasionally hold general auditions; spring is the best time to write requesting auditions. Casting breakdowns are available on Castweb. Accepts submissions (with CVs and photographs) from individual actors previously unknown to the company, sent by post or email. Invitations to view showreels and to attend other productions are also accepted. Will consider applications from disabled actors to play disabled characters, but in practice rarely has the opportunity to cast them.

Imagine Theatre Ltd

2 Brandon House, Woodhams Road,
Middlemarch Business Park, Coventry CV3 4FX

tel 024 7630 7001
email casting@imaginetheatre.co.uk
website www.imaginetheatre.co.uk
Managing Director Stephen Boden *Business Director* Sarah Boden

Production details: Imagine Theatre (since 2009; formerly Wish Theatre) produces pantomimes and children's theatre for No. 1 tours, including *The Tweenies* and *Fun Song Factory*. Venues for pantomime include: Eden Court, Inverness; Beacon Arts Centre, Greenock; Adam Smith, Kirkcaldy; Palace Theatre, Kilmarnock; Southport Theatre; Victoria Theatre, Halifax; Grimsby Auditorium; Palace Theatre, Newark; DeMontfort Hall, Leicester; Belgrade Theatre, Coventry; Spa Centre, Leamington Spa; Hexagon, Reading; Grand Pavilion, Porthcawl and Queen's Theatre, Barnstaple. Also tours Santa Shows. Offers in-house contracts ("enhanced Equity") and does not subscribe to the Equity Pension Scheme.

Casting procedures: Casts mainly in house. Holds general auditions; actors should email the company in March-May to request inclusion. Casting breakdowns are not published except on Spotlight. Welcomes CVs and photographs from actors previously unknown to the company; prefers these to be emailed rather than posted. Will consider applications from disabled actors to play disabled characters. "Panto isn't a cop-out: it's a serious business. We use actors who can engage with the audience and have fun. It is really useful if actors can indicate their location/home town, which helps with accents and knowing if an individual is local to one of our pantomime venues. Please do not send showreels or invitations to view websites."

Owen Money Productions
4 Westgate Close, Porthcawl CF36 3NP
tel 07896 258893
email owen.money@btinternet.com
Director Owen Money *Company Manager* Roger Bell

Production details: Established in 2000. Produces 3-4 family pantomimes a year, touring to 7-8 theatres and community venues around Wales between the end of November and the end of February. Also produces a Brian Rix-style 'adult' panto in April (2007 production was *Buttons Undone*). Offers non-Equity contracts and does not subscribe to the Equity Pension Scheme.

Casting procedures: Casts in-house. Casting notices are published in *The Stage*. Actors wishing to audition for the company should write (with CV and photograph) between November and January. Does not welcome unsolicited CVs and photographs by email. Happy to receive appropriate showreels and invitations to view individual actors' websites. Will consider applications from disabled actors to play disabled characters.

New Pantomime Productions
27 Shooters Road, Enfield, Middlesex EN2 8RJ
tel 020 8363 9920

email simonbarry@nppltd.freeserve.co.uk
Director Simon Barry

Production details: Produces pantomimes at 7 venues: Theatr Colwyn, Colwyn Bay; Brindley Arts Centre, Runcorn; Southport Theatre; Kings Theatre, Southsea; Princess Theatre, Torquay; Grand Opera House, York. Offers non-Equity contracts and does not subscribe to the Equity Pension Scheme.

Casting procedures: Casts in house. Holds general auditions; actors should write in July to request inclusion. Casting breakdowns are not publicly available. Welcomes emails only (with CVs and photographs) from actors previously unknown to the company. Does not welcome showreels or invitations to view individual actors' websites. "Make sure you're suitable for the job you're applying for. We have employed disabled actors – and not just to play disabled characters. So long as the actor is good, that's all that matters."

Pantoni Pantomimes
205 Bexhill Road, St Leonards on Sea, East Sussex TN38 8BG
tel 01424 443400 *fax* 01424 714847
email david@pantoni.com
website www.pantoni.com
Directors David Lee and Rita Proctor

Produces pantomimes for the Doncaster Civic Theatre; Empire Theatre, Consett; New Floral Pavilion, New Brighton; The Leatherhead Theatre; Library Theatre, Luton; and Octagon Theatre, Yeovil.

Qdos Entertainment (Pantomimes) Ltd
2nd Floor, 161 Drury Lane, Covent Garden, London WC2B 5PN
tel 020 7430 7900
email pantoadmin@qdosentertainment.co.uk
website www.qdosentertainment.co.uk
Casting Director/Producer Jonathan Kiley *Producer/ Managing Director* Michael Harrison

Production details: The largest of the commercial pantomime producers with 35 pantomimes across the UK: His Majesty's, Aberdeen; Grand Opera House, Belfast; Hippodrome Theatre, Birmingham; The Alhambra, Bradford; The Bristol Hippodrome; The Churchill Bromley; New Theatre, Cardiff; The Lyceum, Crewe; Civic Theatre, Darlington; The Orchard, Dartford; Kings Theatre, Edinburgh; Kings Theatre, Glasgow; SEC Glasgow; White Rock, Hastings; Beck Theatre, Hayes; Wycombe Swan, High Wycombe; Hull New Theatre; The Empire, Liverpool; Venue Cymru, Llandudno; The London Palladium; The Opera House, Manchester; Milton Keynes Theatre; Theatre Royal, Newcastle upon Tyne; Derngate Theatre, Northampton; Theatre Royal, Nottingham; Theatre Royal, Plymouth; The Richmond Theatre; Cliffs Pavilion, Southend; Mayflower Theatre, Southampton; The Regent Theatre, Stoke; Grand Theatre, Swansea; Wyvern

Theatre, Swindon; Grand Theatre, Wolverhampton; The New Wimbledon Theatre; New Victoria Theatre, Woking.

Casting procedures: Actors should send CVs and photographs by post to Jonathan Kiley from March (star-casting only in February). Welcomes performance notices. Send to: Qdos Entertainment (Pantomimes) Ltd, 2nd Floor, 161 Drury Lane, Covent Garden, London WC2B 5PN.

Spillers Pantomimes
The Old Post Office, Honey Tye, Leavenheath, Suffolk CO6 4NX
email bev.berridge@btinternet.com
Managing Director John Spillers *Casting* (Mr) Bev Berridge

Production details: Established 1989. Produces pantomimes for Alexandra Theatre, Bognor Regis; Epsom Playhouse; Woodville Hall Theatre, Gravesend; Motherwell Theatre; Majestic Theatre, Retford; Civic Theatre, Rotherham; The Music Hall, Shrewsbury; Pavilion Theatre, Weymouth. Offers actors non-Equity contracts and does not contribute to the Equity Pension Scheme.

Casting procedures: Casting is done in house. Holds general auditions. Best time for actors to write (with CV and photograph) to request inclusion is March/April. Casting breakdowns are published in *The Stage*. Welcomes CVs and photographs from actors previously unknown to the company, sent by post or email. Will consider applications from disabled actors to play disabled characters.

UK Productions
Brook House, Mint Street, Godalming, Surrey GU7 1HE
tel 01483 423600
email mail@ukproductions.co.uk
website www.ukproductions.co.uk
Managing Director Martin Dodd

Production details: Established 1995. Produces pantomimes, musicals and plays for No. 1 national and international touring. Also set, costume and production hire. (See entry under *Independent managements/theatre producers* on page 178.) Offers non-Equity contracts.

Casting procedures: Casting is done in house. Does not hold open auditions. Casting breakdowns are distributed via Spotlight. Welcomes performance notices but not any other unsolicited form of correspondence. Will consider applications from disabled actors to play characters with disabilities.

IN-HOUSE PANTOMIMES

Buxton Opera House
Water Street, Buxton, Derbyshire SK17 6XN
tel 01298 72050 *fax* 01298 27563

email admin@boh.org.uk
website www.buxtonoperahouse.org.uk
Chief Executive Officer Paul Kerryson *Theatre Secretary* Pat Russell

Production details: A receiving theatre presenting around 450 performances each year including dance, comedy, children's shows, drama, musical concerts, pantomime and opera as well as Fringe Theatre and Community and Education Programme. Edwardian theatre designed by Frank Matcham, restored in 2001.

Casting procedures: Commissions Channel Theatre Company to produce its annual pantomimes. Philip Dart, Artistic Director of Channel Theatre, is responsible for casting. Please see the entry under *Middle and smaller-scale companies* on page 183.

Cambridge Arts Theatre
Programming & Production Department, 6 St Edwards Passage, Cambridge CB2 3PJ
tel 01223 578903
email info@cambridgeartstheatre.com
website www.cambridgeartstheatre.com
Assistant to the Chief Executive Lucy Tregear

Production details: Seating capacity 665. A receiving theatre which presents a wide range of work, including children's theatre, music, dance and drama. Produces in-house panto annually.

Casting procedures: Engages a freelance director who, together with the producer and choreographer, is responsible for casting the panto. Actors should contact the theatre to request an audition for the pantomime in March/April. These submissions will be forwarded to the director, and marked for the attention of Sue Lowe. Actors are employed under Equity-approved contracts. Invitations to see actors in other productions are only welcomed from actors in whom the director has already shown interest. Will consider applications from disabled actors to play disabled characters.

The Capitol
North Street, Horsham, West Sussex
tel 01403 756080 *fax* 01403 756092
website www.thecapitolhorsham.com
General Manager Nick Mowat

Production details: Seating capacity 423. Produces a professional pantomime each year. Offers TMA/Equity-approved contracts.

Casting procedures: Uses in-house casting director. Optimum time to write requesting an audition is in spring/summer. Casting breakdowns are publicly available on the website, or by postal application (with sae). Accepts letters (with CVs and photographs) from individual actors previously unknown to the company, sent by post or email. Also welcomes invitations to view showreels and to attend other productions. Will consider applications from disabled actors to play disabled characters.

The Theatre, Chipping Norton
2 Spring Street, Chipping Norton,
Oxfordshire OX7 5NL
tel 01608 642349 *fax* 01608 642324
email administration@chippingnortontheatre.com
website www.chippingnortontheatre.com
Director John Terry

Production details: The Theatre is a pivotal part of the artistic life of the area, and takes care to programme as diverse a range of performances – theatre, film, dance, comedy and opera – as possible. Its Community & Education programme takes film and opera out to village halls.

An intimate space, it seats 217 (including 4 wheelchair spaces) in either proscenium (end-on) or in-the-round configurations. While predominantly a receiving house, The Theatre produces an annual pantomime which runs for around 80 performances over the Christmas period, as well as occasional smaller ventures. Recent productions include: *Mother Goose* and *Puss in Boots*, new pantomimes by Simon Brett; and *Taste*, a new play which toured Normandy. The Theatre offers TMA/Equity-approved contracts and subscribes to the Equity Pension Scheme.

Casting procedures: Does not use casting directors. Welcomes unsolicited CVs and photographs from actors unknown to the company, as well as invitations to view actors' websites. Casting breakdowns for the pantomime are available March and September via Spotlight; this is the best time to write to request inclusion. Actively encourages applications from disabled actors, and promotes the use of inclusive casting.

City Varieties
Swan Street, Leeds LS1 6LW
tel 0113 391 7777
email info@cityvarieties.co.uk
website www.cityvarieties.co.uk
General Manager Ian Sime

Production details: Seating capacity 467. Grade II* listed building, built in 1865. World-famous as the home of BBC TV's *Good Old Days*. Produces a professional pantomime each year, running from the end of November to mid-January. Also continues to produce *Good Old Days* music hall entertainment. Actors are employed under Equity-approved contracts and the theatre subscribes to the Equity Pension Scheme.

Casting procedures: Optimum time to write requesting an audition is between January and June. Accepts submissions (with CVs and photographs) from individual actors previously unknown to the company. Invitations to attend other productions are also welcome, depending on distance.

Connaught Theatre
Union Place, Worthing, West Sussex BN11 1LG
tel 01903 231799

website www.worthingtheatres.co.uk
Admin Officer Rosie Gray

Production details: Seating capacity 506 with 6 wheelchair spaces. The Connaught Theatre was built in 1914, but was originally called the Picturedrome. For 20 years it was an early cinema, until 1935 when the Worthing Repertory Company outgrew its own premises and came into the venue, bringing with it the name Connaught Theatre.

Casting procedures: Casting enquiries should be through Chris Lillicrap at The Proper Pantomime Company.

The Courtyard
The Courtyard Centre for the Arts, Edgar Street, Hereford HR4 9JR
tel 01432 346500
email ian.archer@courtyard.org.uk
website www.courtyard.org.uk
Chief Executive & Artistic Director Ian Archer

Production details: Seating capacity 436. The Courtyard opened in September 1998 and was the first Lottery-funded theatre to be built in England. It provides "an eclectic programme of work, from produced to received, and offers something for the whole community". Produces a professional pantomime each year, from the end of November to mid-January. Provides actors with Equity-approved contracts as negotiated through UK Theatre.

Casting procedures: Uses in-house casting directors; actors may write in June to request an audition. Casting breakdowns are available from the website, or via CastNet and Castweb. Welcomes letters (with CVs and photographs) from individual actors previously unknown to the company, sent by post or email. Also accepts showreels and invitations to visit other productions. Actively encourages applications from disabled actors and promotes the use of inclusive casting.

Cumbernauld Theatre
Kildrum, Cumbernauld, Glasgow G67 2BN
tel 01236 737235 *fax* 01236 738408
email info@cumbernauldtheatre.co.uk
website www.cumbernauldtheatre.co.uk
Artistic Director Ed Robson

Production details: Established in 1978. A year-round producing theatre with a broad range of artist development and creative learning programmes. Produces a professional pantomime each year, together with other in-house plays, musicals and 'seasons'. Recent productions include: *The Wasp Factory* by Iain Banks.

Casting procedures: Casting is done by the Artistic Director. Auditions are held all year round; actors should obtain casting breakdowns from the website only. Welcomes letters (with CVs and photographs) from individual actors previously unknown to the company, sent by post or email. Will consider invitations to visit other productions, but requests that no showreels be submitted. Actively encourages applications from disabled actors and promotes the use of inclusive casting.

The Customs House Trust Ltd

Mill Dam, South Shields, Tyne & Wear NE33 1ES
tel 0191 454 1234 *fax* 0191 456 5979
email mail@customshouse.co.uk
website www.customshouse.co.uk
Executive Director Ray Spencer

Production details: Seating capacity 441. Established in 1994 as an arts centre, gallery, cinema and theatre. Produces approximately 6 in-house shows each year, and is a member of the North East Theatre Consortium. Stages a professional pantomime in early December which runs through to the first week in January, as well as new writing and occasional new musicals. Provides actors with Equity-approved contracts as negotiated through TMA.

Casting procedures: Uses both in-house and freelance casting directors. The pantomime is cast in June, and CVs are received all year. Welcomes letters (with CVs and photographs) from individual actors previously unknown to the compay, sent by post or email. Also accepts invitations to visit other productions. Advises actors to "find out about the venue via our website. Mention our work; it makes us feel important and makes you look as if you care!".

The Everyman Theatre

Regent Street, Cheltenham,
Gloucestershire GL50 1HQ
tel 01242 572573 *fax* 01242 224305
email admin@everymantheatre.org.uk
website www.everymantheatre.org.uk
Creative Director Paul Milton *Chief Executive* Mark Goucher

Production details: Seating capacity: main house 668, studio 60. Built in 1891. A receiving theatre which presents a wide range of work, from stand-up comedy to children's theatre and including live music, dance and drama. Also works with many emerging and established theatre companies from Gloucestershire and beyond, creating partnerships and productions that are performed at the Everyman and on tour across the county. Produces in-house plays and pantomime as well as promoting new writing.

Casting procedures: A freelance director is engaged to direct the panto. This director is responsible for the casting process and will choose how and where the casting breakdowns are made available. Actors should write in February to request auditions for the panto, as auditions are held in March and April. Submissions (photos and CVs) are welcomed from actors previously unknown to the company for both panto and new writing projects; these should be

marked for the attention of Millie Krstic-Howe (Theatre Secretary). The Everyman also runs an Actor's Lab, providing professional training and opportunities to meet and work with established directors. The Everyman Theatre is an equal opportunities employer and gives due consideration to applications from all sectors of the community.

The Gatehouse

Eastgate Street, Stafford ST16 2LT
tel 01785 619080
website www.staffordgatehousetheatre.co.uk
Artistic Programme Manager Derrick Gask

Production details: Celebrated its silver jubilee in 2007. A receiving theatre which presents a wide range of work, from stand-up comedy to children's theatre, and including live music, dance and drama. Usually produces its own in-house panto, with the occasional co-production.

Casting procedures: Casting is done by freelance casting directors. Breakdowns are available via Spotlight to agents only. Will consider applications from disabled actors to play disabled characters.

The Gatehouse also produces the Stafford Festival Shakespeare. See entry under *Festivals* on page 301.

Hackney Empire

291 Mare Street, London E8 1EJ
tel 020 8510 4500 *fax* 020 8510 4530
email susie.mckenna@hackneyempire.co.uk
website www.hackneyempire.co.uk
CEO Claire Middleton *Creative Director/Pantomime Director* Susie Mckenna

Production details: Grade II listed Frank Matcham theatre built in 1901. Recently renovated and refurbished. Provides a wide range of productions for the local community and London as a whole. Seating capacity is up to 1,280. Produces an immensely popular and critically acclaimed traditional pantomime, eschewing 'celebrities' in favour of the core elements of traditional pantomime: a well-conceived narrative line, spectacular sets and costumes, magical spectacle, music, dance and slapstick comedy. Offers TMA/Equity-approved contracts.

Casting procedures: Casting breakdowns are not publically available, but actors wishing to audition for the pantomime should contact Susie Mckenna, by post or email, in August/September. Happy to receive appropriate showreels and invitations to view individual actors' websites. Actively encourages applications from disabled actors and promotes the use of inclusive casting.

macrobert

University of Stirling, Stirling FK9 4LA
tel 01786 467155 *fax* 01786 466600
email info@macrobert.org
website www.macrobert.org
Artistic Director & Chief Executive Liam Sinclair

Production details: A busy multi-venue arts centre seating 472, with particular emphasis on work with and for young people. Produces several professional shows per year, in November and December. Offers Equity-approved contracts as negotiated through TMA. Subscribes to the Equity Pension Scheme.

Casting procedures: Uses freelance and in-house casting directors; actors may write in April and May to request inclusion. Welcomes letters (with CVs and photographs) from individual actors previously unknown to the company, sent by post or by email. Accepts showreels and invitations to visit other productions. Rarely (or never) has the opportunity to cast disabled actors.

Millfield Theatre

Silver Street, Edmonton, London N18 1PJ
tel 020 8887 7301
website www.millfieldtheatre.co.uk
Arts Centre Manager and Producer Ralph Dartford

Production details: Produces panto in house. Has been a receiving theatre but is now starting to co-produce a couple of productions each year with partners such as Face Front Inclusive Theatre (**www.facefront.org**).

Casting procedures: Casting is done by liaising with show director and in-house producer. Breakdowns for the panto are sent out to agents via Spotlight Link. Contracts offered are negotiated directly with actors or their agents. Actors can write in May to request an audition for the panto, addressing their submission to Ralph Dartford. At present only welcomes submissions (with CVs and photographs) from actors previously unknown to the company at the time of casting the panto (May). As co-productions are still relatively new to the theatre, is considering developing the website to include a casting page. Will only view showreels if they have been requested. Welcomes invitations to see actors in other productions in the Greater London area. Will consider invitations to shows at The Edinburgh Festival. Encourages applications from disabled actors and promotes the use of inclusive casting.

Theatre Royal, Bury St Edmunds

Westgate Street, Bury St Edmunds, Suffolk IP33 1QR
tel 01284 829945
email Sharron@theatreroyal.org
website www.theatreroyal.org
Artistic Director and CEO Karen Simpson

Production details: Seating capacity 358. Built in 1819, the theatre is the only surviving Regency theatre in the country. Produces an annual pantomime at Christmas and 2 other shows a year – a rural tour in the spring and an in-house production in the autumn, often from or about the Regency period. Offers non-Equity contracts.

Casting procedures: Casting breakdowns are published via Spotlight only. Actors wishing to be considered for the pantomime should write to the theatre in August. (The spring and autumn shows are cast in January/February and June/July respectively.) Only welcomes letters and emails (with CVs and photographs) from actors previously unknown to the company during these casting periods. Does not welcome showreels, but is happy to receive performance notices. Rarely or never has the opportunity to cast disabled actors.

Theatre Royal, Margate

Addington Street, Margate, Kent CT9 1PW
tel 01843 292795 (Box Office)
and 01843 296111 (Admin)
email pam.hardiman@yourleisure.uk.com
website www.margate-live.com
Programme Manager Pam Hardiman

Production details: Seating capacity 465. A grade 2 star listed Georgian Theatre in the heart of Margate town presenting a year-round programme of mixed incoming professional and locally produced community work. Thriving youth theatre and strong relationships with local arts organisations and associate companies. Owned by Thanet District Council, managed by Your Leisure.

Theatre Royal, Norwich

Theatre Street, Norwich NR2 1RL
tel 01603 598500 *fax* 01603 598501
email j.walsh@theatreroyalnorwich.co.uk
website www.theatreroyalnorwich.co.uk
Programming Director & Executive ProducerManager Jane Walsh

Seating capacity 1300. Produces an annual pantomime and is a receiving house for the rest of the year, so very little scope on casting. Actors wishing to audition for the pantomime should contact Jane Walsh **j.walsh@theatreroyalnorwich.co.uk** from March/April. Welcomes emails (with CVs and photographs) from actors not previously known to the company. Does not welcome showreels or performance notices. Will consider applications from disabled actors on the same basis as for non-disabled actors.

Theatre Royal, Nottingham

Theatre Square, Nottingham NG1 5ND
tel 0115 989 5500 *fax* 0115 950 3476
email enquiry@royalcentre-nottingham.co.uk
website www.royalcentre-nottingham.co.uk
Managing Director Mr Robert Sanderson

Production details: Seating capacity 1186. Pantomimes are produced by Qdos Entertainment; those produced in house are by its education-based Royal Company, which includes members of the community. Offers actors Equity-approved contracts but does not subscribe to the Equity Pension Scheme.

Casting procedures: Casts in house. Actors wishing to request an audition should contact Jimmy

Theatre

Ashworth in April/May. Casting breakdowns are not publicly available. Welcomes letters and emails (with CVs and photographs) from actors previously unknown to the company. Happy to receive appropriate showreels and performance notices. Actively encourages applications from disabled actors and promotes the use of inclusive casting.

Theatre Royal, Winchester

Jewry Street, Winchester, Hampshire SO23 8SB
tel 01962 844600 *fax* 01962 810277

website www.theatreroyalwinchester.co.uk
Director Mark Courtice

Production details: Seating capacity 400. A receiving theatre which presents a wide range of work, from stand-up comedy to children's theatre and including music, dance and classic plays. The theatre was re-opened in 2001 following a major refurbishment. Produces panto in house.

Casting procedures: Casting is done by the director of the show. Breakdowns are available publicly in mid June.

The art and craft of pantomime

Iain Lauchlan

Pantomime in the UK has naturally evolved; it has been altered enormously by many generations of performers and producers over the years – from its roots in Commedia dell'arte, which came to this country in the 17th century, to the modern panto we know and love today.

If you are a young actor trying to make your way in the business and you believe that panto is not for you (or indeed think it beneath you), then I suggest you look again at this very popular form of entertainment. I say this because when you get to know pantomime as an art form and become familiar with its challenges and traditions, I'm sure you will find a type of panto that will suit you as a performer.

In my experience, there are three main types of panto on offer in this country: the large-scale commercial panto; the 'rock and roll' panto; and the small- to mid-scale family panto.

Large-scale commercial pantomimes

These tend to be staged in 1000-seat-plus theatres by large commercial producers who use TV personalities to front them. They are more like large-scale light entertainment shows, which rely on a 'name' to sell tickets up front and then shoe-horn the celebrity's persona into the story.

Commercial pantomimes are very popular, but quality can range from poor to spectacular because the show is totally dependent on its star being able to do the job of playing the lead character – and it has to be said that some personalities are just not up to the 'live' challenge. The story also tends to be very thin and the supporting characters, who are normally played by jobbing actors, have a tough job driving the narrative because the shows tend to revolve around the personalities and speciality acts that are hired for their quirky entertainment value.

That said, whilst the quality of these shows tends to vary, there are several around the country that give the audience a really good, glitzy night out.

'Rock and roll' pantomime

These shows tend to be mid-scale and, as the name suggests, have a strong rock and roll element. They rely on actor musicians who can play the characters required for panto but also play an instrument. Although such pantos are often very entertaining and the rock and roll music uplifting, the characters and story tend to suffer a little: this is because all pantomime has three main elements which are equally important – music, story and routines. With music being such a key element in a rock and roll panto, the story may be altered and trimmed to fit more songs in, and the number of routines cut down to accommodate them.

The other issue with this style of panto is that scenery and props tend to be cut back, as there always has to be room for the drum kit or piano and guitars. This means fewer scene changes and does lead to a poorer visual experience. It also feels odd, to me, that the Dame or fairy, for example, suddenly picks up a saxophone or guitar to play for another character.

Traditional family panto

The third type of panto is the small- to mid-scale traditional family show, which is often performed in mid-scale theatres or community halls around the country. This is the model

I prefer, and I am responsible for 11 such pantos every season. For an actor, this type of pantomime offers the best opportunity to use a combination of storytelling, musical and comedy skills.

Some family pantos do use personalities, but because of limited budgets these tend to be jobbing actors who have made a name for themselves on TV or radio and are therefore able to play a story character – rather than diluting the narrative by over-using their TV persona.

The main elements you need in order to create a traditional family panto are:

1. **A strong story**. The foundation on which the entire panto is based. This strong narrative will serve the show well, as it provides a solid framework on which to hang the comedy routines, special effects and characters. It also offers something tangible that the audience members, young and old, can hold onto and follow while the fun and controlled anarchy unfolds onstage.

2. **A good cast.** The lead characters – whether they are Jack, Aladdin, Cinderella, Carabosse or Abanazar – must deliver the story whilst remaining clear, strong and rounded. Good three-dimensional characters will drive the narrative and allow the comedy personalities, like the Dame, Simple Simon, the squire or the baddie sidekick, to weave around the story and have the freedom to play the comedy.

3. **Great comedy routines.** Many traditional panto routines have been tried and tested over the years; some are rather dated and some a bit wordy, but all can be adjusted for today's audiences. The important ingredients of good comedy routines are slickness, clarity, surprise and good contact with the audience. The mirror routine, the wallpapering routine, the mop, or the busy bee can all be inserted into a pantomime to enhance the story.

4. **The music.** I am a great believer in a mix of covers and original songs written specially for the show. Audiences do like to know the songs, or at least to have heard them before; covers fulfil this need, but often fail to push the story on and develop it. Songs may be inserted because of their popularity but then have to be forced into the narrative, which may grind to a halt while the song is sung. If covers are used then they must be chosen wisely.

Character songs written specially for the show may not be known by the audience, which can be a negative, but they are perfect for the moment and enhance the plot and punctuate the story. I like to give the baddies their own specially written song, if possible, so that they can use it to further build on their character and share their evil plans with the audience.

The most difficult song to find is the panto opener. This needs to be an upbeat chorus number that sets the scene and opens the show with a huge burst of energy. It is really difficult to find a cover that will serve this function well, but equally it is one of the most difficult to write as often a new song will not have the impact of a well-known standard.

5. **Finally, the characters.** It is essential that these tell the story, fulfil the expectation of the audience and connect with them to sell the comedy and narrative.

In a traditional panto the Dame is key to both the plot and the comedy. 'She' is often a downtrodden mother who is doing her best against all the odds, and is played by a man in a frock. The Dame is completely different from an ugly sister; she is a good character and must be warm with a matronly quality. This character has to play off the Simple Simon character, who tends to be her youngest son and is a little slow but endearing and vulnerable. These two characters carry the bulk of the comedy routines, whilst Simple Simon has to be our link to the younger element in the audience.

The principal 'boy' or the hero should be played by a tall and shapely young woman who has a boyish quality and inner strength onstage. 'He' will have to drive the narrative through, whilst the comedy characters around him are causing chaos (albeit controlled and rehearsed chaos). It is traditional that this character will fall in love with the princess or principal girl, and will probably sing a ballad with her at some point in the show.

The panto baddie is essential to the story and is often set against the good fairy. This 'good versus bad' is another key element of panto and must be explored as the story develops. There are many different panto baddies; most of them male. Abanazar from Aladdin is the most evil of them all, followed closely by Carabosse, the evil fairy in Sleeping Beauty, and the wicked Queen in Snow White. There are also comedy baddies such as King Rat from Dick Whittington, the Demon King from Mother Goose, and the ugly sisters from Cinderella.

The good fairy can be played in many different ways, from straight traditional fairy to quirky fruit fairy or the 'cockney sparra' from Dick Whittington. She is always good and always on the side of the Dame, the principal boy and Simple Simon characters.

What does it take to succeed in pantomime?

Whatever part you may be asked to play in a panto, it should be an exhausting and uplifting experience, as it requires commitment, courage, skill and warmth to satisfy the many hundreds of thousands of audience members who pitch up to see a panto each year, expecting to be thoroughly entertained by one of our most loved and supported entertainment genres.

It's your choice: large-scale, glitzy, commercial panto with limited rehearsals but larger budgets? Rock and roll panto that will challenge your musical and acting skills? Or traditional mid-scale panto that tells a strong story and relies on tried-and-tested comedy routines? Whichever you may choose, make sure at the auditions that you are prepared to move and learn a short dance routine, and have a well-rehearsed song that shows off your voice. Do not learn one the night before! And remember, if you are asked to read for a part, that panto is a broad, larger-than-life genre of theatre which relies on audience contact. Make your performance big but light, and forge a connection with your audience.

Always keep in mind the 'three Cs': Clarity, Comedy and Contact.

Iain Lauchlan has been involved with children's television since 1980, when he became a presenter on *Playschool* for the following eight years. During this time he also presented *Fingermouse* and a selection of children's radio programmes. Iain later became the Producer of three of the daily *Playdays* programmes – *Why Bird Stop*, *Roundabout Stop*, and *Poppy Stop* – and has also run his own TV production company, which created children's programmes such as *The Tweenies*, *Boo*, *BB3B* and latterly *Jim Jam and Sunny*. During most of this time he has tried to keep his acting career going, and is now Creative Director for Imagine Theatre, producing 11 pantos each year and performing in one as the Dame.

Theatre

English-language European theatre companies

This small section seems to be populated by companies set up by enthusiasts who have kept on going with very little subsidy – and sometimes with none at all. Although living away from home and isolated from auditions, it can be fun working for such companies. It is important to note that the work often involves educational projects and/or touring.

Dear Conjunction Theatre Company

6 Rue Arthur Rozier, 75019 Paris
tel +33 (0) 1 4241 6965
email dearconjunction@wanadoo.fr
website www.dearconjunction-paris-theatre.com
Artistic Directors Leslie Clack, Patricia Kessler

Production details: Founded in 1991, this bilingual company is composed of professional actors, directors and writers who are resident in Paris and who present productions in both French and English. Past productions include: Pinter's *Ashes to Ashes* and *The Hothouse*; and *Someone Who'll Watch Over Me* by Frank McGuinness.

Casting procedures: Welcomes letters and emails (with CVs and photographs) from actors previously unknown to the company. Contact Leslie Clack for more information.

English Theatre Frankfurt

Kaiserstrasse 34, D-60329 Frankfurt
tel +49 69 242 31615 *fax* +49 69 242 31614
email mail@english-theatre.org
website www.english-theatre.org
Artistic and Executive Director Daniel John Nicolai

Production details: Founded in 1979. Presents contemporary plays, musicals and classics. 5 productions performed in the main house each year, totalling 260 performances.

Casting procedures: Uses London-based freelance casting directors. Does not hold general auditions. Actors should write in April to request inclusion. Casting breakdowns are only available via Spotlight.

The English Theatre of Hamburg

Lerchenfeld 14, 22081 Hamburg
tel +49 40 227 7089 *fax* +49 40 229 5040
email ethamburg@onlinehome.de
website www.englishtheatre.de
Contacts Robert Rumpf, Clifford Dean adn Paul Glaser

Production details: Founded in 1976 by 2 Americans, Robert Rumpf and Clifford Dean, who originally trained and worked professionally in the USA. They share general management

responsibilities, plan the artistic programme and direct some of the productions. Since 1981 the theatre has occupied its present premises at Mundsburg, 22081 Hamburg. Performs 8 times per week from September to June. A typical season at the English Theatre includes a classic American or British drama, a comedy and thriller or modern classic. Recent productions include: *Fat Pig*, *The Whipping Man*, *Orphans*, *Othello* and *April in Paris*. Also produces educational material.

Independent English Theatre Associazione Culturale

Via dell'Acquedotto Felice 36, 00178 Rome
tel +39 349 6703331
email director@independentenglishtheatre.com
website www.independentenglishtheatre.com
Artistic Director Sandra Paternostro

Production details: A professional English-speaking theatre company based in Rome. Started producing its own work in 2011, with its first production: *Betrayal* by Harold Pinter.

Casting procedures: Uses in-house casting directors and is always happy to hear from English-speaking actors who have a base in Rome. Casting breakdowns are available via the website. Welcomes CVs and photographs if sent by email; will also accept showreels and invitations to view individual actors' websites if the actors are in Rome.

Light Nights – The Summer Theatre

Baldursgata 37, IS-101 Reykjavik
tel +354 551 9181 *fax* +354 551 5015
website www.lightnights.com
Artistic Director Kristín G Magnús

Production details: Runs a summer theatre show at the Idnó Theatre in Reykjavik. Previous productions have included: *Light Nights* and *On The Way to Heaven*.

Casting procedures: Sometimes holds general auditions. The best time to write requesting inclusion is February/March. Casting breakdowns are not publicly available. Welcomes letters (with CVs and photographs) from actors previously unknown to the company, but not via email. Does not welcome showreels, but is happy to receive invitations to view actors' websites. Offers non-Equity contracts; rarely (or never) has the opportunity to cast disabled actors.

London Toast Theatre

Kochsvej 18, DK 1812 Frederiksberg C. Denmark
tel +45 3322 8686
email mail@londontoast.dk
website www.londontoast.dk
Managing Director Søren Hall

Production details: Founded in 1982. The largest English-speaking theatre company in Northern Europe. Presents theatre productions and provides corporate entertainment, stand-up comedy and Murder Mystery shows in Scandinavia and abroad. The company's voice-over bureau, 'Speaker's Corner', provides English and American voices for films and commercials. Recent productions include: *Shakespeare's Ghost, Hamlet* at Kronborg Castle, *Planet Rump - The Farce Awakens, Fogg's Off, Oh Baby -- It's Cole!* and *The Three Brexiteers.*

Merlin International Theatre

Gerlóczy Utca 4, Budapest 1052
tel +36 (1) 3179338 *fax* +36 (1) 2660904
email info@merlinszinhaz.hu
website www.szinhaz.hu/merlin/english
Director Laszlo Magacs *Associate Director* Emma Vidovsky

Production details: Founded in 1991; Hungary's first and currently its only international theatre. Recent productions include: *The Importance of Being Earnest, Don't Drink the Water, Stones in His Pockets* and *Twelfth Night.* Resident companies at the Merlin Theatre are the Atlantis Company, Junion Group and Madhouse.

Prague Shakespeare Festival

Divadlo Kolowrat, Kolowratsky palac,
Ovocny trh 579/6, Prague 1, 110 00
tel +420 603 968 536
email info@pragueshakespeare.org
website www.pragueshakespeare.org
Artistic Director Guy Roberts

Production details: Founded in 2008. The Festival presents professional theatre productions, workshops, classes, lectures and other theatrical events, of the highest quality, conducted primarily in English by a multinational ensemble of professional theatre artists, with an emphasis on the plays of William Shakespeare. Stages 12-18 productions annually, and holds workshops and classes on an ongoing basis. Recent productions include: *Amadeus, The Winter's Tale, Macbeth, Richard III* in association with the National Theatre at the Estates Theater and Venus in Fur, *Macbeth, Much Ado About Nothing* on international tours to the United States and Egypt.

Casting procedures: Casts in-house; check the website for annual casting and breakdowns.

Welcomes approaches (with CVs and photographs) from actors by post and by email, and accepts showreels and invitations to view individual actors' websites. Actively encourages applications from disabled actors to play characters with disabilities, and promotes the use of inclusive casting.

Simply Theatre

Centre Choiseul, Avenue de Choiseul 23a,
1290 Versoix, Switzerland
tel +41 22 860 0518
email academy@simplytheatre.com
website www.simplytheatre.com
Directors Thomas Grafton and Jenna Melling

Company details: Founded in 2005. Offers English theatre for young people and families featuring professional actors, and an English-speaking Drama Academy for students. A professional English theatre for Switzerland and Continental Europe; and an English-speaking Drama Academy. Predominantly stages family-orientated theatre and shows for children.

Casting procedures: Casting breakdowns are available from Spotlight and Casting Call Pro.

Theatre From Oxford

Suite 251, 266 Banbury Road, Oxford OX2 7DL
tel 0790 544 4495
email fm.oxford@gmail.com
Artistic Director Robert Southam

Production details: Founded in 1984, the main aim for the past 32 years has been to introduce audiences on the continent to the best of theatre in English. The company has toured plays by Shakespeare, Shaw, Wilde, Willy Russell, Tennessee Williams and Arthur Miller, among others. Touring for 3 months from September to Christmas in 7 European countries, the company plays in anything from the best theatres to school gyms – but nearly always to full houses. Tours again in the spring to many of the same venues, providing theatre workshops. Half of the spectators are students; the other half, adult theatregoers. The company is shortly to have its own theatre in France.

Casting procedures: Actors are advised that the tours are enjoyable but demanding, and that the company seldom accepts anyone straight from drama school. Casts often include actors with RSC and RNT experience. Recently has been working with African, Asian and Latin American actors and writers, which has meant less work for British and American actors. Casting breakdowns are available by postal application (with sae) and actors are welcome to write letters or emails with their CVs and photographs. Showreels, however, are not welcomed. Offers non-Equity contracts. Will consider applications from disabled actors to play characters with disabilities.

Vienna's English Theatre

UK address: VM Theatre Productions Ltd,
c/o Hutchinson Rowntree Ltd,

The Deptford Mission, 1 Creek Road,
London SE8 3BT
020 3355 8567
email casting@gmail.com
Theatre address: Josefsgasse 12, A-1080 Vienna
tel (0043) 1 402 1260 26 *fax* (0043) 1 405 4121 261
website www.englishtheatre.at

Production details: Founded in 1963; the oldest
English-language theatre in continental Europe.
Stages 5 shows each year in the main house and sends
5 Theatre-in-Education tours around the schools of
Austria. The season runs from September to July each
year.

Casting procedures: Casting breakdowns are
occasionally posted on the website and actors may
email the UK address above with their CV and
photograph at anytime. Showreels are not accepted.
"Contracts are especially written for us by Equity."

White Horse Theatre
Boerdenstrasse 17, 59494 Soest, Germany
tel +49 2921 339339 *fax* +49 2921 339336

email theatre@white-horse-theatre.eu
website www.white-horse-theatre.eu
Artistic Directors Peter Griffith and Michael Dray

Production details: Founded in 1978. Tours schools
in Germany with occasional visits to neighbouring
countries and to Japan and China. Contracts are for
10-11 months. 9 companies of 4 actors each perform
3 plays. Recent productions include: *The Glass
Menagerie, Oliver Twist, Hamlet, Twelfth Night* and
numerous plays for 14-16 year-olds, for 10-13 year-
olds, and for primary school pupils.

Casting procedures: Does not use freelance casting
directors. Holds general auditions; actors should
write in April requesting inclusion. Casting
breakdowns are available through the website, email
application, Equity Job Information Service and
Mandy. Welcomes postal and email enquiries from
actors previously unknown to the company.
Invitations to view individual actors' websites are also
accepted. Contracts are approved by GDBA (the
German equivalent of Equity). Rarely has the
opportunity to cast disabled actors since "all our
actors must take part in 3 different plays, and they
must also cope with the rigours of touring".

A touring actor's survival guide

Maev Alexander

Touring is more tiring, harder work, more all-consuming and more relentless than playing in one house. In order to give your best to it and get the best from it, you need to be thoroughly organised and disciplined. The main differences are, of course, the travelling and the accommodation. If you arrange these well in advance, you're on your way to having a happy and rewarding experience and saving yourself angst and money.

Getting there

At the beginning of rehearsals, or even before, you'll be given a schedule of dates and venues and a sheaf of digs lists. Work out as early as you can how you will travel and where you will stay.

If you have your own transport you can plan your journeys on a week-by-week basis, pulling maps and route finders and estimated journey times off the Internet – if you have access – both to digs and to theatres. A good company manager will supply maps of town centres with the venue clearly marked. A satnav can be reassuring, but don't rely on it in big town centres – we had to hold the curtain for a leading lady in Sheffield when her instructions were impossible to follow in a new road layout, so it's a good idea to keep your map-reading skills honed. It's amazing how they improve when you *have* to find digs and theatres within a tight timeframe.

If you don't have your own transport, ask around the company and find out if anyone lives close enough to you, and is willing, to give you lifts. Make it clear that you will contribute to petrol costs, be punctual and not bring too much luggage. If you are using public transport, book as far in advance as you can: Apex (or the equivalent) on trains and low-budget airlines will save you huge amounts of money. The touring company will expect you to do this, and will calculate the amount they give you in fares as economically as possible. Be aware that fares are worked out from venue to venue, and not to your home and out again. Remember also that you may get stuck on a Saturday night if your show comes down after the last train, which is more likely than not; this may add to your accommodation expenses. It also eats into your only day off; most No. 1 tours play Monday to Saturday, running for a week in each venue.

The rule for fares and touring allowance is: outwith 15 miles of your permanent base to qualify for fares only, and 25 miles to qualify for touring allowance. This is calculated from postcode to postcode – not by the most convenient or quickest route. Equity has negotiated sharp rises in the level of touring allowance over the last few years, and this is now reasonable. It's meant to cover accommodation and living expenses – and if you're frugal and careful, it can. You have to balance the level of comfort and convenience with which you need to live happily with the budget on which you have to do it.

Finding the right digs

Digs lists cover hotels, guesthouses, self-contained flats, houses for sharing, B&Bs and rooms in private houses. They normally tell you the price (per night or per week), the type of accommodation, the facilities, the prohibitions (i.e. no smoking, no pets), the extras (TV, kettle in room) and the distance from the theatre. The headliners can probably afford

Theatre

to stay in hotels (and many hotels do deals for touring actors), but other ranks will have to juggle their priorities. If you can feel comfortable in a room in a private house, sharing a bathroom and having access to a kitchen, you can do so remarkably cheaply. If you can't do without an en suite or need to be self-contained, this will obviously be more expensive, and so on up the scale; but read the list carefully and you will find something that will tick most of your boxes without too much compromise. The people who do the letting are generally friends of the theatre in some way, and the standard of accommodation is usually pretty high. I have heard horror stories of rooms booked in hotels on last-minute websites – all-night disco music and overpowering 'room fragrancers'.

Start ringing the most promising-sounding digs as soon as possible, before everyone else does. Good options are places within a 15-minute walk (obviating cabs or long, lonely walks or parking problems), or a house or cottage that is further out, possibly in country-side, to share with fellow company members, both in terms of rent and transport. Beware of landlady-speak for 'a 15- to 20-minute walk' – some landladies clearly have seven-league boots! The level of rates varies from place to place: locations like Bath and Malvern tend to be more expensive across the board than, say, Southampton and Coventry. In big centres like Glasgow, Manchester, Birmingham and Leeds you will probably have to travel to the outskirts unless you can afford hotels.

When you've agreed terms with a landlord/lady, write to confirm the booking and the dates, and arrange to ring a couple of days in advance of the stay to negotiate a mutually convenient time to arrive (leave half an hour's leeway so you don't panic about getting lost). It's wise to at least drop off your luggage before the show so that you know you know where the place is, have keys and don't disturb anyone at a late hour – especially on the first night when there are likely to be drinks front-of-house afterwards. Sorting out digs gets easier the more you tour and the more contacts you acquire. If you're new to it, do ask experienced tourers – most actors are very generous about sharing the secrets of top digs. For future reference, keep records of where you've stayed and what it was like. Pay up front, and remember to leave keys when you leave; get a receipt and behave well enough for the landlord/lady to wish to stay on the digs list. You represent future tourers.

What to take

It's important to pack well. Travel as light as you can, and have as much of your luggage on wheels as possible. You need enough clothes for a week, or longer if you need to go straight to the next venue; keep it simple, remembering to have something warm and something cool (because this is Britain) and something smart for the first-night drinks often provided by the host management or friends of the theatre. A towelling robe doubles as a dressing gown and post-shower gear. Take comfortable, reasonably weatherproof shoes, since you'll spend a lot of time walking. Remember your phone charger (it's worth having a spare for touring), and a toothbrush charger and adapter in case there are no shaving points. It's also worth having an emergency kit containing plasters and painkillers and cold remedies. In most places towels are provided, but pack a hand towel just in case. Travel with a hottie in winter: the only miserable digs I've had were very smart but *freezing*. I complained – do complain; you're not paying to freeze. A pocket torch is useful for unfamiliar, unlit keyholes. Don't forget comforts like books or a radio or iPod.

If you have to be away from your base for extended periods, negotiate doing your laundry with the wardrobe department. If you're home on Sunday, it saves time and hassle if you've put what needs washing into a separate bag in your case so that repacking is straightforward and quick. I was told early in my career that no proper actor has less than three weeks' worth of underwear!

You can generally transport your make-up and other dressing-room necessities, comforts and amusements in a bag or box on the truck transporting the set and props, etc. This is not an automatic right, though, so check with your company manager. Some reasonably rigid receptacle is optimal to avoid breakage; label it clearly with the name of the production and your own name, and do not expect anyone else to lug it to or from your dressing room week by week. Pack it as soon as you can on Saturday night, and check where you can leave it so it's not in the way of the get-out.

Eating and drinking

It's easy to be lazy about eating sensibly on tour – financially and nutritionally. Even if there are cooking facilities in your digs, it's not always convenient to be there and it's tempting to eat out all the time or grab burgers. You're going to need all your energy, so make a point of eating healthily.

In most theatres you'll have access to a microwave and possibly a fridge: ring the stage door and check. They're often in the crew room, so ask if you may use them and be considerate about clearing up after yourself. Making an interesting dressing-room picnic is a worthy challenge even if everything has to be cold. Supermarkets do better and better ranges of salads and sushi. Invest in a mini kettle for your touring box and pack a plate, a mug and cutlery. Set yourself a daily budget for food and then you'll know if you can splash out on a restaurant meal.

It's also tempting to do a great deal more after-show drinking when you're away from home: it can feel as if you're living in a bubble, out of the real world. Ask yourself if you're getting jaded/broke, and limit alcohol to within sensible limits. (The same sense of not being quite in the real world can lead also to the most unlikely affairs: be discreet, whether it involves other people or yourself.)

Bonding and recreation

After-show company meals, weekly or fortnightly, are good bonding exercises providing you all get on. Remember that it's not only part of your job to get on, but also in your best interests. It's even more important in the living-in-each-others'-pockets world of touring to be a good company member; leave your troubles firmly at the stage door and don't moan or gossip. If there's someone you find tricky, keep out of their way. In my experience, touring companies bond well and form even more of a parallel family than usual.

That said, getting away by yourself for a time is restoring. Find the local Tourist Information Office and find out about places of interest and specialist shopping. There's bound to be something that appeals to you, even if you're not a galleries/museums/castles/cathedrals person (the ABC of touring is famously, "another bloody cathedral"). I am lucky – and not alone – in regarding touring as being paid to go sightseeing. Stage door, or your company manager, can tell you of gym and leisure facilities and often arrange temporary membership; they can also point you in the direction of the nearest supermarkets and best-value restaurants.

Sussing out the theatre

One of the interesting and rewarding things about touring is playing the same show in lots of different theatres – from 900-seaters to 2000-seaters; from raked stages to flat ones;

Theatre

from Victorian to modern; from those with acres (seemingly) of orchestra pit to those where the front row is looking up your nose. You'll be called early in the first day of each new venue, generally at about 5 or 6pm, to walk the stage, get to know the backstage layout and take note of significant differences. The presence or lack of a rake may mean more or fewer steps on a staircase, for instance; furniture may be closer together or further apart; wing space may be tight; prop tables may be in different places; dressing rooms will be varying distances away and you may be sharing in one venue and by yourself in another. Take time to absorb these differences, test the acoustic and plan how you're going to accommodate any changes you personally will have to make. Discuss these changes too with anyone else they may affect. Bear in mind that the audiences are always different, as well: it's amazing that what makes people laugh or weep in Cardiff is not the same as what makes people laugh or weep in Hull.

Find out when stage door opens; most theatres allow you access to your dressing room from quite early in the day, which is useful for dumping shopping or 'nesting' when it's tipping with rain. A few don't open until much later, though, which is a great bore and makes it good to have digs close by.

Money matters

On a business level, keep a work diary and note down all your expenses (and mileages if you're driving). Have an envelope or plastic wallet in which to file all your receipts and payslips: it's easy to lose track of these when you're away from home.

Tax offices vary in what they will allow you to claim on tour. Travel and accommodation expenses above your allowances are OK, but some accept claims for all eating expenses (again over and above), some for restaurant/cafe receipts only, and some – including my own – clearly expect you not to eat at all.

Research a mobile phone tariff that will let you keep in touch with family and friends, and your agent, as cheaply as possible.

Finally ...

More and more of the available work involves touring at some level. You might just as well maximise your chances of having a good time and making a decent profit. Regard it as an adventure.

Maev Alexander trained at the Royal Scottish Academy of Music and Drama and has been working in theatre, television and radio for 40 years. She has performed in Rep all over the country, playing everything from Cleopatra to a French poodle, been a member of the RSC, and holds the record as the longest-serving Mollie in *The Mousetrap*. She has starred in two TV series and guested in many others, presented the Newsdesk on *That's Life*, and played in dozens of radio dramas. After completing her 7th No. 1 tour in as many years, and transferring the last but one – *A Man for All Seasons* – to the Theatre Royal Haymarket in 2006, she has filmed *Death Defying Acts* with Catherine Zeta Jones and Guy Pearce, and recorded the second series of *The Eliza Stories* for BBC Radio 4.

Editors' note There are a number of websites that can help you plan your journeys to and from the locations on your tour; they may also save you money. Here are some of the major ones:

• *Maps*: **www.streetmap.co.uk**, **www.multimap.com**, and **maps.google.co.uk**. If you have a mobile phone capable of web browsing, point it to **www.google.co.uk/mmp** to access Google Maps for Mobile. Rather cleverly, if you tell it where you are, it can even give you directions to all the nearest pubs. (If you're going to be using this a lot, check how much

Internet access you have on your call plan. Google does not charge you for the service, but you may find yourself with some hefty Internet usage bills if you're not careful.)

• *Driving*: **www.theaa.com** and **www.rac.co.uk** both offer route-planning and maps, as do Google Maps and Google Maps for Mobile (see above).

• *Trains*: **www.nationalrail.co.uk** for timetables and **www.thetrainline.com** for booking the cheapest tickets available. Also worth looking at **www.megatrain.com** to check for promotional fares. In addition to these, **www.traveline.org.uk** is a good way of exploring options (train, coach, plane, etc.) for getting to a location. And of course, the number that the 118 companies get the most requests for: National Rail Enquiries is **08457 48 49 50**; if it's not in your phone already, why not put it there now?

• *Coaches*: **www.nationalexpress.co.uk**, **www.citylink.co.uk** (Scotland), **www.megabus.com/uk** (which often has promotional fares), and **www.eurolines.com** (destinations around Europe). In addition there are some local companies offering low-cost services to major cities such as London, which a little research should uncover.

• *London Transport*: **journeyplanner.tfl.gov.uk** or, from your mobile, text 60835 (60TFL) with 'a to b' (where 'a' and 'b' are stations, stops or postcodes in London) to find out the best way – tube, train or bus – of getting to where you're going. For example: 'Clapham Junction to The Old Vic'. Common sense and some knowledge of the geography of London may need to be applied to the directions given: in this example the text service recommends a bus journey from Waterloo Station to The Old Vic – a walk of three minutes at most.

• *Flying*: **www.travelsupermarket.com** or **www.skyscanner.net** will search out all available flights to a given destination, sorted by price.

Theatre

Fringe theatres

Essentially, the idea of 'fringe theatre' began at the Edinburgh Festival more than half a century ago. It really started taking off (especially in London) in the late 1960s as an arena for 'alternative' and 'experimental' theatre. The 1990s saw a huge expansion in the number of venues being used, and a downturn in the exploration of theatre forms: the 'fringe' became more commercial and much more competitive – and not just in London and Edinburgh. Today, the terms 'alternative' and 'experimental' are far less frequently used, and the Fringe is now largely seen as a way for actors, directors and writers to showcase their work.

Casting for Fringe productions is usually advertised by one or more of the casting information services, and agents and casting directors do scout for new talent in them. However, it's highly unlikely that you will make any money from participating in such a production – you might end up with a net loss after deducting your expenses. Also agents and casting directors get blitzed with so many invitations that the chances of getting one of them to see you are not high. The only reasons for being in a Fringe production are (a) you might be 'seen'; (b) you fundamentally believe in the production's potential; and (c) it could help keep your acting-juices flowing. But you might find classes less time-consuming and possibly more beneficial.

The Edinburgh Fringe Festival

There is a real sense that every actor should try this 'Carnival of theatre' experience – 'the biggest theatrical lottery in the world' – at least once. You'll meet lots of new people, make contacts and it's a great few weeks, even if your own production doesn't hit the heights.

Good advice on mounting a production on the Edinburgh Fringe Festival is available from the Festival Office (details below).

The listings that follow are restricted to the more 'established' venues, with performance spaces for hire. Some Fringe theatres only programme in work known to them.

Note If you are thinking of mounting a Fringe production and/or starting your own theatre company, start researching and planning well in advance. It is well worth consulting the Independent Theatre Council (ITC) – **www.itc-arts.org**.

UMBRELLA ORGANISATIONS

Edinburgh Festival Fringe
The Fringe Office, 180 High Street, Edinburgh EH1 1QS
tel 0131 226 0026 *fax* 0131 226 0016
email admin@edfringe.com
website www.edfringe.com

The Edinburgh Fringe Festival started in 1947 and the Fringe Society was formed in 1959 to coordinate publicity and ticket sales, and offer a comprehensive information service both to performers and to audiences. It compiles information about venues, press and suppliers, and produces a series of publications designed to answer frequently asked questions. Its brochure contains details for Fringe venues and shows in Edinburgh. The office is open all year round and the staff are available to help by phone, email or personal appointment.

OffWestEnd.com
email info@offwestend.com
website www.offwestend.com https//offies.london
Twitter @OffWestEndCom

OffWestEnd promotes the exciting and innovative work performed in the 100+ theatres outside London's West End, and organises the annual Offies awards. Tickets are sold directly from these Off West End theatres, with no fees and no commission being charged.

Society of Independent Theatres (SIT)
website www.sitgb.org

The Society of Independent Theatres (SIT) is a recently established alliance of small independent theatres in London. "We welcome contact from all venue owners, venue managers and artistic directors of independent theatres. Although we are currently looking for members in London, we will eventually widen our catchment area to the rest of Great Britain and Northern Ireland. Our objectives are as follows:

• To raise the profile of small/independent/fringe/pub style venues within the theatre industry and with the general public.
• To encourage the development of the performing arts within independent venues.
• To exchange information on theatre companies and suppliers.
• To exchange ideas and proposals for marketing, promotion and audience development.
• To provide a better understanding of employment laws relevant to our sector of the industry.
• To liaise with Equity and other organisations over issues affecting our industry.

LONDON FRINGE VENUES

The Albany
Douglas Way, Deptford, London SE8 4AG
tel 020 8692 4446
email boxoffice@thealbany.org.uk
website www.thealbany.org.uk
Chief Executive Gavin Barlow

Production details: A multi-use arts centre programming music, spoken word, dance, comedy and family shows. The Albany is an artistic and community resource with a fully equipped theatre space, studio theatre, café and rehearsal and meeting rooms for hire. Has a strong commitment to working collaboratively with the diverse communities of London and encouraging participation, especially by young people and isolated older people and those least likely to engage in the arts. As well as programming performances, the Albany programme and manage two external venues in Lewisham and Southwark. The centre is home to 25+ resident organisations and the national Fun Palaces and Family Arts Campaign movements. It is a social hub and facilitator for partnership working. The Albany co-chairs Future Arts Centres with ARC, Stockon, runs a major partnership with Social Housing providor Lewisham Homes and recebtly launched a campaign to provide free theatre tickets to every 5-year-old child in Lewisham.

Seats 300 (500 standing); 2 secondary spaces seat 60 or 70. Performances also take place in the café – capacity 80. All spaces have fully configurable seating; there is also seating on the balcony. Shows usually run from 1 night to 2 weeks. Hire rates may be subsidised depending on community or charity status – see website for rates of different spaces. There is disabled access. Recent productions developed in partnership with the Albany include Tiata Fahodzi's *Good Dog*; Belarus Free Theatre's *Tomorrow I Was Always a Lion*; Teatro Vivo's *The Residents* and *Muhammad Ali and Me* from Majisola Adebayo, plus seven regular platforms for neew work. *Lipsticks and Lollipops* by Deafinitely Theatre; *A Warwickshire Testimony* by April de Angelis (Mountview Theatre School); and transfer from the Royal Court of *Gone Too Far!* by Olivier Award-winner Bola Agbaje.

Casting procedures: Does not produce in-house shows.

artsdepot
5 Nether Street, North Finchley, London N12 0GA
tel 020 8369 5454
email info@artsdepot.co.uk
website www.artsdepot.co.uk

The only professional arts venue in the London Borough of Barnet. Committed to providing a diverse range of high-quality visual and performance arts for everyone. artsdepot has brand new, state-of-the-art facilities in the form of the large Pentland Theatre, smaller Studio Theatre and Education Spaces, for the provision of drama, dance and visual arts, and a gallery, as well as an excellent café and bars.

Barons Court Theatre
The Curtain's Up, 28A Comeragh Rd, West Kensington, London W14 9HR
tel 020 8932 4747
email londontheatre@gmail.com
Artistic Director Ron Phillips

A central London 62-seat theatre in the basement of the Curtain's Up public house and restaurant. Offers 1- to 5-week runs and can be booked up to 12 months in advance at a moderate rental. Also available for 1-day actors' showcases.

Battersea Arts Centre
Lavender Hill, London SW11 5TN
tel 020 7223 2223
email programmingenquiries@bac.org.uk
website www.bac.org.uk
Artistic Director Tarek Iskander *Senior Producers* Bethany Haynes Catherine Nicolson

Battersea Arts Centre's (BAC) mission is to inspire people to take creative risks to shape the future. Each year the organisation works with over 400 artists to develop new forms of theatre and connect with audiences and participants. The emphasis is on devised rather than script-based work. BAC is the original home and foremost pioneer of Scratch, a model that has transformed the way in which people make and experience theatre. Scratch is a shared space in which ideas are exchanged between artists and audiences as a way to develop the work. Finished shows are then performed throughout the centre's old town hall building and often go on to more unusual spaces across London, the UK and the world.

Work is rarely programmed on the strength of a proposal alone, and unsolicited scripts are not accepted. Instead they prefer to build up a relationship with artists over time. Typically, one of the producers might see a show or workshop by a company at another venue and then start a conversation. A significant exception to this is Freshly Scratched – once or twice a year, BAC programme a week of short 10-minute Scratches by artists who have never presented their work at BAC before, purely on the basis of paper applications.

For more information visit **bac.org.uk/ howweprogramme**. Contact Amy Sutters (Producing Assistant) with programming enquiries at **programmingenquiries@bac.org.uk**.

Blue Elephant Theatre

59A Bethwin Road, Camberwell, London SE5 0XT
tel 020 7701 0100
email info@blueelephanttheatre.co.uk
website www.blueelephanttheatre.co.uk
Facebook www.facebook.com/blueelephanttheatre
Twitter @BETCamberwell
Co-Artistic Directors Niamh de Valera and Jo Sadler-Lovett

The only theatre in Camberwell. A vibrant arts venue aiming to nurture new and emerging artists across the performing arts. Promotes cross-artform work and all types of theatre, from physical and dance to new writing and classics.

Co-produces all shows and is particularly interested in supporting new and emerging London-based artists across the perfoming arts with work that complements the black-box performance space. Those interested in bringing a project to the Blue Elephant should submit a written proposal with suggested dates and a full background to Jasmine Cullingford.

The Bridewell Theatre

Bride Lane, Fleet Street, London EC4Y 8EQ
tel 020 7353 3331
website www.sbf.org.uk

The Bridewell Theatre is a versatile space, which provides both an atmospheric entertainment venue and an unique conference facility in the heart of the City. In addition to a 12x8m performance space, there is a modular tiered seating system that in standard configuration can accommodate a raked audience of 134 people. The theatre also offers dressing rooms with en suite amenities, as well as a box-office/reception area and a fully equipped bar. All areas of the theatre are accessible to disabled users via a lift.

The Broadway Studio Theatre

Catford, London SE6 4RU
tel 020 8690 0002

email helen@broadwaytheatre.org.uk
website www.broadwaytheatre.org.uk
Operations Manager Carmel O'Connor *Sales and Events Manager* Helen Haylett

Originally opened in 1932, the venue is Grade II listed by English Heritage as a beautiful example of 1930s art deco architecture. There are 2 venues: the Main Theatre seats 800, and the Studio Theatre seats 100. "The Broadway Studio Theatre has extremely limited availability; please contact Helen Haylett to check availability and prices."

The Bunker Theatre

53a Southwark Street, London SE1 1RU
tel 020 7403 1139
email info@bunkertheatre.com
Twitter @BunkerTheatreUK
Artistic Director Chris Sonnex *Executive Director* David Ralf

Production details: Housed in a former underground parking garage, The Bunker is a unique 110-seater deep beneath the pavements of Southwark Street. An eclectic mix of seating surrounds a large, square thrust stage on three sides, and a craft beer bar stays open long after performances while audiences mingle with artists in the auditorium. With ambitious, emerging artists at the centre of its work, The Bunker's programming has included the world premieres of award winning sell-out *Skin a Cat* by Isley Lynn, *Devil in a Blue Dress* by Kevin Armento, *Abigail* by Fiona Doyle, *Eyes Closed, Ears Covered* by Alex Gwyther, *31 Hours* by Kieran Knowles.

In spring 2019, Chris Sonnex joined The Bunker as Artistic Director with an aim to programme revolutionary theatre and to continue enabling and championing artists and theatre makers from under-represented backgrounds. His first season included the provocative festival of letter-writting *My White Best Friend*, a new show *Welcome to the UK* by mixed refugee ensemble Borderline, a double bill of working- and benefits-class plays *Killymuck* and *Box Clever*, a new version of Sacha Voit and Jessica Butcher's *Boots*, as well as the London transfers of Emma Dennis-Edwards' award-winning *Funeral Flowers* and Joana Nastari's love letter to sex workers *F*ck You Pay Me*. In 2019, The Bunker also launched its Writers' Snug, a free to use space in the theatre for playwrights with one desk reserved for writers from under-represented backgrounds.

Camden People's Theatre

58-60 Hampstead Road, London NW1 2PY
tel 020 7419 4841
email admin@cptheatre.co.uk
website www.cptheatre.co.uk
Twitter @camdenPT

A central London space dedicated year round to supporting early-career artists making unconventional theatre. In particular, those whose work explores issues that matter to people now.

Canal Café Theatre
Delamere Terrace, Little Venice, London W2 6ND
tel 020 7289 6056 (Box Office) 020 7289 6054
email mail@canalcafetheatre.com
website www.canalcafetheatre.com

A comedy and new writing 60-seat theatre situated above the Bridge House pub in Little Venice. Home to NewsRevue.

Charing Cross Theatre (formerly New Players Theatre)
The Arches, Villiers Street, London WC2N 6NG
tel 020 7930 5868
website www.charingcrosstheatre.co.uk

The recently renovated New Players Theatre is a valuable addition to the London theatre scene and business community in the heart of the West End. Already a popular and well-known venue within the theatre, music and entertainment industries, the New Players now offers producers the opportunity to present a diverse and eclectic range of productions in an Off-Broadway-style, well-equipped, high-specification theatre, complete with on-site bars and a restaurant. It is also a distinctive setting for screenings, conference and corporate hires.

Chelsea Theatre
World's End Place, King's Road, London SW10 0DR
tel 020 7352 1967 *fax* 020 7352 2024
website www.chelseatheatre.org.uk

A 110-seat theatre which can be booked up to 6 months in advance. Particularly welcomes new writing.

The Cockpit
Gateforth Street, London NW8 8EH
tel 020 7258 2925
email mail@thecockpit.org.uk
website www.thecockpit.org.uk

Theatre seats 240 (60 seats on 4 sides) or 180 (60 seats on 3 sides) and should be booked 6 months in advance. Welcomes classics, foreign-language theatre and other niche market work.

The Courtyard Theatre
Bowling Green Walk, 40 Pitfield Street, London N1 6EU
020 7729 2202
email info@thecourtyard.org.uk
website www.thecourtyard.org.uk

Flexible seating arrangements, 2 theatres, rehearsal rooms.

Etcetera Theatre
Above the Oxford Arms, 265 Camden High Street, London NW1 7BU
tel 020 7482 4857
email admin@etceteratheatre.com
website www.etceteratheatre.com

A black-box studio space with 42 raked seats, this intimate theatre is perfect for everything from new writing to comedy and cabaret all the way through to acoustic music. Open 7 days a week with an early and late slot. Available for one-off bookings as well as week runs and any number of shows in between. The Etcetera is also available during the day for rehearsals, auditions and workshops with rates starting from just £10 an hour.

Finborough Theatre
118 Finborough Road, London SW10 9ED
tel 020 7244 7439
email admin@finboroughtheatre.co.uk
website www.finboroughtheatre.co.uk
Artistic Director Neil McPherson

Founded in 1980, the multi-award-winning Finborough Theatre presents plays and musical theatre, concentrated exclusively on vibrant new writing and unique rediscoveries from the 19th and 20th centuries. The programme is unique — never presenting work that has been seen anywhere in London during the last 25 years.

The main theatre space has completely flexible seating for 50 in a variety of formats. The normal run of a show is 4 weeks.

Hire rates: rental for the theatre is £1,500/week, equivalent to £6,000 for a four week run.

Many productions transfer to New York and the West End.

Produces in-house shows but does not hold general auditions. Casting breakdowns are available through the Spotlight Link casting service. Letters (with CVs and photographs) from previously unknown actors are not welcomed, neither are unsolicited CVs or showreels sent by email. Invitations to other productions are welcome. Welcomes applications from disabled performers but there is no wheelchair access to the theatre.

See entry for Concordance, its resident company, under *Middle and smaller-scale companies* on page 190.

Hackney Empire Studio Theatre
291 Mare Street, London E8 1EJ
tel 020 8510 4500 *fax* 020 8510 4530
email info@hackneyempire.co.uk
website www.hackneyempire.co.uk
Chief Executive Claire Middleton *Creative Director* Susie Mckenna

80-seat studio attached to the historic, Grade II listed, Matcham-designed Hackney Empire. Contact Frank Sweeney for booking details.

Hen & Chickens Theatre
Above Hen & Chickens Theatre Bar,
109 St Paul's Road, Islington, London N1 2NA
tel 020 7704 2001
website www.unrestrictedview.co.uk

Theatre

A 60-seat theatre welcoming new writing. Directly opposite Highbury and Islington station. Offers 3-to 4-week runs with Monday nights available separately.

The Hope Theatre

Hope & Anchor Pub, 207 Upper Street, Islington, London N11 1RL
email info@thehopetheatre.com
Artistic Director Matthew Parker

Production details: The multi-award-winning Hope Theatre is a place for audiences and companies to explore big ideas. The company nurtures and develops new producing models, working with exciting companies to present a mix of new writing, lost gems from well-known writers, re-polished classics and innovatively staged musicals. Although The Hope Theatre receives no public subsidy, it was the first Off West End venue to open with a house agreement with Equity, to ensure a legal wage for all actors, stage managers and box office staff working at the theatre.

Matthew Parker was named Best Artistic Director at the Off-West End Awards 2017 for his work at The Hope in 2016.

2019 productions included: *Thrill Me: The Leopold & Loeb Story, The Censor, Starved, River in the Sky*.

Casting procedures: please note does not accept actor CVs or expressions of interest by email. All in-house productions are cast via Spotlight and each casting breakdown will be posted there and application handled via Spotlight. Please do not send CVs for casting.

The Jack Studio Theatre

410 Brockley Road, London SE4 2DH
tel 020 3490 5060
email admin@brockleyjack.co.uk
website www.brockleyjack.co.uk
Facebook www.facebook.com/BrocJackTheatre
Twitter @BrocJackTheatre
Artistic Director Kate Bannister *Theatre Producer* Karl Swinyard

Production details: A vibrant award winning performance space situated in South East London, offering a diverse theatre programme throughout the year. Home also to the Write Now Festivals, Scratch nights, and the Jack Writers' Workshop. Provides high-quality, accessible and affordable productions for South London and beyond, with seasons of both innovative revivals and dynamic new writing. Comfortable cinema-style raked seating for 50; can be configured end-on or on 3 sides or in the round. The performing space is step-free and wheelchair accessible but the rehearsal room is not. Recent productions include: *Kes, Queen of the Mist, Taro, Gentleman Jack, Sweet Like Chocolate Boy, Lifeboat* and *Radiant Vermin*.

Casting procedures: Produces in-house shows; uses both in-house and freelance casting directors. Casting

is generally by invitation. Does not welcome unsolicited submissions from actors, but will accept invitations to view individual actors' websites and to visit other productions. Actively encourages applications from disabled actors and promotes the use of inclusive casting.

Jacksons Lane Arts Centre

269A Archway Road, London N6 5AA
tel 020 8340 5226
email admin@jacksonslane.org.uk
website www.jacksonslane.org.uk

Rooms are available for hire on a daily or hourly basis for private parties, rehearsals and performances. Studio 1 holds up to 120; Studio 2 holds 80; Space 3 holds up to 35; Space 4 holds up to 40; Space 5 holds up to 25, and the Theatre seats up to 166.

Jermyn Street Theatre

16B Jermyn Street, London SW1Y 6ST
tel 020 7434 1443 (Executive Director: Penny Horner) and 020 7287 2875 (Box Office)
email info@jermynstreettheatre.co.uk
website www.jermynstreettheatre.co.uk
Artistic Director Tom Littler

Hire rates: Theatre seats 70, 5 rows facing, 2 rows on side. Stage space is 8 metres long x 4 metres deep x 3.5 metres high (to grid), 2 dressing rooms with fridges, sofas, microwaves, kettles, iron + ironing board. The theatre is air conditioned.

• Main Shows – The theatre is now a fully programmed producing house. However, some weeks can be rented as a receiving house. Weekly rent is £3,000 (this includes get-in, fit-up time, technician operating/rigging, also operates sound as well as lights). A 30% non-refundable deposit is required when the contract is signed.
• Showcases/Rehearsed Readings/Seminars – £90 per hour. Theatre is available on Tuesdays/Wednesdays/Thursdays between 10am and 4pm (includes technician).
• Sunday Nights (Cabaret Evenings) – £395 for the evening, available from 6.30pm on the night for 8pm show, includes rehearsal Friday before (includes technician).

King's Head Theatre

115 Upper Street, Islington, London N1 1QN
tel 020 7226 8561
website www.kingsheadtheatre.org
Artistic Director Adam Spreadbury-Maher

Famous for helping to launch the careers of many new writers, directors and actors including Stephen Berkoff, Anthony Sher and Victoria Wood. The theatre is situated at the back of a public house with flexible seating for up to 120.

The Landor Theatre

70 Landor Road, London SW9 9PH
tel 020 7737 7276

email info@landortheatre.co.uk
website www.landortheatre.co.uk

A 60-seat theatre situated above a public house.

Lion & Unicorn Theatre

42-44 Gaisford Street, Kentish Town,
London NW5 2ED
email info@giantolive.com
website www.giantolive.com and
www.lionandunicorntheatre.com

The Lion & Unicorn is the home of Giant Olive
theatre company. Founded in 2008, the company has
quickly developed a reputation for high-quality and
imaginative theatre and dance. Giant Olive produces
classical productions as well as supporting and
developing new work and talent. "The Lion &
Unicorn Theatre Space is available to hire at the 'Best
Fringe Theatre Rates in London'. Giant Olive doesn't
just offer a black box, they can provide full
production support, with everything from rehearsal
space to flyer and poster design. For prices and
details, and to view the venue, please contact
info@giantolive.com."

New Diorama Theatre

15-16 Triton Street, Regent's Place,
London NW1 3BF
tel 020 7916 5467
email hello@newdiorama.com
website www.newdiorama.com
Artistic and Executive Director David Byrne

New Diorama is an 80-seat theatre located in central
London. "We host and support theatre companies,
both emerging and established, presenting a variety of
productions ranging from comedy to drama. We
want to find and support the next generation of
Complicites, Kneehighs, Headlongs whilst also
offering a space to established companies wanting to
work in intimate spaces."

Old Red Lion

418 St John Street, Islington, London EC1V 4NJ
tel 020 7833 3053 *fax* 020 7833 3053
website www.oldredliontheatre.co.uk
Artistic Director Nicholas Thompson

Founded in 1979, the Old Red Lion Theatre is a 60-
seater Fringe theatre primarily dedicated to new
writing. Companies wishing to hire the venue should
post a script, some company information and a
production proposal to the Artistic Director.
Normally programmes 3 months ahead.

Omnibus Theatre

1 Clapham Common Northside
tel 020 7622 4105
email marie.mccarthy@omnibus-clapham.org
Artistic Director Marie McCarthy

The heart of Omnibus Theatre's ambitious
programme, inspired by their building's literary
heritage, lies in both classics re-imagined and
contemporary storytelling. Provides a platform for
new writing and interdisciplinary work, aiming to
give voice to the underrepresented and challenge
perceptions. 'We believe in affordable tickets and
theatre for all.'

Since opening in 2013 notable in-house productions
include: *Woyzeck* (2013); *Macbeth* (2014); *Colour*
(2015); *Mule* (2016); *Spring Offensive* (2017); *Zeraffa
Giraffa* (2017); *To Have To Shoot Irishmen* (2018);
Perfect (2018) and *Lipstick: A Fairy Tale* (2019).
Registered charity and receives no core funding.

Our venue is home to the 90–110 seat Theatre and
the Studio Upstairs (80 seats), a café/bar and two
more performance and rehearsal spaces.

Oval House Theatre

52-54 Kennington Oval, London SE11 5SW
tel 020 7582 0080
email rachel.briscoe@OvalHouse.com
email rebecca.atkinson-lord@OvalHouse.com
website www.ovalhouse.com
Director Deborah Bestwick

Comprises 2 spaces; the downstairs theatre is a black
box studio with semi-permanent rake seating,
capacity 150. The upstairs theatre is an intimate black
box studio with adjustable seating, capacity 50.
Presents a diverse programme of work.

Pentameters

28 Heath Street, Hampstead NW3 6TE
tel 020 7435 3648
website www.pentameters.co.uk
Founder and Producer Léonie Scott-Matthews

Located in the heart of Hampstead village, among an
abundance of cafés, restaurants, bars, pubs and shops
and just a minute's walk from Hampstead tube. Aside
from the choice of venues to have pre- or post-
theatre drinks or dinner, Hampstead is also well-
known for its artistic character, offering a supportive,
interactive and thriving local community, making it
an ideal spot to promote live theatre and creative arts
events. To discuss requirements, please telephone
Léonie Scott-Matthews directly on the above number:
"Please leave a message, and we will respond."

The Playground Theatre

Latimer Road, London W10 6RQ
tel 020 8960 0110
email info@theplaygroundtheatre.london
Co-Artistic Directors Peter Tate, Anthony Biggs

The Playground Theatre, formerly a bus depot, was
set up as a creative space for innovative theatre artists
of all disciplines to come and 'play' with their
imaginative ideas. One such project, 'Terrific Electric'
won the Samuel Beckett Award for Innovative
Theatre and was part of the Bite season at the
Barbican Theatre. The decision to become a public
theatre was born from the desire to bring the

Theatre

exceptional artists work, who 'played' with the company, to full production. Continues to work with both established and emerging artists from the UK and internationally. The ethos is one of cross-fertilisation between different forms and different cultures in search of a universal language that speaks to all. Many international artists were invited to experiment with the Playground Theatre including Poland's Henryk Baranowski, winner of Poland and Russia's top award as best director, Salius Varnus from Lithuania, and Hideki Noda, currently head of Japan's National Theatre. From the UK, the company has worked closely with Marcello Magni, co-founder of Theatre De Complicité, along with his colleague Linda Kerr Scott. Programme includes international plays, classical concerts, dance, and film. The Playground Theatre is located within a very diverse community and its work will reflect this.

Pleasance Theatre Trust

Carpenters Mews, North Road, London N7 9EF
tel 020 7609 1800
email info@pleasance.co.uk
website www.pleasance.co.uk
Facebook ThePleasance
Twitter @ThePleasance
Director Anthony Alderson

Founded in 1984, the Pleasance has 3 versatile spaces: the Mainhouse, seats between 200–250; and the StageSpace, created to nurture the best in new theatre writing and emerging comedy talent, seats 54.

The standard configurationof the Main House and StageSPace are end on but the seating is completely flexible in both spaces. Shows are programmed for various lengths of run from 1 night to 6 weeks. There is no programme of shows in London during August, during which the Pleasance operates 3 sites at the Edinburgh Festival Fringe. The Mainhouse and Downstairs are fully accessible, however, unfortunately the StageSpace is not wheelchair accessible. Please visit the Pleasance website for hire rates and more information.

RADA Studios

16 Chenies Street, London WC1E 7EX
tel 020 7307 5060
email venuehire@rada.ac.uk
website www.rada.ac.uk/about-us/venue-hire/
Events and Hires Manager Caitlin Richards *Events and Hires Coordinator*

RADA Studios is a receiving theatre located in Chenies Street at the heart of the west end. The Studio Theatre is a hugely versatile space, and we currently host a large variety of work, including theatre, musicals, dance, opera, radio recordings and screenings.

We also have four studio spaces within the RADA Studios building, perfect for castings, read-throughs, rehearsals or fittings in a vibrant and creative atmosphere that continues to inspire future

generations of actors, writers, directors and technicians.

Rich Mix

35-47 Bethnal Green Road, London E1 6LA
tel 020 7613 7490 *fax* 020 7613 7499
email info@richmix.org.uk
website www.richmix.org.uk
Chief Executive Jane Earl

A 132,000 square foot flagship arts and cultural centre, boasting "the best in art, performance, fashion, design, music, dance, film, theatre and comedy – 5 floors of vibrant creativity and excellence".

Rosemary Branch Theatre

2 Shepperton Road, London N1 3DT
tel 020 7704 6665
email unattendededitems@gmail.com
website www.rosemarybranch.co.uk

The Rosemary Branch Theatre is managed by interactive performance company Unattended Items. The theatre holds about 61 seats including a "royal box". Presents a diverse programme including opera, classics, new writing, puppetry and just about any genre you care to mention. Affordable rehearsal space available in the Pink Room as well as the theatre during the day. The theatre offers all visiting companies lots of support and goodwill. One-offs, part week and full week rentals all considered.

The Space

269 Westferry Road, London E14 3RS
tel 020 7515 7799
email info@space.org.uk
website www.space.org.uk
Artistic Director Adam Hemming; *Theatre Manager* Isabel Dixon; *Duty Manager* Keri Danielle Chesser

The Space was founded in 1996 and is managed by the registered charity, St Paul's Arts Trust. In a converted church hall, The Space provides an atmopheric yet flexible Off West End setting. Certainly not a tylical 'black box' theatre, a number if staging options are achievable including end-on, in the round, traverse and thrust.

The Space programmes three seasons a year: in spring (Jan-April), summer (May- Aug), adn autumn/wonter (Sept-Dec). In each season they aim to schedule a minimum of 2 three-week runs alongside shorter runs. The Space offers a range of theatre events within each season, including a mixture of classics, new writing, revivals, puppetry, physical theatre, immersive theatre and musicals. It programmes drama and comedy and works with new, emerging and established companies.

The in-house company Space Productions produces 1-3 shows a year and has received six Off West End nominations to date. Also runs a community theatre company, SpaceWorks, which engages with childen and adults in the local area.

In 2015, a new performance space, Crossrail Place Roof Garden, was inaugurated and operates in the summer only. Performances at this new outdoor amphitheatre ideally run for an hour. Tickets at the Roof Garden must be free so a commission is paid to companies (between £600-£1,000).

The main theatre space seats between 45 and 90 depending on configuration. End on: between 60 (large playing space) and 90 seats (small stage area only, suitable for recitals and solo performances). The end-on configuration can also be reversed, with audience seating on stage. This configuration tends to seat 65 audience members; traverse: between 40-60 seats; thrust: 50-60 seats; in the round: 50-60 seats.

Viewing and speaking with one of their team is recommended before applying.

The normal duration of a show is between 1 and 3 weeks on a box office split basis. Runs shorter than a week will usually be programmed ona straight hire basis, although this is occasionally negotiable.

The main space is used all year round and open submissions are three times a year, announced on the wensbite. Roof Gadren Perforamcne Space is sed in the summer only.

Discounts are offered on block bookings for rehearsals.

Hire rates: rehearsals (10am–6pm) £15/hr + VAT, £12/hr + VAT (when 10+ hrs are booked in one go); workshops (10am–6pm) £20/hr + VAT; performances £150 + VAT per performance (inclusive of inclusion of all of The Space's marketing, full use of lighting/sound equipment and a full box office service). Application for shows on a 50/50 box office split three times a year.

Premises are accessible to disabled performers.

Recent productions include: The Lighthouse by Rachel Claye; The Collector, an adaptation of John Fowles's novel performed by the visiting company Blink and the One Festival — a celebration of solo performers now in its fourth year.

The Space also produced in-house productions. General auditions are advertised on a project-by-project basis, actors can amial Isabel Dixon (isabel@space.org.uk) to be added to the mailing list for casting opportunities. Jobs are also posted on Spotlight and Casting Call Pro. Welcomes letter (with CVs and photos) from individual actors previously unknown to the company. Also welcomes showreels, unsolicited CVs and photos sent by email and invitations to view individual actors' websites and to visit productions. Actively encourages applications from disabled actors and promotes the use of inclusive casting.

Tabard Theatre

2 Bath Road, Turnham Green, London W4 1LW
tel 020 8995 6035
website www.tabardtheatre.co.uk
General Manager Simon Reilly

Situated within the Tabard building with own independent entrance, close to Turnham Green tube.

Offers 3-4 week runs which are programmed 4-5 months ahead.

Theatre503

The Latchmere, 503 Battersea Park Road, London SW11 3BW
tel 020 7229 8530 *fax* 020 7229 8140
email info@theatre503.com
website www.theatre503.com
Artistic Director Lisa Spirling

Situated above a public house, Theatre503 aims to provide a venue for new playwrights, comedians and directors to develop their shows. It has a working relationship with television commissioners and producers, literary managers of established theatres and literary agents, and tries to offer a stepping-stone from Fringe to 'big' theatres.

Theatro Technis

26 Crowndale Road, London NW1 1TT
tel 020 7387 6617 *fax* 020 7383 2545
email info@theatrotechnis.com
website www.theatrotechnis.co.uk

Theatro Technis' ideas and policies are realised for anyone who is interested in the development of individuals and communities. The theatre maintains a balance between classic and contemporary work, and serves to embrace a variety of diverse artforms, ranging from theatre and dance to art, photography, music and film.

Toynbee Studios

28 Commercial Street, London E1 6AB
tel 020 7247 5102
email admin@artsadmin.co.uk
website www.artsadmin.co.uk/toynbee-studios

Toynbee Studios is run by Artsadmin for the development and presentation of new work. Toynbee Studios comprises a 280-seat theatre, rehearsal spaces, technical facilities, and the Arts Bar & Café, hosting rehearsals, meetings, performances and events throughout the year. Office facilities are also provided for a range of arts organisations.

Toynbee Studios has 6 spaces for hire ranging from the intimate to larger high-spec dance and theatre studios. Requests for public events will be reviewed alongside Artsadmin's artistic policy. Spaces are usually hired daily/weekly Monday-Friday 10am-6pm. Occasional evening and weekend hires are available on request.

Artsadmin was founded in 1979 and has been based at Toynbee Studios since 1995. Artsadmin produces bold and inventive art, touring it to audiences across the UK and around the world. They also work to support artists at all stages of their careers with advice mentoring and bursaries.

Tristan Bates Theatre

1A Tower Street, London WC2H 9NP
tel 020 3841 6611 (box office); 020 3841 6610 (for show submissions)

Theatre

email tbt@actorscentre.co.uk
website www.tristanbatestheatre.co.uk
Theatre Programme Manager Will Mytum

The Tristan Bates Theatre (TBT), established in 1994, is an acclaimed, intimate studio theatre in the heart of the West End, with a commitment to showcasing and supporting the best new contemporary theatre and new writing alongside regional and international touring work. The artistic policy reflects the mission of the Actors Centre to provide a home for artists' continuing professional development, with the TBT providing a launchpad for performers to develop their craft and careers to the next step.

Black box studio theatre has a maximum capacity of 75; end-on and thrust configurations are possible. Stage space approx 6.4 x 6.2m. Air conditioned.

Hire rates: main shows: programmed in quarterly seasons. Weekly rental ranges from £1,200 to £3,000 depending on exclusivity rights (includes get-in/get-out times, basic tech support and venue marketing/box office services), though rental/deal varies during festivals and in-house events. Daytime hires for showcases/readings/seminars/film screening are available on top of/around evening performances; approx. £450 for a 10am–5pm day, not including tech support. Monday evenings are sometimes available for one-off performances around main shows. Festivals include the Camden Fringe (August). The building also houses the John Thaw Studio, a small flexible space used for scratch performances and previews, and home to the John Thaw Initiative, a seasonal programme which offers curated support for work-in-progress pieces on a financially risk-free deal. Further submission info is available online.

Union Theatre
204 Union Street, Southwark, London SE1 0LX
tel 020 7261 9876 *fax* 020 7261 9876
email sasha@uniontheatre.freeserve.co.uk
website www.uniontheatre.freeserve.co.uk

Primarily a new writing venue, the theatre aims to present a diverse programme featuring the best new talent. Guest performances are supplemented by regular in-house productions. Normally offers 3-week runs.

Upstairs at the Gatehouse
The Gatehouse Pub, North Road, London N6 4BD
tel 020 8340 3488
email events@ovationproductions.com
website www.upstairsatthegatehouse.com
Directors John Plews, Katie Plews

Seats 122 (140 in cabaret style). See also the entry for Ovation Productions under *Middle and smaller-scale companies* on page 206.

White Bear Theatre
138 Kennington Park Road, London SE11 4DJ
tel 020 7793 9193

website www.whitebeartheatre.co.uk
Artistic Director Michael Kingsbury

An L-shaped studio space with seating for up to 50. Generally prefers new writing but occasionally accepts revivals.

Wimbledon Studio Theatre
In Wimbledon Theatre, 103 The Broadway, London SW19 1QG
tel 0870 060 6646 (Box Office)
tel 020 8545 7900 (Admin) *fax* 020 8543 6637
email sambain@theambassadors.com
website www.ambassadortickets.com/Wimbledon-Studio

A black box studio theatre with flexible seating for up to 80. Normally offers 1-2 week runs which are programmed 6 months ahead. The auditorium is wheelchair-accessible.

EDINBURGH FESTIVAL FRINGE VENUES

Many of these venues are only available for hire during the Edinburgh Festival Fringe in August. For a full list of venues, see **www.edfringe.com/venues**.

Assembly Rooms
Assembly Theatre, 250 George Street, Edinburgh EH2 2LE
tel 0131 624 2442 *fax* 0131-624 7131
email info@assemblyrooms.com
website www.assemblyrooms.com

The Assembly Rooms have presented more than 1,000 productions featuring most of the major names in British comedy – as well as a huge array of theatre, dance and music events which have been seen by more than 1.5 million people over the last 20 years of the Edinburgh Festival Fringe. The daily programme runs from 11am to 3.30am with exhibitions, a café, 2 public bars and a club bar. Aims to programme a balance of theatre, comedy and new work.

Augustine's
Augustine United Church, 41 George IV Bridge, Edinburgh EH1 1EL
tel 0131 220 1677

During the rest of the year this venue is known as Augustine United Church. It is adapted during the Festival to house 2 performance spaces (the upper venue seats 110; the lower venue seats approximately 105). Programmes theatre, musicals, dance and children's theatre from the UK and elsewhere.

Bedlam Theatre
11B Bristo Place, Edinburgh EH1 1EZ
tel 0131 225 9873

email info@bedlamtheatre.co.uk
website www.bedlamtheatre.co.uk

A 90-seat black-box theatre in central Edinburgh housed in a neo-gothic church. The theatre is available for hire when not in use by the Edinburgh University Theatre Company.

C venues

(Administration Office): C venues Limited, 5 Alexandra Mansions, Chichele Road, London NW2 3AS
email info@cvenues.com
website www.cvenues.com

C venues programmes and hosts over 200 productions and events at the Edinburgh Fringe each August at multiple venue locations in central Edinburgh. Buildings include original Fringe venues from the first days of the Fringe and some of the newest venues on the Fringe. Alongside a broad theatre-based programme incorporating drama, new writing, physical theatre, musical theatre and children's theatre, C has developed a speciality programming immersive, interactive and site-specific theatre, and in hosting cabaret, circus theatre, performance art and cross-genre work. C's productions have come from and toured around the world, and have won Fringe First, Total Theatre and other awards. C venues is a founder member of Edinburgh's Associated Independent Venue Producers.

Greyfriars (Studios 1 and 2)

Greyfriars Kirk House, 86 Candlemaker Row, Edinburgh EH1 2QA

Studio 1 (upstairs, seats 60) and Studio 2 (seats around 40) are intimate spaces suited to 1- to 3-handers, storytelling or poetry. Applications should be made by February for hire during the Festival Fringe.

Hill Street Theatre

Hill Street Theatre, Universal Arts, 12 Edina Place, Edinburgh EH7 5RP
tel 0131 478 0195
email admin@universal-arts.co.uk

Presents a programme of well-known works alongside new writing, musicals, dance, mime and physical theatre. Theatrical production includes comic writing but not stand-up comedy. The main theatre seats 120 while the studio theatre is a more intimate space, seating a maximum of 60. Suited to 1-handers, the studio can accommodate up to 8 performers comfortably.

The Netherbow Scottish Storytelling Centre

43-45 High Street, Edinburgh EH1 1SR
tel 0131 556 9579

website www.scottishstorytellingcentre.co.uk

Intimate 100-seat theatre presenting drama, poetry, storytelling and puppetry events. Offers a strong programme of family shows. The whole building, being new-build from 2005, is very wheelchair-friendly both for the public and for actors.

The Pleasance

The Pleasance Courtyard: 60 The Pleasance, Edinburgh EH8 9TJ; The Pleasance Dome: 1 Bristo Square, Edinburgh EH8 9AL; The Pleasance Administration Office: Carpenters Mews, North Road, London N7 9EF
tel 020 7619 6868
website www.pleasance.co.uk
Facebook ThePleasance
Twitter @ThePleasance

The Pleasance presents more than 220 shows across 3 sites and 33 venues during the 4 weeks of the Festival Fringe. With more than 500,000 visitors every year, it remains one of the most popular venues of the Fringe, offering a diverse mix of comedy, theatre, dance, music and everything in-between.

Traverse Theatre

10 Cambridge Street, Edinburgh EH1 2ED
email linda.crooks@traverse.co.uk
website www.traverse.co.uk
Executive Producer Linda Crooks

Centre for new plays in Scotland. All-year-round venue in underground purpose-built theatre with 2 auditoria and off-site rehearsal facilities. Has staged many premieres, including work by Stef Smith, Rob Drummond, Gary McNair, David Greig, David Harrower, Rona Munro, Zinnie Harris and Gregory Burke.

The Underbelly

Edinburgh Permanent Office: 26 Frederick Street, Edinburgh EH2 2JR
tel 0131 5102270
email marketing@underbelly.co.uk
website www.underbelly.co.uk
Underbelly Directors Ed Bartlam, Charlie 'wood

Comprises 23 Frnge spaces over 5 sites with multiple bars. Venues cater for audiences of 60-900 with different seating configurations available. Programmes new writing, theatre, dance, circus and comedy.

OTHER FRINGE LOCATIONS

Komedia

44-47 Gardner Street, Brighton BN1 1UN
tel 01273 647101 *fax* 01273 647102
email info@komedia.co.uk
website www.komedia.co.uk

Komedia host around 700 performances of comedy, music, cabaret and kids shows and club nights.

All taking place under one roof, Komedia incorporates two unique performance spaces with flexible set-ups and a kitchen serving freshly prepared food at most seated shows.

Komedia's programme features the international and national performers and includes a unique range of Komedia-grown resident shows such as the *Krater Comedy Club*, *Comic Boom* and *Bent Double*.

Sevenoaks Stag Theatre

London Road, Sevenoaks, Kent TN13 1ZZ
tel 01732 451548
email enquiries@stagesevenoaks.co.uk

The theatre can seat up to 453 and has provision for wheelchair-users. Companies should book the space up to 6 months in advance. Programmes a wide range of theatre and dance events.

Watermans Arts Centre

40 High Street, Brentford, Middlesex TW8 0DS
tel 020 8232 1019
email info@watermans.org.uk
website www.watermans.org.uk

West London's leading arts centre comprising a 236-seat theatre (plus 2 wheelchairs), 121-seat cinema (plus 3 wheelchairs), a gallery and 2 studios, used for rehearsals, workshops and small-scale performances. There is also a restaurant and bar with river views of the Thames. The programmes covers a range of different artforms including cinema, theatre, cabaret, dance, new media arts and participative arts.

Theatre

To fringe, or not to fringe

Simon Dunmore

Although it is generally regarded as 'professional' work, there is a tendency in Fringe productions for professional standards (and facilities) to be somewhat lacking – and that is sometimes an understatement. Poor technical back-up, indifferent front-of-house arrangements and general unreliability are too often the case, almost inevitably damaging the quality of the final product.

Some potential problems to watch out for

• *The ego trip.* A number of productions are set up by individuals wanting a starring vehicle for themselves – much like the old actor-managers. It is generally better to avoid such enterprises unless you can be fairly sure that the central 'ego' will not be damaging to your contribution. Ask around for objective advice before accepting a part in such a production.

• *What else will you have to do?* Will you have to do other things – like paint the set, distribute posters, help with the get-in, and so on? You may think that you can make time to do things like this, but are you sure you want to be thus distracted in the last few days before opening night?

• *Is the script good enough?* There really is no point in doing a production that's flawed before it leaves the page.

• *Can you work well with the director?* This is a highly subjective judgement, but since you are not being properly paid, it is important that you feel as sure as you can be that it'll be a worthwhile experience.

• *Can you actually afford to do it?* There is no point in taking time out from paid work in order to rehearse and perform a Fringe production unless you really think that you'll get something out of the experience. (It can be worth asking if your rehearsal-calls can be arranged around your work commitments.) Also, check whether your participation will affect your benefits in any way.

• *Your agent.* If you have one, will s/he be happy for you to do the production?

• *Contracts.* In 2005, Equity published a set of guidelines (working hours, etc.) and a suggested contract for Fringe producers. This is not intended as an alternative to Equity's other agreements; rather, it is designed to help Fringe companies develop good employment practices. Some companies issue their own contracts; it is important to read these carefully and check with Equity if you have any doubts.

• *Will the production get reviews?* A good review equals good publicity – important for any production. Some productions in the most prestigious venues get reviewed in national newspapers. However, because there are so many productions at any one time, the press has strict rules (length of run, for instance) about what they will send reviewers to. It is important to note that the perceptiveness of some of the latter is somewhat shallow (that's not sour grapes; it's a fact).

• *Will the publicity and marketing be sufficient?* After the cost of hiring the venue, publicity and marketing represent the next major cost of a Fringe production. Too many productions try to skimp on these. In such a competitive environment, they are very, very important.

• *Does the venue have a good reputation?* It is much, much harder to get people into less prestigious ones.

Theatre

• *Promises*. While enthusiasm for a project is wonderful, beware of promises when they seem over-the-top. Too much optimism can blind people to important practical realities.
• *Is it going to be properly organised?* There is far more to putting on a production than most actors realise (see below). Ask questions based on the above and, if you don't feel sufficiently satisfied, politely back away. There is no point in being miserable, as well as unpaid, for several weeks.
• *If I'm not being paid, can I not just pull out if something better comes along?* Legally, you can; morally and professionally it's an extremely dubious thing to do without the full understanding of your fellow participants – and you never know who, among them, might gain 'casting clout' in the future.

Setting up your own production

Too many people think that mounting a production is just a matter of getting a few friends together, borrowing some props and costumes, and getting on with it. What about the costs of hiring a venue, a rehearsal space, the publicity and marketing, the author's royalties (if still in copyright), and so on?

You may be lucky enough to get some, or even all, of these for free, or you might find a rich auntie. But however you fund the above essentials, you have got to do a lot of careful planning before rehearsals start. Will the playwright (and/or translator) allow you to do a production of the play in the first place? Just because a play is in print, it doesn't mean that anyone can perform it. Is the rehearsal room available for enough of the time? What is the deadline for getting the poster design to the printers, so that they can get the result back to you in time for the distributors to get them displayed in good time before opening night? And so on, and so on, and so on ... Oh, and it is essential to plan and budget with contingency in both time and money – there are always several things that take more time than you'd thought, and several things that cost more than you'd thought (or forgotten to budget for in the first place).

Doing it yourself is far more complex than most people realise, but can be incredibly satisfying if you succeed. For a technically simple production you probably need to find at least £5,000 – and that's without paying any of the participants. The chances of recouping this through the box office are very low; the average audience on the Fringe is about 30 per cent. A recent report stated that: "Theatres are among the most over-regulated businesses in the UK." Legal requirements like Health & Safety, VAT and performance rights cannot be neglected.

Note: For interesting discussion on the whole business of working for little or nothing, go to **http://actorsminimumwage.wordpress.com**.

Simon Dunmore has been directing productions for over 30 years – nearly 20 years as a resident director in regional theatres and, more recently, working freelance. In that time there have been over 200 productions (of all styles, colours, shapes and sizes) – recently: several Drama School Showcases, Maugham's *Home and Beauty* and new plays about sex, WB Yeats' up-and-down relationship with Maud Gonne, one set inside a pyramid and another about Bismarck. Past favourites include: *The Promise* (Alexei Arbuzov), *Antigone* (Jean Anouilh), a seven-handed version of *Antony & Cleopatra* and too many others to mention. He also teaches acting and has worked in many drama schools and other training establishments around the country. He has written several books: *An Actor's Guide to Getting Work* (fifth edition, 2012), the *Alternative Shakespeare Auditions* series and was formerly the Consultant Editor for *Actors' Yearbook*.

Edinburgh or bust: is it worth it?

Shane Dempsey

The Edinburgh Festival Fringe was established in 1947 and has grown into one of the world's most renowned and diverse arts festivals. From its humble beginnings as an alternative to the Edinburgh International Festival, the Fringe has continued to increase and multiply, and, despite the growing costs to companies and performers alike, it still remains high on the agenda of many. The Fringe can be incredibly daunting and at times even crippling. My aim is not to shatter you, but to ensure that you are armed with as much knowledge as possible before you decide if it's worth it.

In 2009 there were 2098 shows performed in Edinburgh and an estimated 18,901 performers in 265 venues. These figures give you an idea of the level of competition for audiences during the three weeks of August. This is an aggressive and over-saturated market. In the Fringe environment, the efforts of many go unrewarded and often even unnoticed. So, can you break through with your production?

Evaluate your work honestly and realistically

The first thing to do is evaluate the production itself. Ask yourself, "What is the appeal of my particular production? What is it about my show that will make it stand out from the crowd? Do I have permission from the author or their estate to perform the piece? If so, what percentage of my overall income will this take, and what are the possibilities of extending this performance licence post-Edinburgh?"

If the piece is new writing or devised then there are fewer issues with performance rights, but it is crucial to discuss billing and authorship, as these can potentially cause problems later. Circumstances change, so with new work it is essential to secure written agreement over the intellectual copyright of the piece – and this also extends to directorial concepts and vision. Get it down on paper so you always know where you stand and can avoid or deal with any issues that may arise.

As well as fledgling companies taking new work to Edinburgh, the festival is also a testing ground for many established, heavyweight companies and producers. They have years of experience, and they have the economic power to invest large sums in PR and marketing. So ask yourself what will bring an audience to your venue, and why. The reality is that you are in direct competition with these established companies as well as with the other thousands who are newer to the game.

Choose the right venue

There are many venues associated with the Fringe. You need to be clear about the kind of work they are interested in programming; some are very specific as to their requirements, while others have a broader remit. Consider not only the price, but also the reputation and the location of a venue, as they vary considerably.

Your time slot is another point of negotiation: late evenings tend to be dominated by comedy, and a great deal of theatre now plays during the day and late afternoon. A general rule is that the more established venues have the best reputations and tend to charge significantly more for their services than smaller, up-and-coming venues. All venues will require you to sign a contract, and you need to be aware of the small print, as it has been known for companies to skim over this only to discover that they were not aware of all the terms and conditions.

Consider venue costs and other expenses

Many venues offer either a box-office split or ask for a flat fee. Almost all will require a deposit in advance. The average cost of mounting a production in Edinburgh is £8,0-00–10,000, and deposits will often be required months in advance – so unless you have access to sufficient funds, consider seriously if there is a more cost-effective way of getting your work out there.

And there are other expenses, including music performance rights, public liability insurance and VAT. Accommodation costs soar during the festival, and local landlords take advantage of the influx of artists and tourists, but if you're organised it is possible to secure a deal by booking early. Many companies choose to stay in Glasgow, which is an hour-long commute, but the time and energy required to do this needs to be weighed up against the convenience and cost of staying in Edinburgh.

What do you want from the experience?

Ask yourself early on what you want to achieve out of the experience. Too often this is not given enough thought, so that it is difficult, if not impossible, to achieve any significant outcomes. Remember that Edinburgh is a massive arts market, and that within any market you need to be specific about your audience – be it the general public or producers who can potentially remount your work post-Edinburgh.

If you want a London transfer, regional tour or international tour, target your promotions pack specifically to relevant individuals and always research their programming tastes. Invite them to the show, ensure that they are given complimentary tickets and try to set up a meeting after they have seen your work. Many international producers are seeking work that would be programmed two to three years after the festival, so you have to have a long-term plan for the production and ensure that it has the necessary factors that will support its longevity.

Network!

Many deals in Edinburgh are set up over late-night drinks and midnight meetings, often to fit in with the schedules of producers who are seeing work all day long. They can be fairly informal, but keeping your professional hat on is essential to any success. There are incredible opportunities to meet new people in Edinburgh, and there are numerous events specifically aimed towards networking, including the Producers' Breakfast.

In addition you can take part in a range of informal activities in which you can make connections that may lead to future work and collaborations. This is often triggered by seeing a company's work: the research trip I made recently to Russia to investigate ensemble practice has been greatly aided by contacts I met in Edinburgh. The key to any networking is to find the common links between you and the other practitioner, and then to develop them into a cohesive relationship. Be honest about what you do and why you do it, and people will usually respond positively.

Press officers have essential contacts with the media and could be a valuable asset to your production. They can not guarantee that your work will be reviewed, but having a person working on your behalf can give you a major advantage over the competition. If, like many companies, you are bringing the show to Edinburgh on a very tight budget, allocate one member of the company to be the designated press officer as this makes life a lot easier for all parties. Again, reputation means a lot in the world of the press and some papers will hold more influence than others. Target the ones that you believe will be interested in your work and be sure to read the reviews every day to get a flavour of what the festival has to offer.

Design, marketing, and word-of-mouth

In a market such as the Fringe, the role of good graphic design and web design is often overlooked, but it is essential to ensure that your work is seen – and seen at its best. Ensure that your production pack has strong imagery. The old cliché of a picture painting a thousand words still rings true, especially to overtired editors at the busiest time of their year. The array of flyers that are seen on the streets of Edinburgh is mind-boggling, but eye-catching design can really aid your marketing campaign.

Over and above marketing, however, is word-of-mouth – one of the key influences in persuading people to see your show. Such recommendations are difficult to achieve, and are dependent on your getting healthy, happy audiences early in your run. The majority of companies spend their days marketing their work, sending emails, chasing the press and leafleting: this is the Fringe, and if you're not prepared to do this to the point of exhaustion, stay at home!

For inclusion in the much-coveted Fringe Brochure you will be asked to submit 50 words of copy to describe your production. Keep it simple and clear, and remember that you are going to have to live with this for the life of your show in Edinburgh, so make sure it really sums your work up. It can be useful to have a quote in there from previous work – after all, everybody wants to see a show from a five-star company – but if it's not true, don't claim it to be so! Fabrication rarely, if ever, helps. The Fringe website provides comprehensive guidelines on producing work in Edinburgh: see **www.edfringe.com/take-part**. The information is there if you look for it, so take the time to investigate. It could save you much stress and money.

Dreams can come true ...

The likelihood of your company or show being picked up for a transfer or tour is extremely slim. The financial burden on companies is very high, and you have to weigh this up against the potential exposure and the possibility of gaining other work after the festival. There has been a recent rise in smaller fringe festivals happening outside of the main Fringe, partially in response to its overtly commercial nature. Notably, the Free Fringe and the Big Red Door are proving to be hugely popular and offer far better deals to the artists. Fragments' production of *The Bay* by Hannah Burke was performed at the Big Red Door, Te-Pooka; we also managed to be seen by representatives of the Traverse, Manchester International Festival, and were transferred into London's prestigious Theatre 503. So yes, dreams can come true ... but only after a serious amount of hard graft, and no little luck too.

Shane Dempsey trained as a director at E15 Acting School and runs Fragments, an international ensemble of theatre and video artists (fragments.ie). His work has been staged in Ireland, London, Scotland and Belgium. In 2008 he filmed the groundbreaking documentary *Mothers of Modern Ireland*. His production of *The Bay* toured extensively in 2009, and he is currently preparing to stage a new adaptation by Hannah Burke of Mikhail Bulgakov's *The Master & Margarita*. He has strong Russian connections, and was invited to observe rehearsals by Lev Dodin of the Maly Theatre of St Petersburg in Paris, November 2009 as well as observing acting workshops at GITIS and Vakhtangov Institute, Moscow 2010.

Theatre

Open Book: fairer finances for fringe theatre

Piers Beckley

What is 'Open Book Theatre'?

Most fringe theatre productions don't make a profit. And as a large number of fringe productions offer only a profit-share as financial recompense for the actors performing in them, this can be a big problem.

Something that can be especially galling for an actor is to perform in front of a house filled with people, and still not receive any money at the end of the run because the production hasn't made a profit. But if half of those tickets are paper to fill the house in early shows in order to help word of mouth, then the number of people that you see in the audience may not give an accurate measure of how much money is actually coming in.

If the tickets were priced too low, or the producer failed to get a good deal on the advertising, or any number of other things, it's very easy for a production to make a loss. And without financial transparency throughout the process, there can always be the niggling suspicion that something, somewhere, has gone horribly wrong that need not have.

By its nature, fringe theatre will never have as much money to spend on props, print, advertising, design, or on actors as a fully professional production. But if a company can't provide the cold hard cash which we all desire, the very least that they can provide is transparency in recording what money goes in and comes out, so that everything is fair and above board, and is seen to be so.

Open Book Theatre is a new way of running the financial books for a fringe production, so that every member of the cast and crew can see the business of putting on a show. In an Open Book production, the budget is viewable by anyone involved – from first draft through to final income statements. This means that as well as knowing that they've been treated fairly throughout the entire process, everyone will be able to see how the production is doing – and, if all goes well, exactly how much of the profit-share pot they'll receive when the money comes in from the theatre.

Open Book Management is a set of techniques that have been used by companies across the world over the last 30 years. It's all about giving the people involved a stake in the outcome, and then giving them the tools to affect what that outcome is. In a business environment, the stake is most often shares in the company, while in Open Book Theatre (at least at the fringe level) it usually consists of a portion of the profit from the show.

What does Open Book Management involve?

Free access and exchange

There are three main points at the heart of an Open Book production:
• Free access to all financial information
• Regular updates on changes
• Listening to suggestions and implementing them

So how would you go about bringing this to life?

One of the easiest ways of sharing information is to use budget spreadsheets showing estimated outgoings and income, which are later updated as the real figures come in. These spreadsheets can be placed on a password-protected website, or emailed to the cast and crew every week to show exactly how much money has come in and gone out.

Because the budgets are available for all to see, as well as knowing exactly where the money has gone on advertising, design, print – all of the things that are necessary to a production, but which generally don't cross an actor's desk – then everyone involved can help suggest improvements.

Perhaps someone has a photographer friend who'll be able to take publicity shots in exchange for a credit or a lower fee. Or perhaps they will know a way to get the fabric needed by a costume designer more cheaply. If everyone knows the cost of the things that make up a production, and how those will affect the profits, then they can suggest ways to make things better for all.

As the financial spreadsheets are regularly updated throughout the show, then everyone involved can see the clock ticking towards breakeven – that magical moment when income from sales and advertising rises above what's been spent on the production, and everyone knows that they're going to be taking some money home with them. It's also nice to be able to celebrate when your production reaches a milestone – for example, when half-way to breaking even.

As well as making the budget documents visible to all, an Open Book production will ensure that all of the documents that are legally required are on display: the insurance schedule, health and safety policy, venue contract, and risk assessment documents. Seeing this information proves that you're dealing with a professional company and a professional production – not just one person's vanity project.

Fair profit-share: the 'tronc system'

In a fringe production, the final part of the Open Book story comes with the division of the profit-share pot. After all costs have been paid (and everyone will know what they are, because they can look at the income and expenditure of the show at any point throughout the production), then any gross profits can be divided between those who brought the show to life.

One way of doing this fairly and equitably is to use what's known as a tronc system, based on the tips system used in many bars and restaurants. In a tronc, everyone involved in the production is allocated a certain number of points depending upon their involvement. So the director and writer might have two points each, while each member of the ensemble cast has one point. It's important to be up front about how any profits will be divided – for example, if the star of the show is to receive more points than the other actors.

After the gross profit has been worked out, the value of each point can be derived by simply dividing the profit by the total number of points – and then everyone is paid that amount for each point that they have.

Control and visibility for everyone involved

Taken all together, these practices mean that everyone involved in a show can see exactly where the money flows from and to, and can be assured of the honesty and integrity of everybody involved in the process.

Theatre

While some producers have been known to say that their books are open if the financial information for the production is published at the end of the show – or even the end of the year – that's not going to help the members of the production get involved. As well as the honesty of the system, Open Book Theatre relies on helping everyone to see the implications of creative decisions, and that means they need to be able to see what's going on throughout the course of production – not just take a look at a spreadsheet at the end.

The Open Book model, especially at the level of fringe theatre, shouldn't be seen as an attempt in any way to replace an Equity contract, which we would always recommend using. What Open Book Theatre should do, though, is provide some protection for actors working in those profit-share productions which currently are not in a position to use Equity contracts.

Running your productions on the Open Book model means more control and visibility for everyone involved, ensuring that you can be confident that things are under control – or, at least, as under control as they get.

Hopefully within ten years the question won't be, 'What is Open Book Theatre?', but rather, 'Why did we ever do things differently?'

Piers Beckley is a writer and producer. He's been a production manager, stage manager, project manager, line manager, extra, actor, web producer, copywriter, interviewer, sub-editor, video editor, and director. Writing credits include *The Treason Show, NewsRevue, Week Ending, Splendid, Spooks Interactive*, and acclaimed productions of *A Christmas Carol* and *Oliver Twist* for the Lion and Unicorn Theatre. He produced *The Just So Stories* and *Hans Christian Andersen's Fairy Tales* for Red Table at the Pleasance Theatre. You can generally find out what he's up to at his website **fatpigeons.com** or on Twitter as @piersb.

Children's, young people's and theatre in education

Paul Harman

Work in this very large sector of employment for actors in the UK varies greatly – both in the style of theatre created and presented, and in the wages and conditions offered by employers. Anyone taking work in the field should always be clear about the aims and status of their prospective employer.

Most producing theatres offer plays for young audiences as part of a season, and Christmas shows and pantomimes are mounted by a large number of receiving theatres and commercial touring companies. Some 200 independent touring companies regularly present original theatre productions, usually in schools, reaching a total audience of at least five million annually. Smaller touring companies may operate for profit, or as profit-share partnerships. Companies which are members of ITC (Independent Theatre Council) offer pay and conditions agreed with the performers' trade union, Equity.

Reality check

There is no official agency that collects reliable statistics or regulates the quality of what is offered. Your work may never be publicly reviewed – and it can be hard and demanding. Casts are often small, and living conditions on the road are sometimes difficult. The work may involve a lot of driving (if you are over 25 and insurable) as well as humping sets in and out of vans. However, the rewards for good-quality work conscientiously presented lie in the warmth of welcome from audiences and bookers alike, and a directness and openness of audience response which is often less evident at more formal, adult-orientated theatre events. In schools, you will perform in daylight, very close to children – so it helps if you like them. They can see every blemish on you, and you can see every reaction on a hundred faces.

You will need physical stamina; the ability to play many parts convincingly; and the facility to hit a peak of performance two or more times in a day, six days a week. You may need skill in playing a musical instrument. In addition, other aptitudes may be called upon. A play may be preceded or followed by workshop activity with young people – from 'hot-seating' in character to involving children in a performance. An understanding of drama education techniques is therefore an advantage, and experience of Youth Theatre useful.

What shows?

For good economic and marketing reasons, most theatre for children presented in larger houses is based on well-known stories by established authors, or on characters from TV shows. Companies may receive financial support from official agencies to present plays on health and social issues. Plays related to the National Curriculum, such as science topics, are in great demand from schools.

Theatre in Education (TIE) is a term commonly used to mean many kinds of theatre in schools. In the strict sense, TIE implies an extended theatre event, combining performance and participatory elements and designed to engage pupils in exploring their own

Theatre

knowledge, feelings and attitudes. This is quite a different process from explaining how magnets work, or presenting an account of an historical event. Very few companies nowadays can afford the time and staffing needed to support real TIE, but there are many opportunities to create and present challenging educational plays on a wide variety of subjects.

Independent touring companies receiving public subsidy from Arts Councils in England, Wales, Scotland and Northern Ireland generally aim to present original, commissioned drama. A small group of writers specialises in this field, addressing personal and social topics, from fear of the dark or the break-up of families to genetics and migration. This group of companies – whose aims are primarily artistic, rather than just to entertain or deliver educational messages – find like-minded companies in 70 countries through ASSITEJ (International Association of Theatre for Children and Young People). Overseas tours and international collaborations are increasing.

Above all, don't look upon this field as an easy step towards something else. Your first experiences may well be tough, but an apprenticeship served with a supportive company will open an area of work that you can return to with growing enjoyment and professional satisfaction.

Paul Harman has worked as an actor and director in professional theatre since 1963. He joined Belgrade Theatre in Education team in 1966, headed Education work at Liverpool Everyman from 1970, and founded Merseyside Young People's Theatre Company in 1978. In 1994 he became Artistic Director of CTC Theatre, Darlington and is now the Chair of TYA (Theatre for Young Audiences) – the UK Centre of ASSITEJ.

Children's, young people's and theatre-in-education companies

Notes:
• Some of the companies listed are members of the Independent Theatre Council (ITC) – **www.itc-arts.org**.
• The Criminal Records Bureau (CRB) is now called the Disclosure and Barring Service (DBS); CRB checks are now termed DBS checks.

Action Transport Theatre
Whitby Hall, Stanney Lane, Ellesmere Port, Cheshire CH65 9AE
tel 0151 357 2120 *fax* 0151 356 4057
email info@actiontransporttheatre.org
website www.actiontransporttheatre.org
Artistic Director Nina Hajiyianni

Production details: "A new writing company creating brave, collaborative theatre for, by and with young people." Stages 3 projects annually, with around 60 performances in 10 venues including schools, arts centres, theatres and community venues across the UK. In general 4-5 actors go on tour, playing to family (5+) and adult audiences. Incoming actors should have singing, musical instrument and physical theatre skills, and may be expected to lead workshops. Recent productions include: *My Mother Told Me Not to Stare*, *10 Tiny Plays* and *Four for the Port*.

Casting procedures: Holds general auditions and actors may write at any time to request inclusion. Casting breakdowns are available from the website, by postal application (with sae), through Equity Job Information Service and Casting Call Pro, and in *The Stage*. Welcomes letters (with CVs and photographs) from individual actors previously unknown to the company, sent by post or email. Will consider invitations to view individual actors' websites. Offers Equity-approved contracts as negotiated through ITC. Actively encourages applications from disabled actors, and promotes the use of inclusive casting.

Actionwork Creative Arts
Ground Floor, 6 The Centre, Weston-super-Mare, North Somerset BS23 1US
mobile 01934 815163
email admin@actionwork.com
website www.actionwork.com

Production details: Actionwork is a theatre and film company that seeks to promote empowerment and reduce bullying and violence in schools. They are committed to producing work through a number of different mediums in order to promote understanding of youth conflict and violence. 3 recent productions include: *Million a Week* (2013),

Theatre

Out of the Box (2013) *Cyber Tears* (2014), *Power For Good* (2015), *Silent Scream* (2016) and *CYBER* (2017). Winner of the Anti-Bullying Flame Award.

Each production consists of 3 actors and, on average, the company present 6-10 productions per year to audiences aged between 4 and 17. This equates to over 300 performances at over 150 venues across the UK, ranging from schools to community spaces, art centres and churches. Cast members are sometimes expected to lead workshops and activity sessions and it is advantageous for them to have a driving licence and some singing and dancing ability.

Casting procedures: Uses in-house casting directors and holds general auditions during September. Casting breakdowns are available through PCR and Bristol Online. Welcomes both CVs and letters from actors previously unknown to the company and unsolicited CVs and photographs. These should be sent via email. Also welcomes invitations to view individual actors' websites, but does not welcome showreels. Actively encourages applications from disabled actors.

Aesop's Touring Theatre Company

The Arches, 38 The Riding, Woking, Surrey GU21 5TA
tel 01483 724633 *mobile* 07836 731872
email info@aesopstheatre.co.uk
website www.aesopstheatre.co.uk
Director Karen Brooks

Production details: Established in 1999, a professional Theatre in Education company specialising in National Curriculum based plays for the nursery and primary age range. Tours extensively on a daily basis performing interactive plays and associated drama workshops. Plays are mostly performed in schools but also embrace theatres, community centres, village halls, arts centres and party venues. On average stages 300 performances each year, in 225 venues across London, in the Home Counties and further afield. 2 actors usually go on tour, plus occasionally a driver or stage manager. Applicants should be fit, versatile all-round actors and must have their own transport to easily reach bases in Weybridge or Woking, Surrey for very early morning starts. Applicants will be expected to drive the company estate car. A current DBS is essential.

Casting procedures: Auditions are held in May and actors may write in at any time: 'We reply to all enquiries'.

Arty-Fact Theatre Co.

27 Mount Drive, Nantwich CW5 6JG
tel 01270 627990
email yvonne@arty-fact.co.uk
website www.arty-fact.co.uk
Artistic Director Yvonne Peacock *Co-director* Brian Twiddy

Production details: Has been performing in schools since 1993, running history workshops, original plays and classics. Performs 6-7 projects annually, with an average annual total of 500-600 performances in 200-300 schools across England. In general 2-4 actors go on tour and perform to audiences aged 7-18. Physical theatre skills and a driving licence are required. Actors may be expected to lead workshops. Recent productions include: *The Time Capsule 1914*, *A Christmas Box* and *Let's Eat Grandma*.

Casting procedures: Holds general auditions twice a year; actors are advised to write in April and July to request inclusion. Casting breakdowns are available via the website, Equity Job Information Service, and Castcall. Welcomes letters (with CVs and photographs) from individual actors previously unknown to the company sent by post or email.

Big Wheel Theatre in Education

PO Box 18221, London EC1R 4WJ
tel 020 7689 8670
email info@bigwheel.org.uk
website www.bigwheel.org.uk
Artistic Directors Roland Allen, Jeni Williams

Production details: Since 1984 has developed interactive theatre for use in education and training in the UK and abroad. Normally tours 15 projects each year, with an average annual total of 500 performances and 250 different venues. Venues include schools, universities, conferences and training centres across the UK and Europe. In general 2 actors go on tour and play to audiences aged 7 upwards. Actors are required to hold a driving licence and to lead workshops. Experience in teaching or training is also useful. Recent productions include: *Introduction to Shakespeare*, a gameshow-based interactive workshop; *Breakfast with Big Wheel,* a show to teach English abroad; *Go! Go! Go!*, a show about sustainable transport; and shows in French and Spanish: *Voulez Vous?!* and *Siesta Fiesta!* Also presents a variety of workshops for the NHS and university postgrads about communication, service improvement, and presentation skills.

Casting procedures: Sometimes holds general auditions; actors may write at any time requesting inclusion. "Best to have a good look at the website. Particularly interested in performers with fluent French and Spanish."

Big Wooden Horse (UK) Ltd

30 Northfield Road, London W13 9SY
tel 020 8567 8431
email info@bigwoodenhorse.com
website www.bigwoodenhorse.com
Artistic Director Adam Bampton-Smith

Production details: Aims to present high-quality theatre to younger audiences across the UK and to represent the best of British theatre craft abroad. Strives both to entertain and to inform young people, drawing from different cultures and traditions. On average 3 actors tour 3 projects annually, with 400 performances at around 80 venues including arts centres and theatres in the UK, US, Canada and the Far East. Audiences range from 2 to 8 years. Recent productions include: *Aliens Love Underpants, STUCK, The Way Back Home, Don't Let the Pigeon Drive the Bus!* and *The Night Before Christmas*.

Casting procedures: Casting breakdowns are available from Spotlight, Castnet and Castcall. Welcomes approaches from actors previously unknown to the company, sent by email only.

Bitesize Theatre Company
8 Green Meadows, New Broughton, Wrexham LL11 6SG
tel 01978 358320 *fax* 01978 756308
email casting@bitesizetheatre.co.uk
website www.bitesizetheatre.co.uk
Artistic Director Linda Griffiths

Production details: Founded in 1992, the company strives to provide high-quality, entertaining theatrical productions for young people, from children's classics to Shakespeare and pantomime to new works. Also runs Theatre in Education projects and bespoke workshops across the UK. The company performs in schools and community venues across the Northwest. Rehearsals take place in North Wales. Between 3-6 actors work on each show and play to audiences aged 3-19 years. Actors are required to be able to sing, dance and drive and may also be expected to participate in workshops. Recent productions include: *Robin Hood, Aladdin, Snow White* and *Sleeping Beauty*.

Casting procedures: The company holds general auditions; actors requesting inclusion in these should write in July. Casting breakdowns are available from Spotlight and Castcall. Happy to receive email enquiries to **casting@bitesizetheatre.co.uk**. Mainly takes actors from recognised drama schools; actors aged over 25 years are preferred for jobs requiring driving. All employees must pass a DBS (Disclosure and Barring Service) check for work with children. Offers non-Equity contracts. Actively encourages applications from disabled actors and promotes the use of inclusive casting.

Blue Moon Theatre Company
20 Sandpiper Road, Blakespool Park, Bridgewater, Somerset TA6 5QU
tel 01278 458253
email info@bluemoontheatre.co.uk
website www.bluemoontheatre.co.uk
Company Manager Steve Apelt *Artistic Director* Kerrie Seymour *Writer* Mark Scott-Ison

Production details: A producing "fun-packed" children's theatre with lots of participation and involvement – mainly incorporating workshops and after-show discussions. Stages on average 2-3 projects annually. In general 4 actors go on tour, staging around 50 performances for young audiences at 40

UK venues including schools, arts centres, theatres, outdoor and community venues. Singing and physical theatre skills are required, as well as a clean driving licence.

Casting procedures: Sometimes holds general auditions, with casting breakdowns publicly available. Welcomes letters (with CVs and photographs) from individual actors previously unknown to the company, sent by post or email. Also welcomes showreels, and invitations to view individual actors' websites. Offers Equity-approved contracts. Actively encourages applications from disabled actors and promotes the use of inclusive casting.

Blue Star Productions
7-8 Shaldon Mansions, 132 Charing Cross Road, London WC2H 0LA
tel 020 7836 6220/4128 *fax* 020 7836 2949
email Hopkinstacey@aol.com

Production details: Blue Star Productions specialises in first-class children's musicals and Songbook Concerts. These shows tour theatres nationally. They include 8-10 performers, beautiful costumes and scenery, and always feature 'live' music. Recent productions include: *The Wonderful Wizard of Oz, The Adventures of Pinocchio, Tales from the Jungle Book, Alice in Wonderland, Snow White and the Seven Dwarfs* and many others. Songbook Concerts include at least 4 singers, depending on venue and finance. One-man shows include: *Life Upon the Very Wicked Stage*, an audience with Barrie Stacey. Barrie Stacey and Blue Star Productions were voted Best Children's Show Producer of the Year 2009 and 2010 at the *Encore Magazine* Theatre Awards.

Casting procedures: All casting is done in-house through Blue Star Associates, also at the above address. Holds general auditions annually, or for specific productions. Welcomes letters with CVs and photographs, and also email submissions.

Box Clever Theatre Company
@ The Oval House Theatre, 52-54 Kennington Oval, London SE11 5SW
tel 020 7793 0040 *fax* 020 7357 8188
email admin@boxclevertheatre.com
website www.boxclevertheatre.com
Artistic Director Michael Wicherek

Production details: Founded in 1996, the company produces contemporary theatre for young people: new plays, contemporary adaptations of classic texts, and issue-based and educational work. 6 major national tours are staged each year with an average annual total of approximately 600 performances in 500 different venues. The company performs to more than 60,000 young people every year. Venues include arts centres, theatres, and educational and community venues nationwide. Approximately 3 actors are involved in each production. Recent productions include: *Time for the Good Looking Boy* (for theatres); *The Buzz, Driving Ms Daisy, The Hate Plays* and *Boxed Macbeth* (for secondary schools); and *Car Story* for primary schools.

Casting procedures: Does not use freelance casting directors. Casting breakdowns are available via Equity Job Information Service and the website (normally June/July and October/November). Welcomes submissions (with CVs and photographs) from actors previously unknown to the company if sent by post and if in response to casting breakdowns only. Advises actors that the company receives a huge response to advertisements, and is therefore unable to return photographs or respond in writing to applicants not invited to audition. Non-Equity contracts "in line with ITC". Considers applications from disabled actors to play characters with disabilities.

Brief Candle Theatre

Oaker View, Wenslees, Darley Bridge, Matlock, Derbyshire DE4 2JZ
tel 01629 735576
email office@briefcandle.co.uk
website www.briefcandle.co.uk
Artistic Director David Shimwell *Writer/Director* Paul Whitfield

Production details: Established in 2002. Produces high-quality Theatre in Education and theatre for young people and family audiences. On average performs 5 projects each year, with 450 performances in 100 venues including schools, colleges, theatres, community venues and occasionally outdoor performances and festivals. Areas covered: Derbyshire, South Yorkshire, Lincolnshire and Wigan. On average 4 actors go on tour, playing to audiences aged 11 to adult. "We seek to work with actors who are committed to working with young people, and who have the skills required to build fast, effective working relationships with company and audience." Actors may be required to lead workshops. Recent productions include: *The Tower* – a play looking at domestic abuse and power in relationships; *Tight* – a play for 14 year-olds, looking at use and misuse of alcohol; *An Evening with Mallet and Ming* – a dark comedy for adults and older children, set in a Victorian Music Hall; and *No Place for Dreams* – a family show for the Edinburgh Festival.

Casting procedures: Holds general auditions and actors may write in at any time; the company keeps all submissions for consideration. Casting details are available via Spotlight Link and from the website. Prefers email applications. An approved Manager member of the ITC; all contracts are ITC Equity-approved. Encourages applications from all actors, regardless of ability or disability, and promotes the use of inclusive casting.

C&T

University College Worcester, Henwick Grove, Worcester WR2 6AJ

tel 01905 855436
email info@candt.org
website www.candt.org
Artistic Director Paul Sutton

Production details: Founded in 1988. A theatre company incorporating performance, learning and digital media. Works in schools, colleges and universities in the UK and across Europe. Normally tours 2-3 projects each year with an average annual total of 50-100 performances at 50-100 different venues. In general 2-3 actors go on tour and play to audiences aged 5-65. Dance/physical theatre skills, proficiency with computers and digital media, and a driving licence are required. Actors are also expected to lead workshops. Recent productions include: *Living Newspaper.com*, a docu-drama project online for schools.

Casting procedures: Sometimes holds general auditions; actors should write in September requesting inclusion. Accepts submissions (with CVs and photographs) from actors previously unknown to the company sent by post or email. Will also accept showreels and invitations to view individual actors' websites.

Cahoots NI

109-113 Royal Avenue, Belfast BT1 1FF
tel 028 9043 4349
email info@cahootsni.com
website www.cahootsni.com
Facebook www.facebook.com/CahootsNI
Twitter @CahootsNI
Artistic Director Paul Bosco Mc Eneaney

Production details: Creates world-class theatre for young audiences. Aims to expand the imagination of children, and to stimulate their artistic creativity through the visual potential of theatre and the age-old popularity of music, magic and illusion. Tours productions to schools, respite centres, councils, arts centres and theatres both nationally and internationally. Actors should have singing, musical instrument, physical theatre, circus and magic skills, and are sometimes required to lead workshops. Recent projects include: *Under the Hawthorn Tree, Milo's Hat Trick, Penguins, Shh! We Have a Plan, Nivelli's War, Egg, Danny Carmo's Mathematical Mysteries, The Incredible Book Eating Boy, Duck, Death and the Tulip* and *The Snail and the Whale.*

Casting procedures: Sometimes holds general auditions; actors may write at any time to request inclusion. Welcomes letters (with CVs and photographs) from actors previously unknown to the company sent by post or email, and is happy to receive showreels. Does not welcome invitations to view individual actors' websites. Actively promotes the use of inclusive casting.

Changing Faces Theatre Company

PO Box 57877, London SE26 9AN
tel 020 8776 8706 *fax* 020 8778 4079

Theatre

email info@changingfacestheatre.com
website www.changingfacestheatre.com
Artistic Director Nicholas Kessler

Production details: A not-for-profit theatre company that is young, vibrant and ready to bring the highest quality of interactive, literacy-based theatre and workshops to primary-aged children. With classroom experience, a passion for language, a little bit of glue and a lot of imagination, Changing Faces was formed as a direct response to the challenges of teaching literacy in the classroom in the 21st Century. On average stages 6-10 projects per year, with around 300 performances and 250 workshops in 100-150 schools, community venues, theatres and libraries in London and the South East. In general, 2 actors perform an interactive, audience-actor collaborative show and /or workshop, working with audiences aged 4-11. Musical instrument, vocal and physical theatre skills are required, as is a clean driving licence. Puppetry, workshop skillls and classroom experience are an advantage.

Casting procedures: Sometimes holds general auditions. Casting breakdowns are available via Spotlight. Rarely or never has the opportunity to cast disabled actors.

The Children's Touring Partnership

2nd Floor, National House, 60-66 Wardour Street, London W1F 0TA
tel 020 7292 8896
email info@childrenstouringpartnership.com
website www.childrenstouringpartnership.com

Production details: Established in 2010. Stages 1-2 productions annually, with around 60 performances in 12 large and mid-scale theatres UK-wide. In general 12 actors are involved in each production. Recent productions include: *Goodnight Mister Tom* and *Swallows & Amazons*.

Casting procedures: Uses freelance casting directors. Does not welcome unsolicited approaches from actors previously unknown to the company, but will consider visiting other productions, and accepts invitations to view actors' websites. Actively encourages applications from disabled actors.

Creaking Door Productions

Rhys Jones House, St Peter's School, Harefield, Lympstone, Devon EX8 5AU
tel 01395 264877
email office@creakingdoor.co.uk
website www.creakingdoor.co.uk
Artistic Director Tom Sherman

Production details: Established in 2005. Specialises in small-scale children's theatre productions in schools and venues throughout the South West; in 2010 the company implemented its new Education Programme. Stages 2-4 productions annually with around 40 performances. In general 2-4 actors go on tour, playing to audiences aged 4 to 13, plus family

audiences. Incoming actors should have singing and good basic movement skills, as well as a current driving licence. Actors may be expected to lead workshops. Recent productions include: *Cindarella*; *The Life and Times of Isambard Kingdom Brunel*; KS2 History workshops – *From Time to Time*; *Just So Stories*; *Frogs, Kings and Golden Wings*; *Tales of Bread and Golden Thread* and *Beauty and the Beast*.

Casting procedures: Sometimes holds general auditions; actors may write in July and October to request inclusion. Casting breakdowns are available from the website, via Equity, and from Theatre Bristol and Theatre Devon. Welcomes letters (with CVs and photographs) from individual actors previously unknown to the company, sent by post only. Rarely or never has the opportunity to cast disabled actors.

Cwmni Theatr Arad Goch

Stryd Y Baddon, Aberystwyth, Ceredigion SY23 2NN
tel 01970 617998 *fax* 01970 611223
email post@aradgoch.org
website www.aradgoch.cymru
Facebook www.facebook.com/aradgoch
Twitter @AradGoch
Artistic Director Jeremy Turner

Production details: Founded in 1989. Main focus of work is theatre. Normally tours 6 projects each year with an average annual total of 200 performances and more than 100 different venues. Venues include schools, theatres and community venues across Wales and occasionally abroad. In general 3-6 actors go on tour and play to audiences of all ages. Singing ability, proficiency with a musical instrument, fluency in Welsh and a driving licence are required. Actors may also be expected to lead workshops. Recent productions include: *SXTO*, a performance for secondary school pupils written by Bethan Gwanas; *Cysgu'n Brysur*, an ambitious, large-scale musical drama; *Diwrnod Hyfryd Sali Mani*, a Welsh-language stage play for 3-7-year-olds and families based on Mary Vaughan Jones's classic, timeless characters; *Hola!*, the story of Welsh emigration to Patagonia 150 years ago; *King Hit*, the story of two boys at a party — where a bit of fun escaltaes into a fight with serious consequences. The company also performed works from their repertoire at various venues in Europe. Offers ITC/Equity-approved contracts and does not subscribe to the Equity Pension Scheme.

Casting procedures: Holds general auditions every year; actors requesting inclusion should send submissions (CVs and photographs) to the company bu post or email. Will also accept showreels and invitations to view individual actors' websites. Will consider applications from disabled actors to play disabled characters.

Fevered Sleep

Shoreditch Town Hall, 380 Old Street, London EC1V 9LT

tel 020 7922 2988
email admin@feveredsleep.co.uk
website www.feveredsleep.co.uk
Artistic Directors David Harradine and Samantha Butler

Production details: Established in 1996. Creates original performances, installations, films, books and digital art for adults and for children. Fearless about experimentation and passionate about research, develops projects that challenge people to rethink their relationships with each other and with the world. Work appears in very diverse places across the UK and beyond, from thatres, galleries and cinemas, to parks, beaches and schools, and the spaces of everyday life; in people's homes, on phones, online. "Whatever we make and wherever it's experienced we're driven by an ambition to present otstanding and transformative art."

Tours 3 projects annually, in around 10 venues (theatres, arts centres, galleries, and site-specific) in the UK, internationally and in London. In general, 3-5 performers go on tour, playing to audiences of all ages. Incoming artists may be expected to lead workshops, and may require dance, physical theatre and/or musical instrument skills, depending on the project. Recent productions include: *Men & Girls*, *Dusk* and *Stilled*.

Casting procedures: Sometimes holds general auditions, artists may write at any time. Welcomes CVs by email only from individual performers previously unknown to the company, sent by post or email, as well as invitations to view individual artists' websites – but prefers not to receive showreels. Offers Equity-approved contracts as negotiated through ITC. Will consider applications from disabled actors "in line with our equal opportunities policy".

Freshwater Theatre Company

St Margaret's House, 21 Old Ford Road, Bethnal Green, London E2 9PL
tel 0844 800 2870
email info@freshwatertheatre.co.uk
website www.freshwatertheatre.co.uk
Directors Helen Wood, Carol Tagg

Production details: Established in 1996 with the aim of offering high-quality, affordable, innovative drama opportunites to primary school children and teachers and MFL workshops for secondary schools. Runs workshops and storytelling sessions addressing a range of curriculum areas including history, geography, Shakespeare, citizenship, multicultural studies, maths, science, cross-curricular and modern foreign languages and the needs of early years pupils. Also runs drama in-service training courses for teachers. Does not tour, but provides over 100 difference sessions all year round at nurseries, schools, libraries and community venues in Greater London, South West, Essex, the West Midlands conurbation, and Greater Manchester. Around 70

freelance facilitators work with audiences aged 3 to 12. Relevant experience is required, and actors are expected to lead workshops. Recent workshops include: *Mary Seacole*, *The Three Musketeers*, and *Great Fire of London*.

Casting procedures: Holds general auditions once a year; actors may write in at any time. Welcomes letters (with CVs and photographs) sent by post or email, but only from experienced workshop facilitators. Does not accept showreels or invitations to view individual actors' websites. "We only engage dedicated, experienced workshop leaders to undertake our drama sessions, and will only consider those who can provide regular and ongoing availability within the areas we cover."

Gazebo Theatre in Education Company

Bilston Town Hall, Church Street, Bilston, West Midlands WV14 0AP
tel 01902 497222 *fax* 01902 497244
email admin@gazebotie.org
website www.gazebotie.org
Artistic Director Michael O'Hara *Strategic Director* Pamela Cole-Hudson

Production details: Founded in 1979. Normally tours 3-5 projects each year plus workshops, with an average annual total of 300 performances and 250 different venues; these are mainly schools and community venues in the West Midlands and South Shropshire. In general between 1 and 3 actors go on tour and play to audiences aged 4-25. Musical ability and movement skills are sometimes required, as is a driving licence. Actors may also be expected to lead workshops. Recent productions include: *Billy No Mates!* (Special Needs); *If you see a crocodile* (Nursery & Reception); *Presents from the Past* (KS2); *Doing our Bit* (KS3).

Casting procedures: Casting breakdowns are sometimes available by postal application (with sae) or through Equity Job Information Service. The company website will also show details of auditions and artists opportunities. Accepts submissions (with CVs and photographs) from actors previously unknown to the company if sent by post. Open auditions take place over the summer months. Will accept invitations to view individual actors' websites. Does not welcome unsolicited emails. Offers non-Equity contracts. Actively encourages applications from disabled actors and promotes the use of inclusive casting.

Gibber Theatre Ltd

The Old Library, 2A Woodleigh Road, Whitley Bay, NE25 8ET
tel 0191 252 2039 *fax* 0191 252 4833
email hello@wearegibber.com
website www.wearegibber.com
Twitter @wearegibber
Artistic Directors Victoria Blackburn, Tim Watt

Theatre

Production details: Founded in 1999. An educational theatre company specialising in innovative multimedia performances for young people of all ages. The company has built a reputation for making a difference in education, by delivering high-quality, hard-hitting interactive performances that effect positive changes in attitudes and behaviours. On average performs 10 projects each year, with approximately 400 performances in schools across the UK and Australia. In general, 3 actors go on tour, playing to audiences aged 5 to 16. Actors may be required to lead workshops, and should have singing and physical theatre skills as well as a driving licence.

Recent productions include environmental education tours: *Super Splash Heroes* (primary) and *The Waste Watchers* (secondary), *Smashed*, an alcohol education awareness tour of Australian high schools, and several careers education tours in both the UK and Australia.

Casting procedures: Sometimes holds general auditions; actors may write at any time. Any specific breakdowns are posted on the company website and social media. Welcomes letters (with CVs and photographs) from actors previously unknown to the company, sent byemail. Accepts showreels and invitations to view individual actors' websites. Will consider applications from disabled actors to play characters with disabilities.

Greenwich & Lewisham Young People's Theatre (GLYPT)

The Tramshed, 51–53 Woolwich New Road, Woolwich, SE18 6ES
tel 020 8854 1316
email info@glypt.co.uk
website www.glypt.co.uk
Artistic Director Jeremy James *Education Officer* Claire Newby.

Production details: GLYPT creates theatre for, with and by young people. It runs Youth Theatre workshops for 8-21 year-olds, and specialist programmes for young people with learning difficulties. The company also runs a comprehensive programme of workshops for young refugees and new arrivals. Tours 2 productions a year to young audiences across South East London and beyond; these visit schools as Theatre in Education programmes, and also play at community and arts centres and at theatres. The work explores current and provoking issues that affect the lives of young audiences, and offers a platform for aesthetic and educational debate. Recent productions have included: *The Inquiry*, *Mud City*, *SK8 Angel* and *Master Juba*.

Casting procedures: Operates the ITC/Equity contract and works with actors committed to the young people's theatre sector. "We actively encourage applications from disabled actors and promote the use of inclusive casting." Welcomes letters and emails (with CVs) from actors and skilled workshop facilitators.

Half Moon Theatre

43 Whitehorse Road, London E1 0ND
tel 020 7265 8138
email admin@halfmoon.org.uk
website www.halfmoon.org.uk
Facebook halfmoontheatre
Twitter @halfmoontheatre
Director Chris Elwell

Production details: Established in 1990, Half Moon is a local organisation with a national remit, based in Tower Hamlets, East London. The company gives young people from birth to 18 (25 for disabled young people) an opportunity to experience the best in young people's theatre, both as a participant and as an audience member. Half Moon tours its own productions nationally, as well as a portfolio of work through its producing arm Half Moon Presents to venues including theatres, libraries, schools, community spaces and festivals. The portfolio covers a range of work from artists and companies drawn from all the genres of theatre, spoken word, new writing and dance, reflecting the UK's contemporary, diverse communities. Half Moon has ethical status with ITC and offers ITC/Equity-approved contracts.

Casting procedures: Casting breakdowns are available through the company's website, circulated to agents and through Spotlight. Actively encourages applications from disabled actors and promotes the use of inclusive casting.

Hopscotch Theatre Company

2nd Floor, 7 Water Row, Glasgow G51 3UW
tel 0141 440 2025
email info@hopscotchtheatre.com
website www.hopscotchtheatre.com
Artistic Director Ross Stenhouse

Production details: Founded in 1988. A Theatre in Education company touring to primary schools, theatre and community venues across Scotland.

Casting procedures: Accepts CVs, photographs and covering letter from actors previously unknown to the company sent by post or email. Will also accept showreels.

In Toto Theatre Company

97 Upper Ground, London SE1 9PR
tel 020 7261 9187
email sarah@in-tototheatre.co.uk
website www.in-tototheatre.co.uk
Artistic Director Sarah Carter *Associate Director* Lennie Charles

Production details: Founded in 1989 and became a charity in 2000. Provides inclusive theatre for all ages using a combination of puppetry, live music, storytelling and dance. Specialises in creating 'total theatre' by, with and for young audiences – "a highly visual musical style of theatre approach which is inclusive and accessible to a wide range of ages and abilities". Also runs participatory arts activities for families, children and young adults to make their own performance. Has completed 7 projects to date with an average of 50 performances in up to 30 venues (schools, community venues and outdoor festivals, including site-specific). On average 2-3 performers/actors tour in the company's small-scale productions devised for age groups from 18 months upwards. An additional skill is usually required of actors; playing a musical instrument and puppetry are especially valued.

Casting procedures: Does not hold general auditions. Will accept email enquiries, but unsolicited letters by post are not welcomed. Sometimes advertises casting breakdowns via Arts Jobs or Equity information line. Rather than showreels, prefers to receive links to actors' websites by email. Offers Equity-approved contracts through ITC. Actively encourages applications from disabled actors and promotes the use of inclusive casting.

"We usually recruit artists with an interest and proven experience in making theatre collaboratively, with an interdisciplinary approach. Being able to facilitate workshops is a very important requirement, and those with a background in arts therapy, social work, education or working with special needs, in addition to professional performance or visual arts training, are far more likely to be considered."

Jack Drum Arts

St Cuthberts Centre Crook, Church Hill, Crook, County Durham DL15 9DN
tel/fax 01388 765002
email info@jackdrum.co.uk
website www.jackdrum.co.uk
Co-Directors Paddy Burton, Helen Ward, Julie Ward

Production details: Founded in 1986. Delivers a strong programme of participatory arts for all sectors of the community, often linked to the production of touring theatre. Historically, toured 2 theatre projects annually with an average annual total of 40 performances at up to 40 different venues, including schools, arts centres, theatres, outdoor venues and community venues across the UK and abroad, with a focus on rural touring and schools. In general, productions involve 3-4 actors, playing to audiences of pre-school age and upwards. Singing ability, proficiency with a musical instrument and a driving licence are required for some shows. Actors may also be expected to lead workshops.

Recent productions include: 3 new shows for young audiences created as part of Children & the Arts START scheme, and a co-production with Mad Alice Theatre Company of a play for family audiences inspired by the Lindisfarne Gospels and the stories of the Northern Saints. Other projects include large-scale community play productions, which are created

with local communities working in tandem with professional practitioners and film/media projects. For the First World War commemoration the company is looking to retour its adult production *Set in Stone* by David Napthine, which was originally created in 1999 to coincide with the Millennium Pardon Campaign and is mentioned in Hansard.

Casting procedures: Accepts submissions (with CVs and photographs) from actors with a North East connection. "We like to know who is around in the North East, especially if based in County Durham. Can help access local networks and professional development." Offers Equity and non-Equity contracts. Rarely (or never) has the opportunity to cast disabled actors, but would be interested in developing projects which can make this possible. Particularly interested in actors who have BSL skills.

Kazzum

Oxford House, Derbyshire Street, London E2 6HG
tel 020 7749 1123
email info@kazzum.org
website www.kazzum.org
Artistic Director Daryl Beeton

Production details: Established in 1989. "We create playful theatre and participative arts activities for young people, using art forms that reflect diverse cultural influences." Stages 1-2 productions each year, with around 40-70 performances in 30 arts centres, theatres, and outdoor and community venues across the UK. In general 3 actors go on tour, playing to audiences aged 4-8 and 10+. Incoming actors should have singing, musical instrument, dance and physical theatre skills and may be expected to lead workshops. Recent productions include: *The Boy Who Grew Flowers, Hunt, The Sorcerer's Apprentice,* and *Beginning with Blobs*.

Casting procedures: Actors may write in March through to May to request inclusion. Casting breakdowns are available from the website, through Equity Job Information Service and Arts Jobs. Welcomes letters (with CVs and photographs) from individual actors previously unknown to the company, sent by post or email. Also accepts showreels and invitations to view individual actors' websites. Offers Equity-approved contracts as negotiated through ITC. Actively encourages applications from disabled actors, and promotes the use of inclusive casting.

Kinetic Theatre Company

Suite H, The Jubilee Centre, 10-12 Lombard Road, London SW19 3TZ
tel 020 8286 2613
email sarah@kinetictheatre.co.uk
website www.kinetictheatre.co.uk
Producer/Writer Graham Scott *Artistic Directors* James Austin-Harvey (Casting Director), Bridget Lambert, Rachel Hickson, Julie Kinsella, Andy Byron

Theatre

Production details: Established in 1988. One of the country's most prominent Theatre in Education companies. Performs plays geared to the National Curriculum for Science, to schools and theatres throughout the UK. Has 9 shows, 4 of which are on the road at any one time. All shows are self-contained musical comedies, all being very different in style. On average performs 12 tours every year with around 900 performances in 600 venues in England, Scotland, Wales and Northern Ireland. All shows are 2-handers, and actors play to audiences aged 5 to 12. Actors require reasonable singing and dancing skills and a driving licence is essential. Recent productions include: *The Hospital Force, Down to Earth, Lady Cecily's Sound Box*, and *Robin & the Withering Wood*.

Casting procedures: Does not hold general auditions; lets actors know when to write in, via the usual casting breakdown sites. Casting breakdowns are widely available: consult the website for full details. Contracts are based on Equity/ITC guidelines for small-scale touring. Will consider applications from actors with disabilities to play characters with disabilities. "We cast for our productions 3 times a year, usually around February, June and October, and we always put out castings for our workshop-style auditions. We cannot consider applications outside these times and due to limited space do not hold details on file. Please do not send unsolicited CVs/photos as it will just waste your money. We recommend that actors check the auditions page on our website for general information on when auditions are coming up, and also for more detailed information to prepare for our auditions."

Krazy Kat Theatre Company
173 Hartington Road, Brighton BN2 3PA
tel 01273 692552
email krazykattheatre@ntlworld.com
website www.krazykattheatre.co.uk
Artistic Director Kinny Gardner

Production details: A children's theatre company founded in 1982, specialising in highly visual forms of theatre that are accessible to Deaf children. Normally tours 2 projects each year with an average annual total of 50 performances and 35 venues. Venues include schools, arts centres, theatres, outdoor venues and community centres throughout UK. In general 2 actors and a technician go on tour and play to audiences aged 3-7. Singing ability, physical theatre skills, British sign language and a driving licence are required. Actors may also be expected to lead workshops. Recent productions include: *A (Midsummer Night's) Dream,Petrushka, The Pied Piper*, a Victorian *Mikado*and *The Very Magic Flute*.

Casting procedures: Sometimes holds general auditions; actors can write at any time requesting inclusion. Accepts submissions (with CVs and photographs) from actors previously unknown to the company if sent by post. Does not welcome

unsolicited emails. Will also accept invitations to view individual actors' websites. Offers non-Equity contracts but at Equity and ITC rates. Actively encourages applications from disabled actors and promotes the use of inclusive casting.

The London Bus Theatre Company
37 Chestnut Close, Hockley, Essex SS5 5EQ
tel 01208 814514 *fax* 01208 814514
email kathy@londonbustheatre.co.uk
website www.londonbustheatre.co.uk
Principal Chris Turner

Production details: The London Bus Theatre Company increases young people's confidence, self-esteem, employability and life skills through a range of drama and filmmaking activities.

It provides councils, NHS Trusts, Essex Police, youth organisations and schools and colleges with drama workshops and DVDs on issues such as bullying, drugs, alcohol and antisocial behaviour and job interview techniques. Approximately 16,000 young people benefit from the workshops in schools every year. From 2009–2011 the group was awarded the largest grant from Essex Community Foundation to run a three-year filming and drama project for the residents from the Craylands and Fryerns East estates, Basildon, and Queen's Park estate, Billericay, under the Fair Share programme. This resulted in employment and volunteering opportunities for over 300 young people on the estates to produce the feature film Angels vs Bullies. The film was screened at cinemas in 2014 and 2015. In 2017, it was awarded funding for a new three year drama project in Harwich – Dock Town Story.

The London Bus Theatre Company has received sponsorship from BP, Tesco, Umbro and KeyMed. The award-winning anti-bullying play Nutter has been filmed by the BBC and is sold by the National Theatre. The Kick It DVDs used in Citizenship programmes produced from 2002–2017 have outsold the BBC and Channel 4 equivalents.Their young actors regularly gain places at RADA, LAMDA, The Bristol Old Vic and The Poor School as well as the National Youth Theatre.

Casting procedures: Holds general auditions and actors may write in at any time. Welcomes letters (with CVs and photographs) from individual actors previously unknown to the company, sent by post or email. Accepts showreels and will consider invitiations to view individual actors' websites. Considers applications from disabled actors to play characters with disabilities.

Loudmouth Education & Training
The Friends' Institute, 220 Moseley Road, Highgate, Birmingham B12 0DG
tel 0121 446 4880 *fax* 0121 440 3940
email info@loudmouth.co.uk
website www.loudmouth.co.uk
Facebook /loudmoutheducationandtraining/

Twitter @LoudmouthUK
*Company Director*s Chris Cowan, Eleanor Vale

Production details: Founded in 1994. Supplies interactive education and training programmes for young people on personal, social and health education issues, and accessible training for adults to aid personal and professional development. On average we work in around 800 UK venues each year; venues include schools, colleges, community venues and youth centres. Actors are expected to lead workshops and must have a full driving licence. Recent productions include: *Working for Marcus* – an interactive theatre programme focusing on child sexual exploitation and grooming.

Casting procedures: Holds general auditions. Welcomes letters with CVs and photographs from individual actors previously unknown to the company. Will accept unsolicited CVs and photographs sent by email. Does not welcome showreels or invitations to view individual actors' websites. Rarely or never has the opportunity to cast disabled actors.

M6 Theatre Company

Studio Theatre, Hamer County Primary School, Albert Royds Street, Rochdale OL16 2SU
tel 01706 355898 *fax* 01706 712601
website www.m6theatre.co.uk
Artistic Producer Dorothy Wood

Production details: M6 Theatre Company specalises in producing and touring high-quality, accessible and emotionally engaging theatre for young audiences. Founded in 1977, the company tours 3-5 productions each year, through approximately 300 performances/workshops. Touring venues include theatres, schools, festivals, prisons and early years settings across the North West and nationally. Cast sizes are generally 2-4; actors may be expected to participate in workshops accompanying productions. Recent productions have included: *One Little Word* (a sensitive and moving production for children aged 3+ exploring friendship and conflict resolution, underscored with original music and with only 1 spoken word); *Sunflowers and Sheds* (a heart-warming tale of friendship, family and fun on the allotment, for ages 5+ and anyone who's ever made a friend); *Mavis Sparkle* – touring Spring 2013 (this delightful new production mixes illusion, animation and laughter to discover the magic and wonder in the universe, each other and ourselves – ages 5+). M6 also creates and delivers an exciting participatory programme of creative, free time; theatre-arts based workshops and sharing events – ACT NOW! A diverse range of young people from Rochdale (8-18s) participate in and lead activities at M6's purpose-built Studio Theatre and at a range of outreach community settings in Rochdale. ACT NOW! is an ambitious extension of M6's participatory workshop programme, building on proven successful experience, practice and

partnerships. Participants' involvement and achievements will be shared with the local community regularly throughout the 3-year project (Big Lottery Reaching Communities funded) and will culminate in a high-profile showcase event/Youth Theatre Festival in 2014.

Casting procedures: Accepts submissions (with CVs and photographs) from actors previously unknown to the company. Unfortunately the company is unable to return photos. Actor contracts are ITC/Equity-approved.

Magic Carpet Theatre

18 Church Street, Sutton on Hull, East Yorkshire HU7 4TS
tel 01482 709939
email jon@magiccarpettheatre.com
website www.magiccarpettheatre.com
Facebook @magiccarpettheatre
Artistic Director Jon Marshall

Production details: Professional touring children's theatre company presenting shows and workshops in the UK and abroad. Tours 3-4 productions annually, with around 250 performances in 250 venues including schools, arts and community venues, and festivals. In general 3 actors go on tour, playing to audiences aged 5-11. Actors may be expected to lead workshops. Recent productions include: *Mr Albert's Big Finish; The Wizard of Castle Magic* and *Magic Circus.*

Casting procedures: Does not hold general auditions; actors may write in the autumn to request inclusion. Advises actors to "ring us rather than sending CVs, etc., to see when we are casting".

MakeBelieve Arts

The Cartoon House, 1a Bradford Road, Corsham, Wilts SN13 0QR
tel 020 8691 3803
email info@makebelievearts.co.uk
website www.makebelievearts.co.uk
Artistic Director Trisha Lee

Production details: Established in 2002 and gained charitable status in 2006. A leading provider of high-quality arts and education programmes, for Foundation Stage and Primary school pupils and their parents and teachers. Based in Wiltshire but works in other counties across the UK. In general 4-6 actors stage 1 project a year, with around 100 performances at 50 schools. Skills required depend on the production, and actors may be asked to lead workshops. Recent productions include: *The Woman Who Cooked Everything, Gulliver's Travels, Giant Tours* and *Journey to the Centre of the Brain.*

Casting procedures: Holds general auditions. Casting breakdowns are available from the website and in *The Stage.* Welcomes letters (with CVs and photographs) from individual actors previously unknown to the company, sent by post or email. Does not however accept showreels or invitations to view individual actors' websites. Offers Equity-approved contracts negotiated through ITC. Rarely has the opportunity to cast disabled actors.

Moby Duck

12 Reservoir Retreat, Birmingham B16 9EH
tel/fax 0121 242 0400
email info@moby-duck.co.uk
website www.moby-duck.com
Artistic Director Guy Hutchins

Production details: Founded in 1999. Performs 2 projects annually, with more than 50 performances at the same number of schools, arts centres, theatres and community venues across all regions. In general 3-4 actors go on tour, playing to audiences aged 4 to 80. Requires actors to have "an understanding of the other cultures we work in". Actors may be expected to lead workshops. Singing, musical instrument, dance and physical theatre skills are an advantage, and actors should hold a clean driving licence. For details of recent productions, see the website.

Casting procedures: Sometimes holds general auditions, and actors may write at any time to request inclusion. Welcomes letters (with CVs and photographs) from individual actors previously unknown to the company, sent by post or email. Also welcomes showreels and invitations to view individual actors' websites. Offers Equity-approved contracts as negotiated through ITC. Rarely or never has the opportunity to cast disabled actors.

Newfound Theatre Company

mobile 07753 237209
email newfoundtheatre@gmail.com
website www.newfoundtheatre.co.uk

Production details: Theatre in Education company touring/performing several projects each year, with around 200 performances annually to schools in London and the North West. In general, 3 actors go on tour playing to audiences aged 5 to 16. Actors are sometimes expected to lead workshops. Recent productions include: *Making Monologues*, *Rewind* and *Thinspiration*.

Casting procedures: Uses in-house casting directors; does not hold general auditions. Casting breakdowns are available via Casting Call Pro. Welcomes unsolicited CVs and photographs from actors previously unknown to the company if sent by email; also accepts invitations to view individual actors' websites. Encourages applications from disabled actors and promotes the use of inclusive casting.

Nimble Fish

30 Wilton Square, London N1 3DW
mobile 07939 522518
email getnimble@nimble-fish.co.uk
website www.nimble-fish.co.uk
Directors Samatha Holdsworth, Greg Klerkx

Production details: Since 2006, award-winning Nimble Fish have been developing and producing projects that explore important social issues as well as engaging audiences that feel the arts have little or nothing to do with them. Recent productions include national tours of *Lost in Blue* by Debs Newbold (2016) and *My Father and Other Superheroes* by Nick Makoha (2015). *You, Me and Everyone in Portsmouth* (2013) became the UK's biggest-ever collaborative storytelling project. In 2007, their production of *The Container* by Clare Bayley won an Amnesty International Freedom Award and an Edinburgh Fringe First.

Casting procedures: Sometimes holds general auditions. Does not welcome unsolicited approaches from individuals not previously known to the company. Offers Equity-approved contracts via ITC. Actively encourages applications from disabled actors and promotes the use of inclusive casting.

Nottingham Playhouse Participation

Nottingham Playhouse, Wellington Circus, Nottingham NG1 5AF
tel 0115 947 4361
email enquiry@nottinghamplayhouse.co.uk
website www.nottinghamplayhouse.co.uk

Production details: Participation creates 1-2 small-scale productions per year. These are performed mostly in East Midlands schools, with some performances in small theatre venues – including own studio at Nottingham Playhouse. Employs 3-6 actors each year, on contracts usually lasting from 6 to 12 weeks. Actors are usually multi-skilled. Singing and physical theatre are essential for many of the productions, and actors often have workshop skills and/or play a musical instrument as well. A driving licence is helpful. The company has a specialism in creating theatre for young people with profound learning difficulties and autism, and Makaton signing skills are very welcome for these productions.

Casting procedures: Casting, which is inclusive in every sense, is carried out by the director of the production, usually in collaboration with the Playhouse's Casting Director, Sooki McShane. Welcomes CVs by email or permanent web link, marked for the attention of the Associate Director. Offers ITC/Equity contracts.

Oily Cart Company

Smallwood School Annexe, Smallwood Road, London SW17 0TW
tel 020 8672 6329 *fax* 020 8672 0792
email oilies@oilycart.org.uk
website www.oilycart.org.uk
Artistic Director Ellie Griffiths

Production details: One of the leading theatre companies in the UKcreating highly interactive multi-sensory performances for and with the very young (6 months to 6 years) and young people (aged

3–19) with complex needs and/or who are on the autistic spectrum. Tours national and international venues like theatres and arts centres with early years shows, and takes its special-needs work to special schools around the UK.Recent productions include: *In A Pickle* (sheep's-eye view of Shakespeare's *The Winter's Tale* for under 5s); *Hippity Hop*; *Kubla Khan* and *Splish Splash* – an interactive show performed in hydrotherapy pools

Casting procedures: Casting breakdowns are available on the website **www.oilycart.org.uk** and the Arts Jobs website **www.artsjobs.org.uk**. Offers ITC/Equity-approved contracts. Actively encourages applications from D/deaf or disabled actors and promotes the use of inclusive casting.

Onatti Productions Ltd

The Old Chapel, Yorkley Slade, Yorkley, Gloucestershire GL15 4SB
tel 01594 562033 *fax* 0870 164 3629
email info@onatti.co.uk
website www.onatti.co.uk

Production details: Produces foreign-language productions performed at Primary and Secondary schools throughout the UK, France and Spain. Plays are produced in French, German, Spanish and English; all are written by the company and used as an exciting way of promoting and enhancing languages in schools. Onatti produces around 8 tours each year. Employs native foreign actors for contracts from 3 to 10 months. Actors are sourced from the UK and Europe.

Passe-Partout

13 Stanford Avenue, Brighton BN1 6AD
tel 01273 557595
email p@sse-partout.com
Artistic Director Michele Young

Production details: Founded in 1986. "Theatre for social change – assisting people to have a voice about an issue which concerns them." Normally tours 3 projects each year, with an average annual total of 20 performances and 20 different venues including schools, outdoor centres, community venues and office spaces in the UK and abroad. In general 4 actors go on tour and play to audiences of all ages. Any additional skills that actors may have will be put to use. Actors may also be expected to lead workshops. Recent projects include: *Anti-bullying Strategy Development* (prisons, UK); *Social Capital* (various schools, Europe); *Street Children* (Nairobi, Kenya); *Bio-diversity* (Toulouse, France) and *Silkworm Journey* (France). Has an alliance with Inedit Films to produce 3-minute dramas (fact-based) for educational purposes.

Casting procedures: "We cast from the group of people who have proposed an issue they want to take forward. We sometimes build-in 1 or 2 people from outside that group who have interest and energy."

Pied Piper Theatre Company

1 Lilian Place, Coxcombe Lane, Chiddingfold GU8 4QA
tel 01428 684022
email tina@piedpipertheatre.co.uk
email info@piedpipertheatre.co.uk
website www.piedpipertheatre.co.uk
Artistic Director Tina Williams *Associate Director* Nicola Sangster

Production details: Founded in 1984, Pied Piper creates exciting, high quality magical plays for children. Tours to schools, theatres and arts centresin the UK, Europe and Asia, specialising in new writing or new adaptations of favourite stories or books. Funded by Arts Council South East. ITC/Equity contracts. Ethical Member.

Pilot Theatre

York Theatre Royal, St Leonard's Place, York YO1 7HD
tel 01904 635755
email info@pilot-theatre.com
website www.pilot-theatre.com
Artistic Director Marcus Romer

Production details: A national mid-scale touring company producing a programme of education resources for young people. Stages on average 3-6 projects annually, with 150 performances in 20 arts centres and theatres across the UK. In general 6-10 actors go on tour, playing to audiences aged 11-25. Actors are sometimes expected to lead workshops.

Casting procedures: Actors may write in May and August to request inclusion. Casting breakdowns are available on the website or via Spotlight. Welcomes unsolicited CVs and photographs if submitted by email. Also accepts showreels and will consider invitations to view individual actors' websites. Offers Equity-approved contracts as negotiated through TMA/ITC. Actively encourages applications by disabled actors and promotes the use of inclusive casting.

The Play House

c/o Birmingham Repertory Theatre, Centenary Square, Broad Street, Birmingham B1 2EP
tel 0121 265 4425 *fax* 0121 233 0652
email info@theplayhouse.org.uk
website www.theplayhouse.org.uk
General Manager Rebecca Wass *Head of Programmes* Juliet Fry

Production details: Established in 1986. An educational theatre charity that uses uses participatory theatre and drama to stimulate and support the language and learning of children and young people. Best known for its *Language Alive!* theatre-in-education tours, which bring the curriculum to life for 3-11 year olds and a range of issue-based projects as well as INSET and CPD for teachers. Tours an average of 10-15 projects annually,

Theatre

with around 1,000 performances in 60-70 schools, outdoor and other venues in the West Midlands. In general 2-3 actors go on tour, performing to young audiences aged 3-18. Skills required vary according to the project and a clean driving licence is required. Actors may be expected to lead workshops.

Casting procedures: Sometimes holds general auditions; actors should write in when these are advertised. Rarely or never has the opportunity to cast disabled actors.

Playbox Theatre (Generator)

The Dream Factory, Shelly Avenue,
Warwick CV34 6LE
tel 01926 419555 *fax* 01926 411429
email stewart@playboxtheatre.com
website www.playboxtheatre.com
Artistic Director Stewart McGill *Directors* Emily Quash, Mary King

Production details: Established in 1986, Generator is the professional acting company of Playbox Theatre, reworking classic drama for contemporary audiences. 2 productions staged annually, touring nationally to arts centres, theatres, outdoor venues and educational venues. Based in Warwick. Up to 12 actors used in each production. Offers Equity approved contracts. Recent productions include: *A Doll's House* and *Henry VI – The Wars of the Roses.*

Casting procedures: Accepts submissions (with CVs and photographs) from actors previously unknown to the company sent by post or by email. Actively encourages applications from disabled actors and promotes the use of inclusive casting.

Playtime Theatre Company

18 Bennell's Avenue, Whitstable, Kent CT5 2HP
tel 01227 26648 *fax* 01227 266648
email Playtime@dircon.co.uk
website www.playtimetheatre.co.uk
Artistic Director Nicholas Champion

Production details: Established in 1983 with the aim of bringing imaginative and innovative professional theatre and workshops to children and young people. Has grown to become "one of the leading children's theatre companies in the South East", and tours both nationally and internationally. Normally tours 2-4 projects each year with an average annual total of 200 performances and 190 venues. Venues include schools, arts centres, theatres, community venues and festivals. Tours have covered the South East, Yorkshire and various countries in Europe and the Middle East. In general 2-4 actors go on tour and play to targeted audiences of 5-7, 4-11, 7-11, 9-13 and 14+. Actors are expected to offer 1-2 additional skills. Singing ability, proficiency with a musical instrument, physical theatre, puppetry and mime skills and a driving licence are all useful. Actors may also be expected to lead workshops. Recent productions include:*The Jackdaw*, a history play set

during the Napoleonic Wars; *The Dark Castle*, an interactive medieval adventure story, *TUI*, a road and cycle safety play and *A Silent Song*, a WW1 play looking at pacifism. We also run an extensive Drama Workshop programme. These can be an adjunct to a performance or bespoke.

Casting procedures: Holds general auditions; actors should write in August requesting inclusion. Casting breakdowns are available through the website, postal application (with sae), Equity Job Information Service, *The Stage* and, Casting Call Pro Castcall. Welcomes submissions (with CVs and photographs) from actors previously unknown to the company sent by post or email. Also accepts showreels and invitations to view individual actors' websites (if actor is shown performing). Advises actors to: "Be truthful. Tell us about the things that make you stand out. Tell us briefly why you want to work in children's theatre and why you like touring. Seriously consider the implications of living away from your base for months on end!" Offers non-Equity contracts. Will consider applications from disabled actors to play characters with disabilities. Also looking for stage managers.

Polka Theatre

240 The Broadway, Wimbledon, London SW19 1SB
tel 020 8545 8320 *fax* 020 8545 8365
email stephen@polkatheatre.com
website www.polkatheatre.com
Artistic Director Peter Glanville

Production details: Established in 1979. A theatre for children aged 0-14. 6 productions staged annually with 700-800 performances per year. The following skills are required from actors: singing, musical instruments, dance, puppetry and physical theatre. Offers TMA/Equity contracts.

Casting procedures: Casting breakdowns sometimes available. Actors are invited for specific shows. Accepts submissions (with CVs and photographs) from actors previously unknown to the company if sent by post, but not by email. Showreels and invitations to view individual actors' websites are also accepted. Actively encourages applications from disabled actors and promotes the use of inclusive casting. "Find out in advance what we're doing, come and visit Polka and see the work."

Pop-Up Theatre

27A Brewery Road, London N7 9PU
tel 020 7609 3339 *fax* 020 7609 2284
website www.pop-up.co.uk
Artistic Director Michael Dalton

Production details: Founded in 1982. Produces and tours theatre for young people to an annual audience of more than 25,000 across theatres, arts centres, schools and nurseries both in the UK and overseas. Normally tours 3 projects each year, with an average annual total of 150 performances at 75 different venues. In general 2-4 actors go on tour and play to audiences aged under 11.

Casting procedures: Accepts submissions (with CVs and photographs) from actors previously unknown to the company sent by post or email. Also accepts invitations to view individual actors' websites. Offers ITC\Equity-approved contracts. Actively encourages applications from disabled actors and promotes the use of inclusive casting.

Q20 Theatre

Creative Arts Hub, Dockfield Road, Shipley,
West Yorks BD17 7AD
01274 221360
email info@q20theatre.co.uk
website www.q20theatre.co.uk
Facebook Q20 Events (@q20eventsuk)
Artistic Director John Lambert

Production details: Tours in excess of 10 projects each year with an average annual total of 350+ performances. Venues include outdoor venues, corporate workspaces and shopping centres throughout the UK. In general 2 or more actors go on tour and play to audiences of all ages. Singing ability and dance/physical theatre skills are required. Recent productions include: *Duelling Wizards* for National Media Museum; 'Snail Sex' Show for Natural History Museum; *Get Thinking About Your Drinking* for NHS Kirklees; *Superheroes* at Metrocentre; *Beatrix Potter* for Bradford Litertaure Festival; Potter-inspired characters for Alnwick Castle; *Pirates and Princesses Parade* for Falkirk Delivers.

Casting procedures: Does not hold general auditions – auditions are for specific productions only. Will accept submissions (with CVs and photographs) from actors previously unknown to the company, preferably by email. Will also accept invitations to view individual actors' websites.

Quantum Theatre

The Old Button Factory, 1-11 Bannockburn Road,
Plumstead SE18 1ET
tel/fax 020 8317 9000
email office@quantumtheatre.co.uk
website www.quantumtheatre.co.uk
Artistic Directors Michael Whitmore, Jessica Selous

Established in 1993. 15 productions performed annually. National touring productions visit schools, arts centres, theatres and outdoor venues. Casting breakdowns available. Holds general auditions. Accepts submissions (with CVs and photographs) from actors previously unknown to the company – email idea. Showreels, voicereels and invitations to view individual actors' websites are also accepted. Operates own contracts based on TMA Equity terms and conditions.

Quicksilver Theatre

The New Diorama Theatre, 15-16 Triton Street,
Regents Place, London NW1 3BF
tel 020 7419 2000
email talktous@quicksilvertheatre.org
website www.quicksilvertheatre.co.uk
Artistic Directors Guy Holland, Carey English

Production details: Founded in 1977, Quicksilver, since 2008, produces 1 new production every 2 years, which is presented at a London venue as well as at partner venues around the UK, mostly small- and middle-scale. Cast numbers change from production to production and vary between 1 and 5. Most of the work is aimed at young audiences, and skills required from actors vary depending on need; may include the playing of musical instruments, singing, puppeteering and dance. Actors may also be expected to lead workshops, as Quicksilver has in recent years expanded its artistic and education projects involving participation by children. Recent productons include *Winter's Tale* (2007, adapted by None Shepphard); *Water Colours* (2007); *Primary Voices* (2007 and 2009, a playwriting project with children and professional actors; and *Ladidada* (2008 and 2010, a co-production between Quicksilver and Indefinite Articles).

Casting procedures: Casting breakdowns are available through the website, by postal application (with sae), and as advertisements in *The Stage*. Accepts submissions (with CVs and photographs) from actors previously unknown to the company sent by post or email. Will also accept showreels and invitations to view individual actors' websites.

Replay Theatre Company

East Belfast Network Centre,
55 Templemore Avenue, Belfast BT5 4FP
tel 028 9045 4562
email info@replaytheatreco.org
website www.replaytheatreco.org
Artistic Director Janice Kernoghan-Reid

Production details: In 2018, Replay turned 30. Started from a spare bedroom in 1988, Replay has grown up to become one of the leading theatre companies in Northern Ireland. Makes innovative, quality work for everyone under the age of 19: from the tiniest babies to the oldest teenagers, for disabled children and young people, for school groups, for families, for festivals. Tours locally, nationally and internationally - from Belfast to Broadway and lots of places in between.

Replay ignites imaginations through leading-edge theatre adventures, creating fun, asking questions and starting conversations; it encourages empathy and creates a climate of aspiration, it speaks to children about their concerns and promotes imagination.

Casting procedures: Replay holds open auditions on a bi-annual basis. From these auditions a list of potential actors will be registered and contacted when appropriate work becomes available. All auditioning opportunities are announced on the website and social media.

Theatre

S4K International Ltd

Oxted Production Office, PO Box 287, Oxted,
Surrey RH8 8BX
tel 01883 723444
email carolyn@s4kinternational.com
website www.s4kinternationalcom
Producer and Director Julian Chenery *Producer*
Carolyn Chenery

Production details: S4K International produces 4
musical theatre productions, including Shakespeare 4
Kidz shows, each year. Performances are now touring
mainly to the Middle East and play to 200,000+
students and children each year. The Touring
Company consists of between 8 and 20 actors,
technicians and musicians, and plays to audiences
from 5 years old upwards. S4K now uses mainly
actor/musicians with strong singing ability and
dance/physical theatre skills. Recent productions
include: *Snow White, Peter Pan, Beauty and the Beast,
Jungle Book, The Snow Queen; Aladdin; Pinocchio;
S4K's Romeo and Juliet; S4K's Hamlet; S4K's A
Midsummer Night's Dream* and *S4K's Macbeth.*

Casting procedures: Holds general auditions
throughout the year. Casting breakdowns are
available through the website and Spotlight. Accepts
submissions (with CVs and photographs) from actors
previously unknown to the company sent by post or
email. Will also accept showreels and invitations to
view individual actors' websites.

Scene Productions

54 Weybridge Mead, Yateley, Hampshire GU46 7UX
email info@sceneproductions.co.uk
website www.sceneproductions.co.uk
Artistic Directors Kelly Taylor-Smith

Production details: Founded in 2004 by Kelly Taylor-
Smith and Katharine Hurst, Scene Productions is a
physical theatre company which creates vibrant, fast-
paced and immersive adaptations of classical texts as
well as their own devised work. Their unique style
combines mask, puppetry, movement, sound, text
and tightly-choreographed movement sequences.

The company became the associate company of
Redbridge Drama Centre in 2010 and the associate
company of South Hill Park in 2013. They have
worked extensively in over 400 schools, arts centres
and theatres throughout the UK, Ireland and
Belgium, and their style and approach to theatre is
studied in schools nationwide.

In 2009 they performed a 3-week run of *The Other
Side,* a devised physical theatre piece based on true
stories from the Israeli/Palestinian conflict, during the
Edinurgh Fringe. In 2013 they were commissioned by
South Hill Park to co-produce and direct the
centenary production of *Oh! What a Lovely War!* in
association with Bracknell Forest Council. With their
love of promenade-style theatre, they have just
finished their promenade production of *Alice in
Wonderland* in the grounds of South Hill Park.

Their work includes a strong focus on learning,
and the company lead a variety of workshops offering
students and adults the chance to re-discover theatre
in fresh, bold and imaginative ways. The company
also offers work experience to students, and
collaborative and participate in workshops with other
theatre companies.

Casting procedures: Sometimes holds general
auditions and actors may write in May to request
inclusion. Welcomes letters (with CVs and
photographs) from actors previously unknown to the
company, sent by post or email. Does not accept
showreels, but will consider invitations to view
individual actors' websites. Rarely (or never) has the
opportunity to cast disabled actors.

Sixth Sense Theatre for Young People

c/o The Wyvern Theatre, Theatre Square,
Swindon SN1 1QN
tel 01793 614864 *fax* 01793 616715
email sstc@dircon.co.uk
website www.sixthsensetyp.co.uk
Artistic Director Benedict Eccles *Education and
Outreach Leader* Laura Barnes

Production details: Founded in 1986. Tours to
schools and small-scale venues in the South and
South West, and increasingly nationally. Receives
funding from Swindon Borough Council and Arts
Council England, South West, and has an "excellent
reputation in the region". Normally tours 3 projects
each year with an average annual total of 150
performances across 90 venues. Venues include
schools, arts centres and community venues. In
general 3-5 actors go on tour and play to audiences
aged 5-18. Singing ability, proficiency with a musical
instrument, dance skills and a driving licence may be
required. Actors are usually expected to lead
workshops. Recent productions include: *Bob the Man
on the Moon* (2012) and *Splosh!* (2012).

Casting procedures: Accepts submissions (with CVs
and photographs) from actors previously unknown
to the company sent by post or email. Will also
accept invitations to view individual actors' websites.
Issues ITC/Equity contracts for 5- to 10-week tours.
"Happy to receive actors' details but can't always
respond. Please don't chase us; if we're interested
we'll contact you."

Sky Blue Theatre Company

14 Hayfield Avenue, Sawston, Cambridge CB22 3JZ
tel 01223 529491 *mobile* 07941 012293
email info@skybluetheatre.com
website www.skybluetheatre.com
Directors Anne Bartram, Frances Brownlie, John
Mitton

Production details: Founded in 2007. A company
touring new plays, Shakespeare productions and
workshops. Founded the British Theatre Challenge,
an international playwriting competition. Works with

young people through its own theatre school and with colleges developing skills in performing arts. Stages productions for young people's theatre and TIE annually, giving around 130 performances in 60 venues nationally. In general, 4 actors go on tour, playing to audiences aged 7 to 18. Actors are sometimes expected to lead workshops. Recent productions include: *Much Ado About Nothing, Real Love – A New Musical*, and *Romeo and Juliet* workshops.

Casting procedures: All casting is done in house. Holds general auditions, for which breakdowns are available via Mandy Network and the website. Welcomes letters (with CVs and photographs) from individual actors previously unknown to the company, sent by email. Does not accept showreels, but will consider invitations to view actors' websites and performances. Will consider applications from disabled actors for any role.

Small World Theatre

Bath House Road, Cardigan, Ceredigion SA43 1JY
tel 01239 615952
email sam@smallworld.org.uk
website www.smallworld.org.uk Instagram @smallworldtheatre
Facebook www.facebook.com/SmallWorldTheatre
Directors Ann Shrosbree and Bill Hamblett *Marketing Manager* Sam Vicary

Production details: Small World Theatre creates unique, flexible puppet theatre performance that tours to small/mid-scale venues across Wales, the UK and internationally. These include schools, arts centres, theatres, outdoor spaces, community venues, and festivals. It makes giants for large-scale outdoor and site specific performances. The work is environmentally sensitive and socially engaging.

In general 3-4 actors go on tour, playing to audiences of all ages. Actors are generally expected to be skilled in areas such as puppetry, mime, singing and physical theatre. They must perform in Welsh and English and be able to facilitate creative/drama workshops.

Small World Theatre also manages a near zero carbon venue in Cardigan, West Wales. The venue and its creative programme of events and classes are a reflection of Small World Theatre's values and provides an accessible, welcoming, sustainable example for other groups working towards a zero carbon future. Most recent production is *The Lightning Path/Y Llwybr Mellt*, supported by Arts Council Wales.

Casting procedures: Uses in-house casting directors. May hold general auditions and advertise casting breakdowns. Will consider submissions (letters, CVs and photographs) from actors and invitations to view indiividuals' details online. No unsolicited showreels. Small World Theatre casts actors with disabilities in inclusive roles.

Solomon Theatre Company

The Grange, High Street, Turvey MK43 8DB
tel 01722 786845
email office@solomontheatre.co.uk
website www.solomontheatre.co.uk
Artistic Director Mark Hyde

Production details: Founded in 2003. Specialises in communicating messages that result in crime reduction, improved community safety and the promotion of healthy schools and healthy lifestyles. Has performed award-winning plays to tens of thousands of people in schools and community locations across the country, as well as producing films and support material for national programmes. Performs around 7 tours annually in more than 300 venues, including schools, theatres and community venues in the South West, South East, Midlands, Wales and Northern Ireland. On average 12 actors go on tour, performing to audiences aged 12-16. Likes to hear from actors with a driving licence, this would be great be not essential and may be required to lead workshops. Recent projects include: *Last Orders* (alcohol education); *Trickster* (burglary education); *Gemma's Wardrobe* (drugs education) and *Power of Love* (domestic violence education) and *Skin Deep* (knife education).

Casting procedures: Holds general auditions; actors may write in July, November and April to request inclusion. Welcomes letters (with CVs and photographs) from actors previously unknown to the company sent by post or email. Also welcomes showreels and invitations to view individual actors' websites. Does not offer Equity-approved contracts but does offer Equity rates. Will consider applications from disabled actors to play characters with disabilities.

Spare Tyre Theatre Company

The Albany, Douglas Way, Deptford, London SE8 4AG
tel/fax 020 8692 4446 (ext 273)
email info@sparetyre.org
website www.sparetyre.org
Artistic Director Arti Prashar

Production details:

• Work with older people aged 60+, outreach workshops for older people, and interactive storytelling for people with dementia. Work with carers.
• Work with people with learning disabilities.
• Work with women who have experienced violence.

London and nationwide. Skills required from actors include workshop-leading and facilitation skills, experience of working with community groups and a sensitivity to, and understanding of, relevant issues.

Casting procedures: Casting breakdowns are published and on the website. Unsolicited approaches at other times – including CVs, showreels and invitations to view individuals' websites – are discouraged. Offers ITC/Equity-approved contracts. Actively encourages applications from disabled actors and promotes the use of inclusive casting.

Splendid Productions

The Dairy, 5 Marischal Road, London SE13 5LE
tel 020 8318 6469 *fax* 0871 750 2166
email info@splendidproductions.co.uk
website www.splendidproductions.co.uk
Artistic Director Kerry Frampton

Production details: Founded in 2003. A theatre company and an education company creating "challenging, vibrant theatre for young people". Also provides expert training in all areas of drama, from practitioner theory to presentation skills. In the last 12 years the company has gained an excellent reputation for the inventiveness of its performances and the clarity of its teaching. Tours 1 main project per year (September through to March), staging on average 130 performances in 130 venues across England and Wales, including schools, arts centres and theatres. 3 actors go on tour, playing to audiences aged 13 years and beyond. Actors require singing skills, strong physicality and a driving licence; workshop-leading experience is desirable. Recent productions include: *The Odyssey, Medea, The Trial, Dr Faustus, Woyzeck, Good Woman of Szechuan, Antigone, Animal Farm* and *The Resistible Rise of Arturo Ui.*

Casting procedures: Does not hold general auditions. Actors may write during April/June to request inclusion. Welcomes letters (with CVs and photographs) from actors previously unknown to the company, sent by post or email. Does not accept showreels but is happy to receive links to individual actors' websites. Will consider applications from disabled actors to play characters with disabilities. "We work hard and are very passionate about working with young people. You need to be flexible, approachable and keen to create good theatre in education. Look at our website to see what we do before getting in touch."

The Take Away Theatre Company

10 Millbank Street, Dalrymple, Ayrshire KA6 6FE
tel 0800 158 3840
email admin@takeawaytheatre.co.uk
website www.takeawaytheatre.co.uk
Artistic Director Lee O'Driscoll

Production details: Founded in 2007. A theatre-in-education company delivering "high-impact and dynamic drama projects in schools and other venues throughout the UK". Tours 9 projects annually with 270 performances at schools, arts centres, theatres and community venues. In general 4 actors go on tour, playing to audiences aged 1 to 101. Actors may be expected to lead workshops and should hold a current driving licence; singing, musical instrument,

dance and physical theatre skills are an advantage. Recent productions include: *The Jungle Book, Scotland (an' a' that), The Wind in the Willows* and *Hansel and Gretel.*

Casting procedures: Sometimes holds general auditions; actors may write at any time to request inclusion. Casting breakdowns are available via the website, by postal application (with sae), and from Casting Call Pro and CastNet. Welcomes letters (with CVs and photographs) from individual actors previously unknown to the company, sent by post or email. Also accepts showreels and invitations to view individual actors' websites. Will consider applications from disabled actors to play characters with disabilities.

Tall Stories Theatre Company

Somerset House, West Wing, Strand,
London WC1R 1LA
tel 020 8348 0080
email info@tallstories.org.uk
website www.tallstories.org.uk
Artistic Directors Olivia Jacobs, Toby Mitchell
Producer Lucy Wood *General Manager* Charlotte Lund, *Creative Coordinator* Natalia Scorer, *Finance Officer* Sheila McClenaghan, *Production and Digital Marketing Officer* Lucy Troy

Production details: Founded in 1997, Tall Stories creates entertaining and imaginative performances for audiences of all ages, with their productions characterised by a blend of storytelling, music and laughs. Recent productions include: *The Gruffalo* (UK and international tours, West End), *The Snail and the Whale* (UK and international tours, West End) and *Wilde Creatures* (West End, Sydney Opera House). Performers are expected to have good singing and devising abilities, and experience of physical theatre, and the ability to play an instrument is useful. Performers may be expected to lead workshops, but training will be given. Each production consists of 3-4 actors and, on average, the company undertakes 3 UK and 5-6 international tours per year. This equates to over 1,500 performances at around 650 venues, ranging from schools and arts centres to West End theatres.

Casting procedures: Tall Stories holds 3-4 workshop auditions a year for up to 75 actors. Actors can send in a CV and covering letter at any point during the year for consideration. Casting breakdowns are occasionally posted on Spotlight, but the company prefers to invite actors via agent recommendations or those that have directly written to them. Offers contracts based on ITC, UK Theatre or SOLT guidelines. Welcomes applications from disabled actors and promotes inclusive casting.

Ten Ten Theatre

Chester House, Pages Lane, London N10 1PR
0345 388 3162 0345 3883167

email office@tententheatre.co.uk
email casting@tententheatre.co.uk
website www.tententheatre.co.uk
Artistic Director Martin O'Brien

Production details: Established in 2006. An award-winning theatre company, specialises in young people's theatre in primary schools, secondary schools, young offender institutions and the local community. Stages 4-6 productions annually with around 400 performances in 200 schools, arts centres, theatres and community venues across England, Scotland and Wales. In general 2-4 actors go on tour, playing to audiences aged 5 to 21. Actors may be expected to lead workshops. Recent productions include: a 6-month tour of secondary schools with 3 separate plays; and a 1-week residency at Feltham Young Offender Institution. Also produces film productions and co-productions with mainstream theatre companies.

Casting procedures: Does not hold general auditions; actors may write at any time to request inclusion. Casting breakdowns are available from the website or via Equity Job Information Service and Spotlight. Welcomes letters (with CVs and photographs) from individual actors previously unknown to the company, sent by post or email, and will accept showreels and invitations to view individual actors' websites. Offers Equity approved contracts as negotiated through ITC. Will consider applications from disabled actors to play characters with disabilities. "Please view our website to look at our projects and ethos before sending details."

Theatr Iolo

The Old School Building, Cefn Road,
Cardiff CF14 3HS
tel 029 2061 3782 *fax* 029 2052 2225
email admin@theatriolo.com
website www.theatriolo.com
Artistic Director Kevin Lewis

Production details: "Formed in 1987, Theatr Iolo aims to produce and programme the best of live theatre, making it widely accessible to children and young people in Cardiff and the Vale of Glamorgan to stir the imagination, inspire the heart and challenge the mind. Theatr Iolo works alongside teachers and advisers to enhance teaching and learning across the curriculum." Normally tours 5 projects each year with an average annual total of 150 performances across 120 venues. Venues include schools, arts centres and theatres in Wales and occasionally England, and international festivals. Cast sizes vary, playing to audiences aged 3-18. Singing ability, proficiency with a musical instrument, dance/physical theatre skills and a driving licence are frequently required. Actors may also be expected to lead workshops. Recent productions include: *Grimm Tales* by Carol Ann Dufy; *Lenny* by Francis Monty (trans. Paul Harman) and *Under the Carpet* by Sarah Argent.

Casting procedures: Sometimes holds general auditions; actors should write in June requesting inclusion. Casting breakdowns are available through Equity Job Information Service. Accepts submissions (with CVs and photographs) from actors previously unknown to the company if sent by post. Emails are also welcome, as long as the file is not too big. Offers ITC/Equity-approved contracts. Actively encourages applications from disabled actors and promotes the use of inclusive casting.

Theatr na nÓg

Unit 3, Millands Road Industrial Estate,
Neath SA11 1NJ
tel 01639 641771 *fax* 01639 647941
email drama@theatr-nanog.co.uk
website www.theatr-nanog.co.uk
Artistic Director Geinor Styles

Production details: Theatr na nÓg was established in 1982 to produce theatre for a wide spectrum of audiences throughout Wales in a variety of venues and locations, in both languages. "The literal translation of Theatr na nÓg is theatre of eternal youth and this encapslutates the ethos of the company by creating theatre that has the power to excite and engage audiences of all ages." The company is a regular provider of main stage work throughout the country and continues to expand its portfolio of venues. Theatr na nÓg continues to evolve from being a company that solely produces work for schools to being recognised by the Arts Council of Wales as one of their producing theatre companies that will be encouraged to produce work to a variety of audiences throughout Wales and beyond. Theatr na nÓg is now an Associate Company to the Wales Millennium Centre. This enables it to produce new work for a broad range of audiences, and to raise its profile on the international stage.

Casting procedures: Although most casting goes through Spotlight and casting agents, Theatr na nÓg still holds general auditions (depending on the project); actors may write at any time requesting inclusion. Acceps submissions (with CVs and photographs) from actors previously unknown to the company sent bu post or email. Will also accept invitations to view individual actors' websites.

Theatre-Rites

Unit 206, E1 Business Centre, 7 Whitechapel Road,
London E1 1DU
tel 020 7164 6196 *fax* 020 7928 4347
email info@theatre-rites.co.uk
website www.theatre-rites.co.uk
Facebook www.facebook.com/TheatreRites
Twitter @TheatreRites
Artistic Director Sue Buckmaster

Production details: Committed to creating challenging productions which push the boundaries of theatrical form by experimenting to combine different artistic disciplines. Highly imaginative visual experiences for families to share together. Stages 2 productions annually, with around 45 performances in 12 arts centres and theatres across all English regions, in Scotland and internationally. In general 5-8 actors go on tour, playing to audiences of various ages, often 5+. Actors are sometimes expected to lead workshops; singing, musical instrument, dance, physical theatre and puppetry skills may all be advantageous, depending on the project. Recent productions include: *Beasty Baby The Broke'n'Beat Collective, Recycled Rubbish, Bank On It, Mischief* and *Hang On.*

Casting procedures: Sometimes holds general auditions; actors may write at any time to request inclusion. Casting breakdowns are available via the website and Spotlight. Welcomes letters (with CVs and photographs) from individual actors previously unknown to the company, sent by post or email. Also welcomes showreels and invitations to view individual actors' websites. Offers Equity-approved contracts as negotiated through ITC. Actively encourages applications from disabled actors, and promotes the use of inclusive casting. "The work is devised and often physical, so we frequently look for performers with previous experience of this kind."

Theatre Centre

Shoreditch Town Hall, 380 Old Street, London EC1V 9LT
tel 020 7729 3066
email admin@theatre-centre.co.uk
website www.theatre-centre.co.uk
Facebook Theatre_Centre
Twitter @TCLive
Instagram @theatrecentre
Artistic Director Natalie Wilson

Production details: Theatre Centre brings world-class theatre straight into the heart of schools. Productions present big ideas and difficult questions that can help young audiences make sense of a complex and changing world. Uses the power of stories, writing and performance to support students and teachers in their learning across a range of subjects to build confidence and aspirations.
  "Our vision is that children and young people are empowered in their activism and leadership through theatre, using their voices and ideas to make change in themselves and the world around them."
  Offers ITC/Equity and ITC/WGBB contracts. Subscribes to the Equity Pension Scheme.

Casting procedures: Casting breakdowns are available through the website, Spotlight and agents.

Theatre Company Blah Blah Blah!

Interplay Theatre, Armley Road, Leeds LS12 3LE
tel 0113 426 1394
email admin@blahs.co.uk
website www.blahs.co.uk
Facebook www.facebook.com/theatreblahs

Twitter @theatreblahs
Artistic Director Deborah Pakkar-Hull

Production details: A Leeds-based theatre company, founded in 1985, which specialises in participatory theatre for children and young people, performing in schools, community settings and theatres. The company usually tours 1 performance each year, regionally and nationally, accompanied by associated project activity. Offers Equity minimum contracts; does not subscribe to the Equity Pension Scheme.

Casting/recruitment procedures: Opportunities are advertised through the company's website, social media and through industry outlets.

Theatre Exchange Ltd

114 Station Road East, Oxted, Surrey RH8 0QA
tel 01883 724599
email theatre.exchange@freedom-leisure.co.uk
website www.theatre-exchange.org.uk
Artistic Director Katy Potter *Associate Director* Andrew Mulquin

Production details: An educational theatre company focusing on the creative exchange between young people, artists and those who work with young people. Works on up to 21 projects each year, with an average annual total of 650 performances across 400 different venues. Venues include schools, arts centres, theatres and community venues across the South East of England. In general 6 actors go on tour and play to audiences aged 4-13. Interest in and some experience of working with young people is necessary; a driving licence is also useful. Actors are also expected to lead workshops. Recent productions include: *Only a Game?, Our June's Midsummer, Luverly Jubilee* and *The Greeks.*

Casting procedures: Holds general auditions; actors requesting inclusion should write between May and July. Casting breakdowns are available by postal application (with sae), on Equity Job Information Service and through advertisements in *The Stage.* Accepts submissions (with CVs and photographs) from actors previously unknown to the company sent by post or email. Will also accept invitations to view individual actors' websites. "Please send a letter detailing why you are interested in working with young people, along with your CV."

Theatre Hullabaloo

The Hullabaloo, Borough Road, Darlington DL1 1SG
tel 01325 405680
email info@theatrehullabaloo.org.uk
website www.theatrehullabaloo.org.uk
Artistic Producer Miranda Thain

Production details: Founded in 1979. A specialist producer of theatre for young audiences. Tours regionally, nationally and internationally for audiences aged 0 to 16 years, with an emphasis on theatre for early years. Recent productions include: *Bear & Butterfly* (4-7 and families) and *Luna* for 2-4 year olds.

Casting procedures: General auditions are sometimes held and casting opportunities are adverised mainly through social media. Welcomes letters (with CVs and photographs) from individual actors previously unknown to the company but who have a demonstrabletrack record in TYA, sent by post or email. Also accepts showreels and invitations to view individual actors' websites. Offers Equity-approved contracts as negotiated through ITC.

Tin Shed Theatre Company

46 Lennard Street, Newport NP19 0EJ
mobile 07921 366038 or 07511 139773
email tinshedtheatre@gmx.com
website www.tinshedtheatrecompany.com
Company Directors Georgina Harris, Justin Cliffe, Antonio Rimola

Production details: Established in 2008. Specialises in devised theatre which lends itself to performance in unusual spaces. High-energy, high-impact work that focuses on many different genres.

Tours 1 project annually, with around 30 performances in 20 venues, including schools, arts centres and theatres. In general 7 actors go on tour, performing to audiences aged 11 to 16. Actors are required to lead workshops. Recent productions include *Of Mice and Men* by John Steinbeck.

Casting procedures: Uses freelance directors, actors may write at any time to request inclusion. Casting breakdowns are available from the website. Welcomes unsolicited approaches by post and email, and accepts showreels and invitations to view individual actors' websites/visit other productions. Encourages applications from disabled actors and promotes the use of inclusive casting.

Travelling Light Theatre Company

Barton Hill Settlement, 43 Ducie Road, Barton Hill, Bristol BS5 0AX
tel 0117 377 3166
email info@travellinglighttheatre.org.uk
website www.travellinglighttheatre.org.uk
Twitter @tl_theatre
Artistic Producer Heidi Vaughan; *General Manager* Dienka Hines

Production details: Since 1984 the company has produced innovative and inspiring work for young audiences using live music, visual and physical performance in its work. Produces on average 2 tours each year with an average annual total of 200+ perfomances across 50+ different venues, and at least one Christmas show with an extended run. Venues include theatres, arts centres, community venues, local schools and festivals across the UK, as well as touring internationally in China and the US. Target audiences vary from 0-adult. Casts are usually 1-5 actors.

Singing ability, proficiency with a musical instrument and physical theatre skills are often required; most plays are devised with the cast. Recent touring productions include: *Boing* (age 2- 5); *Three Kings* (age 5+) and *Into the West* (age 7+).

Casting procedures: Castings are listed on the company website, Arts Jobs and Disability Arts Online. Accepts submissions (with CVs and photographs) from actors previously unknown to the company, and will accept invitations to view individual actors' websites.

Unicorn Theatre

147 Tooley Street, London SE1 2HZ
tel 020 7645 0500 *fax* 020 7645 0550
email admin@unicorntheatre.com
website www.unicorntheatre.com

Production details: The Unicorn Theatre was founded by Caryl Jenner as a touring company in 1947, with a commitment to giving children a valuable and often first-ever experience of quality theatre, and a philosophy that "the best of theatre for children should be judged on the same high standards of writing, directing, acting and design as the best of adult theatre".

Today, the Unicorn is the national home of theatre for children and young people. Its purpose-built premises at London Bridge contains 2 theatres, 4 floors of public spaces and 2 rehearsal studios dedicated to producing and presenting work for and about audiences aged up to 21. It is an Arts Council National Portfolio Organisation. Offers TMA and ITC/Equity-approved contracts and subscribes to the Equity Pension Scheme.

Casting procedures: Generally by invitation via agent, but will read CVs and photographs from actors previously unknown to the company if sent by email.

Whirlwind Theatre for Children

The Kings House, Phoenix Street,
Lancaster LA1 1DD
tel 01524 812480
email enquiries@whirlwindtheatre.org.uk
website www.whirlwindtheatre.org.uk
Artistic Directors Myette Godwyn, Mike Whalley
Associate Artistic Director Alistair Ganley *Patron* David Wood OBE

Production details: Formed in 2000 to produce a community play for the Museum of Cannock Chase in association with Illyria Theatre Company and a South of England tour of a music-based show for children age 5-10 – *Goldie Locks and the Three Bears*. The company has close ties with the Palm Court Theatre Orchestra, and productions are period-music-based with physical and visual performance aimed at the 4-10 year age-group. Whirlwind runs a performance summer school; also has a Saturday youth theatre club and a programme of workshops.

Normally undertakes 2-3 projects each year with a total of around 150 performances. Venues include churches, arts centres, fields, schools, theatres, outdoor and community venues across England. In general 3 actors go on tour and play to audiences aged 4 upwards. Actors must be proficient in workshop-leading for this age-group; will also need singing, dance/physical theatre skills and preferably the ability to play an instrument to a high standard. A driving licence is also required and actors must be prepared to help with get-ins and get-outs. Whirlwind Theatre has a strong Christian ethos, and most rehearsals and community work are carried out at King's Community Church in Lancaster. Although the company welcomes applications from actors of all beliefs and backgrounds, they should feel at ease with this when applying. Recent productions include: *King's New Clothes* (TIE) and *Hamish Bear and Storytelling Magpie* (TIE) and *Toad of Toad Hall* (summer-school production in Ryelands Park, Lancaster).

Casting procedures: Sometimes holds general auditions; these are always held in Lancaster. Welcomes letters and emails (with CVs and photographs) from actors previously unknown to the company. All actors are required to be DBS checked.

Wizard Theatre Ltd

Blenheim Villa, Burr Street, Harwell, Oxfordshire OX11 0DT
tel 0800 583 2373
email info@wizardtheatre.co.uk
website www.wizardtheatre.co.uk
Facebook @WizardTheatre
Twitter @WizardTheatre
Artistic Director Leon Hamilton *Associate Producer* Oliver Gray *Production Manager* Richard Tall

Production details: Established in 2002. Performs in schools, theatres and conferences across the country. Message-based shows are commissioned annually. Works with various organisations, from the Met Police to Drug Action teams. Provides many drama therapy classes in schools. The winter show tours in theatres: 2019's production is *Dr Dolittle*.

Stages 7+ projects annually, with more than 600 performances in 400 venues across London, the Home counties and Shropshire. In general 2-4 actors go on tour, playing to audiences aged 4-18. Actors may be required to lead workshops. Good singing, musical instrument, driving and stage combat skills are useful. Recent productions include: *The Wind in the Willows, Choices* and *On the Right Road*. We are always looking for excellent facilitators and drama teachers. The Pupil Premium Project also always requires goood actor/teachers to join the team.

Casting procedures: Sometimes holds general auditions; actors are welcome to write in at any time. Casting breakdowns are available via Casting Call Pro and on the Equity Job Information Service. Welcomes unsolicited approaches by actors/facilitators/teachers by post or email. Also accepts showreels and will consider invitations to view individual actors' websites. Does not offer Equity-approved contracts: "Usually we pay well above Equity rates." Rarely or never has the opportunity to cast disabled actors.

Young Shakespeare Company

213 Fox Lane, Southgate, London N13 4BB
tel 020 8368 4828
email youngshakespeare@mac.com
website www.youngshakespeare.org.uk
Artistic Directors Christopher Geelan and Sarah Gordon

Production details: One of the longest-established and most respected educational theatre companies in the UK. Currently performs Shakespeare to more than 100,000 young people each year, working in schools and theatres to provide a year-round programme of performances and workshops. On average stages 10 productions each year, with around 1,000 performances in theatres and schools throughout England. In general, 5 actors per show perform to audiences aged 6-16. Actors may be expected to lead workshops. Recent productions include: *Twelfth Night, Romeo and Juliet, Macbeth, The Tempest, Hamlet* and *A Midsummer Night's Dream*.

Casting procedures: Holds auditions every June for autumn season and every November for spring season. Casting breakdowns are available via Spotlight link. Also welcomes emails from individual actors previously unknown to the company.

Shakespeare changes prisoners' lives

Bruce Wall

'Correction and instruction must both work 'ere the rude beast will profit.'
William Shakespeare, *Measure for Measure*, III ii

If prisons really worked there would be fewer of them. Certainly, there were would be fewer people than the 86,000 plus currently locked in British cells. Whereas UK criminal justice regimes have historically failed institutionally, success has been captured by peeking through the keyhole of individual arts successes. They serve as role models. They deserve to be cherished.

The Prison Reform Trust in 2017 reported that the overall number of staff in UK prisons has fallen from 45,000 in 2010 to just under 31,000 in 2016. Over 7,000 UK prison officers have been cut in but five years. Training programmes have been shredded to an unrealistic minimum.

Over the past quarter century, the UK prison environment has become ever more challenging; ever more violent; ever more drug infested; ever larger and ever more dangerous. It is – as even the Prison Service itself acknowledges – unsustainable. Still the arts work inside endures. Somehow.

Historically, there have been many charities running valuable arts programmes in UK prisons. The oldest – groups like the Koestler Trust, Clean Break (itself founded by two female ex-offenders); Fine Cell Work; Dance United and Music in Prisons – have continued to make inroads. Notwithstanding it has become progressively difficult for arts groups to survive, let alone thrive.

The London Shakespeare Workout (LSW) is a charity I had the privilege to co-found opposite the legendary Dame Dorothy Tutin in 1997. It seeks 'to employ the works of Shakespeare and other major dramatic writers/thinkers as a tool towards effective interaction to (a) create new work and (b) promote confidence through the will to dream for all.' Notice that prison does not feature in its title. Terminology is key. To the men and women, we are privileged to work with that is important. They are serving time for the past. LSW trades in futures.

The word 'drama' in ancient Greek means 'conflict'. It might be argued that the world's greatest dramatic/musical art has itself been created in and around adversity. Assuming that to be correct the climate described above is ripe in its artistic potential to both educate and entertain. The arts can step in where more conventional educational programmes have failed. Over the past two decades, LSW has been privileged to engage with more than 9,000 offenders of every race, gender, orientation, colour and creed. Currently, over 82,000 UK prison inmates are adult males, while women account for fewer than 3,200 places. LSW's production of Lorca's *The House of Bernarda Alba* – originally mounted in one women's prison, HMP Send, in an original version translated by a woman serving a life sentence in another – marked the first time in this country that prisoners had been allowed out to perform in London's West End. In this instance at the Criterion Theatre. This production – as almost all LSW's have been – involved a mix of prisoners and professional actors.

Theatre

Indeed, we've been honoured to work alongside more than 12,000 professional actors or those in training. These sessions/workshops/productions have taken place in venues ranging from 100 different prisons in England alone to Broadway; from the House of Lords to the United Nations; from Yorkshire's Stephen Joseph Theatre to the Royal Opera House; from the RSC's Swan Theatre to the celebrated Stratford Festival in Ontario, Canada.

One example: in a round with a mix of juvenile offenders and professional actors in a correctional estate in fashionable Henley-upon-Thames, a lad – no more than fifteen years old – haphazardly pulls a Shakespearean line from a manila envelope. Visibly shocked at what he sees his chin begins to quiver. Bravely he summons up sufficient courage to haltingly read: 'Thought is free'. At the day's end, he asks me – the person leading the session – if he might keep that slip of paper. I knew full well it was against regulations. He could potentially use that wafer-thin slice to self-harm. Still, I didn't have the heart to take it from him. 'It's yours,' I said. He beamed with pride. Minutes later I stood and watched as an officer undertaking a search remove it from him at the gate outside. For a moment, he looked crestfallen. Then he turned back and looked at me through the hut's window. He grinned. I did the same. He put his thumb up. He knew – in the most real sense – he now owned IT.

A second example: we'd done a number of sessions at HMP The Mount in Hertford-shire. On this day, there were forty in the room; fourteen actors and twenty-six inmates. At one point, we launched into a 'Shakespeare interspersal'. In this exercise, an actor uses the Shakespeare in his head to intersperse with an inmate who responds to the language he/she hears in approximate length of line while addressing a scenario selected by their peers. These lads decided it should be set in a 'church in Brixton'. The actor would be the 'father confessor' and the inmate was 'coming in to confess a murder'. I asked for volunteers. One young black lad (many of the inmates in Southern UK prisons are BAME) put up his hand. (He'd been to other sessions we'd run before but never done any individual work.) 'You,' I said: 'You have a go.' Dutifully, Benson (for that's what the guys called him) entered the circle. 'The tempter or the tempted ... who sins most?' the knelling actor, Alasdair Craig, a War Horse veteran, began. Benson responded well. As Angelo questioned his own conscience in that speech, Benson got the brilliant idea that he'd been duped. It had been the father confessor who'd been the perpetrator of the crime. Masterfully he turned the tables ... but that's not the point of this story.

We went on to do many other activities that day and at the end I noticed a prison officer at the door. She'd obviously been crying. Concerned, I went over to her and said I hoped that she had not taken any offence as I was sure none had been intended. She grabbed me. 'You don't understand,' she pointedly said, 'that boy [gesticulating at Benson] has been in this prison for three years and he has never, ever, made a sound.'

Still, why *this* language? 'Why Shakespeare?' I'm asked that question more than any other. One, then twenty-three-year-old, London inmate gives the best answer I've ever heard. In but fifteen minutes, he pens a sonnet in answer to the query. It begins: 'It's addictive. First time's never enough/You wanna taste it again and again.' His final couplet – in perfect scansion – sings out:

> Do you wanna taste this drug? Go on 'ere
> Don't worry. It's harmless. It's just Shakespeare.

He's enrolled in LSW's year-long (2005/6) – precedent setting – drama school lodged in HMP Brixton, the first within a UK prison walls. (For an entire year previously I was entitled to travel to male prisons throughout the country doing workshops and moving men to Brixton who showed aptitude and commitment.) These inmates will study voice with Cicely Berry and text with the likes of Olivier, BAFTA, Tony and Oscar-winning Mark Rylance and Dame Janet Suzman. The lads call it the 'Dream Factory' For many that's what it is.

Today, Dream Factory graduates have worked for, among others, the RSC and the Globe. One leads a film unit in Berlin and another one of the UK's leading youth arts programmes. Of those who were released during the programme's tenure none has reoffended. Throughout the Dream Factory's history, lads take part in countless Shakespeare Workouts with actors from 'the outside'. For the prisoners, these become the equivalent of a ballet dancer's morning class. They instil discipline into their studied craft. Many guests will be recent drama school graduates. Many will later note that this theatrical interaction remains 'profound' in terms of their professional work. Still more will say this experience was 'life changing'.

LSW has worked in a similar light not just in the UK but throughout the world aside a vast array of international talent. The positive response remains universal in locales ranging from Chile to China; from India to Afghanistan. Now LSW dreams of a prison interaction for every UK drama student being aware – as we are – that this is a vital part of their training as future communicators. For the past eighteen years, LSW has been privileged to share prison interactions with graduating students from the Royal Academy of Dramatic Art (RADA). In 2017, we were particularly honoured when this outreach work was embedded as part of every RADA student's core BA curriculum. Indeed, in the 2017 RADA graduating class there is an ex-offender who once defined himself as 'a career criminal'. Today he is a talented actor.

Twenty years of forging history in this arena has taught us that for a performing artist – any performing artist – there are very few things one can do where you immediately know that what you do is vitally important; is socially critical. This incentive offers just such an opportunity. It holds, as t'were, a mirror up to many and contrasting natures; your own as much as anyone else's. To this end, LSW and HMP Pentonville have created the 'Linked Up Initiative' or LUP for short. We've coined a new word much as the Bard often did. It is an ACTIVE verb: 'To LUP' means 'to bring disparate bodies together in hope'. Linked up thinking – or 'lupping' – is not something often celebrated inside prisons but Shakespeare always celebrates community. It is his magnet that melds: It lups.

Yesterday, one eighteen-year-old young offender currently housed within HMP Pentonville, an adult prison, told me that he 'now' knew 'why' he'd been sent to prison. 'It was to do this.' I, myself, know full well we learn from each other.

As usual Shakespeare unifies in whole: 'We are such stuff as dreams are made on'.

Having toiled from childhood onwards as an actor and later a director in the theatre and other media in London, New York and elsewhere, **Bruce Wall** additionally plied his talents as a Director of the Harkness House for Ballet Arts, for the Metropolitan Opera and in 1983 – as the youngest Artistic Director of a LORT (League of Regional Theaters) theatre in the USA – created the first international exchange on a fully fair contractual basis between an American and British actor. Happily, that precedent continues to this day. Dr Wall co-founded the London Shakespeare Workout and remains its Executive Director. Perhaps most aptly the NY Times christened him 'a theatrical missionary'.

Theatre

Festivals

These are populated by all kinds of companies listed in previous sections. Some are hired-in by a festival's organisers; others 'hire' space in order to participate – the latter predominate at the most famous festival of all, in Edinburgh. Participation in a festival can be enormous fun, and a great opportunity to meet other actors and see other productions. However, the chances of such a production transferring, let alone making money, are limited.

UMBRELLA ORGANISATIONS

British Arts Festivals Association (BAFA)
Office 24944, PO Box 6945 London W1A 6US
07756 309844
email bafa@artsfestivals.co.uk
website www.artsfestivals.co.uk
Facebook www.facebook.com/BritArtsFests
Twitter @BritArtsFests

Provides information and a professional network for the festivals movement in the UK, working to promote the profile and status of arts festivals. As well as providing a festival directory on the website, BAFA produces an advance festivals press pack each January and May, and is the British hub for the prestigious European Festivals Association. Members have the opportunity to attend BAFA conferences, access to partnership deals and discounts and vital festival resources. Membership is open to all arts festivals in the UK and associate membership to other arts organisations, universities, students and agents.

The European Festivals Association
General Secretariat, Kleine Gentstraat 46,
B-9051 Gent, Belgium
email info@efa-aef.eu
website www.efa-aef.eu

The European Festivals Association is the umbrella organisation for festivals across Europe and beyond. The oldest cultural network in Europe, it was founded in Geneva, Switzerland, in 1952 as a joint initiative of the eminent conductor Igor Markevitch and the great philosopher Denis de Rougemeont. Since its foundation, the Association has grown from 15 festivals into a dynamic network representing more than 100 music, dance, theatre and multidisciplinary festivals, national festival associations and cultural organisations from 40 countries.

UK ARTS FESTIVALS

Arundel Festival
tel (01903) 883474
email arundelfestival@btopenworld.com
website www.arunundelfestival.co.uk

For 10 days each August, the market town of Arundel is host to a multi-arts festival which began in 1977. Street theatre and a festival Fringe are regular features, as are concerts, exhibitions, fireworks and jazz. The festival culminates in an open-air production of a Shakespeare play in the grounds of Arundel Castle. Each production is led by a cast of experienced professional actors, and extended with members of the local community, who work with the professionals throughout the 6-week rehearsal period.

Barbican
Barbican Centre, Silk Street, London EC2Y 8DS
tel 020-7638 4141
email theatre@barbican.org.uk
website www.barbican.org.uk
Facebook /BarbicanCentre
Twitter @BarbicanCentre

The Barbican showcases international theatre, dance and performance by leading companies, auteurs and emerging artists that challenge the idea of what theatre can be. It invests in the artists of today and tomorrow through the commissioning of new work, showcasing emerging talent and collaborating with their Artistic Associates - Boy Blue Entertainment, Cheek by Jowl, Michael Clark Company ad Deborah Warner.

Belfast Festival at Queens
Ulster Bank Belfast Festival at Queens,
8 Fitzwilliam Street, Belfast BT9 6AW
email n.murphy@qub.ac.uk
website www.belfastfestival.com
Festival Director Shan McAnena

Founded in 1963, the Belfast Festival is an annual 3-week international arts festival held in October and November each year. The largest festival of its kind in Ireland, it covers all artforms including theatre, dance, classical music, literature, jazz, comedy, visual arts, folk music and popular music, attracting more than 50,000 visitors. Theatre performances in 2004 included: the Belfast Theatre Company's production of *A Most Notorious Woman*; Theatre Royal Bath's production of *Blithe Spirit* with Penelope Keith. Artists wishing to participate in the festival should submit a written proposal to the address listed above.

Birmingham ArtsFest

Events Section, Birmingham City Council,
Alexander Stadium, Walsall Road, Perry Barr,
Birmingham B42 2LR
tel 0121-464 5678
email artsfest@birmingham.gov.uk
website www.artsfest.org.uk

ArtsFest is one of the UK's largest free arts festivals
and is held in venues across Birmingham for 2 days
in September. It programmes a range of free
performances including theatre, jazz, opera and
dance events. Street theatre also features heavily, with
musicians, jugglers, visual artists and stand-up
comedians all presenting their work outside. There
are also a variety of workshops on offer, ranging from
screenwriting to Bollywood dancing. *Note*: Because of
the need for budget cuts, the future of this festival is
uncertain.

Brighton Festival

email info@brightonfestival.org
website www.brightonfestival.org

Founded in 1967. For 3 weeks in May, there are more
than 300,000 attendances at 800 separate arts events
taking place in venues across Brighton and Hove.
Artists from a number of different countries are
represented in theatre, dance, music, opera, books,
events and outdoor spectaculars.

Running alongside Brighton Festival, Brighton
Festival Fringe (previously called 'the Open') has
been in existence for 37 years, and is the biggest in
England, showcasing a variety of artforms and
activities. Applicants for the Fringe should first read
the 'How to be in Brighton Festival Fringe' document
available on the website, and then register online.

Canterbury Festival

8 Orange Street, Canterbury, Kent CT1 2JA
tel (01227) 452853
email info@canterburyfestival.co.uk
website www.canterburyfestival.co.uk

One of the UKs longest established arts festivals, the
Canterbury Festival takes place over 2 weeks in late
October/early November. Classical concerts in
Canterbury Cathedral, world music of all kinds plus
circus and cabaret in the beautiful Spiegeltent, the
programme also includes theatre, dance, science,
talks, walks and exhibitions. Spanning school half-
term, there is a wide range of events for families and
young people. With over 200 events in the fortnight,
the Festival is the highlight of Canterbury's cultural
calendar – and a marvellous time to visit the historic
city. Festival guests in the past have included Van
Morrison, Sir Bryn Terfel and the Tallis Scholars,
while the year-round public engagement programme
works with more than 2,000 young people annually.

Dumfries and Galloway Arts Festival

Gracefield Arts Centre, 28 Edinburgh Road,
Dumfries DG1 1JQ

tel (01387) 259627
email info@dgartsfestival.org.uk
website www.dgartsfestival.org.uk

Established in 1979. Scotland's largest perfoming Arts
Festival – runs for 10 days at the end of May. The
festival programme includes a diverse programme of
world class events covering music, contemporary
dance, theatre, comedy and spoken word. Events take
place in a wide range of venues throughout the
region including arts centres, pubs, theatres and
village halls.

Also runs Dumfries and Galloway Arts Live,
established in 2016. A network of venues, promoters
and performing artists set up to bring quality live
events to venues throughout Dumfries and Galloway
year-round. Organised by the Dumfries and Galloway
Arts Festival team.

Edinburgh Festival Fringe Society

Edinburgh Festival Fringe Society, 180 High Street,
Edinburgh EH1 1QS
tel 0131-226 0026 *fax* 0131-226 0016
email admin@edfringe.com
website www.edfringe.com

The Fringe began in 1947, when 8 theatre companies
decided to perform uninvited alongside the first
Edinburgh International Festival. It is now the largest
arts festival on the planet, with over 45,000
performances of over 2,800 shows in more than 250
venues across Edinburgh each August. The Fringe is
still entirely open-access and anyone who wants to
bring a show can do so.

The Fringe Society was formed in 1959 to provide a
comprehensive information service both to
performers and to audiences. You can contact the
Society year round with general questions and advice
on how to take part.

Edinburgh International Festival

The Hub, Castlehill, Edinburgh EH1 2NE
tel 0131-473 2001 *fax* 0131-473 2003
email eif@eif.co.uk
website www.eif.co.uk

Founded in 1947, the Edinburgh International
Festival is an annual event held over 3 weeks in
August, using venues across the city. With music,
opera, classical music and dance, the festival is
recognised as one of the world's most important
celebrations of the performing arts. Also offers a
programme of year-round education and outreach
activities. Performance at the Edinburgh
International Festival is by invitation only, issued by
the Festival Director.

Fierce Festival

Unit 3, Minerva Works, 158 Fazeley Street,
Birmingham B5 5RT
email contact@wearefierce.org
website www.wearefierce.org

Theatre

Biennual festival of live art in theatres, bars, clubs, galleries and public spaces across Birmingham and the West Midlands. The festival takes place in October with smaller events and artist development opportnuities throughout the year.

Grassington Festival

The Festival Office, Grassington Festival, Grassington, North Yorkshire BD23 5AT
tel (01756) 456007
email kate@grassington-festival.org.uk
website www.grassington-festival.org.uk
Festival Director Kate Beard

An annual multi-disciplinary festival featuring contemporary and classical music, theatre, poetry and film, and taking place in the last 2 weeks of June.

Greenwich and Docklands International Festival (GDIF)

Pepys Building, 2 Cutty Sark Gardens, London SE10 9LW
tel 020-8305 1818 *fax* 020-8305 1188
email admin@festival.org
website www.festival.org

Taking place over the 4 weekends of July, the Greenwich and Docklands International Festival programmes multi-disciplinary arts events around East London each summer. As well as programming large-scale, visually impressive work, the festival places emphasis on educational projects and participatory arts.

HighTide

24A St John Street, London EC1M 4AY
tel 020-7566 9765
email info@hightide.org.uk
website www.hightide.org.uk
Artistic Director Steven Atkinson *Incoming Artistic Director* Suba Das

HighTide theatre company produces new plays throughout the UK, and runs a festival in Suffolk. It is internationally renowned in its field for finding new playwrights and in the vanguard of staging theatre productions. Its programming influences the mainstream.

Hotbed: Cambridge New Writing Theatre Festival

Cambridge Junction, Clifton Road, Cambridge CB1 7GX
tel (01223) 403361
email office@menagerie.uk.com
website www.menagerietheatre.co.uk

Produced by: Menagerie Theatre Company

Following the success of the original Hotbed 2002, Menagerie Theatre Company (**www.menagerietheatre.co.uk**) and Cambridge Junction (**www.junction.co.uk**) joined forces to

present Hotbed 2004 and 2006, Cambridge's New Writing Theatre Festival. Over 3 weeks in July, venues around Cambridge – including CB2, Cambridge Drama Centre and Cambridge Arts Theatre's Playroom – hosted a variety of new plays by a selection of regional and national writers. Productions ranged from 15-minute lunchtime shorts to full evening performances, with a selection of workshops, talks, masterclasses and seminars also included in the programme.

In 2014/2015, the festival will present opportunities both for writers and for actors to get involved. Writing opportunities are advertised on the Menagerie website (**www.menagerie.uk.com**). A repertory company based around the members of Menagerie Theatre Company supports the festival, and actors are welcome to audition for the company a few months in advance. For further information about the next Hotbed and how to get involved, contact Paul Bourne at **office@menagerie.uk.com**.

Lichfield Festival

7 The Close, Lichfield, Staffordshire WS13 7LD
tel (01543) 306270
email info@lichfieldfestival.org
website www.lichfieldfestival.org
Festival Manager Peter Bacon

Annual 10-day multi-arts festival in early July, Literature Festival in September/October, plus occasional seasonal events.

London International Festival of Theatre (LIFT)

Toynbee Studios, 28 Commercial Street, London E1 6AB
email info@liftfestival.com
website www.liftfestival.com
Facebook /theLIFTfestival
Twitter @LIFTfestival
Editor Instagram @liftfestival
Artistic Director/Joint CEO Kris Nelson *Executive Director/Joint CEO* Beki Bateson

Started in 1981, LIFT is a biennial summer festival introducing some of the world's most exciting artists and theatre-makers to London. LIFT events have been staged in more than 50 London venues as well as in a number of site-specific venues such as cemeteries, car park roofs, disused buildings, the river, parks and open spaces.

LIFT also runs developmental and educational programmes exploring the nature of exchange and creativity for a range of audiences including schoolchildren and industry leaders.

London International Mime Festival

Somerset House (South Wing), Strand, London WC2R 1LA
tel 020-7637 5661
email direction@mimelondon.com
website www.mimelondon.com
Directors Joseph Seelig, Helen Lannaghan

Founded in 1977 by Joseph Seelig and Nola Rae, the London International Mime Festival presents contemporary visual theatre. Events are non-text based and can include circus theatre, puppetry, mask, mime, clown and live art. Most work will be either a UK or a London premiere.

The festival takes place each January with the deadline for submissions is 1st June. Participation is by invitation only. To be considered, email Helen Lannaghan and Joseph Seelig at the address above.

Ludlow Festival

email info@ludlowfestival.co.uk
website www.ludlowfestival.co.uk

Running for more than 45 years, the Ludlow Festival takes places over 2-3 weeks in June/July with a range of music, theatre and exhibitions on offer. Each year it features open-air Shakespeare productions which are staged in the grounds of Ludlow Castle.

Manchester International Festival (MIF)

Blackfriars House, Parsonage, Manchester M3 2JA
tel 0161-817 4500 *fax* 0161-839 2662
email info@mif.co.uk
website www.mif.co.uk

Manchester International Festival (MIF) is a biennial leading festival of original, new work, created by a wide range of major international artists. The first festival took place in June-July 2007; the sixth edition will take place in July 2017. Strengthening Manchester's reputation as a leading cultural city, the Festival features work across all art-forms, including MIF Creative, a programme of innovative community-based commissions.

The Mayor's Thames Festival

website www.thamesfestival.org

The Mayor's Thames Festival is a free annual event that takes place on and around the River Thames between Westminster and Southwark Bridges. Using the river as a powerful unifying symbol for the whole of London, one of the festival's main aims is to enable more collaborations between artists and community groups. Over 1 weekend in September it programmes events such as night carnivals, fireworks spectaculars, mass choirs, music stages, a range of participatory activities, and both artist-led and river-orientated events.

Merseyside International Street Festival

tel 0151-709 3334 *fax* 0151-709 4994
email info@brouhaha.uk.com
website www.brouhaha.uk.com

Established in 1990, the Merseyside International Street Festival brings a mix of dance, drama, acrobatics, music, comedy, puppetry and street theatre to around 30,000 spectators in Liverpool each July/August.

Minack Theatre Summer Festival

Porthcurno, Penzance, Cornwall TR19 6JU
tel (01736) 810694 *fax* (01736) 810779
email info@minack.com
website www.minack.com

Founded in 1932. An annual, 20-week summer season of plays, musicals and opera held at Minack's unique open-air theatre carved into the Cornish cliffside. Created in 1932 by Rowena Cade and her gardener Billy Rawlings, the Minack lends itself to large-cast plays. Most companies involved are amateur, although approximately 3 each year are professional.

Pulse Fringe Festival

c/o The New Wolsey Theatre, Civic Drive, Ipswich IP1 2AS
website www.pulsefringe.com

Founded in 2000, Pulse Fringe is "a bright snapshot of contemporary theatre and performance, comprising finished shows, work in progress and new ideas". The festival brings an exciting blend of artists embracing a wide variety of performance arts to Ipswich, offering a unique opportunity to see a wide range of top-quality, emotionally charged and entertaining work and innovative thinking.

Stafford Festival Shakespeare

c/o Gatehouse Theatre, Eastgate Street, Stafford ST16 2LT
tel 01785 253595
website www.staffordfestivalshakespeare.co.uk
Artistic Programme Manager Derrick Gask

As well as an annual pantomime, The Gatehouse Theatre, generally a receiving house, produces the Stafford Festival Shakespeare, an open-air production at Stafford Castle every summer. Casting breakdowns for The Festival Shakespeare are sent out in January and casting is done by freelance casting directors; rehearsals start in June. Photos and CVs sent to the theatre by actors wishing to be considered for audition will be forwarded to the casting director. Invitations to see actors in other productions are welcomed and should be addressed to Derrick Gask. Will consider applications from disabled actors to play disabled characters.

See entry under *In-house pantomimes* on page 240 for details of the annual pantomime.

The Sunday Times National Student Drama Festival (NSDF)

Woolyard, 54 Bermondsey High Street, London SE1 3UD
tel 020 7036 9027
email info@nsdf.org.uk
website www.nsdf.org.uk
Facebook @nsdfest
Twitter @nsdfest

Theatre

Director James Phillips *Adminstrator* Lizzie Melbourne

For over 60 years, NSDF has been at the heart of the British Theatre. NSDF selects and presents work created by young people and empowers and inspires young talent – providing masterclasses, workshops and year-round practical advice from experienced professionals including a core team of selectors.

The NSDF has a remarkable alumni including Olivia Vinall, Ruth Wilson, Alex Jennings, Lucy Prebble, Simon Russell Beale, Meera Syal, Kate Mellor, Steve Pemberton and many, many more.

For all information, please visit the website. NSDF is an Arts Council England National Portfolio Organisation.

Role-play companies

Actors have long used their craft in promotional areas like selling products and services over the phone and in department stores; work opportunities in these fields are advertised in *The Stage*. More recently, the idea of using theatre skills deeper inside the world of business (and the service professions, like medicine) has grown considerably. Essentially, the high level of co-operation ('interactivity') and the excitement, creativity and inspirational power of good theatre is being grasped by hierarchies 'outside the proscenium arch'. Role-play practitioners today are using techniques evolved by the Theatre in Education movement in the 1960s and 70s – but with far better-paying 'customers'.

The established companies – mostly created by actors – have built up a great deal of expertise in this new world, and do not take on new 'role-players' lightly. It is therefore especially important to research each individual company's *modus operandi* before spending time and money in contacting them. However, this is a world well worth exploring as an exciting and lucrative alternative area of work.

aardvark productions ltd
Withywinds, Mill Hill, Edenbridge TN8 5DQ
tel 0800-3285 766
email info@aardvarkproductions.biz
website www.aardvarkproductions.biz
Facebook aardvarkproductions1
Twitter @aardvarkprods
Directors Daniel Kerry, Angela Youngs

Production details: Formed in 1991, aardvark creates themed events for corporate and private clients. They also supply historical characters to museums, country houses and schools for education and entertainment as well as performing murder mysteries for any kind of event.

Casting procedures: Uses in-house casting directors, but only holds auditions as and when people apply. Welcomes both CVs and letters from actors previously unknown to the company and unsolicited CVs and photographs. Also welcomes invitations to view individual actor's websites and showreels. Happy to consider disabled actors for all roles. However, a lot of their roles would be difficult to manage for those with disabilities. Currently, there are 4 actors with differing disabilities working for aardvark.

Acting Out Ltd
Regal Chambers, Cavendish Street,
Chesterfield S40 1UY
tel (01246) 520014 *mobile* (07852) 320788
fax (01246) 558396
email acting.out@btinternet.com
website www.acting-out.co.uk
Artistic Director Claire Ashcroft, BA (Hons)

Company's work: Supplies professional role-play actors for training for all kinds of staff, from medical and legal to bar staff and corporate training. All actors must have professional role-play experience. Clients include: NHS Trust and the National Trust.

Recruitment procedures: Periodically extends its actor-base, monthly to annually, via agents, websites and Equity. Welcomes letters (with CVs and photographs) from actors previously unknown to the company sent by post or email; is happy to receive showreels and invitations to view individual actors' websites. Will consider applications from disabled actors to play characters with disabilities.

Activation
Riverside House, Feltham Avenue, Hampton Court, Surrey KT8 9BJ
tel 020-8783 9494 *fax* 020-8783 9345
email info@activation.co.uk
website www.activation.co.uk
Director Paul Gilmore

Company's work: A leading provider of bespoke interactive training. Services include forum theatre, role-play, scriptwriting and performance and the design and delivery of training programmes. Incoming actors are trained by the company, according to the requirements of the project. Strong acting and listening skills are required of all the actors. Recent clients include: Diageo, Barclays and Lloyds TSB.

Recruitment procedures: Periodically extends its actor-base, often by word-of-mouth but also using the Internet. Welcomes letters (with CVs and photographs) from actors previously unknown to the company if sent by post, but not by email. Does not welcome showreels, but is happy to receive invitations to view individuals' websites. Will consider applications from disabled actors to play characters with disabilities.

Theatre

Actors in Industry Ltd (Aii Training)

5 Risborough Street, London SE1 0HF
tel 020-7234 9600 *fax* 020-7357 0915
email enquiries@actorsinindustry.com
website www.actorsinindustry.com
Directors Carry Clubb, Roger Ayres, Lorraine Brunning

Company's work: Established in 1992. "We are the foremost interactive training company in the UK, using role-play, facilitation and interactive training and coaching to create meaningful skills improvement and behavioural change for individuals and organisations." Requires incoming recruits to possess a good knowledge of business, giving feedback, and the ability to understand the perspective of delegates on training programmes. Provides training for associates in the form of an induction, group workshops and one-to-one sessions. Recent clients include: PWC, Amey, Linklaters, Astellas, Barclays, Lilly, Kraft, Johnson & Johnson, RBS, IBM, Jones Lang Lasalle, Mercer and Ernst & Young.

Recruitment procedures: Interviews twice yearly, and recruits via emailed CVs (business and role playing) and covering letter. Advises recruits to be honest about experience; over-elaboration will be discovered very quickly. When submitting files with an application, please make sure that all file names contain the name of the applicant, e.g. NOT roleplay CV but John Smith roleplay CV.

Adhoc Actors

Lordhoill House, Mill Street, Whitchurch, Shropshire SY13 1SE
tel 0161-2360 618
email info@adhocactors.co.uk
website www.adhocactors.co.uk
Artistic Director Guy Hepworth

Company's work: Founded in 2005, Adhoc Actors have worked mainly in the public and private sector business for the last 14 years. They have provided training, writing, drama, entertainment and educational workshops to a number of different organisations. The company requires its actors and performers to have excellent feedback skills and experience of working in corporate role-play, as well as being skilled at improvisation, and comfortable with interactive/immersive performance. However, there is a thorough briefing before any job is undertaken. Clients include: Merseyside Police, Penguin Random House, Macmillan Cancer Support, Next and Arrow Global (Breathe POD).

Recruitment procedures: Uses in-house casting directors but does not hold general auditions. Casting breakdowns can be available from the Equity JIS and Mandy websites. Welcomes letters (with CVs and photographs) from individual actors previously unknown to the company and unsolicited CVs with photographs, sent by email. Will consider invitations

to view individual actors' websites and performance notices. Also welcomes showreels. Will consider applications from disabled actors to play characters with disabilities.

AKT Productions

262 Waterloo Road, London SE1 8RQ
tel 020-7620 0843
email info@aktproductions.co.uk
website www.aktproductions.co.uk
Director Marc Bolton

Company's work: Established in 1996. Provider of theatre-based learning resources, developing quality learning and development programmes. Incoming actors are expected to have experience of corporate role-play. Actor-base is extended every 8-12 mionths via recommendations and applications.

Recruitment procedures: Accepts submissions (with CVs and photographs) from actors previously unknown to the company. Prefers CVs and photographs sent via email. Invitations to view individual actors' websites are also accepted. Applications from disabled actors are considered.

Apropos Productions Ltd

53 Greek Street, London W1D 3DR
tel 020 7739 2857 *fax* 020 7739 3852
email info@aproposltd.com
website www.aproposltd.com
Director Paul Dubois

Company's work: Established in 2004. First feature film completes post-production August 2015, *Dark Signal* (executive producer Neil Marshall). Short films: *The Juror*, *X-Why* and *Cocktail*. Web series: award-winning web series: *A Quick Fortune* and *Le Method* (2016). Script events include *My German Roots are Showing* at the Arcola Theatre, London, starring Miriam Margolyes.

Provides training for local, national and international clients. Key focus is on Organisational Behaviour. Training is provided for incoming actors. Corporate experience is useful but not essential. Actor-base is extended annually through agents, the website and Equity Job Information Service. Clients include: SKANKSA, Sony Computer Entertainment, House of Commons, UBM and the Discovery Network.

Recruitment procedures: Accepts submissions (with CVs and photographs) from actors previously unknown to the company. Disabled actors regularly form part of its teams and are actively encouraged to apply.

Michael Browne Associates Ltd

The Cloisters, 168C Station Road, Lower Stondon, Beds SG16 6JQ
tel/fax (01462) 812483
email hello@mba-roleplay.co.uk
website www.mba-roleplay.co.uk
Directors Michael Browne, Angie Smith

Company's work: Established in 1997. Holds an extensive database of more than 750 professional, corporate actors. Works closely with clients to cast, devise, manage and interpret events and assessments to inform, challenge, develop, assess and train. Will provide training for incoming actors on particular clients' material as and when required. Actors should have professional drama training and experience in the corporate world using role-play for assessment, training and development. Clients include: MoD, KPMG, Nationwide, NHSBT, UKTI, FCA, RBS, DVLA and Open University.

Recruitment procedures: Periodically extends its actor-base when required "via interview/workshop after personal application and recommendation". Welcomes letters (with CVs and photographs) from actors previously unknown to the company, sent by post or email. Accepts showreels and invitations to view individual actors' websites. Will consider applications from disabled actors for specific projects.

CentreStage Partnership

South Hill Park, Ringmead, Bracknell,
Berkshire RG12 7PA
tel (01344) 304305
email info@cstage.co.uk
website www.cstage.co.uk
Contact Pippa Shepherd

Company's work: A leading development consultancy specialising in the use of drama to enhance learning.

Recruitment procedures: In the first instance, actors should send a CV outlining their acting and business experience, along with a recent photograph and covering letter, to Pippa Shepherd via **info@cstage.co.uk.**

Characters

12 Stillness Road, Honor Oak Park,
London SE23 1NG
tel 020-8856 4005 *mobile* (07710) 493483
website www.characters.uk.com
Contact Catherine Hamilton

Company's work: A well-established role-play company with 14 years' experience. Owned by Catherine Hamilton, whose background combines a professional acting career with community health experience. Initially, the company focused on working with police forces and social services departments. It has now begun to expand into the NHS and private sector, more than doubling its client base.

Dramanon

email info@dramanon.co.uk
website www.dramanon.co.uk
Directors Melanie Nicholson, Steven Brough

Company's work: A leading provider of live and multi-media training and consultancy in the UK, Europe and India. Dramanon uses a blend of forum theatre and role-play bespoke to each client to enable the most productive training experience. Have been in operation since 1985. The company has built up a large client base including the public sector, law firms, retail, construction, financial and pharmaceutical companies. Dramanon has expanded its activities to providing immersive theatre and a full repertoire of activities at company conferences. Having moved to Twickenham Film Studios in 2015 they now offer full film production and company TV support.

Frank Partners

website www.frankpartners.co.uk
Key contacts Neil Bett, Anna Carus-Wilson

Company's work: "We work in a variety of ways, including role-play, forum theatre, facilitation, games, coaching, making films ... in fact, any kind of creative, bespoke intervention from fronting conferences (at Deloitte) to enabling creative, strategic thinking (at BBC Worldwide)."

Instant Wit

6 Worrall Place, Worrall Road, Clifton,
Bristol BS8 2WP
tel (0117) 974 5734 *mobile* (07808) 960826
email info@instantwit.co.uk
website www.instantwit.co.uk
Facebook /groups/49979367942/
Twitter @InstantWit
Directors Chris Grimes, Stephanie Weston

Company's work: "A quick-fire comedy improvisation show packed full of sketches, gags, songs, surreal situations, flying packets of 'Instant Whip' and prizes! The show is completely improvised and shaped around audience suggestions. Because of this, each show is unique and takes the form that you – the audience – want it to take."

Interact

138 Southwark Bridge Road, London SE1 0DG
tel 020-7793 7744
email operations@interact.eu.com
website www.interact.eu.com
Directors Derek Hollis, Ian Jessup *Company Administrator* Jamie Wright

Company's work: Through the skill of expert consultants, behavioural specialists and linguistic analysts, Interact creates immersive practice-based training for the corporate world. Real-to-life scenarios coupled with the latest thought leadership provides participants with an exponential level of development. Practice, when delivered hand-in-hand with evidence-based forensic feedback gives participants the opportunity to develop new perspectives, develop skill, and take ownership for their own learning.

Role-play assessments for medical colleges, for example the Royal College of General Practitioners

Theatre

and the College of Optometrists constitutes about 20% of our work. Associates delivering these assessments are trained specifically for these exams. Our bespoke programmes for corporate clients, have included workshops for Allianz, Sainsbury's and Transport for London. These deliveries require actors to go through Interacts Accreditation Programme to become an Interact Certified Professional.

Periodically Interact will interview and recruit new actors that have contacted us directly, responded to an advertisement or have been recommended. For all prospective associates fluency, confidence, strong acting and improvisation skills are required. Business and forum theatre experience is also an advantage.

An email including a cover letter, CV and current headshot is preferred. Those with previous experience are most likely to be invited to interview.

Maynard Leigh Associates (MLA)

3 Bath Place, Rivington Street, London EC2A 3DR
tel 020-7033 2370
email info@maynardleigh.co.uk
website www.maynardleigh.co.uk

Company's work: MLA is essentially a community of about 25 people who share common values, are committed to their own and other people's personal growth, and are passionate about their work affecting an increasing number of individuals and organisations. Associates are required to be expert workshop leaders with an interest in the psychological aspects of human potential development. Clients include: Aviva, DHL, Hewlett Packard, Ernst & Young, BBC TV, Barclays and Visa.

Recruitment procedures: All new consultants and leaders go through a rigorous and lengthy process, regardless of their professional experience. It can take up to 18 months of participation in Maynard Leigh activities before being allowed to represent the consultancy with clients. There are regular personal development sessions. As Maynard Leigh invests heavily in its existing associates, its pace of growth is limited. Professional actors with a good working knowledge of business and corporate life should submit their details by email.

Pearlcatchers Ltd

Claremont House, 70-72 Alma Road, Windsor SL4 3EZ
tel (01753) 670187 *fax* (01753) 830855
email enquiries@pearlcatchers.co.uk
website www.pearlcatchers.co.uk
Director Sharon M Young *Key personnel* Melanie Wright (Business Operations Manager), Karen Hanley (Business Development Manager)

Company's work: An event and training consultancy offering a fresh approach to learning, team-building and conferences. Provides actors with opportunities to shadow at events, and offers regular training afternoons and briefing sessions. Requires business

skills/knowledge and prior experience in role-playing and forum theatre. Clients include: AWE, BT, Tesco, London Underground, Cisco, BUPA, DVLA and the RAF.

Recruitment procedures: Extends its actor base every 2 years, recruiting via *The Stage*. Welcomes letters (with CVs and photographs) from individual actors previously unknown to the company, sent by post or email. Does not accept showreels or invitations to view individual actors' websites. Considers applications from disabled actors for specific projects.

The Performance Business

78 Oatlands Drive, Weybridge, Surrey KT13 9HT
tel (01932) 888885
email info@theperformance.biz
website www.theperformance.biz
Directors Michael McNulty, Lucy Windsor

Company's work: Provides incoming actors with personal assessments and one-to-one coaching. Requires excellent feedback skills and experience of working in business. Clients include: organisations in the financial, pharmaceutical, engineering, and manufacturing & public sectors.

Recruitment procedures: Periodically extends its actor-base, recruiting via the website and CastNet. Welcomes letters (with CVs and photographs) from individual actors previously unknown to the company, sent by post or email. Will consider invitations to view individual actors' websites. Actively encourages applications from disabled actors and promotes the use of inclusive casting.

Role-Players NGA Ltd

tel 020-7394 3221 *mobile* (07984) 471512
email info@role-players.co.uk
website www.role-players.co.uk
Proprietor Nick Gasson

Company's work: Established in 2003. Provider of professional actors as corporate role-players to the industry, in both the private and public sector. Incoming actors are expected to have experience of corporate role-play. Clients include accountancy and law firms, property development companies and management consultancies.

Recruitment procedures: Applications are accepted throughout the year, but mostly through personal recommendation from the company's existing actor list, and through potential actors applying having seen their website. Prefers CVs and photographs sent via email and does accept unsolicitied CVs and photographs via the same method. Invitations to view individual actors' websites are also accepted.

Roleplay UK

Suite 453 South Bank House, Black Prince Road, London SE1 7SJ
tel (0333) 121 3003
email actors@roleplayuk.com
website www.roleplayuk.com
Director James Larter *Creative Director* Andy Blair

Company's work: Established in 1994. Drama-led communications and training. Provides training for incoming actors in the form of workshops.

Recruitment procedures: Periodically extends its actor-base every 6 months or every year, depending on demand. Recruits via Equity Job Information Service. Does not welcome unsolicited approaches by individuals unknown to the company, but actively encourages applications from disabled actors and promotes the use of inclusive training.

Simpatico UK Ltd
63 Petworth Road, London N12 9HE
mobile (07759) 085132
email admin@simpaticouk.com
website www.simpaticouk.com
Managing Director Amanda J. Band

Company's work: Founded in 2003. Focuses on medical role-play. Specialising in communication skills.

Steps Drama Learning Development
Suite 10, Baden Place, Cosby Row, London SE1 1YW
tel 020-7403 9000 *fax* 020-7403 0909
email mail@stepsdrama.com
website www.stepsdrama.com
Account Managers Robbie Swales, Simon Thomson, Mark Shillabeer, Gary Bates, Caitlin Morrow, Jack Rebaldi

Company's work: Founded in 1990, the company supplies training to a wide variety of corporate companies through the use of drama. The work includes role-play, forum workshops and drama facilitation. Incoming actors receive training in the areas of feedback skills, forum workshops, coordinator workshops, facilitation skills and 'train the trainer'. Clients include: Network Rail, BaE Systems, and Virgin Active.

Recruitment procedures: Extends its actor-base on a needs basis. Actors should submit their CV via the website; they should have excellent improvisation skills and be able to present themselves realistically as part of the business world in both their dress and language. Requires actors to behave in a professional manner both in their dealings with Steps and with its clients. Must be organised, reliable and good team players.

Theatre&
25 Queen Square Business Park, Huddersfield Road, Honley, West Yorkshire HD9 6QZ
tel (01484) 664078 *fax* (01484) 660079
email cmitchell@theatreand.com
website www.theatreand.com
Directors Kath Hirst, Russell Watters *Casting and Service Delivery Manager* Clare Mitchell

Company's work: Founded in 2005. An innovative training, development and creative presentation

company working all over the UK. Designs and develops a variety of learning and communications interventions, which incorporate drama-based training techniques in order to deliver the client's desired outcomes. Live Drama training focuses on public and private sector organisations; Educational Presentations work within the education sector, delivering issue-based information to schools. Offers some training to incoming actors, who should ideally possess some touring or corporate training experience, strong improvisation skills, and the ability to use a variety of accents. Clients include a range of public- and private-sector organisations.

Recruitment procedures: Regularly holds auditions to increase its database of actors, and employs up to 100 actors per year. Contract lengths range from a week to 6 months. "Please send your CV and a photo along with a covering letter detailing why you think you are a suitable candidate. We are unable to respond to everyone, but will be in touch to invite you to audition if you are successful." Accepts showreels and invitations to view individual actors' websites, and will consider applications from disabled actors for specific projects.

Theatre Without Walls
Forwood House, Forwood, Gloucesterhire GL6 9AB
mobile 07962 040441
email hello@theatrewithoutwalls.org.uk
website www.theatrewithoutwalls.org.uk
Directors Genevieve Swift, Jason Maher

Company's work: Established in 2002. Award-winning producing theatre company with an active training/corporate wing, working in the public and private sector. Also produces television and corporate films. Clients include: National Trust, Gloucestershire Local Authority, Apollo, BBC and The Prince's Trust. Training is provided for incoming actors in the form of workshops and rehearsals in forum, role-play and interactive drama. Incoming actors require good improvisational skills.

Recruitment procedures: Actors are recruited through agents and Equity Job Information Service. Disabled actors regularly form part of the team and are actively encouraged to apply. See also the company's entry under *Middle and smaller-scale companies* on page 218.

Trainerpool
Hartham Park, Corsham, Wiltshire SN13 0RP
tel 0845-2302 880
email info@trainerpool.co.uk
website www.trainerpool.co.uk
Director Andy Collett

Company's work: Provides corporate training, workshops, coaching, facilitation, roleplay, events and speakers and presenters for corporate events. Requires actors to have prior knowledge and experience of corporate roleplay work. Clients include: BMW, Hill Group and RSM International.

Recruitment procedures: Extends its actor-base on a quarterly basis, recruiting via direct approach and word-of-mouth. Welcomes letters (with CV and photograph) from individual actors previously unknown to the company, sent by email. Also welcomes showreels. Happy to receive unsolicited CVs and photographs via the same method. Will consider performance notices and invitations to view individual actors' websites. Does not generally recruit disabled actors unless this is specifically required for a role by a client.

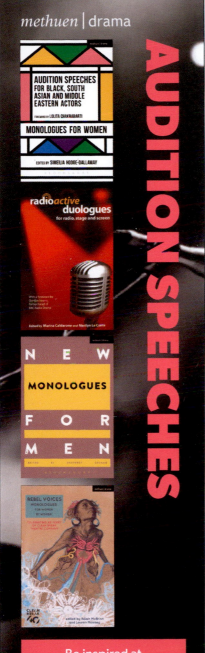

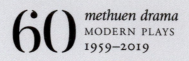
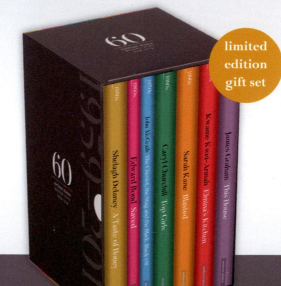

This is ... The Voice Republic

* We are a Voice Talent Directory
* We have Affordable Voiceover Recording Studios
* We produce Voice Reels (and have been for 20 years)
* We produce Singing Reels (a must have for singers)

Membership is on a quarterly subscription basis and there are 3 options, each designed to be affordable without compromising quality. Membership is from £12 per quarter.

An easy to use Voice Casting Breakdown and Audition service will launch late 2019, this has been designed to increase your voiceover opportunites. Our rates tracker will stop clients advertising low-paid jobs - helping ensure you're paid a fair rate.

www.thevoicerepublic.com/ayb2019

I use the studios on a regular basis, they're so much better than a home studio and offer what I cannot, which is the ability for clients to attend sessions. The sound is great and the engineers can edit very quickly so clients leave with a clean take. It's like having your own professional studio.
Dev Joshi, Professional Voiceover Artist

I've popped in here a few times to record auditions for jobs. It means my auditions are broadcast quality, which has done nothing but good in my quest to pick up more voice work. The better the audition the better chance you stand in winning the work. I use the self-operating option, which is a bargain!
Jordan Cunningham, Voice Actor.

As an older actor, getting on with digital devices and technology is a little stressful, so I just hop on the bus to do my demos at The Voice Republic. The guys are really helpful and direct the session so I know I'm giving my very best performance. I use the 'with engineer' option, it costs a little more, but it takes the stress away from doing it myself. They even send it on to the client so I don't have to.
Arthur Willman, Nonogenarian Actor!

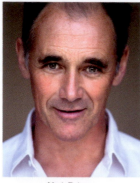

Professional role-playing

Robbie Swales

In 1992 an actor rang me and asked if I would do a job with him, which he had been offered through another actor. The job was to do a role-play with some accountants. I said, "What's role-play?" My friend explained that I had to role-play a demotivated worker, and that the purpose of the role-play was to help the accountants learn how to motivate members of their team. I did the job and enjoyed it. Since then – my first experience of role-play – this area of work for actors has expanded enormously. Although there are still networks of individual actors gaining role-play assignments, the bulk of the work for actors is provided by drama-based training companies, which provide organisations with role-players and actor/facilitators.

So why has this sector grown, and why is there a need for drama-based training companies, rather than individual actors applying directly to the end-user to offer their acting skills?

Trainers and developers within organisations have discovered that when they deliver behavioural skills training, an experiential interactive session provides better learning opportunities for the participants than the traditional talk-and-chalk approach. Because actors can put different behaviours on and take them off like a coat, they have become a valuable resource to the trainers; they make the sessions lively, interesting, interactive and memorable. Participants remember the learning, and then go on to use the skills in the workplace. Training and development in the workplace is only carried out if a company or organisation believes that it will improve efficiency, and therefore productivity. The use of actors for training is no exception; they help to make the behaviour of people in organisations more effective.

Drama-based training companies are what one might call one-stop shops. If an organisation, such as a high street bank, wants to employ actors to role-play on a series of development centres, the training department in the bank will find it easier to approach a role-play company. The trainer from the bank can explain their needs, check how that role-play company guarantees the quality of their actors, and then negotiate a fee. The role-play company can book the actors, brief them appropriately, and arrange for them to be in the right place at the right time.

The field of drama-based training is growing more and more sophisticated, and some of these companies are becoming more like consultancies, with entire interactive theatre programmes being researched, designed, written, rehearsed and delivered by the drama-based company. For such companies to be effective at this type of work, they need a core team of full-time staff, while maintaining a freelance team of actors trained in the appropriate skills whom they can employ on a project-by-project basis.

There are, very broadly, two types of role-play work: role-playing one-to-one with a participant; and role-playing with another actor in front of an audience, with whom the actors then interact. Most role-play work is improvised; however, there are some types of interactive theatre which kick off the session with a scripted scene, before the actors then start improvising the suggestions of the audience.

One-to-one role-play

The range of work performing one-to-one role-play with a participant requires different levels of skill from the actor. An example of the simplest type of role-play is improvising a patient for an assessment centre, where no feedback is required from the actor to the participant. The Royal College of Anaesthetists requires candidates for their anaesthetist qualifying exams to role-play with a simulated patient (an actor), so that the communications and empathetic skills of the candidate can be assessed. The role-play lasts about five minutes and is not complex.

An example of a one-to-one role-play at the more challenging end of the scale would be role-playing a Senior Tax Manager being interviewed for a job. It is important to remember that an actor is used, primarily, to display different types of behaviour (e.g. being nervous, arrogant, aggressive, etc.). However, for the actor to be a convincing Senior Tax Manager for a behavioural role-play, they need to have an overall grasp of what the job entails, and they may need to throw in a few technical phrases to add reality to the situation. This kind of role-play requires a day of training for the actor, so that they can learn about the role of the Tax Manager, memorise a few key technical words and phrases and rehearse the role-play encounter.

Actors are also required to give each participant with whom they role-play some high-quality feedback about their performance. At this highly sophisticated level of role-play, being able to deliver such feedback is an essential skill. Remember to frame the feedback with affirmative and supportive language.

The skills required to be a good one-to-one role-player are: the ability to go into character instantly; the ability to improvise well; the ability to understand and interpret the brief; the ability to memorise some technical terms; the ability to adjust your performance in relation to the quality of the input from the participant; and the ability to give feedback that is communicated sensitively and is useful to the participant.

Delivering an interactive theatre session

This technique has been used in schools by Theatre in Education companies for many years, and is now being used increasingly in the workplace. There are many different variations in the way that interactive theatre, or forum theatre, is delivered, but the principle is quite simple. Actors playing a scene will break out from that scene and talk to the audience, in character, asking for advice. This advice is then taken back into the scene by the actor and played out to see if it is effective.

Many aspects of development and learning can be addressed via interactive theatre: managing difficult conversations; feedback skills; diversity awareness; assertiveness skills; customer service; influencing skills; leadership; performance management; coaching; recruitment; and employment law awareness.

The skills necessary for performing high-quality forum theatre are: good improvisational skills; the ability to gain a thorough understanding of the objectives of the programme; being an able facilitator in order to confidently handle the responses from the audience; and the ability to hang onto a character while improvising and facilitating.

Applying for work

There are many different types of role-play/drama-based training companies. When we created Steps in 1992, we were one of only a handful of role-play companies; I have now lost count of the number of similar organisations! They all have different cultures and different ways of approaching the work, and each individual company's style probably reflects the personalities of their creators. Some companies may only provide actors to do one-to-one role-play, while others may concentrate on providing interactive theatre. Companies may have a large database of actors; others may have a small pool of actors who work on a fairly regular basis.

My advice would be to browse through the websites of the companies listed and get a feel of what they all claim to be offering. Find out from other actors who have worked in this area about their experiences. Ask them what they think of the company who employed them. At Steps we look at all actor CVs that we receive, and run audition workshops as, and when, we need to select new actors onto our team.

Role-playing for learning is no less a professional activity than professional acting. Punctuality, wearing the appropriate business/work clothes, maintaining confidentiality, interacting in an exemplary way with clients and participants, and working effectively as a member of a high-performance team with fellow role-players, are all behaviours that are required during a role-play assignment.

Being a role-player is a fascinating way for an actor to use their skills in between acting assignments while maintaining an income. Also, from the feedback I have received from role-players, the benefits are not only one-way: actors can learn a great deal from the organisations in which they role-play. The work they do can build their confidence and help them to discover new ways of managing their own careers.

Robbie Swales attended the Bristol Old Vic Theatre School from 1968 to 1970. During the 1970s he acted in Rep, toured and appeared in the West End; during the 1980s he made most of his income from TV commercials. In 1994 Robbie joined Steps – Drama Learning Development, and is now one of six directors who manage the company. In 2002 and 2003 Steps was one of the hundred fastest-growing inner-city companies in the UK, appearing on the HM Treasury-sponsored Inner City 100 Index.

Theatre

Media
Introduction

The last few decades have seen incredibly rapid advancements in recording technology, computers, digital media and the Internet. There has also been an enormous growth in the principal broadcasting companies contracting-out much of their output; this in turn has led to an increase in the number of independent companies employing actors. (There are also companies whose output does not include drama – these have not been included in the listings.)

Most film and television companies use casting directors (usually freelance), and it's usually a waste of time and money writing to anyone else unless you have a personal contact. It is worth remembering that many companies do work for businesses – training and promotional films, for instance.

Student films may be a somewhat poor relation to Hollywood blockbusters, in terms of pay (if any) and exposure, but they can provide useful experiences, be a good addition to your CV, and have the potential to lead onto something that is properly paid and much more prestigious. Extracts from such a film could also be useful for your showreel.

Casting for radio is much more akin to that for theatre, although often without the use of a casting director.

Television companies

These almost always use casting directors who, in turn, will circulate casting breakdowns to agents they trust. However, a carefully timed (and crafted) submission from an individual can occasionally excite interest.

BBC NETWORK TELEVISION

BBC Northern Ireland

BBC Broadcasting House, Ormeau Avenue, Belfast BT2 8HQ
tel 028 9033 8000
website www.bbc.co.uk/ni
Head of Drama Stephen Wright

BBC Northern Ireland produces a broad spectrum of radio and TV programmes, both for the BBC's networks and for its home audience. Output includes news and current affairs, documentaries, education, entertainment, sport, music, Irish-language and religious programmes. It also has a thriving drama department which reads unsolicited scripts across all genres, i.e. single, serials, series, feature films and the short-film scheme Northern Lights, which is aimed at new talent from within Northern Ireland.

In addition to making network radio programmes, broadcasting on BBC Radio 1, 2, 3, 4, and 5 Live and BBC World Service, BBC Northern Ireland also makes programmes for its local radio listeners.

BBC Scotland

40 Pacific Quay, Glasgow G51 1DA
tel 0141 339 8844
website www.bbc.co.uk/scotland
Head of Drama, Television Christopher Aird *Head of Drama, Radio* Bruce Young

BBC Scotland is the BBC's most varied production centre outside London, providing BBC TV and radio networks and BBC World Service with pivotal drama, comedy, entertainment, children's, leisure, documentaries, religion, education, arts, music, special events news, current affairs and political coverage. Internet development is also a key element of production activity.

In addition to making network output, more than 850 hours of TV programming per year are transmitted on BBC1 Scotland and BBC2 Scotland. BBC Radio Scotland is the country's only national radio station, and is on air 18 hours a day, 7 days a week. Local programmes are also broadcast on Radio Scotland's FM frequency in the Northern Isles, and there are daily local bulletins for listeners in the Highlands, Grampian, Borders, and the South West. BBC Radio Nan Gaidheal provides a Gaelic service on a separate FM frequency for around 40 hours a week.

The BBC Scotland offices are wheelchair accessible.

BBC Wales

BBC Broadcasting House, Llandaff, Cardiff CF5 2YQ
tel 029 203 22000
website www.bbc.co.uk/wales
Head of Drama Faith Penhale

BBC Wales provides a range of services in both English and Welsh, on radio, television and online.

The Drama department produces programmes for local and network BBC television channels and local and network radio stations. Notable recent successes of the department include *Doctor Who*, *Torchwood*, *The Sarah Jane Adventures*, *Life on Mars* and *Ashes to Ashes* for television, and the serialised and single dramas for radio, *The Wooden Overcoat*, *Investigating Mr Thomas* and *Solo Behind the Iron Curtain*.

INDEPENDENT TELEVISION

ITV (**www.itv.com**) is the biggest commercial television network in the UK. It is made up of a network of 15 different regional licences, each with its own set of obligations and conditions designed to reflect the particular character of their region and the interests of their viewers. Eleven of the licences in England and Wales are owned by ITV Plc (**www.itvplc.com**), formed in 2004 following the merger of Carlton and Granada. SMG owns the two Scottish licences, Scottish Television and Grampian; UTV and Channel Television own the licences for Northern Ireland and the Channel Islands respectively.

Note: Many companies commission from independents, so don't have casting departments.

Channel Television

The Television Centre, St Helier, Jersey JE1 3ZD
tel 01534 816816 *fax* 01534 816777
website www.channelonline.tv

Provides programmes for the Channel Islands during the whole week, relating mainly to Channel Islands news, events and current affairs. Does not produce any in-house drama.

ITV Yorkshire (YTV)

The Television Centre, Leeds LS3 1JS
tel 0113 243 8283 *fax* 0113 244 5107
website www.itv.com/yorkshire
Casting Director Faye Styring

Established in 1968, YTV is one of the biggest ITV companies. Following the new Communications Act and the merger of Granada and Carlton, it is part of the new single ITV plc which began life on 2nd February 2004.

YTV continues to produce a range of drama and light entertainment programmes, including: *A Touch of Frost; Emmerdale* (shown on the network every weekday night) and *Heartbeat* – ITV1's most popular long-running drama series. In 2003 a new sister programme, *The Royal*, attracted 11.3 million viewers and a 41.3% share of the television audience. In addition to its drama series, YTV has made a number of one-off dramas for the ITV network, including: *Booze Cruise* and *Brides in the Bath*. With an audience of 9.7 million viewers and a 44% audience share, *Booze Cruise* ranked as the best performing Single Drama from any channel for the whole of 2003.

The Casting Department generally works through agents, but will accept submissions (with CVs and photographs) from actors previously unknown to the company if sent by post. As the Department is very busy it cannot guarantee to acknowledge all submissions, but advises actors to enclose an sae for a quicker response. Prefers not to be contacted by telephone or email.

ITV Tyne Tees & ITV Border

Television House, The Watermark, Gateshead, Tyne and Wear NE11 9SZ
tel 0844 881 0100
website www.itv.com/tynetees; www.itv.com/border

Broadcasts to the North of England 7 days a week, 24 hours a day.

ITV Wales & ITV West

ITV Wales, The Television Centre, Culverhouse Cross, Cardiff CF5 6XJ
tel 0844-881 0100
ITV West, Television Centre, Bath Road, Bristol BS4 3HG
tel 0844 881 2345
website www.itv.com/wales; www.itv.com/west

Provides programmes for Wales and the West of England during the whole week. Produces programmes for home and international sales.

The ITV West Television Workshop, aimed at young people (up to 26), offers experience in the performance and production skills required for TV, film, theatre and radio. See **www.itvworkshop.co.uk** for more information.

ITV Meridian

Forum One, Solent Business Park, Whiteley, Hants PO15 7PA
tel 08448 812000
website www.itv.com/meridian

The ITV franchise-holder for the South and South East coast of England. Does not produce any in-house drama.

ITV Central

Gas Street, Birmingham B1 2JT
tel 0121 643 9898 *fax* 0121 643 4897
website www.itv.com/central

Provides ITV programmes for the East, West and South Midlands every day.

ITV Anglia

Anglia House, Norwich NR1 3JG
tel 0844 881 6900 *fax* 0844 556 3931
website www.itv.com/anglia

Provides programmes for the East of England, daytime discussion programmes, documentaries and factual programmes for UK and international broadcasters. Does not produce any in-house drama.

ITV London

South Bank, London SE1 9LT
tel 020 7827 7000
website www.itv.com/london

See ITV Yorkshire and ITV Granada for casting contacts.

ITV Granada

Orange Tower, MediaCity UK, Salford M50 2NT
tel 0161 952 1000
email casting@itv.com
website www.itv.com/granada
Casting Director Gennie Radliffe

The ITV franchise-holder for the North West of England. Produces programmes across a broad range for both its region and the ITV network.

Welcomes submissions (with CVs and photographs) from actors previously unknown to the company sent by post and email. As the Casting Department is extremely busy, it cannot guarantee to respond to all submissions. Advises actors to call to find out what projects are being cast, and to send in their details as and when appropriate.

SKY UK Ltd

Sky Entertainment, NHC1, Grant Way, Isleworth, Middlesex TW7 5QD
tel 0333 100 0333
email skypress@sky.com
website www.skygroup.sky/corporate/home
Chief Executive Jeremy Darroch *Head of Entertainment* Zai Bennett *Head of Drama* Anne Mensah *Drama Senior Commissioning Editor*

Cameron Roach *Executive Producers* Jo McClellan, Lizzie Gray, Anna Ferguson *Joint Drama Head of Development* Beverley Booker *Joint Head of Drama Development* Lindsay Salt *Drama Development Editor* Anna Hargreaves

Casting procedures: Sky UK Ltd does not have its own casting department, production companies hire freelance casting directors, for example, Rebecca Wright (*Delicious 2*).

STV Productions

STV Central, Pacific Quay, Glasgow G51 1PQ
tel 0141 300 0300
STV North, Television Centre, Graigshaw Business Park, West Tullos, Aberdeen AB12 3QH
tel (01224) 848848
website www.stv.tv
Head of Drama Eric Coulter

STV Productions (formerly SMG Productions) is the television production arm of STV Group Plc, and incorporates Ginger Productions. Its client list includes all terrestrial networks and major satellite and cable channels. Output includes drama, factual/factual entertainment, entertainment and children's programming.

The Drama Department has more than 20 years' experience of producing network drama for ITV1. Credits include: *Taggart, Dr Finlay, Rebus* and *Goodbye Mr Chips*. The Drama team is based at Glasgow offices. Casting procedures differ from project to project; generally uses independent casting directors, but also accepts letters from actors 'on spec' (with CVs and photographs). Where appropriate these will be passed on to a relevant programme or project.

UTV

Havelock House, Ormeau Road, Belfast BT7 1EB
tel 028 9032 8122 *fax* 028-9024 6695
email info@u.tv
website www.u.tv

Provides programmes for Northern Ireland. All drama is produced by the ITV network.

Media

Media

Casting for television

Janie Frazer

There are now many casting directors working in television, and each will have their own way of working. This is my own viewpoint and may not be shared by others, but I hope it may be helpful.

I came into casting by way of the theatre. When I was a schoolgirl I fell in love with the theatre and, being good at English, thought perhaps I could become a drama critic. However, some wise person suggested that before writing about the theatre I should work within it, and so I managed to get a job – at first unpaid, sweeping the stage and as a dresser, and subsequently as an ASM and then handling publicity for the Citizens Theatre Glasgow. I had also been involved in the big auditions held at the start of each season for the Citizens, and had come to realise that the actors were the thing that interested me most about the theatre. Subsequently I moved to London and incessantly badgered LWT for a job as a casting assistant, which finally transpired. I have worked there, through several mergers which have resulted in the company currently known as ITV, for many years. I have cast for all types of television productions; mainly drama, comedy drama and situation comedy, but also sketch comedy, factual drama, hidden camera, animation (voice-over), and various others programmes which defy definition.

Each production has its own specificity, but there are basic requirements that apply to all of them.

The script

This is the first principle and the foundation for everything else, even though the script may change beyond recognition during the process of getting the production to the screen. The script contains the characters, their descriptions, and the dialogue; from this, in consultation with the director and producer, I will put together a list of suggested actors for the roles.

Casting for television carries with it certain commercial considerations. The casting of the main characters is often crucial to a programme getting commissioned in the first place, since in commercial television the advertisers need to be assured of getting a specific audience for the programmes around and within which they buy advertising space. This is the reason for the often-heard grumble that the same well-known faces crop up again and again, and the reason for it is that they have good form – i.e., the programmes they appear in produce good viewing figures, which is what both ITV and the BBC are striving to maintain.

Beyond the 'name' casting, the casting for other roles involves interpreting the director's vision, style, ideas and the tone of the piece, to come up with suggestions that will best express the way in which the director wants to portray the material. Therefore, the same script may elicit different suggestions from me, according to the individual director.

Suggestions for actors

How do I arrive at these? I have many lists, and many files, sorted in an idiosyncratic fashion over the years and added to constantly after seeing actors' work on stage and screen. Also there is *Spotlight*, which is the casting director's invaluable and indispensable tool. If there was only one piece of advice I could offer to an actor, it would be to appear in *Spotlight*, and to keep one's entry accurate and up to date. I now use *Spotlight* almost exclusively via the Internet, as the information contained on the website is wonderfully comprehensive and well organised, and allows me to do cross-reference searching (e.g. for a 30-year-old Punjabi speaker with a Manchester accent) which is extremely swift and useful. The information contained on the site does however rely entirely on the input of the actors who subscribe to *Spotlight*, and it is therefore very important that they keep their credits and personal details current.

Also and most importantly, their photographs. To state the crashingly obvious, television is a visual medium. It's vital that an actor's photograph is up to date and actually looks like them. Vanity should not be the issue, as television requires all types and ages to be portrayed; moreover, an inaccurate photograph can be misleading and time-wasting. Spotlight's website has now progressed to offer audio and video clips of each actor, and I have found that these can be really useful to play to a director when discussing casting. Therefore, I would strongly recommend that actors make full use of all the opportunities offered by *Spotlight* to show their wares.

Via the Spotlight Link I am also able to send out a breakdown of characters to the agents, who then relay back their suggestions, which I can order, prioritise and follow up. I will discuss with the director and producer the various suggestions we have made between us, and those that have come from agents; I will then arrange casting sessions for the various roles.

Getting in touch

I would love to be able to say that receiving letters with photos and CVs, or emails with all those attachments, is always a boon – but I'm afraid it's not usually the case. More useful is to be notified of actors' forthcoming performances: even if it's not always possible to cover these, it's good to know what work you are doing, and one may ask other casting directors if they have seen you in the piece.

Showreels can be useful to view as examples of an actor's work, but tend not to be so significant if they arrive unsolicited – there are simply not enough hours in the day to watch everything that is sent in. I find I am most likely to watch them if they are directly relevant to a current project (for instance, if I am looking for young Northern actors, or working on a sketch comedy show, I will select to watch those that might fall into the relevant categories).

When you are called for audition

Almost invariably now, casting sessions for television dramas and comedy are video-taped. This allows for greater scrutiny of the actor, and assessment of their presence on screen away from the social context of the audition. It does not mean that the actor has had to produce a flawless reading, but many things emerge from watching an actor on screen which may have been missed during the live reading. The camera is sensitive to minute changes in thought-processes and expression as the actor is being filmed in close-up; this is something the actor needs to bear in mind during a television casting audition – that the performance will be watched at close hand, and therefore a loud voice and large expressions will convey considerable impact and may need to be scaled down.

Whatever an actor's looks, the most important feature on screen is the eyes. The people casting the programme need to see yours. Therefore, it will help enormously if you are able to absorb, familiarise yourself with, or, best of all, learn the scene so that you are able to raise your eyes from the script. Almost all 'sides' or scenes for reading will have been emailed to your agent or yourself prior to audition. Make sure you have an email address. Acquaint yourself with script formats such as Final Draft (at the time of writing, a free download for viewing scripts in Final Draft format is available from the website **www.finaldraft.com**). If you wear glasses, print the scene in a large font so that you can still read it if at the casting they would prefer to see you without glasses.

Other basic things to bear in mind are to arrive on time; make sure you know the specific whereabouts of the casting venue, and how long it is likely to take you to get there. You may be unavoidably kept waiting, in which case make sure you let the casting director know if you have another appointment you need to attend. If you can, do some prior research, both about the project, and also about the producer and director of the pro-gramme. You can find out about their previous work via the IMDb website, **www.imdb.com** – and since they will after all be looking at your CV, they may be impressed and flattered if you also know something about theirs.

Spend some time thinking about the material you've seen, so you have something to say about it. Many actors would be surprised at how much their observations have con-tributed to the final version of the script. In television as in film, time is money. Pre-production periods have been reduced to the minimum, which means that there is often very little time for rehearsal once shooting begins. Directors often therefore use the casting process to try out ways in which they would like to scenes to play – this can be rewarding for the actor, and useful even if they do not finally land the part; often directors keep their interview lists, and bear actors in mind whom they've liked but who haven't been quite right for the part in question.

If you look good, I look good

Sometimes actors view casting interviews as an exam, or as some sort of test they have to pass. However, there is at least one person in the room who is completely on your side – the casting director. The casting director's reputation relies on the calibre of the actors invited for interview, and if the actors aren't up to it then the casting director is the one who's on the line. Therefore, by getting you in for audition, the casting director is dem-onstrating faith in your ability and rightness for the part.

Know your value

Everyone has their own USP – their unique selling point. Even if you are Mr/s Ordinary, then that's it. It's valuable. Get to know what it is that is most intriguing about you, and play to your strengths. Ask your colleagues for constructive criticism and listen to it. Emphasise your strengths and don't pretend to be what you are not. Whereas the theatre can thrive on disguise and artifice, the camera takes no hostages and is ruthless in its exposure.

Did you get it?

If you got the part, then congratulations! But an actor is often confused as well as disap-pointed about not getting a part. They will ask: should I have done it like this, dressed like that, what did I do wrong? It's hard to explain to an actor that the choice is not dependent on something they did or didn't do, but often is the result of someone else being more right for the part than they are. This is a nebulous assessment which I can appreciate is very unsatisfactory to hear, but it is nevertheless the truth. Those actors who have ever been on the other side of the casting process often remark how they now understand what this means, but it doesn't help much with the feeling of frustration. One can only suggest that, by the law of averages, eventually the part will come up for which you are the most right; that you've done pretty well to get the interview in the first place; that the director may well have clocked you for the future – and that the whole experience stands you in good stead.

For most of her professional life **Janie Frazer** worked as a casting director for ITV Productions, the programme-making division of ITV. She is now working freelance. Janie's career in casting has covered all the genres of single drama, drama series, continuing drama, factual drama, comedy drama, situation comedy, single comedy and sketch comedy. Amongst the many productions she has cast are *Spaced*, the cult comedy series with Simon Pegg; *Coronation Street*, Britain's longest-running soap; and *Blue Murder*, the detective series starring Caroline Quentin.

Auditioning for camera
Nancy Bishop

'The camera is your friend' is the first lesson I teach in my courses on auditioning for camera. The ironic truth is that many theatre actors who feel perfectly comfortable performing in front of thousands of people become timid in front of a small piece of electrical equipment. The antidote to camera fear is to practise on screen as often as possible. Own a camera, use it, grow comfortable with the lens, love it – and it will love you back.

What's the difference between auditioning for film and auditioning for theatre?

In theatre, you are often asked perform a prepared monologue, while in film, you read from 'sides' (short scenes from the actual screenplay.) In theatre, you can find yourself reading with another actor, while in film you might end up reading with a talentless casting director.

Actors are deluded in thinking that if they were actually on location, with all of the props and sets, it would be easier than acting in an empty casting studio. ("If I had the actual laser gun then I could act it so much better.") But acting in a dull audition room or in front of a green screen in a film studio is not so different from acting during Shakespeare's time. The Globe didn't have elaborate sets, which is why characters say obvious lines such as, "Well, this is the Forest of Arden." There was no forest on stage … just a wooden O. So the actors had to use their imagination.

It's the same now. When you're doing a horror film, the oozy monster doesn't perform with you. He's created by a computer geek later on. *Actors must use their imagination.* This includes imagining that you have a brilliant scene partner to play off, even when you only have a casting assistant in a bad sweater.

What can I expect at an on-camera audition?
Slating and introduction

Your first audition is likely to be a screening process, or 'pre-read'. Often the director will not be there, so the casting director will need to 'slate' – which means slipping a name card in front of camera and asking you to turn both profiles. Yes, it feels like a prison shot, and every casting director has heard that joke before.

Next the casting director may ask you to introduce yourself, for the benefit of the absent director. For some reason, this trips up a lot of actors. They feel perfectly comfortable playing some one *else*, but when they have to be *themselves* for a few minutes they stumble around. The introduction, however, may be the most interesting part for the casters. We want to see who you *really* are, your personality. It's the alchemy between the actor's unique energy and the screenwriter's written word that creates the character.

It's best to have some kind of pithy introduction semi-rehearsed so that you don't corpse for camera when the casting director asks you to introduce yourself. Remember that it's all about spin. This is your opportunity to sell yourself for the role. Be enthusiastic and be yourself. Here are a few examples of good and poor introductions.

If you already have professional credits:

• Poor spin: "I had a tiny role on *Inglorious Bastards*. I waited on set forever and I think my line didn't make it to the final cut."

• Good spin: "I had a great time working with Quentin Tarantino on my last project."
   If you are new to the business:
• Poor spin: "I haven't really played any big roles before. I'm just out of drama school."
• Good spin: "I'm just out of drama school and can't wait to land my first job. I really like this project. I've always wanted to work on a World War II film."

   These are the kind of personal details you might include in an introduction (such things humanise you; it's interesting to us if you're a mother, if you like to travel, etc.):
• "I just celebrated my daughter's third birthday;"
• "I just got back from a fascinating trip to India;"
• "I work part time in a homeless shelter."

   It's better not to include such comments as "I'm working as a temp in an office right now and I hate it." This tells us that you're not really a professional. True, you might have to work a day job to support yourself, but you don't have to emphasise it.

How do I best play to camera?

You should ask the camera operator about frame size. It's a perfectly professional question. What does the camera see? Is it wide, medium or close? If it's a close-up, you're wasting your energy with hand gestures. Be careful not to pop out of frame, and calibrate the performance in your face, where the camera will detect inner monologue.

   Calibrating a performance to frame size can be one of the trickiest parts of screen acting. Often the actor's fear is that the camera will amplify their performance so that they will appear to be over-acting. In my screen-acting courses, actors sometimes become discouraged when they watch the play-back and realise that they haven't hit the right level; they see themselves either popping out of the screen, or plagued by the opposite problem which I call *dead face* – when a performance is boring and dead. Nice house but nobody is home.

   Theatre actors often fall prey to dead face because great screen actors create the illusion, to the unstudied eye, that they are 'doing nothing'. It's a great misnomer. In a close-up, the actor becomes a talking head, and the only thing that matters is the information communicated by the face. Therefore the performance may have to be even intensified in the eyes and face. The antidote to dead face is an active and ever-changing inner monologue. The camera photographs thought and it loves to watch a character thinking.

   This is true of acting in any medium, but in screen acting, listening and reacting become more than half of the performance. One of the most common mistakes in an audition is when an actor reads along with his or her scene partner's lines rather than truly listening and reacting in the moment.

Where do I look? Directly into camera?

The answer is no. Unless specifically asked, you only look directly into camera when you are introducing yourself. There are exceptions, like in the mock-documentary genre. In the US TV series *Modern Family*, for example, the characters speak directly into camera as if questioned by an imaginary interviewer. It's the modern form of Shakespeare's soliloquy; the character speaks his/her thoughts out loud to the audience. That is the exception, not the rule. Most film and TV genres still assume the removal of the fourth-wall type of realism, wherein the characters go about their lives, not knowing that they are being observed.

   The best place to focus is somewhere near the lens. This will give the viewer a three-quarter view of your face. You want to be as generous as possible about playing towards the camera. We won't cast you if we can't see you. Placing an off-screen reference on the floor will only bring your eyes down. Hopefully the casting director will help you with this by placing the reader directly next to the lens. But if not, you can focus on a fixed point, rather than on the reader. Know your best side for photography and play accordingly.

How can I prepare for a project when I only have a few pages of text?

You can ask for information. The casting director should provide a summary, but if they don't, then ask for information or ask to read the script. Sometimes it's available and sometimes not, but a question never hurts. If you can't get the script, then you need to make decisions about the pages according to the information you have. If the script wasn't available to you, then it wasn't available to other actors either, and you have an even playing field. Start with the basic Stanislavski questions:

- *Who am I?*
- *Where am I?*
- *Who am I talking to?*
- *What do I want?*

I also encourage actors to add:

- *What are the stakes?* Make the stakes as high as possible, and this will drive the dynamics of the performance.

Answering these questions is one of the basic tenets of acting, yet many actors (even experienced ones) forget to do this for an audition, and they find themselves floating in a sea of too many possibilities. Anchor yourself in the 'W' questions; this will guide your performance.

In order for actors to develop their onscreen skills and comfort level, they must practise. Screen acting is like driving a car. No one gets in a car the first time and just drives. You have to learn how to give the car gas and ease up on the clutch so that the car doesn't jerk. This is why I encourage actors to own a camera, practise with it and take on-camera courses. Modern smart phones with cameras are equally useful for practice and self-filmed auditions, which are increasingly prevalent.

Last of all, I always advise actors to have fun and enjoy the process. If you're enjoying yourself, then so will we, the casters. Love the camera – it will love you back.

"Good actors are good because of the things they can tell us without talking." Cedric Hardwicke

Nancy Bishop is an Emmy-award nominated CSA casting director who casts from Prague. She has cast large-scale studio pictures such as *Mission Impossible IV* and *Prince Caspian*. She also coaches actors and teaches master classes on audition technique throughout Europe and the US. She is the author of Methuen's *Secrets from the Casting Couch.*

Self-taping auditions

Ros Hubbard

Time is the enemy! When we set up Hubbard Casting in London in 1976, we had much more time and money (!) available to us. Now with film budgets under far more pressure there are more and more time constrictions. We have been forced to come up with a solution to actors being considered all over the world for parts: self-taping. The positive development that has influenced the simultaneous growth in numbers of actors to be considered for any one role is that there is much more of an international focus. Films have been enhanced by the growth of international audiences and their taste for more broadly based stories with multinational casts, so there is a greater chance of more actors being considered. The facility of self-taping cuts out so much delay caused by booking a live audition, when wanting to take a first look at an actor.

Once I have accepted your agent's recommendation that you be considered for a role, self-tapes allow me to see your acting even if you are working in a different country or elsewhere in the UK, on a theatre job, another film shoot, or even on holiday. Several well-known actors self-taped behind their agent's backs for *The Lord of the Rings* and *The Hobbit*. It is worth chancing your luck by submitting unsolicited self-tapes. I do look at these, but make sure you are brilliant, if you want to catch and hold my attention. However you cannot ring to see if they have arrived, as casting directors do not have the time to respond to such requests. Similarly, if you have been rejected from an arranged submission, you just have to accept it. Do not attempt to open a dialogue about it. You may be called to a live meeting from self-tapes but actors are rarely cast directly from them. Sam Underwood is one of the exceptions we have just cast at the time of writing (summer, 2014).

Now, I may actually physically meet only three to five actors per character, but I like to be inundated by possibilities, and will publicise my search anywhere I think I may discover a new talent. But this itself can demand a big investment of hours, weeks, months. For a film with ten speaking characters, I can watch up to 600 actors on tape. Recently, I was thrilled to be asked to cast John Carney's (director of *Once*) *Sing Street*. With two Irish mid-teens at the centre of the film, my nets would have needed to be cast wide and deep for one of my favourite challenges: hunting the unknown. Regrettably, calculating existing commitments, I knew I could not afford to employ my usual tactics and had to decline the offer, because it would have involved a huge amount of internet searches and self-tapes.

Much of what I have to say about making self-tapes may seem plain common sense, but each piece of advice I give here is based on scores of bad examples seen in the thousands of self-tapes sent to Hubbards in the very few years in which self-taping has become the most prevalent form of first-level audition.

1. The simplest way of self-taping is on an iPhone – it is also very effective. Laptops' sound reproduction is not so good. You can enhance the quality of the filming by using a camera placed on a tripod, but a friend filming you on an iPhone should really be quite sufficient. You should use a closed room, not the corner of a hall or passageway, which is more likely to pick up extraneous noise. If shooting for an American show, try to hire a room at Spotlight. They will put the video on a link for you.

2. Be off-book! No paper should be in view. Margie Haber in LA says you do not need to be off-book in the US, but you would have to be amazing not to be. She runs workshops in on-book auditions, but US auditions can be as many as up to seven a day, so it is impossible to learn that many for one day. You should allow at least one night to prepare. Form a group of actor friends to read in during preparation and filming, so you can support each other and know that at least one of them will always be available to work with you.

3. Remember to have the phone/camera mic as close to you as possible: a foot between your legs is ideal. We embarrass ourselves and the actors ramming the camera and mic close up, but it is the difference between being heard and not being heard. Casting offices are as noisy as chip shops. All four members of the Hubbard family have at least their associate caster working with them at any one time. In the summer of 2014 Amy Hubbard was casting the fourth series of *Homeland* and had just finished *24*, so had a team of ten assistants whirling around the office. The actor on the tape needs to be heard above all that racket. It does not matter if your recording level sounds unnaturally loud – it can always be lowered.

4. Shoot from an angle that shows more of you, with your head and chest occupying the centre of the image – keep it close. It's your soul they are after. A director may later call for an actor to reshoot the scene as full length. Try to shoot in daylight, but *don't sit in front of windows or all we will see is your silhouette*. Filming on camcorders in electronic light is much less effective. Keep your eyes level with the camera. Looking down on the floor or the script will kill the opportunity. Do not look directly at the camera. You should look at your just-off-camera scene partner. If the scene demands physical contact, then you can use a certain amount of movement. Some part of the partner can be visible, but just indicate the action, do not try to be sensational. American casters never use any actors to read in – so your partner can sound very flat and you have to really energise yourself. Do not use any props apart from a cup or a cigarette. There should be no people in the background, or any children or pets anywhere in the field of vision. Do not use too much make-up. Electronic signals are hard and make-up makes you look hard and older.

5. If your tape has been solicited and sides have been sent to you to record, you will be handicapped in doing thorough character preparation, if you are not sent the script or given any other guidance. It never harms to ask for a synopsis of the whole story. You don't have to shoot the whole scene. It will be clearly said to your agent or you how much dialogue is required. I am likely to edit tapes before forwarding them to the director. Don't use showreel material in place of a self-tape, but they are a useful addition. Your showreels should only consist of clips from your films and TV productions. Do not use personally manufactured scenes. Look at other actors' showreels before choosing your own selection. There should not be too many other actors in the clips, especially actors, who look like you – very confusing for us old dears!

6. Do not try charming the casting director by using moody talk or blathering on about what you are doing at the moment. Never bring your fears into an audition, live or recorded. Leave them on a coat hook before you enter the room or screen. Your spoken introduction on tape should simply give your full name, height, your agent's details or whether you are representing yourself, the title of the scene and your availability for a

live meeting and the shoot dates. If an accent is required for the scene, use it for your introduction as well, even if it is less than technically perfect because the effort made will impact positively on your performance. Do not read out the stage directions. Do not underscore the tape with music.

7. You must discipline yourself to closely examine the tape. In the first place you may have forgotten something essential. Ask a friend or friends to give their honest opinion of how well your tape serves the scene, and trust it. This will help you avoid subjective judgements such as choosing the tape most flattering of your general appearance, as opposed to what suits the character best. You can send two versions, especially if the scene is short. Do not announce differences between the two takes. Be subtle in your introductory explanation for sending two. In live auditions, I will always listen to an actor, who feels they have not done themselves justice, and would like to rerun their audition. But it is not always possible to get you back and there have been many occasions when an actor has thought that they read badly and got the part – you are your own worst critic!

8. Use a watermark app on your phone to protect the copyright of your self-tape. You may be the next big thing within two to three years, but in any case do not put your self-tapes on YouTube: that would be even more silly. Also, the script is not your property or the public's. You are in a position of trust. The producers can decide against you no matter how good you are for indiscreet behaviour with scripts. I have seen uploads on YouTube before I can get it out to the director and that is where it ends for you.

9. Do not use an ordinary attachment to email your tapes because their downloading time clogs up our inboxes and slows up the casting process even more. Use web transfer services, e.g. Hightail, WeTransfer or Vimeo. Label your file with your name and the character you are playing.

Good luck with your careers!

Ros Hubbard was born in Dublin and ran a model agency there in the late 1960s. She moved to London and became 'Queen of the Commercials', at which point her husband, John, joined her as a casting director. They went on to cast a myriad of films and TV dramas. The company expanded to include both their daughter Amy and son Dan. Ros and John now live in London but they call their real home Dingle, in Co. Kerry, Ireland.

Media

Are you ready for Pilot Season?

Brendan Thomas

It has been suggested that the exodus of British actors, especially young British actors, to Los Angeles each spring is somewhat akin to the 1840/50s Californian Gold Rush. They come to participate in the casting frenzy of Pilot Season. The surge is understandable as the quantity and quality of UK actors in leading roles in American features and TV series appears to be on an ever-rising tide. Despite this increasing visibility of UK actors on American screens, I would advise others against hoping for great outcomes from purely speculative trips to the US before their careers have gained any momentum. However, if such visits are thought of as largely gaining knowledge for the future combined with aspects of a vacation, there is much to be learned if you come with as much information about the American industry as possible. An initial trip could be very useful in determining how difficult your personal negotiation of the increasingly fierce border regulations would be, as well as giving you the opportunity of discovering how compatible you are with life in Los Angeles.

The internet has transformed pilot season in numerous ways. One of those ways is self-taping for auditions. This is used if an actor cannot make an audition, or is out of town etc. A casting director will review the tapes and, if there is interest, pass it along to pro-ducers/ studio/ network. If there is further interest, you may be asked to fly out to test for the role, or in some cases, they will use your original self-tape. You can participate in American pilot season virtually anywhere in the world. For initial contact with a US man-ager, I would recommend a discussion over Skype. Most managers are very amenable to these.

There are a number of different temporary visas that could cover your investigative trip/ participation in Pilot Season. Obviously you would not be receiving a fee for audi-tioning, but the nature of Pilot Season is such that you could be filming within weeks. The audition process could range from three auditions a day to radio silence for a week, you really never know how busy you will be. There are also circumstances where you could be under consideration for several pilots. If you are one of the lucky ones to do so you can only continue as a series regular in one. Most roles are already made as offers to known actors so the wider auditioning process is one for insurance/ back-up in case offered roles are not accepted. This may seem dispiriting but there is a chance that the offered actor's deal may not work out for all sorts of different reasons, leaving room for the newcomer.

The commitment to screen test is really a very heavy one as effectively you will have agreed in advance to film the full series, if you are accepted to test for the pilot. A series can continue for up to seven years, so you have to know that you are legally available, which means having more than a temporary visa. While it is possible to audition for most series regular roles without the appropriate visa (productions will often sponsor if they like the actor enough) there is not time, normally, to sort your paperwork out between accepting a role and filming. This may feel like Catch 22 territory. You will require a O-1B visa petition (as an individual with an extraordinary ability in the arts or extraordinary achievement in the motion picture or television industry) to be filed at least 60 days before you wish to enter the US to avoid delays in the visa processing. This will permit you to accept most roles: star, regular, recurring or guest star, but certain networks in some cases can demand Green Card (permanent residency) status. It is important to note that any entertainer or artist cannot file for a visa on her/his own behalf – your visa application must be lodged by your sponsor or petitioner. The O-1B filing entity must be an employer (the actual production company/ network/ studio that is offering you work), or a US agent or Management company located in the US – meaning they must be an organization or entity that has an American address and an IRS (Internal Revenue Service) Employer tax number. A blanket 0-1B visa, which lasts for three years, costs on average about $5,000. A Green Card can cost up to twice that amount.

Beware of companies that offer to act as a 'middle man' to help secure visas. They say the folk who made the most money in the Gold Rush were the ones selling the shovels. These 'middle men' are charging an unnecessary fee to help secure a visa which is easily done by contacting an American lawyer, and his/her paralegal. Some of these legal services are advertised on the web, but if you are operating without ready access to an American agent or manager, it would probably be safer to take a recommendation from an actor friend who has been through the process.

Pilot Season has served not only as the core mechanism for the American television networks' collective market research for programming their subsequent year's drama productions, but as a huge actor job-seeking convention. It has incorporated the advent of the cable channels joining the process and, so far, the explosion of online streaming companies such as Hulu, Amazon and Netflix's expansion into production of original drama television: Netflix's *House of Cards* being the most prominent example so far, while in June 2015 Netflix announced it would be making its first feature film, *War Machine*, starring Brad Pitt. An increasing number of pilots are being made outside the January–March box with many going year round. Aside from stand-alone pilots, there are many shows that are straight to series, meaning there will be ten episodes set to air as opposed to shooting a one-episode pilot and seeing how that rates.

It is already common practice for shows to engage casting directors in other countries, alongside their lead home casting director, especially as more and more drama is shot abroad or elsewhere in the US. There can be a casting director in Los Angeles, New York, Ireland, London and Canada (Vancouver/Toronto) all for the same series. The magnetism of American television has grown over the last decade, attracting top writers, directors and actors. There is no longer a stigma for marquee actors to do television. Everything is material driven as opposed to where it will be shown or viewed.

For the lone UK actor venturing into Pilot Season without the direct support of a single representative, or even one audition in place, there is a lot of casting information to be gleaned free of charge on the web from the sites of the trade journals such as *Variety*. American agents and managers (and some UK agents) have access to each network's comprehensive grid of the pilots they are seeking to cast, so it is possible to align all the grids and gain an overview of all the roles available. These grids contain far more detail than the related articles that appear in the trade journals. They are used and reorganized differently at each agency, however, they all contain the vital information about projects throughout all stages of development. They show all the elements to each show: network; studio; producers; length of the episode; shoot dates being aimed for; location; number of episodes; logline; the writer, director, actors attached; executives at network/ studio; roles: type, description status; and are updated at each stage of the process.

Having identified a number of roles you think match your casting profile, it is possible to submit your profile to the casting directors through *Breakdown Express*'s Actors Access, part of *Breakdown Services*: a near equivalent to the interactive casting services of the UK's *Spotlight*, but without its link to a comprehensive actor directory. Individual agencies and personal managements can organize all data relating to their clients' acting credits, diaries (including upcoming auditions, rehearsal calls and filming schedules) and vital statistics, on *Breakdown Services* but they cannot access files of *any* other agencies/managements or those of *any* individual actors, who are not their own clients.

Breakdown Services introduced Actors Access via its website to stem illegal trading of *Breakdown Express*'s casting information between represented and unrepresented actors. The latter are able to receive the same breakdowns that agencies/ managements do. However, casting offices have the option to have *Breakdown Services* release their breakdowns strictly to agents/ managers only. The option to release breakdowns to Actors Access is not made clear, so most if not all of the big project breakdowns go straight to agents/ managers and bypass the actors. Nevertheless you should be able to obtain enough information from sources in the public realm (e.g. deducing there would be a role to match your profile from a plot summary), you can research the casting director's address and make a submission via postal services. You may not receive any response to your submitted CV/ resume and/or tape, or you may be asked to go back on tape incorporating the casting director's notes. A manager would monitor your tapes for you, weeding out ineffective material. This reflects the distinction between the roles of the American agents and managers. While both categories submit their joint clients for castings, the agents deal with booking of meetings and contracts, while the manager works more closely with her/his clients, shaping careers and strategies, forming the basis of decision making for accepting roles. As with any American casting, if your tape is successful you will be asked over for a film test, if you are not already in situ for Pilot Season. Your flight will be paid for and you will receive a $60 per diem. The flights used to be booked "business" class until the recent SAG (Screen Actors Guild) agreement rolled the status back to "coach", though this is subject to variation from case to case.

Signing up to a seven-year deal may appear to be the key to Hollywood from where you stand at the moment, but could become a dreary, unfulfilling commitment, which entraps you from taking much more creatively fulfilling and perhaps more lucrative opportunities over those years. On the other hand, you might not be filming continuously. It is possible to combine filming different series on both sides of the Atlantic, for example O.T. Fabengle shot the first series of *Looking* (San Francisco) alongside (but not clashing specific shoot dates) *The Interceptor* (UK) hopping back and forth across the Atlantic in two incredibly diverse roles. However the chances are your best opportunities elsewhere would arise exactly across your annual commitment to an American series.

From the point of view of general experience, auditioning in America is likely to up your game. It is very, very tough over here. There is a massive amount of competition for roles. Preparation is vital but you often don't get a lot of time to prepare your sides, nevertheless the expectation to be entirely off book is universal here, while not always the case in the UK. Your American accent needs to be 100 per cent in place. Expect blunt criticism if it is not right. Some casting directors have advised, if you are meeting producers etc. in the casting, that you should come into the room speaking in an American accent,

Media

otherwise, if you come in speaking in your own accent, and then switch, their attention is focused on what's not right with the accent rather than focusing on the work. Ultimately the choice is yours, but you may need to decide what lessens the odds against you getting the job. See a reputable dialect coach. There are many – generally actors trying to supplement their income – who are not suitably qualified. On the positive side you may sometimes have up to three castings a day in different parts of LA which often entails a lot of driving across often busy freeways. A full driving licence is essential.

Having digested all this information you may feel more secure about striking out alone for next year's Pilot Season, but here is one final warning: the overall chance factor will be against you, but is higher in some years and unpredictable. Which way will the dice fall for you?

Brendan Thomas is one of a number of managers at **Untitled Entertainment** which is led by two partners and has offices on both coasts repping actors, writers and directors. Brendan comes to the UK three or four times a year combining seeing his UK clients in theatre performances or on film/ TV sets and locations, including elsewhere in Europe, while maintaining face-to-face contact with their UK agents.

Independent film, video and TV production companies

Companies in this field start up and close down all the time, and it is very important to have a proper contract if offered work with an independent. If in doubt, check with Equity.

Absolutely Productions

Unit 19, 15 Ingestre Place, London W1F 0JH
email info@absolutely-uk.com
website www.absolutely.biz
Managing Directors Gordon Kennedy

Founded in 1988. Produces scripted drama and comedy for radio, TV and film, and Factual and Factual Entertainment shows for TV and radio. Recent credits include:*Chris* (sitcom pilot ITV), *Reluctant Persuaders* (Radio 4), *The Absolutely Radio Show* (Radio 4) and *Mrs Sidhu Investigates* (Radio 4).

Actaeon Films Ltd

50 Gracefield Gardens, London, SW16 2ST
tel 020 8769 3339 *fax* 0870 134 7980
email info@actaeonfilms.com
website www.actaeonfilms.com
Company Director/Producer Daniel Cormack *Producer* Matt Gunner *Head of Development* Becky Connell

Production details: A London-based production company established in 2004 to develop and produce theatrical motion pictures, both drama and comedy. Recent productions include: the Tiscali Award-winning *Amelia and Michael* (35mm, 2007) starring Anthony Head; the UK Film Council completion-funded *A Fitting Tribute* (HD/Super 8mm, 2007); and the micro-short comedy *Nightwalking* (HD, 2008) starring Raquel Cassidy.

Casting procedures: Uses freelance casting directors. Offers PACT/Equity approved contracts and does not subscribe to the Equity Pension Scheme. Actively encourages applications from disabled actors and promotes the use of inclusive casting. "We welcome invitations to showcases, screenings and theatrical productions and will view showreels, but we don't advise sending CVs/headshots unless in relevant response to a current casting call."

Bentley Productions

Pinewood Studios, Pinewood Road, Iver,
Bucks SL0 0NH
tel 01753 656594 *fax* 01753 652638
website www.all3media.com/companies.php
Managing Director Jo Wright

Specialises in high-quality drama, and has completed productions for both ITV1 and BBC1, including *Midsomer Murders*. Bentley followed the success of *Midsomer Murders* with an action thriller for ITV1, *Ultimate Force*.

Big Bear Films

48 Priory Road, Richmond, Surrey TW9 3DH
tel 020 8332 9765 *fax* 020 8332 9765
email office@bigbearfilms.co.uk
website www.bigbearfilms.co.uk
Producer/Director Marcus Mortimer

Production details: Established in 1998. Makes comedy, drama, and factual entertainment programmes for all networks. Recent productions include: *My Hero* (BBC1), *Get A Grip* (ITV with Ben Elton), *Strange* (BBC1), and *The Hairy Bikers Cookbook* (BBC2).

Casting procedures: Casting is done by freelance casting directors Tracey Gillham and Sara Crowe. Actors are employed under Equity-approved contracts. Actively encourages applications from disabled actors. "Please come to auditions with some knowledge of the part and the production."

Big Red Button Ltd

91 Brick Lane, London E1 6QL
email hello@bigredbutton.tv
website www.bigredbutton.tv
Key personnel John Burns, Pier Van Tijn, Sagar Shah

Production details: Established in 2002. Specialises in short films and music videos. Works in live action, puppetry and animation. Also employs actors in drama, comedy and commercials.

Casting procedures: Holds general auditions and actors can write to request inclusion at anytime. Casting breakdowns are available on the website. Does not offer Equity-approved contracts. Rarely has the opportunity to cast disabled actors.

Big Talk Productions

26 Nassau Street, London W1W 7QA
tel 020 7255 1131
email info@bigtalkproductions.com
Managing Director Matthew Justice *CEO (Executive)* Kenton Allen *Development Editor (Comedy)* Lara Singer *Drama Producer* Luke Alkin

Production details: Big Talk Productions Ltd is a British film and television production company founded by Nira Park in 1994. Big Talk was acquired by ITV Studios in 2013.

Recent films: *The Brothers Grimsby*, 2016; *Baby Driver*, 2017; *The Kid Who Would Be King*, 2019. Recent TV: *Raised by Wolves*, 2013–16; *Houdini and Doyle*, 2016; *Mum*, 2016; *Cold Feet*, 2016–18; *Defending the Guilty*, 2018; *The Imitation Game* 2018–.

Work experience: As an ITV company, offers work experience placements at Big Talk to enable people to experience what it is like to work in a production company and to learn more about the film and television industry in general. Most placements take place at the office on Nassau Street getting involved with development tasks, shadowing runners and assisting them with their varied task load. Provides the opportunity to learn how things operate, meet people in the industry and work on a variety of projects.

Submissions policy: Does not accept unsolicited material. For administrative reasons, does not respond to individual submissions. **Anything sent to Big Talk Productions will not be read and will be destroyed.**

Blakeway Productions

6 Anglers Lane, London NW5 3DG
tel 020 7428 3100 *fax* 020 7284 0626
email admin@blakeway.tv
website www.blakeway.co.uk

Established in 1994. In 2004 the company was bought by Ten Alps PLC and in 2007 it merged with 3BM Television and Ten Alps TV, bringing together strong track records of successful production across the genres of documentaries, docu-dramas, current affairs and factual entertainment formats.

Has produced more than 200 hours of prestigious programming for the BBC, Channel 4, More 4, ITV1 and Five in the UK, and leading US broadcasters including PBS, National Geographic, HBO, The History Channel and Discovery. Recent hits include: the Emmy-nominated docu-drama *9/11: The Twin Towers*, a co-production with Dangerous Films for BBC1 and Discovery; *The Clinton Years* for Radio 4 and the BAFTA-winning docu-drama *Nuremberg: Goering's Last Stand* for Channel 4 and The History Channel.

Blueprint Pictures

32-36 Great Portland Street, London W1W 8QX
tel 020 7580 6915
email enquiries@blueprintpictures.com
Co-Chairmen Graham Broadbent and Peter Czernin
Managing Director Diarmuid McKeown *Head of Production* Emma Mager *Head of Film* Ben Knight *Head of Television* Dominic Treadwell-Collins

Production details: Founded in 2005 by producers Graham Broadbent and Pete Czernin, Blueprint

Pictures develops and produces film and television drama for international audiences.

Internships: Does not currently have an internship scheme.

Submissions: Does not read unsolicited screenplays unless submitted via an agent.

Known for the film: *In Bruges*, 2008. Recent films: *The Riot Club*, 2014; *The Second Best Exotic Marigold Hotel*, 2015; *Three Billboards Outside Ebbing*, 2017; *The Guernsey Literary and Potato Peel Pie Society*, 2018; *The Mercy*, 2018. Recent TV: *The Outcast*, 2015; *The Last Dragonslayer*, 2016; *A Very English Scandal*, 2018.

Bryant Whittle Ltd

49 Federation Road, Abbey Wood, London SE2 0JT
tel 020 8311 8752
email info@bryantwhittle.com
website www.bryantwhittle.com
Directors John Bryant, Amanda Whittle

Production details: An independent production company working in feature-film production, with a slate of live action and CGI animated movies. Also offers a script-editing service. Employs actors in drama and voice-over.

Casting procedures: Uses freelance casting directors, and actors may write at any time to request inclusion; details will be kept on file. Offers Equity-approved contracts.

Cactus TV

1 St Luke's Avenue, London SW4 7LG
tel 020 7091 4900 *fax* 020 7091 4901
email touch.us@cactustv.co.uk
website www.cactustv.co.uk
Joint Managing Directors Amanda Ross, Simon Ross

Specalises in broad-based entertainment, features and chat shows. Since its inception in 1994 Cactus has produced 41 distinct titles in the UK, for 10 different channels.

Calamity Films

16 Carlisle Street, London W1D 3BT
email david@calamityfilms.co.uk
website www.calamityfilms.co.uk
Producer David Livingstone *Development Executive* Emily Bray

Production details: Calamity Films develops and produces feature films and television. David Livingstone was President of Worldwide Marketing and Distribution at both Universal Pictures International and Working Title Films. Emily Bray joined Calamity Films after four years at Independent Talent Group in the agency's Literary Department. She started out in the industry freelancing in development and production and worked on various music videos, short films and features.

Films: *Pride*, 2014; *Judy*, 2019. TV: *Brassic*, 2019.

Carlton Television Productions

35-38 Portman Square, London W1H 0NU
tel 020 7486 6688 *fax* 020 7486 1132
Director of Programmes Steve Hewlett

Comprises Carlton Television Productions, Planet 24 and Action Time. Makes drama programmes for all UK major broadcasters (ITV, BBC, Channel 4, Channel 5 and Sky) and regional programmes for Carlton Central, Carlton London and Carlton Westcountry.

Carnival Film & Television Ltd

6 Agar Street, London WC2N 4HN
tel 020 3618 6600
email info@carnivalfilms.co.uk
website www.carnivalfilms.co.uk
Executive Chairman Gareth Neame *Managing Director* Nigel Marchant, David O'Donoghue

Production details: Founded in 1978. Works mainly in TV production, creating drama with a popular and international feel. Employs actors for drama. Commissioned by major UK broadcasters including BBC, Channel 4 and ITV. Has received various prestigious awards/nominations, including Oscars, BAFTAs, Golden Globes and Emmys. Recent credits include: *The Last Kingdom, Jamestown, Stan Lee's Lucky Man, Downton Abbey* and *The Hollow Crown*.

Casting procedures: Uses freelance casting directors, does not deal directly with actors. Offers PACT/Equity contracts. Will consider casting disabled actors to play disabled characters.

Celador Films Ltd

39 Long Acre, London WC2E 9LG
tel 020 7845 6800 *fax* 020 7845 1147
email mdavies@celador.co.uk
website www.celador.co.uk
Chairman Paul Smith *Managing Director* Christian Colson

Develops and produces high-quality, commercially viable feature films across all genres. Film credits include: *Dirty, Pretty Things; Separate Lies* and *The Descent.* All projects are commissioned and developed in-house. Christian Colson is responsible for the commissioning, development and production of all projects presented to the company. Unsolicited scripts are not accepted.

Works also in television and radio. TV output is mostly non-fiction and light entertainment – e.g. *Who Wants to be a Millionaire?* and *You Are What You Eat* – although the company produced the sitcom, *All About Me,* starring Jasper Carrott and Meera Syal.

"The company is developing a number of other projects, including a further Neil Marshall project for production; BAFTA-winner Adrian Hodges' adaptation of Claire Tomalin's Whitbread Award-winning biography of Samuel Pepys, *The Unequalled*

Self; Farang, a low-budget road movie set in Thailand – a collaboration with writer Richard Cottan and director Peter Webber; an original screenplay from Paul Webb, based on events following the accession of Lyndon Baines Johnson to the United States presidency in the aftermath of Kennedy's assassination and *Big Deal,* a comedy about a hapless English journalist attempting to navigate the shark-infested waters of the international poker circuit."

Celtic Films

1st Floor, 24/25 New Bond Street, London W1S 2RR
tel 020 7727 6049
website www.celticfilms.co.uk

Production details: Established in 1986, Celtic Films has acted as a co-producer for 15 feature-length episodes of *Sharpe* for ITV, and for the award-winning *The Girl from Rio.*

Casting procedures: Accepts submissions (with CVs and photographs) from actors previously unknown to the company if sent by email. Showreels, voicereels and invitations to view individual actors' websites are also accepted. Offers Equity-approved contracts. Will consider applications from disabled actors to play characters with disabilities.

Coastal Productions

c/o 16 The Plantations, Wynyard Woods, Wynyard, Teesside TS22 5SN
tel 01740 644032
email coastalproductions@msn.com
website www.coastalproductions.co.uk

Created in 1997 by Sandra Jobling and Robson Green with the aim of making feature films and TV dramas in the North East of England – and supporting local young people wanting to get into the industry. The company's many production and co-production credits include: *Take Me, Blind Ambition, The Last Musketeer, Touching Evil, Close and True, Grafters 1 & 2, Rhinoceros, Hereafter, Unconditional Love, Rocketman, Wire in the Blood* and *Place of Execution.*

Collingwood & Co.

10-14 Crown Street, London W3 8SB
tel 020 8993 3666 *fax* 020 8993 9595
email info@collingwoodandco.co.uk
website www.collingwoodandco.co.uk
Head of Development Helen Stroud

Founded in 1988. Animation series and specials for children. Does not deal directly with actors: prefers to deal with agents.

The Comedy Unit

The Comedy Unit, Unit D,
Glasgow North Trading Estate, 24 Craigmont Street, Glasgow G20 9BT
tel 0141 305 6666 *fax* 0141 305 6600
email info@comedyunit.co.uk
website www.comedyunit.co.uk
Managing Director Rab Christie

Produces some of Scotland's best-loved television and radio shows, as well as a range of programmes for transmission across network and satellite channels. Formed in 1996, became part of the RDF Media Group in 2006 and part of the Zodiak Media Group in 2010.

Company Pictures
New London House, 172 Drury Lane (2nd Floor), London WC2B 5QR
tel 020 7380 3900 *fax* 020 7831 5601
email enquiries@companypictures.co.uk
website www.companypictures.co.uk
Managing Director John Yorke

Does not accept unsolicited submissions. Proposals should be submitted through agents.

Cowboy Films
40 Langham Street, London W1W 7AS
tel 020 7580 2982
email info@cowboyfilms.co.uk
email charles@cowboyfilms.co.uk
website www.cowboyfilms.co.uk
Managing Director Charles Steel

Until recently, Cowboy Films represented a range of top-quality commercial and music video directors, and also worked on feature films such as *The Hole* and *Goodbye Charlie Bright*. Sister company Crossroads Films in the US has taken over the roster of music video and commercial projects, while Cowboy continues to work on features. Kevin Macdonald's *The Last King of Scotland* is the company's most recent project.

Dalton Films Ltd
127 Hamilton Terrace, London NW8 9QR
tel 020 7328 6169 *fax* 020 7624 4420

Production details: Established in 1987. Working mainly in film drama. Recent credits include: *Oscar and Lucinda, Country Life* and *Madame Sousatzka*.

Casting procedures: Casting is carried out by freelance casting directors. Actors should only make contact in response to announcements in the trade press – does not welcome any form of unsolicited communication from actors. "Do not waste time or postage until a film is actively being cast or being developed." Rarely or never has the opportunity to cast disabled actors.

Don Productions Ltd
2 Foskett Mews, Shackwell Lane, London E8 2BZ
tel 020 7254 0044 *fax* 020 9227 3283
email london@donproductions.com
website www.donproductions.com
Director Donald Harding

Japanese/English bilingual TV and media production company based in London. Produces TV drama, documentaries, news and sports programmes. Clients include: Japan Broadcasting Corporation, Nippon

Television and Channel 4. Recent work includes: *The Life of Charles Darwin*.

The Drama House
email jack@dramahouse.co.uk
website www.dramahouse.co.uk
Chairman/Chief Executive Jack Emery

Produces drama and drama-documentaries for film and TV. Recent credits include: *Inquisition* for Channel 5, one of the first HD drama shoots – starring Derek Jacobi; also *Breaking the Code, Witness Against Hitler, Little White Lies* and *Suffer the Little Children*. Commissioned by major UK broadcasters: BBCTV, Channel 4 and C5. Also international PBS and HBO. Winner of many international and national awards. Hopes that high-profile work will encourage writers and other professionals to come to the Drama House.

Ecosse Films Ltd
Brigade House, 8 Parsons Green, London SW6 4TN
tel 020 7371 0290 *fax* 020 7736 3436
email info@ecossefilms.com
website www.ecossefilms.com
Director Douglas Rae *Head of Drama* Robert Bernstein

Founded in 1988. Works mainly in TV and feature film production and employs actors in dramas and comedies. Recent credits include: *Mrs Brown, Nowhere Boy* and *Wuthering Heights*. Uses freelance casting directors and does not deal directly with actors.

Extra Digit Ltd
Head office: 8 High Street, Brentwood, Essex CM14 4AB. Please do not send application tot his address see website for contact details.
website www.extradigit.com

Production details: Founded in 2002. Works in film and television and employs actors in drama, comedy and documentary. Recent credits include: *Somewhere*, starring Hugh Cornwell, and *Life is a Circus*, starring Steve Ryland.

Casting procedures: Occasionally uses freelance casting directors. Welcomes approaches by actors by post only (please see website for postal contact details), with CVs and photographs. Will accept showreels if these do not require a response. Has no equal opportunities policy: "If you can do the part better than anyone else, you get the job – regardless." Please do NOT contact by phone or email, use current contact details from the 'Recruitment' section on the website.

Eye Film and Television
Room F7, Epic Studios, 112-114 Magdalen Street, Norwich NR3 1JD
tel 0845 621 1133
email production@eyefilmandtv.co.uk
website www.eyefilmandtv.co.uk
Managing Director Charlie Gauvain

Independent producers of film and TV drama and documentaries. Also produces corporate, commercial, education and training material. Clients include: BBC, ITV1/Anglia, Channel 4, Five and First Take Films. Recent credits include: *The Secret of Eel Island* and *POV*.

Feelgood Fiction Ltd
49 Goldhawk Road, London W12 8QP
tel 020 8746 2535 *fax* 020 8740 6177
email feelgood@feelgoodfiction.co.uk
website www.feelgoodfiction.co.uk
Managing Director Philip Clarke *Drama Producer* Laurence Bowen

Producers of film and TV drama.

Flashback Television Ltd
mobile 07952 090884
email mailbox@flashbacktv.co.uk
website www.flashbacktelevision.com
Managing Director Taylor Downing *Creative Director* David Edgar

Flashback Television has been in continuous production since 1982 and is one of the top-rated production companies in the UK. The company has a reputation for the quality of its work, for high visual standards and powerful story-telling. Flashback produces factual, factual entertainment and drama programming for broadcasters in the UK and around the world. In the UK Flashback has worked for all the other major British broadcasters including the BBC, Channel Four, ITV, Five and BSkyB. Recent credits include *Nigella's Christmas Kitchen* (BBC), *Married to the Prime Minister* (C4), *Secrets of the Classroom* (C4) and *Beau Brummell: This Charming Man* (BBC). Flashback also produces many hours of programming each year for the UK Government-backed channel Teachers' TV.

Flashback has a long track record of production in the international market. For over a decade the company has been producing series direct for North American broadcasters Arts & Entertainment Television Networks and Discovery. They have also co-produced several major projects with FR2 in France. Recent credits include *The Lost Evidence* (The History Channel), *Superhomes* (Discovery), *Top Tens* (Discovery), and *Weaponology* (Discovery).

Flashback also produces interactive material including the website *History Quest* for Channel 4 Learning, and educational podcasts for the British Council.

Flashback Television is based in London and Bristol. More information can be found at **www.flashbacktelevision.com**.

Focus Films Ltd
Suite 146, Hampstead House, 176 Finchley Road, London NW3 6BT
mobile 07785 398604

email focus@focusfilms.co.uk
website www.focusfilms.co.uk
Development Producer Adam Polonsky *Executive Producer* David Pupkewitz

An independent feature film development and production company founded in 1982 by David Pupkewitz and Marsha Levin. Early successes with TV documentaries and dramas preceded a transition to feature films in the 1990s. Recent productions include: *The 51st State* with Robert Carlyle and Samuel L. Jackson; *Master Harold & the Boys* with Ving Rhames and Freddie Highmore; *Chemical Wedding* with Simon Callow and *Crimetime* with Stephen Baldwin and Pete Postlethwaite. Upcoming projects include: *Tainted*, *Leroy Purcell* and *Barry*.

Focus Productions Ltd
4 Leopold Road, Bristol BS6 5BS
tel 0117 230 9726
email martinweitz@focusproductions.co.uk
website www.focusproductions.co.uk
Directors Ralph Maddern, Martin Weitz

Production details: Established 1993. Specialises in TV features and documentaries. Employs actors in TV, radio and film; also for presentation and voice-overs. Recent credits include: *The Real Rain Man* (C5), *Painting the Mind* (C4), *The Piano Player* (C5) and *Vivaldi's Fantasia* (film).

Casting procedures: Holds general auditions. Actors are advised to apply requesting inclusion at any time. Casting breakdowns are available by telephone. Welcomes letters (with CVs and photograph) from actors previously unknown to the company if sent by post, but not by email. Also accepts invitations to view individual actors' websites. Offers Equity-approved contracts. Rarely has the opportunity to cast disabled actors.

Mark Forstater Productions Ltd
11 Keslake Road, London NW6 6DJ
tel 020 8933 5475

Works in film and TV production.

Fremantle
1 Stephen Street, London W1T 1AL
tel 020 7691 6000 *fax* 020 7691 6100
website www.fremantlemedia.com

Fremantle is one of the largest and most successful creators, producers and distributors ofunscripted content in the world. A global entertainment powerhouse, Freemantle has an outstanding international network of production teams, companies and labels in over 30 countries. Produces in excess of 12,000 hours of original programming, rolls out more than 60 formats and airs 450 programmes a year worldwide.

The group distributes over 20,000 hours of content in more than 200 countries. Also a world leader in digital and branded entertainment with more than 300 million subscribers across 1,400 social channels and over 100 billion views across all platforms.

Part of the RTL Group, a global leader across braodcast, content and digital, itself a division of the international media giant Bertelsmann.

Funny Face Films Ltd

8A Warwick Road, Hampton Wick, Surrey KT1 4DW
Director Steven Drew

Production details: Works mainly in film/video.

Casting procedures: Uses in-house casting director. Sometimes holds general auditions. Welcomes letters (with CVs and photographs) from actors previously unknown to the company, sent by post or email. Accepts showreels and will consider invitations to view individual actors' websites. Will consider applications from disabled actors to play characters with disabilities.

G2 Entertainment Ltd

16a Beaufort Road, Reigate, Surrey RH2 9DJ
tel 01737 221238
email jules@g2ent.co.uk
website www.g2ent.co.uk
Producer Steve Gammond; *Director* Jules Gammond.

Founded in 1990. Sport and special interest production company.

Galleon Films Ltd

50 Openshaw Road, London SE2 0TE
tel 020 8310 7276
email alice@galleontheatre.co.uk
website www.galleonfilms.co.uk
Chief Executive Alice De Sousa

Production details: An independent film and drama production company.

Casting procedures: Uses freelance casting directors and sometimes holds general auditions. Casting breakdowns are publicly available via all actor-accessible publications and the website. Does not welcome unsolicited letters and CVs or showreels, but will consider invitations to view individual actors' websites. Actors are employed under Equity-approved contracts.

Handle and Spout Ltd

Suite 14, Centre House, Wood Lane,
London W12 7SB
tel 020 7100 2758
email info@handleandspout.com
website www.handleandspout.com
Key contact Paul Shuttleworth *Head of Production* Loretta Cocchi *Development Producer* Jill Kinnaird

Production details: Handle and Spout is a BAFTA-nominated television production company with bases in London and Leeds. Established in 2006 by former BBC executives, Paul Shuttleworth and Loretta Cocchi, to date the company has completed over 50 hours of television and radio broadcasting for the BBC, ITV and Turner Networks.

Comprised of people who have built careers working on children's classics such as *Blue Peter*, *Live & Kicking* and *Record Breakers*, Handle and Spout's specialism lies in making content for children. In addition, team members bring a wealth of experience in working on more mainstream flagship productions such as *The One Show*, *Come Dine With Me* and *How Do You Solve a Problem Like Maria?* The company is currently looking to build on its growing relationship with the commercial sector and is actively working with advertisers to bring new AFP concepts to air. Alongside the core business of television production, Handle and Spout offers consultancy to other broadcasters and production companies, as well as a full range of corporate video services.

Casting procedures: Employs actors in drama, comedy, children's TV, presentation and voice-overs. Recent credits include: *Harry & Toto*, *Farm Camp*, *Go And . . .* Welcomes submissions by post and email, and accepts showreels and invitations to view individual actors' websites. Strives to be an equal opportunities employer and has signed up to the PACT Diversity pledge.

Handstand Productions

13 Hope Street, Liverpool L1 9BQ
tel 0151 708 7441 *fax* 0151 709 3515
email info@handstand-uk.com
website www.handstand-uk.com
Producer Han Duijvendak *Producer* Nicholas Stanley

Working almost exclusively in documentary, film, TV and video production. Rarely requires actors, so please do not submit anything unless a specific casting requirement has been made available on the website.

Hat Trick Productions Ltd

33 Oval Road, London NW1 7EA
tel 020 7184 7777 *fax* 020 7184 7778
email reception@hattrick.com
website www.hattrick.co.uk
Managing Director Jimmy Mulville

Founded in 1986, Hat Trick Productions is one of the UK's most successful independent production companies working in situation and drama comedy series and light entertainment shows. Recent credits include: *The Kumars at No. 42*, *Worst Week of my Life*, *Have I Got News for You* and *Room 101*.

Heavy Entertainment Ltd

111 Wardour Street, London W1F 0UH
tel 020 7494 1000 *fax* 020 7494 1100
email info@heavy-entertainment.com
website www.heavy-entertainment.com
Director David Roper

Production details: Established in 1992. Audio, video and web producers. Areas of work include drama, corporate, commercials, audiobooks and actor showreels (audio and video). Offers Equity-approved contracts.

Casting procedures: Welcomes showreels and voicereels (via agents only), and invitations to view individual actors' websites.

HuRica Productions

89 Birchanger Lane, Birchanger, Bishop Stortford, Herts CM23 5QF
mobile 07941 236871
email HuRicaProductions@gmail.com
website www.wix.com/HuRica/HuRicaProductions
Director Hugh Allison

Production details: Established in 2010. A company founded on the ethos that "Art Is What You Make It". Works in radio and film. Recent credits include: *The Chronicles of Banania* (radio series aired on Radio North), *Call On Me* (short film) and *Shared Accommodation* (short film).

Casting procedures: Does not use freelance casting directors or hold general auditions.

Hurricane Films Ltd

13 Hope Street, Liverpool L1 9BQ
tel 0151 707 9700 *fax* 0151 707 9149
email sol@hurricanefilms.net
website www.hurricanefilms.net
Producers Solon Papadopoulos and Roy Boulter

Founded in 2000,Hurricane Films develop feature films, feature documentaries and TV series. Credits include: *Of Time and the City* (Terence Davies); *Sunset Song* (Terence Davies); *A Quiet Passion* (Terence Davies); *Unsung Hero: The Jack Jones Story* (Solon Papadopoulos); *A Prayer Before Dawn* (Jean Stephane Sauvaire) and *My Letter to the World* (Solon Papadopoulos). BAFTA-nominated twice with six Royal Television Awards.

Jason Impey Films

90 Hainault Avenue, Giffard Park, Milton Keynes, Buckinghamshire MK14 5PE
mobile 07732 476409
email jasonimpey@live.com
website www.jasonimpey.co.uk
Director Jason Impey

Production details: Works mainly in film, making feature horror films. Also employs actors in the fields of drama, comedy and documentary. Recent credits include: *Fluid Boy, Grim Places, VIPCO The Untold Story, Twink, More Sex, Lies and Depravity, Boys Behind Bars, Lustful Desires* and *Sex, Lies and Depravity* (all feature films).

Casting procedures: Uses freelance casting directors and holds general auditions; actors may write in at any time requesting inclusion. Casting breakdowns available via postal application with sae. Welcomes letters (with CVs and photographs) from individual

actors previously unknown to the company, sent by post or email. Also accepts showreels and invitations to view individual actors' websites. Actively encourages applications from disabled actors and promotes the use of inclusive casting. "Always on the lookout for new talent."

Kelpie Media

The Executive Suite, 44 Washington Street, Glasgow G3 8AZ
tel 0800 840 2815
email info@kelpiemedia.com
website www.kelpiemedia.com

Independent production company that produces a range of broadcast and corporate/commercial work, from computer-animated children's programmes to documentaries in the Middle East and low-budget feature films. Credits include: BAFTA-nominated animation, *Cannonman*; Grierson Award-winning documentary, *And So Goodbye*; and large-scale corporate work for global clients such as Shell and the UK Government.

Left Bank Pictures

33 Foley Street, London W1W 7TL
tel 020 7612 3299 020 7612 3132
email info@leftbankpictures.co.uk
website www.leftbankpictures.co.uk
Chief Executive Andy Harries

An independent television and film production company founded in July 2007 by Andy Harries and Marigo Kehoe, and named "Best Independent Production Company" at the Broadcast Awards in 2011. "We continue to work with the UK's leading writing, directing and onscreen talent to produce bold, innovative feature films, television dramas and cutting-edge comedy. We also pride ourselves on nurturing and championing exciting new talent set to create the hits of tomorrow."

Lexitricity Ltd

15-25 Vereker Road, West Kensington, London W14 9JU
tel 0870 840 4466
email alexandra@lexitricity.com
email production@lexitricity.com

Founded in 2006. An independent production company making short films, music promos, documentaries and actors' showreels. Comprises a writer, director, producer and storyboard artist, teamed up with an experienced professional crew employed on a freelance basis. Work includes experience on feature films, BBC dramas and documentaries as well as award-winning short films. Will take clients through the entire production process, from concept and storyboard to a creative shoot and edit. Works closely with photographers, illustrators and graphic artists to produce original marketing material including flyers, posters and DVD cover designs.

LWT and United Productions
London TV Centre, Upper Ground, London SE1 9LT
tel 020 7620 1620
Controller of Drama Michele Buck

Founded in 1996. Producers of TV and film.

MARV Films
71 Queen Victoria Street, London EC4V 4BE
email info@marvfilms.com
Executive Matthew Vaughn

Production details: Matthew Vaughn is best known for starting his career working as a producer for the Guy Ritchie films: *Lock, Stock and Two Smoking Barrels*, *Snatch* and *Swept Away*.

Recent films: *Kingsmen: The Secret Service*, 2014; *Fantastic Four*, 2015; *Eddie the Eagle*, 2015; *Kingsmen: the Golden Circle*, 2017; *Rocketman*, 2019.

Maya Vision International Ltd
3rd Floor, 6 Kinghorn Street, London EC1A 7HW
tel 020 7796 4842 *fax* 020 7796 4580
email info@mayavisionint.com
website www.mayavisionint.com
Producer/Director Rebecca Dobbs *Producer* Sally Thomas *Writer* Michael Wood

Maya Vision International is an independent film and television production company, founded in 1983. Since then it has won many awards, and become renowned for making work of the highest quality.

Specialising in producing "original, landmark documentaries, features and drama for film and television", Maya Vision has developed a unique style, making some of history's great stories accessible to a wider public. Most recently *The Story of China*, a six part series for BBC/PBS and BBCWW written and presented by Michael Wood.

Working alongside many broadcasters and funders, including the BBC, ITV, Channel 4, Five, PBS, UK Film Council, BFI and Arts Council England. Maya Vision's acclaimed catalogue has been screened in more than 140 territories worldwide. Since 2002 the company has been managing the UK Film Festival's successful Short Film Completion Fund, and has helped support nearly 60 titles that have gone on to win more than 150 awards and appeared in at least as many festivals worldwide. See the website for how to apply for funds.

Met Film Production
Ealing Studios, Ealing Green, London W5 5EP
tel 020 8280 9127 *fax* 020 8280 9111
email mfp@metfilm.co.uk
website www.metfilmproduction.co.uk
Managing Director Jonny Persey *Directors* Paul Morrison, Jerry Rothwell *Producers* Stewart le Maréchal, Al Morrow

Enterprise dedicated to the development and production of feature films for national and international audiences. Also produces short films. The company has a number of feature films in development.

Recent credits include: *Deep Water, Wondrous Oblivion* and *Soloman & Gaenor*. Upcoming work includes: *Heavy Load* and *The Pied Piper of Hutzovina*.

Neal Street Productions
26-28 Neal Street, London WC2H 9QQ
tel 020 7240 8890
email post@nealstreetproductions.com
Executive Sam Mendes *Film Executive* Pippa Harris *Head of Development* Julie Pastor *Television and Film Executive* Nicholas Brown *Production Executive* Caroline Reynolds

Production details: Neal Street Productions is one of the UK's most respected production companies, producing film, television and theatre. Set up in 2003 by Sam Mendes, Pippa Harris and Caro Newling, the company celebrated its tenth anniversary in 2013, as Nicholas Brown was appointed to the Board of Directors. In 2015, Neal Street moved under the umbrella of parent company, All3Media, which is owned jointly between Discovery Communication and Liberty Global. Neal Street Productions makes distinctive, popular, award winning projects on both sides of the Atlantic.

Known for *Revolutionary Road*, 2008 and *Call the Midwife*, 2012–18.

Recent TV includes: *Penny Dreadful*, 2016–18; *Britannia*, 2017; *Informer*, 2018; *Project Runaway All Stars*, 2019.

Submissions: Does not accept unsolicited material.

NFD Productions Ltd
21 Low Street, South Milford, Leeds LS25 5AR
tel/fax 01977 681949
email alyson@nfdproductions.com
website www.nfdproductions.com
Director Alyson Connew

Production details: Production company producing feature films specialising in 3D, children and teenage programmes specialising in 3D, and commercials.

Casting procedures: Please send CVs to **alyson@northernfilmanddrrama.com**. We do require a minimum of 4 featured/named roles in either a film or TV series.

Number 9 Films
Linton House, 1 Floor, 24 Wells Street, London W1T 3PH
tel 020 7323 0456
Twitter @number9films
Producers Stephen Woolley and Elizabeth Karlsen
Head of Development Kate Lawrence

Production details: Number 9 Films is a British independent film production company co-founded in 2002 by producers Elizabeth Karlsen and Stephen Woolley, after a long collaboration at both Palace Pictures and Scala Productions. They are best known for *The Crying Game*, 1992; *Interview with the Vampire*, 1994; *Michael Collins*, 1996; *Made in Dagenham*, 2010. In 2005, the company was awarded one of the much sought-after Slate Development Funding schemes by the UK Film Council. The company has gone on to establish itself as one of the UK's leading independent production companies, forging relationships with a wide range of talent in the UK, across Europe and in the States. The company aims to produce between 2 and 3 films a year.

Recent films: *Carol*, 2015; *Youth*, 2015; *The Limehouse Golem*, 2016; *Their Finest*, 2016; *On Chesil Beach*, 2017; *Colette*, 2018.

On Screen Productions Ltd

Ashborne House, 33 Bridge Street,
Chepstow NP16 5GA
tel 01291 636300 *fax* 01291 636301
email action@OnScreenProductions.com
website www.OnScreenProductions.com
Director and Producer Richard Cobourne *Producer and Director* Alison King *Assistant Producer and Production Manager* Esther Prosser

Production details: Established in 1992. Creative, business-led, integrated visual communications company producing the full range of broadcast and non-broadcast TV, video, TV commercials, interactive media, training, live events, conferences, exhibitions etc. Frequently uses actors across many of its productions – the majority of which are non-broadcast (60% for Health and Pharmaceutical companies).

Casting procedures: Casting is done by freelance casting directors as needed, or in-house by Joe Allansen. Accepts submissions (with CVs and photographs) from individual actors previously unknown to the company if sent by post or email (postal submissions are preferred). Invitations to view showreels and individual actors' websites are also accepted. Deals in 'buy out' contracts (except broadcast and theatrical). "We do not discriminate either positively or negatively against disabled actors."

OVC Media Ltd

88 Berkeley Court, Baker Street, London NW1 5ND
tel 020 7402 9111 *fax* 020 7723 3044
email eliot@ovcmedia.com
website www.ovcmedia.com
Director Joanne Cohen

Production details: Established in 1982. Areas of work include TV, film, video and documentary production. Recent credits include: *History of the World Cup*, *African Odyssey* and *My Matisse*.

Casting procedures: Accepts submissions (with CVs and photographs) from actors previously unknown to the company if sent by post, but not by email. Showreels, voicereels and invitations to view individual actors' websites are also accepted. Offers Equity approved contracts and does not subscribe to the Equity Pension Scheme. Will consider submissions from disabled actors to play disabled characters.

Park Village Ltd

1 Park Village East, Regents Park, London NW1 7PX
tel 020 7387 8077 *fax* 020 7388 3051
email peter.ryan@parkvillage.co.uk
website www.parkvillage.co.uk
Producer Pete Ryan

Established in 1972. Commercials production company working mainly in commercials and content/interactive. Casting is done by freelance casting directors. Recent credits include Marks & Spencer Food. Actors are employed under Equity-approved contracts. Will consider applications from disabled actors to play disabled characters.

Picture Palace Films Ltd

13 Egbert Street, London NW1 8LJ
tel 020 7586 8763 *fax* 020 7586 9048
email info@picturepalace.com
website www.picturepalace.com
Producer and Chief Executive Malcom Craddock

Founded in 1972. Works mainly in feature films and TV drama production. Recent credits include: *Sharpe's Peril*, *Sharpe's Challenge*, *Frances Tuesday* and *Extremely Dangerous* (all ITV); *Rebel Heart* (BBC); *A Life for a Life* (*The True Story of Stefan Kizko*) and the *Sharpe* series.

Pinball London Ltd

tel 0845 273 3893
email info@pinballonline.co.uk
website www.pinballonline.co.uk
Director Paula Vaccaro

Production details: Founded in 2009. Independent film production company assembled by creative and business entertainment industry professionals with a common goal of producing independent auteur-oriented films. Film is main area of work, but may do music promos, TV and Internet content. Recent credits include: *A Day in Two Lives* (short); *Margo & Max* (long feature); and Perempay & Dee feat. Shola Ama (DJPLAY music video).

Casting procedures: Uses freelance casting directors. Sometimes holds general auditions; actors may write at any time to request inclusion. Only accepts postal submissions, which *must* include CV, professional actor's reel on DVD, and headshot photos.

The Reel Thing Ltd

20 The Chase, Coulsdon, Surrey CR5 2EG
tel 020 8660 9609
email info@reelthing.tv
website www.reelthing.tv
Key personnel Frazer Ashford, Chris Day

Production details: Established in 2001. Specialising in corporate and business TV production. Working the UK and worldwide for small, local clients and large multinationals. Recent credits include: *Fire Safety* (Homebase Ltd) and *Lake Avalon* (US).

Casting procedures: Does not welcome unsolicited CVs. Offers non-Equity contracts and does not subscribe to the Equity Pension Scheme. Actively encourages applications from disabled actors and promotes the use of inclusive casting.

Replay Film & New Media
25 Museum Street, London WC1 1ST
tel 020 7637 0473
email solutions@replayfilms.co.uk
website www.replayfilms.co.uk
Directors Dave Young, Stuart Slade

Production details: Established in 1990. Activities include: drama, documentary, corporate, e-learning, training, consultancy. Involved in all aspects of film and new media, web design, working mainly in TV, video and computer media production.

Casting procedures: Casting breakdowns are available publicly on the website and Castweb. Invitations to view individual actors' websites are accepted.

September Films
22 Glenthorne Road, London W6 ONG
tel 020 8563 9393 *fax* 020 8741 7214
email september@septemberfilms.com
website www.septemberfilms.com
Chairman David Green

September Films is a leading UK independent television and film production company with offices in London and Los Angeles. It was founded in 1992 by feature film director David Green, who devised the groundbreaking *Hollywood Women* series that launched the company. Having produced over 1,000 hours of primetime television during the last 13 years, September is an established specialist in factual entertainment, features, reality programming and entertainment formats.

Sightline
Guildford, Surrey GU3 1LZ
tel 01483 813311 *mobile* 07554 019436
email keith@sightline.co.uk
website www.sightline.co.uk
Twitter @KTSightline
Senior Producer and Director Keith Thomas

Production details: Fully resourced. Long-established video and interactive content production company specialising in corporate and training videos, media for the Web, animation and 360 video. Employs actors in corporate work.

Casting procedures: Welcomes letters (with CVs and photographs) from actors previously unknown to the company – please send by email, not by post. Invitations to view individual actors' websites are welcome.

Sixteen Films
2nd Floor, 187 Wardour Street, London W1F 8ZB
tel 020 7734 0168 *fax* 020 7439 4196
website www.sixteenfilms.co.uk
Director Ken Loach *Producer* Rebecca O'Brien

Sixteen Films is a film production company run by Producer Rebecca O'Brien and Director Ken Loach. Writer Paul Laverty is the Associate Director.

Speakeasy Productions Ltd
1A Shandon Crescent, Edinburgh EH11 1QE
tel 0131 557 1288
email info@speak.co.uk
website www.speak.co.uk
Company Directors Jonathan Young, Shona Johnstone, Jeremy Hewitt

Production details: Corporate media production company and event management company based in London and Edinburgh. Works mainly in video production, employing actors in documentary, corporate, and commercials. Occasionally holds general auditions. Recent clients include: Lloyds Banking Group, Food Standards Scotland, Student Loans Council, Scottish Enterprise and the Scottish Government.

Casting procedures: Accepts submissions (with CVs and photographs) from actors previously unknown to the company. Will also accept CVs and photographs sent via email. Invitations to view showreels and individual actors' websites are also accepted. Promotes inclusive casting and applications from disabled actors are considered.

Spellbound Productions Ltd
90 Cowdenbeath Path, Islington, London N1 0LG
tel 020 7713 8066 *fax* 020 7713 8066
email phspellbound@hotmail.com
Producer Paul Harris

Small independent production company specialising in feature films and drama for television. Curent projects in development include: 2 animated features, a drama series and other "genre" pieces.

Stagescreen Productions
Suite 92, One Prescot Street, London E1 8RL
tel/fax 020 7481 4810
website www.stagescreenproductions.com
Director Jeffrey Taylor *Development Executive* John Segal

Founded in 1986, Stagescreen is a film and TV production company with offices in London and Los Angeles. Recent credits include: *What's Cooking*, directed by Gurinder Chadha (Lionsgate); *Alexander the Great* directed by Jalal Merhi (ProSeiben) and

Jekyll, directed by Douglas Mackinnon and Matt Lipsey (BBC). Forthcoming work includes *Young Cleopatra*.

Offers PACT/Equity-approved contracts and does not subscribe to the Equity Pension Scheme. Will consider applications from disabled actors to play disabled characters.

Talkback Thames
20-21 Newman Street, London W1T 1PG
tel 020 7861 8000 *fax* 020 7861 8001
website www.talkbackthames.tv

Founded in 1981. Produces TV situation comedies and comedy dramas, features and straight drama. Credits include: *Property Ladder, Jamie's Kitchen, Smack the Pony, The 11 O' Clock Show* and *Da Ali G Show*. TalkBack is part of the FremantleMedia Group. (See the entry for FremantleMedia under *Independent film, video and TV production companies* on page 334).

Tiger Aspect Productions
4th Floor, Shepherds Building Central, London W14 0EE
tel 020 7434 6700 *fax* 020 7544 1665
email general@tigeraspect.co.uk
website www.tigeraspect.co.uk
Co-managing Directors Ben Cavey abd Will Gould

Founded in 1993. Produces TV comedy and drama with the aim of "investing in and working with the leading writers, performers and programme-makers to produce original, creative and successful programming". Credits include: *Ripper Street* (BBC1), *Teachers* (C4), *Good Karma Hospital* (ITV), *Peaky Blinders* (BBC2), *Bad Education* (BBC3), *Benidorm* (ITV) and *Mount Pleasant* (Sky).

Trafalgar 1 Limited
153 Burnham Towers, Fellows Road, London NW3 3JN
tel 020 7722 7789 *fax* 020 7483 0662
email t1ltd@blueyonder.co.uk

Production details: Established 1985. Produces feature films, music videos, documentaries and short films. Recent productions include: *Rough Cut and Ready Dubbed* and *Art of the Critic*.

Casting procedures: Welcomes letters (with CVs and photographs) from actors previously unknown to the company sent by email. Showreels, voicereels and invitations to view individual actors' websites are also accepted. Offers Equity-approved contracts.

Twenty Twenty Productions Ltd
35 High Holborn, London WC1V 6AE
tel 020 7284 2020 *fax* 020 7284 1810
email triciawilson@twentytwenty.tv
website www.twentytwenty.tv
CEO Tim Carter, *Creative Director* Emma Willis, *Head of Production* Hana Canter, *Director of Development* Martha Housden, *Head of Children's* Helen Soden

Twenty Twenty Television is one of the UK's leading independent television production companies, making award-winning documentaries, hard-hitting current affairs, popular drama and attention-grabbing living history series. Its recent primetime children's shows are also bringing success in an exciting and challenging genre. *The Choir* won a 2007 BAFTA Award; the series *That'll Teach 'Em* won an Indie Award and was nominated for a British Academy Award; the *Lads Army* series gained the Royal Television Society primetime features award as well as a BAFTA nomination and the international factual hit *Brat Camp* brought home an International Emmy from New York in November 2004.

Formed in 1982 by 'hands-on' programme-makers, Twenty Twenty Television has always grown organically. Its industry-wide reputation for quality, intelligence and rigour was built in factual programmes. Twenty Twenty remains truly independent and is still run by creative and enthusiastic programme-makers. Its work has been broadcast by networks around the world including the BBC, CBBC, ITV, Channels 4 and Five in the UK, and ABC, The Discovery Channel, Turner Original Productions, Sundance Channel, CNN, The Arts and Entertainment Channel and WGBH in the USA.

Video Enterprises
12 Barbers Wood Road, High Wycombe, Bucks HP12 4EP
tel 01494 534144 *mobile* 07831 875216
email videoenterprises@ntlworld.com
website www.videoenterprises.co.uk
Director Maurice R. Fleisher

Video Enterprises is a UK-based video production and crewing company specialising in broadcast, corporate, industrial, theatrical and social events programme-making.

Walsh Bros Ltd
29 Trafalgar Grove, London SE10 9TB
tel 020 8858 6870 *mobile* 07879 816426
email info@walshbros.co.uk
website www.walshbros.co.uk

Double BAFTA- and Grierson-nominated film company. Productions range from television series and dramas for BBC like *Sofa Surfers*, Channel 4's *Don't Make Me Angry* and feature film productions *Monarch* and *Toryboy: The Movie*. The BBC documentary series *Headhunting the Homeless* was shortlisted for the Grierson Awards.

Wilder Films
21 Little Portland Street, London W1W 8BT
tel 020 7631 3417 *fax* 020 7636 4439
email molliebishop@wilderfilms.co.uk
website www.wilderfilms.co.uk
Managing Director Richard Batty

Production details: Established in 2003. Works mainly in film and video production, especially corporate, brand and short films, and commercials.

Casting procedures: Uses in-house and freelance casting directors and holds general auditions – but "will look for people if needed". Does not welcome unsolicited approaches but may accept invitations to view individual actors' websites.

Working Title Films
26 Aybrook Street, London W1U 4AN
tel 020 7307 3000 *fax* 020 7307 3003
website www.workingtitlefilms.com
Chairmen Tim Bevan, Eric Fellner *President* Liza Chasin *President UK Production* Debra Hayward

Recent films include *Atonement* (with James McAvoy, Keira Knightly, Romola Garai, Saoirse Ronan and Vanessa Redgrave) and *The Golden Age* (with Cate Blanchett and Geoffrey Rush, who reprise the roles they orginated in the award-winning *Elizabeth*, joined this time by Clive Owen).

World Productions Ltd
101 Finsbury Pavement, London EC2A 1RS
tel 020 3002 3113
email enquiries@world-productions.com
website www.world-productions.com
Creative Director Simon Heath, *Managing Director* Roderick Seligman, *Head of Drama* Jake Lushington, *Head of Development* Kirstie MacDonald, *Development Producer* Priscilla Parish, *Script Editor/Producer* Gwen Gorst, *Production Assistant* Freddie à Brassard

Produces TV drama features, series and serials. Recent credits include: *Line of Duty* (BBC2), *The Bletchley Circle* (ITV), *The Great Train Robbery* (BBC1) and *The Fear* (C4).

Media

Media

Film schools

Although the work is minimally paid (if at all), it is well worth contacting film schools for casting consideration. Despite the fact that you'll often find yourself in the hands of a director with no idea about actors and acting, the potential of gaining something from the experience is possibly greater than that of participating in a Fringe theatre production – and the end result could contain material worthy of use in a showreel. Some schools keep files of actors' CVs and photographs for students to refer to when casting.

Castings for many low- or non-paid films are advertised on Shooting People (**www.shootingpeople.org**) – see entry on page 455.

Arts University Bournemouth
Wallisdown, Poole, Dorset BG12 5HH
tel 01202 363049
website www.aub.ac.uk
Key contact Bournemouth Film School: David Munns

Students do not only consider local actors for their short films. Actors are either paid Equity minimum (both MA and BA Film Production Films) or are offered their expenses and a DVD copy. Also needs actors for exercises and workshops. Welcomes enquiries (containing CV, photograph and covering letter) from new actors; actors' details are kept on file.

Brighton Film School
The Brighton Forum, 95 Ditchling Road,
Brighton BN1 4ST
tel 01273 602070
email info@brightonfilmschool.org.uk
website www.brightonfilmschool.org.uk
Head of School Gary Barber *Creative Director* Carol Harrison

Film-industry-recognised. Provides training in all aspects of motion-picture production: screenwriting, directing, cinematography, editing and production management. More than 30 student short films are made each year; students generally recruit actors through Shooting People (**www.shootingpeople.org**). There is no formal agreement with Equity. Students do not only consider local actors. Actors are generally offered their expenses and a DVD copy. Welcomes enquiries (containing photograph and 1-page CV) from new actors if sent by post.

London College of Communication
Elephant and Castle, London SE1 6SB
tel 020 7514 7935 *fax* 020 7514 6843
email info@lcc.arts.ac.uk
website www.lcc.arts.ac.uk
Course Director Emily Caston

A long-established film and television course with both BA and FdA programmes. Students work on

16mm, video and HD, and cast for projects throughout the year. Letters and CVs are welcome. Expenses only are offered, but a copy of finished work is supplied for showreels.

London Film Academy
The Old Church, 52A Walham Grove, Fulham,
London SW6 1QR
020 7386 7711 020 7381 6116
email info@londonfilmacademy.com
website www.londonfilmacademy.com
Facebook www.facebook.com/londonfilmacademy
Twitter @LDNfilmacademy
Instagram London_film_academy
Joint Principals and Founders Daisy Gili, Anna MacDonald

Specialises in professional, practical full-time training and short, specialised courses across all areas of filmmaking. Students make a series of short graduation films and commercials using both professional and non professional actors.

"Students use agents, casting directors, and various Internet websites and paper casting publications to recruit actors". Accepts submissions (with CVs and photographs) from actors previously unknown to them. Actors' details are kept on file for student reference and actors are contacted directly. Payment to actors depends on the individual project budgets. Expenses will usually be paid and the actor will be provided with rushes for their showreel.

The London Film School
24 Shelton Street, London WC2H 9UB
tel 020 7240 0161 *fax* 020 7240 0167
email c.bright@lfs.org.uk
website www.lfs.org.uk
Director Dr Jane Roscoe

London Film School offers a 2-year MA course in the art and technique of filmmaking, with approximately 120-130 student short films being made each year. Students generally recruit actors through Spotlight, Star Now, and Talent Circle. Expenses and a DVD copy of the film are normally offered to actors cast in student films. "The school welcomes enquiries from actors (with CVs and photographs), but asks that students use websites such as Spotlight and CastingCall Pro to recruit their actors. We also have a 1-year MA Screenwriting Course".

National Film and Television School

Beaconsfield Studios, Station Road,
Beaconsfield HP9 1LG
tel 01494 671234
email info@nfts.co.uk
website www.nfts.co.uk

Offers 2-year MA courses in Cinematography; Composing for Film and Television; Creative Business for Entrepreneurs and Executives; Digital Effects; Directing Animation; Directing Documentary; Directing Fiction; Directing and Producing Science and Natural History; Directing and Producing Television Entertainment; Editing; Film Studies Programming and Curation; Games Design; Marketing, Distribution, Assistant Camera (Focus Pulling and Loading); Assistant Directing and Floor Managing; Cameras, Sound and Vision Mixing for Television Production; Creative Producing for Digital Platforms; Directing Commercials; Factual Development and Production; Graphics and Titles for Television and Film; Model Making for Animation; Production Accounting for Film and Television; Production Management for Film and Television; Sound Development; Sports Production; Writing and Producing Comedy.

Students generally recruit actors through casting directors and Spotlight. Has a formal agreement with Equity. Welcomes enquiries (with CVs and photographs) from new actors, which should be marked for the attention of **casting@nfts.co.uk**. Actors are often used throughout the year for workshops and CVs /photographs are kept for this purpose. Graduation projects are cast by external casting directors.

Newport Film School

University of South Wales, City Campus, Newport, Gwent, Wales NP20 2BP
tel 03455 760101
email philip.cowan@southwales.ac.uk
website http://courses.southwales.ac.uk/courses/1393-ba-hons-film
Head of Film School Philip Cowan

A recognised Welsh national institution for the production and development of the audiovisual culture of Wales, through training, education and postgraduate research. On average 60-80 student short films are made each year. Students generally recruit actors through agents, casting directors, Equity Job Information Service and public notices at the Royal Welsh College of Music and Drama. There is no formal agreement with Equity. Actors' details are held on file. Welcomes enquiries (with CV, photograph and covering letter) from new actors. Students at BA and MA level increasingly work in production groupings, and cast professionally. "As the main centre for film education and training in Wales, we seek, encourage and support the casting of professional actors wherever possible."

University of the Creative Arts

Falkner Road, Farnham GU9 7DS
tel 01252 722441
email cbarwell@uca.ac.uk
email swelsford@uca.ac.uk
email rtorr@uca.ac.uk
website uca.ac.uk
Head of Film, Media and Performing Arts Sarah Jeans

BA (Hons) Film Production (email: cbarwell@uca.ac.uk)at Farnham is accredited by the BKKSTS, the International Moving Image Society and CILECT. The course offers students the opportunity to work on 16mm film and HD formats on both fiction and documentary. Students can specialise from the second year in directing, producing, screenwriting, cinematography, editing, sound and production design. Over a 100 short films are produced every year.

BA (Hons) Acting (email: rtorr@uca.ac.uk) based in Farnham, integrates acting for the screen and stage from day one. The course is taught at the university and at our partners Farnham Maltings.

The **BA (Hons) Television Production** course (email: swelsford@uca.ac.uk) CILECT accredited, is based at Maidstone Studios offers students the opportunity to study in a live working studio environment. Actors are recruited through online casting sites such as Casting Call Pro and Stage Castings.

The **BA (Hons) Acting** course (email: rtorr@uca.ac.uk) is based at UCA Rochester, integrates performance and technology and offers collaborative opportunities with Tevelvision Production and Design for Film, Theatre and Performance students.

University of Westminster

University of Westminster, Watford Road, Northwick Park, Harrow, Middlesex HA1 3TP
email P.S.Hort@westminster.ac.uk
website www.westminsterfilmschool.com
Course Director Peter Hort

Westminster Film School

Makes around 40 short films per year, from 3 minutes to 20 minutes in length, on 16mm film and digital. Films regularly win prizes at international and UK film festivals, notably the 2012 Student Academy Award. Expenses and DVD copy of the film to actors. Welcomes letters (including CV and photograph) from actors previously unknown to the school.

Media

Actors and video games

Mark Estdale

As the game industry continues to grow, the demand for actors grow. With over 1,900 games in development in the UK and over 6,000 in the US the opportunities are myriad.

Games have changed the way we are entertained. As a medium they bring together two strands of human leisure; the active nature of playing and interacting, and the passive engagement of being an audience. The essence of the video game experience is choice and consequence.

Games today embrace every genre. And it's no exaggeration to say games are also transforming the way we inform and live our lives. They're in the classroom and they're in your phone, your watch, your car's computer and your workplace. Games are never far away when you go online and they are at the frontiers of Virtual Reality and Augmented Reality. They are everywhere, they are here to stay, and they are brimming with performances. They require actors of all ages, accents and nationalities.

So how does an actor get started in acting for games?

Games currently present actors with two avenues down which work can be found: performance capture and voice acting.

Performance capture

The UK boasts some of the world's most well-known performance capture studios working with games.

Since the technique was first truly brought to public attention with Andy Serkis's definitive performance as Gollum in Peter Jackson's Lord of the Rings, performance capture has grown into a global industry serving hundreds of games and films every year. And as performance capture technology advances, it becomes more accessible cost-wise and more commonplace. The trend is not going to slow down.

Training resources like The Mocap Vaults (Twitter: @themocapvaults) are the perfect place to start a journey into the rapidly expanding world of performance capture. Actors should also look up studios like Audiomotion, Centroid and Andy Serkis's Imaginarium to find out more. The film Avatar and the acclaimed Uncharted series are great examples of this type of work.

Voice acting

For voice acting, the story is a similar one. Ultimately the demand is high and growing, yet recording for games does have its challenges.

A game script is unlike any other. The mapping needed to create player choice and consequence can make a script huge and complex. A game with hundreds of characters and 30,000 lines of dialogue isn't unusual. Imagine any play, TV or film script as a piece of string with a beginning and an end. Pull the ends and you have a straight line. A game script, by comparison can be a huge knot, like a mussed-up, detailed map of London with no street names.

Now add the fact that your performance is in a virtual environment. There's no set, and no audience, and potentially no other actors around to perform against. The skill for the actor is in being true to the moment, however it is presented to you.

Casting

To be cast for a game, the first obvious thing is to be open to taking part in casting and letting your acting and voice agent know you are available and keen to work with games. Some agents still remain blissfully unaware of this $91 billion industry. Spotlight and online services like voicespro.com are worth trawling for opportunities.

Second, it is helpful to have a pertinent showreel. The ideal reel is a dramatic character one with real characters and perfect accents. If you approach the reel as if it were a film casting which is to be shot in close up, you'll be in the right space: real and intimate.

Have no other voice on your reel than yours, and don't use music or sound effects. You may be required to keep in character consistently for weeks in the studio, so don't include performances you cannot sustain. The most common submission error is to think of games as 'games' then produce a reel that is cartoony and heightened.

When casting for a game I think like an intelligence officer selecting an agent to work undercover. If the candidate can be who I want them to be, in an alien environment, and not attract suspicion, they have potential. I look for decisive character choice and flexibility. Good game actors are instinctive. Being true to character whatever is thrown at them is core. Spycraft is a powerful perspective as agents working undercover have no script and there's no scene rehearsal. It is character first.

For an audition you will usually get a short character brief, hopefully with an image and a few lines of text to perform. Make firm decisions and flesh out the character with what you have. After a first run through expect to be asked to interpret the character differently and to be given something to cold read as well. Sight reading is an essential skill as it is rare that you will get a script in advance once hired.

Valuable acting skills that are beneficial to voice acting in most games are strong sight reading, radio drama, ADR and experience. Performance capture that combines movement with voice recording is staged theatrically. It requires precise physical performances where screen, theatre and acrobatic skills come into play.

Pay

An actor adding their voice to a game character is paid well. They normally get more for a few hours in session than they would for a week on the West End. However, being paid well is not quite as simple as it could be as there are no industry pay standards for voice work in video games. It is a buyer's market and as such voice actors are being exploited.

I know of actors being offered credits on IMDb as 'payment' for working on a game. I have also heard of actors being used as pawns in bidding wars between production companies; undercutting their competition by offering to pay significantly less to the cast.

Currently there are no pay guidelines for video games, so below I've created a table based on what I've gathered from the grapevine. I've matched it with corresponding production budgets to give a better overview. At the 'micro', cash-strapped and, to my mind, most interesting and innovative end of the scale you can find openness to the idea of profit sharing in return for services.

Media

Production Budget Type	Production Budget £	1st hour	2nd
Triple A	>1m	£750	£250
Medium Budget	>400k <1m	£450	£200
Low Budget	>100k <400k	£350	£150
Very Low Budget	>30k <100k	£250	£100
Micro Budget	<30k	£100	£50
Average professional rate	NA	£400	£200

The industry is varied like the film industry; it goes from zero budget productions to those with budgets greater than £100m. So if you have to negotiate a fee, a good starting point is to base it on the production budget.

The weighting for the first hour comes from the practice of paying a royalty buyout for the work. However, this is being challenged. The UK stands alone as the most expensive place in the world to hire actors because of it; the UK loses a lot of work as a result. The thinking is towards having a flat hourly rate that is on par with US rates.

There is another pay debate focused on the idea of paying actors by word or line, based on average recording speeds of lines/words per hour. Fundamentally, why should an efficient and fast actor be paid less than someone who is slow? As inexperienced actors are generally slow, when pay is time based there is a disincentive to hiring them. Paying by word or line with a minimum start fee does have its attractions.

If you want to find out more about rates talk to the voice agents, lobby Equity or plug into Facebook, Twitter, LinkedIn and the voice-acting community via groups like The VoiceOver Network (Twitter: @NetworkVO). They may all disagree with the table but the goal here is to stop actors being exploited by having better transparency. A heated debate is better than silence.

If you're still unsure what the games industry can offer you, here are a few statistics. The UK has the largest games-development community in Europe, with the most recent study indicating over 1,900 games-development companies are based here, employing almost 10,000 creative staff. Data from the UCAS web portal for undergraduates demonstrates that there are now 315 specialist video games degree courses in the UK.

And the audience may surprise you. There are more gamers today older than 50 than there are those aged under 18. The average player is in their 30s, and 49 per cent of players are women. Violent crime rates have gone down as game sales have increased. That may or may not be related, but games today are too diverse and established to be the stimulant for aggression that some headlines might have you believe.

According to figures fromNESTA, the games industry is growing at an extraordinary rate. Almost nine out of ten game companies began operations in the 2000s or the 2010s. And between 2011 and 2013, the number of games companies grew at 22 per cent per year, while current estimates indicate the global industry will pass $100 billion in value soon. In 2014 alone, games contributed £1.7 billion to the UK games industry.

To embrace the opportunity in games the willing actor jumps in. Games need actors.

Originally an actor, **Mark Estdale** founded **Outsource Media Ltd** (**OMUK**) in 1996. It is the UK's largest independent production company providing voice casting and recording of video games. Mark also coaches actors for working with games. OMUK has produced audio content for over 600 titles including titles nominated for 18 BAFTA Game Awards since 2004.

Radio and audio book companies

Unlike in the visual media, many radio directors have their roots in theatre and will go to stage productions to inform their future casting. And, unlike their visual media counterparts, they have a far greater understanding of actors and acting, and are far more open to casting against obvious physical type.

The BBC has by far and away the biggest radio drama output, and also uses actors to read poetry, narrations and stories. Some of this 'output' is made in-house; a good proportion is contracted out to independent companies. This is one area of work that doesn't very often use casting directors. It is a good idea to listen to radio drama in order to become aware of its ways – you won't hear much swearing, for instance. Also see 'Voice-over agents' (page 101) and 'Showreel and voice-demo companies' (page 415); some of the latter have excellent advice on making a voice demo on their websites.

INDEPENDENT RADIO COMPANIES

Above the Title Productions
50 Lisson Street, London NW1 5DF
tel 020 7453 1600 *fax* 020 7723 6132
email mail@abovethetitle.com
website www.abovethetitle.com
Senior Producer Brian King *Producer* Matt Willis

Production details: Founded in 1998, Above the Title Productions has made over 500 hours of radio programming covering a range of genres, from comedy to factual programmes, drama, discussion programmes, and music and the arts. See the website for detailed programme credits.

Casting procedures: All casting is done through agents; direct contact with actors is not welcomed. Is no longer able to accept voice demos and CVs, as the company has received such a large number of applications in the past.

Art and Adventure Ltd
5 Darling Road, London SE4 1YQ
tel/fax 020 8692 0145
email rogerjameselsgood@gmail.com
website www.artandadventure.org
Creative Director Roger James Elsgood

Production details: A production company specialising in making high production-value, location-recorded long-form drama for BBC Radio 3, 4 and the World Service with international casts and directors. Recent work includes: *The Two Gentlemen of Valasna* and *The Mrichhakatikaa* for Radio 3, both recorded entirely on location in India; *To the Wedding* for Radio 3 – a collaboration with Complicite; *Shooting Stars*, for Radio 3 (directed by Mike Hodges and starring Michael Gambon, Michael Sheen and Clive Owen); *King Trash*, the second play in Mike Hodges' radio trilogy and *Inferno* with Corin

Redgrave, Alex Jennings and Laurie Anderson, and *Miss Julie* with Sofie Gråbøl, Lars Mikkelsen and Marie Bach Hansen.

Casting procedures: The company is always happy to receive submissions and voice demos from actors, and auditions as necessary. It sometimes offers Equity contracts. Actively encourages applications from disabled actors and promotes the use of inclusive casting. Art and Adventure Ltd is actively working with actors with south Asian and Middle Eastern heritage and welcomes creative relationships accordingly.

The Bunbury Banter Theatre Company CIC
Office 34, 67-68 Hatton Garden, London EC1N 8JY
tel 020 3137 7994
email info@bunbanter.com
website www.bunbanter.com
Artistic Director Ali Anderson-Dyer *Creative Producer* Philip Anderson-Dyer

Production details: Founded in 2006; broadcasts audio plays across the globe. Has a strong education background, and dabbles in theatrical work. In 2008 the company reached the final of the Channel 4 Talent Awards and in 2012 was nominated for a Radio Academy Award. In 2013 the company won a British Public Radio Award for best short drama. Works very collaboratively on a mixture of audio and stage projects. Incoming actors need regional dialects, strong and accurate accents and versatility.

Casting procedures: Casting breakdowns are released via all the usual sites, social media and the company website. Welcomes submissions from individual actors previously unknown to the company, upon receiving a voicereel. Also welcomes email submissions and voice demos, preferably with a lot of variety. The company is completely opposed to discrimination in any form.

The Comedy Unit

Glasgow TV & Film Studio, Craigmont Street,
Glasgow G20 9BT
tel 0141 305 6666 *fax* 0141 305 6600
email info@comedyunit.co.uk
website www.comedyunit.co.uk
Managing Director Rab Christie

Production details: Founded in 1996. Works in TV
and radio productions – has produced approximately
30 hours of TV and 25 hours of radio. Areas of work
include drama, sitcoms, comedy and other light
entertainment. Recent drama credits include: *Ronan
the Amphibian* and *Coming Home*.

Casting procedures: Sometimes holds general
auditions. Actors can write at any time requesting
inclusion. Submissions from actors previously
unknown to the company are accepted, sent by post
or email. Voice demos and invitations to view
individual actors' websites are also accepted.

CSA Word

6A Archway Mews, 241A Putney Bridge Road,
London SW15 2PE
tel 020 8871 0220 *fax* 020 8877 0712
email info@csaword.co.uk
website www.csaword.co.uk
Key personnel Victoria Williams, Clive Stanhope

Production details: Founded in 1991. Producer of
audiobooks, drama, readings, feature programmes
and documentaries for BBC Radios 4, 2 and BBC
World Service.

Casting procedures: Does not hold general
auditions, as the company tends to use agents for
casting. Invitations to view individual actors' websites
are accepted. Equity contracts are not used, "but we
usually pay above Equity minimum." Happy to
consider disabled actors. "We work mainly in speech,
audio and radio work, so there is rarely an issue with
regard to physical disability."

Culture Wise

1 Chiswick Staithe, London W4 3TP
website www.culturewise.org
Key personnel Mukti Jain Campion, Chris Eldon Lee

Production details: Founded in 1988. Areas of work
include TV and radio documentaries.

Casting procedures: Does not hold general
auditions. Invitations to view individual actors'
websites are accepted. The company rarely employs
actors, as the primary focus is on factual output:
actors are generally used for short readings only,
within a feature programme.

Curtains for Radio

1-3 Middle Row, London W10 5AT
tel 020 8964 0111
email contactus@curtainsforradio.co.uk
website www.curtainsforradio.co.uk

Producers/Directors Andrew McGibbon, Jonathan
Ruffle, Nick Romero, Louise Morris

Production details: Established in 2001. Specialises
in comedy, comedy drama, drama, factual, music and
arts in film, television and audio. The ability to
perform in foreign languages, regional dialects and
singing are among the skills required by actors.
Records/films 1 production play annually. Recent
titles include: *With Nobbs On* (2012), *The Pickerskill
Reports* – 4 series (2005-2013), *I Was ...* (2005-2017),
A Waste of Space (2016), *A Call to Art* (2016-2019),
From the Outside In (2016), *Street City Goodbyes*
(2018), *Drawing on Water* (2018), *In Stitches* (2017),
and *Looking for Oil Drum Lane* (2018).

Casting procedures: Casting is carried out by
freelance casting director Rachel Freck and others.
Accepts submissions from actors previously unknown
to the company. Voice demos and invitations to view
individual actors' websites are also accepted. Voice
demos can only be accepted on mp3/wav files. Online links to audio, music or film are accepted. Voice-
over artists are employed under Equity-approved
contracts. Actively encourages applications from
disabled actors, BAME and are committed to
diversity both on and off air.

Fiction Factory Productions Ltd

4 Chevening Rd, London SE10 0LB
tel 020 8853 5100
email production@fictionfactory.co.uk
website www.fictionfactory.co.uk
Key personnel John Taylor

Production details: Founded in 1993. Makes radio
drama and features for the BBC. Areas of work
include drama, documentaries, light entertainment
and voice-overs. Recent drama credits include:
Macbeth for BBC Eduction; Kafka's *The Castle* and
Michael Butt's *Chronicles of Ait: Stay With Me* both
for BBC Radio 4.

Casting procedures: Does not hold general
auditions. Submissions from actors previously
unknown to the company are accepted if sent by
post. Voice demos are also accepted. Does not
welcome email submissions or invitations to view
individual actors' websites. "It is helpful if showreels
contain material appropriate to the kind of work
sought; for example, corporate voice-overs or radio
advertisements don't necessarily show off ensemble
acting skills."

Heavy Entertainment Ltd

111 Wardour Street, London W1F 0UH
tel 020 7494 1000 *fax* 020 7494 1100
email info@heavy-entertainment.com
website www.heavy-entertainment.com
Director David Roper

Production details: Established in 1992. Audio, video
and web producers. Areas of work include drama,
corporate, commercials, audiobooks and actor

Media

showreels (audio and video). Offers Equity-approved contracts.

Casting procedures: Welcomes showreels and voicereels (via agents only), and invitations to view individual actors' websites.

HuRica Productions
89 Birchanger Lane, Birchanger, Bishop Stortford, Herts CM23 5QF
mobile 07941 236871
email HuRicaProductions@gmail.com
website www.wix.com/HuRica/HuRicaProductions
Producer/Director Hugh Allison

Established in 2010. A company founded on the ethos that "art is what you make it." Works in radio and film. Recent credits include: *The Chronicles of Banania* (Radio Series aired on Radio North), *Call On Me* (short film) and *Shared Accommodation* (short film). Does not use freelance casting directors or hold general auditions.

Ladbroke Productions
17 Leicester Road, East Croydon, Surrey CR0 6EB
mobile 07590 555458
email neilgardner@ladbrokeradio.com
website www.ladbrokeradio.com
Producers/Directors Neil Gardner, Richard Bannerman, Neil Rosser, Adam Fowler, Anna Scott-Brown *Assistant Producer* Anna Van Dieken

Production details: Founded in 1975, Ladbroke Productions produces for all BBC networks in many genres, including drama, documentaries, music, light entertainment and features. Its studio and production facilities are also used by BBC Drama, BBC Readings and BBC Factual Learning. Actors are mainly employed by the company in its drama and documentary production. Recent credits include: *Sitting in Limbo* (BBC World Service) and *In the Company of Men* (BBC Radio 3).

Casting procedures: Will accept unsolicited submissions (written or emailed), voice demos and invitations to view actors' websites. April and September are generally better months to write.

Note Ladbroke Productions will soon join with their audiobook production sister company, Ladbroke Audio, to form one enterprise, focusing on the audiobook and archive sales and production market. They will no longer be pitching for BBC radio work.

Loftus Media Ltd
2A Aldine Street, London W12 8AN
tel 020 8740 4666
email office@loftusmedia.co.uk
website www.loftusmedia.co.uk
Director Joanne Rowntree

Production details: Small award-winning audio and radio production company based in West London, specialising in features, documentaries and readings

for BBC Radio. Requires plain narration and poetry from actors. Records several audiobooks a year. Recent titles include: *Black Music in Europe - Series 1* and *Meeting the Man I Killed*, both for Radio 4.

Casting procedures: Accepts submissions from individual actors previously unknown to the company. Will also accept submissions sent via email. Straight narration is preferred on voice demos and should be sent as an MP3. Actors are employed under Equity-approved contracts. Applications from disabled actors are welcomed.

Pennine Productions LLP
17 Crimicar Lane, Sheffield S10 4FA
tel 0161 427 1460
email janet@pennine.biz
website www.pennine.biz
Key contact Janet Graves

Production details: Founded in 2000. Has made documentaries and features for BBC Radio 4 since 2001, and programmes for BBC Radio 3 since 2004. Has produced book readings for Radio 4 since 2005. Broadcasts northern, national and international stories. Main areas of work include documentaries and readings. Recent credits include: *Israel in East Africa*, *When Jesus Rode into Bristol* and *Land of the Oval Ball* (all Radio 4). Offers Equity-approved contracts and does not subscribe to the Equity Pension Scheme.

Casting procedures: "We only welcome unsolicited approaches from actors with significant broadcast experience, particularly of book readings – or other audiobook productions. We are too small to be useful to actors trying to break into the network radio or TV." Happy to consider applications from disabled actors: "radio experience is the over-riding concern".

Pier Productions
8 St George's Place, Brighton BN1 4GB
tel 01273 691401 *fax* 01273 693658
website www.pierproductionsltd.co.uk
Managing Director Peter Hoare

Production details: Founded in 1993, an award-winning Brighton-based company and a significant supplier of factual and drama productions to BBC Radio 4. The company employs actors for drama productions and is keen to work with talent located in Brighton and the surrounding area.

Casting procedures: Does not hold general auditions. Submissions from actors are accepted by post and email, but invitations to view individual actors' websites are not welcomed. It must be emphasised that opportunities in radio drama are limited and that the company does not use the services of voice-over artists.

So Radio Ltd
1 Boundary Row, London SE1 8GN
tel 020 7960 2000 *fax* 020 7960 2095

email info@sotelevision.co.uk
website www.sotelevision.co.uk
Producer/Director Graham Stuart

Production details: Founded in 2003 as the radio arm of So Television Ltd. Recent credits include: *Don't Make Me Laugh with David Baddiel* and *It's that Jo Caulfield Again* for BBC Radio 4. The company has employed actors mainly for light entertainment productions.

Casting procedures: Does not accept unsolicited written submissions. As the company is small it cannot promise to reply to all enquiries. Offers Equity-approved contracts (where applicable). Actively encourages applications from disabled actors and promotes the use of inclusive casting.

Lou Stein Associates Ltd
email info@loustein.co.uk
Producer/Director Lou Stein *Co-Director* Deirdre Gribbin

Production details: Lou Stein founded the Gate Theatre, Notting Hill, and was Artistic Director of the Palace Theatre, Watford 1986-95. Lou Stein Associates was formed in 2002 to continue Lou's interest in new work, adaptations, music theatre and media. Employs actors for drama programmes. Currently Artistic Director, Chickenshed Theatre Company. Recent drama credits include: *Blowin' in the Wind* (Chickenshed); *Trumpets and Raspberries* (Chickenshed); *Kindertransport* (Chickenshed); *Adventure to Oz* (Chickenshed); *The Midnight Gang* (Chickenshed, world premier); *Mr Stink* (nominated for an Offie Award for Best Production Children 8+) *My Month with Carmen* (starring Miriam Colon and Julian Glover); *Embers* (adapted by Lou Stein from the novel by Sandor Marai and starring Patrick Stewart); *The Possessed* (written and directed by Lou Stein from the Dostoevsky novel, starring Paul McGann); *Performances* by Brian Friel (Wilton's Music Hall, starring Henry Goodman and Rosamund Pike) and *Crossing the Sea* (a new opera by Deirdre Gribbin).

Casting procedures: Voice demos and invitations to view individual actors' websites are accepted, but actors are requested to email in first instance. Please note that no reply will be given unless the actor is suitable for immediate casting. Names will be retained on file. Offers Equity-approved contracts. Actively promotes inclusive casting.

Tempest Productions Ltd
6 Woodend Drive, Airdrie ML6 7EA
tel 01236 768795
email info@tempestproductions.co.uk
website www.tempestproductions.co.uk
Producer/Director Dominic Reynolds

Production details: Records around 4 plays in a year. Is interested in good actors who can portray a range of different accents. Recent titles include: *The Meeting*

(BBC Radio Drama) and *The Mighty Jungle* (BBC Radio Sitcom).

Casting procedures: Uses freelance casting directors (EH7 Casting – Morag Arbuthnot; Kathleen Crawford). Will consider approaches from individual actors previously unknown to the company, but stresses that, as a small unit, it is difficult to manage these. Welcomes invitations to view actors' websites. Offers Equity-approved contracts. Welcomes all actors from every walk of life, regardless of race, disability or creed.

Tintinna Ltd
Summerfield, Bristol Road, Bristol BS40 8UB
tel 01275 333128
email tintinna@aol.com
Directors Ian and Sandy Bell

Production details: Founded in 1998. Produces a variety of output, formerly factual documentaries including history, lifestyle and human interest but more recently business-related work.

Casting procedures: Does not hold general auditions. Submissions from actors previously unknown to the company are accepted if sent by post. Voice demos are also accepted. Does not welcome email submissions or invitations to view individual actors' websites.

Unique
50 Lisson Street, London NW1 5DF
Executive Producer: Drama and Entertainment Frank Stirling

Production details: Produces drama, documentaries, comedy and light entertainment for radio. Recent drama credits include: *Zazie* (World Service), *A Confidential Agent, Fragile!* (Radio 4), *Professor Bernhardi, Bajazet* (Radio 3), and *Something Understood* (poetry and prose readings for Radio 4).

Casting procedures: Submissions from actors previously unknown to the company are accepted, sent by post or email. Voicereels are also accepted. Does not welcome invitations to view individual actors' websites. Advises actors to "include radio work on demo". "We regret that we cannot reply to all submissions, but your details will be kept on file."

Whistledown Productions
8A Ayres Street, London SE1 1ES
tel 020 7407 8001
email davidprest@whistledown.net
website www.whistledown.net
Producers/Directors David Prest, Katherine Godfrey, Kevin Dawson

Production details: Founded in 1998. One of the largest independent suppliers to BBC Radio, with a background in features and landmark documentaries, as well as programme strands such as Radio 4's *The Reunion*. Also podcast and online audio producers. Custom-built studio available for commercial hire.

The Wireless Theatre Company

11A Bolton Gardens, London SW5 0AL
mobile 07931 168911
email info@wirelesstheatrecompany.co.uk
website www.wirelesstheatre.co.uk
Twitter @wirelesstheatre
Artistic Director Mariele Runacre Temple *Executive Producers* Cherry Cookson, David Beck

Production details: Multi-award winning London audio production company at the forefront of modern, online audio drama. Provides original audio plays, comedy, stories, sketches and more to be downloaded from the website and produces long form multi-cast audio content for external clients such as BBC Radio 4 and Audible.

The company has worked with more than 500 actors, including Stephen Fry, Dominic West, Bill Bailey, Richard E. Grant, Derek Jacobi, Roger Allam, Max Beesely, Rebecca Hall, Martin Shaw, Russell Tovey, Colin Salmon, Celia Imrie, Brian Blessed, Lionel Blair, Linda Robson, Prunella Scales, Timothy West, Richard O'Brien, Nicholas Parsons and Alsion Steadman.

The company is very keen to hear from versatile actors with a large range of accents and vocal styles. Experience is not essential, but does prefer some sort of audio sample from actors when applying. Records a minimum of 1 new play each month, as well as several live recordings in theatres per year. Recent titles include: *Black Beauty, Treasure Island, Mr Ten Days, The Chief, A Christmas Carol, Les Liaisons Dangereuses, Hedda Gabler, Romeo and Jude, Murder on the Orient Express* and *Arabian Nights*.

Casting procedures: Casting done in-house. Advertises casting through CCP, but once an actor has worked for WTC they become part of the company and are used frequently. Also casts through Facebook and Twitter (@wirelesstheatre). Welcomes submissions by email, at **casting@wirelesstheatre.co.uk**, and all details are kept on file. Prefers applications with voicereels: simple, definitely without long musical introductions (rarely will listen to more than 2 minutes of any voicereel) and with 1 example of natural accent and some other, shorter samples of accents or voices. Welcomes invitations to view individual actors' websites. Roles are paid.

AUDIO BOOKS

Barefoot Audio Books Ltd

123 Walcot Street, Bath BA1 5BG
Director Tessa Strickland *Group Project Manager* Emma Parkin

Production details: Recent titles include: *Mrs Moon, Animal Boogie* and *Tales of Wisdom and Wonder*.

Casting procedures: Does not use freelance casting directors. Accepts submissions from actors previously unknown to the company if sent by post, but does not welcome email enquiries. Voice demos and invitations to view individual actors' websites are also accepted. Singing ability is required from actors, and Caribbean and African voices are needed in particular.

HarperAudio

HarperCollins Publishers, 1 London Bridge Street, London SE1 9GP
tel 020 8741 7070
email audiobooks@harpercollins.co.uk
website www.harpercollins.co.uk
Group Audio Director Jo Forshaw *Senior Audio Editor & Producer* Abigail Fenton *Senior Audio Editor & Producer* Tanya Brennand-Roper *Audio Assistant* Jack Chalmers

Production details: Has produced more than 2,000 titles for both children and adults. Work spans all genres including crime, comedy, literary fiction, mass market fiction, non-fiction and classics. Recent titles include: *The Postcard* by Fern Britton; *All the Light We Cannot See* by Anthony Derr; and *Predator* by Wilbur Smith. Foreign languages and regional dialect skills are required from actors.

Casting procedures: Does not use freelance casting directors. Advises actors to make contact through an agent or studio.

Isis Audio Books

7 Centremead, Osney Mead, Oxford OX2 0ES
tel 01865 250333
email studio@isis-publishing.co.uk
website www.isis-publishing.co.uk
Audio Production Manager Catherine Thompson

Production details: Founded in 1975. Publishes unabridged audiobooks. Recent titles include: *London Rules* by Mick Herron; *Snap* by Belinda Bauer and *The Magnificent Mrs Mayhew* by Milly Johnson.

Casting procedures: Does not use freelance casting directors. Accepts submissions from actors with proven audiobook experience if sent by post or email, but does not welcome telephone enquiries. Actors should have a range of voices and good sight-reading ability. Offers non-Equity contracts and does not subscribe to the Equity Pension Scheme. Actively encourages applications from disabled actors and promotes the use of inclusive casting.

Macmillan Audio Books

20 New Wharf Road, London N1 9RR
Audio Publisher Alison Muirden *Audio Editorial Coordinator* Rebecca Folkard-Ward

Casting procedures: Casts in-house. Accepts submissions from actors previously unknown to the company if sent by post, but does not welcome email enquiries. Voice demos are also accepted. Does not offer Equity contracts or subscribe to the Equity Pension Scheme. Will consider applications from disabled actors to play disabled characters.

Naxos AudioBooks

5 Wyllyotts Place, Potters Bar, Herts EN6 2JD
tel 01707 653326
email info@naxosaudiobooks.com
Producer/Director Anthony Anderson

Production details: Founded in 1994. Produces classic fiction, modern fiction, non-fiction, drama, poetry and children's classics for CD and download. Recent titles include: *The Decline and Fall of the Roman Empire, Remembrance of Things Past, Middlemarch* and *Julius Caesar.* Regional dialect skills are required from actors. Accepts voice demos from agents.

Orion Audio Books

Orion Publishing Group, Carmelite House,
50 Victoria Embankment, London EC4Y 0DZ
tel 020 3122 6876 *fax* 020 7379 6158
email audio@orionbooks.co.uk
website www.orionbooks.co.uk
Audio Publisher Paul Stark

Production details: Established in 1996, Orion Audio draws mainly on the Orion Group imprints to create their audio list, with notable authors such as Ian Rankin, Maeve Binchy, Michael Palin, Michael Connelly, Linwood Barclay, Joe Abercrombie and Patrick Rothfuss. Orion is now firmly established in the digital download market and produces over 200 unabridged audiobooks a year, across all genres.

Casting procedures: Casts in-house. Useful skills include regional dialects and occasionally singing ability. Welcomes submissions and voice demos from actors previously unknown to the company. Happy to receive submissions from disabled and non-disabled actors with the right skills for the job.

Random House Audio Books

20 Vauxhall Bridge Road, London SW1V 2SA
tel 020 7840 8400 *fax* 020 7834 2509
email jlewis@randomhouse.co.uk
Audio Publisher Videl Bar-Kar *Commissioning Editor* Jenni Lewis *Assistant Editor* Ania Duggan

Production details: Created in 1991, the Audio Books division of Random House publishes writers such as James Patterson, Andy McNab, Lee Child, Ian McEwan and Kathy Reichs.

Casting procedures: Uses freelance casting directors. Accepts submissions from actors previously unknown to the company, sent by post. Voice demos and invitations to view individual actors' websites are also accepted.

TalkingPEN books

Global House, 303 Ballards Lane, London N12 8NP
tel 020 8445 5123 *fax* 020 8446 7745
email info@talkingpen.co.uk
website www.talkingpen.co.uk
Producers/Directors R Dutta, DM Chatterji, Henriette Barkow

Production details: Established in 2002. Produces audiobooks, e-books, TalkingPEN books and posters. The ability to perform in foreign languages, singing and storytelling are often required of actors. Records 20 audiobooks annually. Recent titles include: *Hansel and Gretel, Jill and the Beanstalk* and *English Terms Explained.*

Casting procedures: Accepts submissions from actors previously unknown to them. Voice demos and invitations to view individual actors' website are also accepted; voice demos should include short storytelling in English or other language(s). Actively encourages applications from disabled actors.

Acting for radio

Gordon House

Media

I remember once, in a burst of evangelical enthusiasm at having decided never to touch a cigarette again, upbraiding a distinguished member of the Radio Drama Company for her constant disappearances to the Green Room to light up. (Nowadays, of course, all BBC Green rooms are smoke-free, and your poor cigarette-smoking actor has to shiver in the car park.) "My dear man," she wheezed grandly. "The only reason you employ me on the wireless is because of my nicotine-nourished, port-soaked larynx. Living badly has made me the radio actress I am today!"

Well – it's a point of view. Just as the camera relishes certain skin textures, so the microphone may embellish the actor or actress who has lived a little – resulting in, shall we say, an idiosyncratic oesophagus. But as a way of getting a radio part, it's not a course of action I'd recommend. Radio simply doesn't pay enough to sustain a life of alcoholic debauchery.

So how do you get into radio? "It's a closed shop," moaned one actor to me the other day. "You hear the same names, time and again – and there's no way of breaking into this magic circle." I personally have worked with well over 800 actors, so it can't be that much of a closed shop ... although it's true that given the ruthless time constraints of the medium (a 60-minute play will be rehearsed and recorded in two days), there's a natural tendency for producers to work with those actors whom they know can 'deliver' quickly. There's no joy to be had in the seventh take of a difficult scene when your nervous newcomer is finally coming to grips with the ambiguities of his or her character, as well as the technical demands of this strange new medium, while everyone else's performances have long-since peaked and are now beginning to sound tired and lacklustre.

But that said, new writers and new actors are the lifeblood of the medium. And what do you need to be a good actor on radio? It's simple. You need to be a good actor. If you're successful in the theatre, in film, on TV – then of course you can be successful on radio. A good actor is a good actor. It obviously helps if your voice doesn't sound like a creaking door (given that creaking doors are a staple diet of many a radio play), and the medium has no place for prima donnas. With every producer sparingly counting his or her loose change, there's no such happy luxury as a radio 'extra'; so if you're cast as Hamlet, you can also expect to do your fair share of off-mic mumbling in Claudius' court. And if that doesn't appeal, don't do radio.

You also have to be prepared to work fast and make almost instant decisions. Over the years I've worked with a few actors whom I admire hugely; whom I've seen – in other media – give performances of rare charm and intelligence; but who in radio have simply been unable to 'come off the page' – make the character they're playing sound truthful and real. Of course this may simply be attributed to the crass inadequacy of the director. But for some actors the sheer speed at which they have to make decisions about character, motivation, sub-text and so forth is incredibly daunting. And then there's the physical absurdity of much of what they have to do: "How the xxx do you expect me to be 'truthful' when I'm carrying a xxxing great script in my left hand, a glass of water, masquerading as gin, in my right, and you want me to walk through a carpet of scrunched-up audio tape and pretend it's a meadow," shrieked one despairing actor to me a couple of years ago.

And yet that's exactly what we expect – truth. There's no medium as unforgiving for exposing over-acting or over-emoting (or worse – simple 'reading'). A radio play – and particularly a contemporary, naturalistic play – should make listeners feel that they are eavesdropping on real conversation. It's a medium that may owe much to theatre for providing it with great writing and acting talent (though the reverse is equally true), but the technique of radio acting is far closer to that of film than of theatre. "Less is more! Less is more!" as my erstwhile colleague, Martin Jenkins, one of Radio Drama's finest practitioners, used to impress on his casts. (It was Martin, incidentally, who uttered the memorable phrase: "Good Luck – Please!" before the umpteenth take of one particularly stressful scene.)

How do you bring yourself to the attention of radio producers? Well – there's no denying the fact that a lovingly crafted CD arriving on your desk just as you're in the process of casting your next play, and can't for the life of you think who you can get to play the embittered Glaswegian ex-shipbuilder who's contemplating a sex change, can make all the difference. But choose the pieces you record with care – and keep them short. If varied accents are not a speciality, there's no point in doing all sorts of varied accents. Obviously, it's a great asset to be master – or mistress – of many different voices, this being a medium where 'doubling' and 'trebling' is done with impunity. But a CD where the truthfulness of most of your extracts is undone by your game, but doomed, attempt to do a passable Geordie, won't help anyone. Many years ago I remember auditioning Jeremy Sinden for a part. "What accents do you do?" I asked him. "I do two actually," he said. "I do posh. And I do very posh." Well a mere two accents didn't stop Jeremy getting a load of work in every medium – including radio – in his all-too-brief, but exhilarating, career.

Having recorded your tape or (preferably) CD, you can, of course, circulate it to every producer who's ever made a radio play. But my advice would be to be a little more discerning. Listen to some radio plays (a great way of determining for yourself what works and what doesn't) and note the names of the producers whose productions particularly appeal to you. You can then write a personal note to them – you know the kind: "I must say, Mr House, I really enjoyed your fascinating and unusual interpretation of *Hedda Gabler* on Radio 3 last night, and incidentally Hedda is a part I've always yearned to play myself,"(etc.). I'm not saying it will get you a part, but producers are as vain as the next person (I should know) and it may well make them more inclined to slip your CD into the CD player, on the basis that anyone with such discerning judgement as yours must be worth hearing.

Radio is a fantastic and hugely under-rated medium, and actors, by and large, love working for it. It can also be the stepping-stone to fame and fortune. For many years we've been running our own radio bursary scheme for accredited drama schools – the Carleton Hobbs Competition (named after one of the great 20th century radio actors) – and the role-call of actors who have been winners, from Richard Griffiths to Stephen Tompkinson, from Nerys Hughes to Emma Fielding, is hugely impressive. Our new bursary scheme, the Norman Beaton Fellowship, for actors who didn't go to an accredited drama school, is also providing us with some excellent new talent. Details of both these schemes can be found on the BBC website.

And of course we producers don't simply wait to receive your CDs, but are constantly on the lookout for new and exciting talent from wherever we can find it. You may not need to approach us – we may approach you! As World Service Drama producers, Hilary Norrish and myself gave a young actor called Ewan MacGregor his first two professional jobs, having seen him in a drama school showcase. And Ewan – if you ever get to read this – where are the invitations to those glamorous film previews you promised you'd send us when you were famous? Remember – it was radio that gave you your first break!

Gordon House is the former Head of the BBC Radio Drama Department. He joined the BBC as a studio manager in 1972, working in Children's Television and Radio Sport before becoming a drama director. For 14 years he headed the small BBC World Service Drama team, during which time the Unit won more than 30 national and international awards. In 1998 Gordon won the Writers' Guild Special Prize for services for his work with new writers, and has twice won the Sony Drama Award. He is a founder member of The Worldplay Group, a radio association of drama directors from broadcasting stations around the world, which initiates a yearly season of international radios dramas broadcast on BBC World Service, ABC, CBC, RTE, Radio New Zealand and Radio Television Hong Kong.

Media

Media

Media festivals

These are geared towards showcasing directors, rather than actors. However, they can be useful places to network, learn and (if your film is short-listed) to gain extra exposure.

Belfast Film Festival

The Exchange Place, 23 Donegal Street, Belfast BT1 2FF
tel 028 9032 5913 *fax* 028 9032 5911
email info@belfastfilmfestival.org
website www.belfastfilmfestival.org

Normally held in March/April each year, the Belfast Film Festival brings the best of independent, world, local and classic cinema to screens across Belfast. In addition there are panel discussions, workshops, music events and a series of related club events in venues across the city.

Candidates may submit features, shorts, animation and documentaries for inclusion in the festival. The deadline for submissions is normally early December. While all categories will be considered for screening, the only competitive category is the Irish short film. To be eligible for the £1,000 Kodak Short Film Prize, films must have been shot in Ireland during the previous year and last no longer than 20 minutes.

BFI London Film Festival

BFI South Bank, London SE1 8XT
tel 020 7815 1322 020 7815 1323 *fax* 020 7633 0786
website www.bfi.org.uk/lff

The BFI London Film Festival is Europe's largest public film event, screening an average of 280 films from 60 countries in October/November each year. Leading figures in the film industry present their work at the festival, and the programme is supported by a number of interviews, industry and public forums, lectures, education events, Gala films and special screenings promoting the best in cinema across the world.

Bradford International Film Festival

National Media Museum, Bradford BD1 1NQ
tel 01274 203308
email biffenquiries@nationalmediamuseum.org.uk
website www.nationalmediamuseum.org.uk/bradfordinternationalfilmfestival
Directors Tom Vincent, Neil Young

Held each year in March, the Bradford Film Festival presents a number of special guests, tributes, screentalk interviews, masterclasses, spotlights, the Crash symposium and the Widescreen weekend, over a 15-day period.

Features, shorts, documentaries and experimental work submitted for competition must have been completed during the previous 2 years.

Cambridge Film Festival

Arts Picture House, 38-39 St Andrew's Street, Cambridge CB2 3AR
tel 01223 500082 *fax* 01223 462555
email info@cambridgefilmfestival.org.uk
website www.cambridgefilmfestival.org.uk
Facebook www.facebook.com/CambridgeFilmFestival
Twitter @camfilmfest

Established in 1977, the festival is a celebration of film – past, present and future. It's a chance to relive and enjoy past glories, but also to see what's happening in film right now, and reveal new talents who will shape the future of cinema. Screens films from around the world, many of which may not be available elsewhere. The Cambridge Film Festival attracts big names but is nonetheless intimate and approachable.

Celtic Media Festival

249 West George Street, Glasgow G2 4QE
tel 0141 302 1737
email info@celticmediafestival.co.uk
website www.celticmediafestival.co.uk

The Celtic Media Festival celebrates the cultures and languages of Cornwall, Brittany, Ireland, Scotland and Wales in film and in television broadcasting. Awards include: Short Drama Award, Drama Feature Award and Drama Series Award. The festival is attended by producers, directors, commissioning editors, film executives, media students, distributors and schedulers.

Chichester International Film Festival

Chichester Cinema at New Park, New Park Road, Chichester PO19 7XY
tel 01243 786650 *fax* 01243 790235
email info@chichestercinema.org
website www.chichestercinema.org/film-festival
Director Roger Gibson

An 18-day festival in August/September presenting more than 70 feature films, Q&As with visiting directors, and related talks. More than half the films shown are previews and premieres; the remainder form retrospectives on important contributors to the film world.

Encounters (Short Film and Animation Festival)

1 Unity Street, Bristol BS1 5HH
tel 0117 929 9188 *fax* 0117 952 8888

email info@encounters-festival.org.uk
website www.encounters-festival.org.uk

Encounters is an international short film and animation festival which runs in Bristol for 1 week in September. It discovers, supports and develops new talent in filmmaking, providing a platform for emerging and established filmmakers from around the world, and a unique meeting place for the industry. Connecting industry and audiences, the festival celebrates the creativity, diversity and impact of short film. It enjoys excellent links with the prestigious BAFTAs, Cartoon D'Or and European Film Awards. It is a qualifying festival for the Academy Awards. With screenings of diverse new shorts from around the world, alongside special guests and events, parties, awards, seminars, masterclasses and focus sessions, the festival offers insights and advice from industry professionals about every aspect of film. For advice about submitting your work, visit the website.

Foyle Film Festival

The Nerve Centre, 7-8 Magazine Street,
Derry BT48 6HJ
tel 028 7137 3456 *tel* 020 7126 0562
email b.mclaughlin@nerve-centre.org.uk
website www.foylefilmfestival.org
Festival Director Ms Bernie McLaughlin

Established in 1987, the annual Foyle Film Festival is the flagship project of the multi-media Nerve Centre. For 10 days in November, the Foyle Film Festival capitalises on all the technical expertise of the Nerve Centre to produce a unique programme of film, music, digital technologies, and education. The festival delivers a programme of art house cinema: international and local premieres, foreign language, documentaries, classic film, industry workshops, presentations, outreach events, as well as a stand-alone education programme which is curriculum focused, and targets all local primary and secondary schools, colleges, and universities.

The festival competition has received Oscar and BAFTA recognition for its Light In Motion (LIM) Film Awards. Foyle Film Festival is renowned for attracting top industry professionals to the city, with past guests including high-profile names such as: Brendan Gleeson, Ray Winstone, Richard E. Grant, Jim Sheridan, Danny Boyle, Andrea Arnold, Julie Christie, Neil Jordan, Wim Wenders, Kenneth Branagh, Jenny Agutter, Julien Temple, Christiane Kubrick, Andrew Eaton, Brenda Blethyn, Roddy Doyle, Irvine Welsh, Stephen Frears, Ronan Bennett, Jimmy McGovern, Rob Coleman, Sam Taylor-Wood, Kate Adie, Jonathan Rhys Meyers, Cillian Murphy, Ardal O'Hanlon and Dervla Kirwan.

Leeds International Film Festival

Town Hall, The Headrow, Leeds LS1 3AD
tel 0113 247 8398

email filmfestival@leeds.gov.uk
website www.leedsfilm.com
Director Chris Fell

Leeds International Film Festival has been presenting extensive programmes of new and unseen cinema from around the world since 1987, supported by a number of events and workshops for those wanting to get into film and TV. The Yorkshire Short Film Competition highlights emerging new filmmaking talents in the Yorkshire region, while the Louis Le Prince International Short Film Competition promotes some of the best fiction completed around the world in the last year. The key features of the festival include UK Film Week, an annual showcase of emerging talent; Film Festival Fringe, where the bars and clubs of Leeds host human rights films, music documentaries and special events; the Main Programme; and Unique Retrospectives.

The festival is complemented by the Leeds Children's and Young People's Film Festival held in April each year, with an award for National Young Filmmaker of the Year.

London Independent Film Festival (LIFF)

Studio 160, 77 Beak Street, London W1F 9DB
email info@londonindependent.org
website www.liff.org
Festival Director Erich Schultz

The London Independent Film Festival is the premier event for micro-budget and no-budget films in the UK. LIFF offers a fantastic opportunity for indie filmmakers to showcase their achievements, with spaces reserved for first- and second-time filmmakers and for films that have been overlooked by other events. LIFF presents the best of low-budget filmmaking from around the world and mixes it with relevant industry discussions and targeted social networking events. LIFF's audience is London's sizeable independent filmmaking community; it's an indie film festival for indie filmmakers.

London Lesbian & Gay Film Festival

c/o BFI Southbank, Belvedere Road, South Bank, Waterloo, London SE1 8XT
tel 020 7928 3535 020 7928 3232 (Box Office)
website www.bfi.org.uk/llgff
Festival Programmers Jason Barker, Michael Blyth, Nazmia Jamal, Brian Robinson, Emma Smart

The London Lesbian and Gay Film Festival presents the best of British and international Queer Cinema in all its forms – mainstream and avant garde. Features and shorts are complemented by discussions and interviews with writers and filmmakers. The London run of the festival is based at the BFI Southbank (formerly known as the National Film Theatre), with other screenings taking place in Leicester Square. Following this run in March and April, it continues on tour around the UK until the autumn. See the

Media

website for programme details, including the tour schedule, or contact the BFI box office for a brochure of the London run.

Manchester International Short Film Festival

Kinofilm, 42 Edge Street, Manchester M4 1HN
tel 0161 288 2494 *fax* 0161 281 1374
email john.kino@good.co.uk
website www.kinofilm.org.uk
Director John Wojowski

British New Wave and an International Panorama of film provide the main focus to the festival, with a regional showcase, 'Made up North', aimed at promoting films from local and regional filmmakers. Education and Professional Development events are also hosted by the festival and are presented by external curators and organisations.

The festival is open for film submissions each year from January to June, with shortlisted entries being screened at the festival itself in October. Short films on any theme, subject or category and made on any format are eligible, as long as they run no longer than 20 minutes and have been made within the 18 months prior to the festival. The Kinofilm Awards acknowledge outstanding achievements in short film, with awards in many categories. Rules, regulations and application forms are available on the website.

Raindance Film Festival Ltd

10 Craven Street, London WC2N 5PE
tel 020 7930 3412
email info@raindance.co.uk
website www.raindance.org
*Producer*David Martinez

Running for 2 weeks at the end of September and early October, Raindance is the UK's largest independent film festival and is committed to screening the boldest, most innovative and challenging films from the UK and from around the world. Weighted heavily towards new talent, the festival offers more than 100 features (many of which are directorial debuts), 20 shorts programmes and a wide range of events, workshops and parties.

Rushes Soho Shorts Festival

66 Old Compton Street, London W1D 4UH
tel 020 7851 6207
email info@sohoshorts.com
website www.sohoshorts.com

Taking place for 1 week in July/August, shortlisted films are screened free of charge throughout Soho's cafes, bars and cinemas, as well as other special events and screenings being held. In addition, Vue cinemas around the country will also be holding screenings throughout that week. The festival culminates in an awards cremony with winners being announced in the following categories: Short Film, Newcomer, Animation, Music Video, and Title Sequence & Idents. Patrons of the festival include BAFTA and the Directors' Guild of Great Britain.

Films for submission should be no longer than 12 minutes, and should have been produced in the 12 months prior to the deadline.

UK Jewish Film Festival

5.09 Clerkenwell Workshops,
27-31 Clerkenwell Close, London EC1R 0AT
tel 020 3176 0048
website www.ukjewishfilm.org

Established in 1997, the festival is committed to showing a wide variety of films which celebrate the diversity of Jewish cultures and identity, and which reach both Jewish and wider audiences. In addition to film screenings there are education projects and talks with directors. The UK Jewish Film Festival Short Film Fund offers a grant of up to £15,000 for the production of a short film or video (drama, animation or factual) of a Jewish theme and with a significance both to Jewish and to general public audiences. For application details, consult the website.

Disabled actors
Introduction

This section brings together companies and organisations of specific interest to disabled actors. It should also be noted that (a) some agents and companies now welcome enquiries from disabled actors (see listings), and (b) many drama schools have detail on their disability admissions policies on their websites.

In addition, disabled Equity members can add their details to the *Disability Register*, which is published by Spotlight. Casting directors looking for disabled actors can search this register via the Spotlight website.

Note The UK Government recognised BSL as an official language in March 2003, and the Editor acknowledges that many deaf people consider themselves to be members of a linguistic and cultural minority – Deaf with a capital 'D' – rather than disabled people. For the sake of simplicity, however, this book uses a broad definition of disability to encompass Deaf people (although an individual entry will retain the distinction if present in the material provided to us by that company).

The Editor would like to thank Silvie Fisch (of The National Disability Arts Forum) and the staff of Graeae Theatre Company for their help in compiling this section.

TRAINING

Apart from the training offered by drama schools, a number of theatre companies and organisations operate training schemes or courses for disabled actors. Many of these schemes are relatively short – a few days or weeks – but Lawnmower's Liberdade, Chickenshed's BTEC National Diploma and Mind the Gap's Staging Change operate over a longer term. Shorter courses are run by (among others) Birds of Paradise, Candoco, and Oily Cart. (Details for all the theatre companies listed here can be found in the *Sources of work* section below.)

SOURCES OF WORK

Amici Dance Theatre Company
Turtle Key Arts, Lyric Hammersmith, Lyric Square, King Street, London W6 0QL
tel 020 8964 5060
email amici@turtlekeyarts.org.uk
website www.amicidance.org
Artistic Director Wolfgang Stange

Dance theatre company integrating disabled and non-disabled artists and performers.

Anjali Dance Company
Home Farm House, Wigginton,
Banbury Oxfordshire OX15 4JZ
tel/fax 01295 251909
email info@anjali.co.uk
website www.anjali.co.uk
Artistic Director Nicole Thomson

Production details: A professional contemporary dance company. All Anjali's dancers have a learning disability. The company produces and tours performances, and undertakes Educational and Outreach work; it is one of the first of its kind in the world. It aims to show that disability is no barrier to creativity. Stages 1-2 productions a year with up to 10 performances over 6-8 venues around the country, such as the Mill Arts Centre (Banbury), Stratford Circus (London), and the Pegasus Theatre (Oxford).

Casting procedures: Casts in-house, does not issue casting breakdowns, and welcomes letters (but not emails) from individuals previously unknown to the company. Welcomes invitations to view individuals' websites, but not showreels.

Apropos Productions Ltd
53 Greek Street, London W1D 3DR
tel 020 7739 2857 *fax* 020 7739 3852
email info@aproposltd.com
website www.aproposltd.com
Director Paul Dubois

Company's work: Established in 2004. First feature film completes post-production August 2015, *Dark*

360 Disabled actors

Signal (executive producer Neil Marshall). Short films: *The Juror, X-Why* and *Cocktail*. Web series: award-winning web series: *A Quick Fortune* and *Le Method* (2016). Script events include *My German Roots are Showing* at the Arcola Theatre, London, starring Miriam Margolyes.

Provides training for local, national and international clients. Key focus is on Organisational Behaviour. Training is provided for incoming actors. Corporate experience is useful but not essential. Actor-base is extended annually through agents, the website and Equity Job Information Service. Clients include: SKANKSA, Sony Computer Entertainment, House of Commons, UBM and the Discovery Network.

Recruitment procedures: Accepts submissions (with CVs and photographs) from actors previously unknown to the company. Disabled actors regularly form part of its teams and are actively encouraged to apply.

art+power
Centre Gate, Colston Avenue, Bristol BS1 4TR
tel 0117 317 8099
email info@artandpower.com
website www.artandpower.com
Key contact David Richmond

Bristol-based organisation that uses the arts to empower disabled people and build a more equal, inclusive and creative society. art+power produces theatre, dance and live art projects.

Birds of Paradise Theatre Company
105 Brusnwick Street, Glasgow G1 1TF
tel 0141 552 1725
email all@boptheatre.co.uk
website www.boptheatre.co.uk
Artistic Directors Robert Softley Gale

Birds of Paradise is a force for change in Scottish theatre, creating world class projects and performances that place disabled artists centre stage.

Birds of Paradise's artistic vision is of a culture where disabled artists are recognised for the excellence of their work, celebrated for the stories they bring to the stage and are a vital part of the artistic landscape of Scotland.

BOP's purpose is to be an accessible arts company producing world-class productions and projects that place disabled artists centre stage and to develop future generations of disabled arrtists to fulfil their vision. BOP believes that disabled people continue to experience lack of equality and considerable barriers within society, including the arts. BOP's work exists in part to challenge and address these issues.

BOP is the only professional, disability-led theatre company in Scotland and they exist to:

• make world class, innovative and accessible work using Creative Access approaches that are made by disabled and non-disabled artists, writers and theatre-makers drawn from diverse cultures to reach a wide demographic nationally and internationally;
• play a key strategic role in Scotland's theatre ecology, and wider art scene, by supporting the sector to nurture the next generation of disabled artists, performers and audiences through addresing barriers to opportunities and involving disabled people in the processes.

Previous productions include: *Role Shift* by Lesley Hart; *Purposeless Movements* by Robert Softley Gales; *Crazy Jane* by Nicola McCartney; *Wendy Hoose* by Johnny McKnight; *The Farce of Circumstance* by Tom Lannon; *The Resistible Rise of Arturo Ui* by Bertolt Brecht; *Tongues* by Sam Shephard and Joseph Chaikin; *Working Legs* by Alistair Gray; *Playing for Keeps* by Archie Hind; *Merman* by Susan McClymont and Dave Buchanan; *Twelve Black Candles* by Des Dillon; *The Irish Giant* by Garry Robson; *Brazil 12 Scotland 0* by Ian Stephen; and *Mouth of Silence* by Gerry Loose.

Candoco Dance Company
2T Leroy House, 436 Essex Road, London N1 3QP
tel 020 7704 6845
email info@candoco.co.uk
website www.candoco.co.uk
Artistic Co-Directors Charlotte Darbyshire and Ben Wright

Candoco is a world-leading contemporary dance company. Bridging the mainstream and the experimental, Candoco's bold approach and powerful collaborations create distinctive performances and far-reaching learning experiences. The company celebrates different ways of seeing, of being and of making art, putting it at the forefront of conversations around dance and disability. Candoco regularly commissions artists and choreographers to create dance works that tour nationally and internationally. It also runs a variety of training courses, residencies and workshops, and Cando2 – Candoco's Youth Dance Company.

Chickenshed Theatre
Chase Side, Southgate, London N14 4PE
tel 020 8292 9222 (181001 020 8292 9222 Typetalk)
email susanj@chickenshed.org.uk
website www.chickenshed.org.uk
Managing Director Louise Perry *Executive Management* Paul Morrall, Lou Stein

Chickenshed makes beautiful and inspirational theatre, where imagination translates into empowerment. By bringing together people of all ages and from all backgrounds we produce outstanding theatre that entertains, inspires, challenges and educates both audiences and participants alike.

Using the power of performing arts Chickenshed helps people reach their full potential and feel accepted. We create a truly inclusive environment where people don't stigmatise, label or disregard, but accept and welcome difference.

Chickenshed's vision is a society that celebrates diversity and enables every individual to flourish.

For more company information see the Chickenshed Theatre entry in the Middle and Smaller-scale companies' section, page 188.

In addition the company runs:

• An inclusive theatre education workshop programme for nearly 700 members from the ages of 5 upwards
• 3 nationally accredited education courses
• Community Outreach projects in the UK and internationally
• A growing number of satellite 'sheds' nationally and internationally
• Training in inclusive practice through workshops and seminars for a range of professionals from a range of fields including education, social services and health

Dark Horse

Lawrence Batley Theatre, Queen's Street, Huddersfield HD1 2SP
tel 01484 484441 *fax* 01484 484443
email info@darkhorsetheatre.co.uk
website www.darkhorsetheatre.co.uk
Artistic Director Vanessa Brooks

Production details: Established in 2000. Production company exploring a range of projects that include actors with learning disabilities and promote inclusive working practices. Approximately 1 production per year touring to 10-15 venues, including arts centres and theatres in Yorkshire, the North West and internationally. Roughly 5-8 actors are used in each production.

Casting procedures: Occasionally uses freelance casting directors. Does not welcome unsolicited CVs. Actively encourages applications from disabled actors and promotes the use of inclusive casting. Offers Equity-approved contracts.

Deafinitely Theatre

201 Drummond Street, London NW1 3FE
tel 020 7387 3586
email info@deafinitelytheatre.co.uk
website www.deafinitelytheatre.co.uk
Facebook www.facebook.com/deafinitelytheatre
Twitter @DeafinitelyT

Artistic Director Paula Garfield

Established in 2002 to create theatre for deaf and hearing audiences, the company continues to be deaf-led with a bilingual focus - in British Sign Language and spoken English - which means the work remains accessible to both deaf and hearing people. Deafinitely Theatre also runs an extensive education and training programme, which includes a youth theatre and CPD for emerging and established artists, including the relaunch of its innovative Hub

programme in September 2018. It has produced 39 shows across the UK in the past seventeen years. Recent productions include: *4.48 Pyschosis* (New Diorama Theatre and Derby Playhouse, 2018), winner of Broadway World UK Award for Best Direction of a New Production of a Play, *Contractions* (ND2, 2017) winner of the Off West End Award for Best Production.

Graeae Theatre Company

Bradbury Studios, 138 Kingsland Road, London E2 8DY
tel 020 7613 6900
email info@graeae.org
website www.graeae.org
Artistic Director Jenny Sealey

Production details: Founded in 1980 and artistically led by Jenny Sealey, Graeae boldly places D/deaf and disabled actors centre stage.

Graeae's signature aesthetic is the compelling creative integration of sign language, captioning and audio description, which engages with both disabled and non-disabled audiences. Championing accessibility and providing a platform for new generations of artists, Graeae leads the way in pioneering, trail-blazing theatre. Graeae also run an extensive programme of creative learning opportunities throughout the year, training and developing the next generation of D/deaf and disabled artists. These programmes include Write to Play and Ensemble.

Recent productions and co-productions include: *Reasons to be Cheerful, Cosmic Scallies, The House of Bernarda Alba, The Solid Life of Sugar Water, Blood Wedding, The Threepenny Opera, Belonging, Blasted* and *Bent*. Spectacular outdoor productions include *This is Not for You, The Limbless Knight, Prometheus Awakes* and *The Iron Man*.

Graeae are strategic partners on the Ramps on the Moon consortium and are a National Portfolio Organisation (NPO) of Arts Council England.

Hijinx Theatre

Wales Millennium Centre, Bute Place, Cardiff CF10 5AL
tel 029 2030 0331
email info@hijinx.org.uk
website www.hijinx.org.uk
Artistic Director Ben Pettitt-Wade

Production details: Founded in 1981, the company makes professional theatre performed by actors with and without learning disabilities which tours globally.

Offers ITC/Equity-approved contracts and does not subscribe to the Equity Pension Scheme.

Casting procedures: Shows are cast by the Artistic Director. Welcomes letters, CVs and photographs from actors previously unknown to the company. Welcomes applications from disabled and non-disabled actors.

IMPACT Theatre

IMPACT Community Arts Centre,
Ealing Central Sports Ground,
Horsenden Lane South, Perivale UB6 8GP
tel/fax 020 8997 8979
email info@impacttheatre.co
website www.impacttheatre.co
Facebook https//en-gb.facebook.com/
impacttheatreuk/
Artistic Director Kim Mughan FRSA

IMPACT (IMagine, Perform And Create Together)
Theatre was founded in 1999. It was set up by and for
adults with learning disabilities. While not a
professional company, IMPACT helps to develop
skills of performance and self-expression for its
actors, musicians and dancers. IMPACT Theatre
stages original productions featuring up to 60
performers with learning disabilities. In addition to
the disability arts that IMPACT has become known
for in West London, it is now embarking on
innovative inclusive arts work.

Krazy Kat Theatre Company

173 Hartington Road, Brighton BN2 3PA
tel 01273 692552
email krazykattheatre@ntlworld.com
website www.krazykattheatre.co.uk
Artistic Director Kinny Gardner

Production details: A children's theatre company
founded in 1982, specialising in highly visual forms of
theatre that are accessible to Deaf children. Normally
tours 2 projects each year with an average annual
total of 50 performances and 35 venues. Venues
include schools, arts centres, theatres, outdoor venues
and community centres throughout UK. In general 2
actors and a technician go on tour and play to
audiences aged 3-7. Singing ability, physical theatre
skills, British sign language and a driving licence are
required. Actors may also be expected to lead
workshops. Recent productions include: *A
(Midsummer Night's) Dream*,*Petrushka*, *The Pied
Piper*, a Victorian *Mikado*and *The Very Magic Flute*.

Casting procedures: Sometimes holds general
auditions; actors can write at any time requesting
inclusion. Accepts submissions (with CVs and
photographs) from actors previously unknown to the
company if sent by post. Does not welcome
unsolicited emails. Will also accept invitations to view
individual actors' websites. Offers non-Equity
contracts but at Equity and ITC rates. Actively
encourages applications from disabled actors and
promotes the use of inclusive casting.

Lawnmowers Independent Theatre Company

Swinburn House, Swinburn Street,
Gateshead NE8 1AX
tel/fax 0191 478 9200
email hello@thelawnmowers.co.uk
website www.thelawnmowers.co.uk
Arts Director Geraldine Ling

Theatre company addressing issues of concern for
people with learning difficulties, often with an
international dimension. Uses theatre and drama as a
means for people with learning difficulties to explore
and develop ideas, and help plan and take control of
their futures.

Magpie Dance

The Churchill Theatre, High Street,
Bromley BR1 1HA
tel 020 8290 6633
email info@magpiedance.org.uk
website www.magpiedance.org.uk
Artistic Director Avril Hitman

Magpie Dance is a company for people with learning
disabilities. Based in Bromley, Magpie can also deliver
workshops to any region in the UK. With an
emphasis on ability rather than disability, the
company has a national reputation for its exciting
approach to inclusive dance.

Mind the Gap

Mind the Gap Studios Bradford, Silk Warehouse,
Patent Street, Bradford BD9 4SA
tel 01274 487390 *fax* 01274 493973
email arts@mind-the-gap.org.uk
website www.mind-the-gap.org.uk
Artistic Director Tim Wheeler

Production details: Founded in 1988, Mind the Gap
is a theatre company with a belief in quality, equality
and inclusion, and a mission to dismantle barriers to
artistic excellence so that learning-disabled and non-
learning-disabled actors can appear as equals. The
company has 5 main areas of activity:

• National Touring: in 2000, Mind the Gap
progressed from devised work to adaptations of well-
known texts. In recent years the company has
produced: *Of Mice and Men* (2000 and 2005); *Dr
Jekyll and Mr Hyde* (2001); *Pygmalion* (2002); *Don
Quixote* (2003 – collaboration with Northern Stage)
and *Cyrano* (2004). Total audiences for the 2005 tour
were approximately 6,700
• Learning & Skills: each year Mind the Gap runs a
full-time accredited training course for people with
learning disabilities. In addition, as part of the DaDA
awards scheme, the company runs Staging Change –
a residential, nationally recruited training course for
people with learning disabilities, working in
partnership with 5 of the country's leading
mainstream drama schools
• Acting Company: comprising 7 learning-disabled
graduates of Mind the Gap's training courses who
work on National Touring productions and their
own programme of local and regional performance
work and workshops
• Outreach: each year, Mind the Gap's Outreach
programme works with 300 young learning-disabled
people from West Yorkshire on short-term drama
training and performance projects

• Advocacy: Mind the Gap advocates for people who are traditionally excluded or marginalised from mainstream practices. Mind the Gap is also commissioned to do a variety of performance projects: e.g. *Finding their Feet* – a production commissioned by Bradford School of Health Studies; and *Inside Knowledge* – commissioned by Tonic as part of a consultation to provide guidance for the design of a new cancer care centre in Leeds

Stages 1 or 2 national tours annually (25-30 performances each), 1 large-scale regional performance project (3-6 performances) and 1 or 2 regional schools tours (12 performances). The national tour visits 15-20 venues. In 2005 these included West Yorkshire Playhouse; The Theatre, Chipping Norton; Ustinov Studio, Bath; Norwich Playhouse; Rose Theatre, Ormskirk; New Vic, Newcastle-under-Lyme and Jackson's Lane Theatre, London. 3-5 actors are involved in the national tour, up to 7 actors in the schools tour, and over 20 performers in the regional performance project.

Casting procedures: Casts in-house. When seeking to recruit an actor from outside the core company, the company contacts agents, and advertises in *The Stage* and on its website. Casting breakdowns are available on request. Welcomes letters (with CVs and photographs) as well as showreels and invitations to view individuals' websites, "although we do not often employ actors who are not known to us. For national touring work we rarely cast outside our core Acting Company, but we do keep on record details which have been sent to us. We are particularly interested in hearing from disabled artists." Offers TMA/Equity-approved contracts.

Oily Cart Company

Smallwood School Annexe, Smallwood Road, London SW17 0TW
tel 020 8672 6329 *fax* 020 8672 0792
email oilies@oilycart.org.uk
website www.oilycart.org.uk
Artistic Director Ellie Griffiths

Production details: One of the leading theatre companies in the UK creating highly interactive multi-sensory performances for and with the very young (6 months to 6 years) and young people (aged 3–19) with complex needs and/or who are on the autistic spectrum. Tours national and international venues like theatres and arts centres with early years shows, and takes its special-needs work to special schools around the UK. Recent productions include: *In A Pickle* (sheep's-eye view of Shakespeare's *The Winter's Tale* for under 5s); *Hippity Hop*; *Kubla Khan* and *Splish Splash* – an interactive show performed in hydrotherapy pools

Casting procedures: Casting breakdowns are available on the website **www.oilycart.org.uk** and the Arts Jobs website **www.artsjobs.org.uk**. Offers ITC/Equity-approved contracts. Actively encourages

applications from D/deaf or disabled actors and promotes the use of inclusive casting.

Salamanda Tandem

52 Albert Road, Nottingham NG2 5GS
tel/fax 0845 293 2989
email info@salamanda-tandem.org
website www.salamanda-tandem.org
Artistic Director Isabel Jones

Producer of contemporary art works, creative environments and sensory performances, where people can choose to observe or become part of the artwork itself. Works with a wide spectrum of people, and in particular people with disabilities. Strong advocate for ethical practice in arts and health. Publishes articles and conducts training and professional education.

Spare Tyre Theatre Company

The Albany, Douglas Way, Deptford, London SE8 4AG
tel/fax 020 8692 4446 (ext 273)
email info@sparetyre.org
website www.sparetyre.org
Artistic Director Arti Prashar

Production details:

• Work with older people aged 60+, outreach workshops for older people, and interactive storytelling for people with dementia. Work with carers.
• Work with people with learning disabilities.
• Work with women who have experienced violence.

London and nationwide. Skills required from actors include workshop-leading and facilitation skills, experience of working with community groups and a sensitivity to, and understanding of, relevant issues.

Casting procedures: Casting breakdowns are published and on the website. Unsolicited approaches at other times – including CVs, showreels and invitations to view individuals' websites – are discouraged. Offers ITC/Equity-approved contracts. Actively encourages applications from disabled actors and promotes the use of inclusive casting.

StopGAP Dance Company

Farnham Maltings, Bridge Square, Farnham, Surrey GU9 7QR
tel 01252 718664
email vicki@stopgap.uk.com
website www.stopgap.uk.com
Artistic Director Vicki Balaam

A vibrant integrated dance company that includes disabled and non-disabled dancers. It challenges traditional notions about dance by using each dancer's physical and intellectual potential as a starting point for creating new work. "We work from a philosophy of physical, psychological and social integration. In so doing, we recognise and celebrate individuality and the differences between people, while continually seeking artistic and technical excellence in all that we do."

Theatre Without Walls

Forwood House, Forwood, Gloucesterhire GL6 9AB
mobile 07962 040441
email hello@theatrewithoutwalls.org.uk
website www.theatrewithoutwalls.org.uk
Directors Genevieve Swift, Jason Maher

Company's work: Established in 2002. Award-winning producing theatre company with an active training/corporate wing, working in the public and private sector. Also produces television and corporate films. Clients include: National Trust, Gloucestershire Local Authority, Apollo, BBC and The Prince's Trust. Training is provided for incoming actors in the form of workshops and rehearsals in forum, role-play and interactive drama. Incoming actors require good improvisational skills.

Recruitment procedures: Actors are recruited through agents and Equity Job Information Service. Disabled actors regularly form part of the team and are actively encouraged to apply. See also the company's entry under *Middle and smaller-scale companies* on page 218.

Theatre Workshop

34 Hamilton Place, Edinburgh EH3 5AX
tel 0131 225 7942 *fax* 0131 220 0112
email afleming@twe.org.uk
website www.theatre-workshop.com
Artistic Director Robert Rae

Production details: Founded in 1965; stages 4 productions a year with around 60 performances across 2 theatre venues. Occasionally tours internationally. Employs an average of 5 actors on each production, using ITC/Equity-approved contracts. Recent productions include: *The Jasmine Road* (No Limits International Theatre Festival, Berlin) and *The Threepenny Opera* (Edinburgh Festival Theatre & Tramway, Glasgow).

Casting procedures: Casting breakdowns are available from the website and Equity Job Information Service. Welcomes letters and emails (with CVs and photographs) from individuals previously unknown to the company. Also happy to receive showreels and invitations to view individuals' websites. Encourages applications from disabled actors and promotes the use of inclusive casting. "Theatre Workshop casts both disabled and non-disabled actors in all our productions."

Touchdown Dance

Waterside Arts Centre, Sale M33 7ZF
tel 0161 912 5760 *fax*
email info@touchdowndance.co.uk
website www.touchdowndance.co.uk
Director Katy Dymoke

Touchdown Dance provides dance workshops for visually impaired and sighted people of all ages and ability, ranging from 'jam' weekends to more intensive courses.

Louise Dyson at VisABLE People Ltd

31 Broad Street, WR10 1BB
tel 020 3488 1998 *mobile* 07729 738317
email office@visablepeople.com
website www.visablepeople.com
Agents Louise Dyson and Kate Ellison

Founded in 1994, VisABLE is the world's first agency representing only disabled people for professional engagements. It represents artistes with a wide range of impairments and in every age group, including children. 2 agents represent around 150 artistes in all areas of acting, including presenting.

Does not welcome performance notices: "Sorry, usually no time to get out and see them; unless existing clients." Happy to receive applications from disabled actors via VisABLE website only. Showreels should always be via a l ink sent by email. Also happy to receive invitations to view individual actors' websites. Recommends the photographer Richard Bailey. *Commission*: 10%-17.5% (commercials: 20%)

Wolf + Water Arts Company

The Plough Arts Cebtre, 9/11 Fore Street, Torrington, Devon EX38 8HQ
tel 01805 938147
email office@wolfandwater.org
website www.wolfandwater.org
Co-founders Peter Harris, Philip Robinson

Since establishing itself independently in 1991, after 3 years as the Beaford Centre's 'Common Sense Project', Wolf + Water Arts Company has brought its creative and therapeutic approaches to a wide variety of groups locally, nationally and internationally. These groups have included people with learning difficulties; people with mental health issues; people in conflict situations; offenders; communities; young people at risk; children with life-threatening illnesses and their families and staff groups working with all the above. The company produces original topical performances for conferences and for tour, and provides a wide range of training courses for those wishing to use drama and arts techniques in special-needs situations. Work has taken the company throughout the UK, the Republic of Ireland, Scandinavia, the Middle East and the Balkans.

ARTS ORGANISATIONS

Ableize Arts

website www.ableize.com/disabled-arts

A selection of disabled arts sites, from theatre and dance to visual arts. The Ableize site also features links, from accommodation and travel to support groups and employment and benefits. A fantastic, wide-ranging site.

Arcadea

2nd Floor, Commercial Union House,
39 Pilgrim Street, Newcastle NE1 6QE
tel 0191 222 0708 *mobile* 07932 304241
email info@arcadea.org
website www.arcadea.org

Arcadea aims to promote the artistic and cultural equality of disabled people in the North East region, serving Co. Durham, Northumberland, Tees Valley and Tyne & Wear.

Artlink Central

Unit 8, The Beta Centre,
Stirling University Innovation Park, Stirling FK9 4NF
tel 01786 450971 *fax* 01786 465958
email info@artlinkcentral.org
website www.artlinkcentral.org

Established in February 1988, Artlink Central is a registered charity founded in the belief that involvement in the arts is life-enhancing and should be available to all. It enables a wide range of disabled and/or marginalised people to work with experienced professional artists on high-quality arts projects in the Stirling, Falkirk and Clackmannanshire areas of Central Scotland.

Artlink Edinburgh

13A Spittal Street, Edinburgh
tel 0131 229 3555 *fax* 0131 228 5257
website www.artlinkedinburgh.co.uk

As Artlink Central, but based in Edinburgh and the Lothians.

Artsline

c/o 21 Pine Court, Wood Lodge Gardens,
Bromley BR1 2WA
tel fax minicom
email admin@artsline.org.uk
website www.artsline.org.uk

Founded in 1981 with the aim of increasing disabled people's participation in the arts, and to provide them with accurate information about access to arts and cultural events in London. In collaboration with the London Disability Arts Forum, it began producing *Disability Arts in London* (*DAIL*) magazine in 1986, and now provides a newly launched access database with details for arts and entertainment venues across London, including: theatres, cinemas, museums, art centres, tourist attractions, comedy, music venues and selected restaurants. For details of other publications, projects and services available, consult the website.

Carousel

Community Base, 113 Queens Road,
Brighton BN1 3XG
tel 01273 234734
email enquiries@carousel.org.uk
website www.carousel.org.uk
Director Liz Hall

Carousel helps learning disabled artists develop and manage their creative lives, true to their voice and vision, challenging expectations of what great art is and who can create it.

Carousel believes that learning disabled artists make a vital contribution to the world we live in. It is an organisation that puts learning disabled people in control of their art, in film, music, performance and production. Carousel's work is planned, managed and delivered by learning dsiabled teams and 50% of the board members have a learning disability.

DaDaFest

The Bluecoat, School Lane, Liverpool L1 3BX
tel 0151 707 1733 *fax* 0151 708 9355
email info@dadafest.co.uk
website www.dadafest.co.uk
Facebook @DaDaFest
Twitter @DaDaFest
Artistic Director Ruth Gould

DaDa-Disability is an innovative and cutting edge disability and Deaf arts organisation based in Liverpool, established in 1984. Its vision is to inspire, develop and celebrate talent and excellence in disability and Deaf arts. The organisation 's work covers the whole of the North West of the UK, as well as operating on an international scale.

Disability Arts Cymru

Sbectrwm, Bwlch Road, Fairwater, Cardiff CF5 3EF
tel 029 2055 1040 *textphone* 029 2055 1040
fax 029 2055 1036
email post@dacymru.co.uk
website www.dacymru.co.uk
Facebook www.facebook.com/disabilityartscymru
Twitter @DACymru
Director Sara Mackay

Disability Arts Cymru is the lead disability and the arts organisation in Wales, and the only organisation in Wales providing Disability Equality Training (DET) specifically for arts providers. DAC works with the arts sector to create career progression routes for emerging/professional disabled artists across all arts forms and to build a future where there is equality of access and opportunity for disabled people. A number of documents are available from its excellent website, which offer advice on a range of subjects including access issues for touring companies.

Disability Arts Online

9 Jew Street, Brighton BN1 1UT
mobile 07941 1824458
email info@disabilityartsonline.org.uk
website www.disabilityarts.online

Aims to assist the professional development of disabled and deaf writers, performers and artists, working across all art forms.

Diverse City

3 Manwell Drive, Swanage, Dorset BH19 2RB
tel 07795 247216
website www.DiverseCity.org.uk

Advocates for and delivers diversity and equality of opportunity in culture and learning.

First Movement

Level Centre, Old Station Close, Rowsley,
Derbyshire DE4 2EL
tel 01629 734848
email fmt@first-movement.org.uk
website www.first-movement.org.uk

First Movement is an experimental arts organisation developing projects which uniquely reflect the experiences, choices and abilities of groups of people with severe and profound learning disabilities. Runs a performance company called Spiral.

Northern Ireland Arts & Disability Forum

Cathedral Quarter Managed Workspace,
109-113 Royal Avenue, Belfast BT1 1FF
tel 028 90 239 450
email info@adf.ie
website www.adf.ie
Chief Executive Officer Chris Ledger

A non-profit-making voluntary organisation that aims to provide:

• Information to disabled people and organisations – both inside and outside the arts sector
• A body that advocates on behalf of disabled people in the arts sector
• A networking, developmental and coordinating body
• A body that identifies and fills gaps in training provisions for disabled people working in the arts
• A focus for campaigning

Also runs a gallery to exhibit the work of disabled artists.

Prism Arts

Carlisle Business Interaction Centre,
4-5 Paternoster Row, Carlisle, Cumbria CA3 8TT
tel 01228 587691
email office@prismarts.org.uk
website www.prismarts.org.uk
Director Catherine Coulthard

Promotes diverse access to creative arts activities in Cumbria. Runs Studio Theatre for learning-disabled performers.

Shape

Deane House Studios, 27 Greenwood Place,
London NW5 1LB
tel 020 7424 7344 *fax* 0845 521 3458
email info@shapearts.org.uk
website www.shapearts.org.uk

Shape's mission is to provide skills, opportunities and support for disabled artists, individuals and cultural organisations and to help build a more inclusive cultural sector.

Zinc Arts

Great Stony, High Street, Chipping Ongar,
Essex CM5 0AD
tel 01277 365626
email info@zincarts.org.uk
website www.zincarts.org.uk
Director Dan Burman, Sonia Cakebread, Lyann Kennedy

Zinc Arts work with people of all ages and abilities, but specialise in working with children, young people and adults who are disabled, learning disabled or are mental health service users. Zinc Arts provides beneficial inclusive opportunities for people to engage with the arts; creatively, educationally and vocationally. Zinc Arts Centre offers an inclusive environment with meeting/training rooms, studio theatre, conferencing and performance facilities, as well as contemporary en-suite accommodation.

RIGHTS, ADVICE AND SUPPORT

Business Disability Forum

Nutmeg House, 60 Gainsford Street,
London SE1 2NY
tel 020 7403 3020 *fax* 020 7403 0404
minicom 020 7403 0040
email enquiries@businessdisabilityforum.org.uk
website http://businessdisabilityforum.org.uk

The leading employers' organisation focused on disability as it affects business. Funded and managed by more than 400 members, the Forum works to make it easier for companies to recruit and retain disabled employees and to serve disabled customers. Umbrella organisation for the Broadcasting & Creative Industries Disability Network (BCIDN), a forum for the UK's major broadcasters to explore and address disability as it relates to the media industry. It is advised by a panel of associates – 14 disabled people with considerable media experience who work in different areas of broadcasting and the media in general.

Directgov

website www.direct.gov.uk/disability

The government's Public Services portal, with links to information and advice on employment, home and housing options, financial support, health, education and training, rights and obligations, transport, travel and holidays, leisure and recreation and caring for someone.

Ouch!

website www.bbc.co.uk/ouch

The BBC's online disability magazine, including weblogs, message board and a monthly podcast.

Skill: National Bureau for Students with Disabilities

Skill closed on April 4th 2011. Following a period of financial difficulty, Skill's Board of Trustees decided it was no longer viable to keep the charity open. Although Skill will not be returning in its previous form, Disability Alliance (**www.disabilityalliance.org**) has been supported by the Department for Business, Innovation and Skills to fill part of the gap. Some parts of the Skill website (**www.skill.org.uk**) will continue to be hosted as a free information archive to disabled people, parents and key advisers.

Opportunities for disabled actors

Jamie Beddard

The plethora of journeys and experiences of disabled performers over the past 30 years has ranged from the lonely, demoralising, and depressing to the downright bizarre. The barriers encountered far outreach the regular obstacles preventing non-disabled actors from learning, and plying their trade. Performance attributes of technique, voice, improvisation and movement seem distant concepts when you cannot get through the doors of drama school, producers baulk at the idea of employing disabled performers, and most training and employment opportunities are based around strict notions of 'the classical actor'. This is altogether surprising in the creative industries, which should surely celebrate uniqueness, individuality and diversity. However, where once black actors were denied access to stage and screen, so those with different bodies have fought similar battles for opportunity, acknowledgement and representation. This, against a backdrop in which esteemed, non-disabled actors regularly pick up Oscars for their touching portrayal of characters with disability: Daniel Day Lewis in *My Left Foot*; Jamie Foxx in *Ray*; John Voight in *Coming Home*; Tom Hanks in *Forrest Gump* – there's a long list, and they are one-dimensional replications of impediments, far outweighing any considerations around full and meaningful characterisations. Authenticity has been a label seldom attached to the portrayal of disability in the mainstream.

Personal anecdotes are perhaps best served by exploring the issues faced by disabled performers, as, until recently, there have been no formal routes of progression into the industry. Those few who have made the periphery have tended to have random and short-lived paths, based around such indeterminates as maverick directors, word of mouth or, as in my particular case, luck. The groundbreaking film *Skalligrigg* – a road movie in which a rag tag of disabled characters take to the road on a mythical quest – threw my staid career path into chaos, and levered a window (previously boarded up!) into performance. In the absence of disabled actors, many first-timers with no experience were suddenly thrust onto a film set; I thought the sound-boom was a cheap prop! 'Rough diamonds' probably most accurately described those of us fortunate enough to get such a break, and, for me, the film opened up a completely new, and exciting, world. A mixture of bluff, wide-eyed enthusiasm and no little begging had to suffice in the absence of any formal training.

This 'new and exciting world' was also populated by baffling and disheartening prejudices, and initial enthusiasm soon became tinged with disappointment and anger. A casting director for *Eastenders* once informed me that a disabled character – played by a disabled actor, heaven forbid! – would place the programme in the realm of freak show. So much for diverse communities and gritty realism! This attitude is unfortunately still painfully prevalent, and theatre directors are worried that their audiences will be put off by seeing a disabled person on stage.

I contacted Graeae Theatre Company – a company that had been going since the early 1980s, and was run by, and for, actors with sensory and physical disabilities. Graeae had become accustomed to (and was hardened by) irksome battles against prevalent prejudices and barriers. I found a group of like-minded individuals who were challenging these ridiculous, outdated and offensive attitudes, and were determined to pursue careers considered impractical and unrealistic. They were developing, writing and performing theatre as does any small-scale company; sometimes very good, and sometimes not so good. However, the normal critical faculties brought to bear on other companies seemed strangely absent from assessment of Graeae's work, with emphasis on the 'oh so strange impairments' rather than art. The *Independent*, when reviewing Graeae's 2002 production – *Peeling* – came up with such helpful insights as, "Beaty is four feet tall; Coral has tiny limbs and a torso about the same size as her head." Apart from gross inaccuracies, the obvious offence to the individual actors involved and the banality of such revelations, what relevance has this to the art? Hopefully, the paying public didn't recoil in shock at this assembled collection of bizarre physical specimens!

I always yearned for a bad – rather than ignorant, ill informed and avoiding – review, because this would suggest a considered judgement based on the same criteria as any other performer. Undoubtedly, I have been involved in a few 'turkeys', and they should be recognised as such! However, fascination with individual impediment always seems the central tenet of any assessment of performance. Perhaps it would be interesting to apply such criteria to the wider acting fraternity – solely judging Woody Allen on his glasses, Tom Hanks on his stature, or Kenneth Williams on his nasal inflection.

Over the years, the profile of Graeae, and of disabled performers in general, has grown, and there has been a gradual acceptance that it is no longer acceptable to marginalise their talents, aspirations and contributions. In many ways the Arts have lagged behind society in taking the first steps towards embracing and committing to diversity. Although, there has, in many quarters, been a genuine will to broaden participation, the stick of the Disability Discrimination Act has been instrumental in initiating fundamental appraisal and change. The possibility of legal challenges has shaken many organisations, venues and makers from their comfy inertia. Even tokenism is preferable to apartheid!

Drama schools, in particular, have found the concept of students with disability difficult to grasp, but the introduction of the Dance & Drama Awards (DaDAs) has started the process of drama schools thinking not only about the physical access to their buildings, but also about the attitudinal access, and ways to promote inclusive teaching. This is very exciting, and will no doubt pave the way for young disabled people to go through mainstream training rather than be reliant on Graeae.

While the process of change will take time (especially the attitudinal aspect), Graeae has had to respond to the obvious demand by setting up the training course in conjunction with London Metropolitan University. This course offers all the elements found in drama schools, and provides the skills, disciplines and training that were denied people of my age. Lack of sufficiently trained and experienced disabled actors has long been an excuse for the 'cripping up' of non-disabled actors, while training providers continually stress the unlikelihood of disabled graduates sustaining careers in the industry. A classic chicken-and-egg situation, in which aspirant disabled performers are denied entrance at all levels. However, the percentage of those who have graduated through Missing Piece, and have gone into the industry, compares favourably with other drama schools, and Graeae is frequently approached by casting directors looking for disabled talent. So, young people with disabilities do share the same aspirations as any others; there is an increasing demand for such actors; and the institutions are failing to shoulder responsibility.

Missing Piece is fulfilling this vacuum, and has now been running since 2000. The nine-month (September to May) intensive training allows disabled students to work with a wide

Disabled actors

range of theatre practitioners – both specialist and mainstream. The course can act as a foundation course to further education or drama school – access and will permitting! – or, as is often the case, a direct gateway into the industry. Academic and practical elements of performance are covered, and opportunities for showcasing and touring afforded. Recent years have culminated in professional touring productions of *Mother Courage* and *George Dandin*, and many relationships have been brokered between Graeae's performers and directors, producers and casting directors. There is a crossover with the Performing Arts degree at London Metropolitan, with disabled performers working alongside, and in collaboration with, tutors and students at the University. As well as the main Missing Piece course, Graeae run a series of taster workshops throughout the year for prospective actors.

So strides are being made by Graeae, and by other companies; the excuses and barriers preventing inclusion are slowly being dismantled. There are viable careers for those with the talent, determination and thick skin when necessary.

BBC has set up a talent fund for disabled actors to try and address dated attitudes, and to encourage writers to write storylines which are not always hospital-based or about the whole 'disability thing'!

However the failure of mainstream films such as *Inside I'm Dancing*, which continue to propagate stereotypes and exclusion – with all the main disabled characters played by non-disabled actors – will hopefully mark a sea-change in attitudes and imaginations among creators. The existing, and perspective, body of talent out there no longer allows for petty excuses or wilful misrepresentation. Disabled people, like any others, can make good, bad or indifferent performers, and should be judged as such. However, we have a right to expect the same opportunities, treatments and prospects as all. Banging the door down has become boring – just let us in. It's not rocket science!

Jamie Beddard is an actor, writer and director. Involved with Graeae since 1991, he was Associate Director of the company for some years. He is currently working as a freelance director and co-editor of *DAIL* magazine. Graeae productions 2006/7 include *Blasted* by Sarah Kane, touring March to May; *Once Beyond These Walls, A Girl* by Richard Cameron, touring October to November; and *Whiter Than Snow* by Mike Kenny – a co-production with Birmingham Rep, touring February to April 2007. For full details, visit the website **www.graeae.org**. For information on Missing Piece, contact: **ellie@graeae.org**.

Resources
Introduction

This section covers those practical items (and sources of more detailed help and advice) that are, to the actor, what tools and a first-aid kit are to a carpenter. Some may be irrelevant to you – for instance, you may feel as though you could never have the organisational skills to set up your own company. Others are essential to all actors: good photographs, for example. Whatever your needs, time taken to formulate clearly your requirements before approaching any of the contacts listed below will be time well spent.

Equity

Equity is the only Trade Union to represent performers and people working creatively across the entire spectrum of arts and entertainment, both live and recorded. The main function of Equity is to negotiate minimum terms and conditions of employment throughout the whole world of entertainment, and to endeavour to ensure that these take account of social and economic changes. We look to the future as well, negotiating agreements to embrace the new and emerging technologies which affect performers – so satellite, digital television, new media and so on are all covered, as are the more traditional areas. We also work at national level by lobbying government and other bodies on issues of paramount importance to the membership. In addition we operate at an international level through the Federation of International Artists which Equity helped to establish, the International Committee for Artistic Freedom, and through agreements with sister unions overseas.

As well as these core activities, Equity strives to provide a wide range of services for members so that they are eligible for a whole host of benefits which are continually being revised and developed. These include helplines, job information, insurance cover, members' pension scheme, charities and others. (For more information, visit the Equity website **www.equity.org.uk**. For details of Equity's Job Information Service, see entry under Spotlight, casting directories and information services.)

Equity
Head Office, Guild House, Upper St Martins Lane, London WC2H 9EG
tel 020 7379 6000 *fax* 020 7379 7001
email info@equity.org.uk
website www.equity.org.uk

See www.equity.org.uk/contact-us/equity-helpdesks for specific helpdesk telephone numbers.

Regional offices:

Midlands
Office 1, Steeple House, Percy Street, Coventry CV1 3BY
tel (02476) 553612
email midlands@equity.org.uk

North East
The Workstation, 15 Paternoster Row, Sheffield S1 2BX
tel 0114-275 9746
email northeastengland@equity.org.uk

North West and Isle of Man
Express Networks, 1 George Leigh Street, Manchester M4 5DL
tel 0161-244 5995 *fax* 0161-244 5971
email northwestengland@equity.org.uk

Scotland and Northern Ireland
114 Union Street, Glasgow G1 3QQ
tel 0141-248 2472 *fax* 0141-248 2473
email scotland@equity.org.uk
email northernireland@equity.org.uk

South East
Guild House, Upper St Martins Lane, London WC2H 9EG
tel 020-7670 0229 *fax* 020-7379 7001
email southeastengland@equity.org.uk

Wales and South West England
Transport House, 1 Cathedral Road, Cardiff CF1 9SD
tel 029-2039 7971 *fax* 029-2023 0754
email wales@equity.org.uk
email southwestengland@equity.org.uk

Act For Change
Kobna Holdbrook-Smith

Why?
Actors' faces and voices ultimately represent the months or sometimes years that go into making a production. In January 2014, a UK broadcaster released a trailer for its coming season. Each room in a warm, bustling house showed scenes or characters from forthcoming dramas. Out of eleven people, none was deaf, disabled or of colour; only three were women, none of whom spoke any words and one was weeping. What made that trailer possible? It had been conceived, collated, approved and aired without anyone noticing the exclusions. Again.

Ideas about art are ideas about society and erasing people from our imaginings and artworks, deliberately or not, is harmful on two levels. Clearly it excludes people from careers or involvement in the arts industries, and there are not many good reasons to carry on with that. The second, deeper level of harm is that this unpeopling of imagined worlds reflects a dark desire for the same thing to happen in real life. That is well worth opposing. The Act For Change Project started when the actor Danny Lee Wynter saw that trailer and felt compelled to gather like-minded people from the industry.

What?
The Act For Change Project works to enhance diversity and inclusion in Britain's live and recorded arts. This includes all the people and characteristics missed from the trailer mentioned above as well as LGBT+ people, those above a certain age and those from varying economic backgrounds and more.

We don't yet have staff, just a board of trustees and our committee. The success of the Act For Change Project, in terms of awareness and visibility, is the direct result of actors, whose faces and voices are loved by many people, donating their time to it. We have been based at the National Theatre (NT) in London since 2015. We were invited there after our Diversity in Theatre event because the NT wanted to commit actively to diversity. The NT fully supported Charlotte Bevan transferring from its casting department to act as lead on inclusion and difference. She has been superb, driven and detailed in the execution of her new role. She set up regular internal talk sessions focusing on a different group or diversity issue each week. They were well attended, well supported and seem to be having a lasting positive effect. Morale appears to be higher as people have found friends and colleagues they might not otherwise have encountered. Charlotte has also sought out disabled actors previously unknown to the NT, calling them in to meet her casting department colleagues, and recording auditions onto a proper database. Look out for our podcast interview with Charlotte so you can hear more about what informs, influences and inspires her to do this work.

How does Act For Change work?
Campaigning keeps supporters and the public informed. We campaign by producing videos of testimonies, interviews and discussions; by publishing our newsletters; by using social media to highlight issues, discuss news and share information; and we work with

Resources

print and online publications to make more formal comment. One of our early hashtags was #KeepTheConversationGoing because conversation is key, rather than each of us in our lonely silos being scared to get things wrong.

Advocacy is behind-the-scenes work, demonstrating and sharing better ways of thinking and working. Because many of us are actors, we have been able to access a wide range of links to different people and groups. It has also meant direct and meaningful contact with TV commissioners, theatres and producers, strong partnership with Equity, and alliances with organisations like Tonic, and Equal Representation For Actresses. These consultations happen on an organisation-by-organisation basis and can be one morning, one day or one month, casual or formal. Some of our activity is published in the Act For Change newsletter along with that of our allies and co-campaigners.

Policy shifts organisational thinking and overlaps with advocacy. Despite many schemes, pledges and initiatives, things only seem to move forward slowly, or they slip back. When we had Jenny Sealey, Artistic Director of Graeae Theatre, on our 2015 event panel she said she had sat on thirty-seven different panels over eighteen years. It shouldn't take that amount of dedication to combat the culture of exclusion. Only policies can really prevent that. They find out how and where to make positive changes, create conditions that support those changes, build them into the running and operations of an organisation.

Monitoring refers to gathering data to inform policy. It shows which groups, people or characteristics are being under- or over-used. It is vital that people fill in equality monitoring forms as ignoring them really bruises the effort. No data, no difference. According to figures released by creative skillset and amplified by Lenny Henry's fine speeches at BAFTA, 2014, and updated at the Houses of Parliament 2017, the British, Asian and minority ethnic (BAME) workforce in the UK TV industry has declined rather than increased, going from 6.7 per cent (2009) to 5.4 per cent (2014) and this is despite 13 per cent of the total UK population being BAME.

Figures for deaf and disabled professionals, whether on or off screen, backstage or on stage, have never been provided. The deaf and disabled workforce is continually marginalised or, even worse, forgotten entirely. In most cases the data, if it's even been recorded, is just not made readily available. And without evidence to show whether numbers have risen or fallen, the reality is avoided. The Creative Diversity Network has a project called Diamond (Diversity Analysis Monitoring Data) that gathers equality and diversity data sets from the BBC, ITV, Channel 4 and Sky. At the time of writing, their results remain unpublished but the characteristics they will focus on are gender, gender identity, age, ethnicity, sexual orientation and disability. Monitoring requires a lot of resources to become effective evidence. We conducted some ourselves, looking at TV, West End plays and later diversity in training for the arts. See the article by Giovanni Benne in our Spring 2017 newsletter where he explains our monitoring project methodology, where we struggled and why we need more.

Events bring campaigning, policy and advocacy together. Each year we hold a discussion event focusing on a diversity-related theme or subject. In 2014, our first event, it was diversity in television, 2015 was diversity in theatre, and 2016 was diversity in training for the industry. We think of provocations or questions that will stimulate debate, choose a relevant panel, ideally from varying perspectives, and fill the venues with as many supporters and change-makers as possible. Events introduce us to partner organisations, invigorate our support base and, most importantly, encourage people to take diversity seriously. What makes us especially proud is the conversations they amplify and the issues which, broached by us, can be discussed when individuals alone might be scared to raise them. We try to unpack complicated issues then disseminate the best thoughts about how, why and when to make changes.

Who?

You. People ask how they can get involved with the charity. We need so much volunteer support. People can be researchers for our monitoring work, they can help to produce, shoot or subtitle our videos, we need podcast help, we need help at our events, social media support, fundraising, development and marketing help. Email us and tell us what you can do.

Do

The best and most powerful things actors do are listen and talk. In that order. It is similar for this. Talk to and involve others, especially those that don't know what you know. The more you share ideas the wider the context becomes. Ask complex questions, especially of people with power; hold your own discussion events, notice difference and look for positive progress. Connecting to culture and events that are new to you is another way of doing. Support work and artists you haven't heard of, just to see. People do it with music all the time – try it with ideas and ways of thinking. These are all simple things you can make happen that, in small ways, fortify diversity and inclusion.

Commit

Passion can wane but commitment (like policy) will outlast that. It all starts with thinking, but you cannot dragoon people into adopting ideas, they can only join willingly. A constant readiness to respond is part of making art, that's how artists can respond but like physical exercise or learning we must listen and ask questions regularly. To become effective let your support become part of you.

Visit **www.act-for-change.com** for podcasts, newsletter and much more.

Kobna Holdbrook-Smith is a stage, screen and voice actor, vice chair of the Act For Change Project, Gate Theatre board member, a National Theatre Associate and chair of trustees at the arts education charity Dramatic Need. Films include *The Commuter, Dr Strange* and *The Double*. Theatre includes *Hamlet* (Barbican), *Edward II* (NT). TV includes *Dark Heart* (ITV), *The Split* (BBC/AMC).

Beyond #metoo

Kelly Burke

#metoo

In October 2017, the *The New York Times* published an article accusing Hollywood film mogul Harvey Weinstein of decades of sexual harassment and assault. The entertainment industry's apparent astonishment caused actress Alyssa Milano to tweet, 'If all the women who have been sexually harassed or assaulted wrote "Me too" as a status, we might give people a sense of the magnitude of the problem.'

Within twenty-four hours, 4.7 million people had engaged with #metoo on Facebook alone.[1] Over eighty women came forward with accusations against Weinstein, and a raft of allegations began to surface against other high-profile figures. It became clear that the magnitude of the problem was great indeed.

Since October 2017, conversations have spread through rehearsal rooms and drama schools, agencies, film sets and board rooms, asking the twin questions: How did we get here? and What can we do about it? In the UK, new safeguarding policies have been implemented industry-wide, starting with rigorous guidelines from Equity, the BFI and the Royal Court, geared towards creating safe workplaces, preventing harassment and holding perpetrators accountable. 'Intimacy direction' (in which sex scenes are choreographed by an outside professional, much like stage fights) and ideas around active consent have been gaining traction in creative spaces. Performers are seeking ways to set boundaries and say 'no' without being regarded as difficult or un-creative.

With thousands of people participating in the conversation, there has inevitably been disagreement about where the line between 'harmless' and 'harassment' is drawn, how much banter is too much banter, and how much safeguarding is too much safeguarding. There is anxiety in some corners of the industry that new regulations will compromise artistic freedom, that allegations will turn into witch hunts, and that the logical conclusion of #metoo (in the arts, at least) will be that we're afraid to touch each other, frisson will disappear from our stages and screens, and our work will be condemned to sexless, frightened monotony.

But this puts us in danger of ignoring two important – if subtle – factors:

1. The implementation of codes of conduct, safeguarding, consent negotiations, etc., is not a call for sex to be eliminated from our industry. Instead, it is an insistence that, where sex *does* come into our work, it is negotiated professionally and openly, with input from all involved. Because, of course:

2. The sexual harassment crisis isn't really about sex. It's about power. It's about work.

Power and parity

After all, the women speaking out against Harvey Weinstein weren't sexually assaulted on dates, or by strangers on the street (which would be bad enough). They were assaulted as a condition of their work, in order to get or sustain employment.

To understand why this is so critical, consider:

• Men outnumber women 2:1 on screen — and 3:1 in children's programming
• Crowd scenes in film use about 17% women[2]
• Women make up just 7% of film directors[3] and 23% of crews[4]
• 16% of working film writers in the UK are female (this statistic *has remained unchanged for the past 10 years*)[5]
• Only 1 in 5 artistic directors funded by Arts Council England is female; women control just 13% of the ACE theatre funding budget[6]

What does this mean?

Well, to start with it means that women at the beginning of their careers are less likely to work than their male colleagues. This means that a disproportionate number of female film- and theatre-makers are confined to self-producing work on the fringe, often at their own expense. It means that most female performers, writers, directors, stage managers, DoPs, etc., will at some point find themselves working for little – or no – pay. And this is before we consider the repercussions of having children (or being over 40) on a woman's career – or the dire impact of intersectionality, which puts BAME women, d/Deaf and disabled women, and queer women at an exponential disadvantage.

Less work overall means a less impressive CV, which leads, again, to less work. It also leads to less opportunity to refine one's craft, so skills start to stagnate and confidence deteriorates. This leads to – less work. In this way, many women's careers can become so precarious that they simply cannot afford to 'speak up', whether to advocate for better pay or to reject unwanted advances.

Even for those women who manage sustainable careers, the work itself can be problematic. Acting jobs overwhelmingly push women into sexually objectified and stereotyped roles, where they are often the victims of violence – and rarely have professional status. (For example, the BFI reports that, although women make up 52% of GPs in the UK, only 15% of on-screen doctors are women. On the other hand, women make up 94% of on-screen prostitutes.[7])

This gives our young people a skewed perception of what to expect from the world, and reinforces the fact that a woman's sexuality ultimately determines her (box office) value. It teaches our aspiring film- and theatre-makers that the stories worth telling are men's stories, which results in more work for men – and the cycle repeats itself.

Encouragingly, there are more and more exceptions to this kind of programming, and every day companies are making commitments towards shifting the paradigm. Indeed, if we truly want to eliminate sexual harassment *as a condition of work*, then the content of our work – and the content-makers – will have to change.

Navigating the grey area

In the meantime, we are suspended between the old industry and a hopeful but as-yet-unrealised one. So, what can we do?

Get involved. Campaigns like ERA 50:50, Time's Up UK, and Act for Change are all doing exciting, proactive work to change the landscape of the industry.

Be proud and professional. We can often feel so relieved to be employed that we put up with things which are deeply unprofessional. It can be frightening to say 'no', whether in the context of turning down underpaid work or unwelcome advances. But we must remember that we are professionals and expect to be treated professionally, with respect and dignity. This means:

Don't work for free. Unless there's a really good reason (i.e. we've written a solo show for ourselves or are doing our best friend a favour), we should insist on being paid for our work – like professionals in any other industry. It is *illegal* to employ people for less than the minimum wage: we are likely to be much more vulnerable in projects which have already engaged us on dubious terms.

Know your rights. It is essential to understand our contracts so that we know what we are agreeing to – in everything from working hours to nudity. We should also know what can and *cannot* be required of us in an audition.[8] If we have questions about a contract, we can call Equity to talk us through it.

Talk about it. Having a conversation with our colleagues to set down expectations and parameters before starting intimate work can be enormously freeing and reassuring. It allows us to navigate sensitive work by making conscious choices, rather than resorting to unexamined, automatic ones.

Be clear about boundaries. In our industry, where the line between fiction and reality sometimes blurs, there will be inevitable moments of ambiguity, even discomfort. It is important to recognise within ourselves when we are uncomfortable versus when we are *unsafe*, when we are willing to push our boundaries and what consists of a violation of those boundaries.

Know where to go for help. If something untoward does happen, contact Equity immediately (main switchboard: 020-7379 6000, harassment/bullying helpline: 020-7670 0268) or, if needed, the police. Anyone you work for has a duty of care, but if you don't feel able to talk to someone in the company, remember that your venue is also responsible for your well-being and approach someone in the building. There are more avenues for support and intervention than we might think.

Don't be a bystander. If you see something inappropriate happening, report it.

Remember, it's up to all of us. Men are also subjected to sexual harassment and assault, and are as straight-jacketed as women by gender stereotypes. Our industry leaves almost no place for our trans and non-binary colleagues. The work towards gender equality is everyone's work, and benefits everyone. But we must be sensitive to each other's experiences along the way, and be compassionate with each other when we fail.

Join Equity. The performing arts union, Equity, is our professional safety net. Not only can they provide support in situations of harassment or bullying (including legal support), they can answer contract questions, protect us on vulnerable jobs, and make sure we're paid correctly. Equity also negotiates the terms of our contracts with the industry's biggest employers and campaigns for equal and diverse representation across the performing arts. The more of us are part of the union, the stronger it is and the better supported we are. It is our industry family.

Lastly:

Let's make the work we want to see. We can start changing the industry *by changing the industry*. Write new stories, work with people who excite you, find ways to be nourished by the work you do.

There's no going back from #metoo now. If we insist on parity and respect – and if we make a commitment to looking after one another – we have the chance to turn our industry into something infinitely richer than the one we've inherited.

See you out there.

[1] www.theguardian.com/world/2017/oct/20/women-worldwide-use-hashtag-metoo-against-sexual-harassment
[2] https://seejane.org/research-informs-empowers
[3] https://seejane.org/symposiums-on-gender-in-media/gender-bias-without-borders
[4] https://stephenfollows.com/gender-of-film-crews
[5] https://writersguild.org.uk/women-shut-out-of-top-screenwriting-jobs-for-over-10-years
[6] www.thestage.co.uk/opinion/2018/sphinx-theatres-sue-parrish-we-must-break-down-barriers-to-gender-parity
[7] www.bfi.org.uk/news-opinion/news-bfi/announcements/bfi-filmography-complete-story-uk-film
[8] For example, the Equality Act states that one should not be asked about age, gender, ethnicity, disability, pregnancy, health or other 'protected characteristics'. Nor should you be asked to undress to any extent without warning and without a mutually agreed third party present. For more information, visit **www.equity.org.uk/getting-involved/campaigns/manifesto-for-casting** or call 0207 379 6000.

Kelly Burke is an actor, singer and writer. She trained at RADA and is Chair of Equity's Women's Committee, an Equity councillor, and part of the team that drafted the union's Agenda for Change. **www.kellyburke.com**

Spotlight, casting directories and information services

Spotlight is a fundamental part of the fabric of the acting profession and it is essential to have an entry. (It is a false economy not to have one.) The growth of the Internet has seen a rise in companies offering similar services – usually for a lower subscription. Once again it is important to research thoroughly the value to you of investing in one of these. As well as trying to assess whether such an investment will really enhance your visibility to employers, an essential part of that research is to read the 'small print' properly.

With some exceptions (major musicals, for instance), many employers do not openly advertise the properly paid acting work they have to offer. It's simpler to contact agents whom they know and trust for casting suggestions. This limits the number of submissions, largely prevents time-wasting via unsuitable applicants, and goes some way towards ensuring that those suggested for consideration are really suitable for the parts available. Consequently, the time required to consider all the CVs and photographs submitted is contained within reasonable limits. It can take a day's work to go through a thousand submissions to select whom to interview; it can take another day's work to interview just 30 of these.

Casting information services – often allied to Internet casting directories – glean their information from all kinds of sources. The important thing to remember is that some of the information about 'properly paid acting work' is of a second-hand nature – that is, it was not sent directly to them in the first instance. Consequently, it is important to research reputations for accuracy (and 'up-to-dateness') before committing your funds to such companies. However, many Fringe production and student film opportunities are directly advertised in such publications and such opportunities might lead on to 'properly paid acting work'.

Actors Centre

1A Tower Street, London WC2H 9NP
tel 020 3841 6600
email reception@actorscentre.co.uk
website www.actorscentre.co.uk
Facebook www.facebook.com/TheActorsCentre
Twitter @TheActorsCentre
Instagram theactorscentre
General Manager Amanda Davey

Details of casting information services: Founded in 1978, the Actors Centre runs workshops and courses from its venue in the heart of the West End. The Centre boasts five studios, a Green Room Cafe and Bar, and incorporates the Tristan Bates Theatre. With established links within the industry, it offers opportunities to network with other actors and industry professionals. The Centre also runs workshops and courses for non-members, programmed throughout the year and on a bespoke basis. Please see website for more information.

ArtsJobs

website www.artsjobs.org.uk

Freely advertises a range of opportunities within the arts sector, including positions that require specialist knowledge and skills, and unskilled positions at arts organisations.

Castcall

106 Wilsden Avenue, Luton LU1 SHR
tel 01582 456213
email info@castcall.co.uk
website www.castcall.co.uk

Details of casting information services: Established in 1986. The service is available by email, to professional actors with regular updates throughout the week. Charges from £10 per month. Actors can put subscriptions on hold if required and to resume when appropriate. Also offers general advice and free image scanning.

Sources of casting breakdowns include: Crocodile Casting, Mark Summers, Pippa Ailion, Heather

March, Hannah Birkett, Sharon Lawrence, Tree Petts, Nicci Topping, Beverley Keogh, Debbie O'Brien, David Graham, Louise Kiely, Belinda King, Natasha Gane and many production companies in theatre, video, film and TV.

Casting Networks
website www.castingnetworks.co.uk

Details of casting information services: Casting Networks is one of the biggest casting websites in the USA, but has only recently opened up in the UK. Like others, it offers casting professionals a means to distribute breakdowns and receive submissions, but Casting Networks also provides a very different suite of tools for streamlining, simplifying and facilitating the subsequent casting process: straightforward actor check-in; integration of audition video-recording into online casting tools; software for handling the scheduling and arranging of auditions – these are just a few examples.

Casting Networks is a commitment-free site, where actors have the choice to pay if and when they find value in the services on offer – this equates to no mandatory yearly upfront payment. If and when you choose to pay, payments are made monthly and operate as various ad-ons. The Media Hosting ad-on, for example, allows you to add, delete and update your videos as much as you wish. Anything you upload can also be attached to your CV, meaning you or your agent can tailor your CV for a job in just a few clicks.

"Casting Networks continuously improves the casting process through the application of innovative solutions, cutting-edge technologies, and superior customer support, making a career in the entertainment and advertising industries more efficient, accessible, and fun for everyone involved."

CastNet Ltd
tel 0333 800 0250 (local rate)
email admin@castnet.co.uk
website www.castnet.co.uk
Twitter @CastNetLtd
Key contact Fran Gillett

Details of casting information services: Established in 1997. The information service is only available online, with casting information circulated to members by email and uploaded to the website throughout the day. Casting information is tailored to the exact requirements of the actor; if an actor is not interested in working in certain areas, such as student films or TIE, they will not be sent details of those projects. Information is also filtered according to the skills and physical characteristics of actors. When suitable casting opportunities do arise, CastNet will send actors free text messages and emails. Actors may make a submission for any project via the website; CastNet will then send their CV, headshot and a covering letter to the casting director.

All reproductions of photos and postage costs are included in the subscription charge. Sends a weekly summary report by email, detailing every production for which actors have been submitted. CastNet receives casting breakdowns from a range of clients including Fringe theatre, mainstream films and TV.

Details of actors' Internet directories: All actors must meet the following criteria to be included: have graduated from an NCDT (now Drama UK) accredited course; have a minimum of 3 professional theatre, film or acting credits (does not include extra or drama school work); be able to use 1 UK-based accent to a 'native' standard; have full membership of Equity (or be eligible); have a professionally taken publicity photograph; and be at least 18 years old at the time of application.

Admits new members daily. CastNet has more than 4,000 casting professionals registered on the site, and supports the casting of around 2,500 productions each year. Actors' CVs are included on the website, with instant messaging facility for casting directors to contact them by email or text message. Will also include photos, showreels and voicereels at no extra charge. All members receive a free personal website which they can tailor to their own needs and preferences, from a wide range of designs and styles. Anyone can access the online directory. Members' online details are updated daily. For details of current clients (both actors and casting professionals), consult the website.

The weekly subscription rate varies depending on the pricing plan selected and includes all the services listed above.

See also the entry for CastNet Websites under *Showreel, voicereel and website services* on page 416.

Castweb
7 St Luke's Avenue, London SW4 7LG
tel 020 7720 9002
email info@castweb.co.uk
website www.castweb.co.uk
Key contact Patrick Warrington

Details of casting information services: Established in 1999. A daily information service is available online, with casting breakdowns circulated to subscribers throughout the day. Subscription starts at £19.95 per month. Castweb has circulated casting opportunities for over 3,000 production companies and casting directors and subscription is strictly for the use of professional actors and established agents only. It is now received by more than 1,000 agents across Europe, as well as over 400 in the UK. At just 44p per day, it remains the essential source of casting opportunities for professional performers and agents in the UK.

Dramanic
website www.dramanic.com

Dramanic, developed in 2009, is an online resource for professional actors only, helping them find work opportunities at theatre companies in London and other major towns and cities throughout the UK. "Anyone new to the business will find that keeping tabs on different theatre companies is challenging and time-consuming, and marrying that with your normal lives leaves you no time to effectively find acting work. Dramanic takes all the hassle out of that by alerting you when opportunities arise at the hundreds of theatre companies in our system. We cover a huge variety of theatre companies, big and small, touring and non-touring, and arts council – or otherwise – funded companies. The good news for actors is that such companies would usually pay Equity/ITC minimum wages."

Other features include:

• Casting calendar – know what theatre companies are casting well in advance
• Theatre company research profiles, giving you up-to-date information about company personnel and actor-relevant news
• Contact details of UK actor agents, personal managers and casting directors updated throughout the year
• Swap plays/books with other dramanic.com users
• Look for casual employment in between acting jobs

Equity Job Information Service (JIS)
Guild House, Upper St Martin's Lane,
London WC2H 9EG
website www.equity.org.uk
Facebook www.facebook.com/EquityUK
Twitter @EquityUK

Details of casting information services: It is available free of charge to all full Equity members. The service provides details of job opportunities in the wide range of fields in which Equity members work. Users of the service can search for jobs in acting, singing, dance, variety, light entertainment and circus and in non-performance work such as stage management. All the work listed is at least reasonably paid (although not necessarily at full Equity-agreed rates), thoroughly checked for accuracy and the job-providers checked for their record of fair treatment of employees.

Internet Movie Database (IMDb)
website www.imdb.com

This is not just a comprehensive database of film and television around the world, but also an opportunity for actors to post their photos and CVs ('resumés') for a fee (currently, $15.95 per month) if they have a profile of work listed there. Once you've subscribed, you also have access to a huge international contact database of people and companies, and the facility to track film and television projects from development to post-production.

The Mandy Network
Angel House, Angel Mews, Islington,
London N1 9HH

tel 020 7288 7404
email emails@mandy.com
website www.mandy.com

Details of casting information services: Formerly Casting Call Pro and established in 2004, The Mandy Network is one of the world's leading casting directories, designed with the actor in mind. Featuring over 70,000 professional members in the UK alone, the site is updated daily with a wide range of casting breakdowns including film roles, theatre tours, corporate work and commercials. Mandy also provides a wealth of resources for actors, including a directory of photographers, agents and guides. Additional services include a lively forum, news service and free surgeries with top casting directors. All members have an entirely free profile in the online directory, which is used by thousands of employers and casting directors. Additionally, Mandy offers a Premium Service with a wider range of features. The Mandy Network also includes services for dancers, singers, musicians and voice over artists. To discover more about the benefits of using Mandy as well as current subscription rates and latest updates to the service, please visit the website at **www.mandy.com**.

Shooting People
email contact@shootingpeople.org
website www.shootingpeople.org
Co-founders Cath LeCouteur, Jess Search *Casting Editor* Andrew Robertson

Shooting People allows thousands of people working in independent film to exchange information via a range of daily email bulletins, including a daily UK Casting Bulletin. This allows actors to discuss their craft and receive casting calls from directors, producers and casting directors. Shooting People's overall membership is currently more than 38,000. Actors can create a public casting profile as well as getting significant discounts off key film products and services.

Full membership costs £35 per year and entitles users to a range of other services. See entry under *Publications, libraries, references and booksellers* on page 455 for further details.

Spotlight
Head Office, 7 Leicester Place, London WC2H 7RJ
tel 020 7437 7631 *fax* 020 7437 5881
email info@spotlight.com
website www.spotlight.com

Spotlight was founded in 1927 and has since become world-famous for its casting directories. Today more than 30,000 performers appear in the book and Internet versions of Spotlight, including actors and actresses, child artists, presenters, dancers and stunt artists. As the industry's leading casting resource, Spotlight is used by TV, film, radio and theatrical companies throughout the UK, and many worldwide.

Its Internet casting services have become an essential communication tool, uniting actors, agents and production professionals more quickly and easily than ever before.

Membership of Spotlight means that a performer is promoted to casting opportunities in a number of ways. Firstly, each artist has a photo and contact details in the Spotlight Directories, which are printed once per year. Their details are also held on an Artists' Records telephone database, so that casting/production professionals know immediately where to call when they want to get in touch.

Additionally, every performer is promoted on Spotlight Interactive (**www.spotlight.com**) – the online version of Spotlight. Here, casting professionals can search performers' details according to very specific criteria. For example: "Show me all actors with black hair, aged 35-40, who can speak French and play the guitar." In 2006, the Spotlight website received over 1 million artist searches, and actor CVs were viewed a total of 5,753,312 times.

Performers can upload showreels, voice-clips and additional photos to enhance their online CVs, which is a far quicker and more cost-effective way of promoting themselves than sending out endless copies to casting directors and agents in the post. Artists are also issued with a pair of unique PIN numbers which allow them to access their CV whenever they wish – keeping credits and skills up-to-date – and to email a link to their Spotlight CV to others.

Spotlight is also used on a daily basis by production professionals sending out casting briefs to agents. In 2006, a weekly average of 160 casting breakdowns was sent out via Spotlight link, with more than 33,370 artists submitted weekly for an average of 541 individual roles, spanning a wide variety of TV, film, theatre, radio and commercial work. This makes Spotlight by far the busiest casting service in the UK. Spotlight also offers a job information service which goes directly to artists themselves: see the website for the latest details.

Spotlight also publishes *Contacts* every November. This is a directory of companies and individuals working across TV, film, stage and radio.

To join Spotlight, visit the website **www.spotlight.com**, call 020-7437 7631, or email **info@spotlight.com** for application forms. Entry is strictly limited to professionally trained and/or professionally experienced performers, and applications are always vetted.

The Stage

47 Bermondsey Street, London SE1 3XT
tel 020 7403 1818 01858 438895 (Subscriptions)
email newsdesk@thestage.co.uk
website www.thestage.co.uk
Managing Director Hugh Comerford *Acting Editor* Alistair Smith

Online and weekly print publication for the entertainment industry. Established in 1880. Advice, news, reviews, features and recruitment for theatre, entertainment, opera, dance, TV, radio, backstage and technical, management, education and training. *The Stage* is also available on iPad, Android, Kindle and other tablet devices. *The Stage* Castings, the company's online casting service (**www.thestage.co.uk/castings**), offers access to hundreds of jobs for all kinds of performers.

Talent Circle

website www.talentcircle.org

Details of casting information services: Established in 2003. Provides a free online casting information service and resource where emails are circulated to members on a daily basis.

Details of actors' Internet directories: Directory is open to all actors free of charge and is publicly accessible. Casting directors can select level of experience required at sign-up, as no minimum criteria are demanded of members. Members can update their own entry (to include photograph, voice sample and CV) at any time.

To Be Seen

website www.tobeseen.co.uk

To Be Seen is an online community for the entertainment industry, with 2 membership options:

• Basic (free): a unique web page for your photos and showreel
• Premium (£5.99, £6.99 or £7.99 per month): the benefits of a Basic membership, plus the facility to apply for as many jobs as you like and be searchable in the directory

There are no set-up fees or extra hidden charges; you can stay a member as long as you like, upgrading or downgrading your account at any time.

'Point me in the right direction': navigating the casting services

Isabelle Farah

The hardest battle for an actor has and will always be 'where do I find my next job?' Different services will suit different actors. Some gear themselves more to certain media and some cover all areas with varying degrees of success. My advice, seven years into a career, is to work out what you want from your subscription – is it to make your living exclusively from performing if that includes corporate work, children's parties, etc., or are you looking to expand/improve your show-reel? Do you only want to work in theatre? I hope that this can provide you with some insight as to which might be best for you.

There's no denying that Spotlight is the market leader and has been forever. It's expensive and can feel (particularly if you don't have an agent) like a lot of money with little (or no) payback, but I believe that you cannot be an actor without it. In the US, there is no one market leader and actors are required to pay for several similar services, so while this situation is not ideal, it's definitely not the worst!

It is important to remember that this is your profession, the craft by which you want to make your living. While you may have to accept you have to make money doing something else in between acting jobs and are not going to be employed by Stephen Spielberg straight after graduating from drama school, if you are paying for a casting service, you should expect to get work from it. Ideally paid in cold, hard cash, rather than lukewarm exposure.

The best bit of advice about the services is to be astute about them. Keep an eye on what you're spending (particularly in direct debits) and which services are working for you. Is the cost of the service with the time spent going through it as productive as, say, making your own work, writing a carefully considered letter to a casting director or director you wish to work with or doing a workshop once a month? I believe connections made in person are much stronger than any application via a casting service.

It's worth noting that many will advertise that they have had high-profile work cast through them, but these, with some exceptions, will be the ones that require more niche skills (languages, musical skills, etc.) and will likely be on Spotlight as well.

Many of these services have other features included in the cost, but I have looked solely at their capacity as a casting resource.

Backstage

Cost: £14.95/month

An import from the US, Backstage has been around for a long time and the website is easy to use and navigate. At the time of writing it is offering six months free to new members (don't forget to cancel though if you're not going to continue). There's currently not a lot going through here that isn't elsewhere, but that may change.

Casting Networks
Cost: Registration fee: £10, £5/month for 'Pro Subscription' thereafter
Casting Networks is another import from the US which arrived with a lot of hype a few years ago. Some breakdowns appear here from certain casting directors, commercials and short films most often, though generally not exclusive to Casting Networks. The only advantage to a Pro Subscription appears to be the extra media storage.

Dramanic
Cost: 1 month £11.99; 3 months £34.99 (+1 month); 6 months £54.99 (+2 months); 12 months £99.99 (+3 months)
Rather than advertising jobs as and when casting directors list them, Dramanic gives you as many details as they have about upcoming theatre projects soon after they have been announced. Dramanic takes out a lot of the research hassle involved in writing letters but, as a letter will almost always be needed, is no quick fix solution to getting a job. Most of the work is in theatre, including some regional touring with small but well-known companies as well as the mainstream West End/Off-West End stuff. All jobs I saw had some payment and many looked like they were offering Equity/ITC rates. If your focus is theatre and you don't have an agent, then this comes highly recommended.

Equity
Cost: included in your Equity subscription
Equity's hook here is that all work is paid and in theory you pay your subscription for more than just the jobs board. The work tends to be teaching rather than performing so worth checking if that's what you're after to see you through a month.

IMDb
Costs: $179/year
There are breakdowns here, but not many and usually low/no pay; on the flip side, they tend to be very high quality (the film makers are required to be members themselves, and I don't think you'd bother until you're quite serious). It's not one I'd pay for simply for the breakdowns, but if you reach a point where you think it's useful (when I was in a co-op we'd use it for general research and I found it invaluable as an agent) then it can be worth looking through what's available there.

Mandy
Cost: £20.40/month or £156/year if you want access to paid jobs
Now an amalgamation of the old Mandy and Casting Call Pro, Mandy.com is a stalwart service. The site displays numerous castings. There are some good paid jobs and plenty of unpaid opportunities, including interesting small-scale tours, commercial work, short films and voiceovers. The jobs here are not going to make you a household name, but you can make money from lower-profile jobs and build your CV without an agent using it. Some of the more 'niche' roles in big productions are regularly advertised on here. The premium service includes workshop opportunities, agent and employer directories, and you can upload several photos and reels.

Shooting People
Cost: £7.95/month, £19.95/3 months, £39.95/year

Resources

Shooting People is great for independent film work. The site itself is user-friendly and clean with social network type tagging features. Most of the work advertised is still low/no pay films, but the advantage is that these jobs tend to only be listed here and the yearly subscription rate is good value (there are also often discounts floating around the internet).

Spotlight
Cost: £154/year
Spotlight is where the breakdowns are. I don't think any other service gets as many or from as wide a pool of good casting directors through their sites, let alone exclusive to their sites. Many features (search functions on the Link board, etc.) are not available to actors. Agents see significantly more than you but don't be fooled into thinking there is nothing there. With some pushing, Spotlight will change things that need to be changed. If you want to be in something, it's probably cast here, and your chance of making your money back is far higher here than anywhere else. Make sure your profile is up to date with your skills as casting directors search on here first.

The Stage
Cost: £9/month or £84/year for The Stage Castings; £11/month or £99/year for The Stage Castings and a newspaper subscription
At the time of writing, The Stage is nearly ready to relaunch the casting section of their website. It looks like it will be very easy to use and offer both paid and unpaid jobs. It will also act as a directory for performers, though you will have to link to media hosted on other websites rather than what is uploaded here. Pricing is competitive. They say their target market is actors looking to build their CVs and show-reels at the beginning of their careers or branch into new media.

To Be Seen
Cost: £5.99/month billed £35.94 every 6 months; £6.99/month billed £20.97 every 3 months; £9.99/month billed £9.99 monthly
There are things here, generally corporate or low/no budget films, which aren't available elsewhere.

Work in Europe
Currently, London is where many commercials for Europe are cast and also where many European actors choose to base themselves. There's no denying that it's the industry hub of Europe. This may change over the next year or two, particularly if it is made more difficult for EU nationals to work here or for those with British passports to work in the EU. These two may be useful for anyone who can, does or wants to work in other markets.

enCAST
Cost: £8.40/4 weeks; £20.40/12 weeks; £32.50/6 months
This is relatively new to the market. It covers castings across Europe in all languages so it could well be worth using if you speak another language/s to a high-enough standard. There is a high volume of work advertised but it is spread across all of Europe. France, Belgium, Germany and Italy seem to be the largest players. The jobs are often paid, but it's worth bearing in mind that you are applying as a local, so are unlikely to get travel or accommodation expenses. There is some work in the UK advertised here, but it's likely to

be more useful to those who have contacts, bases or interest in building their networks in other countries. You can look at the breakdowns and apply for unpaid work without paying, but must pay to apply for any paid work.

e-TALENTA
Cost: 89€/year
e-TALENTA is another for Europe-based work. The site looks very shiny and is easy to use, but it does not have a huge volume of work coming through their boards. Its main function is as a platform for CVs with show-reels, photos, voice-reels, etc.

Isabelle Farah is an actor, writer, and comedian. She trained as a serious actor at Drama Studio London and after some pratfalls and upstaging, branched into stand up and character comedy. You can find out more about her work by following her @irresponsabelle but preferably not in real life ...

Be prepared for publicity

Jayne Trotman

Congratulations! You get a great job, meet the director, producer, cast members, start work and then someone asks whether you will you do some publicity for the project. What does that really mean and do you have to do it? If you have been asked, then the answer is most probably yes. Publicity plays a vital role in the marketing process of many film, television and theatre projects. Here are some useful tools to help you navigate the publicity process.

What is publicity?

I have worked with many actors and film makers during publicity for film campaigns – some seasoned household names and others entirely new to publicity. Whilst publicity is an exciting, vital part of the job, and can mean travelling around the globe for weeks (sometimes longer) on end to promote a film, it is hard work. It's essential that you are well prepared and take good care of yourself.

I am sure many of you will have seen an actor sitting next to a mounted film poster, answering questions about what it was like working with their co-star on a soon-to-be-released blockbuster film. Or you will have watched that co-star on a chat-show sofa recounting tales of pranks that said actor played on set before a clip from the film is shown and the audience applaud. To get back to basics, that is all part of the publicity campaign and another skill that actors should appreciate, practise and perfect.

Granted your first job may not be a Hollywood blockbuster; it may well be a touring show or fringe theatre production where local newspaper coverage, radio interviews and podcasts will be the key. Whatever the job is, you should be publicity-ready as you may well be newsworthy, and you'll make many a producer very happy if you are already well prepared.

How can I prepare?

When you play a role you will have researched and honed that character well. This is no different. It's you on your best day with stories aplenty, open and interested to be meeting new people for a good chat. If there are any things you are uncomfortable talking about, think about them in advance and have answers to those questions prepared.

It's definitely worth seeking out those you admire when they are on the publicity trail. Watch them on TV shows (both here and in the US, if you can), read interviews with them and listen to what they have to say if you hear them on the radio. Sometimes interviews don't go quite so well. Those pieces are worth watching and reading as much as the successful ones. Think what *you* might have done in that situation.

Being interviewed is a skill that needs to be worked on – it's hard work at times and some people are just better at it than others. But if you spend time preparing and practising, you will become more adept. I urge you to do your research as much as you can in advance.

It's also important to think about how you look. You may be able to roll out of bed for an early film or television call, know you will have time to get ready and might even have people to help you – but that's not always the case on the press side. Make sure that you look your best and always ask in advance what the set-up will be and what you are expected to be wearing etc. In my years working for major film studios, we have had actors turn up for press days in old crumpled t-shirts (albeit their favourite one), having to call flatmates to go through wardrobes for extra clothes to be sent across. Or, on one occasion, the person arrived for their first major press conference and photo-call with the world's media in a tracksuit and top. On that occasion we kept thinking they would get changed any minute but they didn't. Luckily, we had a budget, an experienced team on hand to help and just enough time to dash to a shop for an outfit change. They looked great in the end and were quite brilliant, but it did not help their nerves (or ours!) in the run-up.

Your publicity moments should and can be enjoyable. I promise it will help if you have done the work in advance.

What am I publicising?

Essentially, the play, TV show, film, event you are in or have created. Make sure you ask for and come armed with all the key facts about the project. If you have not been directly asked to do press, it is always good to check (usually with the producer, director or creator) that it's OK for you to be talking publicly about the piece and that all the key people involved in the project are aware.

You are also publicising brand 'you'. You are a business, so – as we touched on above – please make sure you are bringing the best version of you to work that day. You should also take a moment to consider what people can find out about you if they were doing their research. You are probably on social media. If so, and even if you have not been active for a while, what would people think about you if they looked at your posts online? Brand 'you' and a career path as an actor or performer may not have been on the cards when you first posted on social media. As you are coming into the public eye, you need to start thinking what you are communicating on each channel. You may well have decided to spend time and money creating a stylish new website to help you get work and to promote you as an actor and performer. This will be useful and you can control and curate everything on there. You now need to be mindful of everything you post on social media, may have posted in the past and what friends and family post about you. Your website may be great, but you don't necessarily want a journalist to see everything that happened on that fun night in Ibiza from a social media post. Always think before you post.

Can anyone help me?

Yes, always ask questions and seek out help and advice. If you are working on a project and have been asked to do publicity, your company manager, director or producer should be happy to advise. If you have one, then ask your agent. It's likely they will have other clients well-versed in the publicity circuit. You can also speak to one of your tutors from drama school as they may well be able to help and advise you. Fellow cast members can be very useful too and often more than happy to share their experiences. There will always be someone who can help. Don't be afraid to talk to people: you will be amazed what you can find out when you open up and start asking questions.

Publicists

A high-profile element of the publicity campaign is what is known as a 'press junket'. This is a series of print and broadcast interviews with the cast and film makers, often in a hotel (watch that scene with Hugh Grant posing as a journalist from *Horse and Hound* in the film *Notting Hill*). Many actors are often accompanied by a publicist – someone hired by the actor or film maker to help them navigate publicity requests, promote the film and their role as well as other elements of their careers). You may not need a publicist when you are starting out, unless your first role is on a major high-profile project and, in that case, you may be assigned a publicist to help and advise you. My role as part of a studio's publicity team is to work with the publicist and sometimes directly with the actors, to help and advise them during the publicity campaign. You may well be helped through the process by someone like me if you get cast in a high-profile title.

There are so many additional aspects to the role of being an actor or performer and publicity is often one of the unexpected elements. Please enjoy it, don't be afraid to ask questions, do your research and be prepared. We look forward to seeing the results.

A bit about me: I originally trained as an actor and worked across theatre and television for several years. A colleague I had worked with in a touring theatre company called out of the blue one day and asked if I could help in their London office when their whole team were away covering a film festival. I ended up doing this for many years and, from that and through meeting other people in the industry (and often in between acting jobs), worked for many of the studios before joining Warner Bros as a temp in 1997. I joined the team full time as a publicist, was promoted to Director of Publicity and stepped down as Executive Director of Publicity for Warner Bros UK, having successfully overseen the launch of over 400 films almost 20 years later. I now run my own film and entertainment consultancy.

Photographers and repro companies

Good photographs (and quality reproductions of same) are an essential part of an actor's professional armoury and there is absolutely no point in trying to scrimp on them. ('A picture is worth a thousand words.')

Your photograph is a silent, static, two-dimensional representation of vocal, mobile, three-dimensional you. It should be of your head down to your shoulders, reasonably stylish and well produced without necessarily being too glamorous. It should look natural and have life, energy and personality – especially in the eyes, the most important part of your face. Your photo should say, 'Here I am; I know who I am; I'm OK with who I am.' Also, it is very important that your photograph really looks like you when you arrive for interview.

Crucial to the final result is finding a good photographer (a) who understands the world that the end result is intended for and (b) with whom you can work well. In the listings that follow, you'll find a wide range of prices and deals. It is important to research as many of these as possible, without making cost your prime consideration. Ask friends, teachers and your agent (if you have one) for recommendations, and check through *Spotlight* and websites to see samples of work. Read the details under each listing to get a 'feel' for who might produce the 'goods' for you. Once you have a shortlist of possibilities, phone each with appropriate questions (what to wear, studio or natural light, and so forth) in order to get a sense of how well you might be able to work with him/her. Only *after* you've done all this research should cost be a consideration. Even then, a cheap deal could mean that the photographer will spend much less time, and take fewer photographs, than a more expensive one. You might be lucky with the former, but you'll enhance your chances of getting really good results with the latter.

Note: Allow plenty of time for this research. Also, bear in mind that as the deadline for *Spotlight* gets nearer, photographers become increasingly busy and it becomes more difficult to book a session.

APHP following a photographer's name denotes membership of the Association of Professional Headshot Photographers, a non-profit group of the UK's leading casting photographers. Founded in 2016 on principles of education, expertise and excellence, it establishes new, neutral standards of headshot professionalism, offers a path to qualification for photographers, and promotes the highest standards in casting portraiture.

Copyright

Under the Copyright, Designs & Patents Act 1988, the photographer owns the copyright on any new photograph, even though you've already paid for the original. That means that you have to obtain his/her permission to have new photographs reproduced in *Spotlight* or anywhere else. Your photographer may be happy to approve such reproduction, but may not be so happy about any cropping or other alterations: you must get permission if you intend to do this. The other important new legal requirement is that your photographer must be credited on any reproduction of the original. Some of the repro companies are now doing this as a matter of course.

Repros

You could get subsequent, high-quality reproductions done by your photographer or by someone else nominated by him/her. However, these will be expensive. The specialist repro companies can do this significantly more cheaply with minimal loss of quality. Once again, check with others about the quality (and service and reliability) of individual companies before taking costs into consideration. It is also useful to overestimate the number of copies you might need over the lifetime (generally, about two years) of your chosen photograph – because (a) you'll almost always find that you underestimate that number in the first place, and (b) you can take advantage of cheaper unit costs.

Note: It is often preferable to send a 10x8in (25x20cm) photograph for submissions; however, good-quality 'jpegs' (around 400 pixels wide) inserted into your CV are becoming increasingly acceptable. If you're planning to email a CV containing your photograph, make sure that the total document size is not more than about 200kb, or you'll end up clogging up the casting director's mailbox. (Most image-editing software will have a menu option to allow you to reduce the image size if required.)

It is important to check the current charges of each photographer (and repro company) that interests you, as some will change during the lifetime of this edition.

Abacus Photography

38 Drakes Avenue, Devizes, Wilts SN10 5AZ
tel 01380 829943 *mobile* 07966 551909
email nick@abacus-photography.co.uk
website www.abacus-photography.co.uk

Services & rates: Prices start from £75 in a fully equipped studio. Images supplied on disc so you can make your own prints economically, or email them to casting agents. Discounts available for group bookings.

Established in 1992.

Vincent Abbey

6 Lynton Road, Chorlton, Manchester M21 9NQ
tel 0161 860 6794
email vabbey@yahoo.com
website www.vincentabbey.co.uk

Services & rates: Established in 1995. Charges £90 for a photoshoot, which includes approximately 100 shots and 3 touched up images on CD. Additional images are £8 each. Shoots take place at home studio. Has taken publicity photos for over 2,000 actors.

The Actor's One-Stop Shop

2b Dale View Crescent, Chingford, London E4 6PQ
tel 020 8888 7006 07894 152 651
email info@actorsonestopshop.com
website www.actorsone-stopshop.com

Services & rates: Market leaders in showreels both edited from existing material and filmed. Edited from existing material have a flat rate of £140 or £40 per hour when reels are updated. Filmed scenes can be made from just £110 a scene and includes scripts, location, direction and the hire of professional actors opposite. There are a variety of different packages available.

Stuart Allen

mobile 07776 258829
email info@stuartallenphotos.com
website www.stuartallenphotos.com

Services & rates: Charges £150 for a digital photo shoot which includes 360-500+ images, your own website for proof viewing the whole shoot with email links to you and your agent, contact sheets emailed to you as Adobe PDF files, updated contact sheets emailed to you as you narrow down your selection, cost of retouching 4 images, photos prepared for Spotlight, Casting Call Pro and CastNet, images emailed to Spotlight, Casting Call Pro and CastNet (if applicable). Shoot taken in natural light and typically lasts 2-3+ hours. All the images can be in b&w and/or colour. "The photos are captured in uncompressed high resolution 'raw' format so as to give you the best possible quality and maximum control over the final image. This is the digital equivalent of a negative. It is superior to the other smaller and lower quality digital formats."

Film shoots also available at £130 for 2 36exp films and contact sheets. Competitive print service available. Offers full advice on clothing, makeup and hair.

Areas that are covered in the UK for headshots are London, Bath, Bristol, Brighton, Cardiff, Cheltenham, Guilford, Oxford, Warwick and Winchester. If you do not live near one of these cities please check on availability.

Work portfolio: Stuart studied photography at Salisbury College of Art and Design. Since then he has worked in numerous spheres of the entertainment industry, shooting headshots of actors for almost a decade. His work can be seen on his website, Casting Call Pro website and *Contacts*. Please check website for latest prices.

AM-London Photography

2 The People's Hall, 2 Olaf Street, London W11 4BE
mobile 07974 188105
email studio@am-london.com
website www.am-london.com

Services & rates: Offers 3 types of headshot session; please see details below:

• 1.5-hr Actors Headshot Session at £340 inc. VAT. The package includes: 1.5-hour shoot – in the studio and a range of natural light (outdoor) shots. Variety of headshot styles. Full-length/character/commercial shots (optional). 200+ edited images supplied colour and black & white in high res. 6 retouched 10x8in prints
• 1-hour Actors Headshot Session at £270 inc. VAT. The package includes: 1-hour shoot – studio shots and natural light (outdoor) shots. Variety of headshots. 150+ edited headshots supplied colour and black & white in high res. 4 retouched 10x8in prints
• 40-min Actors Headshot Session at £200 inc. VAT. The package includes: 40-min shoot – studio only. Variety of headshots. 100+ edited headshots supplied in colour and black & white in high res. 2 retouched 10x8in prints

"With all sessions we make sure that you get lots of variety. This means using different lighting set-ups, different backdrops and a number of outfit changes. Each individual set-up will be described and discussed with you in detail. This process allows for you to develop natural reactions and expressions to the different set-ups, altering the mood and intensity as we move through them. The longer session allows time for some additional shots that you may need, e.g. full-length or more commercial shots. After the session we send you a link to download all your high res. images in colour and black & white. These are yours to keep. You then get back to us with your selection. These are retouched and printed 10x8in and sent out to you along with your retouched digital files."

Simon Annand
mobile 07884 446776
email simonannand@blueyonder.co.uk
website www.simonannand.com
established 1986

Services and rates: Charges £350 for a photo shoot, which includes approximately 350-400 shots. Concessionary rate of £310 available for students and the unemployed. The whole session on disc is taken away on the day; after the actor chooses 6 images, Simon will make a second disc with these choices fully photoshopped in colour/b&w. High-end digital cameras are used. Photos are usually taken at home studio with natural light, but can be taken outside if preferred – will travel if necessary. Home studio is wheelchair-accessible.

Work portfolio: With 30 years' experience, has taken publicity shots for around 2,500 actors. Clients include: Eddie Redmayne, Claire Foy, Benedict Cumberbatch, Tamla Kari, Dan Stevens, Jane Asher, Vicky McClure and Clemency Burton-Hill. Advises actors: "There is no time-limit for the session; I see one person a day. Please bring 6-8 different tops and previous photos to discuss." Author of *The Half*; has

worked for the NT, RSC and Royal Court amongst many others.

Ric Bacon
30 Fortis Green Road, Muswell Hill,
London N10 3HN
mobile 07970 970799
website www.ricbacon.co.uk

Services & rates: Charges £280 for a photo shoot which includes photographer's fee, processing of 2 b&w 36exps, 6x4in print of every shot (rather than a contact sheet) and all negatives. Offers reduced rates to students. Shoots in a very relaxed manner, in natural light or studio and offers advice on all aspects including clothing and make-up. Prints are ready to view in 1 hour and will be reviewed with the client, offering advice on selection of images for self-promotion if needed. Happy to look at old photographs of the client that they particularly like or dislike. Works with film or digital.

Work portfolio: Established in 1999. Photographs can be viewed on the website and has a comprehensive portfolio at Spotlight's offices. Has taken publicity shots for around 500 actors.

david bailie photography
tel 020 7460 1105
email davidbailie@davidbailie.co.uk
website http://davidbailie.photium.com

Services & rates: Photographer since 2007. Charges £180 (inc. VAT). Quote ACTORS HANDBOOK for 20% discount. Special discount for students. 2-hour shoot consisting of approx. 120 shots with all contacts saved to disc. Each shoot also includes 4 8x10in or A4 prints, with additional ones available at £15 each. Offers this package at a special rate of £145 (inc. VAT) to actors and £95 (inc. VAT) to students. Uses studio in Kensington and outdoor location for shoots. Only the outdoor location is wheelchair accessible.

Work portfolio: Examples of work can be seen on the website. Has taken photographs for many actors, among them Kevin McNally, Nick Bartlett, Mackenzie Crook, Chris Adamson, Dermot Kelly, Katrina Vasiliev and Patricia Merrick. See also YouTube channel www.youtube.com/user/mdebailes/feed?activity_view=3 - search for mdebailes.

Sophie Baker
tel 020 8340 3850
email sophiebaker@totalise.co.uk

Services & rates: A photographer since 1972 initially working in theatre front-of-house – National Theatre, Royal Shakespeare Theatre and many West End shows; no relation to Chris. Rate is £160 for unlimited digital shots and 4 10x8in printed enlargements. Student rates are £100 for solo sitting and £150 for a shared sitting. Photographs taken in natural light in studio overlooking Hampstead Heath and outside in the park.

Resources

Work portfolio: "As a former student at the Central School of Speech and Drama (after the 1st year I realised that 'acting' wasn't for me – I would be happier behind the camera) I am aware of the discomfort and tensions the sitter can feel so I attempt to empathise and look to make the subject feel as comfortable as possible. The sessions are therefore relaxed and tailored to create a calm atmosphere. I have seen many directors and casting agents looking through books of photographs and therefore aim for a 'bright-eyed and bushy-tailed look' but not to over-glamorise. It is important that a portrait photo attracts the eye of the director but it must be an honest reflection of the sitter. I suggest the client has a good night's sleep beforehand and comes with a mixture of tops and necklines. It is not easy to dictate what will work over the phone."

Taken photographs for as many as 14,000 actors, among them Judi Dench, Ian Holm, Nigel Hawthorne, Ben Whitrow, Hugh Bonneville, Jane Horrocks, Rachel Weisz and John Lynch. "As I have been working for over 35 years the list is long. Over a period of 25 years I was also a film stills photographer working with Ken Loach, Stephen Frears, Louis Malle, Denys Arcand, Atom Egoyan to name a few but now prefer working on my own and not at the dictate of crazy film scheduling hours."

Paul Barrass
Unit 6, Ellingfort Road, London E8 3PA
mobile 07973 265931
email paul@paulbarrass.co.uk
website www.paulbarrass.co.uk

Services & rates: Session price is £120. Includes 4 10x8in prints. Special student rate of £100. All photography is digital. Photos can be taken either in the studio or outdoors. All locations have wheelchair access. Images are viewed during the photo session on a monitor. Has photographed in excess of 1,000 actors.

Pete Bartlett Photography APHP
Kindred Studios, Queen's Park, London W9 3HW
mobile 07971 653994
email info@petebartlett.com
website www.petebartlett.com

Services & rates: Photographer since 2004. Charges £250 for photo shoot, which includes 150-200 digital photographs. A student rate of £225 for a shoot is also available. Shoots from amazing studio with natural light.

Work portfolio: Examples of work can be seen on the website. Has taken photographs for around 2,000 actors; recent clients include: Elliot Knight (*Sinbad*), Jeff and Matt Postlethwaite (*Peaky Blinders*), Matt Milne (*Downton Abbey*), Jo Brand (*Getting On*), Ian Hislop (*Have I Got News For You*) plus many of London's top agents such as United Agents, Independent Talent, Troika and Middleweek

Newton. "I give you 100% to get that killer set of headshots. Please check out my website, drop me an email and we can begin the process today."

Helen Bartlett Photography
Based in London
tel 0345 603 1373
email info@helenbartlett.co.uk
website www.helenbartlett.co.uk
Facebook /helenbartlettphotography
Instagram @helenbartlettphotography

Services & rates: "I specialise in black and white portraits that reflect who you are and show you at your very best. Pictures are taken at my Crouch End studio, using a number of different backdrops to provide a variety of looks. Sessions are a fun and enjoyable experience. There is no pressure to 'smile for the camera'; by chatting and enjoying ourselves, the smiles come naturally and, over the course of the shoot, we will capture a variety of different moods in your set of images." Headshot sessions start at £195 which includes the session, a web gallery of images to choose from and 1 high-resolution digital files for your own printing, additional files are available starting at £55 each.

Richard Battye
Birmingham
mobile 07860 824101
email info@riverstudio.co.uk
website www.riverstudio.co.uk

Services & rates: Charges from £95 for a photoshoot, which includes 30-60 shots with the best 5 edited. 10x8in prints are charged at £9 each. Special packages are available, please call to discuss. Digital photography offered at commercial/advertising rates. Shoots take place at the Birmingham studio and locations around the city, most locations are wheelchair accessible.

Work portfolio: Established in 1990. Has taken publicity shots for around 180 actors. Recent clients include: Birmingham Theatre School, self-employed actors, Sharon Foster Productions and Birmingham Royal Ballet.

Jonathan Bean
mobile 07763 814587
email mail@beanphoto.co.uk
website www.beanphoto.co.uk
Editor Instagram: @beanphotog

Services & rates: Established 2004. Offers a digital service only and charges £125 for a photo shoot, which includes a 1 hour shoot, editing, online contact sheet and choice of 3 selected hi-res files or 10x8in prints. Additional prints or files may be purchased. A discounted 10% rate is available to students. Shoots are either outdoors (on location) or indoors at client's home or chosen venue. Wheelchair-accessible rooms can also be hired (for £15).

Work portfolio: Examples of work can be seen on the website. Portfolio includes many actors, writers and musicians, among them Blake Morrison, Andrew Michael Hurley and John Hegley. "My aim is to make you comfortable and relaxed for natural-looking, great portrait photos that show you at your best."

A Beautiful Image Photography & Design (Debal Bagachi)
31 Church Walk, Brentford, Middlesex TW8 8DB
tel 020 8568 2122 *mobile* 07956 861698
email debal@abeautifulimage.com
website www.abeautifulimage.com

Services & rates: Charges £150 for a photo shoot which includes photographer's fee, studio and equipment costs, processing of 2 b&w 36exps, contact sheets and 2 10x8in prints (either hand- or digitally printed). Occasionally offers 10% discount for clients sharing a shoot. Digital photography is also available at the same rate; images can be supplied on CD-ROM. Also able to provide website and print publicity. Advises actors to keep make-up simple for b&w photography and wear unfussy, unpatterned tops with simple necklines.

Work portfolio: Established in 1994. Photographs can be viewed on the website and at Spotlight's offices. Has taken publicity shots for around 50 actors. Recent clients include: Elizabeth Alexander, Patrick Regis, Fiona Marchant and Diane Cracknell.

Misha von Bennigsen Photography
Harberton Road, London N19 3JR
tel 020 7263 8862
email misha@mishaheadshots.com
website www.mishaheadshots.com

Established in 2009. Charges £180 for a photo shoot, which includes unlimited shots. Prints are charged from 77p each. Student price £120. Offers digital photography at the same rates. Photos are taken outdoors, at wheelchair-accessible locations. Has taken publicity shots for around 30 actors. Recent clients include: Abby Leamon, Polly Banwell, Michelle Miller, Howard Corlett, David Loughlin.

Georgina Bolton King
1st Floor Flat, 51 Sherriff Road, West Hampstead, London NW6 2AS
mobile 07780 866082
email georginaboltonking@gmail.com
website www.boltonkingphotography.com

Services & rates: Charges £80 for a photoshoot (digital only), which includes around 150 shots. 10x8in prints are charged extra, at £10 each. 10% discount for actors/students. Shoots take place at a home studio, in the client's home or in an outdoor location which is wheelchair accessible.

Work portfolio: Established in 2010. Has taken publicity photos for 200 actors. For details of recent

clients, please search at **www.castingcallpro.com/uk/psearch.php**. Advises actors: "Wear neutral make-up. Bring a simple black top (preferably V-necked) and a white top."

Nev Brewer Photography
mobile 07967 993458
email nevbrewer@gmail.com
website www.nevbrewerphotography.co.uk
Instagram @nevbrewer

Services & rates: Photographer for actors and performers since 2013. Offers several photo shoot packages:

• The Theydon Shoot £175 (3+ hours) — For actors who have no time pressures and want a portfolio of both studio lit and natural light images.
• The Classic "Outdoor" £145 (2+ hour) — For actors who have limited time at their disposal and/or want naturally-lit headshots.
• The Classic "Studio" £145 (2+ hours) — For actors who prefer studio-lit images or for those who want to be less dependent of the vagaries of the weather for their headshot session.

All prices include a relaxed pre-shoot discussion. Contact sheets will be supplied within 24 hours and usually 2 to 3 hours after the shoot. Retouched images are supplied in both colour and b&w within a week. These will be in web-ready and print-ready formats. The Theydon Shoot includes up to 300 shots with 4 retouches, The Classic options include up to 200 shots and 3 retouches. Additional images can be retouched at £15 per image. Discounts are available to students. Call or visit the website for more details. The Theydon Shoot includes a studio shoot and natural light shots taken on the local village green.

Work portfolio: Examples of work can be seen on the website. Has taken photographs for around 70 actors to date, among them Paul Beech, Grace Cookey-Gam and Alex Freeborn. "Prior to the headshot session I send out information with recommendations on how best to prepare for the session, what clothing to bring etc. I work hard to ensure that every actor gets a range of great headshots and has a really enjoyable experience."

Marc Broussely
South West London
mobile 07738 920225
email info@10x8headshots.com
website www.10x8headshots.com

Services & rates: Established in 2008. Charges £180 for a photo shoot at home studio: this includes 4 retouched shots and the whole session delivered in high-res. digital files. Optional 10x8in prints are extra at £20 each. Student price is £160.

Sheila Burnett
email sheila@sheilaburnett.com
website www.sheilaburnett-photography.com

website www.sheilaburnett-headshots.com

Services & rates: Charges between £200 and £280 for a photo shoot. Includes 100 colour proofs plus 4-6 highly finished hi res images. Your chosen finished high res images are sent to by WeTransfer. Sessions take place in my home studio and nearby communal gardens. Works with up to 250 actors a year; clients have included Imelda Staunton, Catherine Tate, David Soul, Paul Freeman, Jon Culshaw, Simon Pegg, Anita Harris, Jackie Clune, Caroline Quentin, Jim Carter and Helen Lederer.

APHP approved.

"Appointments can be made either online or by phone. I always advise on what is good to bring with you on the day. You will find a map and travel details on my headshot website. I'm only 20 mins from the West End on the Bakerloo Line, and 30 mins by bus route 6, 414, 16 and 98. I'm open to any questions and happy to have a chat about what it is you want to achieve. My sessions always start with a 10-minute warm-up, everyone has a good side and this gives me the time to find it. Working indoors makes it possible for you to freshen up upon arrival and to change outfits, apply make-up etc., and, for the boys, to shave mid-session if you want. We don't have to cancel if weather is bad as indoors is always available. I have had over 25 years' experience in the industry shooting actors' headshots and theatre productions. Photos are available for you to view in the camera before you go and the proofs are sent to you via email next day. My goal is to make sure you have vibrant natural headshots that stand out from the crowd" Visit the website for further details.

Will C

Pygar Cottage, 31 Oxford Street, Exning, Newmarket, Suffolk CB8 7EW
tel 01638 577535 *mobile* 07712 669953
email billy_snapper@hotmail.com
website www.specialelitepicturelibrary.com
website www.theukphotographerexhibition.co.uk
website www.billysnapper.com

Services & rates: Established in 1968. £160 includes 80 colour, 80 b&w and 2 high-res. CDs with all photos at 14 million pixels, delivered to the client in the studio. All photos are seen at the moment of taking on a large screen. Make-up and hair can be provided in full attendance for the whole photo session for £80. Prints are obtained from an independent printer for £5 (b&w) and £7 (colour). Majority of photos taken in studio (home studio), other location prices are available on request. No wheelchair access to studio.

Work portfolio: Has photographed approximately 6,500 performers, including Dame Judi Dench, Will Young, Charles Dance. Advice: "Neutral colours for clothes, no patterns, simplicity."

Charlie Carter APHP

mobile 07989 389493
email charlie@charliecarter.com
website www.charliecarter.com

Services & rates: Established in 1998. Digital – colour and b&w. Charges £425 for 4.5 hour sessions, tailoring images specifically to you and your casting. Allows plenty of time for many changes of clothing, shaving and reviewing images as the shoot progresses. The shoot includes a web gallery and 4 Spotlight-ready and large file jpegs. Sessions are in a home studio on the 2nd floor, so not wheelchair-accessible.

Work portfolio: Examples of work can be viewed on my website, www.charliecarter.com, my Charlie Carter Photography Facebook page and at Spotlight's offices. Clients include: Kenneth Branagh, Simon Russell Beale, Philip Franks Tom Hollander, Roger Allam, Emily Blunt, Isla Blair, Jemma Redgrave, Jamie Glover, Tom Mison, Cush Jumbo, Chloe Pirrie, Sarah MacRae, Eve Best, Harry Enfield, Eleanor Bron, Martin Shaw, Joanna Van der Ham, Kerry Condon, Jasmine Hyde, Paul McEwan, Serena Evans and Charlie Condou – as well as agents The Artists Partnership, The Richard Stone Partnership, Rebecca Blond Associates, Conway van Gelder Grant, Independent, United, Markham & Froggatt and many others.

"However lovely a photograph is, it has to work. It has to look like you *and* be accurate to your casting - somehow tell the casting directors who to expect will walk through your door. The way I work is totally collaborative – we talk about your casting and what your range is. We look at how you see yourself. We do it together. I suggest you prepare for it as you would for a significant interview by making sure yo do what is necessary to look and feel your best."

Andrew Chapman

198 Western Road, Sheffield S10 1LF
tel 0114 266 3579 *mobile* 07779 861921
email andrew@chapmanphotographer.eclipse.co.uk
website www.andrewsphotos.co.uk

Services & rates: Charges from £125 for a photo shoot, which includes all photography and computer labour charges, studio and equipment costs. The session includes 100+ photos, b&w and/or colour) which are transferred to the computer; you may select any or all images and these are written to a CD for you to take away for immediate use. Prints and contacts are available (e.g. a 10x8in is £15) if required, but in most cases images are emailed directly to Spotlight and for repros. Also gives clients a 'release note' so that photos can be used for PR, repros, agents, Spotlight etc.

Black and bright colours work well in b&w, and higher necklines are usually better than low: "I always advise people on an individual basis. Ideally, allow about 2 hours for the session."

Work portfolio: Has more than 3,500 actors on database as well as singers, dancers, models, martial artists and others. Clients are from agents across the country; they include: Philippa Howell, Sharron Ashcroft, Jane Hollowood, Liberty Management,

David Daly, Direct Line and Act One. "Qualified member of BIPP, SWPP, BPPA with over 25 years' experience."

John Clark Photo Digital APHP
tel 020 8854 4069
email info@johnclarkphotography.com
website www.johnclarkphotography.com

Services & rates: Charges £145 per hour for digital photography.

Work portfolio: Established in 1982. Photographs and advice can be found on the website. Has taken publicity shots for around 500-600 actors. Recent clients include: actors represented by Roger Carey Associates, Collis Management, Crawfords, Rossmore and Langford Associates.

John Cooper Photography
Unit 2, Kelvin Trading Estate, Eastvale Place, Yorkhill, Glasgow
mobile 07803 929091
email studio@johncooperphotography.com
website www.johncooperphotography.com
Facebook @johncooperphotography
Twitter @jcooperphoto

Services & rates: Offers 2 packages at £210 and £280 (all photography is digital). Fee includes 4 or 8 shots, depending on the package, with a 10x8in print of each selected image. Can offer student discount for multiple bookings. Shoots take place at own studio.

Work portfolio: Established in 2005. Has taken publicity photos for hundreds of actors. Recent clients include: Duncan Lacroix (*Outlander*), Grant O'Rourke (*Outlander*), Billy Boyd (*Lord of the Rings Trilogy*), Jordan Young (BBC *River City*), Keira Lucchesi (BBC *River City*), Scottish Opera (emerging artists), Jean-Luc Picard (Assoc. Conductor RSNO), Greg Esplin (In Your Face Theatre, *Trainspotting*),Mark Cox (BBC's *Chewin' The Fat* and *Still Game*), Katrina Bryan (*Taggart* and Children's BBC), Des Clarke (SMTV Live and Capital Radio), Pamela Byrne (BBC River City), Claire Knight (BBC River City). Advises actors: "I think a lot of actors' headshots are very intense and serious looking – because it's easy to do. I help my clients produce contemporary publicity images, with energy and personality, which really improves their casting opportunities."

James Davies Photography
London
mobile 07716 515170
email mail@jamesdaviesheadshots.com
website www.jamesdaviesheadshots.com

Services & rates: Charges £200 for a photoshoot (£165 student rate; special package for those quoting *Actors' and Performers' Yearbook*). Fee includes unlimited shots with no time limit, plus 3 high-res., retouched 10x8in images on a CD. All sessions are

digital. Shoots take place in a studio, and at a private outdoor location which is wheelchair accessible.

Work portfolio: Established in 2007. Has taken publicity photos for around 200 actors. Recent clients include: Jenny Eclair, Amy Lennox, Melissa Suffield, Lauren Samuels, Stephanie Fearon and Robert O'Neil. "I take headshots alongside a career as an agent with a busy theatrical agency. I deal with actors and actresses, as well as casting directors on a daily basis and know exactly what they look for in a headshot."

Nicholas Dawkes Photography APHP
London W4
mobile 07787 111997
email studio@nicholasdawkesphotography.co.uk
website www.nicholasdawkesphotography.co.uk
Facebook @nicholasdawkesphoto
Editor Instagram: @nicholasdawesphotography

Services & rates: Prices start at £305 for headshots. Includes a full consultation, 2-3 hour session in a large fully-equipped studio, shooting in both natural and studio light. Up to 200-300 pictures taken, with full review of images on a large screen. Same-day uploading of images in colour and b&w on private client area, with email links to the client and their agent. Retouching 4 images included in price.

"The aim of my shoots is to show life and character in your headshots through one-to-one direction and explore and capture your different casting brackets."

DF: Photographer/arc172 Ltd
Studio 33, North 6 Flr, New England House, New England Street, Brighton BN1 4GH
mobile 07958 272333
email david@arc172.com
website www.arc172.com (videos: www.youtube.com/arc172tv photos: www.arc172.zenfolio.com)
Photographer David Fernandes

Has worked as a photographer since 1995 and has taken photographs for roughly 500 actors. Charges £85 for a photo shoot including 2 10x8in prints, shooting digitally. Special 'shared sitting' rates are available to students. Works in a studio, outdoors or in the client's home. Shoots and edits actors' showreels; please phone for prices. The studio is not wheelchair-accessible. Advises clients to "bring a selection of tops with different necklines. Not too 'fussy'. A black top always works well".

Sean Ellis
5 Meadow Road, Claygate, Esher, Surrey KT10 0RZ
mobile 07702 381258
email sean@seanellis.co.uk
website www.seanellis.co.uk

Services & rates: Photographer since 1986. Charges £150 for a 2-3-hour photo shoot including 200 shots. All images will be supplied on disc or via email in low-res. format from which 3 can be chosen to be enhanced/retouched and supplied in high-res. digital format. Additional images will be charged at £25 per image. Bespoke 10x8in prints can be supplied at £30 per print. If a large print run is required, this can be arranged at a more economical price. Sean uses a purpose-built studio at his home.

Work portfolio: Examples of work can be seen on the website. Has taken photographs for hundreds of actors, almost all of them have have been for the Buttercup Agency website and their Spotlight entries. "Bring your upbeat, positive self with a clear idea of what you want and we'll do the rest together!"

Elliott Franks Photography Services
mobile 07802 537220
email elliottfrankse@gmail.com
website www.elliottfranks.com

Services & rates: Charges £100 for a location shoot in the London area.

Work portfolio: Established in 1997. Photographs can be viewed on the web gallery. Has taken publicity shots for more than 800 actors. Elliott Franks is one of the UK's leading performing arts press photographers.

Adrian Gibb
44A Wallbutton Road, Brockley, London SE4 2NX
tel 020 7639 6215
email adriangibb@gmail.com
website www.adriangibb.co.uk

Established in 1995. Specialises in headshots/portraits for actors. Charges actors £100 and students £60 for a photo shoot. Digital photo session includes 100-200 images. Price includes 4 b&w 10x8in prints and a CD disc of images. Works at home in studio and/or garden. Studio is wheelchair accessible. Has taken publicity shots for 60-100 actors, including Tamara Beckwith and Sophie Monk.

Chris Giles
5 Waldron Avenue, Brighton, East Sussex BN1 9EF
mobile 07525 752823
email studio@chrisgilesphotography.com
website http://chrisgilesphotography.com

Services & rates: Charges £50-200 for a photoshoot, depending on number of images. Fee includes 80-180 images, usually shot in medium-format digital. Shoots take place at the studio or in the grounds. Home visits are available at extra cost.

Work portfolio: Has taken publicity shots for around 300 actors. Clients include: Tessa Cushan, Verity L. Jones, Gary Phoenix, Katie Green, Alice Christian and Derek Horsham. Advises actors: "Always try to work with nice people, as they tend to rub off on you."

James Gill
6 Hanover Gardens, London SE11 5TL
tel 020 7735 5632

Services & rates: Charges £85 for a photo shoot which includes photographer's fee, studio and equipment costs, processing of 1 b&w 36exps, contact sheet and 2 10x8in (25x20cm) prints. Increases to £130 for 2 rolls and 4 10x8in prints. Extra 10x8in prints are priced at £12.50 each. Advises actors to keep it simple. Will take photos of actors as they wish to be presented and will take all the time necessary.

Work portfolio: Established in 1992. Photographs can be viewed at Spotlight's offices. Has taken publicity shots for around 500 actors and in addition has more than 40 years' experience of working in theatres, both in casting and as company manager.

Greg Goodale
mobile 07768 173503
email greg@gregveit.com
website www.gregveit.com
Facebook www.facebook.com/Greg.Veit.Photography
Twitter @veit_photo

Established in 2009 and has worked extensively in stage photography in the UK and abroad. Charges from £150 for Fringe shows; approx. 100 shots. Works exclusively in digital photography. Most recent clients include the National Theatre, Finborough Theatre, Pleasance Theatre, York Shakespeare Festival. Has on-going projects with Italia Conti Academy of Theatre Arts, Dream Arts and ArtsAdmin.

Greg Goodale was stage photographer of the Gdansk International Shakespeare Festival. His work has appeared in many publications including *The Guardian, The Stage, Exeunt* and *The Telegraph*.

Nick Gregan Photography
The Camera Club, 16 Bowden Street, London SE11 4DS
tel 020 8533 3003 *mobile* 07774 421878
email info@nickgregan.com
website www.nickgregan.com
Facebook /NickGreganHeadshotPhotographer
Twitter @nickgregan
Instagram @nickgregan

Services & rates: Charges £249 for a 2-hour photo shoot, which includes fees, studio (around 300 shots are taken), private web gallery, 3 retouched images and a CD of all saved images in colour and b&w. Students are offered a discount price of £175 on production of a valid student card. Also offers digital photography, for which the same rates apply. Photos are taken in a studio or outdoor location and both are wheelchair-accessible.

Work portfolio: Established in 1992. Has taken publicity photos for over 20,000 clients, including Paul Danan, Lucinda Rhodes and Jenny Powell. "My website offers '7 secrets to a great headshot' – check it out for loads of useful information." Author of *The Headshot Bible - 50 Tips for a Perfect Headshot.*

Charles Griffin Photography
PO Box 36, Deeside, Chester CH5 3WP
tel 01244 535252

email studio@charlesgriffinphotography.co.uk
website www.charlesgriffinphotography.co.uk

Services & rates: Photographer since 1993. Charges £149 for photo shoot, which includes processing of 2 12exps medium-format (high-quality) rolls, contact sheets and 2 10x8in prints. (Offers this service at £92.83 if client mentions *Actors' and Performers' Yearbook* when booking a 2-hour session. Student rates are also available – telephone or email for information.) Digital service also available at the same rates, although an extra charge is made to provide the images on CD. Uses studio and outdoor location (both wheelchair accessible).

Work portfolio: Examples of work can be seen on the website. Has taken photographs for around 250 actors, among them Raquel Lee, Gemma Gray, Sam Gratton and Paul Draw. "Sessions are conducted in a relaxed atmosphere: I will shoot images of actors as they wish. Clients should bring a variety of plain tops: those with high neckline or v-neck in red, grey or black are most useful."

Claire Grogan APHP
18 Calverley Grove, London N19 3LG
tel 020 7272 1845 *mobile* 07932 635381
email claire@clairegrogan.co.uk
website www.clairegroganphotography.com
Facebook www.facebook.com/Claire-Grogan-Photography-105661542805602/
Twitter @ClaireGroganPix
Instagram @ClaireGroganPix

Services & rates: Actors headshots charges – shoot prices from £200-£380, see prices on website for details. Digital shoots outdooor and/or studio. Natural light or flash. Discounted rates for full-time drama students. Offers full advice and help with clothing and make-up. Shoot times range from 2-4 hours in a relaxed environment. Studio and private outdoor space. Time and facilities for changing clothes/hair/make-up or shaving during shoots.

Specialises in capturing shots that really reflect the actor's personality and casting potential, also special TLC for those who normally find having their headshots done difficult.

Work portfolio: Established in 1991, with past clients including Denise Welch, Raji James, Martin Freeman, Stephen Tomkinson, Steve McFadden, Heather Peace. Photographs can be viewed on the website Facebook page, Instagram and Twitter; work updated daily.

Brendan Harrington
Newry, Northern Ireland
mobile 07850 001075
email b.harrington@pobroadband.co.uk
website www.brendanharringtonphotography.co.uk

Services & rates: Charges approximately £70 for a 2-hour session (around 150-225 shots). Fee includes 3 finished images at high res.; small quantities of hand

prints are available at £5 each if required. Shoots take place mainly in the studio, which is wheelchair accessible. Emails web galleries to clients for their final image selection.

Work portfolio: Established more than 25 years ago. Has taken publicity photos for thousands of actors: clients include most Dublin agents as well as Casting Call Pro and Spotlight.

HCK Photography
Based in London
tel 020 7112 8499 (Studio)
email info@hckphotography.co.uk
website www.hckphotography.co.uk

Services & rates: Established in 2007. Specialises in headshots and publicity photography. Charges from £150 for a photoshoot; call friendly staff for more information. Offers student discounts. Studio based. First 10 to mention Actors' and Performers' Yearbook 2019 receive £50 discount.

Work portfolio: Has taken publicity photos for many actors. Recent clients include: Shane Rangi and Kiran Shah.

Headshot Photography by Lynn Herrick
The Studio, 9A Sylvester Road, London N2 8HN
tel 020 8349 3632
email lynnherrick@gmail.com
website www.headshotslondon.co.uk

Services & rates: Charges £80-175 for a photoshoot, which includes 25-60 images. 10x8in prints are available at extra cost. Work takes place in the studio and attached garden. Has taken publicity photos for around 300 actors.

Jamie Hughes Photography
mobile 07850 122977
email jamie@jamiehughesphotography.com
website www.jamiehughesphotography.com/headshots

Services & rates: Charges £285 for a bespoke photo shoot lasting up to 2 hours in a relaxed atmosphere. Over 300 images are shot with the best supplied on CD to take away, plus retouching and processing of 3 10x8in prints and digital originals. Additional prints (including retouching) are available for £15 each. Uses a studio and outdoor location, both of which are wheelchair accessible. Please see website for examples.

Remy Hunter
Flat 2, 9 Belsize Park, London NW3 4ES
tel 020 7431 8055 *mobile* 07766 760724
email remy@remyhunterphotography.com
website www.remyhunter.co.uk

Services & rates: Established in 2003. Charges £190 and £140 for a 4-hour and 2-hour actors' session respectively. Includes 80 digital shots taken for 4-

Resources

hour session and 40 shots for 2-hour session. Also includes CD of all shots given to client at end of session and a further CD of 6 high res. images for 4-hour session and 4 images for 2-hour session. Student discount available as follows: £150 for a 4-hour session and £120 for a 2-hour session. Shared sessions available for half of the above prices per person. Also includes 2 CDs. Studio and outdoor shots available during same session. Free retouching of images where necessary. Uses a studio that is not accessible to wheelchair users.

Work portfolio: Has taken photographs for roughly 500 actors, including (with Spotlight PIN in brackets): Freya Dominic (2211-8979-4470), Gemma Harvey (0615-5643-5877), Julie Pollin (0459-1206-3661) and Jonathan Grace (aka James Dillinger – 2517-8940-4373). Advises clients to "bring a range of tops with varying necklines. Black tends to come out best, so a couple of black tops are a good idea. For make-up bring what you'd wear from day to day".

David James Photography
mobile 07808 597362
email info@davidjamesphotos.com
website www.davidjamesphotos.com

Established 2001. Charges £230 for photoshoot including processing of 2 36exps b&w films and 4 10x8in prints. Also offers digital shoot at the same price. Uses studio, outdoor locations and client's own home for the shoot; the studio is not accessible for wheelchair users. Has taken photographs for around 200 actors including clients of Independent, PFD and Markham & Froggatt.

Nick James APHP
451 Wick Lane, London E3 2TB
mobile 07961 122030
email nick@nickjamesphotography.co.uk
website www.nickjamesphotography.co.uk

Services & rates: Photographer since 2005. Digital service only. Charges £450 for photoshoot, which includes processing of 800 shots taken with 400 taken on contact sheets and 3 images retouched. Student rate available at £400 per session. A 2-hour session is also available for £350, student rate £320. Does not provide prints, but extra photographs are available at £35. Uses studio natural and flash and outdoor location.

Work portfolio: Examples of work can be seen on the website.

Matt Jamie
Newcastle and the North East
mobile 07976 890643
email photos@mattjamie.co.uk
website www.mattjamie.co.uk/portraits

Services & rates: Established in 2000. Digital photography. Cost of photoshoot is £160 (Newcastle), £95 student rate. Shoot includes 1-hour

studio session and 3 final high res images. Extra studio time and images can be purchased. 100% satisfaction promise with no fee charged of you're not happy with the images. Can also shoot at outdoor locations selected by the client, or at collages/dramaschools on request.

Work portfolio: Examples of photography can be seen online. Has photographed hundreds of actors from drama school students to Kevin Spacey. Matt also works as an actor and film maker, so understands the requirements of the shot and the pressures involved. He offers a relaxed, informal shoot. You can bring a variety of different clothes, wigs, friends or anything else you might want with you to make you feel confident on the shoot.

JK Photography
17 Delamere Road, West Wimbledon, London SW20 8PS
tel 020 8946 9549 *mobile* 07816 825578
email jkph0t0@yahoo.com
website www.jk-photography.net

Services & rates: Established in 1997. Sessions start at £160 (studio & outdoor). Includes professional make-up artist and all of your images in high-res. in b&w and colour on disc.

Work portfolio: Has photographed over 500 actors with 15 years of industry experiance. "Our creative team will ensure a relaxed session amd images that are a true representation of your casting needs."

Neil Kendall Photography
19 Oakfield Court, Haslemere Road, London N8 9RA
tel 020 8340 4214 *mobile* 07776 198332
email mondo.nez@virgin.net
website www.neilkendallphotography.co.uk

Services & rates: Charges £135 for a photo shoot which includes photographer's fee, studio and equipment costs, processing of 3 b&w 36exps, contact sheets and 2 10x8in prints. Uses both studio and natural light.

Work portfolio: Photographs can be viewed on the website. Has taken publicity shots for around 30-35 actors. Recent clients include: Vanessa Earl, Peter Ackyroyd, Graham Norton and Liberty X.

Jack Ladenburg Photography
mobile 07932 053743
email info@jackladenburg.co.uk
website www.jackladenburg.co.uk

Services & rates: Established in 2006. Only digital photography. Cost of photo shoot is £205. Includes 6 digital images with basic retouching. Student discount of £30; further discounts for group bookings. Includes high and low res versions of each image. Photos taken in studio or outdoor locations.

Work portfolio: Portfolio is available to view at Spotlight's offices. Has photographed approximately

400 actors. Recent clients include: Roger Moore, Hattie Morahan, Julian Rhind-Tutt, Nicholas Day, Tara Summers and Katherine Tozer. "I place a big emphasis on making sure that my clients are happy and relaxed before we start the shoot, and that they enjoy themselves on the day. I never rush through a session and always devote either a morning or an afternoon to one shoot. I don't set a limit on how many photos I'll take in a session, and make sure we concentrate on the casting needs of each actor."

Carole Latimer
113 Ledbury Road, Notting Hill, London W11 2AQ
tel 020 7727 9371
email carole@carolelatimer.com
website www.carolelatimer.com

Services & rates: Professional photographer for over 25 years. Charge for actors' headshots is £350 inc. VAT (student rate is £300). An electronic contact sheet is provided and up to 5 chosen images are put on to a CD. Photographs are taken in a studio and occasionally outdoor locations. The studio does not have wheelchair access.

Work portfolio: Has provided publicity photos for approximately 2,000 actors, including: Kate O'Mara, Alistair McGowan, Maureen Lipman, Zoe Lucker, and clients from the following agencies: Independent, Conway Van Gelder Grant, Narrow Road. "No large patterns. If it's a b&w shoot, bring at least one black top. Always bring a selection of tops so I have a choice. I have an exceptional daylight studio with full lighting equipment. Good facilities for make-up."

Steve Lawton APHP
134 Randolph Avenue, Maida Vale, London W9 1PG
mobile 07973 307487
email stevelawton2@msn.com
website www.stevelawton.com

Services & rates: Charges £280 for a photoshoot, which includes A3 contact sheets; CD of all shots in colour and b&w; and 4 touched-up 10x8in prints. The same package is offered to students at the reduced price of £260. Additional 10x8in prints are priced at £15 each. A traditional b&w film service is also available. Advises clients not to bring patterned tops; fitted t-shirts and v-necks in blue, grey or black are most effective.

Work portfolio: Established in 2001. Has taken photographs for more than 3,000 actors and is recommended by Curtis Brown, Independent Talent Group, United Agents, Lou Coulson, Jorg Betts, Shane Collins, International Artists and Bronia Buchanan, amongst others. A full portfolio and price information is available on the website.

LB Photography
36 Nutley Lane, Reigate, Surrey RH2 9HS
tel 01737 224578 *mobile* 07885 966192
email lb@lisabowerman.com
website www.lisabowerman.com

Services & rates: Working actress and photographer for 30 years. Charges £190 for a photo shoot (£170 student rate). No VAT chargeable. Includes 40-50 shots, taken in natural light. Price also includes a choice of 7 high-res. and re-touched images, in colour and in addition b&w conversions. Based near Redhill in Surrey – about 30 mins' train journey from Victoria – and the the client can be picked up at station. If the weather's bad the shoot can be rearranged for a different day. For portfolio and more details, visit website.

Pete Le May
mobile 07703 649246
email pete@petelemay.co.uk
website www.petelemay.co.uk/headshots
Twitter @petelemay

Services & rates: Based in London and established in 2002. Typically charges £250 (£200 for students) for a relaxed phorography session lasting 2-3 hours. A disc or download link of all the photographs – allowing you to make as many prints as you want – and retouching of your favourite 6 images. Photos are taken using natural light, both indoors and outdoors. Visit the website for full details and examples of recent work.

Leejay Photography
London N13
mobile 07590 463428
email leejay@leejayphotography.com
website www.leejayphotography.com

Services & rates: Charges £119 for a digital photoshoot, which includes 500 shots with the best 200 images sent to client. 10x8in prints are available at £15 each. Student price is £99. Shoots take place at own studio as well as outdoors.

Work portfolio: Established in 2011. Has taken publicity shots for around 150 actors. Recent clients include: Nick Julian (Independent Talent Group), Lisa Kerr (Conway Van Gelder Grant), Kim Ensor (K Talent), Annabel Lloyd (International Theatre Collective). Advises actors: "I trained as an actor and feel in most cases it takes an actor to take a great actors' headshot."

Murray Lenton
2 Toll Bar Barn, High Hesket, Near Carlisle, Cumbria CA4 OHR
tel 01697 475442 *mobile* 07941 427458
email murray.lenton@btinternet.com

Services & rates: Digital or film as required. Rates to be discussed at time of booking.

Work portfolio: Established as a general photographer in 1983, and as a theatre photographer in 1997. Recent clients include: Tamsin Greig, Simon Dormandy, Luke Sorba and Wild Girls.

James Looker Photography
mobile 07973 566537
email james@jameslookerphotography.com
website www.jameslookerphotography.com

Services & rates: Photographer since 2000. Charges from £150 for up to 2 hours, providing a selection of up to 200 colour/black and white images. From these, 3 will be retouched and cropped to 10x8in/300dpi. Additional retouching £30 each. Student rate is £100 per student if 2 book the same session. Based near Ewell West, Zone 6, location shoots available locally or will travel to client, travel expenses additional. Clients should bring a variety of outfits for their shoot.

Work portfolio: Examples of work can be seen on the website. Has taken photographs for over 500 actors, musicans, directors and performers, among them Mike Leigh, Jarvis Cocker, Karen O and Kanye West.

MAD Photography APHP
200 Gladbeck Way, Enfield EN2 7HS
tel 020 8363 4182 *mobile* 07949 581909
email mad.photo@onetel.net
website www.mad-photography.co.uk

Services & rates: Charges £220 for actors' photoshoot which includes photographer's fee, studio and location shoot, 150 proofs contact sheets emailed same day and 4 high-res. images on disc. Offers discounted rate of £160 to students (includes as above, but with 3 images on disc); also offers student shared shoots at £95 each (includes as above, but with 75 proofs contact sheets and 2 images on disc). Extra 10x8in prints are priced at £20 each and images on disc are £20. "Hair and make-up should be natural. Bring 4 tops in any colours: one v-neck, one collar, one t-shirt and one jacket. No white!"

Work portfolio: Established in 1997. Photographs can be viewed on the website and in *Contacts* and on Casting Call Pro. Has taken publicity shots for over 6,000 actors and student actors. Clients include: Shane Richie, Michelle Ryan, Susan Penhaligon, Michael Knowles, Jessica Wallace, John Partridge, Tom Law, Belinda Owusu, Janie Dee and Phoebe Thomas.

Raymondo Marcus
Marlow, Buckinghamshire
mobile 07831 649 000
email r.marcus@raymondomarcus.co.uk
website www.raymondomarcus.co.uk

Services & rates: Photographer since 2009. Minimum charge £250 (no VAT) full usage licence included. Headshots: Photo shoot at Spotlight Leicester Square, studio in High Wycombe, or location of your choosing. If location is more than 20 miles from Marlow, travel costs will be added to overall fee. Images guaranteed suitable for Spotlight and to meet agreed brief. Performances and events: Can cover performances and has had images featrued in *The Stage*. Testimonials from show business subjects provided on request.

Work portfolio: Examples of work can be seen on his website. Has taken photographs for a number of different actors and actresses, among them Suzanne Kendall, Laura Waddell (*Saving Mr Banks*), Shirley Anne Field, Jo Brand, Emma Thompson, Valerie Leon, Henry Jameson, Claudia Schiffer and Daniel Craig. "I have a good understanding that to generate casting calls is to present you as well as possible but so that there should be no surprises for casting directors i.e. quality images with no reliance on airbrushing."

Kirsten McTernan Photography & Design
Cardiff
mobile 07791 524551
email kirsten@kirstenmcternan.co.uk
website www.kirstenmcternan.co.uk

Services & rates: A professional and comfortable, relaxed session in the studio overlooking Chapter Arts Centre. "We can discuss what you need from your headshot and work towards tailoring it to your needs but most importantly looking like you." Sessions normally last just under an hour and include 2 images from the session in digital format as well as options to purchase the rest if desired.

Work portfolio: Established in 2005. Professional theatre and portrait photographer working exclusively within the arts community. Has taken publicity photos for over 400 actors. Recent clients include major casting agents such as: The Artists Partnership, Regan and Rimmer, Emptage Hallett, Boom Talent and David Chance.

John Need
Studio 147, 1 Summerhall, Edinburgh EH9 1QE
mobile 07756 178947
email pics@johnneed.co.uk
website www.johnneed.co.uk

Services & rates: Charges £125 (+ VAT) for a photoshoot, which includes 200-250 shots. Prints are optional at £15 each. Only shoots digital. Shoots take place at own studio which is wheelchair accessible.

Work portfolio: Established in 2008. Has taken publicity shots for around 400 actors, a collection of which can been viewed on the website. Advises actors: "I know that getting photos right for media is a high priority for any performer. Whether you're in the biz or trying to get into it, get in touch, as I've shot hundreds of actors, presenters and DJs. First impressions count, so give casting directors what they're after – you!"

Paul J Need Photography
5 Metro Business Centre, Kangley Bridge Road, London SE26 5AQ
tel 07860 305327
email pauljneed@hotmail.com
website www.pauljneed.co.uk
Photographer Paul J. Need

Services & rates: Charges £80 for a photoshoot. Photographer has a background in theatre, film, concert and television lighting, as well as teaching lighting design at RADA. Offers digital photography.

Claire Newman-Williams
mobile 07963 967444
email claire@clairenewmanwilliams.com
website www.clairenewmanwilliamsheadshots.com
Twitter @CNWHeadshots

Services & rates: Claire is a fine art and portrait photographer who has worked with actors for 17 years in both the US and the UK, beginning in 1999. Charges £340 for a 3-hour+ photoshoot. All photographs are digital and each session includes unlimited shots edited down to 150 pictures on contact sheets. 2 10x8in retouched digital images are included as part of the session and further copies are available at £30 each. Student rate is also available at £340. Full details about headshot sessions can be seen on the website. Uses a studio for each photo shoot, though this is not wheelchair accessible.

Work portfolio: Has taken photographs for around 2,500 actors, among them Stephen Fry, Tom Hiddleston, Joanna Page, Ben Barnes, Richard Armitage and Kerry Ellis.

Michael Pollard Photographer APHP
Manchester-based
tel 0161 456 7470 *mobile* 07800 989457
email info@michaelpollard.co.uk
website www.michaelpollard.co.uk
Facebook www.facebook.com/michaelpollardphotographer
Twitter @MichaelActors

Services & rates: Charges £120 for around 120 shots to the contact sheet, including the first 5 images chosen in both colour and b&w. Additional images are charged at £10 each. The shoot is unhurried and relaxed and generally lasts up to 2 hours; the shoot can be both outdoors in natural light and in a studio environment to give the widest variety of images possible. As many shots as necessary are taken, which are later carefully edited down to give the actor the very best and most varied images to view. Sets of colour contact sheets are then emailed to the actor and can be sent to their agent also.

"Actors can bring a number of tops ranging from lighter to darker tones. Tops should be simple and comfortable with generally a round- or V-neck, though more character-based shots are now also taken which may involve a wider variety of clothing and styling. Hair generally needs to be tidy but avoid going to the hairdresser the day before to have it cut or styled. For women, make-up should be simple and sparing, avoiding lip liner or lipstick that is too dark or too red. For men, they can arrive with a beard or stubble and shave part way through. The key is to keep things simple and natural and to be positive and be prepared. Think how you want to look and how you don't want to look. Enjoy it and be yourself!"

Work portfolio: Established in 1982 (1993 for actors). Photographs can be viewed on the website. Has taken publicity shots for around 4,000 actors. Recent clients include: Darren Day Lucy-Jo Hudson, Vicky Entwistle, Lee Otway, Peter Armitage.

Will Polley
Unit 2C, 81-85 Wharf Road, Pinxton, Notts NG16 6LH
tel 01773 776379 *mobile* 07766 274205
email info@polleyphotography.com
website www.polleyphotography.com

Services & rates: Photoshoots from £89 for a 30-minute session with 1 digital image retouched in high-res. in colour, b&w and low-res. for web or email. Choose from 5 images (not retouched) selected from all taken at the shoot and viewed on laptop at end of session, image emailed. Prints charged at extra. Special packages and student discounts available, please enquire for more information. Shoots take place at studio and some on location.

Work portfolio: Established in 2005. Recent clients include: Neil Ashley, Darren Richardson and Peter Adcock.

David Price Photography
Hackney, London E5
mobile 07950 542494
email info@davidpricephotography.co.uk
website www.davidpricephotography.co.uk

Services & rates: One of London's leading headshot photographers since 2003. Currently divides his time between Los Angeles and London. Please email for availability. Prices start from £170.

Work portfolio: See website for full details.

Ben Rector
mobile 07770 467791
email ben@benrector.com
website www.benrector.com

Please view my updated portfolio at **www.benrector.com**.

Mat Ricardo
Based in South East London
mobile 07743 494675
email MatRicardo@hotmail.co.uk
website www.MatRicardoPhotography.com

Services & rates: Charges £200 for a photoshoot, which takes 1-3 hours. Also offers digital photography at the same rates. Shoot takes place at a studio, on location, or at a mobile studio.

Work portfolio: Established in 2009. Has taken publicity shots for around 20 actors. Clients include Jenny Eclair, Barry Cryer, Richard Herring and numerous comedy, variety and burlesque performers.

Davey Ross
Central London
mobile 07956 302894

Resources

email davixuk@hotmail.com
website www.davidrossphotography.com

Services & rates: Photographer since 1982. Davey is happy to discuss specific pricing over the phone, and charges a student rate of £300. Uses a studio, or is happy to arrange an outdoor location or travel to client's home.

Work portfolio: Examples of work can be seen on the website. Has taken photographs for hundreds of actors, among them Anne Stafford, Fiona Cuskelly and Christopher Sciueref.

Scott Rylander
South East London
mobile 07775 785250
email contact@scottrylander.com
website www.scottrylander.com

Services & rates: Digital only. Charges £170 for headshots (£150 for students) and from £200 (£180 for students) for publicity stills (e.g. for websites), depending on requirements. Stage advertising and production photography also offered: rates negotiable. Fee for headshots includes a sub-selection of 60-100 unretouched shots, and 3 retouches; for publicity stills the fee covers 5-8 retouches, depending on requirements and the nature of the job, plus sub-selection as necessary for the shoot. For 10x8in prints, recommends that clients use one of the several London printers who can offer far more competitive rates for actors. Shoots take place at a studio or outdoor location, or (for publicity stills) wherever is agreed with the customer.

Work portfolio: Established in 2010. Has taken photographs for around 80 actors. Headshot clients include: Actors Direct Associates, Alliston & Foster and Jessica Carney Associates. Clients for production and stage advertising include: English National Opera and Tarento Productions Ltd. Advises actors: "With many actors setting up their own websites and building their presence on Facebook, the types of photos they need are changing. Headshots will always be hugely important for casting, and my approach is to focus on your personality, not to make everyone look the same. But creative publicity stills – shot with more freedom for you to wear different clothes and do different things – are becoming just as necessary. I take a very relaxed approach to both: we take as long as we need until we have the right look for you."

Robin Savage Photography APHP
North London
mobile 07901 927597
email contact@robinsavage.co.uk
website www.robinsavage.co.uk
Facebook Robin Savage Photography
Twitter @robinsavagepics
Editor Instagram: robin_savage_headshots

Services & rates: A London-based actors' headshot photographer. Has been in business for over 10 years.

Has worked with actors who have appeared in the West End, the National Theatre, the RSC and theatres all around the world who have worked in feature films, major TV dramas, soaps, sitcoms, sketch shows and commercials. Sessions are £260 (£230 for students). Visit the website for more information and to get in touch.

Howard Sayer Photography
tel 020 8123 0251 07860 559891
email howard@howardsayer.com
website www.howardsayer.com

Services & rates: Casting headshots £195 (inc. VAT) for 90-minute sitting; includes images posted to web gallery for viewing and high-res. download. Studio in Surrey able to travel to client location (supplement applies).

Karen Scott Photography
London
mobile 07958 975950
email info@karenscottphotography.com
website www.karenscottphotography.com

Services & rates: Charges £225 for Actors Headshot Shoot. Unlimited images are taken during a relaxed and unhurried shoot (with outfit changes as necessary) and edited to approximately 100 proofs. All proofs are b/w and colour and cropped to 10x8in. High quality contact sheets of the proofs are then emailed to you, after which your chosen 4 images are fully finished including contrast and tonal adjustments and retouching. The 4 finished images in colour and b/w are then uploaded to a private folder, these are high resolution downloadable and printable files. Outdoor or indoor locations used using natural light. Student rates are available.

Work portfolio: Portfolio of images can be viewed on the website, please check for details of contemporary shoots for models, dancers, musicians, etc. Production, publicity and live shoots are also possible – check website for details.

Catherine Shakespeare Lane
The Monsell Stores, 43 Monsell Road,
London N4 2EF
tel 020 7226 7694
email catherineshakespeare.lane@gmail.com
website www.csl-art.co.uk

Services & rates: Charges £310 for a photoshoot which includes photographer's fee, studio and equipment costs, processing of 2 b&w 36exps, contact sheets and 4 10x8in prints. Offers a student package for £270 (1 roll of 36 and 2 10x8in prints). In special circumstances this package is also available to non-students for £280. Uses natural light inside and favours a natural look. "My aim is to show my clients at their most interesting."

Work portfolio: Established in 1975. Photographs can be viewed at Spotlight's offices and in *Contacts*. Has taken publicity shots for more than 2,000 actors.

Michael Shelford

London Bridge
mobile 07753 610784
website www.shelfordheadshots.com

Services & rates: Charges £330 for a standard photoshoot; student discount of rate £300. A portfolio shoot is £450. Studio is at the Biscuit Factory in Bermondsey, South London.

Work portfolio: Has taken publicity photos for 900-plus actors. Recent clients include: David Adjala (Independent Talent Group), James Norton (Artist Partnership), Alexandra Roach (Gordon and French), Nick Hendrix (Ken McReddie), Daniel Ings (The Rights House), James Rastall (Rebecca Blond), Antonia Thomas (Curtis Brown), Theo James (Markham & Froggatt) and Shazid Latif (Lou Coulson).

Alan Sill Photography

43 Surtees Road, Peterlee, County Durham SR8 5HA
tel 0191 518 1677 *mobile* 07977 141809
email alansillphotography@hotmail.co.uk
website www.alansillphotography.com

Established in 1990. Charges £90 for a photoshoot, which includes as many shots as it takes to complete the assignment. Prints are charged at £20. 20% discount for students with a valid student union card. Rates for digital photography are the same. Works on location, at the client's home or at a home studio, which is wheelchair accessible. Member of the National Union of Journalists.

Peter Simpkin

Apartment 13, Stefan House, London N21 3RF
email petersimpkin@aol.com
website www.petersimpkin.co.uk

Services & rates: Charges £350 for a photoshoot which includes photography fee, studio and equipment costs, processing of 3 contact sheets with a minimum of 100 shots, and 6 10x8in prints (also supplied with a CD). Student price is £300.

Work portfolio: Photographs can be viewed on the website. Has taken publicity shots for thousands of actors. Recent clients include actors represented by most leading agents and many students from the big 10 drama schools.

Rosie Still

391 Sidcup Road, London SE9 4EU
tel 020 8857 6920 *mobile* 07597 946252
email contact@rosiestillphotography.co.uk
website www.rosiestillphotography.co.uk

Services & rates: A professional photographer for 40 years. Charges a special price for actors of £190 (normally £240) to be photographed in 4 tops, or £145 (normally £180) to be photographed in 2 tops. This includes session fee, changes of tops and the entire shoot (minus any unflattering ones!) all cropped to 10x8in in both colour and b&w as large, high-res. Spotlight-ready jpegs. For more details please check out the Acting page of the website. Also offers a special reduction for students of £95 (normally £120) to be photographed in 2 tops, which includes all of the above. Takes as many shots as are necessary, depending on the client's needs. All sessions are carried out in own South London studio, approx. 15 minutes' train journey from London Bridge station and with parking spaces directly outside. The studio is wheelchair accessible.

Work portfolio: Portfolio includes many famous actors, presenters, musicians and pop stars from the 70s onwards. Examples of work and testimonials can be seen on the website. "Ladies should keep make-up to the minimum as if going out for the evening, nothing heavier. Men should wear none at all. My priority is to finish a shoot with the client 100% satisfied with their results."

Faye Thomas Photographer

Camden/Highgate, North London
tel 020 7684 6465 *mobile* 07813 449229
email faye@fayethomas.com
website www.fayethomas.com
Facebook www.facebook.com/
fayethomasphotography
Editor Instgram: fayethomasphoto

Services & rates: Charges £340 for a photoshoot (all digital). Images supplied on digital web gallery (average 500-800 images taken);include 3 retouched digital copies (does not do prints). Student rate is £320; more details of additional packages are available from the website. Rates subject to change. Shoots take place in an outdoor location or studio – neither is wheelchair accessible. Advance booking recommended.

Work portfolio: Established in 2005. Recommended by top London agencies including Hamilton Hodell, Troika, Conway Van Gelder Grant, Curtis Brown, United Agents, 42, (Independent Talent Group, The Artists' Partnership, Markham Froggatt & Irwin and many more. High profile clients include: Hayley Atwell, Michelle Dockery, Sam Heughan, Jodie Whittaker, Maisie Williams, Bradley James, Joseph Morgan, Victoria Hamilton, Evanna Lynch, Emily Beecham, Matt Ryan, Charity Wakefield, Tuppence Middleton, Tom Riley, Lauren Cohan, Marc Warren, Kieran Bew, Lucy Griffiths, Lisa Dwan, Ramin Karimloo, Hannah New, John Light, Michelle Fairley, Gethin Anthony, Shaun Evans, Samuel Barnett, Cara Theobold, Jemima Rooper, Elliot Cowan, Alex Hassell, Sam Spiro, Dervla Kirwan, Freddie Highmore, Cressida. See portfolio.

TM Photography & Design

Suites 14 & 15, Marlborough Business Centre, 96 George Lane, South Woodford, London E18 1AD
tel 020 8530 4382

email info@tmphotography.co.uk
website www.tmphotography.co.uk

Services & rates: Established in 1995. All photography is digital. Cost of photoshoot is £70. The cost includes a 10x8in print which can be taken away on the day of the shoot. Images can be viewed by the client as they are taken. Images are loaded on to a private webpage to be viewed. Orders can be placed online. Student photoshoot is discounted at £40. Photos taken in studio or outdoor locations or client's home. Studio is wheelchair accessible.

Work portfolio: Has photographed approximately 3,000 actors, walk-ons and background artists. Has photographed many of the clients of Allsorts Agency, Ray Knight, G2 and Guys & Dolls. Actors photographed include: Fraser Hines and Antonia Okonma. Photoshoots can be booked at short notice. Also offers repro service and promotional products such as websites, model cards and CV creation.

Tony Blake Photography
68 Watergate Street, Chester CH1 2LA
mobile 07974 8044403
email tony@tonyblakephoto.co.uk
website www.tonyblakephoto.co.uk
Twitter @tonyblakephoto
Director Tony Blake

Established in 2001, Tony Blake is based in the north west of England and shoots natural light headshots in a relaxed studio environment. Offers standard and bespoke packages for actors.

Prices start from £150 depending on shoot length which is normally between one-and-a-half and two hours. Check the website for full details. Clients receive contact sheets of all edited-down images to select their favourites for re-touching and [rpcressing

Clients receive contact sheets of all edited-down images to select their favourites for re-touching and processing. Digital files only. Photographs are taken in natural light studio. Studio is not wheelchair acccessible.

A portfolio of images can be viewed on the website.

Steve Ullathorne
London
tel 07961 380969
email steve@steveullathorne.com
website www.steveullathorne.com

Services & rates: Charges £250 for a digital photo shoot; this covers all fees, studio costs and contact sheet. Will offer a discount to students, negotiable at the time of booking. All clients receive an online contact sheet with a web address that they can pass on to their agent. Prior to the shoot, clothing and locations will be discussed with the client on the telephone. All photos are retouched in Photoshop to remove any blemishes plus any other light retouching required by the actor. Email proofs are sent of each

chosen image. Rather than specifying a number of images, prices are dictated by duration of the shoot, which is 2 hours. Actors usually end up with more than 100 shots to choose from, in colour and b&w.

Work portfolio: Please see website for samples. Agency recommendations include: Brown, Simcocks and Andrews, RBM, PBJ, Noel Gay, Troika, DAA and Q Talent.

Vanessa Valentine Photography
mobile 07904 059541
website www.vanessavalentinephotography.com

Services & rates: Headshots. Based in London. Please see the website for more details.

Luke Varley
mobile 07711 183631
email luke@lukevarley.com
website www.lukevarley.com
website www.headshotsbylukevarley.com

Services & rates: Established in 2004. Charges £295 for a photo shoot, which includes approximately 130 shots and 4 retouched high-res. files for printing and web use. Shoots take place in a studio that is not wheelchair accessible.

Work portfolio: Has taken publicity photos for several hundred actors, including for the following agencies: 42, Troika, and Cole Kitchenn. He also shoots production, press and unit stills for film, TV and theatre.

Greg Veit Photography
mobile 07768 173503
email greg@gregveit.com
website www.gregveit.com
Facebook www.facebook.com/greg.veit.photography
Twitter @veit_photo

Services & rates: Prices start from £180 for 2 shots. Works exclusively in digital photography. Photographs taken in studio or on location. Studio has wheelchair access.

Work portfolio: Established in 2009. An experienced headshot and stage photographer; has photographed 500 actors. Recent clients include Jane Paul Gets, Sandra Meunier, Tristram Kimborough, James Arama and Giorgio Borghes.

Ana Verastegui Photography
mobile 07818 067557
email anaphotography@me.com

Services & rates: Charges £170 for a photo shoot, which includes approximately 150 shots and 3 10x8in prints. Student rate is £140. Also offers digital photography at the same rates. Shoots take place mainly outdoors in wheelchair accessible locations.

Work portfolio: Established in 2008. Has taken publicity photos for over 100 actors. Clients include: Cordelia Bugeja, Polly Maberly, and Hannah Melbourn.

Vincenzo Photography
tel 020 8372 0428 *mobile* 07962 338289
email info@vincenzophotography.com
website www.vincenzophotography.com

Services & rates: Photographer since 2000. Charges £230 for a 2-hour photoshoot, which includes 8 high-res. digital files, 4 each in b&w and colour. Offers a student rate of £200 per session. Uses a studio with garden for external shots or is happy to arrange another location of a client's choosing.

Work portfolio: Examples of work can be seen on the website. Has taken photographs for many actors, among them Ken Stott, Hayley Atwell and Paul Nicholas.

Philip Wade
88 Englefield Road, London N1 3LG
tel 020 7226 3088 *mobile* 07956 599691
email pix@philipwade.com
website www.philipwade.com

Services & rates: £175, £125 and £50 Spotlight packages. Up to 250 images, you choose six images, these are adjusted in colour and b/w. Sessions are in the studio and outside with a wide variety of backgrounds, time for six changes of tops, your personal online gallery to view images. Images to Spoltlight standard supplied in high and low resolution.

Work portfolio: Has taken publicity shots for hundreds of actors. Recent clients include: PHM, Abacus, Imperium, Shepherd Management and Sandra Boyce.

Caroline Webster
North London
mobile 07867 653019
email caroline@carolinewebster.co.uk
website www.carolinewebster.co.uk

Services & rates: Established in 2009. Charges £150 for studio or outdoors shoot, and £200 for both studio and outdoors shoot. Approximately 100 digital shots are taken, and final photos provided in colour and b&w, as high-quality jpegs on disc. Offers a student rate of £120 for a studio or outdoors shoot, and £150 for both.

Work portfolio: Has taken publicity photos for over 1,000 actor clients, including Maureen Beattie, Paul Merton, Geraldine Fitzgerald and Kate Duchene.

Michael Wharley Photography APHP
Waterloo, London, Zone 1
mobile 07961 068759
email michaelwharley@michaelwharley.com
website www.michaelwharley.com

Services & rates: Established in 2006. Shoots in digital, featuring studio-lit and outdoor, colour and b&w shooting as standard. Two-hour 'Pro' shoot suitable for all actors. Between 150 and 400 photos taken. Photos supplied in industry-standard web- and print-optimised formats. See website for full details of packages and approach.

Work portfolio: Has taken hundreds of photos for each edition of Spotlight – 'Top Theatre Photographer' (*The Stage*). Works for actors and agencies across the spectrum of the industry. Recent clients have been represented by agencies such as United, Angel & Francis, Curtis Brown and Felix de Wolfe, studied at drama schools like RADA and Central, and worked on high-profile film, theatre and TV projects. Also writes regularly on headshot and digital trends in the acting industry (see **www.wharleywords.co.uk**).

Alex Winn Photography
Studio 6B, The Electricians Shop,
Trinity Buoy Wharf, 64 Orchard Place,
London E14 0JW
tel 020 3432 4408 *mobile* 07816 317038
website www.alexwinn.com
Twitter @alexwinn

Services & rates: Photographer since 2006. Offers 3 packages priced between £200-£325 for sessions starting at 2hrs up to 4hrs. Depending on package selected, they include either 2, 4 or 6 professionally retouched images delivered via digital download and most include two 10 x 8in prints. Contact sheets are made available online 24 hours after each session in both b&w and colour. All sessions are shot and delivered digitally. Studio and outdoor location (both wheelchair-accessible).

Work portfolio: Examples of work can be seen on the website. Has taken photographs for several hundred actors, among them Elizabeth Carling (Curtis Brown), Rafe Spall (Troika), Preeya Kalidas (Cole Kitchenn), Richie Campbell (AHA Talent), Claire Hope-Ashitey (United Agents), Arnold Oceng (Troika), Martin Jenson (Simon & How), James Farrar (Cole Kitchenn), Olly Yellop (A&J Management), Michael Rivers (Marcus & McCrimmon) and Wil Johnson (CAM). "I operate in a relaxed but professional way to ensure that everyone can feel as comfortable as possible in front of the camera. I think good headshots are the result of a collaboration between myself and the actors I work with so each session is tailored accordingly."

Robert Workman
Studio 32, West Kensington Mansions,
Beaumont Crescent, London W14 9PF
tel 020 7385 5442
email bob@robertworkman.demon.co.uk
website www.robertworkman.demon.co.uk

Services & rates: Casting portrait session £250, which includes the session with portraits taken both in the studio and outside in a nearby park, a web gallery of the results, the client's choice of 5 retouched 10x8in prints, and a CD of jpegs ready for digital submissions to casting directors and Spotlight online.

Resources

Work portfolio: Photographs can be viewed on the website or in a portfolio kept in Spotlight's offices. Has been taking around 200 publicity shots for actors every year for nearly 30 years.

REPRO COMPANIES

Denbry Repros trading as Studio 57 Ltd
6 The Old Chapel, 69 Primrose Hill,
Kings Langley WD4 8HX
tel (01442) 242411
email info@denbryrepros.com
website www.denbryrepros.com

Please refer to the website for current details and prices. Other services include a studio for casting photography, downloading images from the Internet and supplying images on CD in colour or b&w.

Denman Repros
Burgess House, Main Street, Farnsfield,
Nottinghamshire NG22 8EFF
tel (01623) 882272 *fax* (01623) 882272

Initial scan of a 10x8in print is free. Can also work with CDs, negatives and transparencies.

Repros of a b&w 10x8in are priced as follows:
£48 for 100, £64 for 250 and £88 for 500.

Repros of a b&w postcard print are priced as follows:
£34 for 100, £39 for 250 and £64 for 500.

Note: Please ring for latest prices for colour repros.

Faces Prints
10 Avondale Road, Carlton, Nottingham NG4 1AF
tel (0115) 847 5640 *fax* 0115-847 5640
email facesprints@ntlworld.com

Initial scan is free.

Repros of b&w 10x8in are priced as follows:
£28 for 25, £43 for 50, £56 for 100, £73 for 200, £85 for 250 and £99 for 500.

Repros of a b&w postcard print are priced as follows:
£22 for 25, £32 for 50, £37 for 100, £49 for 200, £59 for 250 and £85 for 500.

Will also provide a free gloss on quantity of 25, free photo retouch, free design on 'z-cards', and email proofing and free name/caption insertion.

Image Photographic
6 Stonehouse Street, Plymouth PL1 3PE
01752 202929
email spectrum91@yahoo.co.uk
website www.imagephotographic.com

Image Photographic is now part of Spectrum Photo Labs Ltd.
    Various print sizes available. File upload facility and online ordering with secure payment facility available. Please email or phone with any queries.

Moorfields Photographic
2 Old Hall Street, Liverpool L3 9RQ
tel 0151-236 1611
email info@moorfieldsphoto.com
website www.moorfieldsphoto.com

Established in 1981. Please refer to the website for full details.

Profile Prints
Unit 2, Plot 1A, Rospeath Industrial Estate,
Crowlas TR20 8DU
tel (01736) 741222 *fax* (01736) 741255
email sales@courtwood.co.uk
website www.courtwood.co.uk

One-off charge of £2.75 for negative from email, CD or original. All media accepted.

Repros of 10x8in b&w or colour are priced as follows:
£29.75 for 24, £52.25 for 50, and £94.25 for 100.

Credit card-sized self-adhesive 'minis' (great for CVs):
£13 for 50, and £18.25 for 100.

Produces all sizes, postcards and z-cards. Prices include P&P and VAT.

Visualeyes Repro Ltd
F167 Riverside Business Centre, Bendon Valley,
London SW18 4UQ
tel 020-8875 8811
email imaging@visualeyes.co.uk
website www.visualeyes.co.uk
Facebook www.facebook.com/pages/Visualeyes-Repro/32217334051
Twitter @visphoto

Dedicated reproduction of performers' photographic headshots. Free postage. Print sizes: 6x4in; 10x8in; 12x8in (A4); 16x12in (A3). *Other services include*: retouching, captioning, online ordering. Standard or 5-day economy service. Multi-run print discount and individual student or group discounts available. See website for details.

Getting the most from your photographs

Angus Deuchar

When searching for actors, most casting directors or directors start with a pile of photographs. Their time is limited, so they really only want to see the people who stand a chance of being right for a part – and the picture will be a vital part of their decision-making process. It's important therefore, to ensure that the photographs you use are as good as they can possibly be.

Have a flick through *Spotlight*. As well as being compulsive entertainment for any actor, it can be a great way to decide what works and what doesn't. If *you* were the casting director, who would (and wouldn't) you see? Try it for different types of production: a musical, a Shakespeare play, a TV drama. You may be surprised at the assumptions you make based on the photographs.

I'm going to look at what makes a good actor's photograph; help you think through how to choose a photographer; and discuss how you can get the best results from a photo session. Here is a list of, in my opinion, some important qualities to look for in a good headshot. It should be:

- **Honest.** This to me is the key to a good actor's photograph. Decisions at interviews are often largely made in the first few seconds, so it's important that the person who walks through the door is the person they saw in the photograph. If an actor looks different in some way, the interviewer's first reaction may well be disappointment. Which can't be a good start!
- **Well lit.** The face and hair should be well lit. If there are excessively bright areas or shadows on the face, the photo is probably not doing the actor any favours.
- **In focus.**
- **A good connection with the eyes.** These are possibly the most important feature, as these are what we generally look at first. We make a connection with the eyes. They should be well lit, in focus, looking *at* the camera and not squinting. They should also be 'alive' and not glazed over.
- **Well framed.** Ideally just head and shoulders. Not too close up, as it can look a bit overbearing. Likewise, not too far away as the face becomes too small.
- **Nothing 'tricksy'.** No fake hand-gestures, and certainly no props!

Can't I just get my friend to take some pictures in the back garden? Well, you could (in fact, some do). But what kind of image of yourself would that portray? You can always see such pictures in *Spotlight* – the actor looking awkward, squinting into the sunlight or the picture out of focus. Again, if you were the casting director, would you consider that actor to be serious? There's no point in cutting costs here. Decent photographs can more than pay for themselves.

Finding a photographer

Assuming you've decided to employ a photographer, how do you find the right one? Professional photographers are not all alike. Some who may be fantastic at, say, press or

Resources

fashion, may not be good at actors' portraits. It's important that the photographer knows the business of Acting. There are countless listings of specialist actors' photographers – in publications like this one; as adverts in *Contacts*; or on posters in The Actors Centre; but the style of photographs, and the ability of the photographers, are as varied as the prices and packages. It is therefore essential to check out their work for yourself. Have a look at their website if they have one, or at least try to see several different examples of their work.

Don't make a choice based solely on price. The amount a photographer charges is not necessarily an indication of how good (or bad) they are. Wherever possible, make your decision about a photographer based mostly on the *work* they produce, rather than how much they charge. It's important ultimately that you get the best possible photographs.

Find out the following:

• **Studio or natural light?** Studio light is easier to standardise and can be used at any time of the day or night and during any weather. It can be made to flatter someone, but won't necessarily show what they will look like in 'real life'. I prefer natural light, as I believe it to be generally more honest. Good natural light can still show someone at their best, but it won't deceive. It can also be more relaxing for the subject to be outside for the session. Casting directors often prefer natural light as it gives a better indication of who is actually going to walk through the door.

• **Film or digital?** Digital technology has moved on to such an extent that the quality of either format is comparable. Digital tends to produce a cleaner, less grainy image *and* you can check the results as you go along. It is essential however, that whoever is preparing the final photograph knows how to convert the image into a good-quality black and white print, with decent contrast and without loss of detail. This takes a reasonable amount of skill and know-how.

• **How much do they charge?** Does that include VAT? If relevant, you may want to ask about concessions for students.

• **How many photos do I get?** Find out how many photos will actually be taken at the session and how many different, finished 8x10 prints you can choose.

• **How will I view my proofs?** Some photographers will put your proofs onto a website enabling you to view them blown up on the screen. You may prefer a paper contact sheet, which, although much smaller to view, is more portable. If you want both, you may need to pay extra – so ask.

• **How long until I see my proofs?** Websites can often be published the same day as the session, while a paper contact will usually need to be produced and posted, so will take a few days. Some photographers will show you pictures on a computer straight away. This can be useful as a guide, but you probably shouldn't try to make final decisions without a bit of time to think.

• **How long will it take until I get my finished prints?** Try to get an indication of how long you should expect to wait after placing your final order. Hopefully, no more than a few days.

• **Do I get a CD?** As well as the prints, a few electronic versions of the final photos are extremely useful. They can be used on a website, to send a submission via email, to send to Spotlight, to print out yourself, or to act as the master-copy for your 'repros'. Find out if the photographer will provide you with a few different versions on a CD, and if it's included in the price.

The session itself

Here are some important things to prepare before – or think about during – your photo session.

• **Your 'look'.** Do you want to appear neutral or as a particular 'type'? For instance, earrings (on men especially) or other piercings, may limit you to modern or even 'alternative' characters. A formal jacket might suggest a business person or MP. Any of these looks may be fine, as they can make you 'ideal' for a particular type of role – but it's likely that that's all you'll ever be seen for while using that photograph! You decide – it really depends upon how you are marketing yourself.

• **Make-up and hair.** Preferably little or no make-up, but certainly no more than you would wear normally, day to day. Some photographers provide a 'hair and make-up' service but I would strongly discourage actors from using this. Don't confuse actors' portraits with having a glamorous photo to stick on top of the piano! If someone else prepares you, you're unlikely to look like the 'normal' you and it may be difficult to recreate that look in the future. Likewise, if you're planning to get a new hairstyle before your session, do so several days in advance to give you a chance to get used to it.

• **What to wear.** Concentrate on the neckline. Wear something you feel comfortable in, but avoid distracting patterns or logos. Most colours are fine, and black often works well. Bright white can affect the exposure so is less helpful. A jacket of some sort for some of the photos can often work well. Jewellery can be distracting so is usually best avoided.

• **Facial expression.** A big smile is often great for musicals or front-of-house pictures, but for other casting purposes it can seem a little over the top. Any kind of 'emoting' can seem over-earnest or, worse, corny. I tend to favour a good neutral expression with 'spark' behind the eyes. A kind of a relaxed, open look with the smallest hint of a smile.

Ultimately, photographs play an important part in helping you get a foot in the door. But once you've been called for the interview, it's over to you.

Angus Deuchar trained as an actor, during which time he subsidised his grant by taking photographs of his fellow students. When he left drama school in 1987 he soon realised that this was an ideal way to make a living between jobs! He pursued both careers for the first seven years, but has continued with just the photography since then. A website showing examples of his work can be seen at **www.actorsphotos.co.uk**.

Making money from your voice

Marina Caldarone

Clichés and misconceptions abound! 'It's a closed shop'; 'agents won't take you on in this climate'; 'you need an agent to stand any chance of getting work'; 'it's impossible to get into radio drama'; 'audio book recording is really badly paid'; and, the best one, 'you can earn a fortune making voiceovers'. That last bit can be true, incidentally, but it's far from the full story. The voiceover industry seems to be booming; there are more voiceover agencies appearing every year. But only a select few actors are lucky enough to make a living solely through their voiceover work: more likely, the latter supplements the former.

So, it doesn't matter what you look like, it's what you can sound like, it's about your ability to lift the text from the page, to bring it to life, often without rehearsal.

The following is a Users' Guide to debunking some of the myths, and setting the record straight on how to make money from your voice.

A glossary

A **Voiceover CD** or **Voicereel** is the full version of your recording, generally averaging 6-10 tracks in length, each track lasting anything from a 20-second commercial to a 90-second piece of documentary narration. It should be professionally edited to include music and effects where appropriate; it should not be a series of dry recordings of you reading, but rather should play to your strengths. It should *not* include 'everything' you think should go on – the reel itself needs to be about diversity within your natural range, not about you showing every accent you can do. Focus on the different colours and weights and drives within your natural voice.

The reel needs to include some factual material/documentary commercials and maybe fiction/audio book too – and I think, though this is a moot point, a drama track also. This should be delivered to you post-recording in two formats – an audio CD which you can copy and play on your computer/car stereo/CD player, and a data CD, so that the audio (mp3 files) can be sent electronically, as individual tracks.

The **Voice-clip** is a 'best of' compilation of excerpts of your full CD (sometimes called a 'megamix', or 'montage'). This should be delivered to you in the same two formats as the voicereel. Voice-clips are (usually) 2 x 1-minute in length (one clip being all commercial excerpts, and the other covering everything else), or 1 x 2-minute maximum compilation of the whole CD.

Copyright clearance does not need to be obtained for any of the material used, as it is for 'critical review' purposes only. So just tick the box that Spotlight asks you to check to confirm that you have clearance; it's often a formality.

Copy is the script. This can be emailed to you before the recording – although it may not be, if it is still being worked on.

A **Contacts Brochure** is something that all voiceover CD production companies should offer you, at no additional cost. It lists hundreds of potential employers, from the studios that make commercials, to advertising agencies, to Independent Radio Drama production companies.

A **Rate Card** specifies what each voiceover artist charges for the work. There is a minimum rate set by Equity; however, the rates aren't always adhered to. And some voiceover agents, in an attempt to get their client the job, will undercut that rate. It's not difficult to see where this leads to – fees spiralling lower for all.

The **Basic Studio Fee (BSF)** is what each voiceover agent will set for their clients. Most rates start at around £200 an hour.

The **Buyout Fee** is a variable based on many other criteria, such as distribution, whether there is web usage, global coverage, amount of airtime and whether the campaign is local or national.

The most commonly asked questions – answered
If I make a voicereel, will I get work?
Without a voicereel which can be sent by email, and which can be uploaded onto your Spotlight page, it is unlikely that you will get work. There is certain amount you can do to promote your voice, even without a voiceover agent; with your voice-clip costing nothing to send, this just takes application and energy – and time, of course. You can appreciate that a CV is great to back up your CD, but it won't replace it if you are looking for audio work.

So how do I select a company to make my CD?
Do your research, check out their credentials and their website. Listen to examples of their work, some of which should be online. Do they provide a Producer/Director, or just an engineer, and what is the quality of their edit? Who are their previous clients? Look at testimonials. All companies will recycle the same scripts, but to what extent? They should be able to tell you. If it looks too good to be true, it generally is.

How do different companies make the CDs?
Each company will have a house style, of sorts. For example, do you want an opening spot where you introduce yourself? For many companies, that is now old-fashioned, whilst for others it's a feature. The first voices we hear on both clips should be the ones that are closest to your natural voice; that is undisputed. Some companies, at very little cost, will just make a voice-clip for you, but you will have no full CD recorded to back those clips up. Others will invite you on to their website for you to select your own choice of material from their online archive, adjusting that choice on the recording day if it isn't quite right for you. Some will have a chat with you on the phone, get the measure of your voice and email you relevant material; others will meet you for a one-on-one consultation before the recording day, go through scripts and make a selection for you to take away and prep. Some companies keep you in studio from the start of the record through the edit to the mastering, so you walk away with the CD; others keep you in studio just for the recording and will send you the fully edited CD soon after.

What should I expect to pay to have a voicereel made?
Anything from £130 for just a voice-clip to £500 for the full CD with added extras (each company's website should give clear information about what you get for whatever rate).

I am interested in animation – what then?
An animation reel is very different. It comprises lots of different voices, heavily edited with effects and music to pack a punch. It might be that you make an animation track on your regular CD: this could be, say, 12 different 4-second-average sentences (these don't have to be connected but should be funny, caricature-ish and extreme, rather than just good

accents). You would need more time to record this, so there would be an extra cost, otherwise you could include a couple of character voices in one of your commercials.

I have an existing CD, but it's a bit tired and old fashioned. What should I do?

Upgrade it. But check out whether there is anything there you can recycle before getting rid of it all. Send it to the company you are making the CD with; they will listen to it and recommend whether there is anything there you could keep for the new voice-clip.

What do I do if my agent doesn't represent clients for voiceover?

You go hunting for a specific voiceover agent. Always start with your regular agent, as they may have a specific connection with a particular voiceover agent, so you're approaching them by personal recommendation, which is always good.

How do I approach voiceover agents about representation?

Research who they currently have on their books. Your opening gambit, with your voice-clips and CV attached, should be that you note they don't already represent anyone like you. Do not approach anyone who has 'your voice' already. Chase them for a response, carefully, after a few weeks/a month with maybe one other email – but do not hound them, it will backfire.

So I've got a job for a commercial, what does the employer expect?

For you to be efficient, precise, imaginative, and *quick to take and interpret direction into a new reading*. To be positive, upbeat, someone who won't let their irritation show when asked to repeat the same sentence 30 times, with the only direction being, 'Can you try something different?' Someone who will be fine about running a little over the studio booking. If that really is an issue, take it up with your agent, after the booking; they will know how and whether to act on it. Studio etiquette is paramount, this can't be overstated.

Should I include a Radio Drama track?

Being a really strong actor does not mean you will necessarily be a good voiceover. The skills are quite different. The pay rates are different, the representation is different, and your 'regular' agent would put you forward for it, not your voiceover agent. So in spite of some agents saying that there is no need for the actor to have any drama on the CD, this feels like a wasted opportunity. You need to play to your natural casting, as long as it offers an alternative take on your voice.

Marina Caldarone is a Director with Crying Out Loud (**www.cryingoutloud.co.uk**), a company that has been making voiceover CDs for actors since 1999. She is a Radio Drama Producer, a Theatre Director and Acting Coach and is co-author with Maggie Lloyd Williams of the bestselling *Actions – An Actors' Thesaurus*. She has been a tutor in actor training since 1984, which makes her older than she would care to admit to.

Showreel, voicereel and website services

The rapid developments in recording and computer technologies have seen an explosion of such actor-marketing tools over the last decade. There has also been a significant increase in the amount of (sometimes contradictory) advice offered on content, length, and so on. Much of this 'advice' is available on individual service-providers' websites, where you can usually find samples of their work.

Voicereels (also known as 'voice demos' and, sometimes confusingly, 'showreels') have been around for several decades, and a good one could attract the attention of a voice agent. However, the world of voice-overs is hard to break into and so a quality-produced 'reel' is very important. Showreels (applied to videoed performances) are a more recent innovation and are not yet quite the 'norm' – some agents and casting directors insist on seeing you perform live. However, a good one might just tip the balance in your favour.

Personal websites (for actors) are becoming more popular, but are still far from being essential. After all, you should already have a 'web presence' via Spotlight's website – and, possibly, elsewhere.

If you intend to travel down these routes, check the details (including pricing) of each possible company and the quality of their work. You should also assess whether the financial investment(s) involved could produce sufficient return. These additional 'calling cards' need to be of broadcast quality and professionally packaged to have any impact. As with photographers, it is very important to research as thoroughly as possible before committing your meagre funds. Is there a real possibility that one (or more) will enhance your chances of acting work?

Note: It is very important that you have permission from the copyright-holders of any material that you intend to use, and some companies will help with this. It is also important to check the current charges of each company that interests you, as some will change during the lifetime of this edition.

Accent Bank
420 Falcon Wharf, 34 Lombard Road,
London SW11 3RF
tel 020 7223 5160
email enquiries@accentbank.co.uk
website www.accentbank.co.uk
Director Lisa Paterson

A voice-over portal distributed to an international market. Acts as a shop window for experienced voice-over talent specialising in authentic regional and international voices. "Accent Bank provides bespoke one-on-one coaching and workshops for those new to the business. We pride ourselves on a very personal service, using the best coaches and directors, original material and excellent production facilities to bring out the best in your voice. For more information, or to have a chat, contact us by phone or email."

Actor Showreels
51 The Cut, South Bank, London SE1 8LF
tel 07853 637965
email post@actorshowreels.co.uk
website www.actorshowreels.co.uk
Key contact Hugh Montini Lee

Showreel services: The actor works with an editor to select the material from pre-existing clips. The edited material is uploaded online, so that the actor's agent can also view the edit. The editing/upload process continues until the actor is totally satisfied with the final edit. The average duration of a showreel is 3.5 minutes. Average cost per showreel is £175. Recent clients have included: Claire Goose (Independent), Gina Bellman (Independent), Tulisa (Cole Kitchenn), Kerry Ellis (Cole Kitchenn), Colin Salmon (Curtis Brown) and Jennifer Hennessy (Curtis Brown).

Actors Apparel

London based – travels to clients
mobile 07738 876295 07877 142823
email contact@actorsapparel.com
website www.actorsapparel.com

Showreel services: Established in 2010. Charges £780 for a Popular Showreel, £980 for an Exclusive Showreel. Tailor-made showreels; originally written scenes tailored to client's brief. HD footage, montage clips, editing and high-quality sound. Online links and hard copies included. Charges £50 per hour for producing a showreel from existing material only. Popular Showreel includes 3 free hard copies, Exclusive Showreel includes 6 free hard copies. Both packages include online conversion for Spotlight and Casting Call Pro. Editing from existing material, £50 per hour. Average showreel duration is 3-5 minutes. Discounts offered for dual bookings. Please see website brochure for more details and special offers. Also offers Short Film Packages. Recent clients include: Max Fowler (Eamonn Bedford Associates), Katie Redford (Red Canyon Management), Verity Hewlitt (Hoxton Street Casting), Nick Lavelle (SCA Management), Cherice Mckenzie-Cook (Top Talent Agency), Thea Cantell (Sandra Boyce Management), Katie Redford (Red Canyon Management), Max Fowler (Macfarlane Chard Associates) and Carla Nicholls (Lynda Ronan Personal Management).

The Actor's One-Stop Shop

First Floor, Above the Gate Pub, Station Road, London N22 7SS
tel 020 8888 7006 *fax* 020 8888 9666
email info@actorsonestopshop.com
website www.actorsonestopshop.com
established 1997

Showreel services: Offers broadcast-quality, professionally packaged reels. Scenes are crafted like film/TV excerpts rather than being 'audition pieces'. Actors can choose either monologue or dialogue scenes, in any combination they wish. A single scene (monologue) reel costs £310 (including final copy in box DVD presentation).

Also edits reels from past work at a cost of £60 per hour; clients sit-in on the edit and receive the finished product the same day. Price includes full archiving of material so that the reel can be easily and affordably updated in the future. The company also supplies 'streamed' copies for agency and Spotlight websites.

Recommended by several agents, Spotlight and Casting Call Pro. See website for reel samples.

Bolt Tight Showreels

Based in South East London
mobile 07533 353836
email info@samanthabolter.com
website www.vimeo.com/bolt
Facebook www.facebook.com/BoltTightReels
Twitter @BoltTightReels
Key contact Samantha Bolter

Showreel services: Established in 2004. Charges £100 per showreel edit (which includes 1 DVD copy, Internet files and DVD cover). Motto is the '3 M's' - "no Montage, no Monologues to camera and no longer than 3 Minutes!" £400 daily fee to shoot scenes (price can be split between actors; roughly 2-3 scenes can be shot in a day. Price negotiable for updates to existing reel(s). Packages offered: 20% off edit (total £80) and shoot price (total £320 per day) for students, recent graduates and Equity members. Also see Bolt Tight's Facebook page (**BoltTightReels**) or follow the company on Twitter (**@BoltTightReels**).

Does not supply scripts though will happily give advice on how/what to pick. Rehearsal and direction given on day of shoot. Professional directors, sound and camera operators on every shoot (all on IMDb, please contact for details). Editing equipment is portable to locations within London or Brighton. Recent clients include: Russell Floyd, Kimberley Adams and Brad Glen.

CastNet Ltd

20 Sparrows Herne, Bushey, Hertfordshire WD23 1FU
tel 020 8420 4209 *fax* 020 8421 9666
email support@castnetwebsites.co.uk
website www.castnetwebsites.co.uk
Key Contact Fran Gillett

Founded in 2007, CastNet Websites offer affordable and adaptable website building services, designed specifically for UK performers.

Website services: Offers a basic website building service which is free, but standard templates start from £2 per week or £7.45 per month. Premium templates start from £4 per week or £17.45 per month. Standard packages include hosting and domain name registration, email addresses, search engine optimisation and a facility for clients to update their own site. Premium templates include integrated blog, Twitter feed, unlimited video and audio clips, visitor statistics and private document storage. Recent clients include Will Wollen (Steve Nealon Associates), Morven Macbeth (Regan Rimmer Management) and Sophie Cartman (MSFT Management).

See also the entry for CastNet Ltd under *Spotlight, casting directories and information services* on page 381.

Ben Crowe

2 Gladstone Close, Hove BN3 7PD
mobile 07952 784911
email bencrowe@hotmail.co.uk
Key contact Ben Crowe

Charges £75 for producing a Spotlight voicereel from scratch (or £65 with Spotlight card, and for students).

Includes 2 additional CD copies. Average duration of the reel is 60-90 minutes. "Select 4 30-second speeches for Spotlight voice clips."

Crying Out Loud Productions

Chester House (1:12), 1-3 Brixton Road,
London SW9 6DE
mobile Simon: 07809 549887;
mobile Marina: 07946 533108
email simon@cryingoutloud.co.uk
website www.cryingoutloud.co.uk
Key contacts Simon Cryer, Marina Caldarone

Voicereel services: Established in 1999. Charges from £325 plus VAT to produce a bespoke voicereel from scratch; this includes a face-to-face consultation with Marina Caldarone to select material, studio time with both producer and director, full editing and production, a copy of the voice only files, a two-minute megamixe for online service and a 2-year archive.

Clients will record a selection of material consisting of a mixture of commercials, narrative, documentary, corporate, animation and drama as well as any other content they may wish to add to best suit their strengths.

Both are practitioners in the industry - Simon Cryer (Voice Director and Producer and owner of Damn Good Voices Agency) and Marina Caldarone (Director of BBC's *The Archers* and a major UK soap). Limits recording sessions to 20 clients per month - demand is high so book early.

Cut Glass Productions

Tides, Britwell Drive, West Lulworth
tel 01929 400758
email phil@cutglassproductions.com
website www.cutglassproductions.com
Producer Phil Corran

Voicereel services: Two package options:
• £210 'Revive' – created for artists who wish to update or make changes to an existing showreel.
• £250 'Create' – for actors/artists who need a completely new reel. A lot of support and advice is given to beginners. Includes script consultation and 4 hours' studio time.
• £350 'Raw Talent' – this package is for complete newcomers to the voice industry who feel they are going to need the freedom of unlimited time in the studio.

Once each actor's showreel expectations are established, there is a detailed pre-consultation by phone – this enables Cut Glass to get to know you and select material suitable for your playing age/range. Cut Glass doesn't recycle scripts – each piece (4-5 commercials, 2 narrations or documentaries, maybe an animation/story piece) will be unique to you. There is also a detailed consultation on the day to discuss selected material. The recording session itself is a creative experience in terms of ideas and performance, with Phil Corran directing and producing the session. You will be guided throughout the production and go home with your mastered reel and 1 extra copy. Showreels are around 4 mins long, with an option to produce a 90-second punchy 'montage' which sits at the beginning of your reel and can be emailed to casting directors as an MP3 or used on Spotlight.

As well as specialising in creating high-quality voice-over showreels, Cut Glass is a digital voice-over production studio and creative voice agency. As such, the company has a diverse range of clients – both professional voice-over jobs and showreel customers – and works with animation/computer games companies, corporates, the BBC and independent production companies. It regularly produces audio guides and comedy podcasts, and produces showreels for other agencies as well as its own. See the website for examples of 'montages' of the agency's showreels.

Advice to beginners: As voice-over agents, Cut Glass recommends that your showreel be no longer than around 4 mins; any longer and you will have lost the casting director/agent's attention. Talk to people who work in the voice industry, and listen to recommendations. It's so important to get your showreel production spot-on, because it's your one chance to showcase your vocal talent.

Opus Productions Ltd

9A Coverdale Road, London W12 8JJ
tel 020 8743 3910 *fax* 020 8749 4537
website www.opusproductions.co.uk
Key personnel Claire Bidwell, Neil Wilkes

Established in 1999. Works mainly in computer media production. Specialises in video and audio encoding, DVD authoring, video editing, graphic design and website design. Will edit, produce and encode video and DVD showreels for actors.

Pelinor

Harberton Road, London N19 3JR
tel 020 7263 8862
email support@pelinor.com
website www.pelinor.com
Key contact Misha von Bennigsen

Showreel services: Established in 2003. Charges £150 for producing a showreel with existing material only, which includes 1 DVD; extra copies are charged from £1. Average duration of a showreel is 3 minutes. Offers 10% off for CCP and TAG members. Recent clients include: Samantha Robinson (Curtis Brown), Margo Stilley (Curtis Brown), Dave Berry (Troika) and Sharon Duce (JAA).

Website services: Charges £450 for designing and setting up a basic website (£360 for existing clients). Offers a bespoke 'from scratch' design. Package includes hosting and domain name registration, email addresses, search engine optimisation, and facility for clients to update their own site. Updates charged at £40 per hour. Material is usually selected from existing headshots, biographies/CVs, publicity stills, showreels and voicereels.

Popcorn Hub
London UK
mobile 07900 133303
email bookings@popcorn-hub.com
website www.popcorn-hub.com
Twitter @PopcornHub

Services: A boutique production company that offers video production, social media promotion and showreel services.

Packages include 'The Reel Deal'™ and 'Seal the Real'™. For more details and up to 20% off visit the website and enter the code #YEARBOOK19. Also offers studio, crew and photography hire.

The social media department specialises in YouTube, Facebook and Instagram.

The Reel Deal Showreel Co.
6 Charlotte Road, Wallington, Surrey SM6 9AX
tel 020 8647 1235
email info@thereel-deal.co.uk
website www.thereel-deal.co.uk
established 2003

Showreel services: Has 2 rates for editing a showreel: £199 for a full day's editing, which includes 2 free hours in the first year to update the reel, and 2 free DVDs; or the hourly rate of £35 for actors who don't have a lot of material. A discount of 15% is offered if you mention this publication when booking your edit. Clients include: James McAvoy, Rory Kinnear, Rula Lenska, Shane Richie and Shobna Gulati, among others.

Replay Film & New Media
25 Museum Street, London WC1 1ST
tel 020 7637 0473
email solutions@replayfilms.co.uk
website www.replayfilms.com
established 1991

Showreel services: Although Replay can record presentations and performances from scratch, for most clients the task is to produce a carefully constructed compilation of highlights from existing TV and film performances. Advises that the correct selection and juxtaposition of these clips is essential, and it is therefore vital that clients sit in on the editing process to ensure that they are happy with the final result. Most showreels last 4-7 minutes. Will supply scripts if requested, but does not organise for copyright clearance.

As most showreels take around 4 hours to edit, Replay has put together the following package for a fixed fee: up to 4 hours in the edit studio with the editor (digitising existing clips from VHS, capturing digitised clips onto an Avid editing suite, editing the captured clips and inserting titles where required). The digital master will be archived at 2 sites. Exact prices are available on application only. Discounted rates are available to actors, presenters, students and non-commercial theatre companies. Overtime (anything over 4 hours) is charged at approximately 50% of the commercial editing rate.

Recent clients include: Donald Standen, Julian Hanshaw, Justine Waddel, Michael Mears, Patsy Kensit, Shared Experience Theatre Company and Vicky Johnson.

The Showreel Ltd
Soho Recording Studios, 22-24 Torrington Place, London WC1E 7HJ
tel 020 7043 8660
email info@theshowreel.com
website www.theshowreel.com
Facebook www.facebook.com/groups/theshowreel
Twitter @theshowreel

Showreel services overview:

• Get started in voiceovers with our Intro Workshops
• Release the voices in your head with our Character Workshops
• Learn to make money from home with our Home Studio Workshop
• One-to-one personal training plans to increase your skills
• Agents' Demo to get a voiceover agent
• Drama Demo for the BBC
• Character Demo for games and animation
• Audio Book Demo for RNIB, Audible, iTunes and Amazon.

For other services, please visit the website.

Showreel Editing by Anthony Holmes
17 Knole Road, Crayford, London DA1 3JN
tel 020 8144 8835
email anthony@showreelediting.com
website www.showreelediting.com
Facebook www.facebook.com/anthonyholmes.showreelediting
Twitter @showreelediting
Instagram @showreelediting
Key contact Anthony Holmes

Showreel and voicereel editing service for talent with existing footage. Clients include: Sir David Jason, Shohreh Aghdashloo and Cas Anvar. Charges £80 per hour billed in half-hourly increments (minimum charge one hour). Showreel provided as a digital file for direct upload to Spotlight or other casting websites. Able to record material broadcast on television on request, and to download/record material from streaming services such as Netflix, iPlayer and YouTube (where client has permission to do so). Showreel material archived for easier updates. Average duration of a showreel is 3 minutes. Those who quote *Actors and Performers Yearbook* when booking, will receive a 10% discount. Also offers assistance with selection of material for existing footage if required. Does not record voicereels, but is able to edit from radio, animation and videofame material and from existing voicereels if required.

Showreelz.com

51 Cranbrook Road, London W4 2LJ
mobile 07885 253477
email showreelz@yahoo.com
website www.showreelz.com
established 1998

Showreel services: Showreelz.com has been editing showreels for performers since 1999. The company is based in Chiswick, London W4. Editing rates are £75 for the first two hours and then £30 per hour for additional time.

Offers a 15% discount on editing to actors mentioning this publication.

Voicereel services: Rates are set at £75 for the first 2 hours. Normally produces voicereels lasting 2-3 minutes. Will offer a 10% discount to actors quoting this publication.

Silver-Tongued Productions

tel 020 8309 0659
email contactus@silver-tongued.co.uk
website www.silver-tongued.co.uk
Twitter @STP_Voicereels

Voicereel services: With over 20 years of experience recording and producing high-quality voicereels at a competative price. "We guide you through the whole process of recording your voicereel, from choosing your scripts to directing you during the recording session, making it as simple and as easy as possible. Our voicereels are truly bespoke, so are as individual as you are." Visit the website for full details of services.

Silvertip Films Ltd

20 Enterprise House, Foundry Lane, Horsham, West Sussex RH13 5PX
tel 01403 221068 *mobile* 07786 331502
email info@silvertipfilms.co.uk
website www.silvertipfilms.co.uk
Key Contact Geoff Cockwill

Showreel services: Established in 2005.

Shoot and Edit 1 is £400 + VAT + any expenses – this is a half day shooting 3 scenes, either monologue or duologue and editing the scenes for the reel plus any existing material you have.

Shoot and Edit 2 is £800 + VAT + any expenses. This is as above but a full day shooting up to 4 scenes plus editing, including any existing material.

Editing existing material only is £250 + VAT + any expenses. This is a half-day edit and includes transfer of existing material on DVD or from online and editing the reel either using either notes or direct input from the client. The reel is sent to the client for approval and any reasonable changes will be made where possible.

A discount of 10% is available to readers of *Actors and Performers Yearbook*. Packages include reel in web HD format, HD data file and a DVD or BluRay copy. Additional copies at £1.50 (inc. P&P). Silvertip also upload the reel to their YouTube channel and CCP page. The average length of a showreel is 3-4 minutes

Silvertip's previous clients include: Jessica Jay (cre8 talent), Alexis Peterman (United Artists), Dar Dash (Hobsons), Heather Skermer (Red Hot Entertainment) and Libby Gore (Imperium Management).

SonicPond Studio

70 Mildmay Grove South, Islington, London N1 4PJ
tel 020 7690 8561
email martin@sonicpond.co.uk
website www.sonicpond.co.uk
Key contact Martin Fisher

Showreel services: Editing of existing material only. Charges £200 (£180 for students) to edit a showreel from existing material, uploaded directly to Spotlight for you. The average duration of a showreel is 3-4 minutes. Clients include: Annie Cooper (Felix de Wolfe); Zoe Lister (*Hollyoaks*) and Sid Owen (*EastEnders*). Advises actors: "Don't worry that you may not have enough material; you most likely do. Less is truly more with showreels. Also, don't wait for that copy of the student film you have been waiting to be sent; think of the reel as an organic growing thing which you will add to and change for the whole of your career. Just get it started."

Voicereel services: Supplies scripts for actors to use if desired. Charges £345 to produce a commercial voicereel from scratch; working from existing material the rate is £50 per hour. Broadcast quality MP3s of all files are included in the package. Nine pieces recorded, commercial and narrative, with a 90-second montage included. Students: £320 for a full voicereel. Game/animation reels £ 295. Voice clients include: Bob Golding (Hobsons); Nicholas Keith (Yakety Yak); Kellie Bright (Sue Terry Voices); Sam & Mark (Harvey Voices); Ronan Vibert (Harvey Voices) and James Alexandrou (Earache). Advises actors: "Don't worry about the pieces, we will work together to find you the best material. It's much more about finding the tone for each piece, and material that suits you perfectly, rather than the best copy. In the meantime, listen to as much voice-over as possible, and think about why any particular voice is used for any piece."

Sound

Sound, Pembroke House, 7, Brunswick Square, Bristol BS2 8PE
tel 0117 9245 853
email kenwheeler@mac.com
website www.soundat7.com
Key Contact Ken Wheeler

Voicereel services: Established in 1987. Charges £300 (+ VAT) to produce a bespoke voicereel from scratch.This includes a pre-production meeting to select material suitable for the artist and they will be provided with copies for familiarisation and rehearsal before any recording takes place. Sound are happy to provide scripts and organise copyright clearance issues. Editing existing material will cost £110 (+ VAT).The average length of a voicereel is 15 minutes and CD copies of the final recording are available for purchase at 75p each.

Sound's recent clients include: Jaguar, Virgin Media, DFS, Really Useful Theatres Group and Stihl.

Sounds Wilde
Wood Green, London N22
mobile 07930 689132
email kirsty@soundswilde.com
website www.soundswilde.com
Twitter @soundswilde
Instagram @soundswilde
Key contact Kirsty Gillmore

Character voicereel services: Established in 2010. Amination Character Voicereel Package: £350 inc. VAT (clients record 8-12 characters, mixed into a 90-sec master montage with copies of all clips).

Gaming Character Voicereel Package: £350 inc. VAT (clients record 6-10 characters which are mixed into a 90-sec master montage, with copies of all individual clips).

Radio Drama Reel Package: £295 inc. VAT (clients record 8 scripts, mixed into a 2-3 minute reel, with copies of all individual clips).

The UK's only character voicereel specialist. Supplies bespoke scripts (gaming and animation reels) written to character descriptions discussed in an initial personal consultation. Voiceover Services Provider of the Year 2019

Recent clients include: Joanna Lee (Best Animation Demo, One Voice Awards 2019), Dominic Carter (*Game of Thrones*) Christos Lawton (*The Terror*). Advises clients: "Come prepared for your voicereel session – be familiar with your scripts (but not over-practiced), fully warmed up and ready to work hard. Your voicereel producer will offer fully direction you need, but don't be afraid to ask questions or add your own input. Only include character voices and varying accents if you are 100% comfortable with them."

Take Five
37 Beak Street, London W1F
tel 020 7287 2120 *fax* 020 7287 3035
email info@takefivestudio.com
website www.takefivestudio.com
Key contact Charlie Lort-Phillips
established 1995

Showreel services: Charges £70 per hour for filming and £45 per hour for editing (this includes all studio and equipment costs). VHS copies are priced at £6

each, DVDs at £13 each and CDs at £6 each. Discounts are offered for bigger quantities.

A script consultation is held with each actor, preferably 7 days prior to filming. Scenes can be shot in the studio or on location, and benefit from professional direction, lighting and cameramen. Most showreels last around 5 minutes. The company advises actors who are sending in existing material only to cue scenes on the tape or to have the timecodes written down to speed up the capturing process.

Recent clients include: Siobhan Hewlett (Hamilton Hodell), Harry Eden (Independent), Lee Ingleby (Conway van Gelder Grant) and Tim Barlow (Paul Becker).

Twitch Films
22 Grove End Gardens, 18 Abbey Road, London NW8 9LL
tel 020 7266 0946
email post@twitchfilms.co.uk
website www.twitchfilms.co.uk

Established in 2006; offices are fully wheelchair accessible. Working with existing material, charges a flat fee of £200, which includes editing, design of DVD interface and discprint, 10 professionally printed and packaged DVDs, digital files for use on the Internet, websites and for emailing and full archiving. For shorter edits and updates the hourly rate is £40; additional discs can be ordered from £2.50 each, depending on quantity. The average duration of a showreel is 3-5 minutes.

"We advise recording material from scratch only in exceptional circumstances, primarily when an aspect of the actor's range, which would be key to their castability, is under-represented in their existing footage. We do not provide scripts, but will give detailed advice on what scripts may be appropriate, and assist in making the selection." Recent clients include: Darren Boyd and Eleanor Matsuura (Amanda Howard Associates); Colin Salmon (GMM); Jane Perry (Andrew Manson Personal Management); Kevork Malikyan (United Agents) and Trevor White (Price Gardner Management).

Voiceover Kickstart
North London
mobile 07973 445328
email guy@voice-reel.com
website www.voice-reel.com
Facebook www.facebook.com/VOkickstart/
Twitter @VOkickstart
Key contact Guy Michaels

Voicereel services: Charges from £300 inclusive. All voiceover demos are created from scratch. Strict 2 client a week limit ensures a bespoke service.

Clients receive all full versions of the tracks in addition to the compilation. Full guidance/online client area. Sourcing and choosing material is a collaborative process. Scripts are written and tailor-made for gaming demos. Does not arrange copyright clearance.

Has clients worldwide and with all major agencies including Excellent Talent, Lip Service, Soho Voices, Rhubarb Voices, Sue Terry Voices and many more. Full voice-over training facility and free 4-week course available at **www.voiceoverkickstart.com**.

Ken Wheeler
28 Wellington Terrace, Clevedon,
North Somerset BS21 7PT
tel 01275 879799
email kenwheeler@mac.com
website www.soundat7.com

Established in 1987. Supplies scripts. Recent clients include: Virgin, Asda, DFS, Sainsburys, Parampara, Jaguar, The Co-Op, Alfa Romeo, Scholastic Education and Bristol City Council.

Voicereel services: Normal hourly rate is £100. For an inclusive cost of £350, including direction, recording, editing and mixing, we will produce a voicereel from scratch. During a pre-production meeting, scripts (commercials, corporate, narration, prose and poetry) will be selected that are suited to the particular voice to provide a varied and balanced reel.

Resources

Showreels: creation and maintenance

Anthony Holmes

What is a showreel, and why does an actor need one?

A showreel, also known as a demo reel or acting reel, is a short video showcase featuring an actor's best clips.

The key objective of a showreel is career development; a reel isn't a compilation of every character an actor has ever played, but a tool with which to help get cast. As such, your primary audience for a showreel should be casting directors, whose job it is to cast or shortlist actors in film and television. Always think of this audience when editing a showreel; will it help the casting director cast you? Have you used your best clips, and are they appropriate for the roles you're applying for? Think like a casting director. Your showreel should represent you as you are now, and reflect your current vital statistics and casting age. A showreel is successful if it fulfils the primary objective; helping the actor get more work. A showreel by itself won't necessarily secure an actor a role (although there have been many cases of actors being cast on the strength of their showreel alone), but it's a crucial part of the mix which leads to casting success.

Many actors have a main general-purpose showreel, and then additional reels to help them target specific roles, e.g. a commercials reel and a comedy reel, ensuring their reel is always relevant to the specific submission.

Once you have your showreel, how is it best used? Spotlight's interactive services have a near monopoly status for professional productions in the UK, although there are a number of other casting websites used, particularly by low budget or no budget productions, which are unlikely to have a casting director on board. Your agent will submit your application through Spotlight for a particular role, and the casting director will view your CV, headshot and showreel on Spotlight, and consider your suitability for the role. You can also send your Spotlight link directly to casting directors, but unless you're responding to a specific open casting call, please check first that the casting director accepts cold submissions. Never send the showreel file itself (or any other large file such as a headshot), but send a link to your Spotlight profile – large files clog up email inboxes and the last thing you want to do is annoy a casting director!

It's also becoming more important to have an active social media following; a large and active fan base will make you more attractive to producers, particularly for high-profile US-produced television shows and major features. Many actors like to promote their showreel on social media, although opinions among agents are mixed; some prefer to keep their clients' reels away from general public view, and prefer to keep them for the eyes of casting directors and other stakeholders only. Shorter clips or 'sizzle' reels are becoming increasingly popular, however, both with actors and agents, and can be used effectively on social media to help promote an actor's appearance in a film or television series, and help the actor to build and maintain a fan-base.

If you're just starting your career, you may not have much in the way of scenes from film and television to include in a showreel. It can be useful to increase the number of your showreel scenes by applying for lower budget short films and student films. These productions may not have a budget to employ a casting director, and you are likely to be applying directly to the director or producer.

Your headshot will persuade a casting director to look at your CV, and your showreel will persuade them to call you in for an audition. Once you're in the room, your performance and personality can persuade the casting director you're the right person for the job.

You will maximise your opportunities and your chances of being cast if you use the right selection of clips in the right way. A skilled and experienced showreel editor will be able to advise on this.

The general-purpose showreel

Your main showreel should showcase your range, a variety of different roles, and some different looks, but also bear in mind that consistency and suitability for type can be attractive to casting directors.

You may wish to demonstrate your ultimate acting ability by including a range of roles. You should certainly include a good contrast of scenes in your showreel, but bear in mind many casting directors are looking for a type, and you're making their job easier to cast you if you don't try to be all things to all people. This is a difficult balance to strike, especially if you do not wish to be known as a one-trick pony. Theatre casting directors may appreciate a greater contrast of roles than film or television directors, but I do not advise including filmed scenes of theatre work given than the greater part of actor employment is for the screen. If you pride yourself on being a good character actor, you could benefit from a separate reel for each type of character you know you can play, but a more common approach is to edit your general tape for specific submissions, including the most appropriate scenes for that job.

The duration of your main showreel will depend on the experience you have, and the footage you have. Many showreels are around two to three minutes. It's better to have a shorter and tighter showreel featuring the best of the best, rather than padding things out. Casting directors are busy people; if they don't see what they're looking for in the first few seconds, they'll move on – so make the most of your time!

Some actors present an opening montage of moments from the scenes that are to follow. This is generally not recommended. An opening montage to a general reel wastes valuable screen time and a majority of casting directors don't like them. Don't waste time at the start – jump straight into a substantial scene with dialogue. Remember that casting directors want to hear you and see you interact with others, so don't spend long on a moody visual opening shot. Always open with your strongest material. Make it clear who you are, and avoid any confusion; where possible, your showreel should open with a close-up of you rather than a group scene or a close-up of another actor, and be wary of opening your showreel with a scene including another actor of the same gender and age range.

Prioritise your higher profile footage and scenes with better production values. If you have the experience and material, casting directors prefer to see how you handle yourself in the real world, in a fully professional environment; be wary of using 'shot-for-showreel' scenes which often don't reflect a typical working environment, which are likely to have lower production values than even a typical student film, and in which you may be acting with less talented and less experienced actors, dragging down the tone of the showreel and making it less attractive to casting directors. Self-tapes are the way forward for individual castings, but don't belong in your general showreel.

Resources

A showreel, like your CV, is an on-going process; keep it up-to-date with your latest footage. If it's not getting you called in for appropriate castings, tweak the edit until it does. Your showreel is all about you. An existing scene can be re-edited to reduce the screen time of other actors, and refocus the scene more on you. Don't forget, though, that casting directors don't just want to see you act, they want to see you react to other actors.

It's important to always focus on your objective; getting cast. Different casting directors and different talent agents often have different preferences, tastes and expectations from a showreel – if you know you're applying for a specific job, and you know what that casting director likes, then tweak your showreel appropriately. Once again, this is where a specialist showreel editor can advise; a good editor will have experience of what is most likely to work best, and will be interacting with a network of agents and casting directors on an ongoing basis.

Specialist showreels

Action reel: this is often more visual, focusing on your physicality. It may be either full action scenes, or a montage of action clips set to music, depending on your skillset and experience.

Comedy reel: this showcases your physical and verbal comic timing and delivery, and may be appropriate if you would like to work in sitcoms and film comedy. Stand-up comedy may be included, but as the skill sets are quite different, with different target audiences, it may be advisable to keep stand-up in a separate reel.

Commercial reel: this includes clips from your commercials, and is crafted specifically to get more work in commercials. A commercials reel is often shorter than your main showreel, with a greater emphasis on visuals rather than dialogue, as would be expected. Creating the right mood both appropriate for and respectful of each brand included in the commercial reel is important, as your audience in this case is not just the casting director but the advertising agency commissioned to represent the brand.

Demo reel: a showreel is known as a demo reel in the US. Quite rapidly, the differences between US demo reels and UK showreels are narrowing, but if you're applying for roles in US-produced drama, your general showreel may benefit from some slight tweaks to make it more attractive to US productions, such as making it a little more 'glam', and emphasising your looks. A demo reel can be important for career development, as it opens you up to higher profile work. Even if you don't want to work in the US, many American productions are shot in the UK.

Dramatic reel: this is often less visually active than the general reel, and focused on character relationships.

Public reel or 'sizzle' reel: unlike your main reel and most other specialist reels, which are aimed primarily at casting directors, your public reel is used on your website or social media channels to help build and maintain a fan base. A sizzle reel can take many forms, but generally has more action than dialogue and is more fast-paced than other reels, often (but not always) well under a minute long. It can feature shortened scenes or short sound-bites (along the lines of a film trailer), or can be a visual montage set to appropriate music. This positive encouragement to consider sizzle reels should not be confused by the dis-approval of montages at the beginning of general reels. The general/main reel and the sizzle reel serve very different purposes.

Voiceover reel: actors' use of audio voice reels for their narration/voiceover work is long established, but recently it has become more popular to have a video reel to place their work in context, and to show examples of their work as transmitted, though many casting directors still prefer voice reels. Examples of video voiceover reels include an animation, narration and videogame reels.

Actors can also use visual voiceover reels on their websites and social media to help build and maintain a fan-base. It's also easy to provide an audio-only MP3 file from a video voice reel to provide to casting directors who only want an audio reel; it's not easy to simply add video to an existing voice reel. Starting off with a video voice reel means you have a lot of flexibility for use.

You may prefer to specialise in a specific skillset, or develop latent ability as your career advances necessitating the creation of dance reels, modelling reels or presenting/hosting reels.

All rules are made to be broken! The advice given in this article is applicable to many situations, but there will often be occasions where individual situations require different approaches, particularly as the world of online casting is ever-changing. Your showreel editor will be able to advise on the best approach for your situation. To view some examples of the different styles of showreels and demo reels that are available to actors, visit **www.showreelediting.com.**

Anthony Holmes has nearly twenty years' experience as a specialist editor of showreels, working with actors, agents and casting directors in the UK, US, Canada and Europe. Anthony has edited reels for actors at every stage of their careers; from young actors (under 16s) and recent graduates, all the way to Emmy Award winners and Oscar nominees. A good showreel editor knows what works, and Anthony has helped to develop the television and film careers of hundreds of actors, from recurring roles on television to major roles in Academy Award-winning films.

Digital wellbeing for actors

Essentially, digital wellbeing is using the web to work better, not longer; making smart digital choices that work for you. Here, Sinead Mac Manus looks at some of the ways in which you can harness the power of the social web without suffering the burnout.

Getting a web presence

Having a dedicated web presence is increasingly important for any freelance actor. Your personal website can act as a central place on the web for potential employers or collaborators to find you. With free platforms such as WordPress[1], Posterous[2] or Flavors[3], it's never been easier to raise your profile online.

Your domain name

The first step before choosing a web platform is to register your own domain name. Even if you never use it, for the cost of a few pounds each year it is worth owning your own .com and retaining control of your name online. Use a site such as Netnames[4] to search for your professional name and check that it is available. 123-reg[5] is a company with a good reputation for domain name management in the UK, or you can buy your domain name with your web hosting package (see below).

Now you have your domain name secured, how can you build your web presence?

Building a WordPress site

WordPress's easy-to-use and powerful Content Management System (CMS) makes it perfect for freelance artists wanting to create their own website. The platform is free to install and adapt; the only expenses incurred are registering a domain name and paying for web hosting. The CMS of WordPress is easy to get to grips with: in fact, anyone at ease with Microsoft Word will be able to publish a website using WordPress.

Before you start building your site, have a think about what content you want on it. Suggested pages could be Biography, Photography, Credits, Reviews and Contact Me. With WordPress you can easily add a blog to your website with updates of your work.

For a practical step-by-step guide to using WordPress to build your web presence, do read my two-part series on WordPress written for the London Theatre Blog[6]. Part One covers the basics, and Part Two goes into more detail about design, themes, widgets and plug-ins.

Zen Tip: Use a WordPress approved web hosting service to install the WordPress software in one click, rather than going through the complicated manual process.

Do I need a blog?

Blogging can be a great way of building your personal brand as an actor. Through text, images, video or sound, you can demonstrate, reflect and comment on your artistic process. Writing a blog is also a powerful learning tool, promoting critical and analytical thinking, as well as being a powerful audience development and marketing tool.

Microblogging platforms such as Posterous[2] and Tumblr[7] are simple and free ways of starting a blog. Easier to set up than a WordPress blog, these platforms really come into their own when blogging on the go; perfect for freelance actors on tour. Both platforms allow you to post snippets of text, photos, quotes, links, dialogues, audio, video and slideshows from the web or direct from your smart phone.

For a look at the multimedia capabilities of Posterous in action, go to my blog *From Apps to Zen*.[8]

Zen Tip: Use the scheduling feature of Posterous or Tumblr to queue your posts for autoposting during busy tour periods.

Other platforms

Flavors[3] is a relative newcomer to the platform scene, but a fantastic way of creating a personal portal for all your online content in minutes. Simply register your Flavors name (or use you own custom domain), design your layout and background, and then add your choice of 30 social websites. You can pull in tweets from your Twitter Feed, your Wall activity from your Facebook Page, videos from YouTube or Vimeo, posts from your Posterous, Tumblr or WordPress blogs, or photos from Flickr or Instagram[9].

Have a look at some of the wonderfully creative sites on the Flavors' Directory[10] for inspiration.

Zen Tip: Use the Promote tab to add a Search Engine Optimised (SEO)[11] title and description of your page to ensure you are easily found in the search engines.

Using social media

There is a wide range of social media networks and platforms that you can use to communicate and connect with people in the creative industries. Social networks such as Facebook and Twitter, as well as multimedia platforms such as YouTube and Flickr, can help you market yourself, raise your profile and connect with potential employers.

Getting started on social media is relatively easy as the entry barriers are low, both technologically and financially. Social media also harnesses the most highly prized of the marketing methods: word of mouth. It allows you to exponentially expand your marketing potential and reach many more potential audience members or clients than you could using solely an offline approach.

All good so far … But if social media is so effective and easy to use, why isn't every artist jumping on board?

The number one reason why creative people do not get engaged with social media is lack of time, and specifically a fear that if they do engage, it will eat up large chunks of an already busy day. Questions to consider are: do you have the time to plan how you are going to use social media in your work? Do you have the time to set up profiles and start connecting with people? Do you have the time to maintain your online presences and maximise the return from these sites?

I think social media has a bad reputation for being a source of time-wasting. Many of us are guilty of having spent too much time on Facebook or YouTube when we could have been doing something more productive! However, social media does not have to be an unnecessary drain on your time. Rebecca Coleman, a Canadian PR consultant in the performing arts, has written an excellent guide to getting started in social media[12]. She recommends that artists create a Social Networking Marketing Plan, outlining what they want to achieve with social media; what platforms and tools they will focus on; and lastly, how much time they are going to dedicate to being online. Think of social media like email: a brilliant innovation which, when used strategically, can enhance your business and increase opportunity. Of the social media-savvy people I know, many deliberately limit their time online to one or two hours a day for this very reason.

Resources

LinkedIn

My first recommendation would be to set up a LinkedIn[13] profile for your professional name. LinkedIn is a popular social networking site for professionals, featuring high in the search engine rankings, so you can use it as an opportunity to shine.

Setting up a LinkedIn profile is easy. A great profile picture is essential, and an easy one for actors – you can use one of your headshots.

Next, add a juicy-sounding headline that highlights your talents, e.g. "Freelance Actor, Facilitator & Workshop Leader specialising in Site-Specific Theatre". Add Current and Past employments, bearing in mind that LinkedIn lists these in order of start date with the latest position appearing at the top. Claim your 'vanity' URL, i.e. http://uk.linkedin.com/in/yourname by clicking on the Edit link beside it.

Spend some time writing a Summary for your profile. Have a search for other actors on LinkedIn for inspiration. Highlight any noteworthy achievements or credits. Use the Specialities section to summarise any particular talents or skills that you have, e.g. workshop facilitating, fluent Spanish speaker, trained ballet dancer, mask skills, etc.

Recommendations on LinkedIn are a powerful example of what's called 'social proof' – proof to your potential clients that others have already gone before and had a positive experience working with you. No one wants to be the guinea pig!

Now you are ready to start connecting. Use the Add Connections button to find people through your email contacts or through LinkedIn's recommendations. I make a point of connecting on LinkedIn with people I meet socially or at networking events to keep them in my network.

LinkedIn can be a great way of getting introductions to a particular person, e.g. a director or agent that you want to connect with. The more you build your network on LinkedIn, the more likely it is that someone in your network might know them and can provide an introduction.

Twitter

Twitter is one of those social networking sites that divides opinion. To the Twitterarti, it's a way of keeping abreast of what's going on in their industry as well as a way to connect and boost their online profile. To everyone else, it seems like a complete waste of time! But its reach is growing exponentially.

Once you have set up a Twitter account by registering a Twitter name and posting some information about yourself, you can start 'tweeting'. Other users can choose to 'follow' your tweets – they are called 'followers', and you can search for and follow others using the Find People tab. The best way to learn how to use Twitter is to use it: get an account, search for people you think are interesting to follow, and watch and learn how people interact. The Arts Council England digital strategy programme AmbITion has a free Twitter for Beginners ebook[14] on their website, which is a great guide to getting started.

For me, the number one strategic use of Twitter is the constant sharing of valuable information. Following others in your industry or sector allows you to have a network at your fingertips to share ideas and conversations, to find answers or to keep updated on great blog posts and resources. The beauty of Twitter is the brevity of the medium. No essay-style blog posts here, just up-to-date, relevant and interesting conversation that can be skimmed through in minutes. Andrew Girvan[15] on his blog has a great article on 129 people to follow in theatre, crossing venues, companies, news feeds and commentators, and is a good place to start to build your Twitter community.

Zen Tip: Use a free Twitter application such as Tweetdeck[16] to provide a one-stop shop dashboard for managing all your social media use.

Video sharing

The practical application of being able to upload and share video on the web to someone working in theatre is fairly self-explanatory. With video cameras built into almost everything, it's inexpensive to make high-quality videos to showcase your talents.

There are many different video hosting and sharing sites, but a handful do stand out from the rest. YouTube[17] is the world's most popular video sharing site, and it is easy to see why. The site is free to use and, once you have set up an account, videos are easy to upload either singly or in batches. YouTube videos, now that the company is owned by Google, also rate highly in the Google search engine, and therefore clever tagging of your videos can help potential customers and audiences find your work. Another good video sharing site is Vimeo,[18] which features a lot of content from creative people.

The mobile office

An actor's life is sometimes a nomadic one, and therefore it is essential to be able to access your email and important documents wherever you go. I find a combination of Gmail[19] as my email client and file storing and sharing site Dropbox[20] fulfils all my needs when I am away from the office for any period of time.

Using Gmail on your smart phone can mean that you don't need to travel with a laptop and you can process your emails on the go. Similarly, with Dropbox, you can access all your important documents for reading, forwarding or printing direct from your smart phone.

Final thoughts

The social web can provide many benefits to the jobbing actor. It can provide an online showcase for your work, connect you to potential clients, and be used to manage your work.

With mobile computing so readily available, the social web is not going to go away. The smart actor can use these free tools to promote her/himself above the rest of the bunch.

[1]http://wordpress.org; [2]https://posterous.com; [3]http://flavors.me; [4]http://www.netnames.co.uk; [5]http://www.123-reg.co.uk; [6]http://www.londontheatreblog.co.uk/category/articles; [7]http://www.tumblr.com; [8]http://www.fromappstozen.com; [9]http://instagr.am; [10]http://flavors.me/directory; [11]http://en.wikipedia.org/wiki/Search_engine_optimization; [12]http://www.rebeccacoleman.ca; [13]https://www.linkedin.com; [14]http://www.getambition.com/resources/twitter-for-beginners; [15]http://andrewgirvan.com/100-theatre-people-to-follow-on-twitter; [16]http://www.tweetdeck.com; [17]http://www.youtube.com; [18]http://vimeo.com; [19]www.gmail.com; [20]www.dropbox.com

Sinead Mac Manus is founder of 8fold (**www.eightfold.org**), a digital well-being company that helps busy people work better. She writes about mindful 21st-century working at her blog *From Apps to Zen* (**www.fromappstozen.com**) and is the author of *From Apps to Zen: 26+ Ideas for Building a Business with Balance*. Sinead has worked for, consulted and provided training for organisations as diverse as the Independent Street Arts Network, London Metropolitan University, CreativeCapital and the Anne Peaker Centre for Arts in Criminal Justice. Sinead's activity in developing new business models around the idea of e-learning for creative entrepreneurs, using web 2.0 tools and social media, led her to be selected in 2009 as one of the Courvoisier: Future 500 to watch.

Accountants

Alexander & Co.
17 St Ann's Square, Manchester M2 7PW
tel 0161 832 4841 *fax* 0161 832 2539
email info@alexander.co.uk
website www.alexander.co.uk
Accountants John McCaffery, Stephen Verber

Established in 1976. Charges start at £250 depending on complexity. Supports clients via meetings, phone calls and email and written correspondence. Can provide document or spreadsheet templates as required, all of which are Windows compatible. Clients include 20 actors and entertainment industry professionals; the firm is recommended by Equity. "Our tax experts can give strategic planning advice to ensure that you make the most of the opportunities within the current tax system and an introduction to further specialist advice as and when required."

Alexander James & Co.
Upper Deck, Admirals Quarters, Portsmouth Road, Thames Ditton, Surrey KT7 0XA
tel 020 8398 4447 *fax* 020 8398 9989
email actors@alexanderjames.biz
website www.alexanderjames.co.uk
Accountant Andrew Nicholson

Established in 1991. Fees vary according to complexity and completeness of information supplied. Costs are on average between £375 and £500 per annum. First meeting is free, with ongoing support by phone and email and regular email newsletter. Entirely UK-based staff accustomed to working with media industry clients. Advisory work during the year is billed on completion; rates vary depending on requirements. Standard spreadsheet template provided, and online accounts support available. Around 10-15% of clientele are actors or other entertainment industry professionals. Home or workplace visits can be arranged.

Bambridge Accountants LLP
London Office: 7 Henrietta Street,
London WC2E 8PS,
UK; New York Office: 44 Wall Street,
New York NY 1005, USA
tel 020 3829 3492 (UK); 646 781 8929 (US)
email info@bambridgeaccountants.co.uk
website www.BambridgeAccountants.com
Accountants Alistair Bambridge, Jessica McKechnie, Callie Marles

With over 10 years' experience, Bambridge Accountants is an award-winning creative industry tax accountancy firm based in New York and London. Bambridge employs their specialist knowledge to minimise the tax and maximise the profit of actors, performers and other creative professionals. Quote *Actors and Performers Yearbook* to receive an exclusive 25% discount on Bambridge Accountants services.

Bells Hamilton Stewart & Co.
1A Little Roke Avenue, Kenley, Surrey CR8 5NN
tel 020 8763 1711 *fax* 020 8645 9550
email accounts@hamiltonstewart.co.uk
website www.bellshamiltonsyewart.co.uk
Accountant Joanne Bell

Established in 1972. Charges £420 (+ VAT) to prepare an actor's annual accounts for Self-Assessment Return for HMRC or £200 (+ VAT) to prepare a Self-Assessment Return only. Provides first contact face to face, but continued contact may be by email or post – whatever is reasonably required for a client's circumstances. Additional services, such as payroll or VAT Return processing, are negotiated by mutual agreement. Spreadsheet templates can be prepared for Microsoft Excel; this software is suitable for Windows 10 and can be ported to Mac. There is also a free smartphone app available through Apple and Android app stores. Has approximately 107 actor clients.

Breckman & Company
London office: 49 South Molton Street,
London W1K 5LH
tel 020 7499 2292
email info@breckmanandcompany.co.uk
Brighton office: 95 Ditchling Road, Brighton BN1 4ST
tel 01273 929350
website www.breckmanandcompany.co.uk
Accountants Kevin Beale, Graham Berry, Richard Nelson

Established for more than 50 years. Costs are dictated by complexity and time spent. Initial meeting is free during which the fee structure will be discussed. Client support includes face-to-face meetings, phone and email.

P O'N Carden
56-58 High Street, Ewell, Surrey KT17 1RW
tel 020 8394 2957 *fax*
email info@poncarden.com
website www.poncarden.com
Facebook www.facebook.com/poncarden
Accountants Philippe Carden, Mondane Carden, Andrew Fairmaner

Founded in 1977. Charges £400+VAT ("in the early years") for a complete set of accounts and tax return for sole traders. "Time and complexity increase this. Tailor-made packages for complex cases and limited companies." Provides face-to-face meetings in central London. "Our actor clients make clear how much support they feel they need, and the programme of work is tailored accordingly." Provides Excel spreadsheets appropriate to the client's needs. 50% of clients are actors and performers; 35% are other entertainment industry professionals. The offices are not wheelchair accessible, but meetings can be held in wheelchair-accessible locations. Advises actors *not* to "just give your accountant bags of receipts. Provide information about why you are claiming particular expenses. Do be obssessive about keeping payslips and remittance advices". A "Making Tax Digital" ready firm!

Mark Carr & Co. Ltd

Chartered Certified Accountants, 90 Long Acre, Covent Garden, London WC2E 9RZ
tel 020 7717 8474
email mark@markcarr.co.uk
63 Lansdowne Place, Hove, East Sussex BN3 1FL
tel (01273) 778802
website www.markcarr.co.uk

'We have over 450 clients who range from those starting out to those with celebrity status'. Providing Tax and Accounting services (including online accounting). Fees are always competitive and can be paid by a fixed monthly amount. First meeting is free of charge. Represents the Actors Centre with regular Tax Surgery. Very popular free downloadable Excel spreadsheets available from the website to clients and non-clients alike. The London office has wheelchair access.

ClearSky Accounting

Optionis House, 840 Ibis Court, Centre Park, Warrington WA1 1RL
tel 0800 0149 596
email accountinginfo@clearskybusiness.co.uk
website www.clearskybusiness.co.uk/entertainment
Accountant Alex Fielding

Established in 1995. ClearSky is very experienced in dealing with entertainment accountancy and provides advice and recommendations on all tax issues, ranging from completing a standard self-assessment return to dealing directly with agents regarding VAT and payments. Fees start from £35 per month (+VAT) and there are a number of different packages available – details can be found on the website. The company offers support via telephone and email and is happy to provide Excel templates for book keeping, if required. The company's office is wheelchair accessible. "Our team of qualified experts have specialist knowledge of all Equity, PACT & BECTU rules and regulations – giving peace of mind that our work is fully compliant."

Count and See Ltd

219 Macmillan Way, London SW17 6AW
tel 020-8767 7882

email info@countandsee.com
website www.countandsee.com

Charges an annual fee of £250 (+ VAT) upwards, depending on the amount of work involved. Provides actor clients with face-to-face, phone and email support. The trading office is wheelchair accessible. "Before setting up my own practice, I worked for a number of firms specialising in the entertainment industry, so I have experience in advising such clients."

Crowe Clark Whitehill

St Bride's House, 10 Salisbury Square, London EC4Y 8EH
tel 020 7842 7100
website www.crowehorwath.net
Accountants David Ford, Tim Norkett

Established in 1982. Provides flexible solutions to clients' tax problems; initial meeting is offered free of charge. Supports clients via meetings, phone and email. Will supply software and/or spreadsheet templates that are tailor made to individual requirements. Current client list includes 20 actors and 20 other entertainment industry professionals. Offices are wheelchair accessible. Fees vary according to the complexity of the service(s) required: £400 (+ VAT) is the minimum. "The better the quality of the client's recordkeeping, the lower the fees."

Dub & Co.

7 Torriano Mews, Torriano Avenue, London NW5 2RZ
tel 020 7284 8686 *fax* 020 7284 8687
email office@dub.co.uk
website www.dub.co.uk
Accountants George Dub, Joyce Davies

Chartered, certified accountants established in 1979. Charges from £400 (+ VAT) for preparation of accounts for a tax return. Face-to-face meetings, phone and email support included in this fee. Does not provide software or spreadsheet templates to clients. Handles the tax and accountancy affairs of around 50 actors and 100 other entertainment industry professionals. The company's offices are wheelchair accessible.

Dunbar & Co.

70 South Lambeth Road, London SW8 1RL
tel 020 7820 0082 *fax* 020 7820 0806
email mason@equitax.co.uk
Accountants Nick Mason (Senior Partner), Bob Long

Founded in 1896. Fees are on a time-cost basis, depending on the complexity of the client's tax affairs, but a typical fee range for an actor would be £330-£420 per annum. Support is provided via various means, including face-to-face meetings, phone and email. Provides spreadsheet templates for clients, which require Microsoft Excel. 50% of clients are actors, with a further 15% other entertainment-industry professionals. Offices are wheelchair accessible.

"We offer a full accountancy service, including bookkeeping, VAT, tax returns, tax advice, assistance with Revenue investigations, limited company accounts, personal and corporate tax planning. Our sister company, Sandford Dunbar, is authorised by the FSA as an independent financial adviser specialising in personal financial and pension planning."

eStage Accounting

71-75 Shelton Street, Covent Garden,
London WC2H 9JQ
tel 020 7112 8903
email chat@estage.net
website https://accounting.estage.net
Accountant Sarah Hawkings

Established in 2015. Fees start from £300 depending on complexity. Prices may increase due to international work, large or complicated income and specialist tax relief. Prefers meeting clients face-to-face to gain a full understanding of their need but also provides telephone, email on online chat support. Support from eStage is included in the fee unless additional work is required. Offers a number of software options from online bookkeeping software to simple Microsoft Excel template. Online software can be used on any computer or mobile device. All clients are entertainment industry professionals.

Offices are wheelchair accessible and eStage is always happy to meet clients at a location convenient to them.

Fisher Packman & Associates in association with Simia Wall

Devonshire House, 582 Honeypot Lane, Stanmore, Middlesex HA7 1JS and Sir Robert Peel House, 178 Bishopsgate, London EC2M 4NJ (Simia Wall)
tel 020 8732 5500 *fax* 020 8732 5501
email nik@fisherpackman.com
website www.fisherpackman.com
Accountant Nik Fisher FFA FCCA

Established in 2005. Charges between £250 and £750 on average, depending on the amount of work involved. Offers actors face-to-face and email/phone support: "as much as they require; our policy is to teach actors how best to keep their books and records, to save on accountancy fees." Provides spreadsheet templates in Excel and for VAT analysis, suitable for a range of software platforms. Around 15% of clients are actors, and 25% other professionals in the entertainment industry.

Jonathan Ford & Co.

The Coach House, 31 View Road, Rainhill,
Merseyside L35 0LF
tel 0151 426 4512

email info@jonathanford.co.uk
website www.jonathanford.co.uk
Accountant Jonathan Ford

Charges from £275 to £450, depending on the level of bookkeeping the client has done themselves. All fees are agreed in advance. Client service is comprehensive and includes face-to-face meetings, telephone and email support, all included within the fee. "Using the Internet we can meet the needs of clients all over the country." Supplies Excel spreadsheet templates, so MS Office is required; the software is suitable for all operating systems. Has around 10 actor clients and 40 other entertainment industry professionals. Offices are not wheelchair accessible. Advises actors to "see our 10 tax commandments!"

Goldwins

75 Maygrove Road, London NW6 2EG
tel 020 7372 6494 *fax* 020 7624 0053
email aepton@goldwins.co.uk
website www.goldwins.co.uk
Accountant Anthony Epton

Established in 1987. Specialises in the entertainment industry, handling the tax and bookkeeping affairs of around 200 actors. Charges around £400 for preparation of an actor's tax return, although this can vary from £250 up to £1,000 depending on the complexity of the job. Face-to-face meetings, phone and email support included in this price. Does not provide software or spreadsheet templates. The company's offices are wheelchair accessible.

Goodman Jones LLP

29/30 Fitzroy Square, London W1P 6LQ
tel 020 7388 2444 *fax* 020 7388 6736
email jrf@goodmanjones.com
website www.goodmanjones.com
Partner Julian Flitter

Founded in 1934. "Each person is different and we tailor our support to the clients needs, so costs can range from £250 to £500 for more complex returns involving international aspects and multiple categories of income." This amount would include any support required in the form of face-to-face meetings, phone calls, letters and emails. "The range of services we offer includes tax compliance services from personal tax returns and VAT returns, advice on whether or not to incorporate as a limited company, when to register for VAT, how to deal with working abroad, bookkeeping services, preparation of financial accounts (limited company, sole trader, LLP or partnership) as well as full personal tax planning and company secretarial and payroll services." Can supply software templates to clients as required, but recommends "keeping it simple". Offices are wheelchair accessible.

H and S Accountants Ltd

90 Mill Lane, West Hampstead, London NW6 1NL
tel 020 3174 1905

email hstaxplan@gmail.com
website www.hstaxplan.com
Accountants David Summers, Chet Haria

Established in 1982. Charges start from £300 (+ VAT) for preparation of annual self-employed accounts and the self-assessment tax return. A quote is given at the initial meeting, which is free of charge. The services offered also include preparation of limited company accounts and corporate tax returns, VAT registration, payroll, tax-planning advice, etc. Client support includes face-to-face meetings, phone, email, and dealing with day-to-day queries as they may arise (all included in the price). Approximately 10% of clients are actors or members of the entertainment industry. "We tailor advice to each individual's requirements."

Harris Coombs & Co.
5 Jaggard Way, London SW12 8SG
tel 020 8675 6880 *fax* 020 8675 7017
email mailbox@harriscoombs.co.uk
website www.harriscoombs.co.uk

Partners Graham Harris FCCA, Richard Coombs FCA

Charges to prepare actors' accounts for annual HM Revenue & Customs tax returns range from £500-£1,000. Charges vary depending on figures and VAT. Client support includes: face-to-face meetings, phone, email (all included in the price). Personal service in all financial matters: tax, NI, VAT etc. Of client base 15% are actors and 20% are other entertainment industry professionals.

Harvey Mead & Co. Ltd
The Old Winery, Lamberhurst Vineyard, Lamberhurst, Kent TN3 8ER
tel 01892 891572 *fax* 01892 891892
email lynette@harveymead.co.uk
website www.harveysllp.com
Accountants Damian McGee, Lynnette Lawrence

Established in 2008. Charges £600 (+ VAT) per annum. Client support includes face-to-face meetings, telephone and email, as well as fee protection insurance and freepost record envelopes. Accounts support is charged at £40 per hour; tax compliance at £60 per hour; and partner at £90 to £150 per hour. Supplies clients with MS Excel spreadsheet templates suitable for Windows XP and Vista. 50% of the client base comprises actors, and 30% other entertainment industry professionals. Offices are wheelchair accessible.

Hayles & Partners Ltd
39 Castle Street, Leicester LE1 5WN
tel 0116 233 8500 *fax* 0116 233 7288
website www.hayles.co.uk
Accountants Geoff Banks, Amanda Jelley

Charges from £150 for preparation of a basic tax return. Provides face-to-face meetings, phone and email support. Initial consultation or advice is offered free of charge. Does not supply software or spreadsheet templates to clients. Advises actors to "open a separate business bank account and identify all receipts and payments, retaining all supporting documentation".

Hogbens Dunphy Ltd
First Floor, 104-108 Oxford Street, London W1D 1LP
tel 020 7016 2450 *fax* 020 7637 8219
email anything@hogbensdunphy.co.uk
website www.hogbensdunphy.co.uk
Director Richard Wadhams

Established in 1921. Offers complete support to actors and other theatre professionals in dealing with their business, accounting and taxation needs. Prices are dependent on each individual client's needs.

HW Lee Associates LLP – Accountants to the Creative Sector
New Derwent House, 69-73 Theobalds Road, Holborn, London WC1X 8TA
tel 020 7025 4600 *fax* 020 7025 4666
email rhusband@hw-lee.com
email srawal@hw-lee.com
email nstammers@hw-lee.com
website www.hw-lee.com
Accountants Robert Husband, Sudhir Rawal, Neil Stammers

Established in 1978. Charges in the region of £400 to prepare a set of accounts, depending on the complexity and condition of the information supplied. Package and ongoing support tailored to suit each client's requirements, and clients have access to their client partner by mobile at any time. Provides templates for clients to record their accounts information and expenditure, and also gives advice about setting up IT systems. Is able to work with any system used by the client. A creative-focused firm with about 50% of its client base from the creative sectors and 10% directly linked to the entertainment industry. Offices are wheelchair accessible. "Our role is to anticipate the advice you need and help you implement it. Thereafter, managing and maintaining your relationship with the Inland Revenue will be our focus so that you can concentrate on enjoying your roles and performances."

Lees
26 Great Queen Street, London WC2B 5BL
tel 020 7242 1134
email a.mccarthy@leesaccountants.co.uk
website www.leesaccountants.co.uk
Accountants Mrs A. McCarthy, Mr P. Skinner, Mr G. Lyon

Established in 1925, charges from £450 to prepare actors' accounts for the tax return, depending on the complexity of the accounts. Provides a face-to-face initial meeting; support thereafter is as convenient to the client and this is included in the fee. Provides a complete range of accounting services – VAT, income tax, PAYE, business support, book keeping *et al.* Software and/or spreadsheets are provided to the client as required. Offices are not easily wheelchair accessible. Advice to actors: "Seek a *qualified* accountant."

MHA MacIntyre Hudson

New Bridge Street House, 30-34 New Bridge Street, London EC4V 6BJ
tel 020 7429 4100
email david.coppard@mhllp.co.uk
website www.macintyrehudson.co.uk
Twitter @MHUpdates
Accountants David Coppard, Matt Coward

Established in 1880, MHA MacIntyre Hudson acts for over 2,000 individuals in the media and entertainment industry, with 12 national offices and extensive overseas support throughout the Baker Tilly International Network.

They offer a full accountancy service from cloud accounting advice to high-end tax solutions. A fee structure is set out at the first complimentary meeting when media and entertainment specialists will discuss tax needs; arrangements can include monthly payments. They are happy to support clients through face-to-face meetings, telephone or email.

Offices are wheelchair accessible.

Nyman Libson Paul

Regina House, 124 Finchley Road, London NW3 5JS
tel 020 7433 2400 *fax* 020 7433 2401
email entertainment@nlpca.co.uk
website www.nlpca.co.uk

75 years in the entertainment industry.

Performance Accountancy

6 Pankhurst Drive, Bracknell, Berks RG12 9PS
tel 01344 669084
email louise@performanceaccountancy.co.uk
website www.performanceaccountancy.co.uk/Actors
Accountant Louise Herrington

Established in 2012. Charges from £250 +VAT for early years tax returns based on the client's bookkeeping records; if bookkeeping done by the company then £55 +VAT per hour is charged. If Equity number is quoted, then price starts at £175 +VAT for the return and £40+VAT per hour for

bookkeeping. For more established actors and performers who may have more complex returns, such as overseas income, the charge can go up to £450 +VAT. Provides Excel Workbook for clients to use for bookkeeping records. Offers an e-book and support by phone, Skype, webinars and video. Offers face-to-face meetings when starting out, either in Bracknell or Egham. First 30 minutes consultation is complimentary. Offers monthly services to handle bookkeeping and accounting requirements for the self-employed or those who operate through a company. This will help prepare for quarterly digital accounts starting in April 2020. Range of services in addition to personal self-assessment return include company accounts and company tax, bookkeeping, payroll, VAT, strategic planning and help with managing your money. Investment advice not offered. Excel workbook is supplied to actors and performers with typical categories of spend. Software offered works with Windows, but not so well with Mac. Clients are mainly actors, musicians and others in the entertainment inductry. The company is recommended by Equity and is the preferred supplier of tax returns for the Incorporated Society of Musicians.

Premises not suitable for wheelcahirs but face-to-face meetings can be arranged in wheelchair accessible location.

Theataccounts Ltd

49 Greek Street, London W1D 4EG
tel 01905 706050 *fax* 01905 799856
email info@theataccounts.co.uk
website www.theataccounts.co.uk
Twitter @theataccounts
Accountant Alex Dyer

Specialist Entertainment Industry Accountants established in 1967. Charges are based on a sliding scale according to each client's requirements. Basic package can start from £150. Offers unlimited support to clients through face-to-face meetings, phone, email, Skype, etc. No particular software is provided unless required. All clients are actors and other entertainment industry professionals.

Wise & Co. Chartered Accountants & Business Advisers

Rm 245 Pinewood Studios, Pinewood Road, Iver, Bucks
tel 01753 656770 01252 711244 *fax* 01252 737221
email info@wiseandco.co.uk
website www.wiseandco.co.uk
Accountants Colin Essex, Mandy Cornelius, Tom Mason

Established in 1972. Provides a full accounting service, business advice plus tax returns and staff payroll – "a personal, discreet and friendly service tailored to the needs of each individual". Prices vary, please phone to arrange a free initial consultation.

Office at Pinewood Studios as well as in Farnham, Surrey. Works with Windows and MS Office, so Excel is widely used; spreadsheet templates can be provided if required. Offices at Farnham are wheelchair accessible. Coffee shop and restaurant at Pinewood.

Wyatts Partnership
247 Church Street, London N16 9HP
tel 020 7241 6779
email office@wyatts.uk.com

Friendly and clear accounting service. Specialists with actors, artists and performers. Reasonable and transparent scaled fees and charges. Client base is 100% arts and entertainment industry professionals. Offices are wheelchair accessible.

Tax and National Insurance for actors

Philippe Carden

Actors are treated as self-employed for income tax purposes, but can benefit from certain advantages not generally available. Many actors choose to instruct an accountant to benefit from those advantages, and to avoid the attendant pitfalls.

The income tax advantages include being able to claim a deduction for expenses against income in arriving at taxable net profit (or allowable loss), provided that those expenses are incurred 'wholly and exclusively for the purposes of the trade'. *The Equity Tax and National Insurance Guide,* available free of charge to its members, provides a very helpful list of usually allowable expenses, with suitable notes to restrain the enthusiasm of actors to stretch definitions to their limits. Self-imposed restraint in claiming for expenses is sensible in minimising the risk of being selected for an enquiry by HM Revenue and Customs (HMRC). Some accountants produce their own list of generally allowable expenses.

It is helpful to assess the types of expense according to the risk of being challenged by the Revenue. Here are some examples:

Low risk or No risk
- Commission paid to agent (including VAT)
- Annual subscription to Equity
- Travel and subsistence on tour
- Photographs and publicity (repros, Spotlight entry)
- Classes to maintain skills, e.g. voice, movement
- Business stationery and postage
- Fee paid to accountant

Medium risk
- Professional library – scripts, books, CDs
- Publications – *The Stage, Empire magazine*
- Travel and subsistence when not on tour
- Visits to theatre and cinema

High risk
- Home as office
- Cosmetic dentistry

Very high risk
- Wardrobe – renewal, dry cleaning and repair
- Hairdressing and make-up – before auditions reduces the risk
- Gratuities to dressers and stage door-keepers
- Osteopathy and other treatments – lower risks for circus performers and stunt persons

Do not risk
- Gym membership – unless relevant preparation for a specific role
- Television licence

As the risk rises, so too must the care taken in deciding which to claim and which to discard. Engaging an accountant to use his or her experience, skill and judgement in carrying out a review of expenditure claims is a source of considerable reassurance to many actors. It is worth noting that entertaining, as in paying a meal for another person (even if a casting director), is never allowed.

An accountant's review may also be key in calculating the business proportions of motor car expenses, landline and mobile telephone charges (including internet access), television and film hire, including subscriptions to Sky, Netflix etc. An accountant's help in computing capital allowances for expenditure on capital items (computer, motor car, musical instruments) is appreciated by all but the most self-confident.

The emphasis so far has been on the income tax advantages of being self-employed. Whilst many actors are happy to register themselves as self-employed, others enlist the help of an accountant, even at that stage, to help with form-filling and provide a buffer-zone between themselves and the HMRC. Once registration is done, a Unique Taxpayer Reference (UTR) will be issued, often still referred to as a Schedule D number except by the HMRC. This registration is also for payment of Class 2 National Insurance ('NICs') calculated at the weekly flat rate, currently £3.00 a week. This is paid as part of the self-assessment process administered by HMRC.

If an actor achieves only a very modest net profit from his or her self-employment, say less than £6,365 net profit or so, the actor is not charged Class 2 NICs. It is important to remember, however, that paying Class 2 NICs is a cheap way of securing entitlement to certain basic state benefits such as maternity allowance and the state pension. If you are below the threshold at which you pay Class 2 NICs you can make voluntary payments via the tax return to preserve benefit entitlements. This option was under threat in 2018. The government's intention was to increase the cost of voluntary payments by requiring such payments to be made via Class 3 which currently costs £15.00 per week (£780 over a year). This increase would have hit particularly hard those struggling to gain a foothold in the profession or those going through a lean period. However, the government rowed back on this following extensive lobbying from many organisations including Equity.[1] So it remains the case, if one is below the Lower Profit Limit of £6,365, but one still wants to accrue a qualifying year for state pension, one can make voluntary payments of Class 2 NICs via the self-assessment tax return.

For the sake of completeness, Class 4 NICS are payable by actors if their annual net profit rises above the threshold: currently £8,632. That class of NIC is the earnings-related charge borne by self-employed people in addition to the flat-rate Class 2. It confers no benefits to the payer and is collected by the HMRC as part of the self-assessment system.

The complexities of the NI regime, and especially the interaction of its different classes, encourage co-operation between actor and accountant almost as much as does the application of the criteria for acceptability of expenses for income tax purposes.

Core services provided by an accountant include the following:

• Annual income and expenditure account
• Capital allowances computations
• Completion of the annual Tax Return
• Preparing a tax calculation and checking the Revenue's version
• Applying to reduce income tax payments on account, if appropriate

Resources

Additional services would include completing quarterly returns for actors successful enough to be registered for VAT, and advice on the tax and NIC implications of performing abroad. Student loan repayments and (what used to be) tax credit deadlines can also be discussed and planned. Universal credit has replaced a whole range of means-tested benefits including tax credits (other examples are income-based jobseeker's allowance, income support, income-related employment support allowance). It's problematic for the self-employed because the DWP (Department of Work and Pensions) assume an income for those they decide are 'gainfully self-employed'. This assumed income is called the 'Minimum Income Floor' (MIF). Equity provides expert advice for those claiming UC so members are advised to contact their Advice and Rights Helpline before claiming given all the difficulties with the MIF and other aspects of UC.

Most accountants charge according to time spent and the seniority and expertise of the persons doing the work. Here is an example of how this might work in practice for a young actor: he would need five hours of a bookkeeper, an hour for a manager's review and tax return and finally half-an-hour of the principal's/partner's time for overall review and quality control. With perhaps a few telephone calls and shortish meeting, the annual fee would typically be £400 plus VAT, i.e. £480. Accordingly, careful sorting of expenses by expense type can save both time and money.

In my experience, as the cost of the initial meeting is rarely charged for, I make a loss in year one of a new client. I break even in year two, and only make a profit in year three and subsequent years. It is not a surprise, therefore, that I see my relationship with a client as a long-term one – one which has time and effort invested in it by both actor and accountant.

To an actor in the early years of his career, the accountant's annual fee of about £480 represents a significant expense. The decision to instruct an accountant is a personal one. Some actors are much more comfortable and confident than others in dealing with money matters, taxation and National Insurance. Others shy away from such a course of action and choose to have an ally in the form of an accountant.

In general terms, for an actor with gross earnings of less than £25,000 but who still makes a profit, having an accountant is optional. For one with smaller earnings and who makes a loss, having an accountant could be worthwhile to relieve that loss and seek a refund of income tax. For those with gross earnings in excess of £25,000, the choice is compelling. For those with low earnings and perhaps suffering hardship, advice from Tax Aid can be invaluable. Tax Aid is a charity which helps people on low incomes with their tax problems: http://taxaid.org.uk. Helpline 0300 200 3300.

Having made the decision to use an accountant, choose the firm carefully. The most desired method is word of mouth. A personal recommendation from another actor, from your drama school or indeed from the company manager works well. It is important that the accountant selected knows about the taxation and NIC of actors rather than being a general practitioner. It is also important that the accountant be a member of one of the professional bodies of accountants as an indication of quality – and just in case a dispute arises which cannot be resolved amicably. Most of the institutes have a system of arbitration for fee disputes, for example, which can be used as a last resort.

Another factor in the choice of accountant is the size of the firm. The range is huge: from a sole practitioner to a multinational firm employing thousands. The former will be suitable for an actor of modest means, while the latter might be a good match for a performer with very considerable earnings and royalties from several countries around the world. In between those extremes are smaller firms with one to five partners which specialise in the tax affairs of those who work in theatre, television and film, and larger firms which have an entertainment and media department with a similar specialism. The smaller firms are likely to provide a more personal service and lower fees. The larger are likely to have access to a greater breadth of related expertise (such as film finance, production accounting) but fees will be correspondingly higher.

Each accountant will have his or her favoured way for actors to keep records. The most important point is that an actor must co-operate with his or her accountant to save time and maximise the return on effort. Here are some guidelines and handy hints:

• Keep all agent's remittance advices, payslips and invoices.
• Only claim expenses incurred 'wholly and exclusively for the purposes of the trade'.
• Use the Equity list of usually allowable expenses for guidance.
• Keep receipts for all expenses and write explanatory notes on them (for example, 'for audition with X')
• File away, carefully, details of any other income such as interest or dividends received, P60/P45s from employments (for example, bar work), rental income as well as Gift Aid payments made and any other item which may be needed to complete your tax return.
• Deliver your accounts papers to your accountant *as soon as you can* after the end of the tax year (5th April) – never leave it until close to the 31st January deadline! The sooner your return is submitted, the earlier the warning of any tax liability payable 31st January and of any other payments on account due for the following year.

Watch this space! A glimpse into the future

HMRC introduced Making Tax Digital (MTD) in April 2019 for VAT registered businesses, whose turnover exceeds the VAT threshold of £85,000. This involves quarterly reporting of income and expenses to HMRC. However, MTD for income tax is shelved now until at least April 2021. The latest view is that HMRC is determined to introduce MTD for income tax: only staff shortages are delaying its introduction.

[1] https://www.parliament.uk/business/publications/written-questions-answers-statements/written-statement/Commons/2018-09-06/HCWS944

Philippe Carden is a chartered accountant specialising in the taxation of actors and other individuals working in theatre, film, television and dance, onstage and backstage, artistic and technical. He co-wrote *Investing in West End Theatrical Productions* (Robert Hale, 1992) and has written articles for the *Guardian*, *The Stage* and other publications.

Resources

Equity Pension Scheme

Andrew Barker @ First Act

Auto-Enrolment, what is it?

Since October 2012, new legislation has gradually applied to all UK employers to ensure that they provide a suitable pension product for their workers. This legislation includes actors and is calledAuto-Enrolment (AE). If you are aged over 22 and below State pension age there is a probability that any production company that you work for *will* auto-enrol you into their chosen pension scheme. They are legally bound to enrol you. You have no choice on being auto-enrolled, but you can choose to opt out afterwards. The nature of your occupation could result in you ending up with many separate pension pots over the time span of your career.

However, there is an alternative and a way to avoid AE: the Equity Pension Scheme (EPS). The EPS has been in existence since October 1997. Designed and administered by First Act (the preferred insurance advisers to Equity and its members), it has become the pension scheme of choice for actors. If you are engaged on an Equity Agreement, whether it be in theatre, television, film or radio, the production company has an obligation to contribute to the EPS on your behalf and at rates that are higher than those that apply to AE.

The EPS' status as a qualifying workplace pension scheme will ensure that if you are an EPS member, and you inform each company manager of the production companies you work for, they will *not* auto-enrol you into their AE scheme resulting in you having one pension receiving all your contributions.

The EPS provides access to a market-leading pension product for all those working in the creative arts sector (Equity membership is not required). It is the ideal way to start or improve your personal pension arrangements.

Here is how it works

If you are working under an Equity agreed contract you could get your manager to contribute to your EPS.

Current qualifying contracts are issued by: BBC, ITV, PACT & TAC, SOLT, UK Theatre Commercial, UK Theatre Sub Rep, ITC, RSC, RNT, Disney Theatrical, plus a number of in-house arrangements.

Equity Pension Scheme – questions and answers

Q How does the EPS work?

A The funds are managed by AVIVA, one of the UK's largest and most respected pension providers. The EPS has access to over 280 investment funds catering for all attitudes to investment risk, including ethical and sustainable funds.

You have total flexibility. You contribute when you are working, and when you are not, you can take a break. The EPS is penalty-free and currently has a base charge on the core funds of 0.7% cent per annum i.e. £0.70 for every £100 in your personal pot.

Q How do I make payments into the EPS?
A You can make contributions in several ways:
• You can make contributions related to your engagement only; this way you can pay in when you are working but freeze payments when you are not.
• You can make additional regular personal payments by direct debit on a monthly basis.
• You can make additional single personal contributions on-line or by cheque.

Q How does the EPS work in theatre?
A As an EPS member you benefit from a contribution paid by your employers, equal to a percentage of your weekly wage. To qualify, you agree to make a contribution from your weekly wage. The employer contribution is added to your wages and then deducted together with your personal contribution. The employer contributions are sent directly by the employer to First Act, for investment on your behalf. Once with Aviva, basic rate tax relief is added.

Q Which theatrical managers contribute to the EPS?
A Most theatrical employers now contribute to the scheme.
West End managers (SOLT), Disney Theatrical and Shakespeare's Globe
Managers will contribute an amount equal to 5% of your weekly rehearsal or performance wage up to a maximum of 5% of 1.75 x the minimum performance wage. Two years' continual employment with the same manager increases this to 7.5%, 10% after 5 years.
    You pay a 3% personal contribution, rising to 3.75% and 5%.

Subsidised repertory theatres (UK theatre)
The manager will contribute an amount equal to 5% of your weekly rehearsal or performance wage up to a maximum of 5% of 1.5 x the appropriate middle-range salary level (MRSL).
    You pay a 3% personal contribution.

Commercial theatre (UK theatre)
Managers contribute an amount equal to 5% of your weekly rehearsal or performance wage.
    You pay a 2.5% personal contribution.

Independent Theatre Council (ITC)
Managers contribute an amount equal to 5% of your weekly rehearsal or performance wage.
    You pay a 3% personal contribution.

Royal National Theatre
You have a choice of:
    1. RNT pay 5%; you pay 3%
    2. RNT pay 5.5%; you pay 4.5%
    3. RNT pay 6%; you pay 6%
    4. RNT pay 7.5%; you pay 7.5%

Royal Shakespeare Company
The RSC contribute an amount equal to 5% of your weekly rehearsal or performance wage.
    You pay a 2.5% personal contribution.

Q How does the EPS work in television?

A Basically, the scheme works in the same way in television as it does in theatre, but your contribution will be based on either your episode fee or weekly fee, whichever basis brings you the most benefit. It is the responsibility of the artist to notify the producer prior to the engagement that they are a member of the EPS and to provide their pension membership number in the space provided in the form of engagement.

Q Which TV and film managers contribute to the EPS?

A Most TV and film employers will contribute to the scheme.

BBC Television and ITV companies will contribute an amount equal to 5% of your engagement/episode fee or weekly fee.

You pay a 2.5% personal contribution.

PACT and TAC independent TV production companies will contribute an amount equal to 5% subject to a maximum per engagement/weekly/episode fee.

You pay a 2.5% personal contribution.

Film companies will contribute an amount equal to 6% of your fee, subject to a reviewable maximum per production.

You pay a 3% personal contribution.

BBC Radio will contribute an amount equal to 5% of your engagement/weekly/episode fee.

You pay a 2.5% personal contribution.

Details of the current minimum engagement fees/wages for your production company are available from Andrew Barker at First Act 020 8686 5050, by e-mail eps@firstact.co.uk or at firstact.co.uk.

Q How can I join the EPS

A On-line at firstact.co.uk, by email eps@firstact.co.uk or by telephone 0208 686 5050.

Andrew Barker is a Director of Hencilla Canworth Ltd (First Act). Hencilla Canworth is an independent insurance intermediary having facilities with the UK's leading insurers and underwriters. It specialises in insurance products for performing arts companies and groups. He was part of the original team that designed and introduced the EPS in 1997 and has continued to oversee its management to this day.

Physical and mental fitness for actors

Alex Caan

The instrument or tool of the actor is the body. Like a musical instrument, if it is left idle it will become out of tune and lose its ability to function effectively.

Actors need to constantly develop their instrument to get the best out of it. Unlike a musical instrument, we carry our tool with us every day. With good habits and practice we can alleviate many of the problems that need to be fixed before they start. The work required to have a positive ongoing effect is not as great or as demanding as one would expect. Before we look at what we can do to make our bodies outstanding, let's look at what our bodies really are.

In a person of average weight and build, 70 per cent of the mass of the body is muscle and bone. Therefore we can have a large effect on our bodies, by focusing on our muscles and bones. Before we can affect change in our muscles and bones we need to understand how they work and what relationships they have with each other.

The structure of the body is extremely complicated but can be viewed in quite a simplistic manner. Originally we would have walked on all fours, which is why our upper limbs have very similar corresponding joints to our lower limbs. Each hand has five digits, with a dominant thumb; our corresponding lower body part is the opposite foot, with the big toe as the dominant digit. The wrist and ankle are similar multi-directional joints, whereas the elbow and knee are both hinged joints. The shoulder and hip are ball and socket joints.

The upper and lower limbs are also connected by corresponding groups of muscles. The quads, which are in the front of the thigh, are related to the upper body through the triceps, which are in the back of the upper arm. The hamstrings, at the back of the upper leg, are related to the biceps. The gluteus or buttocks are related to the pectorals or chest muscles. So rather than looking at muscular activity in isolation, we must see muscles as groups working together.

When the body moves forward, the opposite arm and leg swing. The combination of muscles working together propels our bodies. Muscles move limbs by shortening.

Muscles work together synergistically, and in a healthy, well-maintained body are balanced. If bad habits occur, this simplicity of movement can lead to long-term health problems by over-use of some muscles, and under-use of others. This constant over-use/ under-use will lead to a tired or sore body part in a specific area, often one side of the neck or lower back.

As we move forward, the chain of movements pass through the centre of the body. This passing through the centre is a clue to the focus of long-term fitness and wellbeing for the actor.

The centre of the body is the place where all life stems from. It is here that a baby is connected to its mother through the placenta, that later becomes the belly button. In the centre of the body is the diaphragm, from which, through correct training, all breath should originate.

The movement of our bodies creates heat and energy. Contrary to what some directors believe, we are not beings that live in our head or brain space. We live in our bodies, and movement produces powerful emotional responses. This is encapsulated in the phrase 'Motion creates Emotion'. This is why actors talk about getting the walk of the character, because this allows them to get into the body of the character, which in turn allows them to get into the personality of the character. Some actors do this instinctively, but it is and can be a learned skill.

Actors communicate thoughts in the vast majority by speaking. There are, of course, actors who use mime and dance to communicate, but mainly thoughts are communicated verbally, using speech or song. Words are merely a manipulation of breath using the tongue, mouth and vocal cords. Without breath we have nothing to carry our thoughts over large theatrical space.

Coincidentally, breath or oxygen is the most important nourishment our bodies need. Without food one can live for 40 days or more; without water one can live for 7-10 days; but if you don't breathe for five minutes you will die.

Using this as our guide, the focus of the actors' fitness should be built around the development of a robust powerful tool that can create large amounts of powerful breath. Not just large volumes of breath, but outstanding control of the mechanism that delivers that breath.

The mechanism that delivers the breath is the lungs and diaphragm and their supporting muscles. These muscles need to be strong, but also need to be mobile and have excellent endurance.

Lastly, the value of water cannot be underestimated. A 5 per cent drop in hydration can lead to mild dehydration, which can lead to a large drop in bodily function, both mental and physical. Even a 2 per cent drop in hydration can have a very damaging and negative effect on our voice. In temperate climates we lose 2.5 litres of water throughout an average day. If we are performing, rehearsing or undertaking strenuous physical activity we will use much greater amounts of water than this. Therefore we must monitor our bodies and increase water intake when needed. Passing clear urine is a good indicator of hydration – if not first thing in the morning, then definitely throughout the day.

So where does one start in the nitty-gritty of training the actor's body? Actors come in all shapes and sizes. I am not advocating that all actors try to become slim and pert: who would play all the non-slim, non-pert roles? Equally, I am not advocating that all actors develop muscular physiques. We need to be limber in the joints and muscles, but there is no point in the serious actor developing big muscles at the expense of range of movement. I believe that you can be tall, short, slim, rotund, lanky or squat and at the same time be very fit. Olympic shot putters are very large but all can run great distances and move like ballet dancers.

Fitness for actors doesn't require a massive overloading of the body. To reach Olympic-standard fitness we would need to break the body down systematically over a period of time, in order to allow the body to regenerate stronger than before. This regeneration occurs during periods of rest. But this overloading is not really needed for general fitness for actors.

In all of our fitness development we need to place breath control and posture at the forefront. The ideas and concepts of the Alexander Technique are pivotal to this. Its values are based on excellent posture and good use of muscles, rather than overuse and bad postural habits. So when performing any movement, be aware of the alignment of the head, neck and back. Often actors strain their voices because they are tight in another part of their body, which pulls the head and neck out of alignment, resulting in a sore throat or strained voice. For those of you who are not familiar with the Alexander Technique, I would recommend that an awareness of posture and balance is vital to long-term fitness.

A simple starting point for general fitness for actors is walking. Walking is the most underused and undervalued exercise we can do. It involves a good pair of training shoes and a place to go! Between 20 and 60 minutes' continuous walking a day will increase lung capacity and make our heart a great deal stronger. I know many actors say that they walk at least that in a day – going shopping, walking to the bus or train, and so on. I am not discounting that, but I am advocating a steady brisk walk with arms swinging back and forth in time with the opposing leg. By doing this, the whole body is being exercised, and the core muscles through the centre of the body are activated. It is akin to the phase of human development that we know as crawling. The same benefits cannot be achieved through passive day-to-day walking.

Walking has a very effective return for the amount of effort expended, because there is little detrimental impact on the joints of the lower limbs. The swinging of opposing arms and legs also helps reinforce correct neurological pathways. This helps us to move our bodies more effectively and efficiently as a kinetic chain, rather than as disjointed isolated movements.

A walking regime three days a week is a good place to start. You will not only build your lungs and heart, but also the tissues around your joints in the legs, arms and back. These need time to adapt and grow to the new stresses being placed on them. Taking a day off in between will allow the tissues throughout your body to regenerate during the periods of rest.

If you are a fitness novice, then building up to an hour-long walk is an achievable goal. Start with a ten-minute walk that builds systematically over a period of between four and six weeks, rather than blazing into a brisk hour-long walk initially. Increasing your walks by three minutes each walk will let you achieve an hour-long walk from a ten-minute starting point in just six weeks. Three minutes may sound a lot, but since it requires adding just one and a half minutes to your outward journey, it is not an unrealistic amount.

Swimming is also an excellent way to work the heart and lungs without placing any stress on the joints, as it is a non-weight bearing form of exercise. However, it is important to swim using the front crawl and backstroke rather than predominantly using the breast stroke, so that we continue to move opposing upper and lower limbs to work our core muscles. A mixture of all swimming strokes would be best to work the greatest range of muscle groups and minimise the likelihood of housemaid's knee (a common breast stroke-related injury)! Learning to swim with your head partially submerged in the water is vital, in order to maintain correct alignment of the spine.

The same incremental approach to developing fitness through walking, as recommended above, should be applied when undertaking a swimming regime. Rather than using the increment of time, the number of lengths swum is a very simple starting point. Do bear in mind the length of each pool that you may swim in may vary! It is likely that the more often you swim, the quicker you will become. So increasing the number of lengths that you swim each session may require little or no extra time in the pool.

We have exercised the heart and lungs with walking and swimming. We need now to develop our range of movement and strength. Basic Yoga movements are also a simple and effective way to increase inner strength and develop range of movement and good posture. I am not looking at the more physical jumping around or sauna types of Yoga. I am advocating basic Yoga moves.

Yoga has many positive effects, which include large ranges of movement and mobility. By getting into certain Yoga positions, we are not only stretching the muscles, but also massaging the internal organs. Yoga also has the benefit of establishing excellent breath control. The breath floods into the centre of the body and has to be released with control and in a sustained manner. This has a very relaxing and meditative effect. This helps us switch off our overactive minds, the value of which cannot be underestimated.

Buying a book or DVD on Yoga or joining a Yoga class is an excellent place to start. If Yoga doesn't appeal to you, then Pilates is an excellent alternative. Both Yoga and Pilates are fantastic for developing breath control and posture control techniques.

Let us look at a sample week's exercise programme – for example, walking or swimming on Monday, Thursday and Saturday, with Yoga or Pilates on Tuesday and Friday. This gives you two days off, on Wednesday and Sunday, which follow either two or three days of activity. Rest is vital to regeneration. We only become fitter and stronger by allowing our bodies to recover and grow. These days off give the individual physical downtime, which can

> **Further information**
>
> For more information about any of the suggested forms of exercise, see the websites listed below:
>
> Alexander Technique **www.alexandertechnique.com**
>
> Walking **www.thewalkingsite.com**
>
> Swimming **www.britishswimming.org**
>
> Yoga **www.bwy.org.uk** (British Wheel of Yoga)
>
> Pilates **www.pilatesfoundation.com**

then be filled with mental stimulation of some kind, including meditation, vocal and singing practice, reading or other pursuits that aid the actor's development as a whole.

This is a brief overview of the most suitable and simple exercises to cover what is required for the stresses and strains of most acting jobs. All of these suggestions can be carried out from home or on tour. The time and effort required to train in this manner will not be detrimental to the actor's performance. By starting small, and increasing gradually, the actor will feel more invigorated and energised from undertaking an exercise programme.

The actor's body should be viewed as a communication tool. Bodies require stimulation to develop. Without stimulus, the body and mind will deteriorate. Permitting this to happen is an injustice to the craft of acting. We all only have one body, and we need to look after it and maintain it for our specific needs.

Alex Caan was an international athlete before training at RADA for three years. Since graduation, he has worked extensively in theatre, TV and radio. As a consultant Alex teaches business people powerful communication through effective use of the body. As a sports coach Alex has coached Premiership football and rugby players to international level. He has coached sportsmen and women to Olympic and World level in a range of different athletic disciplines. He is currently National Event Coach for High Jump in the UK, and prepared the group of talented high jumpers for the London 2012 Olympics.

Funding bodies

The competition for funding is so fierce that it is important to allow sufficient time for research, planning and proper presentation of your proposed project. It is well worth checking to see what information is available on the websites listed in this section. Many funding bodies are happy to advise on form-filling, what kind of projects stand a chance and what could constitute a realistic amount to ask for. It is also well worth going on one (or more) of the Independent Theatre Council's (ITC; see page 460) courses for assistance in the complex world of funding applications.

Bodies that offer individual funding should be approached with similar care and attention.

NATIONAL ARTS COUNCILS

Arts Council England

The Hive, 49 Lever Street, Manchester M1 1FN
tel 0845 300 6200 *fax* 0161 934 4426
textphone 020 7973 6564
email enquiries@artscouncil.org.uk
website www.artscouncil.org.uk
Facebook www.facebook.com/artscouncilofengland
Twitter @ace_london

Arts Council England champions, develops and invests in artistic and cultural experiences that enrich people's lives. It supports a range of activities across the arts, museums and libraries - from theatre to digital art, reading to dance, music to literature, and crafts to collections. "Great art and culture inspires us, brings us together and teaches about ourselves and the world around us. In short it makes us better."

Between 2018 and 2022, we will invest £1.45 billion of public money from government and an estimated £860 million from the National Lottery to help create these experiences for as many people as possible across the country.

Application forms, guidance notes and information sheets can be downloaded from the website. A wide range of resources, publications, links and information about other funding sources is also accessible on the website.

Arts Council of Northern Ireland

Linen Hill House, 23 Linenhall Street,
Lisburn BT28 1FJ
tel 028 9262 3555
email info@artscouncil-ni.org
website www.artscouncil-ni.org

The prime distributor of public support for the arts, the Arts Council of Northern Ireland is committed to increasing opportunities for artists to develop challenging and innovative work. In addition to funding schemes for organisations and community groups, the council has developed a special programme of schemes to extend support for the individual artist. This programme includes the General Arts Award, which provides funding for specific projects, specialised research and personal artistic development; and the Major Individual Award, which supports established artists in the development of ambitious work.

Arts Council of Wales

Bute Place, Cardiff CF10 5AL
tel 0845 8734 900 *fax* 029 2044 1400
email information@artscouncilofwales.org.uk
website www.artscouncilofwales.org.uk

Responsible for funding and developing the arts in Wales, using money from Welsh Government and the National Lottery. Provides arts organisations and individuals in Wales with the opportunity to apply for funding towards clearly defined arts-related projects. Scheme Guidelines for the funding programmes are available on the website.

Creative Scotland

249 West George Street, Glasgow G2 4QE
tel 0330 333 2000
Waverley Gate, 2-4 Waterloo Gate, Edinburgh EH1 3EG
tel 0330 333 2000
website www.creativescotland.com

In April 2010 the Scottish Arts Council merged with Scottish Screen to become Creative Scotland. Creative Scotland is the national leader for Scotland's arts, screen and creative industries. It helps "Scotland's creativity shine at home and abroad . . . We invest in talented people and exciting ideas. We develop the creative industries and champion everything that is good about Scottish creativity."

Resources

REGIONAL ARTS COUNCIL OFFICES

Arts Council England, East
Eastbrook, Shaftesbury Road, Cambridge CB2 8BF
tel 0845 6200 *fax* 0870 242 1271
Twitter @ACE_southeast

Area covered: Our East office covers Bedfordshire, Cambridgeshire, Essex, Hertfordshire, Norfolk and Suffolk.

Arts Council England, East Midlands
St Nicholas Court, 25-27 Castle Gate,
Nottingham NG1 7AR
tel 0845 300 6200 *fax* 0115 950 2467

Area covered: Derbyshire, Leicestershire, Lincolnshire (excluding North and North East Lincolnshire), Northamptonshire, Nottinghamshire, Rutland.

Arts Council England, London
14 Great Peter Street, London SW1P 3NQ
tel 0845 300 6200 *fax* 020 7973 6564

Area covered: Greater London.

Arts Council England, North East
Central Square, Forth Street,
Newcastle upon Tyne NE1 3PJ
tel 0845 300 6200 *fax* 0191 230 1020
textphone 0191 255 8585

Area covered: Durham, Northumberland, Tees Valley, Tyne and Wear.

Arts Council England, North West
The Hive, 49 Lever Street, Manchester M1 1FN
tel 0845 300 6200 *fax* 0161 934 4426
textphone 0161 834 9131

Area covered: Cheshire, Cumbria, Greater Manchester, Lancashire, Merseyside.

Arts Council England, South East
Sovereign House, Church Street, Brighton BN1 1RA
tel 0845 300 6200 *fax* 0870 242 1257
textphone 01273 710659

Area covered: Berkshire, Buckinghamshire, East Sussex, Hampshire, Isle of Wight, Kent, Oxfordshire, Surrey, West Sussex.

Arts Council England, South West
Senate Court, Southernhay Gardens, Exeter EX1 1UG
tel 0845 300 6200 *fax* 01392 498546
textphone 01392 433503

Area covered: Cornwall, Devon, Dorset, Gloucestershire, the Isles of Scilly, Somerset, Wiltshire; unitary authorities of Bath and North East Somerset, Bournemouth, Bristol, North Somerset, Plymouth, Poole, South Gloucestershire, Swindon, Torbay.

Arts Council England, West Midlands
82 Granville Street, Birmingham B1 2LH
tel 0845 300 6200 *fax* 0121 643 7239
textphone 0121 643 2815

Area covered: Herefordshire, Shropshire, Staffordshire, Warwickshire, Worcestershire; metropolitan authorities of Birmingham, Coventry, Dudley, Sandwell, Solihull, Walsall, Wolverhampton.

Arts Council England, Yorkshire
21 Bond Street, Dewsbury,
West Yorkshire WF13 1AX
tel 0845 300 6200 *fax* 01924 466522
textphone 01924 438585

Area covered: Yorkshire and the Humber, which includes North and North East Lincolnshire.

NATIONAL FILM AGENCIES

Northern Ireland Screen
3rd Floor, 21 Alfred House, Belfast BT2 8ED
tel 028 9023 2444
website www.northernirelandscreen.co.uk

Northern Ireland Screen is the national screen agency for Northern Ireland. Its aim is to accelerate the development of a dynamic and sustainable screen industry and culture in Northern Ireland.

Wales Screen Commission
1st Floor North, QED Treforest Ind. Est.,
Pontypridd CF37 5YR
tel 0300 061 5634
email enquiry@walesscreencommission.co.uk
website www.walesscreencommission.com

The Wales Screen Commission is the location service for Wales, offering comprehensive information and support on locations, facilities, crew and local services throughout Wales.

REGIONAL FILM AGENCIES

EM Media
Antenna Media Centre, Beck Street,
Nottingham NG1 1EQ
tel 0115 993 2333
email info@em-media.org.uk
website www.em-media.org.uk

EM Media is the Screen Agency for the East Midlands region of England, and invests in East Midlands based creative talent, supporting and developing projects and activities that meet its business aims.

Film London
Suite 6.10, The Tea Building,
56 Shoreditch High Street, London E1 6JJ
tel 020 7613 7676 *fax* 020 7613 7677
email info@filmlondon.org.uk
website www.filmlondon.org.uk

Film London is the capital's public agency for feature film, television, commercials and other interactive content, including games. "Our aim is simple: to ensure that London has a thriving film sector that enriches the capital's businesses and its people." The government has charged Film London with developing and managing a national strategy to generate inward investment through film production via a public-private partnership with key industry bodies, following its decision in July 2010 to abolish the UK Film Council.

Northern Film & Media

Baltic Centre for Contemporary Art,
South Shore Road, Gateshead NE8 3BA
tel 0191 440 4940
email info@northernmedia.org
website www.northernmedia.org

Northern Film & Media is the screen agency for the North East of England. "Our vision is to create a strong commercial creative economy in the North East, by investing in talent and ideas."

Screen South

The Wedge, 75-81 Tontine Street, Folkestone,
Kent CT20 1JR
tel 01303 259777 *fax* 01303 259786
email info@screensouth.org
website www.screensouth.org

Screen South is the film and media agency for the South East of England. "We aim to be a resource that helps people get their ideas off the ground, whether they want to make a short film, learn how to write successful scripts, set up a film festival or shoot a major movie here. We promote talent, preserve our film heritage and find ways of presenting exciting film to new audiences. Screen South is a Lottery distributor."

Screen Yorkshire

Studio 30, 46 The Calls, Leeds LS2 7EY
tel 0113 236 8228
email sally@screenyorkshire.co.uk
website www.screenyorkshire.co.uk
Twitter @screenyorkshire

Screen Yorkshire champions the film, TV, games and digital industries in Yorkshire and the Humber. Screen Yorkshire offers production financing through its Yorkshire Content Fund. Since it launched in February 2012, Screen Yorkshire has invested in 38 film and TV projects including: *Official Secrets, Ghost Stories, Yardie, Hope Gap, National Treasure, Dad's Army, Sawallows and Amazons, Dark Angel, Journeyman, Dark River, Black Work, The Great Train Robbery, Peaky Blinders, Jonathan Strange and Mr Norrell* and *Testament of Youth*. Screen Yorkshire also develops talent by designing and delivering industry schemes.

OTHER SOURCES OF FUNDING

Additional information about various entertainment charities and benevolent funds can be found on the website of The Actors' Charitable Trust

www.tactactors.org. Unless explicitly mentioned, most of the organisations listed below and on the TACT website do not provide assistance with drama school fees or maintenance.

Actors' Benevolent Fund

6 Adam Street, London WC2N 6AD
tel 020 7836 6378 *fax* 020 7836 8978
email office@abf.org.uk
website www.actorsbenevolentfund.co.uk

Since 1882 the Actors' Benevolent Fund has provided support to professional actors, actresses and stage managers unable to work due to poor health, an accident or old age.

Equity Charitable Trust

Plouviez House, 19-20 Hatton Place,
London EC1N 8RU
tel 020 7831 1926 *fax* 020 7242 7995
email info@equitycharitabletrust.org.uk
website www.equitycharitabletrust.org.uk

The Equity Charitable Trust provides educational bursaries to performers and industry professionals with a minimum of 10 years' professional adult experience who are looking to retrain, develop new skills and obtain valuable new qualifications. Depending on your circumstances, grants can cover a portion of your course costs.

We also provide benefit and debt advice to industry members who are experiencing a financial or medical setback and who may qualify for a one-off financial grant. For information and to download an application form for either a Welfare or Education Grant please visit the website **www.equitycharitabletrust.org.uk** or email **info@equitycharitabletrust.org.uk**

Evelyn Norris Trust

Plouviez House, 19-20 Hatton Place,
London EC1N 8RU
tel 020 7831 1926
website www.equitycharitabletrust.org.uk/
evelynnorris.php
Secretary Keith Carter

The Evelyn Norris Trust is a charity that accepts applications for grants from members of the concert and theatrical professions. The Trust aims to help with the cost of convalesence or a recuperative holiday following illness, injury or surgery.

First Light

Studio 28, Fazeley Studios, Fazeley Street,
Birmingham B5 5SE
tel 0121 224 7511
website www.firstlightonline.co.uk

First Light is the UK's leading initiative enabling young people to realise their potential via creative digital film and media projects. It operates a number of youth funding schemes, including:

• The Young Film Fund – the BFI's Lottery-funded filmmaking initiative for 5-19 year olds.
• Mediabox – a Department for Children, Schools & Families fund to help young people establish a positive voice in the media. It offers disadvantaged 13-19 year olds the opportunity to develop and produce creative media projects using film, print, television, radio or online platforms. There are grants of up to £40,000 available now.
• Second Light – a talent development scheme which, through production-based training, will give 30 talented young people aged 18 to 23, from BME backgrounds, supported opportunities to move into the film industry.

The Foyle Foundation

Rugby Chambers, 2 Rugby Street,
London WC1N 3QU
tel 020 7430 9119
email info@foylefoundation.org.uk
website www.foylefoundation.org.uk

The Foundation operates a Main Grants Scheme supporting charities with a core remit of Arts or Learning and a Small Grants Scheme covering small charities in all fields. It has supported tours, festivals and education projects and helped to develop new work. It will also consider funding the building or updating of arts facilities. The majority of main grants are in the range of £10,000 to £50,000. Capital projects seeking more than £75,000 are considered twice per year. Application forms and guidelines are available to download from the website.

Jerwood Charitable Foundation

171 Union Street, London SE1 0LN
tel 020 7261 0279
email info@jerwood.org
website www.jerwoodcharitablefoundation.org

Jerwood Charitable Foundation is dedicated to imaginative and responsible revenue funding of the arts, supporting professional artists to develop and grow at important stages in their careers. It works with artists across art forms, from dance and theatre to literature, music and the visual arts. For more information on Jerwood Charitable Foundation, please visit the website.

The Oxford Samuel Beckett Theatre Trust Award

PO Box 2637, Ascot, Berks SL5 8ZN
email OSBTTA@barbican.org.uk.com
website www.osbttrust.com
website www.barbican.org.uk/theatre/abouttheatre/award

The purpose of this annual award is, in particular, to help the development of emerging practitioners in the field of innovative theatre/performance and, in general, to encourage the new generation of creative artists. Artists from all disciplines are encouraged to apply.

The award is for a company or individual to create a show either for the Pit Theatre, Barbican, London, or a site-responsive, non-traditional show to take place in London. The winning show, either at the Pit or, if site-responsive, elsewhere, will be part of the Barbican Theatre season.

Performance Initiative Network

email contact@kerryirvine.co.uk
website http://kerryirvine.co.uk/consultancy/performance-initiative-network
Contact Kerry Irvine

Supporting the professional small theatre company and theatre artist to make and produce their work. Runs the GroundWork Festival, eVolve, and the PiLab series of projects.

The Ralph and Meriel Richardson Foundation

c/o Burlingtons LegalLLP, 38 Hertford Street, London W1J 7SG
mobile (07733) 688120
email manager@sirralphrichardson.org.uk
website www.sirralphrichardson.org.uk

The Foundation was established by Lady Meriel (Mu) Richardson after the untimely death of the Richardsons' only son, Charles, to relieve the need, hardship or distress of British actors and actresses who have professionally practised or contributed to the Theatrical Arts (on stage, film, television or radio) and their spouses and children.

The Foundation has made grants for wheelchairs, for hospital treatment, residential care, surgeons fees, medication and a variety of short-term help to a large number of those seeking assistance. An applicant's request for a grant (with a CV and letters in support) is assessed on its merit in light of the objects of the Foundation. A majority of the Trustees is required for approval of every application. Applicants must have been active in the profession for a minimum of 15 years, save in exceptional circumstances.

The Royal Theatrical Fund

11 Garrick Street, London WC2E 9AR
tel 020 7836 3322
email admin@trtf.com
website www.trtf.com

The Royal Theatrical Fund helps people from *all* areas of the entertainment industry. The Fund makes grants which will alleviate the suffering, assist the recovery, or reduce the need, hardship or distress of theatrical artists or their families/dependants. To be eligible to receive a grant, a person must be unable to work due to illness, injury or infirmity, and to have professionally worked in the theatrical arts (on stage, radio, film or television) for a minimum of 7 years.

Sophie's Silver Lining Fund

c/o Marion Cooper, at Aplin Stockton Fairfax,
36 West Bar, Banbury, Oxon OX16 9RU
tel 01295 251234
email office@sslf.org.uk
website www.sslf.org.uk

Provides assistance with the cost of their training to
needy acting and singing students. "Please note that
regretfully, we are no longer able to accept
applications for funding from individual students.
Awards are only made to students put forward by a
small number of drama and music colleges selected
by the trustees."

The Wellcome Trust

Arts Awards, 215 Euston Road, London NW1 2BE
email arts@wellcome.ac.uk
website www.wellcome.ac.uk/arts

The Wellcome Trust Arts Awards is the Trust's
funding scheme that supports arts projects which
engage with biomedical science.

"The Arts Awards provide funding for a range of
projects that bring together any art form and any area
of biomedical science. Projects must involve the
creation of new artistic work and have biomedical
scientific input into the process, either through a
scientist taking on an advisory role or through direct
collaboration. 2 levels of funding are available –
small- to medium-sized projects (up to and including
£30,000) and large projects (above £30,000) –
primarily for artists or organisations with an existing
track record with the Wellcome Trust or Wellcome
Collection. Full details are available on our website,
including details of pending deadlines for large and
small grants, application guidelines, examples of
previously funded projects, and the online
application portal."

Resources

Publications, libraries, references and booksellers

This section lists the major sources for scripts and sheet music – and routes to finding that elusive script or score. While Internet search engines can be extremely useful in such a quest, it sometimes requires some lateral thinking to find what you want. It is possible to find out-of-print plays via libraries or book-finding services and by combing second-hand bookshops. Some publishers (even a few playwrights' agencies) will organise a photocopy – for a fee. Also, the British Library (in theory) has a copy of every play ever performed in this country, but there can be complications in actually getting hold of a copy. Start with your local library if you're determined to find a specific play; if they don't have it, they may well be able to get it from another library (via the inter-library loan system), but be prepared for it to take a long time. Another route is to try to find a theatre at which the play has been performed: they may be able to help.

AbeBooks.com

website www.abebooks.com

Excellent website which will search the catalogues of hundreds of second-hand booksellers in this country and around the world.

Actorsandperformers.com

Actors & Performers is a professional networking site for the acting community, containing must-have career information, and with authors, casting directors, actors and industry practitioners such as Richard Eyre appearing as guest bloggers and contributors, offering advice and insight into the profession.

Actors & Performers provides a community for actors to share events, ask questions, network, comment on blogs and events, and obtain career advice for free.

Register free for Actors & Performers at **www.actorsandperformers.com**.

Amazon.co.uk & Amazon.com

website www.amazon.co.uk or www.amazon.com

Remarkably useful not just for what is currently in print, but also for links to second-hand retailers who may have that out-of-print play or score you are seeking.

Barbican Library

Barbican Centre, London EC2Y 8DS
tel 020 7638 0569
website www.cityoflondon.gov.uk/barbicanlibrary

Situated on level 2 of the Barbican Centre, this is the largest lending library in the City of London. In addition to the general library, the strong arts and music sections reflect the Barbican Centre's emphasis on the arts. The library is fully accessible to wheelchair users. *Opening hours*: Monday and Wednesday: 9.30am–5.30pm; Tuesday and Thursday: 9.30am–7.30pm; Friday: 9.30am–5.30pm; Saturday: 9.30am–4pm.

Bookbarn International

Units 1-2, Hallatrow Business Park, Hallatrow, Bath & Avon BS39 6EX
tel 01761 452178
website www.bookbarninternational.co.uk

"The UK's largest used book warehouse," with many thousands of cheap second-hand scripts and a searchable catalogue online.

The British Library

St Pancras Building, 96 Euston Road,
London NW1 2DB
tel 0330 333 1144 (switchboard), 020 7412 7676 (reader information, St Pancras), 01937 546070 (reader information, enquiries, Boston Spa), 020 7412 7831 (humanities, librarianship, information science service), 020 7412 7513 (maps and manuscripts)
Legal Deposit Office: The British Library, Boston Spa, Wetherby, West Yorkshire LS23 7BQ
tel (01937) 546268
email legal-deposit-books@bl.uk
website www.bl.uk
Facebook www.facebook.com/britishlibrary
Twitter @britishlibrary

The British Library is the national library of the United Kingdom and contains a substantial collection of plays and manuscripts from the UK and Ireland, as well as from other parts of the world. The sound archive also includes just about everything from the sound of Amazonian tree frogs to classic recordings of Shakespeare's plays. Users need a Reader's Pass (details on how to acquire same are on the website) to access and read particular publications. The library will, for a fee, allow photocopying – subject to copyright legislation.

Contacts

See the entry for Spotlight under *Spotlight, casting directories and information services* on page 382.

Doollee.com

website www.doollee.com

An excellent online guide to modern playwrights and theatre plays which have been written, or translated, into English since the production of *Look Back in Anger* in 1956. It costs £5 per week for access or £25 for a year.

Dress Circle

tel 020 7240 2227
email info@dresscircle.co.uk
website www.dresscircle.co.uk

Dress Circle formerly had a shop in London's Covent Garden; it now operates online only. It aims to supply the widest selection of musical theatre and cabaret-related products from around the world – CDs, DVDs, posters, cards, mugs, collectibles and more. "If we can't get it – no one can!"

Fourthwall (incorporating The Drama Student)

3rd Floor, 207 Regent Street, London W1B 3HH
tel 020 3371 0995
email editor@fourthwallmagazine.co.uk
website www.fourthwallmagazine.co.uk
Editorial Director Phil Matthews *Editor* Josh Boyd-Rochford

Fourthwall covers the whole journey, from auditioning for drama school through to graduation and beyond. Believes that to succeed in this industry, it is important that we constantly challenge ourselves, and often that means the training never leaves us. *Fourthwall* is at the forefront of that passion, delivering a magazine that is informative, amusing, intelligent, thought provoking, accessible and challenging. "Above all, we're a publication that is passionate about careers in the performing arts."

Samuel French Bookshop at the Royal Court Theatre

Sloane Square, London SW1W 8AS
tel 020 7565 5024
email bookshop@royalcourttheatre.com
website www.royalcourttheatre.com/your-visit/bookshop

Offers a diverse selection of contemporary plays as well as publications on the theory and practice of

modern drama. The staff specialise in assisting with the selection of audition monologues and scenes. Playtexts for current Royal Court productions typically cost just £4 and past production texts cost £5. The Bookshop is situated on the first floor. *Opening Hours*: Monday to Saturday: 11am–5.30pm. On performance nights, there is a smaller bookstall in the downstairs bar from 6pm until curtain.

Nick Hern Books

tel 020 8749 4953
email info@nickhernbooks.co.uk
website www.nickhernbooks.co.uk

Nick Hern Books is the UK's leading specialist performing arts publisher, with plays by writers including Mike Bartlett, Caryl Churchill, debbie tucker green, Lucy Kirkwood, Conor McPherson, Rona Munro, Jack Thorne and Enda Walsh. Also publishes practical books by renowned practitioners such as Mike Alfreds, Peter Brook, Declan Donnellan, Richard Eyre and Harriet Walter.

Offers online discounts and special promotions, plus downloadable extracts, exclusive signed editions and more. Enquiries for performing licences to their plays can also made online. The online Play Finder allows searches by genre, cast size, length and more.

Useful series for actors include *The Good Audition Guides*, which offer classical, Shakespeare and contemporary monologues and duologues as well as guidance on how to perform them; the *So You Want To...?* career guides, giving advice on a range of careers in the performing arts, written by practitioners with a wealth of knowledge and expertise in their field, and *Drama Classics*, offering great plays from around the world by dramatists including Chekhov, Euripides, Ibsen, Lorca, Molière and Wilde, with introductions, plot synopses and author biographies.

Nick Hern Books publishes plays in the English language alongside major professional productions on stage in the UK or Ireland. Submissions can be emailed to the Commissioning Editor at submissions@nickhernbooks.co.uk.

Internet Movie Database (IMDb)

website uk.imdb.com

A comprehensive database and news round-up of film and television around the world.

The Knowledge

Media Business Insight, Zetland House, 5-20 Scrutton Street London EC2A 4HJ
tel 020 8102 0931
email alexandra.zeevalkink@mbi.london
website www.theknowledgeonline.com
Twitter @TheKnowledgeUK

Covering all aspects of production, The Knowledge Online contains contacts and services for the UK film, television, video and commercial production industry. The website features around 18,000 contacts, is free to use and does not require registration. Its new subscription service Production Intelligence features contact details of casting directors and line producers for forthcoming productions.

London Arrangements

tel 020 7096 1801
email enquiries@londonarrangements.com
website www.londonarrangements.com
Facebook /londonarrangements
Director Stephen Robinson

London Arrangements specialise in the production of professional backing tracks ranging from stage and screen, swing and jazz, to classical and easy listening genres. Samples of all tracks can be listened to online, and the majority may be ordered in any key at no extra charge. We also produce bespoke backing tracks, piano rehearsal tracks and piano/vocal sheet music.

London Theatre

website www.londontheatre.co.uk

A website containing news, reviews, events, booking information and seating plans for London's theatre scene plus maps, hotels and general tourist information.

Methuen Drama

50 Bedford Square, London WC1B 3DP
tel 020 7631 5600
website www.bloomsbury.com/academic/academic-subjects/drama-and-performance-studies/
Twitter @MethuenDrama

Methuen Drama covers a wide range of books that examine the works of key practitioners and playwrights including Stanislavsky, Chekhov, Laban, Bertolt Brecht, Noël Coward, Simon Stephens, Caryl Churchill, Edward Bond and many more. Also publishes books that run the gamut of theatre and performance studies: from movement to directing, voice to playwriting, the list features original material for everyone with an interest in drama, whether a student or a professional. The popular series Student Editions and Student Guides make the most prominent plays and playwrights accessibe to students studying theatre at A level through to undergraduate, whilst Modern Classics, Modern Plays and play anthologies feature the best in new writing and classic contemporary theatre.

Accepts unsolicited play scripts and are pleased to consider proposals for theatre and performance studies textbooks and monographs. For submission details go to the website www.bloomsbury.com/uk/company/contact-us/

Music Theatre International

website www.mtishows.com

A great resource for researching songs – some of which can be partially listened to and read about on this site.

Musicroom

email info@musicroom.com
website www.musicroom.com

The world's largest online retailer of sheet music, tutor methods, instructional DVDs & videos, music software and instruments & accessories.

National Theatre Bookshop

National Theatre, South Bank, London SE1 9PX
tel 020 7452 3456
email bookshop@nationaltheatre.org.uk
website http://shop.nationaltheatre.org.uk/
Twitter @ntbookshop
Instagram @ntbookshop

Britain's leading specialist theatre bookshop. An inspiring selection of books, plays and design-led gifts. *Opening Hours*: Monday to Saturday: 9.30am – 10.45pm (this varies on certain public holidays); 12pm – 6pm on Sundays when there is a performance.

PlayDatabase.com

website www.playdatabase.com

US site that helps theatre-lovers find monologues and plays for production.

Project Gutenberg

website www.gutenberg.org

An online library of more than 18,000 books – and many classic plays – which have gone out of copyright in the US. Also a growing collection of music recordings and scores. Possibly the largest of its kind in the world.

Screen International

Greater London House, Hampstead Road, London NW1 7EJ
tel 020 7728 5000
email mike.goodridge@emap.com
website www.screendaily.com

International news and features on the film business. Subscriptions cost £175 per annum for:

• Screen International – 12 monthly issues delivered to your door
• ScreenDaily.com – instant access to the latest news, reviews and industry moves available online
• Global box office data available online – structured by territories, films and distributors
• Screen Base – the new online, interactive database providing vital production and financing information for the top five European territories

Script Websites

Although subject to rules on copyright, a number of websites make the scripts for films and television shows and suggestions for audition speeches available online. These sites tend to come and go, but here are some that are current at the time of going to press:

- www.script-o-rama.com
- www.sfy.ru
- www.imsdb.com
- www.playscripts.com
- www.simplyscripts.com
- www.whysanity.net/monos
- www.singlelane.com
- www.filmsite.org/bestspeeches.html

The Sheetmusic Warehouse

email pianoman@globalnet.co.uk
website www.sheetmusicwarehouse.co.uk

Specialists supplying old music, rare music, music from the shows, musicals and operetta, popular music, wartime music, jazz music, Deep South American music, music hall music, classical music, modern music . . . "You name it, we've probably got it. Music to play, music to sing to or music to frame and hang on your wall!"

Shooting People

PO Box 51350, London N1 6XS
email contact@shootingpeople.org
website www.shootingpeople.org

Shooting People allows thousands of people working in independent film to exchange information via a range of daily email bulletins. These include:

• Daily UK Filmmakers Bulletin – for directors, producers and crew to share information on the latest technologies, get advice, find crew, locations, production deals, events & screenings, training and more. Currently more than 22,000 members
• Daily UK Screenwriters Bulletin – writers all over the UK use this email network to discuss writing, share ideas and hear about competitions, opportunities and training. Currently more than 13,000 members
• Daily UK Casting Bulletin – for actors to discuss their craft and receive casting calls from directors, producers and casting directors. Currently more than 14,000 members
• Weekly UK Script Pitch Bulletin – a weekly collection of script pitches offered to producers and directors by the writers on the Screenwriters Network. Currently more than 11,000 members

Both part- and full-membership are available. Part-membership allows subscribers to receive email bulletins only, and is free. Full-membership costs £20 per year and entitles users to a range of other services. Full-members can create an actor's personal profile with a photograph and be listed in the online directory, post to any bulletin and download guides on various confusing aspects of film-making such as actor contracts, health and safety and distribution. They are also entitled to create member cards and to browse other member cards to find potential local collaborators.

Shooting People also organises a number of parties, screenings, workshops and other events for which full members receive advanced notice.

Skoob Books

66 The Brunswick, Marchmont Street,
London WC1N 1AE
tel 020 7278 8760
website www.skoob.com

An excellent resource for the peforming arts. Large collection of second-hand plays, including many translated works and as-new titles at half RRP. Strong theatre, film, music and TV sections in a very large basement bookshop. All academic areas covered, and masses of paperback fiction. Lift access and knowledgeable, friendly staff. Skoob is the leading UK supplier of books to TV, film and theatre productions; please contact our Didcot office for hire enquries at skoobhire@pyschobabel.co.uk.

The Stage

47 Bermondsey Street, London SE1 3XT
tel 020 7403 1818 01858 438895 (Subscriptions)
email newsdesk@thestage.co.uk
website www.thestage.co.uk
Managing Director Hugh Comerford *Acting Editor* Alistair Smith

Online and weekly print publication for the entertainment industry. Established in 1880. Advice, news, reviews, features and recruitment for theatre, entertainment, opera, dance, TV, radio, backstage and technical, management, education and training. *The Stage* is also available on iPad, Android, Kindle and other tablet devices. *The Stage* Castings, the company's online casting service (**www.thestage.co.uk/castings**), offers access to hundreds of jobs for all kinds of performers.

Theatre Record – The continuing chronicle of the British Stage

Southernhay, 22 Carlton Road South,
Weymouth DT4 7PR
tel 07777 697270
email editor@theatrerecord.com
website www.theatrerecord.com

Established in 1981 as *London Theatre Record*. *Theatre Record* publishes the complete, unabridged reviews of all new shows in the UK covered by national press and leading magazines. As well as reviews, each show is represented by a full listing of cast, technical credits and, usually, production photographs. Issued fortnightly. Each annual volume is supplemented by a detailed Index which enables searching by production title or artist's name. *Theatre Record* is available in a print or digital version. The complete archive of all theatre records is also available.

Theatrevoice

website www.theatrevoice.com

The leading site for audio content about British theatre, featuring journalists from across the UK press, and practitioners from across the theatre industry. It was set up in 2003 to see if theatre could be talked about in a new way – critics to be more expansive than what the usual space constraints of the print media allowed; to enable actors, writers, directors and designers to be heard talking in detail and at length about their work; and to help members of the public interact more directly with theatre-makers and commentators. The Theatre Museum, now V&A Theatre Collections, which provided technical assistance and a place for recording from the site's inception, assumed management responsibilities for the site in the summer of 2005, to ensure that Theatrevoice's growing archive of material would be preserved for posterity. In April 2008, V&A Theatre Collections and Rose Bruford College agreed to support the site in partnership. Theatrevoice acknowledges with gratitude all the input that has been and still is freely given.

Theatricalia
website theatricalia.com

Theatricalia is aiming to become "the repository of theatre productions on the Internet". In doing so, it will enable people to discover theatre that is going on around them, follow actors they have seen in previous productions and record memorable events of productions they have seen.

UK Theatre Network
PO Box 3009, Glasgow G60 5ET
tel 0870 760 6033 *fax* 0870 760 6033
email editor@uktheatre.net
website www.uktheatre.net

Established 2001. A weekly magazine in PDF, Kindle and eBook format is circulated to members by email. In addition the company offers webmail, website hosting, reviews, contacts and listings of what's on.

All services are provided free of charge. New members should contact **subscribe@uktheatre.net**.

Virtual Library of Theatre & Drama
website www.vl-theatre.com

Lists online versions of plays and resources in more than 50 countries.

Westminster Reference Library
35 St Martin's Street, London WC2H 7HP
tel 020 7641 6200
website www.westminster.gov.uk/libraries-opening-hours-and-contact-details#westminster-reference-library

West End public library specialising in arts and business, with 15,000 volumes, (5,000 of which can be borrowed), on the performing arts, including Spotlight and *The Stage*. There are regular talks, workshops, performances in support of the collections, with the library open to suggestion for future events. Opening Hours: Monday to Friday: 10.00am – 8.00pm; Saturday: 10.00am – 5.00pm.

Wikipedia
website en.wikipedia.org

A free, online encyclopedia with over 1 million articles. Originally created by an army of volunteers in 2001, it can be added to or edited by anyone at all – a very democratic publication. This democracy can sometimes mean that contentious or politically sensitive issues are not always presented in the most balanced way, although some measures are in place to prevent flagrant abuse of the system. Occasionally the editing process makes for some slightly disjointed articles. However, as a free source of information on just about any topic, it is unsurpassed. The theatre section can be accessed via: **en.wikipedia.org/wiki/Theatre**.

Organisations, associations and societies

This section contains details of all kinds of ways (not listed elsewhere) of getting involved, sourcing useful information, learning, finding interesting lectures, networking, and simply keeping in touch with what's going on. It is important for the 'jobbing' actor to keep up-to-date with developments within the industry, and getting involved in related activities can pay dividends in the future.

The Actors' Guild of Great Britain
website www.actorsguild.co.uk

The Actors' Guild is a community of professional actors who meet with leading acting tutors, casting directors, directors, artistic directors, producers and agents to develop their craft, maximise their career development and benefit from the professional networking opportunities that membership brings.

The Guild was formed as an antidote to the increasing number of enterprises that seemed to be taking advantage of actors. Providing a haven, a support network and the opportunity to work with the very people you meet in the audition room.

"Our unique set-up means we are able to swing the pendulum of power firmly back to the actor. Our programme is dictated purely by feedback from our membership; we never ask you to book casting director workshops in 'blocks', and believe quality does not have to cost the earth – workshops start at just £22 and never exceed £30 for a 3-hour workshop.

"We also offer an exclusive range of industry discounts for members; a bursary scheme which pays for all the essentials an actor could need for a year; a forum; and a support network that brings this often disparate, nomadic community together."

The Agents' Association (GB)
54 Keyes House, Dolphin Square,
London SW1V 3NA
tel 020 7834 0515
email association@agents-uk.com
website www.agents-uk.com

Established in 1927 to represent and enhance the interests of entertainment agents in the United Kingdom and to standardise practice. The membership covers all fields of the entertainment industry.

ASSITEJ (International Association of Theatre for Children and Young People)
Preradoviceva 44, 10000 Zagreb
tel +385 (0) 1 4667034 *fax* +385 (0) 1 4667225

email sec.gen@assitej-international.org
website www.assitej-international.org

ASSITEJ International (Association Internationale du Theatre pour l'Enfance et la Jeunesse) states: "Since the theatrical art is a universal expression of mankind, and possesses the influence and power to link large groups of the world's people in the service of peace, and considering the role theatre can play in the education of younger generations, an autonomous international organisation has been formed which bears the name of the International Association of Theatre for Children and Young People." Also see Theatre for Young Audiences (TYA), below.

ASSITEJ (International Association of Theatre for Children and Young People)
The Birmingham Repertory Theatre Ltd, Broad Street, Birmingham B1 2EP
email secretary@tya-uk.org
website www.tya-uk.org
Contact Catherine Rollins

TYA-UK (UK Centre of ASSITEJ) is a network for makers and promoters of professional theatre for young audiences, linking the UK to theatres, organisations and individual artists around the world. Works for a fuller awareness of the value of theatre for young audiences.

BAFTA
195 Piccadilly, London W1J 9LN
tel 020 7734 0022
email reception@bafta.org
website www.bafta.org
Chief Executive Officer Amanda Berry OBE

Founded in 1947, BAFTA is the UK's pre-eminent independent charity bringing the very best work in film, games and television to public attention, and supporting the growth of creative talent in the UK and internationally. BAFTA does this by identifying and celebrating excellence, discovering, inspiring and nurturing new talent, and enabling learning and

Resources

creative collaboration. BAFTA's awards are awarded annually by its members to their peers in recognition of their skills and expertise. In addition, BAFTA's year-round learning programme offers unique access to some of the world's most inspiring talent through workshops, masterclasses, lectures and mentoring schemes, connecting with audiences of all ages and backgrounds across the UK, USA and Asia.

British Association for Performing Arts Medicine (BAPAM)

7-9 Breams Buildings, London EC4A 1DT
tel 020 7404 8444 (Helpline), 020 7404 5888 (Admin)
website www.bapam.org.uk

The British Association for Performing Arts Medicine is a unique medical charity helping performing arts professionals and students with work-related health problems, both physical and psychological.

BAPAM provides:

• Free confidential clinical advice from medical practitioners who have specialist understanding of industry professionals' needs
• Directory of Performing Arts Medicine Practitioners – a list of clinical specialists and practitioners in many branches of healthcare who have an interest in treating performing arts professionals
• Health-information resources enabling you to understand what you can do to keep in peak condition throughout a demanding career
• Healthy Performance talks and training for a wide range of audiences, including introductory sessions for student groups and educational institutions. Bespoke sessions for clients including performers, teachers, clinicians and employers.

British Council

Arts Group, 10 Spring Gardens, London SW1A 2BN
tel 020 7389 3194 *fax* 020 7389 3199
email arts@britishcouncil.org
Norwich Union House, 7 Fountain Street, Belfast
BT1 5EG
tel 028- 9024 8220 *fax* 028 9023 7592
email nireland.enquiries@britishcouncil.org
The Tun, 3rd Floor, 4 Jackson's Entry, Holyrood
Road, Edinburgh EH8 8PJ
tel 0131 524 5714 *fax* 0131 524 5714
email scotland.enquiries@britishcouncil.org
1 Kingsway, 2nd Floor, Cardiff CF10 3AQ
tel 029 2092 4300 *fax* 029 2092 4301
email wales.enquiries@britishcouncil.org
website www.britishcouncil.org/arts

The British Council is the UK's public diplomacy and cultural organisation, and works in 100 countries, in arts, education, governance and science. The Arts Group supports around 2,000 arts events every year, encouraging international collaborations, performances and exchanges with some of the top UK artists. In addition they support arts-based workshops, seminars and online events.

The form of support which is offered varies according to the project. In most cases the Council acts as an advisory body, and brokers partnerships with overseas contacts such as artistic programmers and producers, venues, choreographers and festival directors. Although most work is geared towards young people aged 16-35, this isn't an exclusive emphasis, and classic or traditional work is supported, especially if it has a modern slant.

Resources available on the website include an annual directory of UK drama, dance, live art and street art companies that have work suitable for overseas touring; specialist information about drama/ performing arts education in the UK; and *Britfilms* **www.britfilms.com** – a portal site for the UK film industry with information about international film festivals, UK film directors and films, making a film in the UK, training and careers advice.

Not open to the public except by appointment. Write, phone or email to establish contact, or get in touch with an artform specialist.

British Film Institute (BFI)

21 Stephen Street, London W1T 1LN
tel 0207 255 1444
BFI Southbank, Belvedere Road, South Bank,
Waterloo, London SE1 8XT
tel 020 7928 3535
website www.bfi.org.uk

Established in 1933, the BFI strives to increase the level of understanding, appreciation and access to film and television culture. In addition to the BFI Reuben Library, which provides access to the largest film archive in the world, the organisation runs BFI Southbank (formerly the National Film Theatre) , BFI Flare: London LGBT Film Festival and the London Film Festival (see entry under Media festivals). It also publishes books, releases films in cinemas, on DVD and via its VOD platform BFI Player, runs educational programmes, and has one of the largest collections of film stills and film posters in the world. The BFI also awards Lottery funding to film production, distribution, education, audience development and market intelligence and research.

British Music Hall Society

45 Mayflower Road, Park Street, St Albans,
Herts AL2 2QN
tel 01727 768878
website www.music-hall-society.com
Secretary Daphne Masterton

Founded in 1963, and with offices across England, the society aims to preserve the history of music hall and variety, to recall the artistes who created it and to support entertainers working today. Members receive copies of the society's quarterly magazine *The Call-Boy* containing news, views and information about the sector; they also have the opportunity to attend evening and weekend study group meetings. Arranges live theatre shows, and it is possible for members to take part in such performances on these occasions.

Casting Directors Guild of Great Britain and Ireland
website www.thecdg.co.uk

A professional organisation which represents casting directors working in film, television, theatre and commercials. The Casting Directors Guild aims to standardise professional working practice and to enable the exchange of information and ideas between members.

Election to the Guild is at the discretion of the Committee. Full members must have worked in one or more areas of the industry for at least 5 years, and are entitled to use the initials CDG after their name. Probationary members must have worked as an assistant to a casting director for 3 years.

Members are listed on the website with information about their areas of work and recent credits.

Casting Society of America
website www.castingsociety.com

The Casting Society of America is the premier organisation of theatrical Casting Directors in film, television, and theatre. Although it is not a union, its members are a united professional society that consistently set the level of professionalism in casting on which the entertainment industry has come to rely. Its more than 350 members are represented not only in the United States, but also in Canada, England, Australia and Italy.

Co-operative Personal Management Association (CPMA)
email cpmauk@yahoo.co.uk
website www.cpma.coop

Founded in 2002, the CPMA works to further and promote the interests of its members, who are acting agencies located across the UK. Backed by Equity, it seeks to raise the profile of co-ops with both employers and actors, and to represent the interests of co-ops with external bodies. Also works with members to identify and assist in solving the unique problems of a co-operative, to enourage good practice, to develop training skills and opportunities, and to act as an advocate for co-operative working.

The John Colclough Consultancy
tel 020 8873 1763
email john@johncolclough.com
website www.johncolclough.com

Practical independent guidance for actors and actresses. When Spotlight decided to end their advisory service in March 2005, John Colclough elected to carry on an 'advisory' service independently, using the knowledge he had gained at Spotlight and also from his shop-floor experience as an actor, director and producer.

Sessions take place over the telephone. Please refer to the website for current charges. Payments may be made by Internet Banking or by cheque after the consultation had taken place. Telephone calls are free to landlines. Calls to mobiles will be charged for, unless the caller offers to return the call. For a consultation, telephone John on 020-8873 1763.

Conservatoire for Dance and Drama
Tavistock House, Tavistock Square,
London WC1H 9JJ
tel 020 7387 5101
email info@cdd.ac.uk
website www.cdd.ac.uk

The Conservatoire for Dance and Drama is eight specialist schools delivering world-leading vocational training within higher eduction. On stage and screen and behind the scenes, graduates are the actors, dancers, circus artists, choregoraphers, stage managers and theatre technicians shaping the indutry today.

All the Conservatoire Schools are small institutions with international reputations for high-quality training in dance, drama or circus arts. Publicly funded through the Higher Education Funding Council for England and students new to higher education can access Student Finance like other UK students. The Conseratoire Schools have strong traditions of providing student care and support services. Committed to admitting and supporting disabled students; warmly encourages students to inform the Schools so appropriate support can be put in place as soon as possible. Recruits on the basis of talent and potential, irrespepective of background.

The Conservatoire Schools are: Bristol Old Vic Theatre School, Central School of Ballet,London Academy of Music and Dramatic Art (LAMDA), London Contemporary Dance School, National Centre for Circus Arts, Northern School of Contemporary Dance, Rambert School of Ballet and Contemporary Dance, Royal Academy of Dramatic Art (RADA).

Culture.Info
website www.culture.info

The aim of Culture.Info is to be the first port-of-call for users seeking cultural information on a particular topic. Each Culture.Info sub-portal provides a carefully researched set of listings of links to information that is more focused and useful than can usually be obtained from the vast majority of existing listings or search engines.

Directors UK
3rd & 4th Floor,22 Stukeley Street,
London WC2B 5LR
tel 020 7240 0009
email info@directors.uk.com
website www.directors.uk.com

Resources

Facebook https//www.facebook.com/Directros-UK-115062731847454/
Twitter @Directors_UK
Instgram @directors_uk/

Directors UK is the professional association for screen directors. It is a membership organisation representing the creative, economic and contractual interests of over 7,000 members - the majority of working TV and film directors in the UK. Directors UK collects and distributes royalty payments and provides a range of services to members including campaigning, commercial negotiations, legal advice, events, training and career development. Directors UK works closely with fellow organisations around the world to represent directors' rights and concerns, promotes excellence in the craft of direction and champions change to the current lanscape to create an equal opportunity indusry for all.

Drama Association of Wales

64 Top Llan Road, Glan Conwy,
Colwyn Bay LL28 5ND
email chair@dramawales.org.uk
website www.dramawales.org.uk
Facebook @DramaAssociationOfWales?
Twitter @DramaWales
Key contact Shirley Betts (Chair)

Founded in 1934 and a registered charity since 1973, the Drama Association of Wales aims to increase opportunities for people in the community to be creatively involved in high-quality drama.

Its main activities include a mail-order library service for DAW Publications and training courses in all aspects of theatre, including a 5-day residential summer school.

Also runs a playwriting competition and workshops. Organises the Wales National Drama Festival from March to June, culminating in the Wales Final Festival of One Act Plays at the beginning of June.

UK membership costs £15 per year for individuals and £25 for groups, both professional and amateur. Overseas members are very welcome: contact Shirley Betts for details.

Dramaturgs' Network

c/o 10 Fonthill House, 66 Russell Road,
London W14 8JD
email info@dramaturgy.co.uk
website www.dramaturgy.co.uk
Facebook www.facebook.com/dramaturgsnetwork/
Twitter @dramaturgs_net

The Dramaturgs' Network is an organisation for UK theatre practitioners committed to developing dramaturgy and supporting practitioners' development in the field. Founded in 2001, it is a volunteer arts organisation created to share ideas, knowledge, resources and skills in current dramaturgical practices. The network aims to provide support for theatre makers functioning in the role of dramaturg and/or literary manager and educational professionals involved in dramaturgical practice. Every other year it bestows the Kenneth Tynan Award, which recognises excellence in the field of dramaturgy.

Euclid

website www.euclid.info

Euclid provides a range of European and International information, research and consultancy services. It has been appointed by the UK Department for Media, Culture & Sport and the European Commission as the official UK Cultural Contact Point, in particular to promote the EU's funding programmes for culture.

Federation of Scottish Theatre

c/o Royal Lyceum Theatre, 30B Grindlay Street,
Edinburgh EH3 9AX
tel 0131 248 4842
email info@scottishtheatre.org
website www.scottishtheatre.org

The Federation of Scottish Theatre is the membership and development body for professional dance, opera and theatre in Scotland, bringing the sector together to speak with a collective voice, to share resources and expertise, and to promote collaborative working.

Highlands & Islands Theatre Network (HIN)

c/o HI-Arts, Suites 4 & 5, 4th Floor,
Ballantyne House, 84 Academy Street,
Inverness IV1 1LU
tel 01463 717091
website www.hitn.co.uk

HITN has the following agreed aims:

• To promote the advancement of education and the arts in the Highlands and Islands of Scotland area for the benefit of the public
• To promote the professional theatre sector in the Highlands and Islands of Scotland area at regional, national and international levels
• To work with other organisations to encourage wider access to theatre across the Highlands and Islands of Scotland area

Independent Theatre Council (ITC)

c/o The Albany, Douglas Way, London SE8 4AG
tel 020-7403 1727
email admin@itc-arts.org
website https://www.itc-arts.org/

Founded in 1974, the Independent Theatre Council (ITC) is the management association and political voice of around 450 performing arts professionals and organisations. ITC provides its members with legal and management advice, training and professional development, networking, regular newsletters and a comprehensive web resource.

Working across a variety of art forms, including drama, dance, opera, music theatre, puppetry, mixed media, mime, physical theatre and circus, ITC members usually operate on the middle- and small-scale, and are dedicated to producing innovative work, often in unconventional performance spaces.

ITC has commissioned a wide range of publications which offer guidance on potentially difficult aspects of working in the performing arts, advice on good practice and further sources of information. For more than 20 years the Independent Theatre Council has been organising training for managers and staff across the performing arts.

For details of how to join and other benefits available to members, consult the website.

International Casting Directors Network (ICDN)

website www.shootingstars.eu/en/casting_directors_network.php

The idea for an informal international network was floated during a meeting of casting directors during European Film Promotion's ShootingStars event at the Berlinale. Until then, casting directors had only been organised in national associations, but ICDN offers them "the chance to exchange ideas on an international level about their different ways of working, to take advantage of synergies with international co-productions, and to attract greater attention to the work of casting a film".

International Federation of Actors (FIA)

Rue Joseph II 40, Box 4, B-1000 Brussels
tel +32 (0) 2 234 56 53 / +32 (0) 2 235 08 65 / +32 (0) 2 235 08 74 *fax* +32 (0) 2 235 08 70
email office@fia-actors.com
website www.fia-actors.com

The FIA currently represents 90 performers' unions and guilds in 66 countries around the world. Membership is limited to unions, guilds and professional associations – individual actors may not join. FIA works internationally to represent and co-ordinate the interests of performing artists and their professional organisations.

Services: Lobbying at European and international level on behalf of performers; defence of artists' freedom; trade union development; information exchange through confrences and meetings; networking.

Objectives: To promote a better understanding of performers' concerns and challenges around the world; to ensure that all main decision-making processes take due consideration of the specific needs of performers; to contribute to improve the social and professional conditions of performers worldwide; to facilitate the sharing of knowledge and experience on all issues of common interest between member organisations.

Irish Theatre Institute

website www.irishtheatreonline.com

A comprehensive guide to professional theatre, dance and opera in Ireland, north and south.

National Campaign for the Arts

4th Floor, 17 Tavistock Street, London WC2E 7PA
tel 020 7240 4698
email nca@artscampaign.org.uk
website www.artscampaign.org.uk

The National Campaign for the Arts is the UK's only independent organisation campaigning for all the arts. Since 1985 they have worked to protect and promote the UK's world-class arts scene and acted as a powerful and effective advocate for the sector, able to influence the people who matter. With a growing UK-wide membership, the NCA is driven by the needs of the arts sector. "We believe that only speaking with a united voice can the arts truly be heard."

National Rural Touring Forum (NRTF)

email admin@nrtf.org.uk
website www.ruraltouring.org

The NRTF is the organisation that represents a number of mainly rural touring schemes and rural arts development agencies across the UK. "Our touring scheme members work with local communities to promote high-quality arts events and experiences in local venues."

North American Actors Association (NAAA)

mobile 07873 371891
email admin@naaa.org.uk
website www.naaa.org.uk
Administrator Kelly Jeffreys

The North American Actors Association is an association promoting and supporting North American actors based in Britain, and is the largest non-Americas-based casting resource and database of genuine North Americans for the entertainment industry.

Membership is open to genuine North American professional actors who can work on both sides of the Atlantic without restriction, are full members in good standing of at least 1 entertainment union and have proof of professional contracts. Not an agency, but through the website provides agent and other contact details of members to those involved in casting.

Northern Ireland Theatre Association (NITA)

c/o The MAC, 10 Exchange Street West, Belfast BT1 2NJ
email info@nitatheatre.org
website http://nitheatre.com
Coordinator Charlotte Smith

Resources

NITA is the representative body for professional theatre in Northern Ireland.

Pact (Producers Alliance for Cinema and Television)

3rd Floor, Fitzrovia House,
153–157 Cleveland Street, London W1T 6QW
tel 020 7380 8230
email info@pact.co.uk
website www.pact.co.uk
Twitter @PactUK
Chief Executive John McVay

The UK trade association that represents and promotes the commercial interests of independent feature film, television, animation and interactive media companies. Headquartered in London, it has regional representation throughout the UK, in order to support its members. An effective lobbying organisation, it has regular and constructive dialogues with government, regulators, public agencies and opinion-formers on all issues affecting its members, and contributes to key public policy debates on the media industry, both in the UK and in Europe. It negotiates terms of trade with all public service broadcasters in the UK and supports members in their business dealings with cable and satellite channels. It also lobbies for a properly structured and funded UK film industry and maintains close contact with other relevant film organisations and government departments.

Personal Managers' Association (PMA)

tel 0845 602 7191
email info@thepma.com
website www.thepma.com

The PMA is a membership organisation for agents who represent actors, writers and directors working mainly in film, television and theatre. Established in 1950, the PMA aimed to encouragegood practice among agents by encouraging better communication between agents and better communication from agents to the industry – an ethos that remains true to this day.

AudioUK

c/o Kim Mason (Administrator), 21 Pembroke Road, London N10 2HR
email admin@audiouk.org
website www.audiouk.org
Twitter @WeAreAudioUK

A non-profit-making trade body funded through membership fees and other fundraising activities, representing the interests and needs of the UK's independent audio and radio production industry. Formed in July 2004, AudioUK currently represents over two-thirds of the industry. Membership continues to grow – to over 100 companies, from globe-spanning commercial giants through to one-person companies and partnerships. As well as

representing members' and the industry's needs in negotiations with the BBC, commercial radio, other groups and the government, AudioUK offers support, resources, information, access and training. Its aim is to bring together the knowledge of the thousands of dedicated and skilled people in the independent audio production sector, making as much of it as possible available to all.

Royal Television Society (RTS)

3 Dorset Rise, London EC4Y 8EN
tel 020 7822 2810 *fax* 020 7822 2811
email info@rts.org.uk
website www.rts.org.uk

Provides the leading forum for discussion and debate on all aspects of the television industry, with opportunities for networking and professional development for people at all levels and across every sector. The RTS has 14 national and regional centres in the UK, which draw up an annual programme to suit the needs of their members.

Events organised by the RTS include dinners, lectures, conventions, conferences and awards ceremonies. In addition it produces a monthly magazine, *Television*, outlining key industry debates and developments.

Scene & Heard

Theatro Technis, 26 Crowndale Road,
London NW1 1TT
020 7388 9009
email mail@sceneandheard.org
website www.sceneandheard.org
Twitter @SceneandHeardUK

Scene & Heard is a unique mentoring programme that partners the inner-city children of Somers Town, London, with volunteer theatre professionals, to give them an experience of quality one-to-one adult attention and to enable them to write and sometimes perform their own plays.

The fundamental purpose of the project is to boost the self-esteem of the children involved by giving them a public platform for their voice and by providing a personal experience of success.

By introducing the children to a new way of working with language, Scene & Heard also strives to improve attitudes towards learning and literacy skills. Only accepts enquiries from professional actors, directors, writers and producers. The best way to get in touch is to go and see a performance.

The Society of Teachers of the Alexander Technique (STAT)

Unit W48, Grove Business Centre,
560-568 High Road, London N17 9TA
tel 020 8885 6524 *fax* 020 8808 2135
email office@stat.org.uk
website www.alexandertechnique.co.uk
Facebook @AlexanderTechUK

Instagram @alexandertechuk

The Alexander Technique has been taught for more than 100 years. In 1958, the Society of Teachers of the Alexander Technique (STAT) was founded in the UK by teachers who were trained by FM Alexander. STAT's first aim is to ensure the highest standards of teacher training and professional practice.

Teaching members of STAT are registered (MSTAT) to teach the Technique after completing a 3-year, full-time training course approved by the Society or one of the Affiliated Societies overseas; they are also required to adhere to the Society's published *Code of Professional Conduct and Competence* and are covered by the professional indemnity insurance.

There are currently more than 2,500 teaching members of STAT and its affiliated societies worldwide. Graduates of STAT training courses are assessed by a system of external moderation; the Society also runs a postgraduate programme of Continuing Professional Development. STAT's further aims are to promote public awareness and understanding of the Alexander Technique, and to encourage research. The Society publishes a regular newsletter, *STATNews*, and *The Alexander Journal*.

Society of London Theatre (SOLT)
32 Rose Street, London WC2E 9ET
tel 020 7557 6700 *fax* 020 7557 6799
email enquiries@soltukt.co.uk
website www.solt.co.uk

Founded in 1908 by Sir Charles Wyndham, the Society of London Theatre is the trade association which represents the producers, theatre owners and managers of the major commercial and grant-aided theatres in central London.

Today the Society combines its long-standing roles in such areas as industrial relations and legal advice for members, with a campaigning role for the industry, together with a wide range of audience-development programmes to promote theatre-going.

The Stephen Sondheim Society
265 Wollaton Vale, Wollaton, Nottingham NG8 2PX
email administrator@sondheim.org
website www.sondheim.org
Chairman Craig Glenday *Administrator* Lynne Chapman

The Stephen Sondheim Society is a registered charity promoting the works of the composer and lyricist Stephen Sondheim. Keeps track of all productions (professional and amateur) of Sondheim's musicals, publishes a newsletter, arranges theatre visits, runs an annual student competition and has an extensive archive housed at Kingston University.

At the time of writing, UK membership is £27 (single), £22 (concession) or £32 (joint), £17 (student/Equity/MU/ISM) and £37 (for international membership) but please consult the website for the latest rates.

Stage Directors UK
Exchange at Somerset House, South Wing, Strand, London WC2R 1LA
020 7112 8881
email info@stagedirectorsuk.com
website www.stagedirectorsuk.com
Facebook www.facebook.com/StageDirectorsUK
Twitter @StageDirectors

Stage Directors UK is the professional trade association for stage directors across the UK. SDUK represents the interests of stage directors, campaigning and lobbying for better rights and working conditions. SDUK provides a sense of community and a unifying network for its members, and offers support, training and professional development. "SDUK is *By Directors, For Directors*", moving directing culture towards a greater spirit of collaboration and mutual support.

StartaTheatreCompany.com
email admin@startatheatrecompany.com
website www.startatheatrecompany.com

An online guide to starting and developing a performing arts company. An e-learning course with 6 comprehensive modules, covering all you need to know about building a successful and sustainable enterprise. Delivered through fortnightly video and audio lessons, the guide is presented by tutor Sinead Mac Manus. Sinead has many years of experience working with and training performing arts companies, and has brought this experience to the world of e-learning.

Studio Salford
King's Arms, 11 Bloom Street, Salford M3 6AN
website www.studiosalford.com

Studio Salford is an umbrella group representing and promoting several theatre companies, raising the profile of Salford as a viable artistic location, and promoting artists from all over Salford and Manchester. Their performance venue is the intimate and unique upstairs space at The King's Arms.

Theatre Chaplaincy UK
St Paul's Church, Bedford Street, London WC2E 9ED
tel 020 7240 0344
email actorschurchunion@gmail.com
website www.actorschurchunion.com
Administrator Libby Shaw *President* Bishop Jack Nicholls *Senior Chaplain* Rev'd Lindsay Meader

Provides pastoral support for all members of the entertainment world, regardless of beliefs. Runs a network of voluntary chaplains for theatres, clubs and studios, in the UK and overseas. Also runs a charitable trust for children of parents in entertainment.

Theatre in Wales
website www.theatre-wales.co.uk

"The only comprehensive Welsh theatre and performance website."

Theatres Trust

22 Charing Cross Road, London WC2H OQL
tel 020 7836 8591
email info@theatrestrust.org.uk
website www.theatrestrust.org.uk
Twitter @TheatresTrust

We are the National Advisory Public Body for theatres, we are a statutory consultee on theatres in the planning system, and also operate as a charity. We champion the future of live performance, by protecting and supporting excellent theatre buildings which meet the needs of their communities. We do this by providing advice on the design, planning, development and sustainability of theatres, campaigning on behalf of theatres old and new, and offering financial assistance through grants.

We promote the quality and design of existing and new theatres and protect important historic theatres so that they can be used as theatres in the future. The Trust also advises to ensure theatre buildings meet the current needs and demands of the theatre industry and the audiences they serve.

Total Theatre

University of Winchester, Faculty of Arts,
Winchester SO22 4NR
tel 01962 827107
website www.totaltheatre.org.uk

Total Theatre is a national agency with an international focus, developing contemporary theatre for both theatre makers and theatre audiences.

UK Theatre Association (TMA)

32 Rose Street, London WC2E 9ET
tel 020 7557 6700 *fax* 020 7557 6799
email enquiries@soltukt.co.uk
website www.uktheatre.org
Chief Executive Julian Bird *Head of UK Theatre* Cassie Chadderton

The UK Theatre Association is a membership organisation for theatre and the performing arts organisations. Its members includes theatres, arts centres and presenting venues, producers, opera, ballet and dance companies and supports individuals who work professionally in the performing arts at all stages of their career. There are also membership schemes for sole traders, suppliers of goods and services to the industry and concert halls. Members benefit from access to a range of professional services, high-quality training and events, and networking opportunities. As well as running the only awards scheme to recognise excellence in theatre throughout the UK, UK Theatre leads on audience development programmes and actively campaigns on behalf of theatres and their audiences.

UK Theatre shares a common staff with the Society of London Theatre (SOLT).

University of Bristol Theatre Collection

Vandyck Building, Cantocks Close, Bristol BS8 1UP
tel 0117 331 5086
email theatre-collection@bristol.ac.uk
website www.bris.ac.uk/theatrecollection

The University of Bristol Theatre Collection is one of the world's largest and most significant collections relating to the history of British theatre. It is an accredited museum, accredited archive service and research facility that is open to the public. Its collections cover all aspects of theatre from the seventeenth century up to the present day and includes original documents, photographs, artwork and artefacts.

V&A Department of Theatre & Performance (formerly The Theatre Museum)

tel 020 7942 2697
email tmenquiries@vam.ac.uk
website www.vam.ac.uk/collections/theatre-performance

The V&A's Department of Theatre & Performance holds the UK's national collection of material about live performance in the UK since Shakespeare's day, covering drama, dance, musical theatre, circus, music hall, rock and pop and other forms of live entertainment. In 2009, the Theatre & Performance galleries at the V&A opened to the public. The galleries replaced those at the Theatre Museum in Covent Garden, which closed in 2007. The displays explore the process of performance, from the initial conception, through the design and development stages, to audiences' reactions.

Women in Film and Television (UK) (WFTV)

92/93 Great Russell Street, London WC1B 3PS
tel 020 7287 1400
email admin@wftv.org.uk
website www.wftv.org.uk
Chief Executive Kate Kinninmont

The leading membership organisation for women working in creative media in the UK. With more than 1,500 members including writers, actors, producers and directors, the WFTV promotes the interests and diversity of women working at all levels in these industries. Offers a network of national and international contacts with an online directory of members and provides a number of social forums, workshops, seminars and preview screenings.

WGGB - The Writers' Union

First Floor, 134 Tooley Street, London SE1 2TU
tel 020 7833 0777
email admin@writersguild.org.uk
website www.writersguild.org.uk

WGGB (Writers' Guild of Great Britain) is a trade union for professional and aspiring writers in TV, radio, film, theatre, books, poetry, comedy, animation and video games with 2,300 members; affiliated to the Trades Union Congress. WGGB negotiates collective minimum terms agreements with the main broadcasters and trade bodies for film, TV, radio and theatre – these cover fees, advances, royalties, residuals, pension contributions, rights, credits and other matters. WGGB members have access to free contract vetting, legal advice and representation in work-related disputes, and the Writers' Guild Welfare Fund gives emergency assistance to members in financial trouble. Members receive a weekly email bulletin containing news and work opportunities.

Resources

Bibliography

Books for aspiring, student and young actors

Margo Annett, *Actor's Guide to Auditions and Interviews* (Methuen Drama, 2004). Now in its third edition, this useful guide outlines the techniques needed to achieve success in the challenging process of getting work, covering all aspects of casting, including gaining a place on a drama course, landing a part in film, TV, commercials or theatre, and becoming a radio or TV presenter.

Clive Barker, *Theatre Games* (Methuen Drama, 2010). A guidebook to improvisational games for actors, and a comprehensive exploration of acting techniques.

Tom Cantrell and Christopher Hogg (eds.), *Exploring Television Acting* (Methuen Drama, 2018). A collection of eleven essays from internationally distinguished researchers, actor trainers and early-career advisers bring together scholarly and practical perspectives on acting for television for the first time.

Louise Dearman and Mark Evans, *Secrets of Stage Success* (Nick Hern Books, 2015). Two of the biggest musical-theatre stars working today offer advice on training, auditions, finding an agent, building your career, staying healthy and more

Simon Dunmore, *Alternative Shakespeare Auditions for Men* (A & C Black, 1997). A collection of 50 less-well-known speeches for men.

Simon Dunmore, *Alternative Shakespeare Auditions for Women* (A & C Black, 1997). A collection of 50 less-well-known speeches for women.

Simon Dunmore, *MORE Alternative Shakespeare Auditions for Men* (A & C Black, 2002). Another collection of 50 less-well-known speeches for men.

Simon Dunmore, *MORE Alternative Shakespeare Auditions for Women* (A & C Black, 1999). Another collection of 50 less-well-known speeches for women.

Vanessa Ewan with Kate Sagovsky, *Laban's Efforts in Action* (Methuen Drama, 2018). An accessible textbook for students and teachers looking for new ways to facilitate the creation of embodied and physically ambitious performance.

Niki Flacks, *Acting with Passion* (Methuen Drama, 2015). A revolutionary new approach to the age-old problems of the actor: dealing with nerves, engaging the body, quieting the inner critic, auditioning, creating a character, and even playing comedy.

Helen Freeman, *So You Want To Go To Drama School?* (Nick Hern Books, 2012). A clear and honest guide, written by a teacher and audition panellist with a lifetime's experience of the audition process.

Alison Hodge (ed.), *Twentieth Century Actor Training* (Routledge, 2000). A valuable introduction to the lives, principles, and practices of fourteen of the most important figures in twentieth-century actor training.

Kelly Hunter, *Cracking Shakespeare* (Methuen Drama, 2015). A book that demystifies the process of speaking Shakespeare's language, offering hands-on techniques for drama students, young actors and directors who are intimidated by rehearsing, performing and directing Shakespeare's plays.

Andy Johnson, *The Excellent Audition Guide* (Nick Hern Books, 2013). An engaging, upbeat guide for any student thinking of applying to drama school, this book demystifies the often scary-looking process, leading you through every step with reassurance and encouragement.

Ellis Jones, *Teach Yourself Acting* (Hodder & Stoughton Ltd, 1998). A good overview of acting and the profession.

Samantha Marsden, *100 Acting Exercises for 8–18 Year Olds* (Methuen Drama, 2019). Offers acting exercises to be used with young people in the classroom or by individuals, many based on the teachings of Meisner, Stanislavski and Brecht.

John Matthews, *Training for Performance* (Methuen Drama, 2011). An innovative introduction to the concept of 'askeology' – a field of study that dissolves divisions between disciplines and their exercises – and identifies four meta-disciplinary categories in the process of training that are common to all institutional contexts: vocation; obedience; formation and automatisation.

Jennifer Reischel, *So You Want to Tread the Boards: The Everything-you-need-to-know, Insider's Guide to a Career in the Performing Arts* (JR Books Ltd, 2007).

Anna Scher, *Desperate to Act* (Lions, 1988). Brilliant, basic advice for those so 'desperate', from a lady who should know.

William Shakespeare, *Hamlet, Prince of Denmark*. Especially Hamlet's advice to the players (Act 3, scene 2), which is some of the best advice on acting ever given.

Malcolm Taylor, *The Actor and the Camera* (A & C Black, 1994). Another good 'primer' for the beginner.

Other career advice books for actors

Laura Barnett, *Advice from the Players* (Nick Hern Books, 2014). A host of tips and guidance on every aspect of the actor's craft, direct from some of the best-known stars of stage and screen, including Zawe Ashton, Jo Brand, David Harewood, Mark Gatiss, Lenny Henry, Lesley Manville, Simon Russell Beale and Julie Walters.

James Calleri and Robert Cohen, *Acting Professionally* (7th edition, Palgrave Macmillan, 2009). The first edition was published in 1972, and is now regarded as godfather of this genre in the USA.

Paul Clayton, *The Working Actor* (Nick Hern Books, 2016). A guide to putting yourself in the best possible position to get work, to keep getting it, and to make a living from it. Written by the Chairman of the Actors Centre, with over forty years' experience as an actor himself.

Jane Drake Brody, *Actor's Business Plan* (Methuen Drama, 2015). A smart approach that offers a method for the achievement of dreams through a five-year life and career plan giving positive steps to develop a happy life as an actor and as a person.

Simon Dunmore, *An Actor's Guide to Getting Work* (5th edition, Methuen Drama, 2012). Honest, humorous and thorough, this practical, comprehensive guide draws on the author's rich experience in the field and offers invaluable information and advice to enable actors to succeed in the business.

Ed Hooks, *The Audition Book* (3rd edition, Back Stage Books, 2000). Excellent reading if you're thinking of trying your hand in the USA. It's also worth looking at Ed's website for his excellent 'Craft Notes' (**www.edhooks.com**).

Felicity Jackson and Lianne Robertson, *Surviving Actors Manual* (Nick Hern Books, 2015). A no-nonsense breakdown of the day-to-day essentials you need to succeed in the industry – including establishing a personal brand and business plan, dealing with agents and casting directors, networking and managing your money – from the team behind the internationally successful Surviving Actors conventions.

Peter Messaline and Miriam Newhouse, *The Actor's Survival Kit* (3rd edition, Simon & Pierre, 1999). Well worth reading if you're thinking of trying your hand in Canada.

Andy Nyman, *The Golden Rules of Acting* (Nick Hern Books, 2012). An honest, witty and direct treasure trove of advice, support and encouragement that no performer should be without.

Robert Ostlere, *The Actor's Career Bible* (Methuen Drama, 2019). A career guide for the modern actor filled with wisdom and inside knowledge from industry experts: key organisations, casting directors, agents, producers, directors and most importantly, actors, at different stages in their careers. Backed by online resources.

Jon S. Robbins, *The Actor's Survival Guide* (Methuen Drama, 2019). Completely revised and updated, this new edition is the perfect business handbook and guide to living and working in Hollywood.

Donna Soto-Morettini, *Mastering the Audition* (Methuen Drama, 2012) and *Mastering the Shakespeare Audition* (Methuen Drama, 2016). These thorough handbooks coach the actor to master the audition experience for contemporary and classical speeches, allowing them to master their fear and gain a deeper understanding of the ideas and skills involved.

Books for any actor

Mike Alfreds, *Different Every Night* (Nick Hern Books, 2007). A top ranking director sets out his rehearsal techniques in this vital masterclass.

Glenn Seven Allen, *The Singer Acts, The Actor Sings* (Methuen Drama, 2019). An essential handbook for actors and singers looking to combine great acting with great singing technique.

Brian Bates, *The Way of the Actor* (Century Hutchinson, 1986). Very interesting insights into the inner workings of the actor's psyche.

Nancy Bishop, *Secrets from the Casting Couch* (Methuen Drama, 2009). A practical workbook written from the point of view of a very experienced casting director.

Giles Block, *Speaking the Speech* (Nick Hern Books, 2014). An authoritative, comprehensive book on understanding and performing Shakespeare's language, by the 'Master of Words' at Shakespeare's Globe. Foreword by Mark Rylance.

Peter M. Boenisch, Thomas Ostermeier, *The Theatre of Thomas Ostermeier* (Routledge, 2016). The German director presents his advanced contemporary directorial approach to staging texts, for teh first time.

Anne Bogart and Tina Landau, *The Viewpoints Book* (Nick Hern Books, 2014). The Viewpoints are an improvisation technique: a set of names given to certain principles of movement through time and space – they constitute a language for talking about what happens on stage.

Bertolt Brecht, *Brecht and the Writer's Workshop: Fatzer and Other Dramatic Projects* edited by Tom Kuhn and Charlotte Ryland (Methuen Drama, 2019). A collection of previously uncollected texts from major unfinished dramatic projects dating from all periods of Brecht's creative life.

Bill Britten, *From Stage to Screen* (Methuen Drama, 2014). A handbook for the professional actor packed with advice on how to make the transition from theatre and fully prepare for a film role.

Peter Brook, *The Empty Space* (Penguin, 1990). Written in the 1960s, but still essential reading.

Adrian Cairns, *The Making of the Professional Actor* (Peter Owen Publishers, 1996). A fascinating study of the history, and possible future, of the art of acting.

Simon Callow, *Being an Actor* (Penguin, 1995). Autobiographical books by famous actors are generally useless in terms of practical career advice. However, this one – part autobiography and part advice – has a great deal of down-to-earth common sense. His famous 'manifesto' on directors' theatre is spot on.

Dee Cannon, *In-Depth Acting* (Oberon Books, 2012). An essential guide to mastering the Stanislavski technique, filtering its complexities and offering a dynamic, hands-on approach.

David Carey and Rebecca Clark Carey, *The Shakespeare Workbook* (Methuen Drama, 2015). A unifying approach to acting Shakespeare that is immediately applicable in the rehearsal room or classroom.

David Carey and Rebecca Clark Carey, *The Dramatic Text Workbook and Video* (Methuen Drama, 2019). A new edition of The Verbal Arts Workbook, now featuring detailed online supplementary video.

Mel Churcher, *Acting for Film: Truth 24 Times a Second* (Virgin Books, 2003). Invaluable insights into the specific techniques involved.

Mel Churcher, *A Screen Acting Workshop* (Nick Hern Books, 2011). An excellent and comprehensive training course in screen acting which includes a DVD showing the work in action.

Alex Clifton, *The Actor's Workbook* (Methuen Drama, 2016). Essential and clear, this workbook for actors, actors in training and teachers of acting and drama provides a step-by-step guide to learning techniques in acting through a system of exercises which will develop core acting skills and offer techniques for developing an authored role and models for devising new work.

Michael Clune, *Gamelife: A Memoir of Childhood* (Text Publishing, 2016). This is a history of an intellectual awakening told through the medium of video games.

Martin Constantine, *The Opera Singer's Acting Toolkit* (Methuen Drama, 2019). A step-by-step guide detailing how to create character, from auditions through to rehearsal and performance and formulate a successful career.

Declan Donnellan, *The Actor and the Target* (Nick Hern Books, 2005) A fresh approach to the actor's art from the artistic director of Cheek by Jowl.

Daniel Dresner, *A Life-coaching Approach to Screen Acting* (Methuen Drama, 2018). This handbook combines effective life-coaching techniques with screen acting tools to enable actors to approach their characters and their work with self-confidence.

David Edgar, *How Plays Work* (Nick Hern Books, 2009). The distinguished playwright examines the mechanisms and techniques, which dramatists throughout the ages have employed to structure their plays and to express their meaning.

Paul Elsam, *Acting Characters* (Methuen Drama, 2011). Fundamentally practical, this introductory handbook for the aspiring actor helps them create, present and sustain a believable character using different voice and body language.

Vanessa Ewan, *Actor Movement* (Methuen Drama, 2014). A textbook and video resource for the working actor, this book inspires confidence in the actor to make fully owned physical choices and develop a love for movement.

Gabriella Giannachi and Mary Luckhurst, *On Directing* (Faber & Faber, 1999). Twenty-one directors with very different styles, all working in the UK are interviewed to ascertain how they begin work on a play or performance, what methods they use in rehearsal and answer the question: 'is the modern director an enabler, collaborator or dictator?'

John Gillett, *Acting Stanislavski* (Methuen Drama, 2014). Offering a clear, accessible and comprehensive account of the Stanislavski approach, this book demsytifies the practitioner's key words and concepts from the actor's training to final performance.

Bernard Graham Shaw, *Voice-Overs, A Practical Guide* (A & C Black, 2000). A useful guide which explains and teaches the skills of voicing radio and television commercials.

Uta Hagen, *A Challenge for the Actor* (Macmillan, 1991). One of the best books on acting ever written.

Paul Harvard, *Acting Through Song* (Nick Hern Books, 2013). Takes the techniques of modern actor training – including the theories of Stanislavsky, Brecht, Meisner and Laban, amongst others – and applies them to the fundamental component of musical theatre: singing.

Julie Hesmondhalgh, *A Working Diary* (Methuen Drama, 2019). Reveals the numerous projects and preoccupations of a year in the life of one of Britain's best-loved actresses.

Sidney Hoffman and Brian Rhinehart, *Comedy Acting for Theatre* (Methuen Drama, 2018). A textbook for actors and acting students seeking to learn how to be funny on stage.

Stephen Jeffreys, *Playwriting: Structure, Character, How and What to Write* (Nick Hern Books, 2019). For over two decades, Stephen Jeffreys's remarkable series of workshops attracted writers from all over the world and shaped the ideas of many of today's leading playwrights and theatre-makers. Now, with this inspiring, highly practical book, you too can learn from these acclaimed Masterclasses.

Angela V. John, *The Actors' Crucible: Port Talbot and the Making of Burton, Hopkins, Sheen and all the Others* (Parthian Books, 2015). Dr John presents the emergence of these famous actors as part of a rich culture and commitment to drama long embedded in the town's history.

Keith Johnstone, *Impro: Improvisation and the Theatre* (Faber & Faber, 1979); and *Impro for Storytellers* (Faber & Faber, 1999). Keith Johnstone suggests a hundred practical techniques for encouraging spontaneity and originality by catching the subconscious unawares.

Paterson Joseph, *Julius Caesar and Me: Exploring Shakespeare's African Play* (Methuen Drama, 2018). A casebook of the RSC's African production of *Julius Caesar*, with audience reactions and a detailed evaluation of the position of ethnic minority actors in Shakespeare productions in general.

David Mamet, *True and False* (Faber & Faber, 1998). This book cuts through much of the mythology that surrounds acting.

Lorna Marshall, *The Body Speaks: Performance and Expression* (Methuen Drama, 2001). Lorna Marshall enables actors and performers to recognise and lose unwanted physical habits and discover new possibilities for the body.

John Matthews, *The Life of Training* (Methuen Drama, 2019). In this follow-up to *Anatomy of Performance Training* (2014) John Matthews makes a compelling argument that training not only takes time, but also makes time. Employing the mature philosophy of Hannah Arendt.

Dick McCaw, *Training the Actor's Body* (Methuen Drama, 2018). A practical book that draws on recent research into neurophysiology to illuminate key principles in the movement training of actors.

Kelly McEvenue, *The Alexander Technique for Actors* (Methuen Drama, 2001). The Alexander Technique is a method of physical relaxation that reduces tension and strain throughout the body. F.M. Alexander (1869-1955) was an actor who developed this technique to conquer his habit of straining his voice. This book's exercises are linked to accurate anatomical drawings, showing where stress is most pronounced in the body.

Ros Merkin (compiler), *The Liverpool Everyman Theatre: Liverpool's Third Cathedral* (Liverpool and Merseyside Theatres Trust Limited, 2004). This book offers brief encounters with some of the people, the plays, the on-and-off stage dramas of the Everyman's first 40 highly eventful years.

Ros Merkin (ed.), *Liverpool Playhouse: A Theatre and its City* (Liverpool University Press, 2011). From its opening in 1911, Liverpool Playhouse has reflected the history of Liverpool – and at times the city itself has appeared on stage as a key character.

Bella Merlin, *Facing the Fear* (Nick Hern Books, 2016). An insightful, empowering and reassuring guide to stage fright: why it happens, how it manifests itself, and how to overcome it.

Jeannette Nelson, *The Voice Exercise Book* (National Theatre Publishing, 2015). The Head of Voice at the National Theatre shares the voice exercises she uses with many of Britain's leading actors to help to keep their voices in shape.

Patrick O'Kane (ed.), *Actors' Voices: The People Behind the Performances* (Oberon Books, 2012). Twelve experienced actors share their process, comment on their experiences and consider their role as theatre artists in the broader spectrum of Art and Culture.

Chris Palmer, *Voice and Speech for Musical Theatre* (Methuen Drama, 2019). A workbook with online video resources, which combines traditional voice training for actors and musical training, allowing performers to train their spoken voice specifically for musicals.

Simon Parkin, *Death by Video Game* (Serpent's Tail, 2016). The writer and games critic Simon Parkin offers an enlightening and well-informed survey of developments in the medium, attempting to explain what it is that drives people to these virtual worlds and what keeps their interest when they get there.

Litz Pisk, with introduction by Ashe Taskiran, *The Actor and His Body* (Methuen Drama, 2017). In this seminal book, Pisk quests to find expression for the inner impulse that motivated actors to move and subsequently offer insight on the specific craft of the actor and the relationship between movement and imagination.

Theresa Robbins Dudeck, *Keith Johnstone: A Critical Biography* (Methuen Drama, 2013). A fascinating account of Keith Johnstone's early years at the Royal Court Theatre and teaching at RADA, and a good assessment of his approach and contributions to theatre and improvisation.

Resources

Patsy Rodenberg, *The Actor Speaks* (Methuen Drama, 2019). A brand new edition of legendary voice coach's work on voice for actors with excellent advice and exercises to develop the performer's voice.

Sinéad Rushe, *Michael Chekhov's Acting Technique* (Methuen Drama, 2019). Provides a complete overview of Michael Chekhov's method, offering clear explanations of the principles, practical exercises and application of the exercises to dramatic texts.

Neil Rutherford, *Musical Theatre Auditions and Casting* (Methuen Drama, 2012). A performer's guide viewed from both sides of the audition table.

Michael Sanderson, *From Irving to Olivier – A Social History of the Acting Profession* (Athlone Press, 1984). A very expensive, but nevertheless fascinating, study of the actor's world over the last century.

Edda Sharpe and Jan Haydn Rowles, *How to Do Any Accent: The Essential Handbook for Every Actor* (Oberon Books, 2007).

Michael Shurtleff, *Audition* (Walker & Company, 1984). An American book which should be read. It contains brilliant insights and thoughts to help any actor.

Spotlight, *Contacts* (Spotlight, annually in October). Contact details for everything you can think of (and more) that relates to actors and performers.

Jane Streeton and Phillip Raymond, *Singing on Stage: An Actor's Guide* (Methuen Drama, 2014). Singing should be an essential part of every actor's toolkit. This book encourages each actor to explore their own authentic voice as opposed to offering a 'one-size-fits-all' or 'quick fix' approach.

Steve Waters, *The Secret Life of Plays* (Nick Hern Books, 2010). Covers the key elements of dramatic writing – scenes, acts, space, time, characters, language and images – to show how a play is more than the sum of its parts.

Victoria Worsley, *Feldenkrais for Actors* (Nick Hern Books, 2016). A fascinating guide to the Feldenkrais Method, and how it can help actors with presence and posture, emotion, voice and breath, avoiding injury and more.

Webography

What follows is a selected collection of the most important websites for aspirants and professionals, and some others which the editors have found extremely useful, but don't quite fit elsewhere in this book.

Important websites for aspirants and professionals

www.actorscentre.co.uk – Actors Centre London
www.agents-uk.com – Agents' Association of Great Britain
www.bbc.co.uk – BBC homepage
www.bbc.co.uk/soundstart – advice on how to get work in radio drama
www.thecdg.co.uk – Casting Directors Guild
www.cpma.coop – The Co-operative Personal Management Association
www.cukas.ac.uk – Conservatoires UK Admissions Service (CUKAS) provides the facilities to research and apply for practice-based music, dance and drama courses at some UK conservatoires
www.edfringe.com – Edinburgh Festival Fringe
www.eif.co.uk – Edinburgh International Festival
www.equity.org.uk – Equity
www.federationofdramaschools.co.uk – Federation of Drama Schools
www.imdb.com – Internet Movie Database; catalogues all sorts of information on more than 250,000 films and the 900,000 people who helped to make them
www.itc-arts.org – Independent Theatre Council homepage with links to member companies' websites
www.thepma.com – Personal Managers' Association
www.spotlight.com – Spotlight publishes the most important actors' directories
www.thestage.co.uk – *The Stage*, contains news, information and job advertisements which are updated each Thursday
www.ucas.ac.uk – UCAS, the central organisation that processes applications for full-time undergraduate courses at UK universities and colleges

Other useful websites

http://accent.gmu.edu – the speech accent archive uniformly presents a large set of speech samples from a variety of language backgrounds
www.artsline.org.uk – Arts-Line, provides disability access information on arts venues
www.britfilms.com – an extensive source of information on the UK film industry
www.britishtheatreguide.info – lots of articles, reviews and links about British theatre
www.companieshouse.gov.uk – Companies House: useful for checking background details (like date of foundation) of individual companies
www.dialectsarchive.com – the International Dialects of English Archive (IDEA) is a useful collection of English-language dialects and English spoken in the accents of other languages
www.edhooks.com – contains some interesting articles on acting
www.excellentvoice.co.uk – information and advice for voice-over artists with examples of good voicereels online

Resources

www.its-behind-you.com – seemingly a comprehensive list of pantomimes and their producers

www.officiallondontheatre.co.uk – Society of London Theatre website with news, reviews and booking information

www.royalist.info – a database that provides biographical details of thousands of individuals who have either belonged to, or been connected with, the royal family of England and Scotland during more than 1,000 years of history

www.shakespeare-online.com – electronic copies of the plays and poems, along with other related material of interest. These copies of the texts should be checked against published editions before use in audition or performance, in order to gain the benefit of modern scholarship

www.shakespeareswords.com – an excellent resource for understanding Shakespeare

http://sounds.bl.uk/Accents-and-dialects – the British Library's archive of accents and dialects

www.theatredigs.com – a site aimed solely at touring professionals within the UK entertainment industry

www.theatrenet.com – news, events and special offers and links to agents, producers, theatre companies, venues and more

www.uksponsorship.com – an online database of UK sponsorship opportunities

www.uktw.co.uk – UK Theatre Web, with information, events and tickets for theatre in the UK

www.usefee.tv – a site which lets performers, their representatives and employers quickly calculate the appropriate use fee for featured players in TV commercials based on the established, industry-endorsed method approved by the Personal Managers' Association, the Association of Model Agents and Equity

www.visit4ads.com – a site where you can see recent television and cinema commercials and get details of the companies who created them

www.vocalist.org.uk – a site for singers, vocalists, singing teachers and students of voice of all ages, standards and styles. The site contains useful information on aspects of singing, performance, plus free online singing lessons and articles for vocalists related to singing and getting into the music industry

www.voiceovers.co.uk – a forum for voice-over artists to advertise themselves

www.wefund.co.uk – a fundraising platform for creative projects where people offer perks in exchange for pledges

www.whatsonstage.com – a UK theatre listing service with search facilities, a ticket-ordering service, reviews, news and debate

Index

20 Stories High   183
21st Century Actors Management   89
42 PMA   55
59 Productions   135
1623 Theatre Company   183
1927   136
1984 Personal Management Ltd   89

A&J Management   55
aardvark productions ltd   303
Abacus Photography   392
Chris Abakporo   55
Abbey Theatre Amharclann na
    Mainistreach   138
Vincent Abbey   392
AbeBooks.com   452
ABI Acting   43
Ableize Arts   364
Above the Title Productions   347
Absolutely Productions   330
Academy of Creative Training   32
Academy of Live and Recorded Arts
    (ALRA)*, The   14
Academy of Performance Combat
    (APC)   32
Accent Bank   101, 415
accents   354
Access Artiste Management Ltd   55
Accidental Theatre   184
accountants   437, 439
Act For Change   373
Actaeon Films Ltd   330
Acting Audition Success (Philip Rosch)   43
Acting Coach Scotland   43
Acting Out Ltd   303
Action Transport Theatre   274
Actionwork Creative Arts   274
Activation   303

Actor Showreels   415
Actor Works   32
Actors of Dionysus (AOD)   184
Actors Alliance   90
Actors Apparel   416
Actors' Benevolent Fund   449
Actors Centre   33, 380, 410
Actors Centres   32
Actors' Creative Team   90
Actors Direct Ltd   90
Actors File, The   90
Actors' Group, The   90
Actors' Guild of Great Britain, The   457
Actors in Industry Ltd (Aii Training)   304
Actors International Ltd   55
Actors Network Agency   90
Actor's One-Stop Shop, The   392, 416
Actors Temple   33
Actors Touring Company (ATC)   184
Actors World Casting   55
Actorsandperformers.com   452
Actorum Ltd   91
Ad Voice   101
Jo Adamson-Parker   106
Adhoc Actors   304
ADR   345
Aesop's Touring Theatre Company   275
AFA Associates   55
Agency PMA, The   55
agents   53–54, 96, 126–128, 313, 323–324,
    415, 439
  rates of commission   54
  voice-over work   101
Agents' Association (GB), The   457
AHA Talent Ltd PMA   56
Pippa Ailion CDG   106
AKT Productions   304
Albany, The   255
Alexander James & Co.   430

Alexander & Co.   430
Alexander, Maev   249
All Talent Agency Ltd   56
Stuart Allen   392
Almeida Theatre   138
Alpha Actors   91
Anita Alraun Representation   56
Jonathan Altaras Associates Ltd PMA   56
ALW Associates   56
AM-London Photography   392
Amazon   327
Amazon.co.uk & Amazon.com   452
Ambassador Theatre Group (ATG)   170
Amber Personal Management Ltd PMA   56
American Agency, The   56
American Musical Theatre Academy London
    (AMTA)   14
Amici Dance Theatre Company   359
Dorothy Andrew Casting CDG   106
Angel & Francis Ltd PMA   57
Anjali Dance Company   359
Simon Annand   393
Christopher Antony Associates   57
ANU productions   136
APL Theatre Ltd   184
APM Associates   57
Apropos Productions Ltd   304, 359
ARC Theatre Ensemble   185
Arcadea   365
Arcola Theatre   138
Arena Personal Management Ltd   91
ARG (Artists Rights Group Ltd) PMA   57
Argyle Associates   57
Yvonne Arnaud Theatre   139
Art and Adventure Ltd   347
art+power   360
Artists Partnership PMA, The   57
Artlink Central   365
Artlink Edinburgh   365
Arts University Bournemouth   342
Arts & Business, 'Business in the Arts'
    programme   225
Arts Council England   447
Arts Council England, East   448

Arts Council England, East Midlands   448
Arts Council England, London   448
Arts Council England, North East   448
Arts Council England, North West   448
Arts Council England, South East   448
Arts Council England, South West   448
Arts Council England, West Midlands   448
Arts Council England, Yorkshire   448
Arts Council of Northern Ireland   447
Arts Council of Wales   447
Arts Councils   274
Arts Emergency   5
artsdepot   255
ArtsEd*   14, 34
ArtsJobs   380
Artsline   365
Arty-Fact Theatre Co.   275
Jonathan Arun Group (JAG) PMA   57
Arundel Festival   298
Ashton Hinkinson Casting   106
Asquith & Horner   58
Assembly Rooms   262
ASSITEJ (International Association of
    Theatre for Children and Young
    People)   274, 457
associate caster   324
Associated Studios Performing Arts
    Academy   34
Associated International Management (AIM)
    PMA   58
Attic Theatre Company   185
audition   345
Audition Doctor   43
auditions   126–128, 157, 227, 316–317,
    323–325
  self-taping   323
augmented reality   344
Augustine's   262
Auto-Enrolment (AE)   440
Avatar   344
AXM (Actors Exchange Management
    Ltd)   91

Backstage   384
Ric Bacon   393

Badapple Theatre Company   185
Shaheen Baig Casting CDG   107
david bailie photography   393
Sophie Baker   393
Amy Ball CDG   107
BAM Associates (UK) Ltd   58
Bambridge Accountants LLP   430
Baracke   134
Barbican   298
Barbican Library   452
Barefoot Audio Books Ltd   351
Barker, Andrew   440
Gavin Barker Associates Ltd PMA   58
Andy Barnes Productions   171
Derek Barnes CDG   107
Briony Barnett Casting CDG   107
Barons Court Theatre   255
Becca Barr Management   58
Paul Barrass   394
Becky Barrett Management PMA   58
Pete Bartlett Photography APHP   394
Helen Bartlett Photography   394
Battersea Arts Centre   255
Richard Battye   394
BBC   316
BBC Northern Ireland   313
BBC Scotland   313
BBC Wales   313
Jonathan Bean   394
Lesley Beastall Casting   107
Lauren Beauchamp Casting   107
A Beautiful Image Photography & Design
    (Debal Bagachi)   395
Beckley, Piers   270
Rowland Beckley   107
Beddard, Jamie   368
EBA (Eamonn Bedford Agency)   59
Bedlam Theatre   262
Belfast Festival at Queens   298
Belfast Film Festival   356
Belgrade Theatre   139
Olivia Bell Management PMA   59
Bells Hamilton Stewart & Co.   430
Misha von Bennigsen Photography   395

Bentley Productions   330
Barbara Berkery   44
Leila Bertrand Casting CDG   107
Jorg Betts Associates PMA   59
Lucy Bevan CDG   107
BBC Drama Series Casting   108
BFI London Film Festival   356
Big Bear Films   330
Big Red Button Ltd   330
Big Talk Productions   330
Big Telly Theatre Company   185
Big Wheel Theatre in Education   275
Big Wooden Horse (UK) Ltd   275
Billboard PM Ltd   59
Sarah Bird CDG   108
Birds of Paradise   359
Birds of Paradise Theatre Company   360
Birmingham ArtsFest   299
Birmingham Repertory Theatre   139
Birmingham Stage Company (BSC)   139
Birmingham Theatre School, The   15, 34
Nancy Bishop Casting   44, 320
Bitesize Theatre Company   276
black actors   368
Blakeway Productions   331
Nicky Bligh CDG   108
Rebecca Blond Associates PMA   59
Bloomfields Welch Management PMA   59
Bloomsbury Alexander Centre, The   34
Blue Star Productions   171
Blue Elephant Theatre   256
Blue Moon Theatre Company   276
Blue Star Associates   59
Blue Star Productions   276
Blueprint Pictures   331
Boden Studios   34
Bolt Tight Showreels   416
Georgina Bolton King   395
Bookbarn International   452
Border Crossings   185
Borderline Theatre Co.   186
Boundless Theatre   186
Box Clever Theatre Company   276
Sandra Boyce Management PMA   59

Siobhan Bracke CDG   108

Bradford International Film Festival   356

Irene Bradshaw   44

Michelle Braidman Associates Ltd PMA   60

Breakdown Express   328

Breckman & Company   430

Nev Brewer Photography   395

Bridewell Theatre, The   256

Eva Bridge Management   60

Bridge Theatre Training Company, The   15, 139

Bridges: The Actors' Agency Ltd   91

Brief Candle Theatre   277

Andy Brierley CDG   108

Brighton Festival   299

Brighton Film School   342

Bristol Old Vic   139

Bristol Old Vic Theatre School*   15

British Academy of Dramatic Combat   35

BAFTA   457

British Academy of Stage & Screen Combat, The   35

British Arts Festivals Association (BAFA)   298

British Association for Performing Arts Medicine (BAPAM)   458

British Council   458

British Film Institute (BFI)   458

British Library, The   452

British Music Hall Society   458

Broadway Studio Theatre, The   256

BROOD PMA   60

Valerie Brook Agency   60

Marc Broussely   395

Brown, Simcocks & Andrews LLP PMA   60

Michael Browne Associates Ltd   304

Bruiser Theatre Company   186

Brunskill Management Ltd   60

Bryant Whittle Ltd   331

BBA Management Ltd   60

Jo Buckingham Casting CDG   108

Bunbury Banter Theatre Company CIC, The   347

Bunker Theatre, The   256

Burke, Kelly   376

Burnett Crowther Ltd PMA   60

Sheila Burnett   395

Burningham Associates   61

bursary schemes, radio   354

Bush Theatre, The   140

Business Disability Forum   366

Buxton Opera House   238

BWH Agency Ltd PMA, The   61

Paul Byram Associates (THE AGENCY) PMA   61

Aisha Bywaters Casting CDG   108

C venues   263

Will C   396

Caan, Alex   443

Cactus TV   331

Cahoots NI   277

Cahoots Theatre Company   186

Calamity Films   331

Caldarone, Marina   412

Calypso Voices   101

CAM (Creative Artists Management) PMA   61

Cambridge Arts Theatre   238

Cambridge Film Festival   356

Cambridge Shakespeare Festival   187

Camden People's Theatre   256

Ross Campbell   44

Canal Café Theatre   257

Candid Casting   108

CandoCo   359

Candoco Dance Company   360

C&T   277

Cannon, Dudley & Associates   108

John Cannon CDG   109

Canterbury Festival   299

Capitol, The   238

Cardboard Citizens   187

P O'N Carden   430, 436

Carey Dodd Associates PMA   61

Carlton Television Productions   332

Jessica Carney Associates PMA   61

Carnival Film & Television Ltd   332

Carousel 365
Mark Carr & Co. Ltd 431
Anji Carroll CDG 109
Charlie Carter APHP 396
Castaway Actors Agency 91
Castcall 380
casting 342, 345, 347
  breakdown 128
  for musical theatre 128
  for television 316
  for the stage 126
Casting Angels (London and Paris),
  The 109
Casting Assistant 126
casting assistants 316
casting breakdowns 313
Casting Couch Productions Ltd 109
casting directors 53–54, 126–127, 312–313,
  323–325, 347, 409–410, 415
  in television 316
Casting Directors Guild (CDG) 106
Casting Directors Guild of Great Britain and
  Ireland 459
Casting Networks 381, 385
casting sessions 317
Casting Society of America 459
Castle Players, The 187
CastNet Ltd 381, 416
Castweb 381
Suzy Catliff CDG 109
CBL Management PMA 61
CCM 92
CDA PMA 62
CDs 410
CDs, sent to radio producers 354
Celador Films Ltd 332
Celtic Films 332
Celtic Media Festival 356
Center Stage Agency 62
Central Line 92
CentreStage Partnership 305
Chain Reaction Theatre Company 187
Urvashi Chand CDG 109
Changing Faces Theatre Company 277

Channel Television 313
Chaplins Entertainment Ltd 235
Andrew Chapman 396
Characters 305
Charing Cross Theatre (formerly New
  Players Theatre) 257
charities, registered 225
Esta Charkham Associates 62, 110
Sharry Clark Artists 62
Cheek by Jowl 187
Chelsea Theatre 257
Chichester International Film Festival 356
Chichester Festival Theatre 140
Chickenshed Theatre 188, 360
  BTEC National Diploma 359
Children's Touring Partnership, The 278
children and young people, theatre for 273
Theatre, Chipping Norton, The 239
Christmas shows 273
Jonathan Church Productions 171
Mel Churcher 44
Cinetea 62
Circuit Personal Management Ltd 92
Citizens Theatre 140
Citizens Theatre Glasgow 316
City Lit 15
City Actors' Management 92
City Lit, The 35
City Varieties 239
Andrea Clark Casting 110
John Clark Photo Digital APHP 397
Claypole Management 62
Sam Claypole 110
Clean Break 188
ClearSky Accounting 431
Clic Agency 62
Clod Ensemble 189
Close for Comfort Theatre Company 189
Cloud Nine Theatre Productions 189
Co-operative Personal Management
  Association (CPMA) 99, 459
Coastal Productions 332
Elspeth Cochrane Personal
  Management 62

Index

Cockpit, The   257
Ben Cogan   110
John Colclough Consultancy, The   459
MJ Coldiron   45
Cole Kitchenn Personal Management Ltd
    PMA   62
Coliseum Theatre   140
Collingwood & Co.   332
Shane Collins Associates PMA   62
Jayne Collins CDG   110
Colman, Geoffrey   28
Comedy Unit, The   332   348
Common Players, The   189
Communicado Productions   189
Company Pictures   333
Complicité   189
Concordance   190
Confident Voice, The   45
Connaught Theatre   239
Conservatoire for Dance and Drama   459
consultants   225
Contact Theatre   140
Contacts   235, 410, 453
Contemporary Stage Co   171
contracts   54, 330
Conway Van Gelder Grant PMA   63
Conway Van Gelder Grant   101
Howard Cooke Associates (HCA) PMA   63
Alistair Coomer   110
John Cooper Photography   397
Anna Cooper   110
Cooper Searle Personal Management
    Ltd   63
copyright   415
  on photographs   391
Lin Cordoray   110
Clive Corner Associates   63
Irene Cotton Casting   110
Lou Coulson Associates Ltd PMA   63
Coulter Management Agency PMA   63
Count and See Ltd   431
Court Theatre Training Company   15
Courtyard, The   239
Courtyard Theatre, The   257

Covent Garden Management   64
Cowboy Films   333
Cowley, Knox & Guy   64
Jerry Cox, MA BA PGCE   45
CragRats Theatre   190
Kahleen Crawford Casting CDG   111
Margaret Crawford   111
Creaking Door Productions   278
Creation Theatre Company   190
Creative Scotland   447
Crescent Management   92
Crocodile Casting   111
Sarah Crowe Casting CDG   111
Ben Crowe   416
Crowe Clark Whitehill   431
Crying Out Loud Productions   417
CSA Word   348
CUKAS   13
Culture Wise   348
Culture.Info   459
Cumbernauld Theatre   239
Curtains for Radio   348
Curtis Brown Ltd PMA   64
Curve   141
Customs House Trust Ltd, The   240
Cut Glass Productions   417
CVs   128, 317
Cwmni Theatr Arad Goch   278
Cygnet Training Theatre*   16

DaDaFest   365
Dalton Films Ltd   333
David Daly Associates   64
Damn Good Voices   101
dance   128
Dance and Drama Awards (DaDAs)   14, 369
Dark Horse   190, 361
Elizabeth Davies Associates   64, 397
Chris Davis Management PMA   64
Davis Bishop Associates   64
Gary Davy CDG   111
Gabrielle Dawes CDG   111
Stephanie Dawes CDG   111

Nicholas Dawkes Photography APHP 397
Kate Day CDG 112
Bridget de Courcy 45
Jane de Florez, LGSM PGDip 45
Paul De Freitas CDG 112
Dead Earnest Theatre 190
Deafinitely Theatre 361
Dear Conjunction Theatre Company 246
Dempsey, Shane 267
Denbry Repros trading as Studio 57
    Ltd 408
Denman Repros 408
Denmark Street Management 93
Denton Brierley PMA 65
Derby Theatre 141
Deuchar, Angus 409
Devine Artist Management 65
DF: Photographer/arc172 Ltd 397
Diamond Management PMA 65
digital wellbeing 426
digs 249
Direct Personal Management 93
Directgov 366
directors 54
    radio 347
Directors UK 459
Directory of Social Change 226
Dirty Market Theatre Company 191
disabilities, actors with 359
    opportunities for 368
Disability Arts Cymru 365
Disability Arts Online 365
Disability Discrimination Act 369
Diverse City 366
Antonia Doggett 45
Don Productions Ltd 333
Donmar Warehouse 127, 141
Doollee.com 453
Dorset School of Acting, The 16
Kate Dowd Casting CDG 112
DQ Management 65
Drama Association of Wales 460
Drama Centre London* 16
Drama House, The 333

Drama School Auditions 46
drama school shows 127
drama schools 127, 359, 369
    accredited 354
Drama Studio London (DSL)* 17, 36
Dramanic 381, 385
Dramanon 305
dramaturg 134–135
dramaturgs 134
Dramaturgs' Network 460
Dress Circle 453
Dub & Co. 431
Carol Dudley CDG, CSA 112
Julia Duff CDG 112
Maureen Duff CDG 112
Jennifer Duffy CDG 112
Dukes, The 142
Dumfries and Galloway Arts Festival 299
Dunbar & Co. 431
Dundee Rep and Scottish Dance Theatre
    Ltd 142
Dunmore, Simon 51, 157, 265
DV8 Physical Theatre 191

e-TALENTA 387
E15 Acting School* 17, 36
Earache Voices 101
Kenneth Earle Personal Management 65
earnings, annual 438
Susi Earnshaw Management 65
Irene East Casting CDG 112
East Riding Theatre 142
Eastern Angles Theatre Company 191
École Internationale de Théâtre Jacques
    Lecoq 17, 36
Ecosse Films Ltd 333
Edge Theatre, The 191
Edinburgh Festival 298
Edinburgh Festival Fringe 254, 267
Edinburgh Festival Fringe Society 299
Edinburgh International Festival 299
Daniel Edwards CDG 112
Ben Eedle 46
EJ Casting 112

Elite Talent   65
Sean Ellis   397
EM Media   448
Emptage Hallett PMA   66
enCAST   386
Encounters (Short Film and Animation Festival)   356
English Theatre Frankfurt   246
English Theatre of Hamburg, The   246
English Touring Theatre   192
June Epstein Associates   66
Equity   32, 51, 98–99, 330, 346, 372, 385, 439
Equity Charitable Trust   449
Equity Job Information Service (JIS)   382
Equity Pensions Scheme (EPS)   440
Equity Tax and National Insurance Guide, The   436
Ernst Busch Theatre Academy   135
eStage Accounting   432
Jane Estall Agency, The   66
Estdale, Mark   344
ET Casting Ltd.   112
Etcetera Theatre   257
Euclid   460
European Festivals Association, The   298
European Theatre Company   192
Stephanie Evans Associates   66
Evans, Nick   8
Richard Evans CDG   113
Evelyn Norris Trust   449
Everyman Theatre, The   240
Evolution Productions   235
Extra Digit Ltd   333
Extravaganza Productions   235
Eye Film and Television   333

Faces Prints   408
Faction, The   192
Farah, Isabelle   384
Paola Farino   66
Fawn Casting Ltd   113
Feast Management PMA   66
Federation of Drama Schools   13

Federation of Drama Schools (FDS)   28
Federation of International Artists   372
Federation of Scottish Theatre   460
Feelgood Fiction Ltd   334
festivals   298
Fevered Sleep   278
Fiction Factory Productions Ltd   348
Fierce Festival   299
Susie Figgis   113
Bunny Fildes Casting CDG   113
Film London   448
film schools   342
Finborough Theatre   257
Sally Fincher CDG   113
First Act Personal Management   66
First Family Entertainment   236
First Light   449
First Movement   366
Fisher Packman & Associates in association with Simia Wall   432
fitness, physical and mental   443
Flashback Television Ltd   334
Flatlined Talent   67
Fluellen Theatre Company   192
Focus Films Ltd   334
Focus Productions Ltd   334
Kerry Foley Management Ltd   67
Mark Forstater Productions Ltd   334
Forbidden Theatre Company   193, 225
Forced Entertainment   193
Jonathan Ford & Co.   432
Vanessa Ford Productions Ltd   171
Foreign Versions   101
Forest Forge Theatre Co.   193
James Foster Ltd   67
Found Theatre   193
Fourth Monkey   17
Fourth Monkey Actor Training Company   36
Fourthwall (incorporating The Drama Student)   453
Julie Fox Associates   67
Robert Fox Ltd   172
Foyle Film Festival   357

Foyle Foundation, The 450
Frank Partners 305
Elliott Franks Photography Services 398
Frantic Assembly 179, 193
Frantic Theatre Company 194
Frazer, Janie 316
Rachel Freck CDG 113
Freedom Studios 194
Sonia Friedman Productions 172
Fremantle 334
Samuel French Bookshop at the Royal Court
    Theatre 453
Freshwater Theatre Company 279
Fringe productions 254, 265
Fringe theatre 254, 342
Frontline Actors' Agency 93
Fruitcake London 113
funding 225, 228
    bodies 447
fundraising 226
Caroline Funnell 113
Funny Face Films Ltd 335

G2 Entertainment Ltd 335
Hilary Gagan Associates PMA 67
Galleon Films Ltd 335
Galleon Theatre Company Ltd 194
Galloways PMA 67
game industry 344
games 346
Gardner Herrity PMA 67
Garricks PMA 68
Gate Theatre 142
Gatehouse, The 240
Gazebo Theatre in Education
    Company 279
Adrian Gibb 398
Gibber Theatre Ltd 279
Martin Gibbons Casting 114
Gift Aid 225
Gilbert & Payne Personal Management 68
Giles Foreman Centre for Acting, The 17,
    36, 398
James Gill 398

Prue Gillett Actor Training 46
Tracey Gillham CDG 114
Global Artists PMA 68
Goat and Monkey 194
Nina Gold CDG 114
Goldwins 432
Gomito Productions 194
Miranda Gooch 114
Greg Goodale 398
Goodman Jones LLP 432
Gordon & French PMA 68
Graeae Theatre Company 195, 361, 368
    Missing Piece 359, 369
David Graham Entertainment Ltd 172
Graham, Scott 179
Grandage, Michael 127
Michael Grandage Productions 172
Derek Grant Organisation, The 172
Grantham-Hazeldine Ltd PMA 68
Grassington Festival 300
Grassmarket Project 195
Darren Gray (Management) 68
John Grayson 46
Green Ginger 195
Jill Green CDG 114
Greenwich and Docklands International
    Festival (GDIF) 300
Greenwich & Lewisham Young People's
    Theatre (GLYPT) 280
Greenwich Theatre 142
Nick Gregan Photography 398
Greyfriars (Studios 1 and 2) 263
Grid Iron Theatre Company 195
Charles Griffin Photography 398
David Grindrod CDG 114, 128
Claire Grogan APHP 399
Angela Grosvenor CDG 114
GSA, Guildford School of Acting* 18, 37
Louise Gubbay Associates 68
Guildhall School of Music & Drama* 18,
    37

H and S Accountants Ltd 432
Haber, Margie 324

Hackney Empire 240
Hackney Empire Studio Theatre 257
Half Moon Theatre 280
Hall James Personal Management 69
Janet Hall 114
Hamilton Hodell Ltd PMA 69
Hamilton Hodell Ltd 102
Hammond Cox Casting 115, 236
Louis Hammond CDG 115
Hampstead Theatre 143
Gemma Hancock CDG 115
Handle and Spout Ltd 335
Handstand Productions 335
Happystorm Theatre 196
Julie Harkin Casting CDG 115
Harman, Paul 273
HarperAudio 351
Brendan Harrington 399
Harris Agency Ltd, The 69
Harris Coombs & Co. 433
Martin Harris 46
Harrogate Theatre 143
Hartshorn Hook 173
Harvey Mead & Co. Ltd 433
Harvey Stein Associates Ltd 69
Hat Trick Productions Ltd 335
HATCH Talent Ltd PMA 69
Hatton McEwan Penford PMA 69
Cheryl Hayes Management 69
Judi Hayfield CDG / Judi Hayfield Ltd 115
Hayles & Partners Ltd 433
HB Casting 115
HCK Photography 399
Head, Chris 232
Headlong Theatre 196
Headshot Photography by Lynn Herrick 399
Heavy Entertainment Ltd 335, 348
Hen & Chickens Theatre 257
Henry's Agency 69
Nick Hern Books 453
Hesmondhalgh, Julie 5
Hidden Talent Productions Ltd 196
Highlands & Islands Theatre Network (HIN) 460

Highly Sprung Performance Company 196
HighTide 300
Hijinx Theatre 196, 361
Serena Hill 115
Hill Street Theatre 263
Lotte Hines CDG 115
Hiss & Boo Theatre Company Ltd 173, 236
Historia Theatre Co 197
HM Revenue and Customs (HMRC) 436
Hobson's Actors 70
Hobson's Voices 102
HofeshShechter 136
Daniel Hoffmann-Gill 46
Hogbens Dunphy Ltd 433
Hoipolloi Theatre 197
Holdbrook-Smith, Kobna 373
Hollow Crown Productions 197
Jane Hollowood Associates Ltd 70
Paul Holman Associates 173, 236
Holmes, Anthony 422
Thelma Holt Ltd 173
HOME 134, 136, 143
Jennifer Jane Hooker 47
Polly Hootkins Casting CDG 116
Hope Theatre, The 258
Hopscotch Theatre Company 280
Julia Horan CDG 116
Horse + Bamboo Theatre 197
Juliet Horsley 116
hot-seating 273
Hotbed: Cambridge New Writing Theatre Festival 300
House, Gordon 353
HR Creative Artists (HRCA) 70
Hubbard Casting 116
Amy Hubbard CDG 116
Hubbard Casting 323
Dan Hubbard CDG 116
Hubbard, Ros 323
Nancy Hudson Associates PMA 70
Mark Hudson 47
Steve Hughes Management Ltd 70
Jamie Hughes Photography 399
Charlie Hughes-D'Aeth 47

Hull Truck Theatre 143
Hulu 327
Remy Hunter 399
Hunwick Associates PMA 70
HuRica Productions 336, 349
Hurricane Films Ltd 336
HW Lee Associates LLP – Accountants to the
    Creative Sector 433

IAMBE Productions Ltd 70
iCan Talk Ltd 102
Icarus Theatre Collective 198
Ichiza Theatre Company 198
Icon Actors Management 71
iD Agency Limited 71
IDAMOS Agency 71
Identity Agency Group (IAG) PMA 71
Image Photographic 408
Image Musical Theatre 173
Imagine Theatre Ltd 236
IMDb 318, 345, 385
IML 93
IMPACT Theatre 362
Imperial Personal Management Ltd 71
improvisation 345
Impulse Company, The 38
In Toto Theatre Company 280
Incisor 198
Independent Talent Group Ltd PMA 71
Independent English Theatre Associazione
    Culturale 246
independent television 313
Independent Theatre Council (ITC) 183,
    225, 273, 447, 460
Colin Ingram Ltd 173
Inspiration Management 93
Instant Wit 305
Inter Voice Over 102
Inter-City Casting 71
Interact 305
interactive theatre 310
International Actors London (IAL) 71
International Casting Directors Network
    (ICDN) 461

International Committee for Artistic
    Freedom 372
International Federation of Actors
    (FIA) 461
International School of Screen Acting 19,
    38
Internet 317
Internet Movie Database (IMDb) 382, 453
InterTalent Rights Group PMA
    (incorporating Cole Kitchenn
    Management Ltd) 72
Irish Actors London Ltd 72
Irish Theatre Institute 461
Isis Audio Books 351
Italia Conti Academy of Theatre Arts* 19
ITV 313–314, 316

Jack Studio Theatre, The 258
Jack Drum Arts 281
Sue Jackson 116
Trevor Jackson CDG 116
Jacksons Lane Arts Centre 258
Janis Jaffa Casting 116
Jam Theatre Company 198
Nick James APHP 400
James Grant Media 105
Matt Jamie 400
Jason Impey Films 336
Jasperian Theatre Company 199
Jina Jay CDG 116
JB Associates 72
Jeffrey & White Management Ltd PMA 72
Jendagi Productions Ltd 174
Victor Jenkins Casting CDG 117
Lucy Jenkins (Jenkins McShane
    Casting) 117
Rebecca Jenner 117
Jeremy Hicks Associates Ltd 105
Mark Jermin Management 72
Jermyn Street Theatre 258
Jerwood Charitable Foundation 450
Jewell, Wright Ltd 72
JK Photography 400
Priscilla John Casting CDG 117

Gareth Johnson Ltd 174
Johnston & Mathers Associates Ltd 73
Desmond Jones 47
Sam Jones CDG 117
Sue Jones CDG 117
Andy Jordan Productions Ltd 174
Richard Jordan Productions Ltd 174
JPA Management PMA 73

Kabosh 199
KAL Management 73
Kali Theatre Company 199
Roberta Kanal Agency 73
Kate and Lou Casting 117
Kazzum 281
Keddie Scott Associates PMA 73
Robert Kelly Associates PMA 73
Kelpie Media 336
Neil Kendall Photography 400
Steve Kenis & Co PMA 73
Anna Kennedy Casting 117
Bill Kenwright Ltd 174
Beverley Keogh CDG 117
Kew Personal Management 74
Key Theatre 144
Kiln (formerly Tricycle Theatre), The 144
Kinetic Theatre Company 281
Belinda King Creative Productions 118
King's Head Theatre 258
Kneehigh Theatre 199
Jerry Knight-Smith CDG 118
Knowledge, The 453
Kogan Academy of Dramatic Art 19, 38
Komedia 263
Suzy Korel CDG 118
Krazy Kat Theatre Company 282, 362
Kushner, Tony 134

LA Management 74
Ladbroke Productions 349
Jack Ladenburg Photography 400
Laine Management 74
Lawrence Lambert 47

LAMDA (London Academy of Music & Dramatic Art)* 19, 38
Landor Theatre, The 258
Langford Associates Ltd 74
Language Laid Bare Productions 200
Carole Latimer 401
Lauchlan, Iain 243
Lawnmowers Independent Theatre Company 362
Steve Lawton APHP 401
LB Photography 401
Pete Le May 401
Nina Lee Management PMA 74
Leeds International Film Festival 357
Leeds Playhouse (formerly West Yorkshire Playhouse) 144
Leejay Photography 401
Lees 433
Left Bank Pictures 336
Mike Leigh Associates 74
Leno Martin Associates Ltd 74
Murray Lenton 401
Lexitricity Ltd 336
Lichfield Festival 300
Light Nights – The Summer Theatre 246
Lime Actors Agency & Management Ltd 75
Limelight Productions Ltd 174
Karen Lindsay-Stewart CDG 118
Linkside Agency 75
Lion & Unicorn Theatre 259
Lip Service 102
LipService 200
Live Theatre 145
Liverpool Everyman & Playhouse Theatres 145
Liverpool Institute for Performing Arts (LIPA)*, The 20
Loftus Media Ltd 349
London Bus Theatre Company, The 282, 357
London Academy of Radio, Film & TV 20, 39
London Actors Theatre Co. 200
London Arrangements 454

London Bubble Theatre Co. 200
London College of Communication 342
London Film Academy 342
London Film School, The 342
London International Festival of Theatre (LIFT) 300
London International Mime Festival 300
London Lesbian & Gay Film Festival 357
London Metropolitan University 369
London School of Dramatic Art 20, 39
London School of Musical Theatre 20
London Shakespeare Workout (LSW) 295
London Studio Centre (LSC) 21
London Theatre 454
London Toast Theatre 247
Eva Long Agents 75
Gina Long (Longrun Artistes) 75
James Looker Photography 401
Lord of the Rings 344
Louche Theatre 201
Loudmouth Education & Training 282
Lovett Logan Associates PMA 75
LSW Promotions 75
Ludlow Festival 301
Lurking Truth 201
LWT 316
LWT and United Productions 337
Lyric Hammersmith Theatre 145
Lyric Theatre 145

M6 Theatre Company 283
Mac Manus, Sinead 228, 426
MacFarlane Chard Associates PMA 75
MacFarlane Doyle Associates 76
Cameron Mackintosh Ltd 175
Macmillan Audio Books 351
macrobert 240
Mad Dogs and Englishmen 201
MAD Photography APHP 402
Made in Dagenham 134
Magic Carpet Theatre 283
Magnetic North Theatre Productions 201
Magpie Dance 362
Kay Magson Casting CDG 118

John Mahoney Management 76
MakeBelieve Arts 283
MANACTCO (formerly Manchester Actors Company) 201
Management 2000 76
Manchester International Festival (MIF) 301
Manchester International Short Film Festival 358
Manchester School of Acting 39
Manchester School of Theatre at MMU* 21
Mandy 385
Mandy Network, The 382
John Manning 118
Manor Pavilion Theatre 145
Johnny Mans Productions Ltd 175
Marcus & McCrimmon Management 76
Raymondo Marcus 402
marketing 157
Markham, Froggatt & Irwin PMA 76
Ronnie Marshall Agency 76
Scott Marshall Partners PMA 76
MARV Films 337
Guy Masterson Productions 202
Maya Vision International Ltd 337
Maynard Leigh Associates (MLA) 306
Mayor's Thames Festival, The 301
Marj McDaid 47
Martin McKellan 48
Bill McLean Personal Management 77
McLean-Williams Ltd PMA 77
Carolyn McLeod 118
McMahon Management 77
Chrissie McMurrich 119
Anne McNulty CDG 119, 126
MCS Agency 77
Sooki McShane (Jenkins McShane Casting) 119
Kirsten McTernan Photography & Design 402
Debbie McWilliams CDG 119
Alison Mead 48
Meadow Rosenthal Limited 175
Meeting Ground Theatre Co. 202

Menier Chocolate Factory   145
Mercury Theatre   146
Merlin International Theatre   247
Merseyside International Street Festival   301
Met Film Production   337
Method Acting London   39
Methuen Drama   454
#metoo   376
Thea Meulenberg Casting   119
MHA MacIntyre Hudson   434
Michael Chekhov Studio London   39
Middle Ground Theatre Co.   175
Middleweek Newton Talent Management
    PMA   77
Midland Actors Theatre (MAT)   202
Equity   372
Mikron Theatre Company   202
Milburn Browning Associates PMA (MMB
    Creative)   77
Mill at Sonning Theatre, The   146
Hannah Miller   119
Robin Miller   48
Millfield Theatre   241
Mimbre   203
Minack Theatre Summer Festival   301
Mind the Gap   362
    Staging Change   359
Mischief Theatre   175
Mitchell Maas McLennan Ltd   77
Moby Duck   284
Mocap Vaults, The   344
Owen Money Productions   237
Kate Moon Management   102
Moorfields Photographic   408
Stephen Moore CDG   119
Morello Cherry Ltd   78
Lee Morgan Management   78
Morley College   39
Sally Mortemore   48
Mountview*   21, 40
MR Management PMA   78
Mrs Jordan Associates PMA   78
MSFT Management PMA   78
MTA (The Musical Theatre Academy),
    The   21

Elaine Murphy Associates   78
Music Theatre International   454
musical supervisor   129
musical theatre, casting for   128
Musicroom   454
MV Management   93

National Association of Youth Theatres
    (NAYT)   2
National Campaign for the Arts   461
National Curriculum   273
National Film and Television School   343
National Rural Touring Forum
    (NRTF)   461
National Theatre   146
National Theatre Bookshop   454
National Theatre of Scotland (NTS)   146
National Theatre Wales   147
National Youth Arts Wales (NYAW)   2
National Youth Music Theatre (NYMT)   2
National Youth Theatre of Great Britain
    (NYT)   3
Naxos AudioBooks   352
Neal Street Productions   337
Steve Nealon Associates PMA   78
Paul J Need Photography   402
Nelson Browne Management Ltd PMA   79
NESTA   346
Netflix   327
Netherbow Scottish Storytelling Centre,
    The   263
New Wolsey Theatre, The   147
New Diorama Theatre   259
New Pantomime Productions   237
New Perspectives Theatre Co.   203
New Shoes Theatre   203
New Vic Theatre   147
Newfound Theatre Company   284
Claire Newman-Williams   403
Newport Film School   343
Benjamin Newsome Casting   119
NFD Productions Ltd   337
Nimble Fish   284
NITRO   203

No Limits Theatre   203
North West Actors – Nigel Adams   79
North American Actors Association
      (NAAA)   461
North of Watford Actors Agency   94
Northern Broadsides   204
Northern Film & Media   449
Northern Ireland Screen   448
Northern Ireland Arts & Disability
      Forum   366
Northern Ireland Theatre Association
      (NITA)   461
Northern Lights Management   79
Northern Stage (formerly Newcastle
      Playhouse)   147
NorthOne Management   94
Norwell Lapley Productions Ltd   176
Nottingham Playhouse   147
Nottingham Playhouse Participation   284
NS Artistes' Management   79
NTC Touring Theatre Company   204
Nuffield Southampton Theatres   148
Number 9 Films   337
Nyland Management   79
Nyman Libson Paul   434

Octagon Theatre   148
OffWestEnd.com   254
Oily Cart   359
Oily Cart Company   284, 363
Okai Collier Company Ltd, The   204
Old Red Lion   259
Old Vic, The   148
Omnibus Theatre   259
OMUK   346
On Screen Productions Ltd   338
on-book workshops   324
Onatti Productions Ltd   285
Open Air Theatre   148
Open Book Theatre   270
Open Clasp Theatre Company   204
Opus Productions Ltd   417
James Orange Casting CDG   120
Orange Tree Theatre   148

Oren Actors Management   94
Original Theatre Company, The   205
Orion Audio Books   352
Orti, Pilar   224
Otto Personal Management Ltd   79
Ouch!   366
Out of Joint   183, 205
Outsource Media Ltd (OMUK)   346
Oval House Theatre   259
Ovation   205
Ovation Productions   206
OVC Media Ltd   338
Oxford Samuel Beckett Theatre Trust
      Award, The   450
Oxford School of Drama*   21, 40
Oxford Shakespeare Company, The   206
Oxfordshire Theatre Company   206

Pact (Producers Alliance for Cinema and
      Television)   462
Paines Plough   206
Helena Palmer   120
Pan Artists Agency   79
pantomime   243, 273
Pantoni Pantomimes   237
Park Theatre   149
Theo Park Casting   120
Park Village Ltd   338
Frances Parkes   48
Susie Parriss Casting   120
Passe-Partout   285
Paul Pearson – London Theatrical   80
pay   345–346
Pearlcatchers Ltd   306
Peeping Tom   136
Pelham Associates PMA   80
Pelinor   417
Pemberton Associates Ltd   80
Pendle Productions   206
Pennine Productions LLP   349
Pentabus Theatre Company   206
Pentameters   259
People's Theatre Co, The   207
People Show   207

Simone Pereira Hind Casting CDG   120
Performance Business, The   306
Performance Accountancy   434
Performance Actors Agency   94
performance capture   344
Performance Initiative Network   450
Personal Managers' Association (PMA)   96, 462
Perth Theatre, Horsecross Arts   149
Philippe Quesne   136
Frances Phillips PMA   80
photographers   391, 409
photographs   128, 409
Piccadilly Management   80
Picture Palace Films Ltd   338
Pied Piper Theatre Company   285
Pier Productions   349
Pilot Season   326
Pilot Theatre   207, 285
Pinball London Ltd   338
Pineapple Dance Studios   40
Piper, Andrew   166
Pitlochry Festival Theatre   149
Kate Plantin CDG   120
Janet Plater Management Ltd   80
Play House, The   285
Playbox Theatre (Generator)   286
PlayDatabase.com   454
Playful Productions   176
Playground Theatre, The   259
Playtime Theatre Company   286
Pleasance, The   263
Pleasance Theatre Trust   260
Point Blank   208
policy, artistic   224
Polka Theatre   286
Michael Pollard Photographer APHP   403
Will Polley   403
Gilly Poole CDG   120
Poor School   22, 40
Pop-Up Theatre   286
Popcorn Hub   418
Popular Productions Ltd   176
Powerhouse Theatre Company   208

Prague Shakespeare Festival   247
Premier Acting   80
Morwenna Preston Management   80
David Price Photography   403
Price Gardner Management PMA   81
Primecut Productions   208
Principal Artistes   81
Prism Arts   366
Carl Proctor CDG   120
producers
    independent   170
    radio   354
Profile Prints   408
Project Gutenberg   454
Proteus Theatre Company   209
Andy Pryor CDG   121
publicists   389
publicity   388
publicity interviews   388
David Pugh & Dafydd Rogers   176
Pulse Fringe Festival   301
Punchdrunk   209
Pure Actors Agency & Management Ltd   81
Purple Fish Productions   209
Pursued by a Bear Productions   209
PW Productions Ltd   176

Q20 Theatre   287
Qdos Entertainment (Pantomimes) Ltd   237
Qtalent PMA   81
James Quaife Productions   177
Quantum Theatre   287
Queen's Theatre   149
Questors Theatre Ealing, The   40
Quicksilver Theatre   287

RBM Actors   81
Rabbit Vocal Management   102
RADA (Royal Academy of Dramatic Art)*   22, 40, 260
Gennie Radcliffe CDG   121
AudioUK   462

radio, acting for   353–354
radio companies   347
radio drama   345, 347
Raindance Film Festival Ltd   358
Raised Eyebrow Theatre Company   210
Ralph and Meriel Richardson Foundation,
    The   450
Random House Audio Books   352
Ravenhill, Mark   134
RbA Management Ltd   94
Real Circumstance Theatre Company   210
Really Useful Group Ltd, The   177
Ben Rector   403
Red 24 Management   105
Red 24 Voices   102
Red Ladder Theatre Co.   210
Red Room, The   210
Red Rose Chain   211
Redeeming Features   81
Redroofs Associates   81
Redrush Talent   82
Reel Deal Showreel Co., The   418
Reel Thing Ltd, The   338
Leigh-Ann Regan Casting (LARCA)
    Ltd   121
regional theatre   127
Nadine Rennie   121
REP College, The   22
Replay Film & New Media   339, 418
Replay Theatre Company   287
repro companies   391
Reveal Theatre Company   211
Simone Reynolds CDG   121
Rho Delta Ltd   177
Kate Rhodes-James CDG   121
Rhubarb Voices   102
Mat Ricardo   403
Rich Mix   260
Lisa Richards Agency PMA   82
Vicky Richardson CDG   121
Richmond Drama School   41
Richmond Productions   211
Riding Lights Theatre Company   211
Rifco Theatre Company   211

Roberts, Howard   96
Rocket Theatre   212
Danielle Roffe Casting   121
Rogues & Vagabonds Management   94
role-play companies   303
Role-Players NGA Ltd   306
role-playing   309
Roleplay UK   306
Jessica Ronane CDG   121
Room 3 Agency Ltd   82
Rose Bruford College*   22, 41
Rose Theatre Kingston   149
Rosebery Management Ltd   95
Rosemary Branch Theatre   260
Davey Ross   403
Rossmore Management PMA   82
Rourke, Josie   127
Annie Rowe CDG   121
Royal Academy of Music   22
Royal & Derngate Theatres   150
Royal Birmingham Conservatoire*   23   41
Royal Central School of Speech and Drama*,
    The   23, 42
Royal Conservatoire of Scotland*   23
Royal Court Theatre   150
Royal Exchange Theatre   150
Royal Lyceum Edinburgh   151
Royal Shakespeare Company   151
Royal Television Society (RTS)   462
Royal Theatrical Fund, The   450
Royal Welsh College of Music and
    Drama*   23
Royce Management   82
Rushes Soho Shorts Festival   358
Neil Rutherford Casting   121
Richard Ryder   49
Scott Rylander   404

S4K International Ltd   288
St James's Management   82
Salamanda Tandem   363
Jane Salberg   122
Saraband Associates   83
Robin Savage Photography APHP   404

Savages Personal Management   83
Howard Sayer Photography   404
Scamp Theatre Ltd   212
Scarlet Theatre   212
Scene & Heard   462
Scene Productions   288
Scene Three Creative   212
Schaubuhne   134
Ginny Schiller CDG   122
Karen Scott Photography   404
Laura Scott CDG   122
Tim Scott   83
Scottish Youth Theatre   3
Screen International   454
Screen South   449
Screen Yorkshire   449
script   316
Script Websites   454
scripts, Final Draft format   318
SDM (formerly Simon Drake
    Management)   83
Searchers, The   122
Dawn Sedgwick Management   83
Nadira Seecoomar CDG   122
Select Casting Ltd   122
Select Management   83
self-employment   437
self-taping   323, 326
Rebecca Semark   49
September Films   339
Sevenoaks Stag Theatre   264
Shakespeare at The Tobacco Factory   212
Catherine Shakespeare Lane   404
Shakespeare's Globe   151
Shape   366
Shared Experience   212
Sharkey & Co. Ltd PMA   83
Phil Shaw   123
Sheetmusic Warehouse, The   455
Sheffield Theatres   151
Michael Shelford   405
Shepherd Management Ltd PMA   83
Shepperd-Fox PMA   84
Sheringham Little Theatre   151

Sherman Theatre   151
Shining Management Ltd   103
Shooting People   382, 385, 455
Shopping and Fucking   134
Showcase Entertainments Productions
    Ltd   177
showcases   355
showreel   345, 418
Showreel Editing by Anthony Holmes   418
showreels   54, 317, 324, 342, 347, 422
    companies   415
Showreelz.com   419
sight reading   345
Sightline   339
Alan Sill Photography   405
Silver-Tongued Productions   419
Silvertip Films Ltd   419
Ros Simmons   49
Simpatico UK Ltd   307
Peter Simpkin   405
Simple8 Theatre Company   213
Simply Theatre   247
Marc Sinden Productions Group of
    Companies   177
Rebecca Singer Management   84, 105
Sandra Singer Associates   84
Sixteen Films   339
Sixth Sense Theatre for Young People   288
Skill: National Bureau for Students with
    Disabilities   367
Skoob Books   455
Sky Blue Theatre Company   213, 288, 314
Camilla Storey Management   84
Small World Theatre   213, 289
Smart Management   84
Michelle Smith CDG   123
Suzanne Smith CDG   123
So Radio Ltd   349
Society of Teachers of the Alexander
    Technique (STAT), The   462
Society of Independent Theatres (SIT)   255
Society of London Theatre (SOLT)   463
Soho Theatre   152
Sole Purpose Productions   213

Solomon Theatre Company 289
Stephen Sondheim Society, The 463
SonicPond Studio 419
Sophie's Silver Lining Fund 451
Sound 419
Sounds Wilde 420
Southwark Playhouse 152
Space, The 260
Spanner in the Works 214
Spare Tyre Theatre Company 289, 363
Speakeasy Productions Ltd 339
Spellbound Productions Ltd 339
Sphinx Theatre Company 214
Spillers Pantomimes 238
Splendid Productions 290
Spotlight 51, 126, 128, 316, 323, 328, 345,
     380, 382, 384, 386, 391, 409
   Disability Register 359
Paul Spyker Management 84
Squaredeal Productions Ltd 177
Helen Stafford 123
Emma Stafford 123
Stafford Festival Shakespeare 301
Stage, The 32, 138, 214, 235, 303, 383, 455
   producing 138
Stage Centre Management Ltd 95
Stage Directors UK 463
Stage, The 386
Stagescreen Productions 339
Stanhope Productions Ltd 178
Stanton Davidson Associates PMA 84
Stanton, Sophie 130
StartaTheatreCompany.com 463
Lou Stein Associates Ltd 350
Stephen Joseph Theatre 152
Stephens, Simon 134
Ed Stephenson Productions 214
Steps Drama Learning Development 307
Robert Sterne 123
Gail Stevens & Rebecca Farhall Casting 123
Stevenson Withers Associates PMA 85
Sam Stevenson CDG 123
Rosie Still 405
Stirling Management Actors Agency 85

Stiven Christie Management 85
Liz Stoll CDG 123
Katherine Stonehouse Management 85
StopGAP Dance Company 363
Storyhouse 152
Studio Salford 463
STV Productions 315
Suffolk Summer Theatres (Southwold &
     Aldeburgh) 152
Sunday Times National Student Drama
     Festival (NSDF), The 301
Suspect Culture 214
Swales, Robbie 309
Syson Grainger Casting 124

Amanda Tabak CDG 124
Tabard Theatre 261
TABS Productions 215
Take Away Theatre Company, The 290
Take Five 420
Taking Flight Theatre Company 215
Talawa Theatre Company 215
Talent Agency Ltd, The 85
Talent Artists Ltd 85
Talent Circle 383
British Talent Agency 85
Talkback Thames 340
Talking Heads 103
TalkingPEN books 352
Tall Stories Theatre Company 290
Tamasha Theatre Company 215
Tara Theatre 216
Tauscher, Petra Jane 134
Tavistock Wood PMA 85
tax 225, 436
   expenses 252, 436
   IRS (Internal Revenue Service) 327
Giles Taylor 49
TCG Artist Management Ltd 86
television, casting for 316
television companies 313
Tempest Productions Ltd 350
Ten Ten Theatre 290
Sue Terry Voices Ltd 103

Library Theatre, The   153
Theataccounts Ltd   434
Theatr Pena   216
Theatr Clwyd   153
Theatr Genedlaethol Cymru   216
Theatr Iolo   291
Theatr na nÓg   291
theatre   127, 133, 251, 323
Theatre Absolute   216
Theatre Alibi   217
Theatre Broad   217
Theatre By The Lake   153
Theatre Centre   292
Theatre Chaplaincy UK   463
theatre companies/managements, starting
     your own   224
Theatre Company Blah Blah Blah!   292
Theatre Exchange Ltd   292
Theatre From Oxford   247
Theatre Hullabaloo   292
Theatre in Education   273, 303, 310
Theatre in Wales   463
Theatre Is   217
Theatre Lab Company   218
Theatre Record – The continuing chronicle
     of the British Stage   455
Theatre Royal Bath   153
Theatre Royal, Bury St Edmunds   153, 241
Theatre Royal Haymarket Masterclass
     Trust   42
Theatre Royal, Margate   241
Theatre Royal, Norwich   241
Theatre Royal, Nottingham   241
Theatre Royal Plymouth   153
Theatre Royal Stratford East   153
Theatre Royal, Winchester   242
Theatre Royal Windsor   154
Théâtre Sans Frontières   218
Theatre Set-up   218
Theatre Without Walls   218, 307, 364
Theatre Workout Ltd   42
Theatre Workshop   219, 364
Theatre-Rites   216, 291
Theatre503   261

Theatre&   307
Theatres Trust   464
Theatrevoice   455
Theatricalia   456
Theatro Technis   261
Third Party Productions Ltd   219
Lisa Thomas Management   86, 405
Katie Threlfall Associates PMA   86
Tiger Aspect Productions   340
Tildsley France Associates PMA   86
Tilted Wig Productions   219
Tin Shed Theatre Company   219, 293
Tinderbox Theatre Company   220
Tintinna Ltd   350
TM Photography & Design   405
TMG London   86
To Be Seen   383   386
Tobacco Factory Theatres   154
Paul Todd   49
Told by an Idiot   220
Tongue & Groove   103
Tony Blake Photography   406
Topps Casting   124
Torch Theatre   154
TOSG Gaelic Theatre Company   220
Total Theatre   464
Total Vanity Ltd   86
Touchdown Dance   364
touring productions   249
Tourist Information Office   251
Moira Townsend   124
Toynbee Studios   261
Trafalgar 1 Limited   340
Trainerpool   307
training, for actors with disabilities   359
training, drama-based   309
Travelling Light Theatre Company   293
Traverse Theatre   154, 263
Trestle Theatre Company   220
Jill Trevellick CDG   124
Triangle Theatre Company   220
Tricycle Theatre   154
Triple A Media   105
Tristan Bates Theatre   261

Troika PMA   86
Tron Theatre   154
Trotman, Jayne   388
TTA (Top Talent Agency)   86
Twenty Twenty Productions Ltd   340
Twitch Films   420
Two's Company   221
TYPE (The Yellowchair Performance
   Experience)   221

UCAS   13, 346
UK Theatre Association (TMA)   464
UK Arts International   221
UK Jewish Film Festival   358
UK Productions   178, 238
UK Theatre Network   456
Steve Ullathorne   406
Ulster Theatre Company   178
Uncharted   344
Underbelly, The   263
understudying   166
Unicorn Theatre   293
Union Theatre   262
Unique   350
Unique Taxpayer Reference (UTR)   437
United Agents PMA   87
Universal Artists   87
University of Bristol Theatre
   Collection   464
University of the Creative Arts   343
University of Westminster   343
Unlimited Theatre   221
Unrestricted View   221
Upstairs at the Gatehouse   262
Urban Talent   87
USP (unique selling point)   318
UTV   315
UVA Management   87

VSA Ltd PMA   87, 464
Roxane Vacca Management PMA   88
Vanessa Valentine Photography   406
Anthony Vander Elst Productions   178

Vanguard Productions   222
Luke Varley   406
Sally Vaughan CDG   124
Greg Veit Photography   406
Ana Verastegui Photography   406
Video Enterprises   340
video games   344–345
Vienna's English Theatre   247
Vincenzo Photography   407
Virtual Library of Theatre & Drama   456
virtual reality   344
Louise Dyson at VisABLE People Ltd   88,
   364
Visualeyes Repro Ltd   408
Vocal Confidence with Alix Longman   49
Vocal Point   103
voice acting   344
voice actors   345
VoiceBank Ltd   103
voice demos   101, 347
   companies   415
Voice Shop   103
Voice Squad   103
voice work   345
voice-clips   412
voice-over, agents   347, 412
Voicebank, The Irish Voice-Over
   Agency   103
Voiceover Gallery, The   104
Voiceover Kickstart   420
VoiceOver Network   346
voicepro.com   345
voicereels   412
Volcano Theatre Company   222
Anne Vosser   124
VSI (Voice & Script International)   104

Suzann Wade PMA   88, 407
Waking Exploits   222
Wales Screen Commission   448
Walk the Plank   222
Wall, Bruce   295
Walsh Bros Ltd   340
Genevieve Walsh   50

Walter Meierjohann   134
Jo Wander Management   105
Waring & McKenna Ltd PMA   88
Watermans Arts Centre   264
Watermill Theatre   155
Watford Palace Theatre   155
Caroline Webster   407
Fiona Weir CDG   124
Janet Welch Personal Management   88
Wellcome Trust, The   451
West Central Management   95
West End International   178
West End productions   170
June West   124
Mark Westbrook – Acting Coach
    Scotland   50
Matt Western   124
Westminster Reference Library   456
Meredith Westwood Management Ltd   88
Michael Wharley Photography APHP   407
Ken Wheeler   421
Whirlwind Theatre for Children   293
Whistledown Productions   350
Keith Whitall   223
White Bear Theatre   262
White Horse Theatre   248
Wikipedia   456
Wilde Management   88
Wilder Films   340
Williamson & Holmes   89
Willow Personal Management   89
Wiltshire Creative   155
Wimbledon Studio Theatre   262
Alex Winn Photography   407
Wintersons PMA   89

Wireless Theatre Company, The   351
Wise & Co. Chartered Accountants &
    Business Advisers   434
Anne Wittman   50
Wizard Theatre Ltd   294
Wolf + Water Arts Company   364
Felix de Wolfe PMA   89
Women in Film and Television (UK)
    (WFTV)   464
Tessa Wood   50
Tara Woodward   125
Worcester Repertory Company   155
Working Title Films   341
Robert Workman   407
World Productions Ltd   341
Wrestling School, The   223
WGGB - The Writers' Union   464
Wyatts Partnership   435
Edward Wyman Agency   89

Y Touring Theatre Company   223
Yakety Yak All Mouth Ltd   104
Yellow Earth Theatre   223
York Theatre Royal   155
Young Shakespeare Company   294
Young Vic   127, 156
Youngblood   42
Youth Music Theatre UK   3
Youth Theatre   273
Youth Theatre Ireland   4

Jeremy Zimmermann Casting   125
Zinc Arts   366